GREAT
AMERICAN TRIALS

CONTRIBUTORS

Hendrik Booraem

John S. Bowman

Michael Burgan

Rodney Carlisle

Stephen G. Christianson

Kathryn Cullen-DuPont

Teddi Di Canio

Colin Evans

Ronald J. Formica

Elizabeth Gwillim

Ronald Lansing

Douglas Linder

Buckner F. Melton, Jr.

Carol Wilcox Melton

David I. Petts

Bernard Ryan, Jr.

Thomas C. Smith

Mark A. Thorburn

William Weir

B.J. Welborn

Edward W. Knappman, Editor

Gale Group staff

Kathleen Droste
Project Coordinator

Dean Dauphinais, Robert Duncan, Mary Grimes, David Oblender, Pamela A. Reed
Imaging and Multimedia

Jennifer Wahi
Production Design

Rita Wimberley
Senior Buyer, Manufacturing

Front cover photos: Salem Witchcraft Trial (Bettman/Corbis); Dred Scott (Library of Congress); Clarence Darrow at the Scopes "Monkey Trial" (Library of Congress); Newspaper collage of President Bill Clinton impeached (AP/Wide World Photos).
Back cover photo: Al Capone (Library of Congress)

Published by
Gale Group Inc.
27500 Drake Rd.
Farmington Hills, MI 48334-3535

ISBN 0-7876-4901-5

Printed in the United States of America
10 9 8 7 6 5 4 3 2 1

Highlights

Great American Trials provides an abundance of information on the most significant and celebrated trials in U.S. history, from 1637 to the present. Included are brief and accurate summaries of trials known for their historic or legal significance, political controversy, public attention, legal ingenuity, or literary fame. *Great American Trials* covers a broad scope of trials, including:

- Salem Witchcraft Trials (1692)
- Dred Scott Trial (1856)
- Lizzie Borden Trial (1893)
- Triangle Shirtwaist Fire Trial (1911)
- Leopold and Loeb Trial (1924)
- Teapot Dome Trials (1926)
- Hollywood Ten Trials (1948–50)
- Trial of Julius and Ethel Rosenberg and Morton Sobell (1951)
- Brown v. Board of Education (1954)
- Charles Manson Trial (1970–71)
- Roe v. Wade (1973)
- Ted Bundy Trials (1976 & 1979)
- John Demjanjuk Denaturalization Trial (1981)
- Jim Bakker Trial (1989)
- Mike Tyson Trial (1992)
- O.J. Simpson Trials (1995–1997)
- Bill Clinton Impeachment (1998–99)
- 2000 Presidential Election Trials (2000)
- and many more—378 courtroom cases in all

Each trial begins with the facts—setting up the key players, the charges, and site of the trial, followed by a narrative that explains the circumstances that led to the trial, pre-trial maneuvers, the trial itself, the judgment, appeals (if any), and any subsequent implications of the trial.

Special features:

- Chronological arrangement of trials shows the developmental pattern of law: today's cases apply yesterday's precedents
- Most entries end with suggestions for further reading, enabling the user to easily continue research on a particular trial
- Three tables of contents—chronological, alphabetical, and categorical—provide easy access to any specific trial
- More than 240 subject-specific photographs and drawings
- Glossary defining legal terms
- Comprehensive index lists key figures, subjects, and areas of law

CONTENTS

In Chronological Order
(by date of trial)

1930–1939

1940–1949

1970–1979

1990s

CONTENTS

In Alphabetical Order
(by name of trial)

A

D

M

T

U

V

W

CONTENTS

In Subject Order
(by the crime[s] charged)

Corruption

**Court-Martials
& Military**

Fraud

**Freedom of
Speech & Press**

Heresy

**Rape &
Sex Crimes**

PREFACE

Great American Trials provides readers and researchers with brief, accurate, and readable summaries of the most significant and celebrated trials in U.S. history.

As with any encyclopedic undertaking, the selection process was a complex one and inevitably involved some subjectivity given space limitations. Since the settlement of Jamestown in 1607, literally millions of civil and criminal trials have been conducted in American courts. Many thousands of these had some historic or legal significance or attracted wide public attention for one reason or another. From these, I have selected the 378 I judged best met the following criteria:

Historic Significance: Did the trial have a major impact on the course of American history? Trials such as *Scott v. Sanford* (the Dred Scott case), which was a fateful step on the road to the Civil War, and the Boston Massacre Trial, which set the stage for the American Revolution, are included under this criterion.

Legal Significance: Did the trial result in an important legal precedent or a landmark Supreme Court decision? Examples of such trials include those of Dr. Sam Sheppard, which established a significant precedent concerning pre-trial publicity, *In Re Baby M*, which affected the validity of surrogate motherhood contracts, and *Gideon v. Wainwright*, which led the Supreme Court to rule that states had to provide free counsel to indigent defendants in criminal trials.

Political Controversy: Did the trial crystallize or generate a national political controversy? Among the trials included under this criterion are the Sacco–Vanzetti murder trial, which was tainted by hostility to radicals and immigrants; the Julius and Ethel Rosenberg treason trial; the trial of the Chicago Seven for instigating disruptive anti-Vietnam War demonstrations; and the Clinton impeachment trial which polarized American political life.

Public Attention: Because of the fame of the participants or the nature of the alleged crime, many trials in our history have been national sensations. The trial of Bruno Hauptmann for kidnapping the Lindbergh baby falls under this category, as do the trials of Daniel Sickles, Lizzie Borden, Harry Thaw, Jean Harris, Patty Hearst, and Charles Manson.

Legal Ingenuity: Some trials earned a place in this book because the courtroom skills demonstrated by one or more of participating lawyers have become legendary. Among the trials included under this criteria are *Martinez v. Del Valle,* the occasion of Joseph Choate's most famous cross-examination; the Leopold and Loeb murder trial, featuring Clarence Darrow for the defense; and the Triangle Shirtwaist Fire trial, where Max Steuer won an acquittal few thought possible.

Literary Fame: Trials have inspired novelists, playwrights, screenwriters, non-fiction writers, and even songwriters. Their works have often left a greater impression on the public than the original trial. Among the trials that have been immortalized in literature are the Chester Gillette murder trial, the Salem Witchcraft trials, Joe Hill's murder trial, the Scopes "Monkey" trial, and the Richard Hickok/Perry Smith murder trial.

In my selection process, I have intentionally applied these criteria more leniently to recent trials than to those from the more distant past. This was done to serve the needs of readers who, I suspect, are far more likely to need or desire information on recent trials.

Because the important decisions of the Supreme Court are adequately covered in a host of other standard reference works, I have intentionally minimized the number of such decisions in **Great American Trials.** Only those that resulted from an actual courtroom trial (*Buck v. Bell*), had an impact on the way trials are conducted in this country (the *Miranda* decision), or marked critical turning points in American history (*Roe v. Wade*) have been included.

While another editor might have included some trials that I have not or omitted some that I included, the vast majority of trials would make any editor's list of the most important trials in our history. Several precautions were taken to avoid oversights and omissions. The legal editors of this volume—Lisa Paddock and Stephen Christianson—assisted me in compiling and evaluating the list of trials as did several members of the editorial staff at The Gale Group. Although their assistance has been very helpful, the responsibility for any omissions is mine.

Each entry begins with a set of basic facts about the trial. This is followed by a narrative explaining the circumstances that led to the trial, pre-trial maneuvers, the trial itself, the judgment, and any subsequent appeals. We sought to entertain as well as inform. We have tried to provide the maximum amount of accurate information in the space available.

The extent of sources consulted varies considerably with the trial. Some trials, such as Lizzie Borden's and Sacco and Vanzetti's, have produced shelves of well-researched histories. Others are barely mentioned in secondary sources. Our contributors have dug as deep into the sources as necessary to establish the essential facts of each trial. However, for some 17th-, 18th-, and early 19th-century trials, the surviving records are sparse, failing even to note the full names of judges or lawyers.

All but a few entries end with suggestions for further readings. Contributors were asked to include their suggestions for further reading the most readily and widely available sources of additional information. As the intended audience for this book is general readers rather than legal researchers, we have excluded legal citations.

The trials are presented in chronological order. This was chosen as the most logical sequence for several reasons. First, the law evolves chronologically; today's cases apply yesterday's precedents. Second, many trials are emblematic of a particular historical period and are directly or indirectly connected (the various espionage and anti-Communist trials of the late 1940s and early 1950s, for example.) Third, there is no preferable alternative. Without a generally accepted convention for naming trials, an alphabetical arrangement would be of little benefit to readers. As *Great American Trials* contains three tables of contents—chronological, alphabetical, and category—plus a comprehensive index, readers will have little difficulty in locating any specific trial.

In editing this book, I have made a determined effort to translate legalese into plain English. Unfortunately, there are some legal terms that defy translation; the definition is so particular to the law that no plain English equivalent exists and any paraphrase would risk distorting the meaning. Such terms have been defined in the glossary found at the end of the volume.

For the revised edition, we have added 178 new trials and revised 17 trials from the first edition. The revisions were made either because additional information became available—for example, the opening of archives in the former Soviet Union produced new revelations about Alger Hiss and Julius and Ethel Rosenberg—or because there were new developments, such as the release from prison of Jean Harris.

Many people made vital contributions to the planning, writing, editing, and production of *Great American Trials:*

Chris Nasso of Gale Research provided indispensable support, encouragement, and wise counsel when this book was in its formative stages. Charles A. Bayne and Alan Nichter deserve special recognition for their roles as advisors to the book.

Steve Christianson and Lisa Paddock, the book's legal editors, together scrutinized the manuscript and corrected many misinterpretations of trial procedures and misstatements about the intricacies of the American legal system.

The writers who contributed to *Great American Trials*— Hendrik Booraem, John S. Bowman, Michael Burgan, Rodney Carlisle, Steven G. Christianson, Kathryn Cullen-DuPont, Teddi DiCanio, Colin Evans, Ronald J. Formica, Elizabeth Gwillim, Ronald Lansing, Buckner F. Melton, Jr., Carol Wilcox Melton, David I. Petts, Bernard Ryan, Jr., Thomas C. Smith, Mark A. Thorburn, William Weir, and B.J. Welborn— were dogged researchers, skilled word smiths, and astonishingly conscientious about meeting their tight deadlines. Larry Hand and Susan Paruch copyedited this book with exceptional skill and diligence.

Susan Brainard helped me manage this project day-in, day-out, over two years with unfailing good humor and care. Jil Nelson Kaplan tracked down the illustrations for the first edition, a task that proved far more difficult than either of us imagined when we began, and Vicki Hanlon developed the picture recommendations for the revised edition.

Finally I owe special thanks to my wife and partner, Elizabeth Frost Knappman, who has tolerated my foibles and helped me over the rough patches for 35 years, and to my daughter, Amanda, who brightens the days.

—Edward W. Knappman
August 2001

INTRODUCTION

Trials have been the ultimate means to resolve disputes in American society from Colonial times to the present. Many of the great turning points in the nation's history have occurred in courtrooms—from John Peter Zenger's trial for allegedly libeling the British governor of Colonial New York through *Roe v. Wade*, which barred states from prohibiting abortions in the early months of pregnancy.

Trials have been a prime source of popular entertainment, public ritual, and real-life human drama. In person and through the news media, Americans have flocked to courtrooms to be titillated, scandalized, uplifted, inspired, educated, and just plain amused. Before the age of mass communications, the local courthouse provided one of the few diversions available to a largely rural population. Indeed, judges, preachers, and editorial writers have so long and frequently denounced the "circus-like" atmosphere prevailing at many locally or nationally celebrated trials that the phrase has become a cliché of courtroom journalism. In more recent times, real and fictional trials have become a staple of movie producers and television programmers. Today, cable television's Court TV network enables trial junkies to perpetually indulge themselves without ever changing the channel.

As compelling as trials may be as drama, they fill a far more serious purpose in our society: they offer a mechanism for maintaining public order when one person, or other legal entity such as a corporation, violates the legally protected rights of another person or society at large. In this sense, a trial fulfills the human need for retribution, providing even the losing side with a sense that he or she at least has had an opportunity to air grievances, or has had his or her "day in court."

Trials, therefore, are the central focus of American jurisprudence. However, the process of resolving disputes through a trial of the facts—litigation—is only one area of legal practice. Only a fraction of those cases filed by litigators ever goes to trial. Indeed, most efforts of the vast majority of lawyers who are not litigators are devoted to avoiding trials by advising clients how to stay on the right side of the law and by drafting legal documents, such as contracts.

Fundamentals of the Law

To appreciate what made many of the trials described in **Great American Trials** "great" requires some familiarity with the branches of the law, the history and contours of the American system of jurisprudence, and the rules of procedure and evidence that govern the way trials are conducted. While the editors and contributors have attempted to translate legalese into plain English whenever possible, for some legal terms there is no common word or phrase with an identical meaning. Readers will find a glossary of such terms at the end of this book.

Perhaps the most important factor about a court is that it is a public body. In each case, a court must determine the facts, but in determining their legal significance, the court is performing a service not just to the litigants, but to the larger community as well. In deciding a particular controversy according to the law, courts provide guidance to others who may in the future confront similar issues, thereby ideally forestalling at least some potential litigation.

This evolutionary method of devising so-called judge-made law— as opposed to legislation—is a natural by-product of common-law systems of jurisprudence like ours, in which current cases are decided in accordance with precepts derived from earlier cases. This "common law" is a body of complex rules formulated out of thousands of decisions reached by generations of judges, beginning in England during the Middle Ages. As such, common law predates the creation of legislative bodies, whose primary function is drafting the rules interpreted and applied by modern courts to the cases tried before them.

"Civil law," by contrast, grew out of a written code of Roman laws and today is the system of laws prevailing in Western Europe (except for the United Kingdom, of course), as well as the state of Louisiana. Although today the number of statutes regulating both public, or criminal, law (in which the government has the most direct interest) and private, or civil, law (directly involving the interests of individuals) continues to grow, the common-law system predominates in the rest of our nation.

The Roots of the American Court System

The British judicial system was transplanted wholesale to the American colonies. In 17th-century America, lawmaking and judging were regarded as one and the same. As in England, Parliament was regarded as the highest court. The colonies, however, began to develop their own layered court systems. At the top of the hierarchy stood colonial legislatures, which served primarily as courts of appeals. Beneath them was a network of superior courts, which often included colonial governors among their presiding judges, and which mainly heard appeals in civil matters first tried in lower courts. Superior courts also tried criminal cases. The third level of local courts saw most of the trials in colonial America. These local courts performed governmental functions as well, such as levying and collecting taxes, and provided townspeople with an opportunity to socialize, conduct business, and discuss politics.

A modified version of this three-tier system remains the structure of the various state court systems today. Trials are held in the lowest level of courts; a level of appellate courts reviews all appeals from the trial courts; and a supreme court considers appeals on important issues of law.

As the population of the colonies grew, so did the length of court trial dockets. Courts dealt with increasing demand for their services largely by increasing the formality of their proceedings. When courts began to enforce procedural requirements, fewer cases were filed, and many of those were dismissed. This trend was reversed by the early 18th century with an increase in the number of trained lawyers.

Judges, by contrast, were often appointed lay persons unschooled in the law. This lack of a trained judiciary increased the importance of juries. At the trial of John Peter Zenger for seditious libel (1735), the jury found the defendant not guilty despite the clear import of the judge's instructions to the contrary. This helped establish the principle that juries could exercise considerable discretion in interpreting judicial instructions. Later in the 18th century, however, judges gained the power to order new trials in the face of verdicts that were, in their opinion, contrary to the weight of the evidence. Today, in trials conducted without a jury—so-called bench trials—judges settle questions of both law and fact. In jury trials the roles are apportioned so that jurors decide the facts of the case, while decisions about the law are left to judges.

The use of fictitious litigant names, a common practice by the time of *Roe v. Wade* (1973), first appeared in the late 1680s in a case involving "John Doe" and "Richard Roe." Obscuring the real names of the plaintiff and defendant meant the case would be decided on its specific merits rather than on the influence and connections of the contestants, which was a pattern that had encouraged many plaintiffs to hope that quick, rough justice would be administered in their favor.

The Courts under the Constitution

Article III of the United States Constitution, together with the first Judiciary Act (1789), established three types of federal courts, roughly modeled on the tripartite structure then operating in individual states. The two lower tiers, consisting of trial and appeals courts, are organized along regional lines, with the former vastly outnumbering the latter. District courts were and still are trial courts, each manned by a single district judge. Circuit courts, now federal appellate courts, employed three-judge panels then, as they do now. While circuit courts were then primarily trial courts, today the circuit courts of appeals are devoted to reviews of district court decisions. The Supreme Court was then mainly—and is now almost exclusively—devoted to reviewing decisions of lower appellate courts, both federal and state,[1] and consists of nine justices sitting *en banc*, or altogether.

The principles of Federalism recognized by the framers of the Constitution mandated that the states retain important rights. While the federal government concerned itself with national affairs, such as foreign relations and commerce among the states, states retained under their traditional police powers the right to govern matters of public health, safety, and morality.[2] Consequently, throughout the 19th century, development of many areas of the law was left to individual state legislatures and courts. To this day, important differences exist among states as to contract law, criminal law, and the law of torts, or non-criminal injuries.

In contrast, federal courts' jurisdiction, or power to hear and decide cases, was limited to hearing cases between citizens of different states, admiralty cases, and cases arising under federal law. This third area of empowerment led to the development of federal common-law doctrines and embraced the authority to interpret constitutional and statutory provisions, or even overturn them, as in *Marbury v. Madison* (1803), which established the principle of judicial review.[3] When federal courts hear cases between citizens of different states, known as diversity cases, they must apply the substantive law of whichever state has the strongest interest in the outcome.

Trial Procedures

Each state court system has its own set of procedural rules, but since 1938 and 1945, respectively, federal courts have followed their own rules of civil and criminal procedure, which often differ sharply from procedures observed by state courts.

Rules of procedure govern not just the trial itself, but also all the legally significant events leading up to it. They may, for example, govern the form in which the plaintiff in a civil case files his set of pleadings, customarily called a complaint, which initiates the lawsuit. These rules will ordinarily stipulate the time by which the defendant must respond to the plaintiff's charges in a formal answer. These rules are multitudinous and complex, as they must impose order on the vast array of legal weapons in a litigation attorney's arsenal, the majority of which are deployed before the trial ever begins. In fact, most litigators rarely see the inside of a courtroom. Instead, they spend their time negotiating with the opposing side (always, if that party is represented by counsel, through his or her attorney[4]) and drafting motion papers. Motions can pertain to such things as the pretrial testimony of potential witnesses and the exchange of documents and information that are a prelude to trial. Collectively, this is known as "discovery." Attempts to have an opponent's case dismissed on various grounds before trial also are made in the form of motions.

The purpose of discovery is to preserve evidence that might not be available at trial, such as the testimony of an infirm witness, to ascertain the issues actually in controversy, and to prevent either side from being taken off guard—by surprise evidence, for example. It seems fundamental that both sides should be in possession of all information relevant to the case before proceeding to trial, but the disclosure afforded by discovery is a relatively recent innovation. Discovery only became a vital part of the litigation process with the adoption of the Federal Rules of Civil Procedure. It has since become the focus of much of the debate about the delay and costs associated with modern-day litigation.

Once discovery is complete and rulings are made on motions by the two sides, more precautions are taken to ensure trials are conducted fairly. Both plaintiff's and defendant's counsels submit draft pretrial orders to the court. The pretrial order includes such items as lists of all witnesses the party intends to call and of all documentary evidence, or exhibits, the party intends to present at trial. The parties then proceed to select a jury if the trial is a criminal prosecution or if the plaintiff in a civil case has elected to have a jury trial. This selection process is called *voir dire* and, particularly in recent years, is a crucial stage of the trial, as each opposing counsel subtly maneuvers to get a trial (or *petit*) jury sympathetic to his or her case.

In some criminal prosecutions, a grand jury has already heard the case. Traditionally composed of 23 jurors (as opposed to the six- to 12-person juries used in trials), the grand jury's purpose is to determine whether the facts and accusations presented by the prosecutor warrant an indictment and eventual trial of the accused. Others accused of criminal acts can face other types of juries convened before trial to hear only prosecution testimony. For example, although because of her age she did not herself appear, Cheryl Christina Crane, the 14-year-old daughter of film star Lana Turner, was the subject of a 1958 inquest by a coroner's jury into the murder of her mother's lover. Because the coroner's jury returned a verdict of justifiable homicide, criminal proceedings against Crane were discontinued.

The Sixth Amendment to the Constitution guarantees the accused the right to a trial by a jury of his or her peers, a concept as old as common law itself. The Sixth Amendment also guarantees the accused the right to be tried by an impartial jury, thus making the process of jury selection even more stringent in criminal trials. While voir dire always permits the attorneys for either side to excuse potential jurors for cause or for no cause at all (called a peremptory challenge), the Sixth Amendment mandates that this process result in a jury that represents a fair cross-section of the community and does not discriminate against any class of potential jurors. Disputes about a potential jury's racial balance can be central to the trial strategy of either side, as it was for the defendant's attorney in the 1968 murder trial of Black Panther activist Huey P. Newton. If excessive publicity surrounds the case, the court may take additional measures to make sure the jury remains impartial: sequestering the jury, delaying the trial, even granting a change of venue, as in the 1967 trial of mass murderer Richard Speck.

Trials begin with opening arguments delivered by attorneys for both sides, beginning with plaintiff's counsel—which in the case of most criminal prosecutions will be the government's attorney, such as a district attorney. (A defendant may reserve the right to present an opening statement until after the plaintiff's presentation of its case is complete.) These arguments present the judge and jury with an overview of the evidence each side intends to present and of their respective theories of the case. Plaintiff's counsel then presents his or her case. That starts with direct examination of the plaintiff's designated witnesses, which can include so-called expert witnesses who do not testify about the facts of the case, but about matters requiring specialized knowledge. Documentary or concrete evidence is introduced in the course of direct examination. Each side is permitted to ask open questions only of its own witnesses, unless that witness proves to be hostile, in which case he or she may be asked leading questions and even be cross-examined.

Cross-examination is generally reserved for counsel for the opposing side, who can question each witness before he or she steps down. The purpose of cross-examination is to discredit the witness or cast testimony already given in a light more favorable to the party represented by the cross-examiner. If cross-examination elicits testimony damaging to the party presenting its case, that party may seek to rebut or clarify it through redirect examination of the witness.

When the plaintiff has presented all of its evidence, the defense presents its case using the same process. After both sides have made their cases to the judge, or to judge and jury, plaintiff's counsel, then defendant's, delivers a closing statement summarizing his or her client's case. If it is a jury trial, the judge will then instruct the jurors on the applicable law, including which side has the burden of proof and what the measure of that burden is. There are three standards for the measure of proof that the party bearing the burden must meet to win the case. Most civil cases use the "preponderance of the evidence" standard, which means that the fact finder must be convinced that the fact at issue is more probably true than not. Some civil cases, such as those involving fraud, require proof by clear and convincing evidence, i.e., that there is a high probability that the fact at issue exists. The highest standard applies to criminal prosecutions, in which the defendant's guilt must be established beyond a reasonable doubt.

Juries deliberate, sometimes for weeks on end. Judges acting as finders of both law and fact sometimes deliberate or sometimes rule immediately from the bench. If the trial is criminal in nature, the verdict must be unanimous. Its delivery often is followed by a long delay before the trial court pronounces judgment and holds a sentencing hearing.

Rules of Evidence

Formal rules govern the introduction of both testimonial and documentary evidence. While not all states have codified their evidentiary rules, the Federal Rules of Evidence, which became effective in 1975, govern civil and criminal cases in most federal courts. As might be expected, additional rules apply in criminal cases. For example, if the state wishes to introduce the confession of a defendant at a criminal trial, the court must conduct an examination outside the presence and hearing of the jury (also called *voir dire*). This is done to determine if the statements were voluntarily obtained in compliance with the defendant's Miranda rights,[5] and therefore constitutionally admissible.

Attorneys can attempt at trial to introduce whatever new evidence—largely witness testimony—they feel will help their clients' cases; it is their opponents' job to object to and thus prevent the evidence from being admitted. The most common of these objections are relevance, hearsay, and privilege.

Relevance pertains to the link between the proposed evidence and the proposition it is supposed to support. Relevant evidence, whether direct or circumstantial, must tend to prove a fact that is material to the issue. Even relevant evidence may be excluded if its probative value is outweighed by the danger of unfair prejudice, confusion of the issues, or misleading of the jury.[6] Certain categories of relevant evidence, such as proof that a person was insured against liability in a case where his or her negligence is an issue, are never admissible.

The rule against hearsay is probably the most important—certainly the most complex—exclusionary rule of evidence. The Federal Rules define hearsay as "a statement, other than one made by the declarant while testifying at the trial or hearing, offered in evidence to prove the truth of the matter asserted." In other words, a witness's testimony about what someone else said or wrote or communicated nonverbally is not considered credible evidence of the content of that communication. The reason for the hearsay rule is that the witness's credibility is key to determining the truthfulness of his or her testimony. Without the adverse party's ability to cross-examine the communicant and without the jury's ability to scrutinize his or her demeanor, there is no adequate basis on which to judge the accuracy of the statement. An additional question arises in criminal cases in that the Sixth Amendment grants the accused the right to confront and cross-examine all the witnesses against him or her.

There are numerous exceptions to the hearsay rule, generally based on how trustworthy the statement at issue is and the necessity of making the exception. A witness's recital of a dying individual's declarations, for example, is generally admissible on the theory that a dying person has nothing to gain by lying,[7] and because this is the only method whereby such statements can be admitted as evidence after the speaker dies. As might be expected, exceptions in criminal trials are usually narrower to provide the defendant—who may have his or her life or liberty at stake—with additional safeguards. This is not always the case, however. One state-law exception permits statements made by one conspirator to be admitted against co-conspirators even if the statements are made after all conspirators are in custody. This has been ruled constitutional even though the usual rule is that this co-conspirator exception does not apply to any post-custody utterances.

The third common ground for objecting to admissibility is privilege, which applies to communications taking place in the context of legal or other confidential relationships, such as that between husband and wife, priest and penitent, physician and patient.

There is also, of course, a person's right under the Fifth Amendment to the Constitution to refuse to testify against himself or herself, the privilege against self-incrimination.

Appeals Procedures

The time in which an appeal from the trial court's decision is permitted begins to run after the verdict has been reached and, in a criminal case, the sentence pronounced. In a criminal case, the decision or the sentence can be appealed. The executions of Julius and Ethel Rosenberg after their 1951 espionage trial were delayed for two years, while both the conduct of their trial and the severity of their sentences were appealed.

There are two potential stages of appeal in federal and in most state court systems: from the trial court to the intermediate appellate court, then to the supreme court. While losing parties customarily have an automatic right to appeal to the intermediate courts, in most superior courts of appeal, appeals are usually heard only at the discretion of the court. (Appeals almost always reach the U.S. Supreme Court after a petition has been filed for a writ of *certiorari*.)

In the early stages of development of common law, both in England and in America, courts were divided into two types: courts of law and courts of equity. Courts of law ruled according to accepted common-law principles, but when injuries occurred for which law courts had no ready remedy, equity courts were able to address these issues according to general principles of fairness. An appeal in equity subjected both facts and law to review and retrial. Now, however, the two types of courts have been merged. Appeals seek a reversal of the lower court's opinion or a retrial, based almost exclusively on some misapplication of the law— such as in the judge's instructions to the jury regarding the law pertinent to the case—or on procedural error.

Criminal and civil appeals generally follow similar courses. One significant area of difference, however, falls under the rubric of double jeopardy. The principle of double jeopardy, applicable only in criminal prosecutions, is fundamental to common law and finds its expression in the Fifth Amendment, which provides that "No person . . . shall . . . be subject for the same offense to be twice put in jeopardy of life and limb." This principle operates at the federal and state levels. It prevents a second trial unless the first ended in a mistrial—one declared void prior to verdict, usually because the jury is deadlocked—or the defendant appeals a conviction, as Claus von Bülow did after being found guilty in 1982 of attempting to murder his wife. Von Bülow was acquitted of all charges after his second trial in 1985. For defendants less fortunate than von Bülow, double jeopardy also prevents double punishment and even makes the imposition of any higher penalty on retrial subject to increased judicial scrutiny.[8]

Legal Skills

Few, if any, attorneys are so versatile that they are equally adept in all facets of legal practice. Appellate practice often requires a keener grasp of legal technicalities than is required of a trial attorney. Often, a trial attorney's skill rests instead on keen intuitions about human nature. In the Triangle Shirtwaist Trial (1911), for example, defense attorney Max Steuer was able to secure a not-guilty verdict in the face of enormous odds because he understood the psychology of the jury.

Two manufacturers were on trial for the deaths by fire of 146 of their workers, owing to the fact that the doors to the New York City sweatshop where they worked were locked on the defendants' orders. As unsympathetic as these defendants' case appeared, however, Steuer was able to overcome the jury's emotions by appealing to their intellect. Steuer had the principal prosecution witness, a young female survivor of the fire, repeat her testimony three times. The first two recitals were identical; in the third she changed one word. Steuer won the case by making sure that the jury recognized that the witness had been rehearsed.

Other trial attorneys—Daniel Webster immediately comes to mind—succeed not so much on the basis of their examination technique, but on the eloquence and persuasiveness of their oratory. When great trial skills are combined with great issues, memorable trials result. Although the issue at stake in the 1925 Scopes "Monkey Trial," the teaching of evolution, was of great social significance, what made the trial most unforgettable was Clarence Darrow's clever examination of Fundamentalist politician William Jennings Bryan, whom the defense called to the stand as an expert on the Bible—an unorthodox maneuver, given that Bryan was also acting as plaintiff's counsel.

The Scopes trial was memorialized in a play and subsequent film, both entitled *Inherit the Wind*. Other trials, like the 1943 Errol Flynn rape trial, are famous because they featured an irresistible combination of celebrities and scandal. Some trials become infamous because the public perceives them to be a miscarriage of justice, like the 1979 Dan White case, where the accused was convicted of voluntary manslaughter rather than murder—in part because of the success of the unconventional "Twinkies Defense," which argued that White's intake of junk food was the real culprit.

Some trials are celebrated, though, not because they feature notable parties, salacious facts, or incomparable trial tactics. As noted at the outset of this essay, what matters most about the American court system, ultimately, is its public nature. While spectacle certainly is one aspect of many great trials, perhaps the "greatest" one in American history, the one which arguably has had the most profound and lasting effect on our people, is *Brown v. Board of Education* (1954). *Brown v. Board of Education* was finally decided by the U.S. Supreme Court, and the attorney for the winning side, Thurgood Marshall, was himself later to become a Supreme Court justice. But the case revolved around a modest individual's attempt to gain recognition of his child's right to a good education. By overturning the "separate but equal" doctrine that had up to that time made ours a legally segregated society, *Brown v. Board of Education* fueled a social revolution that has changed the lives of every one of us.

—Lisa Paddock, Esq.

[1] The Supreme Court, however, has been known to give state sovereignty great deference. For example, in *Buck v. Bell* (1927), the Court upheld the constitutionality of a Virginia statute permitting the forced sterilization of 18-year-old Carrie Buck, whose mother had been feebleminded.

[2] With increased emphasis on civil rights in the latter half of this century, many of the states' attempts to regulate morality were overturned. In *Griswold v. Connecticut* (1964), for example, the Supreme Court found unconstitutional an 1879 state statute prohibiting the use or distribution of or advisory services concerning contraceptives. While the justices found no basis in the Bill of Rights for voiding the statute, they explained their decision in terms of a newly explored right, the right of privacy, which was further expanded in such cases as *Roe v. Wade*.

[3] The only other instance before the Civil War in which the Supreme Court struck down a federal law occurred in the more infamous *Scott v. Sanford* (1856), in which the Court found the Missouri Compromise unconstitutional and the plaintiff, a slave, consequently not a citizen.

[4] Parties in civil actions—and even in some criminal cases—can appear *pro se*, that is, represent themselves. In *Gideon v. Wainwright* (1963), however, the Supreme Court ruled that every defendant in a felony trial had a right to counsel, and that if the defendant could not afford to hire his or her own lawyer, the state had to provide one. This decision makes impossible situations such as that prevailing during the second treason trial of John Fries in 1800, in which Justice Samuel Chase acted from the bench—much to the defendant's detriment—as Fries' counsel after the defendant's attorneys withdrew in the face of Chase's open hostility toward their client.

[5] Such rights are named for the landmark case of *Miranda v. Arizona* (1967), which ruled that at the time of their arrests, suspected criminals had to be read their rights to remain silent, to know that anything they said could be used against them, and that if they were indigent the state would provide them with counsel.

[6] The persuasiveness and prejudicial possibilities of circumstantial evidence are well illustrated by the 1955 kidnapping and murder trial of Burton Abbott, who was sentenced to death in the gas chamber largely because the district attorney managed, despite the lack of any real foundation, to introduce the victim's unwashed undergarments and overwhelm the jury with their sight and smell.

[7] For an example of the questionableness of this rationale, one need turn no further than the Finch-Tregoff trial of 1960, in which one of the accused murderers was permitted to recite in open court his dying wife's apology for her own killing.

[8] Under the U.S. system of federalism, states and the national government are considered separate "sovereigns." Therefore, each can try a defendant for the same actions under different laws without violating the prohibition against double jeopardy. This principle permitted the federal government to prosecute four Los Angeles police officers in 1993 for violating the civil rights of Rodney King even though the defendants had been acquitted the prior year on state charges of using excessive force.

Trial of Julius and Ethel Rosenberg and Morton Sobell: 1951

Defendants: Julius and Ethel Rosenberg and Morton Sobell
Crime Charged: Conspiracy to commit wartime espionage
Chief Defense Lawyers: Alexander Bloch, Emanuel H. Bloch, Fyke Farmer,
John Finerty and Daniel Marshall for the Rosenbergs; Edward Kuntz and
Harold Phillips for Sobell **Chief Prosecutors:** Roy M. Cohn, John Foley,
James Kilsheimer III, Myles Lane, and Irving H. Saypol **Judge:** Irving R.
Kaufman **Place:** New York, New York **Dates of Trial:** March 6–29, 1951
Verdict: Guilty **Sentences:** Julius and Ethel Rosenberg: Death by
electrocution; Sobell: 30 years imprisonment

SIGNIFICANCE

The Rosenberg case, coming at the height of the anti-Communist hysteria in
America, produced the harshest result possible: the deaths of two defendants
who, as U.S. Supreme Court Justice Felix Frankfurter put it, "were tried for
conspiracy and sentenced for treason."

O n September 23, 1949, four years after the United States dropped atomic
bombs on Japan to end World War II, President Harry S. Truman announced that an atomic explosion had occurred in the Soviet Union. Until then,
most Americans had been confident that the Soviets, allies in World War II but
opponents in the Cold War that developed after 1946, could not make an atom
bomb. The resulting hysteria found Americans digging basement bomb shelters
and teaching schoolchildren how to duck under classroom desks.

The following February, a German-born nuclear physicist, Dr. Klaus
Fuchs, who had worked in America's Manhattan Project developing the atom
bomb, was arrested in England. In a "voluntary confession," he said he had
transmitted atomic information to the Soviet Union. He was tried and sentenced
to 14 years' imprisonment.

Meantime in America, former Communist spy Elizabeth Bentley told a
federal grand jury that one Harry Gold had been her successor as liaison with the
Soviets. Arrested on May 24, Gold confessed that he had served as courier in the

United States between Klaus Fuchs and the Soviets' New York Vice Consul, Anatoli Yakovlev, in 1944 and 1945.

Invited to Engage in Espionage

Gold implicated David Greenglass, who operated a machine shop in New York City with his brother-in-law, Julius Rosenberg. While in the army, Greenglass had worked in the Manhattan Project in Los Alamos, New Mexico, where the atom bomb was being constructed. Arrested, Greenglass confessed that he had accepted an invitation to engage in espionage presented by Rosenberg and his wife, Ethel, and conveyed to him by his own wife, Ruth, during a visit to New Mexico in 1944.

The Federal Bureau of Investigation (FBI) figured out that two of Julius Rosenberg's college classmates, Max Elitcher and Morton Sobell, had been part of a spy ring. Elitcher confessed, implicating Rosenberg and Sobell. The FBI also learned that Rosenberg had belonged to the Communist Party but apparently had dropped out of the party when his unit was dissolved in 1944.

Julius was arrested, then Ethel. Sobell, on a vacation trip to Mexico City with his family, was abducted by Mexican secret police, "deported" across the Texas border, and arrested.

Rather than espionage itself, the Rosenbergs and Sobell were charged with conspiracy to commit wartime espionage. The distinction was important. The standards for a conviction on conspiracy to commit wartime espionage are less onerous: Each conspirator may be liable for the acts of all the others, even without specific knowledge of them, and it is necessary only to prove that they conspired toward a given end, not that they succeeded.

Prosecution Witnesses Provide Details

The trial that opened on March 6, 1951, found both Rosenbergs and Morton Sobell as defendants. Sobell, however, never took the stand. The first prosecution witness, Max Elitcher, connected him with Julius Rosenberg, and another witness testified that the Sobell family trip to Mexico was actually a flight from the United States in which they used aliases.

At the outset, prosecutor Irving H. Saypol warned defense attorney Emanuel H. Bloch, "If your clients don't confess, they are doomed." Saypol's assistant, Roy Cohn, questioned David Greenglass, the first prosecution witness against the Rosenbergs. Greenglass testified that, while stationed at Los Alamos, he gave Julius Rosenberg crude sketches of two lens molds used to focus high-pressure shock waves converging in an implosion—molds that were "new and original" in 1945 and that still merited classified status in 1951.

Greenglass further related how he had obtained a "pretty good description" of the bomb that was dropped on Nagasaki for his brother-in-law. Altogether, he had written a dozen pages of description and drawn several sketches, for which Julius paid him $200.

Prosecutor Cohn proposed to introduce one of the sketches as Exhibit 8. Defense attorney Emanuel Bloch immediately demanded that the sketch be impounded "so that it remains secret from the court, the jury and counsel." Judge Irving R. Kaufman cleared the courtroom of press and spectators—thus encouraging the jury to think it was hearing "the secret of the atom bomb." Bloch admitted later that his move was made in the desperate hope of impressing the jury with his clients' concern for national security. The impounded testimony remained under security wraps until 1966.

Ruth Greenglass testified to Ethel Rosenberg's telling her in January 1945 that she was tired from typing David's notes for Julius Rosenberg, whom she said had promised to give the Greenglasses $6,000—and actually provided $5,000—for travel.

Judge Kaufman: Who was as it coming from?

Ruth: From the Russians, for us to leave the country.

Witness Harry Gold, who already had been convicted of espionage and sentenced to 30 years, testified that he had received orders from Soviet Vice Consul Yakovlev to go to Albuquerque, New Mexico, to meet a new contact named Greenglass. On a piece of paper that Yakovlev had handed him were the words: "Recognition signal. I come from Julius." He had picked up an envelope from Greenglass, he said, and taken it back to Yakovlev in Brooklyn, New York. In addition, he revealed that Greenglass had given him a telephone number, that of his "brother-in-law Julius," where Greenglass could be reached during his next furlough in New York.

With this strong testimony on the connection between the defendants and a Soviet agent, spectators and journalists alike looked eagerly to the defense attorney. But Bloch declared, "The defendants Rosenberg have no cross-examination of this witness."

Ex-Communist Elizabeth Bentley testified that, as confidential assistant to Jacob Golos when he was chief of Soviet espionage operations in the United States, she had received several phone calls as early as 1943 from a man who said, "This is Julius," and who wanted Golos to get in touch with him.

A Jell-O Box Cut in Two

Taking the stand in his own defense, Julius Rosenberg denied a number of accusations made by prosecution witnesses. A Rosenberg console table that both Greenglasses charged had been a gift from the Russians, and which they said was adapted for microfilming, had been purchased at Macy's department store for "about $21." He testified that he had not given Ruth $150 for a New Mexico trip in November 1944, had not received information on the atom bomb from Greenglass, and had not introduced Greenglass to a man in New York who sought details of the bomb. He denied introducing a neighbor to Greenglass as an espionage courier. He had not cut a Jell-O box into two irregularly shaped pieces and given one to Ruth to be used as a recognition signal if she was succeeded by another courier, and had not said, "The simplest things are the cleverest," when David admired the idea. When Judge Kaufman asked whether he had ever belonged to "any group" that had discussed the Russian system of government, he said, "Well, your Honor, I feel at this time that I refuse to answer a question that might tend to incriminate me."

On cross-examination, Rosenberg defended his denials. But in response to questions from prosecutor Irving Saypol about his conversations with David Greenglass about money, he referred to "blackmail." Judge Kaufman asked about that word.

> Rosenberg: He threatened me to get money. I considered it blackmailing.
>
> Kaufman: Did he say he would go to the authorities and tell them you were in a conspiracy to steal the atomic bomb secret?
>
> Rosenberg: No.

The defendant's choice of words, jury members said afterward, seemed like an admission of guilt.

Ethel Rosenberg tersely denied all accusations. Like her husband, she took the Fifth Amendment when asked any questions about the Communist Party. Following cross-examination, defense attorney Bloch said no more witnesses would be called.

On rebuttal, Saypol produced a surprise witness. Found by the FBI only the day before, photographer Ben Schneider testified that in June 1950 the Rosenberg family, saying they were going to France, had him shoot a large order of passport pictures. Another rebuttal witness testified that the Rosenbergs had told her the console table was "a gift from a friend," and that, despite the fact that it was their finest piece of furniture, they had kept it in a closet.

Ethel and Julius Rosenberg, separated by wire, following their conviction in March 1951. (AP/Wide World Photos)

(It was not put into evidence because the Rosenbergs said they did not know where it was at that time.)

The jury deliberated from late afternoon until nearly midnight, and for an hour the next morning, before finding both Rosenbergs and Sobell guilty as charged. A week later, on April 5, 1951, Judge Kaufman sentenced Sobell to 30 years and the couple to the electric chair.

Appeals Extended Two Years

The executions were stayed pending appeal. In February 1952, the U.S. Circuit Court of Appeals affirmed the convictions. In October, the U.S. Supreme Court refused to review the case, with Justice Hugo L. Black dissenting. December brought a motion for a new trial based on the contentions that photographer Schneider had committed perjury and Saypol had conducted an unfair trial. The motion was denied.

A motion to reduce the sentences as "cruel and excessive" because the charge was not treason and the indictments did not include "intent to injure the U.S." was denied.

In January, the executions were stayed again pending review by President Harry Truman of a petition for clemency. After Truman left office January 20, President Dwight D. Eisenhower refused clemency. Meantime, the National Committee to Secure Justice in the Rosenberg Case had mounted a worldwide effort to save them. It filled an eight-car train that took protesters from New York City to Ossining, where the Rosenbergs sat in Sing Sing's death row. Three million letters and telegrams flooded the White House. Pope Pius XII twice appealed for clemency. Albert Einstein and atomic scientist Harold C. Urey appealed.

A third execution date was stayed as appeals for clemency poured in from around the world. With Justices Black and William O. Douglas dissenting, the Supreme Court again refused to review the case. New evidence on June 8—the discovery of the missing console table in the apartment of Julius Rosenberg's mother—failed to justify a new trial or a stay of execution.

The Supreme Court again refused to review the case or stay the execution. Then, on June 17, Justice Douglas, questioning whether the defendants were correctly tried under the Espionage Act of 1917, granted a stay. The next day, Eisenhower received clemency appeals from hundreds of organizations representing millions of people in Europe, while U.S. embassies mounted police cordons to hold back the crowds, and the Supreme Court was recalled from vacation into unprecedented session. With Black, Douglas, and Felix M. Frankfurter dissenting, it vacated the Douglas stay. Eisenhower rejected another clemency plea.

The Rosenbergs ware executed precisely at sundown on June 19, 1953. That night, New York's Union Square filled with 10,000 protesters, while throngs in capitals around the world expressed their shock.

For decades after their execution, the guilt of the Rosenbergs remained a topic for discussion in books, newspapers, and magazines. However, in the mid-1990s most of the doubts about Julius Rosenberg's guilt were finally put to rest. In 1997, Alexander Feklisov, a retired KGB colonel, said that Julius Rosenberg served as an undercover agent for the Soviets between 1943 and 1946. Feklisov also said that Rosenberg had recruited other spies for the Soviets. Indeed, he even called Rosenberg a hero of the Soviet Union and "a true revolutionary who was willing to sacrifice himself for his beliefs." Feklisov added, however, that as far as he knew, Ethel Rosenberg was not an active agent for the Soviet Union.

Despite Feklisov's claims about Ethel Rosenberg, many feel that her reluctance to acknowledge her husband's role as a Soviet spy still made her compliant in his espionage.

—Bernard Ryan, Jr.

Suggestions for Further Reading

De Toledano, Ralph. *The Greatest Plot in History*. New York: Duell, Sloan and Pearce, 1963.

Fineberg, S. Andhill. *The Rosenberg Case: Fact and Fiction*. New York: Oceana, 1952.

Gardner, Virginia. *The Rosenberg Story*. New York: Masses and Mainstream, 1954.

Kramer, Hilton. "N.Y. Times Still Trying to Minimize Rosenbergs' Role as Soviet Spies." *Human Events* (May 16, 1997): 14.

Goldstein, Alvin H. *The Unquiet Death of Julius & Ethel Rosenberg*. New York: Lawrence Hill, 1975.

Hyde, H. Montgomery. *The Atom Bomb Spies*. New York: Atheneum, 1980.

Meeropol, Robert and Michael Meeropol. *We Are Your Sons: The Legacy of Ethel and Julius Rosenberg*. New York: Houghton Mifflin, 1975.

Nizer, Louis. *The Implosion Conspiracy*. New York: Doubleday & Co., 1973.

Pilat, Oliver. *The Atom Spies*. New York: G.P. Putnam's Sons, 1952.

Radosh, Ronald, and Joyce Milton. *The Rosenberg File: A Search for the Truth*. New York: Holt, Rinehart and Winston, 1983.

Reuben, William A. *The Atom Spy Hoax*. New York: Action Books, 1955.

Schneir, Walter and Miriam Schneir. *Invitation to an Inquest*. New York: Doubleday & Co., 1965.

Sharlit, Joseph H. *Fatal Error*. New York: Charles Scribner's Sons, 1989.

Sharp, Malcolm P. *Was Justice Done? The Rosenberg-Sobell Case*. New York: Monthly Review Press, 1956.

Sobell, Morton. *On Doing Time*. New York: Charles Scribner's Sons, 1974.

Wexley, John. *The Judgment of Julius and Ethel Rosenberg*. New York: Ballantine, 1977.

Whitehead, Don. *The FBI Story: A Report to the People*. New York: Random House, 1956.

Dennis v. U.S. Appeal: 1951

Appellants: Benjamin Davis, Eugene Dennis, John Gates, Gil Green, Gus Hall, Irving Potash, Jack Stachel, Robert Thompson, John Williamson, Henry Winston, and Carl Winter   **Defendant:** United States

Appellants Claims: That the Smith Act, under which appellants were found guilty, violates the First Amendment and other provisions of the Bill of Rights of the U.S. Constitution   **Chief Defense Lawyers:** Philip B. Perlman and Irving S. Shapiro   **Chief Lawyers for Appellants:** George W. Crockett, Jr., Abraham J. Isserman, and Harry Sacher   **Justices:** Hugo L. Black, Harold H. Burton, William O. Douglas, Felix Frankfurter, Robert H. Jackson, Sherman Minton; Stanley F. Reed, and Fred M. Vinson, (Tom C. Clark not participating)

Place: Washington, D.C.   **Date of Decision:** June 4, 1951

Decision: Provisions of the Smith Act prohibiting willful advocacy of overthrow of government by force or violence, organization of any group for that purpose and conspiracy to violate such provisions were held not to violate the First Amendment or other provisions of the Bill of Rights in a 6–2 decision.

SIGNIFICANCE

The U.S. Supreme Court's review of this case provides a classic example of how the guarantees of the First Amendment must be balanced against the nation's need, as prescribed by Congress, to protect itself. The opinions written by the justices contain memorable expressions of this paradox.

The Alien Registration Act of 1940, known as the Smith Act, made it a crime "to knowingly or willfully advocate, abet, advise, or teach the duty, necessity, desirability, or propriety of overthrowing or destroying any government in the United States by force or violence." Publication or display of printed matter teaching or advocating overthrow of the government was forbidden, as was organizing any group that teaches, advocates, or encourages overthrow of government by force. Also against the law was "knowing" membership in any group dedicated to that end.

In July 1948, Eugene Dennis, general secretary of the Communist Party in the United States, and 10 other party leaders were indicted for violating the

Smith Act by conspiring to organize groups that taught the overthrow of the government. In a sensational trial that lasted nine months and resulted in a record 16,000 pages of testimony, the defendants argued that First Amendment freedom of speech protected them. Finding that the leaders of the Communist Party were unwilling to work within the framework of democracy but, rather, intended to initiate a violent revolution, the jury convicted them all.

"Clear and Present Danger"

They appealed. The U.S. Court of Appeals applied the "clear and present danger test" of free speech that was originated by Supreme Court Justice Oliver Wendell Holmes in *Schenck v. U.S.* (see separate entry) in 1919, when Holmes, writing the opinion of the unanimous court, said:

> The question in every case is whether the words used are used in such circumstances and are of such a nature as to create a clear and present danger that they will bring about the substantive evils that Congress has a right to prevent.

Upholding the convictions, the court of appeals applied a "sliding scale" rule for the clear and present danger test, saying it "must ask whether the gravity of the 'evil,' discounted by its improbability, justifies such invasion of free speech as is necessary to avoid the danger."

The U.S. Supreme Court agreed to review the case from the standpoint of whether the Smith Act "inherently or as construed and applied in the instant case violates the First Amendment and other provisions of the Bill of Rights."

Without Justice Tom C. Clark participating, the eight other justices showed wide disagreement over how to measure the Smith Act's restraints on the freedom of speech and association guaranteed by the First Amendment. Chief Justice Fred M. Vinson, with Justices Harold H. Burton, Sherman Minton, and Stanley F. Reed, found that:

> Congress did not intend to eradicate the free discussion of political theories, to destroy the traditional rights of Americans to discuss and evaluate ideas without fear of governmental sanction [but] the formation of such a highly organized conspiracy, with rigidly disciplined members subject to call when the leaders felt that the time had come for action, coupled with the inflammable nature of world conditions, convince us that their convictions were justified. . . . It is the existence of the conspiracy which creates the danger. . . . If the ingredients of the reaction are present, we cannot bind the Government to wait until the catalyst is added.

> Petitioners intended to overthrow the Government of the United States as speedily as the circumstances would permit. Their conspiracy . . . created a "clear and present danger." . . . They were properly and constitutionally convicted for violation of the Smith Act.

"Beyond These Powers We Must Not Go"

Justice Felix Frankfurter concurred, but wrote:

It is a sobering fact that in sustaining the convictions before us we can hardly escape restriction on the interchange of ideas.

Congress, not the Supreme Court, he wrote, was responsible for reconciling such a conflict of values. The Court's job was to require substantial proof before conviction and to ensure fair procedures in enforcement of the law. "Beyond these powers," he wrote, "we must not go; we must scrupulously observe the narrow limits of judicial authority."

While also concurring, Justice Robert H. Jackson wrote:

The authors of the clear and present danger test never applied it to a case like this, nor would I. As proposed here, it means that the Communist plotting is protected during its period of incubation; its preliminary stages of organization and preparation are immune from the law; the Government can move only after imminent action is manifest, when it would, of course, be too late.

Concluded Jackson: "There is no constitutional right to gang up on the Government."

Dissenters Cite Prior Censorship

Justices William O. Douglas and Hugo L. Black wrote dissenting opinions. Said Black:

The indictment is that they conspired to use speech or newspapers to teach and advocate the forcible overthrow of the Government. No matter how it is worded, this is a virulent form of prior censorship of speech and press, which I believe the First Amendment forbids.

Douglas wrote:

We deal here with speech alone, not with speech *plus* acts of sabotage or unlawful conduct. Not a single seditious act is charged.

Free speech—the glory of our system of government—should not be sacrificed on anything less than plain and objective proof of danger that the evil advocated is imminent. On the record no one can say that petitioners and their converts are in such a strategic position as to have even the slightest chance of achieving their aims.

The majority opinion concluded that the Smith Act "does not violate the First Amendment or other provisions of the Bill of Rights." As a result, not only did Dennis and his fellow appellants serve time in prison, but 121 second-rank U.S. Communist Party officials were prosecuted for conspiracy under the Smith Act. Other individual party members also were prosecuted. In every case tried between 1951 and 1956, convictions were obtained. All were affirmed by courts of appeal. All were denied review by the Supreme Court.

—*Bernard Ryan, Jr.*

Suggestions for Further Reading

Belfrage, Cedric. *The American Inquisition, 1945–1960.* Indianapolis: Bobbs-Merrill Co., 1973.

Fast, Howard. *Being Red.* Boston: Houghton Mifflin, 1990.

Hoover, J. Edgar. *Masters of Deceit.* New York: Henry Holt, 1958.

Klehr, Harvey. *The Heyday of American Communism: The Depression Decade.* New York: Basic Books, 1984.

Mitford, Jessica. *A Fine Old Conflict.* New York: Alfred A. Knopf, 1971.

Witt, Elder. *Guide to the United States Supreme Court.* Washington: Congressional Quarterly Press, 1990.

Gertrude Morris Trial: 1952

Defendant: Gertrude Morris **Crime Charged:** Murder
Chief Defense Lawyer: Jake Ehrlich **Chief Prosecutor:** Norman Elkington
Judge: Harry J. Neubarth **Place:** San Francisco, California
Date of Trial: January 22–February 11, 1952 **Verdict:** Guilty:
manslaughter **Sentence:** 1–10 years

SIGNIFICANCE

In this extraordinary murder trial, a dynamic defense counsel found himself fighting not just the prosecution but his client as well.

On the afternoon of April 10, 1951, Gertrude and Milton Morris were trading barbs at the latter's office in San Francisco. This was nothing new. For the past 10 years their marriage had been a loveless, crumbling union. Today, when Milton, a well-to-do executive, wanted to know why Gertrude refused to drive the new Chevrolet coupe he had just bought her, Gertrude ran off, sobbing hysterically. That evening the fight continued at the Morrises' luxurious Lakeside home, until 6.30 P.M. when Milton announced he was leaving for good and began packing his bags. Before he could reach the door, a .32 caliber slug cut him down.

Gertrude Morris made no attempt to deny murder and when her trial opened on January 22, 1952, she seemed indifferent to her fate, laughing inanely while her counsel, Jake Ehrlich, succeeded in sitting a jury where women outnumbered men 3–1. The entire prosecution lasted only two-and-a-half hours, the briefest ever heard in a capital case at San Francisco's Superior Court. For Norman Elkington, chief assistant district attorney, the facts were plain: Morris admitted shooting her husband in the back, with premeditation, therefore it was first-degree murder.

Inspector Al Nelder told how Morris, when arrested at the crime scene, had been most insistent that there was no other woman involved. Nelder, puzzled, had asked, "Do you realize what you have done?"

"Yes, sir. I do now."

"Are you sorry?"

"I certainly am, because I loved him. Maybe that was my whole trouble, I loved him too much."

Another witness, neighbor George W. Jones, testified that Morris had knocked on his door at 2.00 A.M. and asked him to call the police. This timing was important because, on Morris's own admission, she had shot her husband some seven hours earlier and in all that time she had done nothing to help him. Ehrlich managed to mitigate this apparent callousness somewhat by getting Jones to agree that, in eight years, he had never heard the Morrises exchange a cross word.

Extraordinary Defense Opening

Then came Ehrlich's opening address, surely one of the most remarkable ever made by defense counsel. It amounted to a wholesale impeachment of his client's credibility, as he warned the jury that Morris would shape her story in such a way as to leave them no alternative but to send her to the gas chamber. Twice, in custody, she had attempted suicide, he said; now she was asking the state to finish the job. And contrary to what Morris had told the police, Ehrlich noted, she *did* suspect her husband of infidelity, in particular that he had been "intimate with his secretary."

Throughout all this Morris stared blankly into a handkerchief, emotionless. Then Ehrlich called her to the stand. A plain, plump woman, she sat with a wrinkled coat draped across her shoulders, answering questions wearily. After a few minutes she leaned towards the judge and murmured, "I want to plead guilty to first-degree murder."

Judge Harry J. Neubarth blinked. "What?" When she repeated her request the judge said, "You just tell the story. We'll let the jury decide what the verdict should be."

As Ehrlich fought to bring out details of the argument, Morris began to drift. Striding towards her, finger extended, Ehrlich shouted, "I've told you time and time again that I want you to tell how it happened, and not try to build it up so you'll be executed."

Straight away, Elkington was on his feet, objecting that counsel was leading the witness. In what was always a rowdy trial, the crowded gallery urged the rivals on. Amidst the bedlam, Ehrlich bellowed, "It is my moral duty to protect this woman. This woman is trying to destroy herself!"

Ehrlich explained that Morris's problems stemmed from an overnight train journey she and her husband had taken in 1941. Using a diagram that showed sleeping arrangements on the Pullman car, Ehrlich told how Gertrude had surprised Milton wrestling with the door to the adjoining compartment door. Behind that door was Rose Goolo, Milton's attractive, young secretary. Although Milton insisted that Gertrude had completely misinterpreted his actions, she was not convinced. Ten years on, when questioned by Ehrlich about this incident, Morris muttered, "I still think there was something wrong there."

On cross-examination she lapsed back into a dull torpor, repeatedly answering, "Yes," to every question posed by Elkington. "That's right, keep it up," jeered Ehrlich, "She'll say 'yes' to anything you ask her." When Ehrlich complained that "no man, no lawyer living ever heard anything like this," Morris called him over. "Can't we plead guilty to murder now, and have it over with?"

"No," snapped Ehrlich.

Defendant Flees Courtroom

When Rose Goolo took the stand, Morris fled hysterically into the judge's chambers, the only time she ever showed any interest or animation during the trial. Brought back sobbing into court, she heard Goolo admit that Milton Morris drove her to work, took her out to lunch "three or four times a week," and that he drove her home each night after work.

"What was your relationship with Morris?" demanded Ehrlich.

"I was his secretary."

"Any more than that?"

"No," she said primly, though later she conceded that they were "friends" and that Milton Morris bought her perfume.

In his closing speech it was noticeable that Elkington refrained from asking for the death penalty. But that didn't prevent him from heaping scorn on what he termed "Mr. Ehrlich's story." This prompted the pugnacious Ehrlich to square up to his much bigger opponent and shout, "If you indicate that I make up stories, Mr. Elkington, you are a common, ordinary street liar." Again, the gallery roared its approval.

After calm had been restored, Elkington got back on track. "She shot him . . . she saw him fall. She heard him cry, 'Get a doctor.' And she did not get a doctor. She walked away and let him bleed to death." Then Elkington delivered an earnest plea to the jury to exercise caution when heeding Ehrlich. "He is resourceful. He is an attorney you can count on to come up with an unexpected defense. If it succeeds, you will hear about it in the future as the clever defense in the Morris Case."

Elkington had good cause for concern. Ehrlich's peroration—an emotion-packed saga of a marriage gone wrong—was superb, culminating in a scornful assault on Milton Morris' attempts to placate his distraught wife with offers of jewelry. "What good is it to give a diamond ring if, as Mrs. Morris testified, he never put his arms around her . . . She didn't want any diamond ring, she wanted her husband." More than one juror had to wipe away a tear by the time Ehrlich sat down.

On February 11, 1952, Gertrude Morris was convicted of manslaughter, and she later received a jail term of 1–10 years. Allegedly, upon hearing the verdict, she turned to the flamboyant Ehrlich and said, "You are a very talented man, you missed your vocation on the stage . . . But maybe hanging [sic] would have been the best thing."

—Colin Evans

Suggestions for Further Reading

Ehrlich, J.W. *A Life in My Hands*. New York: G.P. Putnam's Sons, 1965.

Noble, John Wesley and Bernard Averbuch. *Never Plead Guilty*. New York: Farrar, Strauss, Cudahy, 1955.

Robert W. Grow Court-Martial: 1952

Defendant: Robert W. Grow **Crimes Charged:** The compromising of classified security information by failing to provide adequate security for the protection of a personal diary **Chief Defense Lawyer:** Robert E. Joseph **Presiding Officer:** John S. Dwinell **Court:** Hubert D. Hoover and seven other court members **Place:** Washington, D.C. **Date of Trial:** July 23–29, 1952 **Verdict:** Guilty on five counts

SIGNIFICANCE

The Robert Grow trial was the first high-profile court-martial under the new Uniform Code of Military Justice and demonstrated that despite attempts to eliminate it, command influence still affected court-martial proceedings.

Major General Robert W. Grow was a veteran army officer who had commanded an armored division in World War II and had been instrumental in implementing early Cold War containment policy in Iran. In 1950 he became senior U.S. military attache to Moscow. In 1952 he made a mistake that resulted in his court-martial, and became an international cause celebre. East German agents photographed Grow's personal diary while he was in West Germany attending a conference. While in Frankfurt he stayed at a U.S. Army guest house that employed German personnel, and which was later found to have woefully lax security. Grow was charged with displaying poor judgment by keeping a diary that contained classified information without taking proper precautions to secure it.

Parts of Diary Published

The public learned of the problem in a highly embarrassing way. A British defector, Richard Squires, reproduced photographs of parts of the diary in a book published in East Germany called *On the War Path*. Squires claimed that these photographs proved Grow was calling for immediate war against the Soviet Union. Squires highlighted such phrases as, "It seems to me the time is ripe for a blow this year," and the United States should "hit below the belt," to prove that Grow was part of an international conspiracy to unleash another world war.

American newspapers paid great attention to the story of the war-mongering general, to the army's great embarrassment. The Pentagon, rather than dismissing the allegations as propaganda, added fuel to the fire when the army chief of information confirmed the diary's authenticity and declared it had been photographed in "an inside job." He did not reveal, and possibly did not know, that some of the excerpts were total fabrications, and that Squires had twisted others to give a false impression of Grow's views. After consulting the State Department, Lieutenant General Maxwell D. Taylor, deputy chief of staff for operations and administration, and Major General Alexander Bolling, assistant chief of staff for intelligence, decided to investigate. Eventually the army gave Grow the option of voluntary retirement or facing a court-martial. Grow, who did not believe that his diary contained any classified information, chose court-martial. He argued that the Soviets' publication of the extracts proved that the diary had no intelligence value. To Grow's way of thinking there was nothing in his diary not already well-known to Soviet State Security. Instead, he believed that publication was a ploy to get him out of Moscow because of his success as an intelligence observer.

Grow Is Charged

The army chose not to challenge the truth of Squires's account. The chief of staff had ordered Grow not to make any public statements, so there was no official contradiction of Squires's accusations. The lack of any rebuttal led to public and congressional pressure to remove Grow from the army. In April, despite the opposition of the State Department and the Central Intelligence Agency (CIA), Grow was charged under Army Regulation 380–5. The case against Grow was classified as "secret," which allowed the army to exclude the press from the trial. The army publicly stated that it had charged Grow with improperly recording classified information in private records and failing to safeguard that information.

Grow selected a Judge Advocate General (JAG) Corps attorney, Colonel Robert E. Joseph, to defend him, even though the recently enacted Uniform Code of Military Justice allowed him to have a civilian attorney. Joseph immediately ran into trouble in mounting a defense. His request to declassify the charge sheet without deletion or alteration so he could prepare for trial was denied, as were his repeated requests to be temporarily transferred to Europe to interview potential witnesses. During the pretrial investigation—a form of preliminary hearing—Joseph attacked the army's case on two points. He alleged that the inspector general had improperly taken the diary from Grow in violation of his Fourth Amendment rights, and that the officer who signed the charge sheet, Colonel C. Robert Bard, was not Grow's actual accuser. When Joseph asked Bard who had told him to sign the charge sheet, Bard replied that Ernest Brannon, the judge advocate general, had ordered him to do it, but Brannon refused to say who had ordered him to proceed against Grow, claiming this information was covered by attorney-client privilege. Joseph insisted that Grow had the right to know the identity of his real accuser, but this argument got him nowhere. Other shadows arose. When Joseph questioned Bard about the specifications he had prepared concerning the classification of military information, Bard quickly admitted he was not a security expert and that he was an "Indian" and not a "Chief," which further suggested improper command influence over the proceedings.

Joseph faced other roadblocks, although the pretrial investigation was supposed to be a "thorough and impartial investigation of all matters." Joseph was unable to view all the pertinent documents, and several of his requests for copies were denied. He moved, unsuccessfully, to suppress and return the diary, pointing out that Generals Dwight Eisenhower, Mark Clark, and Omar Bradley had all kept—and published—personal journals. He also questioned General Bolling about his or General Taylor's influence over the proceedings. Bolling refused to answer any questions about his conversations with Taylor, and Taylor was equally uncooperative.

After the pretrial investigation, the army filed an additional charge against Grow, saying his recording of reported plans of the Soviet Far Eastern Revolutionary Committee for a large offensive in Korea in April 1951 by the Chinese Army was a violation of Article 134 of the UCMJ. On May 31, 1952, Colonel Frederick Matthews, the pretrial investigating officer, recommended a general court-martial. Like the pretrial hearing, the court-martial was closed to the public.

During the trial, Joseph was unable to call General Bolling, who was said to be "unavailable," and he only received a prepared stipulation from General Taylor. The trial proceeded along the same lines as the pretrial investigation. Grow's counsel moved to dismiss all charges and specifications for lack of jurisdiction, claiming that the convening authority, General Brooks of the Second Army, was inferior in rank and command to the actual accuser, (Bolling, Taylor, or the Secretary of the Army). The law officer, General Hubert Hoover, denied both motions. During the trial, Grow's counsel again objected to the diary's being entered into evidence. The prosecutor maintained that Grow had surrendered it voluntarily, so that there had been no unlawful seizure. The law officer agreed that the diary was admissible.

Debate on the Classification of the Diary

From this point on, argument about the security classification of the diary dominated the proceedings. Prosecution witnesses maintained the contents were "secret" and defense witnesses claimed they were common knowledge in Moscow diplomatic circles. On July 29, Grow himself took the stand, swearing that he had not recorded anything that was not widely known. "I treated the diary in about the same manner as you would treat a personal letter," he commented. "I did not treat it in the sense of a military document, but rather in the sense of a personal classified document." But this statement, coupled with his January 18, 1952, remark that the diary had been photographed "in Germany when my security was lax," counted against him. With deliberations of less than an hour, the court convicted him of two counts of dereliction of duty and two counts of security infractions. He was reprimanded and suspended from command for six months. Only after the trial did the public discover that many of the sentiments that Squires attributed to Grow were forgeries. The case was appealed and ultimately came before President Eisenhower in 1957, who approved the findings but remitted the sentence.

Grow's trial took place during the Korean War and the Red Scare. It displayed the army's lack of finesse in dealing with the effects of Soviet espionage and propaganda, and its desire to be seen to act severely against security breeches. It also demonstrated the persistence of command influence over military proceedings.

— Carol Willcox Melton

Suggestions for Further Reading

Aycock, William B., and Seymour W. Wurfel. *Military Law under the Uniform Code of Military Justice.* Chapel Hill: University of North Carolina Press, 1955.

Generous, William T., Jr. *Sword and Scales: The Development of the Uniform Code of Military Justice.* Port Washington, N.Y.: Kennikat Press, 1973.

Hofmann, George F. *Cold War Casualty: The Court-Martial of Major General Robert W. Grow.* Kent, Ohio: The Kent State University Press, 1993.

Reynolds v. Pegler: 1954

Plaintiff: Quentin Reynolds **Defendants:** Westbrook Pegler, The Hearst Corporation, and Hearst Consolidated Publications **Plaintiff Claims:** That a certain column published by the defendants on November 29, 1949 libeled the plaintiff **Chief Defense Lawyer:** Charles Henry
Chief Lawyers for Plaintiff: Walter S. Beck, Paul Martinson, and Louis Nizer
Judge: Edward Weinfeld **Place:** New York, New York
Dates of Trial: May 10–July 22, 1954 **Verdict:** Against all defendants: Reynolds awarded $1 in compensatory damages and $175,000 in punitive damages

SIGNIFICANCE

The lopsided award of a huge amount of punitive damages in connection with an award of only nominal compensatory damages was the largest in history at the time. The decision sent a clear signal to the publishing industry that it would be held accountable for the libelous acts of its writers and reporters.

William Randolph Hearst, the publishing magnate, built an empire by publishing newspapers that had stories the public wanted to read. Hearst made sure that his papers had the best editors, writers and reporters money could buy. One of Hearst's favorite writers was Westbrook Pegler, who wrote articles for the King Features Syndicate of The Hearst Corporation, which in turn sold the articles to other Hearst papers. In particular, King Features sold Pegler articles to the *New York Journal-American,* a New York City newspaper owned by Hearst Consolidated Publications.

Hearst died in 1945, nearly 90 years old, but Pegler remained with the Hearst organization. Pegler's articles could be very vindictive and biting, and in 1949 Pegler was accused of using his writing ability to hurt an old friend. On November 20, 1949, a writer for the *New York Herald Tribune Book Review* named Quentin Reynolds wrote a review of Dale Kramer's book *The Heywood Broun His Friends Recall.* Heywood Broun, himself a writer, had once been a friend of Pegler but, during the 1930s, the two men had a falling-out. In 1939, Pegler wrote a scathing attack on Broun's works. According to Kramer, Broun was so upset by Pegler's attack that Broun was unable to recover from a minor illness and died.

Despite the fact that the events described in Kramer's book were over 10 years old, Pegler took offense at Reynolds' review. On November 29, 1949 Pegler's article, "On Heywood Broun and Quentin Reynolds," was published in the *Journal-American*. Pegler's article had little to do with any critique of Reynolds' review, and was instead a wholesale assassination of Reynolds' character. Without any substantiation, Pegler said: that Reynolds and his girl-friend made a habit of appearing nude in public; that on the way to Heywood Broun's funeral Reynolds had proposed marriage to the widow, Connie Broun; that Reynolds had been a profiteer during World War II; that while working as a war correspondent in London, Reynolds had been a coward; and so forth. Pegler also called Reynolds a degenerate who associated with communists, blacks and others Pegler regarded as undesirables.

Judge Edward Weinfeld was convinced that Pegler's articles libeled Quentin Reynolds. (AP/ Wide World Photos)

Reynolds Sues for Libel

After the publication of Pegler's article, Reynolds sued Pegler, The Hearst Corporation and Hearst Consolidated Publications for libel. Reynolds' lawyers were Walter S. Beck, Paul Martinson, and Louis Nizer. The defendants' chief lawyer was Charles Henry, and the judge was Edward Weinfeld. The trial began on May 10, 1954.

Aware that truth was a defense to the charge of libel, Nizer showed that Pegler's allegations in the article could not possibly be true. Nizer presented witnesses who testified that Reynolds could not have proposed to Connie Broun because she had been asleep and in the company of others all the way to the funeral, that Reynolds had not been a war profiteer, that Reynolds' war record in fact showed considerable heroism rather than cowardice, and so on. Weinfeld was convinced, and he instructed the jury that they were to take it as a given that Pegler's article was libelous:

> [T]hat column read in its entirety, I charge you as a matter of law, is defamatory.

Henry tried his best to present plausible justifications for Pegler's accusations, but his excuses came across sounding rather thin. For example, Henry tried to explain away Pegler's charge that Reynolds had proposed to Connie Broun as possibly referring to the same high-minded spirit as Moses's ancient laws, which in biblical times placed:

> . . . upon a brother the duty of proposing to his dead brother's widow.

The jury was not convinced. On July 22, 1954, the jurors returned a guilty verdict against all three defendants. Given the nature of Pegler's article and Weinfeld's instructions, this verdict was not surprising. What was surprising, however, was the amount of damages the jury awarded to Reynolds, which were of two types. The first type was the compensatory damages, which represented compensation to Reynolds for the damage, emotional and otherwise, caused by Pegler's vicious public attack on his character. As is common in such cases, the dollar value of the damage done was hard to determine and so the jury gave a nominal award of just one dollar. The second type of damages was punitive, which represented the punishment that the jury saw fit to impose on the defendants for having published the article.

The amount of punitive damages rocked the publishing industry, for at the time it was the largest award of its kind in American history. The jury awarded Reynolds $100,000 against Pegler, $50,000 against The Hearst Corporation, and $25,000 against Hearst Consolidated Publications, for a total of $175,000 in punitive damages. Although the size of the award was unprecedented, it was financially a drop in the bucket to the massive Hearst organization. The disturbing part, however, was that publishers could now be held financially liable for the libels and other unlawful acts of their writers. The defendants promptly appealed.

On February 16–17, 1955, the U.S. Court of Appeals for the Second Circuit heard the parties' arguments. The court issued its decision on June 7 of the same year. The court not only upheld the verdict against Pegler and the other defendants, but it reaffirmed the principle that publishers could be held accountable for the acts of their writers:

> The mere fact that there was no proof of personal ill-will or animosity on the part of any of the corporate executives toward plaintiff does not preclude an award of punitive damages. Malice may be inferred from the very violence and vituperation apparent upon the face of the libel itself, especially where, as here, officers or employees of each corporate defendant had full opportunity to and were under a duty to exercise editorial supervision for purposes of revision, but permitted the publication of the column without investigation, delay or any alteration whatever of its contents. The jury may well have found on this evidence a wanton or reckless indifference to plaintiff's rights.

Thus, the court was telling the Hearst companies in particular and the publishing industry in general that if writers like Pegler wrote vicious and personal articles, the publishers would be held liable if they did not exercise proper editorial control over potentially defamatory material. The defendants exercised their final avenue of appeal, namely a petition for a writ of *certiorari* to the Supreme Court, which was denied on October 10, 1955.

The case of *Reynolds v. Pegler*, with its stupendous award of punitive damages in relation to the nominal compensatory damages, sent a danger signal throughout the publishing industry. This new awareness of potential liability changed forever the relationship between publishers, writers, and reporters.

From this date forward, publishers and editors would take greater care to make sure that their publications were accurate and nondefamatory.

—Stephen G. Christianson

Suggestions for Further Reading

Farr, Finis. *Fair Enough: The Life of Westbrook Pegler.* New Rochelle, N.Y.: Arlington House Publishers, 1975.

Nizer, Louis. *My Life in Court.* Garden City, N.Y.: Doubleday & Co., 1961.

Pilat, Oliver Ramsay. *Pegler, Angry Man of the Press.* Boston: Beacon Press, 1963.

Reynolds, Quentin. *By Quentin Reynolds.* New York: McGraw-Hill, 1963.

Brown v. Board of Education: 1954

Appellants: Several parents of African-American children of elementary school age in Topeka, Kansas   **Defendant:** Board of Education of Topeka, Kansas   **Appellants Claim:** That the segregation of white and African-American children in the public schools of Topeka solely on the basis of race denied the African-American children equal protection under the law guaranteed by the Fourteenth Amendment   **Chief Defense Lawyers:** Harold R. Fatzer and Paul E. Wilson   **Chief Lawyers for Appellants:** Robert L. Carter, Thurgood Marshall, Spottswood W. Robinson, and Charles S. Scott   **Justices:** Hugo L. Black, Harold H. Burton, Thomas C. Clark, William O. Douglas, Felix Frankfurter, Robert H. Jackson, Sherman Minton, Stanley F. Reed, and Earl Warren   **Place:** Washington, D.C.   **Date of Decision:** May 17, 1954   **Decision:** Segregated schools violate the equal protection clause of the Fourteenth Amendment

SIGNIFICANCE

Brown v. Board of Education held that segregated schools were unconstitutional, overturning the "separate but equal" doctrine of *Plessy v. Ferguson* (1896).

Sometimes in history, events of great importance happen unexpectedly to modest men. Such was the case with Oliver Brown, whose desire that his children be able to attend the public school closest to their home resulted in a fundamental transformation of race relations in the United States.

Brown was born in 1919 and lived in Topeka, Kansas, where he worked as a welder for a railroad. Brown's family literally lived on the wrong side of the tracks: their house was close to Brown's place of work, and the neighborhood bordered on a major switchyard. Not only could the Brown family hear the trains day and night, but because the Topeka school system was segregated, the Brown children had to walk through the switchyard to get to the black school a mile away. There was another school only seven blocks away, but it was exclusively for white children.

In September 1950, when his daughter Linda was to enter the third grade, Brown took her to the whites-only school and tried to enroll her. Brown had no history of racial activism, and outside of work his only major activity was serving as an assistant pastor in the local church. He was simply tired of seeing his daughter being forced to go through the switchyard to go to a school far from home because she was black. The principal of the white school refused to enroll Brown's daughter. Brown sought help from McKinley Burnett, head of the local branch of the National Association for the Advancement of Colored People, or NAACP.

NAACP Takes on Topeka Board of Education

Burnett's organization had wanted to challenge segregation for quite some time, but until Brown came to them they had never had the right plaintiff at the right time. Segregation, in the public schools and elsewhere, was a fact of life in Topeka as in so many other places and few were willing to challenge it. Now that he had Brown, who was joined by several other black parents in Topeka with children in blacks-only public schools, Burnett and the NAACP decided that the time was ripe for legal action.

On March 22, 1951, Brown's NAACP lawyers filed a lawsuit in the U.S. District Court for the District of Kansas, requesting an injunction forbidding Topeka from continuing to segregate its public schools. The court tried the case June 25–26, 1951. Brown and the other black parents testified to the fact that their children were denied admission to white schools. One parent, Silas Fleming, explained why he and the other parents wanted to get their children into the white schools:

> It wasn't to cast any insinuations that our teachers are not capable of teaching our children because they are supreme, extremely intelligent and are capable of teaching my kids or white kids or black kids. But my point was that not only I and my children are craving light: the entire colored race is craving light, and the only way to reach the light is to start our children together in their infancy and they come up together.

Next, the court listened to expert witnesses who testified that segregated schools were inherently unequal because separation sent a message to black children that they were inferior. This stigma could never be eliminated from a segregated school system, as Dr. Hugh W. Speer, chairman of the University of Kansas City's department of elementary school education, testified:

> For example, if the colored children are denied the experience in school of associating with white children, who represent 90 percent of our national society in which these colored children must live, then the colored child's curriculum is being greatly curtailed. The Topeka curriculum or any school curriculum cannot be equal under segregation.

The Board of Education's lawyers retorted that since most restaurants, bathrooms and public facilities in Kansas City also were segregated, segregated schools were only preparing black children for the realities of life as black adults. Segregation pervaded every aspect of life in Topeka as in so many other places, and it was beyond the court's jurisdiction to act on anything in this one lawsuit but the legality of school segregation. The board's argument did not convince the judges. The board was assuming that segregation was a natural and desirable way of life for the races to live.

Next, the board argued that segregated schools did not necessarily result in any detrimental effect. After all, hadn't Frederick Douglass, Booker T. Washington, and George Washington Carver, among other great African-Americans, achieved so much in the face of obstacles far worse than segregated educational facilities? The fallacy in this argument was obvious, however. While some exceptional people were capable of rising above any adversity, for the majority of African-Americans the discriminatory effect of segregation meant a lessening of opportunities. Dr. Horace B. English, a psychology professor at Ohio State University, testified:

> There is a tendency for us to live up to, or perhaps I should say down to, social expectations and to learn what people say we can learn, and legal segregation definitely depresses the Negro's expectancy and is therefore prejudicial to his learning.

On August 3, 1951, the court issued its decision. The three judges noted that the leading Supreme Court opinion on public school segregation was the 1896 case *Plessy v. Ferguson*. (See separate entry.) *Plessy* legitimized the doctrine of "separate but equal" school systems for blacks and whites, and *Plessy* had not been overturned by the Supreme Court or even seriously questioned, despite some nibbling away at the doctrine's edges in a few recent cases. Therefore, regardless of the experts' testimony that separate-but-equal schools were inherently impossible, the court felt compelled to deny Brown and the other plaintiffs their request for an injunction. The court made it clear, however, that it did not relish its role in upholding Topeka's segregation:

> Segregation of white and colored children in public schools has a detrimental effect upon the colored children. The impact is greater when it has the sanction of the law; for the policy of separating the races is usually interpreted as denoting the inferiority of the Negro group. A sense of inferiority affects the motivation of a child to learn. Segregation with the sanction of law, therefore, has a tendency to [retard] the educational and mental development of Negro children and to deprive them of some of the benefits they would receive in a racial[ly] integrated school system.

Fight Goes to Supreme Court

On October 1, 1951, the plaintiffs filed a petition for appeal. Under certain special procedural rules, they were able to go directly to the U.S. Supreme Court instead of going through a federal court of appeals. On June 9, 1952, the Supreme Court put the case on its docket and consolidated it with several other cases from across the country where school segregation policies were being challenged. The Court scheduled a hearing for December 9, 1952, in Washington, D.C., during which the plaintiffs and the board of education would present their arguments.

Harold R. Fatzer and Paul E. Wilson represented the board. Brown and the other plaintiffs had a number of attorneys representing them at both the trial in the district court and now before the Supreme Court, all sponsored by the NAACP. The chief plaintiffs' lawyers were Robert L. Carter, Thurgood Marshall, Spottswood W. Robinson, and Charles S. Scott. The Supreme Court justices were Hugo L. Black, Harold H. Burton, Thomas C. Clark, William O. Douglas, Felix Frankfurter, Robert H. Jackson, Sherman Minton, Stanley F. Reed, and Earl Warren.

The December 9, 1952, hearing ended in a stalemate. After listening to both sides reiterate the arguments they had made before the district court, the Supreme Court ordered another hearing, to take place December 8, 1953. The Court directed the parties to confine their re-argument to certain specific issues that especially concerned the justices, dealing mostly with the ratification of the Fourteenth Amendment by the states in 1868. Since the plaintiffs' lawsuit rested on the equal protection clause of this amendment, the Court wanted to know more about the circumstances surrounding the Amendment's adoption. For example, the Court was interested in the debates in Congress and in the state legislatures, the views of the proponents and opponents of the amendment, and existing segregation practices. Although the NAACP, Brown and the other plaintiffs were disappointed that their case would be on hold for another year, the Court's order for re-argument signaled its willingness to reconsider the separate-but-equal doctrine of *Plessy*.

Chief Justice Earl Warren, who influenced the unanimous outcome *Brown v. Board of Education*. (Courtesy, National Archives)

Court Throws Out *Plessy;* Declares Segregation Illegal

After the December 8, 1953, re-argument, the Court announced its decision on May 17, 1954. According to the published opinion, the re-argument had not revealed anything that shed light on whether the adoption of the Fourteenth Amendment had been specifically intended to preclude segregated schools:

> Even in the North, the conditions of public education did not approximate those existing today. The curriculum was usually rudimentary; ungraded schools were common in rural areas; the school term was but three months a year in many states; and compulsory school attendance was virtually unknown. As a consequence, it is not surprising that there should be so little in the history of the Fourteenth Amendment relating to its intended effect on public education.

Instead, the Court endorsed the plaintiffs' central thesis that segregation was inherently unequal no matter how much effort the school system made to ensure that black and white schools had equivalent facilities, staffing, books, buses, and so forth. The Court reviewed some recent cases in which it had cautiously made an exception to *Plessy* where certain graduate schools were involved. In those cases, the Court said that segregation was unequal because the blacks' professional careers were hurt by the stigma of having attended schools considered to be inferior, and where they did not have the opportunity to make contacts or have intellectual discourse with their white counterparts. With this support, the Court was ready to declare that all segregation in public schools was unconstitutional:

> We conclude that in the field of public education the doctrine of "separate but equal" has no place. Separate educational facilities are inherently unequal. Therefore, we hold that the plaintiffs and others similarly situated for whom the actions have been brought are, by reason of the segregation complained of, deprived of the equal protection of the laws guaranteed by the Fourteenth Amendment.

After nearly 60 years of legalized discrimination, the Court had thrown out *Plessy v. Ferguson*. It would take 20 years for the Court's decision to be fully implemented, however, long after Oliver Brown died in 1961. In 1955, the Court said that all American school systems must desegregate "with all deliberate speed," but most local schools in the South did nothing until they were brought to court one by one. The process dragged on throughout the rest of the 1950s, during the '60s, and into the early '70s. Meanwhile, particularly during the civil rights movement of the 1960s, the Court acted to strike down all the other forms of legal segregation in American society, from bus stations and public libraries to restrooms.

The process was painful and often violent, frequently accompanied by federal intervention and mass demonstrations. By the 1970s, however, legal desegregation was a fact. *Brown v. Board of Education* not only made it possible to demolish segregated public school systems, but it was the landmark that served as a catalyst for further antidiscrimination decision by the Supreme Court.

—Stephen G. Christianson

Suggestions for Further Reading

"The Day Race Relations Changed Forever: U.S. Supreme Court Desegregation Decision of May 17, 1954 Was Hailed by Many as the 'Second Emancipation Proclamation.'" *Ebony* (May 1985): 108–112.

Kluger, Richard. *Simple Justice: the History of Brown v. Board of Education and Black America's Struggle for Equality*. New York: Alfred A. Knopf, 1976.

Orlich, Donald C. "Brown v. Board of Education: Time for a Reassessment." *Phi Delta Kappan* (April 1991): 631–632.

Sudo, Phil. "Five Little People Who Changed U.S. History." *Scholastic Update* (January 1990): 8–10.

White, Jack E. "The Heirs of Oliver Brown." *Time* (July 6, 1987): 88–89.

Samuel Sheppard Trials: 1954 and 1966

Defendant: Samuel Sheppard   **Crime Charged:** Murder
Chief Defense Lawyers: First trial: William J. Corrigan, William Corrigan, Jr.,
Fred Garmone, and Arthur E. Petersilge; Second trial: F. Lee Bailey
Chief Prosecutors: First trial: Saul S. Danaceau, John J. Mahon, and
Thomas J. Parrino; Second trial: John Corrigan   **Judges:** First trial: Edward
C. Blythin; Second trial: Francis J. Talty   **Place:** Cleveland, Ohio
Dates of Trials: October 18–December 21, 1954; October 24–November 16,
1966   **Verdicts:** First trial: Guilty, second-degree homicide; Second trial: Not
guilty   **Sentence:** First trial: Life imprisonment

SIGNIFICANCE
In this most sensational American murder case of the 1950s, pretrial prejudice
and adverse media publicity conspired to deprive the defendant of his constitutional rights.

Balancing First Amendment rights to free speech against a defendant's right
to a fair trial has never been easy, but in covering the Sam Sheppard trial,
Cleveland's major newspapers trampled these distinctions underfoot. The
abominations they perpetrated on a local level, radio columnist Walter Winchell
paralleled nationally, until virtually everyone in America was convinced of
Sheppard's guilt before even a word of testimony was heard. To be sure, his
story sounded unlikely, but improbability does not necessarily imply guilt. Life
is strange and so, very often, is death.

This amazing saga had its beginnings on July 3, 1954, when Dr. Samuel
Sheppard, an affluent 30-year-old osteopath, and his pregnant wife Marilyn,
invited their neighbors, the Ahearns, over for drinks at their home on the shores
of Lake Erie. While the others watched TV, Sheppard dozed on the couch. Just
after midnight the Ahearns left. Sam Sheppard remained sleeping on the couch
while Marilyn Sheppard went to bed.

Sometime later, according to his version of events, Sheppard heard a loud
moan or scream. He rushed upstairs to the bedroom and saw "a white form"
standing beside the bed. Then everything went black. When he regained
consciousness, Sheppard realized he had been clubbed on the neck. He stum-
bled across to the bed where his wife lay unmoving. A sudden noise sent him

racing downstairs. By the rear door he spotted "a man with bushy hair." He pursued the intruder onto the beach and tackled him from behind. During the struggle Sheppard blacked out again. This time when he came to, he was partially immersed in the waters of Lake Erie. Groggily, he staggered back to the house and phoned for help.

Police found Marilyn Sheppard's half-nude body lying in a pool of blood, her head and face smashed to a pulp. Downstairs, a writing desk had been ransacked and the contents of Sheppard's medical bag lay strewn across the floor. Apparently, someone had come to rob the house and ended up killing Marilyn Sheppard.

Meantime, Sam Sheppard had been whisked away by his two brothers to the hospital they owned jointly. It was this incident, more than any other, which unleashed the tidal wave of venomous press coverage that swamped this case, as circulation-hungry editors clamored that the wealthy "Sheppard Boys" had closed ranks to protect their own.

The discovery at the house of a canvas bag, containing Sheppard's wristwatch, key chain and key, and a fraternity ring, gave rise to speculation that he had faked a robbery to conceal murder. When details of an extramarital affair emerged, official suspicion heightened. Urged on by an increasingly vituperative Cleveland press, police arrested Sheppard and charged him with murder.

Samuel Sheppard, the subject of the most sensational murder case of the 1950s. (AP/Wide World Photos)

The Carnival Begins

Amid unprecedented ballyhoo, on Monday, October 18, the state of Ohio opened its case against Sheppard. Judge Edward Blythin set the tone early. A candidate for re-election in the upcoming November ballot, he shamelessly curried favor with the press, issuing handwritten passes for the elite like Dorothy Kilgallen and Bob Considine, even providing them their own special table at which to sit. Blythin presided over a madcap bazaar of popping flash bulbs, vindictive reporters and hideous uproar, what the *New York Times* would later describe as "a Roman circus."

Prosecutor John Mahon made the most of what was a wafer-thin case. In the absence of any direct evidence against the defendant, other than he was in the house when Marilyn Sheppard was killed, Mahon emphasized the inconsistencies in Sam Sheppard's story. Why was there no sand in his hair when he claimed to have been sprawled on the beach? Where was the T-shirt that he had been wearing? Had bloodstains received during the attack forced him to destroy it? And why would a burglar first take the belongings in the canvas bag and then ditch them? Besides which, said Mahon, "Police . . . could find no evidence that anyone had broken in." For motive, Mahon pointed to Sheppard's affair with Susan Hayes, a lab technician at the family hospital, as reason enough for him to want to be rid of his wife.

Initially, the lack of a murder weapon posed problems for the prosecution, but Cuyahoga County Coroner Samuel R. Gerber neatly circumvented this discrepancy by telling the court that a bloody imprint found on the pillow beneath Marilyn Sheppard's head was made by a "two-bladed surgical instrument with teeth on the end of each blade," probably the missing weapon. Inexplicably, the defense attorneys left this vague assertion unchallenged, an omission which caused irreparable damage to their client's case.

Morals, not Murder

Susan Hayes, in her testimony, demurely cataloged a long-running romantic liaison. Asked where the acts of intimacy took place, she replied: "In his car, and in his apartment above the Sheppard clinic. . . . He said he loved his wife very much but not as a wife. He was thinking of divorce." Other than showing that Sheppard was unfaithful, Hayes' testimony proved nothing. But the damage had been done. Sheppard wound up being tried more for his morals than for any crime. Defense attorney Fred Garmone's final question went some way toward salvaging the loss: "Miss Hayes, during all your activities as a technician at the hospital, and your activities with Dr. Sheppard, were you always aware that he was a married man?"

"Yes," she whispered.

"That's all," Garmone said.

Arguably the most potent prosecution witness was Judge Blythin. His antipathy toward the defendant was plain and unvarnished. Early in the trial he had remarked to Dorothy Kilgallen: "Sheppard is as guilty as hell," and throughout the proceedings he had hectored and hamstrung the defense at every turn. Such an attitude on the bench ensured that Sheppard's last chance of receiving a fair trial evaporated. His own appearance on the stand was largely irrelevant. He performed well, but not well enough to overcome the atmosphere in court.

Jury deliberations lasted four days and resulted in a verdict of guilty to second-degree murder. (A rumor that some jurors were unwilling to commit Sheppard to the electric chair and might therefore acquit him, had forced Judge Blythin to dangle the second-degree carrot in front of them, and they'd gobbled it up greedily.) Blythin pronounced sentence: "It is now the judgment of this court that you be taken to the Ohio Penitentiary, there to remain for the rest of your natural life."

A Second Chance

In November 1961, attorney F. Lee Bailey, then a 29-year-old newcomer, took up Sheppard's cause. He filed a stream of motions on Sheppard's behalf and saw every one rejected. His frustration lasted until March 1964, when, by chance, Bailey attended a literary dinner. Among the other guests was Dorothy Kilgallen, and she happened to repeat Judge Blythin's off-the-record remark to her during the trial. Bailey listened intently. If he could demonstrate judicial prejudice then that would be grounds for a new trial.

Four months later a judge ordered Sheppard freed on bail, citing that the carnival conditions surrounding his trial "fell far below the minimum requirements for due process."

The following year Bailey argued his case before the Supreme Court, claiming that Blythin had displayed prejudice and that the trial had been conducted in a manner unbecoming a legal action. The Court agreed. On June 6, 1965, they handed down their decision that Sheppard's 1954 conviction be set aside, because Judge Blythin "did not fulfill his duty to protect Sheppard from inherently prejudicial publicity which saturated the county."

Ohio tried Sheppard again. Media interest remained high but this time was kept in check when the trial opened October 24, 1966, before Judge Francis J. Talty. Prosecutor John Corrigan led witnesses through essentially the same story that they had told over a decade earlier, but they now faced a defense attorney at the peak of his powers. Bailey demolished them, particularly Coroner Samuel Gerber. Referring to the elusive "surgical instrument," Gerber pompously announced that he had spent the last 12 years looking for just such an item "all over the United States."

"Please tell us what you found?" asked Bailey.

Sadly, Gerber shook his head: "I didn't find one."

Bailey scathingly dismissed the prosecution's case as "ten pounds of hogwash in a five-pound bag."

On December 16, 1966, the jury took less than 12 hours to return a verdict of not guilty: Sam Sheppard's ordeal was over.

But liberty proved brief. Sheppard died in 1970.

In 1995, Sheppard's son, Sam Reese Sheppard, initiated action to sue Ohio for the wrongful imprisonment of his father, claiming that recently uncovered DNA evidence pointed to the real killer being the family's former handyman, Richard Eberling, who was then serving a sentence for murder in Florida. (Before his death in 1998 Eberling denied any involvement in the Sheppard case.)

In December 1998, the Ohio Supreme Court ruled that Sam Reese Sheppard could pursue a wrongful imprisonment suit on behalf of his father.

After much delay, testimony got under way on February 14, 2000, before Judge Ronald Suster. Terry Gilbert, attorney for the plaintiff, promised the eight-person jury that "finaly, after 45 and a half years, the truth will be told to you in this courtroom."

Facing potential damage payments running into millions, the state hit back hard, with Cuyahoga County Prosecutor William D. Mason describing

Sheppard as a cad whose affairs create a "powder keg" of tension that exploded when he battered his wife to death.

The much touted DNA evidence proved to be ambiguous. Dr. Mohammed Tahir testified that two blood smears found at the scene did not match blood from either Sheppard or the victim, but could have come from Eberling. However, under cross-examination, Tahir conceded that Eberling was just one of "thousands" whose blood might match the badly degraded DNA sample. In most other respects the testimony was largely a rerun of the two previous trials, just as baffling, and just as contradictory.

On April 12, 2000, for the third time this remarkable case went to a jury. After just three hours of deliberation they decided in favor of the state, saying that the original jury had got it right after all—Dr. Sam Sheppard had murdered his wife.

—Colin Evans

Suggestions for Further Reading

Bailey, F. Lee with Harvey Aronson. *The Defense Never Rests*. New York: Stein and Day Publishers, 1971.

Gaute, J.H.H. and Robin Odell. *The Murderers' Who's Who*. London: W.H. Allen, 1989.

Holmes, Paul. *The Sheppard Murder Case*. New York: David McKay, 1961.

Pollack, Jack Harrison. *Dr. Sam—An American Tragedy*. Chicago: Regnery, 1972.

Sheppard, Sam. *Endure And Conquer*. Cleveland: World, 1966.

Sheppard, Stephen with Paul Holmes. *My Brother's Keeper*. New York: David McKay, 1964.

Tobacco Litigation Trials: 1954–present

Plaintiffs: Smokers, their next of kin, and the state and federal governments
Defendants: Philip Morris Company; R.J. Reynolds Tobacco Company;
Brown & Williamson Tobacco Corporation; Lorillard Tobacco Corporation; The
Liggett Group, Inc.; American Tobacco Company; British American Tobacco,
P.L.C.; and other tobacco-related entities   **Place:** Various
Dates of Trials: 1954–present

SIGNIFICANCE

The tobacco litigation cases represent one of the largest class action movements in legal history; coupled with state and federal action against tobacco companies, the actions reflect a growing condemnation of the tobacco industry that would have been unthinkable until recently, and which may ultimately lead to similar suits against other makers of controversial products.

In the mid-1950s, two decades after university studies began linking smoking to lung disease, smokers began suing tobacco companies on personal-injury grounds. These plaintiffs, most of whom had health problems for which they blamed their smoking habits, based their suits on product liability principles, arguing that tobacco was an inherently dangerous product for which the manufacturer should be held accountable.

The next 30 years saw two waves of unsuccessful tobacco litigation: from the 1950s to the early 1970s, and throughout the 1980s. The plaintiffs in the second wave relied more heavily on the fact that the federal government had begun to speak out against the dangers of smoking. The first major governmental warning was the 1964 Surgeon General's report stating that smoking was a habit-forming health risk. In 1965, the federal government began requiring tobacco products to carry health warnings on its labels, and in 1969 it banned radio and television cigarette advertisements.

Despite the increased public awareness of the dangers of smoking the second wave of tobacco litigation proved to be a defeat for the smoker/plaintiffs, just as the first had been. The smokers faced many strategic, financial, and legal difficulties in their litigation. As individual plaintiffs, they had to rely on attorneys who were often solo practitioners or members of smaller firms to do battle against wealthy corporations and well-funded corporate counsel. The many smokers' lawsuits were not coordinated with one another. The plaintiffs thus lacked financial and legal resources and organization, while the tobacco industry had both in abundance. In legal terms, moreover, almost all of the plaintiffs' arguments had a fatal flaw: the smokers themselves had made the conscious decision to smoke, and so they, and not the tobacco companies, were ultimately responsible for their illnesses in jurors' eyes. The ever growing weight of research and expert opinion that smoking was dangerous made this relatively easy to prove in court. The paradox was that the knowledge of the dangers was becoming so widespread that the smokers had to shoulder even more of the blame for their injuries, since they had known the risks of smoking but had chosen to smoke anyway.

The results of this paradox were striking. From the mid-1950s to the late 1980s, between 300 and 800 plaintiffs filed personal-injury suits against the major tobacco companies. Of these, fewer than 30 went to trial. Of those that did go to trial, plaintiffs won in only a few cases and all of these were reversed on appeal. The tobacco companies' defenses were impregnable.

Plaintiffs Find a New Argument

Beginning in the early 1990s, however, with antismoking sentiment growing stronger, several changes in litigation procedures occurred. Plaintiffs' lawyers, drawing upon their experience in recent class action injury claims—among them the Dalkon Shield and asbestos suits of the 1970s and 1980s—began to apply their lessons to tobacco litigation. They started to coordinate their efforts with other attorneys, and they sought new strategies and new legal tactics to eliminate the roadblocks that earlier smoker/plaintiffs had faced. Many of these attorneys had watched smoker friends and relatives die of lung disease, and the similarity of these diseases to those of asbestos victims made the asbestos cases especially useful.

Among the leaders of the third wave of tobacco cases were Michael T. Lewis of Mississippi, who HAD lost a friend to what he believed was a smoking-related illness; Richard F. Scruggs, a successful Mississippi asbestos litigator; and Wendell Gauthier, a New Orleans class action lawyer whose best friend, Peter Castano, had recently died of lung cancer. Gauthier joined forces with Ronald L. Motley of Charleston, South Carolina; John P. Coale of Washington, D.C., who had recently sued Union Carbide on behalf of 60,000 people in the wake of the Bophal, India, chemical disaster; and other tobacco and class action litigators. Together the group formed a coalition of attorneys from 60 firms, each of which pledged $100,000 to help cover litigation costs. They decided that their principal tactic would be a federal class action lawsuit on behalf of the tens of millions of addicted smokers in the United States. The case agreed upon was that of Peter Castano, Gauthier's friend, which they filed in March 1994.

The new legal strategy was not to be product liability but instead deception leading to addiction. In 1998, Surgeon General C. Everett Koop had stated that smoking was addictive. But even earlier in 1994, the Food and Drug Administration (FDA) began investigating the charges that tobacco companies had secretly and deliberately increased cigarettes' nicotine content to enhance their addictive quality. This charge eliminated the weakness in earlier plaintiffs' arguments to the effect that they had known of all the dangers from smoking. According to the arguments in the Castano case, the tobacco companies had concealed the full dangers, and so the plaintiffs could not have been responsible for their contracted illnesses.

Given the resources that the attorneys now had, and the potential payout amount involved, the plaintiffs could now meet the tobacco industry on its own terms with a realistic hope for victory and leverage enough for a possible settlement. But the Castano case opened the attorneys to the usual criticism of class action lawsuits: the lawyers would get rich leaving not much for the plaintiffs, who would not be able to file individual suits in the event of a class action victory or settlement. As a result of these criticisms, some attorneys, such as Norwood Wilner and Gregory H. Maxwell of Florida, continued to sue individually, though they also worked to some degree with the Castano attorneys.

State Governments Seek Payback

During this time, Lewis discussed the tobacco litigation with his friend Michael Moore, who was attorney general of Mississippi, and Richard F. Scruggs. The men knew that state governments were spending huge sums of money, through state Medicaid programs and in other ways, to pay for the health hazards of smoking. Also, they realized that individuals could make a decision to smoke despite the risks, but the states had never had the opportunity to make the choice to pay for individuals' ill health. With funding from some of the Castano attorneys, the state of Mississippi—which several other states soon joined—sued the major tobacco companies to recover the costs of smoking that it had borne for its citizens. Deception and addiction again were the key arguments. Mississippi filed the complaint in May 1994, two months after the beginning of the Castano case. Eventually, nearly every state in the country became a party to the litigation.

In the Castano case, the courts ultimately refused to certify all addicted American smokers as a single class and the Castano attorneys soon filed a group of smaller class action lawsuits in various state courts. But in early 1996, before the Castano trial came to an end, the Liggett Group, one of the nation's largest tobacco companies, broke ranks with the others to reach a settlement. This landmark breach in the wall of tobacco company liability required Liggett to pay more than $1 billion to cover some state health care costs for smokers and to fund smoking-cessation programs, in exchange for immunity from future addiction suits.

Still facing concerted action from the state governments, the tobacco companies as a group agreed to another settlement in 1998. In exchange for immunity from future lawsuits, the companies agreed to pay almost $250 billion to the states over a period of 25 years; to limit tobacco advertising; and to take various steps to reduce youth access to tobacco products.

During all of these maneuverings, individual suits continued, made more potent by new evidence from "whistleblower" industry executives, government investigations, and tobacco company documents that the Castano and the states' suits had brought to light. These new revelations indicated that tobacco companies had indeed known of nicotine's addictive qualities and that they had tried to hide that knowledge. Because of these revelations, juries began to believe (and reward plaintiffs accordingly) that smokers had not really known the risks involved in choosing to smoke. A few months after the Castano settlement with Liggett, a Florida jury found the Brown & Williamson Company liable for causing the plaintiff's lung cancer, awarding him $750,000. In 1999, a California jury awarded another smoker punitive damages of $50 million from the Philip Morris Company.

The Feds Hop on Board

With the impregnable wall crumbling rapidly, U.S. Attorney General Janet Reno announced in September 1999 that the federal government would sue the tobacco companies on grounds similar to those of the state governments. The federal case would also invoke RICO (Racketeer Influenced and Corrupt Organizations Act) because of what Reno called the industry's "concerted efforts . . . to defraud the public."

Reno's decision, the settlement of the state claims, and the states' assertion of those claims to begin with, as well as the Castano class action lawsuit, all raised concern in Congress, among the state governments, and in the private sector. Some feared that the settlements went too far in punishing an industry that played such a large role in the American economy and that paid considerable state and federal corporate taxes; others claimed that they did not go far enough. Still others observed that large-scale litigation by states and private parties had transferred a massive effort at social and economic regulation from the state legislatures into the domain of the courts, putting it to a degree under private control. Many observers wondered what this development might mean for gun manufacturers and health maintenance organizations (HMOs). As of this writing, it is unsure what the future will bring regarding these and other similar groups, or how and in what way the tobacco industry itself will be affected. By the mid-1990s, however, the tobacco companies had begun in increase cigarette sales to foreign countries and had started diversifying their holdings in light of the growing apprehension that tobacco would soon be a bad investment.

—Buckner F. Melton, Jr.

Suggestions for Further Reading

Kluger, Richard. *Ashes to Ashes: America's Hundred-Year Cigarette War, the Public Health, and the Unabashed Triumph of Philip Morris.* New York: Alfred A. Knopf, 1996.

Orey, Michael. *Assuming the Risk: The Mavericks, the Lawyers, and the Whistle-Blowers Who Beat Big Tobacco*. Boston: Little, Brown and Co., 1999.

The People vs. Big Tobacco: How the States Took on the Cigarette Giants. Princeton, N.J.: Bloomberg Press, 1998.

Pringle, Peter. *Cornered: Big Tobacco at the Bar of Justice*. New York: Henry Holt, 1998.

Burton Abbott Trial: 1955

Defendant: Burton W. Abbott   **Crimes Charged:** Murder and kidnapping
Chief Defense Lawyer: Stanley D. Whitney   **Chief Prosecutors:** Frank
Coakley and Folger Emerson   **Judge:** Wade Snook   **Place:** Oakland,
California   **Dates of Trial:** November 7, 1955–January 25, 1956
Verdict: Guilty   **Sentence:** Death

SIGNIFICANCE
Shrewd advocacy and the marshaling of highly charged emotions overcame
evidential limitations in one of California's most sensational murder trials.

On April 28, 1955, 14-year-old Stephanie Bryan failed to return home after school in Oakland, California. Apart from finding a school textbook, the police had little to go on. A statewide search proved fruitless until July 15, when Georgia Abbott reported that she had found some of Stephanie's personal effects—a purse and ID card—in the basement of her Alameda home. When police searched the basement more thoroughly the next day, they dug up yet more books belonging to Stephanie, also her spectacles and a brassiere. Neither Georgia Abbott nor her 27-year-old husband, Burton, an accounting student, could explain how the effects came to be there. Burton Abbott told police that at the time Stephanie disappeared, he was en route to the family's vacation cabin, 285 miles away in the Trinity County mountains. On July 20, the battered body of Stephanie Bryan was found lying in a shallow grave, just 335 feet from Abbott's cabin. Soon afterwards he was charged with murder and rape.

Emotion over Evidence

When Abbott's trial got under way November 7, 1955, his guilt seemed a foregone conclusion. Certainly the Bay Area newspapers thought so, judging from the virulent campaign they had waged against the defendant all summer long, but it was soon clear that the case against Abbott was purely circumstantial: not one direct piece of evidence existed to link him to the death of Stephanie Bryan.

Fully aware of the shortcomings in the state's case, yet determined to secure a death verdict, District Attorney Frank Coakley opted for emotion over evidence. He ran into immediate opposition. Prosecution efforts to introduce a particularly gory photograph of the victim brought defense counsel Stanley D. Whitney to his feet, protesting that it was presented "for no other reason than to inflame the jury and raise prejudice against the defendant." Judge Wade Snook sided with Whitney on this point but did allow Coakley to show clothes taken from the dead girl's body. The stench from these unwashed clothes, which had been kept in a closed box, was so bad that several spectators hurriedly vacated the courtroom. The jury, denied any such opportunity, was forced to endure the ordeal, but the effect on them was palpable.

Amused Defendant

Just about the only person unaffected by these antics was the defendant himself. Throughout the trial, Abbott maintained an air of detached amusement. A man of some refinement—he played better than average chess, enjoyed crosswords and created haute cuisine dishes—Abbott didn't bother to stifle his contempt for all that was happening. He displayed that same cockiness on the witness stand, openly scoffing at prosecution charges that he had first attempted to rape Stephanie Bryan and then killed her when she resisted. It was all a "monstrous frame-up," he said, reiterating the stance he had taken from the beginning. As for the articles found in his basement, Abbott said that in May the basement served as a polling station. Dozens of people would have had access to it. Any one of them could have planted the incriminating evidence.

The subject of rape was one which Assistant District Attorney Folger Emerson pursued stridently. Sidestepping earlier pathological testimony that advanced decomposition made it impossible to determine if sexual assault had taken place, Emerson declared,

> I think it time to say from the evidence in this case that the original intent of the defendant when he kidnapped Stephanie Bryan was to commit a sex crime. . . . I think that what happened to Stephanie before she was killed was worse than death itself. . . . If ever there was a crime that fitted the punishment of death, this is it.

Emerson then concluded with one of the strangest and most garbled appeals ever to a jury:

> The state endeavors to take a life in the most humane way possible. Wouldn't it have been a blessing to Stephanie that if she had to die that she could have died that way than the way she did?

Coakley's syntax was less tangled and more effective. Brandishing the dead girl's brassiere and panties, he shouted, "You've heard the defense counsel ask 'What is the motive for this crime? What is the reason? Why? Why? Why?'" He offered the underwear in mute reply, branding Abbott a "typical psychopath and a pathological liar."

The only surprise after this was that it took the jury seven days to reach their verdict: guilty of first-degree murder. But in that delay were perhaps sown the seeds of the future doubt that would assail this case. After Judge Snook passed sentence of death, Abbott was taken to San Quentin to await execution. For more than a year his lawyers fought for commutation, but on March 15, 1957, Abbott was strapped into the gas chamber. Just minutes later a stay of execution was phoned through to the prison, but by then it was too late. The cyanide fumes were already creeping up around Abbott's face. Minutes later he was dead.

The manner and circumstances of Burton Abbott's execution sparked a renewal of the debate over whether society has the right to take life, especially on circumstantial evidence alone. It is an argument that shows no signs of abating.

—Colin Evans

Suggestions for Further Reading

Crimes And Punishment. Vol.16. England: Phoebus, 1974.

Gaute, J.H.H. and Robin Odell. *The Murderers' Who's Who.* London: W.H. Allen, 1989.

Marine, Gene. *The Nation* (May 19, 1956): 424–426.

Newsweek (February 6, 1956): 29.

Time (March 25, 1957): 25.

Wilhelm Reich Trial: 1956

Defendants: Wilhelm Reich, Michael Silvert, the Wilhelm Reich Foundation
Crime Charged: Criminal contempt of court
Chief Defense Lawyers: Wilhelm Reich and Michael Silvert, representing themselves; William Moise, representing the Wilhelm Reich Foundation; on appeal, Charles Haydon **Chief Prosecutors:** Joseph L. Maguire, Peter Mills
Judge: George C. Sweeney **Place:** Portland, Maine **Date of Trial:** May 3–7, 1956 **Verdict:** Guilty **Sentences:** Reich: two years imprisonment; Silvert: one year and one day imprisonment; Foundation: $10,000 fine

SIGNIFICANCE

The judge in this case told the jury, "It's probably the first time in the annals of jurisprudence that the government has presented a case only to have the defendants come in and say they did it." The fact is that, while the Food & Drug Administration succeeded in proving that its injunction had been violated, it has never brought further legal action against the defendants' Public Orgonomic Research Exchange (PORE), which continues to function.

Born on a farm in Austria in 1897, Wilhelm Reich early developed an interest in natural science. Following service in World War I (1914–1918), he entered medical school and soon caught the attention of the well-known psychiatrist, Sigmund Freud, who welcomed him into his Viennese Psychoanalytic Society and, in 1922, made Reich his clinical assistant.

While administering clinics on sexual hygiene, Reich became sensitive to the problems of working-class people. His interest in the social causes of neurosis led him to activity in the Socialist Party. Over a decade, he published papers that compared Marxian and Freudian concepts, married a patient and produced two daughters, and became vice director of Freud's clinic.

Discovers "Orgone"

Before 1930, Reich published his book, *The Function of the Orgasm*. It theorized that physical and mental health were founded on the circulation through the body of a biological energy he called "orgone," repression of which led to physical or mental disease. While Freud's theory of libidinal energy established the libido only as a metaphorical concept, Reich insisted that the orgone was a physical reality.

Reich broke with Freud in 1930. Moving to Berlin, he established a lucrative psychiatric practice and became involved with the German Communist Party until its leadership declared his books, which emphasized sexual health rather than the class struggle, counter-revolutionary. Then, as the Nazis included his articles and books in their public book-burning in 1933, Reich fled to Vienna. There his wife dissolved the marriage, taking the children with her.

Reich moved to Norway, establishing an open marriage with Elsa Lindenburg, who had been in his Berlin Communist cell. There he conducted seminars in psychotherapy and published his findings on biogenesis. The year 1937 brought vicious attacks by the press on his "Bion Experiments," which he said revealed building blocks of life—pulsating microscopic material—that came from inorganic matter. Leaving Lindenburg, Reich next accepted an offer from the New School for Social Research in New York City to teach medical psychology. He sailed in August 1939, two weeks before the Nazis invaded Poland to start World War II (1939–1945).

Invents "Accumulator"

On Christmas day, 1939, Reich married Ilse Ollendorf. She became his laboratory assistant as he experimented further, labeling the bion energy with his earlier name, "orgone." This energy, he theorized, existed not only within living organisms but also in the atmosphere. In 1940, he devised a six-sided box for a person to sit in. Its alternating layers of organic material (plywood or cotton) and metallic material (sheet metal or steel wool) would, he said, attract the energy and radiate it to the box's center. The human sitting in the box, added Reich, would absorb the energy, with a resultant healing effect. Reich called the box the "orgone accumulator."

For nearly 10 years, Reich developed and tested his theories. He created smaller boxes and blanket-like orgone accumulators that could enwrap a human arm or leg. His reports announced that the accumulator could reduce and eliminate cancer tumors, relieve heart and arthritis pain, heal burns, reduce or eliminate the need for prescription medication, and tone up the immune system against disease.

Reich and Ilse moved to Rangeley, Maine, building a laboratory and research center called Orgonon. There they supervised the manufacture and nationwide sale, by mail order, of the orgone accumulator. Meantime, Reich had his attorney, Peter Mills, incorporate The Wilhelm Reich Foundation to own the Orgonon laboratory.

Word of Reich's work reached journalist Mildred Brady. In 1947, in *Harper's Magazine,* she published an article that condemned the orgone accumulator as ineffective and fraudulent. Only weeks later, *The New Republic* published her second piece, "The Strange Case of Wilhelm Reich." In Washington, the Food and Drug Administration (FDA) dispatched an agent to Rangeley to investigate.

Builds "Cloud-buster"

For nearly five years, while the FDA was compiling a case, the laboratory sold and rented accumulators. Meanwhile, Reich built a device—his "cloud-buster"—that some credited with causing severe rain in the Arizona desert and with diverting a New England hurricane.

February 10, 1954, brought a Complaint for Injunction, a formal civil action by the FDA against Reich, his wife, and the foundation. It charged them with violating the Food, Drug, and Cosmetic Act by making false and misleading claims and delivering misbranded and adulterated devices in interstate commerce. As plaintiff, the FDA requested the U.S. District Court to "perpetually enjoin" the defendants from continuing to manufacture, distribute, or publicize the orgone accumulator. Peter Mills, formerly Reich's attorney but now U.S. Attorney for the District of Maine, signed the complaint.

Reich decided not to appear in court to contest the complaint. Rather, he wrote a letter to District Court Judge John D. Clifford, Jr. "I shall not appear," he said, "against a plaintiff who by his mere complaint already has shown his ignorance in matters of natural science."

Mary Boyd-Higgins displays a device designed to concentrate the workings of orgone energy, designed by Wilhelm Reich. (AP/Wide World Photos)

On March 19, Judge Clifford issued a sweeping injunction ordering the destruction of all orgone accumulators owned by Reich or leased to others, as well as all printed and graphic material related to the device.

Ignores Injunction

Reich took his cloud-buster to Arizona and allegedly produced rain that, in turn, produced 12-inch-high grass where—the locals said—none had ever sprouted. During his absence from Rangeley, his assistant, psychiatrist Michael Silvert, shipped orgone accumulators to New York City and the foundation continued distributing its books and other printed material. By early 1955, the FDA accused Reich, Silvert, and the foundation of criminal contempt for failing to comply with the injunction.

The trial opened before George C. Sweeney, senior judge of the U.S. District Court, on Thursday, May 3, 1956. Reich and Silvert both served as their own lawyers. Prosecutor Peter Mills first presented witnesses who had built and shipped the accumulators. A Brooklyn, New York, customer testified that he had rented an accumulator after the March 1954 injunction. Ilse Ollendorf testified that income from accumulators in the first four months after the injunction was the same as earlier. Thomas Mangravite told of repairing used accumulators and reshipping them to other customers after the injunction ordered them destroyed. Two Orgonon laboratory office employees testified that literature was distributed and accumulators rented after the injunction.

Reich's opening defense statement emphasized that he had indeed violated the injunction order. Judge Sweeney warned him, "You're practically pleading guilty."

Reich insisted that the injunction "had to be violated." He then introduced witnesses who established that he and his colleagues "were armed constantly" with rifles "to protect our work against espionage."

Defense witness Thomas Ross testified that his orders were to be armed and admit no one to the Orgonon laboratory. "Tell the jury," Reich said to Ross, "if I was ready to die last summer."

"He can't possibly know that," said the judge.

"Did you prepare a grave for me during the time we were armed?" Reich asked the witness.

The prosecution objected, "That is ridiculous."

"It's not ridiculous if you're in it," said Reich.

The judge permitted Ross to say he did dig a grave. But he refused to permit testimony on the defendants' motives in arming themselves and employees, saying the only question for the jury was whether the injunction had been violated.

The three women and nine men of the jury deliberated for 20 minutes before finding Reich, Silvert, and the foundation guilty. Reich was sentenced to two years' imprisonment, Silvert to one year and a day. The foundation was fined $10,000.

On December 11, 1956, the U.S. Court of Appeals upheld the district court verdict, and on February 25, 1957, the U.S. Supreme Court refused to accept the case. Reich was incarcerated in the Lewisburg, Pennsylvania, federal prison, where he was found dead on his cell cot on November 3, 1957. An autopsy reported "myocardial insufficiency with sudden heart failure."

Silvert was released on December 12, 1957, after serving three-quarters of his sentence. In 1958, he committed suicide.

—Bernard Ryan, Jr.

Suggestions for Further Reading

Bean, Orson. *Me and the Orgone.* New York: St. Martin's Press, 1971.

Boadella, David. *Wilhelm Reich, the Evolution of His Work.* London: Vision Press, 1973.

Greenfield, Jerome. *Wilhelm Reich vs. the U.S.A.* New York: Norton, 1974.

Higgins, Mary, and Chester M. Raphael, M.D., eds. *Reich Speaks of Freud*. New York: Farrar, Straus & Giroux, 1967.

Mann, W. Edward, and Edward Hoffman. *The Man Who Dreamed of Tomorrow*. Los Angeles: J.P. Tarcher, 1980.

Ollendorf, Ilse. *Wilhelm Reich: A Personal Biography*. New York: St. Martin's Press, 1969.

Reich, Wilhelm. *The Discovery of the Orgone*. New York: Noonday Press, 1970.

——. *The Mass Psychology of Fascism*. New York: Farrar, Straus & Giroux, 1970.

——. *The Sexual Revolution*. New York: Noonday Press, 1970.

Sharof, Myron. *Fury on Earth*. New York: St. Martin's Press, 1983.

Wilson, Colin. *The Quest for Wilhelm Reich*. Garden City: Anchor Press/Doubleday, 1981.

Matthew McKeon Court-Martial: 1956

Defendant: Matthew McKeon **Crimes Charged:** Drinking in enlisted barracks, oppression of 74 recruits, culpable negligence in the deaths of six recruits, oppression of the six dead recruits, drinking in front of a recruit
Chief Defense Lawyers: Emile Zola Berman, Thomas Costello
Chief Prosecutors: Charles B. Sevier, Frederick M. Haden, William Otten, Jr.
Judges: Edward L. Hutchinson (President), Nicholas A. Sisak, Robert D. Shaffer, Walter Gall, Edwin T. Carlton, John Demas, Hampton Huddard
Date of Trial: July 17–August 4, 1956 **Verdict:** Guilty of involuntary manslaughter and drinking in the barracks **Sentence:** Nine months hard labor, reduction to the rank of private, forfeiture of $30 per month in pay, and a bad-conduct discharge from the Marine Corps; later reduced to four months hard labor and no severance from the service

SIGNIFICANCE
The McKeon court-martial was a public relations nightmare for the Marine Corps, which had to act quickly to reform its training methods in order to rehabilitate its public image.

On the night of April 8, 1956, at the Marine Corps training center at Parris Island, South Carolina, Staff Sergeant Matthew McKeon marched Platoon 71 into the swampy waters of Ribbon Creek. Six of the recruits did not emerge alive.

For five and a half weeks McKeon had been trying to instill the pride and discipline necessary to good marines in his "boots," but he was unhappy with the results he had gotten. In his opinion "about three-fourths of the platoon was squared away, but the remainder were foul balls." Earlier in the day he had decided to straighten out those unsatisfactory recruits by shocking them into working as a disciplined unit.

Panic in the Mud

After sunset McKeon told his platoon that he was going to take it to a place where the non-swimmers would drown and the swimmers would be eaten by sharks. He then marched his men into the flooded marshes leading to Ribbon Creek. McKeon himself had never been into the area before. Once he reached the creek he led the men into water that was knee- to waist-deep and ordered them to move parallel to the bank, pointing out that in combat, staying near the banks was essential to avoiding detection in the moonlight. The creek bed was covered with deep, suction-producing mud, which filled the men's boots.

McKeon then reversed the column's course and moved nearer to the middle of the creek, where the water was shoulder-deep. Ribbon Creek was a tidal stream and high tide had been two hours earlier. The tide was now ebbing, creating a strong undertow that tugged at the recruits who were trying to maintain their balance in the slimy mud. Several men found themselves in an area where the bottom dropped off suddenly. Panic broke out among the men who found themselves in water over their heads. McKeon, who now reacted quickly, was pulling one of the struggling men near him to shore when another one grabbed him and they all went under. Around them several panic-stricken men were latching onto anyone near them in a desperate effort to save themselves. Strong swimmers who tried to help the non-swimmers went under.

McKeon ordered the platoon out of the water. Dripping and disheveled recruits began straggling toward their barracks. Once news of the incident reached the officer of the day, lights were set up along the creek and a full-scale search for missing men began. A head count found seven men missing. One was found shivering on the far bank of the creek. Six remained unaccounted for. McKeon was arrested, and because there was evidence that he had been drinking earlier in the day, he was sent to the medical officer to be checked for signs of intoxication.

The following day the bodies of Norman Wood, Leroy Thompson, Donald O'Shea, Jerry Thomas, and Charles Reilly were pulled from the water. On April 10 a diver recovered the body of Thomas Hardeman.

Was the Drill Sergeant Drunk?

When the Commandant of the Marine Corps, General Randolph Pate, arrived at Parris Island, he responded to a reporter's question by announcing that apparently McKeon had broken regulations and would be punished to the fullest extent of the law. Before all the bodies had been recovered a court of inquiry convened. A military court of inquiry is similar to a civilian inquest or grand jury proceeding. For several days the court heard testimony from 23 of the surviving 69 platoon members, asking several of them if they thought that McKeon had been drinking. Many men praised McKeon's attempts to save the drowning men and his work as a drill instructor. A medical officer testified about the results of the sobriety tests he conducted on McKeon. McKeon himself had said he had consumed "a few shots of vodka that afternoon." Extensive testimony dealt with the issue of whether the swamps were out of bounds for training. The court of inquiry recommended a general court-martial on charges ranging from involuntary manslaughter and oppression of recruits to drinking intoxicating liquor in the presence of a recruit.

During the preliminary hearing, McKeon was represented by his brother-in-law Thomas Costello. Through the intervention of a New York Supreme Court judge, Costello secured the services of Emile Zola Berman, a personal injury lawyer with a large civil practice. Berman accepted the case pro bono, and despite his lack of criminal experience he proved the ideal defense attorney for McKeon. In a case that would be conducted in the full glare of publicity, Berman immediately set to work trying to reform his client's image in the media by characterizing him as a loyal family man and a patriotic marine, rather than as the drunken sadist he currently seemed.

The court-martial was convened on July 17, 1956. The prosecution began an orderly presentation of witnesses to show that nothing was wrong with the Marine Corps training practices and that McKeon was a "bad apple" who deserved conviction for taking men who could not swim into a dangerous area.

Berman's defense was more subtle. He realized that his client was going to be convicted on at least some of the charges. He wanted to get an acquittal on the manslaughter charges in the hope McKeon would lose a stripe and get minimal brig time instead of being sentenced to ten years in prison and a dishonorable discharge. He ignored the alcohol charges and tried to establish that although McKeon may not have used good judgment, he was following a well-established boot camp procedure for instilling discipline in the recruits. He argued that the six men died as a result of panic rather than any circumstance McKeon could reasonably have anticipated.

In presenting the defense Berman hammered away at several themes. First, he claimed that McKeon was guilty of breaking regulations regarding drinking, but that he was not drunk on the day in question. To support this assertion he had the medical officer testify that he had incorrectly circled "yes" instead of "no" on the record next to the term "intoxicated." Second, Berman argued that the charge of oppression should fail because there was no clear definition of the crime. In historical contexts it connoted tyranny and cruelty. He cited Nero and Captain Bligh as examples, and claimed that a man who led his men into danger, shared their peril, and risked his own life attempting to save them could not be oppressing them. He put the defendant on the stand and let him explain his own actions and accept responsibility for them, hoping that McKeon's own remorse and demeanor would impress the court. Berman also introduced evidence to show that taking recruits into the swamps was not unusual or forbidden, but understood to be common practice.

As to manslaughter by negligence, Berman called two famous witnesses to give their opinions of McKeon's conduct. First he called Commandant of the Marine Corps General Pate, who had already publicly condemned the defendant. When asked what punishment he would recommend, Pate said, "I think maybe I would take a stripe away from him. . . . I would have him transferred away for stupidity . . . I would have probably written in his service record book that under no conditions would this Sergeant ever drill recruits again. I think I would let it go at that." The second witness, Lieutenant General Lewis B. "Chesty" Puller, was probably the best-known and most respected living marine. When Berman asked Puller what action he would take in these circumstances, he replied, "I would say that this night march was a deplorable accident. . . . I think from what I read in the papers yesterday . . . [Pate] regrets that this man was ever ordered tried by a general court-martial."

McKeon was found guilty of involuntary manslaughter by simple negligence and of drinking in an enlisted barracks. He was acquitted of the two most serious crimes: oppression and manslaughter by culpable negligence and the lesser charge of drinking in front of a recruit. He was sentenced to reduction to the rank of private, nine months of hard labor, forfeiture of $30 per month in pay, and a bad-conduct discharge from the Marine Corps. This sentence was later reduced by the Secretary of the Navy, who cut the prison term to four months and remitted the bad-conduct discharge.

The Ribbon Creek incident and McKeon's court-martial highlighted some of the more brutal aspects of Marine training and revealed a low level of officers' supervision of recruit training. It ultimately resulted in the reform of marine training practices to rehabilitate the corps' badly damaged public image.

—Carol Willcox Melton

Suggestions for Further Reading

McKean, William B. *Ribbon Creek: The Marine Corps on Trial.* New York: Dial, 1958.

Stevens, John C. III. *Court-Martial at Parris Island: The Ribbon Creek Incident.* Annapolis, Md.: Naval Institute Press, 1999.

Cheryl Christina Crane Inquest: 1958

Defendant: Cheryl Christina Crane   **Crime Investigated:** Homicide of Johnny Stompanato   **Chief Defense Lawyer:** Jerry Geisler
Chief Prosecutor: William B. McKesson   **Coroner:** Theodore J. Curphey
Place: Los Angeles, California   **Date of Inquest:** April 11, 1958
Verdict: Justifiable homicide

SIGNIFICANCE

The explosive plot and star-studded cast of this particular Hollywood spectacle once again showed that the celluloid screen is no match for real life. Movie stars and mobsters-and a 14-year-old girl facing possible charges of murder kept America hanging on the verdict of a Los Angeles coroner's inquest.

Late on Good Friday, April 4, 1958, police were summoned to 730 North Bedford Drive, the Beverly Hills, California home of screen goddess Lana Turner. The report said that someone had died. Lights blazed in the Moorish mansion as two detectives entered. In the bedroom they came across a small group of people trying to pump some life back into the unreceptive body of Johnny Stompanato, latest in a long line of Turner's lovers and bodyguard to notorious gambler Mickey Cohen. All of their efforts were in vain. A single stab wound had severed the aorta. Police Chief Clinton B. Anderson was irked to see Jerry Giesler, the "attorney to the stars," already in attendance. Giesler's reputation as a high-priced lawyer with a knack for winning difficult cases was legendary around Hollywood. Anderson asked to see Turner. Clearly distraught, her first words to him were, "Can I take the blame for this horrible thing?"

"No, not unless you have committed the act, Miss Turner," said Anderson. After more soul-searching she mumbled, "Okay, it was my daughter."

Fourteen-year-old Cheryl Crane, Turner's daughter by a previous marriage, was taken down to the police station. The next day District Attorney William B. McKesson proclaimed himself dissatisfied with Turner's version of events and announced an inquest for the following week, to determine if Cheryl Crane should be charged with murder. Although still a minor, Cheryl faced life imprisonment if found guilty of murder.

Later, Mickey Cohen, looking every inch the mobster in a felt hat and wide-lapeled suit, provided a bizarre interlude when he was asked to identify the body of his former bodyguard. Chewing on a mouthful of gum, the gambler drawled, "I refuse to answer on the grounds I may be accused of this murder," an odd response that nobody understood and nobody bothered to question.

Tale of Star-Crossed Lovers

Cameras from ABC and CBS lined the Los Angeles courtroom on April 11, 1958, ready to film what promised to be the TV event of the year. The radio networks went one better, broadcasting live when Coroner Theodore J. Curphey gaveled the proceedings to order at 9:00 A.M. After the introduction of the autopsy report and other formalities, it was time for Turner to testify.

Turner had played many roles in her life but none more important than this. She walked steadily to the stand. By now all of America was aware of her tempestuous affair with Stompanato, a third-rate hoodlum and professional gigolo. Their relationship had lasted a little over a year, 12 months of roller-coaster emotion and bruising physical battles.

They had been fighting again on the night of Good Friday. "He started shaking me badly," she told the court in a tremulous voice. "He said that if he said for me to jump, I would jump . . . he would even cut my face or cripple me." Under Jerry Giesler's gentle prompting, Turner went on: "As I broke away from his holding me [sic] and I turned around to face the door . . . my daughter was standing there . . . I said, 'Please, Cheryl, please don't listen to any of this. Please go back to your room.' "

When Turner broke down once during her testimony, clicking cameras recorded every emotion on her tear-stained face. Gathering her composure, she described how Stompanato had grabbed a hanger from the closet and made as if to strike her with it. "I said, 'Don't ever touch me again. I am absolutely finished. This is the end. I want you out.' "

What happened next, she said, was a blur. Cheryl came rushing into the bedroom and seemed to punch Stompanato in the stomach. He collapsed onto his back. Only then did Turner realize that he had been stabbed. While Cheryl stood sobbing, her mother ran to the bathroom for a towel. "I didn't know what to do and then I put the towel there [on the wound] and Mr. Stompanato was making dreadful sounds in his throat . . . gasping, terrible sounds."

At this point a deputy sheriff showed Turner the eight-inch kitchen knife that Cheryl had used to stab Stompanato. She stared at it grimly for a second, then looked away.

As Turner left the stand an unidentified man in the public gallery stood up and shouted, "Lies, lies, all lies! This mother and daughter were both in love with Stompanato. . . . All you Hollywood people are no good." Still yelling, the stranger strode from the court and was never seen again.

Cheryl's Statement Introduced

Because of her age Cheryl was not present at the inquest, but part of her statement made to Chief Anderson on the night of the stabbing was read into the record as follows:

Chief Anderson: Tell us what happened.

Cheryl: They had an argument . . . he was threatening Mother.

Chief Anderson: Where was this argument taking place?

Cheryl: First in my bedroom, then in mother's room.

Chief Anderson: Did you go downstairs and pick up a knife in the kitchen?

Cheryl: Yes.

Chief Anderson: Then you took it into the room?

Cheryl: Yes, in case he tried to hurt Mommy.

Chief Anderson: Then you thought your mother's life was in danger?

Cheryl: He kept threatening her and I thought he was going to hurt her, so I went into the room and stuck him with the knife. He screamed and asked me what I was doing. I ran out of the room. Mother called me back into the bedroom to help her again . . . I called Daddy before I went back into the room and told him to get over here fast.

Shortly before noon the 10 men and 2 women of the coroner's jury returned a verdict of justifiable homicide. Afterward, District Attorney McKesson, who had attended the inquest, announced to reporters: "After what I have heard today, and unless some new facts are uncovered, it would not be my inclination to prosecute her [Cheryl] on criminal charges."

Although this concluded the criminal proceedings, Stompanato's family filed a $752,250 civil suit against Lana Turner and Cheryl's father, alleging that parental neglect had caused the death of Johnny Stompanato. Jerry Giesler arranged a settlement of the suit of about $20,000.

Both mother and daughter survived the ordeal well. Oddly enough, the incident revived Lana Turner's flagging movie career. Her next film *Imitation Of Life* was a great box-office success and led to several more. Cheryl Crane, after further but minor skirmishes with authority, settled down and joined her father in his restaurant business.

The inquest into Stompanato's death afforded instructive as well as compelling viewing. For the majority of Americans, Lana Turner's torment yielded a unique opportunity to glimpse an absorbing and critical stage of the judicial process that is rarely reported by the press or understood by the public.

—Colin Evans

Suggestions for Further Reading

Crane, Cheryl And Jahr, Cliff. Detour. New York: Arbor House, 1988.

Crimes And Punishment. Vol. 14. England: Phoebus, 1974.

Munn, Michael. *The Hollywood Murder Casebook*. New York: St. Martin's Press, 1987.

Turner, Lana. *Lana: The Lady, The Legend, The Truth*. New York, Dutton, 1982.

1958

Cheryl Christina Crane Inquest

Charles Starkweather and Caril Fugate Trials: 1958

Defendants: Charles Starkweather, Caril Fugate   **Crime Charged:** Murder
Chief Defense Lawyers: T. Clement Gaughan, William F. Matschullat, John McArthur   **Chief Prosecutors:** Elmer Scheele, Dale Fahrnbruch
Judge: Harry A. Spencer   **Place:** Lincoln, Nebraska
Dates of Trials: Starkweather: May 5–23, 1958; Fugate: October 27–November 21, 1958   **Verdict:** Guilty   **Sentence:** Starkweather: death; Fugate: life imprisonment

SIGNIFICANCE

Can a dysfunctional upbringing ever excuse homicide? That was the question facing jurors in this remarkable saga that changed forever the face of murder in America.

Although he had murdered a few weeks before, Charlie Starkweather, a diminutive 19-year-old garbage truck driver from Lincoln, Nebraska, didn't begin killing in earnest until January 21, 1958. This was the day when he visited the home of his girlfriend, Caril Fugate, aged 14. While awaiting her return, Starkweather got into an argument with Fugate's mother. When she tried to slap him, he grabbed a rifle and shot her. Seconds later, Fugate's stepfather was similarly dispatched. Minutes later Fugate arrived home, at which point Starkweather stabbed her 2-year-old half-sister to death.

Then, after pinning up a notice in the window that read "Every Body is Sick with the Flu," the couple hunkered down for the next six days, watching television, having sex, gorging themselves on fast food. In that time various people visited the house and met the two teenagers. No one noticed anything out of the ordinary.

One week later, alerted by an anxious relative, police officers called at the house and uncovered the massacre. But there was no sign of the wanted couple.

Another week passed before they were captured. In that time they had gone on a killing binge across Nebraska, littering the highway with bodies, until their final tally reached 11 victims. When eventually arrested, Starkweather mugged for the cameras like some psychotic James Dean, cigarette drooping from his mouth—America's first rock 'n' roll killer had just been born. By this time Fugate had already washed her hands of him.

They were tried separately, Starkweather first. He swaggered into court on May 5, 1958, before Judge Harry Spencer, to face a single count of murder, that of Robert Jensen. The facts were not in dispute, and neither was Starkweather's culpability; at issue was his mental state.

Earlier Starkweather had pointedly refused to cooperate with attempts to save his life through a plea of insanity, sneering, "Nobody remembers a crazy man." Now, when his chief counsel, T. Clement Gaughan, told the jury that Starkweather's IQ was "only a point or two above an idiot," the defendant's knuckles whitened as he gripped the desk in rage. Starkweather, it seemed, would rather die in the electric chair than be classified as mentally subnormal.

Tough Background

Once on the stand, he grudgingly told how it was to grow up in an unfeeling family, to be born bow-legged and half blind with a speech impediment, a figure of constant ridicule amongst other children. But it didn't take him long to crush any sympathy this might have engendered. His absurd rationalization and ingrained callousness couldn't help spilling over.

"Why did you kill, Charlie?" asked Gaughan.

"Self-defense."

"Do you feel any remorse for the people you killed?"

"I won't answer that."

Charlie Starkweather and Caril Ann Fugate. (Bettmann/Corbis)

If Starkweather wouldn't help himself, others were prepared to do the job for him. Dr. Nathan Greenbaum, just one of three psychiatrists to testify on the defendant's behalf, told the court that "Charles Starkweather is suffering from a severe mental disease or illness of such a kind as to influence his acts . . . people don't mean anything to him. They are no more than a stick or a piece of wood to this boy."

In his final address, Gaughan spread the blame far and wide. "This boy is a product of our society. Our society that spawned this individual is looking for a scapegoat." Then he touched on a subject that had terrified many Nebraskans, the prospect that, if found insane, Starkweather might one day be released. "Even an act of Congress will not take him out of the state hospital."

County Attorney Elmer Scheele countered by telling the jury, "Let's get back to earth, get our feet on the ground. . . . Can't you see what a hoax it is to persuade you into grasping at the straw of insanity?" He ended by urging them "to protect this community—our families, yours and mine—from the defendant."

When the jury returned from their deliberations on May 23, the verdict was guilty and the sentence was death.

Hostage or Killer?

The trial of Caril Fugate, which began four months after Starkweather was condemned, was in most respects a carbon copy of the first; with many of the same principals, and many of the same witnesses, who gave much the same testimony. Naturally, most interest centered on the defendant's age. At 14, Fugate was the youngest female ever to be tried for first-degree murder in America. Despite this, under Nebraska law, she could still face the electric chair if convicted. Right from the moment of her arrest, she protested her innocence of any involvement in the murders, claiming that she had been Starkweather's abused hostage, nothing more. As her attorney, John McArthur, put it, "This girl was introduced into this horrible sequence of events by opening the door and having a gun stuck in her face."

Starkweather had also toed this line originally, insisting that Fugate had nothing to do with the crimes, but as she turned against him, so his attitude hardened to the point where he agreed to turn state's evidence. While Fugate fixed him with her most withering glare, he told the court of the day he killed her family.

"What did you do after all this happened?" asked Scheele.

"I cleaned up."

"When you were cleaning up, what was Caril Fugate doing?"

"Watching TV."

Desperate to rattle the witness, McArthur read out one of Starkweather's earliest statements in which he maintained that Fugate was his hostage. "Do you recall that?" asked McArthur.

"That's what I said, but it ain't true. That whole statement is a bunch of hogwash," drawled Starkweather.

McArthur also reminded the witness of his much-quoted remark made earlier, that if he "fried in the electric chair" then Fugate should be "sitting in his lap." Did he still feel the same way?

"No, I don't. Now I don't care if she lives or dies."

There were others, besides Starkweather, who linked Fugate to the killings. Most damning of all was Deputy Sheriff William Romer, with his claim that Fugate told him she had actually seen her family being murdered.

In closing arguments it was noticeable that Scheele singularly avoided asking for the death penalty, but he did say, "Even 14-year-old girls must recognize they cannot go on 8-day murder sprees . . . the time has come when she must face the consequences of her actions.''

That day came on November 21, when Fugate was convicted and Judge Spencer sentenced her to life imprisonment.

The final act in this heartland tragedy was played out on June 25, 1959, when Starkweather strolled disinterestedly to his death in the electric chair. His former lover was paroled in 1976.

The notoriety that Charlie Starkweather craved so desperately has lived on, courtesy of two Hollywood movies, *Badlands and Natural Born Killers,* both of which are loosely based on the events of that mad January in Nebraska.

—Colin Evans

Suggestions for Further Reading

Allen, William. *Starkweather.* Boston: Houghton Mifflin, 1977.

Beaver, Ninette, R.K. Ripley and Patrick Trese. *Caril.* Philadelphia: Lippincott, 1974.

O'Donnell, Jeff. *Starkweather.* Lincoln, Ne.: Lee, 1993.

Reinhardt, James. *The Murderous Trail of Charles Starkweather.* Springfield, Ohio: Thomas, 1960.

Raymond Bernard Finch and Carole Tregoff Trials: 1960 & 1961

Defendants: Raymond Bernard Finch and Carole Tregoff
Crime Charged: Murder   **Chief Defense Lawyers:** Don Bruggold, Grant Cooper, Rexford Egan, and Robert A. Neeb, Jr.   **Chief Prosecutors:** First trial: Clifford C. Crail, William H. McKesson, and Fred N. Whichello; Second trial: Clifford C. Crail; Third trial: Clifford C. Crail   **Judges:** First trial: Walter R. Evans; Second trial: LeRoy Dawson; Third trial: David Coleman
Place: Los Angeles, California   **Dates of Trials:** January 4–March 12, 1960; June 27–November 7, 1960; January 3–March 27, 1961
Verdict: First trial: Mistrial; Second trial: Mistrial; Third trial: Guilty—Finch, first degree; Tregoff, second degree   **Sentences:** Both received life imprisonment

SIGNIFICANCE

Despite overwhelming evidence in favor of conviction, a jury deadlocked, primarily because racial tension had pervaded the jury room.

R ampant greed, sex, and a considerable dose of comedy ensured that this trial of a wealthy doctor and his mistress as joint defendants on charges of murder dominated newspaper headlines for months.

By 1959, Finch, 42, a wealthy Los Angeles, California physician, yearned to elevate his affair with 20-year-old Carole Tregoff to something more permanent. Standing directly in the path of this ambition was Finch's wife, Barbara, backed by the formidable California community property laws. Divorce would entitle Barbara Finch to half of Finch's estimated $750,000 fortune. Furthermore, if Barbara Finch could prove adultery—and there was every indication that she intended to do just that—Finch faced financial ruin, since the court could then apportion any percentage of the community property it deemed fit to the aggrieved party.

Unwilling to accept such a calamity, Finch and Tregoff schemed. In Las Vegas, Nevada, where Tregoff had gone to work, they attempted to hire someone, anyone, to seduce Barbara Finch, and thereby provide Finch with evidence for a countersuit of adultery. This notion brought them into contact with self-confessed gigolo John Patrick Cody, a seedy ex-convict entirely untroubled by matters of conscience. Talk of seduction soon turned to plans of murder. Cody assured the couple that homicide was also high on his list of accomplishments. After accepting a down payment of $350 and an airline ticket, Cody departed, ostensibly to kill Barbara Finch in Los Angeles. (Actually he spent the weekend with one of his several girlfriends.) A few days later he resurfaced and told Tregoff that the matter had been taken care of. She paid him the agreed balance of $850, only to learn later that Barbara Finch was still very much alive. Cody professed astonishment, then explained that he must have killed the wrong woman. For another couple of hundred dollars he promised to rectify the error. With this payment in hand, Cody disappeared, leaving Finch and Tregoff sadder, wiser, and infinitely more desperate.

Carole Tregoff and Bernard Finch (left) with their lawyers, Donald Bringgold and Robert Neeb. (AP/Wide World Photos)

At 10:00 P.M. on July 18, 1959, the couple arrived at Finch's opulent house on Lark Hill Drive in suburban West Covina. Barbara Finch was not at home. Just over an hour later, she drove up in her red Chrysler. Finch went across to talk to her. A struggle broke out. At some point in the dispute, Barbara Finch was shot dead by a .38-caliber bullet. For reasons never fully explained, Finch and Tregoff somehow became separated. Finch, after stealing two cars, made his way back to Las Vegas, where he was joined early the next morning by Tregoff. That same day, Finch was arrested and charged with murder. Eleven days later Tregoff was similarly charged.

Fatal Struggle

Their trial began at the Los Angeles County Courthouse on January 4, 1960. Prosecutor Fred Whichello called his first witness, Marie Anne Lindholm, the Finch maid. She told of running to the garage after hearing Barbara Finch scream and seeing Dr. Finch, gun in hand, standing over his semiconscious wife. Finch had then banged Lindholm's head against the garage wall, apparently in an effort to stun her. He'd ordered both women into the car but Barbara Finch had broken free and run. The doctor gave chase. Moments later Lindholm heard a shot, whereupon she ran to the house and called the police.

Equally damaging were Lindholm's allegations that Finch had regularly abused and threatened his wife. Over strenuous defense objections, a letter Lindholm had written to her mother in Sweden before the murder was admitted into evidence. In it she described a beating that Finch had given Barbara Finch, and also his oft-repeated threats that he had hired "someone in Las Vegas" to kill her.

When Cody took the stand, defense lawyers must have felt confident of demolishing his testimony. If so, it was confidence misplaced. Cody's cheerful admissions to just about every form of reprehensible conduct imaginable—he had been a thief, a sponger, and an occasional swindler—gave his testimony a curious verisimilitude, an honesty, that the defense could never quite shake. Attorney Grant Cooper tried hard but it was useless:

Question: What did you do?

Answer: I loafed.

Question: How did you support yourself?

Answer: By my wit.

Question: (Later in reference to one of Cody's girlfriends): Did she support you?

Answer: Yes.

Defense attorney Rexford Egan fared no better:

Question: Would you lie for money?

Answer: (After a long, thoughtful pause) It looks like I have.

Cody also told the court of a homily that he had delivered to Finch in an effort to dissuade him from murder:

Killing your wife for money alone isn't worth it. . . . Let her have every penny. . . . Take Carole . . . up on a mountaintop and live off the wild. If the girl loves you, she's going to stick with you.

But by far the deadliest thing that Cody had to say detailed a conversation with Carole Tregoff, in which she had snapped: "Jack, you can back out. But if you don't kill her, the doctor will; and if he doesn't, I will."

When the prosecution rested, things looked bleak indeed for the doctor and the redhead.

Dying Words

Rumors that the defense had a surprise in store guaranteed a packed courtroom when Finch took the stand. The doctor didn't disappoint. He described how his wife had pulled a gun on him. Regrettably, in his efforts to take the gun away, he had been forced to club her with it, inflicting two skull fractures. At that moment, the maid Lindholm had entered the garage. Finch's misconstrued attempts to placate the maid's obvious distress—already referred to—gave Barbara Finch the chance to snatch up the gun and take off. Finch went in pursuit. Some way up the drive he saw Barbara Finch taking dead aim at Tregoff with the pistol. A further struggle ensued. Finch grabbed the gun. Barbara Finch began running again. Inexplicably, as Finch attempted to toss the gun away, it went off, neatly drilling his fleeing wife between the shoulder blades. Claiming ignorance of this fact, Finch ran across to his prone wife.

"What happened, Barb?" he cried. "Where are you hurt?"

"Shot . . . in . . . chest," she gasped.

"Don't move a thing. . . . I've got to get an ambulance for you and get you to [the] hospital."

Barbara held up a restraining hand. "Wait. . . . I'm sorry, I should have listened."

"Barb, don't talk about it now. I've got to get you to [the] hospital."

"Don't leave me. Take care of the kids."

As Finch described feeling for a pulse and finding none, his voice broke: "She was dead." He wiped away a tear. Sobs could also be heard in the public gallery. Others preferred to concentrate on the likelihood of a murder victim actually apologizing for being killed, and found the story a little thin, to say the least.

Under cross-examination the doctor regained his normal buoyancy. When prosecutor Whichello, referring to numerous affairs with other women before Carole Tregoff, asked him: "Did you tell these women that you loved them?" the doctor responded jauntily: "I think under the circumstances that would be routine."

Seven days on the stand did little to undermine Finch. His story sounded implausible, but he stuck to it and yielded nothing to the prosecution.

They made more headway against Tregoff, whose own account of events bordered on the fantastic. She told of watching the scene unfold, then cowering for five or six hours behind some bougainvillea plants, paralyzed with fear, while police turned the house upside down. Later, she had driven back to Las Vegas, alone. Allegedly, her first knowledge of Barbara Finch's death came via the car radio, information which she passed on to Finch himself. He reportedly shrugged the news off and Tregoff went to work.

Prosecutor Clifford Crail succeeded in making Tregoff look very bad, intent only on saving herself at the expense of Finch. (Since their arrest, Tregoff had spurned all of Finch's letters and advances.) Crail highlighted her leading role in the solicitation of Cody, also her conflicting stories of why the couple had gone to Lark Hill Drive that night. Originally, Tregoff told police that the intention was to talk Barbara Finch out of divorce proceedings. On the stand that evolved into an attempt to convince her to obtain a "quickie" Nevada divorce.

Stunning Verdict

Courtroom observers thought that, at a minimum, Tregoff's performance had guaranteed a berth for Finch in the gas chamber. But after eight days of wrangling, the jury members announced that they were unable to agree on a verdict and a mistrial was declared. It later transpired that racial tension—one jury member was black, another Hispanic—had led to ugly scenes in the jury room, when neither minority juror would yield to pressure exerted by the white jurors.

A second trial began June 27, 1960, and again ended in deadlock November 7, 1960, despite an extraordinary admonition to the jury by Judge LeRoy Dawson, who told them, in no uncertain terms, that they ought not to believe the evidence of either defendant.

The State of California tried for a third time, opening its case January 3, 1961 before Superior Judge David Coleman. By now much of the earlier sensational coverage had dissipated, leaving a noticeably calmer courtroom atmosphere. It showed in the jury deliberations. On March 27 they convicted Finch of first-degree murder, while Tregoff was found guilty in the second degree. Both were sentenced to life imprisonment.

In 1969 Tregoff was paroled. She changed her name and found work at a hospital in the Pasadena area.

Finch, released two years later, practiced medicine in Missouri for a decade before returning to West Covina in 1984.

Given the lurid ingredients, it was hardly surprising that the trials of Finch and Tregoff assumed national prominence. And yet two juries deadlocked over what was almost surely premeditated murder. How much their indecision was prompted by the defendants' attractive appearance and social standing will remain a matter of conjecture.

—Colin Evans

Suggestions for Further Reading

Ambler, Eric. *The Ability To Kill*. New York: The Mysterious Press, 1987.

Gaute, J.H.H. and Robin Odell. *The Murderers' Who's Who*. London: W.H. Allen, 1989.

Kilgallen, Dorothy. *Murder One*. New York: Random House, 1967.

Wolf, Marvin J. and Katherine Mader. *Fallen Angels*. New York: Ballantine, 1986.

Richard Hickock And Perry Smith Trial: 1960

Defendants: Richard E. Hickock and Perry E. Smith
Crime Charged: Murder **Chief Defense Lawyers:** Arthur Fleming and
Harrison Smith **Chief Prosecutors:** Logan Greene and Duane West
Judge: Roland H. Tate **Place:** Garden City, Kansas **Dates of Trial:** March
22–29, 1960 **Verdict:** Guilty **Sentence:** Death by hanging

SIGNIFICANCE

The case provided a classic example of the limitations of the M'Naghten Test by
which defendants are judged mentally fit to stand trial. Truman Capote's book
about the case, *In Cold Blood,* further cemented the author's literary reputation
and brought the debate over capital punishment into focus for millions of readers
worldwide.

The people of Holcomb, Kansas, had not forgotten them, but the trial and
punishment of Richard Hickock and Perry Smith came and went unnoticed
by most Americans. Within months of their execution, however, Smith and
Hickock became two of the most famous murderers in history.

On Sunday morning, November 15, 1959, a successful, respected, and
well-liked Kansas farmer named Herbert Clutter was found in the basement of
his home with his throat cut and his head blown open by a shotgun blast. His
wife Bonnie and their teenaged children, Kenyon and Nancy, were found
bound, gagged, and shot to death elsewhere in the house. There were no clues
nor any apparent motive. "This is apparently the work of a psychopathic killer,"
declared the local sheriff.

The bloody slayings might have remained unsolved without the help of a
convicted thief, who had once shared a cell with a small-time check kiter named
Richard Hickock. The thief had worked on the Clutter farm and described it to
Hickock, who asked if the Clutters had a safe. The thief thought they did.
Hickock declared that he would find the farm, rob the Clutters, and kill all
witnesses, adding that his former cellmate Perry Smith would be just the man to
help. Herb Clutter's former hired hand dismissed Hickock's plan as a fantasy,
but he came forward when he heard of the murders.

Hickock and Smith were soon arrested in Las Vegas, Nevada, for parole violation and passing bad checks. The Kansas Bureau of Investigation dispatched agents to Nevada, where they questioned the suspects separately. Hickock denied any knowledge of the slayings, but a clever interrogation led Smith to confess to having shot the Clutters. Hickock confessed his part in the slayings the next day and the two men were returned to Kansas for trial.

The gruesome confessions and physical evidence made it clear that the accused men were responsible for the killings. Arguing for the death penalty, prosecutor Logan Greene said, "some of our most enormous crimes only happen because once upon a time a pack of chicken-hearted jurors refused to do their duty." The jury deliberated for only 40 minutes before returning a guilty verdict, ironically about a minute for each dollar Smith and Hickock had found in the Clutter home—there was no safe. "No chicken-hearted jurors, they," Smith joked as he and Hickock were led laughing from the courtroom. Judge Roland Tate sentenced the defendants to death by hanging.

Trial Leaves Questions Over Sanity

Yet the way the trial was conducted left lingering questions. A defense motion to have Smith and Hickock undergo comprehensive psychological testing before the trial had been denied by Judge Tate, who appointed three local general practitioners, not psychiatrists, to make the required examination. After a brief interview, the doctors judged the defendants sane.

Defense lawyers had sought the opinion of a more experienced psychiatrist from the state mental hospital, who diagnosed definite signs of mental illness in Smith and felt that Hickock's head injuries in a past

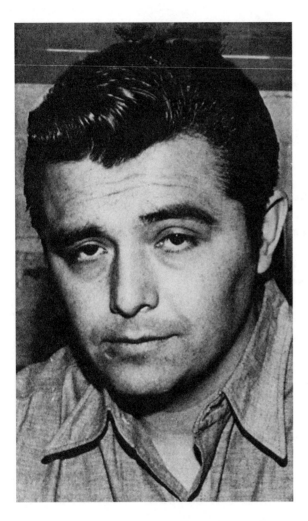

The case of Perry Smith (above) and Richard Hickock brought the debate over capital punishment into focus. (AP/Wide World Photos)

788

auto mishap might possibly have affected his behavior. Yet the diagnosis was never heard in the Finney County courthouse.

Under the M'Naghten Test a defendant is ruled to be sane if he has sufficient mental capacity to know and understand what he is doing at the time he commits a crime, that it is wrong, and that it violates the victim's rights. The M'Naghten Test was applied strictly in the Hickock-Smith trial. By Kansas law, the psychiatrist was allowed only to give his opinion about the defendants' sanity or lack thereof at the time they were in the Clutter house. Under this constraint, the psychiatrist could only answer "yes" when asked if he thought Hickock was sane by the M'Naghten definition and "no" when asked if he could surmise what Smith's state of mind was at the time of the killings. No comment was allowed on the question of whether Perry Smith was mentally able to control his actions, regardless of his knowledge that, they were unlawful.

Appeals Fail to Overturn Conviction

Richard Hickock's complaints to the Kansas Bar Association about the fairness of the trial prompted an investigation. The arguable mishandling of the case by the defense lawyers, failure to move the trial venue outside of Finney County, and the acceptance of a juror who had made questionable statements about the suitability of capital punishment in the case opened the way for four appeals and postponements of the death sentence. Court-appointed federal lawyers tried three times to have the Hickock-Smith case heard by the U.S. Supreme Court, but each time the court declined without comment. Hickock and Smith were hanged at the Kansas State Penitentiary on April 14, 1965, five years after their conviction.

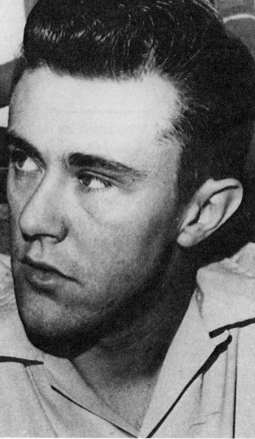

Richard Hickock. (AP/Wide World Photos)

The hangings provided an ending for a book Truman Capote had been working on since the weeks when the Clutter murders were still unsolved. A brief notice of the crime in the *New York Times* had inspired Capote to choose it as the subject for what he called a "nonfiction novel," a factually correct work written with techniques usually employed in writing fiction.

Capote interviewed everyone connected with the case, from the Clutters' neighbors to Hickock and Smith themselves. After the killers were captured, he followed their trials and became their confidant. When his book, *In Cold Blood*, appeared at the end of 1965, the lives and deaths of the Clutters and their killers became intimately known to millions of Americans. *In Cold Blood* was an international best-seller and the basis for a 1967 film.

Capote's experience left him opposed to capital punishment. Instead, he favored the federal imposition of mandatory life sentences for murder. By the time the Supreme Court issued the famous "Miranda Ruling" (see separate entry) in 1966, the writer's celebrity as an authority on criminal matters was such that he was called upon by a U.S. Senate subcommittee examining the court's decision. Capote criticized the high court's opinion that arrested suspects were to be advised of their rights to silence, legal counsel, and the presence of an attorney during police questioning.

Hickock and Smith would have gone "scot-free" under such circumstances because of the lack of clues in the Clutter murders, Capote said. "Any lawyer worth his salt would have advised the boys to say nothing. Had they said nothing, they would not have been brought to trial, much less convicted." Special Agent Alvin Dewey, who had elicited Perry Smith's confession, agreed. Dewey told the subcommittee that investigators abiding by the Miranda rule would be "talking the defendant out of telling us anything."

— Thomas C. Smith

Suggestions for Further Reading

Capote, Truman. *In Cold Blood*. New York: Random House, 1965.

Clarke, Gerald. *Capote: A Biography*. New York: Simon & Schuster, 1986.

Marshall, James. *Intention—In Law and Society*. New York: Funk & Wagnalls, 1968.

Menninger, Karl, M.D. *The Crime of Punishment*. New York: Viking Press, 1966.

Plimpton, George. "The Story Behind a Nonfiction Novel." *New York Times Book Review* (January 16, 1966): 2–3.

Boynton v. Virginia: 1960

Appellant: Bruce Boynton.   **Defendant:** Commonwealth of Virginia
Appellant Claim: Unlawful arrest   **Chief Defense Lawyer:** Walter E. Rogers
Chief Lawyer for Appellant: Thurgood Marshall   **Justices:** Hugo L. Black,
William J. Brennan, Jr., Tom C. Clark, William O. Douglas, Felix Frankfurter,
John Marshall Harlan, Potter Stewart, Earl Warren, Charles E. Whittaker.
Place: Washington, D.C.   **Date of Decision:** December 5, 1960
Decision: Court upheld appellant's claim

SIGNIFICANCE

In the often acrimonious battle between the federal government and individual
states over racial segregation, Bruce Boynton's suit marked a major break-
through. For the first time, Washington sent a clear message that interstate
facilities were for the use of all citizens, irrespective of color.

In 1958, Bruce Boynton, a black student at Howard University Law School in
Washington, D.C., took a Trailways bus from Washington to his home in
Montgomery, Alabama. On a 40-minute layover at the Trailways Bus Terminal
in Richmond, Virginia, the passengers went inside to eat. Boynton entered the
segregated restaurant, sat in the white section and ordered a sandwich and tea.
When asked to move to the colored section he refused, saying that as an
interstate passenger he was protected by federal anti-segregation laws. Declining to leave, he was arrested by local police, charged with trespass, and fined $10.

The Commonwealth of Virginia conceded that the conviction could not
stand if anything in federal law or the Constitution gave Boynton a right to
service in the restaurant. But it found no such right. Lawyers for the National
Association for the Advancement of Colored People (NAACP) petitioned the
Supreme Court on grounds that Boynton *was* entitled to such protection under
the Constitution.

Pleading that case before the Supreme Court on October 12, 1960, was
Thurgood Marshall, who later became the first black Supreme Court Justice. He
maintained that Boynton's arrest placed an unreasonable burden on commerce
and denied him the equal protection of the law, both points with far-reaching
implications. However, the Supreme Court chose not to address this petition
from a constitutional standpoint after the Justice Department, intervening as a

friend of the court, raised the issue of the Interstate Commerce Act, which expressly forbade "unjust discrimination."

For the act to apply, the relationship between restaurant and terminal had to be clarified. When Trailways built the terminal in 1953 it contracted with Bus Terminal Restaurant of Richmond, Inc. for the latter to provide dining facilities for passengers on Trailways buses. The only interest that Trailways had in the restaurant came in the form of the annual rental, $30,000, plus a percentage of the gross profits. So was the restaurant subject to the same federal provisions as Trailways?

Associate Justice Whittaker joined the dissent in *Boynton v. Virginia*, a landmark case, which linked the future of the civil rights movement with the federal government. (Courtesy, National Archives)

No, argued Walter E. Rogers, attorney for Virginia. He contended that the restaurant, as private property, fell outside the scope of the Interstate Commerce Act. Boynton, he said, had been justly convicted.

Court Splits, but for Boynton

On December 5, 1960, the Supreme Court decided 7-2 in favor of Boynton, the first time since 1946 it had divided on a matter of racial segregation. A strong factor in the Court's decision had been the earlier testimony of the restaurant manager who conceded that, although the restaurant received "quite a bit of business" from local people, it was primarily for the service of Trailways passengers. Describing this as "much of an understatement," Justice Hugo L. Black, in writing the majority verdict, added:

Interstate passengers have to eat, and they have a right to expect that this essential transportation food service . . . would be rendered without discrimination prohibited by the Interstate Commerce Act. We are not holding that every time a bus stops at a wholly independent roadside restaurant the act applies . . . [but] where circumstances show that the terminal and restaurant operate as an integral part of the bus carrier's transportation service . . . an interstate passenger need not inquire into documents of title or contractual agreements in order to determine whether he has a right to be served without discrimination.

Anticipating the Supreme Court's decision, Bus Terminal Restaurants, Inc. of Raleigh, North Carolina announced that, as of August 1960, none of its establishments would be racially segregated.

The impact of this case was immense. For the first time a bridge was built between the federal government and the civil rights movement. While many obstacles remained to be conquered in the fight for racial equality, henceforth it would be a struggle fought together.

—Colin Evans

1960
_____

Boynton v.
_____

Virginia

Suggestions for Further Reading

The Negro History Bulletin Vol. 26, 15. New York: Associated Publishers, 1972.

Wasby, Stephen L., Anthony A. D'Amato, and Rosemary Metrailer. *Desegregation From Brown To Alexander.* Carbondale, Ill.: South Illinois University Press, 1977.

Witt, Elder. *Guide To The Supreme Court.* Washington: Congressional Quarterly, 1990.

Clarence Earl Gideon Trials:
1961 & 1963

Defendant: Clarence Earl Gideon   **Crime Charged:** Breaking and entering
Chief Defense Lawyers: First trial: None; Second trial: W. Fred Turner
Chief Prosecutor: First trial: William E. Harris; Second trial: J. Frank Adams,
J. Paul Griffith, and William E. Harris   **Judge:** Robert L. McCrary, Jr.
Place: Panama City, Florida   **Dates of Trials:** First trial: August 4, 1961;
Second trial: August 5, 1963   **Verdict:** First trial: Guilty; Second trial: Not
guilty   **Sentence:** First trial: 5 years imprisonment

SIGNIFICANCE

One man, without benefit of wealth, privilege, or education, went up against the entire legal establishment, arguing that his constitutional rights had been violated. In doing so, he brought about an historic change in American trial procedure: all felony defendants are entitled to legal representation, irrespective of the crime charged, and courts are to appoint an attorney if a defendant is too poor to hire one.

At eight o'clock on the morning of June 3, 1961, a patrolling police officer in Panama City, Florida, noticed that the door of the Bay Harbor Poolroom was open. Stepping inside, he saw that a cigarette machine and jukebox had been burglarized. Eyewitness testimony led to the arrest of Clarence Gideon, a 51-year-old drifter who occasionally helped out at the poolroom. He vehemently protested his innocence but two months later was placed on trial at the Panama City Courthouse. No one present had any inkling that they were about to witness history in the making.

As the law then stood, Gideon, although indigent, was not automatically entitled to the services of a court-appointed defense lawyer. A 1942 Supreme Court decision, *Betts v. Brady*, extended this right only to those defendants facing a capital charge. Many states did, in fact, exceed the legal requirements and provide all felony defendants with counsel, but not Florida. Judge Robert L. McCrary, Jr. did his best to protect Gideon's interests when the trial opened August 4, 1961, but he clearly could not assume the role of advocate; that task was left to Gideon himself. Under the circumstances Gideon, a man of limited education but immense resourcefulness, performed as well as could be expected, but he was hardly the courtroom equal of Assistant State Attorney William E. Harris, who scored heavily with the testimony of Henry Cook.

This young man claimed to have seen Gideon inside the poolroom at 5:30 on the morning of the crime. After watching Gideon for a few minutes through the window, Cook said, the defendant came out clutching a pint of wine in his hand, then made a telephone call from a nearby booth. Soon afterward a cab arrived and Gideon left.

In cross-examination Gideon sought to impugn Cook's reasons for being outside the bar at that time of the morning. Cook replied that he had "just come from a dance, down in Apalachicola—stayed out all night." A more experienced cross-examiner might have explored this potentially fruitful line of questioning, but Gideon let it pass and lapsed into a vague and argumentative discourse.

Eight witnesses testified on the defendant's behalf. None proved helpful and Clarence Gideon was found guilty. The whole trial had lasted less than one day. Three weeks later Judge McCrary sentenced Gideon to the maximum: five years imprisonment.

Gideon Appeals

Gideon was outraged by the verdict, particularly the fact that he had been denied counsel. He applied to the Florida Supreme Court for a writ of *habeas corpus*, an order freeing him on the ground that he was illegally imprisoned. When this application was denied Gideon penciled a five-page document entitled "Petition for a Writ of *Certiorari* Directed to the Supreme Court." (A writ of *certiorari* is an order by an appellate court to hear a particular appeal.) In other words, Gideon was asking the U.S. Supreme Court to hear his case. The suit was placed on the docket under the title *Gideon v. H.G. Cochran, Jr.*, who happened to be the director of Florida's Division of Corrections.

Clarence Earl Gideon argued that his constitutional rights were denied when he was refused an attorney. (AP/Wide World Photos)

Each year the Supreme Court receives thousands of petitions. Most are meritless and don't get heard. Sheer weight of numbers militates against the deserving remainder, and yet, against all odds, the Supreme Court decided to hear Gideon's petition. Abe Fortas, who would himself later sit on the bench, was appointed to plead Gideon's case. Responding for Cochran were Bruce R. Jacob and George Mentz. The date for oral argument was set for January 14, 1963, but before that date Mr. Cochran resigned his position with the Florida Division of Corrections. He was replaced by Louie L. Wainwright—earning for that man an enduring and wholly unwanted place in judicial history—and the case was renamed *Gideon v. Wainwright*.

Fortas, arguing that the restrictive nature of *Betts v. Brady* had treated Gideon unfairly, drew a poignant analogy: "I was reminded the other night, as I was pondering this case, of Clarence Darrow when he was prosecuted for trying to fix a jury. The first thing he realized was that he needed a lawyer—he, one of the country's greatest criminal lawyers." It was time, said Fortas, for the law to change.

Needless to say, Jacob and Mentz stridently disagreed, but the mood of the times was against them, and, on March 18, 1963, the Supreme Court unanimously overruled *Betts v. Brady*, saying that all felony defendants were entitled to legal representation, irrespective of the crime charged. Justice Hugo L. Black wrote the opinion that set aside Gideon's conviction:

> [R]eason and reflection requires us to recognize that in our adversary system of criminal justice, any person haled into court, who is too poor to hire a lawyer, cannot be assured a fair trial unless counsel is provided for him. This seems to us to be an obvious truth.

On August 5, 1963, Clarence Gideon again appeared before Judge Robert L. McCrary in the Panama City Courthouse, and this time he had an experienced trial lawyer, W. Fred Turner, to defend him. All of the publicity resulted in a heavily bolstered prosecution team. In addition to William Harris, State Attorney J. Frank Adams and J. Paul Griffith were on hand to uphold the validity of the first conviction. Henry Cook was again the main prosecution witness but fared badly under Turner's incisive questioning. Particularly damaging was his admission that he had withheld details of his criminal record at the previous trial. Due in large part to Cook's poor showing, the jury acquitted Gideon of all charges.

He died in 1972 at age 61.

Clarence Earl Gideon's petition to the Supreme Court. (Courtesy, United States Supreme Court)

Because one man sat down and wrote a letter, no felony defendant need ever fear facing a court alone. *Gideon v. Wainwright* extended the law's protection to all. More than that, it gave justice a better name.

—Colin Evans

Suggestions for Further Reading

The Guide To American Law. St. Paul, Minn.: West Publishing Co., 1984.

Lewis, Anthony. *Gideon's Trumpet*. New York: Random House, 1964.

Schwartz, Bernard. *History Of The Law In America*. New York: American Heritage, 1974.

John Henry Faulk v. Aware, Inc., et al: 1962

Plaintiff: John Henry Faulk **Defendants:** Aware, Inc., Vincent Hartnett, and Laurence A. Johnson **Plaintiff Claim:** Damages for libel and conspiracy
Chief Defense Lawyer: Thomas A. Bolan **Chief Lawyer for Plaintiff:** Louis Nizer **Judge:** Abraham N. Geller **Place:** New York, New York
Dates: April 23–July 29, 1962 **Verdict:** Award for compensatory damages in the amount of $1 million, plus $2.5 million in punitive damages (at the time, the largest judgment ever returned in a libel suit)

SIGNIFICANCE
The verdict put an end to institutional blacklisting by private groups and individuals who claimed to be experts on Communism, "cleared" artists, and excluded artists from employment in the mass media.

In 1957, radio and television performer John Henry Faulk, a Texan with a penchant for folklore, fought back against blacklisting in the American work place by suing Aware, Inc. and two individuals for libel. In the tense Cold War years following World War II, fear of Communist subversion led to pressure on the movie and broadcasting industries to blacklist anyone suspected of the slightest past or present sympathy with Communist or leftist causes. Afraid of advertiser boycotts, the broadcasting companies buckled under the pressure from self-styled experts on Communism who insisted on their right to screen performers. Hundreds of careers were jeopardized or ruined and some victims of the practice were so distraught they committed suicide.

Despite bankruptcy and humiliation, Faulk persisted in his suit against the blacklisters through six years of pretrial motions, a dramatic trial, and numerous appeals that reached the U.S. Supreme Court.

The Cold War Climate

With the onset of the Cold War in 1946, the federal government and other sectors of American life were purged of those suspected of sympathy with the Soviet Union's Communist government. Blacklists containing the names of anyone who had refused to appear before the House Un-American Activities Committee (HUAC) were circulated to intimidate offending individuals and organizations. By the 1950s, the blacklisters, motivated as much by the desire to make a buck as anti-Communist ideology, had begun to intimidate the private sector—business, higher education, radio, and television.

Performers were systematically "cleared" through paid security consultants. Encouraged and provided with information by the continuing HUAC hearings, they researched a performer's political history. The evidence was often slight or ambiguous. A $5 donation to the "wrong" cause was sometimes sufficient to add a name to a blacklist and jeopardize the "sinner's" livelihood. By 1955, the practice was an integral part of the broadcast industry's hiring procedure.

Faulk Leads Fight Against Blacklisting

John Henry Faulk, who was all Texas charm and folksy humor, was born and reared in Austin and went on to earn a Master's degree in English at the University of Texas, where he lectured on American folklore and English while studying for a doctorate. After the war, during which he served in the Merchant Marine, the American Red Cross, and the U.S. Army, Faulk began appearing on radio and television. By 1953, he was starring in his own talk show, playing popular music and commenting in his distinctive drawl on the news of the day.

His daily afternoon radio program on WCBS, in New York City, had high ratings and solid sponsors such as Libby's Frozen Foods by 1955. Faulk was well-liked by his colleagues and substituted regularly as a panelist on television game shows. He was, in fact, planning a full-time television career.

Like all broadcast performers, he was a member of the American Federation of Television and Radio Artists, known as AFTRA. Formed in 1938, AFTRA's New York local was the largest in the country. It was governed by a 35-member board of directors, elected by the membership every year. In the mid-1950s the board was dominated by an anti-Communist faction supporting Aware, Inc., a political group organized to fight "the Communist conspiracy in entertainment communications." In fact, Vinton Hayworth, the president of AFTRA in 1955, was also an officer of Aware, Inc.

Any performer who found his name in one of Aware's regularly issued bulletins was blacklisted and rendered unemployable in the industry. Sponsors, worried that their products would be linked to those accused of Communist sympathies, canceled advertising spots. Without explanation, performers were denied all opportunities, even 10-minute guest appearances. Careers and lives were quickly ruined. Victims disappeared into obscurity, including Jean Muir, the popular mother on "The Aldrich Family." Others, like Mady Christians and Philip Loeb, committed suicide.

Alarmed by the growing practice of blacklisting, several members of AFTRA, including Faulk, recommended that Aware, Inc. be condemned by the union membership. The vote was carried, 982 to 514, and a new slate was put up for election: Charles Collingwood, a former Rhodes Scholar and then a CBS news commentator; Gary Moore, popular on radio and television; and John Henry Faulk, among others. They called themselves "the middle of the road slate" to oppose Communism and blacklisting alike, to "oppose denial of employment by discriminatory and intimidating practices, especially by outside organizations."

The bitterly fought election brought an overwhelming victory for the "middlers." The highest number of votes went to Faulk, and with it the full force of an Aware assault. In the no-holds-barred, poison-pen campaign that followed, Aware sent letters to CBS executives warning that Faulk had "a significant Communist Front record."

Faulk vehemently denied the allegations. At the urging of CBS executives, he signed an affidavit saying so. Despite the assault behind the scenes, Faulk's show continued to register high ratings. He openly discussed the continued assault on his sponsors and their ad agencies with CBS executives, even urging them to sue sponsors who canceled advertising because of the unfounded accusations. When they refused, Faulk himself filed suit on June 26, 1956. CBS renewed Faulk's contract in December 1956, and in the year that followed, Faulk's earnings were the highest ever and his show was number two in the Nielsen ratings. His friend and manager Sam Slate assured him his job was secure. But in 1957, CBS fired Faulk while he vacationed with his family in Jamaica. The network told him it needed to make format changes and would substitute Arthur Godfrey in his time slot. From that time on, with the exception of a guest appearance on Jack Paar's talk show, Faulk could not get a job. In 1959 he moved his destitute family back to Texas.

The evidence that banished Faulk from the entertainment industry and left him unemployed for 6½ years began with a list of speaking engagements Faulk had made from 1946 to 1949. It stated, "According to the *Daily Worker* (the Communist newspaper) of April 22, 1946, Jack Faulk was to appear at Club 65, 13 Astor Place, N.Y.C.—a favorite site of pro-Communist affairs."

Unlike other Aware victims, Faulk fought back with the help of Louis Nizer, the most respected civil liberties lawyer of the day. Nizer determined first that Faulk's was a case of libel, but Nizer suspected a conspiracy, too. The suit was an opportunity to attack the blacklisting techniques that permeated the industry. To prove the case, Nizer would show how a few private citizens forced the entertainment industry, the fifth-largest industry in the United States, to secretly and illegally boycott its own employees.

The defendants in the case, representing Aware, Inc., were Vincent Hartnett and Laurence Johnson. Johnson, in his 70s, was the prosperous owner of a chain of New York state supermarkets. His criticism of a program or a performer brought anxious network executives to his Syracuse headquarters seeking absolution. Johnson's attack on Faulk took him to the Madison Avenue advertising agencies representing Faulk's sponsors. There he threatened that every supermarket in the country would boycott any product sold on Faulk's show.

Vincent Hartnett was also an entrepreneur, cashing in on the anti-Communist zeal as the principal contributor to *Red Channels*, a book citing the political activities of performers. It became the desktop reference during every casting call. In 1952, Hartnett, with Paul Milton, had formed Aware, Inc., a private consulting firm to screen artists. A former network employee himself, Hartnett charged broadcast networks and ad agencies $5 a head to research a performer's background. Hartnett's alliance with Laurence Johnson added economic muscle to back up the accusations. To deny or protest only brought more controversy for the victim, more letters, more threats. Almost without exception the accused slipped quietly away.

To win the libel suit, Nizer would have to overcome the obvious defense that what was written in the bulletin was true, Nizer had to show that Faulk, as a public figure, was maliciously attacked outside the bounds of fair comment. Although the truth of the speaking engagements was proven, the claim Faulk was a Communist sympathizer was not provable by a mere newspaper listing. Nizer established in pretrial testimony that Aware, Inc., Hartnett and Johnson could not verify any of the accusations against Faulk contained in the lengthy documents they had published and distributed.

In one dramatic pretrial session, Hartnett, in front of his attorney, Godfrey Schmidt, admitted to Nizer that his research consisted of "being sold a barrel of goods." Soon after, Schmidt was replaced by Roy Cohn as the chief defense attorney.

John Henry Faulk fought back when Aware blacklisted him and sought to destroy his television career. (AP/ Wide World Photos)

Trial Witnesses Hard to Find

When the trial finally opened on April 23, 1962, New York Supreme Court Justice Abraham N. Geller immediately impressed upon the members of the jury their right to judge the facts in the case without prejudice and without fear.

The fear of blacklisting was still so great when the trial opened that witnesses whose testimony Nizer needed were hard to find. Both Faulk and Nizer implored individuals to come forward, and those who did were an impressive lot: successful performers, advertising executives, and producers who had had their fill of blacklisting.

Nizer led each one through testimony that described for the court how people were labeled Communists because they were linked to Communist Front activities, often simply because they had made small financial donations to obscure political causes. There were stories of mistaken identity and of guilt by insinuation. Rarely would someone be given the opportunity to deny an allegation, but one witness testified a victim could, if he paid a fee to the consultant, receive a "full report" and concede the wrongdoing.

Actress Kim Hunter told how she couldn't get a job in broadcasting for three years after she'd won an Academy Award in 1949. Her name had not appeared in Aware, Inc. bulletins or on any lists that she knew of, but no one in television would hire her.

Finally in 1956, she traced her lack of employment to Hartnett and sought him out. He told her that his investigation had linked her name with assorted Communist Front activities and she could have a full report for $200.

The actress' former "acts of disloyalty" now valued at $200 were: purchasing for $5 a reprint of the New York Post series entitled, "Blacklist—The Panic in Radio and Television"; lending her name to the "problem of world peace" under the auspices of the National Council of Arts, Sciences and Professions; and signing a petition for the fair trial in Mississippi of Willie McGee, "a Negro."

David Susskind, an experienced producer, testified he had to submit all the names of all the people involved in a production to the ad agency Young and Rubicam for political clearance. No one was hired until approved. In one year alone, Susskind testified he had submitted 5,000 names for approval. One-third were rejected.

Nizer tied this testimony to Hartnett by producing an agreement Hartnett had with Young and Rubicam. For $5 each, Hartnett would check the names of artists submitted to him for Susskind's program. An advertising executive corroborated this by testifying that he came to view Hartnett as a racketeer selling protection.

Apparently no performer had been excluded from the screening process. Nizer produced Hartnett's records in which one entry read, "Santa Claus, $5."

It wasn't Faulk's political sins that got him fired, argued defense attorney Thomas Bolan, who had replaced his associate Roy Cohn. It was Faulk's lack of talent and his loss of popularity. Bolan pointed out that Faulk kept his show for one year after the Aware bulletin was issued—evidence, he said, that it was Faulk's loss of popularity and his own incompetence that cost him his job.

Bolan then accused Faulk of attending Communist Party meetings in the 1940s and associating with known Communists. Faulk denied this on the stand and it gave Nizer an opening to get his client's views before the jury.

"Have you . . . ever been sympathetic to any Communist ideology, directly or indirectly?" Nizer asked. In a tremulous voice, Faulk answered, "No, sir, I have not."

It was Aware, Inc., and the defendants themselves who proved to be the most effective witnesses for the plaintiff. Paul Milton, one of Aware's founders but not included in the suit against the organization, testified for the defense. Under Nizer's questioning, Milton moved from resistance to a reluctant confession, conceding that Faulk's only wrongdoing was opposing Aware, Inc. Nizer also attacked the language of the Aware, Inc. bulletin, which Milton had helped draft. The phrase "according to the *Daily Worker*" made it appear that the Communist newspaper supported Faulk's candidacy. Nizer pointedly asked if news of Faulk's opposition in the union to Aware hadn't appeared in all the daily papers? Milton admitted he had deliberately omitted this fact.

When Hartnett took the stand, Bolan began to lead his client through an impressive-looking pile of documents on which Hartnett claimed he had relied when compiling evidence of Faulk's disloyalty.

Ordinarily notes of this sort are inadmissible, as they cannot be independently verified, but in a libel case an exception is made to permit the defendant to demonstrate a research effort had been made unmotivated by malice. Hartnett began citing the records of the House Un-American Activities Committee hearings, but he was interrupted. These congressional hearings were not admissible in a court of law, Justice Geller told the astonished defense attorney. They did not constitute a judicial finding, and their truth had not been established. With the HUAC hearing records excluded, all that was left of Hartnett's "research" were 13 notes on a file card when Nizer began cross-examination. Of these, only two mentioned Faulk's name, and both were positive references to Faulk's career.

Nizer also proved that Hartnett had attributed a story about Faulk and the "middlers" to the *Daily Worker*, though it had appeared in the *New York Herald Tribune*.

While he was under cross-examination, Hartnett was asked if he could identify Faulk's wife among the spectators. When Hartnett pointed to the wrong woman, Nizer bellowed: "Sir, is that an example of the accuracy with which you have identified your victims for the past ten years?"

Hartnett told the court he investigated individuals only at the request of a client. But no one—not the ad agency Young and Rubicam, not the sponsors, not the network, Nizer showed—had requested a report about John Henry Faulk or the middle-of-the-road slate of officers. This research Hartnett had thrown in for free.

Laurence Johnson never appeared in court to defend himself. Newspaper columnists called him "sick-call Larry," as he traveled from doctor to doctor for exemption. Nizer charged that if Johnson could withstand this many medical examinations, he was sturdy enough to appear in court. The court agreed. But as the trial reached its final days, Johnson checked into a Bronx, New York, motel, where he was found dead of a barbiturate overdose. The news was kept from the jury until both sides finished their summation.

The issue in the trial, Nizer told the jury, was not Communism at all, but private vigilantism and individuals who took the law into their own hands. When a self-appointed group fabricates information about a man, then goes behind his back to deprive him of his livelihood, Nizer declared, it could only be described as a concerted conspiracy. Nizer urged the jury to give by its verdict a "clarion call to the world" that this practice had to stop.

Bolan's defense attacked Faulk's integrity. Faulk, he told the jury, was a liar.

Justice Geller sequestered the jury for the night. The next day he substituted the estate of Laurence Johnson in place of the deceased Laurence Johnson as defendant. One day later, on July 29, 1962, the jury returned a verdict for Faulk along with the largest award in a libel suit to that date. It awarded damages of $1 million against Aware, Inc., Hartnett, and the estate of Laurence Johnson. Finding malice on the part of the defendants, it added $1.25 million in punitive damages against Aware, Inc., and the same amount against Hartnett.

In 1963, an appellate court reduced the damages from $3.5 million to $550,000, deciding that this amount was in line with Faulk's estimated earnings. The decision was upheld the next year in the New York State Court of Appeals.

Hartnett and Aware, Inc. then claimed the verdict violated their First Amendment freedoms and petitioned the Supreme Court for *certiorari*— permission to appeal the constitutional question. The request to be heard was denied with only Justices Hugo Black and William O. Douglas voting to grant it. In one last petition to the Supreme Court, the defendants argued that libel law came from the ecclesiastical law of England and violated the First Amendment separation of church and state. It was unanimously denied. Finally the blacklist and the blacklisters were finished.

—Elizabeth Gwillim

Suggestions for Further Reading

Caute, David. *The Great Fear: The Anti-Communist Purge Under Truman and Eisenhower*. New York: Simon & Schuster, 1978.

Faulk, John Henry. *Fear On Trial*. New York: Simon & Schuster, 1964.

——. "Awareness and Aware, Inc." *Bill of Rights Journal* (December, 1985): 26.

Kanfer, Stefan. *A Journal of the Plague Years*. New York: Atheneum, 1973.

Nizer, Louis. *The Jury Returns*. Garden City, N.Y.: Doubleday & Co., 1966.

Ernesto Miranda Trials: 1963 & 1967

Defendant: Ernesto Miranda **Crimes Charged:** Kidnapping and rape
Chief Defense Lawyers: First trial: Alvin Moore; second Trial: John Flynn
Chief Prosecutors: First trial: Laurence Turoff; second trial: Robert Corbin
Judges: First trial: Yale McFate; second trial: Lawrence K. Wren
Place: Phoenix, Arizona **Dates of Trials:** June 20–27, 1963; February 15–
March 1, 1967 **Verdict:** Guilty, both trials **Sentences:** 20–30 years,
both trials

SIGNIFICANCE

Few events have altered the course of American jurisprudence more than the
1963 rape conviction of Ernesto Miranda. The primary evidence against him was a
confession he made while in police custody. How that confession was obtained
exercised the conscience of a nation and prompted a landmark U.S. Supreme
Court decision.

In the early hours of March 3, 1963, an 18-year-old Phoenix, Arizona, movie
theater attendant was accosted by a stranger while on her way home from
work. He dragged her into his car, drove out to the desert, and raped her.
Afterwards he dropped the girl off near her home. The story she told police,
often vague and contradictory, described her attacker as a bespectacled Mexican, late 20s, who was driving an early fifties car, either a Ford or Chevrolet.

By chance, one week later, the girl and her brother-in-law saw what she
believed was the car, a 1953 Packard, license plate DFL-312. Records showed
that this plate was actually registered to a late model Oldsmobile, but DFL-317
was a Packard, registered to a Twila N. Hoffman; and her boyfriend, Ernesto
Miranda, 23, fit the attacker's description almost exactly.

Miranda had a long history of emotional instability and criminal behavior,
including a one-year jail term for attempted rape. At police headquarters he was
placed in a line-up with three other Mexicans of similar height and build, though
none wore glasses. The victim did not positively identify Miranda but said that
he bore the closest resemblance to her attacker. Detectives Carroll Cooley and
Wilfred Young then took Miranda into an interrogation room. He was told,
inaccurately, that he had been identified, and did he want to make a statement?
Two hours later Miranda signed a written confession. There had been no blatant

coercion or brutality, and included in the confession was a section stating that he understood his rights. When the detectives left interrogation room 2, they were pleased, not realizing the legal repercussions that would result from their efforts.

Tainted Evidence

As an indigent, Miranda was granted a court-appointed defender, Alvin Moore. Moore studied the evidence. The state had an apparently unassailable case, buttressed by Miranda's confession. And yet there was something about that confession that Moore found troubling. Convinced it had been obtained improperly, he intended to move for its inadmissibility.

Only four witnesses appeared for the prosecution: the victim, her sister, and Detectives Cooley and Young. After their testimony, Deputy County Attorney Laurence Turoff told the jury that the victim "did not enter into this act of intercourse with him [Miranda] willfully, but in fact she was forced to, by his own force and violence, directed against her."

Moore responded by highlighting inconsistencies in the victim's story. She claimed to have been a virgin prior to the attack, an assertion discounted by medical examiners, and could not remember the exact chronology of the night's events. Neither did she exhibit any bruising or abrasions after the attack; reason enough for Moore to thunder to the jury, "You have in this case a sorrowful case, but you don't have the facts to require that you send a man to prison for rape of a woman who should have resisted and resisted and resisted, until her resistance was at least overcome by the force and violence of the defendant" (an essential requirement under Arizona law at that time; anything less was regarded as compliance.)

But it wasn't until cross-examination of Carroll Cooley that Moore struck:

Question: Officer Cooley, in the taking of this statement, what did you say to the defendant to get him to make this statement?

Answer: I asked the defendant if he would . . . write the same story that he just told me, and he said that he would.

Question: Did you warn him of his rights?

Answer: Yes, sir, at the heading of the statement is a paragraph typed out, and I read this paragraph to him out loud.

Question: I don't see in the statement that it says where he is entitled to the advice of an attorney before he made it.

Answer: No, sir.

Question: Is it not your practice to advise people you arrest that they are entitled to the services of an attorney before they make a statement?

Answer: No, sir.

This admission prompted Moore to object to the confession as evidence, but he was overruled by Judge Yale McFate, who favored the jury with a well-balanced and eminently fair account of the law as it stood at the time. In 1963, the constitutional right to silence was not thought to extend to the jailhouse.

Consequently, on June 27, 1963, Ernesto Miranda was convicted and sentenced to two concurrent terms of 20-30 years imprisonment.

But Alvin Moore's arguments about the confession had touched off a legal firestorm. Miranda's conviction was appealed all the way to the U.S. Supreme Court. On June 13, 1966, Chief Justice Earl Warren, speaking for a 5-4 majority, for the first time established unequivocal guidelines about what is and what is not permissible in the interrogation room:

> Prior to any questioning, the person must be warned that he has a right to remain silent, that any statement he does make may be used as evidence against him, and that he has a right to the presence of an attorney, either retained or appointed . . .

Conviction Overturned

With Miranda's conviction overturned, Arizona glumly faced the prospect of having to free its most celebrated prison inmate. Without the confession, the chances of winning a retrial were negligible. Ironically, it was Miranda himself who brought about his own downfall. Expecting to be released after retrial, he had begun a custody battle with his common-law wife, Twila Hoffman, over their daughter. Hoffman, angry and fearful, approached the authorities and revealed to them the content of a conversation she had had with Miranda after his arrest, in which he had admitted the rape.

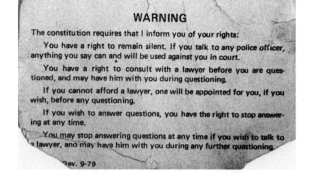

WARNING

The constitution requires that I inform you of your rights:

You have a right to remain silent. If you talk to any police officer, anything you say can and will be used against you in court.

You have a right to consult with a lawyer before you are questioned, and may have him with you during questioning.

If you cannot afford a lawyer, one will be appointed for you, if you wish, before any questioning.

If you wish to answer questions, you have the right to stop answering at any time.

You may stop answering questions at any time if you wish to talk to a lawyer, and may have him with you during any further questioning.

Rev. 9-79

The Miranda warning ensures that the accused is informed of certain rights after being arrested. (Connecticut State Police)

This fresh evidence was all Arizona needed.

Miranda's second trial began February 15, 1967. Much of the case was argued in the judge's chambers. At issue: Could a common-law wife testify against her husband? Yes, said County Attorney Robert Corbin. Defense counsel John Flynn, who had pleaded Miranda's case before the Supreme Court, bitterly disagreed. After considerable legal wrangling, Judge Lawrence K. Wren ruled such evidence admissible, and Twila Hoffman was allowed to tell her story to the jury. It proved decisive. Miranda was again found guilty and sentenced to a 20-to-30-year jail term.

On January 31, 1976, four years after being paroled, Ernesto Miranda was stabbed to death in a Phoenix bar fight. The killer fled but his accomplice was caught. Before taking him to police headquarters, the arresting officers read the suspect his rights. In police vernacular, he had been "Mirandized."

The importance of this case cannot be overstated. Denounced by presidents from Richard Nixon to Ronald Reagan, the Miranda decision has withstood all attempts to overturn it. Framed originally to protect the indigent and the ignorant, the practice of "reading the defendant his rights" has become standard operating procedure in every police department in the country. The practice is seen so frequently in television police dramas that today the words of the so-called "Miranda Warning" are as familiar to most Americans as those of the Pledge of Allegiance.

—Colin Evans

Suggestions for Further Reading

Baker, Liva. *Miranda: Crime, Law and Politics.* New York: Atheneum, 1983.

Graham, Fred P. *The Self-Inflicted Wound.* New York: Macmillan Co., 1970.

Skene, Neil. "The Miranda Ruling." *Congressional Quarterly* (June 6, 1991): 164.

Tucker, William. "The Long Road Back." *National Review* (October 18, 1985): 28–35.

Onion Field Murder Trials: 1963–69

Defendants: Gregory Ulas Powell, Jimmy Lee Smith
Crime Charged: Murder **Chief Defense Lawyers:** John Moore, Kathryn McDonald, Ray Smith, Gregory Powell, Irving Kanarek, Charles Maple, William A. Drake, Charles Hollopeter **Chief Prosecutors:** Marshall Schulman, Philip Halpin, Joseph Busch, Raymond Byrne, Sheldon Brown, Dino Fulgoni
Judges: Twelve judges, the most important being Mark Brandler, Alfred Peracca, Arthur Alarcon, Thomas LeSage, Harold Sheperd **Place:** Los Angeles, California **Dates of Trials:** First trial: July 15–September 12, 1963; new trial hearing: October 31–November 13, 1963; second trial: April 1–November 6, 1969 **Verdicts:** Guilty **Sentences:** Death for both in first trial; life imprisonment for Smith, death for Powell in the second. But Powell's sentence was commuted to life imprisonment in March 1972, when the California Supreme Court decided that death was cruel and unusual punishment.

SIGNIFICANCE

In March 1963, two small-time thieves kidnapped two Los Angeles police officers. They murdered one, but the other escaped. The killers were quickly captured and were convicted of murder. With appeals, interminable pretrial motions, and new trials, however, the case dragged on for another six years. Smith's original death sentence was changed to life imprisonment. Powell's death sentence was found unconstitutional in 1972 and changed to life in prison. The case outraged a Los Angeles police officer, Joseph Wambaugh, who wrote a best-selling book about it, *The Onion Field.* The book was a major factor in the restoration of the death penalty in most of the United States.

O n March 9, 1963, two Los Angeles plainclothesmen, Ian Campbell and Karl Hettinger, approached a car with a pair of suspicious-looking men in it. The men were Gregory Powell and Jimmy Smith, two stick-up men preparing to commit a robbery. The crooks surprised the officers by drawing guns, disarming them, and taking them out of the city. They drove them to an onion farm about 90 miles north of Los Angeles. They shot Campbell, but Hettinger ran and reached the safety of a farm house.

The crooks split up to pursue Hettinger. Smith, driving the car, left his partner and fled. Powell stole a farmer's car but was arrested by two cops who identified the vehicle as stolen. He confessed to the murder and told them Smith was his accomplice.

Hettinger returned to duty. But because he had given up his gun to save his partner, his superiors in the LAPD considered him a coward—treatment that enraged his colleague, Joseph Wambaugh, as much as the fate of the two murderers.

Start of a Legal Marathon

Murder trials in California are bifurcated. The first part focuses, on the guilt of the defendants and the second, on the sentence. After being found guilty, Powell fired his attorneys, John Moore and Kathryn McDonald, and conducted his own defense in the sentence hearing. But, like Smith, he was sentenced to death. He immediately filed an appeal. Jimmy Smith fired his attorney, Ray Smith, and hired a new lawyer, Irving Kanarek. Kanarek had defended Charles Manson, the mass murderer. Kanarek, too, moved for a new trial. When the hearing for a new trial began, Kanarek wasted many days trying to prove that a juror in the first trial—a woman who was obviously insane—had been unjustly replaced because she favored the defense. He followed that with numerous irrelevant motions that moved the prosecutor, Marshall Schulman, to beg the judge to hold Kanarek in contempt. Judge Mark Brandler would not do that, but on November 13, he again sentenced Powell and Smith to death.

But there was another trial, decisions by the U.S. Supreme Court were the cause. In 1964, the Court found in favor of Danny Escobedo, who confessed to a murder after he had asked for, and not received, advice from a lawyer. The next year, the California Supreme Court reversed the conviction of Robert Dorado because the police had not warned him that he had the right to remain silent and be represented by counsel. And the year after that, the U.S. Supreme Court, in the case of Ernesto Miranda, made such a warning mandatory in all cases. Smith and Powell again appealed. While the appeal was pending, Powell tried to escape, but was captured before he could get over the wall.

The escape attempt did not matter. The California Supreme Court ordered a new trial for both defendants on the grounds that they had not been advised of their rights.

Once again, Irving Kanarek represented Jimmy Smith. Public defender Charles Maple represented Gregory Powell. A new prosecutor, Philip Halpin, presented the state's case, and a new judge, Alfred Peracca, presided. The defense, particularly Kanarek, turned this trial into even more of a circus than the preceding trial. Kanarek, during his marathon of pretrial motions, falsely accused Halpin of intending to assault him and then of carrying a gun into the courtroom, meanwhile interrupting the judge and ignoring objections. While this was going on, Powell and Smith made another escape attempt. Judge Peracca had to be removed from the case after he had a heart attack.

Peracca's replacement, Arthur Alarcon, finally removed Kanarek from the case for incompetence, replacing him with William A. Drake. Three months later, the California Supreme Court reversed Alarcon's decision. Kanarek came back. Judge Alarcon left the case.

Exit Kanarek

No judge in Los Angeles wanted to touch the case. Thomas LeSage, a brand-new judge, was assigned to it. When he asked if there were any pretrial motions, Kanarek launched his patented barrage of irrelevancies. It culminated when he accused Halpin of mouthing an obscenity. The prosecutor's patience broke. He grabbed Kanarek by the shirt and screamed, "I will not permit this man to say that about me!" Kanarek demanded that the prosecutor be arrested for assault.

Halpin was removed from the case. So was—finally—Irving Kanarek. Kanarek's dismissal came after a motion by Jimmy Smith to fire his lawyer. Smith became so hostile to his defense attorney that he shoved Kanarek away from him and threw a chair at him. A Pasadena attorney named Charles Hollopeter was assigned to advise Smith. Kanarek maintained that his client was unable to think clearly. He further argued that the judge had no right to ask Jimmy Smith about his choice of lawyers. He charged that the judge was proceeding illegally. The judge, however, ruled that the hostility between Smith and his lawyer prevented the defendant from having the representation by counsel required by law. He relieved Kanarek of his duties. That ruling was final. The next day, he ordered separate trials for the two defendants.

With Kanarek gone, jury selection for the Gregory Powell trial was able to proceed. This time, the confessions and all incriminating statements by the defendants were inadmissible. To a large extent, the case depended on Karl Hettinger, the policeman who had escaped. Hettinger, however, was not the man he was six years before. Practically accused of cowardice, he had been taken off patrol and assigned to drive the chief of police. Colleagues shunned him. Mental and emotional troubles mounted. He had become a kleptomaniac and had been dismissed from the force. By the time he was called as a witness, his memory of events on the night of the shooting was blurred. Prosecutors Joseph Busch and Raymond Byrne were able, however, to present enough evidence to get a guilty verdict. In the penalty hearing, prosecutor Sheldon Brown convinced the jury to prescribe the death sentence. During the trial, Powell tried to escape again, and at one time attacked a spectator while leaving the courtroom.

In his new trial, Jimmy Smith was defended by Charles Hollopeter, while Dino Fulgoni represented the state. After a short time it appeared that Smith didn't like Hollopeter much better than he liked Kanarek. Although Smith, as well as Powell, had actually fired bullets into Campbell, his defense was that he had nothing to do with the shooting. Hollopeter bolstered this defense by calling Powell as a witness. Powell answered almost all questions by invoking the Fifth Amendment. But Powell was a "scary dude." Jurors treated to his malevolent glare were convinced that he was the evil leader of the Powell-Smith partnership. The jurors found Smith guilty but voted for life imprisonment on November 6, 1969. On December 3, 1969, the twelfth judge to be involved with the "Onion Field" case sentenced Gregory Powell to death. But the case wasn't over yet.

Death Penalty Decision

In March 1972, seven years after the murder, the California Supreme Court, considering the trial of Robert P. Anderson, ruled that the death penalty was cruel and unusual punishment. All death sentences were automatically commuted.

The next year, Joseph Wambaugh, a Los Angeles detective sergeant who had published two previous police procedural novels, wrote another book. That book, *The Onion Field*, was what author Truman Capote called a "non-fiction novel." It was a powerful indictment of both the judicial system and the LAPD hierarchy. It became a best-seller and a major factor in the trend toward reinstating the death penalty in the United States.

— William Weir

Suggestions for Further Reading

Wambaugh, Joseph. *The Onion Field*. New York: Delacorte Press, 1973.

Georgetown College v. Jones: 1963

Plaintiff: Georgetown College, now known as Georgetown University
Defendant: Jessie E. Jones **Plaintiff Claim:** That the courts should
overrule Jones' refusal to permit a blood transfusion for his wife, who was
being treated in the school's hospital **Chief Defense Lawyers:** Ralph H.
Deckelbaum and Bernard Margolius **Chief Lawyers for Plaintiff:** Peter R.
Taft, Harold Ungar, and Edward Bennett Williams **Judge:** J. Skelly Wright
Place: Washington, D.C. **Date of Hearing:** September 17, 1963
Decision: That the hospital should be allowed to give all necessary blood
transfusions

SIGNIFICANCE

Despite the expansion of civil liberties by the courts in the 1960s, the judicial
system refused to recognize any right to refuse medical treatment for purely
religious reasons.

One of the many Christian religious sects is a group called the Jehovah's
Witnesses, which is several centuries old. Followers of the sect believe in
the imminent end of the world, and in strictly following the literal words and
commands of the Bible. One of these biblical commands is contained in Genesis
chapter nine, which states that the consumption of blood is forbidden:

> And God went on to bless Noah and his sons and to say to them: "Be fruitful
> and become many and fill the earth. And a fear of you and a terror of you will
> continue upon every living creature of the earth and upon every flying
> creature of the heavens, upon everything that goes moving on the ground,
> and upon all the fishes of the sea. Into your hand they are now given. Every
> moving animal that is alive may serve as food for you. As in the case of the
> green vegetation, I do give it all to you. Only flesh with its soul—its blood—
> you must not eat."

In keeping with their literalist approach, the Jehovah's Witnesses traditionally would not eat blood sausages or blood puddings. They never had any
serious conflicts with the medical profession until the 1940s, when blood
transfusions and the technology of blood storage in blood banks became standardized and commonplace. In 1945, a Jehovah's Witness publication called *The
Watchtower* stated that blood transfusions were akin to consuming blood.

813

Crisis Develops at Georgetown Hospital

In September 1963, a young man named Jessie E. Jones brought his wife into the hospital operated by Georgetown College in Washington, D.C. Georgetown College is now Georgetown University, whose hospital is a world-famous institution. Mrs. Jones, age 25 and mother of a 7-month-old child, had suffered a ruptured ulcer and lost two-thirds of her blood. The Joneses were both Jehovah's Witnesses. When Dr. Edwin Westura, the chief medical resident, said that Mrs. Jones (first name unavailable) would die unless given a blood transfusion, Jones refused to permit it.

Responsible for Mrs. Jones' life, Georgetown had its lawyers, Peter R. Taft, Harold Ungar and the famous Edward Bennett Williams, go to the courts for permission to give the necessary blood transfusions without Jones' consent. On September 17, 1963, the attorneys went to Judge Edward A. Tamm's chambers at the U.S. District Court for the District of Columbia and asked for an emergency order allowing the hospital to save Mrs. Jones' life. Judge Tamm refused. At 4:00 P.M. on the same day, the attorneys went to the chambers of Judge J. Skelly Wright of the U.S. Court of Appeals for the District of Columbia Circuit, asking for an immediate review of Tamm's decision.

Judge Wright telephoned the hospital, and Dr. Westura confirmed that Mrs. Jones would die without a blood transfusion. Wright then went to the hospital with the attorneys, where he met Jones. Jones remained firm in his refusal to grant consent. Father Bunn, Georgetown's president, even came to plead with Jones, to no avail. Westura and the other doctors assigned to the case tried without success to explain that a transfusion is completely different from drinking blood. At 5:20 P.M., Wright signed the orders prepared by the attorneys, and Mrs. Jones was given blood transfusions that saved her life.

On September 19, 1963, Wright filed a memorandum concerning his actions, which recited various legal precedents permitting courts to act in preservation of human life, and ended by stating:

> The final, and compelling, reason for granting the emergency writ was that a life hung in the balance. There was no time for research and reflection. Death could have mooted the cause in a matter of minutes, if action were not taken to preserve the status quo. To refuse to act, only to find later that the law required action, was a risk I was unwilling to accept. I determined to act on the side of life.

On October 14, 1963, Jones' attorneys, Ralph H. Deckelbaum and Bernard Margolius, filed a petition for rehearing before the full court of appeals to quash Wright's September 17 order. On February 3, 1964, the Court of Appeals denied Jones's petition because Mrs. Jones had long since recovered and left the hospital. There was a spirited dissent, however, by Circuit Judge Warren Burger, who subsequently became chief justice of the U.S. Supreme Court. Burger felt that the fact that Jones had signed a release upon bringing his wife to the hospital took the case out of the court's jurisdiction: in effect, the college had to rely on the release for legal protection without court help. Jones appealed to the

U.S. Supreme Court, but his attorneys' petition was denied without comment on June 15, 1964.

Even though the 1960s was an era of increasing civil liberties, the Supreme Court under Chief Justice Earl Warren refused to overturn the court of appeals' *de facto* approval of Judge Wright's actions to save Mrs. Jones' life. Although the Supreme Court and the judicial system were increasingly sensitive to the rights of religious minorities, they drew the line when religious sensibilities meant that modern medical technology would be denied to a person in need.

—Stephen G. Christianson

Suggestions for Further Reading

Evan, Thomas. *The Man to See: Edward Bennett Williams.* New York: Simon & Schuster, 1991.

Kelly, David F. *Critical Care Ethics: Treatment Decisions in American Hospitals.* Kansas City, Mo.: Sheed & Ward, 1991.

Marty, Martin E. and Kenneth L. Vaux. *Health/Medicine and the Faith Traditions: an Inquiry Into Religion and Medicine.* Philadelphia: Fortress Press, 1982.

Penton, M. James. *Apocalypse Delayed: the Story of Jehovah's Witnesses.* Buffalo, N.Y.: University of Toronto Press, 1985.

Rosenthal, Elisabeth. "Blinded by the Light." *Discover* (August 1988): 28–30.

U.S. v. Hoffa: 1964

Defendants: James R. Hoffa   **Crimes Charged:** First trial: jury tampering;
Second trial: mail and wire fraud, conspiracy   **Chief Defense Lawyers:** First
trial: Harry Berke, James Haggerty, Jacques Schiffer, and Harvey Silets;
Second trial: Daniel Ahearn, James Haggerty, and Maurice Walsh.
Chief Prosecutors: First trial: John Hooker and James Neal; Second trial:
William Bittman and Charles Smith   **Judges:** First trial: Frank W. Wilson;
Second trial: Richard B. Austin   **Places:** First trial: Chattanooga, Tennessee;
Second trial: Chicago, Illinois   **Dates of Trial:** First trial: January 20–
March 12, 1964; second trial: May 11–August 17, 1964.   **Verdicts:** Guilty,
both trials   **Sentences:** First trial: 8 years imprisonment and $10,000 fine;
second trial: four concurrent five-year terms

SIGNIFICANCE

U.S. Department of Justice prosecutions of union leader Jimmy Hoffa gave the
nation a series of sensational corruption trials and a debate over the acceptable
limits to which the government should investigate an individual.

The U.S. government's attempts to curtail the influence of organized crime in
labor unions by prosecuting International Brotherhood of Teamsters president Jimmy Hoffa failed for nearly a decade. By the time Hoffa finally went to
prison, numerous trials had cost both sides a great deal of money and arguments
over the ethics of the government's pursuit of Hoffa were commonplace.

The genesis of the Hoffa trials lay in the investigative work of the U.S.
Senate Select Committee on Improper Activities in the Labor or Management
Field. During the late 1950s, the so-called McClellan Committee (chaired by
Arkansas Senator John G. McClellan) put crooked union leaders, crime bosses,
common thugs, and their victims before the public in televised hearings. Many
of the most contentious exchanges took place between the committee's chief
counsel, Robert F. Kennedy, and the feisty Hoffa, who was in line for the
presidency of the powerful Teamsters union.

Even as the hearings began, Hoffa was indicted for illegal possession of
McClellan Committee documents. Hoffa had allegedly handed attorney John
Cye Cheasty $1,000 and promised thousands more if he would infiltrate the
committee to obtain information. Instead, Cheasty revealed the bribery attempt

to committee counsel Kennedy, who arranged to have Cheasty pass a list of witnesses to Hoffa while FBI cameras rolled.

A reporter asked Kennedy what he would do if Hoffa was not convicted. "I'll jump off the Capital dome," replied Kennedy, who was convinced that the filmed transaction gave the Justice Department a perfect case. When the trial ended with a hung jury, Teamsters attorney Edward Bennett Williams offered to send Kennedy a parachute. The growth of a mutual animosity between Kennedy and Hoffa was clear to an entire nation watching their public feud.

"Get-Hoffa Squad" Assembled

Robert Kennedy was appointed U.S. attorney general in 1960 by the newly elected president, his brother John F. Kennedy. Indicting Jimmy Hoffa was a high priority with the new attorney general, who claimed that Hoffa used extortion, bribery, and physical violence to rule the Teamsters. Robert Kennedy was equally sure that Hoffa used the threat of labor trouble to bully employers for personal profit. A small Justice Department unit of lawyers and investigators, informally known as the "Get-Hoffa Squad," was assembled to uncover and prosecute any unlawful activity within organized labor. By the time they disbanded, their conviction rate was impressive.

Yet Robert Kennedy's campaign against union corruption, and Hoffa in particular, raised questions about the role of an attorney general in prosecuting crimes. The constant investigations resembled a vendetta to those who suspected Kennedy's motives. Some thought the attorney general was dogging Hoffa out of personal spite. Others questioned the ethics of the nation's chief law enforcement officer aggressively investigating an individual before evidence of wrongdoing presented itself.

Civil libertarians were concerned by Hoffa's never-proven but steady protests that he was a victim of illegal surveillance and paid government perjurers. The debate also included his union cronies, politicians under his control, and enemies of the Kennedys, all of whom exploited the situation.

One of the first major indictments against Hoffa focused on a Florida real estate development called Sun Valley. Federal prosecutors knew that Hoffa and others had secretly loaned union money to finance the project and secured further loans from local banks by promising them large union accounts. Sun Valley was promoted as a sunny retirement community for union members. In fact, Hoffa and his associate Owen Bert Brennan held an option to buy 45 percent of the development. By risking union funds, Hoffa and Brennan stood to make personal fortunes if the development proved successful.

Instead, Sun Valley remained an undeveloped disaster area. Hoffa was indicted for mail fraud and conspiracy, but the indictments were dismissed in 1961 when a Florida judge ruled that the grand jury issuing them had been improperly impaneled (a second set of indictments was approved but dropped as investigators incorporated their evidence into Hoffa's 1964 Chicago fraud trial).

Hoffa was next indicted for violating the Taft-Hartley Act, which prohibits employee representatives from accepting illegal payoffs from employers. The government charged that a Michigan trucking firm, Commercial Carriers, had organized a Nashville, Tennessee, business called Test Fleet for the sole purpose of avoiding labor trouble with Hoffa's union. As soon as the new business was incorporated—in the maiden names of Hoffa's and Brennan's wives—Commercial Carriers leased all of Test Fleet's trucks and assumed all of their operating expenses, making the venture's income a pure profit for its "owners."

Hoffa claimed that putting the business in his wife's name was a legal tax move. The 1962 case ended with a mistrial when jurors could not agree on a verdict. Yet Hoffa and five others were immediately indicted for tampering with the jury. The new case was moved to Chattanooga, Tennessee, in early 1964 when Hoffa's attorney was arrested (and ultimately convicted) for trying to bribe a police officer into offering a prospective juror $10,000 to ensure another hung jury.

Government Succeeds

The most damaging witness in the Chattanooga trial was Ed Partin, a Teamster officer and government informant. Partin had secretly told investigators that Hoffa had spoken to him about killing Robert Kennedy. Prosecutors were wary of Partin's motives and credibility, for he was under indictment for embezzlement in Louisiana. They nevertheless decided to trust him after he passed a lie detector test.

Partin's presence in Chattanooga was kept a secret until the moment he walked to the witness stand. As Hoffa visibly paled, Partin recalled the union president speaking in detail about how the Nashville jury had been tainted.

The defense protested that the government had placed Partin in the midst of the Hoffa camp to violate Hoffa's rights by spying for prosecutors in the Test Fleet case. The government noted that Hoffa himself had invited Partin to Nashville and that Partin's information has prompted investigations that led to the present trial only. "That son-of-a-bitch is killing us!" Hoffa shouted at his lawyers outside the courtroom.

Hoffa's lawyers fiercely cross-examined Partin about his own criminal record and tried to suppress his testimony, accusing him of being a paid government informer (prosecutors denied this). The defense grew abrasive, accusing the Justice Department of stealing union documents and accusing Judge Frank W. Wilson of bias in favor of the government. The judge kept his composure in spite of apparent attempts to prod him into losing his temper and forcing a mistrial.

Federal prosecutor James Neal called the bribery conspiracy "one of the greatest assaults on the jury system the country has ever known." Neal might have said the same thing about the current trial, for amazing stratagems were being used to force a mistrial. Defense lawyers eavesdropped on the jury room. Bribed bellhops falsely swore that the sequestered jurors were drunk.

Hoffa's attorney, James Haggerty, called the government's case "a foul and filthy frame-up" designed by the "Get-Hoffa Squad." Defense attorney Jacques Schiffer threw a handful of coins at government prosecutors. "Take these thirty pieces of silver and share them—you have earned them."

While two of his co-defendants were acquitted, Hoffa and three others were found guilty. "You stand here convicted of seeking to corrupt the administration of justice itself," Judge Wilson told Hoffa before sentencing him to eight years in prison and fining him $10,000. Defense attorney Schiffer was sentenced to 60 days in prison for contempt.

Two months later, Hoffa went on trial in Chicago, Illinois, for fraud and conspiracy. Prosecutors charged that he and seven co-defendants had approved $20 million in loans from the Teamsters pension fund to real-estate developers. In returns, the developers paid $1.7 million in kickbacks when the loans were approved. The scheme was originated to pay off Sun Valley's creditors. The Chicago trial, however, revealed that Hoffa and the others had not restricted their activity to repaying the union's hidden loss in the Florida fiasco.

After 13 weeks of complex testimony, Hoffa was found guilty on four of the 20 counts against him. Judge Richard B. Austin sentenced him to five years imprisonment on each count, to run concurrently after he finished the eight-year jury-tampering sentence.

Hoffa appealed all the way to the Supreme Court without success. He entered a federal penitentiary in 1967 and served five years before President Richard Nixon commuted his sentence in 1972.

Hoffa paid minimal attention to a condition of his parole forbidding involvement in any union activities until 1980. He disappeared in Detroit, Michigan, on July 30, 1975, and was presumed to have been murdered. His body has never been found.

The Hoffa name did not disappear from the ranks of the Teamsters when Jimmy Hoffa vanished. His son, James Hoffa, a Detroit lawyer, ran for the presidency of the union in 1996, but was narrowly defeated by Ron Carrey. However, Carrey was forced out of the presidency after a federal investigation revealed that his campaign had benefited from illegal fund-raising schemes. James Hoffa ran again in 1998 and was easily elected to head the union his father had once made so powerful.

— Thomas C. Smith

Suggestions for Further Reading

Hutchinson, John. *The Imperfect Union: A History of Corruption In American Trade Unions.* New York: E.P. Dutton, 1970.

Kennedy, Robert F. *The Enemy Within.* New York: Harper & Brothers, 1960.

Navasky, Victor S. *Kennedy Justice.* New York: Atheneum, 1971.

Sheridan, Walter. *The Fall And Rise of Jimmy Hoffa.* New York: Saturday Review Books, 1972.

Jack Ruby Trial: 1964

Defendant: Jack Leon Ruby   **Crime Charged:** Murder
Chief Defense Lawyers: Melvin Mouron Belli, Phil Burleson, Robert B.
Denson, Elmer Gertz, Tom Howard, William Kuntsler, and Joe Tonahill
Chief Prosecutors: William F. Alexander, Jim Bowie, Henry Menasco Wade,
Jr., and Frank Watts   **Judge:** Joe Brantley Brown   **Place:** Dallas, Texas
Dates of Trial: March 4–14, 1964   **Verdict:** Guilty

SIGNIFICANCE

The significance of the Jack Ruby trial is simple and obvious: this was the trial of
the man who killed the man who killed President John Fitzgerald Kennedy.

A t 12:30 P.M. on Friday, November 22, 1963, nightclub manager Jack Ruby was at the *Dallas Morning News* turning in his advertising copy for the weekend editions. Word of gunshots in nearby Dealey Plaza burst into the room. Stunned, Ruby and newspeople there tuned into their television sets to learn of the shooting of President John Fitzgerald Kennedy. Ruby instantly raced to Parkland Hospital's emergency room. There he and a handful of reporters heard acting White House Press Secretary Malcolm Kilduff announce that the president had died.

A Police Buff

Newspeople were not surprised to see Ruby there. Nor were Dallas policemen when he turned up Friday evening and again on Saturday at the police station where the accused assassin, Lee Harvey Oswald, was being held. They knew Ruby as a police buff who liked to hang around and hear what was happening on the police blotter. He often made financial contributions to police causes. As they worked through Saturday evening, he brought them sandwiches and helped out-of-town reporters identify key officers.

That Sunday morning, November 24, the police were ready to move Oswald to the county jail, a mile away. At 11:20, as millions of viewers glued to their TVs watched in amazement, Captain J. Will Fritz led two detectives escorting Oswald through a basement garage toward a car. Suddenly, Jack Ruby lunged from the mob of detectives and reporters and fired a handgun point-blank at Oswald's chest. Oswald died at 1:07 P.M.

Most Jurors Saw the Shooting

Nationally known lawyer Melvin Belli, planning to write a book and produce a movie about the trial, undertook the defense of Jack Ruby free of charge. Belli tried but failed to get a change of venue from Dallas. Ultimately he had to accept, among the 8 men and 4 women jurors, 1 who, watching television at that instant, had witnessed Ruby's act.

Twenty prosecution witnesses testified during the trial. Of those, Detective James R. Leavelle, who had been handcuffed to Oswald, testified that as he lay bleeding, Ruby said, "I hope the son-of-a-bitch dies." Officer D.R. Archer testified that he told Ruby, "I think you killed him," and Ruby's reply was, "I intended to shoot him three times."

Officer Thomas D. McMillon testified that he heard Ruby say, "You rat son-of-a-bitch, you shot the president." A review of television tapes, however, showed that, as Ruby fired at Oswald, McMillon was far to the rear and looking away from the action and therefore couldn't have heard anything.

Sergeant Patrick T. Dean's testimony was damaging. Ten minutes after the shooting, he said, Ruby told him that on Friday night, "when he noticed the sarcastic sneer on Oswald's face," he thought he would kill him.

Psychomotor Epilepsy

The defense set out to prove that Jack Ruby had a troubled mind. Attorney Belli first called Little Lynn, a 19-year-old stripper, who said Ruby "had a very quick temper. He'd fly off the handle." Another stripper, Penny Dollar, told of Ruby's fighting with a taxi driver, beating his head on the sidewalk, then stopping suddenly and asking, "Did I do this?"

Jack Ruby under escort.
(AP/Wide World Photos)

Next came testimony from the experts. Dr. Roy Schafer, associate clinical professor of psychiatry and psychology at Yale University, had performed psychological tests on Ruby. "I determined that he did have organic brain damage," Schafer said. "The most likely specific nature of it was psychomotor epilepsy." He added that Ruby suffered from "mood swings" and "impulsiveness."

Would Ruby be subject to states of rage? asked Belli. "Yup," said Schafer. What might set him off? "Very strong emotional stimulation . . . states of fatigue . . . certain kinds of light stimulation, a certain kind of flickering light."

Dr. Martin L. Towler, neurologist at the University of Texas in Galveston and a court-appointed expert who had examined Ruby, testified to the defendant's history of head injuries and probable "psychomotor variant epilepsy." During a seizure, asked Belli, "Will he know what he is doing?"

"No," replied the witness. "He is behaving as an automaton. Most patients will be amnesic."

Dr. Manfred S. Guttmacher, chief medical officer of the Supreme Court of Baltimore and an expert on criminal psychology, testified, "I don't think he was capable of knowing right from wrong or understood the nature and consequences of his act. I think he was struggling to keep his sanity . . . I think he had an unusual degree of involvement in the whole tragedy . . . [there was] disruption of his ego, a very short-lived psychotic episode in which the hostile part of his makeup, which is very strong, became focused on this one individual. Homicide was the result."

EEG Tracings

Late on the afternoon of Thursday, March 12, the prosecution presented its rebuttal of findings on Ruby's electroencephalograph (EEG) testified to by a leading expert, Dr. Frederic A. Gibbs of Chicago. His written conclusion had been that the EEG recordings "show seizure disorders of the psychomotor variant type." Gibbs had refused earlier invitations to appear in person as a witness. Now, hearing disagreement on his opinion, he flew to Dallas that Thursday evening and testified the next morning without a fee. Standing before the jury with the EEG tracings, he said, "Jack Ruby has a particular, very rare, form of epilepsy. The pattern occurs only in one-half of one percent of epileptics. It was a distinctive and unusual epileptic pattern."

Prosecutor William Alexander tried to get Dr. Gibbs to say that psychomotor variant epilepsy was not a disease. "I say it is a disease," said the doctor, "that is diagnosable from a brain-wave reading."

Judge Joe Brown's charge to the jury and defense and prosecution closing arguments went to well past 1:00 A.M. on Saturday, March 14. That afternoon, the jury deliberated for only two hours and 19 minutes before finding Jack Ruby "guilty of murder with malice, as charged in the indictment, and [we] assess his punishment at death."

More than two and a half years of appeals followed. On October 5, 1966, the Texas Court of Criminal Appeals found that Ruby's statements to police immediately after shooting Oswald should not have been admitted as evidence and that he should have been granted a change of venue.

A new trial was scheduled for Wichita Falls, Kansas. However, when that city's sheriff traveled to Dallas to get Ruby in December 1966, he found him too sick to move. Jail doctors had not taken Ruby's stomach complaints seriously, but Parkland Hospital physicians now found cancer in his liver, brain, and lungs. He died on January 3, 1967, before being able to receive a new trial.

—Bernard Ryan, Jr.

Suggestions for Further Reading

Belli, Melvin M. with Maurice C. Carroll. *Dallas Justice: The Real Story of Jack Ruby and His Trial*. New York: McKay, 1964.

Hartogs, Dr. Renatus and Lucy Freeman. *The Two Assassins*. New York: Crowell, 1965.

Hosty, James P., Jr. with Thomas Hosty. *Assignment: Oswald*. New York: Arcade, 1996.

Kantor, Seth. *Who Was Jack Ruby?* New York: Everest House, 1978.

Kaplan, John and Jon R. Waltz. *The Trial of Jack Ruby*. New York: Macmillan, 1965.

Posner, Gerald. *Case Closed: Lee Harvey Oswald and the Assassination of JFK*. New York: Random House, 1993.

Scott, Peter Dale. *Deep Politics and the Death of JFK*. Berkeley: University of California Press, 1993.

New York Times Company v. Sullivan: 1964

Appellant: The New York Times Company   **Appellee:** L.B. Sullivan
Appellant Claims: That the Supreme Court of Alabama's affirmation of a libel judgment against the *Times* violated the free speech and due process rights as defined by the First and Fourteenth Amendments of the Constitution and certain Supreme Court decisions; also, that an advertisement published in the *Times* was not libelous and the Supreme Court should reverse the decision of the Alabama trial court.   **Chief Defense Lawyers:** Sam Rice Baker, M. Roland Nachman, Jr., and Robert E. Steiner III
Chief Lawyers for Appellant: Herbert Brownell, Thomas F. Daly, and Herbert Wechsler   **Justices:** Hugo L. Black, William J. Brennan, Jr., Tom C. Clark, William O. Douglas, Arthur J. Goldberg, John M. Harlan, Potter Stewart, Earl Warren, and Byron R. White   **Place:** Washington, D.C.
Date of Decision: March 9, 1964   **Decision:** The Alabama courts' decisions were reversed.

SIGNIFICANCE

The U.S. Supreme Court limited for the first time states' authority to award libel damages based on individual state laws and defined "actual malice" as a national standard for determining libel cases involving public figures.

On March 23, 1960, an organization calling itself the "Committee to Defend Martin Luther King and the Struggle for Freedom in the South" paid the *New York Times* to publish a certain advertisement. The ad took up one full page and was a call for public support and money to defend Rev. Martin Luther King, Jr. and the civil rights struggle in the South. Bearing the caption "Heed Their Rising Voices" in large, bold print, the ad was published in the March 29, 1960, edition of the *Times*.

The ad criticized several Southern jurisdictions, including the city of Montgomery, Alabama, for breaking up various civil rights demonstrations. No individual was mentioned by name. Further, the ad declared that "Southern violators of the Constitution" were determined to destroy King and his movement. The reference was to the entire South, not just Montgomery and other localities, and again no individual was mentioned by name.

Over 600,000 copies of the March 29, 1960, *Times* edition carrying the ad were printed. Only a couple hundred went to Alabama subscribers. Montgomery City Commissioner L.B. Sullivan learned of the ad through an editorial in a local newspaper. Incensed, on April 19, 1960, Sullivan sued the *Times* for libel in the Circuit Court of Montgomery County, Alabama. Sullivan claimed that the ad's reference to Montgomery and to "Southern violators of the Constitution" had the effect of defaming him, and he demanded $500,000 in compensation.

On November 3, 1960, the Circuit Court found the *Times* guilty and awarded Sullivan the full $500,000 in damages. The Alabama Supreme Court affirmed the Circuit Court judgment on August 30, 1962. In its opinion, the Alabama Supreme Court gave an extremely broad definition of libel:

> Where the words published tend to injure a person libeled by them in his reputation, profession, trade or business, or charge him with an indictable offense, or tends to bring the individual into public contempt [they] are libelous per se. . . . We hold that the matter complained of [by Sullivan] is, under the above doctrine, libelous per se.

Supreme Court Protects the Press

The *Times*'s chief lawyers, Herbert Brownell, Thomas F. Daly, and Herbert Wechsler, took the case to the U.S. Supreme Court. Sullivan's chief lawyers were Sam Rice Baker, M. Roland Nachman, Jr., and Robert E. Steiner III. On January 6, 1964 the two sides appeared at a hearing in Washington, D.C., before Supreme Court Justices Hugo L. Black, William J. Brennan, Jr., Tom C. Clark, William O. Douglas, Arthur J. Goldberg, John M. Harlan, Potter Stewart, Earl Warren, and Byron R. White.

On March 9, 1964, the Supreme Court unanimously reversed the Alabama courts' decisions, holding that Alabama libel law violated the *Times*'s First Amendment rights. Justice Brennan stated for the Court that:

> We hold that the rule of law applied by the Alabama courts is constitutionally deficient for failure to provide the safeguards for freedom of speech and of the press that are required by the First [Amendment] in a libel action brought by a public official against critics of his official conduct.

The Court was in fact only recognizing what Alabama's own newspapers had been saying, namely that Alabama's libel law was a powerful tool in the hands of anti-civil rights officials. The *Montgomery Advertiser* had even printed an edition (before the Sullivan case went to the Court) with the headline "STATE FINDS FORMIDABLE LEGAL CLUB TO SWING AT OUT-OF-STATE PRESS," reporting that "State and city authorities have found a formidable legal bludgeon to swing at out-of-state newspapers whose reporters cover racial incidents in Alabama." The Court's decision invalidated Alabama's overly broad libel law so that it couldn't be used anymore to threaten freedom of the press.

Next, Justice Brennan stated what the Court had determined was the proper basis of libel law under the First Amendment in cases involving publications concerning public officials:

> The constitutional guarantees require, we think, a federal rule that prohibits a public official from recovering damages for a defamatory falsehood relating to his official conduct unless he proves that the statement was made with "actual malice."

Sullivan hadn't proven that the *Times* acted with actual malice, so even if Alabama's libel law wasn't unconstitutional, his lawsuit still had to be rejected. What constitutes actual malice? The Court defined it as:

> knowledge that it was false or with reckless disregard of whether it was false or not.

In certain libel lawsuits after *New York Times Company v. Sullivan*, the Court expanded the First Amendment's protection. For any "public figure" to sue for libel, he or she would have to prove actual malice. The Court has said that public figures include anyone widely known in the community, not just public officials. Further, anyone accused of libel is protected by this actual malice requirement, not just newspapers like the *Times*. The *Sullivan* case was a tremendous advance for personal as well as press freedom of speech, and it prevented legitimate criticism and social commentary from being suppressed by the threat of dam-

Associate Justice Brennan defined actual malice as "knowledge that it was false or with reckless disregard of whether it was false or not." (Courtesy, Library of Congress)

aging libel lawsuits. *Sullivan* has not, however, become a license to print anything that the papers see fit: as in *Reynolds v. Pegler* (see separate entry), defendants who do act with actual malice are subject to severe penalties.

—Stephen G. Christianson

Suggestions for Further Reading

Bain, George. "A Question of Honor, Malice and Rights." *Maclean's* (October 1984): 64.

Friedman, Robert. "Freedom of the Press: How Far Can it Go?" *American Heritage* (October–November 1982): 16–22.

Hopkins, W. Wat. *Actual Malice: Twenty-Five Years After Times v. Sullivan.* New York: Praeger, 1989.

Lewis, Anthony. *Make No Law: the Sullivan Case and the First Amendment.* New York: Random House, 1991.

Winfield, Richard N. *New York Times v. Sullivan: the Next Twenty Years.* New York: Practicing Law Institute, 1984.

Griswold v. Connecticut: 1964

Appellants: Charles Lee Buxton and Estelle Griswold   **Defendant:** State of
Connecticut   **Appellants Claim:** That Connecticut's birth-control laws
violated its citizens' constitutional rights   **Chief Defense Lawyer:** Joseph B.
Clark   **Chief Lawyers for Appellants:** Tom Emerson, Fowler Harper, Harriet
Pilpel, and Catherine Roraback   **Justices:** Hugo L. Black, William J.
Brennan, Jr., Tom C. Clark, William Douglas, Arthur J. Goldberg, John M.
Harlan, Potter Stewart, Earl Warren, and Byron R. White   **Place:** Washington,
D.C.   **Date of Decision:** May 11, 1964   **Decision:** Reversed Griswold's and
Buxton's lower court convictions for providing contraceptive information to
married couples and struck down all state laws forbidding the use of
contraceptives by such couples

SIGNIFICANCE

The decision articulated a constitutional "right to privacy," which would later be
interpreted as protecting the right of unmarried persons to use birth control
(*Eisenstadt v. Baird,* 1972) and the right of women to terminate their pregnancies
(*Roe v. Wade,* 1973).

Connecticut's anticontraceptive law, passed in 1879, was simple and unambiguous:

> Any person who uses any drug, medicinal article or instrument for the
> purpose of preventing conception shall be fined not less than fifty dollars or
> imprisoned not less than sixty days nor more than one year or be both fined
> and imprisoned. (General Statutes of Connecticut, Section 53–32.)

> Any person who assists, abets, counsels, causes, hires or commands another
> to commit any offense may be prosecuted and punished as if he were the
> principal offender. (Section 54–196.)

The Planned Parenthood League of Connecticut first brought the law
before the U.S. Supreme Court in 1942, with a physician as plaintiff. The court
ruled that the doctor lacked standing to sue, since his patients—and not he—
suffered injury due to his inability to legally prescribe birth control. In June
1961, declining to rule in a suit brought by several women, the Supreme Court
called the normally unenforced law "dead words" and "harmless empty shadows." Estelle T. Griswold, executive director of the Planned Parenthood

League of Connecticut, and Dr. C. Led Buxton, chairman of Yale University's obstetrics department, decided to test the "death" of the 1879 law: On November 1, 1961, they opened a birth-control clinic in New Haven. Dr. Buxton cited the June decision and explained to the press: "This leads me to believe that all doctors in Connecticut may now prescribe child spacing techniques to married women when it is medically indicated."

1879 Law Alive and Well

Griswold and Buxton were arrested and their center closed on November 10, 1961. On December 8, 1961, the opening day of the Sixth Circuit Court trial, defense attorney Catherine G. Roraback argued that Connecticut's birth-control law violated their clients' constitutional right to freedom of speech. Judge J. Robert Lacey, saying he wished to study the defense's brief, continued the case indefinitely.

On January 2, 1962, the trial took place. It lasted only six hours. Julius Martez was the Sixth Circuit Court prosecutor who had requested warrants for Griswold's and Buxton's arrests. He now called his witnesses. John A. Blasi, a New Haven police detective who had entered the clinic on its third day of operation, testified that six women were in the waiting room at the time; that Estelle Griswold freely told him that the facility was, indeed, a birth-control clinic; and that Griswold had offered him contraceptive information and devices. Another detective offered similar testimony.

Dr. Buxton testified that he and his medical colleagues believed that "this type of advice" played a crucial part in women's health care.

Prosecutor Martez said that Griswold and Buxton had broken the law and that the Connecticut legislature, not the court, was the proper forum for anyone objecting to the 82-year-old statute.

Judge Lacey agreed with Martez. He described the statute as "absolute," and he emphasized that it had been upheld three times by the Connecticut Supreme Court of Errors. Rejecting defense attorney Catherine Roraback's free speech argument, he characterized the prohibition of a physician's prescription of birth-control devices as a "constitutional exercise of the police powers of the State of Connecticut." Griswold and Buxton were then convicted of violating Connecticut's birth control law, and each was fined $100.00.

Ten days later, defense attorneys Roraback and Harriet Pilpel filed their clients' appeal with the Appellate Division of the Sixth Connecticut Circuit Court. A three-judge panel heard the case October 19, 1962, and upheld Griswold's and Buxton's convictions on January 18, 1963. However, citing questions "of great public importance," it certified the case for a review by the State Supreme Court of Errors.

That court upheld the convictions on May 11, 1964. Associate Justice John Comley's opinion declared: "We adhere to the principle that courts may not interfere with the exercise by a state of the police power to conserve the public safety and welfare, including health and morals."

On to the Supreme Court

The first action Planned Parenthood took in preparing *Griswold v. Connecticut* for the U.S. Supreme Court was to replace its female attorneys, Roraback and Pilpel, with two male attorneys: Fowler Harper and, upon his death, Thomas I. Emerson, both professors at Yale Law School.

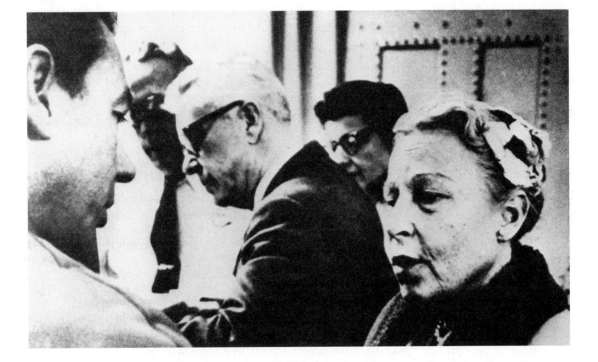

Estelle Griswold and Dr. Charles Lee Buxtom. (Courtesy, Planned Parenthood of Connecticut)

Oral argument began before the Supreme Court on March 29, 1964. Emerson argued that Connecticut's birth-control law deprived his clients and their clinic's patients of the First Amendment right to free speech and of their right to liberty, which according to the Fourteenth Amendment, could not be abridged without "due process of law." Moreover, he claimed that his clients had a right to privacy, which was guaranteed by the Ninth Amendment to the Constitution: "The enumeration in the Constitution, of certain rights, shall not be construed to deny or disparage others retained by the people."

Emerson characterized the Connecticut law as an effort to erect "a principle of morality" by declaring it "immoral to use contraceptives even within the married relationship." This was, he continued, a "moral judgment" that did not "conform to current community standards."

Both Emerson and Connecticut's attorney, Thomas Clark, were questioned about the presumed "under-the-counter" availability of birth-control devices in Connecticut. Clark classified it with clandestine bookmaking on racehorses—available, but not in the open. Emerson said the devices were simply termed "feminine hygiene" items. Clark was then asked whether it was permissible to prescribe contraceptives to prevent the spread of disease. Clark called this a "ludicrous argument" and explained that sexually transmitted disease was not present in married couples, who were claimed as clients of the Planned Parenthood clinic. As the *New York Times* summarized Clark's reasoning, "Connecticut requires applicants for marriage licenses to take venereal disease tests, and . . . Connecticut also has laws against fornication and adultery. Thus, [Clark] indicated, there would be no reason to believe that any such disease would spread."

The next day, Justice Potter Stewart asked Clark to explain the purpose of the statute. "To reduce the chances of immorality," he said. "To act as a deterrent to sexual intercourse outside marriage."

Justice Stewart replied, "The trouble with that argument is that on this record it [the clinic] involves only married women."

A little later in the questioning, Clark declared that Connecticut had the right to guarantee its own "continuity" by prohibiting contraceptives.

Justice Arthur J. Goldberg returned to the statute's alleged role in preventing intercourse outside of marriage, and he asked why Connecticut's laws banning fornication and adultery were not sufficient. Clark replied that "it's easier to control the problem" with the addition of anti-birth control laws.

Decision Reverses Convictions

The Supreme Court, in a 7–2 ruling, reversed Griswold's and Buxton's convictions, invalidated the 1879 law, and enunciated a constitutional "right to privacy." The majority opinion, written by Justice William O. Douglas, declared that the "specific guarantees in the Bill of Rights have penumbras, formed by emanations from those guarantees that help give them life and substance" and cited the Constitution's First, Third, Fourth, Fifth, Ninth, and Fourteenth Amendments. The Ninth Amendment, Douglas quoted in its entirety: "The enumeration in the Constitution, of certain rights, shall not be construed to deny or disparage others retained by the people." The enforcement of the Connecticut birth-control law would require gross violation of privacy, which was presumably a right "retained by the people." "Would we allow the police to search the sacred precincts of marital bedrooms for telltale signs of the use of contraceptives?" Douglas asked. He characterized such action as "repulsive to the notions of privacy surrounding the marriage relationship" and reversed the lower court convictions.

Justices Black and Stewart issued dissenting opinions. Black wrote:

> The Court talks about a constitutional "right of privacy" as though there is some constitutional provision or provisions forbidding any law ever to be passed which might abridge the "privacy" of individuals. But there is not. . . . I cannot rely on the Due Process Clause [of the Fourteenth Amendment] or

the Ninth Amendment or any mysterious and uncertain natural law concept as a reason for striking down this state law.

Griswold, Applied Outside the Marital Bedroom

Before *Griswold,* the Ninth Amendment had usually been interpreted as reserving to the state government any right not specifically granted to the federal government; Douglas' literal interpretation, that the Ninth Amendment reserved such rights *to the people,* formed the basis of two other successful challenges to state reproduction laws.

In *Eisenstadt v. Baird* (1972), single people won the right to purchase and use contraceptives. Justice William J. Brennan, a concurring justice in Griswold, delivered the majority opinion:

> If under *Griswold* the distribution of contraceptives to married persons cannot be prohibited, a ban on distribution to unmarried persons would be equally impermissible. It is true that in *Griswold* the right of privacy in question inhered in the marital relationship. Yet the marital couple is not an independent entity with a mind and heart of its own, but an association of two individuals each with a separate intellectual and emotional makeup. If the right of privacy means anything, it is the right of the *individual,* married or single, to be free from unwarranted governmental intrusion into matters so fundamentally affecting a person as the decision whether to bear or beget a child.

The following year, in its controversial *Roe v. Wade* (see separate entry) decision, the Court held that the "right of privacy . . . is broad enough to encompass a woman's decision whether or not to terminate her pregnancy."

— Kathryn Cullen-DuPont

Suggestions for Further Reading

Carey, Eve and Kathleen Willert Peratis. *Woman and the Law.* Skokie, Ill.: National Textbook Co. in conjunction with the American Civil Liberties Union, New York, 1977.

Countryman, Vern, ed. *The Douglas Opinions.* New York: Random House, 1977.

Cushman, Robert F. *Cases in Constitutional Law,* 6th ed. Englewood Cliffs, N.J.: Prentice Hall, 1984.

Davis, Flora. *Moving the Mountain: The Women's Movement in America Since 1960.* New York: Simon & Schuster, 1991.

Faux, Marian. *Roe v. Wade.* New York: Macmillan Co., 1988.

The *New York Times.* October 27, 1961; November 3, 1961; November 4, 1961; November 11, 1961; November 13, 1961; November 25, 1961; December 2, 1961; December 9, 1961; January 3, 1962; January 13, 1962; October 20, 1962; January 18, 1963; May 17, 1963; May 19, 1963; May 12, 1964; December 9, 1964; March 30, 1965; March 31, 1965; June 8, 1965; June 9, 1965; June 10, 1965; June 13, 1965; and June 15, 1965.

Lenny Bruce Trial: 1964

Defendants: Lenny Bruce, Ella Solomon, and Howard L. Solomon
Crime Charged: Obscenity **Chief Defense Lawyers:** Martin Garbus and Efraim London **Chief Prosecutor:** Richard H. Kuh **Judges:** J. Randall Creel, John M. Murtagh, and Kenneth M. Phipps **Place:** New York, New York **Dates of Trial:** June 16–December 21, 1964 **Verdict:** Lenny Bruce: Guilty; Howard L. Solomon: Guilty; Ella Solomon: not Guilty
Sentence: Lenny Bruce: 4 months imprisonment; Howard L. Solomon: $1,000 fine or 60 Days Jail

SIGNIFICANCE

Freedom of speech is a cherished right. But just how far should that right extend? For many, comedian Lenny Bruce stepped way beyond any reasonable interpretation of free speech. That belief resulted in the costliest, and certainly the most controversial obscenity trial in American history.

On April Fool's Day, 1964, two plainclothes New York City police officers mingled with the audience at the Cafe Au Go Go, a Greenwich Village coffeehouse, and watched comedian Lenny Bruce at work. It was a typical Bruce performance, funny, scatological, bitingly accurate, laced with Anglo-Saxonisms, and all recorded for posterity on a concealed wiretap worn by one of the officers. Two nights later, April 3, just before he was due on stage, Bruce was arrested and charged with using obscene language. Also arrested was club owner Howard Solomon.

Bruce was no stranger to controversy. He had several times been cited for obscenity and twice convicted, but this was easily his highest profile arrest yet. He continued his engagement at the Cafe Au Go Go after posting bail. Four nights later, he and Solomon were arrested again. This time police also took Solomon's wife Ella into custody and charged all three with obscenity.

Just days before their trial commenced, a statement signed by more than one hundred prominent members of the arts community was issued to the media. In it, the signatories pledged support for the beleaguered Bruce, but more especially for the principle of free speech.

Herbert S. Rune, an inspector with the NYC Department of Licenses, was the final witness called to testify. He had watched Bruce perform, jotting down surreptitious notes. Over defense objections, he read out an edited version of Bruce's act that highlighted the language used and virtually ignored the context. Worst of all was Rune's assertion, bitterly denied by the defense, that Bruce had fondled the microphone in an obvious and suggestive manner.

This allegation was reiterated by the next witness, Patrolman Robert Lane, who with his partner, William O'Neal, had recorded Bruce. That tape, scratchy, hissing and difficult to make out, was played in court. Wherever the original words were inaudible, a prosecution transcript provided damaging substitutions.

Adjournment For Illness

Two days into the trial, Bruce had to be hospitalized with pleurisy. When the trial resumed June 30, his chief attorney, Efraim London, a veteran of more than 250 censorship and obscenity cases, including notable victories on behalf of *Lady Chatterly's Lover* and *Tropic of Cancer*, moved for a dismissal, arguing that the prosecution had not proved a *prima facie* case having sufficient evidence obscenity. This stimulated a vigorous counter-assault by Assistant District Attorney Richard Kuh. Fulminating against Bruce's "anthology of filth," Kuh demanded that the trial continue. The three-member panel of judges agreed.

London had assembled an all-star cast of witnesses to plead Bruce's cause, including jazz critic, Nat Hentoff. Calling the defendant a brilliant social commentator, Hentoff hinted darkly of "a national movement to harass Lenny Bruce." Further support came from Dr. Daniel B. Dodson, associate professor of English at Columbia University, who compared Bruce favorably to Jonathan Swift and François Rabelais.

The star defense witness was supposed to be columnist Dorothy Kilgallen. She started off well enough, saying, "He [Bruce] goes from one subject to another, but there is always the thread of the world around . . . whether he's talking about war or peace or religion or Russia or New York." But Kilgallen faltered under Kuh's relentless questioning. After praising Norman Mailer and Jim Jones, writers who both employed earthy language, she slipped badly by blasting another recent book *Naked Lunch*, "which I couldn't even finish reading. . . . I think the author should be in jail."

Prosecutor Kuh grasped this gift with both hands, purring, "Unfortunately we can't do everything at once."

Adjourned for Vacation

Yet another adjournment—this time so that Judge John Murtagh could take his summer vacation—gave the prosecutor ample time to line up his own witnesses. When the trial reopened, John Fischer, editor of *Harper's* magazine, and the Reverend Daniel Potter, executive director of the Protestant Council, both opined that Bruce's work was obscene. Testimony concluded July 28, after

One year before his obscenity trial in New York, comedian Lenny Bruce is denied entrance to England "in the public interest." (AP/Wide World Photos)

which Judge Murtagh instructed counsel that the bench would consider written briefs instead of the customary oral closing arguments.

On November 4, the court reconvened to deliver its verdict. Bruce, who had remained silent throughout, chose this moment to dismiss his lawyers and belligerently insist that he be allowed to conduct his own defense. Judge Murtagh denied the request and read the verdict. "The court, Judge Creel dissenting, finds the defendants Lenny Bruce and Howard Solomon guilty. The court by unanimous vote finds the defendant Ella Solomon not guilty." Sentencing was deferred until December 21, 1964, at which time Bruce received four months Solomon was fined.

The verdict seemed to unhinge Bruce. He became obsessed with appellate litigation. Those legal wheels were still grinding when, on August 3, 1966, he was found dead in his Hollywood home, a hypodermic syringe nearby. An autopsy revealed the presence of morphine. Death was recorded as accidental.

Lenny Bruce's trial attracted immense publicity, a torrent of self-righteous indignation from protagonists on either side of the debate, and still no firm understanding of what constitutes obscenity. At its conclusion, Bruce's life and career were in shambles—vivid proof that free speech is never free, and often costly beyond measure.

—Colin Evans

Suggestions for Further Reading

Bruce, Honey and Dana Benenson. *Honey*. Chicago: Playboy, 1976.

Goldman, Albert. *Ladies And Gentlemen—Lenny Bruce!!* New York: Random House, 1974.

Moretti, Daniel S. *Obscenity And Pornography*. New York: Oceana, 1984.

Morgenstern, Joe. "Lenny Lives!" *Playboy*, (August 1991): 82ff.

Thomas, William Karl. *Lenny Bruce*, Hamden Conn: Archon, 1989.

The Whitmore Confessions and Richard Robles Trial: 1965

Defendant: Richard Robles   **Crime Charged:** Murder
Chief Defense Attorneys: Frederick H. Block and Jack S. Hoffinger
Chief Prosecutor: John F. Keenan   **Judge:** Irwin D. Davidson   **Place:** New
York, New York   **Dates of Trial:** October 18–December 1, 1965
Verdict: Guilty   **Sentence:** Life imprisonment

SIGNIFICANCE

The notoriety of two murders for which Robles was eventually convicted contributed to the legal problems of George Whitmore, Jr., who was initially arrested for the crimes. Whitmore's arrest had a profound effect upon the nature of police interrogations, earning it a mention in the U.S. Supreme Court's Miranda decision.

In the early morning of April 23, 1964, a police patrolman chased away a man assaulting Elba Borrero on a dark Brooklyn, New York, street. When the officer returned to the scene later, he found George Whitmore, Jr., standing in a doorway. The young black man asked if the officer had been the same one shooting at the woman's attacker earlier and volunteered a description of the fleeing suspect.

Similarities between the assault on Borrero and the recent murder of Minnie Edmonds in the same neighborhood convinced detectives that they should have another talk with Whitmore. He was brought to the 73rd precinct on April 24. After questioning him for 22 hours without the presence of an attorney, detectives announced that Whitmore had confessed to both the Borrero assault and the Edmonds killing.

Whitmore also signed a more spectacular confession. Eight months before, Janice Wylie and Emily Hoffert were found tied together and stabbed to death in their Manhattan apartment. A Brooklyn detective familiar with the case thought that a photo of an attractive blonde found in Whitmore's wallet resembled Wylie and had begun the interrogation leading to the confession. The police announced to the press that the bloody "Career Girls Murder" was now solved beyond a doubt.

Confessions Discredited

Brooklyn authorities immediately charged Whitmore with the Borrero and Edmonds crimes. Manhattan District Attorney Frank Hogan's office, however, was slow to indict Whitmore in the Wylie-Hoffert murders. Manhattan prosecutors noticed that every detail in Whitmore's lengthy confession was known to police beforehand. Investigators quietly collected evidence showing the confession to be false. The blonde in the photo was located alive in southern New Jersey, not far from the garbage dump where Whitmore initially claimed to have found the picture.

After Whitmore's confession was discredited, Hogan's office did not immediately dismiss the indictment against him, even though the prosecutors secretly knew that police had a new suspect. With Brooklyn authorities, the public, and even the jury still assuming that Whitmore was a confessed murderer, he was tried in November 1964 for attempting to rape Elba Borrero. She identified Whitmore as her attacker, although she acknowledged that he was the only suspect police had shown her. She also admitted that she had discussed a $10,000 reward offered for the conviction of Janice Wylie's killer with a lawyer. Brandishing Whitmore's ragged raincoat and a leather button Borrero had torn from her attacker's coat, the prosecutor asked the jury, "Haven't we nailed George Whitmore right on the button in the truest sense of the word?"

Whitmore was found guilty, but he was granted a new trial because racial prejudice and knowledge of the Wylie-Hoffert indictment had swayed the jury. The prosecutor also admitted to withholding an FBI report stating that the threads on Whitmore's coat did not match those on the celebrated button.

Richard Robles Arrested

On January 26, a man named Richard Robles was arrested for the Wylie-Hoffert murders. Upon Robles' arrest, District Attorney Hogan petitioned the courts to release Whitmore from the murder indictment on his own recognizance. Despite Robles' arrest, however, Hogan did not request complete dismissal of the Whitmore indictment. This controversial technicality allowed other prosecutors to rebuff defense claims that Whitmore's confessions to the Edmonds murder and Borrero assault were as unsound as his invalid Wylie-Hoffert confession.

In May 1965, the New York State Legislature outlawed capital punishment. Their decision was influenced by public concern over the false confession that nearly electrocuted George Whitmore. Yet Whitmore's legal troubles were far from over. With the Manhattan district attorney still refusing to clear him entirely in the Wylie-Hoffert case, Whitmore went to trial for murdering Minnie Edmonds, solely on the evidence of his "confession."

After a stormy trial marked by Whitmore's accusation that his confessions had been beaten out of him, police denials, and open feuding between the judge and the defense attorney, the jury could not agree on a verdict. Several days after the Edmonds mistrial was declared, Whitmore was finally cleared in the Wylie-Hoffert case.

Nevertheless, when Robles was tried in the autumn of 1965, his attorneys attempted to buoy the credibility of Whitmore's Wylie-Hoffert confession to create a reasonable doubt that their own client had committed the crime.

Prosecutor John F. Keenan replied by summoning Whitmore and the detectives who had arrested him. Whitmore's testimony was erratic, but Keenan's grueling questioning of the detectives illuminated the sloppy analysis of physical evidence that had put Whitmore under suspicion. Whitmore's claims of physical abuse remained in dispute, but threats and trickery had clearly helped elicit his "confession." His guilt was assumed on racist grounds like one detective's belief that "you can always tell when a Negro is lying by watching his stomach, because it moves in and out when he lies."

Robles' attorneys were unable to translate doubts about police interrogation methods to their own client's advantage, despite testimony that Robles had confessed to the Wylie-Hoffert murders while suffering from heroin withdrawal and without his attorney present. He was found guilty, largely on the basis of secretly tape-recorded conversations about the murder. Observers debated the verdict because Robles' self-incriminating statements were made to a fellow junkie, who became an informant and testified in return for immunity in an unrelated homicide.

Whitmore Retried in Assault Case

George Whitmore was retried for attempted rape in March 1966. Borrero's shaky but impassioned identification and Whitmore's confession were the prosecution's only evidence. Whitmore's attorney argued vehemently to introduce the Wylie-Hoffert episode in court, attempting to illustrate the tainted atmosphere in which the confession was obtained. When the judge agreed with the prosecution that past charges against the defendant should not be discussed before the jury—ironically reversing the protective nature of this rule to Whitmore's disadvantage—the defense attorney remained mute in protest for the rest of the trial. Whitmore was found guilty.

On June 13, 1966, the U.S. Supreme Court handed down the Miranda decision regarding the rights of crime suspects. The court acknowledged that coercive interrogations could produce false confessions. "The most conspicuous example occurred in New York in 1964," stated a footnote, "when a Negro of limited intelligence confessed to two brutal murders and a rape which he had not committed. When this was discovered, the prosecutor was reported as saying: 'Call it what you want—brain-washing, hypnosis, fright. The only thing I don't believe is that Whitmore was beaten.' "

The Miranda decision eliminated Whitmore's retrial for the Edmonds murder because his confession was the only evidence against him. When the high court voted not to apply the Miranda rule retroactively, however, Whitmore's attempted rape conviction stood. It was later overturned when an appellate court decided that preventing testimony about the Wylie-Hoffert "confession" had put the defense at a disadvantage.

Whitmore Convicted Again, then Released

On the sole evidence of Borrero's persistent accusations, Whitmore was tried and convicted a third time in May 1967. He returned to prison, sentenced to maximum sentences for attempted rape and assault. An attempt to seek a fourth trial faltered when his conviction was upheld in July 1970.

Meanwhile, Whitmore's defenders located Borrero's sister-in-law Celeste Viruet in Puerto Rico and returned with an affidavit stating that Borrero's courtroom testimony was contradicted by what she told her family shortly after the attack. Viruet had seen the attacker from her window, but police had never asked her to look at Whitmore. Borrero also had identified a different man in a "mug shot" notebook before police had shown her Whitmore.

On April 10, 1973, after four years in prison and nine years of trials, Whitmore was released and all charges against him were dismissed. He attempted to sue the city for $10 million for improper arrest and malicious prosecution. The suits were dismissed on technicalities. "They wrecked my life," Whitmore said bitterly, "and they still won't admit they did anything wrong."

—Thomas C. Smith

Suggestion Further Reading

Cunningham, Barry with Mike Pearl. *Mr. District Attorney: The Story of Frank S. Hogan and the Manhattan D.A.'s Office.* New York: Mason/Charter, 1977.

Lefkowitz, Bernard and Kenneth G. Gross. *The Victims.* New York: G.P. Putnam's Sons, 1969.

Raab, Selwyn. "Justice vs. George Whitmore." *The Nation* (July 2, 1973): 10–13.

Shapiro, Fred C. *Whitmore.* Indianapolis: Bobbs-Merrill Co., 1969.

——. "Department of Amplification." *The New Yorker* (June 9, 1973): 80.

Collie Leroy Wilkins Trial: 1965

Defendants: William Orville Eaton, Eugene Thomas, and Collie Leroy Wilkins, Jr. **Crime Charged:** Felony conspiracy to deny a citizen's constitutional rights **Chief Defense Lawyer:** Arthur Hanes **Chief Prosecutor:** John Doar **Judge:** Frank M. Johnson, Jr. **Place:** Montgomery, Alabama **Dates of Trial:** November 29–December 3, 1965 **Verdict:** Guilty **Sentence:** 10 years imprisonment

SIGNIFICANCE

Twice frustrated in attempts to convict Collie Leroy Wilkins for the murder of Viola Liuzzo, federal prosecutors successfully prosecuted Wilkins with an 1870 law for depriving Liuzzo of her civil rights.

On March 25, 1965, thousands of civil rights marchers converged on the Alabama state capitol in Montgomery, demanding an end to obstacles to black voter registration. The day of speeches ended a 54-mile march from Selma, where civil rights protesters had been gassed and beaten by police, arrested, and murdered during the previous three months.

That evening, a white volunteer from Michigan named Viola Liuzzo and LeRoy Moton, a black teenaged civil rights worker, ferried marchers back to Selma, then headed toward Montgomery for another carload. Near the rural town of Hayneville, a car traveling at nearly 100 miles per hour overtook them. As Liuzzo looked at the men in the car speeding alongside her, one of them shot her in the face, killing her. Her Oldsmobile drifted off the road into a ditch. Terrified but unharmed, LeRoy Moton saved his life by pretending to be dead when the attackers returned to look for survivors.

Gary Thomas Rowe Jr., Eugene Thomas, William Orville Eaton, and 21-old Collie LeRoy Wilkins, Jr., were quickly arrested. All four were members of the Ku Klux Klan. Unbeknownst to the others, Rowe was also a paid FBI informer, a fact which hastened their arrest and was to figure prominently in their trials.

Wilkins was tried first on a state murder charge. His attorney was Matt J. Murphy, Jr., a Klan lawyer or "Imperial Klonsel." Robert Shelton, "Imperial Wizard" of the United Klans of America, sat at the defense table until the judge ordered him to move to a spectator's seat.

LeRoy Moton quietly described the high-speed chase. Interrupted by laughter from Klansmen in the Hayneville court, he endured a cross-examination in which Murphy implied that Moton had shot Liuzzo to rob her. Prosecutors replied with an FBI ballistics report linking the bullet that killed Liuzzo to a revolver found in Eugene Thomas' house.

Gary Rowe described how the four Klansmen had noticed Liuzzo and Moton at a traffic light. Thomas, who was driving, suggested that they "get 'em." As their car gained on Liuzzo's on a desolate stretch of highway, Thomas handed his pistol to Wilkins. Wilkins said that forcing the other car off the road was too risky, for telltale paint scrapes could land them in jail. He told Thomas to speed up. When the cars were even, Wilkins fired twice.

"Shoot the hell out of it," Thomas ordered. Rowe claimed he stuck his weapon out the window, but only pretended to fire with Wilkins and Eaton.

Murphy cross-examined Rowe angrily. He recited part of the oath in which Klansmen swore to die rather than divulge secrets, resisting any "bribe, flattery, threats, passion, punishment, persecution, persuasion, [or] any other enticements."

"Did you hold up your hand before God and swear to these matters?" Murphy said.

"Yes, I believe I did," Rowe replied.

Murphy did not call Wilkins to testify. He did, however, give a vitriolic hour-long summation mingling Old Testament references with Klan doctrine. Murphy raged against blacks, Jews, Catholics, Communists, miscegenation, President Lyndon Johnson, and the National Association for the Advancement of Colored People. He called Rowe a perjurer, "a pimp," and "a white nigger."

Prosecutors told jurors that regardless of how they felt about the civil rights movement, this was a case of cold-blooded murder. Alabama Assistant Attorney General Joseph Gantt quoted segregationist Governor George Wallace, who had called Liuzzo's murder "a cowardly act that should not go unpunished."

The jury returned deadlocked, with 10 members voting for conviction. Some had stared at their hands in embarrassment during Murphy's closing speech. "He must have thought we were very, very ignorant to have been taken in by that act," said one juror. The two holdouts belonged to the white racist Citizens Council. One would not accept Rowe's testimony because the Klansman "swore before God and broke his oath" by becoming a paid informer.

When Wilkins' retrial convened, Alabama Attorney General Richmond Flowers took over the prosecution. He questioned potential jurors about their racial attitudes. Of 30 white males called for jury duty, 11 believed that white civil rights workers like Liuzzo were inferior to other whites.

Alabama law allowed Flowers to disqualify only six jurors with peremptory challenges. Because he was allowed limitless challenges "for cause-removal based on a distinct reason affecting a juror's fitness to serve;" Flowers declared that racial bias was a reason to disallow jurors. "How can the State of Alabama expect a fair and just verdict in this case from men who have already sat in judgment on the victim and pronounced her inferior to themselves?''

The Alabama Supreme Court rejected Flowers' argument. Wilkins' retrial proceeded with former Birmingham mayor Arthur Hanes replacing Murphy, who had been killed in a traffic accident. The testimony echoed the first trial. The jury, which included 10 present or former Citizens Council members, found Wilkins innocent in less than two hours.

Ku Klux Klansman, Collie Leroy Wilkins (center) arriving at court. (AP/Wide World Photos)

The U.S. Justice Department then pressed an indictment against Wilkins, Thomas, and Eaton, using a Reconstruction-era law. The 1870 statute made it a felony "to conspire, to injure, oppress, threaten, or intimidate any citizen in the free exercise or enjoyment of any privilege secured to him by the Constitution or laws of the United States."

Federal prosecutor John Doar argued that the law applied to Viola Liuzzo because the Selma-to-Montgomery Freedom March had been sanctioned by a federal court order after state officials tried to prevent it. Ironically, the court order had been signed by U.S. District Judge Frank M. Johnson, Jr. who would preside over the conspiracy trial.

Gary Rowe testified that he and the defendants had spent March 25 looking for marchers to harass upon orders from their Klan superiors. Defense attorney Hanes accused Rowe of fabricating his story for money and repeated the strategy of reading portions of the Klan's secrecy vow aloud.

When Rowe agreed that the words were "part of the oath" he had taken, Judge Johnson instructed Hanes to read the rest of the oath. Hanes unwillingly read the entire pledge, in which "knowledge of rape, treason against the United States, [or] malicious murder" voided the vow of silence, enjoining Klansmen to "help, aid, and assist" law enforcement officers.

After a day of deliberations, the jury told Judge Johnson that they were "hopelessly deadlocked."

"You haven't commenced to deliberate long enough to be hopelessly deadlocked," the judge replied. He lectured the jurors on the cost and seriousness of the case, adding that it had to be decided eventually. He then delivered an "Allen charge"—also known as a "dynamite" or "shotgun" charge—asking minority-decision jurors to examine the reasoning by which they arrived at a decision contrary to the majority.

Four hours later, the jury returned with a guilty verdict. "If it's worth anything to you," Judge Johnson said, "in my opinion, that was the only verdict you could possibly reach in this case and reach a fair and honest verdict. I couldn't tell you that before. It wasn't my job." Johnson ordered the defendants to be imprisoned for 10 years, the maximum sentence.

William Eaton died of a heart attack three months later. After Wilkins and Thomas served their sentences, they appeared before a 1978 grand jury investigating Rowe's involvement in other violence against civil rights workers in the 1960s . They accused Rowe of shooting Viola Liuzzo. Testimony by the two convicted Klansmen and others resulted in Rowe's indictment for first-degree murder. In 1980, however, the indictment was overturned and Rowe remained in the federal witness protection plan.

—*Thomas C. Smith*

Suggestions for Further Reading

Dees, Morris with Steve Fiffer. *A Season For Justice: The Life and Times of Civil Rights Lawyer Morris Dees.* New York: Charles Scribner's Sons, 1991.

Kempton, Murray. "Trial of the Klansman." *New Republic* (May 22, 1965): 10–13.

Kennedy, Robert F., Jr. *Judge Frank M. Johnson, Jr.* New York: G.P. Putnam's Sons, 1978.

"Liuzzo Case Jury Retires for Night Without A Verdict" and "The Imperial Klonsel." *New York Times* (May 7, 1965): 1, 25.

O'Reilly, Kenneth. *"Racial Matters"—The FBI's Secret File On Black America, 1960–1972.* New York: Free Press, 1989.

"Pictorial Summation of a Tragicomic Mistrial." *LIFE* (May 21, 1965): 32–39.

Wade, Wyn Craig. *The Fiery Cross: The Ku Klux Klan In America.* New York: Simon & Schuster, 1987.

Candace Mossler and Melvin Lane Powers Trial: 1966

Defendants: Candace Mossler and Melvin Lane Powers
Crime Charged: Murder **Chief Defense Lawyers:** Henry Carr, Percy Foreman, Walter E. McGwinn, Marian Rosen, Harvey St. Jean, and Clyde Woody **Chief Prosecutors:** Richard E. Gerstein, Arthur E. Huttoe, and Gerald Kogan **Judge:** George E. Schulz **Dates of Trial:** January 17–March 6, 1966 **Verdict:** Not guilty

SIGNIFICANCE

Millions of dollars were at stake in this trial, one of the most sensational in years. There was talk of sexual variations, suspected contract-killers, and police corruption in this tale of greed and brutal murder.

For 12 years Candace and Jacques Mossler lived together in seeming harmony. Mossler, a multimillionaire Houston, Texas, businessman, lavished attention and money on his beautiful wife and was rewarded with her apparent devotion, until 1961. In that year, Melvin Powers, Candy Mossler's 20-year-old nephew, came to live with the couple. Not long afterwards, according to Mrs. Mossler's testimony, Jacques Mossler was struck down by a mysterious illness that left him a homosexual. Shattered by this discovery, Candy Mossler turned to her sister's son for companionship, despite their 21-year age difference. When Jacques Mossler found out, he fired Powers from the company and moved to Miami, Florida.

Candy Mossler and Melvin Powers remained in Houston until the summer of 1964, when she took her four adopted children to visit her husband in Florida. Once there, she began chauffeuring the children on a series of suspicious midnight car rides. On June at 1:30 A.M. she drove them to a nearby hospital emergency room. Just minutes later, someone broke into the Mossler household, struck Jacques Mossler over the head and stabbed him 39 times. The murder time was established by neighbors who heard loud barking from the Mossler's dog, and cries of "Don't! Don't do that to me!" A "dark-haired man in dark clothing" was also seen fleeing. Police believed that man was Melvin Powers, acting in collusion with Candy Mossler. The couple was charged with murder 12 months later.

Jury selection began January 17, 1966, and took several days. At its conclusion Arthur E. Huttoe presented the state's case against Candy Mossler and Melvin Powers, detailing a "sordid, illicit, love affair." The motive, Huttoe said, was money: with her husband out of the way, Candy Mossler would inherit millions plus control of his business.

Sexual Perversions

A fortune of that magnitude meant that Mossler and Powers were able to afford the very best in legal talent. Legendary Texas attorney Percy Foreman was imported to head the powerful defense team. He maintained that Jacques Mossler's sexual appetites—"transvestitism, homosexuality, voyeurism and every conceivable type of perversion, masochism, sadism,"—had caused his own death; he was murdered, said Foreman, by a slighted homosexual lover. In support of this claim, Foreman referred to a human hair found on Mossler's body, which, despite exhaustive investigation, had never been identified. Foreman later broadened his scope of potential killers to include disaffected business partners, saying that as "mastermind" of a great financial empire, Mossler was hated by "thousands of people."

Prosecutors believed otherwise. Their version had Powers flying into Miami on the night of the murder, killing Mossler, then leaving at eight o'clock next morning. And they had plenty of witnesses to back up the claim. Mary Alice Domick, a National Airlines ticketing agent in Houston, recalled selling Powers a ticket to Miami on June 29, 1964. Stewardess Barbara Ann Barrer confirmed that Powers was aboard, carrying just a brief case; and the manager of a lounge near Mossler's home placed Powers in his bar between 7:00 and 8:30 P.M. on the night of the killing.

At Miami International Airport, police found Candy Mossler's abandoned 1960 Chevrolet. Fingerprint expert Robert Worsham testified that of 55 prints found in the car, six belonged to Powers. Foreman wasn't impressed. "You do not know whether Melvin Powers drove that car in June, May, or April in Miami, do you?" he asked.

"No," admitted Worsham.

Another fingerprint specialist, David Plowden, wasn't so easily dismissed. He had located Powers' palm print on the kitchen counter in the murdered man's home. Mossler's handyman Roscoe Brown testified that he had wiped that counter down just hours before the killing. Brown also disclosed a telephone conversation with Candy Mossler after the murder, in which she said, "You've got to say you didn't clean that sink . . . remember, a man's life is at stake, anything you say can hurt him."

Defense attorney Clyde Woody struggled to salvage the situation. "Didn't Mrs. Mossler tell you, 'Don't let them put words in your mouth?'"

"Right," said Brown.

"Didn't she say, 'I would do the same for you if I thought you were innocent?'"

"That's right," Brown answered.

Earlier in the trial, Freddie Duhart, a colorful ex-convict from Houston, testified that Powers had offered him $10,000 to find a hired killer. "I told him you could get someone from Mexico and put the body in the trunk of the car—nobody checks the trunk of a car at the border—and give a man $50 to $100 to take the body back up in the mountains and throw if off a volcano."

Candace Mossler, wearing a neck brace, was accused of murdering her husband with the help of her nephew, Melvin Powers. (AP/Wide World Photos)

Galveston, Texas, resident Edward Diehl also swore that Powers had solicited him to kill Jacques Mossler, with the promise that "there's $5,000 in it for you."

Yet another convicted felon, Billy Frank Mulvey, pointed the finger of suspicion at both defendants. After stating that, in a jailhouse confession, Powers had admitted murdering Mossler to him, Mulvey further claimed that two years earlier Candy Mossler had paid him "seven grand" as a down payment to kill her husband. At this, Candy Mossler cried out across the courtroom, "I've never seen or heard of this man," an outburst that brought a stern rebuke from Judge George E. Schulz.

Mulvey continued: "I told her it wasn't enough."

"What did you do with the $7,000," asked Foreman.

"I stashed it." Mulvey replied, adding, "I'm a thief—not a burglar." According to several defense witnesses, Mulvey was also a heroin junkie, pathologically incapable of telling the truth, and a police informant willing to say anything to beat an upcoming habitual criminal rap and possible life sentence.

Preparing an Alibi

In closing arguments prosecutor Gerald Kogan submitted that Candy Mossler's strange nocturnal visits to the hospital, all between the hours of midnight and 7:00 A.M., were undertaken to establish an alibi. He further submitted that the evidence, although circumstantial, could lead to only one reasonable conclusion: Powers and Candy Mossler had conspired to kill Jacques Mossler.

From among the several of defense lawyers, it was Percy Foreman who commanded center stage. In his closing 6½ hour speech Foreman laid the blame for Mossler's death everywhere except at the door of Melvin Powers. He blamed the police for entering into a "monetary conspiracy" with the dead man's daughter; he blamed "Dade County justice"; he accused police of buying testimony from "a lifetime thief and other ex-convicts"; he recited passages from the Scripture and Shakespeare. He concluded the masterly, if somewhat discursive, oration by thundering, "Let him among you without sin cast the first stone." Then Foreman sat down, smiling, confident he had won over the all-male jury.

And so it proved. After 16 hours and 44 minutes of deliberation on March 6, 1966, they returned a verdict of not guilty. State Attorney Richard Gerstein received the news in grim silence. Later, watching Candy first embrace Powers, then several of the jurors, he remarked, "I don't agree with the verdict, but this is the American system."

More Unsolved Mysteries

Following the trial, Melvin Powers returned to Houston and became a successful real estate developer. Candace Mossler continued to attract controversy. In 1971, she married Barnett Garrison, 19 years her junior. The following year Garrison suffered brain damage in a fall from the roof of the Mossler mansion in Houston. Apparently Mr. Garrison, wearing a pistol in his belt, had tried to gain access to his wife's third floor balcony window when he lost his footing and plunged 40 feet onto a concrete patio. Police ruled the fall accidental. Three months later the couple divorced.

In May 1974, Candy Mossler told police that a masked intruder had broken into her home, chloroformed her, then made off with $396,000 in jewelry and money. She had reported a similar theft in Miami Beach two weeks earlier. On that occasion a thief "with soft hands" had taken $200,000 in gems. Carelessly, Mrs. Mossler reported the same item—a $160,000 diamond—stolen in each robbery. Neither case was solved.

In October 26, 1976, Candace Mossler died in her sleep at the Fontainbleau Hotel in Miami Beach. She was 55 years old.

Florida's rush to prosecute Candy Mossler and Powers highlights the weakness of any case based solely on instinct and suspicion. At no time did the circumstantial evidence ever approach the degree of cogency necessary for conviction.

—Colin Evans

Suggestions for Further Reading

Axthelm, Pete. *Newsweek* (November 8, 1976).

Crimes and Punishment. Vol. 12. England: Phoebus, 1974.

Taylor, Gary. *National Law Journal* (May 22, 1989): 29ff.

Carl Anthony Coppolino Trials:
1966 & 1967

Defendant: Carl Anthony Coppolino   **Crime Charged:** Murder
Chief Defense Lawyers: Joseph Afflitto, F. Lee Bailey, and Joseph Mattice
Chief Prosecutors: First trial: Vincent Keuper; second trial: Frank Schaub
Judges: First trial: Elvin R. Simmill; second trial: Lynn Silvertooth
Places: First trial: Monmouth County, New Jersey; second trial: Naples,
Florida   **Dates of Trials:** First trial: December 5–15, 1966; second trial:
April 3–28, 1967   **Verdicts:** First trial: Not guilty; second trial: Guilty,
second-degree homicide

SIGNIFICANCE

The two trials of Dr. Carl Anthony Coppolino are case studies in the importance juries attach to an ostensibly discredited witness. In the first trial they chose to disbelieve a self-confessed accessory to murder and were swayed instead by the welter of contradictory forensic evidence. A second jury, confronted by much the same forensic testimony alone, arrived at a very different verdict.

In 1966 a conversation between two women in Florida sparked one of the most hotly contested debates in American legal history: Did Dr. Carl Coppolino murder his wife and his ex-lover's husband, or was he merely the hapless victim of jealous revenge? Two trials, in two states, arrived at very different answers.

At age 30, Coppolino, a New Jersey anesthesiologist, had been declared medically unfit for work because of a heart condition. Supported by a disability benefit, royalties from writing, and the salary of his wife Carmela, also a physician, Coppolino began a torrid affair with 48-year-old housewife Marjorie Farber, a vivacious woman who looked much younger than her years. Marjorie Farber's husband William Farber, at first tolerated the liaison, then grew resentful.

On the evening of July 30, 1963, Marjorie Farber telephoned the Coppolinos in a state of panic. William Farber was unconscious in the bedroom. Could Carl come over immediately? Coppolino, wary of losing his benefits if caught practicing, sent Carmela Coppolino instead. She found Farber dead. Apart from being "all blue down one side," there was no outward sign of distress to the body. At Coppolino's urging, she signed the death certificate, citing coronary thrombosis as the cause.

Over the next 18 months Coppolino's affair with Farber waned, and, in April 1965, the Coppolinos moved to Longboat Key, Florida. Disaster struck when Carmela Coppolino failed the Florida medical examination. Coppolino, in desperate need of money, began dating a wealthy divorcee named Mary Gibson.

At 6:00 A.M. August 28, 1965, the Coppolino family physician, Dr. Juliette Karow, was awakened by a phone call. She heard Coppolino tearfully describe how he had just found his wife dead, ostensibly from a heart attack. Karow was puzzled when she arrived at the house—young women in their 30s rarely suffer coronary failure—but she found no evidence of foul play and duly signed the certificate. Forty-one days later Coppolino married Mary Gibson.

Marjorie Farber, who had pursued Coppolino to Florida in hopes of resurrecting their romance, was incensed by this turn of events. She went to Dr. Karow and unburdened her soul. It was a sensational tale, one that would fill front pages across the nation for months: how she had been hypnotized into attempting murder, then stood by, a helpless onlooker, as her husband was smothered to death by Dr. Carl Coppolino.

Both New Jersey and Florida ordered exhumations. The autopsies were performed by Dr. Milton Helpern, New York's chief medical examiner. He found evidence of succinylcholine chloride, an artificial form of curare used by anesthesiologists, in both bodies. Also, Farber's cricoid—a cartilage in the larynx—was fractured, indicating that he had been strangled. These findings led to dual charges of homicide being filed against Coppolino.

Round One

After considerable interstate wrangling, Coppolino stood trial in New Jersey for the murder of William Farber. Prosecutor Vincent Keuper declared that Coppolino had not only broken the commandment "Thou shalt not covet thy neighbor's wife," but also "Thou shalt not covet thy neighbor's life."

Defense attorney F. Lee Bailey knew his only hope lay in totally discrediting Marjorie Farber. Break her testimony and Helpern's words would fall on deaf ears. His opening address contained a ringing indictment:

> This woman drips with venom on the inside, and I hope before we are through you will see it drip on the outside. She wants this man so badly that she would sit on his lap in the electric chair while somebody pulled the switch, just to make sure that he dies. This is not a murder case at all. This is monumental and shameful proof that hell hath no fury like a woman scorned.

When Bailey sat down, the battle lines had been drawn. Now it was time for the first prosecution witness: Marjorie Farber.

She told of being under Coppolino's spell ever since he had first hypnotized her to get rid of a smoking habit. She was powerless to deny him anything, especially when he told her repeatedly, ". . . that bastard [Farber] has got to go." Coppolino had given her a syringe filled with some deadly solution and instructions to inject Farber when he was asleep. At the last moment her nerve failed, but not until she had injected a minute amount of the fluid into Farber's leg. When he became ill she summoned Coppolino to the house. He first administered a sedative, then attempted to suffocate Farber by wrapping a plastic bag around his head. As the two men struggled, Marjorie begged Coppolino to stop. Instead, he smothered Farber with a pillow.

Devastating Cross-Examination

Bailey rose to face the witness. What followed was brutal and at times belligerent. It also remains a classic of cross-examination. Bailey began sarcastically. There had been no murder at all; everything she said had been a lie, a figment of her malicious imagination, instigated by an evil desire for revenge on the man who had ditched her. Wasn't that right? Over a torrent of prosecution objections, Bailey pressed on: "This whole story is a cock-and-bull story, isn't it?"

Sustained.

"Didn't you make this all up, Mrs. Farber?"

Sustained.

"Did you fabricate this story?"

Sustained.

Shifting tactics, Bailey ridiculed Farber's claim of having been an unwilling but helpless participant in the murder, saying he would produce medical testimony to prove such obeisance impossible. He hacked away, constantly reminding the jury of her adulterous and jealous behavior and, most of all, her age. "This 52-two year-old woman . . ." was a repeated theme, as if this were reason enough to explain Farber's vitriolic accusations. Perceptibly, the mood of the court swung against her. At the end of a two-day ordeal, she limped from the stand, her credibility in tatters.

She was replaced by Milton Helpern. Even this seasoned courtroom veteran reeled under the Bailey bludgeon. At issue was whether William Farber had suffered from terminal heart disease, and if the cricoid fracture had occurred before or after death. Helpern was emphatic on both points, although Bailey drew from him the grudging admission that there was no bruising about the neck, as would normally have been present if strangulation had occurred. Bailey speculated that rough handling of the body during disinterment, in particular a clumsy grave-digger's shovel, had caused the cricoid fracture. Helpern scoffed at such an idea. But Bailey had his own expert witnesses and they thought otherwise.

Doctors Joseph Spelman and Richard Ford, both experienced medical examiners, expressed the view that, not only was the cricoid fracture caused postmortem, but that William Farber's heart showed clear signs of advanced coronary disease, certainly enough to have killed him.

With the verdict still very much up in the air, Bailey called his star witness, Carl Anthony Coppolino. Slim and sleekly groomed, he answered his accusers well and without any noticeable guile. Coppolino came across as confident without seeming cocky, helpful but not obsequious.

Summing up, Judge Elvin Simmill commented on the vast array of conflicting medical evidence and stressed to the jury that they must be satisfied of Coppolino's guilt "beyond a reasonable doubt." It was an admonition that they took to heart. After deliberating for less than five hours they returned a verdict of not guilty.

Florida Fights Back

Coppolino's second trial opened in Naples, Florida before Justice Lynn Silvertooth on April 3, 1967. State Attorney Frank Schaub, recognizing that there was no direct evidence to link Carl Coppolino with the death of Carmela Coppolino, piled up a mountain of inconsistencies and motives for murder that the defense couldn't counter. High on the list was money. Schaub leaned heavily on the fact that Coppolino was running short of cash. He portrayed the doctor as a heartless philanderer, determined to wed Mary Gibson for her considerable fortune. But Carmela Coppolino's refusal to grant him a divorce had blown that idea sky-high. Instead, Coppolino began eying his wife's life insurance policy, $65,000. With that and Gibson's bank account, he would be set for life. "There's your motive," Schaub trumpeted.

Persuasive as Schaub's case was, other, perhaps more significant, forces were at work on his behalf. Coppolino's reputation had preceded him. Nothing was said, of course, but this particular jury gave Milton Helpern a far more favorable hearing than their New Jersey counterpart. His task was much the same as before, to explain the presence of succinylcholine chloride in Carmela Coppolino's body, and this he did in lucid terms that anyone could understand.

Marjorie Farber testified to overhearing Coppolino on the phone after his wife's death, saying, "They have started the arterial work and that won't show anything." Further questioning clarified that this referred to the fluid used by embalmers to replace the blood. It was damning stuff.

Once again F. Lee Bailey performed brilliantly, but each witness stood firm. And this time he received no assistance from the defendant. Unaccountably, Coppolino refused to testify on his own behalf. Bailey was stunned, later calling it "a terrible mistake."

Certainly the jury thought so. On April 28, 1967, they found Coppolino guilty of second-degree murder, a curious verdict that has never been fully explained; under Florida law, murder in the second degree implies a lack of premeditation on the part of the killer, and anything more calculated than willful poisoning is hard to imagine. Whatever the reasoning, their decision saved Coppolino from Death Row. Instead, the slender ex-doctor who thought he had carried out the perfect murder was led away to begin a life sentence at the state prison at Raiford, Florida.

After serving 12½ years, Carl Coppolino was paroled in 1979. Coppolino holds a unique position as the only person ever charged with two entirely separate "love triangle" murders. Either case, taken on its own, might have resulted in acquittal, but coming in such quick succession, the two proved insurmountable. Juries are not prepared to extend coincidences quite that far.

—Colin Evans

Suggestions for Further Reading

Baden, Michael M. *Unnatural Death*. New York: Random House, 1989.

Bailey, F. Lee with Harvey Aronson. *The Defense Never Rests*. New York: Stein and Day Publishers, 1971.

Block, Eugene. *Fabric of Guilt*. New York: Doubleday & Co., 1968.

Coppolino, Carl A. *The Crime That Never Was*. Tampa, Fla.: Justice Press, 1980.

Holmes, Paul. *The Trials Of Dr. Coppolino*. New York: New American Library, 1968.

MacDonald, John D. *No Deadly Drug*. New York: Doubleday & Co., 1968.

Wilson, Colin and Donald Seaman. *Encyclopedia of Modern Murder*. New York: G.P. Putnam's Sons, 1983.

Albert Henry DeSalvo Trial: 1967

Defendant: Albert Henry DeSalvo **Crimes Charged:** Armed Robbery, Sex Offenses **Chief Defense Lawyer:** F. Lee Bailey **Chief Prosecutor:** Donald L. Conn **Judge:** Cornelius J. Moynihan **Place:** Cambridge, Massachusetts **Date of Trial:** January 11–18, 1967 **Verdict:** Guilty **Sentence:** Life Imprisonment

SIGNIFICANCE

When Albert DeSalvo stood trial in Massachusetts courtroom for armed robbery and sexual assault, everyone present knew they were looking at the self-confessed "Boston Strangler." Aware that legal complexities prevented DeSalvo's indictment as the Strangler, his lawyers used the enormity of those crimes to bolster their claim that DeSalvo was insane and therefore not culpable on the present charges.

Boston, Massachusetts, was a city under siege in January 1964. A reign of terror had left 13 women, ranging in age from 19 to 85, dead at the hands of a killer known as the "Boston Strangler." All of the victims were slain in their own homes by a person who seemed able to gain entrance to strange apartments at will and was possessed of an ability to elude his pursuers. And then as abruptly as they began, the killings stopped.

Fears of the Strangler were beginning to fade when, on October 27, 1964, a young Cambridge housewife called police to complain of a knife-wielding intruder who had bound and molested her. Afterwards he had loosened her bonds, mumbled, "I'm sorry," and fled the apartment. Detectives recognized the victim's description of her attacker as that of 32-year-old Albert DeSalvo, known as the "Measuring Man" from his habit of coaxing women into letting him take their measurements with a tailor's tape, under pretext of working for a modeling agency.

Following DeSalvo's arrest, it came to light that he was also the "Green Man," a mass rapist so-called because of the green slacks he wore. Psychiatrists diagnosed DeSalvo as "potentially suicidal and quite clearly overtly schizophrenic," and on February 4, 1965, he was committed to Bridgewater State Hospital "until further order of the court."

It was while in Bridgewater that DeSalvo first began hinting that he was the Boston Strangler. A fellow inmate contacted attorney F. Lee Bailey and asked him to visit DeSalvo. What Bailey heard convinced him that DeSalvo was truthful. Under hypnosis and a promise of immunity from prosecution, DeSalvo made a series of tape-recorded confessions in which he gave graphic accounts of the Strangler murder scenes, including details that only the killer could have known.

These confessions posed an awkward legal problem. Because they were uncorroborated, and because DeSalvo had already been adjudged mentally incompetent, the state was reluctant to proceed against him on the stranglings. Instead, a compromise was worked out. DeSalvo would stand trial for his "Green Man" offenses and receive a mandatory life sentence. Bailey, determined those years should be spent receiving treatment, set out to prove DeSalvo insane.

Sanity Hearing

At a pretrial competency hearing on January 10, 1967, DeSalvo declared that he was not seeking his freedom and would "go anywhere necessary to receive proper treatment." Asked by the prosecutor, Assistant District Attorney Donald L. Conn, why he had retained F. Lee Bailey, DeSalvo answered:

> To defend me, to bring out the truth, rather than let me be buried somewhere where they'd never get at the truth. . . . I'd like, myself, to know what happened . . . to bring out what's inside of me that I couldn't understand.

At the end of the day-long hearing. Judge Cornelius J. Moynihan found De-Salvo competent and announced that his trial would commence the next day.

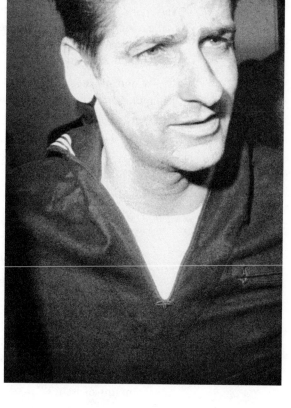

Albert DeSalvo, self-proclaimed "Boston Strangler." (Bettmann/Corbis.)

It began with testimony from four women, all of whom had been attacked by DeSalvo in their homes. Two spoke of awakening to find DeSalvo, an experienced burglar, in their bedroom. One said he had pretended to be a detective before tying her up and committing the offense. As he was leaving, she said, "he asked me to forgive him and not to tell his mother."

Dr. James A. Brussel, associate commissioner of the New York State Department of Mental Hygiene, recounted DeSalvo's grim upbringing. His father had beaten the children repeatedly and often forced his wife to have sexual relations in front of them. The experience left DeSalvo morbidly preoccupied with sex, and with his own wife unable or unwilling to satisfy his voracious appetite, he looked elsewhere. Molestation led to rape, and ultimately to murder.

Prosecutor Conn, who had argued unsuccessfully to have all mention of murder excluded from this case, disputed Dr. Brussel's diagnosis of DeSalvo as a man reacting to an "irresistible drive." What did that mean? After much thought, Brussel replied, "He thought he was God in his own self-created world."

Conn wasn't so sure. He produced another Bridgewater inmate, Stanley Setterland, who said that DeSalvo had bragged of a cunning strategy: he would make a lot of money from his confession, then hire a good lawyer. The lawyer would have him placed in a hospital for a brain operation, after which he would be declared sane and freed.

Conn pushed Setterland hard, determined to expose DeSalvo as a schemer, perfectly aware of his actions. "What did he [tell you he did] after the killings?"

"He wiped everything . . . so he wouldn't leave fingerprints."

When Dr. Ames Robey, medical director of Bridgewater, took the stand, Bailey grilled him about several contradictory diagnoses of DeSalvo. First, Robey had declared DeSalvo sane, then changed his mind, then reverted to his original opinion.

"Why did you change the diagnosis?" asked Bailey.

"I felt I had been taken in."

"Are you saying Albert conned you?"

"I'm afraid so," the doctor conceded.

Robey also admitted that his latest change of heart had been inspired in part by Setterland's own performance on the stand. Bailey looked askance and produced Bridgewater records showing that Robey had once diagnosed Setterland as a patient capable of "a considerable degree of lying on an enormous amount of issues."

"When did you decide Setterland was a man of truth?" he asked with sarcasm.

Flustered, Dr. Robey said that Setterland was "looking a great deal better" after his recent discharge from Bridgewater, and that his testimony given just days previously confirmed Robey's current belief that DeSalvo was manipulative and an "attention grabber," a patient with an "extensive need to prove what a big man he was."

Final Arguments

Bailey closed with an impassioned plea on DeSalvo's behalf. He wasn't asking for freedom for this "dangerous uncontrollable beast" indeed "DeSalvo wants society to be protected from him," but he demanded a verdict of insanity so that DeSalvo could receive proper treatment instead of being locked away.

Prosecutor Conn saw things quite differently. He saw DeSalvo as just one more cunning criminal who had feigned the symptoms of mental illness to avoid the consequences of his actions. He told the jury:

> It's my duty to my wife, to your wife, to every woman who might conceivably be a victim of this man, to stamp his conduct for what it is—vicious, criminal conduct. Don't let this man con you right out of your shoes!

In his final charge to the jury, Judge Moynihan reminded them they were to purge all thoughts of the Boston Strangler from their minds and decide this case on its merits alone.

On January 18, 1967, they did just that, finding Albert DeSalvo sane and guilty on all 10 counts. He was sentenced to life imprisonment.

To reporters later, Bailey commented, "Massachusetts has burned another witch. No fault of the jury's, of course. It's the fault of the law."

On February 24, 1967, Albert DeSalvo and two other inmates escaped from Bridgewater. Murderer Frederick E. Erickson, 40, and armed robber George W. Harrisson, 35, were recaptured that same day, but for 24 hours the city of Boston cringed, waiting for the Strangler to strike again. It didn't happen. The next day DeSalvo was arrested in a clothing store in Lynn, Massachusetts, claiming to have escaped only to draw attention to his case. Nervous authorities decided that in the future DeSalvo would be housed in the maximum-security Walpole State Prison.

Eight months later Albert DeSalvo received an additional 7–10 years for escaping. His brothers, Richard, 32, and Joseph, 37, were each given one-year suspended sentences for aiding in the escape.

On November 26, 1973, Albert DeSalvo was stabbed to death by another inmate at Walpole State Prison. His killer was never apprehended.

Despite his many confessions, Albert DeSalvo was never tried as the Boston Strangler. Some feel that he fabricated the whole story, relying on his contact with the actual killer (allegedly another Bridgewater inmate) for the details of the crimes. Oddly enough, none of the eyewitnesses who saw the Boston Strangler identified DeSalvo as the killer, but one fact is undeniable: Boston's reign of terror ended with the incarceration of this strange and troubled man.

—Colin Evans

Suggestions for Further Reading

Banks, Harold K. *The Strangler!* New York: Avon, 1967.

Brussel, James A. *Casebook Of A Crime Psychologist.* New York: Grove, 1968.

Frank, Gerald. *The Boston Strangler.* New York: New American Library, 1966.

Gaute, J.H.H and Robin Odell. *The Murderers' Who's Who.* London: W.H. Allen, 1989.

Richard Franklin Speck Trial: 1967

Defendant: Richard Franklin Speck   **Crime Charged:** Murder
Chief Defense Lawyers: Gerald Getty, James Gramenos, and Jerome Wexler
Chief Prosecutor: William Martin   **Judge:** Herbert C. Paschen
Place: Peoria, Illinois   **Dates of Trial:** February 20–April 15, 1967
Verdict: Guilty   **Sentence:** Death, later commuted to 8 life terms
imprisonment

SIGNIFICANCE

Nothing like the testimony of Corazon Amurao had ever graced an American courtroom. Witnesses to murder are rare enough; witnesses to the kind of wholesale slaughter she described were unheard of. Richard Speck's killing spree sent shockwaves around the world.

At 6:00 A.M. on July 14, 1966, the early morning calm of Jeffrey Manor, a middle-class South Chicago, Illinois, suburb, was shattered by screaming. Neighbors tracked the disturbance to a two-story townhouse occupied by nurses who worked at the nearby community hospital. They found Corazon Amurao, a diminutive Filipino nurse, perched on a second-floor window ledge, in tears and hysterical. "My friends are all dead, all dead," she cried. "I am the only one alive." Investigation of the townhouse confirmed the grim truth. Someone had turned the place into an abattoir. Eight nurses lay dead—stabbed, strangled, and mutilated.

Amurao told detectives of an armed stranger, smelling strongly of alcohol, who had forced his way in the previous night, ostensibly looking for money. Then he began systematically killing everyone present. Only by hiding beneath a bed and remaining silent was she able to avoid the carnage. She described the killer as tall and blond, and having a "Born to raise hell" tattoo on one arm.

Because of the unusual knots used to tie the victims, police theorized that they were looking for someone with nautical connections. This led them to a nearby branch of the seaman's union. Mention of the killer's tattoo produced a name: Richard Speck, a 24-year-old sailor and habitual criminal, with a long record of drug abuse and drunken violence. A photo and description were circulated throughout the Chicago area.

In the early hours of July 17, a man who unsuccessfully attempted suicide was admitted to Cook County Hospital with slashed wrists. When doctors wiped away the blood, they saw the distinctive tattoo and called police.

Trial Moved

Because of the intense local media coverage, Richard Speck's chief attorney, Gerald Getty, requested a change of trial venue. When the trial opened in the morning of February 20, 1967, it was in Peoria, Illinois, some 140 miles from Chicago. Getty also won another important victory by having all eight murder charges consolidated into one trial with one verdict and one sentence. Assistant State Attorney William Martin had wanted the cases tried individually. That way, even if Speck was acquitted on one count, there were still seven others to trap him. Despite this setback, Martin remained confident that the state had sufficient evidence for conviction.

For two days he carefully laid the groundwork of his case. His first witnesses, sailors Dante Bargellini and George Mackey, both placed Speck in the vicinity of the nurses' house just before the murder and also confirmed his expressed desire to return to New Orleans. Other witnesses testified to seeing Speck on a day-long drinking binge, brandishing a gun and a knife.

It wasn't until the third day of testimony that Martin produced the prosecution's prime witness: Corazon Amurao. She described being awakened by four knocks at her bedroom door. "I went to the door, . . . I unlocked it, . . . then I saw a man . . . with a gun in his right hand pointed towards me and I noticed that he had marks on his face . . . and his hair was blond."

The atmosphere was electric as Martin asked, "Now, Miss Amurao, if you see that same man in the courtroom today, . . . would you please step down and point him out." Amurao didn't hesitate. She crossed to the defense table, raised her hand and pointed directly at Speck. "This is the man."

Next, Amurao told how Speck herded all six girls present in the townhouse into the bedroom, then tore strips off a sheet and tied them up. Later, when three other nurses returned home, they too were made captive. She described Speck's peculiar ambivalence towards his prisoners, smiling a lot, almost friendly. "Don't be afraid," he said while tying one of the girls, "I'm not going to kill you."

Minutes later he began doing just that.

Using a scale model of the townhouse and eight wooden blocks to represent the murder victims, Martin asked Corazon Amurao to describe the events. Richard Speck, she said, went across to Patricia Wilkening, untied her ankles, and led her from the room.

"After Speck had taken Wilkening from the south bedroom, did you hear anything?" asked Martin.

"After about one minute I heard Miss Wilkening say 'Ah.' It was like a sigh."

"Did you hear anything after the noise you just described?"

"No."

But after the next two victims were removed from the bedroom, Amurao *did* hear something: "water running in the bathroom, as if Speck was washing his hands."

The macabre process continued. Speck would enter the bedroom, lead one of the girls away with him, then return several minutes later for his next victim. When the girls tried to hide, Speck found them all—except Corazon Amurao. Eventually, only she and Gloria Davy were left.

Frozen with fear in her hiding place beneath the bed, Amurao could only watch in horror as Speck stripped Gloria Davy and raped her. It later transpired that Davy, the only victim of sexual assault, was very similar to Speck's estranged wife, whom he hated and had threatened on several occasions to kill.

"Was your head down at that time?" asked Martin.

"Yes."

"When did you next look up?"

"About five minutes after the bedsprings stopped. I looked up and saw that Davy and Speck was [*sic*] not there anymore."

Amurao's account of her five-hour ordeal, made all the more poignant by her faltering English, was devastating. When Public Defender Gerald Getty rose to cross-examine, he faced the toughest task of his career. Not once had he lost a client to the electric chair; no one present in court expected that record to survive.

Richard Speck (right), with his lawyer, public defender Gerald Getty. (AP/Wide World Photos)

Mistaken Identity?

It had been Getty's contention throughout that Richard Speck was completely innocent, that Corazon Amurao, in her traumatized and hysterical state, had identified the wrong man. But he had to tread carefully. Amurao had obviously impressed the jury and won their sympathy as well, any suggestion of bullying could backfire badly. But no matter how he tried, Getty could not shake the young Filipino nurse. She steadfastly continued to insist that Richard Speck was the killer.

There was plenty of other evidence to support her claim. Two T-shirts found at the crime scene were of the type that Speck was known to wear. And then there were the fingerprints. Three experts testified that prints found in the townhouse matched Speck's, a pronouncement hotly disputed by assistant defense counsel James Gramenos. He avowed that the prints were too smudged for positive identification. The experts disagreed. Gramenos persisted, though he was conspicuously unable to provide his own expert to back up this claim.

But the defense was not finished yet. Murrill and Gerdena Farmer, both workers at Kay's Pilot House, a tavern several blocks away from the townhouse, swore that Speck was in the bar until 12:30 A.M. on the night in question. Prosecutor Martin sought to demonstrate that the couple had made an honest mistake, but he could not budge them.

Richard Speck remained a spectator to all of this, choosing not to testify on his own behalf. Earlier he had told his attorneys that the events of July 13–14, 1966, were a blur of drugs and alcohol; he could remember nothing.

On April 15, 1967, after just 49 minutes of deliberation, the jury found Speck guilty and recommended death. Confirmation came June 6, 1967, when Judge Herbert C. Paschen sentenced Speck to the electric chair. When U.S. Supreme Court rulings in other cases called into question all death sentences recommended by trial juries, Speck's sentence was commuted to eight terms of life imprisonment.

Speck maintained his innocence until 1978 when he was quoted as telling a newspaper, "Yeah, I killed them. I stabbed them and choked them." After spending 24 years in prison, Richard Speck died of a heart attack on December 5, 1991. He was 49 years old.

—Colin Evans

Suggestions for Further Reading

Altman, Jack and Marvin Ziporyn. *Born to Raise Hell.* New York; Grove Press, 1967.

Crimes And Punishment. Vol. 13. England: Phoebus, 1974.

Felsher, Howard and Michael Rosen. *Justice, U.S.A.* New York: Crowell, Collier & Macmillan, 1967.

Wilson, Colin and Donald Seaman. *Encyclopedia of Modern Murder.* New York: G.P. Putnam's Sons, 1983.

Rubin "Hurricane" Carter Trials: 1967, 1988

Defendant: Rubin "Hurricane" Carter **Crime Charged:** Murder
Chief Defense Lawyers: First Trial: Raymond Brown; Second Trial: Myron Beldock; Federal Court Appeal: Myron Beldock, Leon Friedman, Lewis Steel
Chief Prosecutors: First Trial: Vincent Hall; Second Trial: Ronald Marmo; Federal Court Appeal: John Goceljak **Judges:** First Trial: Samuel Larner; Second Trial: Bruno Leopizzi; Federal Court Appeal: H. Lee Sarokin
Place: First Trial: Paterson, New Jersey; Second Trial: Paterson, New Jersey; Final Appeal: Newark, New Jersey **Date of Trials:** First Trial: April 7, 1967–May 26, 1967; Second Trial: November 11, 1976–December 20, 1976; Final Appeal Filed: February 13, 1985; Heard, July 26, 1985; Decision, November 7, 1985 **Verdicts:** First Trial: Guilty on three counts of first-degree murder; Second Trial: Guilty on three counts of first-degree murder; Final Appeal: Overturned the state's case, trial, and judgment on grounds of withholding evidence and an unacceptable charge of a motive
Sentences: First Trial: two consecutive life sentences, one concurrent life sentence; Second Trial: Two consecutive life sentences, one concurrent life sentence; Final Appeal: Carter released from prison

SIGNIFICANCE

This would have been one of the more publicized legal cases of its era if only because it involved three murders and an alleged murderer who was a nationally-ranked boxer, but what struck such a controversial note were its undertones of racial prejudice and its overtones of celebrity charisma. Beyond its two major trials, a series of appeals, and numerous lives caught up in its wake, the case generated several books, a well-known song, and a powerful movie. And to this day, because the original prosecutors would not accept the final verdict of the courts, the case is officially "unsolved."

Shortly after 2 A.M. on June 17, 1966, two men entered the Lafayette Grill, a dreary bar in a working-class neighborhood of Paterson, New Jersey. One of the men carried a12-gauge shotgun; the other had a .32 caliber handgun. With little warning and no apparent provocation, the men shot and instantly killed the bartender and a man at the bar and shot and seriously wounded another male and female patron (the woman died of complications a month later). All the victims were whites; the two gunmen were black. When the police arrived on the scene, two witnesses reported that they had seen two black men flee from the bar and drive off in a white car.

Rubin "Hurricane" Carter, the man whose case generated two major trials, a series of appeals, several books, a song, and a powerful movie. (AP/Wide World Photos)

Moving in on Carter

Immediately the radio call went out to police in Paterson to look for a white car with two black males. About 2:40 A.M., a policeman stopped a white car, but it had three black men; one of them was well known to the policeman, so they were allowed to drive on. But about one half hour later, after one of the men had been left off at his home, the car was stopped by police again. This time, the two remaining men were taken to a hospital where one of the wounded patrons was asked if either of these two were the men who had shot up the bar. He shook his head emphatically no. Back at the police station, the two men were given a lie-detector test, and when it was announced they had passed, they were released. But on October 14, the Paterson police arrested the two black men, John Artis and Rubin "Hurricane" Carter, and charged them with the three murders.

Artis was a 19-year-old who had been a track and football star in high school; soon to be drafted into the army, he was hoping to get a track scholarship to a college; he had no criminal record and had never been in trouble with the police. Carter had a totally different resume. As a young man he had been in frequent trouble with the law, even serving several years in prison; but in the army he had taken up boxing and after leaving prison in 1961 he became a professional. His ferocious manner in the ring earned him the nickname "Hurricane," and by the time of his arrest he was regarded as a potential contender for the middleweight championship of the world.

More significantly for what lay ahead, Carter was an individual who refused to adhere to any of the constraints expected of a black man at that time and in a community like Paterson. He carried on in a flamboyant way—shaved and polished his head, dressed in a flashy style and drove conspicuous cars, frequented nightclubs, played around with women. He also had spoken out bluntly against the injustices visited upon African Americans. All this had earned him the enmity of many white people in Paterson, and the New Jersey police and FBI were known to constantly shadow and harass him. Now Rubin "Hurricane" Carter was charged with three murders.

First Trial Ends in Conviction

The trial took place in the Passaic County Court in Paterson, New Jersey, and it came at a time when there was great unrest in the African-American communities across the United States. Just finding a jury willing to deal with the controversial Carter took three weeks. In the end, the 14 jurors (this included two substitutes) included only one person of color—a West Indian. In his opening statement, the prosecutor claimed that the police had found an unspent shotgun shell and .32 caliber bullet in the car Carter was riding in that evening—yet this evidence had never been cited during the four months between the police's search of his car and his arrest. Carter's lawyer announced that this would be challenged, and it later turned out that neither the shell nor the bullet was of the same kind found at the crime scene.

Long before this, Carter's lawyer lit into the first witness called by the prosecution—the one surviving bar patron, William Marins. He was the man who on the night of the murders had told the police that Carter and Artis were not the men who had shot him and the others. Before he was through, the lawyer established that Marins had on more than one occasion testified that the two gunmen were tall and light-colored men, and that one had a moustache. Neither Carter nor Artis fit that description; Carter in particular was short, very dark, wore a beard—and above all, had his unmistakable trademark, his polished bald head.

The rest of the state's evidence was equally weak. The murder weapons had never been found; there were no bloodstains on Carter's or Artis's belongings; the police had not taken any fingerprints nor conducted paraffin tests of the defendants' hands (for traces of gunpowder). One of the witnesses, a woman who lived above the bar and claimed she had a good view of the get-away car's taillights, described lights different from those on Carter's car that night.

There had been talk of the state's producing "mystery witnesses," and this they did. They were two small-time crooks, Alfred Bello and Arthur Dexter Bradley, who freely admitted that on the night of the murders they were engaged in trying to rob a nearby business. Bradley simply testified that he had seen Carter running down the street after the shooting, but Bello produced an elaborate story. He had seen three black men cruising in a white car before he decided to go into the bar to buy a pack of cigarettes. As he approached the tavern, he heard shots and saw two black men emerge with a shotgun and pistol; he got a clear look at them and fled as the two got into the white car and drove away. Bello then went into the bar and saw all the bodies, but he simply stole $62 from the cash register. Confronted with the fact that on the night of the murders, he had not identified Carter or Artis when they were brought to the bar or the police station, Bello claimed he had been afraid that his life would be in danger.

When it came to the defense case, all Carter and Artis could do was to provide accounts of their activities that night and witnesses to support their versions of events. Typical of Carter, though, he took the stand in the same cream-colored sport coat he was wearing the night of the murders. This was to highlight the fact that the same woman who said she had a good view of the getaway car's headlights had also described the two fleeing black men as wearing dark clothes.

In the end, though, the jury was not influenced by any of the evidence that might clear Carter and Artis. They apparently accepted the prosecution's claim that Carter and Artis had committed these slayings to revenge the murder of a black barkeeper by a white man earlier that evening—only a few blocks from the Lafayette Grill. After only two hours of deliberation, the jury returned with a unanimous verdict: guilty of all three counts. The jury's only act of moderation was to recommend life imprisonment instead of execution. And although Artis got the same judgment as Carter, it was quite clear to all involved that the prosecution was most pleased that it had finally put Carter away for life.

Second Conviction Overturned on Appeal

But Carter was not your typical prisoner—he was even given a $10,000 advance from a publisher for an autobiography he soon published under the title *The Sixteenth Round*. His case had attracted the attention of numerous prominent individuals, including a reporter for the *New York Times* who located the two petty crooks, Bello and Bradley, who had claimed to have seen Carter and Artis running from the bar. They now recanted their testimony, admitting that they had lied to gain favorable treatment from the police. By 1975 the Hurricane Trust Fund had been started and a host of celebrities were lending their names to his cause—everyone from Burt Reynolds and Stevie Wonder to Muhammad Ali and Coretta Scott King. Perhaps the biggest boost to the campaign to get a new trial for Carter came when Bob Dylan wrote a song, "Hurricane," and proceeded to sing it across the country.

Then in March 1976, the New Jersey Supreme Court overturned the convictions of Carter and Artis on the grounds that the prosecution had withheld a tape recording of an interview with Bello that revealed the state had promised Bello favorable treatment in return for his testimony. The two men were freed on bail (most of it posted by Muhammad Ali) but the New Jersey prosecutor soon re-indicted them. By the time the second trial began in November 1976, Bello had once again changed his story and he became the prosecution's chief witness. This time he took the stand and insisted that not only had he seen Carter and Artis running from the bar, he had told the police so that night. Equally damaging to the defense, the judge allowed the prosecution to introduce testimony about the angry blacks that had gathered outside the bar that evening, the bar where a white man had shot the black bartender. This fortified the state's claim that Carter and Artis had shot the four in retaliation.

The second jury convicted Carter and Artis on the same three counts of first degree murder. The two went back to prison, and it took another nine years and a frustrating series of appeals before a federal judge in New Jersey, H. Lee Sarokin, set aside the convictions, on the grounds that the state had violated the constitutional rights of Carter and Artis by failing to disclose the results of a lie detector test given to Bello and by introducing the claim that the killings were motivated by racial revenge. On August 21, 1987, the Federal Third Circuit Court upheld Judge Sarokin, and on February 27, 1988, the state of New Jersey formally announced it would not seek to re-indict Carter. The long trial of Rubin "Hurricane" Carter had finally ended.

—John S. Bowman

Suggestions for Further Reading

Carter, Rubin "Hurricane." *The Sixteenth Round: From Number 1 Contender to #45472*. New York: Viking Press, 1974.

Chaiton, Sam, and Terry Swinton. *Lazarus and the Hurricane*. New York: St. Martin's Griffin, 2000.

Hirsch, James. *Hurricane—the Miraculous Journey of Rubin Carter*. Boston and New York: Houghton Mifflin, 2000.

Price and Bowers Trial: 1967

Defendants: Cecil Price and Sam Bowers, Jr.   **Crimes Charged:** Conspiracy to violate civil rights   **Chief Defense Lawyers:** Clayton Lewis, H.C. Watkins, and Laurel Weir   **Chief prosecutors:** John Doar, Robert Hauberg, and Robert Owen   **Judge:** William Harold Cox   **Place:** Meridian, Mississippi **Dates of trial:** October 7–20, 1967   **Verdict:** Guilty   **Sentence:** Bowers, 10 years imprisonment; Price, 6 years imprisonment

SIGNIFICANCE

This trial's historic outcome marked a turning point in the long and often bloody struggle for civil rights that bedeviled Mississippi in the 1960s.

On the morning of June 21, 1964, two committed civil rights campaigners, Michael Schwerner and James Chayney, drove into Neshoba county, Mississippi, to investigate the burning of a church. With them was Andrew Goodman, an anthropology major who had arrived from New York the previous day. That afternoon the trio was arrested for speeding just outside the small town of Philadelphia by local sheriff's deputy Cecil Price. Around 10:00 P.M., after paying a $25 fine, they were released. All three then disappeared. Forty-four days later, following massive federal intervention, their murdered bodies were recovered from beneath a dam.

It soon became clear that a gang made up of local police officers and Ku Klux Klan members had carried out the killings. Equally obvious was the fact that chances of obtaining murder convictions were nonexistent. For this reason the federal government chose to proceed against those implicated on lesser charges of violation of civil rights. When the trial finally came to court 17 men were under indictment, but public attention had concentrated on just two:, Deputy Sheriff Cecil Price and local KKK Imperial Wizard Sam Bowers, Jr.

After three years of delays, the trial opened on October 7, 1967. The prosecution team led by the U.S. Justice Department's head civil rights attorney, John Doar, looked positively skimpy when arrayed against no less than a dozen defense attorneys, but the Justice Department case was damning. Doar contended that, while the three men were still in his custody, Price had contacted local KKK members under Bowers' leadership, and that a carefully orchestrated ambush was put into effect. After their release, Schwerner,

Chayney and Goodman were again stopped on the highway by Price, who then delivered them into the hands of his co-conspirators. One of those present, James Jordan, testifying for the prosecution, described how all three men were gunned down, then dumped into a prepared grave, which was bulldozed over.

Defense Tactics Fail

The defense's key strategy, made plain from the outset, centered around an attempt to enlist the sympathy of Judge William Cox, whose record on civil rights was less than exemplary. Their constant maneuvering for a postponement or mistrial, however, drew this stern rebuke from the judge: "I don't want this to be a pattern for this trial, gentlemen, because we are not going to have a big show out of this case. I don't run a court like that. We are going to try this case, we are going to get rid of it. It's not going to be interminable, so you can just get that out of your minds." Judge Cox's words sent a chill across the defense table as, perhaps for the first time, the accused realized that they might actually be convicted.

Another major miscalculation came when defense attorney Laurel Weir, cross-examining a prosecution witness, the Reverend Charles Johnson, asked if it was true that he [Johnson] and Schwerner had tried to "get young Negro males to sign statements that they would rape one white woman a week during the hot summer of 1964 here in Mississippi." Cox angrily interrupted, saying he found the question "highly improper—I'm not going to allow a farce to be made of this trial and everybody might as well get that through heads, including every one of the defendants."

Delmar Dennis, another renegade Klansman, testified that Bowers bragged to other Klan members of his involvement in the Neshoba killings, crowing: "It was the first time that Christians had planned and carried out the execution of a Jew." Dennis also provided details of a loosely coded letter written by Bowers, in which he had attempted to cover up details of the killings. But perhaps Dennis' most startling revelation came when he identified one of the defense attorneys, Clayton Lewis, as a Klan sympathizer. Laurel Weir's vociferous demands for a mistrial were overruled by Judge Cox.

In closing arguments Doar assured the jurors that "the federal government is not invading Philadelphia or Neshoba Country [but rather] these defendants are tried for a crime under federal law in a Mississippi city, before a Mississippi federal judge, in Mississippi courtroom, before twelve men and women from the state of Mississippi." This was a shrewd move on Doar's part. Throughout the trial he had wisely avoided turning this case into an indictment of the state: he knew his best chance of victory lay in appealing to sound common sense. Then he reminded the jurors:

This was a calculated, cold blooded plot. Three men, hardly more than boys, were the victims. The plot was executed with a degree of self-possession and steadiness equal to the wickedness with which it was planned.

Answering defense complaints that the turncoat Klansmen had been paid sums of money by the government to testify, Doar commented that such actions were necessary on occasion. As he put it, "Midnight murder in the rural area of Neshoba County provides few witnesses."

By contrast, defense attorney, H.C. Watkins excoriated the paid informers, then attempted to blacken the character and intentions of Schwerner, Chayney and Goodman:

> It well be that these young men were sacrificed by their own kin for publicity. So far as I have been able to determine, they had no authority to be in Neshoba County. They broke the laws of that county by speeding and they violated the American Constitution by messing in local affairs in a local community. Mississippians rightfully resent some hairy beatnik from another state visiting our state with hate and defying our people.

Jury Reaches Tough Decision

On October 18 the case went to the jury. After a day they declared themselves deadlocked, but Judge Cox refused to declare a mistrial and ordered a return to deliberations, reminding them of the expense of another trial and the necessity for them to reach a verdict. The admonishment worked. On October 20 the jury found Price and Bowers and five other defendants guilty. They could reach no verdict against four other defendants; the remainder were acquitted.

Announcing himself in complete agreement with the verdicts, Judge Cox set December 29 as sentencing day. At that time he imposed a 10-year jail term on Bowers, and six years for Price. The other convicted men received sentences of 3–10 years.

History had been made. For the first time a Mississippi jury had convicted white officials and Klansmen of crimes against black people or civil rights workers. In 1988, these events were captured in the movie *Mississippi Burning*. While the factual accuracy of the film was often called into question, few doubted that its searing portrayal of bigotry and blind hatred was anything other than authentic.

—Colin Evans

Suggestions for Further Reading

Blaustein, Albert P. and Robert L. Zangrando. *Civil Rights And The American Negro*. New York: Trident, 1968.

Cagin, Seth and Philip Dray. *We Are Not Afraid*. New York: Bantam, 1988.

Huie, William Bradford. *Three Lives For Mississipppi*. New York:

Kornbluth, Jesse, "The Struggle Continues." *New York Times Magazine* (July 23, 1989): 16ff.

Alice Crimmins Trials: 1968 & 1971

Defendant: Alice Crimmins   **Crimes Charged:** First trial, murder; Second trial, murder and manslaughter   **Chief Defense Attorneys:** First trial: Marty Baron and Harold Harrison; Second trial: William Erlbaum and Herbert Lyon.
Chief Prosecutors: First trial: Anthony Lombardino and James Mosely; Second trial: Thomas Demakos and Vincent Nicolosi.   **Judges:** First trial: Peter Farrell; second trial: George Balbach   **Place:** New York, New York
Dates of Trials: First trial: May 9–27, 1968; second trial: March 15–April 23, 1971   **Verdicts:** Guilty   **Sentences:** First trial: 5 to 20 years; second trial: life plus five to 20 years.

SIGNIFICANCE

Appeals in this sensational New York case led to a ruling that courtroom errors are only prejudicial when there is a strong probability they have influenced a jury's verdict.

To millions of New Yorkers, Alice Crimmins was a tramp responsible for an unspeakable crime. To others, Crimmins was a victim of what one of her lawyers called "trial by innuendo," a woman persecuted for her defiant anger at a justice system more concerned with her social behavior than in solving the murder of her children.

On the morning of July 14, 1965, Edmund Crimmins reported that his two children were missing from the Queens apartment where they lived with his estranged wife Alice. Police searched the neighborhood, hoping to find 5-year-old Eddie Crimmins, Jr., and 4-year-old Alice Marie "Missy" Crimmins alive. In early afternoon, Missy's dead body was found in a vacant lot.

The ground-floor window of the children's room was open, but police were more interested in Alice Crimmins' reputation as a "swinger." Faced with a dearth of physical evidence, detectives felt that her sexual affairs and her failure to break into tears immediately upon viewing her daughter's body made her a suspect.

Both parents endured intense police questioning about their broken marriage. A court hearing over custody of the children was to have started on July 19. Instead, the badly decomposed body of Eddie Jr. was found that day in scrub near the busy Van Wyck Expressway.

Trial Begins Three Years Later

Mutual resentment grew between Alice Crimmins and the police who suspected her. She angrily accused them of not working to find the real killers and stopped cooperating. Detectives and district attorneys viewed her hostility as evidence of guilt. Wiretaps, electronic surveillance, and hundreds of interviews with her neighbors and friends failed to produce any evidence. The district attorney's office tried twice to convince grand juries to indict her. Secret testimony made a third attempt successful. Alice Crimmins was accused of murdering Missy—there was not enough left of Eddie Jr.'s body to support a murder charge.

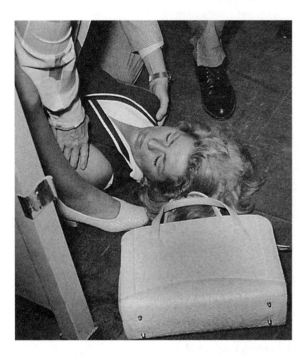

Alice Crimmins fainted at the Queens Police Station where she faced charges of killing her two children. (AP/Wide World)

Her trial began in May 1968, nearly three years after the Crimmins children disappeared. Prosecutors called Dr. Milton Helpern to the stand. The renowned forensic pathologist testified that Missy Crimmins was strangled. He held that food in the child's stomach could not have been ingested more than two hours before her death. Helpern's testimony was irreconcilable with Alice Crimmins' insistence that she fed both children at 7:30 P.M., two hours before she put them to bed, and over four hours before midnight when she last saw them alive.

One of Alice Crimmins' lovers, a contractor named Joe Rorech remembered her telling him a month before the expected custody battle that "she would rather see the children dead" than allow her husband to take them. The night of the disappearance, Rorech claimed to have called her apartment twice, receiving no answer at 2:00 A.M.

More damaging was Rorech's claim of a tearful admission in a Long Island restaurant 14 months after the children were found. "She said there was no reason for them to be killed, it was senseless," Rorech uneasily told the prosecutor. "I said Missy and Eddie are dead," and she said, "Joseph, please forgive me, I killed her."

"Joseph, that isn't true!" Crimmins cried from the defense table. When Judge Peter Farrell restored order, Rorech said that his conscience had later moved him to testify. He admitted to drinking heavily the day he called the apartment, opening the possibility that he might have dialed a wrong number. Rorech was a married man with seven children. The defense attacked him as a spiteful rejected lover, a perjurer whose marital and business problems were being exploited by the district attorney's office.

Observed from Above

The second surprise witness was housewife Sophie Earominski, whom police had discovered to be the author of an anonymous letter offering information. From her third-floor window, Earominski claimed to have seen a woman outside at 2:00 A.M., about the time Rorech supposedly phoned the Crimmins apartment. The woman carried a bundle of blankets and was walking with a man and a little boy. The man tried to hurry the woman, who had a dog on a leash. Earominski said the woman replied that the dog was pregnant and protested when the man threw the bundle into the back of a car. "Does she know the difference now?" the man said.

"Don't say that," said the woman, whom Earominski identified as Alice Crimmins. "There was agony in her voice. She was nervous, she sounded frightened." Earominski said the man snapped, "Now you're sorry!"

Alice Crimmins screamed in the courtroom, "You liar!"

The defense portrayed Earominski as a pathetic individual with an overactive imagination who enjoyed the celebrity of being a witness, adding that no one knew the Crimmins dog was pregnant until well after the killings.

Alice Crimmins' cold attitude broke when she was questioned about her children. She sobbed uncontrollably on the stand. The next day she returned to face prosecutor Anthony Lombardino. As Lombardino sarcastically questioned her about the whereabouts of her children during her numerous affairs, Crimmins' anger flared. The histrionics of the lawyers were so loud that a juror twice told Judge Farrell that the proceedings were inaudible because of the shouting. Noise from spectators was no less distracting. When Judge Farrell finally instructed the jury, he warned them, "We are not trying here a case involving sex morals. We are trying a homicide case."

On May 27, an all-male jury found Alice Crimmins guilty. As Judge Farrell prepared to sentence her, Crimmins turned her wrath on the district attorneys. "You want to close your books! You don't give a damn who killed my children!"

A New Trial

An unauthorized visit to Earominski's building by three jurors during the trial and the judge's disallowance of evidence that might have cast doubt on Rorech's and Earominski's testimony led an appeals court to overturn Crimmins' conviction in December 1969.

Six months later, she was indicted again. Under the double-jeopardy rule preventing defendants from being tried more than once for the same crime, she could not be charged twice with murdering Missy. She was charged instead with manslaughter and indicted for murdering Eddie, largely Rorech's new claim that she had "agreed to" her son's death.

The second trial revealed how sloppily detectives had handled the investigation. Potential evidence from the Crimmins apartment was not kept. Psychiatric doubts about Sophie Earominski's mental fitness were introduced. Joe

Rorech expanded his testimony, saying that Crimmins told him that a convicted bank robber named Vinnie Colabella had killed Eddie Jr. for her. Prosecutors took Colabella out of prison and put him on the stand. He denied ever seeing Crimmins before. The prosecutor from the first trial, Anthony Lombardino, was called as a witness and admitted that he had once offered Colabella "a deal" in return for testimony.

The defense attacked the only motive prosecutors gave for Crimmins having her children killed, the custody battle with her husband (who stood by her during both trials). Her divorce lawyer testified that he had advised her that she would never lose her children under New York law, regardless of allegations about her moral reputation.

A new prosecution witness, Tina DeVita, remembered glimpsing a woman, a man with a bundle, a boy, and a dog on the night the Crimmins children disappeared, echoing Sophie Earominski's scenario without identifying anyone. After DeVita's testimony, Alice Crimmins appealed to the public for help. A man named Marvin Weinstein came forward and testified that he had been walking in the neighborhood with his dog, his young son, and his wife, who was carrying their daughter in a blanket. Mrs. Weinstein came to court. She resembled Alice Crimmins. When a former business associate testified that the Weinsteins did not visit his home on the night in question, the Weinsteins retorted that the man was a liar. Mr. Weinstein said he had not come forward during the first trial because he had not realized the case depended so much on Earominski's testimony.

The state's case seemed so shaky that shock and weeping filled the courtroom when Alice Crimmins was again found guilty. In May 1971, she was sentenced to life imprisonment, for murder, with a concurrent five to 20 years for manslaughter.

The murder charge was overturned two years later by an appellate division of the New York Supreme Court, which ruled that Eddie's death had not been proven beyond a reasonable doubt to have resulted from a criminal act. The manslaughter conviction was also overturned. The court ruled that allowing errors like Joe Rorech's testimony that he had taken "truth serum" and a prosecutor's declaration that Crimmins did not "have the courage to stand up and tell the whole world she killed her daughter" were "grossly prejudicial." The court ordered her to be tried again, but only on the manslaughter charge.

In February 1975, however, the New York State Court of Appeals reinstated the manslaughter verdict. Noting that two juries had found Alice Crimmins "criminally responsible for the death of her daughter," the court ruled that the conviction was fair because there was no "significant probability, rather than only a rational possibility that the jury would have acquitted the defendant had it not been for the error or errors which occurred." Dissenting justices wrote that this decision changed the definition of prejudicial conduct, "dangerously diluting the time-honored standard of proof beyond a reasonable doubt, which has been a cornerstone of Anglo-Saxon jurisprudence."

Alice Crimmins was ordered to finish her sentence. She was paroled in 1977, quietly ending one of the most emotional and troubling cases ever heard in New York courts.

— *Thomas C. Smith*

Suggestions for Further Reading

Goldstein, Tom. "Appeals Court Finds 'Overwhelming Proof' Mrs. Crimmins Killed Her Daughter." The *New York Times* (February 26, 1975): 34.

Gross, Kenneth. *The Alice Crimmins Case*. New York: Alfred A. Knopf, 1975.

Helpern, Milton with Bernard Knight. *Autopsy: The Memoirs of Milton Helpern, The World's Greatest Medical Detective*. New York: St. Martin's Press, 1977.

Mills, James. *The Prosecutor*. New York: Farrar, Straus and Giroux, 1969.

John Marshall Branion Trial: 1968

Name of Defendant: John Marshall Branion, Jr.   **Crime Charged:** Murder
Chief Defense Lawyer: Maurice Scott   **Chief Prosecutor:** Patrick A. Tuite
Judge: Reginald J. Holzer   **Place:** Chicago, Illinois   **Dates of Trial:** May
15–28, 1968   **Verdict:** Guilty   **Sentence:** 20–30 years

SIGNIFICANCE

The murder conviction of John Marshall Branion, Jr., a prominent black doctor and confidant of Martin Luther King, Jr., was achieved without a single scrap of direct proof, demonstrating that, occasionally, circumstantial evidence is the best evidence of all.

The case of John Branion reads like a best-selling mystery thriller. First there was the crime itself, tortuous, full of twists, and ultimately hinging on one issue: Did the defendant's alibi allow him sufficient time to carry out a murder? And then came the trial, riddled with allegations of racial prejudice and possible judicial corruption. Most extraordinary of all was Branion's flight after conviction. Was he, as some claim, an innocent man escaping injustice, or was this rather the tale of a pitiless killer, desperately fleeing the consequences of his actions?

At 11:30 A.M. on December 22, 1967, Dr. John Branion set off in his car from the Ida Mae Scott Hospital on Chicago's South Side. Five minutes later— after passing his home—he picked up his 4-year-old son from outside a nursery school, then called on a Maxine Brown, who was to have lunch with Branion and his wife. When Brown explained that she was unable to keep the engagement, Branion drove to his apartment at 5054 S. Woodlawn Avenue. His story was that he had arrived at 11:57 A.M. and found his wife Donna lying on the floor of the utility room. She had been shot four times by a .38-caliber automatic pistol. Branion immediately summoned help.

Police treated Branion's story with palpable disdain; already witnesses were coming forward to dispute his version of events. Another factor was Branion's unpalatable detachment. Just two days after his wife's murder he flew to Vail, Colorado, for a Christmas break.

One month later, armed with a search warrant, police recovered two boxes of Geco brand .38-caliber ammunition from a closet in Branion's apartment. One full box contained 25 shells. The other box had 4 shells missing, the same number that had killed Donna Branion. Shortly afterwards Branion was arrested for murder.

Imperfect Alibi

According to prosecutor Patrick Tuite, the story that Branion had told police was correct in every respect save one: chronology. Yes, Tuite said, Branion had gone to pick up his son, then on to Maxine Brown's, but first he had sneaked home and shot his wife, before hastening to establish an alibi. This theory was borne out by Joyce Kelly, a teacher at the nursery school. She testified that Branion had entered the school between 11:45 A.M. and 11:50 A.M., some 10 minutes later than he had claimed. Furthermore, she said that Branion's young son was waiting inside the school, again contradicting the defendant's story.

Detective Michael Boyle described for the court a series of tests that he and another officer had performed, driving the route allegedly taken by Branion. They had covered the 2.8-mile journey in a minimum of six minutes and a maximum of 12 minutes. Time enough, said the prosecution, for Branion to have committed the murder and then gone to pick up his son. Oddly enough, this assertion was never seriously challenged by the defense.

A ballistics expert, Officer Burt Nielsen, stated that the bullets which had killed Donna Branion could only have been fired from a Walther PPK .38-caliber automatic pistol, a very rare make. The prosecution pointed out that Branion, an avid gun collector, had at first denied ever having owned a Walther, until it was shown that he had received just such a gun in February 1967 as a belated birthday present. This had prompted Branion to change his original statement in which he claimed that nothing was stolen from his apartment; now he said that the Walther must have been taken by the intruders who killed his wife. The murder weapon was never found.

Much was made of Branion's peculiar indifference toward the discovery of his wife's body. He admitted not bothering to examine it because he could tell from the lividity that she was dead. (Lividity is the tendency of blood to sink to the lowest extremities in a corpse.) But Dr. Helen Payne testified that when she examined the body at 12:20 P.M. lividity was not present. Branion again altered his story, saying that he had really meant 'cyanosis,' a blue discoloration of the skin caused by de-oxygenated blood.

Illicit Love

To establish motive, the state argued that Branion was conducting an affair with nurse Shirley Hudson and wanted to be rid of his wife. Questioning of Maxine Brown, who had allegedly overheard a compromising conversation between Hudson and Branion one day after the murder, produced the following, seemingly fruitless, exchange:

Prosecutor: Who is Shirley Hudson?

Defense Counsel: Objection.

The Court: Sustained.

Prosecutor: Do you know what, if any, relationship Shirley Hudson bore to the defendant?

Defense Counsel: Objection.

The Court: Sustained.

And so it went: an endless string of improper questions, countered by an equal number of objections, all of which were upheld by the court. But the damage was immense. By such tactics the prosecution was able to establish the likelihood of an illicit relationship, if not the certainty.

Declining to testify on his own behalf, Branion remained mute while the jury convicted him of murder and Judge Reginald Holzer passed sentence of 20–30 years imprisonment. Defense counsel Maurice Scott immediately argued that the trial had been prejudiced by Chicago's recent racial disturbances and vowed to appeal.

Released by Judge Holzer on an unusually low bond of $5,000, Branion took his case to the Illinois Supreme Court. On December 3, 1970, while conceding that the evidence against Branion was wholly circumstantial, the court held that it was sufficient to uphold the guilty verdict, stating:

> To support a conviction based on circumstantial evidence it is essential that facts proved be not only consistent with defendant's guilt, but they must be inconsistent with any reasonable hypothesis of innocence; but the People are not required to establish guilt beyond any possible doubt.

On the Run

In 1971, Branion, sensing that the end was nigh, fled the country. After an amazing jaunt across Africa he found asylum in Uganda, occasionally acting as personal physician to Idi Amin, that country's dictator. Upon Amin's ouster, Branion was arrested and returned to the United States in October 1983.

Yet another stunning twist came in 1986, when Judge Reginald Holzer received an 18-year jail sentence for extortion and racketeering. Branion's lawyers seized this opportunity to charge that Holzer had received a $10,000 bribe during the 1968 trial, paid by the defendant's brother-in-law, Nelson Brown. Prosecutor Patrick Tuite admitted that he had heard rumors of Holzer's intention to overturn Branion's conviction and had gone to see him, urging that the law be allowed to take its course. The speculation is that Holzer, unnerved by Tuite's visit, swindled those who allegedly paid the bribe, then sought to placate them by substituting a ludicrously low bail of $5,000, allowing Branion to escape. Because there was no way of corroborating the story—Brown had himself been stabbed to death in 1983—this final effort to overturn Branion's conviction met with the same fate as its predecessors.

After serving just seven years of his sentence, Branion was released from prison in August 1990 on health grounds. One month later, at age 64, he died of a brain tumor and heart ailment.

Branion's conviction stunned Chicago's black community. Initial outrage over a perceived lack of police effort in apprehending the killer quickly turned to fury when the verdict of the jury was announced.

—Colin Evans

Suggestions for Further Reading

Jet. (October 22, 1990): 18.

Sanders, Charles L. "A Man On The Run." *Ebony* (July 1984): 112–119.

Tuohy, James and Rob Warden. *Greylord*. New York: G.P. Putnam's Sons, 1989.

265 North Eastern Reporter, 2nd Series. St. Paul, Minn.: West Publishing. 1971.

Huey P. Newton Trial: 1968

Defendant: Huey P. Newton **Crimes Charged:** First-degree murder, felonious assault, and kidnapping **Chief Defense Lawyer:** Charles R. Garry
Chief Prosecutor: Lowell Jensen **Judge:** Monroe Friedman
Place: Oakland, California **Dates of Trial:** July 15–September 8, 1968
Verdict: Guilty of voluntary manslaughter; not guilty of felonious assault; kidnapping charge dismissed **Sentences:** 2–15 years

SIGNIFICANCE

While Huey P. Newton's 1968 case was technically a murder trial, it was also one of the most politically charged trials of its era. Defense attorney Charles Garry's use of the *voir dire* provided a model for choosing juries for racially and politically sensitive trials.

Before any evidence was heard, many Americans believed that Huey P. Newton, co-founder and "minister of defense" of the Black Panther Party, had murdered a police officer in cold blood. Others were equally certain that the charge was a trumped-up attempt to crush the militant Black Panther Party.

No group brought the racial tensions of the late 1960s into sharper focus than the Black Panther Party For Self Defense. The Panthers' political rhetoric and advocacy of armed self-defense against police brutality alarmed many citizens and brought down the aggressive wrath of police departments across the nation.

Just before dawn on October 28, 1967, Oakland police Officer John Frey radioed that he was about to stop a "known Black Panther vehicle," a van occupied by two men. A second officer, Herbert Heanes arrived on the scene. Minutes later, officers responding to a distress call found Frey bleeding to death and Heanes slumped in his car, seriously wounded. Police found Huey Newton at a nearby hospital with a bullet wound in his abdomen.

Newton was charged with murdering Frey, assaulting Heanes, and kidnapping a man whose car was commandeered for the dash to the hospital. While Newton recovered from his wound, his attorney, Charles Garry, began his defense with a systematic assault on the grand jury system.

Grand Jury Becomes Issue

Garry's pretrial motions argued that the Alameda County grand jury system was unconstitutional, secretive, and prejudiced against minorities and the poor. He pointed out that black citizens were seldom chosen to serve. Garry argued that trial juries also were unfair. Since blacks were disproportionately under-represented on the county voter registration lists from which jury rolls were compiled, he proposed that providing Newton's constitutional right to a trial by his peers was impossible. Garry's pretrial strategy was unsuccessful but thorough, consuming nine months.

Newton's trial began in July 1968 under massive security. During the *voir dire* questioning of prospective jurors, Garry rigorously probed attitudes about race, the Black Panther Party, the Vietnam War, and the police. Prosecutor D. Lowell Jensen frequently objected that such issues were irrelevant to the case. Garry stubbornly held to the strategy, trying to imply that Newton could not get a fair trial or, at least, to sensitize acceptable jurors to racial problems. Both sides fought hard to determine the final composition of the jury, which ultimately was composed of 11 whites and 1 black.

Black Panther party leader Huey P. Newton. (AP/Wide World Photos)

Prosecutor Jensen claimed that Newton was a convicted felon on probation for a 1964 assault conviction. Newton would claim that he was sentenced for committing a misdemeanor, not a felony, and that he was actually coming home from celebrating the end of his probation when Frey stopped him.

Jensen held that Newton's probation was still in effect when officer Frey decided to arrest him for falsely identifying himself as the owner of the van. Two matchboxes of marijuana were allegedly found later in the vehicle. Although he was not charged with drug possession, nor was any concealable weapon produced, Newton was portrayed as a felon with both a motive and the nerve to kill a police officer rather than face additional felony charges and a guaranteed return to prison. The prosecution's motive theory thus hinged on Newton's disputed probation status.

Officer Herbert Heanes testified that he had been guarding Newton's still unnamed passenger by the van when Newton and Frey began to "tussle." As they struggled on the hood of Frey's car, Heanes was struck in the arm by a bullet. Heanes fired at Newton before blacking out. Yet Heanes did not recall seeing any weapon in Newton's hands. Garry raised the possibility that Heanes had shot fellow officer Frey. A ballistics expert testified that both officers had been struck by bullets from police revolvers.

The prosecution summoned a black bus driver named Henry Grier, who testified that his headlights allowed him to clearly see Newton pull a gun from his jacket and shoot Frey repeatedly. Yet the defense exposed more than a dozen points where Grier's testimony contradicted his initial statement to police. Newton's clothing and physique did not match the description Grier had initially given. When Garry tried to fit a pistol into the pocket of the jacket Newton wore on October 28, the gun kept falling out, weakening the claim that Newton had a concealed weapon.

The prosecution called Dell Ross, who had told a grand jury that Newton and another man had forced him to drive them to a hospital at gunpoint. At the Newton trial, however, Ross refused to answer any questions, citing the Fifth Amendment protection against self-incrimination. Despite a grant of immunity and Judge Monroe Friedman's explanation that Ross was a witness, not a defendant, Ross would not talk.

As the judge prepared to jail Ross for contempt, the prosecutor suggested that if Ross did not remember what had happened on October 28, he should say so. Ross replied that he remembered nothing. Jensen nevertheless had Ross' grand jury testimony about his alleged abduction read before the jury. Garry destroyed the effect of this maneuver by playing a taped conversation in which Ross admitted lying to the grand jury because he was afraid of being arrested for outstanding parking tickets. Judge Friedman dismissed the kidnapping charge.

The closure of Newton's probation remained in dispute. His parole officer could not remember what date he gave Newton as the end of his probation period, leaving the motive for shooting Frey unresolved. The matchboxes of marijuana, which Newton claimed were planted by police, had no fingerprints on them.

After moving unsuccessfully for a mistrial because of death threats mailed to the defense, Garry explored officer Frey's reputation. Several black witnesses recalled Frey's physically abusive and verbally insulting behavior. A white high-school teacher who had taught Frey and later invited him back to speak to students recalled the officer's classroom lecture about "niggers" in the district he was responsible for patroling.

Surprise Witness Surfaces

Garry's next witness stunned the courtroom. Gene McKinney was the man riding with Newton on October 28, but police had never learned his identity. After establishing that McKinney was Newton's passenger, Garry asked, "Did you by chance or otherwise shoot officer John Frey?"

McKinney refused to answer, citing the Fifth Amendment. Prosecutor Jensen furiously demanded that McKinney be forced to reply. Garry had skillfully managed to offer the jury a "reasonable doubt" that Newton had killed Frey. As Newton noted later, if Judge Friedman had then granted McKinney immunity, McKinney could have accepted the blame for Frey's death, freeing both himself and Newton without punishment. Instead, Judge Friedman cited McKinney for contempt and sent him immediately to jail.

When Newton took the stand, he calmly denied shooting Frey or Heanes. For nearly a full day, Garry's questions drew full descriptions of the aims of the Black Panther Party, the historical oppression of black Americans, and police brutality in the Oakland ghetto. The prosecution repeatedly objected that the lengthy answers were irrelevant.

Newton admitted using his own trial as a political forum, but the defense was also trying to establish a context in which to view Frey's harassment of Newton as typical police practice in the Oakland ghetto, particularly employed against members of the Black Panther Party.

Newton testified that he had correctly identified himself to officer Frey, who abusively ordered him out of the van. After searching Newton, Frey pushed him down the street to the parked police cars. When they stopped, Newton protested that the officer had no reasonable cause to arrest him, opening a lawbook he habitually carried. Newton claimed that Frey replied with a racial insult and a punch in the face. Newton fell. As he started to rise, Frey shot him in the stomach. Newton remembered little else after that.

Prosecutor Jensen read Newton's arrest records and political declarations, trying to portray the Black Panther minister of defense as a man fond of violence and guns. Newton responded by contending that police harassment had precipitated each arrest and expounded on the political theories in his writings.

In his summation, Jensen soberly concluded that the evidence showed Newton to be a violent man and, in this case, a murderer. Garry's summation was a broad, impassioned indictment of white racism, characterizing the trial as part of an attempt by the Oakland police to destroy Newton and the Black Panthers.

One day after the jurors began their deliberations, they asked to see the transcript of Henry Grier's initial statement to police. Garry noticed that someone had incorrectly transcribed that Grier "did" see Newton at the shooting, when Grier's voice on the police tape said that he "didn't." After a lengthy confrontation between the attorneys, Judge Friedman ordered the transcript corrected and sent into the jury room without any attached comment on the mistake.

Jury Disappoints All

The jury's verdict was a disappointment to both sides. Newton was acquitted of assaulting officer Heanes. Instead of convicting Newton on the more serious charge of murder, the jury found him guilty of voluntary manslaughter. Because the jury also decided that Newton was still on felony probation at the time of the shooting, the manslaughter conviction carried an automatic sentence of 2–15 years.

The defense appealed with a new concerted attack on the jury systems and an assortment of misrulings by the judge. On May 29, 1970, the California Court of Appeals reversed Newton's conviction because of Judge Friedman's incomplete instructions to the jury. The judge erred by not giving jurors the option of convicting Newton of involuntary manslaughter, a charge consistent with his claim that he was disoriented and unconscious after Frey shot him.

Two More Trials, then a Dismissal

Newton was tried again in August 1971. The charge was changed to manslaughter, but the prosecution presented an identical case. A deadlocked jury produced a mistrial.

When Newton was tried a third time in November 1971, the judge ruled that the disputed 1964 conviction should not be included in the indictment. The prosecution's court case was also weaker, despite reappearances by all of the principal witnesses. Officer Heanes, who had maintained that only Newton and McKinney were present during the 1968 incident, now remembered an unknown third man.

Garry also discredited the testimony of Henry Grier, who claimed to have seen the shooting in his bus headlights. Grier's supervisor explained that the bus schedule placed Grier's vehicle well over a mile from the incident. A hung jury delivered a second mistrial. District Attorney Jensen reluctantly dropped the charges against Newton in December 1970 .

Newton was freed, but neither he nor the Black Panther Party fared well in the ensuing years. Decimated by police shootings and internal strife, the Panthers membership swiftly declined. In 1978, Newton was convicted of possessing an illegal weapon but acquitted of assault after allegedly pistol-whipping his tailor. Charges that he murdered a prostitute were dismissed in 1979 after two mistrials. His studies in social philosophy earned him a doctorate in 1980, but his problems with alcohol and drugs persisted. In 1989, he pleaded no contest to misappropriating $15,000 from a public grant to a Black Panther Party-operated school.

Huey Newton was shot to death by an Oakland drug dealer on August 22, 1989.

— Thomas C. Smith

Suggestions for Further Reading

Frazier, Thomas R., ed. *Afro-American History: Primary Sources*. New York: Harcourt Brace Jovanovich, 1971.

Garry, Charles R. *Minimizing Racism In Jury Trials*. Berkeley, Calif.: National Lawyers Guild, 1969.

Hevesi, Dennis. "Huey Newton Symbolized the Rising Black Anger of a Generation." *New York Times* (August 23, 1989): B7.

Moore, Gilbert. *A Special Rage*. New York: Harper & Row, 1971.

Newton, Huey P. *Revolutionary Suicide*. New York: Harcourt Brace Jovanovich, 1973.

Wood, Wilbur. "Oversupply of Doubt." *The Nation* (September 30, 1968): 300–303.

U.S. v. Berrigan: 1968

Defendants: Philip Berrigan, Daniel Berrigan, and others
Crimes Charged: Willfully injuring government property, mutilating public records, and hindering the operation Selective Service System
Chief Defense Lawyers: Harrop Freeman and William Kunstler
Chief Prosecutors: Stephen H. Sachs and Barnet D. Skolnik   **Judge:** Roszel C. Thomsen   **Place:** Baltimore, Maryland   **Dates of Trial:** October 7–10, 1968   **Verdict:** Guilty   **Sentence:** 3–4 years in prison for Philip Berrigan and 3 years in prison for Daniel Berrigan

SIGNIFICANCE

The courts refused to recognize moral opposition to the Vietnam War as a legal defense to prosecution for criminal acts of defiance, such as the Berrigans' raid on a Selective Service office.

The Roman Catholic Church is usually considered a conservative institution, one that doesn't get involved in American politics except in unusual circumstances. During the late 1960s, however, certain Catholic priests began to take an active role in the protest movement against the increasingly unpopular Vietnam War. Two priests in particular, the Berrigan brothers Philip and Daniel, went so far as to organize acts of disobedience that got them into serious trouble with the authorities.

On October 26, 1967, Philip, Daniel, and three other people entered the Customs House in Baltimore, Maryland, where the federal Selective Service Administration kept some draft records. The Berrigans had planned a media event, and several reporters were present when the Berrigans arrived. Philip, Daniel, and the others proceeded to break into the file area, past the minimal clerical staff, and emptied vials of blood into the file cabinets. They waited peacefully for the police to arrive.

The federal authorities charged the Berrigans and the others with criminal violation of laws against willfully destroying United States property, mutilating public records, and hindering the administration of the Selective Service Act. After having been found guilty of these charges at trial and while awaiting sentencing, the Berrigans instigated another anti-war escapade. On May 17, 1968, they led seven other people into the Selective Service office in

Catonsville, Maryland, seized nearly 400 files, and burnt them in the parking lot with homemade napalm.

Philip and Daniel Berrigan Stand Trial

The Berrigans were promptly arrested, and once again they were charged with violations of federal law. The Catonsville incident, however, sparked a nationwide wave of sympathetic anti-Vietnam demonstrations unlike anything generated by the Baltimore Customs House affair. For example, in Milwaukee, Wisconsin a group of Catholic activists stormed a Selective Service office and burnt over 10,000 files.

The trial began on October 7, 1968 before Judge Roszel C. Thomsen in Baltimore, Maryland. The Berrigans' lawyers were Harrop Freeman and William Kunstler, and the federal prosecutors were Stephen H. Sachs and Barnet D. Skolnik. Philip Berrigan testified that his moral opposition to the Vietnam War led him to participate in the Catonsville incident:

> We have been accused of arrogance, but what of the fantastic arrogance of our leaders? What of their crimes against the people, the poor and the powerless? Still, no court will try them, no jail will receive them. They live in righteousness. They will die in honor. For them we have one message, for those in whose manicured hands the power of the land lies. We say to them: lead us. Lead us in justice and there will be no need to break the law.

Daniel Berrigan's testimony and that of the rest of the "Catonsville Nine" was similar to Philip Berrigan's. They had all entered the Selective Service office and burnt the files because of their belief that America's involvement in Vietnam was wrong. All of the defendants understood that they were breaking the law, but they asserted that their higher purpose in attempting to save human lives justified their actions. The prosecutors scornfully replied in their closing argument that:

> Our problems are not going to be solved by people who deliberately violate our laws, the foundation and support for an ordered, just, and civilized society.

Before the jury retired to deliberate, Daniel Berrigan made an impassioned plea to Judge Thomsen to interpret the law not according to its technical requirements, but according to the dictates of human morality. Berrigan argued that the judge and the jury were responsible to a higher authority than the law, and that if they believed as he did that the Vietnam War was wrong, they could acquit him and the others.

Thomsen was clearly sympathetic to these antiwar sentiments, but he knew that his office as judge was to uphold the law. Thomsen replied to Daniel Berrigan that:

> You speak to me as a man and as a judge. I would be a funny sort if I were not moved by your sincerity on the stand, and by your views. I agree with you completely, as a person. We can never accomplish, or give a better life to people, if we are going to keep on giving so much money to war. It is very unfortunate but the issue of war cannot be presented as clearly as you would

like. The basic principle of the law is that we do things in an orderly fashion. People cannot take the law into their own hands.

On October 10, 1968, after less than two hours of deliberation, the jury returned a verdict of guilty against the nine defendants. Philip Berrigan and another defendant were sentenced to 3½ years in prison, Daniel Berrigan and two other defendants were sentenced to three years in prison, and the remaining four defendants received two-year sentences.

The Berrigans' lawyers appealed the convictions to the United States Court of Appeals for the Fourth Circuit, whose jurisdiction includes Maryland. On June 10, 1969, both sides made their case to the court of appeals, which issued its decision on October 15, 1969. One of the most interesting issues that the court had to consider was the defense's argument that the jury should have been free to acquit the defendants if they chose to do so regardless of the defendants' obvious guilt:

> Concededly, this power of the jury is not always contrary to the interests of justice. For example, freedom of the press was immeasurably strengthened by the jury's acquittal of John Peter Zenger of seditious libel, a violation of which, under the law as it then existed and the facts, he was clearly guilty. In that case Andrew Hamilton was allowed to urge the jury, in the face of the judge's charge, to see with their own eyes, to hear with their own ears, and to make use of their consciences and understanding in judging of the lives, liberties, or estates of their fellow subjects.

However, the court affirmed the Berrigans' convictions, noting that the jury's freedom to do as it pleased had been greatly curtailed in modern times. No matter how noble the Berrigans' cause, the law could not sanction their criminal acts, because the alternative was to permit every group with a particular political viewpoint to do as it pleased:

> If these defendants are to be absolved from guilt because of their moral certainty that the war in Vietnam is wrong, would not others who might commit breaches of the law to demonstrate their sincere belief that the country is not prosecuting the war vigorously enough be entitled to acquittal?

The Rev. Philip Berrigan pouring blood on draft records at Selective Service headquarters to protest the "pitiful waste of American and Vietnamese blood" in Southeast Asia. (AP/Wide World Photos.)

The Berrigans and the rest of the Catonsville Nine went to prison. Their defense, which rested on their moral opposition to the Vietnam War, was not recognized by the courts as a legal defense to criminal conduct. In essence, Judge Thomsen and the judges of the Fourth Circuit had held that there was no place in the law for the belief that "extremism in the defense of liberty is no vice."

—*Stephen G. Christianson*

Suggestions for Further Reading

Berrigan, Daniel. *No Bars to Manhood*. Garden City, N.Y.: Doubleday & Co., 1970.

Casey, William Van Etten. *The Berrigans*. New York: Avon, 1971.

Curtis, Richard. *The Berrigan Brothers: the Story of Daniel and Philip Berrigan*. New York: Hawthorn Books, 1974.

Halpert, Stephen. *Witness of the Berrigans*. Garden City, N.Y.: Doubleday & Co., 1972.

Lockwood, Lee. *Daniel Berrigan: Absurd Convictions, Modest Hopes*. New York: Random House, 1972.

Sirhan Bishara Sirhan Trial: 1969

Defendant: Sirhan Bishara Sirhan **Crime Charged:** Murder
Chief Defense Lawyers: Grant Cooper, Russell Parsons, Emile Berman, and
Michael A. McCowan **Chief Prosecutors:** Lynn D. Compton, John Howard,
and David Fitts **Judge:** Herbert V. Walker **Place:** Los Angeles, California
Dates of Trial: January 13–April 23, 1969 **Verdict:** Guilty
Sentence: Death, later commuted to life imprisonment

SIGNIFICANCE

The stature and prominence of Robert Kennedy guaranteed that the trial of his
killer, Sirhan Bishara Sirhan, would be of historic importance. And yet, had it been
left to the prosecution and defense attorneys, there would have been no trial at all.
Their negotiated plea bargain failed because a judge decided that full disclosure
mattered more than legal expediency.

Flushed with triumph, Senator Robert Kennedy stepped down from the podium at the Ambassador Hotel in Los Angeles on June 5, 1968, having just claimed victory in the California primary election. He was seemingly destined for the White House in November. As he moved through the crowded hotel kitchen, on his way to meet reporters in another room, a young man emerged from the throng and began firing an eight-shot Iver-Johnson .22-caliber pistol. Three bullets struck Kennedy, one in the head. The gunman continued shooting, injuring five bystanders, until he was subdued and taken into custody. His name was Sirhan Bishara Sirhan, a 24-year-old Jordanian incensed by Kennedy's support of Israel. The next day the senator died from his wounds.

That Sirhan murdered Robert Kennedy was beyond dispute—a roomful of witnesses saw him do it—but many doubted that the diminutive Arab would ever stand trial. District Attorney Evelle Younger, armed with a psychiatric evaluation of Sirhan that provided clear indications of mental disorder, readily accepted the defense plea of guilty to first-degree murder in return for a promise of life imprisonment. It was the kind of deal worked out daily in the county court system, vital if the system is to avoid legal gridlock. But this was not an everyday case.

Dominating all else was the specter of President John F. Kennedy's assassination in 1963. The alleged killer, Lee Harvey Oswald, had himself been gunned down before standing trial, leaving forever a labyrinth of doubt and suspicion. Determined to avoid such a recurrence, the judge appointed to try the Sirhan case, Herbert Walker, rejected the plea bargain in favor of trial by jury. This ruling left the defense with no alternative but to plead Sirhan not guilty and hope that they could prove his mental insufficiency.

A Murder Plan

The prosecution's opening statement, delivered by David Fitts on February 12, 1979, was packed with examples of Sirhan's devious and deliberate preparations for murder. Just two nights before the attack, he was seen at the Ambassador Hotel, apparently attempting to learn the building's layout, and he visited a gun range on June 4 to polish his already considerable skills with the pistol. However, the testimony of one prosecution eyewitness to the attack, author George Plimpton, backfired when he described Sirhan as looking, ". . . enormously composed. He seemed—purged," a statement which dovetailed neatly with the defense assertion that Sirhan had shot Kennedy while in some kind of trance. More on track was the testimony of Alvin Clark, Sirhan's garbage collector, who claimed that Sirhan had told him a month before the attack of his intention to shoot Kennedy.

Sirhan Sirhan in custody the day after he shot Senator Robert F. Kennedy. Despite his admission of guilt, a lengthy trial followed. (AP/ Wide World Photos)

Defense hopes of proving that this killing had been the spontaneous act of a deranged mind received a severe setback when Judge Walker admitted into testimony pages from three notebooks that Sirhan had kept. They revealed a mind seriously troubled, but quite calculating and willful. One entry written May 18, 1968, read: "My determination to eliminate R.F.K. is becoming the more and more [*sic*] of an unshakable obsession. . . . Robert F. Kennedy must be assassinated before June 5, 1968."

Sirhan's behavior throughout the trial, always bizarre, reached a self-destructive zenith during some unwelcome testimony about his childhood. He raged: "I . . . withdraw my original pleas of not guilty and submit the plea of guilty as charged on all counts. I also request that my counsel disassociate themselves from this case completely."

Bemused, Judge Walker asked, "What do you want to do about the penalty?"

"I will ask to be executed," Sirhan replied coolly, an announcement which prompted a cavalry charge of reporters for the exits. Judge Walker continued,

"This court will not accept the plea. Proceed with the trial." When Sirhan's counsel then attempted to withdraw of their own volition, Walker denied this also. It was all very confusing. Ultimately, order was restored and Sirhan took the stand.

Defense lawyer Grant Cooper didn't mince any words. "Did you shoot Robert F. Kennedy?"

"Yes, sir."

"Did you bear any ill will towards Senator Kennedy?"

"No."

"Do you doubt you shot him?"

"No, sir, I don't."

Cooper then steered Sirhan into the reasons for his attack on Kennedy, a vicious diatribe about the Middle East conflict between Arab and Jew. So impassioned was Sirhan's anti-Zionist rhetoric that one of his own lawyers, Emile Berman, a Jew, felt compelled to offer his resignation from the defense team. Only soothing words from Cooper made him stay.

Cynical Performance

It took cross-examination by Chief Deputy District Attorney Lynn Compton to expose Sirhan for what he was: self-absorbed and arrogant, a master manipulator.

"Do you think that the killing of Senator Kennedy helped the Arab cause?" asked Compton.

"Sir, I'm not even aware that I killed Mr. Kennedy."

"Well, you know he's dead."

". . . I've been told that."

"Are you glad he's dead?"

"No, sir, I'm not glad."

As an exercise in cynicism it was hard to beat. Certainly the jury thought so. On April 17, 1969, they returned a guilty verdict.

During the penalty phase, Prosecutor John Howard demanded death for Sirhan: "In resolving the question of this defendant's guilt," he told the jury, "you have found him lacking in honesty, in integrity, and even in the courage of his own convictions. You could not have failed to see the smirk . . . when he declared 'I don't know who killed Senator Kennedy.'" Howard ended strongly: "Have the courage to write an end to this trial and to apply the only proper penalty for political assassination in the United States of America."

In pleading for his client's life, Grant Cooper quoted from several of Robert Kennedy's own speeches on compassion, but all to no avail. After 12 hours of deliberation the jury decided that Sirhan would die in the gas chamber.

As it transpired, all of the argument was academic. The U.S. Supreme Court's rulings on capital punishment in other cases resulted in Sirhan's sentence being commuted to life imprisonment. He remains in prison, where he regularly applies for parole and is just as regularly denied.

Interestingly, while Sirhan was being tried, in Memphis, Tennessee, another admitted assassin, James Earl Ray, pleaded guilty to the murder of Martin Luther King, Jr., and was quietly dispatched without trial to prison for 99 years.

—Colin Evans

Suggestions for Further Reading

Christian, John and William Turner. *The Assassination Of Robert Kennedy*. New York: Random House, 1978.

Goode, Stephen. *Assassination! Kennedy, King, Kennedy*. New York: Watts, 1979.

Jansen, Godfrey. *Why Robert Kennedy Was Killed*. New York: Third Press, 1970.

Kaiser, Robert Blair. *R.F.K. Must Die!* New York: Dutton & Co., 1970.

Scheim, David E. *Contract On America*. Silver Spring, MD: Argyle Press, 1983.

Clay Shaw Trial: 1969

Defendant: Clay L. Shaw   **Crime Charged:** Conspiracy to assassinate John
F. Kennedy   **Chief Defense Lawyers:** Irvin Dymond, Salvatore Panzeca,
Edward F. Wegmann, and William J. Wegmann   **Chief Prosecutors:** James
Alcock, William Alford, Jim Garrison, Alvin Oser, and Andrew Sciambra
Judge: Edward A. Haggerty   **Place:** New Orleans, Louisiana
Dates of Trial: January 31–March 1, 1969   **Verdict:** Not guilty

SIGNIFICANCE

The assassination of President John F. Kennedy has become the most analyzed
and dissected murder in history.

By late 1966, public confidence in the Warren Commission's report on the
assassination of President John F. Kennedy was undergoing a serious crisis.
With each new inconsistency, both real and imagined, suspicion grew that, far
from being the work of a lone gunman, the killing in Dealey Plaza had been a
well-engineered conspiracy. The most vocal proponent of this view was Jim
Garrison, the charismatic district attorney in New Orleans, Louisiana. In March
1967, Garrison stunned the world when he announced the arrest of local
businessman Clay L. Shaw on charges of conspiring to assassinate the President
of the United States.

Almost two years later, on January 31, 1969, Garrison finally got to make
these charges in a courtroom. Before Judge Edward A. Haggerty, he fleshed out
the bare bones of his theory in a 42-minute address that dealt with alleged
presidential assassin Lee Harvey Oswald and the time he spent in Louisiana
prior to the Dallas tragedy. According to Garrison, Oswald and the late David
Ferrie, an eccentric ex-pilot, had met with a shadowy figure named Clay
Bertrand. Between them, these three men plotted Kennedy's assassination. It
was Garrison's contention that Clay Bertrand was really the defendant Clay
Shaw, who, Garrison noted, had flown to the West Coast on November 15, 1963,
where he remained until after the shooting, thereby establishing an alibi for
himself. Following the assassination, said Garrison, FBI agents undertook a
"systematic and thorough search for Clay Bertrand" in New Orleans but were
unsuccessful. Garrison would produce conclusive evidence, he said, that the
person they should have been looking for was Clay Shaw.

Garrison: Hands Over the Reins

Oddly enough, after making the opening address, Garrison took virtually no further part in the trial. The task of presenting the state's case was left in the hands of his deputy, James Alcock. Although several witnesses confirmed Oswald's presence in Louisiana—a fact never in dispute—not until the testimony of Vernon Bundy, 30, was a connection between Shaw and Oswald established. Bundy, a heroin addict, told of a trip he had taken to Lake Pontchartrain in June 1963. "I was beginning to use my drugs . . . [when] behind me I noticed a black limousine approaching. A gentleman got out of the car and walked behind me." Concerned that the newcomer might be a narcotics agent, Bundy remained watchful. "I saw a man with a towel approaching from the white section of the beach." Alcock asked Bundy if he saw either one of these men in the courtroom. "I can see one," he replied and pointed to Shaw. When shown a photograph of Oswald, Bundy identified him as the man with the towel.

Next to testify was Charles Spiesel, a New York accountant. He spoke of attending a party in New Orleans in May 1963 at which both Ferrie and Shaw were present. When conversation turned to President Kennedy, Spiesel said that Shaw had laughed when somebody remarked, "Someone should kill that son of a bitch!" Talk of "a high-powered rifle" prompted Shaw to suggest that the gunman could escape in a plane flown by Ferrie.

Taken at face value, Spiesel's testimony was devastating, until chief defense lawyer Irvin Dymond began questioning him. After raising doubts about whether Spiesel had ever actually seen Ferrie (a man of remarkably memorable appearance, with glued-on orange hair and huge, painted eyebrows), Dymond asked: "Isn't it true you filed a suit with New York in 1964 . . . claiming that over a period of several years the police and others had constantly hypnotized you and finally harassed you out of business?"

"That's right," Spiesel said, adding proudly that the suit was for $16 million. When asked how many different people had hypnotized him, Spiesel had to think for a moment: "It's hard to say. Possibly fifty or sixty."

With his next question Dymond drove a stake through the heart of the prosecution. "When you conferred with the District Attorney's office about testifying in this case, did you tell them about these lawsuits and having been under hypnosis?"

Spiesel grinned: "Yes, I mentioned it."

Focus Shifts to Zapruder Film

Without exception, every prosecution witness failed the litmus test of cross-examination. Memories grew vague, identifications less sure. Not until the prosecutors came to the main thrust of their case—a full frontal attack on the Warren report's single-gunman theory—did they catch fire. In grim silence the jury watched Abraham Zapruder's film of the Dallas tragedy. Then the prosecution, supported by various ballistics experts, pursued its efforts to prove a triangulation of gunfire. During all of this, Clay Shaw became a forgotten man. And he remained that way until it came time for him to testify.

Those awaiting the much-anticipated duel between Garrison and Shaw suffered a grave disappointment. Again the district attorney was noticeably absent. James Alcock handled the cross-examination, though anything less confrontational was hard to imagine. Apart from admitting that he had seen Oswald once in New Orleans while Oswald was distributing political leaflets, Shaw denied all other contact with him. He also denied virtually everything that the prosecution witnesses had said about him. Alcock handled Shaw with kid gloves, declining to even quiz him on whether he had participated in a deadly conspiracy. About the best that Alcock could manage was in the following exchange:

"Do you recall a press conference after your arrest where you called Lee Harvey Oswald 'Harvey Lee Oswald'?"

"I recall the conference."

"Was there any particular reason why you would call Oswald 'Harvey Lee'?"

"No, it was purely a mistake."

With everyone poised for the *coup de grâce* that they were sure the prosecution had in store, Alcock stunned court-watchers by abruptly turning to Judge Haggerty after just 65 minutes and saying, "No further questions."

Jim Garrison reappeared to make the state's closing argument. Again it degenerated into an attack on the Warren Commission, full of complaints that the American public had been lied to, duped, kept in the dark. Once, just once, he mentioned the defendant Clay Shaw almost as an afterthought, and then in his final admonition to the jury, Garrison evoked the dead president's memory: "Ask not what your country can do for you, but what you can do for your country."

At six minutes past midnight on March 1, 1969, the jury retired. An hour later they were back. When the verdict of "Not Guilty" was read out, a huge roar of approval swept the courtroom.

Establishing his innocence cost Clay Shaw all of his money and most of his reputation. Many believe the ordeal hastened his death from cancer in August 1974. In all probability, he will remain the only person ever charged with complicity in the death of John F. Kennedy. But that won't stop the discussion, and it won't stop the "conspiracists," as they theorize about what really happened on that afternoon in Dallas.

—Colin Evans

Suggestions for Further Reading

Bethell, T. "Conspiracy to End Conspiracies." *National Review*. (December 16, 1991): 48ff.

Garrison, Jim. *On the Trail of the Assassins*. New York: Sheridan Press, 1988.

Gates, D. and H. Manly. "Bottom Line: How Crazy Is It?" *Newsweek* (December 23, 1991): 52ff.

Kirkwood, James. *American Grotesque*. New York: Simon & Schuster, 1970.

Chicago Seven Trial: 1969

Defendants: Rennard C. Davis, David Dellinger, John R. Froines, Thomas H. Hayden, Abbott Hoffman, Jerry C. Rubin, Bobby G. Seale and Lee Weiner
Crimes Charged: Incitement to riot and conspiracy
Chief Defense Lawyers: William Kunstler and Leonard Weinglass
Chief Prosecutors: Roger Cubbage, Thomas A. Foran, and Richard G. Shultz
Judge: Julius J. Hoffman   **Place:** Chicago, Illinois
Dates of Trial: September 24, 1969–February 20, 1970   **Verdict:** Dellinger, Davis, Hayden, Hoffman, Rubin: Guilty; Froines and Weiner: Not guilty; Seale: Mistrial   **Sentence:** 5 years imprisonment, $5,000 fine

SIGNIFICANCE

This was possibly the most divisive—certainly the most chaotic—political trial in American history.

The 1968 Democratic National Convention marked a watershed in American social unrest, as anti-Vietnam War protesters of every political hue descended on Chicago, Illinois, determined to undermine the convention and provoke a confrontation with authorities. They succeeded beyond their wildest expectations. Pitched battles in the streets led to grand jury indictments against eight conspicuously left-wing radicals: Rennie Davis, David Dellinger, John Froines, Tom Hayden, Abbie Hoffman, Jerry Rubin, Bobby Seale, and Lee Weiner. Each was charged with having crossed state lines to incite a riot, an offense that had been on the statute book less than nine months. Collusion between the accused was clearly not an issue—Seale did not even meet his co-defendants until the trial. More important was the government's resolve to quash antiwar protest with what amounted to an attack on the entire spectrum of political dissent.

Rarely does a member of the bench achieve or desire the celebrity that this trial afforded to Judge Julius Hoffman, who right from day one, September 24, 1969, displayed a pugnacious combativeness that was both ill-considered and wholly unjudicial. Seventy-three years old, humorless, and with a reputation for rulings sympathetic to the government, Hoffman's hostility toward the defendants was all too apparent.

On opening day, when U.S. Attorney Thomas Foran angrily objected because four lawyers listed for the defense were not present in court—all had withdrawn from the case by telegram—Hoffman immediately issued warrants for the arrest of the offending attorneys, then poured oil on troubled waters by temporarily jailing two of them for contempt of court. Such a firestorm of protest from the legal community greeted this action that Hoffman was obliged to rescind the order and allow the lawyers to withdraw.

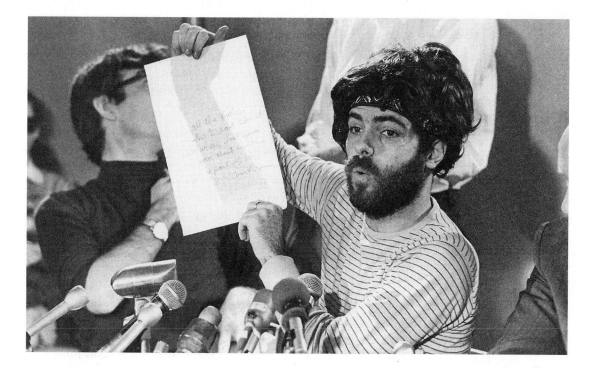

Defense attorney duties were shared by William Kunstler and Leonard Weinglass. Neither had an easy task. Besides battling the bench, they had Bobby Seale to contend with. Seale, a militant black activist, refused to accept either one as his attorney and on September 26 submitted a handwritten note to the court: "I submit to Judge Julius Hoffman that the trial be postponed until a later date when I, Bobby G. Seale, can have the "legal council [*sic*] of choice who is effective,' Attorney Charles R. Garry, and if my constitutional rights are not respected by this court then other lawyers on record here . . . do not speak for me . . . I fire them now." Judge Hoffman, taking exception to being characterized in the note as "a blatant racist," angrily denied the motion.

Jerry Rubin holds up a note from fellow defendant Bobby Seale who had been gagged during the previous day's trial session. (AP/Wide World Photos)

Seale Bound and Gagged

Seale wouldn't be stifled. He continued to disrupt the proceedings, yelling such epithets as "pig" and "fascist" at Hoffman, likening him to a plantation slave owner. Finally, on October 29, Hoffman's thin reserve of patience ran out and he ordered Seale gagged and bound to a chair. As Seale struggled to free himself, court attendants roughly manhandled him, an action that brought Kunstler to his feet in loud protest: "Your Honor, are we going to stop this medieval torture that is going on in this courtroom? I think this is a disgrace."

With the situation fast getting out of hand, Judge Hoffman declared a mistrial as to Seale, thus severing his case from the other seven defendants. Simultaneously he found Seale guilty of 16 counts of contempt and jailed him for four years.

Virtually overshadowed by this extracurricular mayhem was the fact that the prosecution had amassed a formidable case against the remaining accused. Its main witnesses were police officers, each of whom testified to examples of incendiary behavior on the part of the accused.

Robert Murray, an undercover police sergeant, described being in Lincoln Park, scene of one particularly violent clash between police and demonstrators, and seeing defendant Jerry Rubin in conversation with a television newsman. When the reporter had intimated that he was about to leave, Murray claimed that Rubin had called him back, saying, "Wait, don't go right now. We're going out in the ball field. We want to see what these pigs [police officers] are going to do about it."

Prosecutor Foran asked, "How many police officers were standing there?"

"Ten policemen," said Murray, "and one sergeant."

Murray had carefully monitored Rubin's behavior throughout the night.

I saw him walking through the park, walking up to small groups, having a conversation with them and leaving . . . I heard him say that "we have to fight the pigs in the park tonight. . . . we're not going to let them take the park.'

Crucial evidence of intent to riot came with the testimony of newspaper reporter Dwayne Oklepek, who spoke of attending a meeting August 9, 1968, at which defendants Hayden, Davis, and Froines were present. Oklepek told how Davis produced a street map of Chicago and plans for a march on August 28, 1968: "Mr. Davis felt that the separate groups should form up and then attempt to move their way south to the Loop area. . . . He went on to say that he thought these groups should try to disrupt traffic, should smash windows, run through stores and through the streets."

"Do you recall anything else that was discussed?" asked Foran.

"Someone asked Mr. Davis what would occur if it were impossible for the demonstrators to get out of Lincoln Park . . . and Mr. Davis said, 'That's easy, we just riot.' "

In this fashion the prosecution was able to mount a strong case of incitement to riot, at least against some of the defendants, but whether that incitement fell within the provisions of the recent law, with its proviso that a state line had to be traversed, remained in doubt.

Star-Studded Witnesses Appear

To combat allegations of malicious intent, defense attorney William Kunstler had assembled a prodigious list of eminent character witnesses. The roll call included Norman Mailer, Reverend Jesse Jackson, Allen Ginsburg, William Styron, Arlo Guthrie, Country Joe McDonald, Judy Collins, Phil Ochs, Mark Lane, Timothy Leary, even a British Member of Parliament, Anne Kerr.

Apart from their eloquence and name value, there was little that these witnesses could offer the court in the way of direct evidence. Neither did the defendants help themselves. All seemed more interested in advancing their political agenda. Abbie Hoffman's opening remarks set the tone. Asked to identify himself for the record, he said, "My name is Abbie. I am an orphan of America. . . . I live in Woodstock Nation." When defense counsel Leonard Weinglass requested clarification, Hoffman eagerly seized his opportunity. "It is a nation of alienated young people. We carry it around with us as a state of mind." Weinglass concluded his direct examination with a simple question:

> "Prior to coming to Chicago, from April 1968 on to the week of the Convention, did you enter into an agreement with [the other defendants] to come to the city of Chicago for the purpose of encouraging and promoting violence during the Convention week?"

> "An agreement?"

> "Yes."

> "We couldn't agree on lunch!"

Cross-examination by prosecutor Richard Schultz was less conciliatory but equally frivolous, as Hoffman and his fellow defendants refused to recognize the court's legitimacy. Their crude, often childish antics exacted a heavy toll from Judge Hoffman, whose exasperation found ventilation in a litany of unfortunate remarks directed toward the defendants and their counsel.

After months of confusion and much rambling testimony, closing arguments began on February 10, 1970. The final word was left with prosecutor Thomas Foran. Describing the defendants, he said, "They are not kids. Davis, the youngest one, took the witness stand. He is twenty-nine. These are highly sophisticated, educated men and they are evil men." Uproarious laughter greeted this remark. In trying to paint a picture of latent villainy, Foran succeeded only in generating humor.

All things considered, Judge Hoffman's final charge to the jurors was remarkably subdued, and on February 14 they retired to consider their verdict.

Guilty Verdicts Multiply

Judge Hoffman used the hiatus to deal with the numerous contempt of court citations that had accrued throughout the trial. He found all seven defendants and their attorneys guilty of no less than 159 counts. Sentences varied from 2–4 months for Weiner, to four years for Kunstler.

Speculation that the jury would be unable to reach a decision proved unfounded. On February 18, 1970, they adjudged Davis, Dellinger, Hayden, Hoffman, and Rubin guilty, while acquitting Froines and Weiner. Two days later Judge Hoffman passed sentence. Each defendant received the maximum penalty of five years in prison and a $5,000 fine.

A long round of appellate action ensued. It began with the contempt verdicts. On May 11, 1972, the Seventh Circuit Court of Appeals reversed all of these convictions on grounds that, because Judge Hoffman had been targeted by the attack, due process dictated that he should not sit in judgment on the contempt charges.

In November 1972 the appellate court overturned all five incitement to riot convictions, citing numerous errors by Judge Hoffman and the prosecution attorneys. In particular, they denounced Judge Hoffman's "deprecatory and often antagonistic attitude toward the defense." Seale, too, had his conviction overturned.

The government elected not to retry the incitement case, but did proceed on the contempt charges, with the result that in November 1973, Dellinger, Kunstler, Hoffman, and Rubin were again convicted. However, Judge Edward Gignoux signaled an end to the whole unsavory affair by deciding that the imposition of further jail sentences was unwarranted.

By any reckoning the Chicago Conspiracy trial has to be considered a low-water mark in American jurisprudence. Nobody emerged from the conflict untarnished. Ironically, the only victor was the legal system itself. Mocked and derided by the defendants, it bent and on occasion threatened to break, but ultimately it came to the assistance of those who decried it most.

—Colin Evans

Suggestions for Further Reading

Belknap, Michael P. *American Political Trials*. Westport, Conn.: Greenwood Press, 1981.

Clavir, Judy and John Spitzer. *The Conspiracy Trial*. Indianapolis: Bobbs-Merrill Co., 1970.

Epstein, Jason. *The Great Conspiracy Trial*. New York: Random House, 1970.

Goldberg, Stephanie Benson. "Lessons of the 60's." *ABA Journal*. (May 15, 1987): 32ff.

Shultz, John. *Motion Will Be Denied*. New York: William Morrow & Co., 1972.

Curt Flood Trial and Appeals: 1970–72

Plaintiff: Curt Flood   **Defendants:** Commissioner of baseball, presidents of the National League and American League, and owners of all 24 major league baseball clubs   **Plaintiff Claim:** Organized baseball does fall under the definition of interstate commerce and is a monopoly; therefore the trading of baseball players without their agreement is an unreasonable restraint of trade in violation of the Sherman Antitrust Law.
Chief Lawyers for Plaintiff: Trial: Arthur J. Goldberg, Jay Topkis; Supreme Court: Arthur J. Goldberg   **Chief Defense Lawyers:** Trial: Mark Hughes, Victor Kramer; Supreme Court: Lou Hoynes, Paul Porter   **Judge:** Trial: Irving Ben Cooper; Final Appeal: U.S. Supreme Court, Chief Justice Warren Burger presiding   **Places:** Trial: New York, New York; Final Appeal: Washington, D.C.   **Dates of Trial and Final Appeal:** Trial: May 19–June 10, 1970; Decision, August 12, 1970. Final Appeal Heard: March 20, 1972; decision, June 19, 1972   **Decisions:** Trial: Flood's suit rejected. Supreme Court: Lower courts' findings upheld, 5–3

SIGNIFICANCE

Although Curt Flood lost in the trial and in the subsequent Supreme Court decision, his suit to break the reserve clause of organized baseball led the way to the end of this practice within a few years. By his independent and often reviled action, Flood had opened the door for baseball's "free agents," which undeniably led to the late twentieth century revolution in baseball players' salaries and team loyalties.

A mericans had long adopted as one of their national "myths" that baseball played such a special role in their lives and society that even the major leagues differed from all other business operations. In particular, organized baseball's team owners had been able to defy the government's legal prohibition of restraint of trade by maintaining the sanctity of the so-called reserve clause. This refers to the agreement, first adopted by major league teams in 1879, to place their players "on reserve," meaning that so long as they were under contract to one team, they could not move to any other team. Conversely, the team could sell or trade the players at the owners' will. This practice was challenged over the years—by players' unions, by new leagues, by the occasional individual player—but to no avail. In fact, two Supreme Court rulings—one in 1922, the other in 1953—held that the Federal courts were powerless to regulate organized baseball, although in the latter case the justices advised Congress to effect legislation to do so. But not until 1970 was the reserve clause to be put to a true trial by a prominent player with much to lose, Curt Flood.

Flood's Conditioning

Born in Texas in 1938, raised in California, Flood had come up to the majors with the Cincinnati Reds in 1956. After the 1957 season he was traded to the St. Louis Cardinals, and he was soon displaying the skills that would make him a leading player—not only a solid hitter but a superb center fielder. Yet like all ballplayers up to that time, he was totally "under contract" to the owner of his team, and at the end of the 1969 season he was abruptly informed that he had been traded to the Philadelphia Phillies.

Thousands of players before this had quietly packed their bags and moved on to the new team. But something about the way this was handled upset Flood. He had settled into St. Louis and felt at home there. He was a proud man, and a sensitive man—among other things, he was a talented artist: his portrait of Martin Luther King, Jr., hung in Coretta King's home. Perhaps most significantly, Flood was an African American who had been moved by the civil rights struggle of the 1960s. He himself would describe his own reaction to the trade as, "By god, this is America. I'm a human being. I'm not a piece of property."

So Flood decided to challenge the reserve clause. He turned to the Major League Players Association, which not only agreed to finance his suit but also hired Arthur J. Goldberg, the former Supreme Court justice, as his lawyer. On January 16, 1970, he formally filed his suit, taking on the entire baseball establishment.

The Playoffs

The trial opened on May 19, 1970, at the Federal Court of the Southern District of New York, Judge Irving Ben Cooper presiding. Given the role that baseball did play in the nation's life, it was well covered by the media and well attended by people hoping to catch a glimpse of some of the celebrity witnesses. Flood himself was the first to take the stand and at one point he was asked to supply his batting averages during his years in the majors. He was unable to recall these until one of his lawyers handed him a bubble gum baseball card that had the exact statistics. His salary over the years also had to be recorded, and the fact that he was to be paid $90,000 (plus $8,000 for spring training) by the Phillies would be widely cited by those who derided his claim that he was being treated like a slave.

The trial revolved around a basic conflict. Flood claimed that organized baseball exerted a monopolistic hold on all major and minor league teams and that its contracts giving teams total power over the players effectively lowered salaries. The defendants' claim was that this system was essential to the operation and survival of organized baseball, that "the totality of players are better off in the present system," and that to drop it would lead to the destruction of many teams.

Both sides called on numerous witnesses to buttress their sides, and one tactic they both employed was to call upon individuals who might have been expected to oppose their position. Thus in addition to calling up former major league stars such as Jackie Robinson and Hank Greenberg, Flood called on Bill Veeck, former owner of the Chicago White Sox. Flood also called up the heads of the National Basketball Association and National Hockey League, both of which allowed their players more freedom in negotiating contracts. Meanwhile, the defendants, in addition to calling up the then-commissioner of baseball Bowie Kuhn and the presidents of the two major leagues, also called up a former player, Joe Garagiola, who defended the reserve clause. But it was also true that witnesses on both sides showed some flexibility, those for Flood agreeing that the reserve clause should be replaced gradually and partially, those for the defendants agreeing that the present contract system might be somewhat modified.

The trial was not without its lighter moments. Judge Cooper would refer to the occasional recess as a "seventh inning stretch." At one point, when Flood was showing some awkwardness in giving his testimony:

Judge Cooper: You're not finding this as easy as getting up to bat.

Flood: No, sir.

Judge Cooper: Well, you see, other people have their problems, too.

Curt Flood's lawsuit opened the door for baseball's "free agency." (Archive Photos)

Another humorous exchange came when the lawyer for the defendants, Mark Hughes, asked Flood, "What do you think would happen if every player were free after each season?" Flood's lawyer, Arthur Goldberg, immediately objected on the grounds that this was "speculative," but the judge overruled him. When Flood then replied, "They'd have a good chance to renegotiate better contracts," Judge Cooper slyly asked, "Do you want that stricken from the record, counselor?" A smiling Goldberg replied, "No, no, I like that answer."

After the trial ended, the judge took two months before announcing his decision. In his 47-page opinion, Judge Cooper ruled against Flood's suit, basing his position primarily on the legal point that he felt he lacked authority to overturn previous Supreme Court decisions. He also stated that he was not totally convinced that the reserve clause "had occasioned rampant abuse and that it should be abolished," but he did recommend that players and owners cooperate in making the reasonable changes.

Three Strikes . . .

By the time that Judge Cooper issued his decision, Flood himself had gone off to Europe, but his lawyers immediately commenced the appeals process. To the astonishment of many, however, in November 1970, Flood signed a contract with the Washington Senators, accepting the reserve clause but with the provision that this would have no bearing on his legal suit. He had barely started the 1971 season, when on April 7 the 2nd Circuit Court of Appeals issued its opinion upholding Judge Cooper's finding. Then on April 27, citing "very serious personal problems," Flood quit baseball and flew off to Spain. Again, though, the appeals process continued, this time to the Supreme Court.

On March 20, 1972, the full Court heard the oral arguments. This time, the baseball establishment took a new line, arguing that the issue was really one merely of labor-management bargaining. They went even further and said that the true plaintiff in this case should be the Major League Players Association, since it had accepted the terms Flood was opposing. Goldberg, meanwhile, stressed that the Court should uphold their decisions in other related cases involving practices counter to antitrust laws.

The Supreme Court issued its decision on June 19, 1972, upholding the lower court's findings by a decision of 5–3. At least as controversial as the vote itself was the language of the majority's decision, for it sounded less like a jurists' finding than a tribute to the national pastime. It cited dozens of baseball "legends," from Cap Anson and Babe Ruth to "Casey at the Bat" and "Tinker to Evers to Chance." But even though it upheld the reserve clause, the majority described it as an "aberration" and an "anomaly" and concluded, "It is time the Congress acted to solve this problem."

Extra Innings

Curt Flood returned from Europe in 1976 to serve as a sportscaster in California. He had sacrificed his career and a very good chance of being elected to baseball's Hall of Fame (although there remains a movement to get him there). But in the end, he had triumphed. In 1975 the reserve clause was effectively struck down by an arbitrator. And the year after Flood died in 1997, President Bill Clinton signed what Congress had called "The Curt Flood

Law," finally setting aside the exemption that allowed the reserve clause to control players.

—*John S. Bowman*

Suggestions for Further Reading

Flood, Curt. "Why I Am Challenging Baseball." *Sport* (March, 1970): 10–3.

Flood, Curt, with Richard Carter. *Curt Flood: The Way It Is*. New York: Trident Press, 1971.

"Found—An Abe Lincoln of Baseball: Curt Flood's Court Action for Changing the Reserve Clause." *Ebony* (March 1970): 110–11.

"A Loss for Curt Flood." *Newsweek* (July 3, 1972): 67.

New York Times. See Flood, Kurt in the *New York Times Index*, Jan. 17, 25, 1970; May 20, 21, 22, 23, 26, 27, 28, 29, 1970; June 11, 1970; Aug. 13, 1970. Jan. 28, 1971; April 8, 11, 28, 30, 1971; Oct. 20, 1971; Mar. 21, 1972; June 20, 21, 22, 23, 25, 28, 30, 1972; July 1, 1972.

Zimbalist, Andrew. *Baseball and Billions*. New York: Basic Books, 1992.

Charles Manson Trial: 1970–71

Defendants: Charles Manson, Susan Atkins, Patricia Krenwinkel, Leslie Van Houten   **Crimes Charged:** First-degree murder and conspiracy to commit murder   **Chief Defense Lawyers:** Irving Kanarek (for Manson), Daye Shinn (for Atkins), Paul Fitzgerald (for Krenwinkel), Maxwell Keith, Ronald Hughes, and Ira Reiner (for Van Houten)   **Chief Prosecutor:** Vincent Bugliosi and Aaron Stovitz   **Judge:** Charles H. Older   **Place:** Los Angeles, California   **Dates of Trial:** June 15, 1970–March 29, 1971   **Verdict:** Guilty   **Sentence:** Death, later transmuted to life imprisonment

SIGNIFICANCE

The killings for which Charles Manson and his followers were convicted made him one of the century's most infamous murderers. The prosecution's case provided an example of how the U.S. Supreme Court's *Aranda* ruling is applied in cases involving multiple defendants. The trial was one of the longest and costliest in California history.

On August 9, 1969, police in Los Angeles, California, responded to a hysterical call from actress Sharon Tate's housekeeper. When officers arrived at the house rented by Tate and her husband, film director Roman Polanski, they found the corpses of the pregnant actress and three house guests: Jay Sebring, Abigail Folger, and Voyteck Frykowski. All had been stabbed repeatedly. Steven Parent, a friend of the groundskeeper, was found shot to death outside in his car. A day later in another part of the city, Leno and Rosemary LaBianca were found violently stabbed to death in their suburban home. All seven deaths were eventually linked to a scheme whose savagery was surpassed only by the peculiarity of its motive.

The first tips came from motorcycle gang members, who told police about a commune of young people called the "Family" living in the desolate California hills. The commune was led by an ex-convict named Charles Manson, who had bragged of committing murders that resembled the Tate killings. Two prison inmates similarly told authorities that their cellmate Susan Atkins had described to them in horrifying detail how she and fellow members of the "Family" had killed Tate and her guests, the LaBiancas, and others.

In return for a promise of immunity, Atkins repeated her story to a grand jury in December 1969, implicating Manson and others in the Tate-LaBianca killings. Ironically, Manson was already in jail. He had been arrested in October and charged with receiving stolen property. "Family" members Patricia Krenwinkel and Leslie Van Houten were indicted on murder charges and arrested. Charles "Tex" Watson, whose bloody fingerprint was found at the Tate house, was arrested at his parents' home in Texas. Watson's attorney forestalled his extradition for nine months, arguing that pretrial publicity made it impossible for Watson to get a fair trial in California. The Los Angeles district attorney decided to prosecute the others charged in the Tate-LaBianca slayings without waiting for Watson's arrival.

Atkins Reverses Course

Prosecutors lost Atkins' cooperation in March 1970, three months before the case came to trial. After a short meeting with Manson in jail, she retracted her confession and declared that she had invented the story implicating him, Krenwinkel, and Van Houten before the grand jury.

Although the four "Family" members were to be tried together, the prosecution was required to abide by the rules of the U.S. Supreme Court's 1965 *Aranda* decision. Statements made by one defendant, such as the stories Atkins told her cellmates about the "Family's" bloody deeds, could not be introduced as evidence against her co-defendants. The prosecution's task was further complicated by the fact that Manson had not been present at the Tate house the night of the slayings. Deputy District Attorneys Aaron Stovitz and Vincent Bugliosi had to try to convict Manson on the seven murder counts based on the theory that the cult leader had ordered the killings.

Manson's request to be allowed to represent himself was denied. At first angered by this refusal, Manson then accepted Irving Kanarek as his attorney. Kanarek had a reputation in legal circles as an "obstructionist," accused of lengthening trials with pointless or improper courtroom tactics. The prosecution formally protested Kanarek's involvement with prophetic warnings that the complicated trial might last much longer than necessary if he were allowed to

Charles Manson, convicted of the murder of Sharon Tate and six others. (Archive Photos)

participate. Kanarek nevertheless became Manson's attorney. By the end of the trial, even Manson grew annoyed with Kanarek's behavior, which earned the verbose attorney numerous contempt citations.

Worldwide publicity about the case made finding an unbiased jury unusually difficult. When Judge Charles H. Older read a press account of a conference in his chambers, the infuriated judge moved to limit public speculation, about the case. He imposed a "gag order" barring the lawyers and witnesses from speaking to the press about matters not entered as evidence. Stenographers and other court officials were forbidden from giving or selling transcripts of the case to the press.

When testimony began July 24, 1970, Manson arrived in court with an "X" scratched on his forehead. He considered the trial a "game" in which he was being judged by a society unworthy and incapable of understanding him. In protest, he had symbolically "X'd" himself from the world. Atkins, Krenwinkel, and Van Houten followed Manson's example by burning an X into each of their foreheads.

The most damning prosecution witness was Linda Kasabian, a former "Family" member who was granted immunity in return for her testimony. Over protests by the defense, who held that Kasabian's use of LSD and other drugs had made her incapable of distinguishing fact from fantasy, she described sex orgies, drug use, and Manson's domination of all facets of "Family" life. Like other "Manson girls," Kasabian had once believed that Manson was Jesus Christ.

A "Helter Skelter" Scheme

Kasabian explained Manson's bizarre scenario for "Helter Skelter," a scheme to capitalize on a race war between black and white Americans, which he believed was imminent. Manson expected blacks to win, find themselves incapable of governing, and ultimately turn to him for leadership. The Tate and LaBianca murders were committed to provoke the Helter Skelter holocaust.

"Now is the time for Helter Skelter," Kasabian recalled Manson announcing on August 8, 1969. That night he told her to go with Atkins, Krenwinkel, and Watson. The foursome drove to the Tate house, where Watson cut the phone lines and ordered the others to climb over the fence. Watson stopped Parent's car and shot him before ordering Kasabian back to the "Family" car to guard it. As she waited in shock, Kasabian heard screams coming from the house. She ran toward the cries and found Watson stabbing Frykowski on the lawn. When she saw Krenwinkel chasing Folger with a knife, she fled back to the car in horror.

Out of fear for herself and her child, Kasabian drove to the LaBianca home with Manson and other "Family" members the following night. Manson parked and disappeared with Watson. When Manson returned, he said that he had tied up two people in the nearby house. "Don't let them know that you are going to kill them," Kasabian thought she heard him say before he got back into the car and drove away, leaving Watson, Krenwinkel, and Van Houten behind. Kasabian escaped from the "Family" soon thereafter.

Case Draws Presidential Remark

Kanarek's interruptions of Kasabian's testimony were so incessant that Judge Older sentenced him to a night in jail for contempt. Kasabian was about to be cross-examined when the trial was shaken by comment from an unexpected source. President Richard M. Nixon told reporters in Denver, Colorado, Manson was "guilty, directly or indirectly of eight murders." Nixon's remarks were meant to criticize what he perceived as a tendency of the media to glorify criminals, and the White House quickly issued a statement denying any intent to prejudice the case. Nevertheless, Manson's defense, arguing that such a statement by the president made a fair trial impossible, motioned for a mistrial and demanded that the charges against him be dropped. Judge Older denied the motion.

The next day in court, Manson stood and displayed a newspaper with the headline, "Manson Guilty, Nixon Declares." Judge Older questioned the jurors about their reaction to the headline. Satisfied that they would remain impartial, he ordered the trial to resume and sentenced Atkins' attorney, Daye Shinn, to three nights in jail for leaving the newspaper within Manson's reach.

Former "Family" members and visitors to the Manson commune at the isolated Spahn Movie Ranch testified for the prosecution. Danny De Carlo, one of the motorcycle gang members who furnished police with tips, said that Manson had frequently spoken to him of starting a race war. Once again, Judge Older ordered Kanarek jailed for contempt because of his frequent interruptions.

Former "Family" member Barbara Hoyt testified that she had overheard Atkins describing the murders. Juan Flynn, a Spahn Ranch worker, told the court that Manson had tried to frighten him by holding a knife to his throat and saying, "You son of a bitch, don't you know I'm the one who's doing all of these killings?"

On October 5, Manson demanded to be allowed to cross-examine a detective who had just testified. When Judge Older refused, Manson began to argue. Manson leaped toward the judge with a pencil clutched in his hand, screaming, "In the name of Christian justice, someone should cut your head off!" Atkins, Krenwinkel, and Van Houten chanted as bailiffs struggled to subdue Manson. When the trial resumed, the prosecution called Atkins' former cellmates, who described her bloody account of the Tate murders. Under the *Aranda* rule, their testimony was limited to Atkins' participation in the killings.

After nearly four months of testimony by prosecution witnesses, the state rested. Attorney Paul Fitzgerald stunned the court by resting the collective defense without calling a single witness. The three "Manson girls" suddenly announced that they wanted to testify on their own behalf, apparently to free Manson by taking sole responsibility for the murders. Fearing their clients would incriminate themselves, the defense attorneys threatened to quit if the judge allowed the testimony. Judge Older accused the defense of trying to wreck the trial.

Manson Speaks

The impasse was broken when Manson was allowed to speak without the jury present. He gave an angry hour-long statement proclaiming his innocence and condemning society for persecuting him. When he was finished, he told "the girls" not to testify.

As both sides prepared their summations during a Thanksgiving recess, Leslie Van Houten's attorney, Ronald Hughes, disappeared while camping (he was later found dead). The trial was postponed for two weeks to allow Van Houten's new attorney time to study the case. When the trial resumed with final arguments, the prosecution reviewed the abundant testimony about Manson's control over his followers and his messianic "lust for death."

The defense declared that the state had produced no evidence against Manson. Kanarek claimed that Manson was being prosecuted for having a counterculture lifestyle and attacked Kasabian and Watson as the real instigators and murderers. As Kanarek's argument began to consume entire days, Judge Older warned him against using "filibuster" tactics. Kanarek's summation lasted seven days. Van Houten's new attorney, Maxwell Keith, argued more succinctly that the three women should not be convicted if the state's portrayal of them as Manson's "mindless robots" was accurate.

Jury Convicts All Defendants

Manson and his co-defendants were found guilty on January 25, 1971. Under California law, a second trial or "penalty phase" before the same jury then began to determine sentencing. Atkins took the stand and accused Kasabian, not Manson, of ordering the murders. Van Houten and Krenwinkel admitted taking part in the slayings but denied Manson's involvement. After two months of tumultuous testimony, the jury agreed with the prosecution's argument for the death penalty on March 29, 1971.

When the first sentence was pronounced on Manson, he began shouting that he had not been allowed to defend himself. "Better lock your doors and watch your own kids," warned Atkins. "Your whole system is a game," Van Houten exclaimed. The judge ordered all the defendants removed from the courtroom so that the judgments could be read without disruption.

Manson and the others were sentenced to die in the gas chamber. When Tex Watson was tried separately, he also was found guilty and sentenced to death. Yet no Manson case defendants were executed. Their sentences were transmuted to life imprisonment when the state of California abolished its death penalty on February 18, 1972. The U.S. Supreme Court ruled the death penalty unconstitutional under most circumstances later that year.

Long after the Manson case was over, it continued to create legal problems for William Farr, a Los Angeles newspaper reporter. Early in the trial, Farr wrote a story revealing Atkins' tales to her cellmates of "Family" plans to murder celebrities like Frank Sinatra and Elizabeth Taylor. Judge Older summoned Farr to his chambers and demanded to know who had released the confidential information. Farr refused to answer, citing a state law protecting journalists from being forced to reveal their sources.

After the trial, however, the judge learned that Farr was between jobs as a reporter and ordered him back into court to reveal his source or face a contempt charge. Farr said that two of the attorneys had provided the information, but declined to name them. All of the attorneys involved in the case swore under oath that they had not violated the "gag order." The judge ordered Farr to jail to serve an indefinite sentence for contempt. He was confined for 46 days before he was released to appeal the sentence.

The widely debated case was not resolved until 1976, when an appeals court threw out Judge Older's contempt sentence, ending Farr's numerous trips to court and massive legal bills. California laws were amended to protect former reporters as well as currently working journalists.

Leslie Van Houten was granted a new trial on grounds that Ronald Hughes' disappearance had denied her effective representation, but she was convicted again in 1978. Manson continued to charge that President Nixon's statement had tainted the fairness of his trial. Manson also cited a 1975 U.S. Supreme Court decision giving defendants the right to act as their own counsel, but the high court refused to hear Manson's appeal in 1977. In 1985 he was transferred from a state psychiatric prison to the San Quentin penitentiary, where he continues to apply unsuccessfully for parole.

— Thomas C. Smith

Suggestions for Further Reading

Bishop, George. *Witness To Evil*. Los Angeles: Nash Publishing, 1971.

Bugliosi, Vincent, with Curt Gentry. *Helter Skelter: The True Story of the Manson Murders*. New York. W.W. Norton & Co., 1974.

Caldwell, Earl. "Manson Co-Defendants Allowed to Testify After Defense Rests." *New York Times* (November 20, 1970): 22.

Watson, Tex. *Will You Die For Me?* Old Tappan, N.J.: Fleming H. Revell Co., 1978.

Wright, Robert A. "Coast Reporter Ordered to Jail For Refusing to Disclose Source." *New York Times* (November 28, 1972): 36.

William Calley Court-Martial: 1970

Defendant: William L. Calley   **Crime Charged:** Murder
Chief Defense Lawyers: Brookes S. Doyle, Jr., Richard B. Kay, George W. Latimer, and Kenneth A. Raby   **Chief Prosecutors:** Aubrey Daniel and John Partin   **Judge:** Reid W. Kennedy   **Place:** Fort Benning, Georgia
Dates of Court-Martial: November 17, 1970–March 29, 1971
Verdict: Guilty   **Sentence:** Life imprisonment

SIGNIFICANCE
The trial of Lt. William Calley for war crimes is unique in American military history. It provides a unique insight into the horrors of combat and the reaction of ordinary people to extraordinary circumstances.

At first light on the morning of March 16, 1968, 105 soldiers of Charlie Company, a unit of the U.S. 11th Light Infantry Brigade, moved unopposed into the Vietnamese hamlet of My Lai. By midday almost 500 inhabitants had been massacred. All of the victims were unarmed civilians, women, babies, and elderly men. By chance, the scenes of carnage were recorded by an Army cameraman, and it was his pictures that revealed the horror of My Lai to the world. An Army inquiry into the incident resulted in charges of murder against several participants, but evidence suggested that the majority of blame for the tragedy could be laid at the door of a single platoon commander: Lieutenant William Calley.

When the court-martial began on November 17, 1970, Calley was charged with murdering 109 "Oriental human beings." It was the prosecution's contention that Calley, in defiance of U.S. Military Rules of Engagement, ordered his men to deliberately murder innocent civilians. In presenting his case, lead military prosecutor Aubrey Daniel was hamstrung by the reluctance of many soldiers to testify against Calley. Some refused point-blank, citing the Fifth Amendment privilege against self-incrimination. Perhaps the strangest of the holdouts was Paul Meadlo. It had been his televised interview, coupled with Ronald Haeberle's photographs, that had largely inflamed public opinion about My Lai. Yet only after having been ordered into custody by Judge Reid Kennedy, who scathingly derided "the nauseous detail" that Meadlo had provided for television, and being granted immunity from prosecution, would Meadlo describe that day's tragic events. He told of standing guard over dozens of villagers when Lieutenant Calley arrived. "He said 'How come they're not dead?' I said, 'I didn't know we were supposed to kill them.' He said, 'I want them dead.' He backed off twenty or thirty feet and started shooting into the people." Meadlo joined him.

"Were you crying?" asked Daniel.

"I imagine I was," replied Meadlo, confirming other testimony that had the enlisted man with tears in his eyes and a rifle in his hands. Between them, Calley and Meadlo mowed down a hundred villagers.

Barbarous Action Described

Piece by agonizing piece, Daniel painted an almost unimaginable picture of murder, rape, and wholesale devastation. He described how Calley tossed a baby into a ditch and shot it, before opening fire with an M-16, first killing a monk, then cutting a swathe through dozens of villagers cowering in an irrigation channel.

An eyewitness, Dennis Conti, described the bloodbath:

> They were pretty much messed-up. There was a lot of heads had been shot off, pieces of head . . . fleshy parts of the body. . . . I seen the recoil of the rifle and the muzzle flashes and as I looked down, I seen a woman try to get up. As she got up I saw Lt. Calley fire and hit the side of her head and blow the side of her head off.

William Calley arriving at court. (Bettmann/Corbis)

The madness was infectious. One man who had refused to participate in the slaughter, Leonard Gonzalez, told of seeing another soldier herd some women together and order them to strip. When they refused to have sex with him, the enraged soldier fired a single round from his grenade launcher into the group, killing everyone.

Originally it was the defense position that the devastation of My Lai had been caused by helicopters and aerial bombardment. Clearly the prosecution witnesses had proven that premise to be untrue. Calley's only recourse was to fall back on the defense of soldiers since time immemorial: that he was merely acting on orders.

Under the prompting of civilian attorney George Latimer, Calley told his side of the story. He outlined a briefing given one day before the operation by his commanding officer, Captain Ernest Medina, at which, he said, it was made plain that everyone in the village was to be shot. Twenty-one other members of

Charlie Company present at the briefing corroborated Calley's story; others denied that any such order was given. Yet more testified that, while unstated, the intent of the order was plain.

> Calley: I was ordered to go in there and destroy the enemy. That was my job that day. That was the mission I was given. I did not sit down and think in terms of men, women, and children. They were all classified the same, and that was the classification that we dealt with, just as enemy. . . . I felt then and I still do that I acted as I was directed, and I carried out the orders that I was given and I do not feel wrong in doing so.

Some Refused Orders

But not everyone at My Lai that day blindly followed such outrageous orders. Robert Maples told of entering the village and seeing Calley and Meadlo firing into a ditch full of civilians. "[Calley] asked me to use my machine gun."

"What did you say?" Daniel inquired.

"I refused," was the reply.

Another soldier who listened to the dictates of his conscience was James Dursi.

"Did Lt. Calley order you to fire?" asked Daniel.

"Yes, sir."

"Why did you not fire?"

"Because I could not go through with it."

In his final address to the jury, Daniel said, "The defense would ask you to legalize murder," then he invoked the memory of Abraham Lincoln's order to Union troops during the Civil War: "Men who take up arms against one another in public do not cease on this account to be moral human beings, responsible to one another and to God."

On March 29, 1971, after almost 80 hours of deliberation, the six-officer jury—five of whom had served in Vietnam—found Calley guilty of the premeditated murder of 22 villagers at My Lai.

Next came the penalty phase; under military law, Calley faced possible execution by hanging. Latimer pleaded for the life of his client, saying Calley had been a "good boy until he got into that Oriental situation." Latimer reminded the jury of their isolation from the media during the long months of the court-martial. "You'll find there's been no case in the history of military justice that has torn this country apart as this one."

The defendant made an impassioned plea on his own behalf.

> I'm not going to stand here and plead for my life or my freedom. I've never known a soldier, nor did I ever myself, wantonly kill a human being. . . . Yesterday, you stripped me of all my honor. Please, by your actions that you take here today, don't strip future soldiers of their honor—I beg of you.

Daniel was on his feet immediately, reminding the jury, "You did not strip him of his honor. What he did stripped him of his honor. It is not honor, and never can be considered honor, to kill men, women, and children."

The jury mandated that Calley should be sent to prison for life. Three days later he was freed from Fort Leavenworth by President Richard Nixon and returned to Fort Benning where he was held under house arrest pending appeal. On August 20, 1971, the sentence was reduced to 20 years. Calley remained at Fort Benning until February 27, 1974, when he was released on bail. On November 9, 1974, the Army announced that Lieutenant Calley had been paroled.

Following his release, Calley remained in Columbus, Georgia, and as of this writing was a successful jeweler, well-respected in the community.

Four people were tried for war crimes arising out of the My Lai Massacre. Apart from Calley, the most notable was his commanding officer, Captain Ernest Medina. In August 1971 he faced charges of murdering 175 Vietnamese civilians, only to be acquitted after a month-long trial. Calley remains the only man ever convicted for what happened on that morning in Vietnam.

Nothing in its history had prepared the United States for the appalling slaughter at My Lai, and yet the nation's initial revulsion became strangely muted during Calley's protracted trial. Many came to view him as a scapegoat, even a hero, desperately waging the battle against Communism. Time and distance may have dulled the magnitude of his crimes, but not their historical importance.

—Colin Evans

Suggestions for Further Reading

Bilton, Michael and Kevin Sim. *Four Hours At My Lai.* New York: Viking Press, 1992.

Goldstein, Joseph, Burkr Marshall, and Jack Schwartz. *The My Lai Massacre And Its Cover-Up.* New York: Free Press, 1976.

Hammer, Richard. *The Court-Martial Of Lt. Calley.* New York: Coward, McCann & Geoghegan, 1971.

Unger, Craig and Bill Hewitt. *People Weekly* (November 20, 1989): 152–158.

John Hill Trial: 1971

Defendant: John Robert Hill   **Crime Charged:** Murder
Chief Defense Lawyers: Donald Fullenweider and Richard Haynes
Chief Prosecutors: Erwin Ernst and I.D. McMaster   **Judge:** Frederick Hooey
Place: Houston, Texas   **Dates of Trial:** February 15–26, 1971
Verdict: Mistrial

SIGNIFICANCE

Sensational trials are not uncommon in Texas, but the extraordinary sequence of events that followed the death of Joan Hill made this a case without equal.

On Tuesday, March 18, 1969, Joan Hill, a 38-year-old Houston, Texas, socialite, became violently ill for no readily apparent reason. Her husband, Dr. John Hill, at first indifferent, later drove her at a leisurely pace several miles to a hospital in which he had a financial interest, passing many other medical facilities on the way. When checked by admitting physicians, Joan's blood pressure was dangerously low, 60/40. Attempts to stabilize her failed and the next morning she died. The cause of death was uncertain. Some thought pancreatitis; others opted for hepatitis.

Joan's father, Ash Robinson, a crusty and extremely wealthy oilman, remained convinced that his daughter had been murdered. Neither was he reticent about naming the culprit: John Hill. When, just three months after Joan's death, Hill married long-time lover Ann Kurth, Robinson threw thousands of dollars into a crusade to persuade the authorities that his son-in-law was a killer. Noted pathologist Dr. Milton Helpern, hired to conduct a second autopsy, cautiously volunteered his opinion that Joan Hill *might* have been poisoned.

Under Robinson's relentless badgering, prosecutors scoured legal textbooks, searching for a way to indict Hill. They came up with the extremely rare charge of "murder by omission," in effect, killing someone by deliberate neglect. Assistance came in the unexpected form of Ann Kurth. Hill had ditched her after just nine months of marriage. What Kurth told the district attorney bolstered their decision to indict Hill.

Jury selection began on February 15, 1971. Because of the defendant's undeniably handsome appearance, Assistant District Attorney I.D. McMaster aimed for a predominantly male, middle-class panel, one he thought likely to frown on a wealthy philandering physician. His opponent, chief defense counsel Richard Haynes, quite naturally did his best to sit jurors that he thought would favor his client. In this first battle McMaster emerged a clear victor, securing a jury made up of eleven men and one woman. Haynes wasn't that perturbed. In a long and eventful career he'd overcome bigger obstacles, earning a statewide reputation second to none for tenacity and legal acumen. Not for nothing had he acquired the nickname "Racehorse." It promised to be a memorable contest.

Motive: Failed Divorce

Although not required to do so, prosecutors are generally happiest if they can demonstrate to the jury that the accused had a clear motive for committing the crime. McMaster did just this.

> We expect to prove that problems arose in the course of this marriage which resulted in the filing of a divorce petition on December 3, 1968, by the defendant Dr. John Hill. An answer to said petition for divorce was filed by Joan Hill, making the divorce a contested matter which could have resulted in a court trial. . . . Realizing that he had insufficient grounds for divorce and in fear of the adverse publicity in regard to his extramarital activities which might result from a court trial, Dr. John Hill dismissed his divorce case and agreed to a so-called reconciliation with Joan Hill. . . . Having failed to terminate the marriage legally, the defendant began to formulate a plan to rid himself of an unwanted wife.

After detailing Joan Hill's sudden and violent illness, McMaster went on:

> The state expects to show that the defendant, realizing his wife's . . . condition, intentionally and with malice aforethought failed to properly treat Joan Hill and failed to provide timely hospitalization for her in order that she would die.

Haynes listened to all of this, expressionless. He knew that the case, as presented by McMaster was wafer-thin and that, ultimately, everything would hinge on the word of Ann Kurth. But first came Vann Maxwell, a neighbor of the Hills. She testified that, on the weekend before her illness, Joan was planning to reinstitute divorce proceedings against her husband: "The final thing she said about it was . . . would I go with her?"

"How did she appear to you?" Haynes asked casually on cross-examination.

"She seemed in good health," answered Maxwell.

Haynes sat down, pleased. Now it would be up to the prosecution to explain how a healthy, physically fit woman had become a hopelessly sick patient in less than 48 hours.

Effie Brown had worked as a maid for the Hills only a matter of weeks but was well aware of their marital difficulties. "Did anyone tell you that Mrs. Hill was ill . . . that she was sick on Monday?" asked McMaster.

The 69-year-old woman nodded. "I can't recall now who told me . . . but someone did tell that she was ill and not to go into the room."

McMaster turned knowingly to the jury, letting the point sink in of a sick, helpless woman being left deliberately alone. Without actually mentioning John Hill, the inference was clear. But in this statement Haynes saw a chance. His encyclopedic memory recalled something from a deposition that Effie Brown had made, just weeks after Joan Hill's death.

Haynes was courteous as he began cross-examination of the witness. "You went up to her room, didn't you?" he asked. "And you saw Mrs. Hill sitting in the chair, didn't you, ma'am?"

"No," Brown stated positively. At which point Haynes produced the deposition, made two years earlier, and read out a question posed at that time, "On that Monday did you go up and see her? And your answer, 'I went up there one time . . . she's sitting in a big chair'."

Effie Brown shook her head. "Somebody must have put that there. I didn't say nothing."

Haynes paused. At a stroke he had managed to impugn the witness' memory, not implying perjury, just the hazy recollection of an elderly woman caught up in a situation far removed from any other in her experience. He also scored heavily with his last question to Brown. "I suppose you wouldn't hesitate in going back to work for Dr. Hill today?"

"I wouldn't mind going back if he needed me . . . I like him."

On balance this prosecution witness' testimony had been a marginal plus for the defense. Slowly they were managing to chip away at McMaster's depiction of John Hill as a cold and calculating schemer.

Outburst Leads to Mistrial

If Haynes had been discomfited by some of what Effie Brown had to say, then he wanted nothing at all to do with the testimony of Ann Kurth. Indeed, he believed that under Texas law she should not even be allowed to take the stand against her former husband. But his strident and lengthy objections on this point were overridden by Judge Frederick Hooey after the prosecutors had unearthed yet another obscure precedent, this time a case in which a wife had been permitted to testify against her husband. Judge Hooey let it be known, however, that he was uneasy with his own ruling, and had agreed only to Kurth taking the witness stand on condition that he might stop her testimony at any time.

McMaster first led Kurth through her relationship with Hill, then he asked if she had seen anything "unusual" at Hill's apartment during the week of Joan Hill's illness. She told of entering the bathroom and finding three petri dishes—the kind used in laboratories—with "something red in them." Hill had come in and angrily shooed her from the room, saying that it was "just an experiment." The next day she also spotted some unusual pastries in the refrigerator. Hill, again annoyed, told her not to eat them.

But the main thrust of Kurth's testimony was given over to a vivid account of an incident in which, she said, Hill had attempted to kill her. It came just one month into their marriage. They were out driving when, Kurth claimed, Hill deliberately smashed her side of the car into a bridge.

"What happened next?" asked McMaster.

"He pulled a syringe from his pocket and . . . tried to get it into me." Kurth said that she managed to knock the syringe from Hill's hand, but that he then produced another hypodermic needle.

"And what did he do with that one, if anything?" queried McMaster.

Kurth, who several times had to be admonished by the judge for her overly theatrical presentation, crescendoed, "He tried to get that syringe into me!"

Here the prosecutor speculated. "Was he attempting to treat you? Or harm you? Do you know?"

"Yes, I knew." Kurth hesitated, as if unsure what to say next, then blurted out, "Because he told me how he had killed Joan with a needle."

Haynes leapt to his feet, demanding a mistrial on grounds that the defense had not been given an opportunity to prepare themselves against a direct accusation of murder. (This was the first that Haynes had heard of any syringes). Judge Hooey, plainly worried by this turn of events, at first denied the request but did order a recess. During the adjournment, however, Hooey had second thoughts. The tenuous legal precedent by which Kurth had been allowed to testify, and then her foolhardy outburst, convinced him that if he allowed the trial to continue there were clear and palpable grounds for appeal. Accordingly, 11 days into the hearing, he granted the mistrial.

Interestingly enough, the jurors, when polled afterward, indicated that they were inclined to believe John Hill innocent. Ann Kurth's story hadn't impressed them at all.

Retrial Unnecessary

The retrial was set and adjourned another three times until finally being put on the docket for November 1972. But before this could happen, on September 24, 1972, John Hill, by now married for a third time, was gunned down at his mansion in the exclusive Houston suburb of River Oaks, in what had all the hallmarks of a contract killing. After several months of investigation, police arrested three people in connection with the case.

Bobby Vandiver and girlfriend Marcia McKittrick admitted complicity, but claimed that they had been hired by a notorious Houston brothel madam, Lilla Paulus. When Vandiver was shot by police in an unrelated incident, McKittrick, promised a 10-year sentence, agreed to testify against Paulus. Additional testimony was provided by Paulus' own daughter. She told the court of overhearing her mother say, "Ash Robinson is looking for somebody to kill John Hill." Eventually Paulus was convicted and sentenced to 35 years imprisonment in 1975.

This extraordinary case reached its conclusion in 1977 when Hill's surviving wife, Connie, and son, Robert, brought a civil suit against Ash Robinson alleging that he had caused John Hill's wrongful death. On this occasion Lilla Paulus' daughter declined to testify, leaving Marcia McKittrick as the main witness against Robinson. A polygraph examination indicated that she was being truthful in saying that Robinson had caused the death of John Hill. A similar test suggested that Robinson was being truthful when he said he hadn't. Given this welter of confusion, the jury acquitted Robinson of collusion in the death of his son-in-law, and the suit was quashed.

Three trials failed to establish Dr. John Hill's guilt or innocence but did provide one of the most remarkable legal sagas of the 20th century. Had a jury been given the opportunity to hear all of the available evidence against Hill, including his sudden and ominous predilection for plying his wife with unaccustomed pastries in the weeks before her death, in all likelihood he would have been convicted of murder. Whether that verdict would have survived the Texas Court of Appeals is something we shall never know.

—Colin Evans

Suggestions for Further Reading

Kurth, Ann. *Prescription: Murder.* New York: New American, 1976.

Thompson, Thomas. *Blood And Money.* New York: Doubleday & Co., 1976.

Wilson, Kirk. *Unsolved.* New York: Carroll & Graf, 1989.

New York Times Company v. U.S.: 1971

Appellant: The United States   **Defendant:** The New York Times Company
Appellant's Claim: That the government's efforts to prevent the *New York Times* from publishing certain Vietnam War documents known as the "Pentagon Papers" were justified because of the interests of national security
Chief Defense Lawyers: Alexander M. Bickel and William E. Hegarty
Chief Lawyers for Appellant: Daniel M. Friedman, Erwin N. Griswold, and Robert C. Mardian   **Justices:** Hugo L. Black, Harry A. Blackmun, William J. Brennan Jr., Warren E. Burger, William O. Douglas, John M. Harlan, Thurgood Marshall, Potter Stewart, and Byron R. White   **Place:** Washington, D.C.
Date of Decision: June 30, 1971   **Decision:** The government cannot restrain the *New York Times* from publishing the Pentagon Papers.

SIGNIFICANCE

In *New York Times Company v. U.S.,* the Supreme Court held that the government must meet a heavy burden of justification before it can restrain the press from exercising its First Amendment right to publish.

In the Spring of 1971, the Vietnam War was still raging despite the fact that popular opinion was against President Richard Nixon's administration's efforts to keep the United States in the conflict. Opposition to the war spread throughout the armed forces themselves and into what has been called the military-industrial complex. This opposition sentiment affected one man in particular, a former employee of the U.S. Department of Defense who had also worked for the Rand Corporation, an important military contractor. His name was Daniel Ellsberg.

Ellsberg and a friend, Anthony Russo, Jr., stole a copy of a massive, 47-volume study prepared by the Department of Defense titled "History of U.S. Decision-Making Process on Vietnam Policy." The study had more than 3,000 pages, supplemented with 4,000 more pages of source documents. Ellsberg and Russo also stole a one-volume study titled "Command and Control Study of the Gulf of Tonkin Incident," prepared in 1965. These studies were essentially a massive history of American involvement in Vietnam since World War II, and were classified "TOP SECRET-SENSITIVE" and "TOP SECRET" respectively.

Ellsberg and Russo passed these studies on to two newspapers, the *New York Times* in New York City and the *Washington Post* in Washington, D.C. Neither paper was involved in the theft of government documents. In its Sunday, June 13, 1971, edition, the *Times* began a series of articles containing excerpts from the studies, which were dubbed the "Pentagon Papers." The *Times* published more articles on June 14 and 15.

The Government Moves to Stop the Leak

On June 15, 1971, the government asked the U.S. District Court for the Southern District of New York to restrain the *Times* from publishing

any more of the Pentagon Papers. The court refused to issue an injunction against the *Times* but did grant a temporary restraining order against the *Times* while the government prepared its case. On June 18, the *Post* also published portions of the Pentagon Papers, and the government promptly began proceedings in the District of Columbia to restrain that paper as well. The focus of the Pentagon Papers dispute, however, remained with the legal proceedings against the *Times* in New York City.

On June 18, 1971, the district court held a hearing. The government presented five experts on national security, who testified that publication of the Pentagon Papers would compromise the war effort. The next day, district court Judge Murray I. Gurfein issued his decision, in which he again refused to issue an injunction against the *Times*:

Daniel Ellsberg released the highly confidential "Pentagon Papers" to the *New York Times* and the *Washington Post,* thus setting in motion an important freedom of the press decision. (Archive Photos)

I am constrained to find as a fact that the . . . proceedings at which representatives of the Department of State, Department of Defense and the Joint Chiefs of Staff testified, did not convince this Court that the publication of these historical documents would seriously breach the national security. It is true, of course, that any breach of security will cause the jitters in the security agencies themselves and indeed in foreign governments who deal with us. . . . Without revealing the content of the testimony, suffice it to say that no cogent reasons were advanced as to why these documents except in the general framework of embarrassment previously mentioned, would vitally affect the security of the Nation.

Gurfein did, however, prevent the *Times* from publishing any more of the Pentagon Papers while the government hurried to file its appeal with the U.S. Court of Appeals for the Second Circuit (which covers New York). Once the appeal was filed, Circuit Judge Irving R. Kaufman continued the temporary restraint against the *Times* until the government could argue its case, which happened June 22, 1971. Usually, only three circuit judges hear an appeal, but in an unusual procedure all eight second circuit judges were on the bench that day. They listened to the government's claim that the Pentagon Papers' release would hurt national security, and the *Times'* defense that the First Amendment protected its publication of the excerpts.

The next day, June 23, the appeals court refused to give the government the injunction it wanted. On June 24, the government filed a petition with the Supreme Court. On June 25, the Court ordered the government and the *Times* to appear before the Court in Washington on the 26th for a hearing.

The *Times'* lawyers were Alexander M. Bickel and William E. Hegarty. The government's lawyers were Daniel M. Friedman, U.S. Solicitor General Erwin N. Griswold, and Robert C. Mardian. The two sides argued their positions before Justices Hugo L. Black, Harry A. Blackmun, William J. Brennan, Jr., Warren E. Burger, William O. Douglas, John M. Harlan, Thurgood Marshall, Potter Stewart, and Byron R. White.

Supreme Court Throws Out Government's Case

The Pentagon Papers case was a litigation whirlwind, beginning on June 15, 1971, and ending just over two weeks later, after having traveled through three courts, when the Supreme Court issued its decision on June 30, 1971. By a 6–3 vote, the Court slammed the door shut on the government's attempt to stop the *Times* from publishing the Pentagon Papers, with Justice Black stating:

> In seeking injunctions against these newspapers and in its presentation to the Court, the Executive Branch seems to have forgotten the essential purpose and history of the First Amendment. . . .

> Yet the Solicitor General argues . . . that the general powers of the Government adopted in the original Constitution should be interpreted to limit and restrict the specific and emphatic guarantees of the Bill of Rights. . . . I can imagine no greater perversion of history. Madison and the other Framers of the First Amendment, able men that they were, wrote in language they earnestly believed could never be misunderstood: "Congress shall make no law . . . abridging the freedom . . . of the press . . ." Both the history and language of the First Amendment support the view that the press must be left free to publish news, whatever the source, without censorship, injunctions, or prior restraints."

Not only did the Court reject the government's national security argument, but it criticized in no uncertain terms the Nixon administration's attempt to subvert the First Amendment. The role of the federal courts in the division of powers set up by the Constitution, namely as the judicial branch of government charged with the responsibility of protecting individual rights, was also reaffirmed:

> Our Government was launched in 1789 with the adoption of the Constitution. The Bill of Rights, including the First Amendment, followed in 1791.

Now, for the first time in the 182 years since the founding of the Republic, the federal courts are asked to hold that the First Amendment does not mean what it says, but rather means that the government can halt the publication of current news of vital importance to the people of this country.

Chief Justice Burger and Justices Blackmun and Harlan dissented, arguing that the Court should defer to the executive branch's conclusion that the Pentagon Papers leak threatened national security.

The Court also dismissed the government's legal actions against the *Post*. The Pentagon Papers proceedings were not over yet, however. The government obtained a preliminary indictment against Ellsberg on June 28, 1971 for violating criminal laws against the theft of federal property. More formal indictments came against Ellsberg, and Russo as well, on December 30, 1971. In addition to theft, the government charged Ellsberg and Russo with violations of the federal Espionage Act.

Government Thwarts Own Prosecution of Ellsberg

The criminal prosecution involved 15 counts of theft and espionage against Ellsberg and Russo. Ellsberg faced a possible 105 years in prison and $110,000 in fines if convicted. Russo faced a possible 25 years in prison and $30,000 in fines if convicted. The two men were tried in the U.S District Court for the Central District of California, which includes Los Angeles, where they were alleged to have stolen the Pentagon Papers.

The judge was William Matthew Byrne, Jr. The case was stalled for over five months with pretrial procedural activities, but jury selection finally began in June 1972. It took until July 1972 for a jury to be formed and the trial to begin, but the trial was halted almost immediately after it began when it was revealed that the government had been secretly taping the defendants' confidential communications. Supreme Court Justice Douglas, who was responsible for hearing emergency appeals from the Ninth Circuit, which includes Los Angeles, ordered the trial halted until October.

In fact, it was not until January 17, 1973, that the Ellsberg and Russo trial resumed. A whole new jury had to be selected. Further, the case was now overshadowed by the Watergate scandal. On September 3, 1971, G. Gordon Liddy and E. Howard Hunt, Jr., led a group of Cuban exiles in a break-in of the offices of Dr. Lewis Fielding, which were located in Beverly Hills, California. Fielding was Ellsberg's psychoanalyst, and the White House-sponsored break-in team was hoping to discover the identity of other Ellsberg accomplices from Fielding's files. The break-in was a total failure: there was nothing in Fielding's files.

When news of the government-sponsored bugging of the Democratic Party's headquarters in the Watergate hotel and office complex in Washington broke sometime later, it was only a matter of time before the special Watergate prosecutors learned of the Fielding break-in. This information was publicly revealed April 26, 1973, after the Ellsberg and Russo trial had been dragging on for months without any sign of an imminent conclusion.

At first, Byrne didn't want to consider dismissing the charges against Ellsberg and Russo. The government had invested a great deal of time and money in the prosecution. Then, after April 26, there were further revelations that the government had been conducting more illegal wiretaps of Ellsberg's conversations than had previously been admitted. In disgust, Byrne dismissed the entire criminal prosecution against Ellsberg and Russo on May 11, 1973.

Byrne's final dismissal of the charges against Ellsberg and Russo ended the Pentagon Papers affair. The significance of the entire episode is embodied in the Supreme Court's rejection of the government's attempt to prohibit the *Times* from publishing the news. Although the government will not necessarily always lose a case based on the alleged interests of national security, under *New York Times v. U.S.* it must meet a heavy burden of justification before it can restrain the press from exercising First Amendment rights.

—Stephen G. Christianson

Suggestions for Further Reading

Meiklejohn Civil Liberties Institute. *Pentagon Papers Case Collection: Annotated Procedural Guide and Index*. Berkeley, Calif.: Meiklejohn Civil Liberties Institute, 1975.

Salter, Kenneth W. *The Pentagon Papers Trial*. Berkeley, Calif.: Editorial Justa Publications, 1975.

Schrag, Peter. *Test of Loyalty: Daniel Ellsberg and the Rituals of Secret Government*. New York: Simon & Schuster, 1974.

Ungar, Sanford J. *The Papers & the Papers: an Account of the Legal and Political Battle Over the Pentagon Paper*. New York: Columbia University Press, 1989.

Angela Davis Trial: 1972

Defendant: Angela Y. Davis   **Crimes Charged:** Murder, kidnapping, and conspiracy   **Chief Defense Lawyers:** Leo Branton, Jr., Margaret Burnham, Howard Moore, Jr., Sheldon Otis, and Dorris Brin Walker
Chief Prosecutor: Albert Harris   **Judge:** Richard E. Arnason   **Place:** San Jose, California   **Dates of Trial:** February 28–June 4, 1972   **Verdict:** Not guilty

SIGNIFICANCE

A unique mix of murder, race, and politics ensured that this trial could never be anything but memorable.

At 10:45 A.M. on August 7, 1970, a gunman interrupted the Marin County trial of San Quentin inmate James McClains, who was facing a charge of attempted murder. The gunman, Jonathan Jackson, younger brother of George Jackson, one of the so-called "Soleded Brothers," distributed weapons to McClain and two other men, Ruchell Magee and William Christmas. Together, they took Judge Harold Haleys prosecutor Gary Thomas, and three women jurors hostages then attempted to flee in a van. When guards opened fire, Haley, Jackson, McClain, and Christmas were killed. Thomas and Magee sustained serious injuries.

Suspicion that the plot had been connected to the Soleded Brothers, three radical black Soleded Prison inmates, hardened with the abrupt disappearance of Angela Davis, a controversial professor and Soleded supporter, recently fired from the University of California at Los Angeles for her Communist sympathies. She remained at large until her discovery in New York on October 13. Following extradition she was arraigned on charges of murder, conspiracy, and kidnapping, as prosecutors sought to prove that Davis had engineered the escape attempt in a bid to barter hostages for the freedom of her lover, George Jackson.

The task of selecting a jury began before Judge Richard E. Arnason on February 28, 1972. The racial/political overtones made this an especially sensitive issue, but eventually an all-white jury was impaneled, and prosecutor Albert Harris was able to make his opening address. He outlined four elements necessary to establishing guilt through circumstantial evidence: motive, means, opportunity, and consciousness of guilt. "The evidence will show," he said, "that her [Davis'] basic motive was not to free political prisoners, but to free the one prisoner that she loved." The means came on August 5, 1970, when, in the company of Jonathan Jackson, "she purchased the shotgun that was used in the commission of the crime." Harris felt that those days preceding the crime, many of which Davis spent in the company of Jonathan Jackson, provided the opportunity to commit the crime; and finally consciousness of guilt was evidenced by the fact that just hours after the shooting, Davis boarded a flight at San Francisco and went into hiding.

Davis Ridicules Case

Despite having assembled an imposing team of attorneys, Davis chose to make the opening defense address herself. Wisely, she kept the political rhetoric to a minimum, preferring to underscore serious flaws in the prosecution's case—the fact that she had bought the shotgun quite openly in her own name, and, more importantly, her insistence that the Marin shooting had nothing to do with George Jackson. "The evidence will show that there's absolutely no credible proof of what the precise purpose of August 7 was."

This argument was countered by a prosecution witness, news photographer James Kean. He had taken several photographs of the incident and testified to hearing McClain say, "Tell them we want the Soleded Brothers released by twelve o'clock."

Angela Davis, escorted by two FBI agents, October 1970. (AP/Wide World Photos)

Chief defense attorney, Leo Branton cross-examined: "This remark that was made about freeing the Soleded Brothers—it was the last thing that was said just as the group got on the elevator . . . is that a fact?"

"Yes. That's right."

"You never heard Jonathan Jackson say anything about free the Soleded Brothers, did you?"

"No, I did not."

"You didn't hear anybody say it other than McClain and it was the last thing he said as he headed down the elevator; is that right?"

"Yes"

"As though it were a parting gesture, is that correct?"

"That's right."

Branton must have been satisfied, and even more so when Deputy Sheriff Theodore Hughes testified that he had heard some of the escapees shout clearly, "Free our brothers at Folsom, free all our brothers." Again, no reference to Soleded.

Less easy to dispose of was the prosecution's star witness, Gary Thomas. Permanently paralyzed by his bullet wound, he was brought into court in a wheelchair. The key part of his testimony was an insistence that he had seen Magee shoot Judge Haley with the shotgun. Thomas recalled that he "watched the right side of the judge's face pull slowly away from his skull."

Branton had the unenviable task of attempting to prove how Thomas' recollection might have been clouded by the trauma he had suffered. "Isn't it a fact, sir, that the first fusillade of shots that came into the van killed both Jonathan Jackson and McClain, and that you thereupon grabbed the gun that McClain was holding . . . and that you turned around and began firing into the back of the van . . . and that you hit Christmas and you hit Magee, and you possibly even hit Judge Haley?"

Thomas angrily refuted the assertion and Branton had to back down. He made little headway with Thomas, apart from getting the witness to agree that at no time did he ever hear anyone mention the Soleded Brothers.

Mysterious Telephone Number Surfaces

Prosecutor Harris next turned his attention to a piece of paper found on the body of Jonathan Jackson. On it was written a telephone number that corresponded to a public telephone at San Francisco International Airport. Harris contended that this clearly demonstrated a predisposition on the part of Jonathan Jackson to telephone Angela Davis at the airport, and that once Davis didn't receive the call she panicked and took the next available flight out to Los Angeles.

All of this sounded fine but did not bear close inspection. First of all, Branton established that the telephone was in the South Terminal, near the Western Airlines counter. Why, he speculated, had nobody seen Davis waiting by the phone? And why had she left the Western Airlines counter, which operated a convenient hourly shuttle to Los Angeles, and then walked over to the Central Terminal to catch a flight on Pacific Southwest Airlines? It didn't make sense.

In one last desperate effort to salvage their case, the prosecutors fought to introduce into evidence an 18-page "diary" that Davis had kept. While the diary clearly documented the intense love that Davis felt for George Jackson, it did not provide any evidence to support the indictment.

Such a lackluster prosecution hardly merited much of a response. Branton called just 12 witnesses to support his assertion that Angela Davis was entirely innocent, a mere victim of her own notoriety. The case went to the jury on June 2, 1972. They came back two days later with not-guilty verdicts on all three charges.

But for Angela Davis it was a Pyrrhic victory. Six months before she faced her accusers, George Jackson was himself shot to death in an alleged prison break.

Before the trial many, including some on her own defense team, doubted Angela Davis' chances of receiving a fair hearing from an all-white jury. That the jurors were able to separate politics and race from the essential facts of the case speaks volumes for their integrity, making this one of the legal system's finer moments.

—Colin Evans

Suggestions for Further Reading

Aptheker, Bettina. *The Morning Breaks*. New York: International, 1975.

Davis, Angela. *Angela Davis*. New York: International, 1988.

Major, Reginald. *Justice in the Round*. New York: Third Press, 1973.

Mitchell, Charlene. *The Fight to Free Angela Davis*. New York: Outlook, 1972.

Timothy, Mary. *Jury Woman*. San Francisco: Glide, 1975.

Furman v. Georgia: 1972

Appellant & Defendant: William Henry Furman   **Appellee & Plaintiff:** State of Georgia   **Appellant Claim:** That the Georgia death penalty constituted cruel and unusual punishment in violation of the Eight and Fourteenth Amendments   **Chief Defense Lawyers:** Dorothy T. Beasley, Arthur K. Bolton, Harold N. Hill, Jr., Andrew J. Ryan, Jr., Andrew J. Ryan, III and Courtney Wilder Stanton   **Chief Lawyers for Plaintiff:** Anthony G. Amsterdam, Elizabeth B. Dubois, Jack Greenberg, Jack Himmelstein, B. Clarence Mayfield, and Michael Meltsner   **Justices:** Harry A. Blackmun, William J. Brennan, Jr., Warren E. Burger, William O. Douglas, Thurgood Marshall, Lewis F. Powell, Jr., William H. Rehnquist, Potter Stewart, and Byron R. White   **Place:** Washington, D.C.   **Date of Decision:** June 29, 1972   **Decision:** Georgia death penalty statute declared unconstitutional

SIGNIFICANCE

Although *Furman v. Georgia* did not completely abolish the death penalty, it placed stringent requirements on death penalty statutes.

On the night of August 11, 1967, 29-year-old William Joseph Micke, Jr., came home from work to his wife and five children in the city of Savannah, Georgia. He went to bed around midnight. Two hours later, the Mickes were awakened by strange noises in the kitchen. Thinking that one of his children was sleepwalking, William Micke went into the kitchen to investigate. He found William Henry Furman there, a 26-year-old black man who had broken into the house and was carrying a gun. Furman fled the house, shooting Micke as he left. The bullet hit Micke in the chest and he died instantly. Micke's family promptly called the police, who arrived on the scene within minutes. The police searched the neighborhood and found Furman, who was still carrying the murder weapon.

Furman was charged with murder and was tried in the Superior Court of Chatham County, Georgia, on September 20, 1968. Furman was a poor man, and he got a poor man's trial. His court-appointed lawyer, B. Clarence Mayfield, received the court-approved standard retainer for murder cases: $150, which did not include costs. The trial lasted just one day: the jury was selected at

10:00 A.M., the evidence was presented and the judge's instructions to the jury given by 3:30 P.M., and the jury's guilty verdict was returned at 5:00 P.M.

Long before the trial, the court committed Furman to the Georgia Central State Hospital at Milledgeville for psychological examination. Furman had dropped out of school after the sixth grade, and he tested in the lowest 4 percent of the test's intelligence range. The hospital diagnosed Furman as being mentally deficient and subject to psychotic episodes. Nevertheless, the court denied Furman's insanity plea at trial.

Furman Sentenced to Death

Under Georgia law, Furman faced the death penalty. This was despite the fact that Furman had testified that his shooting of Micke was accidental:

> I admit going to these folks' home and they did caught me in there and I was coming back out, backing up and there was a wire down there on the floor. I was coming out backwards and fell back and I didn't intend to kill nobody. . . . The gun went off and I didn't know nothing about no murder until they arrested me, and when the gun went off I was down on the floor and I got up and ran. That's all to it.

Georgia's death penalty statute, however, permitted executions even for unintended killings. So long as Furman had broken into the Micke house illegally, it was irrelevant that his shooting was accidental since that shooting had caused Micke's death while Furman was committing a criminal act. The judge's instructions to the jury made this clear:

> If you believe beyond a reasonable doubt that the defendant broke and entered the dwelling of the deceased with intent to commit a felony or a larceny and that after so breaking and entering with such intent, the defendant killed the deceased in the manner set forth in the indictment, and if you find that such killing was the natural, reasonable and probable consequence of such breaking and entering, then I instruct you that under such circumstances, you would be authorized to convict the defendant of murder and this you would be authorized to do whether the defendant intended to kill the deceased or not.

The Georgia Supreme Court affirmed Furman's conviction and death sentence on April 24, 1969, but on May 3, 1969, Chief Justice W.H. Duckworth stayed the execution so that Furman could file a petition with the U.S. Supreme Court. Furman was no longer represented solely by court-appointed counsel: his case had generated some publicity, and several lawyers were now handling his appeal. Furman's chief lawyers were Anthony G. Amsterdam, Elizabeth B. Dubois, Jack Greenberg, Jack Himmelstein, B. Clarence Mayfield, and Michael Meltsner. The State of Georgia's chief lawyers were Dorothy T. Beasley, Arthur K. Bolton, Harold N. Hill, Jr., Andrew J. Ryan, Jr., Andrew J. Ryan III, and Courtney Wilder Stanton.

On January 17, 1972, the parties argued their case before the U.S. Supreme Court in Washington, D.C. The Court had agreed to hear the case to answer the legal question of whether the death penalty violates the Eighth Amendment to the U.S. Constitution, which states that "Excessive bail shall not be required, nor excessive fines imposed, nor cruel and unusual punishments inflicted."

The Court issued its decision June 29, 1972. By a narrow five-to-four majority, the justices voted to overturn Furman's conviction on the grounds that in his case the death penalty constituted cruel and unusual punishment. The justices were deeply divided over how to interpret the Eighth Amendment, however. All nine justices filed separate opinions stating their legal reasoning, which is highly unusual. For the most part, Justice William O. Douglas' opinion spoke for the five-member majority.

Justice Harry Blackmun opposed abolition of the death penalty in *Furman v. Georgia*. (Archive Photos)

Court Severely Restricts Death Penalty

Douglas reviewed the history of capital punishment under the English common law, from the Norman Conquest in 1066 through the American colonial period and up to the ratification of the Constitution. He noted that English law had evolved to consider the death penalty unfair when applied selectively to minorities, outcasts, and unpopular groups. In America, the Court had already held that discriminatory enforcement of the law violates the equal protection clause of the Fourteenth Amendment. Therefore, if a death penalty statute was applied in a discriminatory manner, it was unfair and constituted cruel and unusual punishment. For Furman, the death penalty was unfair because there had not been enough protection for him at trial. He had gotten a quick one-day trial and he was black, poor, uneducated, and mentally ill:

The generality of a law inflicting capital punishment is one thing. What may be said of the validity of a law on the books and what may be done with the law in its application do, or may, lead to quite different conclusions.

It would seem to be incontestable that the death penalty inflicted on one defendant is "unusual" if it discriminates against him by reason of his race, religion, wealth, social position, or class, or if it is imposed under a procedure that gives room for the play of such prejudices.

The rest of Douglas' opinion reads almost like a professional case study of prisoner treatment throughout the United States. Based on surveys and statistics drawn from a variety of sources, Douglas concluded that the death penalty was disproportionately applied to blacks, the poor, and other groups who are at a disadvantage in society:

Former Attorney General Ramsey Clark has said, "It is the poor, the sick, the ignorant, the powerless and the hated who are executed." One searches our chronicles in vain for the execution of any member of the affluent strata of this society.

Justices William J. Brennan, Jr., and Thurgood Marshall, who had voted with Douglas, wrote opinions that called for the complete abolition of the death penalty for all crimes and under any circumstances. They were in the minority, however, and so Douglas' opinion embodied the impact of the Court's decision: the death penalty could still be imposed, but only if the law bent over backwards to make sure that people like Furman were protected.

While *Furman v. Georgia* was hailed as a landmark decision protecting minorities and other historically oppressed groups, it didn't give the states much guidance on what they had to do to make their death penalty statutes comply with the Eighth Amendment. In the 1976 case of *Gregg v. Georgia*, the Court upheld the death penalty imposed on a convicted murderer under a revamped Georgia statute that required sentencing hearings and other protective procedures. Most states with death penalty statutes have followed *Gregg* and modified their laws so there are procedures to protect the poor, minorities, the mentally ill, and other groups. Further, most states have repealed the death penalty for accidental killings and other crimes less serious than cold-blooded intentional murder.

Furman v. Georgia did not forbid capital punishment, but it did place strict requirements on death penalty statutes, at both the state and federal levels, based on the Eighth Amendment.

—Stephen G. Christianson

Suggestions for Further Reading

Aguirre, Adalberto. *Race, Racism, and the Death Penalty in the United States.* Berrien Spring, Mich.: Vande Vere, 1991.

Congregation of the Condemned: Voices Against the Death Penalty. Buffalo, N.Y.: Prometheus Books, 1991.

Horwitz, Elinor Lander. *Capital Punishment, U.S.A.* Philadelphia: J.B. Lippincott Co., 1973.

Masur, Louis P. *Rites of Execution: Capital Punishment and the Transformation Of American Culture.* New York: Oxford University Press, 1989.

Radelet, Michael L. *In Spite of Innocence: Erroneous Convictions in Capital Cases.* Boston: Northeastern University Press, 1992.

Trombley, Stephen. *The Execution Protocol: Inside America's Capital Punishment Industry.* New York: Crown Publishers, 1992.

Roe et al. v. Wade: 1973

Plaintiff: Norma McCorvey, using "Jane Roe" as an alias and representing all pregnant women in a class-action suit   **Defendant:** Texas District Attorney Henry B. Wade   **Plaintiff's Claim:** That Texas' abortion laws violated McCorvey's and other women's constitutional rights
Chief Defense Lawyers: Jay Floyd and Robert Flowers
Chief Lawyers for Plaintiff: Sarah Weddington and Linda Coffee
Justices: Harry Blackmun, William Brennan, Warren Burger, William Douglas, Thurgood Marshall, Lewis Powell, William Rehnquist, Potter Stewart, and Byron White   **Place:** Washington, D.C.   **Date of Decision:** January 22, 1973   **Decision:** Overturned all state laws restricting women's access to abortions during the first trimester of pregnancy and let stand second-trimester restrictions only insofar as they were designed to protect the health of pregnant women

SIGNIFICANCE

The case was the first to establish that a woman, rather than her physician, might be the party injured by a state's criminalization of abortion. Moreover, the decision was in large measure based on an implied "right to privacy" in the U.S. Constitution, which the majority held was violated by state laws restricting a woman's right to abort a fetus prior to its viability outside her womb.

The Supreme Court's landmark decision legalizing abortion in *Roe v. Wade* aroused more passion than perhaps any other in the Court's history. One segment of the population, energized by Catholic and fundamentalist religious beliefs, held that aborting the unborn was no less than murder. Another segment of the American people was just as convinced and just as adamant that denying a woman's "right to choose" whether or not to bear a child was an intolerable governmental restriction of her freedom and privacy. The decision in 1973 triggered a 20-year battle between its opponents, the self-described "Right to Life" movement who sought to overturn it, and proponents, the "Pro-Choice" advocates who worked to prevent it from being reversed or whittled away. Justice Harry Blackmun, who wrote the majority opinion, had his life threatened and his mailbox filled with letters calling him "Butcher of Dachau, murderer,

Pontius Pilate, [and] Adolph Hitler." Each of the other justices received thousands of letters of condemnation as well.

Support for abortion rights had been growing steadily in the years prior to the decision and continued to increase afterward. In 1968, for example, less than 15 percent of the participants in a Gallup Poll approved "of liberalizing the abortion laws," while 40 percent of Gallup Poll respondents approved in the following year. By mid-1972, the Gallup Poll reported 73 percent of all participants and 56 percent of Catholic participants believed "that the decision to undergo an abortion is a matter that should be left solely to the woman and her physician."

Although they appear to be in a minority, those who object to *Roe v. Wade* do so with a seemingly undying passion; nearly 20 years later, as this is written, their opposition is well organized, well funded and at times even violent. It also has been partially successful: The basic decision still stands, but the high court has narrowed it somewhat by permitting states to regulate abortion for minors and abortions performed in tax-supported institutions.

Norma McCorvey Tests the Law

The "Jane Roe" whose name would be attached to this national divide was actually 21-year-old Norma McCorvey. McCorvey's marriage had ended, and her daughter, age 5, was being reared by McCorvey's mother and stepfather. In the summer of 1969, McCorvey was working as a ticket seller for a traveling carnival; by early autumn she had lost her job and had become pregnant. McCorvey wanted to end her pregnancy, but abortion was illegal in Texas except in cases where it was deemed necessary to save a woman's life. McCorvey's search for an illegal abortionist was unsuccessful.

However, it led her to two young attorneys, both women and both interested in challenging the existing abortion laws: Linda Coffee and Sarah Weddington. Although there was virtually no chance that McCorvey herself would be helped if Coffee and Weddington succeeded in overturning the abortion laws (one could count on pregnancy coming to a conclusion well before any lawsuit simultaneously began), McCorvey agreed to become Coffee's and Weddington's plaintiff in a test case.

Texas had passed its anti-abortion law in 1859. Like other such laws in the United States, it punished only the persons performing or "furnishing the means for" an abortion. This posed a problem for Coffee and Weddington: They knew it could be argued that a pregnant woman, presumably *not* the target of a law restricting medical practice, "lacked standing to sue" regarding that law's supposed unconstitutionality. And if they passed this hurdle with McCorvey's case, they knew they'd face another: When McCorvey gave birth or at least passed the point where an abortion could be safely performed, her case—having resolved itself—might be declared moot and thrown out of court. Linda Coffee prepared and filed the pleading anyway.

Constitutional Issues

Coffee and Weddington decided to attack the constitutionality of the Texas abortion law on the grounds that it violated the Fourteenth and Ninth Amendments to the U.S. Constitution. The due process clause of the Fourteenth Amendment guaranteed equal protection under the law to all citizens and, in particular, required that laws be clearly written. Physicians accused of performing illegal abortions usually cited the Fourteenth Amendment in their defense, claiming that the law was not specific enough with regard to when a woman's life might be considered threatened by pregnancy and childbirth. However, since Coffee and Weddington wanted a decision that rested on a pregnant woman's right to decide for herself whether or not an abortion was necessary, they based their argument first and foremost on the Ninth Amendment, which states: "The enumeration in the Constitution, of certain rights, shall not be construed to deny or disparage others retained by the people." Until 1965, this had usually been interpreted to mean that rights not specifically granted to the federal government were retained by the states. In 1965, however, *Griswold v. Connecticut* reached the Supreme Court and prompted a different interpretation of the amendment. Estelle Griswold, Planned Parenthood League of Connecticut's executive director, and Dr. Charles Lee Buxton had been arrested for providing birth-control information and contraceptives, actions then illegal under Connecticut

Chief Justice Burger voted with the majority in the *Roe v. Wade* decision which affirmed a woman's "fundamental right" to privacy in the area of choosing whether or not to have an abortion. (Courtesy, Library of Congress)

law. Found guilty in the Connecticut courts, the two appealed to the Supreme Court, which overturned their convictions and ruled the Connecticut law unconstitutional. Of particular note to Coffee and Weddington was Justice William O. Douglas' discussion of the Ninth Amendment in his majority opinion. Rights not specifically listed in the Constitution were retained by *the people*, Douglas emphasized, and one of these rights was the right to privacy. This right to privacy, Coffee and Weddington would argue, should certainly protect the right of a woman to decide whether or not to become a mother.

John Tolles was the assistant district attorney chosen by District Attorney Henry Wade to defend his enforcement of the Texas abortion law. Attorney General Crawford Martin chose Robert Flowers, head of the enforcement division, to defend the Texas law itself, and Flowers passed this task on to his assistant chief, Jay Floyd. The state prepared its case primarily on the basis that a fetus had legal rights, which ought to be protected.

State Court Favors Plaintiff

The Three-Judge Court Act of 1910 had created courts in which a panel of three judges drawn from a single appellate circuit might resolve interstate commerce disputes between the federal and state governments. Another act, passed in 1937, required that such a panel hear any case questioning the constitutionality of a state law. On May 23, 1970, Coffee, Weddington, Tolles and Floyd appeared in the Fifth Circuit Court in Dallas, Texas, before Judges Irving S. Goldberg, William McLaughlin Taylor, and Sarah Tigham Hughes, for whom Coffee had once clerked. The courtroom was jammed with concerned women and reporters. Norma McCorvey, or "Jane Roe," not required to be present, stayed home.

Coffee and Weddington had amended their case to a class-action suit so that McCorvey would represent not just herself but all pregnant women. They had also been joined in their suit by an "intervenor," Dr. James Hallford, who had been arrested for performing abortions. Hallford's attorneys, Fred Bruner and Roy Merrill, planned to use the traditional physician's defense, the Fourteenth Amendment.

Coffee spoke first. She had to establish that McCorvey did, indeed, have "standing to sue" and that the question was a serious, constitutional one on which the three judges should rule. At one point she said: "I think the [abortion] statute is so bad that the court is just really going to have to strike it all down. I don't think it's worth salvaging."

Weddington approached the bench next. This was her courtroom debut, and she knew it was an important case. She said she disagreed with the "justification which the state alleges for the state abortion statute, that is, the protection of the life of the child. . . .

"[L]ife is an ongoing process. It is almost impossible," Weddington continued, "to define a point at which life begins or perhaps even at which life ends."

Asked by Judge Goldberg whether the legalization of abortion would promote promiscuity, Weddington said that young women "are already promiscuous when the statute is in effect, and in fact, these are some of the girls who need this right and who have the most socially compelling arguments why they should be allowed abortions—the young still in school, those unable to shoulder the responsibility of a child—these girls should not be put through the pregnancy and should be entitled to an abortion."

Before Weddington stepped down to listen to Fred Bruner's Fourteenth Amendment defense of his physician client, Judge Goldberg asked her one more question. Did she, he wanted to know, think the abortion law was weaker in terms of the Ninth or Fourteenth Amendment? Weddington gave her answer immediately: "I believe it is more vulnerable on the Ninth Amendment basis."

After Bruner addressed the judges, Floyd rose to speak for the state. He claimed that "Roe" must certainly have reached the point in her pregnancy where an abortion would be considered unsafe and therefore had no case. Judge Goldberg flatly disagreed.

Tolles followed for the state, and argued strenuously against a woman's having the right to choose an abortion. "I personally think," he said, "and I think the state's position will be and is, that the right of the child to life is superior to that woman's right to privacy."

The judges did not agree. On June 17, 1970, they issued their opinion: "[T]he Texas abortion laws must be declared unconstitutional because they deprive single women and married couples, of their right, secured by the Ninth Amendment, to choose whether to have children."

Supreme Court Hears the Case

The fifth circuit court had issued *declarative relief*, that is, it had declared the challenged law unconstitutional. It had not, however, issued *injunctive relief*, which would have been an order for Texas to end its enforcement of that law. For this reason, Weddington and Coffee were entitled to appeal directly to the U.S. Supreme Court, which agreed to hear their case.

Forty-two *amici curiae*, or "friend of the court" briefs, were filed in support of a woman's right to choose an abortion from organizations as varied as the New York Academy of Medicine, the American College of Gynecologists and Obstetricians, Planned Parenthood and the California chapter of the National Organization for Women. There was also a "woman's brief," signed by such noteworthy women as anthropologist Margaret Mead; Barnard College President Millicent McIntosh; Oregon's past U.S. senator, Maurine Nuebuerger; and feminist theologian Mary Daly. This brief stated, as Marian Faux summarizes it, "that even if a fetus were found to be a legal person, a woman still could not be compelled to nurture it in her body against her will."

On December 13, 1971, Weddington stood before the Supreme Court and contended the state's ability to compel women to bear children left women without any control over their lives. Then she argued against Tolles' claim that a fetus was entitled to protection. "[T]he Constitution, as I read it . . . attaches protection to the person at the time of birth. Those persons born are citizens."

When Floyd's turn came, he said that "Roe" must surely have given birth by now and thus could not represent pregnant women in a class-action suit. Asked how any pregnant woman could hope to challenge Texas' abortion laws, Floyd replied: "There are situations in which . . . no remedy is provided. Now, I think she makes her choice prior to the time she becomes pregnant. That is the time of the choice. . . . Once a child is born, a woman no longer has a choice; and I think pregnancy makes her make that choice as well."

Floyd was then questioned as to why, if abortion was equivalent to murder, no state had ever punished the women involved. He was also questioned about the fact that doctors who performed abortions were not charged with premeditated murder but "ordinary felony murder," a lesser charge. Finally, he was asked to clarify when life began according to the state of Texas. After several attempts to answer the question, Floyd could only say: "I don't—Mr. Justice—there are unanswerable questions in this field."

Since there had been only seven sitting justices when *Roe v. Wade* was argued, the justices decided such an important case should be re-argued when two newly appointed justices—William Rehnquist and Lewis Powell—joined the Court, restoring the number of justices to nine. Weddington, Coffee, Tolles, and Floyd did so October 10, 1972, repeating their basic arguments.

Landmark Decision

On January 22, 1973, Justice Harry Blackmun read his majority opinion to a room filled with reporters. Reviewing the history of abortion in the United States, he pointed out that "The restrictive criminal abortion laws in effect in a majority of states today . . . are not of ancient or even of common law origin." Instead, he said they seemed to have been passed to protect women from a procedure that was, in the 19th century, likely to endanger their health. That rationale no longer existed, Justice Blackmun declared, since medical advances had made abortion as safe or safer than childbirth for women.

Justice Blackmun next discussed the high court's acknowledgment of a "right of personal privacy" in various decisions, including the recent *Griswold* birth control case. Then he delivered the crux of his decision:

> This right of privacy, whether it be founded in the Fourteenth Amendment's concept of personal liberty and restrictions on state action . . . or . . . in the Ninth Amendment's reservation of rights to the people, is broad enough to encompass a woman's decision to terminate her pregnancy.

Continuing, Justice Blackmun disagreed with Texas' claim that it had the right to "infringe Roe's rights" to protect "prenatal life." He discussed the use of the word "person" in the U.S. Constitution and found that no such use had "any possible prenatal application," and he specifically found that "the word 'person,' as used in the Fourteenth Amendment, does not include the unborn."

However, Justice Blackmun said, neither the woman's right to privacy nor the fetus' lack of a right to the state's protection was absolute:

> [T]he State does have an important and legitimate interest in preserving and protecting the health of the pregnant woman . . . and . . . it has still *another* important and legitimate interest in protecting the potentiality of human life. These interests are separate and distinct. Each grows in substantiality as the woman approaches term and, at a point during the pregnancy, each becomes "compelling."

Finally, Justice Blackmun's decision in *Roe v. Wade* provided the states with a formula to balance these competing interests. During the first trimester of pregnancy, the abortion decision would be "left to the medical judgment of the pregnant woman's attending physician." During the second trimester, a state might "regulate the abortion procedure in ways that are reasonably related to maternal health." From the end of the second trimester "subsequent to viability," a state might "regulate, and even proscribe, abortion except where it is necessary, in appropriate legal judgment, for the preservation of the life or health of the mother."

Justices William Rehnquist and Byron White dissented. Justice Rehnquist, in his brief, said:

> I have difficulty in concluding, as the Court does, that the right of "privacy" is involved in this case. Texas by the statute here challenged bars the performance of a medical abortion by a licensed physician on a plaintiff such as Roe. A transaction resulting in an operation such as this is not "private" in the ordinary usage of that word.
>
> . . . I agree with the statement . . . that . . . "liberty," embraces more than the rights found in the Bill of Rights. But that liberty is not guaranteed absolutely against deprivation, but only against deprivation without due process of law.

Justice White wrote in his dissent:

> At the heart of the controversy in these cases are those recurring pregnancies that pose no danger whatsoever to the life or health of the mother but are nevertheless unwanted for any one or more of a variety of reasons—convenience, family planning, economics, dislike of children, the embarrassment of illegitimacy, etc.
>
> The common claim before us is that for any one of such reasons, or for no reason at all . . . any woman is entitled to an abortion at her request if she is able to find a medical advisor willing to undertake the procedure.
>
> The Court for the most part sustains this position: . . . during the period prior to the time the fetus becomes viable, the Constitution of the United States values the convenience, whim or caprice of the putative mother more than life or potential life of the fetus.

Every state was affected. New York, which had previously permitted abortion until the 24th week of pregnancy, had to extend that period by several weeks, and the laws of Alaska, Hawaii, and Washington required similar amendment. Fifteen states needed a complete overhaul of their abortion laws, while 31 states—including Texas—had strict anti-abortion laws which became immediately and entirely invalid.

In the spring of 1973, with support from the Catholic church, a Committee of Ten Million began a petition drive demanding a "human rights amendment," to ban abortion in the United States. Several proposed constitutional amendments were introduced and discussed in Congress, including proposals for amendments that prohibited abortions even when required to save a mother's life. These attempts failed, and *Roe*'s opponents tried to organize the legislatures of 34 states to call for a constitutional convention; in the mid-1980s, this strategy was abandoned as well.

The Republican party has since adopted the "pro-life" position as part of its party platform, gaining Catholic and fundamentalist members and losing enough support among women to create a 24 percent "gender gap" in the 1988 elections. The Democratic Party—which supports *Roe v. Wade*—also benefitted from the women's vote in the 1992 presidential election, in which Bill Clinton, a supporter of a woman's right to an abortion, was elected president.

Subsequent Developments

Many of the Supreme Court's most liberal members have retired since *Roe v. Wade* was decided in 1973, and their conservative successors have indicated a willingness to re-examine the decision and its implications. On June 30, 1980, in *Harris v. McRae,* the high court ruled that neither the federal nor local government was obligated to pay for abortions for women on welfare, even if their abortions were medically necessary. More recently, *Webster v. Reproductive Health Care,* July 3, 1989, granted states new authority to restrict abortions in tax-supported institutions, and *Rust v. Sullivan,* May 23, 1991, upheld federal regulations that denied government financial aid to family planning clinics that provided information about abortion. Yet, for the time being, the effect of the decision remains intact: A state may not prohibit a woman from aborting a fetus during the first three months of pregnancy and may only regulate abortions during the second three months in the interest of the pregnant woman's health.

— Kathryn Cullen-DuPont

Suggestions for Further Reading

Abraham, Henry J. *The Judicial Process,* 4th ed. New York: Oxford University Press, 1980.

Cary, Eve and Kathleen Willert Peratis. *Woman and the Law.* Skokie, Ill.: National Textbook Co. in conjunction with the American Civil Liberties Union, New York, 1977.

Cushman, Robert F. *Cases in Constitutional Law,* 6th ed. Englewood Cliffs, N.J.: Prentice Hall, 1984.

Davis, Flora. *Moving the Mountain: The Women's Movement in America Since 1960.* New York: Simon & Schuster, 1991.

Ehrenreich, Barbara and Deirdre English. *For Her Own Good: 150 Years of the Experts's Advice to Women.* New York: Doubleday, 1979.

Faux, Marian. *Roe V. Wade.* New York: Macmillan Co., 1988.

Faludi, Susan. *Backlash: The Undeclared War Against American Women.* New York: Crown Publishers, 1991.

Petchesky, Rosalind Pollack. *Abortion and Woman's Choice.* Boston: Northeastern University Press, 1984, revised 1990.

Rosten, Leo. *Religions of America: Ferment and Faith in an Age of Crisis.* New York: Simon & Schuster, 1975.

Peter A. Reilly Trial: 1974 & 1976

Defendant: Peter Reilly   **Crime Charged:** Murder
Chief Defense Lawyer: Catherine Roraback   **Chief Prosecutor:** John Bianchi   **Judge:** John Speziale   **Place:** Litchfield, Connecticut
Dates of Trials: Trial: February 28–April 12, 1974; Appeal: March 25, 1976
Verdict: Guilty of manslaughter in first-degree; conviction reversed on appeal
Sentence: More than 6 but no more than 16 years

SIGNIFICANCE

Peter Reilly was convicted on the basis of a confession he made to police after eight hours of questioning. He later recanted the confession, and after extensive community effort, he appealed for a new trial based on new evidence. His petition for a new trial was granted, but the state never brought him to a second trial and he was thus exonerated.

On the night of September 28, 1973, Barbara Gibbons of Canaan, Connecticut, was brutally killed at her home. Her throat was slashed, almost severing her head, and her legs were broken, apparently after she was killed. There was evidence she had been sexually molested. There were multiple cuts to her body, and the bedroom was splashed with blood. Peter Reilly, her son, claimed that he returned home from a teen center meeting and found his mother on the floor of her bedroom, covered with blood and breathing with difficulty. He placed several phone calls, first for an ambulance, then for a doctor, and finally to a hospital. The hospital notified police, who arrived at 10:02 P.M. Reilly explained to the police that after leaving the teen center meeting, he drove a friend, John Sochocki, to his home, then arrived home between 9:50 and 9:55, discovered his mother, made the calls, and waited for the police.

A Son Confesses

State police who questioned Peter Reilly immediately suspected him because he appeared to express no grief. The fact that he claimed to have found his mother alive, and that her legs were apparently broken after she died, raised police suspicions about his involvement. But when police examined him, they found no blood on his clothes or on his body. After his explanation to the police, he was held overnight, then interrogated at state police Troop B in North

Canaan on the following morning. Police then took him to Troop H in Hartford, Connecticut, for a polygraph test.

Reilly requested the test in the apparent belief that its results would clear him of any suspicion. However, he had had no sleep the night before, and as the questioning wore on for more than six hours on September 29, he eventually agreed with the police that he might have killed his mother but then blocked the event from his memory. His interrogation was recorded, and later transcripts revealed that although he was not intimidated or threatened physically, he became more and more confused and eager to please his questioners during the lengthy process. Several times the police informed him that he had a right to an attorney, but he did not insist on one.

Following the long hours of interview, he developed a confession, which he signed.

Jury Opts for Manslaughter

While awaiting trial, Peter Reilly recanted his confession and sought legal assistance. Community support for his cause developed, and as news of the case spread, a number of authors and other celebrities in Connecticut provided financial support. Among his notable advocates were William Styron and Arthur Miller.

At a pretrial hearing, Judge Arthur Armentano ruled that the confession and selections from the tape-recorded interrogation could be admitted as evidence.

At the trial before Judge John Speziale, deputy state medical examiner Ernest M. Izumi described the extensive wounds to Barbara Gibbons. He also testified that it would be possible to inflict the injuries without being spattered with blood. The prosecution established that Reilly sometimes quarreled with his mother, and other witnesses testified that Reilly showed no apparent grief. His confession and excerpts from his statements to the police were introduced. Neither the defense nor prosecution could clearly establish the time sequence of events between the adjournment of the teen center meeting at 9:15, and the phone call from the hospital to the state police at 9:58. The defense introduced several witnesses who saw Reilly at the teen center as late as 9:30, and also John Sochocki, who agreed that Reilly had driven him home, leaving him there at about 9:45.

The jury found it difficult to reach a conclusion, and spent more than 15 hours deliberating the case over a period of two days. They asked several times to have segments of the trial transcript read back. Judge Speziale urged them to reach a unanimous decision, telling the jury to make their own judgments while considering what the majority is deciding. Reilly was convicted of manslaughter in the first degree and sentenced to prison for a term of six to 16 years.

New Evidence Results in Reversal

Community supporters remained convinced that Reilly was innocent, and that his original confession was the result of an impressionable and inexperienced young man led by suggestive police questioning to falsely incriminate himself. A later review of the lengthy transcripts of his interrogation supported this interpretation. Joan Barthel, a journalist who helped bring statewide and national attention to Reilly's cause, included much of the transcript in a book detailing the case.

A smiling Peter Reilly after charges against him were dismissed. (Bettmann/ Corbis)

The support group continued to widen, and the broadcast of a documentary on CBS television brought even more support. An appeal was mounted on three grounds: two citing new evidence, and one contending that the state failed to provide exculpatory material, records, and evidence at the original trial. The full transcript of the interrogation was part of that material. Attorneys for Reilly in the appeal were T.F. Gilroy Daly, Robert M. Hartwell, and John Fiore.

Judge Speziale heard the appeal and rejected the claim that the state had failed to provide exculpatory material at the original trial. But Speziale accepted that the new evidence justified overturning the original verdict. The crucial new evidence consisted of a fingerprint that pointed suspicion at two other individuals, Timothy and Michael Parmalee. At the original trial, Sandra Ashner had claimed that Michael Parmalee was with her on the night of the murder, but in April of 1975 she said she had originally lied, and that Parmalee was not with her. Furthermore, the first person that Peter Reilly called on the night of the murder, Marion Madow, stated that he had called her during a certain moment of the television broadcast of the movie, *Kelley's Heroes*. CBS television was able to determine that that portion of the movie aired at precisely 9:50 P.M. This helped establish the time sequence, raising serious doubts whether Peter Reilly would have had time to commit the crime before calling for help. Since he had dropped off Sochocki at 9:45, and it took five minutes to drive to his home, it seemed evident that he made his first call for help immediately upon arriving home, leaving no time for him to have committed the crime.

Expert testimony from Dr. Herbert Spiegel suggested how Peter Reilly could have been led to confess, due to his difficulty of "integrating a concept of self." Reilly had been unable to distinguish between a statement and an assertion or a question, and could easily be led to accept as a fact something he knew nothing about.

Judge Speziale ruled that the new expert testimony, the fingerprint evidence, and the newly established evidence regarding timing were all sufficient to suggest that an injustice had been done in the original trial. He also ruled that none of that evidence could have been obtained by the defense counsel through due diligence in the first case. Since all three new pieces of evidence would establish a reasonable doubt as to Reilly's guilt, on March 25, 1976, he therefore ordered the release of Reilly pending a new trial. The state of Connecticut never attempted to bring another prosecution and Reilly remained free.

In later years, Reilly became active in popular efforts to question police interrogation methods.

— Rodney Carlisle

Suggestions for Further Reading

Barthel, Joan. *A Death in Canaan*. New York: E.P. Dutton, 1976.

Tony Boyle Trial: 1974

Defendant: W.A. Boyle **Crime Charged:** First-degree murder
Chief Defense Attorney: Charles F. Moses **Chief Prosecutor:** Richard A. Sprague **Judge:** Francis J. Catania **Place:** Media, Pennsylvania
Dates of Trial: March 25–April 11, 1974 **Verdict:** Guilty **Sentence:** 3 consecutive terms of life imprisonment

SIGNIFICANCE

Successful prosecutions of those responsible for the death of Jock Yablonski revealed that his murder had been ordered by the president of his own union and paid for with union funds.

No one assumed that the struggle for leadership of the United Mine Workers of America ended when incumbent President W.A. "Tony" Boyle defeated Joseph "Jock" Yablonski in the bitter December 1969 union election. The reform-minded Yablonski planned to take evidence of massive election fraud to the U.S. Secretary of Labor. Although he would later claim that the challenger was his "very close friend," Boyle and the hierarchy of the powerful union openly hated Yablonski.

In the New Year's Eve darkness of December 31, 1969, Yablonski, his wife, and their daughter were shot to death in their Clarksville, Pennsylvania home. The Federal Bureau of Investigation (FBI) entered the case on the premise that the killings might be related to Yablonski's union activity, thus making the murders a federal crime. A tip led them quickly to the gunmen: Paul Gilly, Claude Vealey, and Aubran "Buddy" Martin. Gilly's wife Annette was arrested soon. So was her father, Silous Huddleston, the president of a UMW district local.

There was no initial evidence to support a hunch that higher union officials were involved. State prosecutor Richard A. Sprague methodically tried the captured killers one by one, allowing the pressure to mount as each of the conspirators tried to escape the death sentence. In June 1971, Claude Vealey pleaded guilty to three counts of murder. Awaiting sentencing, Vealey was summoned as a prosecution witness at Buddy Martin's trial and implicated his fellow gunman. Both Martin and Paul Gilly, who was tried in February 1972, were convicted and faced three death sentences for murdering the Yablonskis in their beds.

Annette Gilly Confesses

Bargaining her way out of the electric chair, Annette Gilly pleaded guilty and confessed that she and her father had arranged Jock Yablonski's murder at the request of UMW officer William Prater. The ailing Silous Huddleston also confessed and pleaded guilty. Huddleston told the FBI that he and Prater were told to kill Yablonski by Albert Pass, secretary-treasurer of the UMW and a member of the union's national executive board.

As the conspiracy unfolded, the evidence began to point toward the union leadership. But Tony Boyle had more immediate legal problems. In March 1972, he was found guilty of making illegal political contributions with union funds. In May, the results of the 1969 union election were overturned. Boyle lost his bid for re-election. In June, the same month that the U.S. Supreme Court declared the death penalty unconstitutional as it was then applied in most states, Boyle was sentenced to two concurrent five-year prison terms and fined heavily. A month later, as Boyle planned his appeal, Prater and Pass were indicted for murder.

William Prater came to trial in March 1973. Still unsentenced and facing three life terms, gunman Paul Gilley testified for the prosecution. He said that Prater had arranged and paid for Yablonski's murder, allegedly on Boyle's orders. Retired miners testified that they had kicked back their pay from a nonexistent union "Research & Information" committee to Prater. The jury was convinced that this $20,000 was used to pay for Yablonski's death. William Prater was convicted on three counts of murder.

Former UMW head Tony Boyle en route to a pre-trial hearing on murder charges in the death of Jock Yablonski. (AP/Wide World Photos)

Albert Pass was tried two months later. In addition to the prosecution's array of forensics experts, manipulated pensioners, confessed killers, and handlers of the blood money, prosecutor Sprague called Prater, who had decided to confess at the urging of his family. The witness implicated Pass, who had told Prater to organize the killing and had paid Silous Huddleston when the plot was in motion. The jury found Albert Pass guilty on three counts of murder.

Unlike other conspirators, Pass did not aid investigators after his conviction, but the case was not dead. On September 6, 1973, Tony Boyle was arrested for instigating the Yablonski murders. Before he could be extradited to Pennsylvania for trial, however, Boyle swallowed an overdose of sedatives. and nearly died. He recovered in the protective custody of a District of Columbia prison hospital, charged with the federal crime of violating Yablonski's civil rights, but still unarraigned on Pennsylvania's charge of murder.

Boyle Balks on Arraignment

On December 20, U.S. marshals attempted to bring Boyle to Pennsylvania for arraignment. Boyle refused to leave his bed and fainted when the marshals tried to force him to his feet. The marshals returned the next day and physically removed the furious old man from his bed. They flew him to Pennsylvania, where he was formally charged, sitting in a wheelchair and still wearing his hospital pajamas. Boyle pleaded not guilty and was sent on his way to a Missouri federal prison to begin his sentence for election fraud.

A change of venue brought Boyle's trial into an eastern Pennsylvania court, far from the coal field region where the Yablonskis had lived, with Judge Francis J. Catania presiding. When the trial began in the spring of 1974, Boyle's attorney, Charles F. Moses, tried to stanch the testimony creeping toward his client by suggesting that Prater and Huddleston had killed Yablonski to hide their embezzlement of union funds.

Testimony by the same witnesses who had appeared at earlier trials laid out the prosecution's case. The chain now extended from the triggermen to Prater, who said that Boyle had visited him in prison and told him to "stick to your story, even if you are convicted."

Even more striking than the now-familiar machinery of the plot was a new witness directly linking Boyle to the murders. The FBI had arrested and secured the cooperation of UMW official William Turnblazer, who recalled standing in a hallway outside the UMW, executive boardroom with Boyle and Pass on June 23, 1969, six months before the union election.

"We're in a fight," Turnblazer quoted Boyle as saying. "We've got to kill Yablonski or take care of him."

Pass, Turnblazer testified, accepted the job. Turnblazer also explained that Pass gave him printed minutes of an executive board meeting at which the "R&I" group was discussed, thus fraudulently documenting the existence of the bogus committee formed to pay for the murders.

On the stand, Tony Boyle protested that he had authorized the union to offer a $50,000 reward for the conviction of the killers of his "very close friend" Yablonski. Boyle claimed that he had seen Prater in prison only at the urging of Prater's attorney, H. David Rothman, who was concerned about his client's health. Boyle recalled that both his own lawyer and Rothman were present during the encounter, which took place outside Prater's cell and lasted less than 10 minutes.

Boyle denied ever seeing the minutes discussing the R&I committee. He denied meeting Turnblazer and Pass in the corridor outside the executive board room after the June 23 meeting, when the order to kill was allegedly given. When Boyle stepped down, three former UMW board members testified that Boyle left the meeting by a side door that night and had never even entered the hallway.

Boyle's Secretary Spoils Defense

Boyle's defense was gutted by the final prosecution witnesses. Boyle's secretary testified that the union reward for Yablonski's killers was her idea. She had proposed a $100,000 sum, but Boyle cut the amount in half. The secretary also explained that there was no side door by which the union president could have avoided the corridor after the June 23 conference.

Attorney Rothman testified that the prison meeting with his client, William Prater, was Boyle's idea. Rothman recalled Boyle and Prater talking for about 20 minutes, alone. Finally, prosecutor Sprague called Charles Groenthal, an FBI fingerprint expert. Sprague handed the agent the minutes discussing the R&I committee and asked if Groenthal had identified a print found on one of its pages.

"Yes, sir, I did," answered the FBI expert. "It was the thumbprint of Mr. Boyle."

Like the conspirators who had carried out his wishes, Tony Boyle was found guilty on three counts of murder. His sentence was the final blow to the corrupt union hierarchy he had sought to preserve by having Jock Yablonski murdered. Boyle died in 1985 while serving three consecutive life terms in a Pennsylvania prison.

— *Thomas C. Smith*

Suggestions for Further Reading

Armbrister, Trevor. *Act of Vengeance*. New York: E.P. Dutton, 1975.

Finley, Joseph E. *The Corrupt Kingdom*. New York: Simon & Schuster, 1972.

Franklin, Ben A. "Case of the Persistent Prosecutor." *New York Times* (September 9, 1973): 2.

Lewis, Arthur H. *Murder By Contract*. New York: Macmillan, 1975.

U.S. v. Nixon: 1974

Plaintiff: United States **Defendant:** President Richard M. Nixon
Plaintiff Claims: That the president had to obey a subpoena ordering him to
turn over tape recordings and documents relating to his conversations with
aides and advisers concerning the Watergate break-in
Chief Defense Lawyer: James D. St. Clair
Chief Lawyers for Plaintiff: Leon Jaworski and Philip A. Lacovara
Justices: Harry A. Blackmun, William J. Brennan, Warren E. Burger, William
O. Douglas, Thurgood Marshall, Lewis F. Powell, Jr., Potter Stewart, and
Byron R. White. William A. Rehnquist recused himself from the case.
Place: Washington, D.C. **Date of Decision:** July 24, 1974
Decision: President Nixon was ordered to turn over the tapes and other
documents to the prosecutors

SIGNIFICANCE

The President is not immune from judicial process, and must turn over evidence
subpoenaed by the courts. The doctrine of executive privilege entitles the president to a high degree of confidentiality if the evidence involves matters of national
security or other sensitive information, but the President cannot withhold evidence.

By the Spring of 1974, the government investigation into the Watergate
break-in and the subsequent coverup was moving fullsteam ahead. Despite
President Richard M. Nixon's repeated denials, it was becoming increasingly
clear to Congress and the public that senior Nixon administration officials, and
probably Nixon himself, had been actively involved in the coverup. On March 1,
1974, a 19-person federal grand jury indicted Attorney General John N. Mitchell
for conspiracy to obstruct justice, and the proceeding was entitled *U.S. v.
Mitchell*. Six other persons, all senior Nixon administration officials employed in
the White House or the Committee to Re-Elect the President (CREEP), were
indicted as co-conspirators: Charles W. Colson, John D. Ehrlichman, H.R.
Haldeman, Robert C. Mardian, Kenneth W. Parkinson, and Gordon Strachan.
Nixon also was included but as an unindicted co-conspirator.

On April 18, 1974, Special Prosecutor Leon Jaworski, charged with the
responsibility of conducting the Watergate investigation for the government,

went to Judge John Sirica of the U.S. District Court for the District of Columbia. In response to Jaworski's request, Sirica issued a subpoena ordering Nixon to produce "certain tapes, memoranda, papers, transcripts, or other writings" related to the specific meetings and conversations detailed in the subpoena. The material was to be turned over by May 2, 1974, for use in the trial, scheduled for September 9, 1974. Jaworski was able to identify the time, place, and persons present at these discussions because he already possessed the White House daily logs and appointment records.

Nixon Fights Subpoena

Nixon turned over edited transcripts of 43 conversations, which included portions of 20 conversations named in the subpoena, on April 30, 1974. On May 1, however, Nixon's attorney, James D. St. Clair, went to Sirica and asked that the subpoena be quashed. Nixon had hoped that the transcripts, which had been publicly released, would satisfy the court's and the public's demand for information without turning over the tapes. Nixon was wrong: Sirica denied St. Clair's motion on May 20, 1974. Sirica ordered "the President or any subordinate officer, official, or employee with custody or control of the documents or objects subpoenaed" to turn them over to the court by May 31, 1974.

On May 24, 1974, a week before Sirica's deadline, St. Clair filed an appeal to the U.S. Court of Appeals for the District of Columbia Circuit. Both sides realized, however, that the critical legal issue of whether the courts could subject the President to subpoenas and other forms of judicial process would ultimately have to be decided by the U.S. Supreme Court. Further, both sides were acutely aware of the political stakes and were anxious to avoid lengthy litigation. Therefore, on May 24, 1974, Jaworski took the highly unusual step of asking the Supreme Court to grant "*certiorari* before judgment," namely to take the case without waiting for the court of appeals to make a decision. The effect of bypassing the court of appeals would be to get a fast and final decision from the Supreme Court, and on June 6, 1974, St. Clair also requested *certiorari* before judgment.

On June 15, 1974, the Supreme Court granted Jaworski's and St. Clair's requests and decided to take the case from the court of appeals. St. Clair represented Nixon, and Jaworski was assisted by Philip A. Lacovara for the government. The case was argued before Supreme Court Justices Harry A. Blackmun, William J. Brennan, Warren E. Burger, William O. Douglas, Thurgood Marshall, Lewis F. Powell, Jr., Potter Stewart, and Byron R. White in Washington, D.C. on July 8, 1974. Justice William A. Rehnquist, a Nixon appointee to the court, recused himself from the case.

There is a popular notion that the judicial system, especially the Supreme Court, is above politics. This is a myth. When Jaworski and Lacovara went into the Supreme Court building on July 8, there were hundreds of cheering spectators on the steps. The justices themselves were obviously very involved as well, and grilled both sides during the oral argument. Justice Lewis Powell questioned Nixon's claim that the tapes had to be kept secret to protect the public interest:

> Mr. St. Clair, what public interest is there in preserving secrecy with respect to a criminal conspiracy?

St. Clair responded lamely:

> The answer, sir, is that a criminal conspiracy is criminal only after it's proven to be criminal.

The government's attorneys were questioned thoroughly as well, particularly on the issue of whether the grand jury set a dangerous precedent by naming the president as a co-conspirator when the prosecutors hadn't even requested an indictment. In response to Justice Powell's concerns, Lacovara stated:

> Grand Juries usually are not malicious. Even prosecutors cannot be assumed to be malicious. . . . I submit to you, sir, that just as in this case a Grand Jury would not lightly accuse the President of a crime, so, too, the fear that, perhaps without basis, some Grand Jury somewhere might maliciously accuse a President of a crime is not necessarily a reason for saying that a Grand Jury has no power to do that.

The Supreme Court issued its decision on July 24, 1974, less than three weeks later. During the intervening time, the justices struggled to write an opinion on which all eight of them could agree. Although Supreme Court justices are free to dissent as they see fit, they wanted a unanimous decision in this case because of the important issues at stake concerning the relationship between the executive and the judiciary. A split decision would weaken the impact of the Court's decision. Although Burger was the chief justice and nominally in charge of writing the opinion, in fact, all eight justices wrote or contributed to portions of the decision.

Nixon Ordered to Release Tapes

After dispensing with some initial procedural issues, the court went to the main issue, namely whether the president was cloaked with immunity from judicial process under the doctrine called "executive privilege." First, the Court restated the principle of *Marbury v. Madison* (see separate entry) that "it is emphatically the province and duty of the judicial department to say what the law is:"

> [Notwithstanding] the deference each branch must accord the others, the judicial power of the United States vested in the federal courts by Article III, section 1, of the Constitution can no more be shared with the Executive Branch than the Chief Executive, for example, can share with the Judiciary the veto power, or the Congress share with the Judiciary the power to override a Presidential veto. Any other conclusions would be contrary to the basic concept of separation of powers and the checks and balances that flow from the scheme of a tripartite government. We therefore reaffirm that it is the province and the duty of this Court to say what the law is with respect to the claim of privilege presented in this case.

Richard Nixon leaving the White House after his resignation. (Official White House photo.)

Next, the court addressed Nixon's two principal arguments in favor of executive privilege. First, St. Clair argued that for the presidency to function, conversations and other communications between high government officials and their advisors had to be kept confidential. Otherwise, if every statement could be made public, advisors would be reluctant to speak freely, and the decision-making process would suffer. Second, St. Clair argued that the very nature of the doctrine of separation of powers gave the President judicial immunity. In rejecting both arguments, the Court stated that while confidentiality was important, it could be maintained by letting a judge review evidence *in camera*, namely alone in his or her chambers:

> The President's need for complete candor and objectivity from advisers calls for great deference from the courts. However, when the privilege depends solely on the broad, undifferentiated claim of public interest in the confidentiality of such conversations, a confrontation with other values arises. Absent a claim of need to protect military, diplomatic, or sensitive national security secrets, we find it difficult to accept the argument that even the very important interest in confidentiality of Presidential communications is significantly diminished by production of such material for in camera inspection with all the protection that a District Court will be obliged to provide.

Further, the court stressed that recognizing Nixon's broad claim of executive privilege could seriously compromise the judicial system's obligation to assure the dispensation of justice in criminal trials:

> The impediment that an absolute, unqualified privilege would place in the way of the primary constitutional duty of the Judicial Branch to do justice in criminal prosecutions would plainly conflict with the function of the courts under Article III [of the Constitution]. . . . In this case the President challenges a subpoena served on him as a third party requiring the production of materials for use in a criminal prosecution; he does so on the claim that he has a privilege against disclosure of confidential communications. He does not place his claim of privilege on the ground they are military or diplomatic secrets.

Given that Nixon had not asserted any specific reason why the courts should not have the tapes in the *U.S. v. Mitchell* trial, the justices ordered Nixon to turn them over to Judge Sirica for in camera inspection.

Ordering a president to do something is one thing; enforcing that order is another. The judicial branch is a co-equal branch of government, but as one of the framers of the Constitution commented, it "possesses neither sword nor purse," meaning that it is without the military power of the executive branch or the taxing power of the legislative branch. The judiciary depends ultimately on its stature and public respect for the democratic system for enforcement of its orders. During oral argument, St. Clair had hinted darkly that Nixon "had his obligations under the Constitution," leaving it unclear whether Nixon would obey the Court's order to turn over the tapes to Sirica.

Nixon was in San Clemente, California, when he received word of the Supreme Court's unanimous decision from his aide, Alexander Haig. Within a day, however, Nixon issued a public statement that he would comply with the Court's order. The relevant part of Nixon's statement was:

While I am, of course, disappointed in the result, I respect and accept the court's decision, and I have instructed Mr. St. Clair to take whatever measures are necessary to comply with that decision in all respects.

Nixon turned over 64 tapes to Sirica, some of which included highly incriminating conversations between Nixon and his aides shortly after the Watergate break-in. Congress was ready to impeach him, and Nixon realized that his presidency was doomed. On August 8, 1974, Nixon announced his resignation and Vice President, Gerald Ford became president at noon on August 9, the effective date of the resignation. Because Ford later exercised his power to pardon Nixon, Nixon never stood trial. Nevertheless, the case established an important precedent, namely that if there is any executive privilege, it does not permit the president to withhold evidence needed by the courts. Finally, the case sounded the death knell for the political career of Richard Nixon, who had formerly been one of America's most popular and successful presidents.

— Stephen G. Christianson

Suggestions for Further Reading

Ball, Howard. *"We Have a Duty": the Supreme Court and the Watergate Tapes Litigation.* New York: Greenwood Press, 1990.

Berger, Raoul. *Executive Privilege: a Constitutional Myth.* Cambridge, Mass.: Harvard University Press, 1974.

Carlson, Margaret. "Notes from Underground: a Fresh Batch of White House Tapes Reminds a Forgiving and Forgetful America Why Richard Nixon Resigned in Disgrace." *Time* (June 17, 1991): 27–28.

Doyle, James. *Not Above the Law: the Battles of Watergate Prosecutors Cox and Jaworski: a Behind the Scenes Account.* New York: William Morrow & Co., 1977.

Friedman, Leon. *United States v. Nixon: the President Before the Supreme Court.* New York: Chelsea House Publishers, 1974.

Jaworski, Leon. *The Right and the Power: the Prosecution of Watergate.* New York: Reader's Digest Press, 1976.

Woodward, Bob. *The Brethren: Inside the Supreme Court.* New York: Simon & Schuster, 1979.

Joan Little Trial: 1975

Defendant: Joan Little **Crime Charged:** Murder

Chief Defense Lawyers: Jerry Paul, Morris Dees, Marvin Miller, Karen Galloway, James Gillespie, and Milton Williamson

Chief Prosecutors: William Griffin, John Wilkinson, and Lester Chalmers

Judge: Hamilton Hobgood **Place:** Raleigh, North Carolina

Dates of Trial: July 14–August 15, 1975 **Verdict:** Not guilty

SIGNIFICANCE

A mix of sex, race, murder, and unprecedented support for the defendant made this a trial of international notoriety. The trial was also one of the first in which "scientific" jury selection was used by defense lawyers to try to insure a favorable outcome.

At 4:00 A.M. on August 27, 1974, officers at the Beaufort County Jail in Washington, North Carolina discovered the body of guard Clarence Alligood in a cell. Nude from the waist down, he had been stabbed 11 times. His trousers were bunched up in his right hand. The fingers of his left hand enclosed an ice pick. The cell's occupant, Joan Little, age 20, had been serving a seven-year sentence for robbery; now she was gone. One week later she surrendered to authorities. The story she told made headlines. Little, a black woman, claimed that the 62-year-old white jailer had forced her into performing a sexual act, and that she had killed him in self-defense.

Even before her trial began July 14, 1975, Joan Little had achieved global celebrity. More than $60,000 in donations flooded in from around the world, enough to mount a prodigious defense. The leader of that six-person team was lawyer Jerry Paul. He was a believer in scientific jury selection and spent much of that hefty defense fund on psychological profiles to determine which juror was likely to be sympathetic and which wasn't. A revolutionary concept at that time, it only heightened public interest in the case, but as the process dragged on into its second week, Judge Hamilton Hobgood's impatience began to show. Paul protested:

> I don't intend to sit or stand here and see an innocent person go to jail. . . . You can threaten me with contempt or anything else, but it does not worry me.

Advised that his outburst could result in a jail term, Paul attempted to soft-pedal his rhetoric during the remainder of proceedings. To no avail. At trial's end, he was given 14 days for contempt.

Sexual Advance Prompts Killing

When the state commenced its case, prosecutor William Griffin argued that Little had deliberately instigated the incident, seducing Alligood, then killing him when she saw her chance to escape. When jail employee Beverly King testified that nothing in Alligood's demeanor that night indicated that he had sex in mind, deputy defense counsel Morris Dees became belligerent. Over repeated warnings from the bench, Dees pressed King on this issue. During a lunch recess he even approached her. The two were seen in earnest conversation. When court resumed, Judge Hobgood demanded to know the nature of this conversation. Sheepishly, Dees admitted exhorting King to repudiate her testimony, a flagrant impropriety that resulted in his expulsion from the trial.

Why Dees felt the need to adopt such tactics is unfathomable: the defense had a strong case. Three former inmates of Beaufort County Jail testified that Alligood often sexually molested the female prisoners. One, Rosa Robertson, claimed to have attempted suicide rather than yield to Alligood's advances, although it was later established that the suicide bid was half-hearted, to say the least.

Joan Little received unprecedented support during her trial from her attorney William Kunstler. (Archive Photos)

Next came Joan Little's testimony.

In the 12 months between crime and trial she had been entirely reshaped by her lawyers. Gone was the promiscuous, street-wise tough girl. In her place was a well-groomed and demure young woman. She told how Alligood had come to her cell. "He said that he had been nice to me and that it was time that I be nice to him." Under guidance from Paul, Little described what happened next.

> He started to take off his shoes outside the corridor . . . he started in towards the cell and I backed off to the back wall . . . he just started taking off his pants . . . I told him no, I wasn't going to do nothing like that . . . he tried to force me towards him . . . that's when I noticed that he had a ice pick in his hand.

Then, Little claimed, Alligood forced her to her knees and made her commit a sexual act. During this act Alligood let go of the ice pick. A struggle broke out. "I got to the pick first," said Little. She struck Alligood several unthinking, unaimed blows with the pick, then ran from the cell.

A Quick Acquittal

It didn't take long for prosecutor Griffin to isolate the weak spots in Little's testimony. How had the ice pick, an item normally kept in an outer office, suddenly materialized in Alligood's hand? She didn't know. How was she able to fight off Alligood? "He was a big man, wasn't he?"

"Yes," admitted Little.

Griffin pushed harder. Why had she not screamed? Why no attempt to fight back? Why, when Alligood was removing his trousers, had she not attempted to escape his clutches then? Little's answers were inconclusive but not incriminating. Nothing she said was inconsistent with her version of events in the cell.

One of the jurors, when the verdict was in, commented, "I thought about it . . . and I decided that these people [the prosecution] hadn't shown me anything to convict her," a sentiment echoed by fellow jurors. After less than 90 minutes of reflection, they found Little not guilty.

Following acquittal, Little was returned to prison to finish her seven-year robbery sentence. On October 15, 1977, she again escaped, but was recaptured and finished out her term. She resurfaced briefly in 1989 when she spent a night in jail on stolen property charges which were later dropped.

There was something in this case for everyone: civil rights activists, church groups, feminists. All made capital from what was a unique situation.

—*Colin Evans*

Suggestions for Further Reading

Harwell, Fred. *A True Deliverance*. New York: Alfred A. Knopf, 1979.

Jet (March 20, 1989): 37.

Reston, James, Jr. *The Innocence of Joan Little*. New York: Bantam, 1977.

In the Matter of Karen Ann Quinlan: 1975

Plaintiff: Joseph T. Quinlan **Defendant:** St. Clare's Hospital
Plaintiff Claim: That doctors at St. Clare's Hospital should obey Mr. Quinlan's instructions to disconnect his comatose daughter from her respirator and allow her to die **Chief Defense Lawyers:** Ralph Porzio (for Karen Quinlan's physicians), Theodore Einhorn (for the hospital), New Jersey State Attorney General William F. Hyland, and Morris County Prosecutor Donald G. Collester, Jr. **Chief Lawyers for Plaintiff:** Paul W. Armstrong and James Crowley **Judge:** Robert Muir, Jr. **Place:** Morristown, New Jersey **Date of Decision:** November 10, 1975 **Decision:** Denied Mr. Quinlan the right to authorize termination of "life-assisting apparatus" and granted Karen Quinlan's physicians the right to continue medical treatment over the objections of the Quinlan family. Overturned by the New Jersey Supreme Court, which, on March 31, 1976, ruled that Karen's "right of privacy" included a right to refuse medical treatment and that her father, under the circumstances, could assume this right in her stead.

SIGNIFICANCE

This case prompted the adoption of "brain death" as the legal definition of death in some states and the adoption of laws recognizing "living wills" and the "right to die" in other states, as well as the formation of "bioethics" committees in many hospitals. In 1985, the New Jersey Supreme Court ruled that *all* life-sustaining medical treatment—including artificial feeding—could be withheld from incompetent, terminally ill patients, provided such action was shown to be consistent with the afflicted person's past wishes.

On April 15, 1975, 21-year-old Karen Ann Quinlan passed out and lapsed into a coma after sustaining bruises which were never satisfactorily explained and ingesting tranquilizers "in the therapeutic range" with alcohol. Unable to breathe on her own, she was placed on a respirator.

By the following autumn, Quinlan's family and doctors had given up hope of recovery. Her parents, Julia and Joseph Quinlan, were devout Roman Catholics. The Quinlans consulted their parish priest, Father Thomas Trapasso, and were told that they could, in good conscience, request that Karen be removed from the respirator. The request was made, but Karen's primary physician, Dr. Robert Morse, refused to end the artificial support. Joseph Quinlan went to court.

By the time the trial began on October 20, 1975, a lawyer, Daniel R. Coburn, had become the court-appointed guardian for Karen Quinlan and both Morris County Prosecutor Donald G. Collester, Jr., and State Attorney General William F. Hyland had intervened, or joined the case, in an attempt to uphold New Jersey's homicide statutes. During pretrial interviews, Attorney General Hyland had portrayed the case as a challenge to New Jersey's long-standing definition of death as the "cessation of vital signs" and one which could result in a new definition based on "cerebral" or "brain death."

The week before the trial, however, it was disclosed that Karen Quinlan did not have a "flat" electroencephalograph, a medical test which would have been evidence of a complete absence of brain-wave activity. She also was capable of breathing on her own for short, irregular periods and had occasionally shown muscle activity which some doctors had described as voluntary. It immediately became clear that the trial would not center on New Jersey's definition of death but on an even more complicated question of whether Karen Quinlan had a "right to die."

Accepted Standards vs. Right to Die

Karen Quinlan's neurologist, Dr. Robert Morse, was the first person to testify. He acknowledged that there was virtually no chance that Quinlan would resume a "cognitive, functional existence." However, he said he saw no medical precedent for disconnecting Quinlan from her respirator and said he would not obey a court order to do so. Dr. Arshad Jarved, Quinlan's pulmonary internist, also had refused to act on Joseph Quinlan's request; he also testified that accepted standards of medical practice did not permit the removal of the respirator.

The Quinlans' attorney, Paul Armstrong, argued that the rights of privacy and religious freedom included a right to die. He explained his clients' religious view that the respirator was keeping their daughter from God and heaven: "[T]he earthly phase of Karen Quinlan's life has drawn to a close and she should not be held back from enjoyment of a better, more perfect life."

Karen Quinlan's court-appointed guardian, Daniel Coburn, saw the matter differently: "This isn't a terminal cancer case where someone is going to die. Where there is hope, you cannot just extinguish a life because it becomes an eyesore."

The following day, Armstrong called as an expert witness Dr. Julius Korein, a neurologist at Bellevue hospital and New York University Medical School. He described Karen Quinlan—by now weighing only 75 pounds—as having signs of severe higher brain disfunction. He testified that she had only "stereotyped" responses, such as blinking or rolling her eyes, to stimuli. "This pattern of reactions," he said, "could, in no way, in my opinion, be related to conscious activity." Dr. Korein also described "an accepted but not spoken-of law," according to which physicians withheld aggressive, invasive treatment from patients who were, for example, "riddled with cancer and in pain." He added: "That is the unwritten law and one of the purposes of this trial is to make it the written law."

Then an emotional Joseph Quinlan then took the stand and asked the court: "Take her from the machine and the tubes and let her pass into the hands of the Lord."

Julia and Joseph Quinlan with a photo of their daughter Karen Ann. (AP/ Wide World Photos)

On the third day, Karen's mother, Julia Ann Quinlan, testified that Karen had made her wishes known on three occasions, saying, "Mommy, please don't ever let them keep me alive by extraordinary means." The statements were made, Mrs. Quinlan said, when two of Karen's friends and an aunt finally died after long battles with cancer. "Karen loved life, and if there was any way that she could not live life to the fullest she wanted to be able to die in her own surroundings, instead of being kept alive for months or years. I visit her every day and as I see her in her present condition I know in my heart as a mother she would not want to be there. We discussed this many times."

Although the defense lawyers objected to such hearsay evidence, Judge Robert Muir, Jr., permitted Karen's sister and one of her friends to give similar testimony. Judge Muir declined, however, to permit a Roman Catholic priest to give expert testimony regarding the church's view of extraordinary medical intervention. "It is not my role to weigh the merits of what a person believes," he explained. "It is enough that I am convinced he has these beliefs."

On October 23, three neurologists—Dr. Fred Plum of the American Association of Neurologists, Dr. Sidney Diamond of Mount Sinai Hospital, and Dr. Stuart Cook of the New Jersey College of Medicine and Dentistry—gave expert medical testimony. The three concurred that Karen Quinlan's lack of higher brain function was "irreversible" and "irreparable." However, all three agreed that Quinlan was alive by both legal and medical definitions and that it would be improper to remove the respirator.

Decision is Appealed

On November 10, 1975, Judge Muir rendered his decision. He refused permission for the removal of the respirator and appointed Daniel R. Coburn to continue acting as the guardian of Karen's "person." Joseph Quinlan was appointed guardian of his daughter's property. Rejecting the Quinlans' plea that their daughter be allowed to pass into life after death, Muir wrote that disconnecting the respirator "is not something in her best interest, in a temporal sense, and it is in a temporal sense that I must operate, whether I believe in life after death or not. The single most important temporal quality that Karen Ann Quinlan has is life," he continued. "This Court will not authorize that life to be taken away from her."

On November 17, 1975, the Quinlans filed an appeal, which the New Jersey Supreme agreed to hear on an "accelerated schedule."

On January 26, 1976, during a three-hour session, the case was argued before the seven justices of New Jersey's highest court. Their unanimous decision-naming Joseph Quinlan guardian and authorizing him to order removal of the respirator—was rendered on March 31. Chief Justice Richard J. Hughes wrote the opinion. He specifically stated that the ruling was not based on the freedom of religion argument favored by the Quinlans: "Simply stated, the right to religious beliefs is absolute but conduct in pursuance therefore is not wholly immune from governmental restraint."

Instead, Chief Justice Hughes cited the Supreme Court's decision in the *Griswold v. Connecticut* birth-control case and based the decision on "Karen's right to privacy." It was a right, he continued, that could "be asserted on her behalf by her guardian under the peculiar circumstances here present."

Lastly, Justice Hughes dismissed the attorney general's and the Morris County prosecutor's contentions that the person removing Quinlan's respirator should be charged with homicide upon her death:

> [T]he exercise of a constitutional right, such as we here find, is protected from criminal prosecution. We do not question the state's undoubted power to punish the taking of human life, but that power does not encompass individuals terminating medical treatment pursuant to their right of privacy.

Neither the hospital, Karen Quinlan's physicians, nor the State of New Jersey chose to appeal the decision to the Supreme Court. Quinlan's respirator was removed in May 1976. She managed to breathe on her own and remained in a coma for 10 more years. She died on June 11, 1985.

—Kathryn Cullen-DuPont

Suggestions for Further Reading

Colen, B.D. *Karen Ann Quinlan*. New York: Nash, 1976.

New York Times: September 14, 16, 17, 20, 22, 23, 24, 25, 26, 28, 1975; October 1, 3, 8, 10, 11, 12, 13, 14, 15, 18, 19, 20, 21, 22, 23, 24, 25, 26, 27, 28, 1975; November 2, 5, 8, 9, 11, 12, 16, 18, 21, 23, 25, 26, 28, 29, 1975; December 7, 12, 17, 18, 19, 22, 1975; January 19, 26, 27, 1976; February 25, 1976; March 9, 1976; April 1, 2, 7, 8, 9, 10, 12, 13, 1976; May 2, 6, 7, 22, 24, 25, 26, 27, 28, 29, 30, 1976; June 12, 1985.

Quinlan, Joseph. *Karen Ann: The Quinlans Tell Their Story*. Garden City, N.Y.: Doubleday & Co., 1977.

Patty Hearst Trial: 1976

Defendant: Patricia C. Hearst   **Crimes Charged:** Bank robbery and use of a firearm in the commission of a felony   **Chief Defense Attorneys:** F. Lee Bailey and J. Albert Johnson   **Chief Prosecutor:** James L. Browning, Jr.   **Judge:** Oliver J. Carter   **Place:** San Francisco, California   **Dates of Trial:** February 4–March 20, 1976   **Verdict:** Guilty   **Sentence:** 7 years imprisonment

SIGNIFICANCE

Observers expected Patty Hearst's trial to illuminate how—or if—a young woman from one of America's wealthiest families was transformed by her own kidnappers into a gun-wielding revolutionary dedicated to provoking a violent class war. Shifting public sympathies resulted in a campaign to obtain a presidential commutation of her sentence.

February 4, 1974, Patricia Hearst was a wealthy apolitical college student living with her fiancé in Berkeley, California. That night she was abducted screaming from their apartment at gunpoint, dressed in her bathrobe. Three days later her abductors released a tape in which Hearst told her parents she was being well-treated. It was accompanied by a message from "General Field Marshall-Cinque" of the Symbionese Liberation Army (SLA).

Before the Hearst kidnapping, little was known about the SLA, a small but violent group on the fringe of radical leftist politics. In November 1973, they killed Dr. Marcus Foster, the superintendent of schools for Oakland, California. The SLA declared that Hearst was a "prisoner of war" to be ransomed for the release of Joseph Remiro and Russell Little, who were charged with murdering Foster. "Field Marshall Cinque"—an escaped convict named Donald De Freeze—demanded their release. As a gesture of "good faith," the SLA demanded that the Hearst family first distribute $70 worth of food to every needy person in California.

Remiro and Little would not be released. Hearst's father, Randolph, chairman of the Hearst media empire, offered to distribute $2 million worth of food to the poor, with another $4 million to follow his daughter's safe release. The first distribution resulted in a near riot as crowds fought to get food from trucks.

Patty Becomes Tania

Two months after her abduction, Patty Hearst announced in a new tape that she had joined the SLA and taken the name "Tania." The message was accompanied by a photograph of Hearst posing with a gun before a poster of the SLA symbol, a seven-headed cobra. Her parents skeptically replied that all the tapes were made under duress.

On April 15, two bystanders were wounded during an armed robbery of the Hibernia Bank in San Francisco. One robber announced to the terrified customers and automatic bank cameras that she was "Tania . . . Patricia Hearst." In a tape released a week later, she said that she had willingly taken part in the robbery.

Federal arrest warrants were issued for eight SLA members. The FBI chose to seek Hearst's capture only as a "material witness" to the holdup. Yet suspicion that she had indeed joined her captors was voiced by U.S. Attorney General William Saxbe, who declared that Hearst "was not a reluctant participant" in the robbery and was thus "a common criminal."

The Hearst family was outraged by Saxbe's comments, but the transformation of Patty Hearst from victim to outlaw in the public mind had begun. It was bolstered May 16 when she fired an automatic weapon from a van, enabling SLA members Bill and Emily Harris to escape a security guard at Mel's Sporting Goods store in Los Angeles. Teenager Tom Matthews told police that his van was then hijacked by the escaping Harrises and Hearst, who told him openly of her part in the bank holdup.

The "wanted" poster for Patty Hearst. (Courtesy of the FBI)

The next day Los Angeles police surrounded a small house commandeered by SLA members. As viewers watched on live television, the ensuing gun battle turned the cottage into an inferno. Patricia Hearst was not among the six bodies found when the fire expired. Three weeks later, another Hearst tape surfaced in which she spoke of her love for Willie Wolfe, one of the dead SLA members. Nothing more was heard of her for 17 months.

Captured and Arrested

On September 18, 1975, FBI agents captured Hearst in San Francisco. Instead of being freed, she was arrested for the Hibernia Bank robbery and hustled off to jail to undergo the first of many psychiatric examinations.

Hearst's parents hired F. Lee Bailey, a Boston, Massachusetts, attorney renowned for winning acquittals for the alleged "Boston Strangler" and accused wife-murderer Dr. Sam Sheppard. Bailey declared that for 20 months, Patty Hearst had been via "prisoner of war" whose actions were entirely governed by her desire to stay alive.

Hearst's trial began February 4, 1976, two years to the day after she had been kidnapped. No one disputed her presence at the Hibernia Bank heist. The jury's real task was to decide whether she had acted willingly. Bailey hoped to confine the trial to the circumstances of her kidnapping, her mistreatment by the SLA, and the robbery itself.

Prosecutor James Browning, Jr., was equally intent on establishing that Hearst's behavior before and after the holdup reflected her voluntary participation in the crime. When Browning began to question her about the "missing year"—the 17 months preceding her capture—Bailey objected. The jury was sent from the courtroom.

Bailey argued that Hearst's claims of willful participation in the robbery were made under duress and should not be admitted. Judge Oliver Carter denied the motion to suppress the government's intended evidence, ruling that "the statements made by the defendant after the happening of the bank robbery, whether by tape recording, or oral communication, or in writing, were made voluntarily." The ruling entitled the prosecution to introduce all the tapes, testimony by Tom Matthews and Mel's Sporting Goods employees, and a confiscated manuscript known as "The Tania Interview," in which Hearst spoke of her conversion to the SLA and denied being brainwashed.

Defendant Takes the Stand

The jury returned to the courtroom. Over her private objections, Bailey put his client on the stand to counter the coming flood of damaging testimony. Hearst described her violent abduction. For nearly two months, she had been bound, blindfolded, and confined in a dark closet, where she was sexually molested by Wolfe and De Freeze. She was constantly threatened, hectored with revolutionary rhetoric, and told that her parents had abandoned her by refusing the SLA's demands. After seeing the May 16 incident on television, she accepted her captors' claims that the FBI would kill her if they discovered her in a SLA hideout.

Hearst explained that SLA member Angela Atwood had written the text of the tape in which "Tania" declared her willing participation in the robbery. Bill Harris had ordered her to tell Tom Matthews about the Hibernia robbery. The Harrises, she said, also dictated the text of the "Tania Interview," which was to have been published to raise funds for the SLA.

Bailey argued that Hearst's actions and words resulted from a constant threat of death. Prosecutor Browning pressed her to explain why she had not taken advantage of numerous chances to escape, particularly during Bill Harris' botched shoplifting attempt at Mel's. She replied that she feared both the SLA and the FBI. Covering the Harrises' escape was a "reflex action" triggered by incessant drilling and the SLA's "codes of war," which stated that anyone who failed to use a weapon to help comrades escape was to be shot.

When Browning insisted that Hearst testify about her actions in "the missing year," the jury was sent from the room again. Bailey accused the prosecution of prodding Hearst to incriminate herself and leave herself open to prosecution in another case. Her only alternative would be to invoke the Fifth Amendment, possibly implying guilt. Browning replied that the Fifth Amendment was applicable only in discussing a crime. He had not suggested a crime had occurred.

Without speaking of it openly in court, each side was well aware of what the other was pursuing. A woman had been killed in a SLA bank robbery in Sacramento during the "missing year." Hearst had not been involved, but Bailey wanted the jury to hear no mention of it.

When Judge Carter allowed Hearst to claim the privilege against self-incrimination, it seemed as though Bailey had won the point. The victory turned out to apply only to the closed hearing. In his formal decision several days later, Judge Carter declared that he would allow questions about the "missing year." Over Bailey's loud objections, the judge ruled that Hearst had waived her right not to testify about the period by taking the stand and talking about events at both ends of the disputed 17 months.

The jury returned to the courtroom. As Browning's questions began, Bailey stood beside Hearst, instructing her not to answer. The Sacramento robbery was not mentioned, but the jury heard Hearst refuse to answer 42 prosecution questions implying her intimate involvement with the SLA. Judge Carter instructed the jurors that they could draw inferences from her silence if they so wished.

Psychiatrists Testify of Brainwashing

Even Judge Carter appeared to doze off during the weeks of psychiatric analysis that followed. Bailey produced three psychiatric experts, who testified that Hearst's behavior was the result of brainwashing or "coercive persuasion" techniques like those used by Chinese Communists on American prisoners of war during the Korean War. Hearst's behavior was diagnosed to be consistent with the traumas she had suffered. The government called its own experts. One felt that Hearst had cooperated with the SLA voluntarily because she enjoyed her new-found notoriety. Another described her as a "rebel in search of a cause" before her kidnapping.

In his summation, Browning methodically cataloged every action that might indicate Hearst's sympathy with the SLA, from the gunfire at the sporting goods store to her possession of a Mexican trinket given to her by Willie Wolfe. The prosecutor found it incredible that she had not tried to escape during all of her time with the SLA. Bailey's final argument was brief and rambling by comparison.

The jury found Hearst guilty of robbery and use of a firearm in the commission of a felony. Judge Carter imposed preliminary maximum sentences for each crime, with a review contingent on the results of yet another psychiatric report. Before it began, Hearst's lung collapsed. The examinations resumed after her recovery. Psychiatrists pressed Hearst to state some remorse for her involvement in the robbery, but she refused, saying that her agreement to accompany the SLA to the bank was the only thing that stopped them from killing her. Under such circumstances, she maintained, she would do the same thing again. Ironically, the government sought and received Hearst's help in gathering information about the SLA, even as it was prosecuting her. She agreed to testify against the Harrises.

On September 24, 1976, after already serving more than a year in jail, Hearst was finally sentenced to seven years imprisonment. She was freed in November on $1.5 million bail pending the appeal of her robbery conviction. She pleaded "no contest" to charges of assault and robbery in the Mel's Sporting Goods incident and was released on probation because she posed no threat to the community.

She returned to prison more than a year later when the U.S. Supreme Court refused to hear her appeal. She changed lawyers. Her new attorney, George C. Martinez, filed motions in federal court, urging that her sentence be reduced to time served and that her conviction be overturned on the grounds that her former attorneys did not defend her adequately. Hearst accused Bailey of being preoccupied with his plans to write a lucrative book about her case.

Hearst has Groundswell of Support

A "Committee For the Release of Patricia Hearst" sent thousands of letters to President Jimmy Carter urging him to commute her sentence. U.S. Representative Leo Ryan of California circulated a petition on her behalf in Congress. It was signed by 48 members, who agreed that "never before in the history of our country has such a bizarre set of circumstances led to such a tragic result: a victim of a violent kidnapping participated in a bank robbery under the direction and motivation of her abductors."

In November 1978, all motions to reduce Hearst's sentence or to set aside the verdict on grounds of insufficiency of counsel were denied. Hearst remained in prison, maintaining her innocence and refusing to discuss parole because of its imputation of guilt.

President Jimmy Carter conditionally commuted Hearst's sentence on February 1, 1979. The White House declared that it was the consensus of all of those most familiar with this case that but for the extraordinary criminal and degrading experiences that the petitioner suffered as a victim of the SLA, she would not have become a participant in the criminal acts for which she stands convicted and sentenced and would not have suffered the punishment and other consequences she has endured.

— Thomas C. Smith

Suggestions for Further Reading

Alexander, Shana. *Anyone's Daughter: The Times and Trials of Patty Hearst.* New York: Viking Press, 1979.

Dershowitz, Alan M. *The Best Defense.* New York: Random House, 1982.

Hearst, Patricia Campbell with Alvin Moscow. *Every Secret Thing.* Garden City, N.Y.: Doubleday & Co., 1982.

Kohn, Howard and David Weir. "Tania's World." *Rolling Stone* (June 11, 1992): 100.

McLellan, Vin and Paul Avery. *The Voices of the Guns.* New York: G.P. Putnam's Sons, 1977.

Murray R. Gold Trials: 1976–92

Defendant: Murray R. Gold   **Crime Charged:** Murder
Chief Defense Lawyers: First and second trials: Victor Ferrante, William Kuntsler, Timothy Moynahan; Third trial: John Williams; Fourth trial: William Collins, Nicholas Serignese   **Chief Prosecutors:** John A. Connelly, Francis McDonald, Walter Scanlon, Marcia Smith   **Judges:** First trial: Robert A. Wall; Second trial: George A. Saden; Third trial: Charles D. Gill; Fourth trial: William Lavery   **Place:** Waterbury, Connecticut   **Dates of Trials:** First trial: February 17–March 31, 1976; Second trial: October 12–November 18, 1976; Third trial: January 8–March 5, 1985; Fourth trial: June 24–July 24, 1986
Verdicts: First trial: Mistrial (hung jury); Second trial: Guilty of first-degree murder; Third trial: Mistrial; Fourth trial: Guilty   **Sentences:** Second trial: 25 years imprisonment; Fourth trial: Two concurrent terms of 25 years to life

SIGNIFICANCE

The long trip of Murray Gold for well over a decade through the criminal courts shows what can happen when a mentally ill defendant fights the system. The facts of the case, many of them disputed by either the defendant or the prosecution, leave the observer to wonder whether Gold was indeed wrongfully accused and convicted.

Shortly after 9:00 P.M. on Thursday, September 26, 1974, Waterbury, Connecticut, police were called to the Fern Street home of 71-year-old attorney Irving Pasternak. They found Pasternak and his wife, Rhoda, dead—Irving stabbed 35 times, Rhoda 25 times. They found a bloodstained knife and bloody footprints bearing the trademark "Cat's Paw."

In the street, two women reported being nearly knocked down by a man "running like the devil and his long hair waving in the wind."

A Former Son-in-Law

Investigators suspected stockbroker Murray Gold, who lived in New York City and had been divorced 10 years earlier from the Pasternaks' daughter Barbara. Police found fresh cuts on two fingers of Gold's left hand. He said they occurred while scraping carrots. And Gold insisted he had spent the evening of the murders with his parents, who said he had been under psychiatric treatment and was paranoid. He was indicted for first-degree murder.

Following the trial's opening on February 17, 1976, prosecutor Francis McDonald called 41 witnesses. They presented circumstantial evidence: All Gold's shoes had Cat's Paw heels, he had had shock treatments in psychiatric hospitals seven months before the murders, his New York-licensed car had been seen parked early in the morning in the Pasternaks' neighborhood three days before the murders, and pieces of plastic found at the crime scene appeared to match a button-fastening kit in Gold's apartment.

Defense attorney William Kuntsler quickly proved the car had been seen three weeks (not three days) before the stabbings, while Murray was visiting his ex-wife's sister, Myrna, in hope of a reconciliation with Barbara. An expert defense witness testified that he could not make a positive identification or match of the plastic pieces.

Murray Gold (center) flanked by his lawyer Timothy Moynihan (right) and detective James Conway (left). (AP/Wide World Photos)

A Dead Culprit?

Kuntsler introduced the name Bruce Sanford, a dedicated Satanist whom Waterbury police and area psychiatric hospitals had long known for his penchant for violent crime. He had committed suicide in December 1974. Earlier that year, in a custody dispute with his ex-wife, Glorianna, over their five children, Sanford had become convinced that attorney Pasternak was advising her, and on the night of the murders Glorianna had infuriated him by ordering him out of her house. Kuntsler lined up a witness who could testify that Sanford threatened to "get Pasternak."

The prosecution objected. Testimony about a dead man would be hearsay. Judge Robert Wall overruled the objections, and a doctor testified that Sanford suffered from "a maladaptation taking the form of frequent acts of hostility." Another witness testified that Sanford said he was sorry he had to kill Mrs. Pasternak.

After deliberating for five days, the jury stood deadlocked. Judge Wall declared a mistrial.

Second Trial

At Trial II, beginning October 12, 1976, 55 prosecution witnesses testified to the circumstantial evidence. On cross-examination, an FBI expert on footprints admitted that the bloody heel print "was not made by any" of Gold's shoes. The defense then proved that in 1974 Cat's Paw had distributed 10,000 pairs of heels in Waterbury.

While prosecution and defense counsels were the same in Trial II as in Trial I, the judge was not. Unlike Judge Wall, Judge George Saden refused to admit testimony about Sanford's confession. The jury found Gold guilty of both murders in the first degree. He was sentenced to 25 years imprisonment.

Gold's parents hired attorney Louis Nizer to handle an appeal. Before Connecticut's Supreme Court, he argued that the judge should have let the jury hear the hearsay evidence of Sanford's confession. The law, he asserted, permitted a hearsay confession because the confessor could not be expected to make an untrue statement that might subject him to punishment for a crime.

The five-judge Supreme Court ordered a new trial.

". . . Waving in the Wind"

Prosecutor McDonald had Sanford's body exhumed, to see if Xrays showed Moreton's syndrome, a condition that would have made him walk with toes pointed outward—to be compared with crime-scene bloody footprints. The opened casket revealed Sanford's once-bald head covered by a woman's long-haired brown wig.

Testimony in Trial I had described Sanford wearing such a wig. The witnesses who had encountered the man running on Fern Street had described "his long hair waving in the wind."

On October 20, 1980, the Supreme Court of the United States, refusing to hear the case, upheld the Connecticut Supreme Court's decision. Prosecutor McDonald offered a "settlement" to Gold: He would be freed on the basis of time served and no third trial would be held if he would accept psychiatric treatment for one year, stay out of Connecticut, and plead guilty to a lesser charge.

Gold refused. He fired Nizer and hired Yale Law School professor John Williams. With Trial III underway, Williams cross-examined the witness who had seen Gold's car in the Pasternaks' neighborhood. He deftly destroyed her recollections of the man she had seen in the car. But Gold startled judge and jury by announcing, "I'll have to get myself another attorney."

Given several days to interview lawyers, Gold forced delays of the trial and demanded that some jurors be dismissed. Prosecutor Walter Scanlon moved for a hearing on Gold's competency to advise an attorney. On court orders, psychiatrist James Merikangas, M.D., examined Gold, finding him convinced "that there was a conspiracy against him and that his attorney was part of the conspiracy. . . . Mr. Gold suffers from paranoia which renders him presently incompetent to stand trial."

The doctor added that if Gold were treated in a mental institution for 18 months he would probably gain competency. More court-appointed psychiatrists agreed on Gold's incompetency. The judge declared a mistrial.

Found Competent

Following administration of the drug Navane, Gold was found competent by June 1986. Trial IV saw the prosecution witnesses again describe the crime scene, including 47 fingerprints. None, cross-examination revealed, were Gold's.

New defense lawyer William Collins called on Glorianna Sanford. Despite her testimony that her ex-husband had asked her on the morning after the murders to drive him to Florida, she seemed defiantly determined to clear him of suspicion of murder. As a defense witness, observers noted, she was an asset to the prosecution.

An emergency-room doctor testified on treating Sanford on the night of the murders for a self-inflicted superficial wound to the neck. Sanford's shirt, pants, and shoes, he testified, showed an "amount of blood excessive for the wound."

Long-time Sanford friend Patricia Morrison testified that he threatened to "get" Pasternak, and that he phoned her on the night of the murders to ask her to help him leave the state, saying he was covered with blood and had done something he could never get out of.

The jury deliberated for three days before finding Gold guilty of both murders in the first degree. He was sentenced to concurrent terms of no less than 25 years nor more than life. Imprisoned, he refused to appeal.

Habeas Corpus

Gold's attorneys petitioned for a writ of habeas corpus to reverse the verdict. Early in 1991, Superior Court Judge Howard Scheinblum heard psychiatrist Dr. Walter A. Borden, who had reviewed trial transcripts and interviewed Gold, conclude that "he is incompetent to stand trial [and] to take care of his person."

The defense tried to call Judge Lavery, who had presided over the fourth trial, to testify on his observations of Gold's demeanor during that trial, but Judge Scheinblum refused to put Lavery on the stand. Two medical experts testifying for the prosecution, however, admitted that three psychiatric reports had found Gold incompetent to stand the trial that brought his conviction.

On March 11, Judge Scheinblum ruled that Gold had not been legally competent during the fourth trial and "had not been afforded effective assistance of counsel" because the defense had "failed to take sufficient care to monitor and evaluate the petitioner's mental health during the course of the trial." The judge granted the writ of habeas corpus and a new trial.

The state appealed. On January 15, 1992, before the five-judge Supreme Court of Connecticut, Assistant State's Attorney James A. Killen argued that Judge Scheinblum had abused his discretion in refusing to allow the trial judge to testify in the habeas proceeding.

On June 9, 1992, the judges agreed, four to one, to reverse Judge Scheinblum's decision, remanding the Gold case for a new habeas corpus hearing. Three years later, on May 16, 1995, Waterbury Superior Court Judge Samuel J. Sferrazza, citing Gold's persistent refusal to appear in hearings and noting that the defense had not been presented in a diligent manner, dismissed Gold's petition for habeas corpus. Gold remained incarcerated.

—Bernard Ryan, Jr.

Suggestion for Further Reading

Nizer, Louis. *Catspaw: The Famed Trial Attorney's Heroic Defense of a Man Unjustly Accused*. New York: Fine, 1992.

Theodore Robert Bundy Trials: 1976 & 1979

Defendant: Theodore Robert Bundy **Crime Charged:** First Trial: Aggravated kidnapping; Second Trial: Murder **Chief Defense Lawyers:** First Trial: John O'Connell; Second trial: Robert Haggard, Edward Harvey, Margaret Good, and Lynn Thompson **Chief Prosecutors:** First Trial: David Yocum; Second Trial: Larry Simpson and Daniel McKeever **Judges:** First Trial: Stewart Hanson; Second Trial: Edward Cowart **Places:** First Trial: Salt Lake City, Utah; Second Trial: Miami, Florida **Dates of Trials:** February 23–March 1, 1976; June 25–July 31, 1979 **Verdict:** Guilty, both trials **Sentences:** First Trial: 1–15 years; Second Trial: death

SIGNIFICANCE

More than any other murderer, Ted Bundy both fascinated and horrified onlookers. Others have killed more, some killed more horribly, but for most Americans, this young man with the movie star appearance remains one of the most notorious. Often overshadowed by his grim charisma was the controversial testimony that eventually undid him. Bundy's ready smile might have been tailor-made for the cameras, but it proved lethal in the hands of those prosecutors determined to convict him.

Between 1969 and 1975 an unprecedented wave of sex-killings swept from California, through the Pacific Northwest, and into Utah and Colorado. All of the victims were strikingly similar—female, young, attractive, and generally with long hair parted in the middle. Some were found dumped in deserted areas, others were never seen again. As the various law enforcement agencies compared notes and suspects, one name kept cropping up: Ted Bundy, a handsome young Seattle, Washington, law student. But nothing could be proved.

And then on November 8, 1974, 18-year-old Salt Lake City, Utah, resident Carol DaRonch was tricked into entering a Volkswagen outside a shopping mall by a stranger claiming to be a police officer. When the man attempted to handcuff and bludgeon her, DaRonch managed to escape from the car. On August 16, 1975, a Salt Lake City police officer arrested a Volkswagen driver who had been acting suspiciously. Inside the car were a crowbar and handcuffs.

The driver turned out to be Ted Bundy. DaRonch identified him as her abductor, leading to charges of aggravated kidnapping.

Bundy Forgoes Jury

The biggest problem facing prosecutor Dave Yocum when Bundy's trial began February 23, 1976, was safeguarding against the possibility of a mistrial. By this time, speculation that Bundy was indeed a mass murderer had grown; any hint of that appearing in this case could bring about a reversal. Bundy opted to forgo trial by jury and put his fate in the hands of Judge Stewart Hanson. Virtually the entire prosecution case hinged on Carol DaRonch. Painfully shy, she gave her testimony, eyes fixed on the floor, a point not lost on Judge Hanson. By her own admission, DaRonch found it difficult to look people in the face. But when Yocum asked her, "Is that man in court today?" she answered, "Yes."

"Where is he seated?"

For the first time, DaRonch looked at Bundy, a fleeting glance. "Right there," she breathed.

On cross-examination, defense counsel John O'Connell highlighted discrepancies in DaRonch's descriptions of her attacker to police. At first she claimed he had a mustache, then he did not, then he did. He also queried her identification of the Volkswagen, drawing attention to the fact that it now looked markedly different. In a quiet voice, DaRonch conceded that her identification of the vehicle had been stimulated by police assurances that it "was supposed to be the car."

Naturally, Bundy denied everything. He was ingratiating and pugnacious by turns, but prosecutor Yocum prevailed. A series of quick-fire questions about the circumstances surrounding his arrest clearly rattled Bundy and culminated in a damaging admission that he had, on occasion, worn a false mustache.

After a troubled weekend of deliberation, Judge Hanson returned a guilty verdict, saying, "I cannot say that there weren't any doubts." Following a prolonged psychological evaluation, Bundy was sentenced to 1–15 years imprisonment.

One year later, in June 1977, after extradition to Colorado on a murder charge, Bundy escaped. He was captured after eight days of living on the run. Incredibly, on December 30, 1977, Bundy escaped again. This time he proved more elusive.

On the Run and Deadly

Two weeks and 2,000 miles later, five female students attending Florida State University (FSU) in Tallahassee were savagely attacked at the Chi Omega sorority house. Two of the girls, Lisa Levy and Margaret Bowman, died. Just a few blocks away, another student was attacked but lived. On February 16, 1978, a man using the name "Chris Hagen" was arrested for driving a stolen vehicle.

Ted Bundy had been captured for the last time. Only later was it learned that just days before his arrest he had killed again: 12-year-old Kimberly Leach, of Lake City, Florida. Her body was found April 7, 1978.

Because of local feeling, Bundy's trial for the FSU killings was moved to Miami. Earlier it had appeared likely that there would be no trial. Faced with the possibility of two lengthy trials—Bundy was scheduled to be tried for the murder of Kimberly Leach later—the prosecutors reluctantly agreed to a plea bargain. Everything was set; Bundy signed a confession, admitting that he had killed Lisa Levy, Margaret Bowman, and Kimberly Leach. In return, he expected that, "Under the terms of this negotiated plea, I will serve seventy-five (75) calendar years in prison before I become eligible for parole." But when Bundy stood in court to deliver this plea, he abruptly changed his mind and stated, "I'm not going to do it." His attorneys looked on aghast as a trial was set.

The Miami trial got under way June 25, 1979. Larry Simpson made the opening prosecution statement, a low-key, workmanlike presentation, long on fact and bereft of emotion. For theatrics, the court had to rely on the self-appointed chief defense counsel: Bundy himself. It wasn't supposed to be that way—the court had appointed a fine team to argue his case—but Bundy's ego would not allow him to leave well enough alone. His cross-examination of Roy Crew, the FSU officer first on the scene at Chi Omega, was inept. Bundy pushed Crew hard to describe the murder scene in graphic detail, as if determined to impress upon the jury the awfulness of the crime.

Bundy—after he was recaptured outside Aspen, Colorado's city limits. (AP/Wide World Photos)

Testimony that Could Kill

However, when Coral Gables dentist Dr. Richard Souviron assumed the stand, Bundy took a back seat. This was testimony that could kill him and he knew it. Lisa Levy had sustained bite marks to the buttocks. By comparing photographs of those teeth marks with an oversize photo of Bundy's mouth, Dr. Souviron was able to show undeniable similarities. Prosecutor Simpson asked, "Doctor, can you tell us, within a reasonable degree of dental certainty, whether or not the teeth . . . of Theodore Robert Bundy . . . made the bite marks?"

"Yes, sir." For the first time, there was actual physical evidence linking Bundy to a murder victim.

Defender Ed Harvey was quick to try and undermine the setback. "Analyzing bite marks is part art and part science, isn't it?" he asked the dentist.

"I think that's a fair statement."

"Your conclusions are really a matter of opinion. Is that correct?"

Dr. Souviron agreed that it was, but the damage had been done. Confirmation came from Dr. Lowell Levine, chief consultant in forensic dentistry to the New York City Medical Examiner, who told the court that dental identification had been admitted into testimony as far back as the late 19th century. This evidence dealt a body-blow to the defense lawyers, one from which they never recovered. Significantly, Bundy, so eager to play the advocate, declined to testify on his own behalf.

On July 23, 1978, Ted Bundy was found guilty on all charges. Even at the end, his personal magnetism didn't desert him. Judge Edward Cowart, after passing sentence of death, felt moved to add a few words: "You'd have made a good lawyer . . . but you went another way, partner. Take care of yourself." It was an extraordinary end to an extraordinary trial.

Bundy received a third death sentence on February 12, 1980, following his conviction for killing Kimberly Leach. After years of appellate pleas, on January 24, 1989, "the most hated man in America" was executed in Florida's electric chair.

More than anyone else, Ted Bundy shattered popular notions of how a crazed killer should look and act. He was not wild-eyed, dirty, or dissolute; on the contrary, he was incredibly charming. And in a society where such a premium is placed on appearance, he remains a reminder that things are often not what they seem, and nothing is unthinkable.

—Colin Evans

Suggestions for Further Reading

Kendall, Elizabeth. *The Phantom Prince*. Seattle: Madrona, 1981.

Larsen, Richard W. *Bundy: The Deliberate Stranger*. Englewood Cliffs, N.J.: Prentice Hall, 1980.

Michaud, Stephen G. and Hugh Aynesworth. *The Only Living Witness*. New York: Simon & Schuster, 1983.

Rule, Ann. *The Stranger Beside Me*. New York: W.W. Norton & Co., 1989.

Gary Mark Gilmore Trial: 1976

Defendant: Gary Mark Gilmore **Crime Charged:** Murder
Chief Defense Lawyers: Michael Esplin and Craig Snyder
Chief Prosecutor: Noall T. Wootton **Judge:** J. Robert Bullock
Place: Provo, Utah **Dates of Trial:** October 5–7, 1976 **Verdict:** Guilty
Sentence: Death

SIGNIFICANCE

Convicted killer Gary Gilmore's craving for self-destruction fueled a re-examination of capital punishment in America and led to a best-selling book, *The Executioner's Song,* and a subsequent movie.

At age 35, Gary Gilmore had spent more than half his life behind bars. In April 1976 he was paroled from the federal penitentiary in Marion, Illinois, and went to live with family members in Utah. On July 19, 1976, he robbed and killed a gas station attendant in Orem, Utah. The next day, he held up a motel in nearby Provo, forced the manager, Ben Bushnell, to lie face down on floor, then shot him through the head. Less than 24 hours later, Gilmore was in custody. Because there were eyewitnesses to the motel killing, it was decided to try Gilmore on the Bushnell murder first.

When the trial began on October 5, 1976, the evidence against Gilmore was overwhelming. Peter Arroyo, a motel guest, described seeing Gilmore in the registration office. Prosecutor Noall Wootton asked, "How far away from him were you at the time?"

"Somewhere near ten feet."

"Did you observe anything in his possession at the time?"

"In his right hand he had a pistol with a long barrel. In his left hand he had a cash box from a cash register."

Moments later Arroyo found Ben Bushnell, shot to death in the office.

Gilmore had accidentally shot himself in the hand while escaping from the motel. When detectives traced the blood spots to some bushes, they discovered a .22-caliber pistol. Gerald F. Wilkes, an FBI ballistics expert, compared a shell casing found there with one from the murder scene. Wootton asked him, "Would you tell the jury, please, what your conclusions were?"

"Based on my examination of these two cartridges, I was able to determine that both cartridge cases were fired with this weapon and no other weapon."

No Defense

In the face of such damning testimony, Gilmore's chief counsel, Michael Esplin, declared that the defense intended to offer no evidence, a decision that did not sit well with the defendant. Gilmore loudly protested that he be allowed to testify. Judge J. Robert Bullock told him, "I want you to fully understand that if you do that then you're subject to cross-examination by the State's attorney. Do you understand that?" Gilmore replied affirmatively.

At this point Gilmore's other attorney, Craig Snyder, stepped in with an explanation of why he and Esplin had offered no defense. Essentially both felt that there *was no* defense. Snyder's argument obviously impressed the mercurial Gilmore who abruptly said, "I'll withdraw my request. Just go ahead with it like it is."

"What?" gulped Judge Bullock, stunned by this turn of events.

Gilmore said it again. "I withdraw my request."

All that was left was for both sides to make their closing arguments. At 10:13 A.M. on October 7, 1976, the jury retired to consider their verdict. Before mid-day they were back with a verdict of guilty. Later that day they unanimously recommended the death penalty. Because Utah had dual methods of capital punishment—hanging and firing squad—Gilmore was given a choice. "I prefer to be shot," he said.

Gary Mark Gilmore.
(AP/Wide World Photos)

When Gary Gilmore went to Death Row, nobody in America had been executed in over a decade, and nobody expected Gilmore to be the first—except Gilmore. He adamantly refused to appeal his conviction or sentence, dismissed both of his lawyers when they did, and insisted that he just wanted to be shot and be done with it. Anything, he said, was preferable to spending the rest of his life behind bars. Two failed suicide bids, on November 16 and December 16, 1977, only strengthened his resolve. Despite frantic legal wrangling by opponents of capital punishment, Gilmore got his wish.

On January 17, 1977, he was strapped to a chair in the Utah State Prison. Five marksmen took aim at the white circle pinned to Gilmore's shirt, then shot him through the heart.

—Colin Evans

Suggestions for Further Reading

McFarland, Samuel G. *Journal Of Criminal Law And Criminology* (Fall 1983): 1014–1032.

Mailer, Norman. *The Executioners's Song.* Boston: Little, Brown & Co., 1979.

White, Welsh S. *University of Pittsburgh Law Review* (Spring 1987): 853–857.

Leonard Peltier Trial: 1977

Defendant: Leonard Peltier   **Crime Charged:** Murder
Chief Defense Lawyers: Bruce Ellison, Lew Gurwitz, William Kuntsler, Elliott Taikeff   **Chief Prosecutors:** Lynn Crooks, Evan Hultman, Robert Sikma
Judge: Paul Benson   **Place:** Fargo, North Dakota   **Date of Trial:** March 16–April 18, 1977   **Verdict:** Guilty   **Sentence:** Life imprisonment (two consecutive terms)

SIGNIFICANCE
Countless observers find in this trial a larger issue: the question of the continuing struggle between the native American Indian and the U.S. government, epitomized by this local skirmish between members of AIM (the American Indian Movement) and the FBI. In the waning days of President William Clinton's administration, supporters of Leonard Peltier urged the president to respond favorably to a petition for clemency, and current and retired FBI agents opposed it just as vociferously, but Clinton did not include Peltier among his many last-day-in-office pardons.

On June 25, 1975, Special Agents Ronald Williams and Jack R. Coler of the Federal Bureau of Investigation (FBI) searched the Pine Ridge, South Dakota, area for a 19-year-old Indian who was wanted on charges of theft and assault with a deadly weapon. Two Bureau of Indian Affairs (BIA) officers accompanied the FBI men.

Unsuccessful, they resumed the search the next day. Before noon, Williams radioed for help, saying he was near Oglala, a community 10 miles from Wounded Knee, and was being fired upon. FBI agents and BIA officers raced to Oglala. The gunfight that followed lasted all day. Coler and Williams were killed at point-blank range beside Williams' car. An Indian was also killed.

Arrest, Escape, Extradition

Some 300 FBI agents and BIA police, believing that 16 Indians had participated in the shootout, looked for evidence and arrested four men. One of them, Leonard Peltier, escaped and fled to Canada, where he appealed for asylum. His petition denied, he was extradited in December 1976. Meantime, two of the other men were tried in Cedar Rapids and acquitted on grounds of self-defense. Charges against the third were dropped.

As the trial of Peltier began on March 16, 1977, defense attorney Elliott Taikeff's opening statement set his own ground rules. "The only question is," he said, "did the defendant participate. That's what this trial is all about. The government doesn't have to prove first-degree murder, we concede first-degree murder."

A key prosecution witness was Mike Anderson, a youth who said he had watched the shootout from a rooftop. He testified he saw Peltier and two other men in Peltier's red-and-white van pursued by two FBI cars. He "saw everybody hop out" of their cars and move out of sight, then heard gunfire.

On cross-examination, Anderson admitted that, while he was jailed in Wichita on another matter since the shootout, an FBI agent had threatened to beat him up if he "didn't give him the answers that he wanted," that his Wichita charges had then been dropped, and that he had disagreements with Peltier, who had been trying to get him to stop drinking.

"It was the Agents . . ."

Another youth on the stand, prosecution witness Norman Brown, was reminded by prosecutor Evan Hultman that he had told the grand jury he had seen Peltier and the other three men near the death scene. "Are you trying to tell me *I* saw them down there?" he responded. "It was the agents who said I saw them." The reply was so confident that the defense welcomed it.

Prosecution witness Angie Long Visitor told the court she heard shots and saw the red-and-white van that she knew Peltier drove. It was parked near junked cars from which, according to both Anderson and Brown, Peltier and others had fired.

FBI Special Agent Frederick Coward testified that, with his rifle's telescopic sight, he saw Peltier running through the haze from the crime scene. The defense produced an expert on telescopic sights who said that, using the same sight at the same distance on a bright day, he would not be able to recognize someone he knew even facing him and standing still. Judge Paul Benson refused a defense request that he and the jury both test the sight.

Ballistics reports introduced by the prosecutors described a .223 shell casing, presumably ejected from the killer's gun into the trunk of agent Coler's car, but could not link the shell precisely to one of the several AR-15 rifles used by both police and Indians in the shootout.

Two Royal Canadian Mounted Policemen who had arrested Peltier after he fled across the border concluded the prosecution testimony. One said the defendant told him he would have opened fire if he had seen them coming. The other said he asked Peltier if he killed the agents at Oglala and Peltier replied, "No, but I know who did."

Myrtle Poor Bear Irrelevant

With the prosecution resting after calling 25 witnesses during 15 days of evidence, the defense called Myrtle Poor Bear. A girlfriend and confidante of

Peltier, she had been a known informant to the FBI on earlier investigations and had received FBI protection. Her affidavits describing the killings had been instrumental in the U.S. Justice Department's gaining the extradition of Peltier from Canada. Now, out of hearing of the jury, she testified as an "offer of proof" by the defense to show the judge why her testimony was relevant and should be heard by the jury. She signed the affidavits, she said, because two FBI men "told me that they were going to plan everything out and if I didn't do it I was going to get hurt." The judge found her false affidavits "irrelevant."

Finally, defense witnesses from the FBI office in Rapid City testified on confusing radio transmissions, during the shootout, about a red pickup truck or red-and-white pickup or red-and-white van and what kind of vehicle was parked where. Cross-examining, the prosecution blamed incompetent record keeping in the office for the inconsistencies.

Ruling before the defense summation, Judge Benson prevented Peltier's lawyers from disclosing the inconsistencies of the ballistics reports. He also prohibited the summations from using direct quotations from the trial's 5,000 pages of transcript, preventing the defense from citing specific discrepancies in prosecution testimony.

On April 18, 1977, after deliberating for six hours, the jury found Peltier guilty on two counts of murder in the first degree. Sentenced to life imprisonment on each count, he appealed. His extradition from Canada had been illegal, argued his attorneys, because it was based on false affidavits "obtained by the government through coercion and deceit and known by the government to be false." The appeal was denied

Hazel Little Hawk speaks at a rally for Leonard Peltier at the federal building in St. Paul, Minnesota. (AP/Wide World Photos)

by the U.S. Court of Appeals. The Supreme Court of the United States refused to hear the case.

Peltier escaped from the federal penitentiary at Marion, Illinois, in July 1978. Recaptured, he was tried on November 14, 1979, in U.S. District Court in Los Angeles. He was acquitted of conspiracy and assault but sentenced to five years for escape and two years for possession of a weapon by a felon, both sentences added to his life terms.

Appeals Denied

The year 1982 brought a motion for a new trial in U.S. District Court in Fargo. Judge Benson refused a motion that he remove himself from the case, then denied the new-trial motion. In October 1983, the U.S. Court of Appeals, however, hearing oral arguments for a new trial, reversed Benson's decision. Following the resulting evidentiary hearing in October 1984, the judge again refused a new trial.

The U.S. Court of Appeals again heard oral arguments in October 1985. Judge Gerald Heaney recalled that prosecutor Lynn Crooks had said Peltier was "the man who came down and killed those FBI agents in cold blood." To another judge's question, Crooks then said, "But we can't *prove* who shot those agents."

The appeal was denied on September 11, 1986. On October 5, 1987, the U.S. Supreme Court again refused to hear the case.

Peltier remains imprisoned.

—Bernard Ryan, Jr.

Suggestions for Further Reading

Churchill, Ward, and James Vander Wall. *Agents of Repression: The FBI's Secret Wars Against the Black Panther Party and the American Indian Movement.* Cambridge, Mass.: South End Press, 1988.

——. *The COINTELPRO Papers: Documents from the FBI's Secret Wars Against Domestic Dissent in the United States.* Cambridge, Mass.: South End Press, 1990.

Matthiessen, Peter. *In the Spirit of Crazy Horse.* New York: Viking, 1991.

Messerschmidt, Jim. *The Trial of Leonard Peltier.* Boston: South End Press, 1983.

Peltier, Leonard. *Prison Writings: My Life Is My Sun Dance.* New York: St. Martin's Press, 1999.

Weyler, Rex. *Blood of the Land: The Government and Corporate War Against the American Indian Movement.* New York: Everest House, 1982.

Randall Adams Trial: 1977

Defendant: Randall Dale Adams **Crime Charged:** Murder
Chief Defense Lawyers: Edith James and Dennis White
Chief Prosecutors: Douglas Mulder, Winfield Scott, and Stephen Tokely
Judge: Donald J. Metcalfe **Place:** Dallas, Texas **Dates of Trial:** March 28–May 3, 1977 **Verdict:** Guilty **Sentence:** Death

SIGNIFICANCE

The tragedy of Randall Adams, recorded in the movie, *The Thin Blue Line,* represents a withering indictment of the dangers that accompany overzealous prosecution.

In the early hours of November 29, 1976, police officer Robert Wood was gunned down on a Dallas, Texas, side street by the driver of a blue car. Car and driver made a clean getaway. Three weeks later a 16-year-old petty criminal, David Harris, was arrested in Vidor, Texas, about 250 miles from Dallas, on charges of stealing a blue Mercury Comet. Harris, who had bragged to friends about shooting a Dallas cop, led police to a swamp where they recovered the murder weapon. Harris admitted witnessing the killing but claimed that the gunman was Randall Adams, a 28-year-old hitchhiker he had picked up. Granted immunity from other charges, Harris agreed to testify against Adams.

Going into the trial on March 28, 1977, prosecutor Douglas Mulder had a 100-percent conviction record in capital murder cases. But on this occasion that record looked in serious jeopardy. Harris' disingeniousness under oath posed serious problems, even for someone of Mulder's considerable skill. When defense attorney Dennis White began cross-examination of Harris, he did so incredulously: "Now, after this murder you are saying that the defendant . . . drove right on home [to his motel] and said forget it?"

"Yes, sir," replied Harris.

"And insofar as you know he went in, went to bed and whatever?"

"Yes, sir."

Shaking his head, White turned to comments Harris made to friends in Vidor. "Is it a fact when the story of the policeman in Dallas came on the television you turned to these people and said, "I wasted that pig'?"

"No, sir."

"What did you say?"

"I told them I was there whenever he got shot, that I did it."

"That you did it?"

"Yes, sir." Earlier, Harris had admitted saying this only to impress his friends: "I thought it was making me big to their standards."

White showed how, prior to the killing, Harris had been on a month-long crime spree and had good reason to shoot Wood. Being caught in possession of a stolen vehicle would have resulted in the revocation of his parole and subsequent return to jail. Adams, by contrast, had no police record whatsoever.

Surprise Witnesses Emerge

With Mulder unable to shake Adams' assertion that he had left Harris two hours prior to the shooting, acquittal seemed a formality. Then, at the 11th hour, three surprise eyewitnesses came forward. R.L. Miller and his wife, Emily, described driving slowly by and seeing everything. Both identified Adams as the driver of the car. (Significantly, one week later, Mrs. Miller's daughter, due to face armed robbery charges, learned that her case had been quietly dropped.)

Another motorist, Michael Randell, claimed to have seen two people in the car. The passenger was indistinct but he had no trouble recognizing Adams as the driver.

White fulminated at the unfairness of these tactics: "Mr. Mulder is trying to convict an innocent man." But his words fell on deaf ears. Judge Donald J. Metcalfe ruled the evidence admissible and, on May 3, 1977, Randall Adams was convicted and sentenced to death.

But the fight continued. In June 1980 the U.S. Supreme Court overturned the conviction on the grounds of improper jury selection. Dallas prosecutors, anxious to avoid a retrial, advised the governor that Adams' sentence be commuted to life imprisonment.

In 1985, David Harris, on Death Row for another killing, began hinting that much of his testimony against Adams had been coached into him by conviction-hungry prosecutors. In a series of taped interviews Harris obliquely admitted culpability. The three eyewitnesses also admitted that their evidence had been compromised.

Another four years would pass before an appeals court ordered Adams' release. While refusing to admit any error, prosecutors declined to retry him. Adams was freed but has still not been fully exonerated.

In 1988, Errol Morris' Oscar-nominated "docudrama," *The Thin Blue Line*, brought the name of Randall Adams to national prominence. A searching examination of Dallas justice, it did more than pave the way for Adams' ultimate release, it exposed the heartless folly of placing ambition over truth.

—Colin Evans

Suggestions for Further Reading

Adams, Randall, William Hoffer, and Marilyn Mona Hoffer. *Adams V. Texas*. New York: St. Martin's Press, 1991.

Bruning, F. "Why Did Randall Adams Almost Die?" *Mclean's* (March 27, 1989).

Carlson, M. "Recrossing The Thin Blue Line." *Time* (April 3, 1989): 23.

Cartwright, Gary. "The Longest Ride of His Life." *Texas Monthly* (May 1987): 124ff.

Marvin Mandel Trial: 1977

Defendant: Maryland Governor Marvin Mandel   **Crimes Charged:** Mail fraud and racketeering   **Chief Defense Lawyers:** M. Albert Figinski, Eugene Gressman, D. Christopher Ohly, and Arnold M. Weiner
Chief Prosecutors: Russell T. Baker, Jr., Daniel J. Hurson, Barnet D. Skolnik, and Elizabeth H. Trimble   **Judge:** Robert L. Taylor   **Place:** Baltimore, Maryland   **Dates of Trial:** June 1–August 21, 1977   **Verdict:** Guilty, later overturned   **Sentence:** 4 years in prison, commuted after 19 months served.

SIGNIFICANCE

The Marvin Mandel trial was a national scandal, exposing massive political corruption at the highest level of Maryland state government. The reversal of Mandel's conviction, however, signaled a limit on the ability to attack state crimes through federal statutes.

On December 31, 1971, a group of businessmen and investors purchased the Marlboro Race Track in Prince George's County, Maryland. Like all of Maryland's horse racing tracks, the Marlboro track was regulated by the state, and it was allotted 18 racing days. Eager to increase their profits, and not too concerned about the means used, the new owners approached Maryland Governor Marvin Mandel and asked for help. Mandel, formerly a strong advocate of strict horse racing regulation, suddenly dropped his opposition to a bill pending in the Maryland General Assembly that would increase Marlboro's racing days from 18 to 36. The bill passed on January 12, 1972. In March 1972, Mandel successfully lobbied the General Assembly to increase the number of racing days again, this time from 36 to 94. Further, Mandel helped the Marlboro owners acquire interests in other Maryland racetracks.

For his help, Mandel received cash and other valuables under the table from the investors. Expensive clothes and jewelry that Mandel purchased were paid for by the racetrack owners, who also gave Mandel a valuable interest in a new Maryland waterfront development called Ray's Point. Federal prosecutors discovered Mandel's activities, however, and indicted him along with racetrack investors Ernest N. Cory, Jr., W. Dale Hess, Irvin Kovens, Harry W. Rodgers III, and William A. Rodgers.

Tried, Convicted, and Ultimately Acquitted

Mandel was charged with violations of federal law and not state law, namely those federal laws which prohibit mail fraud and racketeering. Prosecutors frequently invoke "mail fraud" when anything connected with a crime goes through the U.S. mail system, such as a check mailed by one defendant to another. Mandel's lawyers were M. Albert Figinski, Eugene Gressman, D. Christopher Ohly, and Arnold M. Weiner. The chief prosecutors were Russell T. Baker, Jr., Daniel J. Hurson, Barnet D. Skolnik, and Elizabeth H. Trimble. The trial began on June 1, 1977, before Judge Robert L. Taylor in Baltimore, Maryland.

Jury foreman Howard Davis delivers the guilty verdict to the court clerk in the fraud and racketeering trial of Governor Marvin Mandel. (AP/Wide World Photos)

The trial lasted nearly three months, during which Mandel fought with the prosecutors over virtually every issue. For example, when Skolnik introduced telephone company records into evidence to show the existence of phone calls between Mandel and the other defendants, Mandel even denied knowledge of his own telephone number.

Question: Governor, who in [your personal office suite] had the phone number 267-5901?

Answer: Mrs. Grace Donald.

Question: And who else, sir?

Answer: Mrs. Grace Donald.

Question: Wasn't that your phone number, sir?

Answer: No, sir, that was Mrs. Grace Donald's phone number listed to the executive office. That was her phone. That is the way she handled it.

Exasperated, Skolnik presented a Maryland state government phone directory, which established that Mandel's telephone number was indeed 267-5901.

On August 21, 1977, the jury found Mandel guilty. He was sentenced to four years in prison. Mandel's attorneys appealed and won a brief victory when the U.S. Fourth Circuit Court of Appeals overturned Mandel's conviction. The Fourth Circuit reheard the appeal, however, and decided to uphold the conviction. Mandel went to prison and served 19 months of his sentence, but the rest was commuted. Even after he served his sentence, Mandel continued to fight the conviction to clear his name.

On November 12, 1987, Judge Frederic N. Smalkin of the U.S. District Court for the District of Maryland, where Mandel had been tried, overturned Mandel's conviction. Smalkin did not deny the strong evidence of bribery and dishonesty presented at Mandel's trial, but he insisted that the prosecutors had stretched their interpretation of federal mail fraud and racketeering laws past the breaking point to bring Mandel to trial for what were really state crimes. Thus, although Mandel remains a political pariah, the outcome of his trial was, in fact, a failure for the federal prosecutors.

—Stephen G. Christianson

Suggestions for Further Reading

Jacobs, Bradford. *Thimbleriggers: the Law v. Governor Marvin Mandel.* Baltimore, MD: Johns Hopkins University Press, 1984.

"Marvin Mandel's Life in Prison." *Newsweek* (November 24, 1980): 20–21.

"A New Verdict for Mandel." *Time* (November 23, 1987): 31.

"Parting Shots." *The Washingtonian* (July 1981): 21.

Collin v. Smith: 1977

Plaintiff: Frank Collin, on behalf of the National Socialist Party of America
Defendant: Albert Smith, as president of the Village of Skokie, Illinois
Plaintiff Claims: That Skokie had illegally prevented the American Nazis from holding a political march   **Chief Defense Lawyers:** Gilbert Gordon and Harvey Schwartz   **Chief Lawyer for Plaintiff:** David A. Goldberger
Judge: Bernard M. Decker   **Place:** Chicago, Illinois
Date of Hearing: December 2, 1977   **Decision:** That Skokie could not prevent the Nazis from marching

SIGNIFICANCE

Despite the fact that the Nazis had deliberately chosen a heavily Jewish community to march in, the courts stuck firm to the First Amendment principle that unpopular groups must be allowed to express their political opinions.

Prior to World War II, there was a small yet fairly significant Nazi movement in the United States, which grew out of the German-American Bund. After the war, the movement was discredited, and survived only due to the leadership of George Lincoln Rockwell, who was assassinated in 1967. As with other fringe groups, such as the Ku Klux Klan, hatred and prejudice kept the National Socialist Party of America alive with a small but vocal membership. In the mid-1970s, to generate publicity and attract new members, Nazi leader Frank Collin targeted the Chicago, Illinois, suburb of Skokie as a site for a series of marches and demonstrations.

Over half of Skokie's 70,000 residents were Jewish, and many were survivors of German concentration camps. Seeing Nazi marchers and the swastika was bound to bring back tragic memories. Skokie was initially successful in getting an injunction against any Nazi marches from the Illinois state courts, but the Supreme Court summarily dismissed the injunction as unconstitutionally infringing on the Nazis' First Amendment right to political expression. Determined to protect its Jewish residents, on May 2, 1977, Skokie decided to thwart the Nazis by passing a series of municipal ordinances. The ordinances required any group wishing to stage a public demonstration to obtain $350,000 in liability and property insurance, and forbade the dissemination of racist literature and the wearing of military-style uniforms by group members during such demonstrations. The Nazis promptly took Albert Smith, president of the Village of Skokie, and other municipal officials to court.

Nazis Must be Allowed to March

Ironically, both sides were represented by Jewish attorneys. David A. Goldberger from the American Civil Liberties Union represented the Nazis; Gilbert Gordon and Harvey Schwartz represented Smith and Skokie. The case was heard before U.S. District Court Judge Bernard M. Decker in Chicago on December 2, 1977.

Collin was brutally honest about his party's beliefs. He stated that the Nazis believed blacks were inferior, and that Jews were involved in an international financial and communist conspiracy. Further, Collin testified that the Nazis deliberately copied the military uniform style of the notorious "Brownshirts" of Hitler's Third Reich:

> We wear brown shirts with a dark brown tie, a swastika pin on the tie, a leather shoulder strap, a black belt with buckle, dark brown trousers, black engineer boots, and either a steel helmet or a cloth cap, depending on the situation, plus a swastika arm band on the left arm and an American flag patch on the right arm.

On February 23, 1978, Decker issued his decision. Stating that "it is better to allow those who preach racial hate to expend their venom in rhetoric rather than to be panicked into embarking on the dangerous course of permitting the government to decide what its citizens may say and hear," Decker held that the ordinances violated the First Amendment and were unenforceable.

Skokie appealed to the U.S. Court of Appeals for the Seventh Circuit, and the case was argued on April 14, 1978. On May 22, 1978, the Seventh Circuit refused to overturn Decker's decision:

> No authorities need be cited to establish the proposition, which the Village does not dispute, that First Amendment rights are truly precious and fundamental to our national life. Nor is this truth without relevance to the saddening historical images this case inevitably arouses. It is, after all, in part the fact that our constitutional system protects minorities unpopular at a particular time or place from government harassment and intimidation, that distinguishes life in this country from life under the Third Reich.

Finally, Skokie asked the Supreme Court to review the case, a procedure called "petition for a writ of *certiorari*." On October 16, 1978, the justices of the Supreme Court voted to deny *certiorari*, and so Decker's original decision was upheld. Justices Harry Blackmun and Byron White, however, dissented. Blackmun and White felt that the court should make an official pronouncement on the important First Amendment issues in the Skokie litigation, and not just let the lower court decision stand by default:

> [We] feel that the present case affords the Court an opportunity to consider whether, in the context of the facts that this record appears to present, there is no limit whatsoever to the exercise of free speech. There indeed may be no such limit, but when citizens assert, not casually but with deep convic-

tion, that the proposed demonstration is scheduled at a place and in a manner that is taunting and overwhelmingly offensive to the citizens of that place, that assertion, uncomfortable though it may be for judges, deserves to be examined. It just might fall into the same category as one's "right" to cry "fire" in a crowded theater, for "the character of every act depends upon the circumstances in which it is done." [Quoting *Schenck v. U.S.*, see separate entry]

There was now nothing to prevent Collin and the Nazis, victorious in the courts, from marching in Skokie. Collin, however, abruptly called the march off. Declaring that his aim had been to generate "pure agitation to restore our right to free speech," Collin proclaimed the whole affair a moral victory for the Nazis and never marched in Skokie. Whether the Skokie affair was a victory for the Nazis is debatable, but it was certainly a victory for the right of every minority group, no matter how unpopular, to express its political views without government interference.

— Stephen G. Christianson

Suggestions for Further Reading

Bartlett, Jonathan. *The First Amendment in a Free Society*. New York: H.W. Wilson, 1979.

Downs, Donald Alexander. *Nazis in Skokie: Freedom, Community, and the First Amendment*. Notre Dame, Ind.: University of Notre Dame Press, 1985.

Gross, Alan. "I Remember Skokie: a Cultural Defense." *Chicago* (February 1981): 90–97.

Hamlin, David. *The Nazi/Skokie Conflict: a Civil Liberties Battle*. Boston: Beacon Press, 1980.

Neier, Aryeh. *Defending My Enemy: American Nazis, the Skokie Case, and the Risks of Freedom*. New York: E.P. Dutton, 1979.

The "Son of Sam" Trial: 1978

Defendant: David R. Berkowitz **Crimes Charged:** Second-degree murder, attempted murder, and assault **Chief Defense Lawyers:** Ira Jultak and Leon Stern **Chief Prosecutors:** Eugene Gold, Mario Merola, and John Santucci **Judges:** Joseph R. Corso, William Kapelman, and Nicholas Tsoucalas **Place:** New York, New York **Date of Trial:** May 8, 1978 **Verdict:** Guilty **Sentence:** Six 25-years-to-life terms, with additional 15-and 25-year terms for assault and attempted murder

SIGNIFICANCE

While there was never any question that David Berkowitz committed the crimes with which he was charged, his case fueled debate over the difficulty of determining the sanity of defendants and the culpability of the mentally ill. He also inspired a state law preventing criminals from profiting from books or films about their crimes. The "Son of Sam Law" was overturned by the U.S. Supreme Court in 1991.

From October 1976 to August 1977, fear spread across New York City whenever night fell. Six young people were killed and seven more were wounded by an unknown gunman who seemed to be hunting young women. Hundreds of detectives were assigned to find "the .44 caliber killer," so-called because of the unusually large handgun bullets he used. When police found a bizarre note at the scene of a double murder New Yorkers came to know the killer by his own nickname, the "Son of Sam."

After the killer mortally wounded 20-year-old Stacy Moskowitz and blinded her date Robert Violante in Brooklyn on July 31, detectives got a lead. They discovered a parking ticket issued to a 24-year-old postal clerk named David Berkowitz for parking alongside a fire hydrant near the crime scene. Police located Berkowitz's car at his Yonkers apartment building and found a duffel bag full of guns behind the front seat. Berkowitz was seized when he came outside, carrying a .44-caliber revolver in a small paper bag.

Berkowitz's statement to police left no doubt that he was responsible for the attacks. He described unreleased details in the "Son of Sam" letter and claimed that "Sam" was a 6,000-year-old man inhabiting the body of a neighbor, Sam Carr. "Sam" and other Satanic "demons" had ordered Berkowitz to kill by transmitting commands through the Carr family's Labrador Retriever.

Insanity Issue Arises

Berkowitz was arraigned in Brooklyn for the Moskowitz-Violante shooting, as prosecutors in the Bronx and Queens quickly wrote indictments against him for murders in their boroughs. The primary legal issue immediately became whether David Berkowitz was sane enough to stand trial.

A psychiatric report delivered to New York State Supreme Court justices in all three boroughs on August 30 concluded that David Berkowitz was not mentally capable of assisting in his own defense and did not understand the charges against him. Psychiatrists Daniel Schwartz and Richard Weidenbacher, Jr. felt that Berkowitz was "well aware" of the six murder charges, understood that they were criminal acts, and had "the intellectual capacity" to understand the legal process unfolding against him. Yet the doctors concluded that paranoid psychosis left Berkowitz so "emotionally dead" that he was neither capable of nor interested in assisting in his own defense.

Brooklyn District Attorney Eugene Gold challenged the report, obtaining court approval for Berkowitz's examination by prosecution psychiatrist Dr. David Abrahamsen. A month of interviews convinced Dr. Abrahamsen that Berkowitz's demons were "a conscious invention" he was able to control, not a psychotic disorder which controlled his actions. Abrahamsen declared that Berkowitz could understand the legal process and assist in his own defense if he chose to do so. Justice John R. Starkey agreed at a competency hearing on October 21. A week later, Justice Starkey withdrew from the case amidst a furor over controversial statements he had made to the press about Berkowitz's intention to blame his actions on the demons. A new competency hearing was scheduled for the following spring before a different judge.

At the second hearing, psychiatrists Schwartz and Weidenbacher reversed their original opinion. They reported that Berkowitz's mental condition was improving from treatment. While not suggesting that he was sane at the time he allegedly committed the murders, they agreed that Berkowitz was now able to participate in his defense. Their reversal helped Judge Joseph R. Corso determine that Berkowitz was mentally fit to stand trial.

Cases Consolidated

Throughout the proceedings again, David Berkowitz remained determined to plead guilty, a decision he insisted was his own in spite of the advice of his "demons." His attorneys unsuccessfully tried to persuade him to plead not guilty by reason of insanity. Expectations of a guilty plea were so high that a special agreement was reached to consolidate all of the legal proceedings to a single trial venue for security and to save court costs.

On May 8, 1978, in a Brooklyn courtroom, Judge Corso accepted Berkowitz's guilty pleas for the Moskowitz-Violante shooting. Justice Corso then signed a special administrative agreement allowing Justice William Kapelman of the Bronx to come to the bench. Justice Kapelman similarly turned the proceedings over to Queens Justice Nicholas Tsoucalas after accepting

Berkowitz's guilty plea for three murders in the Bronx. Like the other judges, Justice Tsoucalas asked Berkowitz if he was making the guilty pleas of his own free will and wanted to know if the defendant had meant to cause serious injury to two young women he had wounded in Queens. "Oh, no, sir," Berkowitz replied. "I wanted to kill them." Judge Tsoucalas accepted Berkowitz's guilty pleas for two murders and five attempted murders.

The three judges returned to Brooklyn on May 22, but postponed sentencing when Berkowitz struggled with deputies and screamed, "I'd kill them all again!" On June 12, 1978, he was sentenced to the maximum term of 25 years to life imprisonment for each of the six murders, plus additional terms for assault and attempted murder. The life terms were to run consecutively, but the New York state practice of "merging" sentences would make him eligible for parole as if he had committed only one murder.

Case Inspires New Law

After four months psychiatric treatment, Berkowitz was transferred to Attica State Prison, where he ordered his lawyers to drop all appeals on his behalf. Negotiations for lucrative book and film projects about the case began against his wishes. Berkowitz tried to stop the deals by telling the *New York Times* that his stories of demons were a hoax.

David Berkowitz during an interview in Attica prison. (AP/Wide World Photos)

Ironically, even before his capture, Berkowitz had inspired a law barring him from receiving any money generated by his crimes. Anticipating that anyone committing such gruesome acts might later profit by telling his story, the New York State Legislature passed a statute popularly known as the "Son of Sam Law" in 1977. The law required that an accused or convicted criminal's income from printed or film work describing his crime be deposited in an escrow account, where it would be available to answer possible claims by crime victims for five years. Berkowitz took no interest in the money swirling around his case, but claims by his lawyers resulted in an eight-year legal battle before the New York Crime Victims Compensation Board was able to distribute royalties to his victims and their families.

The "Son of Sam Law" separated memoir royalties' from famous convicted murderers like Jack Henry Abbott, Jean Harris, and Mark David Chapman. In 1986, however, publishers Simon & Schuster contested the compensation board's demand for future royalties plus $96,000 already paid to career criminal Henry Hill for revealing his misdeeds in the book *Wiseguy* (the basis for the film *Goodfellas*). On December 10, 1991, the U.S. Supreme Court unanimously ruled that the law was an unconstitutional "content-based" suppression of the First Amendment right to free expression. The decision left New York and 41 other states searching for acceptable wording for laws meant to protect the rights of crime victims.

While his trial was the legal finale of one of the bloodiest murder sprees in American history, accepting David Berkowitz's guilty pleas meant that the issue of his sanity at the time of his crimes would never be resolved. As he began serving his time, debates over the insanity defense, the role of psychiatric testimony, and ethical questions about trying the mentally ill continued to grow.

— Thomas C. Smith

Suggestions for Further Reading

Abrahamsen, David. *Confessions of Son of Sam*. New York: Columbia University Press, 1985.

——. "Unmasking Son of Sam's Demons." *New York Times Magazine* (July 1, 1979): 20–22.

Goldstein, Tom. "The Berkowitz Legal Puzzle." *New York Times* (May 25, 1978): Section IV, 20.

Klausner, Lawrence D. *The Son of Sam*. New York: McGraw-Hill, 1981.

Salisbury, Stephan. ".44-Caliber Journalism." *The Nation* (May 26, 1979): 591–593.

Bakke v. University of California . . . Appeal: 1978

Appellee: Allan Bakke   **Appellant:** The Medical School of the University of California   **Appellee Claim:** That the California Supreme Court erred in ruling that the school's special-admissions program for minorities violated Bakke's civil rights as a white male when he was denied admission

Chief Lawyer for Appellee: Reynold H. Colvin

Chief Lawyers for Appellant: Archibald Cox, Paul J. Mishkin, Jack B. Owens, and Donald L. Reidhaar   **Justices:** Harry A. Blackmun, William J. Brennan, Jr., Warren E. Burger, Thurgood Marshall, Lewis F. Powell, Jr., William H. Rehnquist, John Paul Stevens, Potter Stewart, and Byron R. White

Place: Washington, D.C.   **Date of Decision:** June 28, 1978

Decision: That the school's special-admissions program was unconstitutional

SIGNIFICANCE

For the first time, the Supreme Court said there could be such a thing as reverse discrimination.

The University of California operates several campuses throughout the state, and it is one of the largest state-sponsored higher education systems. At the university's campus in Davis, California, a medical school was established in 1968 with an entering class of 50 students. Three years later, the entering class size was doubled to 100 students. Originally, there was no preferential admissions policy for minorities. From 1968 to 1970, the school implemented a special-admissions program to increase minority representation in each entering class.

The special admissions program worked separately from the regular admissions program. Sixteen percent of the entering class was reserved for minorities, and minority applicants were processed and interviewed separately from regular applicants. The grade point averages and standardized test score averages for special-admissions entrants were significantly lower than for regular-admissions entrants.

In 1973, a Caucasian male named Allan Bakke applied to the Davis Medical School. Although Bakke got a combined score of 468 out of a possible 500 from his interviewers, his application was rejected. There were 2,464 applications for the 100 positions in the 1973 entering class, and by the time Bakke's application came up for consideration the school was only taking applicants with scores of 470 or better. Four special-admissions seats were left unfilled, however, and Bakke wrote a bitter letter to Dr. George H. Lowrey, associate dean and chairman of the Admissions Committee, complaining about the injustice of the special-admissions process.

Bakke applied again in 1974. That year there was even more competition for the 100 entering class positions: the school received 3,737 applications. Lowrey was one of Bakke's interviewers and gave him a low score, which contributed to Bakke's being rejected once again. Furious, Bakke sued the University of California in the Superior Court of California.

Marchers protesting the Court's decision in *Bakke*. (AP/Wide World Photos)

Bakke alleged that the Medical School's special admissions program acted to exclude him on the basis of his race and violated his rights under the Equal Protection Clause of the Fourteenth Amendment to the U.S. Constitution, the California state constitution, and civil rights legislation. The trial court agreed but refused to order the school to admit Bakke as a student. Bakke appealed to the California Supreme Court, which confirmed the trial court's decision that the school's admissions programs were unconstitutional and also ordered the school to admit Bakke.

Reverse Discrimination Claimed

The School appealed to the U.S. Supreme Court. Its attorneys were Archibald Cox, Paul J. Mishkin, Jack B. Owens and Donald L. Reidhaar, and Bakke's chief attorney was Reynold H. Colvin. The parties argued their case before the Supreme Court on October 12, 1977. Bakke's attorney, Colvin, was making his first Supreme Court appearance, and he faced several experienced attorneys. For example, Cox was a former Harvard Law School professor and had served as Watergate Special Prosecutor. Colvin found himself immersed in an argument with Justice Thurgood Marshall, the only African-American on the court, over whether minorities should be accorded any preference in the school's admissions process:

> Marshall: You are arguing about keeping somebody out and the other side is arguing about getting somebody in.
>
> Colvin: That's right.
>
> Marshall: So it depends on which way you look at it doesn't it? . . .
>
> Colvin: If I may finish . . .
>
> Marshall: You are talking about your client's rights. Don't these underprivileged people have some rights?
>
> Colvin: They certainly have the right to . . .
>
> Marshall: To eat cake.

On June 28, 1978, Justice Lewis F. Powell, Jr., announced the decision of the majority in the 5-4 decision. It held that the school's special-admissions policy constituted reverse discrimination and was thus illegal. The court upheld the decision of the California Supreme Court, and affirmed the California court's order that Bakke be admitted to the school. Further, the Court upheld the California court's determination that the school's special-admissions program had to be scrapped. However, the Court held that schools could continue to give preference to minorities, so long as they didn't exclude whites from a specific portion of the entering class, like the school had. The Court cited Harvard University's program as a model for an acceptable admissions policy that gave consideration to racial status without violating the civil rights of whites such as Bakke:

> The experience of other university admissions programs, which take race into account in achieving the educational diversity valued by the First Amendment, demonstrates that the assignment of a fixed number of places to a minority group is not a necessary means toward that end. An illuminating example is found in the Harvard College program. . . . When the [Harvard] Committee on Admissions reviews the large middle group of applicants who are admissible and deemed capable of doing good work in their courses, the race of an applicant may tip the balance in his favor just as geographic origin or a life spent on a farm may tip the balance in other candidates' cases. A farm boy from Idaho can bring something to Harvard College that a Bostonian cannot offer. Similarly, a black student can usually bring something that a white person cannot offer.
>
> In Harvard college admissions the Committee has not set target quotas for the number of blacks, or of musicians, football players, physicists or Californians to be admitted in a given year.

In a nutshell, the Court had ruled that while schools could give minority applicants some extra preference and consideration, they couldn't set aside a quota of positions for minority students that excluded whites. Such a program, like that at the Davis Medical School, constituted reverse discrimination. Bakke had won his case and would be admitted as a student. It was the first time that the Supreme Court applied civil rights protection to white students seeking admission to a university.

—Stephen G. Christianson

Suggestions for Further Reading

Ball, Howard. *The Bakke Case: Race, Education, and Affirmative Action*. University of Kansas Press, 2000.

"Five Cases That Changed American Society." *Scholastic Update* (November 30, 1984): 19–20.

"Minorities Down at Davis Univ. Since Bakke Case." *Jet* (June 7, 1982): 8.

Mooney, Christopher F. *Inequality and the American Conscience: Justice Through the Judicial System*. New York: Paulist Press, 1982.

O'Neill, Timothy J. *Bakke & the Politics of Equality: Friends and Foes in the Classroom of Litigation*. Middletown, Conn.: Wesleyan University Press, 1985.

Schwartz, Bernard. *Behind Bakke: Affirmative Action and the Supreme Court*. New York: New York University Press, 1988.

The Marvin v. Marvin "Palimony" Suit: 1979

Plaintiff: Michelle Triola Marvin   **Defendant:** Lee Marvin
Plaintiff Claim: That Michelle Triola Marvin was entitled to half of Lee Marvin's earnings during the six years they spent together as an unmarried couple
Chief Defense Lawyers: Mark Goldman and A. David Kagon
Chief Lawyer for Plaintiff: Marvin Mitchelson   **Judge:** Arthur K. Marshall
Place: Los Angeles, California   **Dates of Trial:** January 9–March 28, 1979
Verdict: $104,000 for "rehabilitation" awarded to Michelle Marvin, later rescinded

SIGNIFICANCE

The case established the right of partners in nonmarried relationships to sue for a division of property.

When film actor Lee Marvin married in 1970, his former lover Michelle Triola was not inclined to wish him well. After all, she had lived with the rambunctious, hard-drinking actor for six years and had even legally changed her name to Marvin. At first she accepted the $833 per month he sent to support her while she tried to resume her singing and acting career. When the promised checks stopped, she decided to sue him. Her claim reverberated in divorce courts across America in a decade when the number of unmarried couples living together more than doubled.

Michelle Marvin contacted Marvin Mitchelson, a colorful Los Angeles, California divorce lawyer often hired by Hollywood celebrities. Mitchelson filed a suit charging that, apart from the lack of a $3 marriage license, Lee Marvin and Michelle Triola Marvin were essentially married from 1964 to 1970. Michelle Marvin had given up her career as a singer and an actress to serve as the actor's "cook, companion, and confidante." She claimed that she was entitled to half of what he had earned during their relationship. Her share would be $1.8 million, including $100,000 for the loss of the career she had forgone. Attorney Mitchelson announced he was demanding "palimony" for his client—alimony from a former "pal." While popular usage of the term palimony would result from the case, Mitchelson's real task was to prove that Lee Marvin had reneged on an oral or implicit contract to share his assets.

California had abolished the concept of common-law marriage in 1895. Because the circumstances of the case were so similar to the common-law concept, Michelle Marvin's suit was initially rejected by the courts. On appeal, however, the California Supreme Court endorsed the principle of seeking palimony in 1976, allowing her case to be heard and sparking similar suits in 15 other states. By the time *Marvin v. Marvin* arrived in court in 1979, more than 1,000 palimony suits were pending in California courts alone.

Lee Marvin's lawyers tried to have the case dismissed, but Judge Arthur K. Marshall denied their final motion in January 1979. In Judge Marshall's opinion, only the lack of a marriage license and the absence of a clergyman made the life the two Marvins led together different from that of a married couple.

Trial Enthralls Spectators

Lee Marvin's celebrity and the legal implications for thousands of unmarried couples ensured that the courtroom was packed. Sensation-seeking spectators were not disappointed. Michelle Marvin claimed that Lee Marvin told her early in their relationship, "What I have is yours and what you have is mine." She felt that this and her six years with the actor added up to an implicit marriage contract. The pair had maintained joint bank accounts and were accepted as husband and wife in Hollywood social circles. She offered a packet of love letters from Lee Marvin as evidence and tearfully recalled having several abortions at the actor's insistence because he did not want to become a parent.

Lee Marvin testified that his declarations of love were sexual endearments and denied ever promising to share his assets with his former lover. He dismissed her name change as an act that was entirely her decision, taken in the last days of their relationship. He claimed that he had tried to talk her out of it, joking that she should take the name of a more successful Hollywood star and call herself Gary Cooper. The joint bank accounts were opened as a convenience on movie locations. He had not relinquished sole ownership of his house nor did he and Michelle Marvin co-own any property.

Lee Marvin's lawyers argued that if he had ever intended to marry Michelle Triola during their six years together, he obviously would have done so.

With dramatic flair, attorney Mitchelson unsuccessfully motioned that Lee Marvin should be forced to pay $1 million punitive damages for the fraud of telling the plaintiff he loved her without meaning it.

Career Claim Fails

The picture of a promising career Michelle Marvin claimed to have abandoned faded on the witness stand. Testimony by nightclub owners and singer Mel Torme appraised her talents as being somewhere between mediocre and "slightly better than average." She claimed that her devotion to Lee Marvin caused her to refuse a part in the Broadway musical *Flower Drum Song*, but dancer Gene Kelly denied ever offering her a role.

After 11 weeks in court, Judge Marshall ruled that Michelle Marvin had failed to prove her claim of an oral or implicit contract to share her lover's assets. Under the legal principle of "equitable remedy," however, the judge awarded her $104,000 so that she would "have the economic means to re-educate herself and learn new employable skills." The $104,000 "rehabilitation" figure represented $1,000 a week for two years, the top weekly salary she had earned as a singer before becoming the film star's companion.

The judge stopped short of likening his decision to alimony or property division in conventional divorces. To accept the notion of equal division of property without a marriage contract, he wrote:

> would mean that the court would recognize each unmarried person living together to be automatically entitled by such living together and performing spouse-like functions, to half of the property bought with the earnings of the other nonmarital partner.

Judge Marshall felt that this would come too close to recognizing the long-abolished concept of common-law marriage.

Both sides claimed victory. The only loser appeared to be attorney Mitchelson, who had taken the case on a contingency-fee basis, agreeing to be paid a percentage of the expected million-dollar settlement. *Time* magazine calculated that the years Mitchelson had invested in the case had earned him $6.50 an hour, a miniscule fraction of his normal hourly fee.

Michelle Triola Marvin and celebrity attorney Marvin Mitchelson after her victory in the first "palimony" case. (AP/Wide World Photos)

Mitchelson attempted to have the $104,000 award increased or, at least, to have Lee Marvin pay Michelle Marvin's legal bill. Judge Marshall refused. Mitchelson's only victory was that he had established the right to file a palimony suit, testing the legal property rights of unmarried couples for the first time. "This principle," ruled the judge, "did not come at the expense of the defendant." Mitchelson tried without success to get the State of California to pay him $500,000 for his work.

Observers debated whether Judge Marshall had set forth new legal guidelines for unmarried couples or had arbitrarily awarded an alimony payment under a different name. In 1981, the California State Court of Appeals overturned the $104,000 award, ruling that there was no basis in law for arriving at such a specific figure. The court's decision related only to the sum itself. The basic precedent set by the Marvin case remained, entitling estranged unmarried partners to sue for an equal division of their assets and prompting luckier couples to have legally binding nonmarital contracts drafted to guard against unforeseen future problems.

—*Thomas C. Smith*

Suggestions for Further Reading

Burnett, Barbara A., ed. *Every Woman's Legal Guide.* Garden City, N.Y.: Doubleday & Co., 1983.

Couric, Emily. *The Divorce Lawyers.* New York: St. Martin's Press, 1992.

Van Gelder, Lawrence. "Lawyers Troubled By Rehabilitation Concept In Marvin Decision." *New York Times* (April 20, 1979): 18.

Weitzman, Lenore J. *The Marriage Contract: Spouses, Lovers, and the Law.* New York: The Free Press, 1981.

Zec, Donald. *Marvin: The Story of Lee Marvin.* New York: St. Martin's Press, 1980.

Silkwood v. Kerr-McGee: 1979

Plaintiff: Estate of Karen Silkwood   **Defendant:** Kerr-McGee Nuclear Company   **Plaintiff Claim:** Damages for negligence leading to the plutonium contamination of Karen Silkwood   **Chief Defense Lawyers:** Elliott Fenton, John Griffin, Jr., Larry D. Ottoway, William Paul, L.E. Stringer, and Bill J. Zimmerman   **Chief Lawyers for Plaintiff:** Gerald Spence, Arthur Angel, and James Ikard   **Judge:** Frank G. Theis   **Place:** Oklahoma City, Oklahoma   **Dates of Trial:** March 6–May 18, 1979   **Verdict:** Defendant was found negligent and was ordered to pay $505,000 actual damages, $10 million punitive damages

SIGNIFICANCE

This precedent-setting action between the estate of a dead woman and a giant industrial conglomerate sparked a public uproar about the issue of safety at nuclear facilities and held a company liable for negligence.

Karen Silkwood, a young lab technician and union activist at an Oklahoma plutonium plant operated by the Kerr-McGee Nuclear Company, uncovered evidence in 1974 of managerial wrongdoing and negligence. On November 13, three months after providing the Atomic Energy Commission (AEC) with a detailed list of violations, she was en route to deliver documents to a *New York Times* reporter when her car crashed under mysterious circumstances and she died. An autopsy revealed plutonium contamination, confirming the results of tests taken when she was alive. Speculation among her opponents at that time, was that she had deliberately contaminated herself to embarrass Kerr-McGee, an assertion that Silkwood bitterly denied. When the Silkwood estate announced its intention to sue, Kerr-McGee insisted that its Cimarron plant met federal guidelines and that any contamination Silkwood sustained must have come from elsewhere.

After more than four years of delay, on March 6, 1979, Karen Silkwood's family finally had their day in court against Kerr-McGee. Actually they had three months, the longest civil trial in Oklahoma history. Leading off for the Silkwood estate, attorney Gerry Spence put Dr. John Gofman, a physician and an outspoken critic of lax nuclear regulation, on the stand. In answer to a Spence question about the dangers of plutonium, Gofman replied, "The license to give out doses of plutonium is a legalized permit to murder."

"Was Karen in danger of dying from the plutonium inside her?" asked Spence.

"Yes, she was."

Pressed on Kerr-McGee's skimpy employee training program, Gofman responded: "My opinion is that it is clearly and unequivocally negligence."

The only member of the Kerr-McGee management team to testify against his former employers was ex-supervisor James Smith. While conceding little affection for Silkwood as a person—as a union organizer she had been prickly and combative—Smith corroborated her findings about safety violations at Kerr-McGee. Most alarming was his assertion that there were 40 pounds of Material Unaccounted For (MUF), meaning deadly plutonium that was missing. He dismissed company claims that the MUF was still at the plant. "Let me put it this way," said Smith, who had been in charge of flushing out the system pipes, "if there's 40 pounds still at Cimarron, I don't know where it is."

Another ex-Cimarron employee, now a highway patrol officer, Ron Hammock, told of defective fuel rods, packed full of plutonium pellets, knowingly being shipped to other facilities. "Who told you to ship them?" Spence asked. "My supervisor," the officer calmly replied.

Near Disaster

Three weeks into the trial something happened that raised the question of nuclear safety throughout the United States. A nuclear reactor in Pennsylvania had a near meltdown. For most Americans, the disaster at Three Mile Island was their first experience of the potential for nuclear calamity. The incident cast an inevitable pall over the Silkwood suit, enough for Kerr-McGee chief attorney Bill Paul to move for a mistrial. After careful consideration, Judge Frank Theis denied the request. On hearing this decision, the Silkwood team heaved a vast sigh of relief. Lacking the limitless financial resources of Kerr-McGee, they were fighting this action on a shoestring; any delay would only play into the hands of the $2-billion giant.

Disgruntled, Bill Paul called Kerr-McGee's star witness, Dr. George Voelz, health director at the prestigious Los Alamos Scientific Laboratory. Voelz testified that, in his opinion, the level of contamination displayed by Karen Silkwood fell within AEC standards. Spence thought otherwise. In a cross-examination lasting two days, he drew one embarrassing retraction after another from the frazzled scientist. Central to Voelz's theme was a model used to arrive at the standards. Spence showed how Karen Silkwood in no way conformed to the average person used in the model, she had been less than 100 pounds and a heavy smoker, both factors that influence the chances of contamination. Also, Spence extracted from Voelz the grudging admission that he really didn't know the level of plutonium exposure necessary to cause cancer.

In his final instructions to the jury, Judge Theis spelled out the law: "If you find that the damage to the person or property of Karen Silkwood resulted from the operation of this plant, . . . Kerr-McGee . . . is liable."

On May 18, 1979, after four days of deliberation, the jury decided that Kerr-McGee had indeed been negligent and awarded $505,000 in damages. A gasp swept the courtroom when the jury added on their assessment for punitive damages: $10 million.

It was a huge settlement, one obviously destined for the appeal courts. The litigation dragged on until August 1986, when, in an out-of-court settlement, Kerr-McGee agreed to pay the Silkwood estate $1.38 million, which amounted to less than one year's interest on the sum originally awarded.

Many regarded Karen Silkwood as a nuclear martyr. To this day, the circumstances surrounding her death remain shrouded in mystery. Was she killed to be silenced? That may never be known. What is known is that the Silkwood estate's victory, modest though it may have ultimately been, sent the nuclear industry a clear message: Dangerous sources of energy demand unusually vigilant regulation.

—Colin Evans

Suggestions for Further Reading

Kohn, Howard. *Who Killed Karen Silkwood?* New York: Summit, 1981.

Rashke, Richard. *The Killing Of Karen Silkwood*. New York: Houghton Mifflin Co., 1981.

"Silkwood Settlement." *Science News* (August 8, 1986): 134.

Spence, Gerry. *With Justice For None*. New York: Times Books, 1989.

Stein, J. "The Deepening Mystery." *Progressive* (January 1981): 14–19.

U.S. v. *The Progressive*: 1979

Plaintiff: The United States   **Defendant:** *The Progressive*, Inc.
Plaintiff Claims: That *The Progressive* magazine should be prevented from publishing an article concerning how to build a hydrogen bomb
Chief Defense Lawyer: Earl Munson, Jr.
Chief Lawyers for Plaintiff: Thomas S. Martin and Frank M. Tuerkheimer
Judge: Robert W. Warren   **Place:** Milwaukee, Wisconsin
Date of Hearing: March 26, 1979   **Decision:** Injunction forbidding *The Progressive* from publishing the article

SIGNIFICANCE

The court's injunction, constituting prior restraint on publication, was the first of its kind in American history.

In 1909, Robert LaFollette, the famous Progressive leader from Wisconsin, founded a monthly news magazine in Madison, Wisconsin called *The Progressive*. The Progressive movement enjoyed some success as a third-party movement in American politics into the 1920s, and the magazine enjoyed a wide circulation. After LaFollette's 1924 bid for the presidency, which won 16% of the popular vote, third parties such as the Progressives largely disappeared as a force in American politics until the 1992 campaign of H. Ross Perot. Today, the magazine has a small but loyal audience of approximately 50,000 subscribers.

In 1978, the magazine commissioned freelance writer Howard Morland to write an article concerning government secrecy in the area of energy and nuclear weapons. Energy and nuclear issues were Morland's specialty, and after months of extensive background research Morland wrote "The H-Bomb Secret: How We Got It, Why We're Telling It." On February 27, 1979, Samuel H. Day, Jr., the magazine's managing editor, sent a copy of Morland's draft to the Department of Energy's offices in Germantown, Maryland. Day asked the DOE to verify the technical accuracy of Morland's draft before the magazine published it.

John A. Griffin, DOE's director of classification, and Duane C. Sewell, assistant secretary of energy for defense programs, read the article with alarm. They determined that it contained sensitive material, material that constituted "restricted data" under the Atomic Energy Act. On March 1, 1979, Lynn R.

Coleman, DOE's General Counsel, phoned Day and Erwin Knoll, another editor involved in the Morland article. Coleman asked that the magazine not publish the article, stating that in addition to DOE, the State Department and the Arms Control and Disarmament Agency believed publication would damage U.S. efforts to control the worldwide spread of nuclear weapons. The next day, Sewell met with Day, Knoll, and Ronald Carbon, the magazine's publisher.

Despite the government's efforts, on March 7, 1979, the magazine informed Coleman that it would publish the Morland article. The next day, the government sued the magazine in the U.S. District Court for the Western District of Wisconsin, and asked the court to stop publication.

Government Wins Battle, Loses War

The magazine's attorney was Earl Munson, Jr., and the government was represented by Thomas S. Martin and Frank M. Tuerkheimer. On March 9, the day after the suit was filed, Judge Robert W. Warren in Milwaukee, Wisconsin issued a temporary restraining order against the magazine until a preliminary injunction hearing could be held on March 16, 1979. The hearing was delayed for 10 days, however, and took place on March 26, 1979.

At the hearing, Knoll testified that, despite the government's concerns, the article would actually benefit the United States by promoting public debate free of secrecy:

> [I am] totally convinced that publication of the article will be of substantial benefit to the United States because it will demonstrate that this country's security does not lie in an oppressive and ineffective system of secrecy and classification but in open, honest, and informed public debate about issues which the people must decide.

Judge Warren was in a bind. Under the First Amendment, the injunction that the government wanted constituted a prior restraint on publication, which is difficult to justify legally because of the principle that the law isn't broken until an illegal act is actually committed, not before. However, the government had presented very strong evidence that the Morland article would contribute to the spread of nuclear know-how. Warren balanced the two considerations, and came down on the government's side:

> A mistake in ruling against *The Progressive* will seriously infringe cherished First Amendment rights. If a preliminary injunction is issued, it will constitute the first instance of prior restraint against a publication in this fashion in the history of this country, to this Court's knowledge. Such notoriety is not to be sought. . . .

> [But] a mistake in ruling against the United States could pave the way for thermonuclear annihilation for us all. In that event, our right to life is extinguished and the right to publish becomes moot.

Therefore, Warren signed a preliminary injunction restraining the magazine, its editors, and Morland from "publishing or otherwise communicating, transmitting, or disclosing in any manner any information designated by the

Secretary of Energy as Restricted Data contained in the Morland article." The injunction would last until a full trial could be held.

Having won the first litigation battle, the government ultimately lost the legal war. Inspired by the publicity surrounding the case, other publications such as *Scientific American* began to run articles related to the H-bomb and nuclear power. Neither the Morland article nor any other article, however, contained much more than a general description of how nuclear weapons work and were devoid of the many intricate technical details necessary to design an actual weapon, much less build one. Rather than begin a massive and probably unpopular litigation against the press, the government dropped its proceedings against *The Progressive* before the trial and the Morland article was published. Nevertheless, Warren's injunction, imposing a prior restraint on the article's publication, was the first of its kind in American history.

—Stephen G. Christianson

Suggestions for Further Reading

Born Secret: the H-Bomb, The Progressive Case and National Security. New York: Pergamon Press, 1981.

Knoll, Erwin. "The Good it Did." *The Progressive* (February 1991): 4.

———. "Through the Looking Glass." *The Progressive* (February 1985): 4.

Morland, Howard. "The Secret Sharer." *The Progressive* (July 1984): 20–21.

———. *The Secret That Exploded.* New York: Random House, 1981.

Daniel James White Trial: 1979

Defendant: Daniel James White   **Crime Charged:** Murder
Chief Defense Lawyers: Douglas Schmidt and Stephen Scherr
Chief Prosecutor: Thomas F. Norman   **Judge:** Walter F. Calcagno
Place: San Francisco, California   **Dates of Trial:** April 25–May 21, 1979
Verdict: Guilty, Voluntary Manslaughter   **Sentence:** 7 years, 8 months.

SIGNIFICANCE

Celebrity murder trials inevitably attract massive media coverage. What made the Dan White case unique was the volatile mix of politics, revenge, and homosexual intolerance. Many wondered if that intolerance spilled over into the jury room. How else could they explain such a verdict based on a defense of impaired mental capacity resulting from eating too much "junk food?"

On November 27, 1978, 32-year-old Dan White entered the San Francisco City Hall by crawling in through a basement window. He adopted this unorthodox means of access to avoid negotiating a metal detector in the main entrance, for reasons which would soon become clear. Once inside, White breezed through the familiar corridors of power. He was on a retrieval mission. Earlier that summer, this ambitious young politician had impetuously resigned his post as a city supervisor, citing financial difficulties; now he wanted that job back. Only one man could make that possible: Mayor George Moscone. White reached Moscone's office and was invited in.

The two men talked, or rather argued, for several minutes. As the exchange heated up, Moscone made it plain that he had no intention of re-appointing White, who had become a political liability, whereupon White drew a .38-caliber Smith and Wesson revolver that had been tucked into his belt and pumped four bullets into his former boss. After reloading, White hunted down long-time political foe Harvey Milk, another city supervisor. Five shots ended Milk's life. White ran from the building, only to surrender to the authorities one hour later.

Police guarded White closely, fearing possible retaliation. They had good cause for concern. Milk, one of San Francisco's most militant gay activists, had many supporters, all of whom loathed White and the homophobic attitudes he had espoused when in office. Anything was possible in such a volatile situation.

Double Execution

Prosecutor Thomas Norman sought to diffuse some of that volatility with a calm, orderly representation of the facts when the state opened its case against Dan White on May 1, 1979. He described in simple terms what amounted to a double execution, carried out deliberately and with malice aforethought. It was, he said, a crime deserving of death in the gas chamber.

Former policeman Dan White (right) was suspected in the killings of city Supervisor Harvey Milk (left) and Mayor George Moscone (center). (AP/Wide World Photos)

Few could have envied Douglas Schmidt's task when he rose to make the opening statement on White's behalf; after all, he was representing an admitted double assassin. However, he soon went on the offensive. In a fine speech he skillfully diverted the jury's attention away from the crime itself and onto the emotional traumas that White had undergone since relinquishing his position as city supervisor. "Good people, fine people, with fine backgrounds, simply don't kill people in cold blood," said Schmidt, "it just doesn't happen, and obviously some part of him has not been presented thus far." Schmidt claimed that White's crimes had been the product of manic depression, "a vile biochemical change" over which the defendant had no control. As added insurance, just in case this line of reasoning failed to sway the jury, Schmidt rounded out his opening with some very pointed comparisons between Milk's overtly homosexual lifestyle and White's all-American background.

The prosecution responded with a parade of witnesses, each of whom recounted events leading up to and on the fateful day at City Hall. Chief among them was recently elected San Francisco Mayor Dianne Feinstein. Mayor Feinstein detailed White's frustration with the political system, his inability to make a difference, as a major source of his discontent. Schmidt scored heavily on cross-examination when he asked, "Would it be your opinion that the man you knew [White] was the type of man who would have shot two people?" Over strenuous state objections, she was allowed to respond. "No," she said. "It would not."

At this point the prosecution began to unravel. What was supposed to be the high-water mark of their case—a taped confession made by White within hours of the shootings—turned into disaster. The tape should have sealed his fate. It did no such thing. Jurors heard him whine: "Well, it's just that I've been under an awful lot of pressure lately, financial pressure, because of my job situation, family pressure . . . because of not being able to have time with my family." The killings were hardly mentioned at all, and White's only display of remorse came when describing his own predicament. And yet, several jurors wept openly as they listened to the story of a man pushed beyond his endurance. Prosecutor Norman could not believe the evidence of his own eyes and ears— Dan White had been turned into a martyr, an object of sympathy.

Unique Defense

Schmidt capitalized on what had been a lackluster prosecution by turning the trial into an examination of White's mental state. Several psychiatrists testified that the defendant had not really meant to commit murder but had been driven to it by factors beyond his control. Much was made of White's prodigious intake of junkfood and candy—what came to be known as the "Twinkies Defense"—in which an abnormally high blood sugar count was blamed for the mayhem that he had wrought. It was a novel but effective defense.

But most effective of all were Schmidt's repeated portrayals of White as an upstanding young man, an ex-fireman and ex-police officer, someone who had been defeated by a corrupt system he was powerless to change. Schmidt cunningly marshaled public resentment against both politicians and homosexuals into one neat package. He found nothing unusual in the fact that White was carrying a gun on the fateful day (As an ex-cop, could anything have been more natural?), or that he had crawled in through a window at City Hall to, as one psychiatrist stated, avoid "embarrassing the officer at the metal detector." Dan White, Schmidt said, was acting under an "irresistible impulse to kill," and as such, under California law, was entitled to a verdict of manslaughter.

The jury agreed. On May 21, 1979, they returned two verdicts of voluntary manslaughter. Judge Walter Calcagno handed down the maximum sentence, seven years, and eight months imprisonment. With time off for good behavior, Dan White was looking at freedom in five years.

When news of the verdicts hit the streets, an already incendiary situation exploded. Five thousand gays marched on City Hall to protest, and a full-scale riot ensued. Inside the jail, the target of their rage, Dan White, lay on his cell cot, ears plugged against the bedlam.

Over concerted gay protests, White was paroled in 1984. But liberty proved even more onerous than incarceration. Plagued by demons that just wouldn't leave him alone, on October 21, 1985, Dan White wrote the final chapter in this tragedy by committing suicide.

The Dan White trial became a rallying call for homosexuals all across America. In their eyes, the jury had semi-officially sanctioned gay murder. Overlooked was the fact that George Moscone was a happily married family man. Somehow that got lost in the politics. Even so, it is difficult to dispute their firmly held belief that had White killed Moscone alone, he probably would still be behind bars.

—Colin Evans

Suggestions for Further Reading

Fitzgerald, Frances. "The Castro-II." *New Yorker* (July 28, 1986): 44–63.

Robinson, P. "Gays In The Streets." *New Republic* (June 9, 1979): 9–10.

Shilts, Randy. *The Mayor of Castro Street.* New York: St. Martin's Press, 1982.

Weiss, Mike. *Double Play.* Reading, Mass.: Addison-Wesley, 1984.

Jeffrey Robert MacDonald Trial: 1979

Defendant: Jeffrey Robert MacDonald   **Crime Charged:** Murder
Chief Defense Lawyers: Bernard L. Segal and Wade Smith
Chief Prosecutors: James L. Blackburn and Brian Murtagh   **Judge:** Franklin
T. Dupree   **Place:** Raleigh, N.C.   **Dates of Trial:** July 16–August 29, 1979
Verdict: Guilty   **Sentence:** Life imprisonment

SIGNIFICANCE

The horror of the triple murder and the long delay between the crime and the trial
alone were sufficient to make this one of the most notorious trials in recent
history. The subsequent best-selling book *Fatal Vision* by Joe McGinnis, written
with the cooperation of the murderer, seared the case into the memories of many
Americans. Jeffrey MacDonald's suit against McGinnis for betraying his trust in
writing a book that portrayed him as guilty, raised ethical and legal issues about
"checkbook" investigative journalism.

Few murder defendants have so assiduously courted the media as Jeffrey
MacDonald. Through books, television, newsprint, and even civil litigation,
he made his name a household word. For more than two decades, America
watched and read about this enigmatic ex-Green Beret. Most remained convinced he was guilty as charged, and yet doubts persisted.

The crime was horrible: a young pregnant mother, Colette MacDonald,
and her two young daughters, hacked and battered to death at their home on
Fort Bragg Army Base in Fayetteville, North Carolina, on February 17, 1970.
Immediately suspicion fell on the woman's husband, Captain Jeffrey Mac-
Donald, a 26-year-old medical doctor. He told of being attacked by four hippie-
type intruders: two white men, one black, and a white woman with long blonde
hair who wore a large floppy hat, high boots, and carried a candle. Throughout
the ordeal she chanted, "acid is groovy . . . kill the pigs." To ward off blows from
an ice pick, MacDonald wrapped a blue pajama jacket around his hands. Even
so, he sustained multiple stab wounds.

The superficial nature of MacDonald's injuries—none required stitch-
ing—and the remarkably tidy condition of the room in which he claimed to have
fought for his life, convinced military detectives that his story was false. Also,
they wanted to know how fibers from his blue pajama jacket came to be found
beneath Colette MacDonald's body?

On May 1 the army announced that MacDonald was being charged with three counts of murder. The preliminary hearing began July 6 and soon revealed a seriously flawed investigation into the death of Colette MacDonald and her two daughters. So embarrassing were the disclosures of official negligence that, in October 1970, the army dismissed all charges against MacDonald.

Shortly afterwards, in a remarkable display of nerve, MacDonald appeared on a national TV talk show and lambasted the army for its ineptitude. He came across as indignant about his own mistreatment and indifferent towards the fate of his family. Galvanized by the criticism, detectives resumed their inquiries. The upshot was a mammoth report in 1972, which again concluded that MacDonald was guilty of murder. In July 1974, a grand jury was impaneled and returned three murder indictments against him.

Jeffrey MacDonald after being freed of murder charges. He was found guilty of the crime nine years later. (North Carolina Division of Archives and History)

The Trial, at Last

Bringing the case to court was a laborious process, but in July 1979, 9½ years after the murders, MacDonald finally faced his accusers in a North Carolina courtroom. He came bearing defense fund contributions from many influential supporters who believed in his innocence.

Defense attorney Bernard Segal was confident when the trial opened, but right from day one things went badly. Judge Franklin Dupree refused to admit into evidence a psychiatric evaluation of Mac-Donald which suggested that someone of his personality type was most unlikely to have committed violent crimes. Dupree did this for the soundest of reasons. If the defense were allowed to present their side of the psychiatric argument, then the prosecution would doubtless counter with experts of their own. Because no plea of insanity had been entered, Dupree didn't want the trial bogged down by a mass of what was likely to be contradictory testimony.

Then Dupree admitted into testimony something that the MacDonald camp very much wanted left out: a copy of *Esquire* magazine, found in the MacDonald household, containing a lengthy article about the Charles Manson murders. (In 1969, Manson, a commune leader, had ordered his "disciples" on a killing binge that left seven dead in southern California.) This was a big plus for the prosecution. They intended to suggest that reading this article had implanted in MacDonald's mind the idea of blaming a hippie gang for his own murderous activities.

In a sedate North Carolina courtroom, Segal's wide-open style of combative advocacy did not sit well with Judge Dupree. The two locked horns repeatedly, mostly to MacDonald's detriment. But it wasn't just a clash of personalities that hurt the defendant; there was the evidence as well.

FBI analyst Paul Stombaugh led the jury through a clear exposition of the blue pajama jacket and its relevance. He showed how all 48 holes made by the ice pick were smooth and cylindrical. In order for this to have happened the jacket would need to remain stationary, an unlikely occurrence if MacDonald had indeed wrapped the jacket around his hands to defend himself and was dodging a torrent of blows. Also, by folding the jacket in one particular way, Stombaugh demonstrated how all 48 tears could have been made by 21 thrusts of the ice pick, coincidentally the same number of wounds that Colette MacDonald had suffered. By implication, Stombaugh was saying that MacDonald's story was a tissue of lies; what really happened was that Colette MacDonald had been repeatedly stabbed through the pajama jacket by her enraged husband, who then concocted the story of four intruders to mask his actions.

Drama in Court

A moment of high drama occurred when prosecutors Brian Murtagh and James Blackburn abruptly staged an impromptu re-enactment of the alleged attack on MacDonald. Murtagh wrapped a pajama top around his hands and tried to fend off a series of ice pick blows from Blackburn. For his troubles Murtagh received a small wound to the arm, but two telling points had been made. First, all of the holes in the pajama top were rough and jagged, not smoothly cylindrical as the holes in MacDonald's pajama jacket had been; second, Murtagh was stabbed, albeit not seriously. When MacDonald had been examined at Womack Hospital he did not have a single wound on his arms. The inference was obvious and highly damaging to MacDonald.

The strongest defense witness was supposed to be Helena Stoeckley, 18 years old at the time of the murders, a known liar with a long record of drug abuse and alcoholism. Over the years, she had yielded several confessions to involvement in the slaughter and an equal number of retractions. Segal was at least hoping to establish some kind of link to a "hippie gang," but Stoeckley let him down. On this occasion she denied ever having been inside the MacDonald home. Furthermore, she denied ever having seen MacDonald before that very morning in court.

Segal was furious. He fought for the introduction of evidence from other witnesses to whom Stoeckley had confessed. But Judge Dupree, in the absence of any evidence to connect Stoeckley to the house and unimpressed by her performance on the stand, refused. When Segal persisted in arguing the point he got his comeuppance. Dupree revealed that, over the weekend, he had received two phone calls from Helena Stoeckley. She had talked about hiring a lawyer because she felt herself to be in mortal danger from none other than Bernard Segal. Upon hearing this Segal sank back into his chair and let the matter drop.

Perhaps the most decisive evidence against MacDonald was a tape made during his original 1970 interview with military investigators. Jury members got to hear a man who sounded evasive and indifferent. Worse than that, he sounded arrogant. Describing himself, MacDonald said: "I'm bright, aggressive, I work hard. . . . Christ, I was a doctor!" Later: "I had a beautiful wife who loved me and two kids who were great. . . . What could I have gained by doing this?" By way of an answer, a detective showed MacDonald the photograph of a young woman, just one of MacDonald's many sexual conquests, a side of his nature that he had desperately tried to conceal. MacDonald, rattled by this surprise revelation, said quietly, "You guys are more thorough than I thought." One juror later remarked, "Until I heard that, [tape] there was no doubt in my mind about his innocence. . . . but hearing him turned the whole thing around."

Under Segal's gentle probing, MacDonald performed well on the stand, but as soon as he was subjected to cross-examination that old cockiness began to reassert itself. Whenever asked to explain an awkward fact or statement, he would shrug indifference. In the end, his performance failed to convince those who mattered most: the jury. On August 29, 1979, they found MacDonald guilty. Judge Dupree sentenced him to the maximum allowable under federal law, three consecutive life terms.

After several appeals, in January 1983 the Supreme Court upheld all three convictions. But Jeffrey MacDonald wasn't finished yet.

Murderer Sues Writer

In 1984 one of the most extraordinary civil actions in American legal history began. The plaintiff, MacDonald, a thrice- convicted murderer, claimed breach of contract and fraud against Joe McGinnis, author of *Fatal Vision,* the definitive account of the murders. McGinnis had been contacted prior to Mac-Donald's trial. The intention, as MacDonald saw it, was for McGinnis to write an account that painted him in the most favorable light. The two had signed a contract in which MacDonald agreed to provide material in return for a handsome percentage of the book profits. As is customary, MacDonald signed a release, the third paragraph of which read:

> I realize, of course, that you do not propose to libel me. Nevertheless, in order that you may feel free to write the book in any manner that you deem best, I agree that I will not make or assert against you, the publisher, or its licensees or anyone else involved in the production or distribution of the book, any claim or demand whatsoever based on the ground that anything contained in the book defames me.

As an afterthought Bernard Segal added the following, ". . . provided that the essential integrity of my life story is maintained."

It was this addendum that proved so controversial. No one reading *Fatal Vision* could have been in any doubt that McGinnis thought Jeffrey MacDonald had slaughtered his wife and children. The book, which later became a TV movie, portrayed MacDonald not as an innocent victim but as a heartless murderer. For this perceived betrayal MacDonald cried foul, claiming that McGinnis had taken advantage of his privileged position, and filed suit.

The action was heard in Los Angeles, California in 1987 before Judge William J. Rea. At the heart of the plaintiff's case was a series of letters that passed between MacDonald and McGinnis, in which the writer, right up to the publication of the book, continued to impress on MacDonald a purported belief in his innocence. Attorney Gary Bostwick, appearing for MacDonald, asked McGinnis: "Did you consider yourself [MacDonald's] . . . friend at the end of the trial?"

"I considered myself the author," said McGinnis, "I don't know how you would define 'friend'. It was a professional relationship."

Bostwick tightened the noose.

"Would you look at Exhibit 36A [a letter] again. . . . It says, 'Goddamn it, Jeff, one of the worst things about all this is how suddenly and totally all of your friends—self included—have been deprived of the pleasure of your company.' "

"Well, that was eight years ago," McGinnis replied lamely, "And my recollections were a lot fresher." It only got worse.

You said yesterday, . . . looking at the letters of the first six to nine months after the trial, that you never intended to deceive him. . . . After the first six or nine months, did you intend to deceive him?

"Well, there certainly came a time when I was willing to let him continue to believe whatever he wanted to believe, so he wouldn't try to prevent me from finishing my book."

"Is the answer yes?"

"The answer could be interpreted that way, I suppose."

Such candor did not sit well with the six-person jury. And neither did the testimony of noted authors Joseph Wambaugh and William F. Buckley, both of whom stated that McGinnis' only obligation was to the truth as he saw it. Defense attorney Daniel Kornstein steered them through a high-minded rationale of the journalist's craft. Their testimony, given with the best of intentions, provided Bostwick with just the weapons he needed to portray MacDonald as the injured party. He extracted a painful admission from Wambaugh that duplicity and deception were everyday currency for the investigative writer, wholly acceptable so long as the ends justified the means. Bostwick, in his charge to the jury, concluded simply, "We cannot do whatever is necessary. We have to do what is right."

Undistracted by any of the murder evidence, the jury heard only Bostwick's tale of a gullible subject, duped by an unscrupulous writer. Five members of the jury agreed with his reasoning; one did not. On August 21, 1987, a mistrial was declared. Later, the parties agreed to settle for $325,000, the sum originally requested. Interestingly, afterward, each jury member revealed his or her belief that MacDonald had murdered his family. That they were able to divorce personal bias from their deliberations on a purely civil matter speaks highly of the essential integrity and impartiality of the jury system.

In July 1991, Judge Franklin T. Dupree, after hearing arguments that MacDonald should be granted a new murder trial on grounds of prosecutorial misconduct, denied the petition.

—Colin Evans

Suggestions for Further Reading

Garbus, Martin. "McGinnis: A Travesty Of Libel." *Publishers Weekly* (April 21, 1989): 69.

Malcolm, Janet. *The Journalist And The Murderer.* New York: Alfred A. Knopf, 1990.

McGinnis, Joe. *Fatal Vision.* New York: G.P. Putnam's Sons, 1983.

Taylor, John. "Holier Than Thou." *New York Times* (March 27, 1989): 32–35.

Ed Cantrell Trial: 1979

Defendant: Edward Cantrell   **Crime Charged:** Murder
Chief Defense Lawyer: Gerald L. Spence   **Chief Prosecutors:** Preliminary
Hearing: Robert Bath; Trial: Robert Pickett   **Judges:** Preliminary Hearing:
Nena Stafford; Trial: Kenneth Hamm   **Place:** Rock Springs, Wyoming
Dates of Trials: Preliminary Hearing: November 13, 1978–February 7, 1979;
Trial: November 12–30, 1979   **Verdict:** Not guilty

SIGNIFICANCE

The case demonstrated how media sensationalism, aided by prosecutorial misconduct, could have sent an innocent man to the death chamber. The media's
grudging acceptance of the verdict did nothing to restore the reputation of a man
who had served the public honorably and well for 30 years.

In the 1970s, because of the hunt for new energy sources, Rock Springs,
Wyoming, suddenly became a boom town. The boom attracted gamblers,
prostitutes and dope dealers. Because of this "big city" crime, the investigative
television news program, *60 Minutes*, did two installments on Rock Creek.
Wyoming's governor established a special grand jury.

Then an undercover policeman, subpoenaed by the grand jury, was killed
two days before he was to testify. Arrested for the murder was the director of
public safety, Ed Cantrell.

Cantrell claimed he had shot his own agent, Michael Rosa, in self-defense.
Prosecutors said it was cold-blooded murder. *Newsweek* reported that Rosa had
"a fat brown envelope," with data to convict officials "all the way up to
Washington," and the "fat brown envelope," had disappeared.

The preliminary hearing was interrupted for a couple of months because
Cantrell's lawyer, Gerry Spence, forced a state witness to admit that the prosecutors had threatened him with a murder charge if he didn't cooperate. Spence got
the hearing postponed until the grand jury's term expired. When the hearing
resumed, Spence asked a witness if he were afraid of something.

"It's immaterial whether he's afraid," Judge Nena Stafford said.

"It goes to his credibility," Spence said.

"I'm not interested in credibility," the judge replied. After a heated protest from Spence, she relented. The witness admitted that he was "afraid, terrorized and felt paranoid" because of threats by the prosecutors.

Shredded Evidence

Spence tried to get documents of the grand jury investigation. He was told they had all been shredded. Fred Reed, a grand jury prosecutor, denied he had any evidence. A search of his briefcase, however, produced a loaded pistol and several tapes. On one tape Larry Yonkee, Reed's boss, was telling Reed to "get back and clean up or Spence will impeach us to death."

But the judge bound Cantrell over for trial.

Shredded Prosecution

At the trial, Rosa's wife admitted that in the last few days of his life, Rosa had been taking medicine that robbed him of sleep and made him edgy and suspicious of everyone. He began saying that Cantrell was out to get him.

Brother officers said Rosa was arrogant, quarrelsome, and violent, even pointing a gun at a man with whom he was arguing. He had been fired from the Washington, D.C., police force for threatening his first wife with a knife. Then he had been dismissed from the Prince George's County, Maryland, sheriff's department for undue aggressiveness. He had moved west and joined the Gillette, Wyoming, police department. He had been fired again, but Cantrell admired his fearlessness and hired him on the Rock Springs force.

Policeman Phil Watt, a prosecution witness, said Rosa had a dispute with Sergeant James Callas, his supervisor, over an expense account. Callas, like all Rock Springs officers, was terrified of the grand jury, which had indicted another cop over a $90 expense item. Rosa became convinced that Callas was going to frame him for something. In a tape-recorded telephone call, Watt told Cantrell about it and added, "Rosa's got a real cute stunt planned for Monday. What he's going to do when he gets up in front of the grand jury is cut his own throat and cut up a couple of other people's."

"Am I one of them?" Cantrell asked.

"No," said Watt. "The information that I'm fixing to give you doesn't necessarily pertain to you, but it does to people who work under you, Jim Callas, for one." The tape pretty much wiped out the state's contention that Cantrell shot Rosa because the detective would testify against him. The prosecutors never made it public.

Callas followed Watt to the stand. Callas had said he met Cantrell and Detective Matt Bider after Cantrell had been talking with Watt. Cantrell thought they ought to talk to Rosa. Rosa was at a bar in town.

When Rosa got in the car, Callas, said, he was holding a wine glass. He sat down and put the wineglass between his legs. Callas asked him for his birth date, which was needed for a report to be sent to the FBI, and was writing it down when he heard an explosion. He looked up and saw Rosa slumped over the seat and Cantrell standing outside.

"My God, Ed, what did you do?" he asked.

"He was coming at me. Didn't you see him coming at me?" Cantrell replied, meaning Rosa was drawing his gun.

Spence asked him why someone would put a wine glass between his legs. The prosecution had said Rosa's hands were around the glass.

"So his hands would be free, I guess," Callas said.

Bobby Bath, the county's chief prosecutor, testified he had Cantrell sent to the state hospital for examination. Spence read the report from the state psychiatrists: "He would not likely act impulsively nor be a danger to himself or others. This, of course, precludes a situation in which he saw himself threatened and needed to act in self-preservation."

Spence looked at Bath. "Now in just plain old English, what does that mean?"

"That means some psychiatrist down there says he wouldn't act except where he is threatened. . . . but it doesn't say the psychiatrist was there when it happened."

The "psychiatrist down there," Dr. William Fogarty, was the next witness. He reiterated his opinion that Cantrell, who had never killed anyone in 30 years of law enforcement, would not kill except in self-defense. He added further medical testimony. The wound in Rosa's head, he said, showed that the dead detective had been leaning back, as he'd have to to draw a gun from his holster. Further, he testified, the medicine Rosa was taking "can bring on symptoms akin to psychosis."

Ed Cantrell, director of public safety in Rock Springs, Wyoming, acquited of murder. (AP/Wide World Photos)

When the state rested, Spence called prosecutor Fred Reed and revealed that the state archivist had refused to shred the documents sent to her. The unshredded documents included investigators' reports that Rosa was involved in drug dealing and in contact with gangsters in Salt Lake City and Tucson. The prosecutors, Reed admitted, had not bothered to follow up.

The next defense witness was Christopher Crofts of the state Criminal Investigation Division. Crofts had filed the affidavit charging Cantrell with murder. He had to admit that incriminating "facts" he had sworn to were not true. Rosa's hands were not, as he swore, around a wineglass. The safety strap on his holster was unsnapped, not snapped, as he had sworn. That indicated Rosa had tried to draw his gun.

Fireworks in the Courtroom

In his testimony, Cantrell said his revolver was in his belt, and his hand was resting on it. "That's the way I always sit," he said.

Cantrell's hand was already on his gun, then, when Rosa reached for his. And Cantrell was a quick draw expert. To show what that meant, Spence called a former lawman who knew Cantrell from years of competing against him at shooting events, retired Border Patrol officer Bill Jordan.

Spence brought in two revolvers and loaded them with blanks. He gave one to Jordan, who put it in a holster. He gave the other to a deputy sheriff, loaded and cocked. He instructed the deputy to point the gun at Jordan and fire as soon as the older man started for his gun. After a few moments, Jordan drew and fired. The deputy's mouth dropped open as he stood there holding the unfired gun.

Spence asked Jordan how fast Cantrell was.

"Ed's a mite faster than me," the old lawman said.

The jury found Cantrell not guilty.

Humble Pie Is Hard to Digest

The press found the verdict hard to accept. Texas journalist Molly Ivins, in a special dispatch to the *New York Times*, put a Wild West spin on the story. "An old Western saying is that the first thing to do in a murder case is to determine whether or not the victim deserved to die," she wrote, inventing "an old Western saying." She ignored the implications of the unsnapped holster and the bullet's path, as well as the prosecution's bullying and lies. Her account was fairer than most.

Ed Cantrell was free, but most of Wyoming, knowing only what they read in the paper or saw on television, still thought he was a murderer. For a long time, he couldn't get a job. Eventually he found work as a cattle detective—a private security guard for a group of ranchers.

—William Weir

Suggestions for Further Reading

Holt, Don, and Paul Brinkely-Rogers. "Crime: Wide Open Town." *Newsweek* (August 7, 1978): 35.

Ivins, Molly. "Wyoming Jury Frees Law Official in Killing." *New York Times* (December 1, 1970): 10.

Spence, Gerry, and Anthony Polk. *Gunning for Justice*. Garden City, N.Y.: Doubleday, 1982.

John Wayne Gacy Trial: 1980

Defendant: John Wayne Gacy, Jr.   **Crimes Charged:** Murder, murder during the commission of a felony, aggravated kidnapping, deviate sexual assault, indecent liberties with a minor   **Chief Defense Lawyers:** Sam Amirante, Robert Morra   **Chief Prosecutors:** William Kunkle, Robert Egan, Terry Sullivan   **Judge:** Louis B. Garripo   **Place:** Cook County, Illinois   **Date of Trial:** February 6–March 12,1980   **Verdict:** Guilty

SIGNIFICANCE

John Wayne Gacy was convicted of more murders than any other serial killer. His case focussed attention on the vexing question of the sanity or mental state of sadistic serial killers.

John Wayne Gacy was arrested on December 22, 1978 in connection with the disappearance of a 15-year old boy, Robert Piest. Gacy was 36 years old, twice divorced, and living in a modest suburban home in Des Plaines, Illinois. He was quite well known in his community, liked by his neighbors, and remembered for his performances in clown costume at children's parties. He was active in local politics and had been recognized for his leadership in the Jaycees. He ran his own successful small construction company, specializing in remodeling. Gacy was quickly linked to the disappearance of Robert Piest because immediately before he was last seen the boy had told his mother that he was going to Gacy's home to talk about a summer job. However, this was not Gacy's first arrest, nor was it the first time that he had been a suspect in the disappearance of young men.

In 1968 Gacy had been convicted of sodomy in Iowa, based on the accusations of two teenage boys. He was sentenced to 10 years in prison, but was released on parole in June 1970 and soon returned to the Chicago area where he had grown up. In February 1971 he was arrested after a teenage boy charged that Gacy had forced him to commit sexual acts, but the charges were dropped after the boy failed to appear in court. In August 1975 and again in December 1976, Chicago police questioned Gacy following the disappearances of two young men. The remains of both of them were among those subsequently discovered under Gacy's home. In December 1977 two young men accused Gacy of kidnapping and rape, but charges were not filed.

Gacy Confesses

Following his arrest Gacy was questioned intensively by police, and on January 3, 1979 he confessed to the killing of Robert Piest and six others. He also gave the police information that led to the eventual recovery of the remains of 33 young men and boys. Four were found in the Des Plaines River near Gacy's home, and the rest were buried in the crawl space under his house and under the floor of the garage. Gacy was indicted by a Cook County grand jury on January 8 and the case was assigned to Judge Louis B. Garripo of the Cook County Circuit Court.

Judge Garripo ordered a psychiatric evaluation of Gacy, and Dr. Robert Reifman subsequently reported that Gacy was mentally fit to stand trial and capable of understanding the charges against him. In October the judge ruled that Cook County would bear the expense of Gacy's defense, and appointed Sam Amirante and Robert Morra as his attorneys.

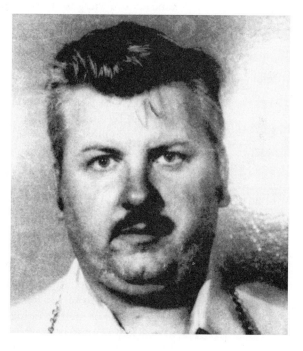

The trial of John Wayne Gacy began on February 6, 1980 in the Cook County Criminal Court Building in Chicago. The prosecution team was lead by William Kunkle, who was assisted by Robert Egan and Terry Sullivan. Simple first-degree murder was not a capital crime under Illinois law, but multiple murders or murder during the commission of a felony were. Therefore, in order to ensure that Gacy would be eligible for the death penalty if convicted, he was originally charged with the seven murders to which he had confessed in January

John Wayne Gacy, sadistic serial killer. (AP/ Wide World Photos)

1979 and with felonies of aggravated kidnapping, deviate sexual assault, and taking indecent liberties with a minor against his last victim, Robert Piest. It was during the months leading up to the trial that excavation under Gacy's house, and dredging of the river near his home, had lead to the finding of the remains of 26 more bodies, 11 of which were unidentified. These victims were added to the original charge, for a total of 33 counts of murder.

Trial Focuses on Gacy's Sanity

Since by the time the trial began Gacy had given three confessions to the police, and had told them where to find the bodies of his victims, the question of whether he had committed the killings was not an issue in the case. Instead, the arguments and testimony on both sides focussed on the question of Gacy's mental state at the time of the crimes. The prosecution argued that Gacy was an entirely sane and calculating, cold-blooded killer. The defense team tried to convince the jury that Gacy was mentally disturbed, possibly as a result of physical abuse by his father during his childhood, and that he was schizophrenic or suffered from a multiple personality disorder. If the jury could be persuaded that Gacy was mentally disturbed and unable to control his actions, he would be placed in a state mental institution, with the possibility of his being subsequently released if found to be mentally stable.

During 13 days of testimony the prosecution questioned 60 witnesses. They began with the frequently emotional accounts of relatives and friends of some of the victims. Former employees of Gacy testified that they had to frequently rebuff his sexual advances and attempts to persuade them to be handcuffed, on the pretext of demonstrating a conjuring trick, a ploy Gacy had apparently used to disable many of the dead victims. Police officers involved in the investigation and forensic experts testified to the circumstances and condition of the bodies recovered, and to the cause of death. Most of Gacy's victims were strangled after a loop of rope had been placed around their necks and tightened by turning a length of pipe or a wooden stick inserted into the loop, like a tourniquet. The prosecutors also brought psychologists as expert witnesses who testified that Gacy was sane at the time of the killings.

The prosecution rested its case on February 20, and the defense began the following day. The first witness was Jeff Rignall, a surviving victim of Gacy's attack. It had been expected that Rignall would testify as a prosecution witness, but for tactical reasons the prosecutors chose to rely on their cross-examination. The defense attorneys hoped that Rignall's description of his experiences would help to convince the jurors that Gacy was insane and not in control of his actions at the time that he attacked his victims. Rignall described having been picked up by Gacy in the latter's car and then rendered unconscious with chloroform. When he came to he was repeatedly raped and sadistically tortured over a period of several hours before being dumped, unconscious, in a Chicago park. Jeff Rignall had been so traumatized by his experience that he became hysterical on the witness stand, began to vomit, and eventually had to be removed from the courtroom. The defense also called Gacy's mother and sister, who described the verbal abuse and beatings he received from his father and his witnessing of the physical abuse of his mother by her husband. Among the 22 witnesses appearing for the defense were six psychologists who testified, as medical experts, that they found Gacy to be mentally impaired by conditions bordering on schizophrenia or multiple personality disorder. They further testified that he was consequently unable to understand the nature of his acts, and therefore, should be held to have been insane when he committed the murders.

During the later days of the trial Gacy appeared to become increasingly detached from the proceedings, and told the judge on several occasions that he did not understand what was happening. However, on March 7 Judge Garripo ruled that Gacy was still fit to stand trial. The defense then completed its case the following day and closing arguments were heard on March 11. The prosecution reviewed in gruesome detail each of the murders with which Gacy was charged, emphasizing that they were all carefully planned and deliberately carried out. The defense again attempted to convince the jury that a finding of insanity was appropriate. They even suggested that if he was not found insane, a unique opportunity might be missed for studying the mind of the serial killer, from which lessons might be learned which could help prevent the repetition of such crimes.

The case went to the jury of seven men and five women on March 12. They deliberated for less than two hours before returning a verdict of guilty. The following day the same jury was asked to consider the sentence, and after deliberating for two and a quarter hours they sentenced John Wayne Gacy to death. Gacy was sent to the Menard Correctional Center where he remained for the next 14 years.

During the long years of the appeals process Gacy was interviewed by several writers, journalists, and others. The reports from those meetings indicate that he consistently contradicted himself. At times he would adamantly insist on his innocence and argue that he had been framed. At other times he would admit guilt for one murder but deny his responsibility for others. Sometimes he would focus on elaborate, supposedly legal arguments as to why his trial had been fundamentally flawed. On other occasions he seemed to be entirely aware of having carried out all the killings over a seven-year period. No consensus appears to have emerged on the question of whether he actually suffered from a mental disorder, or whether his contradictory claims were part of an elaborate and calculated effort to convince others that he did.

After all his appeals failed, John Wayne Gacy was executed by lethal injection on May 19, 1994. In a final statement he proclaimed his innocence.

—*David I. Petts*

Suggestions for Further Reading

Cahill, Tim. *Buried Dreams: Inside the Mind of a Serial Killer*. New York: Bantam Books, 1986.

Moss, Jason. *The Last Victim: a True-Life Journey into the Mind of the Serial Killer*. New York: Warner Books, 1999.

Sullivan, Terry. *Killer Clown*. New York: Grosset & Dunlap, 1983.

U.S. v. Snepp Appeal: 1980

Appellant: Frank W. Snepp III **Appellee:** The United States
Appellant Claims: That a district court erred in ruling that Snepp violated the terms of his Central Intelligence Agency employment agreement by having his book *Decent Interval* published without the agency's prior consent
Chief Lawyers for Appellee: David J. Anderson, Barbara Allen Babcock, William B. Cummings, Brook Hedge, Thomas S. Martin, Elizabeth Gere Whitaker, Glenn V. Whitaker, and George P. Williams
Chief Lawyers for Appellant: Alan M. Dershowitz, Bruce J. Ennis, Joel M. Gora, Mark H. Lynch, Jack D. Novik, John H.F. Shattuck, John Cary Sims, and Geoffrey J. Vitt **Justices:** Harry A. Blackmun, William J. Brennan, Jr., Warren E. Burger, Thurgood Marshall, Lewis F. Powell, Jr., William H. Rehnquist, John Paul Stevens, Potter Stewart, and Byron R. White
Place: Washington, D.C. **Date of Decision:** February 19, 1980
Decision: That Snepp had unlawfully breached the terms of his employment agreement

SIGNIFICANCE

Despite the strong interest in protecting First Amendment rights, the government is entitled to enforce contracts with its employees that prohibit publishing sensitive material without prior consent.

On September 16, 1968, a young man named Frank W. Snepp III took the final step necessary to begin working for the Central Intelligence Agency. The job application process with the CIA is a long one, involving extensive background checks for issuing a security clearance and other procedures. That day for Snepp culminated in signing a secrecy agreement, which obligated Snepp not to "publish or participate in the publication of" any material relating to the CIA's activities during Snepp's term of employment without "specific prior approval by the Agency."

Snepp worked for the CIA for more than seven years. He served two tours of duty with the CIA station in South Vietnam, June 2, 1969—June 21, 1971, and October 4, 1972—April 29, 1975. Snepp became disillusioned with the CIA's conduct in Vietnam, particularly with its role in the final stages of American withdrawal from Saigon. Snepp resigned from the CIA effective January 23, 1976, and was required to sign a termination secrecy agreement reiterating his obligation to obtain the "express written consent of the Director of Central Intelligence" before publishing anything about the CIA.

Snepp Sells *Decent Interval*

Despite the documents he had signed, Snepp went to the publishing company Random House with his manuscript for a book titled *Decent Interval*. The book described the American withdrawal from Vietnam and Saigon and gave unflattering details about the CIA's involvement. Snepp received a $60,000 advance from Random House, and his contract called for potentially lucrative royalties. The book was based on Snepp's experience in the CIA, and he never submitted it to the agency for approval.

Random House published the book in November 1977. On February 15, 1978, the government sued Snepp in the U.S. District Court for the Eastern District of Virginia, which covered Snepp's suburban Washington, D.C., residence. Because the book didn't contain any information that was officially designated as classified, secret or top secret, the government took a conservative approach. Instead of criminal prosecution or seeking an injunction against publication of the book, the government asked the court for all of Snepp's profits as compensation for breach of contract. Snepp stood to lose everything under his contract with Random House.

Frank Snepp III, author of *Decent Interval*, and attorneys leaving U.S. District Court. The case was ultimately heard by the Supreme Court. (AP/Wide World Photos)

The District Court ruled in the government's favor on July 7, 1978, and the U.S. Court of Appeals for the Fourth Circuit largely affirmed the District Court's actions on March 20, 1979. Snepp appealed to the Supreme Court. Both sides had extensive legal teams, because the American Civil Liberties Union and the Authors League of America came to Snepp's assistance.

In an extremely rare procedure, the Supreme Court decided to consider the case, but the Court made its decision solely on the basis of the papers filed by both sides. There was no hearing. In upholding the district court's decision to make Snepp turn over all his proceeds from book sales to the government, the court relied heavily on the testimony of CIA Director Admiral Stansfield Turner before the district court that Snepp's book had hurt CIA operations:

> Over the last six to nine months, we have had a number of sources discontinue work with us. We have had more sources tell us that they are very nervous about continuing work with us. We have had very strong complaints from a number of foreign intelligence services with whom we conduct liaison, who have questioned whether they should continue exchanging information with us, for fear it will not remain secret. I cannot estimate to you how many potential sources or liaison arrangements have never germinated because people were unwilling to enter into business with us.

Snepp's defense was based on the argument that the secrecy agreements violated his right under the Constitution's First Amendment to express himself, a right which cannot be contracted away. In rejecting Snepp's argument, the court held on February 19, 1980, that the government could use employment agreements to bind its employees to vows of secrecy:

> The Government has a compelling interest in protecting both the secrecy of information important to our national security and the appearance of confidentiality so essential to the effective operation of our foreign intelligence service. The agreement that Snepp signed is a reasonable means for protecting this vital interest.

Therefore, despite the court's historic concern for First Amendment rights, it held in a 6-3 decision that the government is entitled to enforce contracts with its employees that prohibit publishing sensitive material without prior consent.

—Stephen G. Christianson

Suggestions for Further Reading

Alter, Jonathan. "Slaying the Message." *Washington Monthly* (September 1981): 43–50.

Mullin, Dennis, and Robert S. Dudney. "When CIA Spies Come in From the Cold." *U.S. News and World Report* (September 28, 1981): 41–44.

Nocera, Joseph. "Finally Proof That Frank Snepp Was Framed." *Washington Monthly* (November 1980): 11–19.

Snepp, Frank. *Decent Interval: An Insider's Account of Saigaon's Indecent End Told by the CIA's Chief Strategy Analyst in Vietnam.* New York: Vintage Books, 1978.

———. "The CIA's Double Standard." *Newsweek* (January 25, 1982): 10.

ABSCAM Trials: 1980 & 1981

Defendants: First trial: Howard L. Criden, Angelo J. Errichetti, Louis C. Johanson, and Michael J. Myers; Second trial: Alexander Feinberg and Harrison A. Williams, Jr.   **Crimes Charged:** Bribery and conspiracy
Chief Defense Lawyers: First trial: Richard Ben-Veniste, Ray Brown, Plato Cacheris, and John Duffy; Second trial: Harry C. Batchelder, Jr. and George J. Koelzer   **Chief Prosecutors:** Edward A. McDonald and Thomas P. Puccio
Judge: George C. Pratt   **Place:** New York, New York
Dates of Trials: August 11–31, 1980; March 30–May 1, 1981
Verdicts: Guilty   **Sentences:** First trial: Myers: 3 years imprisonment, $20,000 fine; Errichetti: 6 years imprisonment, $40,000 fine; Johanson: 3 years imprisonment, $20,000 fine; Criden: 6 years imprisonment, $40,000 fine; Second trial: Williams: 3 years imprisonment, $50,000 fine; Feinberg: 3 years imprisonment, $40,000 fine

SIGNIFICANCE

The sting operation that became known as ABSCAM worked beyond the government's wildest expectations. No previous federal investigation had bagged so many highly placed corrupt political figures or produced so many trials.

In 1978, undercover FBI agents and convicted swindler Melvin Weinberg began posing as American representatives of wealthy Arab businessmen eager to make sizable investments in the United States. Under the auspices of a company called "Abdul Enterprises Limited" (from which the name ABSCAM derived), they let it be known that their clients were willing to pay heavily for influence and favors, especially visas from the Immigration and Naturalization Service (INS). The first politician snared was U.S. Congressman Michael J. Myers, who was videotaped accepting a $50,000 bribe.

As ABSCAM spread its tentacles and word of easy money circulated, more and more politicians fell prey, including U.S. Senator Harrison A. Williams, Jr., and five other congressmen. Geographical considerations and the sheer number of defendants necessitated several trials. The first began in Brooklyn, New York, on August 11, 1980, before Judge George C. Pratt.

In opening his case, Thomas P. Puccio, who would handle most of the ABSCAM prosecutions, brought to the stand Anthony Amorosa, a federal undercover agent. Amorosa and Weinberg had run the sting in a New York hotel room. That videotaped transaction was played to the packed, hushed courtroom. Amorosa handed Myers an envelope containing $50,000, saying, "Spend it well." Myers, who sat next to fellow defendant Mayor Angelo J. Errichetti of Camden, New Jersey, boasted of the influence he wielded in Congress. "As leader of the Philadelphia delegation, I control four and then six when we go into state matters . . . I'm going to tell you something real simple and short—money talks in this business . . . and it works the same way down in Washington."

Four-Way Conspiracy

As the tape rolled, the other two defendants, Louis C. Johanson, a Philadelphia City Councilman, and Howard L. Criden, Johanson's former law partner, watched intently. Both were charged with having conspired with Myers and having shared the money. Myers let slip the names of other prominent Washington politicians, though none was ever charged with wrongdoing. Stifled laughter in court greeted Myers' comment when, leaning across confidentially to the agents, he said, "The key is, you got to deal with the right people," adding a moment later, "I feel very comfortable here."

Next came Melvin Weinberg, a colorful character who provided detailed descriptions of the ABSCAM sting and his efforts to help federal agents. In defense estimations Weinberg was the state's weak link, and they set about undermining his credibility in a three-day grilling. John Duffy, appearing for Johanson, set the tone:

"Are you a con man?"

"I don't know. They say I am."

"Have you spent most of your adult life living by your wits?"

"That's correct."

Richard Ben-Veniste, representing Criden, quizzed Weinberg on the scam he had "franchised to con men all over the world."

"We franchised it," shrugged Weinberg, "but not to con men."

"You were like the MacDonald's of con men?"

Weinberg beamed. "That's correct."

When Congressman Michael Myers took the stand, the 37-year-old Democrat was led through some gentle questioning by his attorney, Plato Cacheris. Cacheris' theme, one adopted by most ABSCAM defense lawyers, was that because there had been no criminal intent, there had been no crime. Myers agreed: "No, it wasn't proper that I accepted this money, but I didn't do anything wrong . . . and didn't intend to do anything wrong . . . It seemed like a chance to pick up some easy money." Myers explained that he had grossly exaggerated his influence during the course of the meeting to get the money.

Less compelling were his attempts to explain away a second meeting, also captured on tape, at which he received an additional $35,000—paid because after dividing up the original payment with his co-defendants, Myers had been left with just $15,000 and felt "entitled" to more. Myers blamed this verbal indiscretion on two bourbons given him by the undercover agents, causing him to say things he didn't really mean.

Prosecutor Puccio had an easy task on cross-examination. The videotape said it all. Pouncing on Myers' assertions that he meant to take the money and then do nothing in return, he asked, "Congressman Myers, did you think it was dishonest to obtain money by false pretenses?"

"No, I didn't think that this was dishonest."

Untrustworthy Witness

In closing arguments each defense attorney fell back on attacking Weinberg's credibility. Ben-Veniste hit the hardest: "Mel Weinberg makes J.R. Ewing look like Peter Pan." He was, said Ben-Veniste, the kind of man that if you shake hands with him, "you count your fingers afterward and then look for your watch."

It was a theme easily countered by Puccio. Myers, he argued, was the man who failed on standards of honesty. "Would a man like that hesitate for one second to lie on the witness stand to get off the hook?"

On August 30, 1980, all four defendants were found guilty. Their attempts to have the convictions overturned were rejected by Judge Pratt on July 24, 1981. In a 136-page decision, he said of the accused:

> Their major defense has been that they were tricked into committing the crime on videotape. The government's need to unmask such conduct more than justifies the investigative techniques employed in these cases. Without question these convictions were reliable, and no constitutional right of any defendant has been infringed.

Sentencing was deferred until August 13, 1981, when Judge Pratt imposed jail sentences and heavy fines on each defendant. But before that, the judge had presided over yet another ABSCAM trial. Puccio was again the chief prosecutor, as the government this time sought to convict the biggest fish caught in their net.

Influential Senator Charged

At the time of his arraignment, Harrison A. Williams, Jr., 61, had been a senator for New Jersey for 22 years and was one of the most powerful men in Washington. He and an associate, 72-year-old lawyer Alexander Feinberg, were jointly accused of scheming to illegally benefit a Virginia titanium mine and processing plant. Williams had allegedly agreed to use his position to obtain government contracts to buy the output of the mine and plant, in which he was to have a secret 18 percent interest.

Assistant prosecutor Edward A. McDonald opened on March 31, 1981, by showing the jury a photograph of Williams aboard a yacht in Delray Beach, Florida, posing with Sheik Yassir Habib, actually Richard Farhart, an FBI agent. "Habib"—supposedly ready to lend $100 million to the titanium project—was also present at an Arlington, Virginia meeting with Williams, which was videotaped. When the conversation turned to matters of influence, Williams assured Habib that he could "go right to the top," and mentioned then Vice President Walter Mondale. Speaking of Mondale, he said, "We have a relationship that will make all of that possible . . . that's all I want to tell you now."

Another ABSCAM victim, Henry Williams (no relation to the senator but a longtime associate) decided to cut his losses and turn state's evidence. He described the senator's tendency and willingness to exploit his position for money. Contrary to what the defense had claimed, Williams said that the senator had been connected with the titanium company since 1976.

To counter this allegation, the defense produced ex-Secretary of the Treasury Henry H. Fowler, now an investment banker. Chief defense counsel George J. Koelzer asked, "Did you feel that Senator Williams was putting any pressure on you to help this enterprise?"

"No."

"Did he indicate . . . that his business could get government contracts?"

Again the answer was no.

Which was the line taken by Williams himself, when he gave evidence on his own behalf.

"Were you guaranteeing government contracts?" Koelzer asked.

"Absolutely not, not at all."

Warning From Bench

At Koelzer's behest, Williams repeatedly and emphatically denied all charges. So often, in fact, that Judge Pratt expressed concern to Koelzer that such repetition might backfire. "You may convince the jury of exactly the contrary of what the witness is saying, simply because he is saying so often. And it may in their view become very artificial and rehearsed." Koelzer, insisting that the technique was necessary to counteract the damaging effects of the tape, then turned to his client and a section on the videotape where the subject of influence was raised. He asked Williams,

"Why didn't you get up and walk out?"

"I respected the man [Habib]."

Prosecutor Puccio wasn't so sure.

"What did you have in mind?"

"To impress the sheik."

"Impress the sheik with what?"

"The baloney, this was the baloney session."

With this answer, Williams went right to the heart of the defense argument of entrapment. Before Habib had arrived, Williams had received coaching from another undercover FBI agent on how to flatter the sheik. None of this would have happened, Williams claimed, had he not been coerced by that instruction.

It was a line of reasoning that failed to impress the jury. On May 1, 1981, they found both defendants guilty. Judge Pratt later mandated jail sentences similar to those in the previous trial.

No Acquittals

There were six more ABSCAM trials and not one defendant was acquitted. The final tally included one senior U.S. senator; six members of Congress; one mayor, who was also a New Jersey state senator; three members of the Philadelphia City Council; an INS inspector; one lawyer; one accountant; and assorted business associates of the public officials. All of the politicians were either expelled from office or else turned out by voters at the next election. By any reckoning, ABSCAM had to be counted a major success.

—Colin Evans

Suggestions for Further Reading

Caplan, Gerald M. *ABSCAM Ethics*. Cambridge, Mass.: Ballinger, 1983.

Eubanks, Brian F. *Stetson Law Review* (Spring 1984): 691–706.

Frey, Richard G. *Criminal Justice Journal* (Summer 1984): 203–250.

Greene, Robert. *The Sting Man*. New York: Dutton, 1981.

Verrone, Patric M. *Boston College Law Review* (March 1984): 351–381.

Jean Harris Trial: 1980–81

Defendant: Jean S. Harris   **Crime Charged:** Second-degree murder
Chief Defense Lawyer: Joel Aurnou   **Chief Prosecutor:** George Bolen
Judge: Russell R. Leggett   **Place:** White Plains, New York
Dates of Trial: November 21, 1980–February 24, 1981   **Verdict:** Guilty
Sentence: 15 years to life

SIGNIFICANCE

Jean Harris' trial was initially famous for the celebrity of the lover she was accused of murdering, but the handling of her defense and the sentence pronounced were debated for years afterward. Her prison writings were among the books prompting review of New York's "Son of Sam" law by the U.S. Supreme Court.

On March 10, 1980, Jean Harris left the exclusive Virginia school for girls where she was headmistress and drove 400 miles to the Purchase, New York, home of Dr. Herman Tarnower. Harris entered the bedroom of her lover of 14 years carrying a bouquet of flowers and a loaded revolver. Her version of what happened next would be emotionally debated in one of the most widely examined trials in the history of New York state.

Bullets from Harris' gun had indisputably killed the 69-year-old Tarnower, author of the popular *The Complete Scarsdale Medical Diet*. Yet Harris' attorney, Joel Aurnou, announced that his client's intended victim had been herself. Despondent over Tarnower's rejection of her for a younger woman and depressed by the pressures of her job at the Madeira School, the 57-year-old headmistress had driven to the cardiologist's house to see him a last time before committing suicide. Harris claimed that Tarnower was accidentally wounded trying to wrest the gun from her.

The Westchester County District Attorney's office proposed that Harris' actions were hardly self-destructive. They accused her of shooting Tarnower in a jealous fury that had been building for years. From the moment her trial began in November 1980, her intent at the time she pulled the trigger was the crucial issue that would determine her fate.

An Awkward Start

The early weeks of the trial went awkwardly for the prosecution. Physical evidence had been mishandled by suburban police, who seemed unaccustomed to following proper procedures amid the novelty of such a bloody situation. Prosecutor George Bolen called Deputy Medical Examiner Dr. Louis Roh, who testified that a bullet hole in Tarnower's hand was consistent with the nature of a "defensive wound," sustained while trying to push away a gun barrel. Roh testified that one of the three bullets found in Tarnower's body had entered through the palm, passed through the hand, and lodged in the chest. Aurnou responded with forensic expert Herbert Leon MacDonnell, who explained how the bloodstains found on Tarnower's bedclothes and pajamas supported defense claims of a struggle over the gun.

Hours turned into weeks as contending medical and ballistics experts testified in numbing detail. Dr. Roh reappeared to testify that tissue found in a chest wound might have been carried from Tarnower's palm by the bullet, bolstering the theory that the victim had raised his hand defensively. Aurnou counter attacked with a succession of pathologists who disputed Roh's palm-tissue theory.

As the prosecution's case wobbled, Aurnou called numerous character witnesses, attempting to portray Harris as "a lady" whose self-control made it impossible for her to commit murder. Madeira School trustees and students testified to Harris' reputation for integrity and discipline, despite her growing signs of depression.

Jean Harris, followed by her son, after her second day on the witness stand in the murder trial of Dr. Herman Tarnower. (AP/Wide World Photos)

Harris Testifies

Aurnou decided to put Harris on the stand. The strain of Tarnower's rejection and the pressures of her career burst forth in emotional exchanges between lawyer and client. Aurnou's probing of Harris' precarious emotional state intended to show that she had been pushed to the point of suicide, not murder. Harris described in detail how she and Tarnower struggled over the gun with which she tried to kill herself.

The defense view of Harris as a stolid, sympathetic figure in control of her behavior despite intense suffering began to blur under prosecutor Bolen's cross-examination. Harris' responses to his questions were haughty and abrasive. She accused other witnesses of perjury. Yet Aurnou's failure to subdue his client's temper was overshadowed by an even graver miscalculation.

Harris testified that she had mailed Tarnower a registered letter on the morning of March 10. She telephoned him later, interrupting his consultation with a patient. Harris told the doctor to throw the letter away when it arrived. After Tarnower's death, the defense team had quickly retrieved the thick envelope from the post office. When the prosecution asked to examine it during the trial, Aurnou theatrically removed it from his pocket and handed it to Bolen, certain that its pleading depiction of Tarnower as a faithless philanderer would win the defense's case.

Instead, the image of a cultivated, quietly suffering headmistress vanished when Bolen read the 11-page "Scarsdale letter" aloud. Pain and bitterness, which the defense had denied was compatible with her character, raged from its page. Harris wrote of her rival for Tarnower's affections, calling her "your whore" and "your adulterous slut." The rambling letter also spoke of Tarnower removing Harris from his will.

Because Harris had voluntarily testified about her March 10 telephone call, Bolen was free to produce the doctor's patient as a rebuttal witness. Juanita Edwards testified that she was with Tarnower when his phone rang that day. The doctor took the call in his office but left the examination room phone off the hook.

"Goddammit it, Jean, I want you to stop bothering me!"

Edwards could hear Tarnower shout angrily at a woman over the open line.

"You've lied and you've cheated!"

Edwards also heard Tarnower say,

"Well, you're going to inherit $240,000!"

Aurnou objected fiercely but to no effect. After more analytical haggling over the tissue found in Tarnower's chest wound, the defense rested. Judge Russell Leggett instructed the jurors that if they found Harris had intended to kill Tarnower at the moment she pulled the trigger, they could find her guilty of second-degree murder. If they decided that she had not intended to kill him, she could be found guilty of either second-degree manslaughter or criminally negligent homicide.

Defense Goes for Broke and Loses

"Don't compromise!" Aurnou told the jury, confident that they would acquit his client completely. It was a disastrous supposition. The jury found Harris guilty of second-degree murder. When Judge Leggett pronounced the mandatory 15-years-to-life sentence, with no possibility of parole until the 15-year minimum had been served, he asked if Harris had anything to say.

"I did not murder Dr. Tarnower," she answered.

"I loved him very much and I am innocent as I stand here. You and Mr. Bolen have arranged my life in such a way that I'll be in a cage for the rest of it, and with irons on my hands every time I go out."

She held up her hands as if they were manacled.

"That is not justice. It is a travesty of justice."

Some spectators applauded when she concluded her statement.

"You have had a fair trial," Judge Leggett replied, expressing regret that "the events of March 10" had ever taken place. The judge hoped that Harris would use her teaching talents to aid fellow prisoners.

Despite her defiant protests that she had been condemned by perjury and an immoral justice system, jurors later revealed that Harris' own testimony convicted her. During eight days of deliberations, the jury tried to re-create the scene in Tarnower's bedroom as Harris described it. They found no way that Tarnower could have been shot through the palm by trying to deflect the pistol from her temple. The jury also was impressed by her lack of any explanation for the other two bullet wounds in Tarnower's body.

Attorney Aurnou appealed for a reversal of the verdict, accusing one juror of possible bias and citing the presence of a police officer during Harris' phone call to a lawyer friend after the shooting. The officer later testified to overhearing Harris say, "Oh my God, I think I've killed Hy." Aurnou also argued that international press coverage had made a fair trial impossible and that the jury's attempt to re-create the shooting during deliberations had been improper.

Westchester County District Attorney Carl Vergari retorted that the "Scarsdale letter" had convinced the jury that Harris was "a liar and that the roots of her hatred for Dr. Tarnower ran to the marrow." Vergari called the letter "an X-ray of Mrs. Harris' state of mind as it existed on March 10" and faulted Aurnou's "go for broke" pursuit of a total acquittal instead of pursuing an "arguably valid defense of extreme emotional disturbance." Many observers including Judge Leggett, agreed that Harris might have gotten a shorter sentence or been acquitted if she had agreed to plead guilty to a lesser charge.

An appeals court unanimously ruled that while Harris' trial was not perfect, it was fair. Judges noted that Aurnou himself had been lax in securing physical evidence. He had not asked for a change of venue and had participated in pretrial publicity. As to the jurors' conduct, the decision noted stonily that "the defendant would appear to be in no position to complain since, in defense counsel's summation, he twice invited the jurors to test Mrs. Harris's version in the deliberation room."

Relentless Appeals Finally Succeed

With the help of prominent sympathizers, Harris continued to appeal. In 1983 she lost a bid for a new trial on grounds that her testimony had been impaired by withdrawal from amphetamines supplied by Tarnower and that

Aurnou had not properly explained the option of presenting a psychiatric defense. Appeals to the New York governor's office for clemency after serving half of her minimum sentence were rejected as premature. In 1992, a federal court ruled that the failure to raise a defense of "extreme emotional distress" was a tactical gamble on which Harris and Aurnou had agreed and lost, not a violation of her Sixth Amendment right to counsel.

Harris wrote two books about her life, her trial, and her prison experiences. She wanted the proceeds to benefit a charity for the children of convicts. The money was instead put in escrow by New York's Crime Victims Compensation Board. Under the state's "Son of Sam law," Harris was forbidden from directing profits gained by writing about her crime. Harris challenged the law. She lost her suit in New York courts, shortly before the U.S. Supreme Court's 1991 ruling that the "Son of Sam law" was unconstitutional.

Harris was paroled from the Bedford Hills Correctional Facility in early 1993. After her release, she became a vocal advocate for the better treatment of female prisoners.

— Thomas C. Smith

Suggestions for Further Reading

Alexander, Shana. *Very Much A Lady.* Boston: Little, Brown and Co., 1983.

——. "Matter of Integrity." *People* (March 9, 1981): 90ff.

Anderson, George M. "Women and Criminal Justice: An Interview with Jean Harris." *America* (March 18, 1995): 10.

Feron, James. "Jurors In Jean Harris Trial Re-enacted Night of Murder." *New York Times* (February 26, 1981): Al, Bl.

"Graduation Day." *Time* (January 11, 1993): 55.

Harris, Jean S. *Stranger In Two Worlds.* New York: Macmillan Co., 1986.

Jones, Ann. "Why Are We So Fascinated By the Harris Case?" *New York Times* (November 8, 1981): 24.

Trilling, Diana. *Mrs. Harris.* New York: Harcourt Brace Jovanovich, 1981.

FALN Terrorist Trial: 1981

Defendants: Elizam Escobar, Ricardo Jimenez, Adolfo Matos, Alfredo Mendez, Dylcia Noemi Pagan, Alicia Rodriguez, Ida Luz Rodriguez, Luis Rosa, Carlos Alberto Torres, and Carmen Valentin   **Crimes Charged:** Seditious conspiracy, interference with interstate commerce by threats or violence, possession of an unregistered firearm, carrying firearms during the commission of seditious conspiracy and interference with interstate commerce by violence, interstate transportation of firearms with intent to commit seditious conspiracy and interference with interstate commerce by violence, interstate transportation of stolen motor vehicles
Chief Defense Lawyers: None   **Chief Prosecutor:** Jeremy Margolis
Judge: Thomas R. McMillen   **Place:** Chicago, Illinois
Dates of Trial: February 3–18, 1981   **Verdicts:** Guilty
Sentences: Imprisonment—Escobar: 60 years; Jimenez: 90 years; Matos: 70 years; Mendez: 75 years; Pagan: 55 years; Alicia Rodriguez: 55 years; Ida Luz Rodriguez: 75 years; Rosa: 75 years; Torres: 70 years; Valentin: 90 years

SIGNIFICANCE
The trial of 10 FALN members in Chicago was one of the most sensational government cases against Puerto Rican nationalist groups accused of violence. The 1999 release of some of those convicted sparked a confrontation between Congress and the White House over the issue of Presidential Executive Privilege.

The 1970s were a troubled decade in the political history of Puerto Rico. Ceded by Spain in 1898 after the Spanish American War, the island became a territory and later an American commonwealth. The island's relationship to the United States has been controversial ever since, with activists advocating options ranging from formal recognition of Puerto Rico as the 51st state to complete independence, obtained by force if necessary.

In the 1970s, groups advocating violence for independence made their presence known with deadly results. Bombs exploded at military facilities and in cities across the American mainland. The worst incident occurred in January 1975, when an explosion tore through Fraunces Tavern in New York City's financial district during lunch hour, killing 4 people and injuring 53 others.

Radical groups credited with such attacks included the FALN or Fuerzas Armadas de *Liberacion Nacional* (Armed Forces of National Liberation). FALN actions were largely limited to bombings that created property damage and temporary takeovers of presidential campaign headquarters in New York and Chicago during the 1980 election primaries. Despite the group's reliance on publicity as a guerilla tactic, however, the group was also covertly linked to August 1977 bombings of the U.S. Department of Defense and Mobil Oil Corporation buildings in New York, in which one person was killed. The FBI suspected FALN involvement in over 100 other bombings nationwide, which, by the end of the decade, had killed 5 people, wounded 80 others, and caused millions of dollars in damage.

A passerby looks at damage inside the New York Stock Exchange, where Puerto Rican terrorist group FALN exploded several bombs. (Bettmann/Corbis)

11 Arrested in Evanston

On April 4, 1980, police in the Chicago suburb of Evanston, Illinois, were staking out a rental truck that had been stolen during an armed robbery earlier that day. When Luis Rosa and Alicia Rodriguez approached the truck, police arrested them. Both suspects were armed and had arrived in stolen vehicles. That afternoon Evanston police were also called to investigate a suspicious parked van. Upon arriving, officers noticed a false mustache slipping from the lip of one of the van's occupants and a pistol was discovered in the purse of another; all nine occupants were arrested. A search of the van revealed a cache of guns.

None of the suspects would give their names. Consultation with the FBI, however, revealed that the Evanston police had at once arrested a major portion of the FALN's membership. Questions about the Fraunces Tavern explosion had landed Carlos Alberto Torres on the FBI's 10-Most-Wanted list, while his wife, Maria Haydee Torres, was suspected in the Mobil Oil bombing. The others were identified as Elizam Escobar, Ricardo Jimenez, Adolfo Matos, Alfredo Mendez, Dylcia Noemi Pagan, Ida Luz Rodriguez, and Carmen Valentin.

Haydee Torres was immediately extradited to New York to stand trial. State weapons and conspiracy charges were filed against all the other suspects, except Rodriguez and Rosa, who were charged with armed robbery, armed violence, possession of a stolen vehicle, and conspiracy.

Because those arrested considered themselves to be prisoners of war, the political overtones were felt at the trials from the start. Rodriguez and Rosa were gagged, then removed from court for incessantly shouting pro-independence slogans. Their defiance was considered a lack of remorse by the judge who, when they were found guilty, added a total of five six-month contempt of court terms to their maximum 30-year sentences. The other FALN defendants received lesser penalties. All were sentenced to three years for conspiracy to commit armed robbery and five years for possessing a sawed-off shotgun. The eight-year sentences meant that each of the defendants would be eligible for parole in four years.

Federal Charges and Trial

Yet the defendants' legal troubles were just beginning. During their trials for breaking Illinois laws, federal charges were being prepared by U.S. government prosecutors. On December 10, 1980, the already jailed FALN members were indicted by a federal grand jury for a variety of felonies, including a rarely employed charge of seditious conspiracy. One of two named but unindicted coconspirators was Maria Haydee Torres. By the time of the indictment, Haydee Torres had already been tried for her involvement in the fatal Mobil Oil bombing and been sentenced to life imprisonment.

When the trial of the 10 FALN members began in Chicago's federal court on February 3, 1981, it was marked by the same political theater that had distinguished the trial for the Evanston incident. When the defendants were brought into court in chains, they loudly demanded independence for Puerto Rico. Carmen Valentin declared war on the United States and called Judge Thomas R. McMillen a "judicial puppet." The judge told the prisoners that they could remain in court and testify on their own behalf, as long as they were not disruptive. The defendants told McMillen that they had no interest in sitting through a proceeding they viewed as "a farce." Although they were accompanied to court by attorney Michael E. Deutsch, they rejected offers of defense counsel.

Judge McMillen entered not guilty pleas for the prisoners and had them removed to a nearby maximum security jail, where they listened to testimony through a loudspeaker. The prosecution produced mounds of confiscated guns, explosives, and ammunition, along with numerous communiqués allegedly discussing FALN bombing and kidnapping plots. The evidence was stacked on the unused defense counsel table. The only signs of the 10 defendants in court were their photographs, which the prosecution mounted and displayed to the jury. Even as the prosecution made its closing arguments, the judge received a dismissive written notice from the defendants, who saw no reason to participate in what they regarded as an illegitimate trial conducted by an occupying government.

After eight days of testimony by the prosecution, the defendants were found guilty on February 11, 1981. On February 18 they were sentenced to lengthy prison terms ranging from 55 to 90 years, to be served consecutively with state sentences stemming from the Evanston incident. Shortly after the trial, another FALN leader named Oscar Lopez-Rivera was arrested on charges similar to those leveled against the Chicago defendants. Lopez-Rivera was accused of plotting to kidnap a government official or one of President Ronald

Reagan's sons to ransom for imprisoned FALN members. To the shock of his family and FALN supporters, the prosecution's star witness in Lopez-Rivera's July 1981 trial was Alfredo Mendez, who became a government witness and entered the federal witness protection program to reduce the 75-year sentence he had received for his conviction in the February trial.

Clinton Grants Clemency

Bombings, robberies, arrests, and trials associated with radical independence groups continued in the 1980s, but by the end of the decade, the crimes were becoming merely painful memories. In the mid-1990s, some of the imprisoned radicals petitioned for early release, claiming that the political motives for their crimes fell under U.S. clemency guidelines and that they had already served disproportionately long sentences. Human rights groups, church leaders, and politicians—including some prominent Puerto Rican politicians who opposed the independence movement—also joined the clemency groundswell and began to lobby the White House.

On September 8, 1999, 11 imprisoned Puerto Rican militants accepted a clemency offer from the Clinton administration and were freed after agreeing to renounce violence and submit to parole restrictions. Eight of the 11 were FALN members convicted in the February 1981 trial; Carlos Alberto Torres was not offered clemency and remained in prison.

Critics of President Clinton accused him of pandering to terrorists and hoping to gain support for his wife's planned campaign for the Senate among New York's Puerto Rican voters. Amid a political furor, Clinton responded that he made the clemency offers in consideration of the lengthy sentences already served by those convicted and on the advice of White House counsel, former president Jimmy Carter, South African Archbishop Desmond Tutu, and others. The explanation did little to satisfy congressional critics, who demanded that the White House turn over records relating to the president's clemency decision, expecting to find evidence that Clinton had rejected FBI and Justice Department advice opposing clemency. When the White House declined to provide the documents on grounds of executive privilege, congressional Republicans responded with an official report critical of the clemency. Like other conflicts typifying the vituperative relations between Congress and the White House in the 1990s, the war of words over the matter was not resolved. The White House, however, agreed to a review of the presidential pardon system to allow the victims of such serious crimes to participate in the process directly.

—*Tom Smith*

Suggestions for Further Reading

Burton, Dan, et al. "Findings of the Committee on Government Reform." http:// www.house.gov/ reform/reports/final_faln_rpt2.htm.

"Suspect in Bombings by F.A.L.N. Is Seized." *New York Times* (April 5, 1980): 1.

"Ten Convicted in Chicago in F.A.L.N Trial." *New York Times* (February 12, 1981): 14.

"Trial without Defendants." *Time* (March 2, 1981): 78.

John Demjanjuk Denaturalization Trial: 1981

Defendant: John Demjanjuk   **Crime Charged:** Illegal procurement of U.S. citizenship   **Chief Defense Lawyer:** John Martin
Chief Prosecutors: Norman Moskowitz and George Parker   **Judge:** Frank Battisti   **Place:** Cleveland, Ohio   **Dates of Trial:** February 10–June 23, 1981   **Verdict:** Guilty   **Sentence:** U.S. naturalization revoked

SIGNIFICANCE

The denaturalization trial of accused war criminal John Demjanjuk marked the beginning of a long and acrimonious legal battle that would be fought out in courtrooms on two continents for more than a decade.

In 1975 the U.S. Immigration and Naturalization Service (INS) began investigating a list of approximately 70 war criminals allegedly living in America. High on this list was a sadistic Ukrainian guard known as "Ivan the Terrible," who had personally gassed thousands of Jews in the Nazi death camp at Treblinka in 1942–43. Evidence suggested that after the war Ivan had entered America illegally and was currently living in Cleveland, Ohio. In 1977, a 57-year-old Ford Motor Company plant mechanic named John Demjanjuk was accused of being Ivan the Terrible.

Demjanjuk arrived in America in 1952. Six years later he was granted citizenship. At this time he also Anglicized his name from Ivan to John. In 1979 INS investigators were shown a photocopied identification card purportedly issued to an "Ivan Denjanjuk" at Trawniki, a German training camp for SS elite guards in Poland. Demjanjuk denied that the card was his. When several ex-Treblinka inmates identified the person shown on the ID card as "Ivan the Terrible," the INS decided to review Demjanjuk's application to find out if he had covered up any concentration camp activities. If this turned out to be the case, his citizenship could be revoked.

The hearing began on February 10, 1981. Prosecutor Norman Moskowitz led off with the expert witnesses. It was their job to verify the disputed ID card. Professor Wolfgang Sheffler, an acknowledge Nazi expert, admitted never having seen a card exactly like it, but he thought the information shown on the

Trawniki card seemed genuine. Heinrich Schaeffer, a former paymaster at Trawniki, declared unequivocally that the card was genuine.

Holocaust Survivors Testify

Next came the victims of Ivan the Terrible's barbarism. Of more than a million prisoners who passed through the gates of Treblinka, fewer than 60 survived to tell the world of the horrors it had housed. Of that 60, only five were left. Four had flown half-way around the world, prepared to swear John Demjanjuk was indeed Ivan the Terrible.

Yehiel Reichman, 65, had seen Ivan daily at Treblinka and had no difficulty in identifying Demjanjuk. Similarly, Pinhas Epstein described Ivan "a big, thickset man" who operated the diesel engine that pumped deadly carbon monoxide into the gas chambers. He also saw Ivan beat prisoners to death with a lead pipe.

Others followed, including Eliahu Rosenberg, who had worked as corpse carrier, clearing the chambers of dead bodies, and Sonia Lewkowicz, a laundress. All had tales to tell, and all identified Demjamjuk as the demon who had murdered thousands. Try as he might, defense counsel John Martin could not budge any of them.

When it came time to testify on his own behalf, Demjanjuk did so briefly and in Ukrainian. His defense was that he had never been at Treblinka at all: it was all a case of mistaken identity. He dismissed the ID card as a KGB forgery (the card had originally surfaced in the Soviet Union). According to Demjanjuk, throughout 1942-43 he was an imprisoned Soviet soldier at a German POW camp at Chelm in Poland.

Demjanjuk is escorted into Israel's supreme court. (AP/Wide World)

The testimony was heard by Judge Frank Battisti, sitting alone without a jury. After lengthy deliberation, in a 44-page decision delivered on June 23, 1981, Judge Battisti found that Demjanjuk had illegally obtained U.S. naturalization by concealing his wartime record and ordered the immediate revocation of his citizenship.

This opened the door for deportation proceedings. Appeals delayed the process until May 23, 1984, when Demjanjuk was given 30 days to leave the country voluntarily. He chose to stay and fight. In February 1985 the INS Board of Appeals ruled that Demjanjuk's background denied him the privilege of voluntary departure and he was imprisoned to await the results of an extradition request made by Israel. On February 27, 1986, Demjanjuk was escorted by two U.S. marshals onto an El Al 747, Israeli airlines jet, bound for Tel Aviv.

Sentenced to Death

John Demjanjuk finally faced his accusers in a Jerusalem courtroom on February 16, 1987. In a emotional trial, the same witnesses who had denounced him in Cleveland repeated their accusations. During testimony Demjanjuk seemed vague and evasive about his past. On April 18, 1988, after 14 months of testimony, Judge Dove Levin read the verdict of the three-member bench: "We determine unequivocally and without the slightest hesitation or doubt that the accused is Ivan [the Terrible]. We therefore find guilty as charged, a) of crimes against the Jewish people; b) of crimes against humanity; c) of war crimes." One week later Demjanjuk was condemned to be hanged.

In January 1992, Israel's Supreme Court announced that it would hear fresh evidence culled from Soviet archives, supporting defense claims of misidentification. The evidence is compelling: 21 former Soviet Treblinka inmates all identified Ivan the Terrible as not Demjanjuk but another Ukrainian, someone strikingly similarly, Ivan Merchanko (present whereabouts unknown). Other evidence strongly suggested that Demjanjuk was a lower-echelon guard at another Nazi camp, not Treblinka.

On July 28, 1993, the Israeli Supreme Court overturned Demjanjuk's conviction, ruling that the totality of the evidence indicated he was not Ivan the Terrible. On February 20, 1998, the Federal District Court of Cleveland reinstated Demjanjuk's U.S. citizenship. However, the court authorized the government to reinstitute denaturalization proceedings if evidence of other offenses by Demjanjuk are ever uncovered.

Eyewitness testimony is notoriously unreliable: memories fade and sometimes fail. If John Demjanjuk is Ivan the Terrible then he is one of the 20th century's worst criminals. If not, he might still be a man with much to hide.

—*Colin Evans*

Suggestion for Further Reading

Loftus, Elizabeth and Katherine Ketcham. *Witness For The Defense.* New York: St. Martin's Press, 1991.

Teicholz, Tom. *The Trial Of Ivan The Terrible.* New York: St. Martin's Press, 1990.

Wagenaar, Willem A. *Identifying Ivan.* Cambridge, Mass: Harvard University Press, 1988.

Johnny Volpato Trials: 1981 & 1986

Defendant: John S. "Johnny" Volpato   **Crime Charged:** Murder
Chief Defense Lawyer: Dick A. Blenden   **Chief Prosecutor:** Ernest Carroll
Judge: Bill Sadler   **Place:** Carlsbad, New Mexico   **Dates of Trials:** First
Trial: September–October, 1981; Second Trial: October 1986   **Verdict:** First
Trial: Guilty; Second Trial: Not guilty   **Sentence:** First Trial: life with no
parole for 30 years

SIGNIFICANCE

Witnesses whom police ignored in the first trial testified during the second trial
with an entirely different outcome. Still, the question remains among the people of
Carlsbad: Is Johnny Volpato guilty or innocent of murdering his wife?

Shortly before midnight on February 5, 1980, Johnny Volpato pulled up to
The Corner Drugstore, which he owned, in downtown Carlsbad. Sitting
beside him in his late-model Datson was his 36-year-old wife, Elaine. The after-
hours drugstore run wasn't unusual for the pharmacist, father of two, and rising
local political star. Volpato often opened his drug store at all hours to fill
customers' emergency prescriptions. In fact, he even ran ads in the local
newspaper with his home phone number so that he could be reached at any
time.

A Robbery Gone Wrong or a Planned Murder?

On this night Volpato had received such an emergency call at home around
11 o'clock. Elaine allegedly decided to accompany him since she needed a few
things from the drug store. Soon after the two walked inside, someone knocked
on the front door. Volpato answered. An Hispanic man came inside and, as he
asked for his prescription, pulled out a gun.

At this moment, Elaine came from the back of the drugstore, saw the gun,
screamed, then ran down a back hallway toward the back door. The gunman
shot her. The 43-year-old Volpato ran to the phone and as he dialed 911, the
gunman also fired at him. A second man entered, and he and the gunman filled a
box with drugs and fled. As Volpato crawled toward the front door he collapsed.
He was wounded in his hand and shoulder.

Emergency personnel rushed the pharmacist to Dallas for emergency surgery; Elaine died. Autopsy reports concluded she was shot four times, twice in her chest and twice in the back.

At first, the folks of Carlsbad rallied around the injured and grieving Volpato. No one seemed to doubt his story that robbers had killed his wife and left him for dead. After all, in the years since he had graduated from the University of New Mexico's pharmacy school in 1961, the father of two had become a social and political pillar in the small desert town. The meticulously dressed, well-spoken Volpato served on the city council, participated in community affairs, and even dispensed free medicine to those in need. The Corner Drugstore became the gathering spot for Carlsbad's movers and shakers.

A Troubled Marriage

But Johnny Volpato had a wild side. Beyond the duties of his drugstore, his family, and his political career, Volpato spent long, boozy hours in Carlsbad's nightspots with his pals. His womanizing exploits became well known, even to Elaine. Not long before her death, Volpato walked out on his wife. She filed for divorce. But after a year of separation, Volpato convinced her to give the marriage another try, and he moved back into their fashionable home on the Pecos River. The Volpatos appeared to be a happy couple again. Still, ugly rumors of Johnny's marital infidelities persisted.

By the time Volpato returned home from his Dallas hospital stay, local police had tough questions for him. Why had the robbers only wounded Johnny in the hand and shoulder, yet shot the fleeing Elaine four times, twice from behind, and strangely, twice from the front? Where was Johnny's own Colt 38 revolver, a gun like the one used to kill Elaine? Why couldn't he produce it for police? Was the popular pharmacist trying to avoid a costly and embarrassing divorce by murdering his wife?

A search of the Volpato home yielded a bullet that proved similar to the bullets lodged in Elaine's body. Careful inspection of The Corner Drugstore revealed a small niche under a wooden staircase, where police believed Volpato could have hidden the Colt 38. Splintered wood suggested that Volpato later pried the gun from its hiding place and disposed of it.

A year after Elaine's death, police arrested Volpato, charging him with first-degree murder. The news divided the people of Carlsbad into warring factions: You were either for Johnny Volpato or against him.

In his trial, Volpato took the stand to claim police framed him. He called the trial a "political execution" maneuvered by the same people who had once befriended him. Prosecutor Ernest Carroll presented a circumstantial case. He described what he termed "silent witnesses," including the incriminating bullets found in Volpato's home, the coroner's report revealing how Elaine died, and the break-up of his marriage.

The jury debated 20 hours before returning a guilty verdict on October 8, 1981. Volpato was sentenced to life in prison without possibility of parole for 30 years.

New Witnesses Testify in Second Trial

Volpato appealed to the New Mexico Supreme Court, which in 1985 granted a new trial. An expanded defense team presented three new witnesses in Volpato's second trial in 1986.

One witness, Delores Looney, testified that she saw two men outside The Corner Drugstore at around midnight on the night Elaine Volpato was murdered. As she continued in her car down the street, she said she heard a sound that she later concluded was gunfire. She testified that she had not gone to police because she was afraid of repercussions against her son, who had troubles with the law.

Two nurses who worked at a nearby hospital also testified that they saw two men running from Volpato's drugstore on the night of the murder. They said at the time that they were sure they had witnessed a robbery and reported their suspicions to police. They said police did not take their report seriously.

The prosecution countered that, after six years, these new witness accounts were not credible.

The jury apparently thought they were. On October 31, 1986, they found Johnny Volpato not guilty of murdering of his wife. Back in Carlsbad, townsfolk still aren't so sure.

— B. J. Welborn

Suggestions for Further Reading

Transcript, *City Confidential: Carlsbad*. A&E Home Video. 1996.

The Trial of Gary Graham: 1981

Defendant: Gary Lee Graham   **Crime Charged:** Murder
Chief Defense Lawyers: Ronald G. Mock, Douglas M. O'Brien, and Chester Lash Thornton; on appeals: Richard Burr, Douglas M. O'Brien, Robert C. Owen, Michael E. Tygar, Mandy Welch, Jack B. Zimmermann
Chief Prosecutors: John H. Holmes, Jr.; on appeals: Dan Morales
Judge: James Richard Travathan   **Place:** Houston, Texas
Date of Trial: October 30, 1981   **Verdict:** Guilty   **Sentence:** Execution

SIGNIFICANCE

Experts on capital criminal trials saw several compelling questions raised by the Gary Graham case, including: Should a jury consider a murderer's youth and background as a mitigating factor that justifies a life sentence rather than execution? Should a governor be empowered to grant more than one stay of execution pending further review? Should a "30-day rule" prohibiting the introduction of new evidence more than one month after a conviction be revoked? Why does Texas perform nearly twice as many executions as other states?

On May 20, 1981, police of Houston, Texas, were called to the home of 57-year-old Lisa Blackburn. They found her holding a .22-caliber handgun she had taken from 17-year-old Gary Graham, who was asleep in her bedroom. Over five hours, she told them, he had collected her valuables, which were piled by her front door, raped her at gunpoint, and threatened to kill her. He had fallen asleep, she said, "So I took his gun, took his clothes, and called the police."

Arrested, Graham admitted that he had recently committed 10 aggravated robberies, pistol-whipping two victims, shooting one in the neck, and striking one with an automobile after stealing it from him. Graham's background, the police found, included a number of petty offenses. The child of an alcoholic father and a mentally ill mother, he was a semi-illiterate seventh-grade dropout who had fathered children when he was 15 and 17.

Witness Identifies Murderer

The police were then investigating the murder, two weeks earlier, of Bobby Grant Lambert, who had been killed by a .22-caliber bullet in the parking lot of a Safeway supermarket during a robbery attempt at 9:30 P.M. Lambert was a known drug trafficker from Tucson, Arizona, who had a criminal record; $6,000 in cash had been found in his pocket.

One witness of that murder, Bernadine Skillern, who had glimpsed the killer from 40 feet away in the darkened parking lot and who had described him to a police sketch artist, now was shown Gary Graham's picture in a photo line-up. She could not positively identify him. Next day, viewing a live lineup, she identified Graham.

Charged with killing Lambert, Graham pled guilty to the 10 counts of robbery, but denied the murder.

Attorney Ronald G. Mock was appointed by the court to defend Graham. Mock was well known in Harris County, Texas, for his availability to represent indigent clients. While the legal community knew that he had been reprimanded or suspended by the bar a number of times, it also knew that he frequently accepted cases turned down by other attorneys. His record—75 percent of his capital case clients went to death row—was the same as the sentencing record of juries in Harris County.

The One-Day Trial

As the trial opened before Judge James R. Travathan on October 30, 1981, prosecutor Johnny Holmes described the arrest of Graham and showed the jury his gun. He did not, however, tell the jury that ballistics tests by Houston police had proved that that gun had not fired the bullets that killed Lambert. Mock, in his opening, did not call attention to that fact or note that neither the gun nor any other physical evidence that could link Graham to the crime had been formally presented. Observers later theorized that Mock was avoiding the fact that Graham had nine other weapons.

The prosecution called several witnesses. Wilma Amos testified that lighting in the parking lot "was good." Daniel Grady, Ron Hubbard, Leodis Wilkerson, and Amos described the shooter they saw as medium height—roughly 5′5″ to 5′9″—but could not identify him as Graham.

Lisa Blackburn, the rape victim who brought about Graham's arrest, testified that he told her, "I have already killed three people and I'm going to kill you," and "I don't have nothing to lose. If I get caught, I burn, and I'm not getting caught." The defense failed to argue that her testimony should be disallowed because no charge of rape had been brought against the defendant.

Another prosecution witness, Richard Carter, Jr., described how Graham, in an earlier robbery, forced him to kneel, put a shotgun barrel in his mouth, and threatened, "I'll kill you. Blowing away another white m----- f----- don't mean nothing to me."

The prosecution introduced Bernadine Skillern. She described how she was sitting in her parked car in the supermarket parking lot at night when she saw a man wearing a white jacket and dark trousers shoot Lambert. She saw the killer, she testified, "full-face" three times, for two to three seconds each, and watched him for a minute or more at distances ranging from 10 to 40 feet. Her further testimony told how she reviewed police photos and picked Graham out of the lineup.

On cross-examination, defense attorney Mock questioned witness Skillern extensively on her angle of sight from her car, on the adequacy of the lighting in the parking lot, and on the length of time she saw the shooter. The light was bright enough and the time was long enough, she insisted, for her to make the positive identification later. The cross-examination testimony ran to 36 pages, yet, said Mock afterward, "I couldn't even get her to flicker."

Mock rested the defense case without calling the defendant or any witnesses. The guilt phase of the trial ended on the day it started. And on the same day, the jury found Graham guilty of capital murder. The sentence was execution.

Demonstrators from the "Campaign to End the Death Penalty" protest the execution of convicted murderer Gray Graham. (Bettmann/Corbis)

20 Years of Appeals

Over the next 20 years, the Gary Graham case and its appeals gained nationwide fame. Among organizations that provided legal assistance and other support were: the Texas Appellate Practice and Educational Resource Center, Inc., which provides direct representation for a limited number of death-row inmates; Amnesty International, which organizes worldwide rallies; the NAACP Legal Defense and Educational Fund, Inc.; the National Coalition to Abolish the Death Penalty; and the Texas Conference of Churches. Hollywood stars, including Danny Glover, Ed Asner, and Mike Farrell, led public appeals. Several Gary Graham Coalitions and legal defense committees were organized.

At a 1987 hearing on Graham's petition for a writ of habeas corpus on a claim of ineffective assistance of counsel, District Judge Donald Shipley deemed the affidavits of four alibi witnesses, who had come forward some years after the crime, as not credible.

In January 1990, the U.S. Supreme Court voted 5–4 against considering the Graham case on the basis of mitigating evidence of his youth and troubled background. It remanded the case to the U.S. Court of Appeals, Fifth Circuit, which concluded that the jury that sentenced Graham to death had not had an opportunity to consider the facts that suggested a lesser sentence. In January 1992, however, the Fifth Circuit reinstated the death sentence. A year later, the U.S. Supreme Court again denied an appeal.

On April 28, 1993, Texas governor Ann Richards granted Graham a 30-day stay of execution only hours before he was to die. By law, the governor was allowed to grant only one such stay. A new execution date, June 3, was set.

On June 2, the Texas Court of Criminal Appeals unanimously granted a new stay, pending the outcome of another Supreme Court case involving the mitigating factor of a youthful defendant's age. In this appeal, Graham's attorneys argued that, while new evidence—the discovery of alibi witnesses—had come to light, it could not be introduced because Texas law demanded its presentation within 30 days of conviction.

August 16 brought another stay from the Court of Criminal Appeals less than six hours before Graham was scheduled to die by lethal injection.

The following April, the same court ruled that Graham was entitled to a hearing on his claim of new testimony from witnesses who had not appeared at the trial. Hearings and pleas for clemency continued well into 2000. By then, Graham's case had been before the U.S. Supreme Court four times, and he had seen 33 judicial or executive reviews and seven stays of execution.

On June 22, 2000, after the Texas Board of Pardons and Paroles voted 12 to 5 to reject a request for clemency, Gary Graham was executed. The case created a brief stir in the 2000 U.S. presidential campaign by focusing criticism on the high number of executions in Texas under Republican Governor George W. Bush, who was running for and would eventually win the presidency. Bush and his supporters, however, largely deflected any criticism by pointing out that under Texas law the governor followed the recommendations of the Board of Pardons and Paroles.

—Bernard Ryan, Jr.

Suggestions for Further Reading

Curtis, Gregory. "Graham-standing." *Texas Monthly Magazine* (October 1993).

Rimer, Sara, and Raymond Bonner. "Texas Lawyer's Death Row Record a Concern." *New York Times Magazine* (June 11, 2000).

Wayne Williams Trial: 1981

Defendant: Wayne B. Williams   **Crime Charged:** Murder
Chief Defense Lawyers: Alvin Binder and Mary Welcome
Chief Prosecutors: Joseph Drolat, Jack Mallard, and Lewis Slaton
Judge: Clarence Cooper   **Place:** Atlanta, Georgia
Dates of Trial: December 28, 1981–February 27, 1982   **Verdict:** Guilty
Sentence: Life imprisonment

SIGNIFICANCE
The trial of the man suspected of being America's worst child-killer was bound to generate immense attention. But did it produce a just verdict?

Beginning in 1979 an unprecedented wave of killings struck Atlanta, Georgia. Over the next two years upwards of 20 young black males were found murdered. In the early hours of May 21, 1981, police staking out the Chattahoochee River, one of the killer's favorite dumping grounds for his victims, spotted a station wagon on a bridge. The driver, Wayne Williams, was questioned but allowed to leave. Two days later, the body of Nathaniel ("Nate") Cater was dragged from the river. Although forensic evidence connected Williams, a 23-year-old black homosexual music promoter, with many of the Atlanta killings, he was charged on only two counts.

Williams' trial began December 28, 1981. Following an adjournment for the holidays, testimony got under way on January 6, 1982. District Attorney Lewis Slaton likened the Atlanta killings to a "jigsaw puzzle with a whole lot of little pieces fitting in." Chief defense counsel Alvin Binder preferred to highlight Williams' solid family background, insisting to the jury: "You don't get a killer from a boy who was raised like this."

Officer Fred Jacobs, part of the surveillance team watching the Chattahoochee River, testified to seeing a station wagon "drive very slowly" across the bridge, moments after hearing a loud splash.

The story was taken up by FBI Special Agent Gregg Gulliland. After being stopped, Williams had given conflicting reasons for being on the bridge, then blurted out, "What's all this about? . . . I know. This is about those boys, isn't it?"

Challenging the defendant's claim that he had not known either victim, Margaret Carter, an acquaintance of Cater's, stated, "I saw Nate sitting on the bench in the park . . . with another fellow." She identified Williams as that man.

Prosecutors Use Microscopic Analysis

But it was the forensic evidence that really undid Williams. Microanalyst Larry Peterson had compared fibers and dog hairs found on the bodies of Cater and second victim Jimmy Ray Payne with examples taken from Williams' house, car, and German shepherd. "In my opinion," said Peterson, "it is highly unlikely any other environment other than that present in Williams' home and car could account for the combination of fibers and hairs I recovered from Mr. Cater and Mr. Payne."

Under cross-examination from Binder, Peterson acknowledged that there was no absolute scientific means of determining the origin of any fiber, and that identification was a subjective judgment on the part of the examiner.

Evidence of Williams' aggressive homosexuality came from two young men who testified that he had made unwanted advances toward them.

Williams Takes the Stand

Other than attack the credibility of prosecution witnesses, there was little the defense could do, except present Williams himself. Describing himself as a "carefree, happy-go-lucky person," Williams went on, "I haven't killed anybody, or thought about it, or plan on thinking about killing anybody."

Assistant prosecutor Jack Mallard pressed Williams on his reasons for being out at 3:00 A.M. Williams said he was searching for the address of a singer with whom he was to meet in the morning. Mallard wondered why he had not asked for directions.

"Me being in Cobb County at three o'clock in the morning?" Williams sounded incredulous. "Sir, they've got the Ku Klux Klan up there'."

Mallard pounced. "If you're so afraid of the Ku Klux Klan, what are you doing in Cobb County at three o'clock in the morning?"

Williams hurriedly mumbled an excuse but soon recovered his composure, insisting loudly, "Sir, I haven't killed anyone!"

The expected lengthy jury deliberation actually took less than 12 hours. On February 27, 1982, Williams was convicted of double murder. That same day, Judge Clarence Cooper imposed two consecutive life terms.

In the years following his conviction, Wayne Williams has maintained his innocence. His conviction ended any further investigation into the murders of the 22 other victims. Since the conviction, Williams has gained support from many unlikely people, including relatives of some of the victims, former investigators who worked on the cases, and even a retired Georgia State Supreme Court justice.

Many of his supporters question the wisdom of closing the cases of all the victims based on Williams's conviction on only two counts of murder. They also dispute the contention that the murders ended with his arrest and incarceration.

Williams continues to fight for a new trial. Bloodstains found in his car could have come from the two victims. New advances using DNA testing could prove conclusively if the blood matches the DNA of the victims. Thus far, many requests to have the bloodstains analyzed have been denied.

—Colin Evans and Ron Formica

Suggestions for Further Reading

Baldwin, James. *The Evidence Of Things Not Seen.* New York: Holt, Rinehart & Winston, 1985.

Fischer, Mary A. "Was Wayne Williams Framed?" *Gentlemen's Quarterly* (April 1991): 228ff.

Koltz, Charles. "The Atlanta Murders." *New Jersey Law Journal* (December 3, 1981): 11ff.

Wilson, Colin and Donald Seaman. *Encyclopedia of Modern Murder.* New York: G.P. Putnam's Sons, 1983.

Jack Henry Abbott Trial: 1982

Defendant: Jack Henry Abbott   **Crime Charged:** Murder
Chief Defense Lawyer: Ivan S. Fisher   **Chief Prosecutor:** James H. Fogel
Judge: Irving Lang   **Place:** New York, New York   **Dates of Trial:** January 4–21, 1982   **Verdict:** Guilty of first-degree manslaughter   **Sentence:** 15 years to life imprisonment

SIGNIFICANCE

The outrage that surrounded Jack Abbott's trial was deep and understandable. Public opinion took the view that, had it not been for influential but naive intellectuals, Abbott would have remained behind bars and one young life would have been saved.

While in jail, convicted killer Jack Abbott began a correspondence with author Norman Mailer. Mailer encouraged Abbott in his writing and helped to find a publisher for these letters which were released, to great critical acclaim, under the title *In The Belly Of The Beast*. Mailer petitioned Abbott's parole board, describing Abbott as "a powerful and important American writer." They promised to review Abbott's record.

Since age 12 (he was then 35) he had spent less than six months out of jail. Minor thefts had led to more serious bank robberies. In 1966 he received an extra 14-year jail term for stabbing a fellow prisoner to death. The board decided to parole Abbott to a halfway house in New York City. Six weeks later, on July 18, 1981, he and two female companions visited an all-night diner. Abbott got into an argument with waiter Richard Adan over use of the staff lavatory. The two took their quarrel outside, where Abbott stabbed Adan once in the heart, killing him almost instantly. Abbott fled. Police traced him to a Louisiana oil field and brought him back to New York to face trial.

Book not Admissible

Following four days of jury selection, assistant District Attorney James H. Fogel opened the state's case on January 8, 1982. He suffered an early setback when Acting Justice Irving Lang refused to admit into evidence excerpts from *In The Belly Of The Beast*, which the prosecution said demonstrated Abbott's predisposition to kill. One passage that Fogel particularly wanted read out contained detailed instructions on how to kill in a knife-fight: "You have to move into total activity from a totally inactive posture to sink a knife in as close to his heart as possible," which, said Fogel, was virtually a blueprint for what had happened to Richard Adan.

It was defense attorney Ivan S. Fisher's contention that Abbott had merely been acting in self-defense, that Adan had grabbed a knife just before the two men left the diner to settle their dispute, a point contradicted by the first witness, Roger Schwarzchild, another waiter at the diner. He said that the only weapons available to Adan were dull butter knives, but that he did not see Adan with a knife of any description. He had seen the two men step outside, then moments later Abbott re-entered the diner and said, "Let's get out of here," to his two companions.

This last statement was corroborated by one of the two women present, a Barnard College student, Susan Roxas, except that in her version Abbott added, "I just killed a man." Once outside, Abbott told the women, "You don't know me," then ran off up the street. Roxas confirmed that Abbott had been carrying a knife earlier in the evening and that all three in the party had been drinking heavily.

Just Like the Book

Another witness, Wayne Larsen, told of seeing Abbott and Adan outside the diner. After a brief dispute, Abbott had lunged at the other man with a knife. Adan staggered back, clutching his chest. Abbott screamed, "Do you still want to continue this?" Adan, bleeding profusely, replied: "God no. Are you crazy? I already told you I don't."

Earlier rumors that Norman Mailer would testify on Abbott's behalf proved erroneous. It was left to Abbott alone to give the court some insight into the rigors of prison life, rigors that he claimed had honed his paranoia to a lethal level. In the midst of tearfully recounting his brawl with Adan, Abbott was caught off guard when the victim's father-in-law, Henry Howard, suddenly leapt up and yelled, "Abbott, you scum! You useless scum! It's just like the book, Abbott, just like in the book." Still shouting, Howard was led away.

Abbott took the interruption coolly, eyes blinking through gold-rimmed spectacles, and continued with his version of events on the fateful night. Adan had approached him outside the diner. "I was going to run, but then I thought, 'You don't do that.'" Adan kept coming. Abbott claimed that Adan went for a knife (none was ever found), that he had tried to block it, and that a brief struggle ensued. "All of a sudden the knife was in his chest and it was dead still. . . . It was one of the most tragic misunderstandings I can imagine."

Abbott's culpability was never in dispute, only the degree. After more than 24 hours of deliberation, the jury adjudged him guilty of first-degree manslaughter, but not murder. On April 15, 1982, Judge Irving Lang sentenced

Abbott to 15 years to life imprisonment. He did so regretfully, blaming Abbott's behavior on "a prison system that brutalizes rather than rehabilitates."

Norman Mailer, asked for his opinion on the verdict, sounded melancholic. "What can I say—the man is used to jail. Jail, sadly enough, is his home."

This case is eerily similar to that of Edgar Smith, when another renowned literary figure, William F. Buckley, took up a murderer's cause with disastrous repercussions. But it also highlights the problem facing all parole boards: balancing humanitarian concerns for the inmate against the public's right to protection from its worst elements. One cannot escape the nagging suspicion that, in this case at least, the weight of celebrity opinion counted for more than common sense.

—Colin Evans

Suggestions for Further Reading

Abbott, Jack. *In The Belly Of The Beast.* New York: Vintage, 1981.

Gaute, J.H.H. and Robin Odell. *The Murderers' Who's Who.* London: W.H. Allen, 1989.

Wilson, Colin and Donald Seaman. *Encyclopedia of Modern Murder.* New York: G.P. Putnam's Sons, 1983.

Claus Von Bülow Trials: 1982 & 1985

Defendant: Claus Von Bülow **Crime Charged:** Attempted murder
Chief Defense Lawyers: First trial: John Sheenan and Herold Price
Fahringer; second trial: Thomas P. Puccio and John Sheehan
Chief Prosecutors: First trial: Stephen Famiglietti and Susan McGuirl; second
trial: Marc DeSisto and Henry Gemma **Judges:** First trial: Thomas H.
Needham; second trial: Corrine Grande **Places:** First trial: Newport, Rhode
Island; second trial: Providence, Rhode Island **Dates of Trials:** First trial:
January 11–March 16, 1982; second trial: April 25–June 10, 1985.
Verdict: First trial: Guilty; second trial: not guilty **Sentence:** 20 years
imprisonment

SIGNIFICANCE
A study in contrasts, the two trials of Claus Von Bülow provide a unique insight
into the excesses and foibles of the super-rich.

For 13 years Claus and Martha "Sunny" Von Bülow had been bulwarks of
Rhode Island's blueblood colony, but by 1979 their marriage was over in all
but name. Around Christmas of that year Sunny slipped into a coma at their
oceanside mansion. Claus dithered over summoning medical attention and only
prompt mouth-to-mouth resuscitation revived the ailing woman. Sunny seemed
as baffled as everyone else as to the cause. Almost exactly one year later, on
December 21, 1980, she again lapsed into a coma and was transferred to Columbia Presbyterian Hospital in New York City, where she remained comatose as of
this writing. A family-inspired investigation led to indictments against Von
Bülow, a Danish-born aristocrat, charging that he had twice attempted to murder
Sunny by injecting her with insulin.

Because of its glittering cast, the trial attracted global attention. The
courthouse in Newport, Rhode Island, jammed with reporters and TV cameras,
reflected this when testimony began February 2, 1982. Prosecutor Stephen
Famiglietti argued that with a $14-million inheritance, the house, and a beauti-
ful young mistress all at stake, Von Bülow had every reason to want Sunny dead.
Describing the delay in requesting medical help, Famiglietti said: "He generally
conducted himself in a manner not consistent with that of an innocent man."

Witness Cites Mysterious Vials

Had it not been for Maria Schrallhammer, Sunny Von Bülow secretary, the prosecution would not have had a case. Making no attempt to conceal her loathing of the defendant, Schrallhammer first outlined the tension that existed between the Von Bülow, then told of entering a closet in February 1980 and finding a black bag that contained several prescription vials made out to the accused. This set her thinking. The preceding Thanksgiving she had found similar vials labeled insulin. Schrallhammer, puzzled because no family member had a history of diabetes, had shown the vials to Prince Alexander von Auersperg, Sunny's son by her first marriage, remarking, "Insulin. What for insulin?" There seemed to be no reason for it to be around—unless, said Famiglietti, Von Bülow wanted to murder his wife. (When doctors examined Sunny they found abnormally high amounts of insulin in her system.) Auersperg's subsequent discovery of a hypodermic needle encrusted with insulin in yet another black bag merely strengthened her story.

Dr. George Cahill, a former president of the American Diabetes Association and one of the world's top experts in blood-sugar disorders, told the court that injected insulin was the only possible explanation for Sunny's coma. Cahill testified with the air of a man unused to having his opinions questioned, shrugging off defense counsel Herald Fahringer's suggestions that the high insulin level could have resulted from other means. "No, that is not correct . . . the sugar levels alone would lead me to suspect insulin."

What was supposed to be the defense's trump card turned into a disaster. By her own account, Joy O'Neill was a close friend of Sunny's and had frequently gone to the house in her capacity as exercise coach. O'Neill testified that during one of these visits in 1978, Sunny had recommended that she try a shot of insulin as a means of losing weight, saying it enabled one to eat "sweets and everything." On rebuttal Famiglietti was able to show that O'Neill had never actually visited Sunny during 1978 and that her reputation for truthfulness was less than sterling.

Claus Von Bülow at his trial (*Providence Journal-Bulletin* Photo)

After what had been the longest trial in Rhode Island history, the jury then set a record of its own by taking the longest time ever to reach its verdict, nearly six days. Many were surprised at the delay—the case seemed so open and shut—but on March 16, 1982, Claus Von Bülow was found guilty.

Seven weeks later Judge Thomas Needham passed sentence of 20 years imprisonment.

New Trial, New Evidence

Freed on bail, Von Bülow engaged the services of noted Harvard law professor Alan M. Dershowitz to organize his appeal. Under Dershowitz's skilled probing, revelations came to light suggesting the strong likelihood that Sunny's coma was self-induced, as friends cataloged a lifetime of drug and alcohol abuse, interspersed with mammoth food binges, a potentially lethal combination for a known reactive hypoglycemic (someone who suffers from low blood sugar). Even more revealing, Maria Schrallhammer's memory was seriously flawed. Dershowitz found some notes made at the time by family attorney Richard Kuh, which unveiled grave inconsistencies in her various statements to police. These and other discrepancies convinced the Rhode Island Supreme Court, on April 27, 1984, to reverse the convictions and order a new trial.

Two days short of a year later it began. Apart from the counsel—Marc DeSisto had taken over as chief prosecutor—the state's case was essentially unchanged. But this time the defense team mounted a far more vigorous campaign. They were led by Thomas Puccio, fresh from his success as a prosecutor in the ABSCAM trials (see separate entry), and now in private practice. He went after Schrallhammer on the vials. "The first time you spoke to Mr. Kuh you didn't tell him about the insulin. Is that correct?"

"That could be. That could very well be, since I was not concerned so much about the insulin."

In fact, Puccio established that Schrallhammer had not mentioned insulin to anyone, not until hearing that doctors had found insulin in Sunny's system. Turning to the vials found at Thanksgiving, Puccio extracted a grudging admission from the witness that she had no idea what they contained because, as she had told Kuh at the time, the labels had been scraped off. It was a telling blow.

Alexander von Auersperg, locator of the insulin-encrusted needle, also came under pressure. Puccio focused on a family meeting held shortly after that discovery. "One of the thing's you discussed at that meeting was a desire on the part of some of the people present to pay your stepfather some money to have him renounce any interest in your mother's estate. Isn't that right?"

Again Kuh's contemporaneous notes gave the witness no escape. He sheepishly nodded, "That's correct," virtually admitting the existence of a family plot to usurp Von Bülow.

Blood-sugar expert, Dr. George Cahill, also was forced to recant some of his former testimony. In a three-hour grilling Cahill now admitted that his previous assertion that only injected insulin could have produced Sunny's symptoms was false; certain prescription drugs might also produce a similar reaction.

The evidence of the encrusted needle was annihilated by Dr. Leo Dal Cortivo, a forensic toxicologist. He dismissed suggestions that it could have been used to inject Sunny, then gave the jury a practical demonstration why. The hypodermic was of the type which employed a separate vial, at no time would it come into contact with any insulin except through its hollow body and tiny aperture at the point. Once the insulin was injected, any residue on the needle would be wiped off by the skin as it was being withdrawn. Dal Cortivo's testimony obviously provoked speculation as to how the needle might have become encrusted. One possible solution was that it had been deliberately dipped into insulin. This theory, raising as it did the specter of Von Bülow being framed, was not one which the defense actively pursued.

Von Bülow's accusers. Left to right (second row): Ala and Franz Kneissl, Maria Schrallhammer, Alexander von Auersperg, and their attorney Richard Kuh. (*Providence Journal-Bulletin* Photo)

They didn't need to. Earlier, with the prosecution faltering, Judge Corrine Grands had almost granted the defense a mistrial, conceding that she was "holding this case together with baling wire."

As in the first trial Claus Von Bülow maintained a lofty silence and did not take the witness stand. Furious family members angrily denounced this as an act of cowardice but other than a certain callous infidelity there was little that the defendant had to answer for. The jury members clearly thought so. On June 10, 1985, they acquitted Von Bülow on all charges.

Considerable anger greeted this verdict, generating the belief that Claus Von Bülow was a guilty man who had bought his freedom. Certainly his own wealth and that of affluent friends enabled him to employ the very best legal and forensic talent available, but it should be remembered that he was up against an equally well-endowed and very determined family, one prepared to spare no cost to see him convicted.

— Colin Evans

Suggestions for Further Reading.

Briton, Tracy. "Von Bülow's Victory." *The National Law Journal* (June 24, 1985): 24ff.

Dershowitz, Alan M. *Reversal Of Fortune*. New York: Random House, 1986.

Frey, Darcy. "Boomerang." *American Lawyer* (November 1986): 36ff.

Lapayowker, Stewart. "Evidence." *Temple Law Review* (Winter 1988): 1561–1586.

Wright, William. *The Von Bülow Affair*. New York: Delacorte Press, 1983.

John Hinckley Trial: 1982

Defendant: John W. Hinckley, Jr.   **Crime Charged:** Attempted murder
Chief Defense Lawyers: Lon Babby, Gregory Craig, Vincent Fuller, and
Judith Miller   **Chief Prosecutors:** Roger Adelman and Robert Chapman
Judge: Barrington Parker   **Place:** Washington, D.C.   **Dates of Trial:** April
27–June 21, 1982   **Verdict:** Not guilty by reason of insanity

SIGNIFICANCE

The insanity plea has always been a gray area with lawyer and layperson alike,
difficult to plead, often difficult to accept. But the outrage caused by this trial
brought into question the very existence of insanity as a defense.

The facts were never in dispute. On March 30, 1981, John Hinckley, Jr., fired six
shots at President Ronald Reagan and his entourage outside the Washington
Hilton Hotel. The President, Press Secretary James Brady, police officer Thomas
Delahanty, and Secret Service Agent Timothy McCarthy were hit. All recovered.
Hinckley was arrested at the scene and later charged with attempted murder.

With the abortive assassination having been captured on videotape and
replayed endlessly on television, Hinckley's trial was expected to be a foregone
conclusion—until the defense attorneys announced their intention to enter a
plea of not guilty by reason of insanity. In this respect they were greatly aided by
Judge Barrington Parker's decision to hear the case under federal procedural
rules, which meant that the prosecution would bear the burden of proving
Hinckley's sanity beyond a reasonable doubt, whereas, under local rule, the
onus would have fallen on the defense attorneys prove their client insane. This
was an important distinction.

Stalking Gunman Fires Six Shots

Senior prosecutor Roger Adelman made his opening address on May 5,
1982. He described how Hinckley had deliberately stalked the President, and
that when the time came to act, he assumed the "crouch position" used by an
experienced marksman cognizant of his own actions. "With six shots, Mr.
Hinckley hit four people," said Adelman, concluding that these were "the
central and critical events" of the case.

Chief defense counsel Vincent Fuller made no attempt to deny the truth of what Adelman had said, but he disputed the motivation. He traced the origins of the assassination attempt back to Hinckley's four-year obsession with movie actress Jodie Foster, an obsession that led to prolonged psychiatric treatment. Frustrated by his inability to meet Foster, Fuller said, Hinckley retreated "into this world of isolation." He began stalking President Jimmy Carter, and later

The scene immediately after John Hinckley's assassination attempt on President Ronald Reagan, March 30, 1981. (Bettmann/Corbis)

President Reagan. On the morning of the shooting Hinckley checked into a Washington hotel and wrote Foster an undelivered letter, clearly outlining his intentions:

> Dear Jodie,
>
> There is a definite possibility that I will be killed in my attempt to get Reagan. It is for this reason that I am writing you this letter now. . . . I am asking you to please look into your heart and at least give me the chance, with this historical deed, to gain your respect and love.
>
> I love you forever.
>
> —John Hinckley

The accused's father, Jack Hinckley, delivered an impassioned plea from the witness stand. Referring to the rancor between himself and his psychologically troubled son—enough to compel Hinckley's banishment from the family home—Jack Hinckley cried,

I am the cause of John's tragedy. I forced him out at a time when he simply could not cope. I wish to God that I could trade places with him right now.

Testimony, quite predictably, developed into a battle of medical opinion. Was Hinckley a helpless victim of his own neurosis, or was he, as prosecutors alleged, a willful assassin? Dipping deep into his sizable fortune, Hinckley's father paid the handsome fees of an impressive array of psychiatrists to argue the former.

Just How Mad?

Dr. David Bear of Harvard University described Hinckley's obsession with the movie *Taxi Driver*, in which Jodie Foster had starred, explaining how Hinckley identified with the leading character, Travis Bickle, and his attempt to shoot a presidential candidate. Bickle's later success with an attractive woman, said Bear, convinced Hinckley that "violence, horrible as it is, was rewarded . . . [he] felt like he was acting out a movie script."

Answering for the government, Dr. Park Dietz characterized Hinckley as a spoiled rich kid, basking in "notions of achieving success and fame in a way that would not require a great deal of effort." Settling on some sensational crime as the easiest means of gaining attention, Hinckley then "thought about a variety of potential crimes and how much publicity each would attract." While conceding Hinckley's abnormality, Dietz insisted that the defendant was never out of touch with reality—the hallmark of psychosis.

Such contradictory and confusing testimony clearly presented enormous problems for the jurors as they retired on Friday, June 18, 1982. They returned the following Monday. Judge Barrington Parker, visibly shaken, read their verdict—not guilty by reason of insanity—to a stunned courtroom. In post-trial interviews some jurors hinted that they had been coerced into this verdict by other jurors. Following acquittal, Hinckley was detained at St. Elizabeth's mental hospital and remains there to the present day.

The most grievously injured victim of Hinckley's havoc, James Brady, lent his name to a bill designed to stiffen gun control regulation but saw his efforts fail to pass the U.S. House of Representatives in March 1992.

In September 1992 a federal judge ruled that Hinckley's insanity did not absolve him of liability for damages to the three presidential aides wounded in the shooting, all of whom had brought suit against the would-be assassin. By the mid-1990s, his doctors felt that after years of therapy and medication, Hinckley was no longer delusional or psychotic. In 1996, Hinckley asked for monthly passes to spend days alone with his parents outside of St. Elizabeth's Hospital. For nearly three years, federal prosecutors opposed such trips. But in August 1999, a three-judge panel decided to allow supervised off-campus visits.

Hinckley's acquittal sparked a vigorous and often misguided debate about the insanity defense. Many sought to curtail its use; others urged total abolition. Sadly, the swell of unrest owed more to the standing of the victims than it did to the facts of the case. John Hinckley had enough peculiarities of mind and behavior to justify the jury's decision.

—Colin Evans

Suggetions for Further Reading

Caplan, Lincoln. *The Insanity Defense.* Boston: Godine, 1984.

Hinckley, Jack and Jo Ann Hinckley. *Breaking Points.* Grand Rapids, Mich.: Zondervan, 1985.

Lindbergh, Tod. "Keep Him Out of the Public Eye." *Insight* (September 4, 1989): 64ff.

Winslade, William J. and Judith Wilson Ross. *The Insanity Plea.* New York: Charles Scribner's Sons, 1983.

Mumia Abu-Jamal Trial: 1982

Defendant: Mumia Abu-Jamal **Crime Charged:** Murder
Chief Defense Lawyers: Anthony Jackson (trial); Leonard I. Weinglass
(posttrial, since 1992) **Chief Prosecutor:** Joseph J. McGill **Judge:** Albert
Sabo **Place:** Philadelphia, Pennsylvania **Dates of Trial:** June 15–July 2,
1982 **Verdict:** Guilty **Sentence:** Execution

SIGNIFICANCE
The trial of Mumia Abu-Jamal raises a number of questions that jurisprudence
must face: How believable is witness? How does a judge handle an unruly
defendant? Is capital punishment justifiable? Abu-Jamal's lingering incarceration
on death row has prompted numerous protests against his execution, many in
countries that have abolished the death penalty. During demonstrations on
February 28, 2000, 185 people were arrested outside the U.S. Supreme Court
building in Washington, D.C., and 164 protestors were arrested at a federal
appeals court building in San Francisco.

At 3:51 A.M. on December 9, 1981, 25-year-old Philadelphia police officer
Daniel Faulkner, a five-year veteran on the force, radioed from his patrol car
for backup at Thirteenth Street and Locust. Arriving seconds later, police found
Faulkner lying dead, his face blown away by a gunshot.

Sitting nearby and bleeding profusely was a man identified later as
Mumia Abu-Jamal. He was a cabdriver. On the ground was a gun he was licensed
to carry.

Black Panther Activist

A Philadelphia native, Abu-Jamal had cofounded a chapter of the Black
Panthers in 1969, when he was 15 years old. Expelled from high school for
radicalism, he had since become a radio journalist, well known for his smooth,
resonant voice and on-the-air ambience. He was also known as a harsh critic of
the police. However, since 1979, when he had joined a local public radio station,
and especially since January 1981, his colleagues had noticed a deterioration in
the quality of his work. He was also accused of biased reporting. Finally, asked
to resign, he took to driving a taxi.

Hospitalized with a severe chest wound from a bullet fired by Officer Faulkner's gun, Abu-Jamal was arrested for murder. The bullet recovered from the policeman's skull was too fragmented to be identified as having come from Abu-Jamal's gun, which held five empty cartridges, but it was consistent with its type.

Trial Begins, Defendant Absent

As jury selection began in June 1982, Abu-Jamal insisted on representing himself. By the third day, however, Judge Albert Sabo disqualified him, ruling that he was taking too long for the voir dire process and intimidating prospective jurors. A court-appointed attorney, Anthony Jackson, took over. In the end, the jury included 10 whites and 2 blacks.

Mumia Abu-Jamal. (AP/ Wide World Photos)

Abu-Jamal was absent during most of the prosecution's seven-day presentation; Judge Sabo had dismissed him from the courtroom because of his continuing and unruly insistence on representing himself. The proceedings were not transmitted to his holding cell, nor was he provided a transcript.

Prosecutor Joseph J. McGill gave a description of the presumed sequence of events of that night: Officer Faulkner had stopped a car, probably for a traffic violation. The driver, who turned out to be Abu-Jamal's younger brother, William Cook, took a swing at the cop, who responded by brandishing his billy club or a flashlight. Abu-Jamal, who had witnessed the altercation from his cab, parked nearby, then dashed from the taxi, firing a shot at Faulkner. Downed and wounded, the officer managed to fire back at Abu-Jamal, who then stood over him and shot him directly in the face.

Four witnesses testified for the prosecution. Cynthia White, a prostitute with 38 arrests to her credit, was the only one who said she had seen Abu-Jamal's gun. Robert Chobert, a taxi driver who had pulled up behind the police car (and who was on probation with his license suspended), said he saw Abu-Jamal make the up-and-down motions of firing a gun. "I know who shot the cop and I ain't going to forget it," Chobert declared. Upon cross-examination the defense reminded him that he had told police he had witnessed the shooter flee before more police arrived, and had described the gunman as over six-foot-two and weighing more than 225 pounds, while the defendant weighed barely 170 pounds.

Policeman Garry Bell testified that he had heard Abu-Jamal say, in the hospital, "I shot that mother-f-----, and I hope the mother-f----- dies." Hospital security guard Priscilla Durham said she had also heard the same, and that she had told hospital investigators about it the next day. But the defense suggested that Bell had invented the confession, pointing out that he had waited to report it until 77 days after the crime. The defense also revealed that a report filed that night by the cop who took the suspect into custody had made no mention of such comments.

Was There Another Shooter?

Witnesses introduced by defense attorney Jackson painted a different picture. A second prostitute who had worked that same corner that night said she, like White, had been offered immunity from arrest in exchange for testimony against Abu-Jamal. A neighborhood resident said he had seen a man run away in the direction cabdriver Chobert described. Altogether, four witnesses, none of whom were acquainted, testified as seeing the shooter flee in the same direction. Was Mumia Abu-Jamal framed, the defense asked, by police who resented his on-air reporting and public insinuations about police brutality?

Meanwhile, court pundits wondered why the suspect's hands had not been checked for residue upon his arrest; why he had not claimed to have shot the officer in self-defense; why the court had allotted only $14,000 for the defense of someone accused of first-degree murder; why Abu-Jamal had been so disruptive that the judge had no choice but to throw him out of the courtroom; and why the defense had not called a ballistics expert or a pathologist to testify.

The defense, however, did call 16 character witnesses to avow that Abu-Jamal, a decent, professional good guy, was not the type to commit such a crime.

The Verdict

Jury deliberations on Friday, July 2, took less than six hours. Mumia Abu-Jamal was found guilty. The next day, as the jury considered whether to impose the death sentence or life imprisonment without parole, the prosecution reviewed his Black Panther experience 12 years earlier. The jury was read a newspaper interview published when he was 16 that included his quoting Mao Tse-tung of the People's Republic of China: "Political power grows out of the barrel of a gun." The jury deliberated for an hour and 53 minutes, and sentenced Abu-Jamal to death.

Since 1982, Abu-Jamal has been on death row while the Pennsylvania Supreme Court has rejected two applications for a new trial; civil disobedience rallies have been held from Philadelphia to San Francisco; prominent writers and artists have spoken out on his behalf; National Public Radio had scheduled him to comment on prison life and crime issues on its *All Things Considered* and then backed off; worldwide opponents of the death penalty have engaged in protests; Abu-Jamal has received honorary citizenships in Copenhagen and

Palermo and an honorary law degree in California; donations to support his legal fees have mounted to well over $200,000; prominent attorneys have taken up his cause; he has written and published several books and numerous essays; and the U.S. Supreme Court has refused to grant him a writ of *habeas corpus* or consider his appeal.

In October 1999, to give defense and prosecution lawyers time to prepare arguments for a new trial, U.S. District Judge William H. Yohn, Jr. suspended a death warrant that had set Abu-Jamal's execution for December 2.

—Bernard Ryan, Jr.

Suggestions for Further Reading

Abu-Jamal, Mumia. *All Things Censored*. San Francisco: AK Press, 1999.

——. *Death Blossoms: Reflections from a Prisoner of Conscience*. Farmington, Penn.: Plough, 1997.

——. *Live from Death Row*. New York: Avon, 1996.

Weinglass, Leonard I. *Race for Justice: Mumia Abu-Jamal's Fight against the Death Penalty*. Monroe, Me.: Common Courage, 1995.

Pulitzer Divorce Trial: 1982

Plaintiff: Herbert Pulitzer, Jr. **Defendant:** Roxanne D. Pulitzer
Chief Defense Lawyers: Joseph D. Farish, Jr., and Louis L. Williams
Chief Lawyers for Plaintiff: Mark T. Luttier and Robert T. Scott
Judge: Carl H. Harper **Place:** Palm Beach, Florida
Dates of Trial: September 20–November 9, 1982 **Verdict:** Divorce
granted, and custody of the children awarded to Herbert Pulitzer

SIGNIFICANCE

While the Pulitzer marriage was dissolved simply under Florida's "no-fault" divorce law, sensational allegations about Roxanne Pulitzer's conduct caused the judge to rule that the state's "tender years doctrine" awarding custody of young children to the mother should not be applied in this case. Some of the testimony at the trial was graphic enough to border on the pornographic, which ensured that the trial received more news coverage than any divorce trial in recent history.

Until it ended, the marriage of Roxanne and Herbert "Peter" Pulitzer looked like a real-life Cinderella story. The couple came from very different worlds. The divorced Pulitzer, wealthy grandson of publishing magnate Joseph Pulitzer, was considered to be one of the most eligible bachelors in the wealthy Florida enclave of Palm Beach. The recently divorced Roxanne Dixon, 21 years younger, was a former cheerleader from a small town in rural New York state. The pair met at a party, married, had twin sons, and seemed to have a happy marriage for 5½ years until things went wrong. To the discomfort of Palm Beach society and the titillation of the rest of the world, tales of what went wrong between the Pulitzers made their televised divorce extremely popular.

When Herbert Pulitzer sued his wife for divorce, he offered her a substantial financial support settlement if she would relinquish custody of their children. Roxanne Pulitzer refused and was initially granted custody of their two young sons in an emergency custody hearing. When the Pulitzers' lawyers took their proposed settlements for child custody and the financial terms of the divorce before Circuit Judge Carl Harper, the case quickly became ugly. To little effect, Judge Harper slapped a "gag order" on all parties involved to prevent the case from being tried in the press. Palm Beach seemed to empty of socialites, many of whom feared being subpoenaed to testify about the Pulitzer marriage.

Herbert Pulitzer accused his wife of wrecking their marriage with adultery and drug abuse. His lawyers called a train of witnesses—many of them Pulitzer employees—whose allegations portrayed Roxanne Pulitzer as an unfit mother by virtue of her heavy cocaine use and alleged affairs with a race car driver, a French bakery owner, and a former nanny's boyfriend, whom the lawyers characterized as a drug dealer.

Both Pulitzers claimed that they had shared in sexual encounters with Jacquie Kimberly, socialite wife of Kleenex heir James Kimberly. Herbert Pulitzer further accused the two women of carrying on a lesbian relationship, a charge which provoked Jacquie Kimberly to retort that Pulitzer was "definitely deranged." When Roxanne Pulitzer counterattacked with accusations that her husband had an incestuous relationship with a daughter by his previous marriage, Pulitzer's daughter appeared on the stand and accused Roxanne Pulitzer of propositioning her.

Several witnesses testified about Roxanne Pulitzer's active interest in the supernatural. A psychic described seances in the Pulitzer bedroom, during which a trumpet lay on the bed. Wondering aloud how it could be relevant, Judge Harper allowed the trumpet to be entered as evidence. Newspapers immediately dubbed Roxanne Pulitzer "the strumpet with the trumpet."

Judge Harper did little to disguise his contempt for what he was hearing. "It surely made me appreciate my wife," said the judge. "I go home every night and give her a big hug."

Judge Harper ultimately ruled in Herbert Pulitzer's favor with a severity that struck many observers as peculiar. Contrasting Pulitzer's "doleful eyes and aging face" with his wife's apparently unconcerned "doodling" on a notepad during the trial (she later claimed she was trying to maintain her composure), the judge proclaimed that Herbert Pulitzer was a hard worker and loving parent who deserved custody of his children.

Judge Harper's decision intimated that Roxanne Pulitzer was a gold digger intent on profiting financially from the divorce. He wrote that her "exorbitant demands shock the conscience of the court, putting the court in mind of the hit record by country singer, Jerry Reed, which laments, 'She Got the Gold Mine, I Got the Shaft.'"

Herbert Pulitzer was ordered to pay his wife's legal fees, return $7,000 she had contributed toward the purchase of his yacht, and pay her $2,000 a month in "rehabilitative alimony" for two years so that she would have a means of support until she could become gainfully employed. All other alimony and financial claims were denied. In view of her husband's wealth, his pretrial offer, and the annual $144,000 alimony payment she had requested, Roxanne Pulitzer's cash award was minuscule. She was given two weeks to vacate the house for which lawyers had fought.

In 1982, Florida's "tender years doctrine" was based on the premise that a child forms a strong emotional bond with its mother during the first three years of age. Courts customarily awarded custody to mothers in divorce suits for fear of breaking this bond and damaging the emotional development of any children involved. Judge Harper, however, declared that Roxanne Pulitzer's "flagrant adultery and other gross marital misconduct" required abandoning the doctrine in her case. He ruled that the children would live with their father. Their mother would be allowed custody two weekends per month, holidays on alternating years, and for an annual four-week vacation.

The decision left Roxanne Pulitzer emotionally shattered. She contacted Los Angeles divorce attorney Marvin Mitchelson, winner of the celebrated "palimony" suit brought against actor Lee Marvin by his former lover Michelle Triola Marvin. The flamboyant and expensive attorney offered to take Roxanne Pulitzer's case without a fee, but bowed out after the ensuing publicity faded, leaving her appeals in the hands of Florida attorneys.

Roxanne Pulitzer's three appeals of the custody ruling were unsuccessful, but she found a way to capitalize on her notoriety. Working as an aerobics instructor and occasionally lecturing in favor of joint child custody policies, she paid her legal bills with the help of $70,000 she received for posing nude in *Playboy* magazine. In 1987, she told her side of the story in *The Prize Pulitzer*, an immediate best-seller whose portrait of the Pulitzer marriage and its dissolution differed greatly from the scenario that emerged from the trial.

Roxanne Pulitzer claimed to be the victim of perjurers and a methodical character assassination that cost her custody of her children. She portrayed her ex-husband as a manipulator whose constant hints of reconciliation led her not to take his divorce action seriously until it was too late. "I had no game plan," she told the *Houston Post* during a promotional interview for the book. "I was sleeping with him right up to the trial and after the trial. And he evidently had a plan that was way beyond me. . . . I was an idiot."

— Thomas C. Smith

Suggestions for Further Reading

Axthelm, Peter. "The Palm Beach Fun Couple." *Newsweek* (January 10, 1983): 69.

Couric, Emily. *The Divorce Lawyers.* New York: St. Martin's Press, 1992.

Pulitzer, Roxanne with Kathleen Maxa. *The Prize Pulitzer.* New York: Random House, 1987.

Thompson, Hunter S. "A Dog Took My Place." *Rolling Stone* (July 21–August 4, 1983): 18–22.

Charles Harrelson Trial: 1982–83

Defendants: Charles Voyde Harrelson, Jo Ann Starr Harrelson, Elizabeth Chagra, Jamiel Chagra   **Crimes Charged:** Charles Harrelson: conspiracy to murder; murder of a federal judge; conspiracy to obstruct justice. Jo Ann Starr Harrelson: conspiracy to obstruct justice. Elizabeth Chagra: conspiracy to murder and conspiracy to obstruct justice; separate indictment on income tax evasion. Jamiel Chagra: separate trial on murder, conspiracy to murder, conspiracy to obstruct justice; drug conspiracy and trafficking charges; separate indictment on income tax evasion   **Chief Defense Lawyers:** Charles Harrelson: Thomas G. Sharpe, Jr.; Jo Ann Harrelson: Charles Champion; Elizabeth Chagra: Warren Burnett; Jamiel Chagra: Oscar B. Goodman   **Chief Prosecutor:** Ray Jahn   **Judge:** William Sessions   **Places:** Charles Harrelson: San Antonio, Texas. Jamiel Chagra's trial moved to Jacksonville, Florida. Jo Ann Harrelson tried for perjury, and Jamiel and Elizabeth Chagra tried for tax evasion in Shreveport, Louisiana.   **Dates of Trials:** October 7, 1982–December 14, 1982 (Charles Harrelson, Jo Ann Harrelson, Elizabeth Chagra); January 10, 1983–February 7, 1983 (Jamiel Chagra); March 1983 (Chagra trials for tax evasion and Jo Ann Harrelson trial for perjury)   **Verdicts:** Charles Harrelson: guilty of murder of federal judge, conspiracy to murder, conspiracy to obstruct justice. Jo Ann Harrelson: guilty of conspiracy to obstruct justice, perjury. Jamiel Chagra: guilty of conspiracy to obstruct justice, drug charges, and tax evasion. Elizabeth Chagra: guilty of conspiracy to murder, conspiracy to obstruct justice, tax evasion, conspiracy conviction overturned February 15, 1985, on appeal   **Sentences:** Charles Harrelson: two life sentences plus five years. Jo Ann Harrelson: 25 years for obstruction of justice and perjury. Elizabeth Chagra: 30 years for conspiracy to murder, two concurrent five year sentences for obstruction of justice and tax evasion. Jamiel Chagra: 15 years and $120,000 fine

SIGNIFICANCE

Charles Harrelson was convicted for a hit-man killing of Judge John H. Wood, the only federal judge to be assassinated in the twentieth century. The trial grew out of one of the largest FBI investigations in history, taking three years and over $5 million. Charles Harrelson's son, the actor Woody Harrelson, later supported a motion for a retrial, based on both the inadequacy of the original defense and the federal government's methods of gathering evidence.

On May 29, 1979, Judge John H. Wood was killed in San Antonio, Texas, by a shot from a high-powered rifle to the back of the head. Judge Wood, known as "maximum John" because of the heavy sentences he had imposed on drug dealers, had presided over the pretrial hearing of Jamiel Chagra, denying 20 defense motions. At the end of the hearing, Jamiel turned to his brother and attorney, Joseph Chagra, and said he would never have a fair trial. He asked if he should have Judge Wood killed. Joseph agreed that he should.

The Chagras were known as key members of a so-called Dixie Mafia, heavily involved in drug smuggling.

The trial of Jamiel Chagra was set for May 29, 1979, but Judge Wood was shot as he left his apartment in Alamo Heights for court.

Investigators suspected that the murder was somehow connected to the growing drug trade in Texas. Assistant U.S. Attorney James Kerr, who had prosecuted several drug cases before Judge Wood, had barely escaped an assassination attempt some six months before Wood was killed. However, there was no physical evidence and investigators had to rely on circumstantial evidence and informants. Investigators questioned several long-term convicts, offering reduced sentences for information about the judge's killing. One, Jerry Ray James, befriended Jamiel Chagra in prison and allowed his conversations to be secretly taped. The government also taped other conversations, including some between Charles Harrelson and his attorney, and others between Joseph and Jamiel Chagra. Agents searched the El Paso homes of the Chagra family. The evidence gathered against Harrelson was somewhat tenuous, and included testimony from Joseph Chagra in return for a reduced sentence, and a letter from Elizabeth Chagra that claimed she had delivered money to Harrelson as a payoff for the murder.

Chagra Testifies for Prosecution

When the murder trial got underway in San Antonio, in exchange for a guilty plea to commit conspiracy to murder and a sentence of 10 years, Joseph Chagra testified against Harrelson, who he claimed was the hit man. Joseph testified as well against his own sister-in-law Elizabeth Chagra, and Harrelson's wife, Jo Ann. Joseph Chagra refused to testify against his own brother Jamiel (Jimmy), however. In addition to the testimony of Joseph Chagra, the government had evidence drawn from more than 1,000 recorded telephone and face-to-face conversations, most of them involving Jamiel Chagra in various prisons. Tapes of Jerry Ray James' extensive conversations with Jamiel spelled out details of the plot to kill the judge. Federal authorities claimed that attorney-client privileges did not protect conversations between Joseph and Jamiel Chagra, because Joseph (the attorney) was himself a suspect in the conspiracy to conceal the crime.

The prosecution charged that Harrelson, who had earlier served five years before being paroled of a 15-year sentence for killing a man for a $2,000 fee, killed Judge Wood in exchange for a promised $250,000 payment by Jamiel Chagra.

Kathryn Wood, the widow of the slain judge, provided a five-page handwritten letter from Elizabeth Chagra, apologizing for her involvement in the murder. In the letter, Elizabeth relayed conversations about plans to kill Wood and told of her own delivery of the payoff money to Las Vegas.

Charles Harrelson in a Federal Penitentiary serving two life sentences for the murder of Judge John Wood. (The Gamma Liaison Network)

Harrelson Alleges Complicated Set-up

Harrelson claimed that he was set up. He claimed that a fellow gambler, George (Pete) Kay had bilked Jamiel Chagra by claiming that Charles Harrelson had killed the judge and should collect the $250,000 fee. In effect, he was being tried for murder, when he claimed that his only involvement was in a con-game to get the murder pay-off money for a killing performed by someone else. Harrelson argued that Kay's wife had purchased a Weatherby hunting rifle of the type used to kill the judge some 12 days before the killing. Jo Ann had purchased the rifle under a false name, Mrs. "Fay King." She had then given the rifle to George Kay. Harrelson also testified that Kay had borrowed his own distinctive gold-colored Oldsmobile, similar to one seen near the judge's apartment on the day of the killing. Harrelson claimed that when the murder took place, he was in Dallas, 270 miles away.

Harrelson said that Kay had about $135,000 of the payoff money delivered to him by Elizabeth Chagra as part of the scam. She, in turn, claimed she thought the payoff was for a gambling debt, and did not believe her husband when he claimed, "This is for the judge."

Verdicts and Convictions

Jamiel Chagra was acquitted of murder and conspiracy to murder but convicted of conspiracy to obstruct justice and conspiracy to possess marijuana; he was later convicted of tax evasion. Jo Ann Harrelson was convicted of conspiracy to obstruct justice and later convicted of five counts of perjury. Elizabeth Chagra was convicted of conspiracy to murder and conspiracy to obstruct justice. The 5th U.S. Circuit Court of Appeals overturned the conspiracy conviction February 15, 1985, on the grounds that the prosecution failed to show premeditation and malice. In exchange for agreeing to testify against

Charles, Jo Ann Harrelson and Elizabeth Chagra faced only the lesser charges. Joseph Chagra pled guilty to the charge of conspiracy to commit murder and received a sentence of ten years. Jamiel Chagra was tried separately, in Jacksonville, Florida and received a sentence of 15 years and was fined $120,000 on the charge of conspiracy to obstruct justice and conspiracy to possess marijuana. Without his brother's testimony, Jamiel was acquitted of conspiracy to murder charges.

Harrelson's jury found him guilty of murder of a federal employee, and he was also convicted on the charges of conspiracy to commit murder and conspiracy to obstruct justice. He was sentenced to two life sentences. His wife received a total of 25 years on the conspiracy and perjury charges; Elizabeth received 30 years on the conspiracy and tax evasion charges.

Harrelson's Son Funds Appeal

Woody Harrelson, the actor who played the part of the affable bartender in the television series *Cheers,* and also the lead in *The People vs. Larry Flynt,* mounted an appeal in 1998, hiring famed criminal attorney Alan Dershowitz. However, after a game of pickup basketball between Woody and Fred Biery, the judge scheduled to hear the case, the judge disqualified himself and the case was continued to the year 2000, to be heard before Judge Orlando Garcia in Denver.

Among other points, Woody said that his father had spent only $7,000 on his defense, compared to the $5 to $10 million spent by the federal government in marshalling evidence. Further, most of the evidence and testimony against Charles Harrelson had been gathered from prisoners who were offered reduced sentences in exchange for implicating Harrelson. As of mid-2001, the appeal remained postponed.

— Rodney Carlisle

Suggestions for Further Reading

King, Wayne. "Three Are Found Guilty of Assassination of Federal Judge." *New York Times* (December 15, 1982).

"The Judge Wood Murder Case." *Newsweek* (June 22, 1981).

"Texas Sniper—The Charge: Murdering a Judge." *Time* (October 25, 1982).

Alcee Hastings Trial and Impeachment: 1983 & 1989

Defendant: Alcee L. Hasting **Crimes Charged:** Trial: Conspiracy to solicit and accept money in return for unlawful influence in the performance of lawful government functions and for corruptly impeding due administration of justice. Impeachment: Fifteen articles detailing charges of conspiracy to accept a bribe and for making false statements and falsifying evidence throughout the investigation and trial; one article for leaking confidential wiretap information; and one article for bringing disrepute to the Federal Courts **Chief Defense Lawyers:** Trial: Alcee Hastings, Patricia Williams; Impeachment: Terry Anderson, Patricia Williams **Chief Prosecutors:** Trial: Reid Weingarten; Impeachment: Six "trial managers" from the House of Representatives, headed by John Bryant (D) of Texas **Judges:** Trial: Edward T. Gignoux; Impeachment: The U.S. Senate, with Senator Robert C. Byrd, president pro tem, presiding **Places:** Trial: Miami, Florida; Impeachment: Washington, D.C. **Dates:** Trial: January 19–February 4, 1983; Impeachment: October 18–20, 1989 **Verdicts:** Trial: Not guilty; Impeachment: Guilty on eight articles, which included charges of conspiracy to obtain a bribe and of committing perjury and falsifying documents during the investigation and 1983 trial. Not guilty of leaking confidential wiretap information **Penalty:** Removed from federal bench

SIGNIFICANCE

This is the only instance in American history where a Federal official was first tried by a criminal court and, after being acquitted, was then impeached by the U.S. Congress for the same crime. What makes it even more extraordinary is that the individual in question then went on to be elected to the very U.S. House of Representatives that had impeached him.

In 1979, Alcee L. Hastings, the son of domestic servants, became, at age 43, the first African American to be named to the federal bench in Florida. As a member and supporter of numerous local and national civic and social organizations, he was understandably the pride of his home state's black community. It came as a special shock, then, when in December 1981, the U.S. Attorney for the Southern District of Florida announced that Hastings was being charged with engaging in a plot to solicit and accept a bribe in return for giving a more lenient sentence to convicted criminals.

The Alleged Plot

Word had gotten through to the FBI that William Borders, Jr., a prominent Washington, D.C., attorney and old friend of Hastings, was claiming that he could arrange for favorable sentences by Hastings in return for a payment. To test this, in September 1981, the FBI had a retired agent named Paul Rico pose as Frank Romano, one of two brothers who in 1980 had been convicted of racketeering in Hastings' court. The Romanos had already been sentenced to three years in prison and $1.2 million of their assets had been seized, but the FBI agent posing as Frank (the brothers were out on appeal) arranged with Borders (who had never seen the Romanos) to get the sentence reduced to probation and for $845,000 to be returned. For this, Borders demanded $150,000, a generous portion of which, he claimed, would go to Hastings.

Immediately after Borders made the deal with Rico/Romano, Hastings did issue an order returning $845,000. But because the government arrested Borders the instant he took possession of the money, the government never could actually prove that any of it went to Hastings.

Borders went to trial in March 1982, was found guilty, and was sentenced to five years in prison. Hastings brought a legal action to establish that a federal judge could not be tried without first having been impeached, but the courts rejected this and he was brought to trial.

The Trial

Hastings lost his motion to remove the trial from Miami, but the presiding judge, Edward T. Gignoux, had come from the federal court in Maine because all the federal judges in the Southeast had disqualified themselves. Hastings, defying conventional wisdom that "a lawyer who defends himself has a fool for a client," chose to serve as co-counsel with Patricia Williams, who was also his fiancée. The government's opening argument compared the case to a "jigsaw puzzle where each piece is subject to debatable interpretation."

In fact, the case against Hastings was built almost entirely on circumstantial evidence. William Borders had already insisted that Hastings was not involved in his scheme, and refused to cooperate in any way, forcing the government to rely on tapes of phone calls between Hastings and Borders. The problem was that neither Romano's name nor any sum of money were ever mentioned, so the government had to argue that instead the two men had spoken in code. Thus, the government claimed that phone discussions about a "letter" for a certain Hemphill Pride was really referring to the court order to return $845,000 to Romano. The government also argued that Hastings' departure from Washington as soon as he got word of Borders' arrest constituted "flight" and suggested wrongdoing.

As his own defense lawyer, Hastings called on 49 witnesses—including his own mother—to counter the prosecution's case or to testify to his own integrity. Then, as the 50th witness, he took the stand for an entire day and effectively guided his inexperienced co-counsel, Patricia Williams, in his own interrogation. He had an explanation for each of the government's charges. The return of the $845,000: he did this because a recent appeals court ruling required it. Hemphill Pride was a real individual, a friend of his and Borders', and the letter was a real one that he considered writing to help get him reinstated to the bar. If his name was merely a code, Williams argued, "How would they distinguish when they were legitimately talking about Hemphill and about bribery?"

Aylcee Hastings testifying during his Senate impeachment hearing. (AP/Wide World Photos)

In summing up, Hastings stated that Borders' claim to the FBI agent posing as Romano was an old lawyer's scam known as "rain-making." The lawyer takes the money to guarantee a decision that he already has reason to believe is coming down—and then if the decision goes otherwise, he returns the money with some excuse about the judge's running scared.

Whatever their reasoning, the jury— 10 white people, two black—after deliberating 17 and one-half hours over three days, returned with a verdict of not guilty. Hastings walked out of the court, still a federal judge. Indeed, on the courthouse steps, he stated, "I think I'm going to be a much better judge than I've ever been." Then he added a typically defiant punch line: "I don't think the Justice Department will ever be able to pull the wool over my eyes."

Phase Two

But his troubles were far from over. Shortly after his acquittal, two of his fellow judges in the Eleventh Circuit filed a complaint with their Judicial Council that led to a three-year investigation of Hastings. After the Council's investigation committee turned in its report concluding that Hastings had broken the law, the full Council endorsed this conclusion and passed it on to the Judicial Conference of the United States. In March 1987, this Conference, composed of federal judges, then informed the House of Representatives that impeachment might be warranted. In May 1988, a special House subcommittee began to examine the case and the evidence. Hastings again tried to stop this, arguing that impeachment would expose him to double jeopardy, and that the whole action was motivated by a racial and political vendetta. But the subcommittee recommended impeachment and on August 8, 1988, the House voted 413 to 3 to accept 17 articles of impeachment. On March 16, 1989, the Senate voted to proceed with all 17 of them.

The Impeachment Trial

Up to this time, there had been only 13 such impeachment trials: one president, one Senator, one cabinet officer, one Supreme Court justice, and nine federal judges. Of these, only five had been convicted—all federal judges. What followed, however, was quite different from the process that Americans later would become familiar with during the impeachment of President Clinton. Concerned that a trial before the full Senate would keep it from more pressing affairs, the Senate set up a special committee composed of six Democrats and six Republicans. Senator Jeff Bingaman (D) of New Mexico was the chairman, while Senator Arlen Specter (R) of Pennsylvania was vice chairman. Meeting sporadically between July 10 and August 3, 1989, this committee reviewed all the facts, considered the evidence, and heard various witnesses, including Alcee Hastings himself. By mid-October the committee submitted a report but did not recommend action in either direction.

On October 18, as the impeachment trial began, Judge Hastings himself addressed the Senate to urge that they cease the proceedings, but the next day, members of the U.S. Senate gathered in a closed session to consider the case. At this time, Senator Specter, the vice chairman of the special committee, released his lengthy personal letter urging the Senate to reject all charges on grounds of insufficient evidence. The next day, the Senate met in open session, and by a vote of 69–26 found Hastings guilty on the first article, then proceeded (by almost the same margins) to find him guilty of seven more articles. The article that charged he brought "disrepute to the Federal Courts" fell seven votes short of the two-thirds majority needed to convict.

Hastings Rebounds

After a federal official has been convicted of one or more articles of impeachment, that individual is automatically removed from office. But the Constitution also gives the Senate the choice to take the additional step of barring that official from ever again holding "any office of Honor, Trust, or Profit under the United States." As it happened, the Senate did not choose to do so for Hastings. So in 1992, Hastings ran for Congress from the 23rd District of Florida—his home base in the Miami area. He was elected to the House of Representatives and then re-elected every two years through at least 2000.

—John S. Bowman

Suggestions for Further Reading

Congressional Record, 101st Cong., 1st sess, 1989.

New York Times. See Hastings, Alcee in the *New York Times Index,* January 19, 20, 23, 25, 27, 28, 29, 1983; February 2, 3, 5, 6, 1983; March 17, 1989; August 11, 1989; October 20, 21, 24, 1989.

Volcansek, Mary L. *Judicial Impeachment: None Called It Justice.* Champaign Ill.: University of Illinois Press, 1993.

Weatherman Brinks Trials: 1983

Defendants: First trial: Cecilio Ferguson and Edward Joseph; second trial: Kuwasi Balagoon, Judith Clark, and David Gilbert   **Crimes Charged:** First trial: Murder, robbery, racketeering, and conspiracy; second trial: Murder and robbery   **Chief Defense Lawyers:** First trial: Jesse Berman, Chowke Lumumba, and William Mogulescu; second trial: The accused
Chief Prosecutors: First trial: Robert S. Litt, Stacey J. Moritz, and Paul E. Summit; second trial: Kenneth Gribetz   **Judges:** First trial: Kevin T. Duffy; second trial: David S. Ritter   **Places:** First trial: New York, New York; second trial: Goshen, New York   **Dates of Trials:** First trial: April 13–September 3, 1983; second trial: July 11–September 15, 1983   **Verdicts:** First trial: Not guilty of murder/robbery, guilty of acting as accessories after the fact; second trial: all defendants found guilty   **Sentences:** First trial: 12½ years; second trial: 25 years to life

SIGNIFICANCE

Political dissent in America has a long, often violent history. Of all the extremist groups that sprang from the seventies, none was more prepared to continue that bloody tradition than a band of black rights activists who called themselves the Weather Underground.

Ten years of Weather Underground politico/criminal mayhem culminated in a botched robbery of a Brinks armored vehicle in October 1981. In making off with $1.6 million, robbers killed one guard and two policeman. After a chase four people were arrested. Over the next 15 months several more suspects were rounded up. The complexity of the case necessitated multiple trials.

In the first hearing, which opened April 13, 1983, Cecilio Ferguson and Edward Joseph stood trial with four other Weather Underground members, none of whom was charged with the Brinks robbery. The government, perplexed by how best to proceed against a gang which had been robbing and killing for much of the preceding decade, had decided on a catch-all federal action against this batch of Weathermen. One component of the prosecution was the Brinks robbery.

Before the trial, defense attorneys William Mogulescu and Jesse Berman won an important victory when they persuaded Judge Kevin Duffy that the prosecution should not be allowed to call two other gang members whose testimony was considered unreliable. However, they were less successful in keeping Tyrone Rison off the stand. He readily admitted his own complicity in the murderous robbery.

"You had the M-16 rifle, is that right?" asked defense attorney, Chowke Lumumba.

"That's correct."

"And you shot the gun at the guard who was on the ground?"

"That's correct."

"A man who was totally disarmed and helpless?"

"That's correct."

And so it went. Defense counsel depicted Rison as a thug who had done a deal with the government in exchange for a 12-year sentence, questioning whether such a man should escape so leniently while the defendants faced a lifetime behind bars?

The jury thought not. On September 3, 1983, they convicted Ferguson and Joseph only of being accessories after the fact, an outcome the defense team jubilantly declared "a defeat for the government."

Judge Duffy had a different view. Sentencing both defendants to 12½ years imprisonment, he commented, "I have never understood juries."

A Straightforward Case

The state trial against Kuwasi Balagoon, Judith Clark, and David Gilbert began on July 11, 1983, and was far more clear-cut. Here the charges related entirely to the Brinks robbery, allowing the jury to concentrate more fully on the facts of one case, rather than be confused by several. At least it should have been that way, until the defendants, declaring themselves "freedom fighters," refused to mount a conventional defense. When Judge David Ritter clashed with Balagoon, the prisoner said, "In that case I'm leaving," and he stormed from the courtroom accompanied by his co-defendants. Gilbert yelled, "All the oppressors will fail." Clark chimed in with, "Death to U.S. imperialism."

Their departure left prosecutor Kenneth Gribetz an open field. Over two weeks he presented 86 witnesses and some devastating evidence. Clark and Gilbert had been arrested on the day of the murder in a car with $800,000 of the stolen money, while Balagoon's palm print was found on bags of the stolen money.

When the prosecution rested, the defendants deigned to return. Their only witness, Sekou Odinga, already convicted of robbery in the preceding federal trial, justified the Brinks murders because the victims had obstructed the "expropriation" of money earmarked to create the black Republic of New Africa in five Southern U.S. states. Odinga further rationalized the theft, saying it was designed "to take back some of the wealth that was robbed through the slave labor that was forced on them and their ancestors."

Both Clark and Gilbert warmed to this theme. Gilbert said, "I just want to meet you, Comrade Odinga, and express my respect for you for twenty years of commitment . . . for the New African people, and all oppressed people." Clark sought reassurance, wondering if white persons, like herself, "have a responsibility to struggle for the rights of oppressed people, for their human rights and self-determination?" Odinga gave ready assent, then was led away to begin his own 40-year jail term.

When the jury returned its guilty verdict September 15, 1983, prosecutor Gribetz's only complaint concerned the sentencing: "We're upset, frankly, that there's no death penalty." On October 6, Judge David Ritter sentenced each defendant the maximum three consecutive life terms in prison without possibility of parole until each had served 75 years.

On June 14, 1984, yet another Weatherman, Samuel Brown, was convicted of complicity in the Brinks murders and later jailed for 75 years.

Ironically, the most notorious Weather Underground member, Kathy Boudin, never stood trial. This daughter of left-wing radicals and a lifelong extremist, plea-bargained her way to a 20-year jail sentence.

These trials reveal how, masquerading under the guise of political activism, the Weathermen slid from committed principle into heartless criminality. In doing so, they trod a well-worn path as agents of change who succeeded only in changing themselves.

—Colin Evans

Suggestions for Further Reading

Castellucci, John. *The Big Dance*. New York: Dodd, Mead & Co., 1986.

Frankfort, Ellen. *Kathy Boudin And The Dance Of Death*. New York: Stine & Day, 1983.

Tell, Larry. "Socialists Sue Over Suspect ID." *The National Law Journal* (December 7, 1981): 3ff.

New Bedford Rape Trial: 1984

Defendants: John Cordeiro, Jose M. Medeiros, Virgilio Medeiros, Victor Raposo, Daniel Silva, and Joseph Vieira   **Crime Charged:** Aggravated Rape
Chief Defense Lawyers: Edward F. Harrington, Judith Lindahl, Kenneth Sullivan, and David Waxler   **Chief Prosecutors:** Ronald A. Pina and Raymond P. Veary   **Judge:** William G. Young   **Place:** Fall River, Massachusetts   **Dates:** February 23–March 21, 1984   **Verdicts:** Cordeiro, Raposo, Silva, and Vieira, Guilty; Jose Medeiros and Virgilio Medeiros, Not guilty   **Sentence:** 6–12 years imprisonment

SIGNIFICANCE

Reports of the crime spurred a national debate as to whether a woman's independent or (as some saw it) compromising behavior made her partially responsible for sexual crimes committed against her; the conviction of four of the men was widely hailed by feminists, who insisted that rapists, and not the character of their victims, should be tried in court.

A gang rape that took place March 6, 1983, in Big Dan's tavern, New Bedford, Massachusetts, quickly became national news. The first reports were of a 21-year-old mother of two raped by a half-dozen men over the course of two hours, while the bar's 15 other patrons cheered. Later investigation of the evidence reduced the size of the cheering squad, but confirmed the other details of the crime. According to eyewitness testimony, two men tried to force the woman to perform oral sex; two others threw her on a pool table and raped her; the bartender was physically restrained from going to a phone; and another nonparticipating man—who first ignored the bartender's instructions to call the police—dialed a wrong number and then didn't bother to try again.

Amid the outrage of women's groups and many of New Bedford's citizens, Big Dan's tavern was closed and its bar cut up with a chain saw. But many members of the town's Portuguese community just as quickly rallied behind the accused rapists, claiming, as one woman put it, "There was guilt by national origin." Throughout the trial and for years afterward, they would express resentment against the woman. "She should have been home in the first place," the *New York Times* quoted one Portuguese-American woman shouting on the day of sentencing. The paper aptly summed up the sentiment:

By their lights she wasn't raped. Rather she got herself raped, a very different crime for which they think the victim must take the blame. She did, after all, enter a bar, drink, flirt—behavior which offends a conservative community like theirs. Those demonstrators may not condone her rapists' behavior, but they are more ashamed of hers.

The New Bedford gang rape trial served as a benchmark for the feminist community characterized by Susan Brownmiller, author of the landmark book *Against Our Will: Men, Women and Rape,* as a "public morality play," the trial was broadcast live on CNN, discussed on op-ed pages and homes across America, and monitored daily by both the Coalition Against Sexist Violence and the Committee for Justice (founded to support the accused).

Who's on Trial?

Originally, David Silva (26), John Cordeiro (23), Joseph Vieira (26), and Victor Raposo (23) were charged with aggravated rape, while Jose Medeiros (22) and Virgilio Medeiros (23)—who were not related—were charged as accessories. By the time the trial began in Fall River, Massachusetts on February 23, 1984, Jose Medeiros and Virgilio Medeiros also were charged with aggravated rape. (As alleged participants in a "joint venture" crime, they could be guilty of aggravated rape if they were found to have aided in or encouraged the crime.) Because some of the men were expected to incriminate the others, the trial was split into separate morning and afternoon sessions: Silva and Vieira in the afternoon, the others in the morning. All six of the defendants and one of the witnesses, Carlos Machado, spoke in Portuguese through interpreters.

Assistant District Attorney Raymond Veary outlined the case against Silva and Vieira for Judge William Young and the jury. The rape of the young woman, he said, took place while bystanders "were cheering like at a baseball game." Defendant Silva, he continued, had pushed the woman onto the pool table, and had held her there and raped her. Then Silva and Vieira "traded places."

The woman—who requested anonymity—began her own testimony the following morning. "I was screaming—I was begging for help. I could hear people laughing and cheering, yelling." She said she had gone out to buy cigarettes after tucking her two young daughters into bed. Two stores were closed, she continued, and she had ended up in Big Dan's. She bought cigarettes from the vending machine and sat beside the only other female patron to order a drink. That woman left. When she herself headed for the door, she said, a man yanked her jacket and she complained: "What the hell do you think you're doing?" Another man took her feet. "They started dragging me across the floor. I started kicking and screaming." She told the court that the men threw her onto the pool table and removed her jeans. She said that one man raped her while another held her down; then the men switched places and she was raped again.

The defense attorneys accused the woman of fabricating a story to make money through the sale of book rights or by suing the bar's owners, charges which the woman denied. The defense lawyers then questioned the woman about her original statement to the police, accusing six men of rape, and her testimony since, which referred to four men. The woman remained calm and said, "It was told when I had not slept and was very upset."

Carlos Machado, the bartender at Big Dan's on the night of March 6, testified that he saw the woman on the floor and heard her screaming while Joseph Vieira and Daniel Silva removed her pants. Jose Medeiros and Virgilio Medeiros, he said, were shouting, "Do it! Do it! That's it! That's it!" One of them, he continued, kept him back from the phone. Victor Raposo and John Cordeiro, then attempted to force the woman to engage in sex. She was then placed on the pool table, Machado concluded, and Daniel Silva "took off his pants and went on top of her."

During cross-examination on March 2, Machado said he'd noticed the woman before the rape occurred. "I had a bad impression of the girl," he said. "She was laughing and talking with the boys, and I wanted to call the police and get her out."

Defense attorney Kenneth Sullivan asked Machado why he wanted the woman to leave. Machado explained: "A group of guys around a girl in such a tight crowd."

Sullivan asked, "That was so unusual that you thought she should be ejected?"

Machado replied, "Yes." He also testified that she had three drinks, not one.

Before resting their case against Silva and Vieira, the prosecution called 19 additional witnesses. Among them was Detective Sandra Grace, who testified about her meeting with the woman shortly after the rape was reported. "She was hysterical and in a state of shock," the officer recalled. Another officer described finding the woman outside of the tavern. She was nude below the waist, he testified, and "said she had been repeatedly raped and abused."

Detective Kenneth Gormley testified that when John Cordeiro arrived at the police station, he "told us that he wanted to tell us what he did." Gormley continued, "He said he was sorry. He said he was drunk, but that was no excuse for what he had done." Cordeiro had admitted that "he and Victor held her legs."

On March 13, 1964, Edward Harrington, defense lawyer for Daniel Silva, offered another version of events. "He was talking to her alone," Harrington claimed. After Silva removed the woman's pants, "both fell on the floor." When Silva placed the woman on the bar, Harrington continued, "His state of mind was that he and she would do something just by themselves. But by then a lot of men came over." Harrington declared that "Whatever he was doing with that girl was between he and she. It was consensual, no screaming, crying or protest."

Harrington called four witnesses on Silva's behalf. One, Lizetta Robida, was a friend of the woman's. She testified that she had "told her she should stay home" and that the woman had consumed two drinks while in her company earlier that evening. Marie Correia was the other woman in Big Dan's on March 6, 1983. She testified that the woman "was bubbly, she was bouncing around the chair. Her pupils were large and her eyes were very glassy." The chief toxicologist for Allegheny County's coroner's office, Charles Winek, then testified that the woman was "clinically poisoned, poisoned with alcohol," according to a blood test taken several hours after the incident.

Silva also testified on his own behalf, saying, "She was, you know, willing." Silva said the woman had asked if he had drugs to share, and that he had said no but offered to "fool around" with her. "She said yes," Silva said. "She looked very happy." He testified that they had kissed and partly undressed when others interrupted them. Contradicting the bartender's testimony, Silva said he had not entered the woman.

Verdicts and Sentencing

On March 17, 1984, Daniel Silva and Joseph Vieira were convicted of aggravated rape by a jury of eight men and four women. Some people in the courtroom cried, "Shame!" When news reached the parking lot, others smashed their fists on cars and shouted obscenities. Women's groups and their supporters sponsored a candlelight march, in which 2,500 people participated.

News of the convictions was kept from the other jury, which convened as scheduled on Monday the 19th. The defense continued to characterize the woman as a drunken liar, and John Cordeiro testified that "she was enjoying herself."

On March 22, the last verdicts were rendered. Virgilio Medeiros and Jose Medeiros were acquitted; John Cordeiro and Raposo were found guilty. There was immediate upheaval in Fall River as 3,000 to 4,000 people attended a candlelight vigil in support of the victim, while 7,000 to 10,000 marchers protested the convictions. Judge Young sentenced the four men to six to 12 years in prison. He also responded to what had become an underlying question. He had not reduced the sentence because the victim had been in a bar, he said, because to do so would "virtually outlaw an entire gender for the style of their dress, the length of their skirts or their choice to enter a place of public refreshment." The four men first asked for retrials and then appealed; all attempts to overturn their convictions were unsuccessful. The woman moved to Miami with her children and was killed in an automobile accident in December 1986.

— Kathryn Cullen-DuPont

Suggestions for Further Reading:

Brownmiller, Susan. *Against Our Will: Men, Women and Rape.* New York: Simon & Schuster, 1975.

Faludi, Susan. *Backlash: The Undeclared War Against American Women.* New York: Crown Publishers, Inc., 1991.

The *New York Times.* March 11, 12, 13, 18, 19, 1983; September 1, 3, 4, 1983; February 6, 24, 25, 28, 29, 1984; March 1, 3, 4, 6, 7, 8, 9, 13, 14, 15, 16, 17, 18, 20, 22, 23, 24, 27, 28, 1984; April 11, 25, 1984; May 7, 1985; October 7, 1986; and December 18, 1986.

John DeLorean Trial: 1984

Defendant: John DeLorean **Crime Charged:** Drug trafficking
Chief Defense Lawyers: Howard Weitzman, Donald Re
Chief Prosecutors: James P. Walsh Jr, Robert Parry **Judge:** Robert
Takasugi **Place:** Los Angeles, California **Date of Trial:** April 18–August
16, 1984 **Verdict:** Not guilty

SIGNIFICANCE

Dubious government witnesses and the ethics of "sting" operations in general
were on trial as much as the defendant in this high-profile drug case.

In 1982 John DeLorean was popularly viewed as one of the auto industry's
most charismatic figures. He was handsome and dashing, and the independent motor company that he had founded and which bore his name was lauded
as a brave attempt to take on the Detroit "big guys." But on Wall Street it was a
different story: whispers of DeLorean's financial difficulties were rampant,
centered on the increasing problems at his Northern Ireland factory, and few
expected the company to remain solvent for long. No one, though, was prepared
for the stunning events of October 19.

That was the day when DeLorean was arrested in Los Angeles and
charged with conspiracy to distribute $24 million worth of cocaine. Federal
officials were cock-a-hoop, crowing that more than 100 hours of audio and video
surveillance had culminated in the 57-year-old automaker being caught on tape
accepting a coke delivery from undercover cops.

Top-Notch Lawyer

When the most eagerly awaited drug trial in years opened on April 18,
1984, the elegant defendant was represented by one of California's top litigators,
Howard Weitzman, and nobody doubted that it would take all of Weitzman's
formidable skill to save his client from prison. The prosecution had amassed a
wealth of electronic evidence. The jurors heard how FBI agent Benedict Tisa,
posing as James Benedict, a crooked banker, had met with DeLorean at a bank
in San Carlos, California, on September 8, 1982. In their taped conversation he
told DeLorean about a prospective investor who had "all these profits from his

cocaine deals," to which DeLorean replied, "It looks like a good opportunity." On a later tape DeLorean was shown raising a glass of champagne and describing cocaine as "better than gold."

Tisa testified that he had heard from James Hoffman, a convicted drug smuggler and government informant, that DeLorean had $2 million "he wanted to invest in a narcotics transaction" that would turn a fast profit. The proposed deal was for DeLorean to invest $1.8 million with Hoffman to buy 34 kilos of coke that they hoped to sell for $5.1 million. Through other Hoffman connections, DeLorean then hoped to raise a $15 million loan routed through the San Carlos bank and parlay his money.

The defense tactics were unconventional. With such a high-profile client, Weitzman shrewdly opted for maximum publicity as a way of demonstrating that DeLorean had nothing to fear. At the end of each trial day, Weitzman held a well-attended press conference outside the federal courthouse. Not only did this allow him to cozy up to the media, it gave him the opportunity to present DeLorean's side of the argument on a day-to-day basis, without fear of cross-examination. In one tape, DeLorean could be heard telling Tisa that he no longer had the money to buy into the deal. Weitzman informed the reporters that this was DeLorean's way of telling Tisa to "get lost . . . It's a clear indication that John doesn't want to participate in a narcotics transaction."

John DeLorean, founder of an independent automobile company, on trial for drug trafficking. (AP/Wide World Photos)

It wasn't all grand-standing for the cameras. Inside the courtroom Weitzman was giving Tisa a miserable time. After extracting an early confession from the witness that he had lied in telling another contact that he had already received money from DeLorean, Weitzman turned up the heat. He wanted clarification of Tisa's case notes, which appeared to show some inconsistencies. Finally, after three days of relentless questioning, Tisa admitted, "I may have rewrote the pages [sic]."

Weitzman, insistent that the only possible reason for such actions was to alter evidence, looked askance. "And you destroyed the original?"

"Yes, a portion of them," confessed the hapless Tisa.

Weitzman threw his hands up in disbelief. "How do we know what you changed, what you added, what you took out and what you threw away? How do we know that?"

It was a bravura performance, one which moved DeLorean to tell waiting reporters that night, "I only got one thing to say [sic], 'Thank God for Howard.'"

For his part, Weitzman admitted that the tapes showed his client discussing coke. "Clearly his judgment was not only poor, it was non-existent," he said, but added that DeLorean, vulnerable and desperate, had been coerced by government pressure.

Witness Sensation

When the informant, James Hoffman, took the stand he did so under a cloud. Tapes already played in court had showed him drinking profusely and making lewd comments about women, none of which did anything to shore up his shaky credibility, and it was widely felt that he would buckle under cross-examination. Despite this perception he managed to resist the best that Weitzman could throw at him.

Then came a sensational development: it emerged that Hoffman was trying to work a deal with the government. Judge Robert Takasugi exploded. Blasting the witness as a "hired gun," Takasugi found it to be "offensive" that the prosecution had failed to reveal sooner that Hoffman had "demanded" a share of any money seized in the case. Although said out of the jury's hearing, this revelation brought about a marked change of courtroom atmosphere.

Suddenly, the prosecution was on the back foot, so much so that Weitzman felt no compunction to call DeLorean to the stand, saying, "We don't believe he [has] anything to defend . . . The burden is on . . . the Government to prove their case beyond a reasonable doubt. I don't think they've done that."

In his closing address, chief prosecutor James P. Walsh, Jr. describing DeLorean as "a man with the conscience of a tomcat," someone prepared to do anything to save his ailing auto company, struggled hard to regain the initiative. But the impetus had been lost and he could only sit and muse reflectively as the defense took control.

Throughout the trial Weitzman had varied his pose, at times friendly and almost folksy, at others bitingly sarcastic; but in closing he was at his most aggressive. He likened the case to the George Orwell novel *1984,* in which "the whole premise is that the government rewrites history, the government controls people, the government stifles people." Even though the United States government knew that DeLorean was in deep trouble, said Weitzman, it went after him anyway. "Somebody should have said, 'Step back here, this is wrong,' " but no, federal officials had approached his client "and promised to save his dream, and there's something wrong with that."

Weitzman piled on the agony. By putting the government on trial, blaming it for his client's transgressions, he clearly struck a chord with the jury, for on August 16, after 29 hours of deliberation, they acquitted DeLorean of all charges.

Talking afterwards, jury members said that they felt the defendant had been entrapped, and that he would not have tried to engage in criminal practices had not the financial carrot been dangled so enticingly by a government more intent on securing a conviction than in upholding the law.

—Colin Evans

Suggestions for Further Reading

DeLorean, John. *On a Clear Day You Can See General Motors.* Grosse Pointe, Mich.: Wright, 1979.

DeLorean, John and Ted Schwarz. *DeLorean.* Grand Rapids, Mich.: Zondervan, 1985.

Fallon, Ivan and James Strodes. *DeLorean, the Rise and Fall of a Dream-Maker.* London: Hamish Hamilton, 1983.

Haddad, William. *Hard Driving.* New York: Random House, 1985.

Westmoreland v. CBS: 1984

Plaintiff: General William C. Westmoreland   **Defendant:** CBS, Inc.

Plaintiff Claim: That a certain television documentary broadcast by CBS concerning the conduct of the Vietnam War libeled the plaintiff

Chief Defense Lawyers: David Boies and Stuart W. Gold

Chief Lawyers for Plaintiff: Dan M. Burt and David M. Dorsen

Judge: Pierre N. Leval   **Place:** New York, New York

Dates of Trial: October 9, 1984–February 18, 1985   **Decision:** None. The case was settled out of court before it went to the jury.

SIGNIFICANCE

The principle of *New York Times v. Sullivan* remains strong: public figures must prove actual malice to win libel suits. Despite strong evidence of press misconduct in this and a related case, namely *Sharon v. Time, Inc.,* both plaintiffs lost.

O n January 23, 1982, CBS Television ran a documentary entitled "The Uncounted Enemy: A Vietnam Deception" The narrator, Mike Wallace, took an aggressive investigative approach in preparing the documentary. The theme of the program was that the effects of infamous Tet offensive, which took American forces by surprise and caused much loss of life, could have been avoided if the actual size of North Vietnam's troop strength had been calculated accurately. The documentary placed much of the blame on the commanding general, William C. Westmoreland, who had been in command in Vietnam throughout the late 1960s and during the Tet offensive.

The CBS report took several liberties with the truth, however. For example, Wallace accused Westmoreland of juggling enemy troop figures to produce an artificially low count and please President Johnson:

> Wallace: Isn't it a possibility that the real reason for suddenly deciding in the summer of 1967 to remove an entire category of the enemy from the Order of Battle, a category that had been in that Order of Battle since 1961, was based on political considerations?
>
> Westmoreland: No, decidedly not. That—that . . .
>
> Wallace: Didn't you make this clear in your August 20th cable?
>
> Westmoreland: No, no. Yeah. No.
>
> Wallace: I have a copy of your August 20th cable.

Westmoreland: Well, sure. Okay, okay. All right, all right.

CBS had succeeded in making Westmoreland look like a liar and a fool, but in fact the cable in Wallace's possession had been sent by another officer in Saigon while Westmoreland was away, a fact known to CBS but not revealed on the program.

Retired General William Westmoreland and his attorney announce his intention to sue CBS for libel. (AP/Wide World Photos)

Incensed, after the program was televised, Westmoreland denied the allegations it raised about his conduct. The Capitol Legal Foundation offered to represent Westmoreland for free, and attorneys Dan M. Burt and David M. Dorsen filed Westmoreland's libel suit on September 13, 1982. CBS's chief attorneys were David Boies and Stuart W. Gold. Before the case went to trial, Boies and Gold succeeded in having it transferred from South Carolina, where the case was originally filed, to New York City, where it was tried before Judge Pierre N. Leval.

The trial began on October 9, 1984. On February 15, 1985, Leval ruled that under such First Amendment precedents as *New York Times Company v. Sullivan* (see separate entry), Westmoreland had to prove by "clear and convincing evidence" that CBS acted with actual malice in preparing a false documentary. Legally, this is a heavy burden of proof for the plaintiff in a libel suit, one which was invoked by Leval because Westmoreland was a famous general and thus a "public figure." Faced with the prospect of a lengthy legal battle against difficult odds, Westmoreland settled his case with CBS out of court on February

18, 1985. Both sides agreed to pay their own legal fees, and of the $120 million for which Westmoreland had sued, he got nothing.

At the same time the Westmoreland case was pending, another prominent military figure was pursuing a libel lawsuit. Israeli general Ariel Sharon sued Time, Inc., which publishes *Time* magazine, for having printed an article on February 14, 1983, that accused Sharon of encouraging certain Lebanese militia forces to massacre some Palestinians in 1982. The case was tried from November 13, 1984, to January 24, 1985, in New York City before Judge Abraham D. Sofaer. The jury found *Time* not guilty due to lack of actual malice, and Sharon dropped his case. However, jury members made a special point of stating that they thought *Time* had acted "negligently and carelessly" in preparing the article.

Generals Westmoreland and Sharon ran into the same obstacle in their cases: despite strong evidence of press misconduct, under the *New York Times Company v. Sullivan* case's standard they couldn't make the difficult showing necessary for public figures to win libel suits.

— Stephen G. Christianson

Suggestions for Further Reading

Adler, Renata. "Annals of Law: Two Trials." (Part 1) *The New Yorker* (June 16, 1986): 42–85.

———. "Annals of Law: Two Trials." (Part 2) *The New Yorker* (June 23, 1986): 34–79.

———. *Reckless Disregard: Westmoreland v. CBS, Sharon v. Time.* New York: Vintage Books, 1988.

Benjamin, Burton. *Fair Play: CBS, General Westmoreland, and How a Television Documentary Went Wrong.* New York: Harper & Row, 1988.

Roth, M. Patricia. *The Juror and the General.* New York: William Morrow & Co., 1986.

Falwell v. Flynt: 1984

Plaintiff: Jerry Falwell   **Defendant:** Larry Flynt   **Plaintiff Claim:** That an ad parody published in *Hustler* magazine was libelous and intended to cause Jerry Falwell emotional distress   **Chief Defense Lawyers:** David O. Carson, Alan Isaacman, and Arthur P. Strickland
Chief Lawyers for Plaintiff: Jeffrey H. Daichman, Norman Roy Grutman, and Harold H. Rhodes, Jr.   **Judge:** James C. Turk   **Place:** Roanoake, Virginia
Dates of Trial: December 3–8, 1984   **Verdict:** That the ad was not libelous but did inflict emotional distress, thereby entitling Falwell to $200,000 in damages

SIGNIFICANCE

This First Amendment battle between long-time adversaries culminated in an unprecedented verdict.

For several years Larry Flynt's magazine *Hustler* had published a bizarre mix of sex, religion, humor and political comment. In the November 1983 issue it spoofed a Campari vermouth ad campaign in which various celebrities were asked to recall their "first time," that is, the first time they tried Campari. *Hustler*'s version had nationally known pastor and political activist Reverend Jerry Falwell describing his "first time" as an incestuous encounter with his mother. The ad further stated that Falwell needed to be drunk to preach. At the foot of the page was a brief and barely noticeable disclaimer, "Ad parody—not to be taken seriously." Falwell, a perennial target of Flynt's irreverence, filed suit for libel, requesting $45 million in damages.

The jury was seated on December 3, 1984 and after opening statements, Falwell's attorney, Norman Roy Grutman, led off with his star witness. Falwell vehemently denied every allegation in the ad. "Have you ever taken alcoholic beverages before going into the pulpit to deliver your message?" asked Grutman.

"Never at any time," responded Falwell.

Over strident defense objections, Grutman inquired, "Mr. G. Falwell, specifically, did you and your mother ever commit incest?"

"Absolutely not."

The reason for the defense objections was simple: it had been their contention all along that the idea of Jerry Falwell enjoying an incestuous relationship with his mother was so preposterous that no one could possibly believe it. Judge James Turk's decision to allow the question dealt a body blow to that argument, as did Falwell's heartfelt comment to the jury, "It is the most hurtful, damaging, despicable, low-type personal attack that I can imagine one human being can inflict upon another."

Larry Flynt and Rev. Jerry Falwell. (Archive Photos)

Flynt Duels with Lawyer

When it came time for Flynt to testify, he did so from the wheelchair to which he had been confined since 1978 when a would be assassin's bullet left him paralyzed. Earlier, the defense failed in its attempt to suppress a foul-mouthed videotaped deposition that Flynt had given to Grutman. That allowed the jury to see Flynt at his worst. Now they had the opportunity to observe the publisher in a far different light. Flynt protested that pain and medication had rendered the deposition meaningless: this, he assured the court, was the real him. "What," asked chief defense attorney Alan Isaacman, "was intended to be conveyed by the ad?"

Well, we wanted to poke fun at Campari . . . because the innuendoes that they had in their ads made you sort of confused as to if the person was talking about their first time as far as a sexual encounter or whether they were talking about their first time as far as drinking Campari . . . . They [the public] know that it was not intended to defame the Reverend Falwell, his mother, or any members of his family, because no one could take it seriously.

Isaacman explored whether Flynt had deliberately intended to damage Falwell's reputation by printing the satire.

Flynt scoffed. "If I really wanted to hurt Reverend Falwell, I would do a serious article on the inside . . . talk about his jet airplane or maybe Swiss bank accounts . . . I don't know if such accounts exist, but if you want to really hurt someone . . . you put down things that are believable. You don't put down things that are totally unbelievable."

The duel between Flynt and Grutman, neither of whom attempted to conceal their poor opinion of the other, was much awaited. They were old protagonists. Grutman had previously represented *Penthouse* magazine in an action against Flynt and lost. Here, as the two crossed swords, Judge James Turk several times had to defuse the rhetoric. But Grutman pounded away. "Mr. Flynt, have you ever said, 'Free expression is absolute?'"

"Yes, I believe free expression is absolute . . ."

"And 'absolute' means that you can say whatever you want?"

"Yes," replied Flynt, adding coolly. "You want to bait me?"

Grutman shrugged off the taunt and played a televised interview in which Flynt charged that his deposition had been a parody of Grutman's conduct in this case. "Do you deny having said what appears to have been uttered by you, as it was shown on that video monitor?"

Flynt sighed. "Yes. It's very difficult to take you seriously."

Jury Verdict Unprecedented

After clarification from Judge Turk on the complex legal issues involved, the jury retired. On December 8, 1984, they rejected the libel suit but found that Flynt *had* intended to cause Falwell emotional distress. For this reason they awarded the plaintiff $100,000 actual damages and $100,000 punitive damages.

Never before had a jury reached such a verdict. Clearly this was a decision headed for appeal, and in February 1988, the Supreme Court unanimously voted to reverse the lower court's verdict. In reaching their decision the Court made no attempt to condone the content of the *Hustler* parody, other than to say it was entitled to Constitutional protection.

Falwell v. Flynt ignited a storm of protest among America's media. Many feared an erosion of First Amendment right to free speech. In upholding this view the Supreme Court implied that while insults to public figures might be painful, denying the right to make them would be intolerable.

—Colin Evans

Suggestion for Further Reading

D'Souza, Dinesh. *Falwell, Before The Millenium*. Chicago: Regenery Gateway, 1984.

Falwell, Jerry. *Strength For The Journey*. New York: Simon & Schuster, 1987.

Martz, Larry and Ginny Carroll. *Ministry Of Greed*. New York: Wiedenfeld & Nicolson, 1988.

Smolla, Rodney A. *Jerry Falwell v. Larry Flynt*. New York: St. Martins' Press, 1988.

Anne Anderson, et al. v. W.R. Grace and Beatrice Foods: 1986

Plaintiff: Anne Anderson et al.   **Defendant:** W.R. Grace and Company, Beatrice Foods, Unifirst Company   **Plaintiff Claim:** Contamination of public water resulting in deaths and serious illnesses
Chief Defense Lawyer: Michael Keating   **Chief Lawyer for Plaintiff:** Jan Schlictmann   **Judge:** Walter Jay Skinner   **Place:** Boston, Massachusetts
Date of Trial: March 10–May 26, 1986   **Verdict:** The jury found W.R. Grace Co. guilty and cleared Beatrice Foods; the judge threw out the verdict and Grace settled with the defendants

SIGNIFICANCE

One of the first high profile suits involving pollution by a major corporation, it also demonstrated the difficulty of proving a direct connection between cancer and specific chemicals.

From 1965 to the early 1980s, residents of Woburn, Massachusetts, particularly children, began contracting leukemia at a rate in excess of the national norm. The citizens of Woburn wondered why, and some felt they had found the cause—industrial pollution. In 1982, Anne Anderson and several other townspeople sued the W.R. Grace Company, Beatrice Foods, and the Unifirst Company, claiming that these corporations were responsible for contaminating wells that supplied water to the town. The plaintiffs were the families of seven children who had contracted leukemia, five of whom were already dead. The parents of these children claimed that the companies' manufacturing operations had polluted two city-owned wells, which in turn caused their children's disease. The parents also claimed that the contamination was responsible for the unusually high number of cases of leukemia among other children in the town of Woburn, as well as cases of liver disease and central nervous system disorders.

Taking on Two Giants

The plaintiffs settled with the Unifirst Company, an industrial dry cleaning business, for one million dollars, and they used the settlement money to continue to press their case against both Beatrice Foods and W.R. Grace and Company. The case was one of the few in which a small group of private citizens was successful in marshaling the resources necessary to take on a major corporation.

In March of 1986 the first phase of the trial began. In an unusual move, the plaintiffs did not ask for a specific amount in damages, but the trial judge, Walter Jay Skinner, characterized the potential award as "astronomical." In his opening arguments before the jury, Jan Schlictmann, attorney for the plaintiffs, promised to call an array of expert witnesses to the stand who would prove that the chemicals found in the aquifer were "toxic and can destroy cells;" that the companies had knowingly dumped them onto Grace and Beatrice property; and that they later seeped into Woburn's water supply through two nearby wells. Lawyers for Grace and Beatrice argued that while solvents were dumped on company land, the dumping had not been reckless or negligent. Both companies contended that chemicals in the city water supply could have come from a number of other sources in the Woburn area, since the town had been an industrial and manufacturing center since the 1850s. Grace's attorney, Michael Keating, claimed that he would present testimony that the land between Grace's Cryovac Division, which made food packaging equipment, and the city wells lay in such a way that none of the chemicals in question—specifically trichloroethylene and tetrachloroethylene—could have reached the wells.

Verdict Is Thrown Out by Judge

For the plaintiffs to prevail, they had to prove that the chemicals repeatedly detected in the wells by the Environmental Protection Agency came from the Grace and Beatrice properties. They then had to prove that drinking water contaminated with these chemicals in the proportions found in the wells could cause leukemia and the other related illnesses. They partly succeeded on both accounts. On May 28, 1986, the six-member jury found that W.R. Grace's plant in Woburn had been negligent in dumping substances regarded as potential human carcinogens that could also cause liver, kidney, and nervous system damage when ingested in high doses, on their property. The jury also found that W.R. Grace was responsible for the contamination of the ground water serving the residents of east Woburn, where the leukemia cases were clustered. But the jury cleared Beatrice Foods and its subsidiary, the J.J. Riley Co., the owner of a tannery in the same area accused of contaminating the ground water. Attorneys for W.R. Grace argued that without a specific date, it was impossible to know whether the chemicals contaminated the aquifer before the illnesses began. The trial judge, U.S. District Court judge Walter Skinner, threw out the jury's verdict against W.R. Grace, holding that the jurors could not know with certainty when the pollutants penetrated the water supply. On September 22, 1986, with an appeal pending, W.R. Grace settled with the Woburn families for a reported eight million dollars. Jan Schlictmann, the plaintiffs' attorney, claimed that the settlement "showed that companies can be made to pay for poisoning their community." In return for the payments the families agreed to drop their suit against W.R. Grace. Michael Keating, the company's chief counsel, said that the settlement agreement did not mean that the company acknowledged any responsibility for the pollution or the deaths. He said that the company settled in order to avoid "additional strain on the families" and to cut further litigation costs.

Judge Denies Request for New Trial

Meanwhile, the plaintiffs asked the U.S. Court of Appeals for the First Circuit for a new trial of the suit against Beatrice Foods on the grounds that defense lawyers failed to disclose a potentially damaging report on the pollution of the property that Beatrice Foods owned. The federal appeals court ordered a new hearing on the issue of the pollution from the J.J. Riley tannery, finding dereliction of duty by the company and its lawyers for failing to supply a 1983 hydrogeologic report that might have confirmed that the tannery had contaminated the ground water. The appeals court claimed that "the record contains clear and convincing evidence—overwhelming evidence, to call a spade a spade—that [Beatrice] engaged in what must be called misconduct" on the tannery issue.

The case returned to the original trial court for hearings on the report, but there Judge Skinner denied the plaintiffs a new trial, saying that it would be "pointless, wasteful and unwarranted." During the hearings Schlictmann charged Beatrice Foods with a massive cover-up of environmental crimes and charged that the J.J. Riley Company had illegally carted off toxic waste from its property to conceal the pollution. In his decision, Skinner chastised Schlictmann for pursuing a retrial, claiming that he lacked "competent evidence." Skinner found that the report in question failed to prove conclusively that chemical contamination committed by Beatrice existed at the tannery. "The chance that a viable 'tannery case' could be developed in any further proceedings is virtually nonexistent," he declared, "even if the plaintiffs were entitled to try." The First Circuit upheld this decision on appeal in 1990, and the U.S. Supreme Court denied certiorari that same year.

But the litigation was not over yet. The struggles of the families in Woburn and their attorney, Jan Schlictmann, were later chronicled in a popular book and a movie, both entitled *A Civil Action*. This prompted a defamation suit against Jonathan Haar, the book's author, and Random House, Inc., its publisher. In still another case, Beatrice Foods sued its insurance companies to recover legal fees.

The Woburn cases demonstrated that eight tragedy-stricken families and a small law firm could successfully challenge two rich and powerful corporations and their attorneys. The cases also raised awareness of the importance of corporations properly disposing of and handling hazardous materials.

—Carol Willcox Melton

Suggestions for Further Reading

Grossman, Lewis, Robert G. Vaughn, and Jonathan Haar. *A Documentary Companion to A Civil Action.* Mineola, N.Y.: Foundation Press, 1999.

Haar, Jonathan, *A Civil Action.* New York: Random House, 1995.

Fells Acres Sexual Abuse Trials: 1986–87

Defendants: Gerald Amirault, Violet Amirault, Cheryl Amirault LeFave
Crimes Charged: Sexual abuse (including rape and indecent assault)
Chief Defense Lawyers: First Trial: Juliane Balliro, Frank Mondano; Second Trial: Joseph Balliro, Juliane Balliro   **Chief Prosecutors:** Both Trials: Patricia Bernstein, Laurence Hardoon   **Judges:** First Trial: Elizabeth Dolan; Second Trial: John Paul Sullivan   **Place:** Cambridge, Massachusetts
Dates of Trials: First Trial: April 15–July 19, 1986; Second Trial: May 28–June 13, 1987   **Verdicts:** Gerald Amirault: guilty of eight counts of rape and seven indecent assaults; Violet Amirault: guilty two counts of rape and three counts of indecent assault; Cheryl Amirault LeFave: guilty of three counts of rape and four indecent assaults.   **Sentences:** Gerald: 30–40 years in prison; Violet and Cheryl: 8–20 years in prison

SIGNIFICANCE

One of a number of similar cases alleging patterns of sexual abuse of very young children in institutional settings, the Fells Acres Day School case was perhaps not the most extreme, but it raised the issues common to so many of these cases: Why did they suddenly emerge on the American scene only at this time? How much of the children's testimony may have been "planted" by the adult questioners? What were average people to make of the contradictory claims of the experts?

In the 1980s, Americans suddenly found themselves reading of charge after charge that individuals attached to various institutions had sexually abused children in both persistent and provocative ways. In particular there were cases involving day-care centers in Miami, Florida; the Bronx, New York; and Manhattan Beach, California: some involved "recovered memory," some involved "satanic rituals," but all shared the charge that adults attached to day-care centers had subjected the children to horrific varieties of sexual abuse. One of these day-care center cases was the Fells Acres Case.

What Went on at Day Care?

The Fells Acres Day School was located in Malden, Massachusetts, a city just north of Boston. Violet Amirault had founded the day-care school in 1966; by 1984, her daughter Cheryl Amirault LeFave was teaching one class, while her son Gerald did everything from maintenance repairs to cooking. When things were busy, he would also pitch in and help the staff with the children.

It was just such an occasion in April 1984, when a four-year-old, new to the school, wet himself during a nap. At a teacher's request, Gerald changed M.C. (as he would be known in the trial) into some dry clothes and put the wet things in a plastic bag that the child took home. As it happened, the boy's parents were in the midst of breaking up and he was exhibiting several behavioral problems at home. At this time, too, M.C.'s mother told him of the alleged sexual abuse of her brother when he was a child; and during that summer, the boy was discovered in sex play with a cousin. This prompted the mother to ask her now-adult brother to question the boy, who, told his uncle that Gerald had taken his pants down. Upon further questioning, his mother would later claim, the boy proceeded to describe how every day at Fells Acres Gerald had led him blindfolded into a "secret room" and there performed sex acts.

At that point, in September 1984, the mother called a hotline and accused Gerald of sexual abuse. The local police were informed and they arrested Gerald and closed the school. Soon numerous Fells Acres children were being interrogated by not only their parents but also by the police, social workers, therapists, and prosecutors. Child after child began to tell stories of fantastic goings on, not only involving sexual acts performed by or in the presence of all three members of the Amirault family, but also incidents involving robots, murdered and buried animals, drinking of their own urine, eating a frog. By 1985, the district attorney indicted the three Amiraults and charged them with sexual abuse of a total of 21 children. Gerald's offenses were regarded as especially horrific and so he was brought to trial first.

Gerald's Trial

The trial was held at the Middlesex County Superior Court in Cambridge, Massachusetts. Because of the pretrial publicity, the jury was actually drawn from people in the Springfield area, 100 miles west of Boston. The trial proper began on April 29, by which time Amirault was charged with 10 counts of rape and 12 counts of indecent assault on a total of 13 children. Prosecutors said that six other children originally part of the case against Amirault had been withdrawn because they could not stand the prospect of testifying against him. Those who did come to the courtroom were protected by their parents from seeing him, and one child was allowed to testify via a videotape. When the children did testify, the courtroom was usually cleared of the public and the press.

The testimony that was then offered by the prosecution was indeed horrific. Several children—now some two years older than when the alleged events occurred—took the stand to recount stories of how "Tooky," as Gerald was known by the children, had taken them to a "secret room" or "magic room." There—usually made-up and costumed as a clown—he did everything from simply touching their genitalia to actually placing his penis in their genitalia, anus, or mouth. One child testified that Gerald and a never-identified "Mr. Gatt" had each inserted a butcher knife in her rectum on separate occasions.

In addition to the children who took the stand, several parents testified about their own conversations in which their children told them of these events. The prosecution also called several specialists on child psychology, pediatric medicine, and sexual abuse. Much of the prosecution's case, however, rested on the intensive interrogations of the children by Susan Kelley, the Fells Acres Day School's own pediatric nurse. In these interviews, she employed a controversial technique: using anatomically correct dolls, she persisted in trying to get the children either to point to parts of the doll or to actually demonstrate with the doll where the alleged sexual acts had occurred. But the potential fallacy of this technique was demonstrated by the prosecutor who used just such a doll to question a child on the witness stand:

Q. I'm going to take the dress off this doll and show it to you . . . [Prosecutor has the child name the body parts.] If I show you this doll, can you tell us or show us on the doll whether or not Tooky did anything to you?

A. [No response]

Q. Can you show us on the doll, yes or no?

A. I don't know.

Q. Was there any time that anyone in the magic room touched you? Yes or no?

A. Yes.

Q. Who touched you?

A. Tooky.

Q. And can you tell us where he touched you?

A. [No response.]

Q. And did he touch you here on the vagina?

A. Yes.

Q. And did he touch you on the legs?

A. Yes.

Q. And did he touch you on the bum?

A. Yes.

In such questioning lay what the defense would attack as the fundamental fallacy of the whole case against Gerald Amirault. From the very first time M.C. and all the subsequent children had been questioned, Amirault's lawyers contended, adults had put ideas and words in their mouths and then coaxed and pressured them until they got the answers they were seeking. It was also pointed out that experiments had shown that young children often claimed to have been touched in their private parts during doctor's visits when videos showed nothing of the sort.

The cumulative detail and consistency of the children's accounts, however, proved to be more than Amirault and his lawyers could overcome, and after 64 and one-half hours of deliberation, the jury returned with its verdict: they found Gerald Amirault guilty on 15 counts of rape and aggravated assault. On August 21, he was sentenced to 30 to 40 years in prison.

Mother and Daughter on Trial

After Gerald's conviction, there was some doubt as to whether the state would move ahead with the charges against Violet and her daughter, Cheryl, but on May 28, 1987, jury selection began for this new trial. The charges against them were of the same nature as those against Gerald: by the time they went to the jury, Violet was charged with two rapes and three indecent assaults and Cheryl with three rapes and four indecent assaults. In the end only four children testified against them but, as with Gerald, they recounted shocking tales: how they had been fondled by the women, had objects inserted in them, had been made to fondle the women, and, in the case of the boy, had oral sex performed on him. Much was made in this trial, too, of the claims that while these acts were being performed in the "magic room" or elsewhere, they were being photographed by Gerald Amirault. The state then charged that the Amiraults did this to sell the photographs to dealers or fanciers of child pornography, although no such photograph of the Fells Acres children was ever produced.

One issue hanging over both trials was how such things could have been going on over a period of time yet none of the children spoke up until well after the initial

Violet Amirault and her daughter Cheryl Amirault LeFave speak with reporters after they were found guilty of child molestation. (AP/Wide World Photos)

claims of M.C. The prosecution got several children to testify that it was because the Amiraults constantly threatened that they would kill them and their parents. The little boy in this trial, for instance, said that Cheryl had "hurt" a bird and a squirrel in front of him and then said that "this is going to happen to your parents" if he ever spoke of what was going on.

When it came time for the defense, they introduced 23 former teachers or teachers' aides at the school and five parents who testified they had never seen any indications of any of the activities described by the children. All testified, in fact, that the children seemed eager to be at the school and that they interacted easily with the Amiraults The most they conceded to the prosecution's cross-examination was that there were times when the defendants were alone at the school with some children.

But once again, a jury chose to believe the stories of the children and returned on June 13 with a verdict that found Violet and Cheryl guilty of all charges. On July 15, the two women were sentenced to 8–20 years in prison.

Aftermath

Not unexpectedly, the Fells Acres case produced a lengthy and complicated series of legal actions. Gerald appealed his case on numerous grounds and in several courts but was never able to gain a new trial, let alone his freedom, and short of a commutation, it appears he will be in prison until at least 2015. Violet and Cheryl, however, were released on an appeal in 1995, and in May 1997, their convictions were overturned on the grounds that the children, while testifying, had not been required to face them. The state appealed this, but that September Violet died. Then in June 1998 Judge Isaac Borenstein ruled in favor of Cheryl's motion for a new trial on the grounds that there was new evidence that testimony of very young children can be drastically distorted by suggestive interviewing techniques of the kind applied in the Fells Acres case. After the Massachusetts Supreme Judicial Court overturned Judge Borenstein's ruling in August 1999, the state negotiated an agreement with Cheryl: in return for ceasing all attempts to clear her name via both the legal system and the media, Cheryl's sentence was reduced to time already served plus 10 years of supervised probation.

But the issues raised by this and similar cases of child abuse still trouble many people—numerous articles, books, television programs, and movies have been based on these day-care cases alone. One such issue was that the parents and others who interrogated these children appeared to have set out with an agenda to prove they had been abused. Another issue was how it was possible for Violet Amirault to have had some 3,000 children pass through her school during 18 years before any such charges surfaced. Equally troubling to logic was another question: how is it that, after the wave of institutional child abuse charges swept across the country in the 1980s, the phenomenon seems to have vanished from the American scene?

—*John S. Bowman*

Suggestions for Further Reading

Boston Globe. April 16, 19, 24, 30, 1986; May 8, 14, 29, 1986; July 21, 1986; August 22, 1986; May 29, 1987; June 2, 4, 6, 9, 14, 1987; July 16, 1987.

http://www.tiac.net/users/hcunn/witch/fells

http://www.ultranet.com/-kyp/amirault

Nathan, Debbie, and Michael Snendeker. *Satan's Silence: Ritual Abuse and the Making of a Modern American Witch Hunt.* New York: Basic Books: 1995.

In the Matter of Baby M: 1987

Plaintiffs: William and Elizabeth Stern   **Defendant:** Mary Beth Whitehead
Plaintiff Claim: That Whitehead—who had entered a "Surrogate Parenting Agreement," become pregnant via artificial insemination with William Stern's sperm, and delivered his and her own biological child—ought to be forced to give up the baby   **Chief Defense Lawyers:** Harold Cassidy and Randy Wolf
Chief Lawyers for Plaintiffs: Frank Donahue and Gary Skoloff
Judge: Harvey Sorkow   **Place:** Hackensack, New Jersey
Dates of Trial: January 5–March 31, 1987   **Verdict:** The Judge terminated the parental rights of Mary Beth Whitehead and permitted Elizabeth Stern to adopt Whitehead's and William Stern's daughter. This verdict was overturned in part by the New Jersey Supreme Court which, on February 2, 1988, granted William Stern custody but invalidated Elizabeth Stern's adoption and restored Whitehead's parental rights.

SIGNIFICANCE

This was the first highly publicized trial to examine the ethical questions raised by "reproductive technology."

On February 5, 1985, three parties entered into an agreement in the offices of Noel Keane's Infertility Center of New York.

Richard Whitehead consented to the agreement's "purposes, intents, and provisions" and acknowledged that his wife, Mary Beth Whitehead, would be inseminated with William Stern's sperm. Since Richard Whitehead would be the legal father of any child born to his wife, he also agreed to "surrender immediate custody of the child" and to "terminate his parental rights." Mary Beth Whitehead agreed to be artificially inseminated, to conceive and bear a child without forming "a parent-child relationship," and to relinquish the child and her own parental rights to William Stern. She also relinquished her right to make a decision concerning an abortion. She promised not to seek one unless the fetus was deemed "physiologically abnormal" or the inseminating physician declared that it was necessary to preserve her "physical health." Moreover, she granted William Stern the right to demand that she undergo amniocentesis testing and agreed "to abort the fetus upon demand of WILLIAM STERN" if the fetus was found to be congenitally or genetically abnormal. Together, the Whiteheads "agree[d] to assume all risks, including the risk of death, which are incidental to conception, pregnancy, [and] childbirth."

William Stern agreed to pay Mary Beth Whitehead $10,000 upon her surrender of the baby. Although the contract stated that its "sole purpose . . . is to enable WILLIAM STERN and his infertile wife to have a child which is biologically related to WILLIAM STERN," it described the $10,000 as "compensation for services and expenses," which should "in no way be construed as a fee for termination of parental rights or a payment in exchange for a consent to surrender the child for adoption." Betsy Stern was neither a party to the contract nor mentioned by name; the Whiteheads did agree, however, "that the child will be placed in the custody of WILLIAM STERN'S wife" in the event of Stern's death prior to the child's birth.

Noel Keane of the Infertility Center was paid a fee of $10,000 from the Sterns.

A Child is Born, and Plans Go Away

Events did not go as outlined on paper. Mary Beth Whitehead gave birth to a daughter on March 27, 1986. She refused the $10,000, named the baby "Sara Elizabeth Whitehead," and took her home. The Sterns demanded the baby and took her home on Easter Sunday, March 30. Whitehead got her back on March 31 and, 12 days later, told the Sterns she could never surrender her daughter. The Sterns, determined to enforce the contract, hired attorney Gary Skoloff. The first time the police showed up, Whitehead presented a birth certificate for her daughter, Sara Elizabeth Whitehead, and the police left without "Melissa Elizabeth Stern." The next time the police knocked on the door, Mary Beth Whitehead passed the infant to her husband through an open window and begged him to run. The battle was on.

By the time the trial commenced on January 5, 1987, a *guardian ad litem*, Lorraine Abraham, had been appointed for the infant. Temporary custody of the child known as "Baby M" had been awarded to the Sterns, and Mary Beth Whitehead had been granted two-hour visits each week "strictly supervised under constant surveillance . . . in a sequestered, supervised setting to prevent flight or harm." She had also been ordered by Judge Harvey Sorkow to discontinue breast-feeding the infant.

The contract itself was considered first. The Sterns' attorney, Gary Skoloff, said: "The issue to be decided in this court is whether a promise to make the gift of life should be enforced. . . . Mary Beth Whitehead agreed to give Bill Stern a child of his own flesh and blood." He then explained that Betsy Stern's multiple sclerosis "rendered her, as a practical matter, infertile . . . because . . . she could not carry a baby without significant risk to her health."

Whitehead's attorney, Harold Cassidy, countered in his own opening remarks: "The only reason that the Sterns did not attempt to conceive a child was . . . because Mrs. Stern had a career that had to be advanced. . . . What Mrs.

Stern has is [multiple sclerosis] diagnosed as the mildest form. She was never even diagnosed until after we deposed her in this case. . . . We're here," Cassidy concluded, "not because Betsy Stern is infertile but because one woman stood up and said there are some things that money can't buy." Dr. Gerard Lehrer, a neurologist with a teaching position at Mount Sinai School of Medicine then testified that Betsy Stern had merely "a very, very, very slight case of MS, if any."

Custody was quickly raised, and Skoloff claimed that his clients were exclusively entitled to the baby, under contract law and because it would serve the child's best interests: "If there is one case in the United States, where joint custody will not work, where visitation rights will not work, where maintaining parental rights will not work, this is it." He appealed directly to Judge Sorkow: "Your Honor, under both the contract theory and the best-interest theory, you must terminate the rights of Mary Beth Whitehead and allow Betsy Stern to adopt. . . . Terminate the parental rights of Mary Beth Whitehead and allow Bill Stern and Betsy Stern to be Melissa's mother and father."

Lorraine Abraham testified that she "knew the day would come when I would have to stand before this court [as *guardian ad litem*] and present a recommendation." She explained that she had consulted three experts while trying to make her decision: Dr. Judith Brown Greif, a social worker; Dr. David Brodzinsky, a psychologist; and Marshall Schechter, a psychiatrist. The three, Abraham continued, "will . . . recommend to this court that custody be awarded to the Sterns and visitation denied at this time." As for her own opinion, Abraham concluded, "I am compelled by the overwhelming weight of their investigation to join in their recommendation."

When Betsy Stern took the stand, she was asked by one of Whitehead's lawyers, Randy Wolf: "Were you concerned about what effect taking the baby away from Mary Beth Whitehead would have on the baby?"

She replied: "I knew it would be hard on Mary Beth and in Melissa's best interest."

Wolf asked her: "Now, I believe you testified that if Mary Beth Whitehead receives custody of the baby, you don't want to visit."

Stern answered: "That is correct. I do not want to visit."

Skoloff then tried to demonstrate that Mary Beth Whitehead would be an unfit mother. Whitehead had fled to Florida and hidden there with the baby for a time. Skoloff characterized this as the action of an unstable person. Then he played a tape recording of a phone conversation between William Stern and Mary Beth Whitehead:

Stern: I want my daughter back.

Whitehead: And I want her, too, so what do we do, cut her in half?

Stern: No, No, we don't cut her in half.

Whitehead: You want me, you want me to kill myself and the baby?

Stern: No, that's why I gave her to you in the first place, because I didn't want you to kill yourself.

Whitehead: I've been breast-feeding her for four months. She's bonded to me, Bill. I sleep in the same bed with her. She won't even sleep by herself. What are you going to do when you get this kid that's screaming and carrying on for her mother?

Stern: I'll be her father. I'll be a father to her. I am her father. You made an agreement. You signed an agreement.

Whitehead: Forget it, Bill. I'll tell you right now I'd rather see me and her dead before you get her.

Mary Beth Whitehead took the stand the next day. Randy Wolf asked her, "If you don't get custody of Sara, do you want to see her?"

Whitehead answered,

Yes. I'm her mother, and whether this court only lets me see her two minutes a week, two hours a week, or two days, I'm her mother and I want to see her, no matter what.

The prominent child psychologist Dr. Lee Salk testified on behalf of the Sterns: "[T]he legal term that's been used is 'termination of parental rights,'" he said,

and I don't see that there were any "parental rights" that existed in the first place. . . . The agreement involved the provision of an ovum by Mrs. Whitehead for artificial insemination in exchange for ten thousand dollars . . . and so my feeling is that in both structural and functional terms, Mr. and Mrs. Stern's role as parents was achieved by a surrogate uterus and not a surrogate mother.

On February 23, Marshall Schechter, one of the experts consulted by Lorraine Abraham, testified. As Abraham had earlier indicated, he thought the Sterns should be awarded custody. Schechter also said that Whitehead had a "borderline personality disorder" and said that "handing the baby out of the window to Mr. Whitehead is an unpredictable, impulsive act that falls under this category." Finally, he testified that Whitehead dyed her prematurely white hair, evidence of a "narcissistic personality disorder."

The next day, Dr. Phyllis Silverman, a Boston psychiatric social worker, defended Whitehead's flight to Florida and "crazy behavior." She testified:

Mrs. Whitehead's reaction is like that of other "birth mothers" who suffer pain, grief, and rage for as long as thirty years after giving up a child. The bond of a nursing mother with a child is very powerful.

Whitehead Gets Support

Other women organized to defend Whitehead's fitness as a mother. Children's author Vera B. Williams, actress Meryl Streep, and writers Margaret Atwood and Susan Sontag were among a group of 121 prominent women who released a letter mocking statements made by Schechter and the other "experts." The letter, entitled, "By These Standards, We Are All Unfit Mothers," demanded that "legislators and jurists . . . recognize that a mother need not be perfect to 'deserve' her child."

In his closing argument on Whitehead's behalf, Harold Cassidy pointed out again that Mrs. Stern was not, as originally represented to Whitehead, infertile. He pointed out that the law permitted a termination of parental rights only in the case "of actual abandonment or abuse of the child." And he predicted that a verdict upholding the contract would result in "one class of Americans . . . exploit[ing] another class. And it will always be the wife of the sanitation worker who must bear the children for the pediatrician."

On March 31, 1987, Judge Sorkow announced his decision: "The parental rights of the defendant, Mary Beth Whitehead, are terminated. Mr. Stern is formally judged the father of Melissa Stern." Judge Sorkow then took Betsy Stern into his chambers and presided over her adoption of Baby M.

Supreme Court of New Jersey Overrules

On February 2, 1988, the Supreme Court of New Jersey invalidated the surrogacy contract, restored Mary Beth Whitehead's parental rights, and annulled the adoption of Baby M by Betsy Stern. "We do not know of, and cannot conceive of, any other case," Chief Justice Robert Wilentz wrote for the unanimous court, "where a perfectly fit mother was expected to surrender her newly born infant, perhaps forever, and was then told she was a bad mother because she did not." After invalidating the surrogacy contract, the justices classified the dispute as one between "the natural father and the natural mother, [both of whose claims] are entitled to equal weight." The court granted custody to William Stern and ordered the trial court to set visitation for Mary Beth Whitehead.

The decision permitted future surrogacy arrangements in New Jersey only where "the surrogate mother volunteers, without any payment, to act as a surrogate and is given the right to change her mind and to assert her parental rights."

By 1992, 16 other states had passed legislation outlawing or restricting commercial surrogacy contracts.

During the appeals process, Mary Beth Whitehead divorced her husband Richard and married Dean Gould. The two have since had two children. Occasionally, Whitehead speaks out in support of other surrogate mothers, hoping to help other women avoid what she went through.

—Kathryn Cullen-DuPont

Suggestions for Further Reading

Chesler, Phyllis. *Sacred Bond: The Legacy of Baby M.* New York: Times Books, 1988.

Davis, Flora. *Moving the Mountain: The Women's Movement in America Since 1960.* New York: Simon & Schuster, 1991.

Evans, Sara M. *Born for Liberty: A History of Women in America.* New York: The Free Press, 1989.

Sack, Kevin, "New York is Urged to Outlaw Surrogate Parenting for Pay." *New York Times* (May 15, 1992).

Squire, Susan. "Whatever Happened to Baby M?" *Redbook* (January 1994): 8-9, 60.

Whitehead, Mary Beth with Loretta Schwartz-Nobel. *A Mother's Story: The Truth About the Baby M Case.* New York: St. Martin's Press, 1989.

Beaulah Mae Donald v. United Klans of America Inc. et al: 1987

Claimant: Beaulah Mae Donald   **Defendants** United Klans of America Inc., Robert M. Shelton, Henry Hayes, Bennie Jack Hays, Thaddeus Betancourt, Frank Cox, William O'Connor, Teddy Kyzar, James Knowles   **Claim:** That defendants were responsible for the murder of Michael Donald
Claimant's Lawyers: Morris Dees, Michael Figures
Chief Defense Lawyer: John Mays (UKA only)   **Judge:** Alex Howard
Place: Mobile, Alabama   **Date of Trial:** February 9–2, 1987   **Verdict:** In favor of claimant   **Sentence:** $7 million damages

SIGNIFICANCE

The Beaulah Mae Donald civil suit bankrupted the largest Ku Klux Klan faction in America, establishing an "agency theory" precedent used successfully in future lawsuits against hate groups.

On March 21, 1981, the mutilated body of Michael Donald was found hanging from a tree in Mobile, Alabama. Local and federal authorities were slow to conclude that the 19-year-old black student's murder was the Ku Klux Klan lynching it clearly resembled. After two FBI investigations of the killing, however, local members of the United Klans of America (UKA) began implicating each other before a grand jury. On June 16, 1983, James "Tiger" Knowles pleaded guilty to one count of violating Donald's civil rights, saving himself from a first-degree murder prosecution. Knowles confessed that he and Klansman Henry Hays had abducted Donald at gunpoint. The two Klansmen had driven the teenager to a secluded rural field where they beat and strangled him to death, cut his throat, and returned to Mobile to hang his body from a tree.

Klansmen Plot Racial Revenge Murder

While the felony to which Knowles confessed was a federal crime, the ensuing murder charge against Hays was prosecuted as a state crime. He pleaded innocent. During Hays' trial, Knowles testified that the killing was planned to avenge a white police officer killed after a Birmingham bank robbery. Knowles and Hays assumed that a predominantly black jury would not convict a black defendant in the Birmingham case. With the approval and assistance of Hays' father Bennie, Frank Cox, Thaddeus Betancourt, and Teddy Kyzar—all members of the United Klans of America—Knowles and Hays planned to kill a randomly selected black person and burn a cross at the Mobile County Courthouse in a symbolic act of Klan strength. To establish alibis, the group threw a party the night the Birmingham case went to the jury. When news of a hung jury was announced on television, Knowles and Hayes slipped away and abducted Donald, whom they found walking alone on a dark street.

Knowles was sentenced to 10 years to life imprisonment for his part in the killing. Henry Hays was convicted of murder on December 10, 1983, and sentenced by the jury to life imprisonment without parole. The jury's sentence was overruled by Judge Braxton Kittrell Jr., who condemned Hays to be electrocuted, making him the second white man in Alabama history to be sentenced to death for killing a black victim.

Civil Suit Goes After Klan

Despite the sentences meted out to the killers, no charges stood against the klansmen who had helped them. The fact that all the plotters were UKA members seemed a legal opportunity to Morris Dees, director of the Southern Poverty Law Center (SPLC). Dees convinced Beulah Mae Donald, Michael's mother, that a civil suit against the UKA would uncover the entire truth about her son's murder. Donald agreed to sue the corporate UKA, its leader "Imperial Wizard" Robert Shelton, and the Mobile Klansmen for $10 million in damages.

The suit was based on "agency theory," which holds that corporations are responsible for the deeds of employees acting according to the corporation's principles. Donald's attorneys attempted to prove that her son's death was not only the result of a conspiracy between the Mobile Klansmen, but also of their acting upon the UKA's violent policies through a semi-military chain of command.

When the Donald suit went to court on February 9, 1987, all of the defendants except Robert Shelton defended themselves. John Mays, the Imperial Wizard's lawyer, tried to distance Shelton and his organization from the Mobile Klansmen. Mays deplored Donald's murder as an "atrocity" and told the jury that there was no evidence whatsoever of his client or any other national officer of the UKA directly participating in the crime.

Dees responded with a copy of *Fiery Cross*, a Klan magazine containing a caricature of a lynched black man with the caption that "All whites should work to give the blacks what they deserve." When Shelton described the drawing as an objectionable mistake by a local editor, Dees made him read the publication's masthead, which listed Shelton as both editor and publisher. Shelton admitted that he had not retracted the cartoon's sentiments in the next issue.

Testimony traced the idea of a revenge killing to Mobile Klan leader Bennie Hays and detailed the contributions of his codefendants to the plot.

"Tiger" Knowles testified about the UKA's command structure. Knowles admitted to Shelton's lawyer that Shelton himself had never ordered him to kill anyone, but added that Klan rules bound him to follow the orders of his superior Bennie Hays, who was answerable to Shelton. Knowles recalled discussing the plot with Henry and Bennie Hays. Dees asked what the Klansmen did when they heard of the mistrial in the Birmingham case.

"Well, Henry Hays and myself went and got Henry's car," Knowles replied. "We had the gun and the rope and we went out looking for a black person to hang." As Beaulah Mae Donald sobbed softly at the prosecution's table, Knowles retold the gruesome story of her son's death. Knowles recalled seeing the lynching drawing in *Fiery Cross* and interpreted it as both a message and an order.

When Dees called the individual members of Mobile's UKA, they implicated each other. William O'Connor and Bennie Hays accused each other of complicity in the plot. Teddy Kyzar recalled Bennie Hays threatening him with death if he spoke to police about the killing. Frank Cox, who was accused of providing the gun and the rope used to hang Donald, repeatedly invoked his Fifth Amendment right against self-incrimination. Cox's mother recalled her son, Knowles, and Henry Hays borrowing rope from her on the pretext of using it to tow Knowles' mother's car. Mrs. Knowles testified that there was nothing wrong with her car on the night of the Donald slaying.

Klan's Violent History Traced

Dees next concentrated on proving that violence was essential to the corporate philosophy of the UKA. He relied heavily on a deposition by Gary Thomas Rowe, a controversial government informer who had been present during the 1965 murder of civil rights worker Viola Liuzzo. As well as detailing UKA sanctions of the Liuzzo killing and describing her murder on a Mississippi highway, Rowe's deposition illuminated Shelton's conspiracy with Birmingham police in 1961 attacks on Freedom Riders and the 1963 bombing of Birmingham's Sixteenth Street Baptist church. Rowe's damaging testimony went uncontested by Mays—although invited, Shelton's attorney had not attended the taking of Rowe's deposition. Consequently, it was read into the trial record unchallenged.

To buttress Rowe's claims that the Klan was institutionally violent, Dees called Randy Ward, a former UKA member living in the federal witness protection program. Ward detailed his own violent past and recalled Shelton inspiring Klansmen with his exploits during attacks on civil rights volunteers in the 1960s. Ward also recalled a telephone conversation with Shelton, during which the Imperial Wizard told Ward that Klansmen implicated in shooting incidents would receive legal and financial aid.

At the end of the trial, the defendants offered no witnesses. In contrast to the lack of contrition among the other defendants, Knowles tearfully asked the jurors to return a guilty verdict and sought Mrs. Donald's forgiveness.

"Son," she replied, "I forgave you a long time ago."

The six members of the all-white jury ruled in favor of Donald, awarding her damages of $7 million. The decision effectively bankrupted the UKA, which mailed the deeds and keys to its property to Donald. Evidence unearthed during the trial resulted in murder charges against Frank Cox and Bennie Hays. Cox was convicted and sentenced to life imprisonment in 1989. Bennie Hays suffered a heart attack during his trial and died before he could be retried. Henry Hays continued to protest his innocence until his execution on June 6, 1997. Most significantly, the SPLC led by Morris Dees pursued civil suits in future murder and assault cases, dismantling hate groups through their bank accounts.

— Tom Smith

Suggestions for Further Reading

"Alabamian Guilty in Killing of Black." *New York Times* (May 20, 1989): 33.

Dees, Morris. *A Season for Justice*. New York: Charles Scribner's, 1991.

Stanton, Bill. *Klanwatch: Bringing the Klan to Justice*. New York: Grove Weidenfield, 1991.

"U.S. Jurors Award $7 Million Damages in Slaying by Klan." *New York Times* (February 13, 1987): A1.

Bernhard Goetz Trial: 1987

Defendant: Bernhard Hugo Goetz   **Crimes Charged:** Attempted murder, assault, reckless endangerment, and criminal possession of a gun
Chief Defense Lawyers: Mark Baker and Barry Slotnick
Chief Prosecutor: Gregory Waples   **Judge:** Stephen G. Crane   **Place:** New York, New York   **Dates of Trial:** March 23–June 16, 1987   **Verdict:** Guilty of criminal possession of a gun; not guilty of all other charges   **Sentence:** 1 year imprisonment, $5,075 fine, 4 years probation

SIGNIFICANCE

How far should an American citizen be allowed to go in the defense of his life and liberty? That was the question facing a jury in this, one of the most highly charged trials New York City had ever seen.

Following a 1981 beating that left him with a permanently damaged knee, Bernhard Goetz, a 36-year-old electrical engineer, took to carrying a gun everywhere he went. On December 22, 1984, while riding a New York City subway train, he was approached by four black youths, one of whom demanded $5. Goetz's response was to yank a revolver from a special quick-draw holster and begin spraying bullets. As two of the youths fled, Goetz shot them in the back. One, Darrell Cabey, fell. Goetz approached him and said, "You seem to be all right; here's another," firing a second open-nosed bullet that severed Cabey's spinal cord. Then Goetz calmly left the scene and disappeared.

Nine days later Goetz gave himself up at a police station in Concord, New Hampshire. Following several lengthy confessions he was charged with 13 various offenses, from attempted murder to criminal possession of a gun.

Bringing the case to court took time—more than two years. Selecting a jury for such an obviously volatile trial proved almost as laborious, as neither side wanted to concede any advantage in this most critical phase of the judicial process. Eventually, after one month, a jury of 10 whites and two blacks was impaneled, and on April 27, 1987, they heard Assistant District Attorney Gregory Waples make the opening presentation. He outlined the salient facts, then said: "These terribly destructive shots . . . were fired not by a typical New Yorker, not by a reasonable person such as yourselves, responding to provocation in an appropriate and limited manner, but by an emotionally troubled individual." Goetz was, said Waples, "a man with a passionate but very twisted and self-righteous sense of right and wrong . . . an emotional powder keg, one spark away from explosion." To drive home this point Waples highlighted Goetz's refusal to wear gloves, even on the coldest winter day, so that he might remain "fast on the draw" should trouble arise. Such an obsession, the prosecutor reasoned, was far more likely to lead Goetz into conflict rather than avoid it.

The Defense Attacks

Quite naturally the defense, led by Barry Slotnick, saw things in an entirely different light. His opening statement left no doubts about their intention to turn this trial into an indictment of the "aggressors . . . this gang of four." Excoriating them as "savages and vultures . . . who got what the law allowed," Slotnick launched into a vitriolic assault on the character and credibility of James Ramseur, one of the alleged assailants. Five months after the Goetz incident, Ramseur had been arrested for participating in the savage gang-rape of a pregnant woman. "And to add insult to injury," thundered Slotnick, "Mr. Ramseur and his friends took her earrings and her ring, and left her bleeding on the rooftop landing." So heavy-handed and graphic did Slotnick's depiction of this rape become that it drew a sharp rebuke from Justice Stephen Crane: "Why don't you get off this, Mr. Slotnick."

But the damage had been done. The impression of the four black youths as rampaging sadists was firmly implanted in the jury's mind. This skillful defense manipulation of proceedings went a stage further when one of the state's witnesses, Detective Michael Clark, referred to "the four victims on the train." Slotnick was on his feet immediately. "Your Honor, I would object to the characterization of the "victim'. That's a decision the jury will have to make." Surprisingly Waples yielded the point, when there was no real need for him to do so, agreeing to the much meeker term "young men." It was another small but important victory for the defense. Slowly Bernhard Goetz was being turned into the victim in the case, not the perpetrator.

Central to the prosecution case was a taped confession that Goetz had made to police. Because Goetz would not take the stand, this was the jury's only opportunity to hear him speak. In a rambling two-hour account Goetz gave his version of the attack. It contained many damaging statements. Most incriminating of all was his clearly expressed intention "to murder them, to hurt them, to make them suffer as much as possible." Also revealed was his aversion to being "played with . . . as a cat plays with a mouse."

Several witnesses from the subway train testified. Through careful questioning Slotnick succeeded in drawing admissions that the action had happened so quickly as to impair their recollection of what actually occurred. In particular Slotnick created doubt about the actual number of shots fired. The intention here was to undermine the prosecution's claim that Goetz had cold-bloodedly stood over Cabey and fired the fifth and most damaging shot. Slotnick desperately needed to demonstrate that this injury had occurred just in random gunfire. By far the most resistant to this line of questioning was Christopher Boucher, a

San Franciscan vacationing in New York at the time of the shooting. Boucher testified that he initially heard gunfire but that his view was blocked. However, he then saw Goetz "standing, looking down at the man in the seat." Waples asked, "How far was the defendant from him [Cabey]?"

Answer: Two to three feet.

Question: Did you see the gun at any point?

Answer: Yes.

Question: And what did the person, who was sitting down, do at the moment the shot was fired?

Answer: Well, he was sitting, grasping the bench, and he just tightened.

Slotnick, aware that this was the most damaging eyewitness testimony yet, did everything in his power to discredit it. He began by implying that Boucher had been unduly influenced by media accounts of the shooting, an allegation that Boucher strenuously denied. Next, Slotnick asked Boucher, had he not been "shaken and traumatized" by the violence, perhaps enough to compromise his memory?

"Actually no," Boucher replied. "That's the funny thing."

Effective Demonstration

Slotnick fared much better with Joseph Quirk, a ballistics expert hired to recreate the crime scene in court. For the purposes of this demonstration Slotnick had engaged the services of four black youths, dressed like street toughs, to act out the parts of the attackers. Had the defense only been interested in demonstrating bullet paths, then the color of the assistants would have been immaterial, but the sight of four black teenagers jostling Quirk, a white man, was highly inflammatory. So much so, that Judge Crane ordered Slotnick to use court employees in the future should he need to carry out any further demonstrations.

Bernhard Goetz leaving court escorted by Guardian Angel Keith Johnson. The Goetz trial addressed the question of a citizen's right to defend himself. (AP/Wide World Photos)

Without meaning to be, prosecution witness James Ramseur was far and away the defense's strongest card. He entered the court in prison dungarees, pugnacious and petulant, determined to face down Slotnick. At first he refused to testify, earning for himself several citations for contempt. When he eventually condescended to take the stand, Ramseur foolishly bandied words with counsel. "When was the last time . . . that you . . . committed a crime against a human being?" asked Slotnick.

"When was the last time you got a drug dealer off?" sneered Ramseur. Three days later, in sentencing Ramseur for contempt, Judge Crane upbraided him for his stupidity:

> Your conduct has played right into the hands of Mr. Goetz's lawyer. He owes you a vote of thanks. . . . The jurors saw your contemptuous conduct. That can never be erased from their minds.

On Friday, June 12, 1987, the jury retired to consider their verdict. By the following Tuesday they had reached agreement on all 13 counts. Twelve times jury foreman, James Hurley, intoned, "Not guilty." Only once did he respond, "Guilty"—to a charge of criminal possession of a weapon in the third degree.

Three months later, on October 19, 1987, Judge Crane passed sentence: six months in jail, plus a fine and probation. Upon review in January 1989, the jail sentence was increased to one year.

The Bernhard Goetz trial opened up many old wounds and left a peculiar sense of public dissatisfaction at its outcome. Many believed that he should never have faced a court; they saw him as acting well within his rights. Others, fearful of vigilantism adding to the problem of already dangerous streets, were outraged by the jury's refusal to convict on all but the least serious charge. In the final analysis, skillful advocacy emerged as the only winner in this case. It wasn't elegant, but it was effective.

Goetz served just over eight months in prison. Freedom, however, brought further problems: a $50 million civil suit, filed by lawyers representing the paralyzed Darrell Cabey. The case finally reached the Bronx Supreme Court on April 8, 1996.

This time Goetz did take the stand. Under tough questioning from Cabey's attorney, Ronald Kuby, his testimony did more harm than good. Callous and unremorseful, Goetz said his actions could be considered a public service, claiming that he opened fire when he saw "that smile" and "that shine" in one of the assailant's eyes.

On April 24, 1996, the jury—four African Americans and two people of Hispanic descent—unanimously found that Goetz had acted recklessly and deliberately inflicted emotional distress. They awarded Cabey $43 million in damages—$18 million for pain and suffering, and $25 million in punitive damages. It was purely a token sum, since Goetz had very little money. In such cases it is common for the court to garnish 10 percent of the defendant's wages for 20 years.

—Colin Evans

Suggestions for Further Reading

Blecker, R. "A Verdict By Their Peers." *The Nation* (October 3, 1987): 334ff.

Fletcher, George P. *A Crime Of Self-Defense.* New York: Free Press, 1988.

Jet (October 22, 1990): 22.

Lesly, Mark and Charles Shuttleworth. *Subway Gunman.* Latham, N.Y.: British American Pub., 1988.

Margaret Kelly Michaels Trial and Appeal: 1987 & 1993

Defendant: Margaret Kelly Michaels   **Crimes Charged:** Aggravated sexual assault, sexual assault, endangering the welfare of children, and terroristic threats   **Chief Defense Lawyers:** Harvey Meltzer and Robert Clark   **Chief Prosecutors:** Glenn Goldberg and Sara Sencer McArdle   **Judge:** William A. Harth   **Chief Lawyers for Appeal:** Morton Stavis and William Kunstler   **Chief Prosecutor:** Clifford Minor   **Place:** Newark, New Jersey   **Dates of Trial:** June 22, 1987–April 15, 1988   **Verdict:** Guilty   **Sentence:** 47 years imprisonment (5 years served)   **Date of Appeals Court Decision:** March 26, 1993   **Decision:** Verdict overturned on the basis that the defendant received an unfair trial

SIGNIFICANCE

The reversal of Kelly Michaels's conviction on appeal reflected a concern with the techniques used to obtain testimony from the young children in this sexual abuse case—an issue raised in other highly publicized abuse trials.

During the 1980s, the Unites States saw a wave of sensational trials involving alleged sexual abuse of children at day-care centers and preschools. The press reported often-lurid charges of bizarre sexual practices committed by day-care workers against toddlers. One child or parent's charge of abuse often snowballed into dozens. Sometimes the allegations involved satanic worship and the ritualistic slaughter of animals. In many cases, prosecutors had little or no physical evidence—just the testimony of small children, some of whom seemed quite loving toward their supposed abusers.

Critics believed the defendants were accused on the flimsiest of evidence, and that young witnesses were coaxed and coached by parents, prosecutors, and child abuse experts. They were concerned that the alleged crimes had no basis in reality. Some journalists and defense lawyers compared the sexual abuse cases to the seventeenth-century Salem witch trials and the McCarthyism of the 1950s.

In 1985, Margaret Kelly Michaels found herself trapped in one of these controversial cases. The year before, Michaels had taken a job at the Wee Care Day Nursery in Maplewood, New Jersey. An aspiring actress, Michaels had always considered the job temporary, and she left Wee Care the following April. She had been considered a good employee, earning a promotion and working well with the children. But a few days after Michaels's departure, suspicions arose about her conduct at the nursery.

From Questions to Indictments

On April 30, 1985, a four-year-old boy who attended Wee Care visited his doctor. During an examination, the nurses took his temperature with a rectal thermometer. "That's what my teacher does to me at nap time at school," the boy said. The teacher he was referring to was Kelly Michaels. The boy's comments prompted his mother to call the New Jersey Division of Family and Youth Services. The boy was also questioned by Assistant Prosecutor Sara Sencer McArdle, head of the Essex County Child Abuse unit.

In that interview, the boy said that Michaels had touched other boys as well. Subsequently, these children were also questioned. One said Michael had touched his penis. A few weeks later, parents of the children attending Wee Care were told by New Jersey authorities to watch for "danger signs" of abuse. Later the parents were instructed to record their observations in a journal. Soon, a deepening pattern of alleged abuse evolved. In June, Michaels was indicted on six counts of child abuse; she pleaded innocent to all charges.

Sexual abuse experts questioned the children, letting them demonstrate with anatomically correct dolls. The children used the dolls to indicate where they had been touched. The charges against Michaels continued to grow including accusations that she played "Jingle Bells" on the piano while naked; she made the children take off all their clothes and roll around on kitchen utensils spread on the floor; and she licked peanut butter off the children's genitals. By December 1985, the indictments reached 235 counts of abuse against 31 children.

Michaels continued to assert her innocence. She noted that none of the children had ever lodged complaints against her while she worked at Wee Care. And she had never spent enough time alone with all the children to carry out some of the more unusual practices she had allegedly committed. Michaels also passed a lie detector test when she was first questioned by police. Still, prosecutors believed the children's stories and pressed on with the case.

Michaels on Trial

The trial began on June 22, 1987. By now, the charges had been reduced to 163 counts involving 19 children. According to trial rules in force at the time, the jury did not have to believe everything the children said to find their testimony credible. Judge William Harth allowed the children to testify via closed-circuit television, a common practice in child sexual abuse trials. But he refused to let defense psychologists interview the children.

One key witness for the prosecution was psychologist Eileen Treacy. She introduced the concept of Child Sexual Abuse Syndrome and testified that many of the Wee Care children showed symptoms of it. She called them "the most traumatized group of children" she had ever seen.

Michaels's defense lawyers tried to raise doubts about the whole process used to extract testimony from the children. Their star witness, Dr. Ralph Underwager, argued that children can easily be coaxed to tell their questioners what they want to hear. However, ultimately the jury believed there was enough evidence against her and on April 15, 1988, Michaels was found guilty on 115 charges. She was later sentenced to 47 years in prison and denied bail pending appeal.

Margaret Kelly Michaels being led into court on child sexual abuse charges. (AP/Wide World Photos)

A Legal Rescue

A number of journalists chronicled the Michaels trial and the controversy that surrounded sexual abuse cases such as hers. One of these reporters was Dorothy Rabinowitz. She wrote a lengthy article for *Harper's* magazine detailing some of the more questionable tactics used by the prosecution against Michaels. The article caught the attention of Morton Stavis, a founder of the Center for Constitutional Rights. Working pro bono, Stavis and a team of law students prepared an appeal for Michaels.

Stavis died in December 1992 before completing the appeal motion. Well-known defense lawyer William Kunstler then took over the case. The appellate brief raised nine points. These included arguments that Michaels was denied due process, since defense experts could not question the children; that Eileen

Treacy's testimony was not scientifically sound; and that the questioning of the children was suggestive and coercive.

On March 26, 1993, the Appellate Division of the Superior Court of New Jersey overturned Michaels's conviction. The three-judge panel ruled that Treacy's testimony about Child Sexual Abuse Syndrome was improperly used by the prosecution. The judges also criticized Judge Harth for his actions during the children's testimony, during which he had sat some of them on his lap, whispered in their ears, and played ball with them. The appellate judges said, "The required atmosphere of the bench's impartiality was lost in this trial."

Michaels was released on bail on March 30, but her case was not over. Essex County Prosecutor Clifford Minor asked the New Jersey Supreme Court to consider an appeal of the appellate decision. In a brief filed with the Supreme Court, 45 social scientists backed the defense assertion that the children's testimony against Michaels was unreliable.

On June 24, 1994, the New Jersey Supreme Court unanimously affirmed the appellate decision, agreeing that the "interrogations that occurred in this case were improper and there is a substantial likelihood that the evidence derived from them is unreliable." The court also said that prosecutors would have to show "clear and convincing evidence" that the questioning methods had produced reliable testimony before asking for a possible retrial. In December 1994, prosecutor Minor decided against a retrial.

Margaret Kelly Michaels has joined a number of other defendants in child sexual abuse cases who have been acquitted or had convictions overturned—but only after suffering years of public personal agony.

—Michael Burgan

Suggestions for Further Reading

Fasion, Seth. "Child-Abuse Conviction of Woman is Overturned." *New York Times* (March 27, 1993): 26.

Gray, Jerry. "Trenton Court Assails '88 Trial of Day-Care Aide." *New York Times* (June 24, 1994): B5.

Nathan, Debbie and Michael Snedeker. *Satan's Silence: Ritual Abuse and the Making of a Modern American Witch Hunt.* New York: Basic Books, 1995.

Rabinowitz, Dorothy. "From the Mouth of Babes to a Jail Cell." *Harper's* (May 1990): 52–63.

Sanderson, Bill. "Day-Care Abuse Case Dropped." *The Record* (December 3, 1994): A1.

McMartin Preschool Trials: 1987–90

Defendants: First trial: Raymond Buckey and Peggy Buckey; second trial: Raymond Buckey **Crimes Charged:** Child abuse and conspiracy **Chief Defense Lawyers:** Raymond Buckey: Daniel G. Davis; Peggy Buckey: Dean R. Gits **Chief Prosecutors:** First trial: Roger Gunson, Ira Reiner, and Lael Rubin; second trial: Joseph Martinez **Judges:** First trial: William R. Pounders; second trial: Stanley M. Weisberg **Place:** Los Angeles, California **Dates of Trials:** First trial: July 13, 1987–January 18, 1990; second trial: May 7–July 27, 1990 **Verdicts:** First trial: Ray Buckey: Acquittal on 39 of 52, hung jury on 13 counts including conspiracy; Peggy Buckey: Acquittal; second trial: Ray Buckey: Hung jury

SIGNIFICANCE

The longest and most expensive criminal trial in U.S. history, the McMartin preschool trials lasted six years from preliminary hearings to acquittal and cost the state of California some $15 million. The case disrupted and adversely affected the lives of hundreds of children, who became convinced they were abused during bizarre rituals. The number of copy-cat prosecutions it engendered cannot be measured, but countless subsequent accusations of sexual and sadistic abuse of children became stereotypical as gullible adults made unfounded hysterical charges. The result has been distrust of the testimony of preadolescent witnesses whose memories of preschool years have been stirred, if not steered, by determined adults.

In 1983, the McMartin Preschool in Manhattan Beach, California, was a long-established school where toddler applicants often waited six months to get in. It was co-owned by its 76-year-old founder, Virginia McMartin, and her daughter, Peggy Buckey.

On the morning of May 12, 1983, McMartin teachers discovered an unknown two-and-a-half-year-old boy at the door. They found him "pre-verbal" and cared for him, assuming that a parent would pick him up later.

In the school yard was a menagerie of brightly painted wooden animals, including rocking horses, a dinosaur, octopus, camel, giraffe, and ducks big enough to sit on. One of the children's favorite activities was crawling through wooden boxes that zigzagged for 18 feet as aboveground "tunnels."

The boy's mother, 40-year-old Judy Johnson, came for him in the afternoon. She told Peggy Buckey she had no money as she had separated from her husband two months earlier. Mrs. Buckey enrolled the new student.

Mother Calls in the Police

Exactly three months later, on August 12, Judy Johnson called the Manhattan Beach Police Department. She said her two-and-a-half-year-old, Billy, had been molested by Ray Buckey, Peggy Buckey's 25-year-old son, a part-time aide at the school. At Johnson's suggestion, the police interviewed a dozen parents of children enrolled at the school. None thought their children had been sexually abused. Additionally, Billy Johnson could not identify Ray from photographs. Nor did medical examinations of the boy reveal any signs of abuse. Searching Ray Buckey's home, the police confiscated ordinary household items—including pictures from *Playboy* magazine—and subsequently arrested him on September 7, 1983. The Los Angeles County District Attorney's office, however, found insufficient evidence for a prosecution.

Shortly thereafter, Manhattan Beach Police Chief Harry L. Kuhlmeyer wrote to 200 parents of current or former McMartin students, telling them of Buckey's arrest and asking them to question their children regarding whether Buckey had engaged them in "oral sex, fondling of genitals, buttocks or chest area, and sodomy." The letter, enclosing a reply form, suggested that "photos may have been taken of the children without clothing," and concluded that "any information from your child regarding having ever observed Ray Buckey to leave a classroom alone with a child during any nap period, or if they have ever observed Ray Buckey to tie up a child, is important."

Parents Demand Action

A television station immediately reported that McMartin Preschool might be connected to sex industries and child pornography rings. Overnight, gossip became panic. Parents demanded action by the district attorney. The D.A.'s child-abuse unit brought in Kee McFarlane of the Children's Institute International (CII), an agency that dealt with abused children.

McFarlane's CII staff videotaped interviews with hundreds of current and former McMartin students. Frightened parents were shown parts of the videotapes and urged to support their children's disclosures.

By March 1984, the CII reported that there was evidence that 360 children had been abused. Astrid Heger, a doctor for the organization, had medically examined 150 of the children and concluded that 120 had been molested. With the town beside itself with anxiety and outrage, enrollment at McMartin Preschool plunged and, after 28 years of community service, it closed on January 13, 1984. Three months later, on February 3—at the start of television's "sweeps" month, during which stations battle for viewers and advertising dollars—KABC reporter Wayne Satz announced that some 60 children "had been keeping a grotesque secret of being sexually abused and made to appear in pornographic films while in the preschool's care—and of having been forced to witness the mutilation and killing of animals to scare the kids into staying silent."

On March 22, 1984, a grand jury indicted Ray Buckey, his mother, grandmother, sister, and three other women on 115 counts of child sexual abuse. Buckey and his mother were held without bail.

Rewarded for "Right" Answers

An 18-month preliminary hearing began on June 6. The chief prosecution witness, Dr. Roland C. Summit, a mental health expert on child sexual abuse, congratulated the media for bringing the issue to the public's attention, theorizing that the publicity had protected countless children from sexual assault. He also defended the interview technique in which McFarlane and her associates rewarded the children for "right" answers.

Because of the children's interviews, the formal charges against the codefendants came to include:

conspiracy to make the preschool the headquarters of an extensive kiddie-porn/prostitution ring producing millions of child-sex pictures;

drugging children and forcing them into satanic rituals and sex games;

exposing the children to encounters with lions, rabbits, turtles, a sexually-abusive elephant, flying witches, space mutants, and bodies (including babies) in mortuaries and graveyards;

taking children via trapdoors through underground tunnels to adjacent garages, thence by train, airplane, and hot-air balloon to secret rituals; and

killing and cutting up animals and threatening to do the same to children's parents "if you tell."

(Years later, in a 1993 broadcast interview, Summit admitted he hadn't viewed any of the 400 videotaped interviews and hadn't read any of the transcripts.)

In March 1985, nearly 50 parents dug up the vacant lot beside the McMartin school in search of an underground room and animal remains. After finding nothing, the district attorney's office hired an archaeological firm to excavate. The dig discovered trash dating back 60 to 100 years, but no tunnels or rooms. The FBI and Interpol conducted a worldwide search for evidence of a kiddie-porn/prostitution ring but found no photographs or films to corroborate the children's stories.

On January 17, 1986, District Attorney Ira Reiner dropped charges against five of the defendants. Having reviewed 100,000 pages of testimony, he said his predecessor had based the case on "incredibly weak" evidence. Yet he found other "strong and compelling" evidence against Ray Buckey and his mother, who were kept in jail. He announced 79 child-abuse counts against Ray, 20 against his mother, and one conspiracy count against both.

Paranoid Schizophrenic

In December 1986, Judy Johnson died of alcohol poisoning. Only then was it revealed that she had been a paranoid schizophrenic. In January 1997, defense attorneys learned that for 10 months prosecutor Lael Rubin and her assistants had not divulged that Johnson had accused the defendants of being witches, and had insisted to investigators that her son had been forced to drink blood from the chopped-open head of a baby and had been molested by a member of the Los Angeles Board of Education. Johnson's bizarre complaints continued from her first report of sexual abuse against her son in May 1983 to March 6, 1985, when it took the help of police to have her committed to a hospital for psychiatric examination. In the end, neither jury in either trial was told of Johnson's emotional problems.

The first trial began on July 13, 1987. Prosecution witnesses included children who testified to playing "naked movie star" games and seeing cats mutilated, as well as a professional "jailhouse snitch" and career criminal put in Ray Buckey's cell to obtain "corroborative" testimony. To show that Buckey was a pedophile, the prosecution provided evidence that he read Playboy and hadn't had any underwear on when he was arrested.

In the circus atmosphere of the courtroom, some child prosecution witnesses refused to testify, causing the judge to dismiss some of the charges. In fact, while the prosecution had assembled charges involving 41 children, it eventually concentrated on only 13—and by February 1989 only 5 had testified. One, a boy now aged 11, said he once saw Ray Buckey kill a horse; however, as defense attorney Dean Gits pressed for details, repeatedly replied, "I don't know."

Bail after Five Years

In February 1989, Ray Buckey's friends raised $1.5 million in bail money—enough to free him after five years' imprisonment. His mother had earlier spent two years in jail before being released on $495,000 bail on January 23, 1986.

Both defendants testified on their own behalf. Peggy Buckey denied that she ever sexually assaulted any student. Ray Buckey repeatedly denied sodomizing the children, playing naked games with them, killing animals before them, or taking pornographic pictures. Typical of the trial's slow pace was a several-weeks-long debate over how a car wash operates—all because one of the charges against Ray was for molesting children in a car wash.

Acquittals and Deadlocks

The jury deliberated from November 2, 1989, to January 18, 1990. Finally, it acquitted Ray Buckey and his mother on 52 counts of molesting young children, but deadlocked on the single count of conspiracy against both and on 12 molestation charges against Ray.

District Attorney Reiner announced he would retry Ray Buckey alone, reducing the charges to five. With Judge Stanley M. Weisberg presiding and newly elected District Attorney Joseph Martinez prosecuting, the new trial began on May 7, 1990. After three months of hearing many of the first trial's witnesses, the jury deliberated from July 9 to July 27, then reported it was "hopelessly and irreversibly" deadlocked. Dismissing all the charges, the judge declared a mistrial.

However, the story took an unexpectedly bizarre turn. In April 1990, as the school building was being demolished, several parents of former McMartin students hired an archaeologist to find evidence of subterranean rooms or tunnels. After the close of the second trial, archaeologist Dr. E. Gary Stickel reported finding a pattern of tunnels. He said they had been constructed after the structure was built in 1966, and were subsequently repacked with soil and artifacts. "The discoveries," he concluded, "stand in stark contrast to the skeptical position that the children only imagined what they described as activities underground."

On August 6, 1990, U.S. District Judge Richard A. Gadbois, Jr., dismissed a $1 million civil suit filed by Peggy Buckey against Los Angeles County. The judge said he understood how Buckey felt but that "being very, very upset does not constitute a cause of action."

—Bernard Ryan, Jr.

Suggestions for Further Reading

Eberle, Paul and Shirley Eberle. The Abuse of Innocence: *The McMartin Preschool Trial*. Buffalo, N.Y.: Prometheus, 1993.

Mann, Abby. Shocking *True Story of the McMartin Child Abuse Trial*. New York: Random House, 1993.

Nathan, Debbie and Michael Snedeker. *Satan's Silence: Ritual Abuse and the Making of a Modern American Witch Hunt*. New York: Basic Books, 1995.

Cipollone v. Liggett Group: 1988

Plaintiff: Estate of Rose Cipollone   **Defendant:** Liggett Group
Plaintiff Claims: That the defendant, a cigarette company, was liable for Rose Cipollone's death from cancer because it failed to warn consumers about the dangers of smoking   **Chief Defense Lawyer:** H. Bartow Farr III
Chief Lawyers for Plaintiff: Alan Darnell, Marc Z. Edell, and Cynthia Walters
Judge: H. Lee Sarokin   **Place:** Newark, New Jersey
Dates of Trial: February 1–June 13, 1988   **Decision:** Jury awarded plaintiff damages of $400,000; reversed on appeal, and lawsuit later dropped

SIGNIFICANCE

Despite encouraging early victories, the lesson of the Cipollone case is that smokers face very burdensome legal difficulties in suing cigarette companies.

Rose Cipollone of Little Ferry, New Jersey, was born in 1926. Like many people of her generation, she took up smoking at an early age, in her case, 16. Although medical studies examining evidence of a link between smoking and cancer began to appear as early as the 1920s, they' were not widely read, and the U.S. Surgeon General didn't look into the issue until 1962. In 1966 the first federal law on cigarette warning labels went into effect, and in 1969 Congress passed a stricter law requiring that the label, "Warning: The Surgeon General Has Determined That Cigarette Smoking Is Dangerous to Your Health," be printed on all cigarette packs.

Decade after decade, the cigarette industry spent billions of dollars on advertising. Newspaper, magazine, radio, and television ads extolled the pleasures of smoking. There was no mention of any risk, and the tobacco companies vigorously fought government regulation in the 1960's and 1970's with studies of their own that denied any health risk from smoking. Meanwhile, Cipollone had been smoking since 1942. Her favorite brands were Chesterfields and L&M, manufactured by Liggett Group, Inc., one of the smaller tobacco companies.

In 1981, Dr. Nathan Seriff diagnosed Cipollone as having lung cancer, caused by smoking cigarettes. Cipollone filed a lawsuit against Liggett on August 1, 1983 in the U.S. District Court for the District of New Jersey in Newark. She was represented by Alan Darnell, Marc Z. Edell, and Cynthia Walters, and the judge was H. Lee Sarokin. Of Liggett's team of defense lawyers, who worked to prevent the case from going to trial for nearly five years, the most prominent lawyer was H. Bartow Farr III . . . Early in the litigation, however, Cipollone won an important victory when Sarokin refused to dismiss the case on the grounds that Liggett's compliance with the federal warning-label law absolved Liggett from further legal liability:

> This case presents the issue of whether cigarette manufacturers can be subjected to tort liability if they have complied with the federal warning requirement. . . . In effect, the cigarette industry argues that such compliance immunizes it from liability to anyone who has chosen to smoke cigarettes notwithstanding the warning, that federal legislation has created an irrebuttable presumption that the risk of injury has been assumed by the consumer. This court rejects that contention.

Cippolone Dies, But Her Case Proceeds

Sarokin's decision was issued on September 20, 1984, and generated enormous publicity about the case. The prospect of successful smokers' litigation sent tobacco company stocks into a tailspin. Unfortunately for her, Cipollone died shortly thereafter, on October 21, 1984. Her husband, Antonio Cipollone, continued the case on behalf of her estate. After years of foot-dragging and delays by Liggett's attorneys, the Cipollone case finally went to trial on February 1, 1988. Just getting the case to trial was an accomplishment: of the 300 lawsuits on record against tobacco companies in the past 40 years, fewer than 10 have actually gone to trial.

Edell, the senior attorney in the Cipollone legal team, described Liggett's legal defenses to the jury as basically a statement to all smokers:

> If you trusted us, if you thought we would test, if you thought we would warn, if you believed our statement in the press, if you believed our advertisements, if you were stupid enough to believe us, then you deserve what you got.

Cipollone's attorneys introduced documents showing that the cigarette companies were aware of smoking-related health risks before the government took any action but failed to disclose these risks to the consumer. For example, one Liggett report from 1961 described certain ingredients in cigarettes as "(a) cancer-causing, (b) cancer-promoting, (c) poisonous, (d) stimulating, pleasurable, and flavorful."

On June 13, 1988, the jury returned its verdict. It was a very conservative finding, mostly based on Liggett's failure prior to the 1966 law to warn smokers like Cipollone about the dangers of smoking. Further, the jury found that Cipollone was 80 percent responsible for her death by smoking, and Liggett only 20 percent responsible. Nevertheless, the jury assessed $400,000 in damages against Liggett, the first such award in tobacco-litigation history.

Liggett appealed, and the case ultimately reached the U.S. Supreme Court on October 8, 1991. During the lengthy appellate process, however, Antonio Cipollone died in 1990. His son, Thomas Cipollone of Grass Valley, California, carried on the case on behalf of both his parents' estates. The Supreme Court required the parties to re-argue the case on January 13, 1992, and issued its opinion on June 24, 1992. Although the court ruled in a 6-3 decision that health warnings on cigarette packs don't shield cigarette companies like Liggett from personal-injury lawsuits, the court did impose tougher evidentiary requirements concerning the companies' advertising and promotions. The case would have to be retried.

Thomas Cipollone and the attorneys had had enough. After nine years of expensive litigation, they were back at square one, facing even more time-consuming hurdles thanks to the Supreme Court's decision. To make matters worse, Judge Sarokin had been removed from the case for comments he had made elsewhere about how he believed that the tobacco industry was hiding evidence. On November 5, 1992, the Cipollone family dropped their case against Liggett. While the initial jury verdict was the first of its kind in American legal history, the ultimate lesson is that the tobacco companies can delay and delay in court until their victims die or give up in despair.

—Stephen G. Christianson

Suggestions for Further Reading

Crudele, John. "The Smoke Clears: Tobacco Liability Suits Decline." *New York* (November 14, 1988): 28.

"For the First Time Ever." *The New Republic* (July 4, 1988): 10–11.

Gostin, Larry O. "Tobacco Liability and Public Health Policy." *Journal of the American Medical Association* (December 11, 1991): 3178–3182.

Spencer, Leslie. "Just Smoke." *Forbes* (December 23, 1991): 41–42.

"Where There's Smoke . . ." *Time* (April 8, 1991): 55.

Hartford Wells Fargo Trial: 1988–89

Defendants: Antonio Camacho Negron, Juan E. Segarra Palmer, Roberto J. Maldonado Rivera, Carlos M. Ayes Suarez, Norman Ramirez Talavera
Crimes Charged: A 17-count indictment that included charges of conspiracy in belonging to a corrupt organization, planning a robbery, transporting the stolen money across state lines, helping the robber to escape, and laundering the money   **Chief Defense Lawyers:** Juan Ramon Acevedo, Linda A. Backiel, James Bergenn, Roberto J. Maldonado Rivera, Leonard Weinglass
Chief Prosecutors: Leonard Boyle, Albert S. Dabrowski, Carmen Espinosa Van Kirk   **Judge:** T. Emmett Claire   **Place:** Hartford, Connecticut
Date of Trial: September 6, 1988–April 10, 1989   **Verdicts:** Ayes: innocent of all charges; Segarra: guilty of 11 counts involving three major charges (conspiracy, planning a robbery, transporting stolen money); Maldonado and Ramirez: guilty of conspiracy; Camacho: guilty of transporting stolen money
Sentences: Segarra: 65 years imprisonment (reduced to 55 on appeal); Camacho: 15 years imprisonment; Maldonado: 5 years imprisonment and $100,000 fine; Ramirez: 5 years imprisonment and $50,000 fine

SIGNIFICANCE

What began with a robbery developed into a trial for conspiracy involving alleged terrorists linked to the decades-old struggle by small groups of Puerto Ricans seeking total independence from the United States. The known perpetrator of the robbery was not present and the government could not establish the true nature of the conspiracy, so there were charges of a political "show trial," although years later the government's position would be considerably vindicated.

About 9:30 P.M. on September 12, 1983, Victor Gerena and a coworker arrived back at the Wells Fargo depot in West Hartford, Connecticut, after a day spent collecting several million dollars from banks and other clients of the armed car service. Their boss had arrived somewhat earlier with his truckload of another $5 million. As they were occupied with various chores, Gerena suddenly pulled the pistol from the boss's holster and ordered the two men to lie on the floor. After handcuffing his boss's wrists and taping and tying up his coworker, he injected the two men with some substance that in fact had no effect. But as the two men lay there powerless for some 90 minutes, Gerena carried some $7.1 million into the beat-up Buick LeSabre he had rented two days earlier, then drove off into the night.

The Perfect Crime?

The next day Gerena's Buick was found abandoned at a hotel lot elsewhere in Hartford. There was no question that Victor Gerena had carried out the robbery. But with whose help? He had no record as a criminal of any sort, so he must have had accomplices. How else could he have vanished without a trail? And why? No one questioned could come up with any explanation for a motive. Of Puerto Rican origin, he had no known affiliation with any organizations, criminal or otherwise. He even left behind a fiancée. Yet somehow this ordinary "joe" had managed to carry off the second largest robbery in American history.

As months, then years, passed, the crime vanished from most people's consciousness. There were rumors that Gerena had somehow escaped to Cuba with his money, but this was based more on speculation than any real evidence. Then suddenly, on August 30, 1985, some 250 FBI agents and U.S. marshals, operating from the U.S. Naval Base at Roosevelt Roads in eastern Puerto Rico, descended on homes and offices across Puerto Rico and arrested numerous individuals. Many of those arrested were soon released, but eventually 19 individuals were charged with conspiracy involving a corrupt organization, Los Macheteros ("The Machete Wielders"), and more specifically, with planning and helping to carry out the 1983 Wells Fargo robbery in Hartford. Victor Gerena, however, was not among those apprehended.

Background to the Robbery

The organization that these individuals were accused of being involved with, Los Macheteros, was one of several in a decades-old struggle by some Puerto Ricans to attain total independence for their island. Leading *independistas* had been imprisoned for violent and/or "seditious" actions since the 1930s. In the early 1980s the U.S. government had begun a major campaign to crack down on groups of Puerto Ricans charged with conducting a series of bombings of U.S. government, military, and corporate targets (one of which killed two U.S. sailors). Los Macheteros, organized by a leading radical nationalist, Filiberto Ojeda Rios, and based primarily in Puerto Rico, actually took credit for some of these actions. When the government rounded up and charged the 19—including Ojeda Rios—with involvement in the Wells Fargo robbery, some of the individuals openly boasted that Los Macheteros had indeed masterminded it.

In proceedings leading up to the trial, nine defendants, including Ojeda Rios, were severed from the others because the government was appealing a ruling that threw out 50 reels of wiretap tapes crucial to their cases. Charges against three others were dismissed. That left seven defendants to face a trial. Two of these, however, would choose to plea bargain with the government before the case went to trial. Luz Berrios Berrios, wife of the leading defendant, Juan Segarra Palmer, pled guilty to sending several thousand of the stolen dollars to Hartford to buy toys for Puerto Rican children and was sentenced to five years. Paul S. Weinberg, a lawyer and college classmate of Segarra pled guilty to a misdemeanor for his connection with the transportation of the stolen money. He was sentenced to a year in prison. With these matters disposed of, the trial of the remaining five defendants proceeded.

Trial Focuses on Conspiracy

The trial began on September 6, 1988, in the federal courthouse in Hartford, Connecticut, with the selection of a jury. After several weeks, a jury of six women and six men had been drawn from Connecticut cities well removed from Hartford; even so, federal judge T. Emmett Claire announced that their names would not be made public to protect them from any possible threats or attacks. (The defense not unexpectedly objected to this and other security measures, claiming it prejudicially associated the defendants with violence.)

Finally on October 11, both sides made their opening statements. The government said it intended to prove that Gerena had been recruited by Los Macheteros to carry out the robbery so that the group could use the money to finance their activities, including acts of violence. Beyond that, the government said it would show that these particular individuals had to varying degrees actually aided in the planning of the robbery and the successful escape of Gerena and the transporting of the money. The defense, while admitting that some of them might be associated with Los Macheteros and even have been aware of aspects of the robbery, said they would show that their clients had no direct involvement in the robbery.

From the very first day of the trial, however, one of the defendants, Juan Segarra Palmer, emerged as the major player in this drama. He was thirty-eight years old, from a Puerto Rican family with a history of resistance to both Spanish and U.S. authorities, a Harvard graduate, and with a longtime and extensive commitment to leftist social and political causes. Segarra admitted freely that Gerena had discussed with him his intention to carry out the robbery and then had turned over most of the $7.1 million to him in Mexico City.

In fact, Segarra seemed almost to welcome the spotlight cast on him by the trial. He seemed anxious to promote the revolutionary goals of Los Macheteros (although it was soon revealed that he no longer belonged to the group— allegedly he was dismissed for being overly independent). Before the trial began, he had announced: "I don't recognize the legitimacy of the court or the whole proceeding. All I am guilty of is opposition to colonialism, which is a crime against humanity, like apartheid."

In the early weeks of the trial, when the government produced tapes of telephone calls between him and Gerena and members of Los Macheteros charged with being involved in the robbery, Segarra always had explanations that attempted to exonerate himself from direct involvement.

The most damaging witness, however, was Anne L. Gassin, also a Harvard graduate and Segarra's onetime girlfriend from his days of lying low in Cambridge after the robbery. She claimed that Segarra had not only hidden the stolen money in Massachusetts for over a year after the robbery, but that he had supervised Camacho, one of the other defendants, in the job of making secret compartments in a motor home so that the money could be taken to Mexico. She also freely admitted to having helped "launder" some of the money in Boston-area banks.

Her most surprising testimony, however, was that Segarra had shown her a 60-page manuscript that he had written, setting forth some of the exact details of the robbery. She said that Segarra claimed it was going to be used as the basis for a film about the robbery. Segarra's attorney tried to shake her testimony:

> Weinglass: You are putting together a screenplay and your discussion and you can't pull them apart.
>
> Gassin: It's not mixed in together. I know what I read and I know what he told me.

The defense never mounted much of a case except to reiterate that there was little or no hard evidence linking any of the defendants to the robbery itself. Even the government's witness, a man who had allegedly sold Segarra the motorcycle that Gerena had then allegedly used to flee from Hartford into Massachusetts, could not pick Segarra out in the courtroom. As a result, after six months of trial (seven including jury selection), the jury returned on April 10, 1989, with a mixed bag of verdicts that allowed both sides to claim victory. Only Segarra was found guilty of the serious charge of planning the robbery; he, Maldonado and Ramirez were found guilty of conspiracy; and he and Camacho were found guilty of helping to transport the money.

Mystery and Controversy Linger On

The robber who was at the heart of this whole case had all but been lost sight of in the course of the trial. The government, even after five years, still had little definite knowledge of just how Gerena came to be involved with Los Macheteros, or how he got away with the money, or where he was. All that would come out many years later: how he had been recruited by Segarra through mutual contacts in the Hartford Puerto Rican community—probably because Gerena's mother was politically active; how soon after the robbery Gerena had been smuggled across the border into Mexico (with about $2 million) in the same motor home later used to get the rest of the money into Mexico; and how Gerena flew from Mexico to Cuba, where he almost certainly remained ever since.

There are numerous claims as to what happened to the $7.1 million. The usual story is that at least $2 million was taken by Gerena to Cuba; Ojeda Rios, founder of Los Macheteros denies that. In fact, the U.S. government claims it has records proving that much of the money was dispensed to various individuals in New England and Puerto Rico. It would also come out later that Cuban agents had given Segarra and the Los Macheteros some $50,000 to support the robbery. Even more unsettling, it was revealed that the U.S. government knew from early on that Cuba had been supporting, even directing, the violent activities of Los Macheteros and other Puerto Rican radical groups but chose not to bring that into the trial.

And in what aroused considerable controversy at the time, in August 2000 President William Clinton issued executive clemency to 16 Puerto Rican radicals involved in various actions on behalf of the Puerto Rican independence movement. Among them were Segarra and Camacho, who had their sentences reduced (although Segarra would have to serve five more years), and Maldonado and Ramirez, who had their outstanding fines forgiven. Because the clemency was conditional on renouncing all further activities and associations with *independistas*, Camacho declined. Meanwhile, the world was still awaiting the final chapter of the Wells Fargo robbery—the fate of Victor Gerena.

—*John S. Bowman*

Suggestions for Further Reading

Fernandez, Ronald. *Los Macheteros: The Wells Fargo Robbery and the Violent Struggle for Puerto Rican Independence*. New York: Prentice Hall, 1987.

Hartford Couran. October 11, 12, 13, 14, 25, 26, 29, 1988; December 1, 2, 3, 1988; January 11, 12, 13, 1989; February 1, 3, 4, 1989; March 28, 29, 30, 1989; April 11, 12, 1989; June 16, 1989.

Joel Steinberg Trial: 1988–89

Defendant: Joel Steinberg   **Crime Charged:** Murder
Chief Defense Lawyers: Ira London and Adrian DiLuzio
Chief Prosecutors: Peter Casolaro and John McCusker   **Judge:** Harold Rothwax   **Place:** New York, New York   **Dates of Trial:** October 25, 1988–January 30, 1989   **Verdict:** Guilty, First degree manslaughter
Sentence: 8½–25 years

SIGNIFICANCE

New York's first-ever televised murder trial held the interest of the nation with its account of chronic child abuse and obsessive love. Initial audience anger and frustration with an adoption system that could allow such a thing to happen soon coalesced into bewilderment over why a seemingly intelligent and upscale couple would resort to such atrocities.

For 12 years criminal lawyer Joel Steinberg and Hedda Nussbaum, a former editor and writer of children's books, shared a one-bedroom apartment in New York City's Greenwich Village. Theirs was a brutal relationship, fueled by cocaine and sado-masochistic sex. Violent beatings often sent Nussbaum to the hospital, but she always returned to the man she loved and their filthy apartment. One observer would later describe it as "a cave." Inexplicably, they sought to introduce children into this nightmare, but they were unable to have children themselves. Steinberg used his knowledge of legal loopholes to "adopt" two babies without filing the necessary paperwork. These loopholes cost one little girl her life.

At 6:35 A.M. on Monday, November 2, 1987, a 911 call from Nussbaum brought paramedics to the apartment. They found 6-year-old Lisa naked and emaciated, unable to breathe, covered with bruises. Steinberg, 47, his knuckles scratched and raw, told the paramedics that she had choked on some food and lapsed into a coma, and he had attempted to revive her with a combination of cardiopulmonary resuscitation and the Heimlich maneuver. Nussbaum, 46, watching from the bedroom, said nothing. Investigators later found the couple's other child, Mitchell, 16 months old, tethered to a makeshift playpen with a rope. He too showed obvious signs of neglect.

The full extent of Lisa's maltreatment became apparent at the hospital. Hardly an inch of her 43-pound-body was unmarked. Guided by the varying discoloration, doctors were able to plot a long pattern of abuse. The examination resulted in Steinberg and Nussbaum being charged with attempted murder. On November 5, when it became clear that Lisa would never recover from the coma, her life-support system was removed. The couple now faced murder charges.

In building their case, prosecutors realized that to secure a conviction against Joel Steinberg, they needed Hedda Nussbaum's testimony. Reluctantly they agreed to drop all charges against her if she would cooperate with their inquiries. She readily agreed.

Joel Steinberg conferring with his attorneys. Steinberg was convicted of murdering 6-year-old Lisa Steinberg whom he had illegally adopted. (AP/Wide World Photos)

A Deadly Relationship

The trial opened October 25, 1988, before Judge Harold Rothwax. In what promised to be an emotional hearing, a cool head on the bench was essential, and Judge Rothwax had a reputation as a jurist of unflappable demeanor. He presided over a courtroom packed with spectators and members of the media. In his opening address, Assistant District Attorney Peter Casolaro made it clear that he would be picking apart the relationship between Steinberg and Nussbaum piece by piece. By this means he hoped to convince the jury of Steinberg's guilt. But first there was the medical evidence.

Dr. Douglas Miller, a New York pathologist, told the court that Lisa had died from a brain hemorrhage caused by a blow to her right temple. He also described two other severe blows. All three, in his opinion, were administered by a large, strong person. Every eye in court fell on the powerfully built Steinberg. He remained impassive. A videotape of Nussbaum, filmed by police on the night of her arrest, showed a battered, frail woman, barely able to walk, let alone capable of beating anyone to death.

Other witnesses testified to the tragedy and traumas of Lisa's brief life, but only Hedda Nussbaum could provide the evidence that would convict Joel Steinberg. When she took the stand, the problem, as prosecutors saw it, was to build her credibility with the jury. For her testimony to be believed, she had to be presented as yet another of Steinberg's victims. Casolaro started off slowly, asking Nussbaum to describe her feelings towards her former lover.

"I thought he was probably the most wonderful man I'd ever met."

"What qualities was it that attracted you to him, Miss Nussbaum?"

"Well, he seemed to be extremely intelligent and bright, and I loved to hear him talk for hours."

Cocaine Rage

But any admiration that she felt for Steinberg soon faded. She catalogued their mutual involvement with cocaine and the fury that it provoked in him. Without any provocation he would pound her unmercifully with his fists. Five times between 1983 and 1985, she fled the house. Casolaro, anticipating the defense, asked why on each occasion she had not taken Lisa with her. Nussbaum's answer was most illuminating. "I thought she would be better off with Joel's care . . . . I thought that he had tremendous insight and ability to handle people, including children, and he was very sensitive, and that I had those problems and obviously caused problems in the house." With these few words, Hedda went to the core of what came to be known as the "Nussbaum Defense," an attempt to show the world a woman whose self-esteem had been so undermined by Steinberg as to make her feel worthless and, by extension, not wholly responsible for her actions.

In her flat voice, Nussbaum described the deadly argument. It began, like nearly all the others, over something inconsequential. Steinberg became incensed because she and Lisa had not drunk any water. From such trivia he routinely manufactured rages that would last for hours. On this occasion he insisted that they both eat slices of hot pepper, then forced them to drink several glasses of water. Later, Nussbaum was in the bathroom. "The next thing was that Joel came into the bathroom carrying Lisa in his arms." She had been beaten senseless. For an hour, Nussbaum said, she and Steinberg attempted to revive Lisa, then Steinberg left to attend a business meeting. When he returned later that night, Lisa was still unconscious. The couple used cocaine and went to bed. At six o'clock the next morning Nussbaum woke Steinberg with the news that Lisa wasn't breathing. Minutes later she dialed 911.

It took no great effort for the prosecutors to depict Steinberg as a villain, but in attempting to portray Hedda Nussbaum as a hapless and helpless victim of abuse, they had fallen short of their goal. Now it was up to defense counsel Ira London to demonstrate that this particular tragedy had more than one villain.

He began by delving into Nussbaum's background. "Do you consider yourself to have had an unhappy upbringing?"

"Not especially."

"Do you consider it to have been uneventful?"

". . . I think it was average."

Unable to make much headway with this line of questioning, London turned to an incident in 1981, when Steinberg had beaten Nussbaum so badly that her spleen had to he surgically removed. The next day, Steinberg showed up at the hospital. Nussbaum admitted that she was pleased to see him. "I was feeling very connected to him, not like he was someone who had hurt me."

London pounced. "Are you familiar with the term masochist?"

Nussbaum acknowledged that she was. London also drew from her an admission that she should have done more to help Lisa on the night of her final beating. When Nussbaum dissolved into tears, London asked who the tears were for. "Hedda," she answered, then added as an afterthought, "and Lisa."

Because Joel Steinberg chose not to testify, we only have Hedda Nussbaum's version of what happened on the night that Lisa was beaten. All Ira London could offer by way of defense was an attempt to prove that it was Nussbaum who had caused Lisa's death, not Steinberg. After 12 weeks of testimony, the jury convicted Steinberg of first degree manslaughter. Steinberg did speak at his sentencing on March 24, 1988, a rambling and incoherent address that did nothing to affect the outcome. Judge Harold Rothwax imposed a prison term of 8½-25 years.

In the wake of this case, New York State passed new legislation in 1988. Called the "Lisa Law," it was designed to seal some of the glaring loopholes in laws affecting private adoptions.

Enormous publicity surrounded the trial of Joel Steinberg. For many people, it was their first indication that child abuse knows no financial boundaries, has nothing to do with social status or income, and can prosper anywhere.

—Colin Evans

Suggestions for Further Reading.

Brownmiller, Susan. "Madly In Love." *Ms.* (April 1989): 56ff.

Johnson, Joyce. *What Lisa Knew*. New York: G.P. Putnam's Sons, 1990.

Volk, Patricia. "The Steinberg Trial." *New York Times Magazine* (January 15, 1989): 22ff.

Wulfhorst, E. and B. Goldberg. "The Steinberg File." *New York* (April 17, 1989): 42ff.

Oliver North Trial: 1989

Defendant: Oliver Laurence North   **Crimes Charged:** Obstruction of justice, corruption, and perjury   **Chief Defense Lawyers:** Barry Simon and Brendan V. Sullivan, Jr.   **Chief Prosecutors:** Michael Bromwich, John Keker, and David Zornow   **Judge:** Gerhard Gesell   **Place:** Washington, D.C. **Dates of Trial:** January 31–May 4, 1989   **Verdict:** Guilty, 3 counts; Not guilty, 9 counts   **Sentence:** $150,000 fine, 2 years probation, 1,200 hours of community service

SIGNIFICANCE

"I was only following orders" has been an excuse of soldiers facing disciplinary action since time immemorial. But the trial of Colonel Oliver North added a new dimension, as a nation wondered, "just who did issue those orders?"

In 1985 the administration of President Ronald Reagan embarked on a plan to secure the release of American hostages by illegally selling arms to Iran. Funds from those sales were channeled to the Contra guerrillas in Nicaragua who were attempting to overthrow that country's leftist government. When news of this deal broke in 1986, a Congressional hearing followed. Under promise of immunity, Oliver North, a Marine Corps lieutenant colonel and member of President Reagan's National Security Council (NSC), provided an account of the U.S. government's role. North's emotional performance captured the public imagination but left doubts about his veracity. A grand jury later charged him with having lied to Congress, obstructed justice, and received kickbacks.

Jury selection and other legal gyrations delayed opening arguments until February 21, 1988. Chief Prosecutor John Keker laid out the government's case, alleging that North had shredded documents and altered computer records, knowing them to be vital to the Iran-Contra investigation, before visiting U.S. Attorney General Edwin Meese III. There, he "met with the attorney general and some of his top assistants, and when they asked him questions about something very important to know, he lied. . . . The evidence in this case is going to show that these were crimes, and the reason for these crimes was that Colonel North was covering up crimes he had already committed."

Defender Brendan Sullivan's response was simple and direct. His client "never broke the law. He acted within the law at all times. He followed the instructions of the highest ranking officials of the United States of America. He protected the secrets that he was ordered to protect, to save the lives of many people, many sources, many relationships. That's what he was ordered to do, and he followed his orders as any Marine Corps officer and any officer that worked at the National Security Council [would do]." Sullivan painted a stirring portrait of North as a Vietnam war hero, whose personal valor under fire had led to the heady promotions that came his way.

Unhelpful Witnesses

The biggest problem facing prosecutors was that most of their witnesses were unswerving admirers of North, with testimony couched in such a way as to impart the facts without leaving any doubts as to which side they were really on. Contra leader Adolfo Calero was typical. "He [North] became sort of a savior. . . . The Nicaraguan people have a tremendous appreciation of this man. So much so . . . that they're going to erect a monument for him once we free Nicaragua." Rarely has a prosecution witness been more accommodating to the defense.

Former NSC advisor Robert McFarlane—North's immediate superior— took the stand, already having pleaded guilty to four separate charges of withholding information from Congress. Reluctant and evasive, McFarlane had a knack for framing his answers in language and syntax so arcane as to render them

National Security briefing in the Oval Office with Oliver North at rear. (Courtesy, Ronald Reagan Library)

incomprehensible. One of his few unambiguous responses came when Keker asked, "Do you ever recall hearing the president of the United States, Ronald Reagan, instruct you or anyone else in your presence to lie to . . . Congress?"

"No," McFarlane replied.

"About anything?"

"No."

Probably the witness more eagerly anticipated than any other was Fawn Hall, North's former secretary. A media favorite, she told of deliberately shredding papers at North's request and also smuggling documents from his office. "I . . . placed them inside the back of my skirt so they were secured there." Those reporters present hoping for elaboration on this last tantalizing tidbit were disappointed; Hall, yet another witness clearly under North's spell, said nothing further to harm him.

When North testified, he did so with the same confidence that had served him so well at the congressional hearing. The first part of his testimony comprised a condensed version of the $25,000-a-night speech that he had been making lately to boost coffers for his defense fund. In a brief geopolitical slide show, North sketched a picture of the United States under assault at every border. He explained how only the efforts of himself and other like-minded Cold War knights kept the Western world safe from communism. Asked by Sullivan how he regarded his position, the defendant replied in the tremulous voice that had become his trademark, "I felt like a pawn in a chess game being played by giants."

Missing Funds

The prosecution, determined to keep the jury's attention on the charges and not allow them to be swayed by appeals to their emotions, began by probing North about $300,000 in travelers checks, which had passed through his hands. "Where would you keep careful track of it, in what kind of book?" asked Keker.

"In a ledger."

"Is that ledger still around?"

"No, . . . it was destroyed."

"Do you know who destroyed it?"

"Yes."

"Who?"

"I did," North grudgingly admitted.

Equally suspicious was the source of $15,000 in cash which North kept at his home. He insisted that it came from his pocket change, dutifully deposited in a metal box every Friday evening over the course of 20 years.

Keker was incredulous. "The change in your pocket grew to $15,000?"

"Yes."

In building their case, prosecutors had compiled a large dossier on North, detailing his occasional economies with the truth. That groundwork paid off. Over four days of cross-examination, Keker repeatedly trapped the defendant in an endless succession of contradictions and deceit, especially on matters of money. When North left the stand, the aura of selfless patriot had been replaced by one of artful dissembler.

In the wake of this mauling, Sullivan did a masterful job of damage control. He returned to and expanded on the theme of North as victim: "I draw the conclusion that the president was using Ollie North as a scapegoat" Sullivan concluded on a biblical note, " 'Greater love hath no man than he be willing to lay down his life for another.' That's Ollie North, that's the kind of man he is."

Now it was up to the jury. They retired on April 20. Twelve days of deliberation produced not guilty verdicts on every count save three. It was a long way from the clear message that the prosecutors wanted to send. Their disappointment only hardened when Judge Gerhard Gesell imposed sentence: $150,000 fine, two years probation, and 1,200 hours of community service. At the very least, the prosecution had been expecting some jail time. North supporters rushed to pay the fine but it was all academic. On July 20, 1990, the U.S. Court of Appeals, citing that evidence used against North had been obtained under immunity, overturned the convictions, wiping the stigma of "felon' from his name.

North has since made a career both as host to and frequent guest on political talk shows. In 1994, he ran as the Republican candidate for senator from Virginia but lost to incumbent Democratic senator, Charles Robb. Despite this loss, North has hinted that he may run for public office sometime in the future.

Hero or villain? Oliver North's astonishing charisma and a carelessly enacted immunity provision pulled him through. Whether that makes his actions excusable is still open to debate.

—Colin Evans

Suggestions for Further Reading

Bradlee, Ben, Jr. *Guts and Glory*. New York: D.I. Fine, 1988.

Meyer, Peter. *Defiant Patriot*. New York: St. Martin's Press, 1987.

North, Oliver L. and William Novak. *Under Fire*. New York: HarperCollins, 1991.

Toobin, Jeffrey. *Opening Arguments*. New York: Viking Press, 1991.

Ohio 7 Sedition Trial: 1989

Defendants: Patricia Gros Levasseur, Raymond Luc Levasseur, Richard C. Williams **Crimes Charged:** Seditious conspiracy to overthrow the government; racketeering; conspiracy to engage in racketeering
Chief Defense Lawyers: Peter Avenia, Robert Boyle, Elizabeth Fink, Kenneth J. King, William Newman **Chief Prosecutors:** David Douglass, Michael K. Loucks
Judge: William G. Young **Place:** Springfield, Massachusetts
Date of Trial: April 21, 1988–November 29, 1989 **Verdict:** All three acquitted of charge of seditious conspiracy; Patricia Levasseur also acquitted of racketeering; mistrial declared for racketeering for Raymond Levasseur and Richard Williams; mistrial declared for all three for conspiracy to engage in racketeering

SIGNIFICANCE

In what was up to that time the longest and most expensive trial in the history of Massachusetts, the federal government chose to try three individuals on what many observers regarded as problematic charges. And in fact, two of the three were already serving long sentences for the basic crimes behind these charges, while the third defendant was merely the wife of one of the others. When the trial ended with no convictions, it also turned out to be one of the most controversial— and highly criticized—trials in the history of Massachusetts.

Of the several underground-activist groups associated with the radicalization of various young Americans in the 1970s—such as the Symbionese Liberation Army and the Weathermen—one of the less publicized was the United Freedom Front (UFF), also referred to as the Sam Melville-Jonathan Jackson Brigade (SMJJ). Operating in the Northeast, led by Raymond Luc Levasseur and composed of a small circle of mainly working-class men and women, its announced targets were American corporations that continued to do business with South Africa, the American government's support for Latin American rightist dictatorships, and anyone it perceived as associated with racism and economic injustice in America.

The Underlying Crimes

During the late 1970s and early 1980s, the UFF was alleged to have conducted a number of bank robberies and bombings in New England and New

York. In one of the latter, a bombing of the Suffolk County Courthouse in Boston, Massachusetts, 22 people were injured, the most serious of whom had to have his leg amputated below the knee. The members eluded authorities until five of them were arrested in Cleveland, Ohio, in November 1984; two more were arrested in Norfolk, Virginia, in 1985. In April 1986, a Brooklyn, New York jury found six of the seven guilty of various bombings and they were sentenced to terms ranging from 15 years to life. The seventh, Patricia Gros Levasseur, was found guilty of the charge of harboring a fugitive—the group's leader, Raymond Luc Levasseur, her husband and father of their three children. In separate trials, one of the members, Thomas M. Manning, was also found guilty of murdering a New Jersey state policeman, while another, Jaan Karl Laaman, was convicted of armed assault in a shootout with a Massachusetts state trooper.

Raising the Stakes

By 1986, all seven individuals were behind bars when the U.S. government decided to indict them on the charges of seditious conspiracy to overthrow the government and also to have engaged in "racketeering." The first charge was based on a law from the Civil War era, designed specifically to round up Confederate loyalists in the North. The second charge was based on the so-called Racketeer Influenced and Corrupt Organizations statute, better known as the RICO statute and drawn up to deal with organized crime. It's not clear why the U.S. government chose to move ahead with this case, considering that the major defendants were already serving long sentences for the actions behind the alleged conspiracy and racketeering. The government appears to have been motivated essentially by the desire to send a warning signal to anyone who might consider underground violence on behalf of such causes.

Although the group would become known as the Ohio 7 because of where five had been arrested, the trial was scheduled to be held in Boston because of the Suffolk County Courthouse bombing. But because of extensive pretrial publicity in Boston, and the realization that security arrangements would greatly disrupt the federal court building there, the trial was relocated 100 miles to the west, to Springfield. Elaborate and expensive security arrangements were put into place there, including the preparations for a new courtroom.

Before the jury selection began in April 1988, the government decided to drop the charges against two defendants, Thomas Manning and Jaan Karl Laaman. Manning was already serving a life sentence without parole and Laaman was serving at least 40 years for their earlier convictions. The government admitted this would help to "simplify" what promised to be a very long trial. The government also decided to hold a separate trial for Barbara Curzi Laaman when a federal court ruled that the evidence seized in the raid of her home was illegal. Then Carol Manning, wife of Thomas, accepted a plea bargain that added a fine to the 15 years she was already serving. In March 1988, Patricia Levasseur was released on parole, having completed 3 and one-half years in prison, but she now faced as many as 60 years along with her codefendants, Raymond Luc Levasseur and Richard Williams.

The Long Road to the Verdicts Begins

The jury selection process began on April 21, 1988, but because of the reluctance of so many people to get involved in what promised to be such a lengthy trial and various other delays, it was not until January 10, 1989, that the trial proper began. Raymond Levasseur, recognized as the leader, chose to represent himself in court, and from the outset freely admitted that he was a revolutionary while denying that he was a criminal or racketeer. Williams's defense was based on essentially the same position although he did not choose to adopt such a defiantly revolutionary stance. But Patricia Levasseur's defense was to be quite different. One of her attorneys, William Newman, in his opening statement, said:

> Proof will not be shown that she ever robbed a bank, cased a bank or drove a getaway care. It did not happen. She wasn't a bomber, a bank robber, or an attempted murderer.

Rather, said Newman, whatever she did was simply out of dedication to her family:

> She did everything you'd expect from a caring mother. She enrolled her children in school, took them to doctors' appointments . . . baked cookies for PTA meetings . . . grew a garden.

Newman also attacked the government's use of charged terms such as "underground," "safe house," and "cell" designed to prejudice the jury:

> Underground? She only joined her husband to be away from the eyes and ears of the government. She didn't live in a safe house. She lived in a home. It wasn't a cell. It was a marriage.

The government called witness after witness—eventually adding up to almost 200—and introduced some 1,700 pieces of evidence. But much of the evidence and testimony was less than convincing. A teller from a bank in Maine that the government alleged had been robbed by members of the UFF, for instance, could only testify that a ski-masked robber had stuck a revolver in her ribs; she could not identify any of the three defendants on trial.

Among the major pieces of evidence were several notebooks in which were recorded the group's concerns and plans; Patricia Levasseur's lawyer, Elizabeth Fink, used a novel argument in her summation to the jury, claiming that at least her client—with three young children underfoot—could not be implicated with this:

> Many of you on the jury know what it is like to raise children and you will understand that the women of this group were the primary caregivers. The children would have fought and needed feeding, and diaper changes, and they would have cried. . . . There would have been a lot of preoccupation with children in this sort of group. Yet none of this is reflected in the notebooks.

In the end, Raymond Levasseur, in summing up his own case for the jury, tried to justify the actions of his "brigade" by a historical analogy:

> Martin Luther King said there is nothing wrong with a traffic light that says you have to stop for a red light. But when a fire is raging, the fire truck goes

right through the red light. He added that people all over the world are bleeding to death from deep social and economic wounds. They need brigades of ambulance drivers who will have to ignore the red lights of the present system.

Expensive Acquittals and Mistrials

Although there was evidence to connect the two men with at least some of the bombings and robberies, it was difficult to prove that these actions added up to "racketeering" as defined by the statute, let alone a consistent plot to overthrow the government. And that is evidently how the jurors saw things. After 18 days of deliberation, they came in with a unanimous verdict to acquit all three on the charge of seditious conspiracy. They also acquitted Patricia Levasseur on the charge of racketeering, but they said they could not agree on that charge for the two men or with the conspiracy to engage in racketeering for the three of them. The judge asked them to go back into session and try to come to some decision. Instead, after another day and a half of deliberation, the jury came back and reported they were "hopelessly deadlocked." The judge thus declared a mistrial on the racketeering charges, and in January 1990, the government announced it would not ask for a new trial. The Springfield trial, including jury selection, had run for over 19 months and—including all associated investigative, legal, and security fees—had cost the government by some estimates as much as $60 million.

—*John S. Bowman*

Suggestions for Further Reading

Boston Globe September 1, 1988; January 9, 1989; March 26, 1989; April 26, 1989; November 5, 26, 28, 30 1989.

Churchill, Ward, and Jim Vander Wall. *The COINTELPRO Papers*. Boston: South Bend Press, 1990.

Hartford Courant (January 12, 1989).

Texas v. Johnson: 1989

Appellant: State of Texas   **Defendant:** Gregory Lee Johnson
Appellant Claim: That the Texas statute against "desecration of venerated objects," in this instance burning an American flag, did not violate Gregory Lee Johnson's constitutional rights   **Chief Defense Lawyer:** William M. Kunstler   **Chief Lawyer for Appellant:** Kathi Alyce Drew   **Justices:** Harry A. Blackmun, William J. Brennan, Jr., Anthony M. Kennedy, Thurgood Marshall, Sandra Day O'Connor, William H. Rehnquist, Antonin Scalia, John Paul Stevens, and Byron R. White   **Place:** Washington, D.C.
Date of Decision: June 21, 1989   **Decision:** Texas statute declared unconstitutional

SIGNIFICANCE

No matter how unpopular it is to burn an American flag, the First Amendment protects that act and other forms of political expression.

Gregory Lee Johnson, nicknamed "Joey," was a fervent supporter of an American communist movement known as the Revolutionary Communist Youth Brigade. When the Republican National Convention met in Dallas, Texas in 1984, Johnson decided to participate in a political demonstration called the "Republican War Chest Tour." The demonstration's purpose was to protest the policies of the Reagan Administration.

On August 22, 1984, Johnson, amidst a crowd of approximately 100 other demonstrators, unfurled an American flag. He splashed it with kerosene and set it on fire, while the other demonstrators chanted. "America, the red, white, and blue, we spit on you." After the flag burned, the demonstrators left, and one of the many shocked onlookers gathered the burnt remains for burial in his back-yard. No one was hurt, and no property other than the flag was destroyed. Both the press and the police were at the scene of the flag burning, and when police reinforcements arrived shortly thereafter they arrested Johnson.

Johnson was prosecuted under a Texas law that made it illegal to "intentionally or knowingly desecrate . . . a state or national flag." Johnson was convicted in Dallas County Criminal Court No. 8 of desecration of a venerated object and sentenced to a year in prison and a $2,000 fine. The prosecutor blatantly asked the jury to convict Johnson for the political symbolism expressed by the flag-burning incident:

> And you know that he's also creating a lot of danger for a lot of people by what he does and the way he thinks.

The Court of Appeals of Dallas, Texas, affirmed Johnson's conviction on January 23, 1986. On April 20, 1988, the Texas Court of Criminal Appeals reversed the court of appeals and the trial court, and threw out Johnson's conviction. The court of criminal appeals rejected the state's argument that the antiflag-burning statute was a valid measure to preserve a symbol of national unity:

> Recognizing that the right to differ is the centerpiece of our First Amendment freedoms, a government cannot mandate by fiat a feeling of unity in its citizens.

The state of Texas appealed to the U.S. Supreme Court. Johnson's attorney was William M. Kunstler, and the state's attorney was Kathi Alyce Drew. The parties argued their case before the Supreme Court on March 21, 1989.

Justice William J. Brennan authored the decision for the majority of the court, which was issued on June 21, 1989. By a 6–3 vote the justices upheld the Texas Court of Criminal Appeals decision, stating that:

> The way to preserve the flag's special role is not to punish those who feel differently about these matters. It is to persuade them that they are wrong. . . . We can imagine no more appropriate response to burning a flag than waving one's own, no better way to counter a flag-burner's message than by saluting the flag that burns, no surer means of preserving the dignity even of the flag that burned than by, as one witness here did, according its remains a respectful burial. We do not consecrate the flag by punishing its desecration, for in doing so we dilute the freedom that this cherished emblem represents.

The Supreme Court's decision sparked a vigorous but brief political uproar, culminating in President George Bush proposing an antiflag-burning Constitutional amendment, which quietly died. The lasting legacy of the Johnson case was to demonstrate that the First Amendment's protection of forms of political expression, extends even to those as unpopular and provocative as burning the national flag.

—Stephen G. Christianson

Suggestions for Further Reading

"The Flag Again." *The Progressive* (February 1989): 8.

Goldstein, Robert Justin. *Flag Burning and Free Speech: the Case of Texas v. Johnson.* University of Kansas Press, 2000.

Grogan, David. "Unimpressed by the Freedom to Burn Old Glory Joey Johnson Still Wants a Revolution." *People* (July 10, 1989): 98–100.

Jacoby, Tamar. "A Fight for Old Glory." *Newsweek* (July 3, 1989): 18–20.

Simpson, Glenn. "Decision Unravels Flag's Very Fabric." *Insight* (July 24, 1989): 8–13.

"Waiving the Flag." *The New Republic* (January 23, 1989): 7–8.

U.S. v. Helmsley: 1989

Defendant: Leona Helmsley   **Crimes Charged:** 47 criminal offenses concerning conspiracy, tax evasion, filing false tax returns, mail fraud, and extortion   **Chief Defense Lawyer:** Gerald A. Feffer
Chief Prosecutors: James R. DeVita and Rudolph Giuliani   **Judge:** John M. Walker   **Place:** New York, New York   **Dates of Trial:** June 26–August 30, 1989   **Verdict:** Guilty on 33 counts   **Sentence:** 4 years in prison and more than $7 million in fines

SIGNIFICANCE

The Leona Helmsley prosecution signaled a new determination by the government to prosecute brazen tax evaders, regardless of their wealth or power.

Leona Helmsley, whose full name is Leona Mindy Rosenthal Roberts Panzirer Lubin Helmsley, married into money. Her husband, Harry Brakmann Helmsley, had been in the real estate business for decades. By the 1980s, his collection of hotels, office buildings, and other properties stretched across more than a dozen states and was worth at least $5 billion.

In 1980, Harry brought Leona into his business activities. He built the massive Helmsley Palace hotel in Manhattan, which became the flagship of the Helmsley Hotels corporation, and handed it over to Leona to manage. Leona not only managed the hotel successfully, but in short order she became the president of Helmsley Hotels, overseeing all 26 of Harry's hotels. As a reward, in 1983, Harry bought Leona an estate called Dunnellen Hall in Greenwich, Connecticut. Dunnellen Hall contained an enormous mansion situated on 26 carefully landscaped acres. Harry gave Leona carte blanche to redecorate it as she saw fit, and that's when her troubles began.

Leona had expensive tastes. She spent millions having a marble dance floor and a custom-built swimming pool installed, on antiques and art for decoration, and on everything from gardening to her personal wardrobe to make Dunnellen Hall live up to her vision of a dream house. Although the cost of remaking Dunnellen Hall was less than one percent of the value of the Helmsleys' fortune, Leona paid the bills through the various Helmsley corporations so that they could be deducted as business expenses. To help cover her tracks, Leona forced suppliers to submit their invoices with phony work descriptions on them under the threat of losing all Helmsley business.

A regional newspaper, the *New York Post*, learned about some of Leona's dubious activities and published an article about her on December 2, 1986. Assistant U.S. Attorney James R. DeVita happened to read the article and promptly initiated an investigation. For the next 2–4 years, the federal prosecutors and their counterparts in the office of New York State Attorney General Robert Abrams pored over the Helmsleys' personal and business records, questioned their employees, and went to the various suppliers and contractors involved. The prosecution's efforts resulted in an indictment against Leona for 47 violations of federal law, relating to her evasion of more than $4 million in taxes from 1983 to 1986, as the result of illegally writing off the estate renovations as business expenses. Leona was even charged with extortion, for having forced suppliers to provide phony paperwork.

"We Don't Pay Taxes. Only the Little People Pay Taxes."

This notorious statement attributed to Leona may go down in history as one of the most ironic on record. For the Helmsleys did indeed pay taxes, and quite a lot of them: usually more than $50 million a year on the income from their vast holdings. Leona would go to jail and see her world shattered because she tried to cheat the government out of a fraction of that.

Leona's trial began June 26, 1989, in New York City before federal Judge John M. Walker. Her chief defense lawyer was Gerald A. Feffer, from the elite criminal defense firm of Williams and Connolly. The chief prosecutors were DeVita and Rudolph Giuliani. The evidence against Leona was overwhelming, and the public animosity toward her for her arrogant attitude on taxes was shared by the former contractors and Helmsley Hotels employees who testified against her. Feffer, who had once headed the criminal tax division of the U.S. Justice Department and was an expert on tax fraud cases, couldn't stem the avalanche. On August 30, 1989, the jury found Leona guilty on 33 of the charges against her.

All that remained was the sentencing. Leona begged the court for mercy:

> I'm guilty of a serious crime. I'm more humiliated and ashamed than anybody could imagine. I feel as though I have been living through a nightmare for three years.

Walker sentenced Leona to four years in prison and a fine of more than $7 million. In his sentencing order Walker made it clear that he found Leona's expression of remorse to be too little and too late given the severity of her crimes. Walker addressed his comments directly to Leona:

> You bear full responsibility for this scheme. It was carried out under your direct orders for your benefit. Unlike many defendants who come before the court, you were not driven to this crime by financial need. Rather, your conduct was the product of naked greed. Throughout its course you persisted in the arrogant belief that you were above the law. Moreover, since the indictment and the trial, you have displayed no remorse or contrition. I trust

that the sentence today will make it very clear that no person, no matter how wealthy or prominent, stands above the law.

Leona hadn't given up yet, however. Helmsley hired the famous criminal defense lawyer Alan M. Dershowitz to assist Feffer in the appeal and subsequent proceedings, such as motions for retrial. Dershowitz is well-known for his role in overturning the murder conviction of socialite Claus Von Bülow and has been involved in several cases concerning wealthy and prominent people. Dershowitz began an aggressive appeal, part of which included a personal attack on Judge Walker.

Leona Helmsley. (AP/ Wide World Photos)

In addition to being a highly respected judge, Walker is extremely well-connected politically. His first cousin is George Bush. Whether because of his abilities or connections, in September 1989, Walker was nominated by President Bush to an opening on the U.S. Court of Appeals for the Second Circuit, which includes New York. Moving from district court to circuit court is a significant career move upward for a federal judge. Dershowitz, however, publicly opposed Walker's nomination. Not only did Dershowitz criticize Walker in the press, but he even appeared at Walker's confirmation hearing on November 7, 1989, before the Senate Judiciary Committee. At that hearing, Dershowitz testified in opposition to Walker's appointment, to no avail.

On December 19, 1989, Walker was sworn in as a judge on the court of appeals. Walker continued to hear post-trial motions on the Helmsley case, however, because he also was still a district judge "by special designation" so that he could continue to preside over the case. On March 27, 1991, Walker denied Dershowitz's request that he disqualify himself and let another judge hear Dershowitz's various post-trial motions. Despite Dershowitz's vehement opposition to Walker's promotion, Walker claimed that he was not biased against Dershowitz. After countless appeals and legal maneuvering, Helmsley finally began her sentence on April 15, 1992—ironically, the day income taxes are due. She served 18 months in jail and was released in October 1993. Harry Helmsley died in 1997 and left his considerable fortune in real estate to Leona. Almost immediately, she began to sell off his real estate holdings.

Leona Helmsley's fall from wealth and arrogance was in many ways another signal that the excesses of the 1980s were over. No matter how rich and prominent you were, the government would prosecute you if you broke the law.

—Stephen G. Christianson

Suggestions for Further Reading

Green, Michelle. "Heartbreak Hotel." *People* (April 1992): 101–102.

Hammer, Richard. *The Helmsleys: the Rise and Fall of Harry and Leona.* New York: New American Library, 1990.

"Leona Helmsley and the Iniquitous 1980s." *Economist* (April 1992): A28.

Moss, Michael. *Palace Coup: the Inside Story of Harry and Leona Helmsley.* New York: Doubleday & Co., 1989.

Pierson, Ransdell. *The Queen of Mean: the Unauthorized Biography of Leona Helmsley.* New York: Bantam Books, 1989.

Jim Bakker Trial: 1989

Defendant: Jim Bakker   **Crime Charged:** Fraud and conspiracy
Chief Defense Lawyers: Harold Bender and George T. Davis
Chief Prosecutors: Jerry Miller and Deborah Smith   **Judge:** Robert D. Potter
Place: Charlotte, North Carolina   **Dates of Trial:** August 21–October 5, 1989
Verdict: Guilty   **Sentence:** 45 years imprisonment and $500,000 fine

SIGNIFICANCE

This trial marked the first prosecution of a television evangelist on charges of duping his followers.

For years Jim Bakker's *Praise The Lord (PTL)* ministry had been the most successful television program of its type. Following the exposure in 1987 of an affair with assistant Jessica Hahn, his financial empire began to crumble. An investigation into the workings of PTL led to 24 indictments charging that Bakker had defrauded the public of millions.

Between 1984 and 1987, PTL supporters paid $158 million to obtain "lifetime partnerships" in Bakker's Heritage USA theme park, Assistant U.S. Attorney Jerry Miller alleged when testimony began August 28, 1989. Miller explained how the $1,000 partnerships were supposed to entitle the contributor to three nights' lodging a year for life at Heritage USA. But with accommodations for just 25,000 vacationers, Bakker oversold an additional 43,000 memberships, diverting $3.7 million to his own personal use. According to Miller, Bakker used PTL to "cheat people out of their money . . . [with] a disdain for all those around him."

George Davis, defending, said that Bakker admitted the facts of the case but denied any wrongdoing. "He was," argued Davis, "a creative, religious genius."

When Bakker's former personal assistant David Taggart, himself previously convicted of fraud, took the stand, he cataloged Bakker's lavish lifestyle: condominiums, houses, mink coats, diamonds, two Rolls Royces, and a Mercedes, all paid for out of donations.

Further evidence of extravagance came from Steve Nelson, an ex-PTL vice president, who also spoke of warning Bakker about the overbooked vacation deals. "I told him that I thought we had some big-time problems. I specifically said, 'Someone could go to jail for this.' He told me not to worry, that there was always room at the inn." Seconds after giving his testimony, Nelson collapsed in court. At the behest of his lawyer, Bakker prayed gently at Nelson's side while paramedics administered treatment.

The next day it was Bakker's turn to require medical attention. He had been found beneath a desk in his lawyer's office, huddled in a fetal position, apparently hallucinating. "Please don't do this to me," he sobbed, as he was led away in shackles for psychiatric evaluation.

One week later Bakker was back in court to hear former aide Richard Dortch agree with prosecution contentions that the partnerships had been a classic "pyramid scheme." Dortch quoted Bakker as saying, "There's no limit to the amount of people we can offer them to, because I can control the crowds of people as they come."

Televangelists, Jim and Tammy Bakker. (AP/Wide World Photos)

Hurricane Interrupts Trial

No sooner had Bakker's defense gotten under way than Judge Robert Potter had to suspend the trial yet again, this time because Hurricane Hugo was imminent. When testimony resumed, Heritage contributor Sam Gassaway, an Atlanta land developer, denied expecting a guarantee of lodging. "I was a partner to help build something, . . . I did not expect title or anything of that nature."

Central to the defense argument was the contention that Bakker had never actually sold anything, that all of the monies he had received were donations, not purchases.

Bakker confirmed this when he testified. He started out in control, but the longer he remained on the stand the more his composure frayed. Prosecutor Deborah Smith lashed him for continuing to receive million-dollar bonuses, despite knowing that PTL was financially troubled.

"I said to them not to give me the bonuses many, many times," insisted Bakker.

"And then you cashed the checks and used them to buy houses many, many times," Smith replied icily.

Alluding to $600,000 in bonuses received over six weeks in 1986, Bakker reiterated the Heritage board credo: "We say that by faith, God will supply the need."

"How about truth?" Smith shot back. "Did you ever tell them the truth of what the financial situation was?"

His voice dropping to a whisper, Bakker went on to blame Jerry Falwell and other evangelists for the PTL debacle. "The real conspiracy to defraud came from the group of people who took over the ministry for their own gain."

In closing, Smith told the jurors, "What you have here is a pyramid on the brink of collapse, a house of cards ready to fall." She concluded by quoting Lord Tennyson: "A lie which is half a truth is ever the blackest of lies. Mr. Bakker is a world-class master of using half-truths."

Both defense attorneys made final addresses. George Davis, apparently pinning all his hopes on a mistrial, urged those jurors with doubts to hold out, "even if it's one versus eleven."

Fellow counsel Harold Bender adopted a more traditional tack. "He [Bakker] doesn't expect you to give him mercy. He doesn't expect mercy. But he does have the right to expect justice under the law."

On October 5, 1989, the jury returned a guilty verdict. Judge Robert Potter, as expected, came down hard. Saying, "Those of us who do have a religion are sick of being saps for money-grubbing preachers and priests," he jailed Bakker for 45 years and fined him $500,000.

Citing federal sentencing guidelines and Judge Potter's inappropriate mention of religion, an appeals court in February 1991 ordered a resentencing. On August 23, 1991, Judge George Mullen reduced Bakker's jail term to 18 years, making him eligible for parole in 1995. Mullen reduced Bakker's sentence again on December 22, 1992, to eight years, making him eligible for parole in 1993.

While Jim Bakker served his time, his wife Tammy Faye filed for divorce. The divorce became official in 1992. Jim Bakker was paroled in 1994, and at the time of his release said that he was not sure if he would ever return to preaching. In 1996, his book, *I Was Wrong*, was published telling his side of the PTL scandal.

Today, Jim Bakker is remarried and living in Los Angeles, California. He teaches Bible classes and preaches at the Los Angeles International Church. Bakker has recently said that he may some day consider a return to televangelism.

Those who expected Jim Bakker's trial to titillate and tantalize came away disappointed. There was hardly a mention of his affairs. Wisely, the prosecution concentrated on Bakker's greed and hubris. Measured against his indifference to those he bilked, any other diversions would have seemed irrelevant.

—Colin Evans and Ron Formica

Suggestions for Further Reading

Fitzgerald, Frances. "Jim And Tammy." *The New Yorker* (April 23, 1990): 45ff.

Martz, Larry and Ginny Carroll. *Ministry of Greed.* New York: Weidenfeld & Nicolson, 1988.

Richardson, Michael. *The Edge of Disaster.* New York: St. Martin's Press, 1987.

Shephard, Charles E. *Forgiven.* New York: Atlantic Monthly Press, 1989.

Pete Rose Trial: 1990

Defendant: Pete Rose **Crime Charged:** Filing false tax returns
Chief Defense Lawyers: Reuven Katz, Roger J. Makley, and Robert
Pitcairn, Jr. **Chief Prosecutors:** G. Michael Crites and William E. Hunt
Judge: S. Arthur Spiegel **Place:** Cincinnati, Ohio **Date of Trial:** April 20,
1990 **Verdict:** Guilty **Sentence:** 5 months' imprisonment, 3 months in a
community treatment center or halfway house, $50,000 fine, and 1,000 hours
of community service

SIGNIFICANCE

This case revealed how a spectacular career as a nationally admired, record-
breaking athlete can be ruined by an addiction to gambling. It also demonstrated
that even national heroes face prison when they stiffarm the Internal Revenue
Service.

On August 23, 1989, long-time Cincinnati Reds player-manager Pete Rose was banished forever from the game of baseball by Baseball Commissioner A. Bartlett Giamatti. Rose, who held the record for more career hits and games played than any other player in baseball history, admitted that he had bet on football and basketball games. His behavior, said the commissioner, had "stained" the game. The evidence before the commissioner led him and, almost immediately, the American public to the conclusion that Rose was a compulsive gambler.

Six months later, a federal grand jury was investigating whether Rose might owe taxes on income from cash he earned at baseball card and memorabilia shows. One newspaper quoted "sources" as saying that the beloved ballplayer had failed to report to the Internal Revenue Service at least $250,000 in income between 1985 and 1987. Witnesses were reported to have seen Rose take cash earned at baseball card shows—where he signed hundreds and hundreds of autographs at $8 each—and stuff it into suitcases and sacks. The implication was that Rose used the huge amounts of cash to support his costly gambling habit.

By mid-April, the news was confirmed. Pete Rose and his lawyers had worked out a plea bargain. He would plead guilty in U.S. District Court in Cincinnati to two felony counts of filing false federal income-tax returns. The bargain was that Rose would not be charged with failing to report income from gambling, despite the fact that one of his associates had been convicted only months earlier of conspiring to defraud the IRS by claiming one of the ballplayer's winning racetrack tickets as his own.

On April 21, Rose appeared before Judge S. Arthur Spiegel. Confirming charges that he had knowingly failed to reveal income of more than $300,000 in 1985 and 1987, he pleaded guilty to the two felony counts. The Statement of Facts, a court document signed by Rose and his attorneys, described him as a "chronic gambler during the years 1984 through 1988, betting substantial amounts of money at horse and dog racetracks, as well as with illegal bookmakers." Said Assistant U.S. Attorney William E. Hunt, who presented the government's case:

> Rose received $129,000 from an individual who purchased his "4,192' bat [the bat with which he broke Ty Cobb's record for career hits] by requesting and receiving [as partial payment] 11 checks for $9,000 and one check for $5,000. These checks were cashed at the bank on separate days in order to avoid the filing of currency transaction reports.

Even more was revealed in the courtroom. In 1987, Rose had filed amended tax returns for the years in question. But they were still false, for he failed to report $51,800 in 1984, $95,168 in 1985, $30,659 in 1986, and $171,552.60 in 1987.

Some Losses Greater than Winnings

Rose's diehard fans were astonished to learn still more. By entering into partnerships on Pick-6 horse-track bets on 10 occasions between 1984 and 1987, an activity that Rose had previously denied, he had won $136,945.30. But the irony was that, while gross income amounts as high as $59,788.40 (in 1984) were not reported, he was not liable for failure to report the figures because his losses were greater than his winnings.

In a jam-packed courtroom on July 19, Judge Spiegel handed down Rose's sentence:

> We must recognize that there are two people here: Pete Rose, the living legend, the all-time hit leader, and the idol of millions, and, Pete Rose, the individual who appears today convicted of two counts of cheating on his taxes. Today, we are not dealing with the legend. History and the tincture of time will decide his place among the all-time greats of baseball. With regard to Pete Rose, the individual, he has broken the law, admitted his guilt, and stands ready to pay the penalty.

The judge then sentenced Pete Rose to five months in a federal correctional institution, to be followed by three months in a community treatment center or halfway house. In addition, he would pay a $50,000 fine and serve 1,000 hours of community service.

Rose said he would not appeal. "I accept my punishment," he said. "I will serve my sentence, pay my debt to society, and get on with my life." The sentence did not permit any parole.

Rose served his five months at the Southern Illinois Prison Camp at Marion. His days were spent in the prison machine shop, where he earned 11 cents an hour fabricating and welding metal. "He gets in there and works just as hard as the rest of them," said the assistant warden.

When released January 7, 1991, Rose began his 1,000 hours of community service, working as an assistant in physical-education programs in five Cincinnati public schools and at recreational centers in the city's lower-income areas.

Pete Rose surrounded by reporters following his conviction for failing to report income on his tax returns. (AP/Wide World Photos)

On January 10, the board of directors of baseball's Hall of Fame voted unanimously that anyone on baseball's permanently ineligible list could not be eligible for the Hall of Fame. The rules change effectively barred Pete Rose, who would have become eligible for election into the hall by the Baseball Writers' Association of America the following December.

However, Rose's popularity with baseball fans gained momentum as the 1990s came to an close. In 1999, he was voted to the All-Century Team—a team of the greatest baseball players of the 20th century—by fans and baseball writers. Despite his ban from baseball, Commissioner Bud Selig allowed Rose to be a part of the ceremony honoring the team at the 1999 All-Star Game in Boston. When Rose was introduced, he received the loudest and longest ovation of any player honored.

Immediately following the ceremony, Rose was interviewed on live television by NBC's Jim Gray. Gray's seemingly antagonistic questions about

Rose's gambling problems upset many fans and players, prompting further sympathy from his fans for Rose's continuing quest to once again be part of Major League Baseball. However, at the start of the 2000 baseball season, that dream remained as elusive as ever.

—Bernard Ryan, Jr. and Ron Formica

Suggestions for Further Reading

Andrews, A.E. "Bittersweet Homecoming." *U.S. News & World Report* (January 14, 1991): 14.

Callahan, T. "Justice for a Baseball Felon." *U.S. News & World Report* (July 23, 1990): 15.

Corelli, R. "The Fall of a Titan." *Maclean's* (July 30, 1990): 38.

Goodman, M.S. "Pete Rose Longs to Rise Again." *People Weekly* (September 2, 1991): 47.

Leerhsen, C. "All is Not Lost in Cincinnati." *Newsweek* (July 30, 1990): 61–62.

Lieber, J. and S. Wulf. "Sad Ending for a Hero." *Sports Illustrated* (July 30, 1990): 22–25.

Reston, James, Jr. *Collision at Home Plate: The Lives of Pete Rose and Bart Giamatti.* New York: HarperCollins, 1991.

Rose, Pete, and Roger Kahn. *Pete Rose: My Story.* New York: Macmillan Co., 1989.

Bensonhurst Murder Trial: 1990

Defendants: Joseph Fama, Keith Mondello   **Crimes Charged:** Riot, unlawful imprisonment, discrimination, murder   **Chief Defense Lawyers:** Mondello: Stephen Murphy; Fama: David DePetris   **Chief Prosecutor:** Paul Burns   **Judge:** Thaddeus Owens   **Place:** Brooklyn, Kings County, New York   **Date of Trial:** May–June 11, 1990   **Verdicts:** Fama: guilty of murder in the second degree (manslaughter), guilty of riot; Mondello: not guilty of manslaughter; guilty of riot, menacing, and unlawful imprisonment   **Sentence:** Fama: 32 and one half years to life imprisonment; Mondello: 4 terms of 1 year 4 months to 4 years to run consecutively for riot in the first degree, with consecutive 90-day sentences for each of 3 counts of unlawful imprisonment. Sentence was later modified on appeal (March 1, 1993) to allow the sentences for unlawful imprisonment to run concurrently with the other sentences. Total sentence: 5 and one-third to 16 years. Note: John Vento found guilty of lesser charges and sentenced to 4 years; other defendants either acquitted or sentenced to community service were Joseph Serrano, Charles Stressler, James Patino, and Steven Curreri.

SIGNIFICANCE

This case brought national attention as a racially motivated "hate crime." The Reverend Al Sharpton led marches in protest against the killing and the justice system; and the case may have contributed to David Dinkins' victory in the New York City mayoral election over Edward Koch.

Yusuf Hawkins, 16 years old, was murdered on August 23, 1989, when he and several other black friends walked down the street in the Bensonhurst neighborhood of Brooklyn near the corner of 68th Street and 20th Avenue. The group was menaced by a largely white gang with baseball bats. At least one in the attacking gang, Russell Gibbons, was black. Hawkins died of two bullet wounds to the chest.

Racial Jealousy Leads to Murder

The killing of Yusuf Hawkins was a case of mistaken identity. Earlier that day, Gina Feliciano had taunted neighborhood boys that she was inviting black and Hispanic boyfriends to her 18th birthday party. Feliciano had a reputation for taking drugs, for numerous sexual liaisons, and for jealous conflicts with others in the Bensonhurst neighborhood. Hearing of her taunts, a group of youths ranging in age through their early 20s, mostly Italian-American, gathered at a nearby schoolyard and armed themselves with baseball bats and golf clubs. Meanwhile, Yusuf Hawkins, who lived in another New York neighborhood, accompanied three friends as one of them sought to follow up in the possible purchase of a used car that had been advertised for sale in the Bensonhurst neighborhood. Neither Hawkins nor any of his small group had ever heard of Feliciano or their assailants.

When the four boys arrived near the schoolyard, looking for the address of the owner of the used car, the gathering gang assumed they were Feliciano's friends, simply because they were black. The large group stalked and then halted and threatened Hawkins and the three others. Suddenly, one in the bat-wielding crowd pulled out a pistol and shot Hawkins twice. When the others realized a shot had been fired, they all dispersed. Police arrived to find Hawkins bleeding to death.

Police Quickly Arrest Suspects

The police immediately decided that the killing fell into the special category of bias crime, and worked quickly to round up suspects. The recognized leader of the group leading the assault was Keith Mondello, whose father was Italian and mother, a Jewish convert to Catholicism. Mondello was arrested late that night. However, as members of the local group were rounded up, several agreed that the Joey Fama, a hanger-on, had fired the gun. Fama himself disappeared for a few days as police mounted a search. They feared he might have fled to Italy. However, after hitchhiking north, he surrendered to authorities in upstate Oneonta. Others in the group were arrested and charged with complicity in the murder, although all agreed that one shooter had done the killing.

Racial Tensions Boil Over

The case immediately drew national news coverage for its racial overtones. It was clear that Hawkins had been assaulted and killed because he was a black youth. The Bensonhurst neighborhood in which the killing took place was largely Italian-American, and many assumed that the neighborhood itself was on trial. The reluctance of witnesses to testify or to identify all of the members of the gang that confronted Hawkins that night probably contributed to the sense of neighborhood solidarity along racial lines.

Hawkins' parents were incensed that the accused youths were released on bail, rather than held in jail. Furthermore, only a handful of those in the attacking group were ever identified, leaving most of the group free and at large in the community. The press charged that a collective "Bensonhurst amnesia" protected most of the gang.

Moses Stewart, the father of Hawkins, was a member of Louis Farrakhan's wing of the Nation of Islam. He approached Reverand Al Sharpton for assistance and advice. Sharpton helped arrange Hawkins' funeral and mounted several marches to the Bensonhurst neighborhood to protest the failure of the police to bring more of the perpetrators to justice. The demonstrations and marches were met by hostility from local white youths, who jeered at the marchers. A massive police presence prevented small episodes of anger from erupting into violence.

The killing took place during a hot summer, when many youths were on the street and racial tensions ran high. Furthermore, it was an election year in which incumbent white mayor Edward Koch was opposed in the Democratic primary election by David N. Dinkins. Dinkins' victory in the primary election in September 1989 has been partially attributed to the heightened political consciousness in the black community brought about by the Yusuf Hawkins case. Both mayoral candidates attended the funeral and both pleaded for calm. Reverend Jesse Jackson participated in the funeral, as did local black community leaders, contributing to the sense that the case had political overtones.

Media coverage often oversimplified the case, highlighting the racial aspects. Some reports suggested that Hawkins was gunned down simply because he was black in a white neighborhood; largely black crowds chanted, "No justice, no peace!" Even peaceful demonstrators were met by white youths holding up watermelons and shouting insults, episodes caught in newspaper photos and on television. Despite such publicity, it was an exaggeration to suggest that blacks could not walk peacefully through the streets of Bensonhurst, and elitist prejudice against working class Italian-Americans appeared behind many of the criticisms of the neighborhood.

However, the fact that crime against blacks, whether perpetrated by whites or by other African Americans, is rarely given much attention in the press had produced pent-up frustration with the American justice system that this case brought to the surface.

Controversial and Complicated Verdicts

The prosecution had difficulty in collecting evidence, since most of those involved in the case refused to testify against each other. Although urged to use a theory of a crime that all in the gang were "acting in concert," jurors only applied that theory to one of the defendants. Attorney Jacob Evseroff, who represented Charles Stressler, one member of the gang, commented that "nobody was ever shot with a baseball bat." That line of thinking appeared to impress two juries, which rejected the acting-in-concert argument for manslaughter against the other members of the gang.

Defense attorney Stephen Murphy argued that Keith Mondello was simply "a jerk" taunted into action by Gina Feliciano and should not be made a victim of racial politics and hysteria. Nevertheless, it was clear that Mondello had organized the group that marched out from the schoolyard to attack Yusuf Hawkins. Even the evidence against Fama was shaky. He had reportedly told two other prison inmates that he had fired the gun. One of the gang, Frankie Tighe, testified that he saw Fama fire the gun, but he later recanted his testimony.

Both the jury hearing Fama's case and the one hearing Mondello's case were racially mixed. The judge in both cases, Thaddeus Owens, was black. Each jury deliberated 11 days.

On May 17, 1990, Joey Fama's jury found him guilty of "depraved indifference" to human life, and therefore guilty of murder, since it had been proven that he was in the crowd that attacked Hawkins. Judge Owens had instructed the jury that if depraved indifference could be proven, a guilty verdict could be returned. Such a decision appeared to imply that all in the gang were guilty, even if only one had fired the shot. Furthermore, the jury did not have to believe, by this logic, that Fama had fired the gun. Members of the press and public assumed that this decision paved the way for the acting-in-concert theory to lead to a group of manslaughter convictions. The next day, a separate jury found the ringleader of the gang, Keith Mondello, guilty of riot, menacing, discrimination, and possession of a weapon. However, Mondello was *acquitted* of manslaughter charges. Judge Owens imposed sentence on June 11, 1990.

Both Fama and Mondello appealed their sentences. Mondello's sentence was modified on March 1, 1993, allowing concurrent service of the terms for imprisonment with the terms for riot as the crime was essentially the same. Fama's sentence and judgment were affirmed on February 5, 1995, in the Appellate Division of the Supreme Court of New York.

John Vento, who had provided evidence against Fama, which he later recanted, was sentenced to four years on lesser charges. Steven Curreri and James Patino were acquitted of all charges; Joseph Serrano was given community service on a weapons charge; Charles Stressler was acquitted after a mistrial was declared in his first trial.

— Rodney Carlisle

Suggestions for Further Reading

DeSantis, John. *For the Color of His Skin: The Murder of Yusuf Hawkins and the Trial of Bensonhurst.* New York: Pharos Books, 1991.

Sullivan, Andrew. "The Two Faces of Bensonhurst." *New Republic* (July 2, 1990).

Marion Barry Trial: 1990

Defendant: Marion Barry, Jr.   **Crime Charged:** Drug offenses (14 counts)
Chief Defense Lawyers: Robert Mance and Kenneth Mundy
Chief Prosecutors: Judith Retchin and Richard Roberts   **Judge:** Thomas
Penfield Jackson   **Place:** Washington, D.C.   **Dates of Trial:** June 4–August
10, 1990   **Verdict:** Guilty on 1 count of cocaine possession; Not guilty on 1
count; Mistrial on remaining 12 counts   **Sentence:** 6 months imprisonment,
$5,000 fine, 1 year probation

SIGNIFICANCE

The sensational arrest of Marion Barry guaranteed that the ensuing trial would be
high drama. But almost no one could have predicted such a remarkable verdict or
Barry's political comeback.

For years Washington, D.C., had buzzed with rumors that Mayor Marion Barry had a drug problem. Concrete proof came January 18, 1990, when Barry entered Room 726 at the Vista International Hotel to keep an assignation with ex-girlfriend Rasheeda Moore. After rejecting Barry's sexual advance, Moore produced a pipe for smoking cocaine. (Barry had earlier given Moore $20 to buy some crack cocaine.) Seconds after Barry put the pipe to his lips, half a dozen FBI agents and other police officers rushed into the room and arrested him. The sting had worked perfectly: Every incident had been captured on videotape.

On June 19, 1990, prosecutor Richard Roberts outlined Barry's six-year involvement with drugs, emphasizing the mayor's hypocrisy:

> "During the course of this trial, you will learn that while the defendant preached "Down with dope!' he was putting dope up his nose. . . . Every person has two sides. . . . This case is about the other side, the secret side of Marion Barry."

The star prosecution witness was Charles Lewis, a confessed drug dealer. He first met Barry in the Virgin Islands in June 1986. "He asked me if I could get some rocks [crack cocaine]. . . . I told me yes." According to Lewis, Barry's drug binge included straight cocaine and marijuana, as well.

Chief defense counsel Kenneth Mundy, deriding Lewis' claim that conscience had prompted his testimony, scoffed, "You didn't wake up and start cooperating [with the authorities] until you got convicted in the Virgin Islands, is that correct?"

"Both things happened at the same time."

"You were facing big time weren't you?"

"The reason I waited. . . ."

"Is that a yes or a no?" barked Mundy.

"Yes," Lewis admitted.

For three days Mundy kept up the attack, extracting one damaging concession after another from Lewis. It was a superb feat of advocacy, one which gave the prosecution pause for thought: Perhaps their case wasn't so airtight after all?

Violent Relationship

Help was at hand—Rasheeda Moore. She detailed a three-year liaison with Barry, plagued with drugs and occasional violence, that put the prosecution back on track. It was during her testimony that the Vista videotape was played. Mundy grilled Moore about her background—hardly exemplary—portraying her as out to get Barry because he had ditched her for another woman. He also scored points with her admission that she had used drugs in April 1990, three months after the Vista sting.

Mayor Marion Barry is escorted by police following his appearance before a federal magistrate. (AP/Wide World Photos)

"It's something I have to deal with everyday," said Moore, referring to her cocaine addiction. When Mundy suggested that the receipt of several thousand dollars from the government had loosened her tongue, Moore demurred. Her decision to set Barry up, she said, had resulted from a revival of religious belief.

Because Barry declined to testify on his own behalf, the defense comprised mainly of witnesses who placed Barry elsewhere at times when he was supposed to have participated in alleged drug deals.

On August 2, 1990, the jury began deliberations. More than a week later they announced themselves hopelessly deadlocked on all except two counts, one guilty, the other not guilty. Judge Thomas Jackson had no alternative but to declare a mistrial on the remaining 12 charges. Later, in a public attack, Judge Jackson suggested that some jurors had been less than forthcoming about their true feelings during the impanelment process, telling a Harvard Law School class that he had "never seen a stronger government case" than the one mounted against Barry.

The final act in this drama came October 26, 1990, when Judge Jackson sentenced Barry to six months imprisonment, a fine and probation. The verdict temporarily derailed Barry's political career, reinforcing the perception in some quarters that that had been the intent all along. After completing his jail term, Barry was elected in November 1992 to Washington's city council.

The most remarkable political comeback in recent U.S. history continued. Apparently perceived by the Washington electorate as more sinned against than sined. Barry stunned his detractors on September 14, 1994, by winning the Democratic nomination for Mayor of the city, the very position he had disgraced just four years earlier. In the primary, he emphatically trounced both of his rivals, including incumbent Mayor Sharon Pratt Kelly who received just 13 percent of the vote. At the November 8 election, Barry's margin of victory was no less impressive as he garnered 54 percent of the vote to doom the mayoral ambitions of Carol Schwartz, a white Republican. Washington, D.C., is an overwhelmingly African American city where registered Democrats outnumber Republicans by more than four to one.

During Barry's four-year term, the city saw it's crime rate increase while the public schools' infrastructure and other public services declined sharply. With a budget deficit of half a billion dollars, the city was soon on the verge of bankruptcy.

In 1995, Congress set up the Financial Control Board to oversee some of the city's day-to-day business. By 1997, municipal authority had been taken away from the city, and the Financial Control Board made most of the decisions, leaving the mayor and the city council virtually powerless. In 1998, in what many observers considered to be a surprise, Barry announced that he would not seek another term as mayor of Washington, D.C.

—Colin Evans and Ron Formica

Suggestions for Further Reading

Agronsky, Jonathan I.Z. *Marion Barry: The Politics Of Race*. Latham, N.Y.: British American, 1991.

Morley, Jefferson. "Crack in the Washington Culture." *The Nation* (February 19, 1990): 221ff.

Puddington, Arch. *Insight* (June 3, 1991): 44–45.

Starr, Richard. *Insight* (February 5, 1990): 22ff.

Central Park Jogger Rape Trials: 1990

Defendants: First trial: Antron McCray, Yusef Salaam, Raymond Santana Jr.; second trial: Kevin Richardson and Kharey Wise   **Crimes Charged:** First trial: Second-degree attempted murder, rape, sodomy, first and second-degree assault, robbery, riot; second trial: all of the above, plus sexual abuse   **Chief Defense Lawyers:** First trial: Robert Burns, Michael Joseph, Peter Rivera; second trial: Howard Diller and Colin Moore   **Chief Prosecutors:** Arthur Clements and Elizabeth Lederer   **Judge:** Thomas B. Galligan   **Place:** New York, New York   **Dates of Trials:** June 13–August 18, 1990; October 22–December 11, 1990   **Verdicts:** First trial: all acquitted of attempted murder, sodomy, and one of five counts of assault, but guilty of all other charges; second trial: Richardson guilty of all charges, Wise guilty of sexual abuse, assault, and riot   **Sentences:** First trial: 5–15 years imprisonment; second trial: 5–10 years imprisonment for Richardson, 5–15 years imprisonment for Wise

SIGNIFICANCE

The violent assault and rape of the woman known as "the Central Park Jogger" resulted in two tense and widely publicized trials that many New Yorkers felt were emblematic of the crime and racial problems characterizing the era.

More than 3,000 rapes were reported in New York City in 1989, but none aroused more fear and anger than an attack on a young woman who became known simply as "the Central Park jogger." The facts sometimes disappeared in chaotic arguments outside the courts—and in the spectators' seats—over the racial politics of dispensing justice in America. Yet most of the trial itself was fought over one point that horrified New Yorkers on both sides of the case: the fact that nearly all of the suspects were legally children.

On the spring evening of April 19, 1989, a loosely knit gang of about 30 adolescents roamed the northern acres of Central Park, terrorizing everyone they encountered. Police grabbed several suspects, including one who blurted, "I know who did the murder!" The confession made little sense until several hours later, when two passers-by heard moans coming from the darkness. A naked woman was discovered lying in the woods. She had been bound, raped, and beaten so severely that doctors expected her to die.

The victim was a white 28-year-old investment banker who enjoyed jogging in the park at the end of long days at a Wall Street firm. The suspects were all black or Hispanic. All but one were 14 or 15 years of age. None had an arrest record, but outrage and sadness ran through the city with reports of the young suspects' apparent indifference to human life. It was just a "wilding," one explained, a night of terror for the sake of fun.

Several suspects were released for lack of evidence or pleaded guilty to earlier assaults in the park. The rape victim remained unidentified by most of the press, who simply called her "the Central Park jogger." Despite their youth, six suspects indicted for the attack were publicly identified in the press. The indicted minors were to be tried as adults, but sentenced as juveniles if found guilty.

Confessions Prove Crucial

To abide by the U.S. Supreme Court's 1965 *Aranda* rule, which forbids testimony in which one codefendant implicates another, three trials were planned to separate youths who had implicated each other in videotaped or written confessions. These incriminating statements quickly defined the case for the defense. After unsuccessfully trying to bar the confessions for nearly a year, defense attorneys continued to challenge their legal and ethical legitimacy throughout the trials.

When defendants Antron McCray, Yusef Salaam, and Raymond Santana, Jr., came to trial in June 1990, they faced prosecutor Elizabeth Lederer, who began by methodically reconstructing the night of violence. Seven victims of earlier harassment, robberies, and beatings in the park testified, although none implicated the three defendants. Doctors who treated the jogger testified that she had lost 75 percent of her blood by the time she was discovered. Her skull had been hammered so violently that the normally wrinkled surface of her brain had been beaten flat. Yet lack of physical evidence remained the weakest part of the prosecution's case. Blood and semen tests of the jogger were inconclusive.

In spite of the seriousness of her injuries, the scarred victim had recovered enough strength to appear in court. She testified briefly about the lingering after-effects of the beating, but she could remember nothing about the assault itself.

The atmosphere changed when video monitors appeared in the court-room. Jurors watched a half-hour videotape in which the prosecutor read McCray his Miranda rights as his parents looked on. On the tape, McCray then described how he and the gang had "charged" the jogger and beaten her to the ground. Someone, he said, hit her with a length of pipe before the gang took turns raping her. McCray admitted dropping his pants and climbing on top of the jogger but denied raping her. "I didn't do nothing to her," he said.

In his signed and videotaped confessions, Santana admitted assaulting other joggers in the park and implicated two youths who were scheduled to be tried later for rape. He confessed that he had held the jogger while Kevin Richardson raped her and Steven Lopez hit her in the head with a brick to stop her screams.

While police denied intimidating the suspects or promising them anything in return for the crucial confessions, detective Thomas McKenna testified that he had tricked a written confession out of Salaam, who denied even being in the park. When the detective falsely told Salaam that his fingerprints were found on the jogger's synthetic running tights, Salaam changed his story.

"Yes, I was there but I didn't rape her," Salaam said.

"How could you possibly do something like this?" the detective asked.

"It was just something to do," Salaam replied. "It was fun." Salaam admitted hitting the jogger twice with a metal pipe and grabbing her breasts, but he said that four others raped the woman, including Richardson and Wise.

McKenna said that Salaam's statement ended when his mother arrived and told police that her son was only 15. Minors were entitled to have a parent or guardian present during questioning, but when police took Salaam into custody, he claimed he was 16 and produced a transit authority pass to prove it. Defense witnesses claimed that the police knew Salaam was a minor and interrogated him anyway. Judge Thomas Galligan allowed the prosecution to introduce Salaam's unsigned statement and instructed jurors to decide for themselves if it was obtained fairly.

Defense Unwittingly Helps Prosecution

Without any physical evidence, the unsigned confession represented all of the prosecution's case against Salaam until his lawyer made a series of strategic blunders. When attorney Robert Burns asked McKenna why he believed the confession was true, the detective replied that he knew none of the particulars of the attack until Salaam revealed details which later turned out to be true. Burns also allowed the detective to mention that an unindicted witness placed Salaam in the park on the night of the attack.

McCray's and Santana's lawyers objected vehemently when Burns decided to put his client on the stand. Salaam denied taking part in the attack and testified that he told police he was only 15 when they questioned him. Under cross-examination, however, his confused explanation for being in the park dissolved into bickering with the prosecutor.

The defense claimed that the entire prosecution case rested on confessions coerced with lies and threats. The prosecution was accused of playing to the jury's emotions by unnecessarily putting the victim on the stand. Burns also suggested that the jogger had freely engaged in sex with an unnamed person before embarking on her run and that no rape had occurred. After 10 days of turbulent deliberations, however, the jury found the defendants guilty.

Details of the confessions had been leaked almost from the moment they were given, producing considerable press commentary that presumed the youths guilty. This bias and the absence of forensic evidence in the trial prompted some black New Yorkers to be suspicious of the verdict. A few activists, including the Reverend Al Sharpton, observed and criticized the trial, ignoring the multiracial jury's insistence that the youths were convicted by their own admissions.

When Kharey Wise and Kevin Richardson came to trial two months later, their supporters rained racial insults on prosecutors arriving at the courthouse. Richardson's attorney, Howard Diller, threatened to ask for a mistrial when Wise's lawyer announced publicly that he would cross-examine the jogger, a move the defense in the first trial had avoided for fear of alienating the jury. Richardson's family responded by trying to fire Diller for not being aggressive enough.

The tense courtroom erupted almost immediately. "That woman, she's lying!" Wise sobbed during prosecutor Lederer's opening argument. "I can't take it anymore!"

Wise's lawyer, Colin Moore, kept his promise to cross-examine the jogger vigorously. He inferred that she had been seeing more than one man and that her boyfriend had attacked her in a jealous fury. Moore's suggestive questions were buried in a hail of sustained objections.

Surprise Witness Surfaces

A subpoena forced one of Wise's friends to testify against her will as a surprise witness for the prosecution. Melody Jackson tearfully recalled Wise telephoning her from the Riker's Island detention center three months after his arrest. He denied raping the jogger, but he said that he had fondled her and helped hold her legs down.

The prosecution introduced two videotaped confessions featuring Wise. In the first, he admitted only that he had watched the rape. The second was more vivid. "It was my first rape," he said. He described how he had hit the jogger repeatedly with a rock. He recalled Salaam laughing while Santana and Lopez raped the victim. Wise claimed that he talked Lopez out of killing the woman. He also accused Richardson of rape, but his references to his codefendant were removed from the tape shown in court.

Wise's mother testified that her son had returned home at approximately the time he was accused of taking part in the rape. When the prosecutor asked if her son had not returned half an hour later, Mrs. Wise refused to cooperate and began screaming at Lederer. The judge ordered Wise's mother to be ejected from the court and told the jury to disregard her testimony.

Wise's own temper flared when he was asked to explain his admissions to police. He stalked off the stand and briefly refused to answer any questions. When he returned, his lawyer asked why he had confessed.

"The detectives told me to put myself in it," Wise replied. "They promised I could go home if I did."

Second Jury Issues Surprise

The verdict was a surprise to both sides. Jurors believed that Wise had been pressured into making the second videotape and convicted him only of sexual abuse, assault, and riot. Richardson, who had confessed to being present during the rape but denied taking part, was found guilty on all counts. The jury decided that physical evidence, including semen in Richardson's underwear and a strand of the victim's pubic hair found on his shirt, was more damning than any of the videotaped confessions. The absence of identical verdicts also disregarded the judge's instructions concerning the concept of "acting in concert," which holds that those who contribute to a major crime are liable to prosecution for its most serious aspects, even if they participate to a lesser degree.

Richardson's family shouted angry insults at prosecutors and the judge, accusing them of racism. ". . . you'll pay for this," Wise spat at Lederer as he was led away amid the uproar.

Richardson received the maximum sentence for minors. Wise, the only defendant who was not a minor when he was arrested, was sentenced as an adult to slightly less than half of the maximum sentence.

Ironically, the suspect accused by the convicted youths of raping and beating the jogger most violently never stood trial. Only Steven Lopez had not given police an incriminating statement. Prosecutors prepared to try him for rape anyway, but the accusations of his codefendants were inadmissible and other witnesses ultimately refused to testify.

A plea bargain allowed Lopez to admit his part in the earlier muggings and plead guilty to a charge of robbery. In sentencing Lopez to 1½–4½ years imprisonment for his part in the "sadistic rampage" in Central Park, Judge Galligan called the conviction "the final chapter of a cowardly attack that will continue to live in the hearts of New Yorkers."

— Thomas C. Smith

Suggestions for Further Reading

Didion, Joan. "New York: Sentimental Journeys." *New York Review of Books* (January 17, 1991): 45–56.

Glaberson, William. "Jogger Case Defense: Scattershot Approach." *New York Times* (July 13, 1990): B1, B3.

Stone, Michael. "What Really Happened In Central Park." *New York* (August 14, 1989): 30–43.

Sullivan, Ronald. "Confessions Lawyers Couldn't Undo." *New York Times* (August 20, 1990): B4.

Turque, Bill and Anne Underwood. "Judgment For the Wilders." *Newsweek* (August 27, 1990): 39.

Mapplethorpe Obscenity Trial: 1990

Defendants: Dennis Barrie and the Cincinnati Contemporary Arts Center
Crime Charged: Displaying obscene material, namely pictures by the artist
Robert Mapplethorpe **Chief Defense Lawyers:** Marc D. Mezibov and H.
Louis Sirkin **Chief Prosecutors:** Richard A. Castellini, Frank H. Prouty, Jr.,
and Melanie J. Reising **Judge:** F. David J. Albanese **Place:** Cincinnati,
Ohio **Dates of Trial:** September 24–October 5, 1990 **Verdict:** Not guilty

SIGNIFICANCE
The acquittal of the Mapplethorpe defendants was a major reaffirmation of First
Amendment freedom of speech protection in the new realm of homosexual art.

In the Spring of 1990, the Contemporary Arts Center (CAC) in Cincinnati, Ohio, held an exhibit of photographs by the late artist Robert Mapplethorpe. The exhibit was controversial from the start because of the openly homosexual nature of much of Mapplethorpe's work and was well covered in the Cincinnati press. There was a great deal of negative public reaction, and rumors spread that the city of Cincinnati would attempt to close down the exhibit under Ohio's obscenity statute, which makes it illegal for any person to "Promote, . . . display . . . or exhibit . . . any obscene material."

The CAC's director, Dennis Barrie, attempted a preemptive strike aimed at heading off an obscenity prosecution. The CAC filed an action for a declaratory judgment, which is a type of civil lawsuit, on March 27, 1990, in Hamilton County (which includes Cincinnati) Municipal Court. CAC asked the court to declare the exhibit not obscene, but on April 6, 1990, the court refused and dismissed the action. The next day, the Hamilton County Grand Jury indicted CAC and Barrie for criminal violations of the Ohio obscenity statute.

Of the approximately 175 pictures in the exhibit, seven were particularly controversial and were the focus of the ensuing trial. Two pictures were of naked minors, one male and one female, with a "lewd exhibition or graphic focus on the genitals." The other five were of adult men in unusual sadomasochistic poses.

Obscenity or Art?

The trial began on September 24, 1990, before a jury of four men and four women with Judge F. David J. Albanese presiding. The lawyers for CAC and

Barrie were Marc D. Mezibov and H. Louis Sirkin. The prosecutors were Richard A. Castellini, Frank H. Prouty, Jr., and Melanie J. Reising.

The prosecutors had to convince the jury that the seven pictures were legally obscene, as "obscene" was defined by the Supreme Court in the 1973 case *Miller v. California*. *Miller* says that material is obscene only if: (1) the average person, applying contemporary community standards, would find that the material as a whole appeals to the prurient interest; (2) the material depicts or describes sexual conduct in a patently offensive way; and (3) the material, as a whole, lacks serious literary, artistic, political or scientific value.

Following the jury's verdict of "pandering obscenity," hundreds of protesters demonstrated outside the Cincinnati Arts Center. (AP/Wide World Photos)

Both the prosecution and the defense wanted Albanese, rather than the jury, to make the decision on particular elements of the *Miller* test. Prosecutor Prouty argued that Albanese should determine what community standards were:

> We're not required to show community standards because the court [Albanese] becomes the community.

For the defense, Mezibov argued that Albanese and not the jury should decide whether the pictures had serious artistic value:

> It would be inappropriate, it would be wrong, I submit, for lay people to guess and to speculate as to what constitutes serious artistic value.

Albanese, however, decided to leave all three elements of the Miller test to the jury, holding that, "The court will not substitute its judgment for that of the jury."

To prove the defense's claim that the seven pictures had serious artistic value, therefore, Mezibov and Sirkin brought in several art experts to testify. The art experts called the pictures the work of "a brilliant artist," with "symmetry" and "classic proportions."

On October 5, 1990, the eight jurors found CAC and Barrie not guilty of the charges of displaying obscene material. Under Ohio law, the case ended then and there, because the state is prohibited from appealing a jury verdict. Although CAC and Barrie were vindicated, the victory was expensive: The trial cost CAC over $200,000 in costs and attorneys' fees.

The acquittal of the Mapplethorpe defendants reaffirmed the obscenity principles of *Miller v. California* and the protection of the First Amendment in a new area. This new area was the field of gay rights and the right of homosexual artists to express themselves. As Mezibov said after the trial:

Yes, we have a Bill of Rights. But it's meaningless unless you fight for it.

—*Stephen G. Christianson*

Suggestions for Further Reading

Cembalest, Robin. "Who Does it Shock? Why Does it Shock?" *Artnews* (March 1992): 32–33.

———. "The Obscenity Trial: How They Voted to Acquit." *Artnews* (December 1990): 136–141.

Gurstein, Rochelle. "Current Debate: High Art or Hard-Core? Misjudging Mapplethorpe: the Art Scene and the Obscene." *Tikkun* (November–December 1991): 70–80.

Light, Judy. "Jury Acquits Museum in Landmark Art Trial." *Dancemagazine* (December 1990): 12–13.

Merkel, Jayne. "Art on Trial." *Art in America* (December 1990): 41–46.

Parachini, Allan. "Year of the Censor: How Photography Became the Focus of Fear and Loathing." *American Photo* (November–December 1990): 39–42.

George Franklin Trial: 1990–91

Defendant: George Franklin   **Crime Charged:** Murder
Chief Defense Lawyers: Douglas Horngrad and Arthur Wachtel
Chief Prosecutor: Elaine Tipton   **Judge:** Thomas McGinn Smith
Place: Redwood City, California   **Dates of Trial:** October 31, 1990–January 29, 1991   **Verdict:** Guilty (overturned on appeal)   **Sentence:** Life imprisonment

SIGNIFICANCE
The trial of George Franklin raised the troubling question of how far courts and juries can rely upon and trust the evidence of formerly repressed memories of traumatic events in deciding a defendant's guilt or innocence.

In January 1989, Eileen Franklin-Lipsker was playing with her young daughter, Jessica, and as the child turned toward her, a memory of another girl in just such a pose sprang into Franklin-Lipsker's mind. The memory was of her childhood best friend, eight-year-old Susan Nason, being raped and killed by Franklin-Lipsker's father nearly 20 years earlier.

Until that moment in 1989, Franklin-Lipsker had had no recollection of being a witness to this horrible scene. Now, suddenly, it came flooding back in graphic and gruesome detail. "Her hands flew up to her head," she later said. "The next thing I heard was two blows. It sounded terrible."

Daughter Goes To Police

This, at least, was the story that Franklin-Lipsker began to tell her friends and family, and eventually the police. After taking a statement from her, the police arrested her father, George Franklin, on November 29, 1989, for the murder. At his home they found a number of pornographic magazines and pictures, including those of young children.

Twenty years earlier, in September 1969, young Susan Nason disappeared from her town of Foster City, California. Her body was discovered outdoors a few months later, showing signs of a violent death, including a crushed skull and a smashed ring that seemed to indicate she was warding off a blow. A bloodstained rock was found nearby. The press reported these and other facts, but police never made an arrest for her murder. Franklin and others were questioned at the time, and Franklin went to visit Susan's graveside on the first anniversary of her death.

Ten years later, Franklin's wife asked him if he had murdered Susan. During their divorce proceedings Franklin-Lipsker's mother said that Franklin had abused his own children, including Eileen, both verbally and physically.

Now, 20 years after Susan's death, Franklin-Lipsker claimed that she remembered being with her father and Susan on the day of the murder. She said that she had watched her father rape and kill Susan, and that he had threatened her, too.

"He said that if I told anyone," she testified, "he would have to kill me. I believed him." Because of the shock of what she had witnessed and her total belief in her father, according to several psychiatrists who were questioned, she had repressed her memories of that day for years. Not until she saw her own daughter in a pose similar to Susan's two decades later, she said, did they resurface.

Daughter Is Star Witness At Father's Trial

The trial opened in late October 1990, and Franklin-Lipsker became the star witness. The prosecution's case revolved almost totally on her account based on the resurfacing of her repressed memories. Leading psychiatrists and psychologists testified on behalf of both the prosecution and defense. The prosecution witnesses explained the theory of the repression of traumatic memories; the defense witnesses argued that Franklin-Lipsker did not fit the profile of those who had such memories, and, indeed, called into question the accuracy of such memories in any event. The defense also argued that all of the facts to which Franklin-Lipsker testified had been reported in the papers; she therefore could have known what had happened without being an eye-witness to the murder.

George Franklin as he was released from jail. (AP/Wide World Photos)

Trial judge Thomas McGinn Smith prevented the defense from introducing newspaper accounts that mentioned the facts that Franklin-Lipsker revealed. However, he did allow the admission of what some would call circumstantial evidence. When Franklin-Lipsker went to visit her father in prison before the trial and asked him to tell the truth, Franklin had said nothing, instead pointing to a prison sign that warned inmates that officials might monitor their conversations. Franklin's silence, said prosecutor Elaine Tipton, in the face of this accusation, was "worth its weight in gold" as an implied admission of guilt.

On November 30, 1990, the jury found Franklin guilty of Susan's murder, although the prosecution had not produced any physical evidence to connect him with her death. The conviction rested almost totally on Franklin-Lipsker's testimony, despite her estrangement from him and the psychologists who challenged the veracity of her claims. On January 29, 1991, Judge Smith sentenced Franklin to life imprisonment, the maximum sentence possible under the law at the time of the 1969 murder. However, in 1995, a federal appeals court overturned the conviction, finding that Judge Smith should have allowed Franklin to challenge his daughter's testimony by being able to introduce the newspaper articles as evidence. The court also found that using Franklin's silence as evidence of an admission of guilt violated his constitutional right to remain silent. Finally, the court noted that the entire subject of repressed memory was a highly controversial one whose accuracy was still subject to debate. Franklin later sued his daughter and the psychologists who had testified against him for conspiracy to present false testimony, but the courts ultimately rejected this suit.

While memories of past events are often used as evidence in civil and criminal trials, the heavy reliance on repressed memory in the Franklin case was unique in American criminal law. Trial courts had long recognized that memories could be faulty, especially when they were of events from far in the past. The federal appeals court here found that the repressed memories of Franklin-Lipsker were no different from other types of memories, and it criticized the trial court for refusing to let the defense test these memories, as it would have been able to test any others.

After being imprisoned for six years, George Franklin was released from jail when his conviction was overturned.

—*Buckner F. Melton, Jr.*

Suggestions for Further Reading

MacLean, Harry N. *Once Upon a Time: A True Story of Memory, Murder, and the Law*. New York: HarperCollins, 1993.

Terr, Lenore. *Unchained Memories: True Stories of Traumatic Memories, Lost and Found*. New York: Basic Books, 1994.

Baby Richard Trial: 1991–95

Plaintiff: Otakar Kirchner   **Defendants:** Jay and Kimberly Warburton
Chief Defense Lawyer: Richard Lifshitz   **Chief Lawyer for Plaintiff:** Loren
Heineman   **Judges:** Dom J. Rizzi and Ann G. McMorrow   **Place:** Chicago,
Illinois   **Dates of Trials:** 1991–1995   **Verdict:** For the plaintiff: custody of
the child Baby Richard awarded to his biological father, Otakar Kirchner

SIGNIFICANCE
The Baby Richard case elicited public outrage against the legal system at its
worst. Outmoded adoption principles and a strict adherence to the law failed to
protect a child whose fate was determined by interests other than his own.
Intervention by the Illinois legislature spotlighted even more media attention on
this sad case.

In the fall of 1989, Otakar Kirchner met Daniella Janikova in Chicago. The two,
both emigrants from the former Czechoslovakia, moved in together, and soon
Daniella became pregnant.

During the pregnancy, Kirchner returned to Europe for a time. Upon
hearing rumors that he had taken up with his previous girlfriend there, Daniella
abandoned her plans to marry him and also decided, without telling Kirchner, to
put her baby up for adoption. She asked her friends and family to tell Kirchner
that the baby had died.

Daniella hired an attorney to begin the process of finding adoptive parents
for her unborn child. The attorney soon found and contacted Jay and Kimberly
Warburton, who were hoping to adopt a baby. The Warburtons and their
attorney were told of Kirchner's existence, but not his identity, since Daniella
would not reveal it. According to later court records, they also knew that Daniella
had planned to tell Kirchner that the baby had died. Four days after the birth of
the child, known as "Baby Richard," Daniella put him up for adoption and the
Warburtons took custody and began adoption proceedings.

Father Attempts to Gain Custody

Kirchner, meanwhile, aware of the due date, had returned from Europe
and tried to learn of Richard's fate, checking with area hospitals, searching

public records for evidence of the birth or death, and frequenting Daniella's neighborhood. However, he apparently did not try to contact Daniella or her doctor directly, or consult an attorney. Despite being told of the baby's death, he kept up his efforts to find out what had happened. Two months after Richard was born, a friend of Daniella's told him the truth, and Kirchner intervened in the adoption proceedings to gain custody of his son.

The ensuing litigation spawned a number of strongly worded judicial opinions, several appeals to state and federal courts, and a great public outcry over Richard's fate. The Illinois Court of Appeals decided the case on the basis of the baby's best interests, which Illinois adoption laws dictated. Judge Dom Rizzi ruled that the interests of the baby would best be served if Richard remained with the Warburtons, since by that time he had been with them for nearly two and a half years, and his biological parents were now utter strangers to him. Rizzi also found that Kirchner was an unfit parent in light of what the judge characterized as feeble efforts to learn the truth about Richard. "There comes a point," stated Rizzi, "when we should not be ignorant as judges of what we know as men and women."

However, the Illinois Supreme Court, in a terse opinion, reversed the court of appeals and Judge Rizzi's ruling and invalidated the adoption, awarding custody instead to Kirchner. Rizzi, the court determined, had done things backwards: under Illinois law, the courts could not even begin to consider Richard's best interests until they first found Kirchner to be an unfit parent, thus terminating his parental rights. One justice noted the public furor surrounding the case and the irresponsibility of the press in stirring up outrage against the courts; he accused one Chicago columnist in particular of "character assassination" and "journalistic terrorism" against the court system.

Illinois Legislature Gets Involved

The Illinois Supreme Court's decision's unpopularity led to an immediate convening of an emergency session of the state legislature, which at once passed a retroactive law requiring a custody hearing in the case. This led Kirchner to seek a writ of *habeas corpus* from the Illinois Supreme Court to gain custody of the child, and the Illinois court promptly granted Kirchner's request. At the same time the court took the legislature to task for trying to reverse, by statute, the court's earlier decision.

The Illinois Supreme Court's second ruling in favor of Kirchner, however, was not unanimous. Breaking away from her peers on the court, Justice Ann G. McMorrow, who had sided with the majority in the first decision, now dissented, denouncing the judicial system that had let the case drag on for four years. She was to be only one of many critics of Baby Richard's court-decreed fate. It was popularly believed that the system had failed Richard; but the court was not alone in the blam—Kirchner, Daniella, the Warburtons and their attorney who had known of Kirchner's existence, social workers, the press—everyone seemed to have played a part in the unpopular ruling.

On April 30, 1995, amid a media circus, Kirchner and Daniella arrived at the Warburtons' house and took Richard home with them. Richard cried pitifully and begged the Warburtons not to make him leave. Kirchner and Daniella later married, but in January 1997 Kirchner moved out, leaving Daniella and Richard—now known as Danny Kirchner—for another woman.

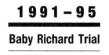

Otakar Kirchner (left) carries his son known as "Baby Richard," as the boy's foster family grieves. (AP/Wide World Photos)

The Baby Richard case epitomized the American legal system at its worst. It was a sorry story of long judicial delay that made the ultimate decision ever harder on Richard; an unpopular decision that called the legal system's legitimacy into question; and an episode that pitted the judiciary against the political branches of government. Most important, it revealed that traditional American notions of stable families consisting of two married parents raising their own biological children was a simplistic view of modern family life.

—*Buckner F. Melton, Jr.*

Suggestions for Further Reading

Zito, Anthony S. "Baby Richard and Beyond: The Future for Adopted Children." *Northern Illinois University Law Review* (Summer 1998): 445–79.

Carolyn Warmus Trials: 1991 & 1992

Defendant: Carolyn Warmus **Crime Charged:** Murder
Chief Defense Lawyers: First trial: David L. Lewis; second trial: William I.
Aronwald **Chief Prosecutors:** Douglas J. Fitzmorris and James A. McCarty
Judge: John Carey **Place:** White Plains, New York **Dates of Trials:** First
Trial: January 14–April 27, 1991; second trial: January 22–May 27, 1992
Verdicts: First trial: mistrial; second trial: guilty **Sentence:** 25 years to life

SIGNIFICANCE

Obsession, deadly and destructive, was never more chillingly illustrated than in this trial resulting from one woman's determination to have the man she craved at any cost.

For several weeks following the January 15. 1989 shooting of Betty Jeanne Solomon in her Westchester County, New York home, husband Solomon was the chief suspect. But when police learned that Solomon's longtime lover, Carolyn Warmus, had been more relentless than ever in her pursuit of the reluctant widower, official attention turned toward this 27-year-old Manhattan schoolteacher. Their investigation revealed a woman with a turbulent history of romantic fixations, most often with unavailable men. But there was other evidence, too, enough to warrant a murder indictment against Warmus. Guaranteed immunity from prosecution, Solomon agreed to testify against his former lover when her trial began January 14, 1991.

In his opening statement, chief prosecutor James A. McCarty described Warmus as driven by a "consuming passion to possess" Solomon. McCarty conceded the lack of any single piece of proof that would on its own prove Warmus guilty, but "like pieces of a puzzle," he said, circumstantial evidence would "reveal a clear picture of the killer . . . Carolyn Warmus."

David L. Lewis, lawyer for the defendant, countered that his client was the victim of a "deliberate, malicious" frame-up, reminding the jury that "love and passion are not on trial here, this is a trial about murder."

The first witness to link Warmus to a potential murder weapon was private investigator James A. Russo. In the fall of 1988, Warmus had come to him, he said, seeking protection from Betty Jeanne Solomon, who was jealous about the defendant's affair with her husband. Russo had suggested a bodyguard. "Her answer was no," he said. "I pushed her to say exactly what she wanted. She said a 'machine gun and silencer,' I said, 'We're not arms dealers.'"

Solomon Tells of Unusual Marriage

When Paul Solomon took the stand he cataloged a bizarre marriage. While acknowledging that neither partner had been faithful—there had been "ups and downs"—he maintained that the union was basically sound. Responding to questions about his affair with Warmus, Solomon said that for some time he had been trying unsuccessfully to terminate the relationship. Even so, he admitted meeting Warmus on the night of the killing and having sex with her in a car. Afterward he had gone home and found his wife murdered. Unnerved by Warmus' subsequent and, he said, unwanted pestering, he confronted her in a bar. "Did you have anything to do with Betty Jeanne's death?" he asked. She replied, "No."

For five days Solomon underwent a battering at the hands of defense counsel Lewis, who insinuated that it was actually Solomon himself who had arranged the murder. "You told your wife you'd be home early, but you didn't come home early because you knew your wife was dead!"

Finally Solomon erupted. "You twist and turn words, manipulate facts . . . to make them what they aren't," he shouted. But Lewis scored heavily when he drew an admission from the witness that he stood to profit significantly from his wife's death, having already signed a movie contract worth $175,000.

The star prosecution witness was yet another private investigator, Vincent Parco. He testified that one week before the shooting he sold Warmus a .25-caliber pistol—the kind used to kill Betty Jeanne Solomon—equipped with a silencer. (The murder weapon was never found.) Parco claimed he had done so only after considerable badgering by the defendant. "Almost every time I'd see her she'd bring it up." The silencer had been his idea, so she could practice in a "house, woods, or garage, and no one would know."

Vigorous Defense Launched

Lewis launched an assault on Parco's credibility, forcing him to admit his own infatuation with Warmus and asserting, without producing evidence, that it was Parco, hired by Paul Solomon, who had shot Betty Jeanne Solomon and then framed Warmus.

Strong circumstantial evidence tying Warmus to the murder came in the form of phone company records, which showed that the defendant had called a New Jersey sporting goods shop on the day of the killing. The prosecution alleged that, using fake identification, Warmus bought some .25-caliber bullets from the store, then shot Betty Jeanne Solomon nine times before keeping her rendezvous with Paul Solomon.

In response the defense produced its own phone record. Not only did this record lack the New Jersey call, but it logged an additional 6:44 P.M. call from Warmus' Manhattan apartment, thereby making it virtually impossible for her to have committed the murder several miles away at 7:15 P.M. But the veracity of this second record was challenged by MCI executive Thomas Sabol, who declared it a forgery.

With Warmus exercising her right to silence, the major defense witness was Joseph Lisella, a building contractor. He claimed to have overheard a conversation between "Parco" and "Solomon" in a Yonkers, New York, bowling alley bathroom less than an hour after the killing. Lisella said, "Paul" handed over $20,000 to the other man, saying, "Count it if you don't believe me." Later, "Vinnie" remarked, "Don't worry about the gun. It's in the deepest part of the river."

During cross-examination McCarty attempted to impugn Lisella's credibility by outlining several house fires connected with the witness. Lisella denied McCarty's charge that "people call you 'Toaster Joe,'" but did admit to contact with Warmus' wealthy father.

Following directions from Judge John Carey, the jurors retired to consider their verdict. Twelve days later they announced themselves irretrievably deadlocked, and a mistrial was declared.

Second Trial Results in Conviction

On January 22, 1992, the state tried again. This time Warmus' defense was in the hands of William I. Aronwald, a somewhat more understated advocate than his predecessor. In essence, he had to deal with much the same evidence, except for one vital difference. Original crime-scene photographs had shown a black bloodstained glove near the body. Somehow it had vanished, only to reappear when Paul Solomon was searching a box in his bedroom closet between trials.

From Warmus' credit card records the prosecution was able to prove that the defendant had purchased just such a pair of gloves one year before the murder. Aronwald fumed, accusing McCarty of "trial by ambush," but the evidence was in and its effect was deadly, especially when forensic expert Dr. Peter DeForest gave his opinion that stains on the glove could be human blood.

Again it was no easy matter for the jurors but after a week of consideration, they convicted Warmus of murder. On June 26, 1992, Judge Carey passed sentence—25 years to life—and the blond-haired defendant was led away without ever uttering a word in her own defense.

—*Colin Evans*

![section divider]

Suggestions for Further Reading

Brady, Diane. "Fatal Attraction." *Maclean's* (April 8, 1991): 44–45.

Colapinto, John. "By Love Obsessed." *Mademoiselle* (August 1990): 188–191.

Hammer, Joshua. "Teacher, Lover, Schemer, Killer?" *Newsweek* (February 25, 1991): 57ff.

Kunen, James S. "A Dangerous Passion." *People Weekly* (April 15, 1991): 34–39.

Pamela Smart Trial: 1991

Defendant: Pamela Smart   **Crime Charged:** Conspiracy to commit murder
Chief Defense Lawyers: Mark Sisti and Paul Twomey
Chief Prosecutors: Paul Maggiotto and Diane Nicolosi   **Judge:** Douglas R.
Gray   **Place:** Exeter, New Hampshire   **Dates of Trial:** March 4–22, 1991
Verdict: Guilty   **Sentence:** Life imprisonment

SIGNIFICANCE

Millions watched this trial on live television, fascinated by the sensational saga of a murderous plot hatched in high school involving sex and the lure of life insurance money.

Just one week before his first wedding anniversary, Gregory Smart, a 24-year-old insurance salesman, was shot dead at his New Hampshire condominium during what appeared to be a botched burglary. Six weeks later William Flynn, 16, Vance Lattime, 17, and Patrick Randall, 18, were arrested and charged with the murder. All three pleaded guilty. In return for reduced sentences the teenagers agreed to testify against the person they claimed persuaded them to carry out the killing: Pamela Smart, wife of the dead man.

When oral argument commenced March 4, 1991, Assistant Attorney General Diane Nicolosi portrayed the teenagers as naive victims of an evil woman bent on murder. Nicolosi claimed that Smart, a 22-year-old high-school teacher, seduced Flynn with the sole intent of duping him into murdering her husband, so that she might avoid an expensive divorce and benefit from a $140,000 life-insurance policy.

Graphic details of the murder were provided by Patrick Randall. He told how Flynn had enlisted his services, together with Vance Lattime, and how all three went to the Smart residence. While Lattime waited outside, Flynn and Randall ransacked the townhouse, then ambushed Greg Smart when he returned home from a sales meeting. Randall admitted holding a knife at Smart's throat as Flynn fired a .38-caliber bullet through the victim's brain. Afterward the two took some jewelry to create the impression of a robbery gone wrong.

Defense counsel Mark Sisti bitterly denounced all of Randall's allegations, noting that only in the course of pleabargaining had he implicated Pamela Smart.

"Pamela Smart didn't make you kill anybody, right?" Sisti asked.

"No," agreed Randall.

"You went to kill Greg Smart for your friend Bill [Flynn], right?"

"Yes."

"Pamela Smart had nothing to do with that, correct?"

"Correct," Randall admitted.

Pamela Smart and her husband on their wedding day. (AP/Wide Worls Photo)

Payoff for Murder: Stereo Speakers and $250

Vance Lattime, driver of the getaway car, told the jury that Smart gave him a pair of stereo speakers and promised an additional $250 for his part in the slaying. He added that, prior to the murder, she asked the other gang members how she should act upon finding her husband's body. "She didn't know whether to scream, run from house to house or call the police. We told her just to act normal." About one point Lattime was adamant: Smart insisted that they shoot her husband rather than stab him, because she didn't want blood splattered all over her white furniture.

When William Flynn took the stand, he tearfully recounted how Smart seduced him, interspersing the sexual blandishments with repeated and ever more urgent stories of physical abuse inflicted by Greg Smart on his wife, especially one incident when he locked her out of the house in winter while she was clad in only her nightclothes. Flynn said, "She started crying and said the only way she could see for us to be together was if we killed Greg." At first Flynn doubted Smart's seriousness, but as her temper and threats worsened, he yielded to her demands. "I was afraid if I didn't do it, she would leave me."

Flynn described to an emotion-packed courtroom how he put the revolver to Smart's head, then uttered, "God, forgive me," before pulling the trigger.

"Why did you say 'God, forgive me?'" asked Assistant Attorney General Paul Maggiotto.

"Because I didn't want to kill Greg," said Flynn. "I wanted to be with Pam, and that's what I had to do to be with Pam."

Of all the prosecution witnesses, none created more of an impact or did more damage than Cecelia Pierce, 16, another Winnacunnet High School student. She repeated a conversation with Smart: "I have a choice: either kill Greg or get a divorce," she quoted Smart as saying. "I told her to get a divorce," Pierce said. Asked how Smart responded, Pierce replied, "She said she couldn't, because Greg would take the dog and the furniture and she wouldn't have any money or a place to live."

Pierce did admit prior knowledge of the murder plot even to the point of aiding Smart in her search for a gun, but she claimed that conscience led her to the police afterward. At their behest she secretly taped several conversations with Smart. In one, Smart ordered Pierce to keep quiet, otherwise they would all "go to the slammer for the rest of our entire lives." On another occasion Smart boasted of committing the perfect murder.

Sisti cast a pall over much of this testimony by revealing that Pierce had sold the rights to her story to a Hollywood production company for a considerable sum of money. "What this all comes down to," he said, "is that you have a shot at $100,000 . . . and you claim to have been Pam's best friend?"

"Yes," admitted Pierce.

The Ice Melts

Throughout the proceedings Pamela Smart had maintained her composure, but contrition took over in the witness box. She claimed that her attempts to break off the affair with Flynn had been thwarted by his threats of suicide. "I was devastated," she said. While conceding the impropriety of their relationship, Smart vehemently denied any suggestion that she had planned murder. "I didn't force anybody to kill Greg!"

Then why, wondered Maggiotto, had she made those statements to Cecelia Pierce?

That had been a subterfuge, Smart said, all part of her own investigation into the murder of her husband.

"What were you going to do," asked Maggiotto, "Make a citizen's arrest?"

"No."

"Or was Pam Smart going to use her own investigation skills . . . and write a report and mail it in?"

"Yes," replied Smart, blaming some medication she was taking at the time for her apparent instability.

It was Smart's position, as it had been for the defense from the outset, that the murder was solely the work of the three teenagers, who now saw a way to ameliorate their sentences by implicating her. "They murdered Greg," she cried. "They're the ones who broke into the house. They waited for him. And they're the ones who brought him to his knees and brought a knife to his throat, before shooting him!"

The jury took 13 hours to decide Smart's fate. She stood emotionless as the guilty verdict was read. When Judge Douglas Gray imposed a life sentence without the possibility of parole, she seemed equally unaffected.

For their involvement in the murder, William Flynn and Patrick Randall each received sentences of 28 years to life. Vance Lattime received 18 years to life. Yet another student who knew of the plot, Raymond Fowler, also pleaded guilty to conspiracy and was jailed for 15 to 30 years.

In 1995, *To Die For,* a film loosely inspired by the Pamela Smart trial and starring Nicole Kidman, was released. In a made-for-television movie, *Murder in New Hampshire,* Pamela Smart was depicted as a scheming architect of murder. While the pertinency of that view is a matter of record, often overlooked is the ease with which her young lover was able to recruit assistants for his deadly mission. In this extraordinary case there was more than enough blame for everyone.

On March 11,1993, it was announced that Smart had been moved from the New Hampshire State Prison for Women in Goffstown, New Hampshire, to Bedford Hills Correctional Facility, 35 miles north of New York City. Although spokesman Donald Veno declined to comment on the move other than to say it was for "security reasons," rumors had reached the media concerning a relationship that Smart was allegedly conducting behind bars. Needless to say, her defense team was less than enthralled by the fact that they had not been told of the transfer beforehand. Commented one sarcastically, "There was a time in this country when prisoners had no rights."

—Colin Evans

Suggestions for Further Reading

Case, Tony. "Trial Coverage Under The Microscope." *Editor & Publisher* (April 20, 1991): 25ff.

Diamond, John N. *Washington Journalism Review* (June 1991): 15–16.

Plummer, William and Stephen Sawicki. *People Weekly* (February 4, 1991): 105–110.

Wanda Holloway Trial: 1991

Defendant: Wanda Webb Holloway   **Crimes Charged:** Solicitation of capital murder and solicitation of aggravated kidnapping
Chief Defense Lawyers: Troy McKinney and Stanley Schneider
Chief Prosecutors: Mike Anderson and Casey O'Brien   **Judge:** George H. Godwin   **Place:** Houston, Texas   **Dates of Trial:** August 23–September 4, 1991   **Verdict:** Guilty   **Sentence:** 15 years imprisonment and a $10,000 fine (later overturned)

SIGNIFICANCE

The case of the "Texas Cheerleader Mom" was one of the most sensational trials of the 1990s.

On January 30, 1991, the people of Channelview, Texas, learned that one of their neighbors had been arrested for trying to hire a contract killer. If the crime itself was not shocking enough, the identity of the suspect, her target, and her motive seemed incredible. Wanda Webb Holloway stood accused of trying to hire a hit man to kill the mother of her daughter's rival for selection to the junior high school cheerleading squad.

The novelty of the charges against the 37-year-old made her case an international media sensation well before her trial began. Holloway allegedly wanted to dispose of Verna Heath, whose daughter Amber had twice been chosen as a cheerleader over Holloway's daughter, Shanna. Prosecutors charged that Holloway had asked her former brother-in-law, Terry Harper, if he could hire someone to kill Verna Heath, presumably to traumatize Amber enough to make her forgo her cheerleading activities. Harper claimed that he had initially brushed aside her request, but later mentioned it to his brother Tony, Holloway's former husband and Shanna's father. Tony Harper insisted that Terry report the incident to the authorities. Although incredulous at first, Houston detectives wired Terry Harper with hidden recording devices. When Holloway and Harper met again, the tape was rolling and enough evidence was gathered to prosecute.

Tapes Lead to Conviction

The trial began on August 23, 1991. Prosecutors called upon school administrators, who testified that Holloway had taken her daughter's rejections from cheerleading far less gracefully than Shanna had. A high school friend of Shanna's brother, Shane, recalled that Mrs. Holloway once asked him if he would kill Verna Heath.

The most damaging witness for the prosecution was Holloway herself, whose voice was recorded during her meetings with Terry Harper. With Harper on the witness stand, prosecutors played the conversations recorded by the Houston police. The tapes revealed Holloway's obsessive hatred of Verna and Amber Heath. She agreed to the price of $2,500 that Harper told her a fictitious hit man would charge to eliminate Verna Heath—$5,000 less than the asking price for killing both mother and daughter.

"You want her dead?" Harper asked.

"I don't care what you do with her. You can keep her in Cuba for 15 years," Holloway snapped. "I want her gone." Holloway gave Harper a pair of diamond earrings as partial payment for the deadly contract.

The defense countered that Harper had plotted with his brother Tony to gain custody of the divorced couple's teenagers. Ironically, this theory was proposed in court by Terry Harper's wife, Marla. Her rambling testimony for the defense, however, merely convinced observers that both her first and second marriage to Harper were acrimonious, drunken disasters. The defense also tried to cast doubt on Terry Harper's veracity by making his police record an issue. These attacks were blunted by the prosecution's opening statement and Harper's own eager testimony, during which no secret was made of his checkered employment history and arrests for driving while intoxicated, disturbing the peace, and drug possession.

When Wanda Holloway took the stand in her own defense, she admitted that she had unwisely said many angry things about the Heaths. She tearfully insisted that the plot to murder Verna Heath had been Harper's idea and that she had not backed out of the plan because she was afraid of him. Under cross-examination by the prosecution, however, she admitted that she had never informed the police about what she claimed were Harper's harmful intentions.

The jury was unconvinced by her histrionics. They found Holloway guilty on September 3 and recommended a sentence of 15 years in prison, intentionally choosing the same number of years she had blithely suggested that Verna Heath might be forced to spend in Cuba. Holloway was also fined $10,000. Despite this attempt at poetic justice, Holloway spent less than a day behind bars. The jurors were unaware that Texas law allows a felon sentenced to a term of 15 years or less to post an appeal bond, making a conditional release possible. Holloway made her $75,000 bond and was free almost immediately.

Plea Agreement Ends Second Trial

The case did not end there, however, and the next twist was even more astonishing. The defense petitioned for a new trial, claiming that Holloway's conviction—her entire trial, in fact—had been invalid. Her attorneys correctly claimed that one of the jurors had been technically ineligible for jury duty because of a felony drug arrest. During the jury selection, Daniel Enriquez had truthfully answered yes when asked if he had been involved in a criminal case, but the judge incorrectly assumed that Enriquez had served his sentence. Furthermore, he had not responded when the judge asked if any of the prospective jurors were on probation, for Enriquez had served on a different jury several months earlier before a judge who had assured him that his legal problems did not render him ineligible for jury duty. Although observers suspected the defense of knowing the truth about the juror's ineligibility all along, the result was the same under Texas law. The entire Holloway trial and its verdict were voided. She was granted a new trial on November 8.

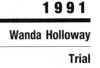
Holloway's peculiar celebrity continued while she awaited retrial. Two made-for-television films were aired about the case, "Willing to Kill: The Texas Cheerleader Story," and a tongue-in-cheek HBO production, "The Positively True Adventures of the Alleged Texas Cheerleader-Murdering Mom."

Eventually, the justice system got around to confronting Holloway with her responsibility for the crime she had planned. On September 9, 1996, a month before her second trial was to begin, she pleaded no contest and was sentenced to 10 years imprisonment. Lawyers on both sides were dissatisfied with the sentence. Holloway's attorneys continued to insist that their client was being jailed unfairly, while prosecutors were irritated by the fact that she could be paroled after serving only six months. The Heaths, who were initially content with the sentence, were less comfortable when the prosecution's prediction came true. After spending half a year in a state prison, Holloway was placed on probation for the remainder of her sentence and ordered to serve 1,000 hours of community service. She was freed and immediately disappeared from the headlines.

Wanda Halloway leaves jail after being freed on probation for trying to hire a hitman to kill the mother of her daughter's cheerleading rival. (AP/Wide World Photos)

"I think it was probably a case of a mother trying to live her life through her daughter," said George Helton, one of the detectives whose investigation led to Holloway's arrest. "Reasonable people like you and me can't understand how in the world cheerleading can be so important, but I think these people are just a bubble off."

— Tom Smith

Suggestions for Further Reading

Balleza, Maureen. "New Trial for Woman Convicted in Plot against Daughter's Rival." *New York Times* (November 9, 1991): A8.

Maier, Anne McDonald. *Mother Love, Deadly Love.* New York: Birch Lane Press, 1992.

Suro, Roberto. "Verdict Is Guilty in Cheerleading Trial." *New York Times* (September 4, 1991): A18.

Manuel Noriega Trial: 1991

Defendant: Manuel Antonio Noriega   **Crime Charged:** Drug trafficking, racketeering, and conspiracy   **Chief Defense Lawyers:** Jon May and Frank A. Rubino   **Chief Prosecutors:** James McAdams, Myles Malman, and Michael P. Sullivan   **Judge:** William M. Hoeveler   **Place:** Miami, Florida   **Dates of Trial:** September 6, 1991–April 9, 1992   **Verdict:** Guilty   **Sentence:** 40 years imprisonment

SIGNIFICANCE

This landmark trial marked the first time that a former head of a foreign government had ever faced criminal charges in an American court of law.

At 45 minutes past midnight on December 20, 1988, U.S. armed forces began the costliest and deadliest arrest mission in history, when 25,000 troops invaded Panama, all looking for one man, General Manuel Antonio Noriega, dictator of that country and suspected conduit for the flow of cocaine into America. After holing up at the Papal Embassy for two weeks, Noriega meekly surrendered and was flown to Miami, Florida, to face charges of drug trafficking.

The five-year running battle between the U.S. Government and General Noriega entered its climactic phase when his trial began September 5, 1991. Following a week given over to the demanding process of jury selection, Michael Sullivan opened for the government. He derided Noriega as a "small man in a general's uniform," who gave his "permission, authorization, and encouragement to a scheme to transform his nation into an international cocaine trafficking and manufacturing center."

In a surprise move, defense counsel Frank Rubino waived his right to deliver an opening statement to the jury, choosing instead to wait until the prosecution had revealed its entire hand before deciding what direction the defense should take.

After various academic witnesses provided some background on Panama's geopolitical history, the prosecution really got into gear when Lieutenant Colonel Luis del Cid, a close aide to Noriega for 25 years, took the stand. Like many of the prosecution witnesses, Cid was himself facing drug charges and had agreed to testify against Noriega only in return for a lighter sentence. Describing himself as Noriega's "errand boy, bodyguard and bagman," he told of suitcases stuffed with cash arriving from Colombia, either as a payoff for Noriega or to be laundered through Panamanian banks. An extraordinary interlude came when Cid, asked to identify the defendant, leapt to attention as his former boss stood up. Those in court half expected the witness to salute.

Cartel Contacts Revealed

Floyd Carlton, Noriega's personal pilot, recounted how two prominent Medellin cartel members, Pablo Escobar and Gustave Gavira, had approached him through an intermediary to "go and talk with Noriega" about an arrangement which would allow Carlton to fly cocaine to Panama under the general's

Former Panamanian dictator General Manuel Noriega being booked in Miami for charges of drug trafficking, conspiracy, and racketeering. (Archive Photos)

authority. Carlton said that Noriega "told me he didn't want his name involved in this type of problem, and that if something happened he would know nothing about it," but, he added later, "Nothing is to be done without notifying me." According to Carlton the cartel originally offered Noriega between $30,000 and $50,000 for each flight of cocaine. When he relayed this news to Noriega the general exploded: "Either they're crazy or you are! Not for that kind of money. I won't allow it to happen for less than $100,000 a flight." Over the years, Carlton estimated that Noriega received $5 million in kickbacks.

When Rubino reproved Carlton because no one else was present at these alleged meetings, the witness snapped back, "Mr. Rubino, this was a cocaine deal, we weren't talking about cookies!" Counsel fared slightly better in getting Carlton to admit that Noriega had been angered to learn of illicit money-laundering flights into Panama.

By far the most prominent witness against Noriega was Carlos Ledher Rivas, the only founding member of the Medellin cartel ever to face charges in an American court. Amid heavy security, Ledher, whose 1988 conviction for drug trafficking brought him a sentence of life plus 135 years, said Noriega offered the cartel a cocaine pipeline to the United States." In addition to paying the general $1,000 for every kilo of cocaine that passed through the country, the cartel agreed to pay Noriega 5 percent of all profits deposited in Panamanian banks—a sum that other witnesses said often amounted to $60 million a week.

Ledher explained the cartel's plight: "We were desperately looking for new routes. We had no point of transshipment for the cocaine that was piling up in Colombia." Under questioning from prosecutor Guy Lewis, Ledher elaborated on Noriega's alleged involvement with Fidel Castro, whom he said was also dealing with the Medellin cartel. The doubtful pertinence of much that Ledher had to say aroused defense suspicions that the witness was testifying very much out of self-interest, prepared to blacken Noriega's name at all costs in hopes of getting his own jail sentence reduced.

After establishing the existence of such a *quid pro quo*, Rubino challenged Ledher about Medellin involvement with the Nicaraguan Contras, a line of questioning that clearly unsettled the witness. With great reluctance, he said, "To the best of my recollection, there was some contribution to the Contra anticommunist movement." When Rubino pushed for an exact figure, Ledher hedged and tried to dodge, until finally saying, "It could have been around $10 million." Rubino was prevented from pursuing this source of potential embarrassment to the U.S. government, which had also been funding the Contras, on grounds that it was not relevant.

Judge Taken Ill

The much-awaited defense strategy had be put on hold when Judge William Hoeveler was stricken by illness and had to undergo open heart surgery. After more than a six-week delay, Noriega's team finally got its chance. The defense attorneys provided few surprises and none of the bombshells that had been predicted. Attorney Jon May portrayed Noriega as one of America's greatest allies in the fight against drugs. The level and quality of cooperation he gave the United States, May proclaimed "unprecedented among the leaders of Central and South American nations. . . . Over and over the U.S. came to General Noriega for assistance," when it served "our national interest to use that relationship in times of crisis."

Some evidence to support that contention came from Thomas Telles, former head of the Drug Enforcement Agency's Panamanian office. He said that Noriega had promised to help the United States in identifying cartel members' bank accounts, monitoring movements of their money, and seizing the chemicals needed to make cocaine.

Further confirming Noriega's ties to U.S. policy was Donald Winters, Central Intelligence Agency station chief in Panama from 1984 to 1986. Over a period of 15 years, he said, Noriega provided Washington with considerable information about Fidel Castro, information deemed so useful that then CIA Director William Casey made a personal visit in 1984 to thank the Panamanian dictator. Asked to characterize the nature of the meeting, Winters said, "I would describe it as something more substantial than a courtesy call."

Throughout the trial Noriega remained impassive and largely silent, He did not take the stand in his own defense. After almost seven months, closing arguments finally began on March 31, 1992. Describing Noriega as "nothing more than a corrupt, crooked and rotten cop [who] sold his uniform, his army and his protection to a murderous criminal gang called the Medellin cocaine cartel," Assistant U.S. Attorney Myles Malman said that Noriega had been responsible for polluting U.S. streets with "tons and tons of a deadly white powder." Malman admitted that many of the prosecution witnesses were less than model citizens, but as he put it, law enforcement officials must use "small fish" to catch "big fish" and Noriega was "the biggest fish of all."

It was an argument bitterly denounced by Frank Rubino. "This indictment stinks," he told the jurors, "It stinks like dead fish. It smells from here to Washington." The case against Noriega, he said, was predicated solely on the theory that "if you throw enough mud against a wall, some of it will stick." He zeroed in on the more than 20 prosecution witnesses already convicted of drug offenses. "They are the scum of the earth. These people are disgusting. What kind of morals do these people have?" He reserved his most acerbic condemnation for Carlos Ledher Rivas, whom he called "the Charles Manson of this case."

Over five difficult and often stormy days, the jury deliberated. At one point the recalcitrance of a single juror threatened to bring about a mistrial, but on April 9 they found Noriega guilty on eight charges, while acquitting him of two.

Two months later, Judge Hoeveler sentenced Noriega to 40 years imprisonment.

In the years since his conviction, Noriega has maintained that he was not given a fair trial. In 1996, he appealed his conviction on the basis that a key witness had been bribed to testify against him. Noriega's attorneys sought a new trial based on the revelation that a key government witness connected to the Cali drug cartel had been paid $1.25 million to testify against Noriega. However, a federal judge ruled that Noriega was not entitled to a new trial.

Noriega was not deterred by this ruling. In 1997, he returned to the public spotlight when his book, *America's Prisoner: The Memoirs of Manuel Noriega,* was published. In the book, Noriega exposed covert dealings with the U.S. government, including dealings with Oliver North and former president George Bush. Still, the book did little to help Noriega's public image within the United States.

In 1999, Noriega's 40-year sentence was reduced to 30 years. He was eligible for parole in mid-2000.

In political, criminal, and economic terms, the trial of General Manuel Noriega is without equal. By some estimates it cost $168 million to convict him. More certain is the expense in American lives: 25 killed in the invasion. What impact Noriega's incarceration has on the flow of drugs into the United States remains to be seen.

—Colin Evans and Ron Formica

Suggestions for Further Reading

Booth, Cathy. "The Trial Of Manuel Noriega." *The Los Angeles Daily Journal* (April 7, 1992): 6ff.

Dinges, John. *Our Man in Panama.* New York: Random House, 1990.

Kempe, Frederick. *Divorcing the Dictator.* New York: G.P. Putnam's Sons, 1990.

Koster, R. Medellin and Guillermo Sanchez. *In the Time of the Tyrants.* New York: W.W. Norton & Co., 1990.

McDonald, Marci. "Threat Of The Beast." *Maclean's* (September 16, 1991): 22ff.

Noriega, Manuel, and Peter Eisner. *America's Prisoner: The Memoirs of Manuel Noriega.* New York: Acacia Press, 1997.

George Russell, Jr. Trial: 1991

Defendant: George Walterfield Russell, Jr.   **Crimes Charged:** Murder
Chief Defense Lawyers: Miriam Schwartz, Brad Hampton
Chief Prosecutors: Rebecca Roe, Jeffrey Baird   **Judge:** Patricia Aitken
Place: Seattle, Washington   **Date of Trial:** September 13–October 18, 1991
Verdict: Guilty   **Sentence:** Life in prison without parole

SIGNIFICANCE
Winning a conviction in Washington State's first serial-murder trial ultimately depended on convincing jurors that the degrading pose of all three murder victims constituted the unique "signature" of a single sociopathic killer.

Folks around wealthy Mercer Island, Washington, just couldn't dislike good old George. Sure, he'd crash your pad, "borrow" your car for days on end, relieve you of a few treasured items. But then he'd turn around and cook you a gourmet dinner, treat your friends to a round of drinks, and give you earnest, religion-tinged advice. All this was done with a big smile, a hug, and silky smooth assurances that "it's cool, hon."

Petty Thief Turned Murderer

George Russell, Jr., was a charming reprobate. But by the time he was 31, his Jekyll-Hyde existence would evolve from a lying, petty thief to a sadistic serial killer. This slender, smart, and sure guy would become a woman-hating murderer seeking sexual satisfaction by degrading and abusing them—dead or alive.

Since moving to the wealthy Seattle suburb as a child, one of only a handful of African Americans on the island, Russell had brushes with the law: stealing from high school lockers, marijuana use, truancy. But he ingratiated himself with police by running errands for them, working as an informant, listening to cops' personal problems. The local police station became Russell's second home; the police his substitute family. Eventually, Russell's escalating crime, pathological lying, and in-your-face toying with the law destroyed that bond.

Troubled Youth

Abandonment was the story of George Russell's life. His college-bound mother left him with a negligent grandmother in Florida when he was six months old. She later remarried. With her dentist husband, she moved to Mercer Island when Russell was in junior high school. His mother and stepfather doted on their own new daughter, but Russell was barely tolerated. Although his gregarious nature earned him many friends at school, he couldn't move beyond shallow popularity to real acceptance among the fickle, indulged white teens of Mercer Island.

As the sense of isolation grew, Russell's crimes became more frequent and serious. At night, he donned dark clothes, usually "borrowed" from pals, and boldly invaded homes as families slept inside. He stole cash, jewelry, and personal mementos. He often stood next to the bed of sleeping women, gazing silently at them. Investigators theorized that the nocturnal burglar plaguing the area gained perverse sexual gratification from his exploits.

From early youth through adolescence, Russell was a one-man crime wave in suburban Seattle. He was incarcerated 24 times, mostly for minor offenses. His intimate knowledge of police procedure and the six-mile-long island helped him allude arrest and avoid conviction for most of his crimes. In a real pinch, he could manipulate people into lying for him, especially the younger, adoring crowd to which he gravitated.

In his 20s, Russell became an affable fixture in the rollicking nightclubs of Bellevue, just east of Mercer Island. He couldn't hold a legitimate job, he carried all his possessions—including a collection of pornographic magazines—in a duffel bag and paper sacks, and his daytime home was the apartment of his latest unsuspecting "best friend." He said he worked as an undercover cop at night. Most who befriended him thought George Russell was a wonderful guy. Those who knew him better thought he showed little emotion, no guilt, and growing hostility toward women. They said he was obsessed with sex. Charming George would hit on anybody.

A Serial Murderer on Mercer Island

When three murdered Bellevue nightclub habitués turned up within two months in the summer of 1990, some, including an ex-girlfriend whom he had beaten after his move to Bellevue, quickly suspected Russell.

The first victim was Mary Ann Pohlreich. Her obviously posed, nude body was found beside a McDonald's restaurant dumpster. Her left foot was crossed over her right ankle, her hands lay over her stomach, clutching a fir cone, as if she were lying in a coffin. An autopsy showed she had been brutally beaten, choked and kicked so hard that her liver had split against her spinal column. She had been raped after her death, a victim of a "sadistic necrophile."

Seven weeks later, the ex-husband of Carol Marie Bleethe found her battered body in the bed of her East Bellevue home. This time the killer showed thought, imagination, and improvisation. Bleethe, mother of two young daughters who were at home when she was murdered, had been struck repeatedly in the head with a weapon. It had sliced her ear and left 13 distinctive Y shapes on her body. She had been bitten and kicked with such ferocity that two broken ribs penetrated the chest cavity. Her head was bound in a plastic dry-cleaning bag.

Although she had been "blitzed" in her sleep, her body lay nude except for red high heels. The killer had positioned her on her king-sized bed so that her crotch faced the bedroom door. He had inserted a Savage .22 long rifle that Bleethe kept under the bed five and a half inches into her vagina. Her favorite diamond ring was missing. Friends later testified that Russell cut pictures of the first two victims—whom he called "skanky sluts"—from the newspaper, taped them to the wall, and bragged that police would not find their killer.

The third body, that of Andrea "Randi" Levine, turned up on September 3, 1990. She too had been "blitzed" in her sleep. The killer had savagely beaten her with an aluminum baseball bat, spraying the room with blood. Her spread-legged body was stabbed and covered from scalp to the bottom of her feet with 231 small knife wounds, some in patterns. They appeared to have been inflicted after death in an uncommon necrophilic perversion known as "picquerism." A plastic vibrator had been stuffed into her mouth. She held a copy of *More Joy of Sex* under her left arm. Her brains leaked out onto the bed.

The killer had wiped down the bat and taken every knife from the house. Police theorized he had used a kitchen knife to violate his victim, then taken them so that the real weapon used in the picquerism couldn't be identified. The victim's favorite amethyst ring was missing.

Authorities Zero in on Russell

Investigators called on an expert in sexualized crime who said that the murders were the work of one man. Although the expert said the serial killer would be a young, white male, police zeroed in on Russell, who grew up in a white, upper middle class neighborhood and "acted white." The challenge of the investigation and of the subsequent trial was connecting Russell to all three victims.

Semen found in Mary Ann Pohlreich matched Russell's blood type. Hair found on all three bodies proved to be "Negroid." Eventually, Russell was tied to missing rings from the bodies of Carol Bleethe and Randi Levine. Small blood stains in a truck Russell borrowed on the night Pohlreich died matched her blood type. Police arrested Russell on January 10, 1991.

During Russell's trial, the prosecution succeeded in admitting into evidence the controversial DNA tests for the hairs, semen, and blood stains. But winning a conviction rested on moving beyond circumstantial evidence and convincing jurors that the degrading pose of all three bodies constituted the unique "signature" of a single sociopathic killer.

Both the prosecution and defense brought experts in sexual homicide and behavioral profiling to the stand. John Douglas, the famous FBI behaviorist, testified that he found a common denominator in the way the victims were "penetrated vaginally, anally or orally with some type of device, foreign object." He also said the close timeframe of the murders pointed to one perpetrator.

Russell Vorpagel, a respected 20-year FBI veteran now private investigator, disagreed. He claimed there were too many differences in the way the women were killed, degraded, and posed to have been the work of one person. He said Pohlreich's body was posed peacefully, Bleethe's body was not raped; a woman could have been the killer. He said the odd stab wounds on Levine's body separated her murder from the others.

Russell's lawyers emphasized the possibility that the wrong man was accused. They hinted that ex-husbands or ex-boyfriends were responsible, not the friendly guy at the defense table.

Russell, smartly dressed in a navy sports coat, gray slacks, white shirt, and tie, appeared alternately bored and bemused. He did not take the stand.

After 22 hours of deliberation, the jury returned verdicts of guilty of the first-degree murder of Pohlreich and aggravated first-degree murder in the cases of Bleeth and Levine. Judge Patricia Aitken sentenced Russell to life imprisonment without possibility of parole. Jurors later told reporters that there'd been little disagreement that Russell was the lone killer. They just took a long time to discuss the bizarre facts.

—B. J. Welborn

Suggestions for Further Reading

Olson, Jack. *Charmer: A Ladies Man and His Victims.* New York: Avon Books, 1994.

Transcript: *City Confidential: Sunny Days, Deadly Nights on Mercer Island.* A&E Home Video.

El Sayyid Nosair Trial: 1991

Defendant: El Sayyid A. Nosair   **Crime Charged:** Murder, attempted murder, and assault   **Chief Defense Lawyers:** William M. Kunstler and Michael Warren   **Chief Prosecutor:** William Greenbaum   **Judge:** Alvin Schlesinger   **Place:** New York, New York   **Dates of Trial:** November 4– December 21, 1991   **Verdict:** Not guilty, murder, and attempted murder; Guilty, assault with a deadly weapon   **Sentence:** 7–22 years imprisonment

SIGNIFICANCE

Never has the unpredictability of juries been more idly demonstrated than in this case of such seeming straight forwardness.

Just minutes after delivering a speech at a New York City hotel in November 1990, Meir Kahane, militant conservative rabbi and former Jewish Defense League head, was shot down by a gunman. As the assassin fled, he wounded a Kahane supporter. Outside the building, El Sayyid Nosair, a 36-year-old Arab, was tackled by an armed U.S. Postal Service officer. Shots were exchanged, and both men were hit. Following treatment for his wound, Nosair was charged with murder.

Violent clashes between extremist Jews and Arabs on the steps of the courthouse marred the trial's opening day, November 4, 1991. Judge Alvin Schlesinger, plagued by death threats, commented sadly, "I have never seen so much hate. It's beyond reason, principle, and cause."

When lead prosecutor William Greenbaum led off for the state he contended that Nosair alone had fired the deadly bullets. Contrary to several pretrial statements in which he called Kahane's murder "a planned political assassination," Greenbaum neglected to attribute any motive to the accused, apparently feeling that the sheer weight of evidence obviated this customary bulwark of most prosecution cases.

Chief defense attorney William Kunstler argued that the reason for this omission was simple: his client was innocent, just someone who had fled the hotel fearing for his own life. According to Kunstler, Kahane had been murdered by a disgruntled supporter in a dispute over money. "You'll have to decide who shot Meir Kahane," he told the jury. "This case is not cut and dried."

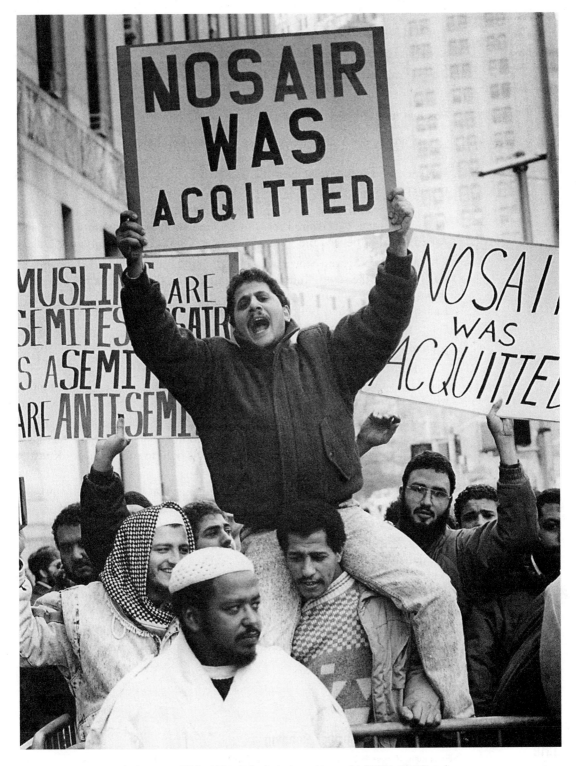
Supporters of El Sayyid Nosair after the jury's surprising verdict. (AP/Wide World Photos)

Michael Djunaedi, a student, placed Nosair with a gun in his hand just moments after the shooting. "I heard some guys yelling, 'He's got a gun!'" Seconds later, Djunaedi said, postal worker Carlos Acosta and Nosair began firing at each other.

Positive Identification Introduced

Corroboration came from Acosta, who, without being asked, stood up from the witness chair, pointed at the defendant, and shouted, "This man shot me!" Kunstler's suggestion that Nosair Chad actually had been fleeing from armed pursuers drew a scoffing response. "My focus was on him, he had the gun."

Another spectator, Ari Gottesman, told of standing between Kahane and "a dark-skinned, dark-haired man," who fired two shots at point-blank range. Asked whether he saw the gunman in court, Gottesman picked out Nosair.

When Dr. Steven Stowe, who had attended Kahane immediately after he was shot, took the stand, Kunstler seized the chance to expand on his conspiracy theory. "Didn't you do everything in your power that night to see that Meir Kahane never reached Bellevue (Hospital]?"

"No, sir," the doctor replied. Later, though, he did concede that he and paramedics had argued over what treatment to give.

Kunstler brushed aside the testimony of a forensic expert, Detective Robert Cotter, positively identifying the Magnum found next to Nosair as the murder weapon. Kunstler claimed it had been "planted" by the real killers of Kahane.

In all, the prosecution presented 51 witnesses. By contrast Kunstler called just six, none of whom supported his vague contention that Kahane had been shot by his own followers. Nosair, exercising his right to silence, heard Kunstler depict him as a tragic victim of circumstances.

Kunstler's eloquence found a ready audience. On December 21, 1991, the jury acquitted Nosair of murder or attempted murder and convicted him only on assault and weapons charges.

Sentencing Nosair to a maximum sentence of 7–22 years, Judge Schlesinger denounced the jury's verdict as "against the overwhelming weight of evidence . . . devoid of common sense and logic." Bemoaning his inability to impose a stiffer sentence, Judge Schlesinger said: "I believe the defendant conducted a rape of this country, of our Constitution and of our laws."

The extraordinary outcome of this case provided compelling proof that the human content in a trial can never be ignored or taken for granted.

—Colin Evans

Suggestions for Further Reading

Friedman, Robert I. *The False Prophet.* New York: Lawrence Hill Books, 1990.

Hewitt, Bill. "A Career Of Preaching Hatred." *People* (November 19, 1990): 48ff.

Kotler, Ya'ir. *Heil Kahane.* New York: Adama Books, 1986.

Masland, Tom. "The High Price Of Hatred." *Newsweek* (November 19, 1990): 48ff.

Rosenbaum, Ron. "The Most Hated Man In America." *Vanity Fair* (March 1992): 68ff.

Charles Keating Trials: 1991–99

Defendant: Charles F. Keating, Jr. **Crimes Charged:** First trial: Securities fraud; Second trial: fraud, conspiracy, racketeering
Chief Defense Lawyers: Stephen C. Neal; several other attorneys have represented him over the course of his many civil and criminal trials
Chief Prosecutor: William Hodgman; several others have prosecuted him at the state and federal level **Judge:** Lance A. Ito **Place:** Los Angeles, California **Dates of Trial:** First criminal trial: November 18–December 4, 1991; second trial: January 3, 1993 **Verdict:** First trial: Guilty on 17 of 18 counts; second trial: guilty on 73 counts **Sentence:** Second trial: 151 months in prison, overturned after Keating had served 50 months of the sentence; over the years, fines of several hundred thousand dollars

SIGNIFICANCE

Charles Keating was convicted for securities fraud in connection with the largest savings and loan collapse in history, which cost the American taxpayers $2.6 billion. The repercussions reached the U.S. Senate, where five senators (Cranston, DeConcini, Glenn, McCain, and Riegle), known as the "Keating Five" were investigated for ethics violations in connection with their helping Keating avoid federal regulators in return for large campaign contributions.

The problems experienced by the savings and loan industry did not begin with the spectacular wave of collapses in the late 1980s. In fact, there have been financial problems with savings and loan (S&Ls) institutions for nearly 20 years before then. In the 1970s, S&Ls chafed under federal restrictions that limited the amount of interest they could pay to depositors, the types of investments S&Ls could make and when they could borrow money. Many of these restrictions made the S&Ls uncompetitive with traditional banking and finance companies.

Congress bowed to S&L lobbying, abolished the interest rate limitations on deposits, and lifted restrictions that previously only permitted S&Ls to invest in single-family home mortgages. Congress believed that deregulation would bring private-sector money into S&Ls and revitalize the industry without federal involvement. In many respects, Congress deregulated the S&Ls rather than spend federal money to bail them out, with disastrous consequences.

Charles F. Keating, Jr., was one of many people who would treat S&L deregulation as a license to steal. Keating was a close associate of Carl Lindner, a wealthy businessman from Cincinnati, Ohio who owned the American Financial Corporation (AFC). In 1976, Keating bought a subsidiary of AFC called American Continental Homes from Lindner, which Keating later renamed American Continental Corporation (ACC). ACC embarked on several ambitious real estate development projects, mostly in Arizona and Colorado. To finance its activities, ACC set up its own in-house mortgage company and was a pioneer in creating the type of financial package and instrument known as the "mortgage-backed security." Keating, however, had his sights much higher.

ACC Buys Lincoln Savings and Loan

On February 24, 1984, Keating's ACC bought Lincoln Savings and Loan for $55 million. Lincoln S&L was one of the largest S&Ls in southern California, with assets at the time of more than a billion dollars. Keating was attracted to Lincoln S&L not only because of its size, but also because California state S&L regulations were very lax.

Keating and ACC installed their own management team to run Lincoln S&L and began to systematically pillage its assets through thinly disguised accounting gimmicks. Millions were funneled into ACC to cover its losses from real estate projects that had turned sour. In additions, Lincoln S&L was used as a conduit to sell hundreds of millions of dollars of ACC bonds to depositors. More than 20,000 people—many of whom were retired and were investing their pensions:embought ACC junk bonds from salesmen who told them that the bonds were federally insured, when, in fact, they were not.

Keating surrounded himself, Lincoln S&L, and ACC with an army of lawyers and accountants who thwarted the few efforts federal and state authorities made to look at ACC's transactions with Lincoln S&L. Finally, however, the house of cards fell in. On April 14, 1989, the Federal Home Loan Bank Board (FHLBB) exercised its authority and appointed a conservator, who took over Lincoln S&L. Unable to sustain itself on Lincoln S&L's assets any longer, ACC went bankrupt in the same month, and the purchasers of ACC bonds lost all of their money. After the conservator found that Lincoln was insolvent by more than $600 million, the FHLBB (later succeeded by the Office of Thrift Supervision, OTS) put Lincoln S&L into receivership on August 2, 1990. Cleaning up Lincoln S&L would eventually cost the taxpayers $2.6 billion.

Litigation Abounds

A myriad of civil litigation and criminal prosecutions followed the collapse of ACC and Lincoln S&L. Civil and criminal trials, followed by countless appeals, went on for nearly a decade. Civil class action suits were filed by the purchasers of ACC bonds against Keating; other officers and directors of ACC; and the banks, lawyers, and accountants who shielded them from regulatory scrutiny for so long. Federal and state criminal charges were filed against Keating and others. There were regulatory actions by the OTS against the same banks, lawyers, and accountants being sued in civil court. In March 1992, the OTS shocked the legal world when it froze the assets of the huge, 400-lawyer law firm Kaye, Scholer, Fierman, Hays & Handler, which had represented Keating. After bringing the firm to its knees, the OTS imposed a $41 million settlement on it.

The only criminal case against Keating occurred when the state of California prosecuted him for 18 separate counts of securities fraud in connection with the sale of ACC junk bonds under the misrepresentation that they were federally insured. This trial took place in Los Angeles before Judge Lance A. Ito. The chief defense lawyer was Stephen C. Neal and the prosecutor was Deputy District Attorney William Hodgman.

The trial began on November 18, 1991. Many of the elderly investors who had purchased ACC junk bonds attended the trial, and yelled angrily at Keating both in the courtroom and as he was being escorted to and from trial. One spectator managed to punch Keating in the arm.

Keating's defense lawyers tried to argue that Keating had no control over what salesmen were telling investors about federal insurance coverage for ACC junk bonds, but after hearing all the evidence, the jury returned its verdict finding Keating guilty of 17 of the 18 counts.

Keating Draws Maximum Sentence

During the sentencing hearing on April 10, 1992, seven small investors testified, and begged Judge Ito to punish Keating to the maximum extent provided by law. One of the witnesses, Harriet Chappuise, stated that "Charles Keating did not steal a loaf of bread. He stole the bread out of the mouths of thousands of old people. Try, Mr. Keating, try living on Social Security checks." Ito sentenced Keating to the statutory maximum of 10 years in prison, and to pay a $250,000 fine, but Keating's lawyers immediately began to appeal the conviction and sentence. Keating's lawyers argued that the number of legal actions against him violated his right to due process under the Constitution. Defense attorney Neal stated:

> You can make a pretty good case that it is overkill and a waste of taxpayers' money.

Joseph W. Cotchett, an attorney representing one of the plaintiffs in the civil cases against Keating, did not concede that there was any due process violation resulting from "overkill" litigation, but agreed that there are too many federal agencies jumping on the bandwagon too late to do any good:

> Where were all the inside-the-beltway bureaucrats when Charley Keating was riding high on the backs of the public?

Keating was prosecuted in a second criminal trial in Los Angeles, this time for violating federal laws against fraud, conspiracy and racketeering. The case went to trial in October 1992, and on January 6, 1993 the jury returned a guilty verdict on all 73 criminal counts against Keating. This trial resulted in a sentence of 151 months in jail. As with the state trial in Los Angeles, Keating's lawyers immediately began to appeal the conviction and sentence. His lawyers argued that the jurors in the federal case were influenced by Keating's conviction at the state court level. After several years of appeals, U.S. District Judge Mariana R. Pfaelzer disagreed with Keating's attorneys but still overturned the conviction, citing a presumption of prejudice and finding that the law compelled her to grant Keating's motion for a new trial. By this time, Keating had already spent nearly 50 months in a federal prison.

Keating Loses in Civil Court, too

The first civil case against Keating was a class action lawsuit filed in federal court in Tucson, Arizona. The lawsuit was filed on behalf of the more than 20,000 people who lost their money after buying ACC bonds. In addition to Keating, there were three other defendants, who had been involved in ACC's real estate schemes: a wealthy businessman in Tempe, Arizona, named Conley Wolfswinkel, Continental Southern, Inc. of Atlanta, Georgia, and the Saudi European Investment Corporation.

The trial began on April 1, 1992, before Judge Richard Bilby. Keating did not appear at the trial or have any lawyer represent him during the proceedings, claiming that he was too busy preparing for the October 1992 federal criminal trial in Los Angeles. The other defendants, however, denied that they had acted jointly with Keating in causing Lincoln S&L's collapse, and the case dragged out for more than three months.

After deliberating for eight days, on July 10, 1992, the jury found Keating and the other three defendants guilty of violating federal antifraud laws. The plaintiffs' lawyers had sought $288.7 million in compensatory damages from Keating alone, but the jury awarded $600 million in compensatory damages, with an additional amount of $1.5 billion awarded for punitive damages. Because the compensatory damages were tripled under federal antiracketeering statutes to $1.8 billion, the total amount of the verdict against Keating was $3.3 billion. The jury rendered similarly large verdicts against the other three defendants as well.

Shadows Fall over Senators

Keating's downfall had repercussions at the highest levels of government. During the height of his power, Keating contributed heavily to the political campaigns and causes of U.S. Senators Alan Cranston, Dennis DeConcini, John Glenn, John McCain, and Donald W. Riegle, Jr. These senators intervened on Keating's behalf several times with federal regulators in the late 1980s to allay growing suspicions about Keating's activities. Cranston was the largest beneficiary, receiving roughly $850,000 in contributions from Keating. When Keating's empire collapsed and the senators' involvement was revealed, they were labeled the "Keating Five" by the press. After an investigation of several months by the Senate Ethics Committee, the committee voted on November 19, 1991, to rebuke Cranston for improper conduct, but did not recommend formal censure by the full U.S. Senate. The other Senators received nothing but minor chastisement.

In reality, the connection between Charles Keating and the senators did little to hurt their political careers. By 2000, the press hardly mentioned John McCain's involvement with the "Keating Five" when the Arizona senator ran for the Republican presidential nomination.

A Final Resolution?

Throughout the 1990s, in trial after trial, Charles Keating never publicly admitted any wrongdoing. This changed in April 1999, when he pleaded guilty to four federal counts of fraud. In doing so, Keating admitted that he had siphoned $975,000 out to the ACC just a few days before the company filed for bankruptcy. A new federal trial had been scheduled to begin in 1999, but Keating's turnaround precluded it.

In announcing the guilty plea, U.S. Attorney Alejandro Mayorka said, "For more than 10 years, Charles Keating has fought us, denied any guilt, and refused to accept responsibility for his illegal conduct. Today, that fight is over."

Keating, 75 years old at the time of the plea, was spared more jail time. He was sentenced to the 50 months he had already spent incarcerated before his conviction was reversed.

—*Stephen G. Christianson and Ron Formica*

Suggestions for Further Reading

Davis, Sally Ogle. "Keating's Folly." *Los Angeles* (November 1991): 58–62.

Fowler, Jack. "The Keating Fizzle." *National Review* (February 1991): 22–23.

Glassman, James K. "The Great Banks Robbery: Deconstructing the S&L Crisis." *The New Republic* (October 1990): 16–21.

"House of Ill Repute." *The New Republic* (December 1990): 7–9.

United States Senate. *Preliminary Inquiry Into Allegations Regarding Senators Cranston, DeConcini, Glenn, McCain, and Riegle, and Lincoln Savings and Loan.* Washington: U.S. Government Printing Office, 1991.

William Kennedy Smith Trial: 1991

Defendant: William Kennedy Smith   **Crime Charged:** Rape
Chief Defense Lawyers: Roy E. Black, Mark Schnapp, and Mark Seiden
Chief Prosecutors: Moira K. Lasch and Ellen Roberts   **Judge:** Mary E. Lupo
Place: West Palm Beach, Florida   **Dates of Trial:** December 2–11, 1991
Verdict: Not guilty

SIGNIFICANCE

The Kennedy family name and the concomitant glare of global media attention
made this nothing less than the most heavily scrutinized rape trial in history.

A chance encounter at a Palm Beach, Florida, nightspot between William
Kennedy Smith and Patricia Bowman led to the couple returning to the
Kennedy compound overlooking the Atlantic Ocean. From the house they
walked down to the beach. What happened next would become the subject of
worldwide headlines. According to Bowman, Smith raped her. Smith maintained
that everything which occurred had been with Bowman's consent. The state,
satisfied that Smith had a case to answer, filed rape charges against him.

When she rose to speak to a jury of four women and two men on December
2, 1991, prosecutor Moira Lasch already had lost an important battle. Judge Mary
Lupo had earlier denied the prosecution's request to admit the testimony of
three other women who claimed that Smith had assaulted them between 1983
and 1988 on grounds that it did not demonstrate the discernible pattern of
behavior required by Florida law for introduction. This meant that Lasch had to
pin virtually her entire case on the word of the accuser.

First, though, Anne Mercer, a friend of Bowman's, who had also been at
the Kennedy house on the night in question, told the court that Bowman was
"literally shaking and she looked messed up . . . she said she had been raped."
When Mercer had confronted Smith to ask him how he could have acted as he
did, his response, she said, was simply to shrug his shoulders.

Tabloid Interview Nets $40,000

In a blistering cross-examination, defense counsel Roy Black knocked gap-
ing holes in Mercer's testimony. He forced a retreat from her earlier assertion to

police that Bowman had been raped twice, and that on one of these occasions Smith's uncle, Senator Edward M. Kennedy of Massachusetts, had watched. Black also got Mercer to admit that she had failed to inform the authorities of details she subsequently revealed for the tabloid TV program "A Current Affair."

Gasps filled the courtroom when Mercer confessed that she had been paid $40,000 for her story. By implication, Black suggested that Mercer's tale had been heavily embellished for monetary gain. It was a stigma that the witness never fully shrugged off. Black drove home his advantage by playing Mercer a taped account she had made earlier for the police that contained several statements that disagreed with the version she had provided the court.

After posting a $10,000 bond, William Kennedy Smith makes a statement to the press. (AP/Wide World Photos)

In a surprise move, prosecutor Lasch produced the accuser early in the trial. To protect her identity, TV cameras obscured Bowman's face with a blue dot. (Following the trial Bowman elected to abandon her anonymity for a TV interview.) Referring to the defendant first as "Mr. Smith," and later as "that man," Bowman described the alleged assault, saying, "I thought he was going to kill me."

When Black chided Bowman for several lapses of memory, she insisted, "The only thing I can remember about that week is Mr. Smith raped me."

Black wasn't impressed. "I know you've been prepared to say that."

Bowman snapped back. "I have not been prepared to say anything."

Throughout his cross-examination Black walked a fine line; how best to undermine the accuser's credibility without wishing to appear bullying or insensitive. On those occasions when his questioning provoked a tearful response, Black immediately backed off and suggested a recess. Under his deft probing, however, Bowman did acknowledge a history of problems with men, resulting, she said, from "having one-night stands."

On rebuttal, Lasch asked Bowman whether she had any ulterior motives for bringing the charge. Bowman replied, "What he did to me was wrong. I have a child and it's not right and I don't want to live the rest of my life in fear of that man. And I don't want to be responsible for him doing it to someone else."

This final comment brought Black to his feet, objecting. Judge Lupo ordered the remark stricken from the record, calling it "inappropriate."

Curiously, the prosecution called Smith's uncle, Senator Edward Kennedy, as its witness. If, as some observers believed, Lasch was attempting to visit some of the senator's perceived foibles upon his nephew, then she sorely miscalculated. For some 40 minutes Senator Kennedy managed to re-create Camelot in a Palm Beach courthouse as he evoked memories of the family's numerous tragedies. Nothing he said was remotely helpful to Lasch's case. Not for the first time the prosecution's strategy showed signs of being ill-conceived and poorly executed.

Much of the defense was built around forensic testimony. Charles M. Sieger, an architect, said that, given the house's construction, had Bowman screamed as she claimed, the sounds would have been clearly audible indoors, yet no resident admitted to hearing anything.

Rather less successful was Professor Jay Siegel's testimony. He stated that sand found in Bowman's underwear most likely came from the beach, which tallied with Smith's version of events, and not the lawn, where Bowman claimed she had been raped. Lasch bored in. "Wouldn't you agree that a 6-foot-2, 200-pound man running up a beach is going to churn up some sand?" Siegel agreed. Lasch went on: "And if the defendant was wet . . . some of that [sand] could stick to his body, couldn't it?" Besides having to concede this possibility, Siegel also was forced to admit that the lawn itself actually contained a significant amount of sand, thus rendering his testimony virtually useless.

Defendant Remains Cool

It took William Kennedy Smith just 29 minutes to tell his side of the story. Black concluded the brief account by asking if he had "at any time" raped his accuser. "No, I did not," Smith replied firmly.

Lasch went on the attack. "What are you saying, that she raped you, Mr. Smith?" Later, in reference to an alleged second sexual encounter, she leered, "What are you, some kind of sex machine?"

Smith weathered the assault coolly. He reiterated his story that the evening had turned ugly when he had inadvertently called the accuser "Kathy." She "sort of snapped . . . she got very upset." Later, he said, Bowman apologized as she was leaving the compound, "I am sorry I got upset . . . I had a wonderful night. You're a terrific guy." Minutes later, however, she was back, crying and claiming that he had raped her, repeatedly calling him "Michael."

Frustrated by Smith's matter-of-fact responses, Lasch adopted a different tack, claiming the Kennedy family was trying to engineer a cover-up. Smith would have none of it. "If you're implying that my family is lying to protect me, you are dead wrong." Someone else less than impressed with this line of questioning was Judge Lupo. "If you ask one more question along these lines," she told Lasch, "you will not get away with it. Failure to abide by this instruction will result in legal action." It was a humiliating rebuke for the prosecutor, coming as it did with Judge Lupo's oblique reference to the fact that she suspected Lasch might be angling for a deliberate mistrial, thus salvaging her case for another day.

In closing, Black said, "they want us to believe that this young man goes up there and rapes a screaming young woman under the open windows not only of his mother, but his sister, two prosecutors from New York, and the father of one of them who is a former special agent for the FBI!" Making no attempt to apologize for his client's self-confessed dishonorable behavior on the night concerned, Black still appealed to the jury to exhibit "general, human common sense."

Lasch could dwell on only inconsistencies. Referring to Bowman, "She didn't know this man. She didn't even have an opportunity to know him. . . . This woman has had a child. She's a high-risk pregnancy. If she was going to have consensual sex on March 30, 1991, she would use birth control."

On December 11, 1991, the case went to the jury. After deliberating for just 79 minutes they returned with a verdict of not guilty.

Millions of viewers watched this drama played out on their television screens. For most it was their first glimpse of the extraordinary problems that attend "date rape" cases. By its very nature this kind of rape will always remain a question of "he said, she said." In such circumstances courtroom demeanor invariably decides the day.

Two years after the verdict, William Kennedy Smith had another brush with the law. He was arrested and charged with assault after he hit a bouncer at a bar in Arlington, Virginia. Smith pleaded guilty to the charge and was sentenced to 100 hours of community service. Since completing his sentence, Smith has returned to a relatively quiet life of practicing medicine and heading an organization he started, Physicians Against Land Mines.

—Colin Evans

Suggestions for Further Reading

Dunne, Dominick. "The Verdict." *Vanity Fair* (March 1992): 210ff.

Fields, Suzanne. "Sexual Revolution Bares Its Flaws." *Insight* (January 6, 1992): 17ff.

McDonald, Marci. "Beyond The Trial." *Maclean's* (December 23, 1991): 16ff.

Stein, Harry. "It Happened One Night." *Playboy* (April 1992): 78ff.

Taylor, John. "A Theory Of The Case." *New York* (January 6, 1992): 34ff.

Richard Lyon Trial: 1991–92

Defendant: Richard Allen Abood Lyon   **Crime Charged:** Murder
Chief Defense Lawyer: Dan C. Guthrie   **Chief Prosecutor:** Jerri Simms
Judge: John C. Creuzot   **Place:** Dallas, Texas   **Date of Trial:** December 2,
1991–January 19, 1992   **Verdict:** Guilty   **Sentence:** Life in prison and
$10,000 fine

SIGNIFICANCE

This murder case had all the elements of a good "whodunit": old money, a marriage gone sour, and arsenic poisoning. The accused husband, a suave Harvard graduate, took the stand in his own defense, almost convincing the jury of his innocence. Then the prosecution brought in a last-minute surprise witness with startling information that sealed Lyon's fate.

An autopsy revealed that when Nancy Dillard Lyon died, she had nearly 100 times the normal amount of arsenic in her body. In other words, the 37-year-old wife, mother, and wealthy Harvard graduate had been poisoned to death. All signs eventually pointed to her adulterous husband, Richard, as her murderer. But was he capable of such a thing?

The first real clue that he was came soon after Richard took Nancy to the emergency room of Dallas's Presbyterian Hospital. For weeks, Nancy had complained of nausea and headaches. Friends noticed her behavior had become increasingly erratic.

Doctor's Suspicions Prompt Investigation

While treating Nancy, a third-year resident, Dr. Ali Begheri, became suspicious about the cause of her symptoms. Begheri testified in Lyon's murder trial that soon after Nancy's admission to Presbyterian, he waited until Lyon left his wife's bedside in the intensive care unit. He lifted Nancy's oxygen mask so she could speak. She whispered how she had become violently ill after drinking foul-tasting wine from a bottle left anonymously on her front porch during her separation from Richard.

Begheri also said that Nancy told him of at least two other means by which she suspected her 34-year-old husband had poisoned her. Richard had given her a horrible-tasting soda with a powdery substance floating in it at a movie. Earlier, he had urged her to take strange pills, which he told her were "vitamins." She told Begheri she feared her husband. Nancy died on January 14, 1991, a few days after Richard had rushed her to the emergency room.

Although the hospital initially reported Nancy had died of natural causes, Begheri's suspicions launched a criminal investigation. When an autopsy revealed that arsenic poisoning had caused her death, Richard Lyon was charged with murder that June.

Lawyer Promises Perry Mason Defense

Before the jury was even seated, Lyon's attorney, Dan Guthrie, publicly characterized Nancy's death as "an honest-to-goodness Perry Mason-style whodunit." The statement hinted at Guthrie's defense to establish reasonable doubt. In the trial, Guthrie attacked local police for ignoring other possible suspects with motives much stronger than Lyon's. Among them: Nancy's older brother, who had sexually abused her in childhood; the Lyons' nanny, who disliked Nancy Lyon; and Nancy's former boss, who had been involved in a litigious, work-related scandal and may have wanted to keep Nancy quiet.

In the courtroom, the defense presented several other theories about Nancy's death. Couldn't this depressed incest victim have committed suicide, then framed her unfaithful husband in a final act of spite? Couldn't overworked emergency room doctors have administered drugs that caused fatal side effects? Wasn't it even possible that Mrs. Lyon had accidentally poisoned herself?

After all, there were plenty of toxic chemicals around the couple's fashionable Park Cities home. Lyon claimed Nancy was working with him to eradicate pesky fire ants mounds from their yard. The project, said Lyon, a professional landscaper, involved mail-ordering a series of chemicals to concoct a homemade ant-killing poison. In fact, Nancy herself had signed the receipt when arsenic trioxide and other chemicals were delivered to their home.

The prosecution whittled away at Lyon's defense with a series of condemning witnesses and a mountain of incriminating documents. Family nanny Lynn Pease-Woods testified that although she and Nancy Lyon had personal difficulties when she was hired in 1987, she eventually loved working for the Lyons. She visited the children after Nancy had quit her real estate job in 1990 to be home with daughters Anna, 3, and Allison, 5.

The nanny also testified that Richard over time had given his wife large "vitimins" from a bottle. The nanny turned the capsules over to detectives after Nancy's death. A toxicologist later testified that two of the pills in the bottle contained barium carbonate, a substance used in rat poison. Pease-Woods said that there were no major ant hills at the Lyon house.

The lead police investigator testified he found store-bought fire ant killer in the Lyons' garage. More damaging, the investigator said that when he questioned Lyon, he initially denied he had ordered any toxic chemicals. Pressed further, Lyon modified his statement.

A Marriage on the Rocks

Prosecutors portrayed Richard Lyon as an undependable, unfaithful, and unscrupulous husband who wanted a financially advantageous way out of his marriage. He killed his wife to be with his lover, with whom he took a long vacation only five weeks after Nancy's death. They presented a paper trail of canceled checks, long-distance telephone records, and invoices for chemical purchases linking Richard to the arsenic that could have been used to kill his wife.

Nancy Lyon's divorce attorney, Mary L. Henrich, testified that Nancy had told her that she thought Richard was systematically poisoning her. She told of the foul-tasting soda he bought for her at the movie. She also described how Nancy became violently ill on the bathroom floor after drinking a nightcap her husband had mixed for her. She said Nancy told her that Richard didn't seem to care that she was ill that night.

Defense attorney Guthrie had Henrich read aloud a poignant letter Nancy had written to Richard on September 12, only months before her death. In the letter, Nancy agonized about her husband's adulterous wanderings, disappearances for days on end, and extravagant spending. She wanted to end their marriage.

"Not only are you free to go, but I need to demand that you go before even more damage is done to the children and to me," the letter stated. The couple separated. Nancy filed for divorce in September 1990.

The defense cited the letter as proof that Nancy was willing to let Richard go. Did he need to kill her in order to be with his lover? No. Guthrie also noted that Lyon had agreed to all of Nancy Lyon's demands during their legal separation. Lyon had offered a fair plan to divide their assets.

Nancy withdrew the divorce petition on January 2, just weeks before her death. Lyon remained beneficiary and executor of Nancy's estate, although he had waived any interest in her property before her death. During the trial, however, it was unclear if Richard realized that Nancy had removed him as beneficiary of a $500,000 life insurance policy and substituted her children. The prosecution claimed he did not; the defense said he was aware of the situation.

Among papers the prosecution subpoenaed from Nancy Lyon's insurance company were three pages of notes penned by the Dallas therapist who treated Nancy from January 1990 to January 1991. Dr. Joanna Jacobus wrote that Richard told his wife he felt trapped by her family money. He said his in-laws considered him inadequate. The Lyons' personal life was in turmoil, punctuated by Richard's affairs, the therapist said. In June 1990, Richard cleaned out their bank account. He failed to pay bills.

In a further attempt to suggest that others might be responsible for Nancy's death, the defense called one of Nancy's former coworkers at Trammel Crow Co. to the stand. Kathleen E. Cunningham testified that Nancy had feared and disliked her ex-boss, David S. Bagwell, whom the company sued in 1987. Cunningham said that before Bagwell settled out of court with Trammel Crow, she and Nancy had received anonymous letters threatening "the wrath of God" if they testified against Bagwell in the lawsuit.

Bagwell took the stand and denied any knowledge of the letter. Nancy's father, William Dillard, Jr., then testified that Bagwell was "a great friend of Nancy's" and visited her in the hospital before she died.

A string of witnesses chronicled how they had signed for a host of chemicals addressed to Richard. The defense countered that Richard could not be directly linked to the purchases. Nancy's sister Susan Hendrickson described how Nancy questioned a canceled check to the Houston-area chemical supplier. Susan called the firm because she thought Nancy's behavioral changes might stem from exposure to the chemicals. She dropped the matter until Nancy mysteriously died.

Handwriting Expert Cinches Guilty Verdict

In a dramatic moment, Lyon himself took the stand. He passionately denied killing his wife, declaring himself a moral, intelligent man who enjoyed life and would not throw everything away by committing murder. Jurors interviewed after the trial said that Lyon had convinced them of his innocence.

But the trial took a turn when a surprise witness took the stand with startling information.

Earlier, the defense had produced a receipt that Lyon said he found in his wife's belongings. The receipt from a Dallas chemical company purported to show that Nancy had signed for a delivery of arsenic trioxide and other chemicals. A defense handwriting expert had testified that the signature was Nancy's.

Near the trial's end, the prosecution brought in its own handwriting expert. The expert testified that Richard himself had penned his wife's signature on the documents, which the Dallas chemical company owner had already described as bogus on the stand. The expert also testified that Richard had forged his wife's name on several other evidential papers.

The jury took three hours to find Lyon guilty of his wife's murder. Judge John C. Creuzot gave him the maximum sentence noting that in his view, Lyon tried "various and sundry chemicals to kill Nancy. The first two didn't work, and you finally finished her off with arsenic, a tried-and-true method of producing death." Then for months, Creuzot added, Lyon coldly watched his wife of nine years die. Lyon had requested that the judge sentence him, not the jury.

In March 1992, Judge Creuzot denied Lyon's bid for a retrial.

—B. J. Welborn

Suggestions for Further Reading

City Confidential: Dallas: Arsenic and Old Money. A&E Home Video.

Slover, Pete. "Lyon Gets Life Term in Slaying." *The Dallas Morning News* (January 18, 1992): 33A.

Yahweh Ben Yahweh Trial: 1992

Defendants: Yahweh Ben Yahweh (Hulon Mitchell); Codefendants (15 in all): Mikael, Absalom, Jesee Obed, Abiri, Isaiah Solomon, Hezion, Hoseah Isaac, Enoch, Aher, Job, Amri, Dan, Ahinadab, Sister Judith (who was Yahweh's second in command), Ahaz (all codefendants had "Israel" as their surname)
Crimes Charged: Conspiracy to commit murder, racketeering
Chief Defense Lawyer: Alcee Hastings   **Chief Prosecutor:** Richard Scruggs
Judge: Norman Roettger   **Place:** Miami, Florida   **Date of Trial:** January 2– May 28, 1992   **Verdicts:** Yahweh and Job, Amri, Dan, Ahinadab, Sister Judith, and Ahaz guilty of conspiracy; other defendants acquitted
Sentences: Yahweh: 18 years in prison; Job, Amri, Dan, Ahinadab, Sister Judith, and Ahaz: 15–16.5 years imprisonment

SIGNIFICANCE

This conviction for conspiracy imprisoned the leader of a black messianic cult, Yahweh Ben Yahweh (born Hulon Mitchell), and exposed a series of crimes committed by members of the cult at his direction. When the state of Florida refused to prosecute, federal prosecutors brought charges against the cult leader and members under the federal Racketeer Influenced and Corrupt Organizations (RICO) statute, the first time the law was employed against a religious organization. Although at least 15 gruesome murders were charged, the complex case resulted in relatively light sentences against the leader and six of his followers, with the others being acquitted.

Hulon Mitchell was born in 1935 in Kingfisher, Oklahoma, the son of a Holiness Pentecostal preacher. He served in the air force after graduating high school and earned a B.A. in psychology from Phillips University in Enid, Oklahoma. In 1965 he earned an MA degree in economics from Atlanta University. In 1967, he became a leader in the branch of the Nation of Islam in Atlanta, Georgia, but Elijah Muhammad soon removed him from his post due to complaints of sexual misconduct and misuse of funds. Mitchell established his own cult in Miami, Florida, in the early 1980s, and over a period of years, acquired a devoted following of several hundred members. His followers lived in a building owned by the religion that they named Liberty City, and turned over their paychecks and welfare checks to the organization. Yahweh Ben Yahweh (God son of God) as Mitchell called himself, appeared to seek absolute power over his followers, often with considerable success.

A Criminal or a Role Model?

Later allegations by members who dropped out included widespread sharing of sexual partners among cult members, intimidation by the cult leader and severe punishments for disloyalty, and a luxurious lifestyle of Yahweh Ben Yahweh himself. An inner circle of bodyguards protected him, standing watch over the entrance and during meetings. Friction with the outside community mounted and in May 1986, a group of Yahwehs, as the members became known, were attacked in a neighborhood of Delray Beach, south of West Palm Beach. In apparent revenge, a group of eight to 15 black men returned in the middle of the night on May 19, 1986, and firebombed four homes in the neighborhood where the cult members had been accosted. Later Yahweh Ben Yahweh denied that any of his members had participated in the firebombing, and he sent checks of several thousand dollars to the victims of the firebombing attack.

Through such gestures, and through the thriving businesses he established, he won widespread support in the Miami political community. His program of investments in real estate and the fact that he recruited and apparently rehabilitated homeless and destitute members of the black community in the period 1988–1990 began to win local and even national recognition. Mayor Xavier Suarez of Miami praised Yahweh for the economic ventures that included a grocery store, motels, and other businesses.

Meanwhile, a series of unsolved crimes in the Miami area had police puzzled. Several murder victims were found in outlying wasteland, some mutilated by having their ears cut off. One murder victim, Aston Green, was decapitated. Another victim, Leonard Dupree, was reputedly beaten to death by a mob at the cult headquarters, on suspicion that he was a police or Black Muslim informant. Rumors spread that the cult leader had sex with many of the female members, some as young as 10 or 11 years old. Murder victim Raymond Kelley, a 61-year-old white mechanic, had one ear partially severed and the other entirely cut off. Later, the police attributed the ear-mutilations to the cult, after defectors from the cult claimed that Yahweh Ben Yahweh urged them to "smite their enemies" and to bring him proof of their action.

A confrontation between the Yahwehs and apartment residents in Opalocka, a suburb of Miami, brought the cult into the news in 1986. The cult attempted to evict tenants forcibly from an apartment complex on 131st Street, leading to an exchange of gun fire and two deaths.

Arrest and Indictment

Bobby Rozier, a former football player with the University of California Golden Bears and with the St. Louis Cardinals, had joined the cult and changed his name to Neariah Israel. He later dropped out and agreed to help the FBI work on building a case against Yahweh. Yahweh excommunicated Rozier from the cult. Rozier became the chief prosecution witness as the federal government built a conspiracy and murder case against the cult, its leader, and several of its members. After developing testimony, the FBI conducted a raid on the headquarters, November 7, 1990, in "Operation Jericho." The FBI coordinated raids on a travelling Yahweh group staying in a hotel in New Orleans, where Yahweh Ben Yahweh himself was arrested. Following the arrest and raid on Liberty City, the FBI questioned former and current cult members, gathered depositions, and sought physical evidence. The indictment included the firebombing in Delray Beach, the extortion and threats against the tenants in Opa-locka, two attempted homicides, and 14 specific murders. A later grand jury finding added an additional murder charge.

Although many witnesses were afraid to testify, several defectors from the cult appeared as witnesses. The trial was complicated by the fact that in addition to Yahweh himself, 15 other members of the cult were charged with conspiracy, extortion, and murder. The mass of evidence, the multiple charges, the lengthy proceedings, conflicting testimony, outbursts during the trial, and intense local media coverage exhausted and confused the jury. Among other defenses offered by Yahweh's attorney was the claim that he had not intended his sermons (protected as religious speech) regarding "smiting the enemy" to be taken literally, and that if followers had done so, he had no knowledge of their actions. Testimony by Rozier and others, however, indicated that he had specifically urged his followers to kill defectors and random whites.

Jury Deadlocks on Several Charges

In May 1992, the jury reported being deadlocked several times, but federal judge Norman Roettger ordered them to continue searching for a verdict. The extortion charge against Yahweh was thrown out, and the racketeering charge against him resulted in a hung jury. He was convicted of conspiracy. Seven of the charged disciples were acquitted: Mikael, Absalom, Jesee Obed, Abiri, Isaiah Solomon, Hezion, and Hoseah Isaac (all followers took the surname "Israel"). The jury deadlocked on two others, Enoch and Aher. Six others were convicted of conspiracy: Job, Amri, Dan, Ahinadab, Sister Judith (who was Yahweh's second in command), and Ahaz. The six convicted disciples each received sentences for 15–16 years, 6 months.

When handing down the sentence to Yahweh, Judge Roettger stunned prosecution attorneys, jury members, and the press by complimenting Yahweh on attempting to be a good community influence. He then reduced Yahweh's sentence to 18 years, with possibility of parole in 9 years. Janet Reno, state attorney general in Florida at the time, dropped state murder charges against Yahweh on the total of 18 or 19 murders attributed to the cult by local authorities. No charges against any of the cult members for sexual abuse of children was ever brought, nor were the financial dealings of the cult ever subject to a comprehensive scrutiny.

— Rodney Carlisle

Suggestions for Further Readings

Anti-Defamation League of B'nai B'rith. "The Yahwehs: Violence and Anti-Semitism in a 'Black Hebrew' Sect." 1991

Freedberg, Sydney P. *Brother Love: Murder, Money, and a Messiah.* New York: Pantheon, 1994.

Jim Mitchell Trial: 1992

Defendant: Jim Mitchell   **Crimes Charged:** Murder, burglary, weapons charges   **Chief Defense Lawyers:** Michael Kennedy, Nanci Clarence **Chief Prosecutor:** John Posey   **Judge:** Richard Briener   **Place:** San Rafael, California   **Date of Trial:** January 13–February 19, 1992   **Verdict:** Guilty of voluntary manslaughter and weapons charges   **Sentence:** Six years, three on voluntary manslaughter and three on weapons charges; paroled in 1997

SIGNIFICANCE

Jim and Artie Mitchell were "pioneers" in the pornographic film industry, bringing the once underground industry into the mainstream. But the success led to drug abuse, money problems and eventually murder.

Brothers Jim and Artie Mitchell had achieved a degree of local and even national fame as the owners of the O'Farrell Theater in San Francisco and as the producers of pornography films. Among the more well-known of their productions were *Behind the Green Door*, *The Autobiography of a Flea*, and *The Grafenberg Spot*. In a number of legal cases, they had fought for the right to make, distribute, and show explicit hard-core pornographic films. They had successfully fought to preserve copyright to their films, and by the 1980s, their reputation as counterculture folk heroes spread beyond California. However, their personal lives became troubled with abusive relationships with numerous women, alcoholism, and drug abuse.

The Falling Out and the Killing

During the late 1980s, the two brothers drifted apart, as Jim, the older brother, rehabilitated himself from drug addiction, and Artie became more abusive of girlfriends and family and sank deeper into alcoholism. Artie's threats to others became increasingly violent, claimed Jim.

Although there were no witnesses to the shooting on the night of February 27, 1991, several gunshots were recorded during a 911 emergency call from Artie Mitchell's home in Corte Madera, California. The call was made by Artie's girlfriend, a beautiful exotic dancer named Julie Bajo, who later testified that she made the call while hiding in a closet, fearful of her life during the burst of gunfire from an unseen intruder. Responding to the call, police found Jim Mitchell outside Artie's home, holding a *.22* rifle and with a loaded pistol strapped in a holster. His car was parked on a nearby street. Physical evidence at the scene was confusing. Altogether seven shots had been fired from the rifle, one of which was in Artie's body. A 9mm bullet, fired from Artie's gun, had penetrated a glass table. Artie had three wounds, including the fatal wound to the head. Furniture, venetian blinds, doorframes, and wall plasterboard, were all marked with bullet holes.

The Trial

In a pretrial hearing, the prosecution called as expert witness Dr. Harry Hollein, an expert in acoustics, who testified that the recorded shot on the 911

Jim Mitchell (right) with his brother Artie in front of the O'Farrell Theater in San Francisco. (AP/Wide World Photos)

tape was fired from the *.22* calibre Winchester rifle owned by Jim Mitchell. Despite efforts by defense attorney Michael Kennedy to discredit the testimony, the judge decided to permit it. Another prosecution witness, Lucien Haag, a ballistics expert, was also allowed to testify.

The prosecution built a case on ballistic and acoustic evidence, supplementing it with a video animation reconstructing the complex routes of the various shots. The video itself was controversial, and only admitted after strenuous debate.

The defense built its case around the warm relationship between the two brothers and character testimony regarding the many acts of charity and public works by both of the Mitchells. The defense brought out the fact that Jim had once saved Artie from drowning. Prosecution witnesses included the 911 operator who had heard the gunshots, police who responded to the call, and the experts who identified the shots and the bullets, as well as the county coroner, and other forensics experts. In addition, Prosecutor Posey introduced friends of Artie Mitchell who testified about the deteriorating relationship between the brothers and about Artie's drug and alcohol problems. However, when Posey questioned Julie Bajo, her testimony was self-contradictory. The jury had other reasons to doubt her veracity, including her admission that she had been rolling a joint when the first shots were fired, and that she later posed topless for a magazine interview regarding the killing. The defense found her testimony so helpful to their side that they chose not to cross-examine.

Video at the Trial

On January 24, 1992, in the second week of the trial, Prosecutor Posey gave to the defense team a copy of a computer-generated video animation of the shooting. In the tape, Artie Mitchell was represented as a robot-like figure that moved through the house during the shooting. The figure opened the bedroom door as the gunfire began, walked down the hall and was shot twice. The figure then entered the bathroom, put its head into the hallway, and was shot the final time in the head before falling to the floor. The presumed tracks of the bullets were shown as red laser beams against a blue background. Defense Attorney Kennedy strongly objected to the film, as it purported to show the order in which the shots were fired, building on opinions of forensic experts. He denounced the video as a fabricated computerized eyewitness to events for which there were no human eyewitnesses. Posey defended the video as simply an animated diagram.

The judge ruled that the high-tech nature of the presentation was legitimate. His only objection was that it showed Artie Mitchell with his hands at his side, not carrying anything. That presentation would leave the jury with the impression that Artie was completely defenseless during the shooting, which was an assumption that could not be confirmed or disputed on the basis of other evidence. He therefore ruled that the figure in the animation had to be presented without showing the positions of the arms. Nevertheless, the fact that the animation would be accepted in modified form impressed journalists and other observers. The animation was the first such video introduced in a murder trial, although similar simulations had already been used in several other trials. When shown at the trial, the video was slightly modified, with an armless figure walking down a hall as the bullet tracks slashed at it.

Admission and Verdict

The defense introduced expert forensic witnesses as well as several friends and relatives of Jim Mitchell, who testified as to his character and to the violent and threatening temper of Artie. When Jim Mitchell testified, he admitted that he had taken the rifle to Artie's house with the intention of bluffing him out of his threatening mood. He also admitted to puncturing the tires on Artie's car to prevent him from driving anywhere. He testified that his brother approached him, threatening with a pistol, and that he fired the rifle. He did not remember anything between the exchange of gunfire and being arrested on the street outside the house. He admitted that he had killed his brother, but insisted he had not intended to do so.

The prosecution asked for a first-degree murder conviction, claiming that Jim Mitchell had visited his brother with the express intention of killing him. However, the jury voted to convict Mitchell on a charge of voluntary manslaughter plus two lesser felonies for unlawfully discharging a firearm and brandishing a firearm to a police officer.

On April 24, 1992, Judge Briener handed down the sentence, after receiving over 100 letters asking for leniency. Political and police figures in San

Francisco, including Mayor Frank Jordan, as well as recipients of Mitchell charity, all argued for a light sentence. The judge sentenced Mitchell to three years on the manslaughter charge and three for using a firearm in the killing. Mitchell was sentenced to 16 months to be served concurrently, for exhibiting the firearm to a police officer. Briener also issued a 4 and one-half year sentence for discharging a firearm in a negligent manner, but he stayed that sentence. Thus the total sentence was six years, of which Mitchell served over four before being paroled. He was not incarcerated while his case went through appeals.

The case was the subject of a book written by Davis McCumber, and of a Showtime movie entitled *Rated X*, starring real-life brothers Emilio Estevez and Charlie Sheen.

— Rodney Carlisle

Suggestions for Further Reading

Kantor, Andrew. "Computing in the Courtroom." *PC Magazine* (February 23, 1993): 23.

McCumber, David. *X-Rated—The Mitchell Brothers: A True Story of Sex, Money and Death*. New York: Simon and Schuster, 1992.

Schroeder, Eric. "3D Studio Gives Crime-solving a New Twist." *PC Week* (March 9, 1992): 51.

John Gotti Trial: 1992

Defendant: John Gotti   **Crimes Charged:** Racketeering; racketeering conspiracy; murder; Illegal gambling; obstruction of justice; and conspiracies to murder, bribe a detective, obstruct justice, commit loan sharking, and commit tax fraud   **Chief Defense Lawyer:** Albert J. Krieger
Chief Prosecutors: John Gleeson and Andrew J. Maloney   **Judge:** I. Leo Glasser   **Place:** Brooklyn, New York   **Dates of Trial:** January 21–April 2, 1992   **Verdict:** Guilty   **Sentence:** Life imprisonment without parole and $250,000 fine

SIGNIFICANCE
Fear, bribery, flawed prosecutions, and his lawyers' obstreperous courtroom behavior helped outspoken mob boss John Gotti avoid prison three times before he was successfully convicted of violating the Racketeer Influenced and Corrupt Organizations Act.

When John Gotti was indicted along with members of the Gambino organized crime "family" in New York in March 1985, law enforcement officials considered him to be a small-time hoodlum who had served short sentences for hijacking and attempted manslaughter. Everything changed December 16, 1985, when Gambino crime family leader Paul Castellano and "underboss" Thomas Bilotti were shot to death outside a midtown Manhattan restaurant.

Leadership of the powerful Gambino organization seemed to shift swiftly to Gotti. Law officers speculated that the new mob boss or "don" had murdered his predecessor before Castellano could have Gotti killed for violating a Gambino family prohibition against narcotics dealing. Gotti's violent celebrity grew quickly. Shortly after Castellano's murder, a terrified refrigerator mechanic who had accused Gotti of assaulting him in a parking dispute lost his memory in court.

Yet Gotti still faced trial for violating the federal Racketeer Influenced and Corrupt Organizations Act, popularly known as the RICO statute. Under the 1970 law, anyone found guilty of two felonies listed in a RICO indictment was considered to be engaged in a pattern of criminal activity and thus open to conviction for violating the RICO law itself. Federal prosecutors began using the statute against organized crime in the 1980's with considerable success.

The most serious charges in the 1985 Gambino RICO indictment died with Castellano and terminally ill Mafia boss Aniello Dellacroce, leaving Gotti to face lesser charges that had little to do with his sudden eminence as a mob boss. The government's case also was hampered by a bitter jurisdictional dispute between several state and federal law enforcement agencies. Each was building its own case against Gotti. None wanted to share witnesses or information for fear of jeopardizing its own chances for a successful conviction.

John Gotti avoided prison three times before he was finally convicted. (AP/Wide World Photos)

Gotti Eludes Conviction

Gotti's RICO trial began in August 1986. The prosecution case relied heavily on testimony by convicted felons. All were admitted liars who agreed under defense cross-examination that they hoped their testimony was buying them shorter sentences. One informer falsely denied ever working for the FBI. Another openly perjured himself, accusing the prosecution of offering him drugs in prison in return for testimony. After a long and acrimonious trial in which the defense repeatedly fired crude personal insults at the prosecutors and outshouted the judge's orders, Gotti was acquitted in March 1987.

Federal prosecutors immediately announced that Gotti would be indicted for a different set of racketeering crimes. When Gotti next appeared in court in January 1990, however, he faced assault and conspiracy charges in the wounding of John O'Connor, an officer of the United Brotherhood of Carpenters. The corrupt union officer had ordered a Manhattan restaurant wrecked for resisting his bribery demands, unaware that the restaurant had ties to the Gambino crime family. Gotti was accused of ordering O'Connor shot in retaliation. If convicted, Gotti faced a sentence of 15 years to life as a thrice-convicted, "persistent felony offender."

Witnesses Weaken Prosecution

The main witness for the prosecution was James McElroy, a former "enforcer" for the Westies, a violent gang based in the Hell's Kitchen section of Manhattan. McElroy claimed that the Westies had done the shooting as a favor to Gotti, who wanted O'Connor "whacked," or killed. Gotti's combative lawyer

Bruce Cutler argued that the Westies' leader was an admitted perjurer and murderer, "a lying bum" trying to bargain his way out of a 60-year prison sentence for racketeering.

Secret tapes which purportedly showed Gotti's desire for revenge were imperfect. Cutler admitted that they reflected Gotti's involvement in Gambino family business, but he argued that his client's promise to "bust "m up" referred to reorganizing Gambino "crews" and was not a description of what he wanted done to O'Connor. The issue was further confused when state and federal prosecutors gave jurors differing transcripts of the same secretly taped conversation between two Westies. The star defense witness was the victim himself, John O'Connor, who denied that he could identify his assailants.

Gotti's supporters and neighbors celebrated with a fireworks display at the news of his third acquittal. Media pundits transformed the stylishly dressed "Dapper Don" into "The Teflon Don," a criminal to whom charges would not stick. "He is a murderer, not a folk hero," replied U.S. Attorney Andrew J. Maloney, who handed down the long-awaited new set of RICO charges in December 1990. Gotti and his top associates Frank Locasio and Salvatore Gravano were arrested and held without bail for multiple felonies ranging from murder to tax evasion.

Tide Changes for Prosecutors

Before testimony began, federal prosecutors succeeded in having Gotti's loud but effective lawyer Bruce Cutler barred from the trial. Judge I. Leo Glasser agreed that secret tapes showed that Cutler and two other attorneys had acted as "house counsels" for the Gambino crime organization. Since playing the tapes would result in the lawyers having to testify about matters the prosecution intended to introduce as evidence, the enraged Cutler was disqualified from working on the case.

Rumors of jury tampering in Gotti's previous trials also helped prosecutors convince the judge that the jury should remain anonymous and be sequestered throughout the trial. But the hardest blow of all came in the announcement that "Sammy Bull" Gravano, Gotti's "underboss," or second in command, would plead guilty and testify as a government witness.

When the trial began in Brooklyn, New York on January 21, 1992, Gotti's new lawyer, Albert J. Kreiger, opened the defense by stating that his client's only crime was the lack of a formal education. Kreiger wasted no time in accusing the admitted murderer Gravano of being the rightful object of the prosecution's attention.

Unruffled government prosecutors had learned from past mistakes. "This is not a complex case," Maloney told the jury. "These defendants will tell you in their own words what it's about." Prosecutors played hours of secretly taped conversations in which Gotti spoke of murders and other crimes. "Anytime you got a partner who don't agree with us," Gotti told Locasio on one tape, "we kill him."

The second source of strength in the government's case was Gravano, who admitted his role in 19 murders, including 10 authorized by Gotti. The former underboss described how he and Gotti waited in a nearby car while Castellano and Bilotti were shot and then drove slowly past the bloody scene. Gravano added that a taped conversation in which Gotti falsely disavowed any part in Castellano's slaying was performed for the benefit of eavesdropping "bugs."

The defense attacked Gravano's description of the Castellano murder and characterized him as "a rat" who was willing to implicate others falsely to obtain a lighter sentence for his own violent crimes. Gravano admitted his hopes for leniency, but his testimony remained unshaken. Prosecutors also submitted evidence that Gotti had bribed a police detective for information and had failed to file income tax returns for six years during which he claimed to work as a plumbing company salesman.

The sole defense witness was a tax lawyer who had advised Gotti to exercise a "legitimate privilege of silence" by not filing returns while under indictment. As Judge Glasser ruled that appearances by all five other defense witnesses would be inappropriate for various legal reasons, Gotti's former cheery bluster eroded completely. He bickered openly with the judge, who threatened to have him removed from court.

In his summation, defense attorney Krieger accused the government of victimizing his client with a case manufactured from Gravano's lies. Prosecutor John Gleeson replied, "these defendants ranted and raved about Salvatore Gravano because he is their nightmare."

The jury agreed. On April 2, 1992, after only 13 hours of deliberations, Gotti was found guilty on all counts. Locasio was convicted of all charges, except one count of illegal gambling. Both career criminals were sentenced June 23 to life in prison without parole. Gotti's supporters protested the sentence by fighting with police and overturning cars in the streets outside the Brooklyn courthouse. Seven protesters were arrested on felony riot charges.

As Gotti was taken to a federal prison to spend the rest of his days in solitary confinement, his former confidante "Sammy Bull" Gravano continued to testify about the Gambino organization's hidden financial assets. Under the seizure provisions of the RICO statute, the FBI moved to confiscate ill-gotten properties owned by Gotti and the nation's largest Mafia family.

Prosecutor Gleeson's courtroom summation seemed to linger as the last word. The attorney who had faced Gotti's sarcastic jibes and hateful stares during both RICO trials told the jury that there were two ways to convict mobsters: "One, catch them talking about their crimes. Figure out a way to find those secret meetings and record them. There's one other way. Get one of them to come in and tell you about the crimes. We did both."

Nevertheless, others were convinced that Gotti tried to retain a surrogate hold on his criminal leadership by designating his son, John A Gotti, as acting boss of the Gambino family. The celebrity status once enjoyed by "the Dapper Don" shone less attractively on his son, however, who was dogged by the media and criminal investigators. New York organized crime families were said to be intensely displeased with Gotti's decision to literally keep his business in the family.

With Gotti imprisoned, federal authorities intensified efforts to dismantle the Gambino organization. The Ravenite Social Club, the notorious headquarters in Manhattan's Little Italy district from which Gotti and his cronies had proudly held court, was confiscated by the government and sold to real estate developers. Waves of arrests and plea bargains in New York and Florida dismantled the alleged command structure of the Gambino mob.

One of the arrests had far-reaching consequences. A 1994 gambling raid in the Bronx mushroomed into a federal massive racketeering indictment against John Gotti, Jr. and 37 other reputed Gambino family associates, who were arrested on January 21, 1998. While his codefendants accepted guilty pleas to avoid testifying and to reduce possible sentences, Gotti Jr. remained in jail for months as his relatives and friends scrambled to accumulate enough money to cover his $10 million bail.

The elder Gotti was furious. He railed to his daughter Victoria that her brother was an "imbecile" for leaving incriminating evidence within reach of investigators and surrounding himself with incompetents. Gotti's tirades in the prison visiting area were videotaped by investigators, who offered them as evidence that "Junior" was deeply involved in the Gambino criminal operation and thus undeserving of bail.

Media reports that Gotti Jr. was ready to strike a plea bargain with the government began to surface, mingling with rumors of his incarcerated father's anger over such a possible move. In the midst of the bedlam, the younger Gotti protested that the government's freezing of his assets made it impossible for him to earn a living or pay his family's enormous security bills. At one point the exasperated defendant asked the judge to send him back to jail to save money.

By April 1999, the pressure was too much for John Gotti, Jr. As his trial for racketeering was about to begin, he pleaded guilty to end what he characterized as government harassment. He hoped to salvage a life with his wife and young children from a devastating amount of potential jail time. Had Gotti gambled unsuccessfully on an acquittal at trial, he might have faced 20 years imprisonment. Instead he pleaded guilty to six charges, including loan sharking, bribery, mail fraud, gambling, tax evasion, and conspiracy to commit extortion.

On September 3, 1999, John Gotti, Jr. was sentenced to almost six and a half years in prison, 10 months less than the maximum requested by prosecutors. The sentence also included enormous forfeitures of money and real estate that Gotti was unable to prove were not obtained by noncriminal means. It was another bitter loss for the Gotti family. As law enforcement agencies continued to attack the Gambino organization, however, it would not be the last time relatives of the once-feared mob boss would face a judge.

— Thomas C. Smith

Suggestions for Further Reading

Chen, David. "Younger Gotti Is Sentenced to Six Years." *New York Times* (September 4, 1999): B1.

Cummings, John and Ernest Volkman. *Goombata: The Improbable Rise of John Gotti and His Gang.* Boston: Little, Brown & Co., 1990.

Dannen, Frederic. "The Untouchable? How the FBI Sabotaged Competing Prosecution Teams In the Race to Nail Mob Boss John Gotti. *Vanity Fair* (January 1992): 26–44.

Fisher, Ian. "Defending the Mob: A User's Guide." *New York Times* (March 26, 1992): Bl, B5.

Goldberg, Jeffrey. "The Godfather Jr." *New York Times Magazine* (January 31, 1999): 25

McFadden, Robert D. "For Gotti Prosecutors, Hard Work Pays off With Conviction." *New York Times* (April 3, 1992): Al, B3.

Mustain, Gene and Jerry Capeci. *Mob Star: The Story of John Gotti.* New York: Franklin Watts, 1988.

Raab, Selwyn. "A Weakness in the Gotti Case." *New York Times* (March 14, 1987): A1.

Mike Tyson Trial: 1992

Defendant: Michael Gerard Tyson   **Crimes Charged:** Rape, criminal deviant conduct, and confinement   **Chief Defense Lawyers:** Kathleen I. Beggs, Vincent J. Fuller, and F. Lane Heard   **Chief Prosecutors:** David Dreyer, J. Gregory Garrison, and Barbara J. Trathen   **Judge:** Patricia J. Gifford
Place: Indianapolis, Indiana   **Dates of Trial:** January 26–February 10, 1992
Verdict: Guilty   **Sentence:** 10 years imprisonment

SIGNIFICANCE

As with his colorful and controversial boxing career, Mike Tyson's trial—saturated with titillating accounts of sex and violent assault—was eagerly followed by fans and foes alike, although subsequent events would return him to the headlines.

At age 25, Mike Tyson had already won and lost the world heavyweight boxing championship. Seemingly on the verge of challenging to regain his crown, in July 1991 he attended the Black Expo in Indianapolis. One of the scheduled events was the Miss Black America pageant and one of the contestants was Desiree Washington, the 18-year-old Miss Rhode Island. Tyson, whose fondness for and occasional problems with attractive young women were well documented, invited Washington to his hotel room. Around 2:00 A.M. on July 19, she agreed. Three days later Washington went to the police. What she had to say resulted in Tyson facing charges of rape and related offenses.

Once the jury was impaneled on January 29, and after Judge Patricia J. Gifford had denied a request from Tyson's chief attorney, Vincent J. Fuller, that the accuser's sexual history be admitted into evidence, it was time for the opening statements.

Prosecutor J. Gregory Garrison delivered a ringing indictment of the defendant. "This man," he said, pointing at Tyson, "is guilty of pinning that 18-year-old girl to a bed and confining her . . . callously and maliciously raping her even though she cried out in pain."

Fuller, on the other hand, depicted a calculating vixen "mature beyond her 18 years," sophisticated and poised and out for money, an educated overachiever more than a match for a high-school dropout like Tyson. To be sure, Washington's level of sophistication had unnerved prosecutors before the trial, but when it came time for her testify she did so in a childlike voice, peppering her speech with expressions like "yukky."

She described receiving a phone call from Tyson at 1:36 A.M. Minutes later, believing herself to be en route to a party, she joined Tyson in his limousine. As soon as she entered the car Tyson grabbed her: "I kind of jumped back because I was surprised that, being who he is, he acted like that and, besides, his breath smelled kind of bad."

Instead of the expected party, they drove to Tyson's hotel. Once inside his room Tyson resumed his advances. At that point, Washington said, she told him that she was "not like the girls he must be used to hanging out with." Tyson, undeterred, pinned her down on the bed with one arm and used his free hand to undress her. All the while, she said, he mocked her efforts to resist, saying, "Don't fight me. Don't fight me."

Brutal Attack

Then the alleged rape took place. Washington described the pain as "excruciating," and that when she began to cry, "he started laughing like it was a game or something, like it was funny." Then she ran from the room, shoes in hand. Outside she saw Tyson's chauffeur who offered to drive her back to her hotel.

Boxer Mike Tyson pleaded not guilty to rape and was released on bond. (AP/Wide World Photos)

When cross-examined, Washington conceded that on several occasions she had the opportunity to leave the hotel room but chose not to do so. Fuller probed reports that after meeting Tyson, she had told other pageant contestants, "He's rich. Did you see what Robin Givens [Tyson's ex-wife] got out of him? Besides, he's dumb." Washington denied that any such exchange had ever taken place. Neither had she sung "Money, money, money, money, money," from the song "For the Love of Money" to a girlfriend later, as alleged.

Partial corroboration of Washington's story came from the chauffeur, Virginia Foster, 44. When Washington returned to the limousine, said Foster, "She looked like she may have been in a state of shock . . . dazed, disoriented. She seemed scared." (Earlier the defense had successfully petitioned to have disallowed as evidence Foster's claim that Tyson had been sexually aggressive toward her also. No charges were ever filed.)

Dr. Thomas Richardson, the emergency room physician who examined Washington more than 24 hours after the incident, confirmed the presence of abrasions "consistent with forced or very hard intercourse."

Earlier prosecution comparisons between Tyson's menacing bulk and Washington's slight 98-pound stature came into stark relief as the defendant took the stand. He began by saying that everything had taken place with Washington's full cooperation and consent. Asked by Fuller if he forced himself upon her, Tyson replied, "No, I didn't. I didn't violate her in any way, sir."

In graphic terms Tyson described the encounter, but denied Garrison's claims that he had willfully misled Washington, insisting she had been aware of his sexual intentions beforehand and had only become annoyed when he remained in bed afterwards and refused to accompany her downstairs. "I told her that was the way it was. I said 'The limousine is downstairs. If you don't want to use the limousine, you can walk.'"

Quizzed by Garrison on why he had urged Washington to wear loose-fitting clothes, Tyson admitted that he had planned to have sex in the limousine, and tight-fitting jeans "would have complicated it."

Ten hours of jury deliberation produced a guilty verdict. On March 26, 1992, Judge Gifford passed sentence: 10 years imprisonment, with the last four suspended. With time off for good behavior, Tyson would be eligible for parole in 1995.

Often, in trial by jury, demeanor is everything. In the words of her deputy defense counsel, Barbara Trathen, Desiree Washington made "a great victim" on the stand, demure, almost adolescent. By contrast, Tyson's untutored responses to questioning came across as brutish and arrogant.

After learning on March 71, 1994, that the Supreme Court had refused to hear his appeal, Tyson applied to the Indianapolis Parole Board. On June 13, 1994, a hearing was convened to consider the application. His lawyers, arguing that their client was a rehabilitated man, produced three witnesses who testified that Tyson's attitude behind bars had undergone a change. Under cross-examination, however, all three said they had never heard Tyson admit to raping Washington. Tyson himself was oddly belligerent on this point when questioned. He told the court, "I have done no criminal conduct. The jury said I did."

It was an attitude that cut little ice with Judge Gifford, who had presided over Tyson's trial. She noted that Tyson had failed to meet the legal requirement of completing an educational or vocational course while in prison, which defense lawyers attributed to the constant stream of visitors that made it difficult for Tyson to concentrate. Without Tyson's acknowledgement of his "inexcusable conduct," Judge Gifford was unprepared to grant his parole request.

In March 1995, having served three years behind bars, Tyson was released with four years' probation. Controversy continued to plague the disgraced fighter when, in April 1996, a young woman claimed he had sexually assaulted her in a Chicago nightclub. However, these allegations were later dismissed.

As expected, Tyson resumed his boxing career and on June 27, 1997, he challenged Evander Holyfield for the world heavyweight title. In front of thousands of appalled live spectators at Las Vegas' MGM Grand Garden arena and millions more television viewers worldwide, Tyson bit a chunk out of Holyfield's ear and was disqualified from the fight. Soon afterward, the Nevada State Athletic

Commission revoked Tyson's boxing license and fined him $3 million (10 percent of his earnings from the fight, the maximum allowable by law).

Just over one year later, on August 31, 1998, Tyson again made the headlines when a car driven by his wife, Monica, was involved in a minor traffic accident with two other vehicles in Gaithersburg, Maryland. An argument broke out between Tyson and the other car operators. One of the drivers, Richard Hardick, 50, alleged that Tyson had attacked him, while the second driver, Abmielec Saucedo, 62, claimed that he had been punched in the face by the boxer. Early speculation that Tyson would settle both incidents out of court proved to be accurate.

Things seemed to settle down for Tyson and on September 9, 1998, he went before the Nevada Athletic Commission, requesting that his license be reinstated. They deferred a decision pending psychiatric evaluations. All five doctors who examined Tyson concurred that he was unlikely to repeat the ear-biting incident, and that he had shown genuine remorse for his actions. Guided by this testimony, on October 19, the Nevada Athletic Commission ruled 4–1 to return Tyson's license, although he was warned by Elias Ghanem, the panel's chairman, "This will be your last chance."

Unexpectedly six days later Maryland state's attorney, Robert Dean, resurrected the August "road rage" incident, declaring his intention of pursuing a criminal case against Tyson. On December 1, Tyson pleaded no contest to misdemeanor criminal charges of assault, aware that he risked being returned to prison.

On February 5, 1999, in a Rockville, Maryland, courtroom, despite Tyson's written plea for mercy and the testimony by his victims that they had forgiven his attack, Judge Stephen Johnson ruled in agreement with the warning of prosecutor Carol Crawford that Tyson was "a time-bomb buried in our own backyard," and handed down two concurrent two-year sentences, with all but one year suspended. He also fined Tyson $5,000 and gave him two years' probation after his release from jail.

How long Tyson would actually spend in prison now rested with the original judge, Patricia J. Gifford. If she decided that this latest offense amounted to a parole violation, he could be returned to Indiana to serve the remainder of his sentence. Following the Maryland Parole Commission's decision on Friday, May 21, 1999, to reduce Tyson's sentence to time served, Judge Gifford announced the following Monday that Tyson's probation for the 1992 rape conviction had ended, thus clearing the way for his immediate release from prison.

—Colin Evans

Suggestions for Further Reading

"Boxer Mike Tyson Convicted of Rape." *Facts On File* (February 13, 1992): 97ff.

Jet (February 24, 1992): 16ff.

Oates, Joyce Carol. "Rape and the Boxing Ring." *Newsweek* (February 24, 1992): 60ff.

Steptoe, S. "A Damnable Defense." *Sports Illustrated* (February 24, 1992): 92.

Los Angeles Police Officers' Trials: 1992 & 1993

Defendants: Theodore J. Briseno, Stacey C. Koon, Laurence M. Powell, and Timothy E. Wind   **Crimes Charged:** First trial: Assault, excessive force by a police officer, and filing false report; Second trial: Violating civil rights
Chief Defense Lawyers: First trial: Paul DePasquale, Darryl Mounger, and Michael P. Stone; second trial: Harland W. Braun, Paul DePasquale, Ira M. Salzman, and Michael P. Stone   **Chief Prosecutor:** First trial: Terry L. White; second trial: Steven D. Clymer, and Barry F. Kowalski   **Judges:** First trial: Stanley M. Weisberg; second trial: John G. Davies   **Places:** First trial: Simi Valley, California; second trial: Los Angeles, California   **Dates of Trials:** First trial: March 4–April 29, 1992; second trial: February 3–April 17, 1993
Verdict: First trial: Not guilty; jury deadlocked on one charge against Powell; Second trial: Koon and Powell, guilty; Briseno and Wind, not guilty
Sentence: Koon and Powell sentenced to 30 months imprisonment each.

SIGNIFICANCE
What was already one of the highest profile cases in American legal history assumed landmark proportions when a second jury had to wrestle not only with questions of guilt or innocence, but how best to assuage outraged civic sensibilities.

In the early hours of March 3, 1991, motorist Rodney King was stopped by Los Angeles, California, police officers following a three mile high speed chase. According to arrest reports filed later, King refused orders to exit the car, then put up such a struggle that officers had to use batons and stun-guns to subdue him. However, unbeknownst to police, the entire incident had been captured on video by a nearby resident, and the resulting 81-second tape told a different story. In it King seemed to offer little resistance as several officers kicked and beat him to the ground while a dozen of their colleagues looked on. Public outrage led to a grand jury investigation and indictments against four officers for assault and use of excessive force.

Because of the extraordinary pretrial publicity, a defense motion to move the proceedings from Los Angeles succeeded, and on March 4, 1992, the trial began in suburban Simi Valley. In his opening speech, chief prosecutor Terry L. White referred to falsified reports submitted after the incident as evidence that the police had realized the illegality of their conduct and had tried to conceal it. But it was the evidence of another California Highway Patrol officer, Melanie Singer, which yielded the most prosecutorial advantage. She testified that defendant Laurence Powell had unnecessarily struck King six times with his metal baton. "He had it in a power swing and he struck the driver right across the top of the cheekbone, splitting his face from the top of his ear to his chin," she said. "Blood spurted out." Singer did say that defendants Koon and Briseno tried to restrain Powell from further beating King.

Laurence Powell with his attorney Michael Stone outside the courthouse, Stacey Koon in the background. (AP/Wide World Photos)

King, a tall, heavyset man and former convict, was never called to the stand by the prosecution, a decision reportedly based on prosecution fears that he would make a poor impression on jurors.

Under questioning, Briseno admitted that he did not consider King's actions to be threatening, and he repeatedly described codefendants Powell and Wind as "out of control." He further blamed Sergeant Stacey Koon, the highest ranking officer present, for not intervening.

It was the defense contention that the officers had believed King to be under the effects of PCP, a powerful hallucinogenic, and therefore extremely dangerous. (King had acknowledged that he had been drinking, but there was no evidence he had taken any drugs.) In his closing statement, defense attorney Michael P. Stone said of the tape, "We do not see an example of unprovoked police brutality. We see, rather, a controlled application of baton strikes, for the very obvious reason of getting this man into custody."

The jury clearly agreed. On April 29, 1992, they returned not-guilty verdicts for all defendants, deadlocking on only one charge against Powell.

A City in Flames

The verdict rocked Los Angeles. Within hours the city erupted in rioting that left 58 people dead and caused $1 billion in damage. In the aftermath of this tragedy the U.S. government filed charges of civil rights violations against the four officers.

Prosecutors Barry F. Kowalski and Steven D. Clymer faced an uphill task when the second trial began in Los Angeles on February 3, 1993: convincing a jury that the officers had *deliberately* intended to deprive Rodney King of his constitutional rights. But first they had to select that jury.

The absence of black jurors in the state trial had kindled a firestorm of criticism, but on this occasion a more ethnically diverse panel was selected. In his opening argument, Clymer declared "Rodney King is not on trial." "The issue of whether he was guilty or innocent that night is not the issue in this trial. What we will tell you is that while he was being beaten while he was on the ground he didn't kick a police officer, he didn't punch a police officer, he didn't grab a police officer, he didn't injure a police officer."

Confirmation of this came from Dorothy Gibson, an eyewitness. "He [King] was lying on the ground, face down with his hands stretched out like a cross shape." Another eyewitness, Robert Hill, described hearing King scream in pain as officers beat him.

Sergeant Mark Conta, an expert on police procedure with the LAPD, condemned the tactics used. "It is my opinion that it was a clear violation of Los Angeles police policy." Conta singled out Koon for special criticism. "He should have stopped this and should have taken care of his officers when they needed him most."

Following the first trial it was widely believed that the prosecution had miscalculated by not putting King on the witness stand. On this occasion he did testify and made an effective witness.

Describing his actions to Kowalski, King said, "I was just trying to stay alive, sir." King admitted that he had responded defiantly when the officers began baiting him, chanting, "What's up, nigger? How do you feel, killer?" "I didn't want them to know that what they were doing was getting to me—I didn't want them to get any satisfaction." He described the baton blows as feeling "like you would get up in the middle of the night and jam your toe . . . on a piece of metal. That's what it felt like every time I got hit."

Throughout a grueling day of cross-examination, King did much to dispel earlier defense depictions of him as a menacing brute. Even when defense attorney Michael Stone drew an admission from him that he had lied to investigators when he denied driving drunk on the night of the beating, King managed to salvage the situation, saying that, as a parolee, he had been afraid of being returned to prison.

Another defense team member, Harland W. Braun, hammered away at King's varied and contradictory versions of events that night, implying that King had appended the assertions of racial epithets to enhance his civil suit against the city of Los Angeles. "You can become a rich man," said Braun, suggesting that King stood to gain $50 million in the suit.

King did admit to a faulty memory: "Sometimes I forget things that happened and sometimes I remember things," conceding an uncertainty about whether the taunts leveled at him had actually included the word "nigger." "I'm not sure. I believe I did hear that." In earlier grand-jury testimony, King had made no mention of racial slurs.

Braun was incredulous. "As an Afro-American who admittedly was beaten, you would forget that police officers called you nigger? . . . The fact is that you were trying to improve your case or lawsuit and really didn't care about the impact it would have on anyone else!"

The assault was continued by Paul DePasquale, attorney for Timothy Wind, who also highlighted King's hazy recollection of events by referring to an interview in which King had erroneously claimed that he was handcuffed all through the beating. Despite these inconsistencies, Rodney King left the stand largely undiminished and having impressed the majority of those present.

In a strange turn of events, officer Melanie Singer was again called, this time for the defense, but the content and manner of her testimony yielded a bonanza for the prosecution. Defense attorneys could only stand aghast as she tearfully condemned their clients' conduct. It was a devastating setback.

Textbook Tactics

Now only the defendants could help themselves. Stacey Koon was first to take the stand. Insisting that his actions were a textbook example of how to subdue an aggressive suspect, the sergeant said, "My intent at that moment was to cripple Rodney King . . . that is a better option than going to deadly force." Koon maintained that "He [King] made all the choices. He made all the wrong choices." In a cool, confident voice, Koon continued, "This is not a boxing match. We had a tactical advantage and we keep the tactical advantage, and we do not give it up. The tactical advantage is Rodney King is on the ground and we are going to keep him on the ground."

The prosecution was denied an important line of inquiry when Judge John G. Davies barred Steven Clymer from raising allegedly racial passages included in a book written by Koon about the incident. Instead, Clymer could isolate only minor inconsistencies in Koon's testimony. "You are exaggerating, are you not, the amount of things you say happened?"

"No, sir," Koon replied firmly. "I am telling you my recollection."

To general astonishment, it was announced that none of the other defendants would testify. Which left only the closing arguments. Following these representations, Judge Davies gave the jury a careful reading of the complex law involved and they retired.

With the media, many public officials, and ordinary citizens predicting another round of riots if the four officers were acquitted, the tension built in Los Angeles as the jurors deliberated. Police officers were put on 12-hour shifts, and California Governor Pete Wilson mobilized National Guard units. Gun stores did business at breakneck speed as shopkeepers and residents set about protecting themselves. One week after jurors began deliberation on April 17, 1993, they were back. Koon and Powell were emotionless as their guilty verdicts were read out, while Briseno and Wind were acquitted. Koon and Powell were each sentenced to 30 months imprisonment on August 4, 1993.

On August 19, 1994, after a well-publicized and well-funded campaign on behalf of the convicted officers, a Federal Appeals Court upheld the convictions against Koon and Powell, and admonished Trial Judge John G. Davies for the leniency of the sentences.

Rodney King's civil suit against the city of Los Angeles concluded on April 19, 1994, when he was awarded damages of $3.8 million. His suit for punitive damages was declined by a jury on June 1, 1994.

Koon and Powell were released from prison in December 1995. Rodney King used some of the money he was awarded to form a record label. In 1996, King was convicted of a misdemeanor domestic violence charge after he tried to throw his wife out of a moving car; he served 90 days in jail.

Few jury decisions have so affected everyday life as the verdicts in these two trials. The first prompted violence on an appalling scale, while an entire city held its breath awaiting the second. And yet, almost unmentioned in all of the turmoil, was the question of possible double jeopardy, and whether the officers should have been retried for essentially the same crime. As puzzling as the first verdict may have been, many felt that the subsequent federal trial was predicated more on outrage than the Constitution.

— *Colin Evans*

Suggestions for Further Reading

Boyer, Peter J. "The Selling of Rodney King." *Vanity Fair*. (July 1992): 78–83.

Duffy, Brian and Ted Gest. "Days of Rage." *US News & World Report*. (May 11, 1992): 20–26.

Koon, Stacey and Robert Dietz. *Presumed Guilty*. Chicago, Regnery Gateway, 1992.

Prudhomme, Alex. "Police Brutality." *Time* (March 25, 1991): 16–19.

Richard Lapointe Trial: 1992

Defendant: Richard Lapointe   **Crimes Charged:** Murder, arson, assault, sexual assault, kidnapping   **Chief Defense Lawyers:** Patrick Culligan, Christopher Cosgrove   **Chief Prosecutors:** Rosita Creamer, Dennis O'Connor   **Judge:** David M. Barry   **Place:** Hartford, Connecticut   **Date of Trial:** May 6–July 6, 1992   **Verdict:** Guilty   **Sentence:** Life imprisonment plus 60 years

SIGNIFICANCE

While the trial itself provoked little attention, Lapointe's conviction became the center of a growing international controversy over the rights of mentally impaired defendants.

On March 11, 1987, 88-year-old Bernice Martin was raped, bound, and brutally murdered in a senior citizens' housing complex in Manchester, Connecticut. Martin's killer set her apartment on fire, presumably to destroy evidence. Police were frustrated by a lack of leads in the case for two years. They eventually focused their investigation on Richard Lapointe, the husband of Martin's granddaughter. Lapointe, a mentally impaired dishwasher, lived nearby and had reported the fire.

A Disputed Confession

On July 4, 1989, Manchester police asked Lapointe to come to their station to be interviewed about the murder. Before he arrived, they arranged a room with fake evidence bearing his name and implicating him in the case. Police read Lapointe his Miranda rights and accused him of the murder when he arrived, but did not arrest him. They falsely told him that his fingerprints and DNA matched that of the killer, when in fact no such evidence existed. They similarly lied that his wife had been told that he committed the murder and she wanted him to confess. After an interrogation lasting nine and one-half hours, police allowed Lapointe to leave. The following day, however, they arrested him at work and publicly announced that he had signed a confession the previous day. Preliminary hearings on August 23 and 25 convinced Hartford Superior Court Judge Harry Hammer that sufficient evidence existed to try Lapointe for Martin's murder.

Unable to post a $500,000 bond or afford an attorney, Lapointe remained imprisoned for two and a half years before his case finally came to Hartford Superior Court on December 16, 1991. His court-appointed attorneys, Patrick Culligan and Christopher Cosgrove, immediately tried to suppress Lapointe's confession, which they argued was coerced. On March 6, 1992, Judge David M. Barry ruled that the confession was admissible.

Lapointe's trial began on May 6. He denied that he had killed Martin and said that the Manchester detectives had supplied the details in three signed confessions. "I figured if I signed the statements, I could leave," he said, explaining that he had signed the first two documents so that he would be allowed to use the bathroom, then recanted when he emerged.

The prosecution offered circumstantial evidence that semen lacking sperm was found at the scene, matching Lapointe's blood type and possibly coinciding with his having had a vasectomy. Yet the prosecution relied almost exclusively on Lapointe's confession. Prosecutors and police witnesses insisted that only the killer could have known certain details in the confession, including a correct description of the knife used to stab Martin, the location of her wounds, and what parts of her sofa had been set afire. They also pointed out that Lapointe told a friend the day after the murder that Martin had been raped. Police did not tell Martin's family about the sexual assault until months after her death. On the stand, Lapointe responded that he had overheard someone mention the rape at a hospital the night Martin was futilely transported for emergency treatment.

Attorneys on both sides sparred over the details in Lapointe's third and most damaging confession. Lapointe confessed to raping Martin with his penis, but medical analysis determined that she was raped with a blunt object. Lapointe confessed to strangling the victim with both hands, but an autopsy revealed that strangulation occurred when an object was pressed into the right side of her neck. Lapointe confessed to raping Martin in her bedroom, then stabbing her on the couch. Forensic investigation at the scene, however, established that Martin was stabbed on her bed. Testimony about the time frame when Lapointe was seen walking his dog in Martin's neighborhood was confusing and inconclusive.

On June 30, the jury found Lapointe guilty of capital felony murder and related charges. Prosecutors sought Lapointe's execution during the penalty phase of the trial, but medical testimony missing from the earlier portion of the trial cast doubt upon Lapointe's mental capacity. The jury decided against capital punishment. On September 6, Judge Barry sentenced Lapointe to life imprisonment without the possibility of parole, plus 60 years.

The sentence satisfied state prosecutors, but it enraged many who had monitored the trial, including attorneys and advocates for persons with mental impairments. A group called "The Friends of Richard Lapointe" began publicizing the view that Lapointe's conviction was based on an invented confession by a brain-damaged man intimidated by threats and tricks. The Manchester police were widely criticized for not recording the sessions that elicited the controversial confessions.

Rights of Mentally Handicapped Raised in Appeal

When Lapointe's appeal was formally filed on February 27, 1995, attorneys John Williams and Norman Pattis sought not only a reversal of Lapointe's conviction, but a new law requiring police to record interrogations that produce confessions. The appeal questioned whether or not the due process clause of Connecticut state law required electronic taping of confessions and advisement of Miranda rights. Two further points directly questioned Lapointe's ability to understand his legal situation during his interrogation. Specifically, attorneys questioned whether the trial court had erred in concluding that Lapointe was not in custody during his second and third confessions and in ruling that Lapointe had "knowingly and intelligently" waived his right to counsel. As the appeal was weighed, the pitch of a public relations battle between Lapointe's defenders and the state justice system rose. International advocates for the mentally handicapped increasingly cited the Lapointe case as an example of a retarded defendant's rights being trampled. Connecticut critics of Lapointe's conviction called publicly for the resignation of chief state's attorney John M. Bailey over his refusal to reexamine the case. Area attorneys and newspaper editorials agreed that regardless of the truth about the Martin murder, Lapointe's trial had been unfair.

On July 5, 1996, the Connecticut Supreme Court voted 5–2 to uphold Lapointe's conviction. The court rejected contentions that taped confessions were a constitutional right and that Lapointe's confession was obtained involuntarily. Lapointe's attorneys had argued that the hydrocephalic condition from which he suffered, Dandy Walker Syndrome, made him liable to confess to whatever he assumed authority figures wanted to hear. The court ruled that there was no evidence that the Manchester detectives had forced the confessions from Lapointe or restrained him against his will during the long interrogation.

The state court's decision was as controversial as Lapointe's conviction itself. Although his supporters continued to petition for his retrial or release, the 1996 decision forced them to argue increasingly finer legal points to make the case for his freedom.

— Tom Smith

Suggestions for Further Reading

Condon, Tom. "Reasonable Doubt." *Northeast Magazine, Hartford Courant* (February 21, 1993).

Jensen, Steve. "Man Guilty in Killing of Wife's Grandmother." *Hartford Courant* (July 1, 1992) B1.

Kauffman, Matthew. "Supreme Court Upholds Lapointe Conviction." *Hartford Courant* (July 6, 1996): A1.

Crown Heights Trials: 1992 & 1997

Defendants: First trial: Lemrick Nelson, Jr.; second trial: Lemrick Nelson, Jr. and Charles Price   **Crimes Charged:** First trial: Nelson: Murder; second trial: Nelson and Price: Violation of civil rights   **Chief Defense Lawyers:** Nelson: Trevor L.F. Headley, Arthur Lewis, Jr., James Neuman, and Christine E. Yaris; Price: Darrell Paster and Anthony Ricco   **Chief Prosecutors:** Valerie Caproni, Zachary W. Carter, David C. James, Sari Kolatch, and Alan M. Vinegard   **Judges:** First trial: Edward M. Rappoport; second trial: David G. Trager   **Place:** Brooklyn, New York   **Dates of Trials:** First trial: September 23–October 29, 1992; second trial: January 16–February 10, 1997   **Verdicts: First trial:** Nelson: Not guilty; second trial: Nelson and Price: Guilty   **Sentences:** Second trial: Nelson: 19½ years imprisonment, plus 5 years probation; Price: 21 years and 10 months imprisonment

SIGNIFICANCE

The significance of the Crown Heights trials depends upon one's point of view. The Hasidic community labeled the riots as "the first pogrom in America." The African-American population said the violence rose from long-standing tensions. The clash dramatized the discrimination felt by both groups: Caribbean immigrants, many without U.S. citizenship and Lubavitchers, an Orthodox Jewish sect whose insular lifestyle made them susceptible to stereotyping. Civil rights were violated and civil disorder was uncontained, if not countenanced, by the police. And finally, political pressure produced a second trial after the first resulted in an apparent mockery of justice. Did this put the defendant in double jeopardy? No, for (as the U.S. Supreme Court has consistently ruled), when the second case is brought by a separate government "sovereign," the Fifth Amendment principle that bars trying someone twice for the same crime does not apply.

At 8:30 on the evening of August 19, 1991, a motorcade carrying Hasidic Jews moved through the Crown Heights neighborhood in Brooklyn. One car ran a red light, hit another car, spun onto the sidewalk, and crashed into a wall. It hit two seven-year-olds, Gavin Cato and his cousin, Angela, pinning them under the car. The Hasidic driver was injured. Gavin, an African-American native of Guyana, was killed. Angela was injured.

Two ambulances, one Hasidic, the other non-Hasidic, arrived on the scene. In the mostly African-American crowd that quickly gathered, rumors spread that the Hasidic ambulance, which got there first, ministered to the Hasidic driver rather than the injured and dying children. As the crowd and rumors grew, people threw bottles and rocks to protest the treatment of the children. At about 11:00 P.M., someone shouted, "Let's go to Kingston Avenue and get a Jew!" A number of black youths then set off toward Kingston, a street of predominantly Jewish residents several blocks away, vandalizing cars and heaving rocks and bottles as they went.

A Bloody Knife and a Riot

One block past Kingston, 29-year-old Australian Hasidic student Yankel Rosenbaum was walking from an evening class, unaware of the nearby accident. The mob spotted him and chased him for three blocks, shouting "There's a Jew, kill the Jew!" Caught, he was stabbed repeatedly and left bleeding.

Finding a bloody knife in his pocket, the police apprehended 16-year-old Lemrick Nelson, Jr. At a "show-up" identification in the hospital, Rosenbaum positively identified Nelson as the person who stabbed him. The victim died the next day, reportedly of a back wound that had not been treated by Kings County Hospital doctors who failed to turn him over. Nelson soon made an oral confession to the police.

Rioting in Crown Heights continued for three days. During this time, according to later reports, Jewish residents were beaten up, cars were overturned and set afire, and stores were looted and firebombed. Police officers, reportedly forbidden by their commanders to respond to calls for help, in some cases were told they would be suspended if they left their posts to protect Jews who were being beaten only yards away. Finally, after three days, hundreds of police in riot gear arrived on foot, motorcycle, and horseback to restore order.

The Democratic administration of Mayor David Dinkins, an African American, was widely blamed for imposing a strategy of inaction by the police. The following year Dinkins lost his re-election bid to Republican Rudolph Guiliani—a result many pundits attributed to Dinkins's inept and belated response to the Crown Heights riots.

"Why Did You Stab Me?"

Nelson's background revealed that he was a special-education student who read at the third-grade level and understood math at the fifth-grade level. He was charged, as an adult, with second-degree murder.

As the trial began, the jury comprised six African Americans, four Hispanics, and two whites. Prosecutor Alan Vinegard called 10 police officers to describe the accident and riots.

The key prosecution witness was officer Mark Hoppe, who said he caught Nelson after seeing him jump a fence near the bleeding Rosenbaum; Hoppe took him back to the victim, who looked up and asked, "Why did you stab me?" Hoppe also said that in Nelson's right front pocket he found a blood-stained knife with the word "killer" painted in red on the handle.

During the cross-examination, defense lawyer Arthur Lewis, Jr., suggested that Hoppe had mishandled evidence by storing the knife and bloody dollar bills from Nelson's pocket in a paper bag he had found "someplace" in the station house.

Two officers testifying about Nelson's oral confession said he told them he had been caught up in the frenzy of the crowd. Others testified that the victim had identified Nelson as his attacker. Three forensic experts described the results of tests indicating that blood on Nelson's knife, his jeans, and the dollar bills matched Rosenbaum's.

Attorney Lewis said the defendant's confession had been coerced and that the evidence was planted by cops eager to make a quick arrest. Observers noted that the African-American defense lawyer seemed to work on the jury's sympathy—putting himself in the role of victim and playing on the vulnerability of the jurors to anti-Semitic appeals—provoking Judge Edward M. Rappoport to berate him for such blatant tactics.

The jury found Nelson not guilty. Interviewed later, jurors said they did not believe police testimony that he had confessed or that he had been read his Miranda rights. They then accepted an invitation to go out to a celebratory dinner with the defendant, with defense lawyer Lewis as host.

In the meantime, Nelson moved to Atlanta, Georgia, to live with friends and go to high school. There he attacked a classmate with a razor blade for telling authorities he had stolen some money. When arrested, he was carrying a hidden scalpel. Charged with aggravated assault and carrying a concealed weapon, he pled guilty and was sentenced to 90 to 120 days in a boot camp program, three years' probation, and expulsion from the state of Georgia.

Civil Rights Charges Brought

Although Nelson could not be tried again on the murder charge, over the next year, Hasidic leaders and Yankel Rosenbaum's brother, Norman, who made many trips from his home in Australia, pressed local politicians to seek justice. In Washington, D.C., Senator Alfonse D'Amato and Congressman Charles E. Schumer worked to pass a Senate appropriations bill that carried an amendment stating ". . . the United States Department of Justice should investigate whether any Federal criminal civil rights laws were violated as a result of (1) the murder of Yankel Rosenbaum on August 19, 1991, and (2) the circumstances surrounding the murder and accompanying riots in Crown Heights." The bill was unanimously approved.

As a result, Attorney General Janet Reno launched an investigation into the affair, and on August 10, 1994, the U.S. Attorney for the Eastern District of New York charged Nelson with violating civil rights, stating that he and others "did willfully injure, intimidate and interfere with . . . Yankel Rosenbaum, an Orthodox Jew, because of his religion and because he was enjoying the facilities provided and administered by a subdivision of the State of New York, namely, the public streets provided and administered by the City of New York, and bodily injury to and the death of Yankel Rosenbaum did result."

The charge included Charles Price, 43, who had been identified as the man who touched off the riots by shouting, "Let's go to Kingston Avenue and get a Jew!"

The Second Trial Begins

Court documentation for the second trial included transcripts of a tape secretly made in 1995 by an undercover informant who got Price to talk about the rioting. Price was quoted describing his reaction when he saw the mortally injured African-American child: "I saw that blood mix with that oil and it was like a bolt of lightning hit me, bam, and I started runnin' my mouth."

Prosecutor Valerie Caproni described for the jury of three African Americans, two Jews, three Hispanics, and four whites the "raw anger" of the attack on the victim. Witness Chaya Popack, who had not been called to testify during the 1992 trial but who had watched the attack from her car said, "I saw them strike him again and again and again." Officer Hoppe repeated his earlier testimony about catching Nelson and finding the bloody knife, adding that he saw a "bald black man"—Price was bald—shouting at the crowd, "Do you feel what I feel? Let's get a Jew." Police

Lemrick Nelson was found guilty of violating the civil rights of Yankel Rosenbaum during the riots in Crown Heights, Brooklyn. (AP/Wide World Photos)

Sergeant Richard Sanossian testified that Price's voice "was the loudest and most angry voice there, and that is the voice I was watching."

Convincing testimony came from Nelson's Atlanta girlfriend, Travionne Shaw, 20. She said Nelson had told her, "The black people in Crown Heights rioted. And some friends and him [Nelson] had been drinking, and they saw this man and were fighting him. And the police were coming, and the guy was holding his shirt, and the guy wouldn't let him go, and he—he stabbed him."

"They . . . Set Him Up"

After two weeks of testimony from 28 witnesses, the prosecution rested. Defense attorney Christine Yaris, describing her client as a "sacrificial lamb," said the police "took the first kid they found and set him up." She asked Nelson to put on the blood-spattered, baggy jeans that police had testified he had worn during the killing. The astonished courtroom saw them fall to Nelson's knees. Then, showing photos of the jeans Nelson had actually worn that night, she noted that the belt loops were empty. "If those pants are the pants in evidence," she said, "they had no visible means of support." In rebuttal, the prosecution detailed how nine police and civilian witnesses would have had to have plotted to frame the defendant. The jury was excused and Nelson was ordered to put the pants on again. This time, they stayed up without a belt.

Price's attorney Darrell Paster described his client as a scapegoat implicated "to carry away the sins of unknown people the government can't find."

After four days of deliberations, the jury found both defendants guilty of violating Rosenbaum's civil rights. Judge David G. Trager sentenced Nelson to 19½ years in prison, plus 5 years' probation. Price received 21 years and 10 months imprisonment. Under federal law, neither could expect parole. Lawyers for both defendants said they would appeal.

Following the trial, New York City Mayor Rudolph Guiliani formally apologized to the residents of Crown Heights and to the Rosenbaum family. The city agreed to a $1.1 million settlement of a lawsuit brought by the Hasidic community for the city's failure to protect its citizens.

—Bernard Ryan, Jr.

Suggestions for Further Reading

Daughty, Reverend Herbert D. *No Monopoly on Suffering: Blacks and Jews in Crown Heights and Elsewhere.* Trenton, N.J.: Africa World Press, 1997.

Fletcher, George P. *With Justice for Some: Victims' Rights in Criminal Trials.* Reading, Mass.: Addison-Wesley, 1995.

Lenowitz, Harris. *The Jewish Messiahs: From the Galilee to Crown Heights.* New York: Oxford, 1998.

Smith, Anna Deavere. *Fires in the Mirror: Crown Heights, Brooklyn, and Other Identities.* New York: Doubleday, 1993.

Amy Fisher Trial: 1992

Defendant: Amy Fisher   **Crimes Charged:** Attempted murder, assault
Chief Defense Lawyer: Eric Naiburg   **Chief Prosecutor:** Fred Klein
Judge: Marvin Goodman   **Place:** Long Island, New York
Date of Trial: September 24, 1992   **Verdict:** Guilty of assault
Sentence: 5–15 years imprisonment; released after 7 years

SIGNIFICANCE

The Amy Fisher/Joey Buttafuoco affair (she being a teenager at the time) showed the extent of tabloid newspapers' and television shows' power in capturing the public's attention and catapulting ordinary people into celebrityhood.

One sunny May afternoon in 1992, Mary Jo Buttafuoco found a teen-aged girl ringing the doorbell of her suburban Massapequa, New York, home. The girl accused Buttafuoco's 36-year-old husband Joey of having an affair with her younger sister. Unimpressed by the story and a T-shirt the teenager offered as proof, Mary Jo Buttafuoco decided that the conversation was over and turned away. As she stepped back into the house, she suddenly fell with a bullet at the base of her skull.

The following year would be enlivened by an antic cavalcade of lawyers, tabloid reporters, Hollywood film makers and the participants themselves—all openly playing with the truth about why Mary Jo Buttafuoco was shot. Conflicting stories became a profitable commodity to be bought and sold in the form of newspapers, magazines, tell-all books, and television shows. By the time the justice system was finished with the affair, Americans would be fascinated or repelled by a story in which nearly all of the action took place out of the courtroom.

When Mary Jo Buttafuoco began to write a description of her assailant for the detectives clustered around her hospital bed, her husband, Joey, suddenly announced that he knew the identity of the attacker. He steered police toward the teenaged daughter of one his customers.

Police quickly arrested 17-year-old Amy Fisher, who claimed that she had been having a sexual affair with Joey Buttafuoco since she was 16 years old. She said she was obsessed with the auto-body mechanic and had gone to the Buttafuoco home to confront his wife. When Buttafuoco's wife refused to take her seriously, Fisher angrily smacked Mary Jo in the head with a cheap handgun, causing it to accidentally discharge and fall apart.

Anyone who assumed that Fisher was merely a smitten teenager confused by the promises of an older lover got a rude shock a week after the shooting. In a secretly made videotape purchased by the tabloid television program *A Current Affair*, Fisher was seen negotiating terms for sex with a salesman in a motel bedroom. The videotape aired on national television the night before her bail hearing. What had been a sordid local story became an instant national sensation.

Calling her a prostitute who had stalked Mary Jo Buttafuoco for months, Nassau County Assistant District Attorney Fred Klein charged Fisher with attempted second-degree murder, first-degree assault, and a host of firearms-related felonies. Klein asked for a record-breaking $2 million bail.

If Fisher were a call girl, replied her attorney, Eric Naiburg, then Joey Buttafuoco was a pimp who had introduced his client to prostitution by setting her up with work at an escort service. Nassau County Supreme Court Justice Marvin Goodman was not convinced by Naiburg's arguments that Fisher was a victim of Buttafuoco's manipulations. The judge agreed to the prosecutor's unprecedented $2 million bail request and sent Fisher off to jail to await trial.

Long Island Lolita

The media latched onto the tale of the "Long Island Lolita" with an obsession that rivaled Fisher's hunger for Buttafuoco's affection. Reporters looking for a fresh angle in the case were rewarded within days. While tending to his recovering wife at home, Joey Buttafuoco dialed controversial talk radio personality Howard Stern to denounce the sensational stories about his involvement with Fisher. Over the airwaves, Buttafuoco announced to the world that he loved his wife and was innocent of any part in her shooting. He declared that Fisher's claims were hallucinations.

Television and press reporters swarmed around Joey Buttafuoco. Was it true that Long Island escort services called him "Joey Coco-Pops" because of his ability to procure cocaine and women for customers? Buttafuoco admitted that he once had a drug problem, but said that it was now behind him. Had he met Fisher for sex at motels, his boat, his auto body shop, and at her parents' house, as she claimed? Had he encouraged her to kill his wife? Absolutely not, repeated Buttafuoco, who blandly insisted that such charges were the lies of a sick young woman. Buttafuoco said that he only knew the teenager from his auto body shop where she had brought her smashed car for repairs. She was such a frequent customer that he had her telephone beeper number.

As Mary Jo Buttafuoco regained her speech, she vigorously defended her husband. "The story is pretty simple," she told the press. "I love my Joey. My Joey loves me." If she suspected her husband of being involved in the shooting, she said, she would castrate him. "I'm no pushover who doesn't know her ass from her elbow," she told the Ladies Home Journal.

Hollywood Deals

With Judge Goodman repeatedly refusing to lower Fisher's huge bail, her attorney went to Hollywood to obtain bail money. Naiburg constructed a deal in which a film production agency secured the rights to Fisher's story by guaranteeing the major portion of her bail. The contract was signed and Fisher was released.

When prosecutors learned that Hollywood had helped finance Fisher's bail bond, they were furious. Since 1977, New York's so-called "Son of Sam" law, named after serial killer David Berkowitz, had barred criminals and defendants under indictment from selling their stories for profit. Six months before Fisher's case, however, the law had been declared an unconstitutional infringement of First Amendment rights to free speech. The state was hurriedly modifying the voided law in a way that would comply with the U.S. Supreme Court's decision, while still making convicts liable to financial claims by their victims. The prosecution charged the defense with improperly funding Fisher's release. However, Fisher remained free, Although under a restraining order to stay away from the Buttafuocos. This was not enough for an angry Mary Jo Buttafuoco, who filed a civil suit against Fisher for over $100 million, including the Hollywood bail money.

Meanwhile, the Buttafuocos were also selling interviews and cutting deals with Hollywood. Partially paralyzed and suffering from impaired vision and hearing, Mary Jo Buttafuoco sold the rights to her side of the story to CBS television for several hundred thousand dollars.

On September 23, 1992, Amy Fisher agreed to plead guilty to the lesser charge of reckless assault rather than face the uncertain outcome of a trial for attempted murder. Mary Jo Buttafuoco was livid over the plea bargaining, which required Fisher to aid investigators still examining the incident. This was a clear indication that Joey Buttafuoco was vulnerable to a statutory rape charge if it could be proved that he had had sex with Fisher when she was 16 years old.

"She tried to kill me and now she's taking my husband and trying to destroy us," said Mary Jo Buttafuoco. "This girl is an attempted murderer, a liar, a prostitute, and the D.A. is accepting her statement that she and Joe were together. Something's wrong here."

Free on bail while awaiting sentencing, Fisher visited a boyfriend, Paul Makely. While she rattled on about marrying Makely so that she could have conjugal visits in prison and about a sports car she hoped her notoriety could buy her, Makely secretly videotaped the conversation. He sold the tape to *Hard Copy*, a national tabloid television show, and Fisher made headlines again. When she saw the tape, she attempted suicide and checked into a psychiatric hospital. After she was released, she voluntarily returned to prison to avoid the media.

By now, police investigators had collected a handful of motel receipts signed by Joey Buttafuoco on dates when Fisher claimed to have met with him. F.B.I. handwriting analysts confirmed that most of the receipts carried Buttafuoco's signature. Yet facing a lack of any other evidence and with Fisher's reputation making her a useless witness, the District Attorney announced that

Buttafuoco would not be indicted. At her sentencing on December 1, 1992, Fisher listened as Mary Jo Buttafuoco told the court of the lifelong pain she would endure as a result of her gunshot wound and the permanent disruption of her life and those of her loved ones.

"A Walking Stick of Dynamite"

When her turn to speak came, Fisher nervously apologized, but continued to insist that Joey Buttafuoco had encouraged her.

Judge Goodman was unmoved. "You are a disgrace to yourself, your family, and your friends," he told Fisher as he imposed the maximum sentence of 5-to-15 years imprisonment. "You were like a walking stick of dynamite with the fuse lit."

The Buttafuocos happily declared they were satisfied with the verdict and used the occasion to once again brand Fisher a liar. Major television networks soon aired the made-for-TV movies whose broadcast rights had floated Fisher's bond and paid the Buttafuocos's medical and legal bills. Local interest in the crime had faded. Ratings for the movies, however, demonstrated that viewers around the nation still had not tired of watching the cheap plot play out.

Joey's Troubles Are Not Over

With Fisher in prison and the television dramas over, the story soon started anew for Joey Buttafuoco. Police questioned a former employee of his body shop who claimed to have heard Buttafuoco boast of having sex with Fisher. On April 15, 1993, nearly a year after his wife was shot, Buttafuoco was indicted on six counts of statutory rape, twelve counts of sodomy, and one count of endangering the welfare of a child. Buttafuoco pled not guilty and left court in a white Cadillac accompanied by his still supportive wife.

That summer, Mary Jo Buttafuoco accepted an undisclosed settlement in her $125-million damage suit against Fisher and Peter Guagenti, who was spending six months in prison for selling Fisher the handgun and driving her to the Buttafuoco house. The New York State Supreme Court, however, denied Buttafuoco's claim to any of the money with which Fisher made bail, ruling that the deal with Hollywood was within Fisher's rights as a presumed innocent defendant who was permitted to raise bail by any lawful means.

The Buttafuocos's frequent press conferences and interviews on television programs like The Phil Donahue Show were viewed by millions, although the couple's version of events wore thin with much of the American public. Joey Buttafuoco's constant claims that he had never slept with Amy Fisher and Mary Jo's feisty denials of her husband's alleged affair provided easy laughs for comedians across the nation. Prosecutors were less jocular about the case. They ordered Buttafuoco to submit to a blood test and physical examination to weigh Fisher's charge that he had given her herpes and her claim to be able to identify hidden birthmarks on his body.

Joey Buttafuoco's wife stayed home with their children when he went to court on October 5, 1993. Flanked by his lawyer, Buttafuoco pled guilty to one count of statutory rape, the most serious charge in a 19 count indictment against him.

"I cannot accept your plea unless you are, in fact, guilty," Judge Jack Mackston told the tense defendant. There was a long pause. "On July 2, 1991, I had sexual relations with Amy Fisher at the Freeport Motel," Buttafuoco finally said.

"Do you mean sexual intercourse?" interjected the prosecutor.

"Yes, sir."

The defense attorney had an explanation for skeptics, to whom the crumbling of Buttafuoco's claim of innocence was no surprise. "There is a family involved here," Attorney Dominic Barbera said of his client. "That's the man he is. He did what he had to do in that courtroom so everybody else's life could go on."

Those wondering if Buttafuoco had committed a noble perjury to save his family more pain looked to the District Attorney's office, who assured Judge Mackston that factual evidence included motel receipts and witnesses to Buttafuoco's boasts about his sexual relationship with Fisher.

Joey Buttafuoco was sentenced to six months in prison and five years probation. He was also fined $5,000. He left prison after serving only 129 days of the sentence, flashing a thumbs-up sign at photographers. His wife threw a welcome-home party for him and several hundred guests attended. Bemoaning the sensationalism surrounding the case, The New York Times printed the party menu and photographed the Buttafuocos celebrating together.

Amy Fisher served her sentence amid tabloid rumors of a romance with a prison guard and later a lesbian affair with a fellow

Amy Fisher in 1996, before her release from prison. (AP/Wide World Photos)

inmate. Meanwhile New York Governor George Pataki eliminated work release for any inmate convicted of a violent felony, thus scuttling Fisher's chance for an early parole.

Joey Buttafuoco considered embarking on a career as an actor, a line of work for which his detractors considered him well-qualified. But Joey's troubles were not over: On May 24, 1995, in Los Angeles, California, he was arrested for—and later pleaded no contest to—soliciting sex from an undercover vice officer. In addition to ordering Buttafuoco to pay $1,715 in fines and take an HIV test, the judge placed Buttafuoco on two years' probation.

Back in Nassau County, Judge Mackston found Buttafuoco guilty of violating his parole and sentenced him to 10 months in prison.

After his release, Joey Buttafuoco spent several years in Hollywood trying his hand at acting. He landed small roles in forgettable movies and for a short time, hosted his own public access cable television talk show.

In May 1999, Amy Fisher was released from prison after serving seven years of her sentence. Her early release from jail was due, in large part, to Mary Jo Buttafuoco's public statements forgiving Fisher. At the time of her release, Fisher's attorney said that she had a job waiting for her in the fashion industry.

—Tom Smith

Suggestions for Further Reading

Barry, Dan. "No Way Out: Still Gawking After All These Years." *New York Times* (May 16, 1999): 12.

Leavitt, Paul. "Buttafuoco Threat." *USA Today* (May 5, 1994): 3.

McQuiston, John T. "Helped by Women She Shot, Amy Fisher May Be Paroled." *New York Times* (March 31, 1999): 1.

——. "Amy Fisher Is Released After Almost 7 Years in Prison." *New York Times* (May 11, 1999): 1.

The Glen Ridge Rape Trial: 1992–93

Defendants: Christopher Archer, Bryant Grober, Kevin Scherzer, Kyle Scherzer **Crime Charged:** Rape **Chief Defense Lawyers:** Kyle Scherzer: Louis Esposito; Christopher Archer: Thomas Ford, Jr.; Kevin Scherzer: Michael Querques; Bryant Grober: Alan Zegas **Chief Prosecutors:** Glenn Goldberg, Robert Laurino, Elizabeth Miller-Hall **Judge:** R. Benjamin Cohen **Place:** Newark, New Jersey **Dates of Trial:** October 15, 1992–March 16, 1993 **Verdicts:** Archer: guilty on two counts of first-degree aggravated sexual assault and guilty of second-degree conspiracy; Grober: acquitted of aggravated sexual assault but guilty of third-degree conspiracy to commit aggravated sexual assault and aggravated sexual contact; Kevin Scherzer: guilty of two first-degree counts of aggravated sexual assault and guilty of second-degree conspiracy; Kyle Scherzer: guilty of one count of first-degree aggravated sexual assault, guilty of second-degree attempted aggravated sexual assault, and guilty of second-degree conspiracy. **Sentences:** Grober: three years' probation and 200 hours of community service; Kyle Scherzer: seven years imprisonment; Archer and Kevin Scherzer: 15 years each.

SIGNIFICANCE

Many consider this case a symptom of the ailments of late twentieth-century American society. It sent to prison three of the stereotypical heroes of a public high school in a stereotypical middle-class suburban community. As it exposed the thoughtless, sordid, and vicious crimes of the defendants, it was almost a textbook case of group abnormal psychology. [NOTE: To protect the victim, her name in news accounts and books has been changed. Here it is Susan Fisher; other names reported are factual.]

In prosperous Glen Ridge, New Jersey, high-school students Christopher Archer, twins Kevin and Kyle Scherzer, and Susan Fisher had been schoolmates since kindergarten. For 12 years, the boys had amused themselves by making things difficult for Fisher, who was, as everybody knew, developmentally challenged.

By March 1, 1989, Fisher was 17. Her IQ was 64. Her mind was considered that of an eight-year-old. That afternoon, Christopher Archer found Fisher on a playground near the Scherzer brothers' home. He urged her to join him and several friends at the Scherzers'. Reluctant at first, she yielded to Archer's promises of a prize and a date later with his brother Paul.

Teens in the "rec room"

In the Scherzers' well-furnished basement, Fisher found a small crowd of Glen Ridge's acclaimed high-school athletes, including Paul Archer, football team co-captains Kevin and Kyle Scherzer, Bryant Grober, Peter Quigley, and another half-dozen teen boys. Within minutes, told to take off her clothes, Fisher was undressed and performing fellatio with Grober as the others cheered. Next, several of the young men used a broomstick, a baseball bat, and a dowel stick to rape Fisher. Finally, Fisher masturbated each of them in turn.

Told she could leave, Fisher was admonished not to tell anyone about the event. But within three days, she confided in her high-school swimming coach that something had happened but that she did not want to betray the boys, who were her friends. Within a week, a social worker told Fisher's mother what the swim teacher knew.

Meantime, the rapists bragged. They planned a second session with Fisher—this one to be videotaped. Gossip elaborated. On March 22, Glen Ridge High School principal Michael Buonomo notified the police. The board of education investigated. But two months passed before the six leaders in the rape were indicted. Peter Quigley and Paul Archer reduced their charges by agreeing to testify and to perform 60 hours of community service. As the trial of the four others began on October 15, 1992, Essex County assistant prosecutor Glenn Goldberg described the victim's childhood, her neurological impairment, intellectual limitations, low IQ, and second- or third-grade achievement in sixth grade. At almost 18, he said, "Her ability to assess social situations, to know what is appropriate, was that of an eight-year-old."

Goldberg told the jurors that a recent New Jersey Supreme Court ruling had found that an act of sexual penetration was punishable if the participant could not understand the right to refuse the act or could not exercise the right. Then he outlined Fisher's personality. "If somebody was nice to her," he said, "that person became a good, maybe even her best, friend."

". . . the People that Teenagers Admired . . ."

The boys Fisher encountered on March 1, 1989, said Goldberg, "were the football players, the wrestlers, the baseball players, the people that teenagers admired for their physical prowess. They were her heroes—the stars."

Defense attorneys Thomas Ford, Michael Querques, Alan Zegas, and Louis Esposito each opened with comments on Fisher's previous sexual experience, theorizing that she knew what was happening and could have said, "Stop."

Prosecution witness Dr. Susan Esquilin, a psychologist expert on sex-abuse victims who had diagnosed Fisher as a mental eight-year-old, testified that "sexuality for her has to do with what somebody asks her to do." Cross-examined, she said, "I don't think she has any capacity to say no."

Also for the prosecution, Dr. Gerald Meyerhoff, former chief of psychiatry at Bergen Pines County Hospital in Paramus, New Jersey, testified that "her search for friends is an important piece of her life." Next, psychiatric nurse and University of Pennsylvania professor Ann Burgess used drawings depicting rape, made by Fisher some months after the attack, to explain the victim's long wait to report the crime and to prove that she was distressed by it. This testimony about rape trauma syndrome was the first ever permitted by a New Jersey judge as trial evidence.

Defendants in Glen Ridge sexual assault trial, from right, Kevin Scherzer, his twin, Kyle, Bryant Grober, Christopher Archer. (AP/ Wide World Photos)

Called as a prosecution witness, Fisher's mother testified on her daughter's learning difficulties and inability to travel alone or handle finances. She described how school officials had told her a group of boys had had some kind of sexual encounter with her daughter.

On cross-examination, defense attorney Thomas Ford established that Fisher's mother had earlier realized that Fisher was sexually active and had obtained birth control pills for her. Bryan Grober's lawyer, Alan Zegas, insisted that Fisher had been removed from her high school "because of her inappropriate conduct." Fisher's mother replied, "The situation was that she was a potential rape victim."

Zegas persisted. "Your reason for getting birth control pills for your daughter was not because she, of her own accord, was having sexual relations with other men?"

"I have never heard that before," came the reply.

"I Still Care about Them"

Susan Fisher was called to the stand. Prosecutor Robert Laurino took her through the events of March 1, including specific details of the rape and of the sex acts she performed on the high-school athletes. "Are those boys still your friends?" asked Laurino.

"Sort of."

"What do you mean, sort of?"

"I mean I still care about them," said Fisher.

Cross-examined by attorney Ford, Fisher admitted that she had made no attempt to leave the Scherzer basement, that no one told her not to leave, and that she would not have performed sexual acts in front of her parents or other adults. Grober lawyer Zegas asked her extensively about her experience with and enjoyment of sex. Scherzer lawyer Querques reminded Fisher of her examination by psychologist Esquilin and concluded, "You are proving right now, because you can answer questions, that you are not retarded?"

"Right. If I was retarded, I wouldn't know what I was talking about."

"Perfect, Susan," said Querques.

The prosecution rested.

The Defense Argues Consent

Defense attorney Michael Querques, representing Kevin Scherzer, argued that Fisher provoked the rape and enjoyed it. "There are some girls," he said, "who are Lolitas." He urged the jury to view defendant Scherzer not as the 21-year-old in the courtroom but as a teenager. To prove that Fisher was obsessed with sex, Querques reviewed doctor's records showing that her mother had had him prescribe birth control pills for her because she was sexually active. And, for two hours, the lawyer lectured the jury on the sexual revolution and the sex lives of today's teenagers.

As its chief witness, the defense introduced defendant Christopher Archer's brother Paul, an eyewitness. He said he saw Fisher "voluntarily doing everything" and added, "She made all the advances. It was all her idea."

The next day, Archer changed his testimony. Now he said Kevin Scherzer actively manipulated the broomstick during the rape of Fisher. During his third day as a witness, Paul Archer admitted lying to investigators in order to protect his pals.

Summing up, prosecutor Glenn Goldberg spent 14 hours and 15 minutes over six days. "This mentally defective girl," he concluded, "can be taunted, teased, abused, poked, and prodded with sticks, but she matters and her life matters, too."

The jury deliberated for 12 days. On March 16, 1993, it found all four young men guilty, to various degrees, of conspiracy to commit aggravated sexual assault and aggravated sexual contact.

On April 23, 1993, Judge R. Benjamin Cohen sentenced Grober to probation. The other three defendants received indeterminate sentences, not to exceed 15 years, in "youthful offenders" prison. The judge then permitted the three to go free on $2,500 bail each while their lawyers filed appeals.

After the Appellate Division of New Jersey Superior Court reduced Kyle Scherzer's sentence to seven years, letting Archer's and Kevin Scherzer's sentences stand at 15 years, all three entered prison. The New Jersey Supreme Court refused to review the case. Kyle Scherzer was paroled in 2000. His twin and Archer remained in prison in 2001.

—Bernard Ryan, Jr.

Suggestions for Further Reading

Brownmiller, Susan. *Against Our Will: Men, Women and Rape.* New York: Simon & Schuster, 1975.

Fairstein, Linda. *Sexual Violence: Our War Against Rape.* New York: Morrow, 1993.

Farrell, Warren. *The Myth of Male Power.* New York: Simon & Schuster, 1993.

Laufer, Peter. *A Question of Consent: Innocence and Complicity in the Glen Ridge Rape Case.* San Francisco: Mercury House, 1994.

Lefkowitz, Bernard. *Our Guys: The Glen Ridge Rape and the Secret Life of the Perfect Suburb.* New York: Vintage, 1998.

Vachss, Alice. *Sex Crimes: Ten Years on the Front Lines Prosecuting Rapists and Confronting Their Collaborators.* New York: Random House, 1993.

Woody Allen–Mia Farrow Custody Trial: 1993

Defendant: Woody Allen **Plaintiff:** Mia Farrow **Plaintiff Claim:** Custody of three children Allen Shared with Mia Farrow
Chief Defense Lawyers: Alan M. Dershowitz, Eleanor B. Alter
Chief Lawyer for the Plaintiff: Elkan Abramowitz **Judge:** Elliot Wilk
Place: New, York, New York **Date of Trial:** March 19–June 7, 1993
Verdict: Petition for custody was denied

SIGNIFICANCE

This custody battle between two very public figures revealed just how painful such fights can be for all involved.

Woody Allen and Mia Farrow are not Hollywood stars—they stay away from the glamour of tinseltown. They are, nevertheless, famous film people, and millions flock to see their movies. The couple was never married, nor did they live together: During their relationship they inhabited separate apartments on opposite sides of Central Park in New York City. Together they had children and they were a family.

On August 13, 1992, the public gasped when Woody Allen filed suit against Mia Farrow for custody of their three children. Although the three children lived with Farrow, Allen was a frequent household visitor. Farrow adopted Moses Amadeus Farrow, 14, a Korean boy, after her divorce from noted symphony director André Previn. Later, Allen also adopted the boy. Dylan O'Sullivan Farrow, 7, a girl, was adopted as a baby by Farrow and Allen together in 1985. The couple's natural son, Satchel O'Sullivan Farrow, was 4 and one-half on that fateful day.

While the legal documents in the suit were immediately sealed, an excited public got the details from the celebrities themselves. Two New York newspapers, The Daily News and The New York Post reported that for the past eight months Allen had been having an affair with Farrow's 21-year-old daughter, Soon-Yi Farrow Previn, a Korean whom the actress had adopted when she was married to Previn. (Altogether, Farrow has 11 children, seven of whom are adopted.) Responding to these reports, Allen put out a press release saying, "It's real and happily all true." About the same time that Allen filed the custody suit, Connecticut State Police disclosed that they were investigating Allen's alleged sexual abuse of Dylan at Farrow's country home in Bridgewater. The well-known movie maker vehemently denied the allegation. He said it was a weapon used by Farrow to counter his efforts to win custody of the children.

Life Imitating Art?

The battle was joined. Legions of fans were both confused and disappointed. The news media, while proclaiming that all its major sources in the story were the principals themselves, also chased every rumor and interviewed whoever had an opinion. Film buffs wondered how tarnished the reputation of their idol, Allen, would become. Cashing in on the publicity, Allen's studio advanced the opening date of his new movie, *Husbands and Wives*, in which he starred with Farrow and which, according to advance notices, mimicked their real-life breakup and custody battle. The studio announced that the film would be released nationally, rather than in only eight cities, as had previously been scheduled.

Woody Allen and Mia Farrow before their breakup. (AP/Wide World Photos)

At a preliminary hearing, New York Supreme Court Justice Phyllis B. Gangel-Jacob turned down Allen's request for visitation rights with the children. She also refused to accept, from Farrow's lawyers, Allen's photographs of Soon-Yi in the nude—pictures that Farrow had found on the mantel-piece in her home and that had tipped her off that the affair was going on.

By October 1992, the case had become fuel for the raging political fires of the U.S. presidential election year—one of whose themes was family values. U.S. Attorney General William P. Barr, quoting an Allen interview in Time, said, "After all, he [Allen] said 'the heart wants what the heart wants.' There you have it. In seven words, Allen epigrammatically captures the essence of contemporary moral philosophy." U.S. Representative Newt Gingrich, known for preaching family values as a Republican strength, told a Georgia audience, "Woody Allen is currently having non-incest with a non-daughter for whom he is a non-father because they have no concept of families . . . it's a weird environment out there."

Next came a wave of hearings and rulings. Acting New York Supreme Court Justice Elliott Wilk ruled that television cameras would be allowed into the court during future hearings and during the trial. Both sides immediately appealed, so Administrative Judge Stanley S. Ostrau barred both TV and radio coverage in his courtroom. Meanwhile, Farrow sued in Surrogate's Court to nullify Allen's adoption of Moses and Dylan.

In a December 15, 1992, hearing, Justice Wilk ruled that Farrow must provide Allen a copy of a videotape in which Dylan reportedly said Allen molested her. Wilk also turned down Farrow's request that Allen's suit for sole custody be put on hold pending the outcome of her suit in Surrogate's Court.

On March 18, 1993, a team of psychological investigators at Yale-New Haven Hospital cleared Woody Allen of sexually molesting Dylan. The findings, which were the results of repeated interviews with Allen, Farrow, Dylan, the child's psychologist, and household servants, were not made public. However, Allen's lawyers reported that the videotape on which Farrow had based the accusation was a result either of the child's imagination or of someone else's manipulation.

The Custody Trial Begins

The next day, on March 19, 1993, the custody trial began before Acting Justice Wilk. Allen testified that after Farrow learned of his affair with Soon-Yi, she cut his head out of family pictures and that "she [Farrow] called me dozens of times a night, raging and screaming, threatening to kill me." He testified further that he once found a note she left by an open window saying, "I've jumped out the window because of what you've done to the children."

The nude photos of Soon-Yi were admitted as evidence in court. Farrow's attorney, Eleanor B. Alter, suggested they were pornographic. Allen testified they were a matter between consenting adults and were intended to be erotic. Attorney Alter read a letter from Moses Farrow, 15, to Allen that said, "You have done a horrible, unforgivable, ugly, stupid thing. I hope you get so humiliated you commit suicide. . . . Everyone knows not to have an affair with your son's sister, including that sister, but you have a special way to get that sister to think that that is O.K." Questioned by Elkan Abramowitz, his own lawyer, Allen responded that Moses was manipulated by his mother and used the same words and phrases that she had used only days earlier.

Farrow then testified that Dylan told her the preceding summer that her father had sexually molested her. Farrow conceded, however, that the child, in her shyness, would not tell doctors of the abuse and that a medical examination produced no signs of it. She explained that she had videotaped the girl's statement because, "I wanted this documented because it had happened before. . . . He would creep up in the morning and lay beside her bed and wait for her to wake up. I thought it was excessive. I was uncomfortable all along." Farrow added that when Allen came to visit, Dylan screamed, "Hide me! Hide me!" to her brothers and sisters.

Clinical psychologist Dr. Susan Coates, who had treated Satchel and met often with both parents, testified that she had been convinced by Farrow's behavior—including sending Allen a Valentine with skewers through the hearts of her children—that she might harm herself or Allen.

More than two weeks went by in the stuffy, crowded New York City courtroom where the paint was peeling from the walls and ancient chairs creaked constantly. Dr. Coates testified that Allen should be allowed unsupervised visits with Satchel but was less certain about his seeing Dylan. The children's nanny testified that Farrow was not always a good mother and had once slapped an adopted son across the face for not finding a dog leash. Allen's sister testified that Farrow taught the children to hate him. Allen produced a surreptitious recording of a phone call from Farrow's Connecticut housekeeper that disparaged Farrow's abilities as a mother. Allen's lawyer, Abramowitz, accused the Connecticut State Police of aiding Farrow's case by allowing her lawyers to see the Dylan videotape but refusing his request to see it. A baby sitter testified that she saw Allen kneeling before Dylan "in a way that bothered" her. In a three-hour shouting match between Farrow's attorney, Alan M. Dershowitz, and Allen's attorney Abramowitz, Dershowitz denied allegations by Abramowitz that he had asked Allen to pay millions of dollars to get Farrow to call off the molestation charge. Justice Wilk criticized New York investigators for subjecting Dylan to the trauma of a second sex-abuse investigation. A doctor who headed the Connecticut investigation said that Dylan's story had "a rehearsed quality" and that Farrow might have encouraged the child to fabricate because she liked to perform.

On June 7, 1993, Justice Wilk, in a stinging 33-page decision, called Allen a "self-absorbed, untrustworthy and insensitive father. It is clear," he continued, "that the best interests of the children will be served by their continued custody with Ms. Farrow." The judge denied Allen immediate visitation rights with Dylan, ruling that a further review be held after Dylan received psychological therapy. Supervised visits, however, with Satchel would be allowed. The judge also acceded to Moses's request not to be forced to see his father and ordered Allen to pay Farrow's legal fees. Finally, the judge questioned the findings of the Yale-New Haven Hospital investigators, noting that whether or not molestation took place, "Mr. Allen's behavior toward Dylan was grossly inappropriate."

In September 1993, Connecticut State Attorney Frank Maco announced that, while he had "probable cause" to prosecute Allen on charges of sexual molestation of Dylan, he was dropping the case to spare her the trauma of appearing in court. Allen filed complaints asking the state bar counsel to disbar Maco and requesting that the State Criminal Justice Commission discipline Maco for making an accusation without producing an indictment. In October, the New York State Department of Social Services dropped its investigation into the child molestation charge. It concluded "that no credible evidence was found . . . that the child named in this report has been abused or maltreated." In November, the Connecticut Criminal Justice Commission voted unanimously to dismiss Allen's complaint against Maco. It said that after four hours of deliberation it could find no evidence that Prosecutor Maco had violated the canon of ethics for lawyers in his remarks during the September news conference in which he announced that he was dropping the charges against Allen. In January 1994, the Connecticut bar's disciplinary panel criticized Maco's handling of the case and found that he might have prejudiced the celebrities' custody battle, but that he did not violate the state's code of conduct for lawyers.

The Aftermath

Over the following year, Allen continued to date Soon-Yi, dining with her in the exclusive Manhattan restaurant, Elaine's, where he and Farrow had often been seen in earlier days. Farrow no longer visited the restaurant. Meanwhile, Farrow informally renamed two of her children, calling Dylan by the name Eliza. Satchell became Seamus. On October 5, 1994, Allen lost an appeal for relief from the custody ruling that forbade his seeing Dylan (Eliza) and Moses and allowed court-supervised visits only with Satchel (Seamus). Both Farrow and Allen went on with their film making. In 1994 Farrow starred with Joan Plowright and Natasha Richardson in Widows Peak, which met with some critical acclaim. Meanwhile, Allen released Bullets Over Broadway, which went on to be heavily nominated for Academy Awards.

Allen and Soon-Yi Previn married in 1997. In April 1999, the couple had their first child, a daughter. However, neither Allen nor Soon-Yi would publicly say whether the child was adopted or if Soon-Yi had given birth to the baby girl.

—*Bernard Ryan, Jr.*

Suggestions for Further Reading

Hewitt, Bill. "No Laughing Matter." *People Weekly*, (June 21, 1993): 85–86.

Marks, Peter. "Allen Loses to Farrow in Bitter Custody Battle." *New York Times* (June 8, 1993): A1, B4.

Seligmann, Jean and Mary Talbot. "A Game for the Whole Family." *Newsweek* (April 12, 1993): 66.

Randy Weaver Trial: 1993

Defendants: Randall Weaver, Kevin Harris **Crimes Charged:** Conspiracy, murder, failure to appear for trial, interference with federal marshals, possession of illegal firearms, resisting arrest, violation of bail
Chief Defense Lawyer: Gerry Spence **Chief Prosecutor:** Assistant U.S. Attorney Ron Howen **Judge:** Edward J. Lodge **Place:** Boise, Idaho
Date of Trial: April 12–July 8, 1993 **Verdict:** Guilty of bail violation and failure to appear for trial, not guilty of all other charges **Sentence:** 18 months in jail, $10,000 fine, 3 years probation

SIGNIFICANCE

In a troubling case that raised the specter of government persecution of innocent citizens for political and ideological reasons, a federal jury, because of misconduct and deception in the government's case, found Randy Weaver not guilty of shooting a federal marshal.

Randall Weaver, according to the U.S. government, was a white supremacist, affiliated with the notorious Aryan Nations, and a dealer in illicit weapons, who was determined to provoke a confrontation with the law even if it meant his death and those of his wife and children. With his wife, Vicki, and his friend Kevin Harris, he carried on a criminal conspiracy over many years to oppose the government and its officers. His home in the remote woods of northern Idaho's Boundary County was a "fortress," filled with automatic weapons. Clearly, he was a dangerous figure, against whom the government was justified in using extreme force.

A Fugitive from Justice

Some question the truth of these statements, and say government spokesmen used it to explain their conduct in the violent confrontation that broke out near the Weaver home on August 21, 1992. The single, undeniably true statement is the location of the home, which was located on an outcropping in the mountainous terrain of Boundary County. It was a simple, uninsulated, home-built cabin with plywood sides. It contained 14 guns of various sorts, not an unusual number for a home in that part of Idaho, especially for a family that obtained much of its food by hunting. None were automatic; some were as much as 70 years old. It also contained a library of books for the four Weaver children, and a large supply of dried and canned food under the house. It was the home of a family who were isolated by choice.

Randy Weaver in August 1992 was technically a fugitive from justice, although he was in his own home. The previous January he had been arrested by federal agents on a weapons charge and freed on $10,000 bail. He had failed to appear for his court date on February 20. His failure is somewhat understandable in view of the charge against him. In 1989 he had been entrapped by Kenneth Fadely, an ex-convict working as an informer for the Bureau of Alcohol, Tobacco, and Firearms (BATF), into selling Fadely two sawed-off shotguns without a federal license to do so. Weaver had been reluctant to make the sale, but he was hard pressed for money, and trusted Fadely as an acquaintance. Not long after the transaction, two BATF agents approached Weaver with tapes of his conversations and threatened him with prosecution and loss of his home unless he collaborated with them to become a government spy on Aryan Nations. Weaver refused, and his arrest followed.

The BATF had considered Weaver a good prospect to spy on Aryan Nations, since he shared many of their racist views. Randy and Vicki Weaver, who had moved to Idaho from Iowa in 1983, were fundamentalist Christians who believed that white people were the true Chosen People of the Bible, favored by God over other races. They had friends in the area, some of whom belonged to Aryan Nations, and had attended gatherings there. Nonetheless, they disagreed with much of the group's stand. Aryan Nations was a white supremacist group with political aims, which recruited ex-convicts, preached violence against minorities, and hoped eventually to seize power; the Weavers were narrowly religious and had no use for revolution.

Learning how the BATF had entrapped them into violating the law, the Weavers became strongly convinced that they were being persecuted by a Godless government, and determined to resist. "We have decided to stay on this mountain," Vicki Weaver wrote to the head of Aryan Nations in 1990; "you could not drag us away with chains."

A Gunfight in the Woods

On August 21, 1992, three armed federal marshals, without a warrant, entered the Weavers' property on a reconnaissance mission. Their rifles had silencers, and at the trial the defense suggested they intended to kill the family dog to permit them to approach nearer to the cabin unnoticed. On the road downhill from the cabin they encountered Randy Weaver, his 13-year-old son Sammy, and family friend Kevin Harris. All were armed and looking for game; the dog's barking had alerted them. The marshals hid in the woods and shouted, "Freeze!" When the Weaver party turned back toward the cabin, a marshal fired, killing the dog. Sammy returned the fire and then ran uphill. A marshal shot him in the back, killing him. Harris and Weaver also fired. At some point in the melee, one of the marshals, William Degan, was killed, and Harris was wounded. The surviving marshals made their way off the property.

The marshals' exaggerated story—that they had been victims of an un-provoked attack and had been pinned down for hours by gunfire from the cabin—led the government to cordon off the entire area and mobilize its heaviest law enforcement resources, including the Federal Bureau of Investiga-tion's (FBI) crack Hostage Rescue Team. The following day, FBI snipers were stationed in the woods above the cabin and a helicopter was sent over. Their purpose was to protect federal agents who would have to approach the cabin. They were ordered to shoot to kill any armed adult male who appeared outside.

In the courtroom, Randy Weaver is holding the shot up door of his cabin. (AP/Wide World Photos)

In the late afternoon, Weaver, Harris, and 16-year-old Sara Weaver emerged from the cabin to retrieve Sammy's body. Weaver and Harris were armed. The snipers fired at them without warning, using a rifle especially designed for precision shooting at long distances, wounding Weaver in the arm. As the three fled back into the cabin, Vicki Weaver, holding her ten-month-old baby Elisheba, came out to hold the door open for them. A bullet fired by Lon Horiuchi, one of the snipers, passed through her temple, killing her.

After a ten-day standoff, Weaver, his remaining children, and Harris were persuaded to surrender to federal authorities, with the promise that Gerry Spence, one of the leading defense lawyers in America, would consider representing Weaver. The prosecutor would be Assistant U.S. Attorney Ron Howen, who had handled Weaver's case ever since the original weapons charge.

After talking with Weaver, Spence agreed to represent him. He stressed, however, that he abhorred Weaver's racist views and was defending him simply as a victim of abusive government. In their interview, Spence began by saying, "I want you to know that I can't stand racists." Weaver replied, "I want you to know that I can't stand lawyers." Nonetheless, they managed to work together.

Prosecution Witnesses Help the Defense

Testimony began on April 12, 1993, and lasted two months. On three occasions evidence was withheld from the defense and revealed later. On the third occasion the judge required the government to pay the defense lawyers' fees for one day as formal punishment. Repeatedly, government witnesses had to retract sworn testimony that contradicted their previous statements. Witnesses called to describe the Weavers' religious and political views ended up, on cross-examination, praising them as a warm, caring, nonviolent family. Three weeks into the trial, Judge Edward Lodge told Spence, "As far as I can see, at least 75 percent of the prosecution witnesses thus far have helped the defense in this case."

Spence agreed; when the prosecution rested, the defense presented no case, but moved immediately to final arguments. On June 15, the case went to the five-man, seven-woman jury, which returned a verdict on July 8. They acquitted Harris on all counts, and Weaver on all but two minor counts. The verdict was a stinging rebuke of government entrapment and violence.

After the trial, Randy Weaver sued the government for damages to himself and his family, and was awarded $3.1 million in a civil action. The Boundary County prosecutor attempted to try Lon Horiuchi for shooting Vicki Weaver, but Judge Lodge ruled in 1998 that Horiuchi was "acting within the scope of his federal authority" and could not be prosecuted.

—Hendrik Booraem V

Suggestions for Further Reading

Bock, Alan W. *Ambush at Ruby Ridge: How Government Agents Set Randy Weaver Up and Took His Family Down.* Irvine, Calif.: Dickens Press, 1995.

Walter, Jess. *Every Knee Shall Bow: The Truth & Tragedy of Ruby Ridge & the Randy Weaver Family.* Acacia Press, 1995.

Masson v. Malcolm et al.: 1993 & 1994

Plaintiff: Jeffrey M. Masson   **Defendants:** Janet Malcolm and the New Yorker magazine   **Plaintiff Claim:** That certain quotes in a profile of the plaintiff written by the defendant and published in the *New Yorker* were libelous   **Chief Defense Lawyer:** Gary Bostwick
Chief Lawyer for Plaintiff: Charles O. Morgan   **Judge:** Eugene F. Lynch
Place: San Francisco, California   **Dates of Trials:** May 6–June 3, 1993;
October 3–November 2, 1994   **Verdict:** For the defendant

SIGNIFICANCE
The long legal battle between psychoanalyst Jeffrey Masson and writer Janet Malcolm resulted in a standard for determining when a misquote is grounds for a libel suit. The conflict also stirred an ethical debate among journalists over what is a legitimate quote.

In 1983, journalist Janet Malcolm wrote a two-part profile for the New Yorker magazine of Jeffrey Masson, a flamboyant psychoanalyst who challenged the traditional tenets of Freudian theory. At one time Masson had served as the projects director at the Sigmund Freud Archives in England, but was fired after advancing his dissident beliefs. Malcolm's unflattering profile of Masson portrayed him as a brash, egotistical man. The New Yorker has always had a reputation for its high journalistic standards, so the publishing world was surprised when the magazine and Malcolm were sued for libel.

After the article appeared, Masson claimed he never uttered some of the quotes Malcolm had attributed to him, and in 1984 he sued both Malcolm and the *New Yorker*, seeking $10 million in damages. Masson also named Alfred A. Knopf in his lawsuit, after the publishing company released the article as a book. Masson's action began a legal battle that took a dozen years to settle.

Back and Forth in the Courts

Masson's case centered around six disputed quotes. In one of the quotes, Malcolm wrote that Masson said he was "like an intellectual gigolo." In another, Masson supposedly said he wanted to turn the house of Anna Freud into a "place of sex, women, fun." Malcolm argued that although some of the quotes were not exactly what Masson had said, they captured the essence of his meaning. She based her article on 40 hours of taped interviews with Masson and typewritten notes from unrecorded conversations. Masson argued that some of the recorded statements were taken out of context, and he denied ever making the comments in the written notes.

A California district court refused to let a jury hear the case, ruling that the six quotes were substantially true or rational interpretations of Masson's intent. The Ninth Circuit Court of Appeals subsequently upheld this judgment. Masson then took his case to the Supreme Court. In *Masson v. New Yorker Magazine, Inc.* (501 U.S. 496, 1991), the court unanimously found that the lower courts had erred in dismissing the case.

The Supreme Court did allow that not all misquotes were automatic grounds for a libel suit. A misquote first had to be false or substantially alter the speaker's meaning. If that were the case, a jury could then decide if the misquote met the grounds for libel against a public figure—that a statement is knowingly false or printed with reckless disregard for its truth and injures the plaintiff's reputation. The Supreme Court ordered the case returned to the district court so a jury could hear the facts on five of the six disputed quotes.

The libel trial finally began on May 6, 1993, with Malcolm and the New Yorker as defendants. Masson was now seeking $7.5 million in damages. Championing the plaintiff's case, Masson's attorney, Charles O. Morgan, questioned Malcolm's journalistic techniques. She admitted that she had combined quotes from interviews made days apart, rearranged words, and relied on memory for one of the disputed quotes.

Journalist Janet Malcolm sued for libel. (AP/Wide World Photos)

In response, defense lawyer Gary Bostwick portrayed Masson as being untrustworthy. Years earlier, he had denied ever making some of the disputed quotes printed in the article, but Malcolm's tapes showed she had indeed quoted him correctly. Masson's image as an egotistical playboy who in the past had burned professional bridges was also used as a defensive ploy.

On June 3, the jury returned with a mixed decision. It found that Malcolm had made up the five quotes, and two of them did meet the standard for libel.

The jury also found that the *New Yorker* had not been responsible for the validity of Malcolm's piece. But the jury deadlocked on awarding damages for Masson. Judge Eugene F. Lynch then ordered a new trial to determine the libel award, saying in this case that liability and damages could not be separated.

Final Decision

The second trial began on October 3, 1994. Morgan again challenged Malcolm's ethics as a journalist. He also hinted that she may have had a bias against Masson because of his anti-Freudian leanings. Malcolm was a known supporter of traditional psychoanalysis and her father had been a psychiatrist. A few weeks later, in his closing arguments, Morgan charged that Masson had lost a promising career after being "shot down by the cruelest language of a skilled writer."

Despite these arguments, the jury this time exonerated Malcolm, finding that two of the quotes were false and one was defamatory, but none was written with a reckless disregard for the truth. A relieved Malcolm burst into tears. Masson indicated he might not appeal the verdict, although he subsequently did. In 1996, the Ninth Circuit Court upheld the verdict of the lower court.

Although Malcolm ultimately won her case, some journalists questioned her professional practices. After the 1993 trial, an editor at *Time* magazine said, "I think it is always dangerous when the public is given any reason to doubt what they have been reading." But when Malcolm was asked if she would change her reporting techniques, she replied, "Absolutely not."

—Michael Burgan

Suggestions for Further Reading

Carmody, Deirdre. "In Trial's Wake, Rethinking What to Put in Quotes." *New York Times* (June 4, 1993): A16.

Greenhouse, Linda. "Justices Refuse to Open a Gate for Libel Cases." *New York Times* (June 21, 1991): A1.

Gross, Jane. "Impasse over Damages in New Yorker Libel Case." *New York Times* (June 4, 1993): A1.

——. "Jury Hears Final Arguments in Analyst's Libel Suit." *New York Times* (May 28, 1993): A10.

——. "On Libel and the Literati: The *New Yorker* on Trial." *New York Times* (May 5, 1993): A1.

Malcolm, Janet. *In the Freud Archives.* New York: Alfred A. Knopf, 1984.

Margolick, David. "Psychoanalyst Loses Libel Suit against a New Yorker Reporter." *New York Times* (November 3, 1994): A1.

Malice Green Beating Death Trials: 1993–2000

Defendants: Larry Nevers, Walter Budzyn, Robert Lessnau
Crimes Charged: Nevers and Budzyn: murder; Lessnau: aggravated assault
Chief Defense Lawyers: Carol Stanyar, James Howarth, Michael Batchelor, John Goldpaugh **Chief Prosecutor:** Kym Worthy **Judge:** Robert W. Crockett III **Place:** Detroit, Michigan **Dates of Trials:** First trial: June–August 1993; Budzyn retrial: April 1998; Nevers retrial: March 2000
Verdict: Nevers and Budzyn: guilty of second-degree murder; Lessnau: not guilty **Sentence:** Nevers: 12–25 years imprisonment; Budzyn: 8–18 imprisonment

SIGNIFICANCE

Shortly after the riots in Los Angeles over the Rodney King beating, the nation watched expectantly as three white police officers stood trial for the assault and murder of a black man in Detroit. Unlike what happened in Los Angeles, two of the officers were convicted of murder.

During the evening of November 5, 1992, Malice Wayne Green, a black, unemployed steelworker, stopped his car to drop off a friend at a house in the inner city of Detroit, Michigan. He was observed by two white police officers, Larry Nevers and Walter Budzyn, who were working under cover and who suspected the location was a drug house. They ordered Green to get out of his car. When he refused, they radioed for backup help; then they dragged him out. Noticing that Green kept one fist clenched, the officers ordered him to open it. When he balked, they started beating his fist with their heavy metal flashlights.

While the policemen were beating Green, five additional officers arrived in response to the backup call. By then, it was later alleged, Nevers and Budzyn were hitting Green on the head with their flashlights. One of the five, a white officer named Robert Lessnau, joined in the beating. Another, Sergeant Freddie Douglas, who was the ranking officer at the scene, and who was black, did not participate in the beating; neither did he intervene to stop it.

Malice Green, 34, died that night. The next day, Detroit Police Chief Stanley Knox suspended Nevers, Budzyn, and the five backup officers from the police force without pay. An autopsy a few days later revealed that Green had died of a torn scalp and as many as 12 to 14 blows to the head, and that he had both cocaine and alcohol in his system at the time of his death. On November 16, Wayne County Prosecutor John D. O'Hair charged officers Budzyn and Nevers with second-degree murder. Sergeant Douglas was charged with involuntary manslaughter and willful neglect of duty for failing to stop the beating, and Officer Lessnau was charged with aggravated assault. All four pleaded not guilty. The three other officers were kept on indefinite suspension, but prosecutor O'Hair said he did not have enough evidence to charge them with a crime.

Officer Larry Nevers, found guilty of the death of Malice Green. (AP/ Wide World Photos)

Detroit held its breath. In a city whose population is 75 percent black, most people were probably thinking of the aftermath of the notorious beating of black motorist Rodney G. King by four Los Angeles policemen only the year before: five days of rioting when the accused officers were acquitted on all but one charge. However, Detroit officials were cautious about suggestion an analogy between the King beating, which had been perceived as motivated by racial hatred, and the Green beating. Police Chief Knox said he did not believe that race was a catalyst in this case. Furthermore, when the Detroit officers were charged, the National Director of Special Projects for the National Association for the Advancement of Colored People (NAACP), Jack Gravely, congratulated the police chief and other officials on their prompt reaction by suspending the officers the very next day after the beating. "What is different in Detroit," said Gravely on November 16, "is the leadership. When we compare what happened in Detroit with what happened [in Los Angeles], it does make a difference. Without it, this city probably would still be burning at its walls today."

On December 23, 1992, Michigan District Court Chief Judge Alex J. Allen, Jr., dismissed the charge of involuntary manslaughter against Sergeant Douglas because the beating of Malice Green had already been under way when Douglas arrived on the scene.

The trials of the three remaining police officers raged simultaneously for three months in the Detroit courtroom of Judge Robert W. Crockett III, who was black, and in the homes of America via cable television's Court TV. The evidence was heard by two separate juries. The Nevers jury comprised ten black and two white members. Budzyn's included 11 blacks and one white. Lessnau, facing the lesser charge of assault, found his fate in the hands of Judge Crockett himself rather than a jury.

The prosecution team was led by 36-year-old Kym Worthy, a black lawyer and a graduate of the University of Michigan and the University of Notre Dame Law School, who was already renowned for her skillful use of courtroom dramatics. With her fingernails painted in multiple colors and her long black hair whipping her shoulders as she tossed her head, she had built a solid reputation by winning 90 out of the 100 jury trials she had conducted in nine years with the Wayne County prosecutor's office.

Officer Nevers testified in his defense that he had been in fear of his life when Malice Green resisted arrest. He admitted that he had hit Green five or six times with his flashlight. Officer Budzyn, on the other hand, denied striking Green and testified that he had not seen officer Nevers or any of the backup policemen club the motorist in the head.

That testimony brought one of the highlights of Prosecutor Worthy's presentation. She pulled a tape measure from her pocket and stretched out two feet of it. "You were this far away from Malice Green and didn't see him being pummeled to death?" she demanded. "You couldn't smell the blood?"

Asked later if such a courtroom stratagem wasn't outside of normal jurisprudence, and if the remark about smelling the blood wasn't inflammatory, Kym Worthy replied, "I don't think it's pushing the lines. I think it's just being thorough. He gave me a story that I didn't think was plausible. I wanted to make sure the jury was able to evaluate it for what it was worth, and I just wanted to show that it wasn't worth too much."

On August 16, Judge Crockett announced that he had reached his decision in the case of Officer Lessnau. August 21 brought the jury's decision in the Budzyn case. Both verdicts, however, were sealed until the end of the Nevers trial. That jury reached agreement on August 23, finding Nevers guilty. Then the Budzyn jury's verdict was also read: guilty. However, the judge found Lessnau not guilty under the charge of assault with intent to cause great bodily harm.

Before they were sentenced, both Nevers and Budzyn apologized to Malice Green's family in the courtroom. Then Judge Crockett pronounced sentence. Larry Nevers, 53, was given 12–25 years in prison, with no parole permitted until he served at least nine years and eight months. Walter Budzyn, 47, was sentenced to 8–18 years, with a minimum of six and a half years. Before they were led from the courtroom, both former police officers asked that they be sent to out-of-state prisons. They said that, as new prisoners, they wanted to dodge any chance of cell block confrontations with prisoners whose incarceration was the result of their work as Detroit policemen. The Michigan Department of Corrections made arrangements for both men to serve their time in Texas.

In the summer of 1997, after serving four and a half years, Walter Budzyn was released from jail after the Michigan State Supreme Court threw out Budzyn's conviction. Among other reasons, the court ruled that the mostly black jury may have been influenced by a showing of the film *Malcolm X* during a break in their deliberations. (The film opens with the infamous Rodney King beating videotape.) A new trial was subsequently ordered for Budzyn, which was conducted in April 1998.

At the retrial, Budzyn was found guilty of involuntary manslaughter. Though the lesser conviction carried a possible maximum penalty of 15 years in jail, prosecutors agreed to a sentence of time served and Budzyn was released from custody.

Larry Nevers was also released from prison in 1997 after a federal judge overturned his conviction. After several delays, Nevers' retrial began in March 2000. On April, 18, 2000, after less than a full day of deliberation, the jury found Nevers not guilty of second-degree murder, but guilty of involuntary manslaughter. He was sentenced to seven to 15 years in prison.

—Bernard Ryan, Jr. and Ron Formica

Suggestions for Further Reading

Bacon, John, et. al. "Manslaughter Verdict in Police Officer Trial." *USA Today* (March 20, 1998): 3.

Dyer, Jim. "Budzyn Gets 4–15 Years in Malice Green Death." *Detroit News* (April 18, 1998): 1.

Linden, Eugene, et. al. "Milestones." *Time* (October 1993): 25.

Menendez Brothers' Trials: 1993–94 & 1995–96

Defendants: Lyle and Erik Menendez   **Crimes Charged:** Murder
Chief Defense Lawyers: First trial: Leslie Abramson, Jill Lansing; second
trial: Leslie Abramson, Jill Lansing, Barry Levin   **Chief Prosecutor:** First trial:
Pamela Bozanich; second trial: David Conn   **Judge:** Both trials: Stanely M.
Weisberg   **Place:** Both Trials: Los Angeles, California   **Dates of Trials:** First
trial: July 20, 1993–January 28, 1994; second trial: August 23, 1995–March
20, 1996   **Verdict:** First trial: Mistrial; second trial: guilty of first-degree
murder with special circumstances   **Sentence:** 2 consecutive life sentences
for both Lyle and Erik Memendez

SIGNIFICANCE

The Menendez brothers' trials, claiming self-defense for brutally murdering their
parents after enduring years of sexual and emotional abuse, revealed another,
more sinister, motive for their crime: a vast inheritance upon their parents' death.

O n the evening of August 20, 1989, with bowls of strawberries and ice cream in
their laps, entertainment magnate José Menendez and his wife, Kitty, were
watching television in the den of their Beverly Hills mansion. Unexpectedly, their
sons Lyle and Eric allegedly burst through the door with 12-gauge shotguns,
killing their parents. Bizarre as it may sound, this bloody "fact" would be the least
disputed feature of one of the most controversial court battles of the decade.

Organized Crime Hit?

Detectives weighing the ferocity of the homicides thought the killings had
the look of an organized crime hit. José Menendez, a 45-year-old Cuban immigrant and self-made millionaire, had dealings throughout the film and music
distribution industry, including a production interest in Sylvester Stallone's
"Rambo" movies. It seemed unlikely that anyone would pump 15 shotgun rounds
into the Menendez couple unless that person were trying to make a statement.

As time passed, however, the police took a closer look at the Menendez
sons, who were heirs to their parents' $14-million fortune. Lyle, 22, and Erik, 19,

spent over a half million dollars on new cars, watches, and a restaurant business soon after their parents' funerals. Suspicious evidence began to accumulate.

In March 1990, police, using search warrants, confiscated the records of Dr. L. Jerome Oziel, the psychotherapist who had been treating the brothers. Lyle Menendez was arrested a few days later. Erik, who had spent part of his inheritance on a personal tennis coach, surrendered to Los Angeles police upon his return from a tournament in Israel. Prosecutors charged that the pampered sons had murdered their parents because of an impatient desire to collect their inheritance.

The most incriminating evidence was said to exist in a tape of one of Dr. Oziel's therapy sessions. A legal battle quickly erupted over whether or not the tape could be admitted as evidence. Under California law, such recordings are confidential under the protection of the patient-therapist relationship. Judge James Albracht, however, ruled that the Menendez brothers had threatened Dr. Oziel's life, thus voiding any claim to confidentiality. After two years of grappling over the issue, the state Supreme Court ruled that only a tape of Dr. Oziel dictating his notes from the session would be admissible as evidence.

If convicted of first-degree murder, Erik and Lyle would face death in California's gas chamber. In an unusual arrangement, the brothers were to be tried simultaneously by the same judge but before two separate juries.

Testimonials of Sexual Abuse

Throughout the three years before the Menendez brothers were brought to trial, they repeatedly denied shooting their parents. A week before the trial began on July 20, 1993, however, the brothers admitted to the killings. Nevertheless, they pleaded not guilty, claiming that they had acted in self-defense after years of suffering sexual and emotional abuse at the hands of their parents.

"We are not disputing where it happened, how it happened, who did it," Jill Lansing, Lyle's lawyer, said in her opening statement. "What we will prove to you is that it was done out of fear."

Lansing and Leslie Abramson, Erik's attorney, called over 30 relatives, neighbors, teachers and sports coaches to the stand. They all described José Menendez as a success-obsessed tyrant who completely dominated his sons' lives, publicly humiliating them whenever he felt their conduct was unsatisfactory. Kitty Menendez was described as depressed, prone to hysterical fits and suicidal over her husband's extramarital affairs. While the Menendez brothers were legally adults when they killed their parents, the defense attorneys consistently referred to them as "children."

After a month of hearing testimony of witnesses who remembered José and Kitty as less than model parents, Judge Stanley M. Weisberg had heard enough. "We're not talking about a child custody case," he snapped. Lansing and Abramson were ordered to put their clients on the stand.

José Menendez had been accused of browbeating his sons to attain excellent grades and high tennis scores. However, when Lyle took the witness stand, he painted a profoundly darker picture of his father's demanding nature. He testified that his father had begun showing the boys pornographic videos and telling them about homosexual bonding rituals between soldiers in ancient Greece when he was six and Eric was three years old. The defense produced nude childhood snapshots of Lyle taken by his father. Lyle recalled his father massaging him after sports practices when he was a child. The rubdowns turned into forced oral sex. When he was seven, Lyle said, his father sodomized him.

"I told my mom to tell Dad to leave me alone, that he keeps touching me," Lyle said. "She told me to stop it, that I was exaggerating, and my dad had to punish me when I did things wrong."

With tears in his eyes, Lyle said the abuse stopped when he was eight, but that his father threatened to kill him if he ever revealed the truth.

In August 1989 Erik confided to his older brother that José had been sexually molesting him for years. Five days before the killings, Lyle confronted his father.

"What I do with my son is none of your business," Lyle recalled his father retorting. "I warn you, don't throw your life away."

Lyle persisted, telling his father that he would expose the abuse if it continued.

According to Lyle, José replied, "We all make choices in life, son. Erik made his. You've made yours." From that moment on, Lyle felt his and his brother's lives were in danger. "I felt he had no choice but that he would kill us, that he would get rid of us in some way because he thought I was going to ruin him."

Lyle and Erik Menendez, found guilty for the murder of their parents. (AP/Wide World Photos)

Kitty became hysterical after the confrontation. She told Erik that if Lyle "had just kept his mouth shut, things might have worked out in this family." The brothers took this as proof that their parents were planning to kill them soon. According to the brothers, things remained tense in the Menendez household for the next few days. When their parents disappeared into the den, the brothers suspected an attack, got their guns, and burst through the door, firing.

Cold-Blooded Killers?

Deputy District Attorney Pamela Bozanich declared that the tales of abuse were nonsense. She made Lyle admit that he had lied to detectives and had discreetly removed shotgun shell casings from his car while police combed the gory crime scene.

The brothers claimed they had bought shotguns for protection. Yet Bozanich established that they had deliberately bought the guns out of town with false identification, paying in cash so that the purchase could not be traced. Bozanich scoffed at Lyle's claim that he placed the muzzle of his shotgun against his fatally wounded mother's cheek and fired because he was "afraid" of her.

On November 3, after Lyle's emotional testimony and Bozanich's fierce cross-examination, the drama halted with a fresh dispute over Dr. Oziel's therapy session tape. Playing of the actual tape had been barred by the pre-trial ruling. During the trial, however, defense attorneys had made the defendants' psychological health a crucial issue. Therefore, Judge Weisberg decided, the tape should be heard.

Battle over Incriminating Tape

In an effort to portray their case to its best advantage before the juries, both sides immediately began battling over which one would be able to introduce the tape in court. The judge ordered that the tape be turned over to the prosecution, but allowed the defense to introduce it as evidence.

On the tape, Lyle and Erik said nothing to their therapist about sexual or physical abuse at the hands of either of their parents. They said nothing about killing for their inheritance. They confessed to the shootings, but identifying the killers was no longer the central mystery it had been when police seized the tape over three years earlier. Both sides agreed that the fate of the Menendez brothers now hinged on their motive for killing their parents. The tape gave no answers.

The case took an odd turn as soon as the tape ran out. Ms. Judalon Smyth, Dr. Oziel's former lover, had helped to launch the prosecution's case. In 1990, she had given police a sworn affidavit claiming that she had overheard the Menendez brothers talk about committing "the perfect killing" and threatening Dr. Oziel because he knew too much.

"I can't believe you did this," Smyth swore she had heard Lyle tell Erik. "I can't believe you told him. I don't really have a brother now. I could get rid of you for this. I hope you realize what we're going to have to do. We've got to kill him and anyone associated with him."

Smyth's tip helped police make the arrest. Knowledge of the threat against Oziel was what had allowed the prosecution to bypass patient therapist confidentiality in introducing the tape.

Now, however, Smyth turned defense witness. Her affair with Oziel, who was married during their relationship, was over. She was suing him for rape, assault, and forcing her to take mind-controlling prescription drugs. When she took the stand at the Menendez trial, she disclaimed her previous statements, saying that the psychotherapist had "brainwashed" her into believing what she told police three years ago. Vexed prosecutors accused Smyth of changing her story in order to take revenge on her former lover.

The defense introduced substantial testimony about the nature of psychological abuse in order to support claims of sexual victimization. Experts explained how the brothers' secrecy, along with their simultaneous attachment to and violence toward their parents, was consistent with the symptoms of "battered wife syndrome."

Closing Arguments

Six months of testimony had passed when closing arguments began on December 8. Prosecutor Bozanich depicted the brothers as "vicious, spoiled brats" who had killed their parents out of greed and then lied repeatedly to cover their tracks. When they were caught, Bozanich continued, the pattern of lies grew into elaborate tales of abuse intended to gain sympathy. Even if the unproved allegations of abuse were true, however, the brothers should not go free.

"We don't execute child molesters in California. Some of you think we should," Bozanich told the jurors. "But the state does not execute child molesters, and these defendants cannot execute them either."

The defense's demonization of José and Kitty Menendez continued into the final arguments. Some legal observers wondered why the prosecution had not pressed the brothers harder to explain why they had killed their allegedly unstable but unthreatening mother.

"It may be hard for you to believe that these parents could have killed their children," Lansing proposed. "But is it so hard to understand that these children believed their parents would kill them?"

Judge Weisberg's final instructions to the twin juries ruled out acquittals. The judge declared that the facts did not support a plea of "perfect self-defense," in which "a reasonable and honest belief that their own lives were in imminent danger" led the brothers to kill.

The jurors had four options. If it was agreed that the brothers had maliciously plotted to kill their parents, a verdict of first-degree murder could warrant the death penalty. Varying sentences could be imposed for convictions of second-degree murder, voluntary manslaughter or involuntary manslaughter. If the brothers were found guilty of "involuntarily" shooting their parents out of a genuine but unreasonable fear, they could be sentenced to a term shorter than the time served since their arrest.

After 16 days of deliberations, Erik's jury told Judge Weisberg that it could not agree on a verdict. Weisberg ordered the jurors to keep talking, but after nearly three weeks of shouting behind closed doors, the jurors gave up. Judge Weisberg declared a mistrial and released the jurors with a warning not to speak to the media. He did not want Lyle's unsequestered jury to be influenced.

However, two weeks later, on January 28, Lyle's jury reported that it was also deadlocked. As weary attorneys on both sides watched, a second mistrial was declared. Los Angeles District Attorney Gil Garcetti immediately announced that the Menendez brothers would face a second trial for first-degree murder, with no possibility of plea bargaining.

Strong disagreements over the sexual abuse claims had scuttled any chance for unanimous verdicts. With both juries stubbornly divided over the brothers' truthfulness, the final votes were scattered over the three most serious verdicts possible, each with its own implicit, differing degree of guilt. Only one of the 24 jurors had voted for the least serious charge of involuntary manslaughter.

Regardless of his intent, Lyle's testimony indicated that he had made most of the decisions regarding the shootings, with his younger brother passively agreeing to participate. Yet Erik's jury had been the most contentious, with an almost even split between men voting for first degree murder and women voting for voluntary manslaughter. The female jurors complained that sexist bullying and male jurors' homophobic suspicions about Erik's sexuality had prevented a serious resolution of the case.

Defense attorney Abramson's tough, flamboyant defense had kindled tension between her and Judge Weisberg throughout the first trial. She continued her public assault on the prosecution after the verdict. She faulted the judge for his handling of the case and declared that no jury would ever be able to agree on a verdict. To prove her point, she invited the sympathetic women jurors to her home for dinner, a telephone chat with Erik, and an interview session with reporters about the stormy deliberations in the jury room.

While her detractors accused her of being a media hound, others marveled at her unabashed willingness to exploit the media on behalf of her client. Both critics and sympathizers agreed that publicizing her post-trial dinner aimed to influence the jury pool, while illustrating to the state that plea bargaining might be preferable to the time and expense of a second trial in which jurors might be no more likely to agree on a verdict.

Prosecutors were not impressed. They declared that the defense strategy used so successfully in the first trial would be easier to counter now that it was known. Those who had questioned the sincerity of the Menendez brothers' tears on the witness stand doubted that the defendants would be clever enough to convince a second jury of their emotional fragility.

Costly Trial

The trials cost the brothers their inheritance; the vast Menendez fortune was now depleted. Public defenders were appointed to represent Lyle. Erik pleaded with the judge for the State of California to pay his legal fees so that he could retain Abramson as his lawyer. The judge refused. After some grumbling about what a sacrifice it would be, Abramson agreed to stay on the case for a reduced fee.

If the Menendez brothers had killed their parents for money, their reward had vanished. In September 1994, the Menendez mansion was sold at auction for $1.3 million. The money was split between creditors and the county, which demanded restitution for the cost of the defendants' lengthy incarceration. Even their notorious celebrity dimmed. Although the trial of Hollywood Madam

Heidi Fleiss and the Menendez brothers' second pretrial hearings were held in the Los Angeles County Courthouse, both legal proceedings were largely ignored by the media, whose attentions had moved en masse to the O.J. Simpson murder trial being held in the same building. Coincidentally, Simpson had visited the Menendez family in the days when he was sprinting though airports in Hertz commercials. José Menendez, then a prominent Hertz executive, invited the former football star to dinner so that his sons could meet him. According to Vanity Fair (February 1995), Simpson and the Menendez brothers did not meet again until "they were all in the celebrity section of the Los Angeles County Jail, all three charged with double murder."

On April 3 Judge Stanley Weisberg ruled that the brothers would be retried together and in front of a single jury. Judicial discipline and shifts in the defense strategy reduced the potential for sensationalism in the second trial, which Weisberg ruled would be heard by a single jury. The judge banned television cameras from the courtroom. By restricting testimony only to events relevant to Erik and Lyle's state of mind just the week before the killings, the judge eliminated a potential parade of defense witnesses who were called in the first trial to bolster the brothers' allegations that their father was an abusive tyrant.

The most damaging blow to the defense was Judge Weisberg's ruling that the principle of "imperfect self-defense," which had previously been argued so effectively, was inapplicable. Citing a footnote in a Supreme Court decision rendered in another case after the first trial, the judge determined that the principle could not be applied to the retrial because the defense had failed to provide sufficient evidence that Kitty Menendez had treated her sons in any way that might have provoked them to kill her. This time neither Erik nor Lyle took the stand, thus eliminating any tearful testimony of abuse by their father and additionally negating the risk of being cross-examined about the truthfulness of such accusations.

On March 20, 1996, after 16 hours of deliberation, the jury found Lyle and Erik guilty of first-degree murder with special circumstances. The verdict left the brothers liable to either life imprisonment or death by lethal injection. The jurors, who had expressed uncertainty over the allegations of child abuse, decided against recommending the death penalty. On July 2, Judge Weisberg accepted the jury's advice. The Menendez brothers were each sentenced to serve two consecutive terms of life imprisonment, thus bringing to a close a long and sad story of familial relations gone terribly wrong.

— Tom Smith

Suggestions for Further Reading

Leavitt, Paul. "Second Menendez Jury Declares Deadlock." *USA Today* (January 26, 1994): 3.

Ross, Kathryn. "Do Cameras Belong in the Courtroom? No." *USA Today* (August 19, 1994): 9.

Stewart, Sally Ann and Gale Holland. "Some See Vindication in Verdict." *USA Today* (March 21, 1996): 3.

Baby Jessica Case: 1993

Defendants: Cara and Dan Schmidt   **Plaintiffs:** Jan and Roberta DeBoer
Plaintiff Claim: The DeBoer's sought to block the order of the Michigan Supreme Court to return Jessica to the Schmidts
Chief Defense Lawyer: Marian Faupel   **Chief Lawyer for Plaintiff:** Scott Bassett   **Justices:** William H. Rehnquist, Harry A. Blackmun, John Paul Stevens, Sandra Day O'Connor, Antonin Scalia, Anthony M. Kennedy, David H. Souter, Clarence Thomas, Ruth Bader Ginsberg   **Place:** Washington, D.C.
Date of Decision: July 30, 1993   **Verdict:** The DeBoer's request was denied

SIGNIFICANCE
The Baby Jessica case caused people to consider the risks and problems inherent in private adoptions.

In 1990, an Iowa woman named Cara Clausen found out that she was pregnant. Single and 29 years old, Cara had recently split with her boyfriend, Dan Schmidt, and was dating a man named Scott Seefeldt. Before the birth, she told friends she couldn't care for the baby on her own and would give it up for adoption. When the child was born on February 8, 1991, she named Scott as the father, and within two days, she and Scott signed papers waiving their parental rights.

In Ann Arbor, Michigan, Jan DeBoer, 37, and his wife, Roberta (known as Robby), 32, were eager to adopt. She had had a hysterectomy some years before, so she could not become pregnant. The DeBoers had spent several years sweating out adoption procedures in Michigan, where adoption was legal only through bureaucratic public services. Iowa permitted legal private adoptions. A Cedar Rapids lawyer who was married to Robby DeBoer's cousin, heard about Cara's pregnancy and her plan to give the baby up for adoption. He put the DeBoers in touch with Cara. Another lawyer, John Monroe, took care of the required paperwork, and on March 2, 1991, the DeBoers took the six-day-old baby home, named her Jessica, and looked forward to becoming full legal custodians in six months.

Biological Mother Regrets Adoption

Almost immediately Cara began to have second thoughts. When her old boyfriend Dan showed up, she told him the baby she had just given up for adoption was his, not Scott's. Cara also attended a support-group meeting of the Concerned United Birth parents. There she listened to the sad tales of mothers who regretted giving up their babies for adoption. Before Jessica was more than a month old, Cara and Dan, who were now living together, filed motions to get her back.

It took six months to process genetic tests to prove that Dan indeed was the father. By the end of 1991, an Iowa court, accepting the proof of Dan Schmidt's parenthood and recognizing that he had never signed away his rights, nullified the adoption before it became final. The court ordered the DeBoers to return Jessica to her biological parents, Clara Clausen and Dan Schmidt.

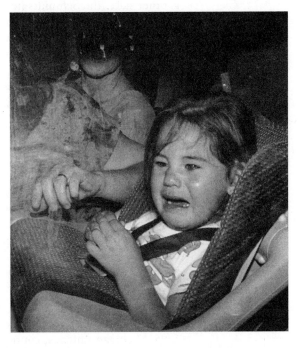

Devastated, the DeBoers decided to fight to keep Jessica. They wrote countless letters to children's rights groups around the country. They contacted reporters. They uncovered the fact that Dan Schmidt had fathered two other children, neither of which he supported, by two other women, neither of whom he had married.

In January 1992, the Iowa Supreme Court agreed to hear the case, which dragged on throughout the year. Meanwhile, Cara and Dan were married in April 1992.

Baby Jessica cries as she is being taken away from her adoptive parents, Jan and Roberta DeBoer. (AP/Wide World Photos)

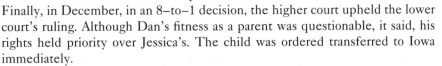

Finally, in December, in an 8–to–1 decision, the higher court upheld the lower court's ruling. Although Dan's fitness as a parent was questionable, it said, his rights held priority over Jessica's. The child was ordered transferred to Iowa immediately.

The DeBoers stood their ground. Despite the Iowa court's finding them in contempt for defying its ruling, they appeared before Judge William Ager, Jr., of Washtenaw County Circuit Court in Michigan. Their lawyer, Suellyn Scarnecchia, argued that Michigan had jurisdiction in the case because Jessica had resided there for at least six months and because the majority of her records and personal relationships were in that state. The judge agreed to assume jurisdiction on behalf of the state of Michigan in order to determine what would be in Jessica's best interest.

On February 12, 1993, citing the testimony of child psychologists that Jessica would bear permanent emotional damage if she were removed from the only parents she had ever known, Judge Ager awarded custody of the child to the DeBoers. Agreeing with their lawyers that there was "much to lose and little to gain" in moving the two-year-old, and turning to the Schmidts, he said, "Think possibly of saying, 'Enough.'" He urged the two couples to keep in touch, but cautioned them not to lead Jessica to believe she had four parents.

The Battle Over Jessica Continues

Arguing that the judge had acted improperly by assuming jurisdiction from another state, the Schmidts headed for the Michigan Court of Appeals. Within six weeks, in a 3–to–0 decision that ruled only on the question of jurisdiction, that court agreed with the Iowa courts. The DeBoers had 21 days to file an appeal to the Michigan Supreme Court.

Meantime, "Baby Jessica" had become a household name and the case caused millions to more closely consider the risks and problems of adoption. In about half of all adoptions, the natural fathers, even if they are known, cannot be located. But what if they turn up demanding their "parental rights?" Who knows—wondered columnists, Op-Ed writers, and talk-show hosts—how permanent any adoption is?

Michigan's seven Supreme Court judges heard the arguments. Representing Baby Jessica, Attorney Scott Bassett said the Schmidts were strangers to the child. "These children don't care about biology," he contended. "They know who loves them and who they love." Schmidt lawyer Marian Faupel insisted that the DeBoers had manipulated delays and appeals in order to buy time to bond with the child—to whom they had no legal right. She added that it was not too late for Jessica to bond with her biological parents, for children are not fragile. "They are somewhere between forged steel," she said, "and delicate teacups."

In June 1993, Cara Schmidt gave birth to a second child, Chloe. On July 2, 1993, Michigan's highest court ruled 6–1, that Michigan held no jurisdiction in the case over Baby Jessica and that she was to be handed over to the Schmidts within one month.

Jan and Robby DeBoer filed a request for the Michigan Supreme Court to stay its ruling until the U.S. Supreme Court could rule on their request to have the case heard there. The court refused the stay, 6–1. Ad hoc "Justice for Jessi" groups began planning bus trips to Washington, D.C., to demonstrate on the steps of the Supreme Court building.

U.S. Supreme Court Justice John Paul Stevens, who handled emergency cases from Michigan for the Court, considered the DeBoers's request to block the order, giving Jessica to the Schmidts. He refused. Their argument, he said, "rests, in part, on the relationship that they have been able to develop with the child after it became clear that they were not entitled to adopt her."

On July 30, 1993, the U.S. Supreme Court refused to lift the deadline for Jessica's return to her natural parents. Justices Harry A. Blackmun and Sandra Day O'Connor dissented. "This is a case that touches the raw nerves of life's relationships," wrote Justice Blackmun. "I am not willing to wash my hands of this case at this stage, with the personal vulnerability of the child so much at risk."

Three days later, the 2 and one-half-year-old was carried, screaming, from the DeBoers's home by their lawyer, Suellyn Scarnecchia, and placed in the back seat of a minivan filled with Jessica's favorite toys, clothing and bedding. With Cara and Dan Schmidt, Jessica flew the 400 miles from Ypsilanti, Michigan, to Cedar Rapids, Iowa, by private plane. She napped during half the trip, then awoke and played contentedly with her toys. When they landed, Baby Jessica had a new name, Anna Jacqueline Schmidt.

Nine months later, Jan and Robby DeBoer successfully adopted a newborn boy. His name is Casey. Meanwhile, child psychoanalyst Lucy Biven, who supervised Baby Jessica's transition to the Schmidt home, where she is now known as Anna Lee, reported that "her adjustment has been so unexpectedly good that I give the Schmidts and the DeBoers a lot of credit." And, a year after the transfer, Cara Schmidt said, "Everyone guaranteed—guaranteed—that she would have short-term trauma, that she wouldn't eat, wouldn't sleep, she'd cry. It didn't happen. She progressed rapidly."

Sadly, the strain of the court cases permanently damaged both marriages. In October 1999, Jan and Robby DeBoer divorced after 17 years of marriage. They released a statement after the divorce, saying that, "The loss of our daughter was more than our mariage could handle." Later that month, Cara and Dan Schmidt also announced their plans to divorce.

Anna Lee and her younger sister Chloe live permanently with their father, Dan. According to Dan Schmidt, Anna at age 9 had no memory of the custody battle that once raged around her.

—Bernard Ryan, Jr.

Suggestions for Further Reading

Gibbs, Nancy. "In Whose Best Interest." *Time* (July 19, 1993): 45–6.

Many, Christine. "Follow-Up: Jessica Turns Nine." *Ladies Home Journal* (February 2000): 17.

Verhovek, Sam Howe. "Michigan's High Court Says Adopted Girl Must Be Sent to Biological Parents." *New York Times* (July 5, 1993): 1.

Ira Einhorn Trial: 1993

Defendant: Ira Einhorn **Crime Charged:** Murder
Chief Defense Lawyer: Norris E. Gelman **Chief Prosecutors:** Lynne Abraham, Joel Rosen **Judge:** Juanita Kidd Stout **Place:** Philadelphia, Pennsylvania **Date of Trial:** September 1993 **Verdict:** Guilty
Sentence: Life imprisonment

SIGNIFICANCE

Philadelphia prosecutors took the unusual step of trying Ira Einhorn *in absentia* more· than 12 years after he had jumped bail and fled the country. Located in France some four years after being convicted, Ira Einhorn successfully resisted extradition until July 2001.

In 1979, Ira Einhorn had held a unique place in the Philadelphia civic community for several years. A self-proclaimed guru of the counter culture movement of the 1960s, he had managed, as the movement faded, to avoid becoming marginalized. Without compromising his commitment to nonviolence, sexual liberation, drug experimentation, and the other trappings of the hippie lifestyle, he had become accepted by a wide spectrum of society's leaders. He worked tirelessly as an organizer, facilitator, speaker, and consultant of sorts, and took great pride in the international network of correspondents he had cultivated. The movements and causes that he supported were an eclectic mix of environmentalism, futurism, the paranormal, and the occult, laced with conspiracy theories. He was a graduate of the University of Pennsylvania, had done some graduate work and teaching, and his credentials and reputation were enough to earn him a prestigious fellowship at the Kennedy School of Government at Harvard University in 1976–77.

An Abusive Relationship Leads to Murder

Einhorn met Helen "Holly" Maddux in October 1972. She was an intelligent, attractive, slightly built young woman of 25. Maddux had grown up in Tyler, Texas, and entered Bryn Mawr as a freshman in 1965. She experienced difficulty in adjusting to the profound differences between life at the elite eastern liberal arts college and that of her small east Texas hometown. She was drawn to the popular counterculture lifestyle of the late 1960s; her academic career suffered, and she did not complete her degree until 1971, at which time she apparently had very little idea of what she wanted to do with her life. She began living with Ira Einhorn in his modest apartment on Race Street in the Powelton neighborhood of Philadelphia soon after their first meeting. It was an open and uncommitted relationship, as befitted the lifestyle they had both adopted. There were several acrimonious separations over the next few years, followed by reconciliation. Mutual friends were aware that Einhorn was physically abusive of Maddux on occasions, but the relationship lasted for almost five years.

In the summer of 1977, however, it appeared that this relationship was about to end, or at least to undergo a significant change. Maddux had become involved with a man, Saul Lapidus, whom she had met on Fire Island a year earlier, and she was planning to move into an apartment of her own in Philadelphia. In September she returned to the city from a visit to Lapidus, and disappeared. Maddux's parents and her friends in Philadelphia became concerned when they heard nothing from her for several weeks. Einhorn told them the same story: she had been with him in September, but one day had gone out to buy some groceries and had not returned. A couple of days later she had called him and told him that she was alright, but he should not try to find her. She said she would call him regularly, but she had not done so. As more weeks went by, including the passage of several family birthdays, which previously Maddux had always remembered, Maddux's parents became increasingly disturbed. In early 1978 they hired a private investigator to try to find her. After more than a year of tracing her movements and interviewing neighbors and friends, the private detectives took their findings to the Philadelphia police, who then obtained a warrant to search Ira Einhorn's apartment at 3411 Race Street. There, on March 28, 1979, they found the decomposed and partially mummified body of Holly Maddux in a locked steamer trunk in a locked closet in the back porch of the apartment. Ira Einhorn was arrested at the scene and charged with murder later the same day.

Defendant Flees the Country

Einhorn appeared at a bail hearing before Judge William M. Marutani on April 3. He was represented by Arlen Specter, who had served two terms as a district attorney in Philadelphia, but who would withdraw from the case shortly afterwards as he began his successful campaign for election to the U.S. Senate. Specter was able to produce such an impressive array of prominent professionals as character witnesses for Einhorn that the judge released him on a $40,000 bond, a remarkably low amount in a murder case. Einhorn consistently and stridently maintained his complete innocence. He knew nothing about the body in the trunk; he expressed doubts that it was that of Holly Maddux. He suggested that the whole affair was a conspiracy by the CIA designed to interfere with important work he was currently engaged in, which had international security ramifications.

The process of preparing for trial was a lengthy one, but a trial date of February or March 1981 was set; Barbara Christie was assigned to lead the prosecution. Norris E. Gelman had taken over Einhorn's defense. The trial did not take place because Einhorn fled, probably in the second week of January 1981. He is believed to have left the country via Canada, and then gone on to Europe. A bench warrant for his arrest was issued on January 14 when he failed to appear for a pretrial hearing. The search to locate him and bring him back to the United States would go on for the next 20 years. Rich diBenedetto, of the extraditions office of the Philadelphia district attorney's office, headed these efforts. Einhorn was located in Ireland late in 1981, and again in 1984 and 1986, but international legal problems prevented his arrest, and he fled again. In 1988 he narrowly escaped arrest in Stockholm, Sweden, and again disappeared.

A Trial without the Defendant Present

Frustrated in their attempts to recapture Einhorn, the Philadelphia district attorney's office decided in 1993 to pursue the unusual course of trying him *in absentia*—that is, in his absence. *In absentia* trials are rare and controversial. The accused is denied what are generally considered fundamental rights of Western judicial procedure: the right to testify in their own defense, to confront their accusers and the witnesses against them, and to consult with their counsel. However, a ruling of the Pennsylvania Supreme Court provided the opportunity for the successful filing of a motion to proceed with a trial *in absentia*. The district attorney argued that the prosecution had an overwhelming case for conviction, but that its strength would be inevitably weakened as time passed: witnesses might die, memories become less reliable. Assistant District Attorney Joel Rosen, with seven years experience of prosecuting homicide cases in Philadelphia, led the prosecution. Norris Gelman continued to represent Einhorn, having been instructed to do so by a Common Pleas judge in 1992. He had been paid from a legal defense fund established by Einhorn's friends. The trial was set for mid-September 1993, in the Court of Common Pleas, before Judge Juanita Kidd Stout.

Gelman was unsuccessful in a pre-trial motion to block the trial on the grounds that the accused had not been notified that the trial was scheduled, and quite possibly did not know about it. He achieved limited success with a motion to exclude as hearsay statements by friends of Holly Maddux that she had told them that Einhorn had beaten her. These witnesses could testify that they had seen Maddux with bruises and red marks on her skin, but they could not accuse Einhorn of causing them. For the prosecution, retired detective Robert Coates described the search of Einhorn's apartment, and the discovery of the body. The former city medical examiner, Halbert E. Fillinger, testified that Maddux had died as a result of at least six blows to the head, delivered with such force that fragments of her skull had penetrated her brain. He ruled out the possibility of these injuries being the result of a fall or other accident.

Friends of Maddux testified to knowing that she intended to leave Einhorn because he was too domineering, and others to having observed her with bruises. A former friend of Einhorn, Joyce Costello, testified that in mid-September she had helped him move the trunk in which the body was found, and that he had told her it contained "Russian documents." Saul Lapidus testified that he had put Holly Maddux on a plane to Philadelphia on September 10, 1977, because she needed to "calm" Einhorn. Rich diBenedetto described the search for Einhorn and the various sightings of him between 1981 and 1988.

For the defense, Gelman was only able to bring witnesses who had been interviewed by the private investigators searching for Holly Maddux who said they had seen a woman who resembled her some months after the alleged killing took place. On September 30 the jury returned a verdict of guilty, and Einhorn was sentenced to life imprisonment. Gelman appealed, but the Pennsylvania Supreme Court ultimately upheld the trial and the verdict.

The search for Ira Einhorn, headed by diBenedetto went on. In June 1997 he was found to be living in France, under the name of Eugene Mallon, with his Swedish wife, and he was arrested. However, a French court turned down the request for extradition on the gounds that a trial *in absentia* violates the European Convention on Human Rights, to which France is a signatory. Einhorn was released after some months in custody, but because he had entered the country illegally, he was required to report weekly to the police. The Pennsylvania Assembly responded to this obstacle by passing a law granting Einhorn a new trial. In February 1999 a three-judge court in Bordeaux ruled that Einhorn could be extradited, provided that he be granted an "equitable" trial with a right to appeal, and that he not be subject to the death penalty. Einhorn's attorneys appealed this ruling, but it was upheld by the French prime minister. In July 1999 a jury in a civil court in Philadelphia awarded $907 million in wrongful death damages to Holly Maddux's family (her parents being now dead).

Finally, on July 20, 2001, Einhorn was extradited to the United States to face a new trial for the murder of Holly Maddux.

—David I. Petts

Suggestions for Further Reading

Caba, Susan. "No Surrender." *The Philadelphia Inquirer, Inquirer Sunday Magazine* (September 12, 1993).

Levy, Steven. *The Unicorn's Secret—Murder in the Age of Aquarius* New York: Prentice Hall Press, 1988.

World Trade Center Bombing: 1993–94 & 1997

Defendants: First trial: Mahmud Abouhalima, Ahmad Ajaj, Nidal Ayyad, and Mohammed Salameh; second trial: Eyad Ismoil and Ramzi Yousef
Crimes Charged: Multiple offenses, including explosive destruction of property, conspiracy, interstate transportation of explosives, and assault on a federal officer **Chief Defense Lawyers:** First trial: Hassen Ibn Abdellah, Atig Ahmed, Austin Campriello, and Robert Precht; second trial: Ismoil: Louis Aidala; Yousef: Roy Kulcsar **Chief Prosecutors:** First trial: J. Gilmore Childers; second trial: Lev Dassin and David Kelley **Judge:** Kevin T. Duffy
Place: New York, New York **Dates of Trials:** First trial: September 14, 1993–May 24, 1994; second trial: August 3–November 12, 1997
Verdicts: Both trials: Guilty **Sentences:** First trial: All defendants: 240 years imprisonment; second trial: Ismoil: 240 years imprisonment; Yousef: Life imprisonment without parole

SIGNIFICANCE
The trials resulted in successful prosecutions for the bombing of the World Trade Center, the first large-scale terrorist attack in the United States of the 20th century.

The tremor felt by tourists at the Statue of Liberty on February 26, 1993, was not an earthquake. The shudder reaching across New York Harbor was the shock of a bomb smashing four underground levels of the World Trade Center, shaking the twin towers of the 110-story complex. Electricity and elevators were cut off, leaving hundreds of office workers and visitors huddling in terror or struggling down dark stairways choked with black smoke.

Six people were killed and over 1,000 were injured by the blast. The United States had seemed immune from such terrorist attacks until this explosion. As a chill of vulnerability touched the nation's cities, investigators crept into the teetering rubble of the World Trade Center's basement, looking for clues.

Van Deposit Leads to Arrests

Forensic investigators soon determined that the blast was caused by common explosives, detonated in a yellow van. They found the vehicle's charred identification number and traced it to a Ryder Rental Company agency in New Jersey. A few days later, the man who had rented the van told a federal agent posing as a rental clerk that the vehicle had been stolen. When the "clerk" refused to return a $400 deposit, the customer left in a huff. Federal agents grabbed him at a nearby bus stop and held him without bail.

Police and firefighters inspect the bomb crater inside the World Trade Center. (AP/Wide World Photos)

The suspect was Mohammed Salameh, a Jordanian living in the United States with an outdated tourist visa. Other arrests quickly followed. Nidal Ayyad, a chemical engineer whose business card was discovered in Salameh's pocket, was also taken into custody. Bilal Alkaisi, who shared a joint bank account with Salameh and Ayyad, surrendered to the FBI. A fourth man, Mahmud Abouhalima, was arrested in Cairo and deported to the United States to face indictment. Abouhalima showed signs of having been tortured by Egyptian police. His American lawyer, William Kunstler, argued unsuccessfully that any admissions obtained by Egyptian authorities from Abouhalima were gotten under duress and should be ruled inadmissible. A fifth suspect, Ibrahim Elgabrowny, was accused of carrying false passports and resisting arrest. He was indicted with Salameh and Ayyad on March 19.

A Palestinian, Ahmad Ajaj, was also arrested, on May 6, 1993. The previous year, he had been detained at Kennedy International Airport for having a doctored passport and military manuals containing bomb-making instructions. After six months in detention, he had been released. When investigators learned that he had traveled to the United States on the same flight as Ramzi Ahmed Yousef—another suspect who had been seen with Salameh in the yellow van and whose fingerprints were found on the pages of the manuals in Ajaj's luggage—Ajaj was arrested again. Yousef, in the meantime, had disappeared. The FBI placed him on its 10-Most-Wanted list and a $2 million reward was offered for information leading to his arrest.

Far-Reaching Conspiracy Alleged

Ajaj, Ayyad, Salameh, and Abouhalima were charged with a total of 38 crimes, including explosive destruction of property, conspiracy, and interstate transportation of explosives. All the suspects except Ajaj were followers of Sheik Omar Abdel Rahman, a blind cleric who preached militant Islamic doctrine from a Jersey City storefront mosque. In late August 1993, Sheik Abdel Rahman and a dozen of his adherents were indicted for plotting "a war of urban terrorism against the United States." Under a rarely used seditious conspiracy law, the sheik was accused of guiding the group, whose alleged targets included the United Nations, New York's FBI office, and the Holland and Lincoln Tunnels connecting New York with New Jersey. The defendants were also accused of planning to kill Egyptian President Hosni Mubarak and American politicians sympathetic to Israel.

Federal authorities declared that the World Trade Center bombing was one of the violent acts within this wider conspiracy. Salameh, Ayyad, Abouhalima, and Ajaj were named as coconspirators in the new case, but no fresh charges were added to those they already faced when their trial began on September 14, 1993. Judge Kevin T. Duffy was sufficiently concerned that publicity about the bombing had been so pervasive that he ordered an extra 5,000 jury duty summonses to be mailed. In fact, a jury was selected in less than a week.

Although none of the accused men had been seen at the site of the explosion, prosecutors attempted to tie them to the crime by sheer weight of circumstantial evidence. An entire month crawled by as hundreds of forensic exhibits were introduced, ranging from macabre photos of dead victims to dry architectural analyses of the World Trade Center's internal structure.

Defendants Tied to Van, Bomb Manuals

Testimony eventually got around to the defendants themselves. Prosecutors produced as evidence the frame of a vehicle that experts placed at the very center of the explosion. The serial number on the charred metal matched that of the yellow Ford van rented by Salameh. Bank officers testified that Salameh and Ayyad shared a joint account funded by undetermined overseas sources. A Jersey City chemical supplier relayed that Salameh and the fugitive, Yousef, had bought thousands of dollars of raw materials, which experts identified as primary components used in homemade bombs. Other witnesses recalled Ayyad ordering tanks of compressed hydrogen gas, which were delivered to a storage locker rented by Salameh and Yousef. When the storage company asked the renters to remove the tanks, the canisters were picked up by a yellow van.

A gas station attendant recalled two customers filling a yellow van's gas tank on the morning of the blast. When asked to identify the men in court, however, the attendant pointed to two jurors. The witness identified Abouhalima and Salameh when he returned to court the next day. Apart from this tenuous connection, the only physical evidence against Abouhalima consisted almost entirely of sulfuric acid burns on shoes found in his home. Prosecutors noted that the chemical could be used to make bombs. Hassen Ibn Abdellah, Abouhalima's attorney, pressed witnesses to admit that the substance could as easily have come from a car battery.

The *New York Times* received a letter from the Liberation Army Fifth Battalion claiming responsibility for the bomb after the blast occurred. DNA testing confirmed with a 97 percent probability that Ayyad's saliva had sealed the envelope. No such scientific evidence was offered in the case against Ajaj. The government, however, contended that Ajaj's possession of military manuals containing bomb-making instructions was sufficient proof of his complicity.

Austin Campriello, Ajaj's attorney, argued that possession of the manuals had resulted in his client's detention by immigration authorities on September 1, 1992 and therefore could not have been used in the bombing plot.

"What he slid over," Campriello said, faulting lead prosecutor J. Gilmore Childers's view of the confiscated manuals, "was that [Ajaj's] material was taken from him that very day and was in the possession of the United States government until the very day the World Trade Center tragedy occurred."

During four months of testimony from 207 witnesses, defense attorneys offered no rebuttal witnesses or evidence of their own. None of the defendants testified on his own behalf.

Verdicts Are Read

During closing arguments, Salameh's lawyer unexpectedly claimed that his client had been manipulated into unwittingly participating in the plot by the fugitive, Yousef. However, defense attorney Robert Precht's gamble did not pay off. After less than a week of deliberations, the defendants were found guilty of all 38 charges.

"Victory to Islam!" Ayyad shouted when the verdict was read.

The defendants dismissed their lawyers while awaiting sentencing. When they returned to court on May 24, 1994, all four were allowed to give statements.

Speaking in Arabic, each defendant protested that the trial was unfair. Salameh, Ayyad, and Abouhalima each gave long, angry political speeches, expressing their distaste for American society and their support for Islamic extremist movements around the globe. Unlike the others though, Ajaj called the bombing "a horrible crime." He then spoke for over two hours about atrocities committed against the Palestinian people. After witnessing and suffering from such violence, he said, he had no wish to act violently toward anyone.

Judge Duffy eventually cut him off. "All you've done in the past two and a half hours is convince me that anything you say is either a reworking of the truth or an out-and-out lie. . . . You were in this plot up to your ears."

Eyad Ismoil (left) and Ramzi Yousef found guilty of bombing World Trade Center. (AP/Wide World Photos)

Although all of the crimes in the case were serious, none was punishable by terms of life imprisonment under New York law. When the judge passed sentence, however, it was clear that the convicted men would spend the rest of their lives in prison.

The judge subtracted the ages of each of the six dead victims from an average life expectancy of 60 years. Together, according to this formula, the deceased had been denied a total of 180 years of possible life. To this sum, the judge added mandatory 30-year penalties for each of the two convictions of assault on a federal officer. The defendants were thus sentenced to 240 years in prison each, with no possibility of parole.

Ajaj appealed his conviction with the help of a new court-appointed attorney. Looking again at one evidentiary notebook on explosives, upon which the government had built much of its case, analysts found that Ajaj's handwriting did not match the incriminating notations in the book.

Ajaj also claimed that he had been planning to mail the other military manuals in his possession to the family of a Jordanian, who had been killed fighting in Afghanistan. He pointed out that the books were only part of a bundle of mail he had agreed to post for other Arabs he had met in Pakistan, whose mail systems to other countries were not as reliable as those of the U.S. Postal Service. Ajaj admitted that he had met Yousef, but insisted that the fugitive had neither revealed his real name nor spoken of any violent intentions.

Philippine Airline Plot

In the ensuing years, other figures in the wider conspiracy alleged by the government were brought to trial. Sheik Rahman was convicted on October 1, 1995, on conspiracy counts brought under the sedition charge and sentenced to life imprisonment without parole. During the sheik's trial, Ramzi Yousef was arrested in Pakistan and extradited to the United States. The indictment against him was so complicated that Judge Duffy divided the charges against Yousef into two separate court cases.

Before Yousef could face trial in the World Trade Center case, however, he stood accused of a potentially bloodier terrorist plan. Prosecutors charged that Yousef, Pakistani pilot Abdul Hakim Murad, and Wali Khan Amin Shah had conspired to detonate bombs aboard a dozen commercial airliners during a 48-hour period in January 1995. By killing an estimated 4,000 passengers en route from the Philippines to Los Angeles, San Francisco, Honolulu, and New York, the bombers hoped to force the United States to end aid to Israel. Shah was accused of testing a timer by leaving a bomb in a Manila theater on December 1, 1994. Yousef was charged with hiding a bomb on a Philippine Airlines flight to Tokyo on December 11 in a similar test; the bomb killed a Japanese passenger and injured 10 others.

Philippine police discovered the airline plot on January 6, 1995, when chemicals Yousef and Murad were mixing started a fire in a Manila apartment. Yousef fled to Pakistan, but Murad was arrested when he returned, allegedly to dispose of nitroglycerine, timers, bomb-making equipment, and manuals, as well as a computer containing details of the plot.

The three defendants pleaded not guilty when the trial began on May 13, 1996. They claimed they were beaten while in custody and that they had not been properly informed of their rights when they gave statements to FBI agents while being transported to the United States to face trial. The incriminating statements included a detailed account by Yousef of how the World Trade Center bomb was made and delivered. The FBI agents also claimed that Yousef had boasted of plots to assassinate Pope John Paul II and President Bill Clinton.

Judge Duffy, also presiding in the Philippine Airlines plot, ruled that these disputed statements were admissible at the trial and rejected a defense motion that the United States did not have jurisdiction in the airline case. Although the plot was to have been executed from the Philippines, Duffy pointed out that U.S. law allowed prosecuting any crime taking place aboard an international aircraft.

In addition to Yousef's admissions and voluminous bomb-related evidence linked to the trio, the most damaging exhibit was the laptop computer found in the Manila apartment. Under the file name "Bojinga," the computer's contents included the targeted jets' flight schedules, money transfers, identification photographs, and a threatening letter explaining that the attack was a response to U.S. financial, political, and military assistance to Israel.

Over the objections of his codefendants' attorneys and warnings from Judge Duffy, Yousef dismissed his court-appointed lawyer, Roy Kulcsar (who would represent Yousef later in the World Trade Center bombing trial). Yousef argued that he had been detained and tortured by Pakistani security forces in November 1994 when he was allegedly organizing the airline plot in Manila, but was contradicted by prosecution records showing that he was not arrested in Pakistan until February 1995.

With little apparent success in forwarding his defense, Yousef cross-examined an airline attendant who identified him as sitting in the seat later taken by the airline bomb victim. He declared that the evidence against him had been fabricated by the Philippine and Pakistani governments. Shah's and Murad's lawyers repeated this charge, pointing to testimony in which Manila investigators admitted filing false reports to justify searching the fire-damaged apartment where the evidence was discovered. Because the search had taken place in the Philippines and was not subject to U.S. rules of evidence, however, the discovery was ruled legitimate.

Boastful Admissions

On September 5, 1996, a jury found the three defendants guilty on all of the counts against them. Before they were sentenced, however, Yousef stood trial for complicity in the World Trade Center plot. When that trial began on August 3, 1997, Yousef's codefendant was a former schoolmate and chemical engineer named Eyad Ismoil. Prosecutors accused Ismoil of driving the explosive-laden van into the World Trade Center's underground garage and helping Yousef set the fuse. Ismoil had flown to Jordan that night, but was later arrested and extradited to the United States. Ismoil pleaded his innocence and protested that he thought the van contained only soap and shampoo.

Prosecutors ridiculed Ismoil's claim. For two months they introduced forensic testimony about residue and fingerprints found at bomb-making sites in New Jersey; telephone receipts; and other evidence linking both defendants to a Jersey City apartment where the bomb had been made.

The most damaging testimony against Yousef stemmed from his alleged boasting to American agents on his flight back to the United States from Pakistan. Aboard the plane, Yousef allegedly claimed that he had masterminded the plot and had initially considered mounting a poison gas attack. He hoped the bomb would topple one Trade Center tower into the other and kill at least 250,000 people. He was disappointed in the results of the blast, but stood on the

New Jersey waterfront to watch the smoke from the fire across the river before he fled the country.

Neither of the defendants took the witness stand in their own defense, leaving the arguments to their lawyers. Defense attorney Kulcsar characterized Yousef's alleged admissions of guilt as illogically self-incriminating. Kulcsar wondered why the damaging confessions had never been recorded. Ismoil's attorney, Louis Aidala, admitted that his client had helped load the van but had been ignorant of its deadly contents.

Final Sentences

On November 12, 1997, Yousef and Ismoil were convicted on all the charges against them, including the lethal use of explosives, which carried a mandatory sentence of life imprisonment without parole. On January 8, 1998, Yousef was sentenced to life imprisonment without parole for participating in the World Trade Center bombing, the airline conspiracy, and causing the death of the Japanese passenger in the latter plot's "test run." Murad received a life sentence and was fined $250,000 so that he could not profit from the case. Shah began cooperating with authorities and was rumored to provide information about Saudi militant Osama bin Laden, whom U.S. authorities accused of being the mastermind behind explosions at two American embassies in Africa on August 7, 1998. Ismoil received a 240-year sentence calculated by the same formula Judge Duffy used in the first bombing trial, plus heavy fines that ensured Ismoil would never profit financially from telling his story.

The World Trade Center trials resulted in the prosecution of all but one of the accused participants, Abdul Rahman Yasin, whom federal authorities had detained but carelessly released after the blast. Yasin was thought to have escaped to Iraq. Despite the trials and convictions, the mystery of who financed the attack, however, still remains.

— Tom Smith

Suggestions for Further Reading

Childers, J. Gilmore. Statement before the U.S. Senate Judiciary Committee Subcommittee on Technology, Terrorism, and Government Information, "Foreign Terrorists in America: Five Years after the World Trade Center" hearing. February 24, 1998. http://judiciary.senate.gov/childers.htm.

Dwyer, Jim et al. *Two Seconds under the World*. New York: Crown Publishers, 1994.

Reeve, Simon. *The New Jackal: Ramzi Yousef, Osama bin Laden and the Future of Terrorism*. Boston: Northeastern University Press, 1999.

John Wayne and Lorena Bobbitt Trials: 1993 & 1994

Defendants: First trial: John Wayne Bobbitt; second trial: Lorena Bobbitt
Crimes Charged: First trial: marital sexual assault; second trial: malicious wounding **Chief Defense Lawyers:** First trial: Gregory L. Murphy; second trial: Lisa B. Kemler **Chief Prosecutor:** Both trials: Paul B. Ebert.
Judge: Both trials: Herman Whisenaut, Jr. **Place:** Both trials: Manassas, Virginia **Dates of Trials:** First Trial: November 8–10, 1993; second trial: January 10–22, 1994 **Verdict:** First trial: not guilty; second trial: not guilty

SIGNIFICANCE

These two trials involving allegations of rape and sexual mutilation captured the attention of the public. In so doing, the nature of what is deemed acceptable for broadcast media changed forever.

When Lorena Bobbitt picked up a 12-inch fillet knife in her kitchen at 5 A.M. on June 23, 1993, she presumably never gave a thought to the gift she was about to bestow on the nation's editors and news anchors: the opportunity to put the unmentionable word "penis" in front-page headlines and on network news by the dinner hour. Was it on her mind to focus world attention on the issue of violence against women? Moments later, with one stroke of the knife, she accomplished both results by severing her slumbering husband from his most cherished possession. This act produced two courtroom dramas.

Lorena and John Bobbitt had met, when she was 19 and he was 21, at a club for enlisted men near the Quantico, Virginia, Marine Corps base, where he was a lance corporal. Raised in Venezuela, she was, at the time they met, a manicurist in Manassas, Virginia. She was slender, 5'2", attractive, with long dark brown hair. She held a U.S. immigration visa that was soon to expire.

John was inexperienced with women. Lorena's strict upbringing had included chaperones tagging along on dates, no premarital sex, and no tolerance of divorce or abortion. "She was pretty," said John later. "She had a cute accent. We thought we were in love. I didn't want her to leave." They were married on June 18, 1989.

Trouble soon began. John drank. He spent money extravagantly. A month after the wedding, when she criticized his erratic driving, he struck her. When they argued over a television program, he broke off the rooftop antenna, knocked her down with his car, and drove off. In another fight, she locked herself in the bathroom. He unscrewed the doorknob. When she dialed 911, he ripped out the phone. Neighbors noted her recurring bruises. Short of cash, Lorena stole money from her employer and stole dresses from Nordstrom's department store.

Upon completing his Marine enlistment, John began working as a bouncer at a Manassas night club. Over their four-year marriage, interrupted by long separations in 1991 and again in 1992, both Bobbitts called the police to break up their disputes several times. In mid-June 1993, Lorena requested a restraining order against her husband. Two days later, at 3 A.M., he came home drunk.

A house guest, John's buddy Robert Johnston, was asleep in the next room. At about 5 A.M., he felt a kick. He looked up. John Bobbitt, naked, a bloody sheet clutched to his groin, calmly asked Robert to get him to the emergency room. Lorena was not in the house. On the way to the hospital, John said, "They better be able to make me a new penis."

Urologist Dr. James T. Sehn examined Bobbitt, explaining to him that, unless the missing penis was found, he would have to sew the stump closed. With Bobbitt on a gurney ready for surgery, Dr. Sehn pushed him toward the operating room.

At that moment the police arrived at the hospital with the missing organ, packed in ice. They had received a call from Lorena Bobbitt, who told them her husband's penis could be retrieved from a field next to the neighborhood 7–11 convenience store. Dr. Sehn immediately called Dr. David E. Berman, a skilled microsurgeon, and in a nine-hour procedure, they reattached John Bobbitt's penis.

Lorena Bobbitt Is Charged

Lorena Bobbitt was charged with malicious wounding. Overnight, the amputation, the reattachment, the couple's record of domestic violence, and Lorena's statement, saying she was raped by her drunken husband at 3 A.M., which was the last straw for her, spread like wildfire throughout the world. Late night talk show hosts David Letterman and Jay Leno began quipping Bobbitt jokes night after night.

With Lorena indicted and women's voices rising, Attorney Paul B. Ebert of Prince William County Commonwealth, Virginia, examined Lorena's police statement. Six weeks later, he indicted John Bobbitt on a charge of marital sexual assault.

By this time, the outraged members of the Virginia chapter of the National Organization for Women (NOW) had set up a support hotline. Dr. Sehn's wife was harassed by women who were angry that her husband's surgery had succeeded. "This is a tragedy, not a comedy," said Phyllis D. Barkhurst of the National Coalition Against Domestic Violence. "It is deeply revealing that it has taken the mutilation of a man to attract attention to the abuse of women," said a New York Times Op-Ed article.

Both Bobbitts quickly hired agents to handle book and movie offers and public appearances. Almost immediately, Lorena's agents got her on ABC's *20/20*, and in *Vanity Fair* magazine. Both Bobbitts filed for divorce.

Lorena Bobbitt arriving at the courthouse for her trial in the malicious wounding of her husband. (AP/Wide World Photos)

John Bobbitt Tried for Malicious Assault

On Monday, November 8, 1993, nine women and three men sat in the jury box in the Prince William County Circuit Court to hear John Wayne Bobbitt tried for malicious assault. Rape was not charged because under Virginia law it applies only to couples living apart or in cases where the victim suffers serious physical injury. Reporters from around the world packed the courtroom. Outside, pushing their way through the hundreds of spectators and reporters who failed to find room inside, hawkers sold nine hundred T-shirts, at $10 each, with the inscription, "Manassas, Va.—A cut above the rest."

On the witness stand, Lorena Bobbitt tearfully described how her husband had come home drunk, woke her, choked her, and raped her for the second time in two days. "I was crying," she testified. "I said, 'You hurt me again and again and again. How much do I have to put up with?'"

She said Bobbitt then fell asleep. She went to the kitchen to get a drink of water. "The refrigerator door was open," she testified, "and that was the only light. And I turned and saw the knife. I took it. I went to the bedroom. I pulled the sheets off, and I cut him." She said she then ran out, threw the knife into a garbage can, jumped into her car, and drove away. When she realized she still held the penis in her hand, she tossed it into the vacant field next to the convenience store.

Bobbitt took the stand, telling the jury, "I felt a pull, a jerk that hurt real bad and I sprang up—like, silent pain. I grabbed my groin area and held myself." John Bobbitt could not recall whether he had had sex that night. A police detective testified that at the hospital John Bobbitt told him, "if he had sex with his wife, then he may have done it while he was asleep, that he did those things very often.''

Stephen Roque, a Prince William County court counselor, told the court that two days before the attack, Lorena Bobbitt had complained of physical and sexual abuse by her husband and had asked about court protection. Told she would have to appear before a judge, she said she would return later in the week.

Called back to the stand, Lorena Bobbitt explained that five days before the attack, her husband had raped her while calling out the names of other women.

In his summation, Prosecutor Ebert said, ''You might say these two people deserve each other.''

After deliberating for only four hours, the jury found John Bobbitt not guilty. Afterward, a juror said the jury had agreed with John's lawyer, Gregory L. Murphy. The case was too circumstantial, and it could not rely solely on Lorena Bobbitt's word. ''If someone had heard her scream,'' continued the juror, ''or if there had been some sort of bruising, that would have made more substantive evidence.''

It would be two months before Lorena's trial would begin. Meanwhile, appetites for the sensational were being well fed. Shock jock Howard Stern put John Bobbitt on a New Year's Eve telethon to raise money to defray $250,000 of his legal and medical fees. People magazine made the Bobbitts its cover story and devoted five full pages of the same issue to the Bobbitts. Late night talk show hosts Letterman and Leno vied to see who could come up with the most jokes. Feminist author Katie Roiphe wrote in The New York Times:

> Lorena Bobbitt has become a symbol of female rage. . . . With that primal cut, she exposed the raw hostility between the sexes that is usually clothed in everyday social interaction. . . . We need to understand the part of the women's movement that yearns for a Lorena Bobbitt.

Lorena Bobbitt's Trial Begins

The trial of Lorena Bobbitt on the felony charge of maliciously wounding her husband opened January 10, 1994. Autographed John Bobbitt T-shirts were selling for $25, all proceeds going to the defense fund. A restaurant offered a Bobbitt Special—a hot dog with French ''cut'' fries. Downtown Manassas was a mass of eager spectators and throbbing diesels powering satellite trucks.

Seven women and five men occupied the jury box. Prosecutor Ebert's opening statement asserted that, temperamental and demanding, Lorena Bobbitt had acted out of pique.

Defense Attorney Lisa B. Kemler described her client as ''a battered woman in the classic sense'' who acted in self-defense out of ''irresistible impulse,'' and who was suffering from mental disorders. ''What we have,'' said Kemler, ''is Lorena Bobbitt's life juxtaposed against John Wayne Bobbitt's penis. In her mind, it was his penis from which she could not escape. At the end of this case, you will come to one conclusion. And that is that a life is more valuable than a penis.''

On the stand, Bobbitt denied he had raped his wife just before the attack. She, he said, had tried to initiate sex when he returned from drinking with a friend, but he was too tired and fell asleep. Then, he testified, "I was bleeding. I hurt real bad. I thought she just, you know, grabbed me, just pulled it out of my body.''

Defense witnesses testified to John's boasting that he enjoyed brutal sex with women, repeatedly hit his wife, pulled her hair, and threw her against the wall.

Lorena's defense traced the disintegration of the Bobbitts's marriage, the increasing violence, and John Bobbitt's use of what she called "Marine Corps torture techniques,'' which included twisting her leg so severely that she was hospitalized. She finally acted, said James Lose, one of her defense lawyers, on "irresistible impulse,'' a form of temporary insanity.

In cross-examination, Lorena testified that she did not remember severing John's penis. Only when she found it in her hand while driving away, she said, did she realize what she had done. But Assistant Commonwealth Attorney Mary Grace O'Brien retorted by quoting Lorena's police statement. "He always have orgasm and he doesn't wait for me to have orgasm,'' it said. "He's selfish. I don't think it's fair, so I pulled back the sheets then and I did it.''

Attorney O'Brien then asked Lorena, "You're saying under oath that you don't remember cutting him?''

"No,'' said Lorena. "That's what I assumed happened.''

A defense psychiatrist testified that Lorena suffered a "brief reactive Psychosis'' under which she attacked "the instrument that was the weapon of her torture.'' A prosecution psychiatrist rebutted by declaring, "she had a choice to make. She chose to amputate that penis, and as such we do not have an irresistible impulse but an impulse she did not resist.''

After six hours of deliberation, the jury concluded that Lorena Bobbitt was temporarily insane when she cut off her husband's penis. It found her not guilty on all criminal charges. Said a male member of the jury, "We didn't believe John Bobbitt.''

Under state law, Lorena underwent five weeks of psychiatric examination in a mental hospital and was released.

John Bobbitt's Troubles Continue

The press announced that John Bobbitt was booked on a worldwide media tour billed as "Love Hurts.'' Within months, he was engaged to marry a former topless dancer, Kristina Elliott. But on May 6, 1994, in Las Vegas, Elliott had Bobbitt arrested for assault, asserting that he had thrown her against a wall. He pleaded not guilty. Out on bail and awaiting trial, he announced complete recovery from his celebrated surgery. "Its like it was before," he said. "There's no problem."

June found Bobbitt in court again in a paternity suit. He pleaded guilty and arranged a settlement with Beatrice L. Williams of Niagara Falls, New York. He said he was "thrilled, excited and blessed" to be the father of a 17-month-old son. Two months later, he was convicted of a misdemeanor against Kristina Elliott, his former fiancée. Observing that Bobbitt had "an attitude problem," Las Vegas Justice of the Peace William Jansen sentenced him to 60 days in jail, then suspended 45 of the days. "Your attitude problem is caused by your drinking," said the judge. He ordered therapy and membership in Alcoholics Anonymous, as John Wayne Bobbitt was led from the courtroom to jail.

In 1994 John Bobbitt starred in an X-rated movie with an all-too predictable title: "John Wayne Bobbitt Uncut."

Releasing Lorena Bobbitt after psychiatric evaluation in a mental health facility, Prince William County Circuit Court Judge Herman A. Whisenant, Jr., ordered her to undergo outpatient treatment weekly and not to leave Virginia without permission.

Both Lorena and John Wayne Bobbitt continue to occasionally popup in the news. In 1996, John was ordained as a minister in the Universal Life Church. His conversion to religion did not last very long. A few years later, he took a job as a greeter at a Nevada brothel. Lorena now works as a manicurist in Virginia. In 1997, she was arrested and charged with assault on her mother. She was later acquitted of those charges.

—*Bernard Ryan, Jr.*

Suggestion for Further Reading

Hewit, Bill and Rochelle Jones. "Slice of Life." *People Weekly* (August 30, 1993): 57–8.

Margolick, David. "Wife Says She Does Not Recall Cutting." *New York Times* (January 15, 1994): B1.

——. "Witness Says Lorena Bobbitt Earlier Threatened to Maim Husband." *New York Times* (January 20, 1994): B1.

The West Memphis Three Trials: 1994

Defendants: Damien Wayne Echols, Charles Jason Baldwin, Jessie Misskelley **Crimes Charged:** Murder **Chief Defense Lawyers:** Val P. Price, Scott Davidson, Daniel Stidham **Chief Prosecutors:** Brent Davis, John Fogleman **Judge:** David Burnett **Place:** Jonesboro, Arkansas **Date of Trial:** January–April 1994 **Verdict:** Guilty **Sentences:** Echols: Death by lethal injection; Baldwin and Misskelley: life imprisonment

SIGNIFICANCE

The conviction of three teenage boys for the sadistic murder of three eight-year-old boys in what the prosecution claimed was a Satanic ritual received national attention largely as a result of a prize-winning documentary film which contributed to doubts about the correctness of the verdict.

In the early afternoon of May 6, 1993, the bodies of three eight-year-old boys were found in a drainage ditch in an area known as Robin Hood Hills, near West Memphis, Arkansas. James Moore, Steven Branch, and Christopher Byers had been last seen playing together in the late afternoon of the previous day. A search had begun in the late evening and had gone on through most of the night. Their bodies were naked and their hands were bound to their feet with shoelaces. Moore and Branch both died from head injuries and drowning. Byers had been more extensively injured and his genitals had been torn or cut off. He had died from a variety of head injuries and from loss of blood, and had been dead before being put in the ditch.

Damien Echols immediately became a suspect in the eyes of the investigators, apparently because he was suggested to them by a juvenile officer, Steve Jones. Echols was 18 years old, and had had a disturbed childhood; although a somewhat isolated young man, he had called attention to himself in his small community by for shoulder-length hair and his penchant for dressing in black, and for liking heavy metal rock bands. Two days after the discovery of the bodies Echols was interviewed by the police. During this interview, he told them that he knew that one of the three boys had been more severely injured than the others. Since this information had not been officially released, police would later claim that only the killer could have known this. However, no charges were pressed at this time.

The Confession of Jessie Misskelley

Early in June police questioned a 17-year-old acquaintance of Damien Echols, Jessie Misskelley. Reports of the length of the interrogation vary from two hours to 12 hours, but it is not disputed that the interrogation was conducted without the presence of counsel, and without any waiver of Miranda rights having been obtained. No record of the interrogation was kept, except for a short recording of the confession that Misskelley gave at the end of it. Misskelley admitted having killed the three boys and implicated Damien Echols and a third boy, 17-year-old Charles Jason Baldwin. This confession, although it contained several factual errors relating to the circumstances of the crime, would constitute the most important evidence against the three teenagers, all of whom were charged with the murders.

Misskelley's trial was separated from the other two, and he was tried first, in January 1994. The prosecution's case relied solely upon his confession. Daniel Stidham, counsel for Misskelley, moved to have the confession held inadmissible, but Judge David Burnett ruled that the confession was voluntary and admissible. Professor Richard Ofsche of the University of California at Berkeley was called as an expert witness on coerced confessions after the judge's ruling, but was not allowed to present all of his prepared testimony as to why he believed the confession was probably coerced. The defense's second expert witness on police interrogation and the use of lie detector tests was also only allowed to give part of his prepared testimony. The jury found Misskelley guilty of one count of first-degree murder and two counts of second-degree murder. He was offered a reduced punishment if he would agree to testify against the other two, but he refused and was sentenced to life plus 40 years in prison.

The Trial of Damien Echols and Jason Baldwin

The trial of Damien Echols and Jason Baldwin began on February 22, 1994, also before Judge Burnett. The prosecution again relied heavily on Jessie Misskelley's confession, but they also went to considerable lengths to try to establish that the murders were part of an occult sacrificial ritual led by Echols. Books had been found at his home in which spells had been written, and pentagrams and upside down crosses had been drawn. Books had also been found indicating an interest in neopagan religions and the history of witchcraft. Attention was drawn to his interest in heavy metal rock music and his liking of black T-shirts with occult designs. Dr. Dale Griffis testified for the prosecution as an expert witness on occult killings. He presented 11 aspects of the murders which he felt indicated that the killings were Satanic in nature. These aspects included such things as the facts that three eight-year-old boys were killed and their bodies found in water, and water and the numbers three and eight have mystic significance in Satanic cults.

A mother and daughter testified to having seen Damien Echols and Jason Baldwin together in a car on the night of May 5, and to seeing Echols and his girlfriend later in the evening walking near a truck stop not far from where the bodies were found. A 12-year-old girl and a 15-year-old girl testified that at a softball game they had overheard Damien Echols say, "I killed the three little boys and before I turn myself in I'm going to kill two more and I already have one of them picked out." Under cross-examination by Val Price, the public defender assigned by the court to represent Echols, the girls admitted that the game was very noisy, and they could not recall anything else they had overheard during it. A young addict, Michael Carson, who had met Baldwin when they were both being held in detention, testified that Baldwin had admitted to him that he had killed the boys. A hunting knife which could have been the murder weapon, was recovered from a lake behind Baldwin's home. Fibers similar to some found on the victims' clothing (which had been discovered near the bodies) had been located in Echols's home, but they were apparently from a widely used fabric. Other than this, no physical evidence was introduced that would link the three accused to the victims.

On April 18, both were found guilty of three counts of capital murder. The following day Echols was sentenced to death by lethal injection, and Baldwin, who was just 16 at the time of the murders, was sentenced to life in prison without parole.

Appeals Fail

Lengthy appeals were filed citing numerous points of law relating to both the conduct of the investigation and the trial, but in 1996 the Supreme Court of Arkansas, in separate opinions, upheld first the Misskelley conviction and then those of Echols and Baldwin. Two years later a hearing was granted in the case of Echols on a motion for a new trial. Ed Mallet, who now represented Echols, argued that Echols had received ineffective counsel during his original trial. This was partly because of the inexperience of the court-appointed attorney in trying cases of this sort, partly because of the lack of resources provided by the court to the defense for the securing of expert witnesses, but also because the defense counsel had entered into a financial arrangement with Joe Berlinger and Bruce Sinofsky, the producer/directors of a documentary film made for the Home Box Office network (HBO). This film was first shown on HBO in June 1996. Reviewers of the film commented on the unusual access that the film-makers were given to the trial preparation process.

Also raised in the motion for the hearing on a new trial was the fact that a forensic scientist, Brent E. Turvey, had identified from autopsy photographs what he considered to be human bite marks on the face of Steve Branch. Mouth impressions had been taken of Echols, Baldwin, and Misskelley, and at the hearing Dr. Thomas David, a forensic odontologist, testified that in his opinion none of the three youths had made the bite mark wounds. The hearing was held before Judge Burnett, who had presided over the original trial. He declined to recuse himself, and ruled against the motion for a new trial. Damien Echols is still under sentence of death, and Jason Baldwin and Jessie Misskelley are serving their prison terms.

—David I. Petts

Suggestions for Further Reading

Berlinger, Joe, and Bruce Sinofsky. *Paradise Lost: The Child Murders at Robin Hood Hills*. Cabin Fever distributors, 1997. Videocassette. (Berlinger and Sinofsky made a sequel, *Paradise Lost: Revisited*, which was shown on HBO in March 2000.)

http://www.wm3.org This website is maintained by supporters of the West Memphis Three, but it includes links to extensive excerpts from the transcripts of the original trial and the complete text of the Arkansas Supreme Court rulings.

Jack Kevorkian Trials: 1994–99

Defendant: Dr. Jack Kevorkian **Crimes Charged:** Assisted suicide, murder, delivering a controlled substance for administering drugs without a license
Chief Defense Lawyers: 1994 and 1996: Geoffrey Fieger, Mayer Morganroth; 1999: David Gorosh, Lisa Dwyer **Chief Prosecutor:** 1994 and 1996: Richard Thompson, Lawrence Bunting, Michael Modelski; 1999: David Gorcyca, Daniel L. Lemisch, John O'Brien, John Skrzynski **Judge:** 1994: Thomas E. Jackson; 1996: David Breck, Jessica Cooper; 1999: Jessica Cooper **Place:** Pontiac, Michigan **Dates of Trials:** April 19–May 2, 1994; February 20–March 8, 1996; April 16–May 14, 1996; March 22–26, 1999
Verdicts: 1994 and 1996: Not guilty; 1999: guilty of second-degree murder and delivery of a controlled substance

SIGNIFICANCE

The name Dr. Jack Kevorkian—also known as "Dr. Death"—has become synonymous with the subject of doctor-assisted suicide. By helping the desperately ill to determine their own fates, Kevorkian has forced the courts to tackle the issue of whether assisted suicide should be an option in some instances. Court ruling based on laws unclear on the subject, as well as Kevorkian's continuing to assist those wanting to die, prompted legislative action by the state of Michigan—and indeed, elsewhere in the country.

In June 1989, 53-year-old Janet Adkins of Portland, Oregon, was diagnosed with Alzheimer's disease—the nation's fourth-leading cause of death, which manifests itself as the irreversible deterioration of brain cells. A Renaissance woman, Janet had taught English and piano, taken up hang gliding when her three sons were grown, traversed the mountains of Nepal, and climbed Oregon's highest peak, Mount Hood. Determined not to put herself or her family through the agony of Alzheimer's, she began to plan her own death.

When Adkins heard about Dr. Jack Kevorkian, a 62-year-old pathologist in Royal Oak, Michigan, who had invented a suicide device, she got in touch with him.

Dr. Kevorkian was known among medics as an eccentric. Officials had forced him out of his residency at the University of Michigan Hospital in 1958 when he proposed medical experiments on death-row prisoners. Since 1982, his ideas on euthanasia had prevented his getting an appointment in a hospital. But, he was still licensed to practice medicine in Michigan and California.

Over several weeks, Kevorkian talked frequently with Janet. He ascertained that her determination to kill herself was clear. But, in Oregon, causing or assisting a suicide was a felony. Michigan had no such statute.

In June 1990, Janet Adkins and her husband flew to Michigan. Over dinner, Kevorkian explained the suicide procedure. Over the next two days he tried to find a motel, funeral home, or vacant office to permit Janet Adkins's suicide on its premises. He explained that he had to tell them what he was doing so they wouldn't sue him later for emotional distress. All efforts failed. Finally, he drove Janet in his own rusty 1968 Volkswagen van to a campsite that had electrical hookups. He attached an electrocardiogram to monitor Janet's heart; next he inserted an intravenous needle into her arm to drip harmless saline solution. Then, as Adkins pressed a button on the machine, stopping the saline and starting the thiopental, which induced unconsciousness, she said, "Thank you, thank you, thank you." A minute later, the machine switched to potassium chloride, which stopped Adkins's heart. The doctor called 911 and, when the police came, told them what he had done. Within hours, his name was being heard in households across America.

The Public Debate over Assisted Suicide Begins

Four days later, a New York Times/CBS News Poll found 53 percent of Americans said a doctor should be allowed to assist an ill person in taking his or her own life. But Judge Alice Gilbert of Michigan's Oakland County Circuit Court ordered Kevorkian to stop using his machine. Talk shows, newspaper and magazine editorials and Op-Ed pages, nursing homes, medical and legal societies all vibrated with the debate over the ethical issue. "I'm trying to knock the medical profession into accepting its responsibilities," explained Kevorkian, "and those responsibilities include assisting their patients with death."

In December, Oakland County prosecuting attorney Richard Thompson charged Kevorkian with first-degree murder. But, Oakland County District Court Judge Gerald McNally found no probable cause that the doctor had committed murder, because Michigan had no law against assisting suicide.

The prosecutor asked the court to forbid Kevorkian to regain possession of his "death machine" from the police, build another like it, or help anyone else build one. Defense lawyer Geoffrey Fieger argued that, since the doctor had been cleared of criminal charges, the prosecution had no legal basis for its request. On February 5, 1991, Judge Gilbert ruled that Dr. Kevorkian could no longer use the machine.

Two days later, on February 7, the doctor told reporters he intended to use the machine again. In October 1991, in a remote cabin outside Pontiac, Michigan, he helped two women kill themselves. One, who had multiple sclerosis, used a somewhat different intravenous device. Instead of pushing a button, as Janet Adkins had done, the MS victim had two strings attached to her fingers.

She pulled the first to activate the anesthetic. Then, as she lost consciousness, her falling arm pulled the second string to start sending sodium Pentothal, a poison, into her system. The other woman, who suffered from a pelvic disease, breathed carbon monoxide, a poisonous gas. Upon hearing of the deaths, Judge McNally commented to an AP reporter, "There is a place for this in society. You can't put this in dark alleys or cabins."

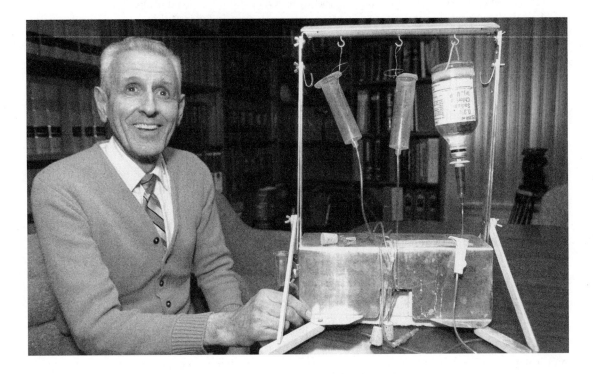

Dr. Jack Kevorkian and his "suicide machine." (AP/Wide World Photos)

Michigan Suspends Kevorkian's License

Within a month the eight-member Michigan Board of Medicine suspended Kevorkian's license indefinitely. The suspension, they hoped, would make it impossible for him to get or prescribe lethal drugs and, if he again assisted a suicide, would expose him to the criminal charge of practicing without a license.

Dr. L.J. Dragovic, the Oakland County medical examiner, ruled that both women's deaths were homicides because "suicide is reserved for self-inflicted death" and "all the evidence indicates these deaths were brought about by another person."

In February 1992, the doctor was indicted on two counts of murder and one of delivery of a controlled substance. Free on $15,000 bond, Kevorkian advised a California dentist by telephone and mail on how to kill himself with a suicide machine. The dentist did in fact proceed with his suicide.

On May 15 in Clawson, Michigan, Dr. Kevorkian provided the canister of carbon monoxide as another multiple sclerosis victim killed herself. Again the medical examiner ruled homicide. On July 21, Michigan Circuit Court Judge David Breck dismissed the earlier murder charges, saying the doctor had merely assisted the suicides, which was not illegal in Michigan.

September and November, 1992, brought two more Kevorkian-assisted suicides. This prompted Michigan's House of Representatives to vote, 72–29, to ban assisted suicide for 15 months while a state commission studied the issue. "It's a bill against one person," said the doctor. "It's like we're still in the Dark Ages."

The ban was to begin March 30, 1993. In January and February, Dr. Kevorkian helped eight more terminally ill patients commit suicide. Each time, the police confiscated the doctor's paraphernalia. And each time he built a new machine. Incensed, the Legislature passed a hurry-up ban for Michigan Governor John Engler to sign on February 25.

The Severely Ill Ask Kevorkian for Help

The public debate grew intense. California suspended Kevorkian's license. From all over America, the hopelessly ill and severely pained called day and night begging the doctor to help them. In May 1993, he was arrested, then released in his lawyer's custody, for merely being present at a suicide.

Then Michigan Circuit Court Judge Cynthia Stephens declared the hurry up 15-month ban unconstitutional because it was passed without public hearings and contained more than one objective.

Helping his seventeenth suicide, Kevorkian dared the authorities to prosecute him under the questionable law, which was under review by the Michigan Court of Appeals. On August 17, 1993, he was indicted. "I welcome going on trial," he said. "It isn't Kevorkian on trial. It isn't assisted suicide on trial. You know what's on trial? It's your civilization and society."

Eight hours after the judge ordered him to stand trial, the doctor helped his eighteenth suicide. Some one hundred Friends of Dr. Kevorkian rallied before his apartment building. Neighbors expressed fond support when the doctor said that, if jailed, he would go on a hunger strike.

In October, the doctor assisted his nineteenth suicide—the first in his own apartment in Royal Oak, Michigan. Arrested and refusing to post bail or walk from the courtroom, he was dragged to jail. After Jack DeMoss, a stranger who opposed assisted suicide, bailed him out, the doctor helped his twentieth suicide.

Courts Grapple with the Issue

December 1993 saw Dr. Kevorkian returned to jail on his third charge of breaking the 15-month ban. He refused to post bond or consume anything but fruit juice, water, and vitamins. After ten days, unshaven, weak and gaunt, he was pushed into the courtroom in a wheelchair for a hearing. Three days later, Wayne County Chief Judge Richard C. Kaufman declared the controversial law unconstitutional. In barring all assisted suicide, he said, the Michigan legislature had passed a statute that was too broad to be consistent with rights guaranteed by the U.S. Constitution. The judge cited a 1990 U.S. Supreme Court ruling that affirmed the right to refuse life-supporting medical treatment and found that "when quality of life is significantly impaired by a medical condition and the medical condition is unlikely to improve" the person has a "constitutional right" to commit suicide. Oakland County Prosecutor Thompson, holding the doctor in jail, said the ruling was not binding in his jurisdiction.

Then, later in December after nearly three weeks in jail, Dr. Kevorkian promised to stop helping suicides "until we get some resolution of this from the courts." A jury trial in the spring of 1994 found him not guilty of violating the ban on assisted suicide even though he admitted to helping a suicide in 1993. Next, the Michigan Court of Appeals reinstated the two murder charges from 1991. The doctor appealed that ruling to the state Supreme Court. Meanwhile, the Court of Appeals found the 15-month temporary ban unconstitutional for technical reasons. Prosecutor Richard Thompson appealed.

Hours after the 15-month ban ended, in his first assisted suicide in more than a year but his twenty-first altogether, Dr. Kevorkian helped a Royal Oak, Michigan, woman commit suicide in her home. She had had both legs and one eye removed because of rheumatoid arthritis and advanced osteoporosis. Two weeks later, the Michigan House of Representatives, in a lame-duck session, rushed through a new bill to take effect April 1, 1995, outlawing assisted suicide. It then moved in an apparent contradiction, for a state-wide voter referendum in November 1996. The state's Senate passed a similar bill but did not call for a referendum. At the same time, the Michigan Supreme Court reversed the Court of Appeals decision and said the Legislature had acted within the constitution in banning doctor-assisted suicides. By this time, the 15-month ban had already expired.

The court also declared that, even without a law, helping a suicide "may be prosecuted as a common-law felony" with a five-year prison term. "This," said Dr. Kevorkian, "is a perfect, clear manifestation of the existence of the inquisition in this state, no different from the medieval one." Attorney Fieger, who had beaten every criminal charge ever brought against the doctor, said "I am ready to take on 21 murder trials, starting tomorrow. No jury will ever convict Dr. Kevorkian. They couldn't even convict him of assisted suicide."

Assisted Suicide also Debated on West Coast

On May 2, 1994, a Michigan jury acquitted Kevorkian of criminal charges in assisting the suicide of Thomas Hyde, a young man suffering from Lou Gehrig's disease. The next day, in Seattle, U.S. District Judge Barbara J. Rothstein ruled in a suit brought by three terminally ill patients, five doctors, and Compassion in Dying—an organization that supports those who seek help to commit suicide. The judge found that a Washington state law that made helping a suicide a felony offense was unconstitutional. Under the 14th amendment to the U.S. Constitution, she decided that adults who are terminally ill and mentally competent have a right to doctor-assisted suicide. The Ninth U.S. Circuit Court of Appeals overturned the ruling. The U.S. Supreme Court, finding that Compassion in Dying arguments were not convincing, upheld the Ninth Circuit Court decision.

Election day, November 8, 1994, found Oregon voters in favor of a law permitting doctors to prescribe lethal drugs to terminally ill patients who ask for them. Scheduled to take effect December 8, the law required the patient to ask for the prescription at least twice orally and once in writing, with a lapse of at least 15 days between the first request and the prescription date. The new law was immediately challenged by a coalition of patients, doctors, and other healthcare providers. U.S. District Judge Michael Hogan put the law on hold while its constitutional aspects could be reviewed. The law was upheld.

From *60 Minutes* to 10–25 Years

By 1999, it was estimated that Kevorkian had assisted in at least 130 suicides over a nine year period of time. Murder charges against him had been thrown out of court twice. Three charges of assisted suicide had come to trial, with acquittals resulting each time. A fourth had ended in a mistrial. In every case, the jury had decided in his favor based on heart-wrenching testimony depicting the pain and agony of those Kevorkian felt compelled to help die. In 1997, as he took office, Oakland County prosecutor David Gorcyca had dropped 13 of the charges filed by his predecessor Richard Thompson, because he found there was not enough evidence to bring the cases to trial successfully.

On September 17, 1998, Kevorkian, apparently determined to force society to deal with the issue of assisted suicide, videotaped the death of 52-year-old Thomas Youk, who was severely incapacitated with Lou Gehrig's disease. But this time, rather than setting up a device to allow Youk to trigger his own death, Kevorkian himself injected a drug into Youk's veins. He then offered the videotape to the CBS *60 Minutes* television program, which aired it in November.

Prosecutor David Gorcyca pounced on the case, charging Kevorkian with first-degree murder, assisted suicide, and delivering a controlled substance (being no longer certified as a doctor, Kevorkian could not legally prescribe or administer drugs). When Kevorkian insisted on acting as his own lawyer, Geoffrey Fieger stepped down succeeded by his associate, David Gorosh.

By the beginning of the trial in March 22, 1999, the prosecutors, hoping to avoid jury-swaying depictions of pain and suffering, withdrew the assisted-suicide charge. Instead, the jury listened to Kevorkian testify that his goal was not to commit murder but to gain a forum for assisted suicide. It viewed the *60 Minutes* videotape but heard from only three witnesses: two policemen (respondents to the 911 call about Youk's death) and Oakland County Medical Examiner Dr. L.J. Dragovic, who said an injection of potassium chloride caused Youk's heart to stop.

Judge Jessica Cooper denied Kevorkian's motion to allow relatives of Youk to testify that the death was a mercy killing. She advised the jury it could return a verdict of first-degree or second-degree murder or manslaughter. As the jury deliberated, Kevorkian withdrew as his own attorney. On Friday, March 26, the former doctor was found guilty of second-degree murder and of delivering a controlled substance.

Cooper sentenced the 71-year-old to 10–25 years in jail, with a concurrent of 3 to 7 years on the drug charge. "You had the audacity to go on national television, show the world what you did, and dare the legal system to stop you," she told the defendant. "Well, sir, consider yourself stopped."

Saying that he had been ill-advised by Gorosh in presenting his defense, Kevorkian requested a new trial. It was refused. As he entered Oaks Correctional Facility as prisoner no. 284797, the state of Michigan, which can legally take up to 90 percent of a prisoner's assets to pay for living costs, siezed a lump sum of $31,155 from Kevorkian's bank account and $364.50 per month from his hospital pension. He was allowed to keep some $77,000 in his legal defense fund.

—Bernard Ryan, Jr.

Suggestions for Further Reading

Brovins, Joan, and Thomas H. Oehmke. *Dr. Death: Dr. Jack Kevorkian's Rx: Death.* Hollywood, Fla.: Lifetime Books, 1993.

Brown, Judy. *The Choice: Seasons of Loss and Renewal after a Father's Decision to Die.* Berkeley, Calif.: Conari, 1995.

Dzwonkowski, Ron, ed. *The Suicide Machine: Understanding Jack Kevorkian, the People Who Came to Him, and the Issue of Assisted Suicide.* Detroit: Detroit Free Press, 1997.

Kevorkian, Jack. *Prescription: Medicide: The Goodness of Planned Death.* Amherst: N.Y.: Prometheus, 1991.

Loving, Carol. *My Son, My Sorrow.* Far Hills, N.J.: New Horizon, 1998.

Paul Cox Trials: 1994

Defendant: Paul Cox **Crime Charged:** Murder
Chief Defense Lawyer: Andrew A. Rubin **Chief Prosecutor:** George L.
Bolen **Judge:** James R. Cowhey **Place:** White Plains, New York
Dates of Trials: First trial: June 1994; second trial: November–December
1994 **Verdicts: First trial:** Mistrial/hung jury; second trial: Guilty of
manslaughter **Sentence:** 16–50 years imprisonment

SIGNIFICANCE

The courts refusal in the Paul Cox trials to extend the privilege of confidential
communications to members of self-help groups such as Alcoholics Anonymous
raised questions about such groups' need for the privilege at a time when they
were becoming increasingly important social forces.

On December 31, 1988, 21-year-old Paul Cox sat drinking with friends in
Garry's Barleycorn Bar in New Rochelle, New York. After downing several
pitchers of beer and mixed drinks, the group went for a drive that ended in an
accident. Cox then walked to his nearby childhood home in Larchmont, which
now belonged to Shanta Chervu and her husband, Lakshman Rao Chervu, both
physicians. Cox broke a window, entered the house, and stabbed both of the
Chervus to death. He left many fingerprints, but because he didn't have a
criminal record the police could not match them with any on file. The double
murder remained a mystery for four years.

Cox, meanwhile, joined Alcoholics Anonymous (AA) and began to follow
its Twelve-Step program, the fifth of which calls for an admission "to God, to
ourselves and to another human being the exact nature of our wrongs." Soon
Cox started to tell fellow members that he thought he might be responsible for
the Chervu killings.

"He told me," one man later said, that "he had gone to a house and killed
two people while they slept." Cox's girlfriend, herself an AA member, gave a
similar account. " 'I don't remember this night,' " she reported him as saying. " 'I
don't know what happened. I don't know what went on. But I might have done
it.' "

Cox said that he had once been diagnosed with patricidal and matricidal
tendencies, and that he feared that he had mistaken the Chervus for his parents

since they were sleeping in his parents' old bedroom. He also recalled finding a bloody knife a few weeks after the murders and throwing it into Long Island Sound.

Confidentiality is crucial in AA meetings. Without it, members would not freely confess their wrongdoings, an important part of the Twelve-Step program. But in 1993, some members contacted the police about what they had been told. As a consequence, Cox was indicted for second-degree murder.

Paul Cox during his trial for murdering two doctors in a drunken haze. (AP/ Wide World Photos)

A Confidantes Testify against Cox

Cox's first trial took place in June 1994. Prosecutor George L. Bolen had a fairly easy case; Cox had admitted his guilt. Cox's attorney, Andrew A. Rubin, meanwhile argued that Cox had been psychotic and temporarily insane during the episode, and thus was not responsible for his actions. Rubin also tried to quash Cox's fellow AA members' testimony, arguing that they should have a legal privilege against testifying about their comembers similar to that of clerics and psychotherapists. AA is to an alcoholic, Rubin maintained, as a priest is to a penitent or a psychologist to a patient. Without a legal guarantee of confidentiality, a person would not speak freely and the meeting would be pointless.

Ultimately, trial judge James Cowhey denied Rubin's motion and allowed the testimony to be admitted. Seven AA members, whose identity, in an ironic twist, the court kept secret, testified under subpoena that they had heard Cox confess to the killings. Despite this evidence, the jury deadlocked at 11 to 1 in favor of a murder conviction.

The government tried Cox for murder again in November 1994 with Judge Cowhey again presiding. Once more Rubin tried to block the admission of the AA members' testimony as evidence, but, as before, Cowhey allowed it. This time the jury convicted Cox of manslaughter; Cowhey sentenced him to 16–50 years in prison.

Although AA took no official position in the Paul Cox case, the court's verdict angered many AA members and other self-help (also known as mutual-aid) groups, and some legal scholars criticized the policy of restricting the privilege against testifying.

"It doesn't seem right," one attorney noted. "It's like he's being punished for recovering." One priest who was also an AA member voiced a widespread concern when he noted that "once you make Alcoholics Anonymous people talk about one thing, what is to stop the authorities from deciding that they can come around for anything?" Another self-help member stated, "This just points out another middle-class hypocrisy—money buys privacy. . . . If you have the money, you can have the protection. A lot of people . . . can't afford a fancy shrink."

The Paul Cox case raised troubling questions about how the legal system should handle confessions that occur in self-help groups at a time when those groups were active and successful. The traditional law of confidentiality is relatively easy to understand and appreciate, but having it applied in such circumstances could lead to a legal quagmire. On the other hand, many people felt that the court's refusal to extend the privilege in this instance was both unjust and a danger to the future success of these programs.

—Buckner F. Melton, Jr.

Suggestions for Further Reading

Reed, Thomas J. "The Futile Fifth Step: Compulsory Disclosure of Confidential Communications among Alcoholics Anonymous Members." *Saint John's Law Review* (Fall 1996): 693–753.

Baby Maranda Case: 1994

Defendant: Jennifer Ireland **Plaintiff:** Steven Smith
Plaintiff Claim: Custody of his daughter, Maranda
Chief Defense Lawyer: Julie Field **Chief Lawyer for Plaintiff:** Sharon-Lee
Edwards **Judge:** Raymond R. Cashen **Place:** Macomb County, Michigan
Date of Trial: June 27, 1994 **Decision:** Custody was granted to Steven
Smith

SIGNIFICANCE

The judge's surprising decision granting custody of Baby Maranda to her father seemed to be a setback for single women struggling to provide a decent education for themselves as well as maintain a family.

Early in the summer of 1990, Jennifer Ireland of Harrison Township, Michigan, was just 15 years old. Her new boyfriend, Steven Smith, was 16. After they dated for two months, they became sexually intimate. Soon Jennifer thought she might be pregnant and thought she should take a home pregnancy test. The result was positive. "I felt like this was just a dream, and I was going to wake up, and it was all going to go away," she said later. "I was a straight-A student, never did anything wrong. This was not happening to me."

Smith couldn't believe it either. After thinking it over for four days, he told Jennifer he didn't have time for a girlfriend. As a star football player, he had to concentrate on the coming season. They agreed that she would have an abortion.

At an abortion clinic two months later, Jennifer, a Roman Catholic, changed her mind. "I saw all these girls talking about it like it was no big deal," she later admitted, "but I started thinking that I was going to burn in hell for even considering this. So I left."

Although most of Steve Smith's and Jennifer Ireland's schoolmates knew who the father-to-be was, Steve steered clear of Jennifer during her pregnancy. When Maranda Kate Ireland Smith was born on April 22, 1991, he went to the hospital to see her and her now 16-year-old mother, but refused to hold the baby. Putting Maranda in foster care for three weeks, Jennifer thought about adoption. She decided to raise the child herself. Her mother, a divorced 46-year-old who was a professional nanny, and her 13-year-old sister agreed to help.

Steve Smith was furious. "He said he didn't want her," reported Jennifer, "and I shouldn't want her. He said I was doing the worst thing in the world."

Jennifer had missed two months of her sophomore year in high school. But now, with her mother and sister baby-sitting, she concentrated on her studies and finished in June 1991 with a 3.98 grade point average.

For about a year, Maranda's father stayed away. Then he began to show up to see her more and more often. During this time, he provided no financial support. Finally, Jennifer filed for child support, but none was forthcoming.

In January 1993, Jennifer obtained a court order garnishing $62 a week from Smith's meager income as a high-school student doing odd jobs. However, he managed to have the child support payments cut to $12.

Alleging that Smith grabbed her by the shoulders, shook her, and shoved her into a wall during an argument over visitation rights on Christmas Eve 1992, Jennifer charged Maranda's father with assault. He countersued for custody of the toddler.

In June 1993 when Jennifer Ireland graduated from Cardinal Mooney Catholic High School in suburban Detroit, she stood third in her class. The University of Michigan awarded her $11,000 in scholarships as an entering freshman. She packed up Maranda, her toddler toys and clothing, and they headed for the college in Ann Arbor. There, using personal savings, Jennifer Ireland placed her child in a day-care center for 35 hours a week while she attended classes full time. The day-care facility was one recommended by the university.

In March 1994, Steve Smith's countersuit for custody came before Judge Raymond R. Cashen of Macomb County Circuit Court. In the hearing, Smith's lawyer, Sharon-Lee Edwards, attacked Jennifer Ireland's behavior as a mother. Her accusations included drug and alcohol abuse and sexual misconduct. Jennifer denied all such allegations.

Judge Cashen appointed two independent experts to appraise Maranda's situation. The Psychodiagnostic and Family Services Clinic found that Maranda looked to her mother for "guidance, discipline, and the necessities of life" and that she had a strong attachment to both parents. The Macomb County Friends of the Court, a social services agency that performed investigations related to court cases, found nothing to condemn in the environment in which Maranda was being raised. Both organizations recommended that the little girl stay with her mother. The judge himself observed that the three-year-old had lived all her life with her mother, who was her primary care giver, and that such a disruption of family life as a change of custody would be disturbing to her. However, the judge ruled on June 27, 1994, that Maranda should be handed over to her father because her mother had placed her in a licensed day-care facility for 35 hours a week in order to attend college classes. "There is no way," concluded the 69-year-old jurist, "that a single parent attending an academic program at an institution as prestigious as the University of Michigan can do justice to their [sic] studies and the raising of an infant child. A child gains the feeling of security, a safe place, by virtue of permanence." The judge added that he was skeptical about how the child's emotional well-being would be affected by the long-term impact of "strangers."

Child-care experts were astonished. "It was unusual," said Henry Baskin, who, as a state bar commissioner, had helped draft Michigan's child custody act, "for the court to ignore a recommendation from two separate agencies who concluded that the child should be with the mother."

In the same week that Judge Cashen's order was handed down, Smith was arraigned on Jennifer's charge of assault. The domestic violence was "not pertinent" to his decision, remarked Judge Cashen. "The parties in their youthful way apparently crashed or mauled one another," he said. "It is all superfluous." The judge also seemed unimpressed by the fact that Maranda's father had sought custody of her only after her mother pressed the domestic violence charge against him and hauled him into court for child support.

The household to which the judge consigned Maranda was that of Smith's parents, with whom he was living while attending Macomb Community College and working part-time cutting lawns. His homemaker mother would take care of the child—a provision, said the judge, that was better than having the child "supervised a great part of the time by strangers. Under the future plans of the father, the minor child will be raised and supervised by blood relatives."

The day after he ordered Maranda handed over to her father, Judge Cashen, himself a Roman Catholic who had seven children and 16 grandchildren, told a reporter that "family values" were his "whole background." The written opinion he sent down, he said, was based not on any allegations regarding behavior, but on the fact that the child was put in day care by the mother even though the father's mother was capable of taking care of her.

Within days, the American Civil Liberties Union (ACLU), the National Organization for Women (NOW), the United Auto Workers (UAW), and several other national groups filed a joint friend-of-the court brief on behalf of Jennifer Ireland. The New York Times ran a major editorial excoriating Judge Cashen. It concluded:

> "Judge Cashen's order . . . stands: an affront and threat to the millions of women for whom day care is the difference between ignorance and an education, poverty and a decent income, dependency and self-reliance. In stigmatizing Jennifer Ireland for her ambition and initiative, Judge Cashen stigmatizes all of them."

After considering the brief, the Michigan Court of Appeals delayed the Judge's order. On August 9, 1994, it granted a stay of the transfer of custody of baby Maranda pending review of the case. In November 1995, the Michigan Court of Appeals reversed the lower court's decision and gave custody of Maranda to Jennifer. 1n 1996, Jennifer dropped out of college to take care of her daughter and to prevent any further custody battles. She has taken classes on a part-time basis.

—Bernard Ryan, Jr.

Suggestions for Further Reading

Helton, Charmagne. "Mom Loses Custody Over Day Care." *USA Today* (July 27, 1994): 1.

Leavaitt, Paul. "Mom Can Keep Tot for Now." *USA Today* (August 8, 1994): 3.

Stone, Andrea. "Custody Cases: Growing Pains-Judges' Jobs Getting Trickier." *USA Today* (July 29, 1994): 3.

Paula Coughlin v. the Las Vegas Hilton: 1994

Defendant: Paula Coughlin   **Plaintiff:** The Las Vegas Hilton
Plaintiff Claim: That the Las Vegas Hilton failed to provide adequate security during the 1991 Tailhook convention   **Chief Defense Lawyer:** Eugene Walt
Chief Lawyer for Plaintiff: Dennis Schoville   **Judge:** Philip M. Pro
Place: Las Vegas, Nevada   **Date of Trial:** September 12–October 28, 1994
Verdict: Against the defendant, awarding the plaintiff $1.7 million in compensatory damages and $5 million in punitive damages. Later reduced to a total of $5.2. million

SIGNIFICANCE

The "Tailhook Scandal" revealed misconduct and sexual harassment on the part of Navy officers at a Las Vegas hotel to be so shocking as to require the intervention by President George Bush and the resignation of Navy Secretary H. Lawrence Garrett. The high public regard for navy officers was severely damaged by the incident and prompted congressional hearings into discrimination against women in the military.

Navy Lieutenant Paula Coughlin was a 30-year-old helicopter pilot when she went to the annual convention of the Tailhook Association at the Las Vegas, Nevada, Hilton Hotel in September 1991. Tailhook was a private organization of active and retired Navy and Marine Corps fliers. Its name came from a device at the rear of a Navy plane that hooks onto a braking cable on the flight deck of an aircraft carrier as the plane lands.

After the weekend convention, Lieutenant Coughlin filed an official complaint, through Navy channels, saying that she had been sexually abused when she found herself "running a gauntlet" of dozens of officers with groping hands in a third-floor corridor of the hotel. At the same time, the Las Vegas Hilton billed the Navy for $23,000 worth of damages suffered during Tailhook's wild party.

With the whistle blown, the Navy announced, on October 30, that it was breaking all ties with Tailhook. It began looking into similar allegations made by several other women.

Seven months later, on May 1, 1992, separate reports were made public by the Naval Investigative Service and the Navy Inspector General. More than 1,500 people who had attended the convention had been interviewed. Fourteen female naval officers and 12 female civilians reported sexual abuse. The convention was described as a beehive of hospitality suites in which alcohol was heavily consumed while the cavorting of nude exotic dancers was punctuated by the screening of pornographic films. Navy Secretary H. Lawrence Garrett III immediately ordered the Navy and Marine Corps to begin disciplinary action against nearly 70 officers, including six who were accused of obstructing the inquiries and 57 suspected of participating in the "gauntlet."

Shortly thereafter, a supplemental report revealed that Secretary Garrett, himself, had been seen in one of the hospitality suites where the scandalous activities had occurred. The Defense Department's Inspector General took over the investigation, Tailhook canceled its 1992 convention, and Admiral Frank B. Kelso, Chief of Naval Operations, promised a service-wide program to train Navy personnel about sexual harassment issues. Admiral Kelso also admitted that he had attended the 1991 convention, but said he "didn't see anything untoward."

The President is Briefed on the Situation

It was not until June 26, 1992, that Defense Secretary Richard B. Cheney briefed President George Bush on the reports. The President invited Lieutenant Coughlin to the White House that day to hear her description of an experience she said left her "the most frightened I've ever been." Within hours, Secretary Garrett resigned. Accepting the resignation that evening, the President did not include the "thank you" usually given a high official who resigns. Three days later, the Appropriations Committee of the U.S. House of Representatives, protesting the "arrogance and obstruction" of the Navy, cut from its defense spending bill the funds for some 10,000 active-duty administrative personnel, and the Armed Services Committee of the U.S. Senate blocked the approval of nearly 4,500 Navy and Marine promotions and transfers.

On July 29 the Los Angeles Times reported that aviators at the Miramar Naval Air Station near San Diego, California, had turned over to the Defense Department Inspector General's Office five rolls of film showing a teenage girl, apparently drunk, being stripped of her clothing by a crowd of rowdy Navy and Marine fliers in the gauntlet corridor at the 1991 Las Vegas Tailhook convention.

The next day, the U.S. House of Representatives Armed Services Committee held a hearing on discrimination against women in the military. Four members of the Joint Chiefs of Staff testified. Admiral Kelso, Chief of Naval Operations, admitted that the Navy had not paid attention to earlier evidence that women in the service were being mistreated.

On April 23, 1993, Pentagon Inspector General Derek J. Vander Schaaf released the Defense Department's three-hundred-page report on the Tailhook convention. Among the subheads of chapters in the report were "Streaking,"

"Mooning," "Butt Biting," "Pornography," "Public and Paid Sex," and "Ballwalking." Citing "the culmination of a long-term failure of leadership in naval aviation," it said that 117 officers were "implicated in one or more incidents of indecent assault, indecent exposure, conduct unbecoming an officer or failure to act in a proper leadership capacity." Of the 117 officers, the report stated that 23 were involved in indecent assaults and 23 in indecent exposure, while 51 lied to investigators. All faced disciplinary action. In addition, the report concluded that "the number of individuals involved in all types of misconduct or other inappropriate behavior" was "more widespread than these figures would suggest." Altogether, it said, several hundred officers concealed information so that "collective 'stonewalling' significantly increased the difficulty of the investigation."

Report Cites 90 Victims

The 90 victims of assault included 7 servicemen, 49 civilian women, 22 servicewomen, 6 government employees, and the wives of 6 conventioneers. According to the report, misbehavior was traditional in "a type of 'free-fire zone'" at the convention, with the fliers acting "indiscriminately and without fear of censure or retribution in matters of sexual conduct and drunkenness." Furthermore, it noted, previous conventions and the triumphs of the Persian Gulf War earlier in 1991 had set up a sort of "can top this" atmosphere at the convention.

The Navy temporarily reassigned six senior officers (all captains and commanders) to desk duty ashore, but it took no disciplinary action against them, while Vice Admiral J. Paul Reason, commander of the Atlantic surface fleet, reviewed the report. A week later, the admiral docked $1,000 from the pay of each of 10 officers—1 lieutenant commander, 2 junior-grade lieutenants, and 7 lieutenants—and gave them letters of admonition.

In a pre-trial hearing in a Marine courtroom in Quantico, Virginia, on August 17, 1993, Lieutenant Coughlin faced Captain Gregory Bonam, the pilot she had recognized, both from a photograph and in a lineup, as her chief molester in the gauntlet. Bonam's lawyer produced a photograph, purportedly snapped the night of the gauntlet, that showed him wearing not the burnt orange T-shirt that Coughlin had sworn she saw him in but a shirt with green and black stripes. No witness testified as to when the picture was taken. Character witnesses backed him as "very moral" and a "very good person." The Marine judge saw no need for a trial.

Six months later, in February 1994, after examining 140 cases of misconduct, the Navy closed the investigation of Tailhook. After a pre- trial hearing, Captain William T. Vest, Jr., a Navy judge, ruled that Admiral Kelso had used his influence as Chief of Naval Operations "in a manner designed to shield his personal involvement in Tailhook." Under oath, the admiral and three of his aides had testified that he did not witness the gauntlet assaults and that he was nowhere near them. But, said Vest, testimony of more than a dozen witnesses proved that the admiral—despite his denial—was present at some of Tailhook's wildest parties and made no effort to stop the sexual assaults. Furthermore, Vest added, Tailhook's reputation for including prostitutes, strippers, porn films, and plenty of alcohol in its festivities should have alerted the admiral that there might be trouble. Having put the blame on Admiral Kelso's shoulders, Vest concluded that charges against three of Kelso's subordinates should be dropped. Since Kelso's retirement was imminent further action was not taken. No trial followed the pre-trial hearing.

The U.S. Senate has the responsibility of approving the retirement rank and pensions of top military officers. By law, Admiral Kelso was entitled to retire with a two-star rank and a $67,000 annual pension. But, following tradition, the Senate's Armed Services Committee voted him four stars and $81,000 a year. For the full Senate's vote on April 19, nine Congresswomen, led by Representative Pat Schroeder (D-Colo.), marched onto the Senate floor to join the seven female Senators (five Democrats and two Republicans) who opposed the committee's recommendation. The vote was 54–43 in favor of Kelso.

Coughlin Sues Hilton

With the investigation closed, Lieutenant Paula Coughlin sued both the Tailhook Association and the Las Vegas Hilton for compensatory damages for emotional distress. Then, citing emotional stress brought on by the lawsuits, and writing that "the covert attacks on me that followed have stripped me of my ability to serve," she resigned from the Navy on February 7, 1994. Her resignation letter made note of a newsletter titled The Gauntlet put out by former Navy pilots who used the pseudonym, "Paul A. Coffin."

On September 8, 1994, the Tailhook Association settled for an undisclosed amount. Four days later, the Hilton suit opened in the Las Vegas courtroom of Judge Philip M. Pro of the Federal District Court before a jury of four men and four women.

During a seven-week trial, Coughlin accused the Hilton Hotels Corporation and its subsidiaries of failing to set up proper security for the Tailhook convention, despite the fact that they had hosted 19 earlier Tailhooks, at many of which drunkenness and debauchery had been exhibited. Witnesses testified that during at least one convention, Hilton security guards found a teenage girl, in a Tailhook hospitality suite, nude from the waist down while in a drunken stupor.

Coughlin's lead lawyer, Dennis Schoville, argued that Tailhook had changed his client's life by bringing on a serious post-traumatic stress disorder. Testimony by psychiatrists and psychologists on both sides observed that she was deeply depressed and Coughlin herself testified that she had become suicidal as a result of the Las Vegas experience.

Hilton Defense Attorney Eugene Walt, however, produced a deposition made in August 1993 by Navy Lieutenant Roland Diaz that said Lieutenant Coughlin had allowed him to shave her legs while she was in uniform the night before she was assaulted in the gauntlet. Coughlin emphatically denied the allegation. Her attorney commented that the Diaz testimony was a setup and that the defense lawyers would do almost anything to win, including "destroying her reputation."

Walt admitted that the gauntlet incident had occurred but said it was overdramatized, and he argued that the post-traumatic stress "appears to be mild and closer to anger and less to a victim who has been sexually molested." Attorney Schoville ridiculed Walt's use of the word "mild," saying, "She feels used and dirty," and implored the jury to award his client $5–$10 million in damages.

As Coughlin ended her testimony, Attorney Walt questioned why she had resigned from the Navy after agreeing in April 1992 to re-enlist for at least six years, enabling her to earn a bonus of $60,750. "I was drummed out of the Navy," she replied.

On October 28, 1994, its second day of deliberation, the jury found the Las Vegas Hilton negligent in failing to provide adequate security during the 1991 Tailhook convention. It awarded the former Navy lieutenant $1.7 million in compensatory damages for emotional distress and $5 million in punitive damages.

Almost six months later, on March 9, 1995, Judge Pro reduced the award. Revealing that the Tailhook Association's settlement, which had not been disclosed in September, was $400,000, the judge ruled that the amount must be subtracted from the $1.7 million compensatory-damages award. Furthermore, citing Nevada law that limits punitive damages to three times compensatory damages, Judge Pro cut the punitive award to $3.9 million. Thus Coughlin's total award stood at $5.2 million. The Las Vegas Hilton and its parent, the Hilton Hotels Corporation appealed the judgment; however, an appeals court upheld both the decision and the award in 1997.

The reputation of the Tailhook Association was damaged but not totally destroyed by the scandal. As the 1990s came to an end, the navy slowly began the process of possibly restoring ties with Tailhook. The navy sought complete guarantees from Tailhook that no sexual misconduct would ever happen again. In early January 2000, satisifed with the organization's public assurances, the navy officially restored ties to the Tailhook Association.

—Bernard Ryan, Jr.

Suggestions for Further Reading

DeArmond, Michelle. "Tailhook Whistleblower Awarded $5 million in Punitive Damages." *Detroit News* (October 29, 1994): A1.

LaCayo, Richard. "Lost in the Fun House." *Time* (February 21, 1994): 45.

Myers, Steven Lee. "8 Years Later, Navy Restores Official Ties to Tailhook." *New York Times* (January 20, 2000): A13.

Florida v. Hill: 1994

Defendant: Paul J. Hill   **Crimes Charged:** Murder, attempted murder, and shooting at an occupied vehicle   **Chief Defense Lawyer:** Paul Hill
Chief Prosecutor: James R. Murray   **Judge:** Frank L. Bell
Place: Pensacola, Florida   **Dates of Trial:** October 31–November 3, 1994
Verdict: Guilty of all charges   **Sentence:** Death by electrocution

SIGNIFICANCE

Paul Hill was the first anti-abortion activist sentenced to die for murdering a doctor who performed abortions. His case also highlighted the growing willingness of some pro-life advocates to use violence to achieve their goal of outlawing abortion.

Protests outside abortion clinics became a common sight during the 1980s and 1990s. Pro-life activists took their message to the streets, trying to dissuade young mothers from having abortions and challenging the morality of the procedure. Some activists also began to target doctors who performed abortions, harassing them or threatening their safety. This new tactic in the anti-abortion movement became extreme in 1993, when 32-year-old Michael Griffin murdered Doctor David Gunn outside a Pensacola, Florida, abortion clinic. When Griffin's trial began in February 1994, one of his most ardent supporters was Paul Hill.

A former Presbyterian minister, Hill had recently joined a radical faction of the pro-life forces that believed that killing doctors who performed abortions was justified in God's eyes. After an appearance on the *Donahue* television show, Hill became the most visible disciple of this faith-based defense of murder. Hill wrote extensively on the issue and called extreme anti-abortion violence "defensive action" to save the unborn. At Griffin's murder trial, Hill carried a sign that summed up his philosophy: "Execute murderers, abortionists, accessories."

Killing at the Clinic

In the following months, Hill became a familiar figure at Pensacola's Ladies Center Clinic, where abortions were performed. As doctors and clinicians worked inside, Hill, using a child's voice, sometimes screamed "Mommy,

Mommy, don't murder me!" Clinic workers wanted Hill arrested under a new federal law, the Freedom of Access to Clinic Entrance (FACE) Act. The law had been passed in the wake of the 1993 Gunn killing. The Justice Department, however, was not willing to use Hill's actions as the first court test of FACE. After another protest, Hill was arrested by local authorities for disturbing the peace, but once again federal officials declined to prosecute under FACE.

On July 29, 1994, Hill returned to the Ladies Center Clinic. This time he did more than shout. At about 7:30 A.M., Dr. John Britton arrived at the clinic with two escorts, 74-year-old Jim Barrett and his 68-year-old wife, June. Jim Barrett was acting as a bodyguard for Dr. Britton, 69, who performed abortions at various clinics in northern Florida including the Pensacola Ladies Center Clinic. As the three prepared to leave their vehicle, Hill pulled out a newly purchased Mossberg shotgun. Hill shot and killed Jim Barrett, reloaded, then fired again, killing Dr. Britton and severely wounding Mrs. Barrett. Hill then put down his gun and walked away. Moments later, he offered no resistance when police apprehended him. Hill told the officers, "I know one thing. No innocent babies are going to be killed in that clinic today."

Anti-abortion activist Paul Hill. (AP/Wide World Photos)

Two Fast Trials

Hill's actions prompted the FBI to investigate whether the growing anti-abortion violence was part of a larger conspiracy. The Britton/Barrett murders also led to Hill's arrest under FACE, as well as state charges of murder, attempted murder, and shooting into an occupied vehicle.

Hill's federal trial began in October 1994, and he chose to act as his own attorney. The judge denied Hill's attempt to argue that the murders were justifiable homicides to prevent the murder of unborn children. Stripped of his defense, Hill did not call or cross-examine any witnesses. He was subsequently convicted and sentenced to life in prison. However, Hill faced an even stiffer sentence on the state charges—the death penalty.

His state trial drew the most public attention. As in the first trial, Hill represented himself and again tried to introduce a defense of justifiable homicide. Judge Frank Bell could only rule against him, since abortion is a legal procedure. Once again, Hill did not call any witnesses or offer any other defense. The trial ran just three days, and the jury needed only 20 minutes to convict him on two counts of first-degree murder as well as the other two charges.

After the trial, federal prosecutors said they would allow the state's punishment to take precedence over Hill's sentence for the FACE conviction. On November 3, the jury recommended that Hill die in the electric chair. Judge Bell, noting that Hill had no sense of remorse and that he had "look [ed] at what he accomplished with pride and satisfaction," agreed with the sentence.

Appeals for a "Martyr"

Under Florida law, Hill's sentence was automatically appealed to the Florida Supreme Court. Hill again wanted to act as his own attorney during this process, but the Florida Supreme Court ruled against him. At one point, Hill said he did not want to appeal the conviction at all, and noted that if he were executed, "I think you could justifiably call me a martyr." In 1997, the Florida high court unanimously upheld Hill's state conviction, and as of this writing he is awaiting execution on Florida's Death Row.

Some pro-choice forces believed that Hill's death sentence would deter future acts of violence against abortion providers. But the attacks continued, including the murder of two Boston abortion clinic workers in December 1994 and bombing attacks against clinics in various cities, including Atlanta and Birmingham. Pro-choice forces have called for increased prosecutions under FACE and more police protection of clinics. Supporters of abortion rights were also disappointed in 1996, when the FBI decided the anti-abortion violence was not part of a vast conspiracy. In the meantime, some pro-life groups have disavowed the use of extreme violence to espouse their cause.

— Michael Burgan

Suggestions for Further Reading

"Death Sentence for Abortion-Doc Killer." *Newsday* (December 7, 1994): A7.

"Florida High Court Upholds Death for Abortion Shooter." *Reuters* (March 6, 1997).

Kuntz, Tom. "From Thought to Deed: In the Mind of a Killer Who Says He Served God." *New York Times* (September 24, 1995): IV, 7.

Navarro, Mireya. "Abortion Foe Is Guilty of Murder in Deaths of Two at a Florida Clinic." *New York Times* (November 3, 1994): A1.

Risen, James and Judy L. Thomas. *Wrath of Angels: The American Abortion War.* New York: BasicBooks, 1998.

Tupac Shakur Trial: 1994–95

Defendants: Tupac Shakur and Charles Fuller   **Crimes Charged:** Sexual abuse, sodomy, and illegal possession of a firearm
Chief Defense Lawyer: Michael Warren   **Chief Prosecutor:** Francine James
Judge: Daniel P. Fitzgerald   **Place:** New York, New York
Dates of Trial: November–December 1994   **Verdict:** Guilty of sexual abuse; acquitted on the two other charges   **Sentence:** Shakur: 18 months to 4 and one-half years imprisonment; Fuller: 4 months imprisonment and 5 years probation

SIGNIFICANCE
To many, the rape trial of Tupac Shakur was proof that "gangsta' rap" promoted violence and that it also demeaned women.

"**G**angsta' rap," as its performers and aficionados call it, is a rhythmic, chantlike musical genre with lyrics that often glorify guns, drugs, and violence. During the peak of its popularity in the early to mid-1990s, one of the most popular "gangsta rappers" was Tupac Shakur. Before his violent death in 1996, Shakur was known to his fans as the king of "gangsta rap."

Almost from the time he first arrived on the music scene in the early 1990s, critics of Shakur's music claimed that his lyrics encouraged violence. As proof, these critics cited a case in which a young man gunned down a Texas state trooper and later told authorities that Shakur's music had been his inspiration. Running for reelection in 1992, Vice President Dan Quayle urged record stores to stop selling Shakur's album *2Pacalypse Now* on the ground that its lyrics condoned violence against the police. Although a number of stores agreed, Shakur's fans continued to buy his music. His popularity as a rapper led to several roles in movies, some of which received critical acclaim.

Whether out of personal inclination or a shrewd publicity sense, Shakur reveled in his bad-boy reputation, once describing himself as the "hardest prick out there" and having the words "thug life" tattooed across his chest. Dismissing the critics, Shakur and his defenders argued that his music was merely a reflection of the cruel reality of life in America's inner cities.

Whether Shakur's music was inspired by or instead determined the course of his life will never be known for sure. What is known is that Shakur eventually lived out the harshness of his lyrics. In 1992, he had the first of several highly publicized and increasingly serious run-ins with the law. He was cleared of charges arising out of a 1993 gunfight with two off-duty Atlanta, Georgia, police officers, but was convicted in 1994 of attacking a man with a baseball bat at a 1993 Michigan State University concert.

Rap Star Tried on Sex Charges

In November 1993, Shakur was arrested after a 19-year-old fan reported to police that she had been with the performer in a New York hotel room when several of his friends came in and, led by Shakur, forced her to perform oral sex on them. Shakur and his road manager, Charles Fuller, were taken into custody and charged with three counts of first-degree sexual abuse, sodomy, and illegal possession of a firearm after police found two guns in the hotel room. (One of the other two men involved was not apprehended, and the fourth eventually faced a separate trial.)

From the beginning of Shakur's trial, which began almost one year after the alleged incident had taken place, everyone involved seemed to expect a sleazy and dramatic courtroom battle. Justice Daniel P. Fitzgerald removed two jurors because they had been overheard voicing their disgust with the defendant and his music. Replacing the two jurors was a minor procedural hurdle for the court, but it was an omen of things to come.

Assistant District Attorney Francine James began the state's case against Shakur by calling the accuser to the stand. (As is often the case in rape or sexual assault cases,

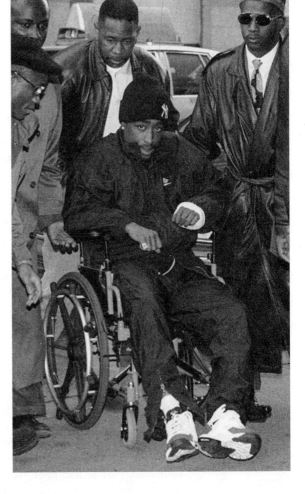

Tupac Shakur, injured in a shooting, arrives at court for his trial. (AP/Wide World Photos)

the media did not report the victim's name to protect her privacy.) She told the jury that she had met Shakur at a Manhattan nightclub several days before the alleged attack. During this first encounter, she acknowledged performing oral sex on Shakur, just half an hour after having met him. Later, the two returned to Shakur's hotel suite for the night. She testified that the next day she called and left a message on his voice mail complimenting him on his sexual prowess from the night before.

Four days after this first encounter, she returned to Shakur's hotel suite to retrieve something she had left there. She testified that she and Shakur had been in his room kissing when three of his friends burst in and attacked her. According to her version of events, Shakur grabbed her by the hair and began tearing her clothes off, while the other three fondled her. Earlier, in a statement given to prosecutors, she had quoted Shakur as telling her that she was "a reward for his friends" and that "millions of other women would be happy to be in her situation." During cross-examination defense lawyer Michael Warren tried to discredit the alleged victim's story, insinuating to the jury that it had been a consensual encounter with jealousy as the motive.

The defense called only one witness to the stand, Shakur's publicist, Talibah Mbonisi. She testified that on the night in question she had returned to the hotel suite and was told that Shakur was with a woman; she heard no noises coming from the adjoining room. Some time later, according to her testimony, he came in and was talking to her when the victim burst in and demanded to know who he was with and why had he just had sex with her if he had someone else waiting for him.

Shakur later told reporters that his accuser was out to get him because she had seen him with another woman. Warren used the same theory in his argument to the jury, contending that the second sexual encounter with the rap star was as consensual as the first and that the allegations were made to punish Shakur for spurning her for someone else.

After both sides finished presenting their arguments, the judge charged the jury, defining for them the elements necessary for each offense to be valid, providing the definition of "beyond a reasonable doubt," and giving them the parameters within which they were required to make their decision. The judge sequestered the jury during their deliberations, so they were unaware of the next event to take place during the trial.

Shakur Shot During Trial

One day after the jury began deliberating the verdict, Shakur and Fuller were entering a recording studio shortly after midnight when they were approached by several men with guns. The robbers ordered the men to give them all their jewelry and to lie on the ground. When Shakur reportedly refused, one of the gunmen shot him five times, and the robbers made off with $40,000 worth of jewelry that he had been wearing. The defendant was taken to the hospital, treated, and held for observation.

Against his doctor's wishes, Shakur left the hospital soon after surgery and, wearing a knit Yankees baseball hat pulled over the top of his heavily bandaged head, returned to the courtroom in a wheelchair. If jury members were startled or curious about the sudden change in the defendant's appearance, Justice Fitzgerald left them to puzzle it out for themselves.

Shakur's courtroom appearance was brief; he was taken back to the hospital for further treatment and was there when the jury rendered its opinion. After only three days of deliberation the jury returned to the courtroom with its verdict: Shakur and codefendant Fuller were found guilty of sexual abuse and acquitted on the other charges. Apparently, the jury had not been convinced that sodomy or illegal possession of firearms had been proven beyond a reasonable doubt.

Shakur's attorney claimed to be "ecstatic" that the rap star had been acquitted on the more serious charges, but quickly added that the defense would appeal the one guilty verdict. One of the grounds for an appeal had been given to the defense several hours before the verdict was reached when James revealed to the court and defense counsel that the prosecution had inadvertently withheld evidence from the defense—photographs of the victim's chest taken the day after the alleged attack had been misfiled and were not found until the morning of the disclosure. While withheld evidence is often sufficient grounds to move for a mistrial, the defense decided to wait until the verdict was announced before determining what action to take.

Judge Imposes Prison Sentence

The sentencing took place on February 8, 1995, and it was no less dramatic than the trial. The proceedings began with the victim explaining how the crime had affected her physically, emotionally, and psychologically.

"He took advantage of his stardom to abuse me and betray my trust," she declared. Since the attack, she said, she had been turned into the villain while Shakur "has been glorified by his peers and fans."

Shakur stared intently at his accuser while she spoke. When she finished, he stood and, with tears in his eyes, apologized, but it wasn't clear for what. "I'm not apologizing for a crime," he declared. "I hope in time you'll come forth and tell the truth—I am innocent."

Addressing Judge Fitzgerald before sentencing, Shakur virtually accused him and the court system of racism. "You never looked into my eyes. You never used the wisdom of Solomon. I always felt you had something against me."

Then, in an about-face, he addressed the youth of America. "I got so involved in my career that I didn't see this coming. I have no shame, I don't feel shame." This statement received a positive response from the many fans in attendance. At one point, a sheriff had to order a young woman back to her seat after she leaned over the railing and kissed the rap star on the cheek.

Justice Fitzgerald then addressed Shakur, "This was an act of brutal violence against a helpless woman." And with that he sentenced Shakur to 18 months to four and one-half years in prison. Noting that Fuller had no criminal record and that Shakur had been the instigator of the attack, Fitzgerald sentenced Fuller to four months in jail and five years probation.

Shakur served nearly eight months in prison and was released in October 1995. His trial and conviction was not a liability for Shakur's career, however. Soon after his release, Shakur was given acting roles in two films, *Gridlock'd and Gang Related*—both of which would be released after his death. The first album released after his prison term, *All Eyez on Me*, debuted at number 1 on the *Billboard* album charts, and went on to sell over five million copies.

Shakur's musical and acting careers appeared to be on the rise. Then, on September 7, 1996, he was shot in Las Vegas, Nevada, shortly after leaving a Mike Tyson fight. He would later die of his wounds on September 13. Although the shooting took place on the very public Las Vegas main strip, no one has ever been arrested for his murder.

— Penelope Petzold and Ron Formica

Suggestions for Further Reading

Alexander, Frank, and Heide Sigmund Cuda. *Got Your Back: My Life in Tupac's Last Year*. New York: St. Martin's Press, 1998.

Scott, Cathy. *The Killing of Tupac Shakur*. Las Vegas: Huntington Press, 1997.

White, Armond. *Rebel for the Hell of It: The Life of Tupac Shakur*. New York: Thunder's Mouth Press, 1997.

Zion v. New York Hospital: 1994–95

Plaintiff: Sidney E. Zion **Defendants:** The New York Hospital, Maurice Leonard, M.D., Raymond Sherman, M.D., Gregg Stone, M.D., and Luise Weinstein, M.D. **Crime Charged:** Medical malpractice resulting in wrongful death **Chief Defense Lawyers:** Francis P. Bensel, Peter T. Crean, Luke M. Pittoni, and Keith C. Thompson **Chief Lawyers for Plaintiff:** David Bamberger, Cheryl Bulbach, Judith Livingston, and Thomas A. Moore **Judge:** Elliott Wilk **Place:** New York City **Dates of Trial:** November 10, 1994–February 6, 1995 **Verdict:** Doctors Sherman, Stone, and Weinstein found negligent; New York Hospital cleared of wrongdoing **Award:** Doctors and hospital to pay Zion family $750,000 (later reduced to $375,000) for pain and suffering, $1 for wrongful death; no award for punitive damages

SIGNIFICANCE

The Libby Zion case led to legislation that has significantly changed the training rules for interns and resident physicians in hospitals nationwide. As a result of this case, most training programs have adopted a maximum workweek of 80 hours (formerly 100 hours), with one day off in every seven-day period. Resident doctors (the step beyond internship) must be more closely supervised, especially in the emergency room, with busy night duty relieved by "float" coverage—a system that permits one intern to catch up on sleep while another covers for him or her—and with fewer patients cared for by a single resident. The Zion case stands also as an example of how one person can compel a long-established institution—the medical infrastructure that encompasses hundreds of hospitals—to re-examine and overhaul its customs and practices.

On Thursday, March 1, 1984, Libby Zion, an 18-year-old freshman at Bennington College in Vermont, had been living at home in New York City for two months under the college's work-study program.

During the previous January, at the suggestion of her mother, Elsa, Libby had begun seeing a psychiatrist. He had prescribed an antidepressant drug, Nardil.

On this particular Thursday, complaining of a cold, Libby visited her pediatrician, who prescribed an antibiotic, erythromycin. Libby then saw her dentist, who extracted a decayed eyetooth and gave her Percodan pills to help alleviate any resulting pain.

The next day, not feeling well, Libby went home early from work. By that evening, she had a fever, and by Sunday afternoon she complained she was "burning up inside." Her mother took her temperature and found that it was 102. Elsa gave her daughter alcohol rubs and checked with the pediatrician, who said to continue the antibiotic. That evening, Libby seemed better and her parents went out to a party.

Around 10 P.M., Libby's brother Adam called his parents asking them to come home, saying Libby was "really bad." They found her skin flushed and her eyes dilated and apparently rolling. Her father, Sidney Zion, phoned Dr. Raymond Sherman, who advised taking Libby to the emergency room at New York Hospital.

There, Dr. Maurice Leonard, a second-year resident in charge of the emergency room, took a full medical history from Libby and her mother. When her parents were out of earshot, he asked Libby if she used marijuana. She said she often did, but not on that day. He asked about other medicines or illegal drugs, including cocaine. She denied taking any. The doctor and the emergency room nurse performed a two-hour evaluation including a chest X ray, cardiac exam, blood tests, and urinalysis. To help control her temperature, they gave her fluids through an intravenous (IV) line. They noted Libby's thrashing, compulsive arm and leg movements alternating with moments of calm. They recorded her dehydration and her temperature climbing to 103.5. Finally, Dr. Leonard turned his patient over to Dr. Luise Weinstein, the intern on duty on the private floors, and her supervisor, Dr. Gregg Stone, the second-year resident on duty. The doctors agreed on a tentative diagnosis of "viral syndrome" and admitted Libby to a semiprivate room.

Libby's agitated shaking continued. Twice her thrashing disconnected her IV. At 2:45 A.M., however, her parents, sensing that she was being cared for, went home.

At 7:45 A.M., Dr. Sherman called Sidney Zion and asked him to come to the hospital at once. While Sidney hurried to get ready, Elsa called Dr. Weinstein and learned that Libby had died at 7:30 that morning.

Formal Complaint Served

Formerly an assistant U.S. attorney, Sidney Zion had been a legal correspondent for the *New York Times* for five years in the 1960s. Since then he had written numerous newspaper and magazine articles.

On July 17, 1985, a formal complaint charging gross negligence was served by "Sidney E. Zion, as Administrator of the estate of Libby Zion, deceased, Plaintiff, against The New York Hospital, Raymond Sherman, M.D., Maurice Leonard, M.D., Luise Weinstein, M.D., and Gregg Stone, M.D., Defendants."

In addition to the complaint, Zion pressed New York County (Manhattan) District Attorney Robert Morganthau to indict the doctors for criminal negligence. On November 20, 1986, a grand jury report "concerning the care and treatment of a patient and the supervision of interns and residents at a hospital in New York County" made history as the first such report in the annals of medicine—without naming Libby Zion or New York Hospital. According to the report, specifically in this case:

Sydney Zion sued New York hospital and four doctors for medical malpractice in the death of his daughter. (AP/Wide World Photos)

no attending physician had performed an examination;

only an intern and junior medical resident had supervised the patient's admission;

those two duty officers had each been working for 18 hours at the time of admission (2:00 A.M.);

physical restraints had been applied without an examination by a physician; and

Demorol had been administered without knowledge of earlier treatment with Nardil.

Making broad recommendations, the report urged legislation to overturn counterproductive medical procedures as:

hospitals interpreting "inadequate and ill-defined laws" to permit resident doctors to act unsupervised;

hospitals overworking their residents, keeping trainee doctors on duty as long as 36 hours without relief;

residents (known as PGY-3s, for postgraduate year) being allowed to serve in emergency rooms;

interns (PGY-1s) and residents (PGY-2s) not being supervised in person by PGY-3s.

The report revealed that, after Libby's parents went home, she was given Demorol and Haldol to help control her agitated movements and was restrained in a Posey jacket (a vestlike garment that leaves the arms free). The report also noted the autopsy's report of trace amounts of cocaine found in Libby's nose.

The autopsy had concluded that Libby had died of bilateral bronchopneumonia caused by a virus or bacteria, adding that she collapsed after receiving Demerol and Haldol.

On March 12, 1987, the New York State Department of Health fined New York Hospital $13,000 for "woeful" treatment of Libby Zion. Admitting that it had not given her appropriate care, the hospital agreed to adopt a remedial program that included monthly evaluation of emergency room procedures.

In April, the New York State Board for Professional Medical Conduct, responding to persistent demands by Sidney Zion, held the first of 30 hearings charging Doctors Weinstein and Stone with gross negligence and/or gross incompetence. After interviewing 33 witnesses over the course of two years, the board unanimously dismissed all charges. The New York State Board of Regents, however, reversed the verdict but concluded that a "censure and reprimand" was adequate punishment. Ultimately the New York State Supreme Court Appellate Division cleared the doctors of the formal censures.

Conflicting Trial Testimony

As the trial opened on November 10, 1994, plaintiff attorney Thomas A. Moore asked for $2 million for Libby's pain and suffering, plus $1 for her wrongful death. He cited a litany of reasons for punitive damages, including:

Dr. Sherman, as attending physician, had failed to appear at the hospital;

the patient's fever was ignored;

her vital signs were not monitored properly;

she was administered Demorol even though her current medications included Nardil;

she was held in restraints;

Dr. Weinstein did not respond to calls from nurses for assistance.

The defense admitted that administering Demerol had been wrong, but insisted that had not caused Libby's death. Eleven hospital witnesses testified that Libby's care had been appropriate.

Judge Elliott Wilk presided, as plaintiff lawyer Moore debated defense attorney Frank Bensel over whether Libby's agitated condition had begun at home or in the emergency room. Dr. Charles Wetli, the hospital's expert in forensic pathology, testified that Libby did not have pneumonia; but its expert in infectious diseases, Dr. William McCormack, testified that early signs of pneumonia were present. The plaintiff's star witness, Dr. Harold Osborn, director of emergency services at the South Bronx's Lincoln Hospital, accused the doctors of doing virtually everything wrong. In an intensive debate over whether Libby's infection had been due to viral or bacterial causes, Dr. Osborn said her white blood cell count indicated that bacteria were present even though none appeared in her urine.

Plaintiff attorney Moore insisted that the combination of Nardil, the antidepressant drug Libby had been using since January, and Demerol, administered in the hospital after the Zions went home, had brought about her death. Defendant Dr. Luise Weinstein admitted that she had failed to notice the phrase "death can result" while checking the *Physicians' Desk Reference* for information on the drug combination. Defendant Dr. Sherman testified that a cocaine-Nardil reaction was a possible cause of her death. And the hospital's expert in standard of care, Dr. Robert Glickman, testified that the cause of Libby's death "was operative before she entered the hospital" because "the events in the hospital are not adequate to explain why she died."

Finally, defendant Dr. Gregg Stone testified, "Based on the evidence and what we've learned over the years, I think cocaine is what killed this poor girl."

Further testimony addressed the issue of whether the intern's and residents' lack of sleep contributed to Libby's death. A defense witness and sleep expert, Dr. Michael Thorpe, said Dr. Weinstein had not been sleep deprived, while the plaintiff's expert witness Dr. Merrill Mitler observed that sleep-deprived doctors are likely to ignore patients' warning signs and may not check medical literature.

Both Demerol and Doctors Blamed

The jury deliberated for four days. Finally it found that Dr. Stone and Dr. Weinstein ordering the administration of Demerol had been a proximate cause of Libby's death. The jury further found that the intern and two residents had been negligent in administering it. Blame was also put on Dr. Weinstein for not personally checking on the patient when called by a nurse at 4:30 A.M., and for not consulting more experienced doctors at that time. The jury found the hospital negligent regarding the workload assigned to Dr. Weinstein. It found that Libby had ingested cocaine at some time on March 4, 1984, and had been negligent in giving her medical history. Because of this, the jury unanimously decided she had been 50 percent responsible for her death, and the hospital also 50 percent responsible.

The jury also said the hospital's system of training and supervising young doctors did not depart from accepted medical practice. It awarded no punitive damages, but ordered the doctors and hospital to pay $750,000 to the Zion family for pain and suffering—plus the $1 for wrongful death. On May 1, however, Judge Wilk ruled that the jury had improperly heard evidence of the cocaine use and threw out the blame allocated to Libby Zion. However, he lowered the total award amount to $375,000.

—Bernard Ryan, Jr.

Suggestions for Further Reading

Asch, D.A., and R.M. Parker. "The Libby Zion Case: One Step Forward or Two Steps Backward?" *New England Journal of Medicine,* (March 24, 1988).

Duncan, David Ewing. *Residents: The Perils and Promise of Educating Young Doctors.* New York: Scribner, 1996.

Gilbert, Sandra M. *Wrongful Death: A Medical Tragedy.* New York: Norton, 1997.

Harr, Jonathan and Marty Asher, eds. *A Civil Action.* New York: Random House, 1996.

Hinckle, Warren and John J. Simon. *Do No Harm: The Libby Zion Case: How Doctors Killed Her and Then Blamed the Victim.* New York: Argonaut Press, 1996.

Macklin, Ruth. *Enemies of Patients: How Doctors Are Losing Their Power and Patients Are Losing Their Rights.* New York: Oxford University Press, 1993.

Nuland, Sherwin B., M.D. *How We Die.* New York: Knopf, 1994.

Robins, Natalie. *The Girl Who Died Twice: Every Patient's Nightmare—The Libby Zion Case and the Hidden Hazards of Hospitals.* New York: Delacorte, 1999.

Werth, Barry. *Damages: One Family's Legal Struggles in the World of Medicine.* New York: Simon & Schuster, 1998.

Zion, Sidney. *Trust Your Mother But Cut the Cards* (fiction). New York: Barricade Books, 1993.

Whitewater Trials and Impeachment of a President: 1994–99

THE WHITEWATER TRIALS

Defendants: Webster L. Hubbell, James B. McDougal, Susan McDougal, and Jim Guy Tucker **Crimes Charged:** McDougals and Tucker: Bank fraud and conspiracy; Susan McDougal: Mail fraud, making false financial statements and entries, civil contempt of court, criminal contempt of court, and obstruction of justice; Hubbell: Tax evasion, mail fraud, and perjury **Chief Defense Lawyers:** McDougals: Mark J. Geragos and Bobby McDaniel; Hubbell: John Nields and Charles Owen **Chief Prosecutors:** Charles Bakaly, Mark J. Barrett, W. Hickman Ewing, Jr., Robert B. Fiske, Jr., W. Ray Jahn, Julie Myers, and Kenneth W. Starr **Judges:** McDougals and Tucker: George Howard, Jr.; Hubbell: James Robertson **Places:** Little Rock, Arkansas, and Washington, D.C. **Dates of Trials:** McDougals and Tucker (bank fraud and conspiracy trial): March 4–May 29, 1996; Susan McDougal (criminal conspiracy and obstruction of justice trial): March 8–April 13, 1999; Hubbell: December 1994; July 1, 1998; June 30, 1999 **Verdicts:** McDougals and Tucker: Guilty of bank fraud and conspiracy; Susan McDougal: Guilty of civil contempt, not guilty of obstructing justice, mistrial on criminal contempt; Hubbell: Pleaded guilty 1994, pleaded guilty with plea bargain 1999 **Sentences:** James McDougal: 3 years imprisonment, $4.2 million restitution, $10,000 fine, 3 years probation; Susan McDougal: For bank fraud and conspiracy, 2 years imprisonment, 3-year probation with 300 hours of community service, $300,000 restitution, $5,000 fine; for contempt of court and obstruction of justice: 18 months imprisonment; Tucker: 4 years imprisonment (suspended because of ill health), 18 months home detention, $25,000 fine, $294,000 restitution and interest; Hubbell: 18 months imprisonment

THE IMPEACHMENT

Defendant: William Jefferson Clinton, President of the United States **Crimes Charged:** High crimes and misdemeanors: Perjury and obstruction of justice (i.e., suborning a witness to lie) **Chief Defense Lawyers:** Gregory Craig, David Kendall, Cheryl Mills, and Charles Ruff **Chief Prosecutors:** Members of the Judiciary Committee of the U.S. House of Representatives: Henry Hyde (R-Illinois), chairman; and Bob Barr (R-Georgia), Ed Bryant (R-Tennessee), Steve Buyer (R-Indiana), Charles Canady (R-Florida), Chris Cannon (R-Utah), Steve Chabot (R-Ohio), George Gekas (R-Pennsylvania), Lindsey Graham (R-South Carolina), Asa Hutchinson (R-Arkansas), Bill McCollum (R-Florida), James Rogan (R-California), and James Sensenbrenner (R-Wisconsin)   **Judge:** William Rehnquist, chief justice of the Supreme Court **Place:** Washington, D.C. **Dates of Trial:** January 7–February 12, 1999 **Verdict:** Not guilty

SIGNIFICANCE

The Whitewater trials and the impeachment and Senate trial of the president pose a number of significant, if perplexing, questions: Can an independent counsel stretch his power as prosecutor to try to bring down a single target? What happens if that target is the president of the United States? Can our criminal justice system work if a witness can ignore the rules? Can criminal contempt be used to further punish a witness who has already served time for civil contempt for the same offense? When does helping someone obtain a lucrative job cross the line to become obstruction of justice? Can a plea bargain end the investigation that raises such questions? The complex history of Whitewater is significant because only two U.S. presidents have ever been impeached. The first was Andrew Johnson, who was tried in 1868 on a charge of conspiring against Congress and the Constitution. He was acquitted by one vote. The second was William Jefferson Clinton. It should be remembered that impeachment is an accusation, not a verdict. The House of Representatives can impeach for conduct unbecoming the office; a simple majority vote is required. The Senate then functions as the trial court. Conviction requires an affirmative vote by two-thirds of the Senate.

In 1978, Arkansas Attorney General Bill Clinton and his wife, Hillary Rodham Clinton, organized the Whitewater Development Corporation with the intention of building vacation homes in the Ozark Mountains of Arkansas. Along with James B. and Susan McDougal, they borrowed $203,000 to buy 220 acres of land. That year, Clinton was elected governor of Arkansas.

Two years later, Bill Clinton lost his reelection bid. James McDougal, who had been Clinton's economic development director, bought a small bank and loaned $30,000 to Hillary Clinton to build a model house on land owned by Whitewater Development. In 1982, Clinton was reelected governor and McDougal bought a small savings-and-loan association: Madison Guaranty.

Regulators In, McDougal Out

In 1984, federal regulators questioning Madison Guaranty's financial stability and lending practices found insider lending, speculative land deals, and sizable commissions paid to the McDougals and others. That year, the voters returned Clinton to the governor's mansion. And in 1985, to help the governor pay off a $50,000 campaign debt, James McDougal hosted a fund-raiser at Madison Guaranty. He also hired the Rose Law Firm, where Mrs. Clinton was a partner, to do his S&L's legal work.

In 1986 McDougal borrowed $300,000 from a company, owned by former Little Rock judge David Hale, that provided federal money on behalf of the Small Business Administration (SBA). Federal regulators, saying McDougal's practices were improper, had McDougal removed as Madison's president but let him keep the ownership. By 1989, the feds had shut down the S&L. Bailing it out cost American taxpayers $60 million.

In addition, McDougal's mismanagement of a real estate subsidiary of Madison Guaranty brought his indictment on federal fraud charges. He was acquitted in a 1990 trial. Investigations continued, however, and in 1992, when Clinton was running for president, the Federal Resolution Trust Corp. (RTC) told the Justice Department that the Clintons were "potential beneficiaries" of Madison Guaranty's illegal activities.

Suicide, Special Counsel, Hearings

Clinton took office as president of the United States. Over the next two and one-half years:

Clinton's deputy counsel Vincent Foster committed suicide after filing three years of delinquent Whitewater corporate tax returns;

the White House agreed to release Whitewater documents to the Justice Department;

Attorney General Janet Reno appointed Robert B. Fiske, Jr., as special counsel to examine the Clintons' involvement in Whitewater;

Webster L. Hubbell, facing allegations over his activities during his earlier partnership at the Rose Law Firm, resigned abruptly (in March 1994) as Clinton's associate attorney general;

the U.S. Court of Appeals refused to reappoint Fiske, citing a conflict of interest in his appointment by Reno, and Kenneth W. Starr, who had been both a federal appeals court judge and a U.S. solicitor general (in the Reagan and Bush administrations) succeeded him;

Whitewater hearings by House and Senate Banking Committees cleared 29 administration officials of any wrongdoing;

a special Senate Whitewater committee, headed by Republican Alfonse D'Amato, conducted hearings that lasted 11 months without significant results;

Hubbell pleaded guilty (in December 1994) to two felony charges of tax evasion and mail fraud for bilking his law firm and clients out of more than $480,000 (six months later, on June 28, 1995, he was sentenced to 18 months imprisonment); and a grand jury investigating questionable loans charged James and Susan McDougal (who by then had divorced) and Arkansas Governor Jim Guy Tucker with bank fraud on August 17, 1995.

The following January, Hillary Clinton's billing records from the Rose Law Firm, which RTC investigators had sought for two years, turned up on a table in the White House living quarters. Starr subpoenaed Mrs. Clinton, and she testified before a grand jury on the discovery and content of the records.

A Woman Named Paula

An article in the January 1994 issue of *The American Spectator*—a conservative magazine backed by a strongly anti-Clinton billionaire, Richard Mellon Scaife—reported that on May 8, 1991, an Arkansas state trooper on duty at the Excelsior Hotel in Little Rock had arranged, at Governor Clinton's request, for him to meet a woman named Paula. The state policeman had escorted her to Clinton's suite. As she was leaving, the trooper said, she told him "she was available to be Clinton's regular girlfriend if he so desired."

The article was brought to the attention of Paula Corbin Jones. She was furious. She had worked at the Governor's Quality Management Conference going on that day at the hotel and (she later said) had naively gone to the governor's suite when state troopers said Clinton wanted to meet her. There the governor, putting his hand on her leg, had tried to kiss her, then exposed himself and asked for oral sex. Rejecting the proposition, she had departed as Clinton said, "You are smart. Let's keep this between ourselves."

The Paula Jones Lawsuit

Reading the magazine piece three years later and resolving to clear her name, Ms. Jones filed a federal civil lawsuit in May 1994. She claimed $700,000 in damages for sexual harassment and said what she really wanted was an apology and an admission by Clinton that he had done what she said he had done.

Clinton's lawyer, Robert Bennett, offered a settlement but no apology. Jones refused it. In December 1994, to delay the suit, Bennett invoked presidential immunity. The U.S. District Court agreed, but the U.S. Court of Appeals ordered the case to proceed. On May 27, 1997, the Supreme Court upheld that opinion, ruling unanimously that a sitting president has no temporary immunity from a civil lawsuit related to an unofficial act.

Hubbell: Allegations and Facts

While the Paula Jones lawsuit was threading its way through the appeals courts in 1995 and 1996, a number of allegations and suspicions began to surface concerning Webster Hubbell, who President Clinton had once described as his closest friend. News reports asserted that the long-missing Rose Law Firm billing records had somehow made their way from Arkansas to the basement of the Hubbell home in Washington before they were found in the White House. Other stories claimed that Clinton friends—among them top administration officials Thomas F. "Mack" McLarty (then White House chief of staff), Erskine Bowles (former White House chief of staff and former SBA chairman), Mickey Kantor (former U.S. Trade Representative), and Washington attorney Vernon Jordan—had tried to get legal business for Hubbell and had helped his family with donations and jobs.

Some reports were more alarming. In 1994, in the nine months between his resignation as number 3 in the Justice Department and his guilty plea, Hubbell had received more than $400,000 in legal retainers and consulting fees. Included were $100,000 from a subsidiary of an Indonesian conglomerate, the Lippo Group, which was controlled by Clinton supporter James Riady; $18,000 from Clinton backer Bernard Rapoport's American Income Life Insurance Company; and an undisclosed amount from Texas oilman and devoted Clinton backer Truman Arnold. Neither Hubbell nor the people paying him could or would disclose what services Hubbell had provided in exchange for these payments. To some, it looked like "hush money" had been paid to keep Hubbell from implicating Clinton or his wife in illegal acts.

One Governor and Two McDougals Convicted

As their trial began on March 4, 1996, Governor Tucker and the McDougals were charged with scheming to obtain $3 million in illegal loans through David Hale's small-business investment company. Hale himself testified that pressure from then governor Bill Clinton to help the Democratic "political family" in Arkansas had prompted his fraudulent loan of $300,000 to Susan McDougal, and that Clinton had asked him to keep his name out of the deal. On April 28, during four hours of videotaped testimony, Clinton (the sole defense witness other than James McDougal) denied the charge. The Whitewater jury watched the tape on May 9 and heard 33 prosecution witnesses over nine weeks. On the 28th, it found Tucker guilty on one count of conspiracy and one of mail fraud but not guilty on five other counts. James McDougal was found guilty on 18 of 19 counts of fraud and conspiracy; Susan McDougal was found guilty of illegally benefiting from a $300,000 loan.

Susan McDougal Jailed for Contempt

On August 20, 1996, Susan McDougal was sentenced to two years in prison for obtaining the illegal loan. Within two weeks, however, after saying she didn't trust her prosecutors because "they always wanted something on the Clintons," she was jailed for civil contempt of court for refusing to testify before yet another grand jury. For seven months, she languished 23 hours a day in a windowless cell. Then, after the American Civil Liberties Union (ACLU) filed suit alleging that Starr's office was keeping her in barbaric conditions to coerce her testimony, she was moved to a federal detention facility.

Meanwhile, on April 14, 1997, James McDougal was sentenced to three years in prison for his conviction on 18 counts of fraud and conspiracy. While the sentence could have been as many as 84 years, Starr had requested a reduced sentence because McDougal had helped the prosecution by offering information "on a wide range of matters, including matters previously unknown to us," leading to additional witnesses and documents. Starr also told the press that he had given Judge George Howard, Jr., under seal, information that influenced the judge's decision to reduce the sentence. The independent counsel refused to disclose what the evidence was. Less than a year later, McDougal died in prison of a heart attack.

Anonymous Phone Calls

By October 1997, the Paula Jones case was getting funding from the Rutherford Institute, a nonprofit organization dedicated to defending civil liberties. That month, Rutherford received three anonymous phone calls from a woman who said President Clinton might have had an affair with a woman named Monica Lewinsky. The Rutherford lawyers realized that such a person could be a valuable witness for Jones regarding Clinton's character and behavior.

The Linda Tripp tapes

Shortly thereafter, on November 24, attorneys for Paula Jones subpoenaed a Pentagon employee named Linda Tripp, and two weeks later they named Monica Lewinsky as a potential witness and served her with a subpoena. A Pentagon public affairs staffer since April, the 24-year-old Lewinsky had been transferred there from the White House Office of Legislative Affairs (where she had worked since November 1995, following a five-month internship) because her superiors thought she spent too much time around the president. During two years at the Pentagon, Lewinsky and Tripp had become confidants.

On December 15, 1997, Jones's lawyers requested that Clinton "produce documents related to communications between the president and Monica Lewinsky." The following January 12, Linda Tripp presented independent counsel Kenneth Starr—who was continuing his investigation of the Whitewater Development Corporation and Madison Guaranty Savings & Loan—some 17 audiotapes she had recorded during telephone conversations with Monica Lewinsky. The tapes were purported to include Monica's graphic descriptions of her sexual affair with the president, as well as implications that she, the president, and Clinton's friend Vernon Jordan had discussed denying the affair.

Meanwhile, in the Jones case, Lewinsky signed an affidavit on January 7, 1998, saying she "never had a sexual relationship with the president." Over the next two weeks, the FBI supplied Tripp with a hidden microphone to record face-to-face conversations with Lewinsky; Tripp received a "talking points" paper from Lewinsky (presumably to guide her in making fraudulent testimony in the Jones case); Starr obtained Justice Department authority to look into the allegations about Lewinsky; and, in a deposition in the Jones suit, Clinton denied having sexual relations with Lewinsky. None of this information, of course, was made public at the time.

The Astounding News Breaks

On January 21, 1998, the *Washington Post* reported that Starr had expanded his Whitewater investigation into an examination of whether the president and his friend Vernon Jordan had encouraged Lewinsky to hide from Paula Jones's lawyers the truth about whether she had had an affair with Clinton. Starr's objective, said pundits, was to learn whether the president had conspired to suborn perjury, make false statements, and obstruct justice.

On January 26, Clinton faced the TV cameras. "I want you to listen to me," he said. "I did not have sexual relations with that woman, Miss Lewinsky. I never told anybody to lie, not a single time—never. These allegations are false."

McDougal Indicted Again

In April 1998 Susan McDougal completed her 18-month sentence for civil contempt of court and started to serve her two-year sentence for fraud. And once more she refused to testify before the Starr grand jury. On May 4, 1998, she was indicted on two charges of criminal contempt and one of obstruction of justice.

Hubbell "performed little or no work"

Just before McDougal's indictment, on April 30, Webster Hubbell—out of prison after serving 16 months of his three-year sentence and in home confinement since January 7, 1997—faced a new barrage of fraud and tax evasion charges by Kenneth Starr. In a 10-count indictment of Hubbell; his wife, Suzanna; his lawyer, Charles C. Owen; and his accountant, Michael C. Schaufele, the independent counsel alleged that Hubbell "performed little or no work" for the legal and consulting fees he was paid in 1994 by friends of the president—a time during which Hubbell was being investigated. The indictment also charged that all four defendants attempted "to evade and defeat the payment of" back taxes, interest, and penalties amounting to more than $894,000 for 1989–1992, 1994, and 1995.

District Judge James Robertson, dismissing the charges on July 1, observed that Starr had been on "the quintessential fishing expedition." The judge noted that Hubbell had given Starr his financial records under an immunity agreement and Starr had then used those records as evidence against him. He also ruled that Starr had overstepped his authority in going after Hubbell without first obtaining approval from Attorney General Janet Reno. Starr filed an appeal to the U.S. Circuit Court of Appeals for the District of Columbia.

Clinton Admits Relationship

During the first seven months of 1998, President Clinton continually denied having a sexual relationship with Monica Lewinsky. On August 17, during four hours of testimony to Starr's grand jury via closed-circuit TV, the president denied perjuring himself in his deposition to the Jones attorneys. But that evening, he appeared on national television. "I did have a relationship with Miss Lewinsky that was not appropriate," he said. "In fact, it was wrong. It constituted a critical lapse in judgment and a personal failure on my part, for which I am solely and completely responsible."

The Starr Report

On September 9, 1998, Starr's 453-page report was turned over to the House of Representatives. It accused Clinton of "abundant and calculating" lies about his relationship with Lewinsky. The document used explicit language and graphic descriptions from the Tripp-Lewinsky recorded phone conversations to describe sexual escapades in and near the Oval Office. It cited nine instances of oral sex, including one during which Clinton spoke on the telephone with certain congressmen. It revealed that DNA in a semen stain on a blue dress—one that Tripp had advised Lewinsky not to have cleaned—matched Clinton's DNA. It itemized gifts from Lewinsky to Clinton and vice versa, with Clinton's secretary Bettie Currie often the deliverer. It detailed phone calls to Clinton by Vernon Jordan timed closely with chats between him and Lewinsky about job interviews, culminating in Lewinsky taking a job at Revlon in New York and Clinton saying "Thank you very much" when Jordan told him about it. It reported Clinton discussing with Currie her memory of interactions with Lewinsky.

Clinton's lawyers immediately wrote a 78-page rebuttal. "This private mistake does not amount to an impeachable action," they said, adding that the report was "nothing but the details of a private sexual relationship told in graphic details with the intent to embarrass."

The Castle Grande Trailer Park

In November, with the appeal pending on the "fishing expedition" ruling against him, Starr obtained a third indictment against Webster Hubbell. This time, citing 15 counts of fraud and perjury, Starr alleged that the lawyer had lied to Congress and to federal banking regulators about a complex real estate deal called Castle Grande and the role he and Mrs. Clinton had played in it. According to the indictment, Hubbell helped the Rose Law Firm obtain profitable legal work from the federal government. It also alleged that he helped conceal from regulators the fact that Castle Grande—an industrial and trailer park development built on 1,100 acres near Little Rock—was created from illegal sales of land and phony loans aimed at enriching the insiders at Madison Guaranty. According to the indictment, Hubbell committed perjury in telling regulators that he had not worked on Castle Grande business and in testifying before a hearing of the House Banking Committee on August 10, 1995, that he didn't know what work the Rose Law Firm did for Madison Guaranty. Said Hubbell to reporters, "I do not know of any wrongdoing on behalf of the First Lady and President, and nothing the independent counsel can do to me is going to make me lie about them."

Jones Settlement

On November 13, 1998, the Clinton legal team reached a settlement with Paula Corbin Jones: the president would pay her $850,000 but would not admit wrongdoing or apologize. Clinton made the payment on January 13, 1999, taking $375,000 out of his and Hillary Rodham Clinton's blind trust, and $475,000 from a personal liability insurance policy. Jones then had to deal with paying her attorneys. Her current law firm held an agreement for at least one-third of the case's proceeds, while a former firm had an $800,000 lien on the case. And the Rutherford Institute was entitled to $400,000 to repay expenses.

Meanwhile, in December 1998, the House Judiciary Committee, led by its chairman, Henry Hyde, went to work. Its task: to determine whether to recommend, to the full House of Representatives, the impeachment of the president of the United States. For seven days, the 37 members of the committee debated and wrangled, with television networks transmitting every histrionic word to every corner of the earth.

Articles of Impeachment Approved

Finally, on December 11 and 12, 1998, the committee approved four articles of impeachment. In brief, they stated:

> Article I. Clinton lied to the Starr grand jury on August 17, 1998, concerning his relationship with Lewinsky, his earlier testimony in the Jones suit, false statements he permitted his lawyer to make during the Jones case, and his "corrupt efforts" to influence Lewinsky's testimony.

Newspaper headlines proclaiming President Bill Clinton impeached. (AP/ Wide World Photos)

Article II. Clinton committed perjury in his Jones-case deposition in denying having had sexual relations with Lewinsky.

Article III. Clinton committed obstruction of justice in both the Jones case and the Starr probe, by encouraging Lewinsky to give false testimony and hide gifts that Jones's lawyers had subpoenaed, by permitting his lawyer to introduce Lewinsky's false affidavit during his deposition, and by trying to lead his secretary, Bettie Currie, to give false testimony.

Article IV. Clinton abused the power of his high office by "frivolously and corruptly" asserting executive privilege.

On Saturday, December 19, Chairman Hyde delivered the articles of impeachment to the U.S. House of Representatives. The House voted, mostly along party lines, to approve the first two articles, but Articles III and IV were rejected. For only the second time in American history, a president had been impeached. Speaking on the White House lawn and surrounded by loyal Democrats, Clinton vowed to stay in office.

The Senate Trial Begins

The world watched on television as Henry Hyde and the 12 other House "managers" of the prosecution opened the trial in the Senate chamber on Thursday, January 7, 1999. U.S. Chief Justice William Rehnquist, attired in a judge's robe of his own design that observers likened to a Gilbert-and-Sullivan operetta costume, presided. Hyde read the two articles of impeachment.

The managers set out to prove a web of deceit woven by the president. After presentations by Hyde and others, Representative Asa Hutchinson detailed how phone calls between Clinton, Lewinsky, and Jordan "became a frenzied and concerted effort to keep the holes plugged in the dike" of obstruction of justice.

The next day, Representative Bill McCollum urged the Senate to call witnesses, including Monica Lewinsky. Senate Democrats argued that the evidence brought in by the House could stand as the official record, without other witnesses. Meanwhile, the major TV networks, which had carried the first day's session, reverted to soap operas and talk shows, and the Senate gallery, jam-packed the day before, found one-quarter of its seats empty.

On Saturday, January 9, Representative Steve Buyer reminded the Senate that, in 1997, 182 Americans were convicted of perjury and 144 were convicted of obstruction of justice. "Where is the fairness for these Americans," he asked, "if they stay in jail and the president stays in the Oval Office?"

Representative Lindsey Graham, striding back and forth on the Senate floor as he spoke without notes, asked whether it was worth it to risk political chaos over lies about sex. "If we can do nothing else for this country," he said, "let's say this behavior is unacceptable. Remove him."

The Clinton Defense

White House Council Charles Ruff opened for the defense on Tuesday, January 19. "We are not here to defend William Clinton the man," he said. "He, like all of us, will find his judges elsewhere. We are here to defend William Clinton, the president of the United States, for whom you are the only judges."

Ruff said that in their "rush to judgement" the managers had become "convinced by their own rhetoric."

White House Counsel Gregory Craig noted that the managers had made "many, many allegations of grand jury perjury that the independent counsel declined to make."

Then Deputy Counsel Cheryl Mills argued that the obstruction-of-justice charge was invalid. "The president's intent," she said, "was to manage a looming media firestorm, which he correctly foresaw." Turning to the allegation that Bettie Currie, the president's secretary, had furtively retrieved gifts that Lewinsky had received from Clinton, attorney Mills observed that "it is an insult to Ms. Currie to suggest that loyalty breeds dishonesty."

Clinton's longtime friend, former senator Dale Bumpers, in a speech charged with emotion, closed the defense by entreating the senators to consider how much personal anguish Clinton's "terrible moral lapse" had caused him. "The American people," he concluded, "are asking for an end to this nightmare."

Starr Wins Appeal in Hubbell Case

January 26, 1999, brought the news that the circuit court of appeals, ruling 2–1, had reinstated the tax evasion case against Hubbell. Starr's theory that he could bring charges based on evidence that the huge payments to Hubbell were hush money, said the court, was sound enough to justify the indictment. But it added that Starr would have to show "reasonable particular knowledge" of Hubbell's financial records before he could subpoena them for any new trial.

Three Witnesses Deposed

On Capitol Hill, after two more days and 16 hours of questions from both Republicans and Democrats, the Senate closed its doors to the public and went into debate. Meanwhile, the House managers interviewed Monica Lewinsky for two hours but, according to her lawyer, learned nothing that was not already on the record. On Wednesday, January 27, after considering 15 potential witnesses and deciding not to risk the political consequences of lengthening so unpopular a trial, the managers said they would call for depositions from only three: Lewinsky, Vernon Jordan, and White House aide Sidney Blumenthal, to whom the president had first denied having the affair with Lewinsky.

On Monday, February 1, Monica Lewinsky was interviewed for six hours by three Democratic and three Republican senators. Lewinsky reiterated her testimony that, while she and the president had discussed cover stories in the Jones case, he had not asked her to lie.

A three-hour interrogation of Vernon Jordan garnered only his insistence that his effort to help find Lewinsky a job was not an attempt to buy her silence. Blumenthal told the senators that he now realized the president had lied in telling him Lewinsky had stalked him and demanded sex and that he had rebuffed her.

Clips of the videotaped testimonies were shown to the Senate on Friday, February 5, with full transcripts.

Closing arguments on both sides reiterated the evidence. The prosecutors urged the senators to put their political courage up front and "let justice roll down" on Clinton. Defense attorneys reminded them that they were participants in a case of partisan politics and retribution.

Clinton Acquitted

The vote on impeachment came on Friday, February 12, 1999. With a two-thirds majority of 100 senators needed to convict, they voted 45 guilty and 55 not guilty on the article of perjury—not even a simple majority—with 10 Republicans voting across the aisle for acquittal. On the charge of obstruction of justice, 5 Republicans joined the Democrats to make an even 50–50 split. Then, immediately following the impeachment vote, a Democratic-sponsored motion for censure was blocked. President William Jefferson Clinton was free of all charges.

Another McDougal Trial

As her latest trial began on March 9, 1999, Susan McDougal's attorney Mark Geragos told jurors that independent counsel Starr's prosecutors had told her she could avoid jail by providing damaging information about the Clintons, saying, "You know who we want. You know what we want."

Tracing bank records, FBI agent Mike Patkus told jurors that a 1982 loan of $27,600 to Clinton was reimbursed partly through the $300,000 loan Susan McDougal obtained via the SBA and partly by Whitewater Development real estate salesman Chris Wade with borrowings from Madison Guaranty. Wade was then reimbursed with a Whitewater check, which was covered by money from a bank loan to the McDougals, and the McDougals then paid off the bank by using money from the $300,000 loan to Susan McDougal. The trial jury viewed a grand jury videotape of testimony by Hillary Clinton, declaring that she "never spent any significant time at all" supervising records of the Whitewater land deal and was not aware of the $27,600 loan to her husband.

McDougal continued to contend that the independent counsel just wanted evidence against the president, and that her refusal to testify had been because of her fear that Starr would indict her for perjury if she did not tell the story he wanted. On March 24, she took the witness stand in her own defense and testified that she "did not hear anything untruthful" in President Clinton's videotaped testimony at her 1996 trial and knew of no illegal actions by him. She also said she began to mistrust Starr after he tried to make dubious bargains with witnesses. Her ex-husband, she testified, had urged her to say she had had a sexual affair with Clinton so that Starr could use that information against the president before the 1996 election.

On April 12, the jury acquitted Susan McDougal of obstructing justice. On the two charges of criminal contempt, they were deadlocked. Judge George Howard, Jr. declared a mistrial.

The Denouement: A Plea Bargain

The Castle Grande real estate deal made the headlines again on June 30, 1999, when Webster Hubbell as part of a plea bargain pleaded guilty to felony charges under the first of a 15-count indictment. The plea bargain dismissed the other 14 charges. It also kept Hubbell from returning to jail and, as part of the deal, Starr agreed not to press criminal charges against Hubbell's wife, his accountant, or his lawyer. In addition, by pleading guilty and eliminating the expected trial, saved Hubbell substantial legal fees. And there was still another benefit: the indictment on Castle Grande had included more than 30 references to Hillary Clinton, implying the possibility that she had been as much involved in illegal activities as Hubbell himself. Starr had her on his witness list, with the trial scheduled for August 9—just when she would have been on her "listening tour" of New York State in anticipation of running for a Senate seat. Altogether, observed commentators, the Hubbell plea bargain amounted to surrender by Ken Starr because it signaled that he feared defeat in another Whitewater trial.

—Bernard Ryan, Jr.

Suggestions for Further Reading

Bennett, William J. *The Death of Outrage: Bill Clinton and the Assault on American Ideals.* New York: Simon & Schuster, 1999.

Beschloss, Michael R. and Bill Clinton. *The Impeachment and Trial of President Clinton: The Official Transcripts, from the House Judiciary Committee Hearings to the Senate Trial.* New York: Random House, 1999.

Cohen, Daniel. *The Impeachment of William Jefferson Clinton.* Brookfield, Conn.: Twenty-First Century Mediacorp, 2000.

Conason, Joe and Gene Lyons. *The Hunting of the President: The Ten-Year Campaign to Destroy Bill and Hillary Clinton.* New York: St. Martin's, 2000.

Coulter, Ann H. *High Crimes and Misdemeanors: The Case against Bill Clinton.* Washington, D.C.: Regnery, 1999.

Evans-Pritchard, Ambrose. *The Secret Life of Bill Clinton.* Washington, D.C.: Regnery, 1997.

Finkelman, Paul. *Impeachable Offenses: A Documentary History from 1787 to the Present.* Washington, D.C.: Congressional Quarterly, Inc., 1999.

Ginsberg, Benjamin and Martin Sheffer. *Politics by Other Means: Politicians, Prosecutors, and the Press from Watergate to Whitewater.* New York: Norton, 1999.

Gross, Martin Louis. *The Great Whitewater Fiasco: An American Tale of Money, Power, and Politics.* New York: Ballantine, 1994.

Lyons, Gene. *Fools for Scandal: How the Media Invented Whitewater.* New York: Harper's Magazine Foundation, 1996.

McDougal, Jim and Curtis Wilkie. *Arkansas Mischief: The Birth of a National Scandal.* New York: Henry Holt, 1998.

Meyer, Wayne, ed. *Clinton on Clinton: A Portrait of the President in His Own Words.* New York: Avon, 1999.

Morris, Roger. *Partners in Power: The Clintons and Their America.* New York: Henry Holt, 1999.

Roberts, Robert N. and Marion T. Doss. *From Watergate to Whitewater: The Public Integrity War.* Westport, Conn.: Greenwood, 1997.

Sheehy, Gail. *Hillary's Choice.* New York: Random House, 1999.

Starr, Kenneth, Monica Lewinsky, and the United States Court of Appeals. *The Starr Evidence: The Complete Text of the Grand Jury Testimony of President Clinton and Monica Lewinsky.* New York: HarperCollins, 1998.

Stephanopoulos, George. *All Too Human: A Political Education.* New York: Little, Brown, 1999.

Stewart, James Brewer. *Blood Sport: The President and His Adversaries.* New York: Simon & Schuster, 1997.

Toobin, Jeffrey. *A Vast Conspiracy: The Real Story of the Sex Scandal That Nearly Brought Down a President.* New York: Random House, 2000.

O.J. Simpson Trials: 1995 & 1996–97

CRIMINAL TRIAL

Defendant: Orenthal James Simpson **Crime Charged:** Murder
Chief Defense Lawyers: Robert L. Shapiro, F. Lee Bailey, Robert Blasier, Johnnie L. Cochran, Jr., Carl Douglas, Robert Kardashian, Peter Neufeld, Barry Scheck, and Gerald Uelmen **Chief Prosecutors:** Marcia Clark, George Clarke, Christopher A. Darden, Hank Goldberg, Rockne Harmon, William Hodgman, and Brian Kelberg **Judge:** Lance A. Ito **Place:** Los Angeles, California **Dates of Trial:** January 24–October 3, 1995 **Verdict:** Not guilty

CIVIL TRIAL

Plaintiffs: Fred Goldman, the estate of Ronald Goldman, Sharon Rufo, and the estate of Nicole Brown Simpson **Defendant:** Orenthal James Simpson
Plaintiff Claim: Liability for assault and battery and for wrongful deaths
Chief Defense Lawyers: Robert Baker, Phil Baker, Bob Blasier, Daniel Leonard **Chief Lawyers for the Plaintiffs:** For Fred Goldman and the estate of Ronald Goldman: Daniel Petrocelli, Peter Gelblum, Tom Lambert, and Ed Medvene; for Sharon Rufo: Michael Brewer and Nick Hornberger; for the estate of Nicole Brown Simpson: John Q. Kelly, Paul Callan, Ed Horowitz, and Natasha Roit **Judge:** Hiroshi Fujisaki **Place:** Santa Monica, California
Dates of Trial: October 17, 1996–February 4, 1997 **Verdict:** Simpson was found liable for the deaths of Nicole Brown Simpson and Ronald Goldman; the Goldman family was awarded $8.5 million in compensatory damages (the Simpson family had not sought compensatory damages); each family was awarded $12.5 million in punitive damages

SIGNIFICANCE

The two trials of O.J. Simpson revealed the challenging paradox that the American legal system does not work and then again does work. The criminal trial proved that a celebrity defendant who is served by determined lawyers can get away with murder. The civil trial proved that indisputable facts adding up to a preponderance of evidence can at least bring a modicum of solace to brokenhearted families.

Just before midnight on June 12, 1994, the brutally slashed bodies of Nicole Brown Simpson and Ronald L. Goldman were found outside Nicole's condominium at 875 South Bundy Drive in the Brentwood section of Los Angeles, California. Nicole was the ex-wife of football hero and TV spokesman Orenthal James Simpson, known as "O.J." Goldman was a friend of Nicole who worked as a waiter.

Before dawn, Detectives Philip Vannatter and Tom Lange of the Los Angeles Police Department (LAPD) Robbery-Homicide Division were named lead investigators. The detectives headed for Simpson's home to notify him of his ex-wife's death. They took along with them Detective Mark Fuhrman.

While waiting to get into Simpson's walled estate (the doorbell was not answered), Fuhrman called Vannatter's attention to bloodstains on a Ford Bronco parked outside the rear gate. Vannatter ordered Fuhrman to climb the wall and let the others in. At a guest house inside the grounds, Brian "Kato" Kaelin (a friend of O.J.'s) referred them to Arnelle Simpson, O.J.'s daughter by his first wife. She told them Simpson had taken a red-eye flight to Chicago at midnight. Detective Ronald Phillips phoned Simpson in Chicago to break the news.

Meanwhile, Kaelin told Fuhrman that at about 10:40 P.M. he had heard thumps on his wall. Checking a passageway behind the guesthouse, Fuhrman found a bloody black glove that looked like a match for one he and Vannatter had seen beside Goldman's body. They observed blood on the driveway, on the path to the front door, and on the house's entryway. The senior detective declared the property a crime scene, and obtained a search warrant. The Ford Bronco was impounded.

When Simpson returned to Los Angeles the next day, the LAPD interviewed him for three hours. Vannatter noticed that Simpson had a bandaged finger. The detective had the finger photographed without the bandage, which revealed two lacerations. Vannatter also had a nurse obtain a sample of Simpson's blood. The next morning, Vannatter told Los Angeles D.A. Gil Garcetti he considered Simpson the prime suspect. By then, the police could not locate Simpson.

The Infamous Chase

That evening, nearly every television station interrupted their regular programming to go live from a helicopter above a Los Angeles freeway. Approximately 93 million viewers watched the scene as the helicopter followed a Ford Bronco. Below, Simpson's friend, Al Cowlings, reported by phone that O.J. was in the car with a pistol to his head, intent on suicide. Police cars and ordinary traffic were moving slowly behind them.

After 90 minutes, Cowlings drove Simpson home, where he was arrested. On Monday, June 20, the Los Angeles County grand jury charged O.J. with the murders. He was held without bail.

At Simpson's arraignment, his attorney, Robert L. Shapiro, was joined by America's perhaps best-known African-American trial lawyer, Johnnie L. Cochran, Jr. Simpson declared that he was "absolutely, 100 percent not guilty."

Chief prosecutor Marcia Clark, a deputy district attorney, was highly proficient in trials involving circumstantial evidence and testing for DNA—deoxyribonucleic acid, a molecule that blueprints inherited traits in every living cell. Assisting Clark was Deputy District Attorney Christopher A. Darden, an African-American prosecutor widely experienced in murder trials. By December 8, 1994, Judge Lance A. Ito had seated the jury and 12 alternates, including 15 African-Americans in all.

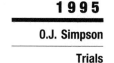

The Trial of the Century Begins

Opening the trial on Monday, January 24, 1995, Clark assured the jury they would hear evidence involving a trail of blood from the death scene to a pair of socks in O.J.'s bedroom. DNA testing would confirm whose blood it was. Prosecutor Darden described the defendant's years of abusive behavior toward his wife. He included 911 tapes of Nicole screaming for help, and police photos of her battered face.

The prosecution recounted the events of June 12, 1994. Karen Lee Crawford, manager of the Mezzaluna Restaurant, testified that Nicole's mother had called about her daughter's left-behind eyeglasses, and that waiter Ron Goldman had departed to return them to her. The Simpsons' neighbor, Steven

O.J. Simpson (right) in court with two of his attorneys, Robert Shapiro and Johnny Cochran. (Archive Photos)

Schwab, recalled walking his dog at 10:30 P.M. and encountering an agitated dog trailing its leash. The dog had bloody but uninjured paws. Schwab's neighbor Sukru Boztepe described taking that dog for a walk to calm it down, only to find it "pulling me harder" near Nicole's home, where "I saw a lady laying down, full of blood." He flagged down a passing squad car.

Officer Robert Riske, the squad car driver, testified, "We observed a white female in a black dress, laying in a puddle." Then he found Goldman's body. Riske described seeing a white envelope (later proved to contain Nicole's eyeglasses), a black glove, and a blue knit ski cap near the bodies.

Detective Mark Fuhrman took the stand. Anticipating the defense's plan to depict him as a racist, the prosecution presented the jury with a good-looking, athletic cop who had neither inclination nor opportunity to plant the glove at Rockingham. Defense attorney F. Lee Bailey grilled him aggressively as he denied making racist statements in 1985.

Kato Kaelin Testifies

Brian "Kato" Kaelin testified that Simpson had told him how, on the evening of the murders, his ex-wife had tried to prevent him from speaking with their daughter after her dance recital, and that Simpson had complained about Nicole's tight dress. Kaelin described accompanying Simpson to a McDonald's earlier that evening, but did not know the defendant's whereabouts between 9:35 P.M. and about 11:00 when Simpson left in his limousine for the airport. He recalled offering to pack Simpson's knapsack in the limo, but the defendant declined, saying, "I'll get it."

Limousine driver Allan Park testified about picking up Simpson and the airport trip. While loading the car, Park said, Simpson tried to get Kaelin away from the knapsack by saying, "No, no. I'll get it."

Criminologist Dennis Fung described gathering and examining the physical evidence—gloves, cap, footprints, and hair and blood samples. He was cross-examined by defense attorney Barry Scheck, a New York lawyer considered an expert on blood-related evidence. Implying that Fung was inept and deceitful, Scheck cited errors in note taking, leaving blood samples in a hot truck, and not conducting tests on bloodstains that Fuhrman pointed out on the Bronco but later filing false reports about them.

May came. By then, the judge had dismissed seven jurors for various reasons. Five alternates remained.

The Scientific Evidence Is Presented

LAPD forensic chemist Gregory Matheson testified that blood on the Bundy walkway could not have come from 99.5 percent of the population but could be Simpson's, and that blood found on socks in Simpson's bedroom could have come from Nicole but not from the defendant. During the cross-examination, defense attorney Robert Blasier repeated a litany of incompetencies: police did not follow proper chain-of-custody procedures for the blood samples; bodies were wrongly covered with improper blankets; officers were late reaching the crime scene; laboratory tweezers were improperly cleaned; 1.5 millimeters of Simpson's blood sample had mysteriously disappeared.

Robin Cotton, director of Cellmark Diagnostics in Germantown, Maryland, said DNA tests confirmed that blood found near the victims was the defendant's, indicating that Simpson cut himself while committing the murders. While cross-examining, defense attorney Peter Neufeld questioned Cotton's estimate that only 1 in 170 million African-Americans and Caucasians showed the same genetic pattern as Simpson. In probability statistics, she replied, numbers "mean what they mean. A number isn't an opinion."

Gary Sims, lead forensic analyst at the California Justice Department's DNA laboratory, testified that blood on the glove found at Simpson's Rockingham estate matched Goldman's blood, and that blood in the Bronco matched both victims' as well as the defendant's. Under cross-examination, Sims minimized the possibility of cross-contamination of blood samples—that is, one being tainted by another—in the laboratory.

Extremely graphic photos of the victims' bodies were presented with the testimony of Dr. Lakshman Sathyavagiswaran, chief medical examiner of Los Angeles County. The doctor described Mrs. Simpson facing her killer's slashing knife and absorbing a severe blow that probably knocked her out. Goldman was then killed, he surmised, before the killer slashed Nicole's throat. Next, Goldman was stabbed more than two dozen times before he died. Dr. Sathyavagiswaran said the deaths occurred between 9:00 P.M. and 12:45 A.M. No pathologist, he concluded, could give a more precise time.

The Gloves and the Shoe Prints

Prosecution witness Brenda Vemich, a glove buyer for Bloomingdale's department store in New York City, identified the expensive brand and size—extra large—of the bloody gloves. Prosecutor Darden asked the defendant to put them on. Wearing latex gloves (to protect the evidence), Simpson pulled and squeezed, then held up both hands with the obviously too-tight gloves only partway on. Critics declared a major prosecution blunder. Defense attorney Cochran said the trial was as good as over because of four words: "The gloves don't fit."

FBI agent William J. Bodziak, a shoe print expert, testified that the bloody print at the crime scene had been traced to a $160-a-pair Italian designer brand, Bruno Magli. They were Simpson's size, and only 299 pair had been distributed in the United States. When cross-examiner F. Lee Bailey proposed that professional assassins had left the imprints, the witness replied, "Ridiculous."

Prosecution witness Richard Rubin, a former executive of the glove manufacturer, Aris Isotoner, testified that moisture could shrink the gloves 15 percent. Prosecutor Darden presented a brand-new, extra-large pair of the same gloves. Simpson easily put them on.

Douglas Deedrick, of the FBI's hair and fiber section, testified that hairs on the ski cap matched Simpson's. Prosecutor Clark evinced testimony that the glove found at Bundy, which had only one of Nicole's hairs, probably fell off the murderer's hand early in the crime, whereas the glove found at Simpson's Rockingham estate stayed on and picked up hair from both victims.

The FBI witness said his microscopes revealed "fibers with knobs," resembling a child's set of jacks, found on the Rockingham glove and the Bundy cap. In analyzing thousands of samples over 17 years, he added, he had never seen such fibers. They matched those from the carpet of Simpson's Bronco.

The Defense Makes Its Case

Simpson family members were the first defense witnesses. O.J.'s sister, Carmelita Durio, and his eldest daughter, Arnelle, both said he was "distraught" when informed of the murders. His 73-year-old mother, Eunice, testified, "He seemed shocked."

The defense called several witnesses who testified that they heard nothing unusual in the Bundy neighborhood during that Sunday evening of June 12. One neighbor, Robert Heidstra, testified that at 10:40 P.M. he had heard two persons arguing. One shouted "Hey! Hey! Hey!" while the second voice was overridden by the frenzied wailing of a dog. Shortly thereafter, a white sport utility vehicle sped south. Cross-examination disclosed that Heidstra had told friends the voices were a younger white man's and an older black man's, and that Simpson's was one.

Johnnie Cochran objected furiously, "You can't tell by someone's voice when they're black. That's racist, and I resent it." Judge Ito sent the jury out and declared a recess as prosecutor Darden and Cochran verbally dueled—an event forbidden in courtroom protocol and one the judge had frequently warned against.

Dr. Robert Huizenga, former team physician for the Los Angeles Raiders, cited injuries he had found while examining the defendant soon after the murders, concluding that "fast walking, slow jogging would be difficult if not impossible."

The prosecutors showed the doctor a Simpson exercise video made shortly before the murders. Deputy District Attorney Brian Kelberg argued that Simpson could have been under the influence of an "adrenaline rush," which would have helped him through the physical stress of committing murder. The doctor agreed. A videotaped workout of O.J. was shown with the jury excused. At one point, Simpson told a trainer, "You got to get your space in if you're working out with your wife, if you know what I mean. You can always blame it on working out." The remark, Kelberg argued, proved "that he thinks beating a wife is of no consequence." Ito admitted the tape as evidence.

LAPD cameraman Willie Ford testified that he hadn't seen any socks in Simpson's bedroom when he videotaped the home at 4:13 P.M. on June 13. On cross-examination, he admitted he had been told to videotape only after the room had been searched. Detective Adelberto Luper said he saw the socks on the floor earlier, at 12:30 P.M.

Josephine "Gigi" Guiran, the Rockingham maid, said Simpson did not leave socks lying around. While cross-examining her, Darden suggested that the defendant's unusual sloppiness—socks on the bedroom floor, a towel on the bathroom floor—was evidence of frantic behavior that night.

To support their theory of a police conspiracy to frame Simpson, the defense called Fredric Rieders, Ph.D., to interpret FBI tests of blood on the socks and on a Bundy gate. The toxicologist said both blood specimens contained EDTA—ethylenediaminetetraacetic acid—a chemical that prevents coagulation of blood, often used for preserving blood samples. Defense witness Roger Martz, chief of the FBI's chemistry toxicology unit, disagreed, saying the bloodstains did not come from preserved blood.

Cross-examined, Martz said EDTA was a preservative in many foods. "If a person is eating EDTA," he said, "some will be in their blood."

On July 28, Cochran asked a North Carolina superior court to order Laura Hart McKinny, a screenwriter who had been advised by Mark Fuhrman, to testify regarding racial slurs Fuhrman had made while they worked on the screenplay. The judge ruled that the writer's conversations with Fuhrman were immaterial to the trial. Cochran filed an appeal.

The defense brought in police nurse Thano Peratis, who said he had obtained between 7.9 and 8.1 milliliters of Simpson's blood on June 13. The defense insisted that 1.5 milliliters had gone missing.

John Gerdes, a molecular biologist, testified that the LAPD laboratory had a "substantial" problem that "created unacceptable risks" of cross-contamination, from using outdated chemicals to wearing the same gloves for more than one test. Under cross-examination, Gerdes admitted he had never examined another laboratory so scrupulously and that he opposed DNA testing.

Detective Fuhrman a Racist

In North Carolina, on August 7, the court of appeals ruled that tape recordings and testimony of McKinny, the screenwriter whom Fuhrman advised, "could make a difference in the trial." This permitted Judge Ito to rule on whether the jury could hear the tapes.

Cochran announced that the transcripts from McKinny disclosed that Fuhrman had used the word "nigger" at least 30 times and that at least 17 times he had referred to lying, covering up for fellow officers, or planting evidence. "I am the most important witness in the trial of the century," said Fuhrman on one tape. "If I go down, their case goes bye."

"And that's what they're faced with—bye," Cochran told the press. "This is a blockbuster. This is perhaps the biggest thing in any case in this decade, and they know it."

Dr. Henry C. Lee, head of the Connecticut State Police Crime Laboratory, took the stand. Defense attorney Barry Scheck focused Lee's testimony on faint marks on the walkway at Bundy. Were the marks from a shoe? One could be from a shoe, said Lee, but not from Bruno Magli shoes. Deputy District Attorney Hank Goldberg's cross-examination tried to dispel Lee's suggestion that more than one assailant might have committed the murders.

On August 29, 1995, Judge Ito permitted screenwriter McKinny to tell the packed courtroom—minus the 14-member jury—how she had audiotaped 16 hours of interviews with Mark Fuhrman. Defense attorney Gerald Uelmen argued that the jury should hear all of the 41 times that Fuhrman—who had testified that he had not used the word "nigger" in the last 10 years—had in fact voiced that word on tape. Prosecutor Clark countered. The real "N word," she said, is not "nigger" but "Nicole." "None of this is relevant," she said. "The admission of this evidence is telling the jury, 'Disregard the case. Look somewhere else.'"

The next day, Judge Ito ruled that the jury would be allowed to hear only 2 of Fuhrman's 41 references to blacks as "niggers."

On September 5, the jury was again excused. Fuhrman took the stand and replied, "I wish to assert my Fifth Amendment privilege" to several questions asked by defense attorney Uelmen. The judge dismissed him, agreeing to instruct the jury that "Detective Fuhrman is not available for further testimony."

Prosecutor Clark objected and filed an appeal. Within three hours, Justices Paul Turner and Orville J. Armstrong of the California Court of Appeals ruled that "the proposed instruction regarding the unavailability of Detective Fuhrman is not to be given."

Rebuttals Get Under Way

The defense requested that Judge Ito either strike Fuhrman's testimony about finding the Rockingham glove or return the detective to the stand. The judge refused. Cochran filed an appeal, refusing to rest his case until the appeal decision came down. Judge Ito then ordered the prosecution to start its rebuttal before the defense had closed.

The California Court of Appeals ruled that jurors could not be informed of Fuhrman's Fifth Amendment plea. Nor might the jury draw adverse conclusions from his absence. The defense appealed to a higher court.

Prosecution witness Gary Sims, of the California Department of Justice, testified that DNA testing proved that blood found inside the Bronco had come from both Goldman and Simpson. FBI agent Deedrick challenged defense witness Dr. Lee's testimony that marks on Goldman's jeans might have come from shoe prints of a second murderer. Rather, they matched the ribbed texture of Goldman's shirt. FBI footprint expert William Bodziak observed that what Dr. Lee had characterized as "imprints" on the Bundy walkway were impressions made in the concrete when it was poured years earlier.

On September 21, 1995, the California Supreme Court rejected the defense appeal to reinstate the judge's instruction to the jury about Fuhrman.

The next day, the defense rested. Then Cochran said his client "would like to make a brief statement." Prosecutor Clark objected. "This is a bid to get material admitted through conjugal visits that is not admitted in court."

Simpson stood up. "I am mindful of the mood and the stamina of this jury," he said. "I have confidence of their integrity . . . that I did not, could not, and would not have committed this crime. . . . I have four kids—two kids I haven't seen in a year. They ask me every week, 'Dad, how much longer . . .?'"

"All right," the judge cut in. He asked Simpson if he understood that he had a right to testify. "Yes," said Simpson.

Both sides rested. Later, a defense lawyer revealed that Simpson, coached by Cochran and attorney Robert Kardashian, had rehearsed his statement for two weeks.

Closing Arguments

Summations began on September 26. Prosecutor Clark took the Fuhrman bull by the horns: "Is he a racist? Yes. But it would be a tragedy if you found the defendant not guilty because of the racist attitude of one police officer."

Clark reviewed the timing of the thumps on Kaelin's wall; the absurdity of defense contentions that blood had been planted; the trail of blood down the Bundy walkway, into the Bronco, and into the Rockingham house; and the DNA evidence that made Simpson "one in 57 billion people that could have left that blood."

Defense counsel Cochran summed up. Referring to the defendant's attempt to put on the glove, he repeatedly said, "If it doesn't fit, you must acquit." He suggested that professional killers were the murderers. He lambasted the "untrained officers" who "traipsed through the evidence." He reminded the jury that the defendant "doesn't have to prove anything." Finally, he compared Fuhrman's racist attitude to Hitler's and advised the jurors that in acquitting Simpson they would become custodians of the Constitution.

Prosecutor Darden told the jury, "I looked in the Constitution, and you know what I saw? The Constitution said Ron and Nicole had the right to liberty, the right to life, the right to the pursuit of happiness. And I looked further to see if it said anything about O.J. Simpson. And it said that a man has no right to kill and get away with it because one of the investigating officers is a racist."

"Ron and Nicole—they're speaking to you," impassioned prosecutor Clark to the jury. "They are both telling you who did it, with their hair, their clothes, their bodies, their blood. They tell you in the only way they can."

It was Friday afternoon, September 29, 1995. Judge Ito briefly charged the jury. They retired to elect their foreman. Deliberations began at 10:00 A.M. on Monday. Less than four hours later, they reached a verdict. Ito said he would announce it the next morning.

The Verdict

On Tuesday, October 3, across the country people learned that the jury had found Orenthal James Simpson not guilty of murder.

In the days following the verdict, while O.J. Simpson promised to find Nicole and Ron Goldman's killer(s), the LAPD and Los Angeles district attorney announced that the investigation into the murders was closed.

The Goldmans and Browns Sue

While the murder trial was going on, three civil suits for wrongful death had been filed against O.J. Simpson: by Fred Goldman, father of Ron Goldman; by Ron's mother, Sharon Rufo, who had divorced Fred when Ron was six years old; and by the Brown family.

California law permitted two kinds of suits. The estate of a dead person could bring a survival suit by the victim's personal representative—parents or other immediate relatives—for punitive damages. The victim's heirs would share any money won by the suit.

The other permissible suit was a *wrongful death claim*. This could be brought by an heir for loss of financial support or loss of emotional support (i.e., loss of a relationship). Fred Goldman filed only for the latter. Although Sharon Rufo had had no relationship with her son since he was six, she filed her own wrongful death suit.

The Brown family decided to bring only a survival suit for the assault and battery that resulted in Nicole's death. They didn't want to put her young children through a wrongful death suit. It would be up to a jury to decide whether Simpson had attacked and battered Ron Goldman and Nicole and whether he had killed Ron; they did not have to determine whether he had killed Nicole.

Simpson and his defense lawyers found the rules and courtroom atmosphere different this time. They lost a motion to seal Simpson's depositions explaining the cuts on his hand and body and ownership of gloves and shoes. Judge Hiroshi Fujisaki allowed no courtroom cameras of any kind, and permitted only an audio feed to reporters who could not be accommodated inside. He issued a gag order to keep the lawyers on both sides from commenting on the trial. He excluded irrelevant and prejudiced evidence that Judge Ito had permitted. He did not sequester the jury.

Plaintiff lawyers Daniel Petrocelli and Tom Lambert brought in all the pertinent witnesses from the criminal trial and took the jury through the evidence. The defense had to admit that lab test results of various bloodstains were valid and proper, and it quickly became clear that no blood had been "planted" anywhere. After glove expert Richard Rubin demonstrated that the bloody gloves could easily fit if latex gloves were not put on first, defense lawyer Robert Baker avoided asking Simpson to try them on. Testimony by Kato Kaelin and limo driver Allan Park destroyed Simpson's alibi that he was napping at home between 10:00 and 11:00 P.M. Telephone records not previously revealed proved that early in the evening of the murders Simpson had received an ego-shattering "Dear John" call from girlfriend Paula Barbieri that probably enraged him. Forensic pathologist Dr. Werner Spitz described in sickening detail how quickly the victims were killed, countering the testimony of defense expert Michael Baden that Simpson hadn't had enough time. An attendant on Simpson's red-eye flight told of his using the lavatory every 10 or 15 minutes yet never flushing the toilet—apparently, the jury was led to believe, treating his bleeding finger.

With the defendant on the witness stand, Petrocelli led him through each moment of the 911-call batterings of Nicole, and made him describe his movements on the day of the murders. During his two-day testimony, Simpson denied committing the murders but could not adequately explain his own injuries or his whereabouts during the time between the McDonald's trip with Kato Kaelin and the limo coming to pick him up.

The defense failed to prove its contention that one photo of Simpson in the Bruno Magli shoes was a fake, then fell apart when 31 pictures of O.J. wearing the shoes by another photographer turned up. It called no DNA expert to question the blood tests that incriminated Simpson. It offered no witness to counter the hair and fiber matches.

The judge instructed the jury that they were not bound by the verdict of the criminal trial. Nor was unanimity required. Rather, 9 of the 12 had to find that a preponderance of the evidence supported their verdict.

The jury deliberated for five days. On Tuesday, February 4, 1997, it unanimously found that O.J. Simpson had willfully and wrongfully caused the death of Ronald Goldman and had maliciously attacked and assaulted Nicole Brown Simpson. It ordered Simpson to pay the Goldman family $8.5 million in compensatory damages, and to pay $12.5 million in punitive damages to each of the two families.

—Bernard Ryan, Jr.

Suggestions for Further Reading

Bugliosi, Vincent. *Outrage: The Five Reasons Why O.J. Simpson Got Away with Murder.* New York: Norton, 1996.

Cochran, Johnnie L, Jr. with Tim Rutten. *Journey to Justice.* New York: One World (Ballantine), 1996.

Darden, Christopher with Jess Walter. *In Contempt.* New York: Regan (HarperCollins), 1996.

Dershowitz, Alan M. *Reasonable Doubts: The O.J. Simpson Case and the Criminal Justice System.* New York: Simon & Schuster, 1996.

Goldberg, Hank. *The Prosecution Responds: An O.J. Simpson Trial Prosecutor Reveals What Really Happened.* Secaucus, N.J.: Carol, 1996.

Petrocelli, Daniel with Peter Knobler. *Triumph of Justice: The Final Judgment on the Simpson Saga.* New York: Crown, 1998.

Schiller, Lawrence and James Willwerth. *American Tragedy: The Uncensored Story of the Simpson Defense.* New York: Random House, 1996.

Shapiro, Robert L. with Larkin Warren. *The Search for Justice: A Defense Attorney's Brief on the O.J. Simpson Case.* New York: Warner, 1996.

Toobin, Jeffrey. *The Run of His Life: The People v. O.J. Simpson.* New York: Random House, 1996.

Uelmen, Gerald F. *Lessons from the Trial: The People v. O.J. Simpson.* Kansas City, Mo.: Andrews and McMeel, 1996.

Colin Ferguson Trial: 1995

Defendant: Colin Ferguson **Crimes Charged:** Murder, attempted murder
Chief Defense Lawyers: Colin Ferguson, Alton Rose
Chief Prosecutor: George Peck **Judge:** Donald Belfi **Place:** Mineola, New York **Date of Trial:** January 26–February 17, 1995 **Verdict:** Guilty on 68 of 93 counts, including murder, attempted murder, assault, reckless endangerment, weapons possession **Sentence:** 6 consecutive 25-years-to-life terms for the murder conviction; 19 additional 25-year sentences for each count of attempted murder

SIGNIFICANCE

In a nationally publicized trial involving a defense that could only be described as bizarre, Colin Ferguson, acting as his own attorney, questioned his alleged victims on the witness stand in an attempt to prove that someone else had committed the crimes.

On December 7, 1993, the daily 5:33 P.M. Long Island Rail Road train left Penn Station in New York City for Hicksville, New York, carrying commuters home. As the train raced into neighboring Nassau County, one of the passengers rose and walked calmly down the aisle, shooting everyone he passed with a 9mm handgun. When the shooter paused to reload, terrified passengers wrestled him down. By then, six people lay dead or dying. Nineteen more were seriously wounded.

The man with the gun was Colin Ferguson, 36, a well-educated, unemployed immigrant from an upper middle-class Jamaican family. His surreal defense would strain debates over mental competency and criminal insanity like few others ever heard in an American courtroom.

Ferguson insisted that he was perfectly sane. In fact, he denied that he was the killer; he claimed that an unidentified white man had done the shooting and then escaped. With a train full of wounded survivors and traumatized onlookers accusing him, Ferguson's claim was clearly either a delusion or a lie.

A court-ordered psychiatric examination determined that Ferguson met both criteria by which defendants are deemed sane enough to stand trial in New York: He understood the nature of the legal proceedings against him and he was able to assist in his own defense. He was also found to have been able to distinguish right from wrong at the time of the shootings.

One month after the shootings, on January 7, 1994, Ferguson was declared mentally competent by Nassau County District Judge Ira Warshawsky. Despite this ruling, Ferguson's court-appointed attorney, Anthony Falanga, said he would still attempt to defend Ferguson on grounds of insanity. Ferguson refused to cooperate with Falanga. After two months of being ignored by his client, Falanga stepped aside when Ferguson agreed to be represented by controversial civil rights attorneys William Kunstler and Ronald Kuby. Ferguson's new lawyers agreed that he was mentally unstable, but they announced that his defense would take a different approach.

When Ferguson was arrested, police found notes in his pockets expressing his hatred of Caucasians, Asians, and "Uncle Tom Negroes." Kunstler and Kuby held that Ferguson's behavior could be tied to a study entitled Black Rage. In this 1968 study, psychologists Price Cobbs and William Grier observed that in order to function in society, African Americans suppress feelings of intense anger over racism. Kunstler and Kuby would try to expand this thesis into a "black rage" defense, arguing that continual racist mistreatment was the catalyst that caused Ferguson's delusions and paranoia to explode into violence.

Critics accused the attorneys of manipulating the sensitive state of race relations in New York in order to excuse the acts of a cold blooded killer. Kunstler and Kuby vowed to press ahead with the "black rage" defense. Their strategy, however, accepted that Ferguson was the killer and that he was mentally unsound. Ferguson rejected both assumptions.

Ferguson then decided to act as his own attorney, against the advice of his lawyers and Nassau County District Judge Donald Belfi. Because Judge Belfi reaffirmed the mental competency finding on December 9, Ferguson was entitled to represent himself, even though he had no legal training. Furthermore, because the defendant was considered legally sane, Judge Belfi was required to provide the indigent Ferguson with county funds to pay for a private investigator to find "the real killer."

"What we will have now is a complete circus," predicted Kuby.

Although Ferguson dismissed Kunstler and Kuby, he continued to telephone them for advice. Nevertheless Ferguson decided that his only legal advisor in court would be Alton Rose, a Jamaican-born attorney who had known the defendant when he was a young man. Since emotions surrounding the case were so high, Rose made a motion to have the trial moved outside of Nassau County. An appeals court refused, holding that Ferguson, not Rose, would have to make such a request.

Opening statements in the trial began on January 26, 1995, in Mineola, New York. Wearing a bulletproof vest under a handsome suit and speaking evenly, Ferguson said that as the commuter train made its way out of New York City, he had dozed off and someone had stolen his gun and opened fire on the passengers. "Mr. Ferguson was awakened by the gunfire and, amid the confusion, sought to protect himself," Ferguson said, speaking of himself in the third person to an increasingly strange effect in the courtroom. Ferguson told the jury that the charges against him were a racist conspiracy.

Prosecutors produced police photos of victims lying in pools of blood, there were shell casings and bullet holes in the railroad car. Averting his eyes from the pictures, Ferguson objected that the photos were prejudicial in nature, but the judge overruled him.

The pistol wrestled from Ferguson was entered as evidence. As prosecutors passed the weapon back and forth in front of the jury, Ferguson objected when he was not allowed to hold the gun. The judge sent the jury out of the room.

"By not being allowed to hold the weapon, the jurors are given the impression that the court has already made up its mind about my guilt or innocence," Ferguson said. "Therefore, I move for a mistrial."

"This is one of the pitfalls of self-representation," replied Judge Belfi. "No defendant can handle a weapon. You were not singled out. Motion denied."

Survivors of the massacre began to testify. Television viewers across the nation watched incredulously as Ferguson questioned the people he was accused of shooting at point-blank range. Far from appearing terrified, however, most of the victims responded to Ferguson's bizarre queries unflinchingly.

Mary Anne Phillips, the first gunshot victim, testified that she had played dead after she was wounded. Ferguson asked if she kept her eyes closed.

"Yes," replied Phillips, "so you wouldn't come back and shoot me again."

Elizabeth Aviles similarly refused to be intimidated by the man who had shot her in the back. When Ferguson pressed Aviles to describe the gunman, she responded angrily, "I saw you shooting everyone on the train, okay?"

As the trial progressed, the eloquence of Ferguson's frequent objections led many to wonder if he was a crazy man mounting an able defense or a sane man cultivating an appearance of insanity, cynically paving the way for future appeals. He accused the Jewish Defense League of conspiring to kill him and said that the prison murder of cannibal serial killer Jeffrey Dahmer was a rehearsal for his own death behind bars.

Ferguson made a request to subpoena U.S. President Bill Clinton, because the president had personally commended the bravery of George Blum, Michael O'Connor, and Mark McEntee—the three men who subdued the killer at the time of the shootings. The request was denied. Ferguson also argued that the indictment against him contained 93 counts only because the shootings occurred in 1993. "Had it been 1925," Ferguson said, "it would have been 25 counts."

Outside of court, a New York exorcist claimed that the CIA had kidnapped Ferguson and implanted a computer chip in his brain, activating it with an order to kill. Ferguson considered calling the exorcist as a witness, but decided against it. Although he was entitled to do so, Ferguson rested his case without calling the defendant he habitually referred to as "Colin Ferguson" to the stand. Carolyn McCarthy, whose husband Dennis had been killed and her son critically wounded in the railroad shootings, described Ferguson as a coward for not taking the stand.

On February 17, the jury considered the case for ten hours. When the jurors returned to court, they acquitted Ferguson on 25 counts of aggravated harassment, but found him guilty of all the other charges, including multiple counts of murder, attempted murder, assault, reckless endangerment, and weapons possession. There had never been any doubt about Ferguson's guilt, said the jury foreman, who explained that the long deliberations concerned the less serious harassment counts.

To attorneys Kunstler and Kuby, Ferguson agreed to pursue an appeal based on grounds that he never should have been found mentally competent to stand trial. To Attorney Rose, however, Ferguson maintained that he was mentally sound. Rose announced that he would not represent Ferguson during any appeals and would ask the state to appoint a public defender to represent his indigent client after sentencing.

On March 21, survivors and family members of the dead filled the court to testify during sentencing recommendations. For two days, people directly touched by the railroad massacre asked Judge Belfi to punish Ferguson severely for the suffering he had inflicted. Robert Giugliano, whom Ferguson had shot in the chest, lunged at the defendant.

"Look at these eyes," shouted Giugliano. "You can't! You're nothing but a piece of garbage!"

When Ferguson accused the wounded of plotting with police against him, victims and their families turned their backs and filed out of the courtroom. Visibly aghast at Ferguson's insensitivity, Attorney Rose asked the judge if he could also leave the room. Judge Belfi denied the request. As Rose sat exasperated beside him, Ferguson declared his innocence in another rambling monologue, which lasted for hours.

"John the Baptist lived in the wilderness, a humble man, and he was put into prison," Ferguson said. "He was beheaded by a criminal justice system similar to this. After his death, we can look back and say with 20–20 hindsight, 'This was a great man.' And as much as I'm hated in Nassau County and America, I believe there are persons that are strengthened by me and my stand."

Judge Belfi saw things differently. "Colin Ferguson, in my almost 21 years on the bench, I have never presided over a trial with a more selfish and self-centered defendant," the judge said before a packed courtroom. "The vicious acts you committed on December 7, 1993, were the acts of a coward."

During the trial the New York State Legislature had re-instituted the death penalty for murder. However, Ferguson would not face execution because his crimes occurred before the law was passed. "Unfortunately, this new law cannot be applied to you," Judge Belfi told Ferguson. "The court is, however, empowered to mete out a sentence equivalent to life without parole."

Noting the killer's "total lack of remorse," Judge Belfi sentenced Ferguson to six consecutive 25-years-to-life terms, one for each count of murder. The judge also gave Ferguson 25-year sentences for each of 19 counts of attempted murder—for a total of 475 years. But prison terms for multiple convictions of attempted murder are limited by New York law to a total of 50 years. Thus, Ferguson's combined sentences added up to 200 years. His victims and their families cheered as the sentence was read.

Ferguson appealed his conviction, asking for legal counsel this time. However, in December 1998, the New York Court of Appeals refused Ferguson's request for a new trial.

Colin Ferguson's killing spree opened the debate on the issue of gun control. The widow of one of his victim's, Carolyn McCarthy, became a crusader for stricter gun control laws. A retired nurse, McCarthy became a fervent activist for the issue and ran for a seat in Congress in 1996. Campaigning primarily on the basis of tighter regulations on the availability of guns, the political novice won, stunning many observers and proving that the populace agreed with her views.

—Tom Smith

Suggestions for Further Reading

Baum, Geraldine. "Long Island Raid Road Shooting a Charade." *Detroit News* (February 13, 1995): 1A, 8A.

McQuiston, John T. "L. I. R. R. Trial Has Adviser Disgusted." *New York Times* (January 31, 1995): B5.

Nieves, Evelyn. "An Anguished Audience in a Theater of the Absurd." *New York Times* (January 31, 1995): B5.

Sheik Omar Abdel Rahman Trial: 1995–96

Defendants: Sheik Omar Abdel Rahman, El Sayyid Nosair, Ibrahim El-Gabrowny, Victor Alvarez, Amir Abdelgani, Fadil Abdelghani, Tarig Elhassan, Ramzi Ahmed Yousef, Rodney Hampton-El, Fares Khallafalla, and Mohammed Saleh **Crimes Charged:** All defendants: Seditious conspiracy; Nosair: Murder and assault; individual charges included solicitation and conspiracy to commit assassination or bombings, violations of the Racketeer Influenced and Corrupt Organizations (RICO) Act, and weapons charges **Chief Defense Lawyers:** Lynne F. Stewart, John Jacobs, Ramsey Clark, and Anthony Ricco **Chief Prosecutor:** Mary Jo White **Judge:** Michael B. Mukasey **Place:** New York, New York **Dates of Trial:** January 30, 1995–January 17, 1996 **Verdicts:** Abdel Rahman: Guilty of conspiracy and solicitation to commit sedition, assassination, and attacks on U.S. military installations; Nosair: Guilty of conspiracy, assault, and murder; Not guilty on 2 counts of bombing conspiracy; El-Gabrowny: Guilty of assault and plotting to aid Nosair; Not guilty on 2 counts of bombing conspiracy; remaining defendants: Guilty of participating in the bombing conspiracy **Sentences:** Abdel Rahman and Nosair: Life imprisonment; El-Gabrowny: 57 years imprisonment; Alvarez, Elhassan, and Hampton-El: 35 years imprisonment each; Abdelgani and Khallafalla: 30 years imprisonment each; Abdelghani: 25 years imprisonment

SIGNIFICANCE

The rarely used antisedition statute was used successfully to prosecute and convict foreign terrorists.

Before a terrorist bomb exploded in the World Trade Center on February 26, 1993, few Americans had ever heard of Sheik Omar Abdel Rahman, a blind cleric who preached militant Islamic doctrine from a Jersey City storefront mosque. He might have been an obscure figure in his New Jersey exile, but the sheik was well known to Islamic fundamentalists and security police in his native Egypt. Abdel Rahman had been acquitted of aiding the 1981 assassination of Egyptian President Anwar Sadat. He later fled prosecution on charges of fomenting a riot and came to the United States in 1990, despite the fact that his name was on a computerized list of suspected terrorists barred from entering the country.

As arrests followed the World Trade Center bombing, it was discovered that all but one of the suspects were followers of the cleric. Sheik Abdel Rahman's virulent anti-American sermons attracted a public scrutiny that was lacking before the explosion in New York. He was constantly surrounded by FBI agents and news hungry reporters. Although it was speculated that Abdel Rahman might be arrested for complicity in the bombing, Attorney General Janet Reno announced that too little evidence existed for an immediate indictment.

Sheik Arrested in Terrorist Plot

On July 2, 1993, however, Sheik Abdel Rahman was arrested after a tense standoff at the Jersey City mosque. He and 10 other men were indicted for plotting "a war of urban terrorism against the United States." Under a rarely used seditious conspiracy law, the Sedition Act of 1918, Abdel Rahman was charged with coordinating the group, whose alleged targets included the United Nations, New York's FBI office, and the Holland and Lincoln Tunnels. The defendants were not charged directly in the World Trade Center bombing case, but prosecutors accused Abdel Rahman of giving final approval for the attack. The defendants were also accused of planning to kill Egyptian President Hosni Mubarak, as well as several American politicians sympathetic to Israel.

Sheik Omar Abdel-Rahman convicted of seditious conspiracy for plotting a "war of urban terrorism against the United States." (AP/Wide World Photos)

Not all of the charges centered on unrealized plots. In a controversial 1991 New York state trial, El Sayyid Nosair had been convicted of gun possession and assault, but acquitted of murdering militant Rabbi Meir Kahane in 1990. By claiming that he was involved in the newly uncovered plot, federal prosecutors indicted Nosair again for the Kahane murder without breaking the double-jeopardy rule against trying a defendant twice for the same crime. Borrowing a legal tactic used successfully against organized crime figures like John Gotti, the government charged Nosair under the Racketeer Influenced and Corrupt Organizations (RICO) Act, contending that the killing was part of a larger pattern of criminal activity.

Soon after the trial began on January 30, 1995, the defense was shaken by the news that Siddig Ibrahim Siddig Ali, Abdel Rahman's translator, would plead guilty. Following a plea bargain agreement, Siddig Ali implicated all but one of his codefendants, including the sheik, whom he accused of approving the bombing targets. Outraged defense lawyers Lynne Stewart, John Jacobs, Ramsey Clark, and Anthony Ricco protested that Siddig Ali's recent deal with the government had denied them a chance to attack his credibility in their opening statements; they were demanding a mistrial when even more sensational news arrived. On the same day that Siddig Ali's plea bargain was announced, Ramzi Ahmed Yousef was arrested in Pakistan. Yousef, the fugitive whom federal officials accused of directing the four men already tried and imprisoned for the World Trade Center bombing, was being returned to the United States to stand trial.

Bomb Factory Described in Testimony

Despite Siddig Ali's defection, the prosecution's case was still expected to be difficult to prove, for it relied heavily upon the testimony of an Egyptian-born U.S. government informant named Emad Salem, whose credibility and motives were fiercely challenged. Salem admitted on the witness stand that he had lied repeatedly to the FBI in order to impress the law enforcement agency of his usefulness. He also admitted demanding large amounts of money for working as an informer.

While under the FBI's employ, Salem had actively helped some of the conspirators, renting a Queens warehouse where he videotaped them mixing fuel oil and fertilizer into explosives. The FBI offered hours of recordings made by Salem in which the defendants implicated themselves in the bombing plot. Despite Salem's proximity to Abdel Rahman's inner circle, however, prosecutors offered as physical evidence only one taped conversation in which the sheik directly approved a terrorist action. Salem told Abdel Rahman that a wave of attacks was being planned and asked if the United Nations was a legitimate bombing target. Abdel Rahman replied that bombing the UN might be bad for Muslims because the institution was perceived to be a center for peace. He then told Salem to "find a plan" to inflict damage on the U.S. Army instead. Salem also spoke of bombing the FBI's New York headquarters, but the sheik told him not to proceed, adding that much preparation would be needed for such a target.

Prosecutors declared that the conversation was proof that Abdel Rahman was directing the plotters and approving targets. The defense responded that it was the informer Salem who was orchestrating the conversations, pointing out that the sheik instructed Salem *not* to carry out the attacks. The defense further argued that Abdel Rahman's suggestions of alternative targets were merely efforts to mollify the apparently excitable Salem, who had been presenting himself as a fervent religious disciple.

Salem's tapes and Siddig Ali's defection were not the only testimony presented against Abdel Rahman. Abdo Mohammed Haggag, a former aide to the sheik and one of the defendants, agreed to a plea bargain that resulted in conspiracy charges against him being dropped. Haggag stated that Abdel Rahman had approved a plot to assassinate President Mubarak, but that the plan was never carried out because the Egyptian president had canceled a trip to the United

States. The defense, in response, accused Haggag of lying to obtain his freedom and to get revenge against the sheik, with whom he had had a falling out.

Defense Claims Religious Persecution

Throughout the trial, the defense argued that Abdel Rahman was a spiritual leader being prosecuted for his speech. The prosecution contended that the sheik had instead acted more like an organized crime boss, approving violent acts against his enemies and trying to ferret out informers from his organization. The trial slowed to a crawl as investigators offered scores of exhibits whose details allegedly proved conspiratorial relationships between the accused.

Defendant Rodney Hampton-El testified that he was lying when he had boasted of being able to obtain bomb detonators for Salem and Siddig Ali. In any case, Hampton-El claimed, he was under the impression that the bomb under discussion was being made to attack a New York warehouse full of weapons being stockpiled illegally for use against Bosnian Muslims, not against domestic U.S. sites named in the indictment against him. Victor Alvarez's attorney defended his client by characterizing him as a mentally handicapped cocaine addict, unable to grasp the full implications of helping fellow Muslims he was trying to impress.

Jury Convicts on 48 Charges

The trial, which involved testimony from 200 witnesses, went to jury deliberations the third week of September 1995. On Sunday, October 1, 1995, the 10 defendants were found guilty on 48 of 50 charges. Nosair and his cousin, Ibrahim El-Gabrowny, were cleared of complicity in the citywide bombing plot. They were convicted, however, of assault and conspiracy charges, including a plot to help Nosair escape from Attica prison and flee the country using fake passports. The other defendants—Alvarez, Hampton-El, Amir Abdelgani, Fadil Abdelghani, Tarig Elhassan, Fares Khallafalla, and Mohammed Saleh—were all convicted of conspiracy and charges relating to the preparation of bombs to be used in the planned attacks.

The defendants remained silent when the verdicts were read. Before they were sentenced on January 17, 1996, however, each took the opportunity to declare his innocence. Sheik Abdel Rahman angrily denounced the United States and the trial proceedings for over an hour and a half before Judge Michael B. Mukasey cut him off. "This case is nothing but an extension of the American war against Islam," protested Abdel Rahman.

The judge was unimpressed. "You were convicted of directing others to perform acts which, if accomplished, would have resulted in the murder of hundreds if not thousands of people," Mukasey said, adding that the bombing of the World Trade Center would have seemed "insignificant" by comparison.

The blind cleric received a life sentence for conspiracy and solicitation to commit sedition, assassination, and attacks on U.S. military installations. Nosair, who was convicted of conspiracy, assault, and the 1990 murder of Rabbi Meir Kahane, also received a life sentence. El-Gabrowny was sentenced to 57 years imprisonment for assault and plotting to aid Nosair. The remaining defendants received sentences ranging from 25–35 years for their parts in the bombing conspiracy.

Controversies over alleged connections between politics, religion, and the legal system continued long after Sheik Abdel Rahman was incarcerated in a federal penitentiary. His supporters continued to press for the diabetic cleric's release on medical grounds, and to protest that he had been framed by the United States as a favor to the Egyptian government.

— Tom Smith

Suggestions for Further Reading

Dwyer, Jim et al. *Two Seconds under the World.* New York: Crown Publishers, 1994.

Fried, Joseph P. "Closing Arguments Start Tuesday In Terror-Bomb Trial." *New York Times* (September 3, 1995): B30.

——. "Sheik and Nine Followers Guilty of a Conspiracy of Terrorism." *New York Times* (October 2, 1995): A1.

Waneta Hoyt Trial: 1995

Defendant: Waneta Hoyt **Crime Charged:** Murder
Chief Defense Lawyers: Robert Miller and Raymond J. Urbanski
Chief Prosecutors: Robert J. Simpson and Margaret Drake **Judge:** Vincent Sgueglia **Place:** Owego, New York **Dates of Trial:** March 30–April 21, 1995 **Verdict:** Guilty on 5 counts of murder **Sentence:** 75 years imprisonment (she died of cancer after serving 3)

SIGNIFICANCE

The Waneta Hoyt case challenged a long-standing medical theory about Sudden Infant Death Syndrome (SIDS) and raised questions about other parents who used the disease as a cover for murdering their own children.

A young child, typically between two and six months old, dies without warning during the night. The baby does not cry out in pain or torment. If an autopsy is performed, the doctor finds no clinical reason for the death. The likely conclusion: the child died of Sudden Infant Death Syndrome. Reports of unexplained "crib deaths" date back hundreds of years, but the term "Sudden Infant Death Syndrome" was not widely used—or systematically studied— until the 1960s.

Waneta Hoyt and her husband Tim seemed particularly hard hit by SIDS. The couple lived in the rural town of Newark Valley, New York. As far back as 1965, Mrs. Hoyt had stood by helplessly as each of her five small children died of SIDS. (A sixth, adopted child, survived infancy.) The youngest was just three months old at the time of death; the oldest just under three years.

The Hoyts' tragedy caught the attention of Dr. Alfred Steinschneider, a local pediatrician studying SIDS. In a famous 1972 article, Steinschneider chronicled the deaths of the last two Hoyt children and introduced the notion that SIDS resulted from a hereditary form of apnea, a condition that cuts off a person's breathing during sleep. Steinschneider's theory and strategies for combating the problem gradually became accepted in pediatric medicine. However, years later, the details of the Hoyt infant deaths began arousing legal suspicions.

Searching for the Truth

In the early 1980s, William Fitzpatrick, an assistant district attorney in upstate New York, investigated a crime of infanticide. He worked on the case with Dr. Linda Norton, a Texas medical examiner.

Norton was familiar with Steinschneider's groundbreaking article—and doubted its conclusions. She handed the article to Fitzpatrick, telling him to read it and saying, "You may decide you have a serial killer here."

Like Norton, Fitzpatrick was struck by the extraordinary odds of one family having five children die of SIDS. The article did not mention the Hoyts by name, printing only their initials, but Fitzpatrick was able to uncover their identity. In 1992, now the district attorney for Onondaga County, he located the Hoyts in nearby Tioga County. He shared his suspicions with his counterpart there, Robert J. Simpson. After studying old medical records, Simpson concluded with Fitzpatrick that Waneta Hoyt had most likely killed her children.

Finally questioned so many years later by state police, Hoyt admitted her crimes, offering details of how she smothered each of the children. "They just kept crying and crying." Hoyt said, ". . . and I just kept squeezing and squeezing and squeezing." On March 23, 1994, Hoyt was charged with 10 counts of second-degree murder—5 for intent to kill and 5 for "creating a grave risk of death."

The Trial

During the opening arguments at Hoyt's trial, the prosecution revealed her confession about the murders. The defense countered that Hoyt's statements had been made under duress, and she had since recanted her confession. As the trial progressed, the prosecutors introduced testimony from nurses who had worked with the Hoyt children and had had suspicions about their deaths. Another prosecution witness was Dr. Michael M. Braden, a forensic pathologist who had examined the bodies of the children after they were exhumed prior to the trial. According to Braden, all five children were deliberately suffocated. He said, "There are no natural conditions, including sudden infant death, that can explain the deaths."

The main witness for the defense was the renowned SIDS expert himself, Dr. Steinschneider. By now he was president of the American SIDS Institute in Atlanta. Steinschneider testified that the deaths of the two Hoyt children he had reviewed were consistent with SIDS. But under cross-examination, he stated that he did not know how thoroughly the police had searched for evidence of foul play. "For all I know," Steinschneider admitted, "they could have been suffocated."

Steinschneider's theory of SIDS had been under close scrutiny since Hoyt's arrest in 1994. Some doctors, such as Dr. Linda Norton, believed the sleep-apnea theory diverted attention away from parents who had killed their children and then claimed SIDS was to blame. Some medical examiners and prosecutors believed that as many as 20 percent of the approximately 7,500 SIDS deaths reported annually resulted from other causes—including murder. Cases similar to Hoyt's had been reported before and at the time of her trial. But many legal and medical officials also stressed that children did indeed die of SIDS, and most parents of dead infants were not killers.

In the end, the jury believed Hoyt's original confession and the other evidence against her were sufficient proof to find Hoyt guilty of murdering all five children. Judge Vincent Sgueglia sentenced her to 15 years for each murder. Already ill at the time of her trial, Hoyt served just 3 of her 75-year sentence, dying of pancreatic cancer in September 1998. Her trial and conviction revealed the necessity for legal and medical officials to look beyond SIDS when faced with the seemingly inexplicable death of a child.

—Michael Burgan

Suggestions for Further Reading

Eftimiades, Cynthia Sanz Maria. "A Mother's Fatal Embrace." *People* (November 9, 1995): 103.

Firstman, Richard and Jamie Talan. *The Death of Innocents: A True Story of Murder, Medicine and High-Stakes Science.* New York: Bantam Books, 1997.

Gruson, Lindsey. "A 25-Year Trail to Five Murder Charges." *New York Times* (March 29, 1994): B1.

Judson, George. "Mother Guilty in the Killings of Five Babies" *New York Times* (April 22, 1995): 25.

Steinberg, Jacques. "Pathologist Says Five Children Died of Deliberate Suffocation." *New York Times* (April 7, 1995): B5.

——. "Defense Begins for Mother in Sudden Deaths of Five Children." *New York Times* (April 11, 1995): B4.

Toufexis, Anastasia. "When Is Crib Death a Cover for Murder?" *Time* (April 11, 1994): 6.

Brandon Teena Murder Trial: 1995

Defendants: John Lotter, Marvin Thomas Nissen   **Crimes Charged:** Murder, kidnap, rape   **Chief Defense Lawyers:** Lotter: Michael Fabian; Nissen: Peter Blakeslee   **Chief Prosecutor:** James Elworth   **Judge:** Robert Finn **Place:** Falls City, Nebraska   **Dates of Trials:** Lotter: May 15–25, 1995; Nissen: February 21–March 3, 1995   **Verdicts:** Lotter: guilty of three counts of first-degree murder and four other charges; Nissen: guilty of first-degree murder of Brandon Teena and second-degree murder in deaths of potential witnesses Lisa Lambert and Philip DeVine; also convicted of burglary **Sentences:** Lotter: death; Nissen: three consecutive life terms

SIGNIFICANCE

Brandon Teena was born a girl. Later Teena decided to change sexual identification, and began to pass as a young man by the name of Brandon Teena. Brandon concealed the fact that he was biologically a woman. When his biological identity was uncovered, two young men who had befriended him as a man forcibly raped him. After Brandon reported the rape to the local sheriff, he did not arrest the rapists. A few days later the two men tracked down Brandon to an isolated farmhouse in Humboldt, Nebraska, where they killed him and two witnesses. Since Brandon Teena had chosen a gender identity different than that he was born with, his murder drew widespread attention. In particular, the transgendered community saw him as a martyr because he chose to be different.

Although born and raised as a girl, Brandon Teena made a conscious choice to live as a man. (Hence the use of the male pronoun to describe him in this entry.) Brandon was originally from Lincoln, Nebraska, and had moved to the Falls City area to take up his life as a man, hoping for an eventual sex-change operation. As a teenager, Brandon had several scrapes with the law over stolen credit cards and forged checks. Brandon passed as a man quite readily, dating a local girl in Falls City, Lana Tisdale, and befriending Thomas Nissen and John Lotter. Brandon would wear a sock in his pants in order to appear more male. John Lotter had previously dated Lana Tisdale.

In December 1993, local police arrested Brandon on a misdemeanor check forgery charge and at that time discovered that Brandon was biologically female. The police released the information. The information was published in the local

Falls City Journal. Apparently both Lotter and Nissen, unsure of their own sexual identity, became enraged that Brandon had won the affection of Lana Tisdale. Lotter and Nissen, both of whom had already served time in the state penitentiary on other charges, had been involved in a variety of unhappy relationships, drank heavily, and had floated from job to job. The issues of homophobia, sexual insecurity, and enraged bigotry against those crossing the gender line came into disastrous confluence.

The Rape and Murder

On Christmas Day, 1993, Brandon was raped and assaulted at a Christmas party by two men whom he identified as Nissen and Lotter to Richardson County sherriff Charles B. Laux. The failure of Laux to immediately arrest the two men became an issue. Brandon's sister, Tammy Brandon, called the sheriff's office to inquire why the two had not been arrested, and said that deputies told her the sheriff was collecting evidence. A Falls City police officer told the two men that they were suspects in the December 25 rape. On New Year's Eve, Lotter and Nissen drove about looking for Brandon. They carried a rope and hatchet in their car, and eventually tracked Brandon to a friend's farmhouse in Humboldt. After killing Brandon, they allowed Lisa Lambert to put her baby in a crib before they shot and killed her. Philip DeVine, who was visiting Lambert at the time, pleaded for his life before he was shot at close range.

Teena Brandon, a woman who posed as a man, was raped and murdered. (AP/Wide World Photos)

The Trials

Marvin Thomas Nissen incriminated Lotter, claiming that he had fired all the shots. He later admitted that he had stabbed Brandon to make sure he was dead. At Nissen's trial, Assistant Attorney General James Elworth, serving as special prosecutor in the case, pointed to evidence of premeditation. Nissen told his wife on December 30, 1993, that he was going to get a power of attorney over his children for his mother. Elworth claimed Nissen had done so because he knew he would be in jail and that he would not be able to take care of his children. Elworth showed through testimony that Lotter and Nissen had gone to the Falls City home of Lana Tisdale, and then drove by the home of a local deputy sheriff to make sure he was home and would not disturb them. Wearing gloves, they then drove to the Humboldt farmhouse where Brandon was staying.

Had they intended only to frighten or intimidate Brandon, they would not have been wearing gloves, Elworth claimed.

The shootings were conducted in execution style, leaving powder burns on the bodies. Although Nissen said that Lotter did all the shooting, he was also legally responsible. Elworth explained to the jury that they could find Nissen guilty of first-degree murder by several lines of logic. Even if he had not premeditated the crime, committing a murder during the course of a burglary, under Nebraska law, was also first-degree murder.

Lotter's attorney, Mike Fabian, tried to pin Nissen down to admitting that he hated Brandon, and that the rape was inspired by hate. But both Nissen and Lotter denied that they hated Brandon.

Peter Blakeslee, Nissen's attorney, argued that Nissen was less involved in the murders than Lotter, and asked the jurors to consider charges less serious than first-degree murder. He claimed the plan was Lotter's and that Nissen was not sure what they were going to do on the night of the murder.

At Lotter's trial, Nissen testified against Lotter, claiming that Lotter had killed all three of the victims, and told police they had thrown the murder weapons in a nearby river. Lotter never confessed, and he denied any part in the murders, claiming he was asleep in the car while Nissen committed the murders. Lotter's attorney claimed that all the evidence against Lotter was circumstantial and unsuccessfully sought to bar Nissen's testimony.

In February 1996, Lotter was sentenced to death. In May of 1997, Nissen's appeals were turned down by the U.S. Supreme Court.

Gender Issues

The Brandon Teena story became a national issue in the gay, lesbian, and transgendered communities. Since Brandon was essentially scorned, raped, and then murdered for his effort to redefine his biological gender, and since he was ousted by local authorities and press, his murder came to symbolize the difficulties facing those ostracized by mainstream society over gender identity issues. Brandon's former girlfriends in Nebraska found themselves stigmatized as lesbians, although they denied that their affairs with Brandon were lesbian in nature. They simply felt that they were innocent victims of sexual deception.

Brandon's mother, Joann Brandon, sued Sheriff Charles Laux in 1998 for not offering her daughter protective custody after Brandon reported the rape by Lotter and Nissen. The lower court ruled against Joann Brandon, saying that because Brandon dressed as a man, he was partly responsible for his own death. However, on April 20, 2001, the Nebraska Supreme Court overturned that ruling and said that Sheriff Laux was negligent for not providing protection to Brandon.

Aphrodite Jones authored *All She Wanted*, a sympathetic true-crime study of the rape and killing, and Jami Floyd, an ABC reporter, put together a television documentary for ABC *20/20* television. A full-length documentary movie, *The Brandon Teena Story*, the popular film *Boys Don't Cry*, together with numerous magazine articles and an Internet website all served as testimony to the compelling appeal of the tale in which this sensitive but troubled young person became a victim of prejudice and violent crime.

—*Rodney Carlisle*

Suggestions for Further Reading

Jones, Aphrodite. *All She Wanted*. New York: Simon and Schuster, 1998.

Muska, Susan, and Greta Olafsdottir. *The Brandon Teena Story*. Zeitgeist Films, 1998.

Susan Smith Trial: 1995

Defendant: Susan Smith **Crime Charged:** Murder
Chief Defense Lawyers: David Bruck and Judy Clarke
Chief Prosecutor: Tommy Pope **Judge:** William Howard **Place:** Union,
South Carolina **Dates of Trial:** July 18–28, 1995 **Verdict:** Guilty
Sentence: Life imprisonment

SIGNIFICANCE

The notion of a mother deliberately killing her own children is particularly
abhorrent, but as this trial revealed, all too often mere facts sometimes only hint
at the full complexities of a tragedy.

At around 9:15 P.M. on October 25, 1994, a young mother, Susan Smith, was driving her two children home in Union, South Carolina, when she stopped at a red light. Suddenly a young black man with a gun allegedly forced his way into the car and ordered Smith to drive off. A few miles later she was thrown from the car, which then sped away, still carrying her two screaming sons, three-year-old Michael and his 14-month-old brother, Alex. Dazed and distraught, Smith ran for help.

A massive search by the authorities failed to uncover any trace of the two boys; nor did numerous television appeals by the grieving mother and her estranged husband, David, result in any answers. Then, nine days after the alleged carjacking, detectives reinterviewed Smith, at which time she recanted her original story and made a confession that she had drowned her two boys. Following her admission to the police, divers searched a nearby lake, and there, submerged just off a boat ramp, they found Smith's missing Mazda. Horrifyingly, the bodies of her two sons were strapped inside. That same day Smith was charged with first-degree murder.

On July 18, 1995, when Judge William Howard banged his gavel to call to order South Carolina's most closely watched trial in decades, solicitor Tommy Pope described the carjacking story as a fabrication, concocted by Smith to hide the fact that she had murdered her children simply because they were obstacles to an affair she was conducting.

The defense, led by David Bruck, took the position that this tragedy had really been a botched suicide attempt by an unstable woman rejected by the man she loved.

A diver for the South Carolina Wildlife Department, Steve Morrow, on the stand as a prosecution witness, described the harrowing scene of how he had found the boys' bodies. He shined his flashlight through the murky water, into the submerged vehicle and, "I was able to see a small hand against the glass." In a voice cracking with emotion, he described the car as having nose-dived into the mud, and he saw the boys' heads hanging downward in their car seats.

Lover Takes Stand

In her handwritten confession, Smith wrote, "I was in love with someone very much, but he didn't love me and never would." The man she wrote about was a graphic artist named Tom Findlay, who enthralled the court with details of a stormy relationship that came to a head on October 25, 1994.

Findlay admitted seeing Smith three times on that fateful day, and that she had been overwrought. According to the prosecution, this despair resulted from Findlay's decision to end their affair, and it was this that had driven Smith to murder. Pope produced as evidence a two-page letter from Findlay to Smith that had been recovered from the submerged car. It said, "There are some things about you which aren't suited for me, and yes, I am speaking about your children. I'm sure that your kids are good kids, but it really wouldn't matter how good they may be. The fact is, I just don't want children."

Alexander and Michael Smith, a month before their death. (AP/Wide World Photos)

Under cross-examination, Findlay spoke compassionately about Smith. "The Susan that I know is very caring, very loving, a good friend to everyone, not just me," and he claimed they had remained on good terms even after their relationship had ended on October 15, when he had seen her kissing another man at a hot-tub party.

Key to the defense's case was Smith's dysfunctional background and its subsequent psychological impact on her. Defense witness Jenny Ward, a caseworker, told the court how, in 1989, she had investigated Smith's allegation that at the age of 15 she had been molested by her stepfather, Beverly Russell, charges that Russell had indeed admitted. "That is child sexual abuse," said Ward. "It is criminal in nature. The child said it, the perpetrator admitted it—that's a case."

Despite this, the Smith family refused to press charges against him, intimidated, Ward believed, by Russell's strong affiliations with the local Republican Party, and the matter was sealed. "That's the only order I've had sealed in 20 years," Ward said.

Her explanation of how sexual abuse in childhood, if not properly treated, can have adverse reactions in later life failed to impress Pope, who drew attention to the forceful manner in which Smith had conducted her relationship with Russell.

Ward was defiant. "I hold adults responsible for adult behavior," she said, but when pressed she was forced to admit that Smith had never appeared troubled or suicidal at the time.

Horrible Choice

Was it murder or a botched suicide? Pope made his opinion very clear. In closing arguments he said, "On the night of October 25, Susan Smith made a choice—a horrible, horrible choice. She chose the love of a man over the love of those boys. . . . This case screams out for a verdict of murder." Letting go of the emergency brake was, he said, like pulling a trigger. "The intent was formed when she pulled the trigger to the car and let it drop down into the lake." Seeking to make the jury visualize the sheer terror of the victims and the wanton disregard shown by their mother he went on, "I submit those children . . . in the car . . . were screaming and yelling and they were calling for their father while she was running up the hill. . . . If she truly wanted to stop the deaths of those boys she could have pulled the brake up."

"Absurd," responded Judy Clarke, who closed for the defense. "Sadness is what brings us together—not evil. . . . The love of Susan Smith for those two boys was unbelievable. There is no evidence of anything but absolute unconditional love. . . . The only two people who loved her unconditionally are gone. She made that decision with a confused mind and a heart that has no hope." Clarke urged the jury to show compassion, repeating her belief that this tragedy had resulted from a failed suicide, in which case the verdict should be involuntary manslaughter.

On July 22, the jury took just two and a half hours to decide that Smith was guilty of murder.

During the penalty phase of the trial, the testimony that would decide whether Smith lived or died again concentrated on the circumstances of her troubled upbringing. The court heard how, following the suicide of her father, Smith had been lured into an intermittent sexual relationship with her stepfather. Now, for the first time, Russell appeared on the stand, to plead with the jury not to take Smith's life. Sobbing, he read aloud from a letter he had written her while she was in jail. "I want you to know you do not have all the guilt in this tragedy. . . . My heart breaks for what I have done to you."

The jury decided that her sad past had influenced her actions, and on July 28 Smith was sentenced to life in prison. She will not be eligible for parole until 2025.

—Colin Evans

Suggestions for Further Reading

Eftimiades, Maria. *Sins of the Mother*. New York: St. Martin's Paperbacks, 1995.

Peyser, Andrea. *Mother Love, Deadly Love: The Susan Smith Murders*. New York: Harper, 1995.

Rekers, George. *Susan Smith: Victim or Murderer*. Lakewood, Colo.: Glenbridge Publishers, 1996.

Smith, David with Carol Calef. *Beyond All Reason: My Life with Susan Smith*. New York: Pinnacle Books, 1996.

Yolanda Saldivar Trial: 1995

Defendant: Yolanda Saldivar   **Crime Charged:** Murder
Chief Defense Lawyer: Doug Tinker   **Chief Prosecutor:** Carlos Valdez
Judge: Mike Westergren   **Place:** Houston, Texas   **Date of Trial:** October 11–23, 1995   **Verdict:** Guilty   **Sentence:** Life in prison with possibility of parole in 30 years

SIGNIFICANCE

The fate of a popular music star's killer hung on one question: Was she a suicidal woman accidentally shooting the object of her adoration, or was she a cold-blooded murderer playing the blame game?

By age 23, Selena Quintanilla Perez had taken the Tex-Mex world of *Tejano* music by storm. Known simply as "Selena," the pretty, diminutive singer with the big voice and squeaky-clean image was poised to take her popular, award-winning sound into the American mainstream. But her violent death at the hands of the woman who organized Selena's fan club and whom the young singer called "mother" bitterly ended those dreams.

A Rising Star

Was Selena's death on March 31, 1995, a cold-blooded murder or was it a tragic accident? This became the consuming question not only for the *Tejano* (Spanish word for Texas) music world, centered largely in Corpus Christi where Selena lived and died, but ultimately in the trial of Yolanda Saldivar.

Saldivar came into Selena's life in 1991, when the mousy registered nurse approached Selena's manager/father Abraham for his blessing to organize the Selena Fan Club. He agreed.

For the next few years, Selena's career blossomed as did the unusually strong bond between Saldivar and the singer. Saldivar tended to Selena's every personal whim and many of her professional needs, eventually controlling access to Selena for everyone but family members. In 1993, Selena named Saldivar manager of her Corpus Christi fashion boutique, Selena, Etc. The shop, one of two that marketed Selena's fashion designs, was the singer's personal creative outlet, one off limits to her controlling father. Or so she thought.

Abraham Quintanilla had directed his daughter's career with a strong hand since she was nine years old. Selena first sang as part of a family band her restaurateur father created, *Selena y Los Dinos*. Quintanilla knocked on closed doors, dogged reluctant record companies, and took Selena out of school in eighth grade to concentrate on a music career. Selena won awards and signed a recording contract with EMI Latin. In 1992, she married a guitarist in her band, Chris Perez. Meanwhile, Saldivar's feelings for Selena progressed from adoring to obsessive. She even gave her an egg-shaped diamond ring.

Selena's talent, good looks, and hard work brought her a dedicated following, but her fame was largely limited to regional Spanish-American audiences. Quintanilla decided to change that. He just had to overcome a few obstacles, including Yolanda Saldivar.

Killing Follows Embezzlement Accusations

Rumors had circulated among boutique staff about Saldivar's mismanagement of money since Selena had elevated her to boutique manager. Bills went unpaid. Books appeared cooked. Saldivar had a record of stealing money from a previous employer and had not paid back loans for nursing school. Selena refused to believe that her faithful confidant was embezzling; Quintanilla was convinced and furious about it.

On March 9, 1995, he confronted Saldivar, demanding to know where missing money had gone not only from the boutique but from the fan club. Saldivar had no answers. Quintanilla threatened to pursue the matter legally.

In response, Saldivar bought a .38-caliber revolver from a gunstore in San Antonio where she lived. Saldivar claimed she bought the gun to protect herself from Quintanilla, who had trumped up the embezzlement charges to get rid of her. During the trial, the defense contended Saldivar bought the weapon to kill herself. She actually had put the gun to her head to do so when Selena arrived at her Days Inn room in Corpus Christi. But in a terrible turn of events, Saldivar accidentally shot the singer instead.

In his opening statement to jurors, court-appointed defense attorney Doug "The Stinker" Tinker said that as Selena entered the hotel room, Saldivar motioned with the hand in which she held the gun for Selena to shut the door. As the singer turned to do so, the gun accidentally discharged. A single bullet struck Selena in the back near the right shoulder.

Trial Focuses on Shooting Aftermath

The prosecution claimed Saldivar deliberately shot Selena as she attempted to flee Room 158. The state claimed Selena had finally been convinced that Saldivar was stealing from her. Selena had come to the motel to fire her employee.

What happened immediately after the shot rang out became fodder for national news media as well as a key question in the murder trial. (Sensational pre-trial publicity led presiding Judge Mike Westergren to issue a gag order, relocate the trial to Houston, and ban television cameras in the courtroom.)

Hotel desk clerk Shawna Vela described how Selena ran into the hotel lobby just after noon that cloudy day, leaving a 390-foot trail of blood. She testified that Selena screamed, "She shot me. She's in room 158. Lock the door or she'll shoot me again." The last word on Selena's lips before she collapsed was "Yolanda." She held in her hand the diamond ring Saldivar given her. Selena apparently had taken the ring off her finger to return to Saldivar.

Fans of slain music star Selena wait outside the courthouse for the sentence of convicted killer Yolanda Saldivar. (AP/Wide World Photos)

Selena died less than two hours later on the operating table at a nearby hospital, where she had been rushed after the shooting. Meanwhile, Saldivar ran to the red GMC pick-up she had borrowed from her nephew for the trip from San Antonio. She drove the truck to the hotel lobby and parked there. As police arrived, she put the gun to her head. She held police at bay for nearly 10 hours. She begged hostage negotiators to shoot her before surrendering.

Days Inn housekeeper Norma Martinez testified for the prosecution how a bloody Selena fled the hotel room as Saldivar ran after her, pointing the gun at the singer and yelling "bitch!" The defense attacked Martinez's testimony, noting that she embellished her story with the accusation that Saldivar yelled "bitch." Martinez, a convicted thief, said she hadn't wanted to use a curse word when giving police her statement.

Tinker also doggedly chipped away at Vela's testimony and that of other hotel employees. Tinker was able to uncover testimony contradictions, but his point seemingly was lost. Every witness painted a picture of Saldivar as a ranting murderess relentlessly pursuing her prey.

The defense claimed the shooting was provoked by Selena's overbearing father, then covered up by overzealous Corpus Christi police doing sloppy work. Prosecutors accused Tinker of using "the squid defense," spreading ink about anyone but the predator herself. If Saldivar had shot Selena accidentally, why didn't she call 911 instead of the motel manager? Why didn't she run after Selena and try to help her after the shooting?

The prosecution presented 122 exhibits and called on 33 witnesses, including the hotel employees. Selena, Etc. staff asserted Saldivar was stealing from the business. Quintanilla family members told of the deteriorating relationship between Selena and her business associate.

The defense presented only five witnesses: three hotel employees; Saldivar's seventh-grade teacher, and the policeman who took Saldivar's confession. Tinker asked investigator Paul Rivera why he didn't consider audiotapes made between police and Yolanda when she held them at bay in her nephew's truck after the shooting. Rivera said he didn't know about them.

The audiotapes stand out as the most riveting portion of the trial. For five hours, police taped exchanges between their negotiators and a distraught, crying and wailing Saldivar as she held them at bay. She alleged Abraham Quintanilla hated her, spread rumors she was a lesbian and a thief, and had raped her. On tape she cried, "I did something very bad. I have disgraced my family." As the audio played in court, Saldivar sobbed.

Tinker claimed that the tapes proved Saldivar's confession was coerced. The tapes showed Saldivar told the truth when she claimed the shooting was accidental, a fact not mentioned in the confession. The prosecution said the tapes only proved that Saldivar was an unstable person and a pathological liar. The defense countered that before the police began recording the negotiations leading to Saldivar's surrender, she had said several times that she did not mean to shoot Selena. Prosecutor Carlos Valdez established that Saldivar never said the shooting was accidental until negotiator Larry Young suggested it.

Judge Westergren instructed the jury to consider only murder, as both sides had agreed. The prosecution wanted to placate public outrage by going for the toughest charge. The defense decided Saldivar's chances for acquittal rested on an all-or-nothing trial. The jury took only two hours to find Saldivar guilty. Although Tinker argued for probation, Saldivar received the maximum punishment of life in prison with no chance of parole until 2030.

In December 1995, Judge Westergren denied Saldivar's bid for a new trial. Saldivar appealed to the 14th Court of Appeals in Houston, which unanimously affirmed her conviction on October 1, 1998.

— B.J. Welborn

Suggestions for Further Reading

Day, Jim, and Mary Lee Grant. "Murder Conviction Upheld in Selena Case; Court Says Evidence Strong Against Saldivar." *Corpus Christi Caller Times* Online (October 2, 1998).

Patoski, Joe Nick. *Selena Como La Flor.* New York: Little, Brown and Company, 1996.

Reinert, Patty. "Saldivar, Convicted in Murder of Selena, Seeking Retrial." *Houston Chronicle* Online:1995.

Snoop Doggy Dogg Trial: 1995–96

Defendants: Calvin Broadus, McKinley Lee **Crimes Charged:** Murder, voluntary manslaughter, conspiracy to commit assault; accessory to murder after the fact (Broadus) **Chief Defense Lawyers:** Broadus: David Kenner, Marcia Morrissey; Lee: Donald Re **Chief Prosecutors:** Edward Nison, Robert Grace **Judge:** Paul G. Flynn **Place:** Los Angeles, California **Date of Trial:** November 27, 1995–February 21, 1996 **Verdict:** Not guilty of murder, assault, and accessory charges; mistrial on voluntary manslaughter charges

SIGNIFICANCE

The arrest of Calvin Broadus a.k.a. Snoop Doggy Dogg for murder coincided with his ascendancy as the most popular rap music star in the United States. The case also fueled a general debate over whether "gangster rap" contributed to or merely reflected gunplay, drug abuse, sexual violence, street gang warfare, and other social ills.

In the afternoon of August 25, 1993, rising rap star Calvin Broadus, better known as Snoop Doggy Dogg, heard a commotion in the street outside his Los Angeles apartment. As Broadus watched, his bodyguard McKinley "Malik" Lee went outside to investigate. Lee found a carload of street gang members arguing with Sean Abrams, one of Broadus's friends. Lee's appearance ended the argument, but as the car departed, Broadus thought he recognized one of the occupants as a man who had recently accosted him with a pistol at a video filming. The gang member was Philip Woldemariam, a 20-year-old Ethiopian immigrant.

A Rising Rap Star

Later that day, with Lee and Abrams accompanying him, Broadus was driving his Jeep past a park when he encountered Woldemariam again. Accounts of the encounter would differ, but there was no dispute over the fact that Lee shot and mortally wounded Woldemariam. Police found Woldemariam's bloody corpse in a nearby carport. Murder charges were filed against Broadus, Lee, and Abrams, all of whom had disappeared into hiding. While Broadus's attorney negotiated the terms of a surrender and bail, the rap star appeared at a televised music awards ceremony on September 2 and shouted his innocence to a cheering audience. He turned himself in later that night.

The killing occurred as Broadus's alter ego, Snoop Doggy Dogg, was becoming the most popular rap star in America. His debut album, *Doggystyle*, released several months after the shooting incident, sold over five million copies. One of its songs, "Murder Was the Charge" was promoted heavily by his record label in a video that featured Snoop as a man who kills someone in self-defense, but is convicted of murder. The notoriety of Snoop Dogg's impending trial

Rap singer Snoop Doggy Dogg talks with reporters as he arrives at the courthouse for his trial. (AP/Wide World Photos)

fed his celebrity and attracted the ire of critics who blamed "gangster rap" for glorifying the gang-related violence plaguing urban communities. Rap artists responded that their work was an accurate reflection of existing mayhem, not its inspiration. Although he was concentrating on his musical career at the time of the Woldemariam shooting, Broadus had served prison time for selling crack cocaine and had been a member of the Long Beach Insane Crips, a long-established Los Angeles street gang. Woldemariam belonged to an upstart gang called the Yerself Hustlers. Police theorized that the shooting incident was just one more of thousands of fatal gang-related confrontations. Other observers proposed that the Woldemariam shooting was a case of Snoop Dogg's life imitating his art.

Murder Was the Charge

Charges against Sean Abrams were dropped by the time the case came to court over two years later. When testimony began on November 27, 1995, the trial immediately centered on the conduct of the Los Angeles Police Department, whose alleged mishandling of evidence in the recently decided O.J. Simpson murder trial had been cited as a major reason for Simpson's controversial acquittal. Prosecutor Edward Nisson tried to minimize any damage to his case by admitting in opening statements that some evidence, including Woldemariam's bloody clothing, a bullet, and a shell casing, had disappeared while in police possession. Jurors, who had been examined about any negative impressions the Simpson case might have had on their opinion of the city's justice system, rolled their eyes at Nison's admissions. Despite the police department's mistakes, Nison persistently argued that Broadus and Lee had hunted down Woldemariam over a gang-related insult and had shot him in the back.

The prosecution's problems were not confined to the missing evidence. The defense held that Lee had fired only in self-defense when Woldemariam ran toward Broadus's Jeep while reaching for a gun in his waistband. Yet no gun had been found on Woldemariam's body. Two fellow gang members who had witnessed the shooting initially told police that the dead man had been unarmed when Lee shot him. By the time the trial began, they recanted their stories and admitted that they had hidden a pistol Woldemariam had been carrying. Defense attorney David Kenner seized the opportunity to discredit the incriminating testimony upon which the murder indictments relied so heavily. Kenner grilled prosecution witness Jason London, who admitted that he and fellow gang member Dushaun Joseph had hidden Woldemariam's gun. London denied that he and Joseph had taken the weapon to make Woldemariam appear to have been a defenseless victim or that they had tried to incriminate Lee and Broadus by denying the gun's existence to police. Nevertheless, the defense had succeeded in bringing this implication before the jury. London also admitted that Woldemariam had a reputation for irrational behavior and that Broadus had played no part in the earlier confrontation at his apartment complex.

The prosecution ridiculed claims that Lee had used his gun to protect himself and Broadus. In the prosecution's scenario, the location of Woldemariam's wounds proved that he was an innocent victim. A Los Angeles County medical examiner was called to confirm that Woldemariam had been shot in the back and buttocks. Under cross-examination, however, the examiner admitted that his report noted that the wounds were "lateral," implying that the bullets that hit Woldemariam traveled sideways through his body, not necessarily from back to front.

Jury Frees Snoop Dogg

On February 20, 1996, after six days of deliberations, the jury returned not guilty verdicts on the murder charges against Broadus and Lee. The defendants sat silently as their supporters cheered, causing Judge Paul Flynn to threaten to clear the courtroom. The jury remained deadlocked on the voluntary manslaughter and accessory charges. On February 21, jurors acquitted Broadus on the accessory charge, but informed Judge Flynn that they remained deadlocked 9–3 in favor of acquittal on the voluntary manslaughter charge and could not agree. Judge Flynn declared a mistrial.

Snoop Dogg expressed his relief at being allowed to return to his career, unhampered by the electronic surveillance ankle bracelet he was ordered to wear after his indictment. The Los Angeles District Attorney's Office declined to try Broadus or Lee a second time on the unresolved voluntary manslaughter charges, but legal issues remained. Woldemariam's family filed a $25 million wrongful death lawsuit against Broadus. The suit was confidentially settled out of court for an undisclosed sum in August 1996, nearly three years to the day Woldemariam died.

— Tom Smith

Suggestions for Further Reading

Dogg, Snoop, with David Seay. *Tha Doggfather*. New York: William Morrow & Company, 1999.

Pertman, Adam. "Simpson Case Comparisons As Rap Star Goes on Trial." *Boston Globe* (November 27, 1995): 21.

Senna, Danzy and Fleming, Charles. "A New Star Gets a Murder Rap." *Newsweek* (September 20, 1993): 54.

White, Michael. "Jury Clears Rapper and Bodyguard of Murder Charge." *Associated Press* (February 21, 1996).

Len Davis Trial: 1996

Defendant: Len Davis   **Crime Charged:** Murder
Chief Defense Lawyer: Dwight Doskey   **Chief Prosecutors:** Constantine
Georges, Michael McMahon   **Judge:** Ginger Berrigan   **Place:** New Orleans,
Louisiana   **Date of Trial:** April 8–April 24, 1996   **Verdict:** Guilty
Sentence: Death

SIGNIFICANCE
This trial blew the lid off police corruption in one of America's major cities.

Even in a city as wearily accustomed to crooked cops as New Orleans, Len Davis stood out. In his six years on that city's police department (NOPD), he'd become known in the housing projects as "Robocop," on account of his highly individualistic style of law enforcement. The subject of more than 20 complaints, mostly for brutality and intimidation, he had once been suspended for hitting a woman on the head with his flashlight. Not that Davis worried overmuch about complaints: most had a way of just fizzling out as terrified witnesses suddenly developed amnesia or else became tongue-tied.

But Kim Groves, a 32-year-old mother of three, was made of tougher stuff, and when, on October 11, 1994, she saw Davis and his partner, Sammie Williams, pistol-whipping a young man named Nathan Norwood, she filed a complaint with the NOPD Internal Affairs Division. Just over 48 hours later, Groves' sense of civic duty was repaid by a bullet in the head, gunned down outside her house by a young man who made his getaway in a blue car.

When Davis was arrested and charged with having ordered the killing, it caused a sensation in New Orleans. The sweep had also netted a couple of known drug dealers, Paul Hardy and Damon Causey, who were suspected of being the actual hitmen, but it was Officer Len Davis who took center stage when the trial opened before Judge Ginger Berrigan on April 8, 1996. Because Davis had used his official position to deny Kim Groves her civil rights, he was tried under federal law. If convicted he faced the death penalty.

It was soon clear that the prosecution, under the stewardship of Assistant U.S. Attorney Constantine Georges, had built its case primarily around the evidence of Sammie Williams, Davis' former partner. He testified that, at about 5:00 P.M. on October 13, 1994, he and Davis were stopped at a traffic light, when a car containing Groves and others pulled up alongside. According to Williams, Groves began mouthing the words, "That's them, that's them," whereupon Davis pointed back and yelled, "I see you too, I see you too."

Williams said this exchange had the effect of infuriating Davis, who reached for his pager and growled, "I could get 'P' to do that whore and we can handle the '30.'" Williams understood this to mean that Davis would get his longtime associate, Paul Hardy, a drug dealer who "looked out for" Davis, to kill Groves. Then it would be up to Davis and Williams to respond to the homicide—or "30" in police code—and dispose of any incriminating evidence.

That evening, continued Williams, Davis met Hardy and gave him details of Groves' appearance and address. He also asked Hardy if he had a gun and was told that he did.

At 10:50 P.M. that same night, Williams got a call from Davis, saying "signal 30 NAT." Williams explained to the jury that "NAT" was police code for "necessary action taken," and he assumed that Groves had been shot.

Undercover Tapes!

In the ordinary course of events, Williams' testimony would have been unsubstantiated, but here the prosecution had cast-iron corroboration—unknown to Davis every word of these conversations had been caught on tape!

For 11 months FBI agents had been investigating allegations of widespread coke dealing in the NOPD, and it just so happened that they had a tap on Davis' phone. Besides the above conversations, the surveillance had also caught Davis gleefully confirming Groves' death to Hardy on the day after the murder, laughing, "Yeah, yeah, yeah, rock, rock-a-bye," an expression used by a drug dealer in the movie *New Jack City* just before shooting people. Davis could be heard adding that if Nathan Norwood persisted with his complaint, it would be "rock-a-bye, baby" for him, too.

Williams, who himself had been indicted on corruption charges, gave some insight into a police force awash with illegal drug money. On the day of Groves' murder, he and Davis had split $16,000 in cash. Asked to explain this transaction, Williams just shrugged. "[I thought] it would be more convenient for us to be partners, given the other things we were involved in."

Next on the witness stand was Steve Jackson who, in return for a deal with the U.S. government, had agreed to give evidence for the prosecution. He told the court of driving Hardy and Causey into the neighborhood where Kim Groves lived. All the while, according to Jackson, Hardy said, "He gots to do this for his nigger," but without specifying who "his nigger" was.

When they reached their destination, Jackson said, Hardy got out, leaving Jackson and Causey in the car. A short while later, Hardy came running back, jumped in, and told him to drive off fast, shouting, "I hit the bitch!" According to Jackson, as they sped away, Hardy threw the barrel of the gun into a canal, switched barrels, then gave Causey the gun to hide. The next day, according to Jackson, Hardy told him "he had to do this . . . Lennie kept bothering him about doing this." Asked by counsel if he knew who "Lennie" was, Jackson replied, "Len Davis."

Ballistics expert James Churchman testified that a 9-mm barrel recovered from the canal over a year later was too corroded to match to the murder weapon, but he did confirm that it fitted a Beretta handgun found at Causey's house.

Defense Fights Back

Although Davis declined to testify on his own behalf, chief defense counsel Dwight Doskey fought hard for his client. So far as he was concerned, it was all a question of mistaken identity. Doskey threw out some heavy hints that Groves had actually been shot by longtime partner, Sylvester "Jimmy" Jones, with whom she shared a violent four-year relationship. Doskey even managed to produce a string of witnesses who described seeing someone close by at the time of the murder who strongly resembled Jones.

But the prosecution would have none of it. In their eyes Davis was "a street killer, a ruthless person." With Assistant U.S. Attorney Michael McMahon making an emotion-packed appeal to the jury not to forget Kim Groves' bravery: "What happened on that day to that poor woman, a citizen of the United States, should not have happened in this country. Maybe somewhere else; not in the United States. Because what the evidence showed, what we proved to you . . . was the existence of a police death squad in New Orleans, Louisiana."

On April 24, Davis was convicted of murder. As was his right, he refused to participate in the penalty phase of his trial, which ended on May 1 with Judge Berrigan sentencing him to death. Hardy also received a death sentence. Causey received two concurrent life terms. On August 16, 1999, Davis and Hardy had their sentences overturned on appeal, and they were referred back to district court for resentencing. (This was still pending in 2001.)

The FBI sting that inadvertently sent Davis to death row also led to convictions for a half-dozen former NOPD officers on drug trafficking charges.

—Colin Evans

Suggestions for Further Reading

"Can I Get a Witness." *Gambit Weekly* (July 28, 1998).

Gleik, Elizabeth. "The Crookedest Blue Line." *Time* (September 9, 1995).

Keegan, V. Paul. "The Thinnest Blue Line." *New York Times* (March 31, 1996).

The New Orleans Times-Picayune. See Groves, Kim, in the *New Orleans Times-Picayune Index* (April 8– November 7, 1996).

Richard Allen Davis Trial: 1996

Defendant: Richard Allen Davis   **Crimes Charged:** Murder, robbery, kidnapping, burglary, attempting a lewd act with a minor, and other charges
Chief Defense Lawyers: Barry Collins and Lorena Chandler
Chief Prosecutor: Greg Jacobs   **Judge:** Thomas Hastings   **Place:** San Jose, California   **Dates of Trial:** April 17–June 18, 1996   **Verdict:** Guilty
Sentence: Death by lethal injection

SIGNIFICANCE

The 1993 abduction and murder of 12-year-old Polly Klaas stunned the nation. Her murderer, Richard Allen Davis, had a string of prior convictions, including two kidnappings. This case helped create public support for tougher sentencing laws for repeat felons. The Klaas kidnapping also focused attention on preventing child abductions and helped law enforcement officials improve their investigative techniques in such cases.

A pretty, dark-haired girl with a dimpled smile, 12-year-old Polly Klaas won fame for all the wrong reasons. Her face appeared in newspapers and on television screens across the country after she was kidnapped from her mother's home in Petaluma, California. On October 1, 1993, while Polly enjoyed a sleep-over with two visiting friends, a man broke into the house and abducted her at knifepoint. Soon, a massive manhunt was under way.

For more than two months, thousands of volunteers combed the woods of Petaluma, looking for any signs of Polly. Fliers went out across America with her picture and a composite sketch of a suspect. The media soon dubbed Polly "America's Child," and the case stirred memories of the kidnapping of Charles Lindbergh's baby in 1932. But unlike that celebrated incident, the Klaas kidnapping did not involve a wealthy, famous family. Polly's abduction reminded the nation that even a "typical" child was not safe in her own home.

The hunt for Polly finally ended on December 4. Police found her body in a shallow grave about 30 miles from Petaluma. She had been strangled. Officers were led to the scene by their chief suspect, Richard Allen Davis, who had recently confessed to kidnapping and killing the young girl.

A Sordid Past

Davis had an arrest record that stretched back more than two decades. He was convicted in 1976 for kidnapping and assaulting a woman and served five years in prison for that crime. In 1984, a second conviction for kidnapping and other charges brought a 16-year sentence; Davis served 8.

Twice after the Klaas abduction, police had had contact with Davis but did not connect him with the crime: About an hour after killing Polly, Davis drove his car into a ditch. Sheriff's deputies from Sonoma County stopped at the scene, and Davis convinced them he was merely a sightseer. The deputies had not received the description of the suspected kidnapper sent out by Petaluma police, and they let Davis go. A few weeks later, Davis was arrested for drunken driving. Police did not associate him with the composite sketch hanging on their office walls.

Police finally caught up with Davis after finding pieces of cloth near the site where Davis drove off the road on October 1. They arrested him on a parole violation. When police told him that a palm print found at Polly's home matched his own, Davis finally confessed to the crime. He told them that a combination of marijuana and alcohol had left him "toasted," and "things got fuzzy after that." Davis described how he let Polly out of the car so she could go to the bathroom. When she returned, he strangled her with a piece of cloth. "She didn't know what hit her," Davis said.

Richard Allen Davis (foreground) sitting in the courtroom after hearing of his death sentence. (AP/ Wide World Photos)

Anger in the Courtroom

Davis's trial for murder, kidnapping, attempted lewd acts, and other charges began two and a half years later, on April 17, 1996. Difficulty in selecting a jury led Judge Thomas Hastings to move the trial from Sonoma County to Santa Clara County. When the trial finally began, Barry Collins, one of Davis's public defenders, admitted that his client had kidnapped and murdered Polly Klaas. But the defense planned to show that Davis had not sexually assaulted Polly in any way. Collins hoped to reduce the chance of Davis's receiving the death penalty. Under California law, a capital murder must be accompanied by "special circumstances"—such as sexual assault and kidnapping. As the trial went on, the defense tried to depict the events of October 1, 1993, as a botched burglary that had gone horribly wrong.

Prosecutor Greg Jacobs, however, stressed the premeditated nature of Davis's crime, including his intent to commit sexual assault. Polly's body was too badly decomposed to yield physical evidence of an assault. Still, Jacobs argued that Davis had stalked Polly, and he called witnesses who testified to seeing Davis in the neighborhood days before the kidnapping.

On June 18, the jury found Davis guilty of 10 felony counts, including the charge of attempted lewd acts. A defiant Davis made an obscene gesture as he left the courtroom. Two months later, the jury recommended that Davis receive the death penalty, having found special circumstances in the case. Judge Hastings accepted this recommendation.

At the sentencing hearing, Davis again shocked the courtroom with his antagonistic behavior. He denied attempting any lewd acts with Polly because, he claimed, the girl had told him her father, Mark Klaas, had sexually abused her. An enraged Klaas rose from his seat and lunged at Davis before being escorted from the court. Since Polly's abduction, Mr. Klaas had become a strong advocate for improving child safety and increasing penalties for criminals who targeted children. He had never been accused before of abusing Polly. After Davis's flip accusation, Judge Hastings said imposing a death sentence was usually very traumatic, but "you made it very easy today by your conduct." As of April 2000, Davis's sentence was waiting review by the state supreme court, as required by California law.

The Polly Klaas case led to important changes in the criminal justice system. In California, the incident kindled popular support for lengthening the sentences for repeat felony offenders. The so-called "three-strikes" law was passed in 1994, requiring that criminals receive 25-years-to-life sentences for a third felony conviction. About 30 other states have since passed similar laws.

For police officials, the case spurred new techniques for tracking lost or abducted children. California now requires all missing children reports and descriptions of suspects to be broadcast on all radio channels, to officers of every jurisdiction. Law enforcement officials also have better access to the records of convicted criminals. On the federal level, the FBI now works more closely with local officials on kidnapping cases, using methods developed during the Polly Klaas manhunt.

—Michael Burgan

Suggestions for Further Reading

Beck, Melinda and Andrew Murr. "The Sad Case of Polly Klaas." *Newsweek* (December 13, 1993): 39.

"Before Being Sentenced to Die, Killer Disrupts a Courtroom." *New York Times* (September 27, 1996): A16.

Bortnick, Barry. *Polly Klaas: The Murder of America's Child*. New York: Pinnacle Books, 1995.

"Klaas Jury Hears Taped Confession." CNN Interactive (May 1, 1996): http://www.cnn.com/US/9605/01/klaas/index.html.

"Lawyer Says Client Is Guilty in Klaas Case." *New York Times* (April 18, 1996): A18.

Rose, Bleys W. "Polly Klaas Abduction-Slaying Has Brought Flood of Reforms." *Dallas Morning News* (October 4, 1998): 7A.

Starr, Jr., Oliver. "The Case of Richard Davis." *National Review* (May 30, 1994): 34.

Jenny Jones Trials: 1996–99

Principal Defendants: Jonathan Schmitz, The *Jenny Jones* television show, and Warner Brothers **Claims/Crimes Charged:** Wrongful death, murder, and committing a felony with a firearm **Chief Defense Lawyers:** Schmitz: James Burdick, Fred L. Gibson, and Jerome Sabbota; Jenny Jones/Warner Brothers: James Feeney **Chief Prosecutors:** Roman Kalytiak and Donna Pendergast **Chief Lawyer for Plaintiff:** Geoffrey N. Fieger **Judges:** First criminal trial: Francis X. O'Brien; second criminal trial: Wendy Potts; civil trial: Gene Schnelz **Place:** Pontiac, Michigan **Dates of Trials:** First criminal trial: October 14–December 4, 1996; second criminal trial: August 9–September 14, 1999; civil trial: March 18–May 7, 1999 **Verdicts:** First criminal trial: Guilty of second-degree murder; second criminal trial: Guilty of second-degree murder; civil trial: $25 million judgment for the plaintiff **Sentences:** First and second criminal trials: 25 to 50 years imprisonment for each

SIGNIFICANCE

The criminal trials of Jonathan Schmitz, and even more so the civil trial of the *Jenny Jones* television show, revealed the tension between the belief that people must take responsibility for their own actions while ill-considered and ever more extreme sensationalism on TV talk shows can push people into violent and tragic behavior.

In 1994, the *Jenny Jones* television show (*Jenny Jones*), a national television talk show, was planning to produce a program on same-sex crushes and was searching for people who would publicly admit to having one. Thirty-two-year-old Scott Amedure, who lived in a Detroit suburb, fit the description, having developed a crush on his 26-year-old friend Jonathan Schmitz some time earlier, and he contacted the show's producers. *Jenny Jones* executives then invited Schmitz to appear as a guest on the program, explaining that someone had confessed to having a crush on him.

The producers later said that Schmitz knew the show was about same-sex crushes and that the person interested in him could be a man, while Schmitz maintained that they had led him to believe that the secret admirer was a woman.

On March 6, 1995, Schmitz walked onto the stage of *Jenny Jones* in front of a studio audience, expecting to find (he later said) his former girlfriend on stage as well. Instead, Amedure was waiting for him and described, on camera, a sexual fantasy involving Schmitz. Schmitz smiled and said to Amedure, "You lied to me." While he seemed to keep his good humor during the taping, he stressed that he was heterosexual and that he was not romantically interested in Amedure.

Schmitz Guns Down His "Admirer"

Three days later, after finding a sexually explicit note at his apartment door, Schmitz bought a 12-gauge pump shotgun and ammunition. He went to the mobile home where Amedure lived and shot him twice in the chest. According to what he told a 911 operator just after the killing, he did it because Amedure had humiliated him on national television. In fact, the show never aired, but the damage had been done. Shortly thereafter Schmitz was charged with Amedere's murder.

The sensationalistic and some would say extreme topics covered by *Jenny Jones* had gotten the show into legal trouble before. This show, like others, was part of a larger phenomenon that people were coming to call "trash TV" or "ambush TV" (labels that such shows obviously resented) since programs of this sort often made unexpected personal revelations about guests during taping. In the wake of the Amedure shooting, public outrage at such tactics grew especially

Jonathan Schmitz argued that the *Jenny Jones Show* drove him to kill Scott Amedure.(AP/Wide World Photos)

vehement. Now the show and its producers, as well as Schmitz, found themselves targets because of the shooting.

In October 1996, Schmitz went on trial for murder. His defense attorneys argued that his humiliation in front of a live audience, coupled with the mental instability that his medical records revealed, had driven him to commit a crime of passion, rather than a slaying after calm deliberation. If they could convince the jury that this was what had happened, the conviction would be for manslaughter rather than murder. The defense also called Jenny Jones herself to the stand to try to prove that she and the show had deceived Schmitz about Amedure's identity and sex. But these arguments and the efforts to put the show on trial did little to help Schmitz, whom the jury convicted of second-degree murder. The Michigan Court of Appeals later overturned the conviction on a technicality, however, Schmitz soon faced the prospect of a new trial.

Jenny Jones Show Sued

Scott Amedure's family, meanwhile, who had settled out of court with Schmitz for a few thousand dollars, sued *Jenny Jones* and Warner Brothers, its distributor, for Amedure's wrongful death. The outspoken attorney Geoffrey N. Fieger, who had often represented right-to-die activist Jack Kevorkian and who routinely won huge civil damage awards, claimed that the show and its negligence had been responsible for Amedure's death.

The show's executives "created a scenario," Fieger said in his opening statement to the jury. "They picked the victim. They deceived him. They picked the murderer and deceived him. They did everything but pull the trigger." The show had put Schmitz in a humiliating position without even trying to discover his past record of mental instability, substance abuse, and suicide attempts. The killing would never have happened, Fieger argued, if the program had not ambushed Schmitz in the manner that it did.

To show how humiliating the experience could be, Fieger put producer Ed Glavin on the witness stand and asked him to describe a sexual fantasy for the jury involving Glavin's own wife, which Glavin refused to do. Fieger also put Jones herself on the stand. Two years after the shooting, she had written a book in which she discussed the tragedy and denied that she or the producers had misled Schmitz. But during questioning, just as at the first criminal trial, the talk show hostess seemed ignorant of the workings of her own series and unable to answer clearly even basic questions about the process of selecting and preparing guests. This put the show in an even less favorable light than before.

Attorneys for *Jenny Jones* countered that Schmitz had known that the topic in question was "Same-Sex Secret Crushes," and that he had been able to make conscious decisions about all of his actions including appearing on the show, buying the gun, and firing it at Amedure. In the end, the jury sided with the Amedures, awarding them $25 million in damages. A few months later a new jury convicted Schmitz of second-degree murder at this second trial. On September 14, 1999, Judge Wendy Potts sentenced Schmitz to 25 to 50 years in prison. This was the same sentence that Judge Francis X. O'Brien had given him after Schmitz had been found guilty in the first criminal trial.

The *Jenny Jones* trials, as they came to be known, spotlighted the long-troublesome issues of personal responsibility in a criminal justice setting. This time, though, the culprit to which the defendant pointed was a new one, a television genre that many people found incendiary and offensive. Some denounced the outcome of the civil trial as a dangerous development that might ultimately threaten First Amendment broadcast rights; others applauded it as a message to powerful, profitable, and irresponsible media that it must begin to show self-restraint.

—Buckner F. Melton, Jr.

Suggestions for Further Reading

Famoso, Robin. "Ambush TV: Holding Talk Shows Liable for the Public Disclosure of Private Facts." *Rutgers Law Journal* (Spring 1998): 579–605.

Alex Kelly Rape Trials: 1996–97

Defendant: Alex Kelly **Crime Charged:** Sexual assault, kidnapping (first trial only) **Chief Defense Lawyers:** Thomas P. Puccio, Hope Seeley
Chief Prosecutor: Bruce P. Huddock **Judges:** First trial: Martin L. Nigro; Second trial: Kevin Tierney **Place:** Stamford, Connecticut
Dates of Trials: October 15–November 12, 1996; April 9–June 12, 1997
Verdicts: First trial: Mistrial; Second trial: Guilty **Sentence:** 20 years imprisonment, suspended after 16 years

SIGNIFICANCE
The Alex Kelly case was notorious for the lurid nature of the crime and public debate over the prosecution of a socially privileged defendant, who had evaded punishment for his crime with the help of his wealthy parents.

On the night of February 10, 1986, Alex Kelly offered 16-year-old Adrienne Bak a ride home from a party in Darien, Connecticut. The next day, Bak told police that Kelly had raped her. Eleven years would pass before the charge was weighed by a jury.

Three days after the Darien incident, while the shaken Bak family was mulling over the consequences of pressing charges, police received a complaint from a 17-year-old girl in nearby Stamford, who accused Kelly of raping and sodomizing her. Kelly was arrested and charged with sexual assault and kidnapping. Some residents of the wealthy suburbs were shocked by the arrest. Darien police, however, found the accusations believable. They also knew of the high school athlete's drug use and had previously arrested him for burglary. Kelly was scheduled to be tried for both alleged rapes simultaneously on February 16, 1987. Three days before his court date, however, he fled to Europe and disappeared.

Arrested After Eight-Year Vacation

Kelly's flight was an expensive decision for his parents, who forfeited a $200,000 bond they had posted for him. They also funneled money to their fugitive son during the next eight years, which he spent skiing and hang-gliding at expensive resorts. In January 1995, Kelly surrendered to Swiss authorities, saying that he wanted to put the accusations in front of a jury to clear his name. Prosecutors believed instead that he knew he was finally about to be arrested.

Although the original sexual assault and kidnapping charges against Kelly remained unchanged, the courts now agreed to weigh the two alleged incidents in separate trials. Jury selection in the Darien case began on October 1, 1996. When testimony began two weeks later, Adrienne Bak Ortolano (she had married after high school) recalled the night she accepted a ride from Kelly. She had reluctantly accepted his repeated offers in order to be home before an 11 P.M. curfew imposed by her parents. Kelly, she said, drove past her house to a dark dead end and pushed her into the back of the Jeep, choking her with both hands. Ortolano tearfully described how the amateur wrestler pinned her in the back of the vehicle and threatened to kill her if she did not stop screaming. After raping her, Kelly drove the bleeding girl home, repeatedly saying he would kill her if she revealed what he had done.

Kelly's attorney, Thomas Puccio, aggressively cross-examined Ortolano, trying to portray her as a willing sexual partner. Puccio stressed that Ortolano had been drinking at the party and implied that she had not resisted Kelly's advances. She repeatedly denied Puccio's insinuations that she had flirted with Kelly. She also protested that she was not drunk, which was corroborated by other partygoers in testimony for the prosecution.

When police officers to whom Ortolano reported the alleged rape took the stand, Puccio asked why they had taken no photographs of her injuries. The police responded that her distraught emotional state made them decide against it. Gynecologist Marilyn Kessler introduced a visible representation of her injuries. Dr. Kessler had not conducted an internal examination at the time of the incident. Consequently, Judge Martin Nigro ruled that Dr. Kessler would not be allowed to testify that a rape had occurred. Yet Kessler did describe the teenager's injuries in detail and offered a medical illustration drawn from her report on the girl's physical condition, infuriating Puccio and his client.

Alex Kelly is led out of court. (AP/Wide World Photos)

Defense Claims Consent

The defense began its case with an appearance by Kelly's girlfriend Amy Molitor, whose family's Jeep Wagoneer he was using on the night of the incident. Molitor was an object of constant fascination to the press and the public, who speculated what was going on in the mind of the attractive young woman who came to court every day with Kelly, holding his hand. To cast doubt on the idea that Kelly would force sex upon anyone, Puccio had Molitor testify that she and Kelly were involved in an intimate relationship during the period when the incident took place. More significantly, Puccio asked Molitor to describe how two hands were needed to lower the back seat of her family's Jeep. Pressing the point without objection, Puccio arranged to have the jury view the vehicle itself and let them examine how the seat-lowering mechanism worked.

Puccio's contention that the sex was consensual was seconded by Joe Kelly, Alex's father, who recalled confronting his son in the middle of the night over a phone call from Adrienne's father. " 'Alex,' I said, 'Mr. Bak says you raped his daughter,' " Kelly testified. "He said, 'Dad, I didn't rape his daughter. We had sex. Dad, go to bed.' " Prosecutor Bruce Huddock objected vociferously while Joe Kelly spoke. Judge Nigro sustained the objection and ordered Kelly's remarks stricken from the record. Puccio concluded his case with medical experts who testified about the effects of alcohol and the sexual behavior of adolescents. He accused Ortolano of willingly and drunkenly losing her virginity to Alex Kelly, then trying to cover up feelings of shame or disappointment. When Puccio presented his final arguments, he presented a scenario in which the "victim" was a liar bent on persecuting his client.

After several days of deliberations, the jury remained deadlocked 4–2 in favor of conviction. Judge Nigro declared a mistrial. The jurors voting against conviction wondered why the Baks had not reported the rape to police immediately. Jurors also realized that Ortolano's claims that Kelly's hands never left her throat and that he had lowered the back seat could not both be true, since the seat release required manual operation. Meanwhile, the public relations brawl surrounding the trial tumbled into the courthouse parking lot. "They came in here totally coiffed and dressed to kill," the abrasive Puccio said of Ortolano and her family. "You might even say they liked being here." Ortolano's lawyer responded furiously, accusing Puccio of pandering to the worst possible stereotypes of rape victims.

When Kelly's retrial began on April 9, 1997, Judge Kevin Tierney had replaced Judge Nigro. Tierney immediately dismissed the kidnapping charge against Kelly on grounds that there was insufficient proof of an abduction. Yet the prosecution was better prepared, both emotionally and in terms of new evidence. Ortolano testified that she had made "a mistake" in the first trial by insisting that Kelly's hands never left her throat as he pushed her into the back of the Jeep. She said that Kelly had removed one hand long enough to flip the seat release. Although Puccio accused her of changing her testimony, her claim agreed with the original statement she gave Darien police.

Despite Ortolano's adamant denials, Puccio charged that she had been smoking pot at the party the night of the incident, lowering her inhibitions. Puccio succeeded in introducing evidence that the blood on her underwear contained traces of marijuana. Puccio strove to destroy Ortolano's credibility, but she was more self-composed than she had been during the first trial. After she described the violent details of the rape, Puccio asked her how long the episode had lasted.

"Forever," she replied.

The defense's credibility problems increased. Thomas Kelly, an unrelated friend of Alex's, testified that Alex told him the day after the incident that the girl had been driven home by her friends, not by him. In retrospect, this was clearly a lie. Asked why he had not given this damaging information in the first trial, Thomas Kelly simply replied that no one had asked him to testify.

The Jury's Verdict

On June 12, the jury took eight hours to find Alex Kelly guilty. He seemed dumbfounded by the verdict. "Are you serious? I'm not guilty!" he said repeatedly to the jury before turning to his accuser. "Why are you doing this to me?" he said.

On June 24, Kelly was sentenced to the maximum term of 20 years imprisonment, to be suspended after 16 years. In contrast to the outburst at his conviction, Kelly apologized to his victim. The sentence, however, stood. So did plans for Kelly's trial for assaulting the identified Stamford woman. Facing a stronger case, which included DNA evidence, the fact that he possessed the woman's underwear when he was arrested, and outstanding charges for fleeing the United States, Kelly pleaded no contest on December 23, 1998. His sentence of 10 years was to run concurrently with his prison term for the Darien rape.

— *Tom Smith*

Suggestions for Further Reading

Glaberson, William. "Alex Kelly Avoids Trial in Second Rape." *New York Times* (December 24, 1998): B1, B6.

"The Jury: It Was Rape." *Associated Press* (June 13, 1997).

Weller, Sheila. *Saint of Circumstance.* New York: Pocket Books, 1997.

Williams, Monte. "In Retrial, Alex Kelly Is Convicted of Rape Committed 11 Years Ago." *New York Times* (June 13, 1997): A1, B6.

Darlie Routier Trial: 1997

Defendant: Darlie Lynn Routier   **Crime Charged:** Murder
Chief Defense Lawyer: Doug Mulder   **Chief Prosecutor:** Greg Davis
Judge: Mark Tolle   **Place:** Kerrville, Texas   **Dates of Trial:** January 6–
February 1, 1997   **Verdict:** Guilty   **Sentence:** Death

SIGNIFICANCE

Young mother Darlie Routier did the unthinkable: she murdered her two sons in cold blood. This grizzly capital murder case, built on detailed, abundant and damning circumstantial evidence, continues to roil emotions, generate national publicity and raise lingering doubts of guilt. Recent findings may lead to a new trial. Meanwhile, Routier awaits death by lethal injection in a Dallas prison. She is one of only a handful of women on America's death row.

W hy would a mother savagely murder her own flesh and blood? The prosecution in the murder trial of Darlie Routier had a simple explanation: Here was an immature, materialistic, manipulating young woman with low self-esteem who saw her lavish lifestyle slipping away. She not only blamed her two young sons for the family's deteriorating economic state, she saw their deaths as a means to turn things around.

So in the middle of the night of June 6, 1996, Routier (pronounced "Rue-teer"), 27, took a butcher knife from the kitchen of their grand, Georgian-design home in a fashionable Rowlett, Texas neighborhood. She tiptoed into the den where sons Devon, 6, and Damon, 5, lay sleeping after watching television late with mom. Then she repeatedly stabbed the boys, tearing into their chests, lungs, and abdomens. Devon died immediately. Damon lay on the floor, painfully struggling for air. Husband Darin, 28, and six-month-old son Drake, asleep upstairs, heard nothing.

Records show that Darlie called Rowlett police at 2:31 A.M., screaming that someone had broken into her home and stabbed her and her children. "My boys are dying!" she said. "My boys are dying!"

A House Stained by Blood

Police officers arrived minutes later and were horrified by the carnage. Routier, clad in a blood-soaked nightshirt, bled profusely from her throat but was still on her feet. Instead of tending to the suffering Damon, as police asked her to do, she kept screaming to police that the attacker might be hiding in the garage. Damon drew his last bloody breath as a paramedic frantically tried to save him.

A K–9 team and police searched the house. Investigators found no one in the garage. A trail of blood went from the den, through the kitchen, and into the garage, but mysteriously disappeared in front of a garage window. Police saw that the window screen had been sliced open, but they found no blood on the windowsill. In fact, dust on the sill lay undisturbed, as did the damp soil just beyond the window.

The gory trail that began in the Routier den then crossed into the kitchen, where a bloody butcher knife lay on a counter—next to Routier's unopened purse and several pieces of expensive jewelry. Blood glistened on a countertop around the sink and on the floor. A vacuum cleaner lay on its side.

Officers immediately noted that the kitchen sink itself appeared suspiciously clean. After they sprayed the area with Luminol and turned off the lights, however, the entire sink basin and surrounding counters glowed with blood. Officers also found a small child's bloody handprint on the leatherette sofa in the den. Someone apparently had wiped it away.

Investigators found no signs of forced entry at the Routier house. They discovered a bread knife in the kitchen that they later believed had been used to slice open the garage window. Police noted the crime scene showed virtually no sign of a violent struggle. They found only a lampshade askew and a bunch of flowers on the den floor. The flowers' fragile stems remained unbroken, as if they had been placed on the floor instead of thrown. Blood *underneath* the vacuum in the kitchen indicated it had been overturned *after* blood was splattered on the floor.

Officers on the scene came to one, unanimous conclusion: There was no intruder into the Routier home on the night of June 6, 1996. Someone had staged the crime scene. Darlie Routier was lying.

On June 18, police arrested Routier for the first-degree murder of her sons. Prosecutors decided to try her only for Demon's murder. If she received a life sentence in that trial, or if she were found innocent, the state then would try her for Devon's killing.

News media swarmed into Kerrville. Judge Mark Tolle issued a gag order, which Darlie immediately violated, granting an emotional radio interview from her jail cell.

Deadly or Doting Mother?

At Routier's trial six months later, police and paramedics painstakingly presented their theory that the woman who seemed the doting mother of two, indulged boys actually was their cunning murderer. FBI special agent Al Brantley also pointed out that an intruder bent on harming an adult simply wouldn't attack vulnerable children first. He believed that "someone who knew these children very well murdered them."

Testimony from staff members at Baylor Hospital where the boys' bodies were taken and where Routier was treated for her wounds, buttressed that conclusion. No one at Baylor saw Routier cry, even when she encountered Damon's nude, mangled body. She never asked about her children.

Coroner Janice Townsend-Parchman testified that Routier's superficial neck wounds appeared inflicted in a slow, hesitant manner, most likely by Routier herself. The deep, multiple wounds on the boys, however, showed the attack on them was personal. An evidence expert testified that the sons' blood on Routier's nightshirt was literally sprayed onto her while she was executing upswing motions, such as stabbing and slicing.

A parade of Darlie Routier's acquaintances revealed the Routiers' dark side. Things apparently weren't happy at the two-story, brick home on Eagle Drive with the Jaguar parked out front, the 27-foot cabin cruiser nearby, and the kids playing happily in the yard. Witnesses testified about the Routiers' marital discord, punctuated by ugly public fights and mutual cheating. Others painted Routier as an impatient, angry mother who often left her children unsupervised. At Devon's fifth birthday party, she shoved a piece of cake in his face when he squirted her with a watergun. She opted for size EE breast implants. Friends called her "Shop-Till-You-Drop Darlie." Routier also suffered postpartum depression after her third son's birth.

Darlie Routier with her husband Darrin and two sons Damon (left) and Devon. (AP/Wide World Photos)

Witnesses testified about the couple's financial crises. Business had dropped at their company, which tested circuit boards for computer manufacturers. Bills were mounting. Their bank recently denied the Routiers a $5,000 loan.

Possibly the most damaging testimony came in the form of a video. Rowlett police had secretly taped a post-mortem, graveside birthday party Routier had thrown for Devon just days after his death. As the minister began a somber eulogy, Routier lightheartedly sprayed a can of silly string over the grave. Laughing and chewing bubble gum, she sang "Happy Birthday."

Expert defense witnesses, however, characterized Routier's bizarre actions as normal for many who are severely traumatized. Forensic Psychologist Dr. Lisa

Clayton also supported Routier's story of the murders. She said Routier exhibited the typical blackouts and distorted memory of people who experience a profound trauma and are forced to give clear descriptions of it soon after the event.

Bexor County medical examiner Dr. Vincent DiMaio skillfully shed doubt on statements that Darlie's wounds were self-inflicted. He said her throat slash came within two millimeters of the carotid artery. Bruises on her arms could indicate she fended off an attacker.

Others who took the stand in Routier's defense were mostly character witnesses. They portrayed Routier as a doting mom, saying she was devastated by her sons' deaths and grieved appropriately.

Unfortunately for Routier's defense, however, the defendant herself took the stand, despite her lawyers' objections. After she told her version of the crime and insisting she was a good mother, Prosecutor Greg Davis tore into her story with a vengeance. He reduced Routier to a sobbing, stuttering, stammering woman.

Jurors deliberated only four hours before returning a guilty verdict. Three days later, Routier was sentenced to death. The young mother had no tears.

In the years since Darlie's conviction, renewed media attention—including an investigation by the television news program *20/20*—has raised questions about her guilt. Among the media findings: Jurors received a trial transcript with 33,000 errors and omissions; jurors never saw photographs of Routier's arm bruises; and an unidentified bloody fingerprint was found on the Routiers' kitchen counter after the murder.

Routier's supporters are fighting for a new trial.

— B. J. Welborn

Suggestions for Further Reading

"Darlie Routier: Doting Mother/Deadly Mother." Crime Library Crime Story Archive, On-Line.

Davis, Barbara. *Precious Angels*. New York: Onyx/Penquin, 1999.

Verhovek, Sam Howe. "Dallas Woman Is Sentenced to Death in Murder of Son." *New York Times* (February 5, 1997): A12.

John E. DuPont Trial: 1997

Defendant: John E. DuPont   **Crimes Charged:** Murder, assault
Chief Defense Lawyer: Thomas Bergstrom   **Chief Prosecutor:** Joseph
McEdigan   **Judge:** Patricia Jenkins   **Place:** Delaware County, Pennsylvania
Dates of Trial: January 21–February 25, 1997   **Verdict:** Guilty of third-
degree murder and assault   **Sentence:** 13–30 years in prison

SIGNIFICANCE

The trial focused national attention on the insanity defense, particularly as used by
wealthy defendants.

In January 1996 a media frenzy began when the news broke that John DuPont, an heir to the DuPont chemical fortune, was holding police at bay at his estate in Newtown Square, Pennsylvania. DuPont had been accused of murdering Olympic wrestling gold-medalist Dave Schultz, and was believed not only to be armed, but possibly to have cached explosives on his farm. For many years DuPont had been an active supporter of Olympic athletes and had run a training facility for pentathletes and wrestlers at Foxcatcher Farm, about 15 miles west of Philadelphia.

The incident began on the afternoon of January 26, 1996, when DuPont shot and killed the 36-year-old Schultz. DuPont, who had recently been displaying animosity towards Schultz, went to the Schultzes' cottage accompanied by his security consultant, Patrick Goodale. Dave Schultz, who was working on his car in the driveway when the men arrived, greeted them. DuPont asked, "You got a problem with me?" and then shot Schultz three times with a .44 Magnum revolver. He also pointed the gun at Goodale and Nancy Schultz, who was watching from the house.

A Standoff with the Police

DuPont then got into his car and fled to his mansion, where he barricaded himself inside, refused to surrender to the police, and held them off for two days. During the standoff he spoke to his attorney on several occasions. Finally police arrested him on January 28 when he left the house to repair his heating system. DuPont had complained that his house was cold and asked for permission to go outside to repair his boilers. What he did not know was that the police had turned off the heat in an attempt to lure him out of the house. Within a few minutes the SWAT team had him under arrest. The police then searched the house and discovered the murder weapon and other small arms, but no explosive devices.

DuPont's Mental Competency Debated

DuPont was charged with murder and assault. In February the court ordered a competency examination, and in September, Delaware County judge Patricia Jenkins ruled that John DuPont was mentally incompetent to stand trial, and ordered that he be sent to a state psychiatric hospital for compulsory treatment. Several psychiatrists eventually testified that DuPont was a paranoid schizophrenic who wove complicated conspiracy theories involving Tibetan Buddhists, the CIA, Nazis, and Jesus. In light of this testimony the judge declared the 57-year-old DuPont psychotic and unable to help his attorneys mount a rational defense. Judge Jenkins chastised both prosecution and defense attorneys for not seeking treatment for the defendant earlier. The judge ordered a hearing on the state of DuPont's mental health every 90 days until he was found competent to stand trial. DuPont's relations then petitioned the county court to obtain control of his finances, claiming he was no longer capable of managing them.

The Trial Finally Begins

Almost exactly a year after the crime, DuPont was found competent and the trial began in suburban Philadelphia. Dupont's lawyers did not deny that he killed Dave Schultz, but they argued that their client was insane at the time of the shooting and was suffering from severe paranoid schizophrenia. The prosecution argued that DuPont did know right from wrong at the time of the shooting. The prosecutor pointed to the fact that DuPont asked to speak to his attorney several times during the police standoff as evidence that he understood what was happening.

Witnesses who knew the defendant testified that his behavior had started to change about the time of his mother's death in 1988. He had become extremely security conscious and hired a firm in 1993 to provide protection on the estate. Despite the implementation of extensive security measures, DuPont claimed on several occasions that he was being spied on and that his life was in danger. That same year he installed razor wire inside the walls of his home to prevent anyone from hiding in the walls. He also hired excavators to dig up the property to search for tunnels be believed were being dug to his home. Several witnesses also told of his increasing drug and alcohol problems between 1988 and 1995. Nevertheless, he continued to manage the daily operations of his training facility during this time. He developed close relationships with some of the wrestlers and their families, and he took a dislike to others.

The defense presented extensive evidence that DuPont was paranoid and schizophrenic. This evidence focused on his delusional beliefs, particularly evident in his statements during the police standoff and at his examination afterwards that he was Jesus Christ, the Dalai Lama, and a Russian czar, just to name a few. The defenses expert witnesses opined that DuPont was legally insane at the time of the shooting. Experts for the prosecution, Drs. John O'Brien and Park Dietz, testified that they believed that DuPont did indeed suffer from mental illness, but that he was not legally insane at the time of the shooting.

Verdict: Guilty but Mentally Ill

On February 25, 1997, the jury found DuPont guilty of third-degree murder and simple assault, under Pennsylvania's guilty but mentally ill statutory scheme. In Pennsylvania, "guilty but mentally ill" means that a defendant who offers a defense of insanity in accordance with the rules of Criminal Procedure may be found "guilty but mentally ill," at trial if the trier of facts finds, beyond a reasonable doubt, that the person guilty of an offense was mentally ill at the time of the commission of the crime and was not legally insane at the time. "Mentally ill" means that as a result of mental disease or defect, a person lacks substantial capacity either to appreciate the wrongfulness of his or her conduct or to conform his or her conduct to the requirements of the law. Whereas, under the more widely known "not guilty by reason of insanity," the person who committed the crime is incapable of understanding the nature of his or her actions, or if he or she does understand them, cannot understand that they are wrong. The statutory maximum sentence for third-degree murder in the state of Pennsylvania is 40 years in prison.

On May 13, 1997, DuPont was sentenced to 13 to 30 years for the murder conviction. He also received a concurrent sentence of three to six months on the assault conviction and was ordered to pay costs incurred by the district attorney's office in connection with his prosecution.

The John DuPont case once again focused attention on the use of the insanity defense and was one of the first high-profile cases to be tried under the new "guilty but mentally ill" statutes that 12 states had enacted following John Hinckley's attempted assassination of Ronald Reagan.

—Carol Willcox Melton

Suggestions for Further Reading

Ordine, Bill, and Ralph Vigoda. *Fatal Match*. New York: Avon, 1998.

Turkington, Carol A. *No Holds Barred: The Strange Life of John E. DuPont*. Atlanta: Turner, 1996.

Frederic Tokars Trial: 1997

Defendant: Frederic Tokars   **Crime Charged:** Murder
Chief Defense Lawyers: Bobby Lee Cook, James Berry, Jerry Froelich, Ed Moriarity   **Chief Prosecutors:** Tom Charron, Russ Parker   **Judge:** James G. Bodiford   **Place:** LaFayette, Georgia   **Date of Trial:** January 30–March 8, 1997   **Verdict:** Guilty   **Sentence:** Life imprisonment

SIGNIFICANCE

Issues of double jeopardy were aroused when this Atlanta lawyer, already serving four life terms on charges arising from the death of his wife, suddenly found himself facing execution as state prosecutors decided to pursue the death penalty.

When Sara Tokars and her two young sons returned to their suburban Atlanta home on November 29, 1992, they were jumped by a gunman who forced them back into their car and made them drive off. Less than a mile away the attacker shot 39-year-old Sara in the back of the head at point blank range with a sawed-off shotgun and fled. The two boys were unharmed.

Initial police theories of a bungled robbery soon gave way to suspicions about the victim's husband. Not only was Fredric Tokars, a former Atlanta prosecutor and prominent criminal defense lawyer, rumored to be in hock to organized crime, but also his marriage had been falling apart for some time. Sara's relatives claimed she had been threatening to expose Tokars' drug-trafficking connections as a prelude to filing for divorce and seeking custody of the children.

Investigators believed that Tokars had coerced a shady business associate, Eddie Lawrence, into finding a hit man to kill Sara. The trail then led to a crack addict named Curtis Rower, who was subsequently convicted of Sara's murder and sentenced to life. Lawrence plea-bargained his way to a 12 and one-half year federal prison term.

In April 1994 Tokars was also convicted on federal charges of racketeering and other crimes related to the death of his wife, and sentenced to four consecutive life terms without the possibility of parole. But this wasn't enough for Cobb County district attorney Tom Charron, a zealous proponent of capital punishment. He wanted Tokars dead. And on January 30, 1997, he finally got to open the state's capital case against the crooked lawyer.

"This is a conspiracy between three people," said Charron. "It is a case of betrayal—betrayal of a marriage and a family and the oath of a husband. . . . It is a case that the evidence will show you deals with ambition, blind ambition, of the defendant wanting to exercise his political power and control people."

Charron told how Tokars had insured his wife's life for $1.75 million, money that he needed to repay $700,000 in missing drug money he was supposed to have laundered for his criminal associates.

Innocent Victim?

Unsurprisingly, Tokars had hired a topnotch defense team, and James Berry wasted little time in portraying his client as an innocent dupe, victimized by corrupt police detectives, an embittered business partner, and a media frenzy fed by Sara Tokars' vengeful family.

"Fred Tokars is the scapegoat in this case," Berry said. "A beautiful young woman is killed . . . and what would be a terrible tragedy, as well, is if Fred Tokars is convicted of something he did not do."

Charron's first witness—Sara's younger sister Joni Ambrusko—testified about her sister's failing marriage. "She would say, 'Please, Fred please, let's figure out how to get a divorce.'" But Tokars always rejected Sara's pleas, saying, "'I'll never let you have the kids.'"

Next came Atlanta prostitute Patricia Williams, who told the court that during her only "date" with Tokars, "he asked me if I did drugs and if I knew any drug dealers who would kill his wife for him . . . he said it was because she was going to divorce him and knew too much."

However, Williams' probity took a big hit when Tracey Gammons, Tokars' receptionist, testified that far from being a stranger to the defendant, as she claimed, Williams had several times called at his office, carrying documents for Eddie Lawrence.

The third member of the alleged murder triumvirate, self-confessed gunman Curtis Rower, did not testify at the trial, but his role in this tragedy was confirmed by his girlfriend, Lashara Bryant. On the night of Sara Tokars' death, Rower allegedly confided to her, "Baby, I shot a white [woman]."

Right from the outset, it had been obvious that Eddie Lawrence would be the state's key witness, their main hope of executing Fred Tokars. The former businessman didn't disappoint. In a matter-of-fact way he outlined the plot to murder Sara Tokars, with every detail planned by her husband over several meetings, the last just hours before the shooting.

On cross-examination, lead defense attorney, Bobby Lee Cook, worked himself up into a lather of indignation over the "sweetheart" deal with prosecutors that allowed Lawrence to escape the electric chair in return for testifying against Tokars, and the fact that after serving his prison term, Lawrence would be given a new identity under the federal Witness Protection Program.

Tempers frayed to breaking point as Cook hit top gear. "You're a flimflam artist, aren't you? You're a liar," he thundered over Lawrence's repeated denials. "You've lied so much, even you don't know when you're lying or telling the truth."

In the end Cook succeeded in extracting an admission from Lawrence that he had frequently lied to business associates. "But I know when I'm telling the truth," Lawrence added defiantly.

Mistrial Demand

The vituperative courtroom atmosphere was not made any better by Judge James G. Bodiford's refusal to grant strenuous defense demands for a mistrial over Court TV's decision not to show Lawrence's face. "I'm not telling Court TV what they can and can't do," the judge said sharply.

Although Tokars chose not to testify on his own behalf, his brother, Andy, took the stand to refute allegations of an unhappy home life. "I was over there a lot. . . . I can honestly say I never saw a fight, I never saw them raise their voices to each other. . . . I never saw any kind of anger towards each of them at all in the many, many years that I had been there."

In closing, Charron said that although Tokars didn't pull the trigger on the sawed-off shotgun that killed his wife, he was the mastermind, he was "the person who had the most to gain."

For Cook it all came down to Lawrence's credibility. "I can say with absolute candor I have never seen such an audacious liar in my life. He can be glib and even defraud smart lawyers when he wants to."

Fellow defense attorney Berry echoed this skepticism. When arrested for the murder, he said, Lawrence was prepared to do "whatever it takes" to escape the electric chair by framing Tokars with information fed to him by his lawyers while he was in jail. Berry likened the case against Tokars to "a chain. If you break one link in that chain—Eddie Lawrence—that chain is going to make you fall. . . . If you don't believe Eddie Lawrence, you can't convict Fred Tokars."

On March 8, the jury decided that Lawrence had been telling enough of the truth to convince them, and they found Tokars guilty of murder with malice. Jubilant prosecutors, confident that this time Tokars would get the chair, saw those hopes crushed just four days later when the jury imposed yet another life sentence.

More than $1 million of Georgia taxpayers' money had been spent and not a thing had changed.

—Colin Evans

Suggestions for Further Reading

Atlanta Journal-Constitution. See Tokars, Sara, in the *Atlanta Journal Constitution Index* (January 31–March 9, 1997).

McDonald, R. Robin. *Secrets Never Lie*. New York: Avon Books, 1998.

Oklahoma City Bombing Trials: 1997–98

Defendants: Timothy J. McVeigh and Terry L. Nichols
Crimes Charged: Murder, conspiracy to use a weapon of mass destruction, use of a weapon of mass destruction, and destruction by explosive
Chief Defense Lawyers: McVeigh: Stephen Jones and Robert Nigh, Jr.; Nichols: Michael Tigar and Ron Woods   **Chief Prosecutors:** McVeigh: Joseph Hartzler; Nichols: Larry Mackey   **Judge:** Richard Matsch
Place: Denver, Colorado   **Dates of Trials:** McVeigh: March 31–June 13, 1997; Nichols: September 17, 1997–January 7, 1998   **Verdicts:** McVeigh: Guilty on all counts; Nichols: Guilty of conspiracy to use a weapon of mass destruction and involuntary manslaughter, acquitted on all other counts
Sentences: McVeigh: Death by injection; Nichols: Life imprisonment, plus 8 concurrent 6-year terms of imprisonment

SIGNIFICANCE

Although they produced a new law allowing the first television viewing of a federal trial and resulted in a rarely imposed federal death sentence, the trials were noted primarily for prosecutions of the worst act of domestic terrorism in U.S. history.

On the morning of April 19, 1995, a state trooper stopped a car without a license plate traveling on an interstate highway near Billings, Oklahoma. Evasive answers about the car's registration and a concealed handgun resulted in the arrest of the driver on weapons and vehicle violations. The routine traffic stop resulted in the arrest, trial, and conviction of two men accused of committing the most destructive terrorist act ever to take place on U.S. soil.

A little more than an hour before Timothy McVeigh was questioned about his missing license plate, the center of Oklahoma City shook with a roar. At 9:02 A.M., a huge homemade bomb exploded outside the Alfred P. Murrah Federal Building, transforming the neighborhood into a hell of jagged glass, bleeding survivors, and frantic rescuers trying to reach the dead and the dying in the rubble. A total of 168 people were killed and over 500 were injured in the explosion. The victims included a roomful of children in the building's daycare center, less than 30 feet from the epicenter of the blast.

Despite a national panic that the devastation was caused by international terrorists or drug cartels, authorities quickly decided that the bombing was a singular act of domestic terrorism. Investigators received a tip that a widely distributed sketch of John Doe no. 1, the driver of a Ryder rental truck whose mangled axle was found at the scene, resembled Timothy McVeigh. The FBI checked the national crime computer database and learned that McVeigh was still in jail in Perry, Oklahoma, for the vehicle and weapons violations. On April 21, two days after the explosion, FBI agents swept into Perry and arrested McVeigh on federal charges.

Other suspects included two of McVeigh's ex-U.S. Army buddies. Terry Nichols turned himself in to Herington, Kansas, police when he heard news reports that he was being sought as a material witness. Evidence found at Nichols's house led to him being charged as a coconspirator with McVeigh. The FBI also held Michael Fortier, a hardware store clerk from Kingman, Arizona, with whom McVeigh and Nichols had served in Kuwait during the Persian Gulf War. All three of the young veterans had obsessions with weapons, ties to anti-establishment militia groups, and a hatred of the federal government.

Oklahoma Grand Jury, Colorado Venue

By the time a grand jury was convened, Fortier and his wife, Lori, had agreed to cooperate with the government. Their testimony, along with the prosecution's evidence and emotional testimony by McVeigh's sister Jennifer, convinced the jury to return an indictment on August 10. Defense attorneys protested that the real bombers might still be at large or could have perished in the explosion.

The indictments against McVeigh and Nichols charged them with one count each of conspiracy to use a weapon of mass destruction, use of a weapon of mass destruction, and destruction by explosive. Despite the loss of life resulting from the bomb, federal law confined prosecutors to seeking murder charges only in the deaths of federal law enforcement officers. The grand jury returned counts of first-degree murder for each of eight Secret Service, Customs Service, Housing and Urban Development, and Drug Enforcement Administration agents who were killed. The two defendants would be tried separately. Prosecutors announced that they would seek the death penalty against both McVeigh and Nichols.

News coverage of the horror in Oklahoma City complicated the task of assembling an unbiased jury. After unsuccessfully trying to arrange a suitable venue in Oklahoma, the trial was assigned to Chief U.S. District Judge Richard Matsch, who moved the case to Denver, Colorado, ruling that McVeigh and Nichols had been "demonized" by media coverage in Oklahoma. Matsch initially barred survivors and victims' family members from attending the trial if they planned to testify. He was later forced to reverse his ruling when Congress passed a law allowing limited public access to the proceedings. Matsch approved a closed-circuit telecast to be shown in a government auditorium in Oklahoma City, but banned the news media from the viewing site.

McVeigh's Trial

Jury selection for McVeigh's trial began on March 31, 1997. When opening statements were made three weeks later, the prosecution charged that McVeigh's hatred for the federal government had escalated into violence after the disastrous federal raid on the Branch Davidian religious compound near Waco, Texas, on April 19, 1993—two years to the day before the Oklahoma City bombing. In order to inspire an uprising against the government, McVeigh had parked a Ryder rental truck containing a 4,000-pound homemade bomb outside the Murrah Building in the erroneous belief that it was the headquarters of the agents who had carried out the Waco raid.

Timothy McVeigh was executed by lethal injection for the Oklahoma city bombing that killed 168 people. (AP/Wide World Photos)

The prosecution couldn't produce an eyewitnesses placing McVeigh at the Murrah Building nor was there any direct evidence that he and Nichols had built the bomb. The key and rental paperwork for the Ryder truck had been recovered, but neither McVeigh's nor Nichols's fingerprints were found on them. The circumstantial evidence against McVeigh was stronger. Traces of PETN, a compound used in detonator cord, were found on his jeans, pockets, and a set of earplugs he was carrying when he was arrested. Phone records tied McVeigh and Nichols to purchases of ingredients identical to those used in the bomb.

Although the evidence was circumstantial, the prosecution's case was bolstered by abundant motive for McVeigh's alleged crimes. When he was arrested, antigovernment propaganda found in his car included an excerpt from *The Turner Diaries*, a white-supremacist novel containing an instructive chapter about blowing up an FBI building with a bomb-laden truck. His sister Jennifer tearfully recalled McVeigh telling her that "something big" was going to happen in the spring of 1995. She also attributed a letter found in her computer to her brother. "You'll swing in the wind one day for your treasonous attacks against the Constitution of the United States," said the letter, which was written to the Bureau of Alcohol, Tobacco, & Firearms. "Die, you spineless cowardice bastards!"

Testifying under immunity, Lori Fortier recalled McVeigh's visits to the Fortiers' Arizona trailer during which he had described the process of building bombs, saying he intended to blow up a government building. She admitted that she and her husband had hidden and sold guns that McVeigh and Terry Nichols had stolen in Arkansas. She had made a fake identification card for McVeigh, using the name "Robert Kling"; a Ryder truck rental manager identified

McVeigh as one "Robert Kling" who had rented the obliterated truck two days before the bombing.

Michael Fortier also recalled McVeigh's bomb-making experiments and testified that he had circled the Murrah Building with McVeigh in December 1994, during a trip to pick up the stolen guns in Kansas. McVeigh had detailed how he planned to blow up the building with a rental truck packed with explosives, hoping to cause a "general uprising in America." When Fortier commented on the potential loss of life, McVeigh allegedly replied that he "considered all those people to be as if they were storm troopers in the movie *Star Wars.* They might be individually innocent, but because they are part of the evil empire, they were guilty by association." Fortier admitted that he might have prevented the bombing by informing authorities.

McVeigh's defense attorneys did not offer an alibi for their client. Instead, they assailed the Fortiers' credibility, playing FBI wiretaps from the days after the bombing. "I can tell a fable, I can tell stories all day long," Michael Fortier was heard telling his brother. "The less I say now, the bigger the price later." Hoping to undercut the impact of his testimony, the defense portrayed Fortier as a methamphetamine addict and opportunist who was willing to lie to obtain lucrative book and film contracts about the case.

Suggesting that the real bomber might have died in the blast, the defense called a pathologist who testified that an unidentified leg found at the Murrah Building could have belonged to someone carrying a bomb. Scientist Frederic Whitehurst testified that the explosives residue on McVeigh's possessions had been examined during a period when FBI laboratory procedures were so flawed that they were later severely criticized by the Justice Department. Whitehurst admitted, however, that he had no specific knowledge that the evidence in the Oklahoma City cases had been tainted.

After almost two weeks of testimony, on June 2, the jury convicted McVeigh on all 11 counts. During the subsequent penalty phase of the trial, the jury unanimously agreed that McVeigh's actions were distinguished by aggravating factors such as premeditation and intent to kill and consequently recommended a death sentence on June 13. On August 14, Judge Matsch formally sentenced McVeigh to be executed by lethal injection. But it wasn't until June 11, 2001 that this execution finally took place in Terre Haute, Indiana.

Nichols's Trial

When the case against Terry Nichols began on September 17, store clerks, testifying as prosecution witnesses, verified receipts for the purchase of an unusually large amount of fertilizer. Although the clerks could not identify Nichols as the buyer, the receipts—which had been found in Nichols's home—were for a purchase of two tons of ammonium nitrate, a primary component of the Oklahoma City bomb.

Michael Fortier testified that he had seen explosives in Nichols's pickup truck, but admitted that he had seen his former friend only infrequently before the bombing. During McVeigh's trial, Fortier testified that Nichols attempted to back out of the plot a month before the bombing. "Tim told me that Terry no longer wanted to help him mix the bomb," Fortier had said. "He went on to say that Terry would have to help him because he's in it so far up 'til now." Fortier did not repeat the claim at Nichols's trial nor did he specifically identify Nichols as the accomplice with whom McVeigh claimed to be planning on blowing up a federal building. As McVeigh's attorneys had done, Nichols's lawyers portrayed Michael Fortier as a lying drug addict whose testimony should not be considered credible.

Nichols's ex-wife was called by the defense as a sympathetic witness. When she testified that she had found a letter in which Nichols urged McVeigh to "go for it" five months before the bombing, however, observers wondered if putting her on the stand had been a defense blunder.

Mixed Verdict

On December 23, Nichols was found guilty of conspiracy to use a weapon of mass destruction, but was acquitted on the two counts related to using such a weapon. The jury settled on convicting Nichols of eight counts of involuntary manslaughter, rather than murder. It appeared that the jury was certain that Nichols was involved in the plot, but chose to convict him only on the counts for which his responsibility seemed clear.

When the jury met again to consider a sentence for Nichols, however, they could not agree on a punishment. On January 7, 1998, they announced to Judge Matsch that they were deadlocked, thus leaving the sentencing to the judge. After their dismissal, jurors revealed that they felt prosecutors had not conclusively proven the extent to which Nichols was involved in the actual bombing. Without unanimous agreement from the jury, the judge was prevented from imposing a death sentence.

In the months that passed before Nichols's sentencing, McVeigh's attorneys filed an appeal. They claimed there was evidence of juror misconduct and argued that emotional testimony by survivors and victims' family members had prejudiced the jury. The appeal also claimed that Judge Matsch had erred in not allowing testimony about possible alternative antigovernment extremist conspiracy theories and by not giving the jury an option of convicting McVeigh of a lesser charge of second-degree murder.

Michael Fortier was sentenced on May 27 for failing to report McVeigh's and Nichols's criminal intentions, lying to the FBI about the case, and various weapons charges. Despite acknowledgments from the prosecution and the judge crediting Fortier's testimony with significantly helping to convict McVeigh and Nichols, federal sentencing guidelines required that Fortier serve 12 years in prison. Fortier's plea bargain also required him to pay $200,000 in fines, including restitution to the Arkansas gun store owner who had been robbed to finance the plotters' bomb-making activities. In contrast to the silent McVeigh and Nichols, Fortier tearfully apologized after his sentencing. Neither the apology nor the sentence was sufficient for victims and family members who spoke before the sentencing, urging the judge to impose a severe penalty upon the man whose silence had allowed the bombing to take place.

On June 4, 1998, Judge Matsch imposed the maximum sentence of life without parole for Nichols's conviction on conspiracy to use a weapon of mass destruction. Nichols was also sentenced to eight concurrent six-year terms for involuntary manslaughter. The judge accused Nichols of attempting to destroy the very institution on whose behalf he had adopted violence.

"What he did was participate with others in a conspiracy that would seek to destroy all of the things that the Constitution protects," Judge Matsch said. "Terry Nichols has proven to be an enemy of the Constitution, and accordingly the sentence I am going to impose will be for the duration of his life."

Although Nichols's sentence appeared to spare his life, he still faced a second trial. Prior to his sentencing, Nichols had rejected an offer of leniency by Judge Matsch in return for information about the bombing, saying that it might put him in jeopardy if the state of Oklahoma pursued charges against him. As expected, in March 1999, the Oklahoma County district attorney charged Nichols with 160 counts of murder for the deaths of the victims who were not federal law enforcement officers. The possibility that he could be executed for his part in the Oklahoma City disaster remained.

— Tom Smith

Suggestions for Further Reading

Hamm, Mark S. *Apocalypse in Oklahoma*. Boston, Mass.: Northeastern University Press, 1997.

Kenworthy, Tom and Lois Romano. "McVeigh Guilty on All 11 Counts." *Washington Post* (June 3, 1997): A1.

Thomas, Jo. "Friend Says McVeigh Wanted Bombing to Start an 'Uprising.' " *New York Times* (May 13, 1997): A1, 14.

United States v. Rita Gluzman: 1997

Defendant: Rita Gluzman   **Crime Charged:** Interstate domestic violence
Chief Defense Lawyer: Lawrence Hocheiser   **Chief Prosecutor:** Deidre Daly
Judge: Barrington D. Parker, Jr.   **Place:** White Plains, New York
Date of Trial: April 30, 1997   **Verdict:** Guilty   **Sentence:** Life
imprisonment without parole

SIGNIFICANCE

Rita Gluzman was the first woman to be convicted under the Violence Against
Women Act 18 USC 2261.

Rita Gluzman, a former chemical engineer living in Upper Saddle River, New Jersey, was convicted for crossing state lines with her cousin, Vladimir Zelenin, killing her husband Yakov Gluzman, and then chopping his body into 65 pieces in his apartment in Pearl River, New York.

Zelenin was arrested while dumping parts of the body in 10 plastic bags into the Passaic River on April 7, 1996, the day after the murder. He was found by police walking along the bank of the river, with bloody hands and blood on his clothes. In nearby cars, bags with body parts, bloody clothes, and tools used in dismembering the body were found. The fingertips of the body had been removed in an apparent attempt to conceal the identity of the victim. On Zelenin's arrest, he confessed, implicating Rita. He said that they had purchased the tools for dismembering the body in New Jersey, then went to the apartment and surprised Yakov when he entered.

Zelenin said they had killed Yakov with two axes, then dismembered the body with hacksaws and a scalpel. Rita's motive in the case, the prosecution would later allege, was that she feared her husband was going to divorce her, and she wanted to preserve her interest in a computer firm, ECI Technologies. Zelenin was employed in the company.

Rita was sought by police for several days, and then arrested April 12 on Long Island, where she had taken refuge in a cabin for visiting scientists at Cold Spring Harbor Laboratories. She was found with travel books and flight information regarding Switzerland. She was first arrested on burglary charges, before federal charges were brought.

From Asylum to Affluence

The Gluzmans had been married for 27 years. Rita had gained some notoriety many years before as part of the Jewish exodus from the Soviet Union. Although she had been able to leave the country, her husband had not been granted an exit visa. She had emigrated first to Israel, and then to the United States, where she sought help to get her husband out. In 1971, she had asked for support from U.S. ambassador to the UN, George H.W. Bush, in her efforts to help her husband emigrate from Russia. She spoke at meetings of the United Jewish Appeal and the American Conference for Soviet Jews, and conducted a personal hunger strike.

Eventually, Yakov was granted an exit visa to emigrate to Israel. The couple then moved to the United States, where Yakov Gluzman continued his work in molecular biology, rising to a position as senior director of molecular research at Lederle Laboratories in Pearl River, Rockland County, New York. Gluzman, a prominent molecular biologist and cancer researcher, had also established the profitable computer firm ECI Technologies, in which he and his wife shared ownership.

Their marriage had become more and more difficult in the years before his death. Yakov claimed that his wife was running the electronics firm into the ground, spending more than $11,000 a month on herself. For her part, she suspected her husband maintained a mistress in Israel. Gluzman filed for divorce four months prior to his death, alleging his wife had become abusive and was spending too much money. Federal authorities later alleged that Rita had gone to Israel to obtain photos of her husband with another woman and had used the photos and illegal telephone taps to try to blackmail him.

Rita Prosecuted Under Federal Statute

After her arrest, Rita was charged by federal prosecutors under the Violence Against Women Act (passed in 1994 by Congress following the O.J. Simpson case). The act contains gender-free language, and Rita was the only woman charged with violation of the new law among the three or four cases brought since it had been passed. The act was used because of the difficulty of bringing charges under New York State rules prohibiting convictions solely based on uncorroborated accomplice testimony. Since her accomplice Zelenin was the only witness against her, the federal charges appeared to be the only way to get a conviction for the murder.

At the trial for the murder, Zelenin admitted he had butchered the body of Yakov Gluzman, but argued that Rita had pressured him into the act. Zelenin agreed to testify in exchange for a lighter sentence, and sought political asylum. Rita Gluzman's defense attorney pointed out that Zelenin, who admitted the grisly crime, and who cursed Rita at the conclusion of his testimony, was an unreliable witness. The defense further pointed out that had Rita wanted to collect life insurance and title to shared property, she would hardly have engaged in a plot to dispose of her husband's body.

However, the prosecution argued that only Rita had a motive for the killing and that Zelenin would gain nothing. Rita had feared her husband would divorce her, move to Israel with his girlfriend, and take the proceeds of their lucrative business.

On April 30, 1997, Judge Barrington Parker convicted Rita of violation of the federal statute against interstate domestic violence and sentenced her to life in prison without parole. The pertinent section of 18 USC 2261 states in language carefully crafted to be gender-free: "A person who travels across a state line . . . with the intention to injure, harass, or intimidate that person's spouse or intimate partner, and who in the course of or as a result of such travel, intentionally commits a crime of violence and thereby causes bodily injury to such spouse or intimate partner, shall be punished. . . ." Although known as the Violence Against Women Act (VAWA), that language of the act very clearly covered the crime charged against Rita Gluzman.

Courts Dismiss Appeals

Rita Gluzman appealed her sentence on several grounds. In *U.S. v. Gluzman* 154 F.3d 49 (2nd Cir. 1998), the Second U.S. Circuit Court of Appeals denied her appeal on August 28, 1998. Then the U.S. Supreme Court denied certiorari on March 22, 1999. In that appeal her attorney Judd Berstein contested the constitutionality of the federal statute, claiming Congress exceeded its power to control interstate commerce by extending the commerce clause to cover domestic violence. Berstein also alleged that the jury selection system in White Plains, New York, by excluding jurors from the Bronx, tended to discriminate against minority representation in the jury pool. U.S. attorney Cathy Seibel argued for the federal government, showing precedents for use of the interstate commerce clause to protect against spousal abuse.

In a later appeal Rita argued that she had received ineffective counsel due to failure to use mental illness as a defense. In a decision on December 7, 2000, Judge Parker dismissed that appeal, noting that her careful planning was not symptomatic of someone insane. Although she might have been distraught at the thought of divorce, there was no evidence she was mentally ill. In his 16-page opinion he scolded Rita Gluzman's lawyers for raising that appeal.

— Rodney Carlisle

Suggestions for Further Reading

Berger, Joseph. "Soviet Emigré Is Guilty in Ax Murder of Husband." *New York Times* (January 31, 1992): B5.

Jesse Timmendequas Trial: 1997

Defendant: Jesse Timmendequas **Crimes Charged:** Murder, kidnapping, rape, sodomy **Chief Defense Lawyers:** Barbara R. Lependorf, Roy B. Greenman **Chief Prosecutors:** Kathyrn Flicker, Lewis Korngut **Judge:** Andrew J. Smithson **Place:** Trenton, New Jersey **Date of Trial:** May 5–June 20, 1997 **Verdict:** Guilty **Sentence:** Death

SIGNIFICANCE

Because of the publicity in the wake of Megan Kanka's murder, most states now require that citizens be notified in advance if a sex offender plans to move into their neighborhood.

In July 1994 seven-year-old Megan Kanka was living in Hamilton Township, New Jersey, with her parents and two siblings. Unknown to them, twice-convicted sex offender Jesse Timmendequas had moved in across the street, along with Brian Jenin and Joseph Cifelli, two men with similar records whom he had met in prison. On July 29, Mrs. Kanka took a nap at about 6:30 P.M. While she slept, Megan went down the street to visit a friend, and when Mrs. Kanka awoke she could not find her. The Kankas began asking their neighbors if they had seen Megan, and a number said that they had seen the girl. Timmendequas told the Kankas he had seen Megan with a friend earlier in the day when they stopped to talk to him about his new boat, which was parked in front of his house. Soon after Megan was discovered to be missing, the Kankas called the police. They arrived at 8:49 P.M., searched the Kankas' property, and questioned the neighbors, including Timmendequas. Now he said that he had seen Megan riding her bicycle about 2:30 P.M. This conflicted with his earlier statement, so the police asked him if he had seen her at any other time that day. He replied that he had also seen her riding her bicycle between 5:30 and 6:00, but that his roommates were out shopping and would not have seen her. At 10:00 P.M. the police searched the house, boat, and property where Timmendequas lived and found nothing.

At 12:30 A.M., detectives got Cifelli's mother's written consent to search the house again, and they also began questioning the three men separately. Although the detectives found nothing incriminating in the house, they became suspicious of Timmendequas because he was sweating and shaking as they questioned him. Timmendequas's nervousness, his lack of alibi for the time of Megan's disappearance, and the fact that he changed his story about when he had seen her prompted the police to take him to the station for further questioning.

Clues and Conflicting Stories Point to Suspect

At the station, Timmendequas waived his right to counsel and agreed to a search of his truck, which he had driven to the police station. It contained a piece of black felt and a brown toy chest. During the search, Timmendequas volunteered that he had cut his hand earlier in the day on a curtain rod in the truck. He did have a wound on his palm, but the police found no blood or skin on the rod.

Timmendequas then went home, promising to return the next day. Meanwhile the police searched his boat and nearby garbage cans. In the trash they found a knotted rope with what appeared to be dried blood on it, and the waistband to a pair of small pants. Mrs. Kanka identified them as fragments of Megan's clothing.

On July 30 police again questioned Timmendequas, who was by now their main suspect. He wrote a second statement about his activities that conflicted with his previous statement written the night before. Detectives questioned him for another six hours. Finally he asked to speak to his roommate, Brian Jenin. When Jenin entered the room he told Timmendequas, "They got you, they got you, they got you. You're going to need a friend on the outside and I'll be that friend." Timmendequas put his head down and said, "She's in Mercer County Park." He agreed to lead the police to the body, which he had dumped near a portable toilet in a weeded area of the park three miles from Megan's home.

Timmendequas Convicted

In May 1997, the 36-year-old Timmendequas went on trial in Trenton, New Jersey. In her opening statement, the chief prosecutor told the jury that Timmendequas had lured Megan into his house by promising to show her his puppy. According to his own statements he started to touch Megan and she screamed and tried to get away. Timmendequas was afraid that Megan would tell her mother so he grabbed her, ripping her shorts, then put a belt around her neck and pulled her back into his room. At some point in the struggle she bit Timmendequas's hand, and she fell and began bleeding. To keep the blood from getting on the carpet, Timmendequas put two plastic bags over her head and stuffed her into a large toy box he had converted into a tool chest.

The medical examiner testified that Megan had been deliberately strangled and sexually assaulted. Police detectives testified that Timmendequas had admitted to sexually assaulting Megan when they confronted him with the medical evidence, and that he had described the assault to police in a "flat and unemotional tone." He had also confessed that he had been "slipping for a while" and had been "getting those feelings for little girls . . . for a couple of weeks or a couple of months."

Timmendequas did not testify or present any witnesses during the guilt phase of the trial. His defense was presented through cross-examination and argument, and he was convicted on all counts.

Defense Pleads Mitigating Factors

During the penalty phase of the trial Timmendequas presented two witnesses: a forensic social worker and a clinical and forensic psychologist, both

Convicted sex offender Jesse Timmendequas is flanked by his lawyers at his trial for the sexual assault and murder of Megan Kanka. (AP/Wide World Photos)

of whom testified to mitigating factors. Each described Timmendequas's childhood as extremely disfunctional. His mother was a promiscuous alcoholic who had had 10 children by seven different men. Several of the children had been placed in foster care or adopted. Timmendequas's brother testified that he and Jesse had both been repeatedly molested by their father, Skip, and that they had both witnessed Skip rape a seven-year-old girl when Jesse was eight or nine.

The psychologist also testified, on the basis of trial testimony, that Timmendequas was under "extreme emotional disturbance" when he killed Megan, that he was "unraveling psychologically," and that his ability to understand the nature of his actions "was very much impaired." Finally, he asserted that the defendant's intent to commit sexual assault did not mean that he intended to murder Megan. He testified that the defendant had killed Megan as a reflexive response to the panic he felt when she attempted to flee. Thus the murder, according to the psychologist, was not premeditated.

The prosecution had consistently argued that Timmendequas had "wanted to kill, meant to kill" Megan from the time he abducted her. It relied on evidence introduced in the guilt phase to support its argument that sufficient aggravating factors existed to warrant the death penalty. The prosecution's expert argued that there was no evidence either of extreme emotional disturbance, or of mental disease or defect that might have been mitigating. The prosecution challenged the defense's portrayal of the defendant's childhood, pointing out that there were no witnesses outside the family who could substantiate the stories of abuse and neglect, and in fact that some witnesses disputed the portrayal of Timmendequas's mother as a drunken slattern. In the end the jury found that the prosecution had proven both aggravating factors beyond a reasonable doubt and sentenced Jesse Timmendequas to death.

After Timmendequas's conviction his attorney appealed the decision, alleging several procedural errors. Among them were the trial court's failure to change the venue for the convenience of the victim's family and its decision to empanel a jury from another county instead of moving the trial, and the jurors' prior knowledge, or suspicion, of the defendant's criminal history. The defense also claimed prosecutorial misconduct, citing the prosecutor's repeated references to the defendant's sexual perversion, lack of emotion, and lack of remorse after the crime, and the prosecutor's overly emotional summation in the guilt phase of the trial. But the New Jersey Supreme Court affirmed both the conviction and the death sentence.

As a result of Megan's death, her mother, Maureen Kanka, began a campaign for laws requiring notification of the presence of sex offenders in communities. "Megan's Law" gained both state and national acceptance, and in 1996 President Clinton signed a bill encouraging states to adopt such notification legislation.

— *Carol Willcox Melton*

Suggestions for Further Reading

Fodor, Margie Druss. *Megan's Law: Protection or Privacy (Issues Forum)*. Berkeley Heights, New Jersey: Enslow Publishers, 2001.

Walsh, Elizabeth Rahmberg. *Sex Offender Registration and Community Notification: A "Megan's Law" Sourcebook*. Kingston, New Jersey: Civic Research Institute, 1998.

Vincent Gigante Trial: 1997

Defendant: Vincent "The Chin" Gigante **Crimes Charged:** Racketeering, murder, conspiracy to commit murder **Chief Defense Lawyer:** Michael Marinaccio **Chief Prosecutors:** George Stamboulidis, Andrew Weissman **Judge:** Jack Weinstein **Place:** New York, New York **Date of Trial:** June 25–July 25, 1997 **Verdict:** Guilty of racketeering and conspiracy to murder **Sentence:** 12 years in prison and $1.25 million fine

SIGNIFICANCE

After finally bringing the elusive "Chin" to trial, the government's case rested on two things: 1) Proving the mobster really was a top crime boss and 2) establishing that he had the mental competence to issue orders and run the family business. Testimony by gangster turncoats, including a riveting one via closed-circuit television, guaranteed justice at last.

For more than 20 years, Vincent "The Chin" Gigante eluded justice with an elaborate and innovative ruse: He acted crazy. The reputed head of New York's powerful Genovese crime family wandered the streets of his Greenwich Village neighborhood in a tattered bathrobe, relieved himself against light poles, and muttered incoherently. Word on the street had it that "The Oddfather" used an umbrella while showering. Gigante even had himself hospitalized 25 times for schizophrenia in the 20 years before his prosecution.

An Elaborate Ploy

Federal authorities claimed that the charismatic ex-boxer Mafia boss committed himself whenever they came close to indicting him. In a seemingly endless series of competency hearings, Gigante's lawyers stalled prosecution for nearly seven years, saying their infamous client was mentally unstable.

Finally in August 1996, a federal judge in New York found "The Chin" competent to stand trial. Gigante, twitching, trembling, and talking to himself in the courtroom, faced 21 charges ranging from racketeering and extortion to the murders of two mob rivals. Federal prosecutors also charged him with ordering several gangster murders as well as conspiring to murder three others. Notorious New York crime boss John Gotti was on Gigante's hit list.

Gigante reportedly plotted the executions because the target mobsters allegedly had violated a Mafia rule against committing murders not sanctioned by mob chieftains.

During his four-week trial in 1997, the question of the 68-year-old Gigante's sanity remained central, along with the issue of whether or not he actually ruled the Genovese family. Prosecutors claimed that Gigante feigned mental illness, all the while directing operations for the Genovese Family. The Genovese reportedly reigned the strongest of New York's Big Five crime families, including the Bonanno, Colombo, Gambino, and Lucchese clans.

Vincent Gigante, reputed head of New York's Genovese crime family. (AP/Wide World Photos)

Gigante's defense told jurors their client whispered to light poles and told psychiatrists he heard the voice of God. They argued that because the mobster clearly was mentally incompetent, he couldn't have the acuity to concoct sophisticated plans for kickbacks, bid-rigging, and murders. They claimed he was unable to issue orders to Genovese soldiers.

Mob Informants Testify about Gigante's Sanity

Prosecutors built their case on the testimony of six mob informants and a dozen law enforcement agents. The defense presented no witnesses; Gigante did not take the stand. He sat in a wheelchair during the proceedings, at times seemingly oblivious to the drama unfolding in the Brooklyn federal courtroom.

First to testify for the prosecution was Peter "Big Pete" Chiodo, a former captain of the Lucchese family. The 400-pound Chiodo, whose bulk may have helped him survive a dozen bullets fired into him during a 1991 hit, said he had heard Gigante referred to as the Genovese family boss on several occasions.

Chiodo also testified that he had angered Genovese family members once when he used Gigante's name in a conversation instead of the word "Chin." Mob bosses, he said, preferred their nicknames and Gigante was emphatic about it. Sometimes, gangsters simply referred to Gigante by stroking their chins. Anthony "Fat Tony" Salerno and former Lucchese crime family captain Al D'Arco related similar stories on the witness stand.

Ex-Gambino family underboss Salvatore "Sammy the Bull" Gravano testified in a thick, Brooklyn accent that "Chin was the boss" of the Genovese family. Gravano had confessed to 19 murders as part of a 1991 deal with the government to testify against reputed mobsters for at least two years. He had spent five years in prison.

But it was turncoat gangster Peter Savino who emerged as the government's most important witness. Savino, a Gigante assassination target, was the only prosecution witness with direct ties to the Genovese family. The 55-year-old mobster testified via closed circuit television, visible to both Gigante and jurors, from an undisclosed location. He was too ill to travel.

Sweating profusely and constantly mopping his brow with a paper towel, Savino testified for a day and a half. Obviously in pain, he frequently asked for breaks, which Judge Jack Weinstein granted. Savino told how he was the Genovese family's man in a vast network of bid-rigging and extortion schemes. He related how the crime family earned millions of dollars in kickbacks from replacement window contracts for New York city housing projects. Savino produced taped conversations to back his story.

Ironically, Gigante might not have taken it on the chin from Savino if he had been able to keep up the stalling tactics that had served him so well for nearly seven years. Only three months after his testimony, Savino died of cancer of the lungs, liver and pelvis.

Defense Accuses Informants of Lying to Save Themselves

In his closing arguments, Gigante's attorney, Michael Marinaccio, branded the turncoat gangsters "psychopaths and liars," claiming they tailored their stories to get favorable government treatment. Assistant U.S. attorney Andrew Weissman countered that the Mafia squealers were telling the truth; if they weren't, they would lose their promised freedom.

"In the old world, lying was a way of life," he told jurors. "After they made a deal with the government, lying risked everything."

Marinaccio produced a series of elaborate charts to remind jurors how many people the government witnesses had admitted killing. He warned the jury not to believe the "words of six madmen." Gigante stared vacantly from his wheelchair.

The panel of eight women and four men deliberated 16 hours over three days before delivering a guilty verdict. Jurors decided Gigante indeed headed a sophisticated bid-rigging and kickback scheme to infiltrate the window-replacement business. He also was convicted of conspiring to kill informer Savino as well as Gambino crime boss Gotti and his brother Gene.

Gigante affected the role of crazy man to the bitter end. At his sentencing on December 18, 1997, Judge Weinstein ordered "The Chin" to shed his sweatpants and don gray slacks and blazer from a stash of used clothes set aside for improperly attired defendants. Looking dazed and confused, Gigante said "Good morning" to the judge and courtroom viewers. He listened glumly as the judge gave him a 12-year prison term and imposed a $1.25 million fine.

With mandated good time, Gigante could be free in 10 years. Noting "The Chin's" sentence could have been as much as 30 years, Judge Weinstein stated he had weighed Gigante's documented hypertension and heart problems against his crimes. Nevertheless, Gigante appealed.

The U.S. Court of Appeals for the Second Circuit affirmed Gigante's conviction in January 1999. He then petitioned the U.S. Supreme Court, claiming he was denied a "face-to-face confrontation" with Savino when the dying man testified via closed-circuit television. He said his Sixth Amendment right to confront his accuser had been violated. In January 2000, the Supreme Court justices let Gigante's conviction stand.

"The Chin" now serves his 12-year term in a Fort Worth, Texas, prison hospital. He reportedly has delegated many mob duties, but continues to call the shots in Genovese family operations, just as he's done for decades.

— *B. J. Welborn*

Suggestions for Further Reading

Capeci, Jerry. "Chin: Dazed, Confused, Guilty." *The Week in Gangland, The Online Column* (July 29, 1997).

Okwu, Michael. "Judge: Mob Boss Fit to Be Tried." *CNN Interactiv* (August 19, 1996).

"Vincent, 'Chin' Gigante Loses Appeal." *USA Today Online* (January 18, 2000).

Mackenzie v. Miller Brewing Co.: 1997, 1999, 2000

Plaintiff: Jerold J. Mackenzie   **Defendant:** Miller Brewing Company and two Miller employees, Robert L. Smith and Patricia G. Best

Plaintiff Claim: Intentional misrepresentation, tortious interference with prospective contract, tortious interference with contract

Chief Lawyer for Plaintiff: Gerald P. Boyle   **Chief Defense Lawyer:** Frank J. Daily   **Circuit Court Judge:** Louise Tesmer

Appeals Court Judges: Ralph Adam Fine, Charles B. Schudson and Ted E. Wedemeyer, Jr.   **Places:** Milwaukee and Madison, Wisconsin

Date of Trial: June 27, 1997–July 15, 1997   **Dates of Appeal:** Oral arguments: August 18, 1999. Opinion filed: February 22, 2000

Verdict: Jury awarded Mackenzie $26.6 million: $24.5 million from Miller Brewing Co.; $1.5 million from coworker Best, and $601,500 from former supervisor Smith. Judge Tesmer set aside judgment against Best and reduced award to $24.7 million. Miller appealed the judgment to Wisconsin Court of Appeals, District I. Appeals Court reversed judgment with orders affirmed in part and reversed in part. Mackenzie has appealed to Wisconsin Supreme Court. Decision expected in 2001.

SIGNIFICANCE

This case ultimately hinged on the simple question: Do employers have the legal right to lie to employees? The Wisconsin Supreme Court has agreed to review the case, which involved a record damage award. The high court could clarify state tort law govering what obligations employers have or don't have to tell at-will employees the truth about their job status.

This case gained national attention as "The Seinfeld Case" because the plaintiff alleged in part that he was fired from Miller Brewing Company after discussing a risqué episode of the television show with a female coworker. But during Jerold Mackenzie's complex five-year court battle, this aspect of the case was dropped early on. Mackenzie maintains, however, that the media frenzy surrounding the sexual harassment allegation labeled him a pervert and precluded job possibilities anywhere in the country.

In his suit, Mackenzie argued that Miller shabbily dismissed him without fairly investigating coworker Patricia Best's claim of sexual harassment. He claimed Best was fraudulent when she reported that Mackenzie's conversation about the *Seinfeld* episode made her uncomfortable.

He also argued in his trial that Miller never told him about his 1989 demotion. Mackenzie claimed his boss lied to him about his job status. When a 1992 memo tipped him off about the secret demotion, Mackenzie claimed he was too old to find a new job, being past "marketable age." This argument became the heart of his case.

Mackenzie said that although he was unaware of his job downgrade, it prohibited him from moving up the corporate ladder. If he had known his grade-level had been reduced, he would have left Miller at the time of the demotion. He suffered behind-the-scenes career sabotage and was summarily fired after Best's bogus sexual harassment complaint. Mackenzie argued that his firing was improper, Best was not harassed, and Miller was looking for an excuse to unfairly get rid of him.

Mackenzie v. Miller involved years of litigation, including a three-week jury trial, a 10,000-page record, more than 300 pages in briefs, national publicity, and nearly $25 million awarded in punitive damages, in part for being improperly fired. In his civil action, Mackenzie had sought damages for lost salary and benefits as well as for the salary he would have received had he become a director at Miller, his career goal. He asked for $9.2 million in compensatory damages.

Corporate Deceit or a Manager's Incompetence?

Here are the events that led to Mackenzie's suit against Miller:

Mackenzie joined Miller in 1974 when he was 31 years old, taking a grade 7 job. He moved often for the company and climbed the corporate ladder quickly. He reached grade level 14 by 1982. He was assigned to corporate headquarters in Milwaukee.

From 1984 to 1990, Miller experienced downsizing and mergers. In the process, Mackenzie's responsibilities were reduced. In 1989, his position was lowered to grade level 13. Mackenzie said he was not told of the downgrade. His benefits and perks had continued, apparently because his $95,000-per-year position had been "grandfathered" in 1989. Miller also considered him for additional management responsibilities during this period. But Mackenzie alleged that his boss, Robert Smith, sabotaged those chances for advancement by bad-mouthing him behind his back.

Mackenzie remained ignorant of his demotion until 1993 when a memo advised him that all "grandfathered" jobs would no longer receive the perks of the higher level. Mackenzie then realized that since he was in fact a grade 13, his goal of rising to grade level 15 was unreachable.

Mackenzie confronted Smith about the downgrading. Mackenzie claims Smith assured him that all was well with his executive job status.

On the morning of March 18, 1993, while conversing with Best, Mackenzie asked the distributor services manager if she had seen the previous night's *Seinfeld* episode. She said she had not. Mackenzie told of the plot in which Jerry Seinfeld could not remember his date's name, but that the name rhymed with a female body part. The date's name was Delores. Mackenzie challenged Best to guess the body part. She could not. He then copied a page from a dictionary that defined the body part and showed the copy to Best. Mackenzie expressed his outrage that the episode had passed censors. Best said she did not want to discuss the TV show further.

On March 24, Best told Mackenzie that he had stepped over the line. Mackenzie said he couldn't believe that Best, who he claimed often used vulgar language, would be offended. Best reported this conversation to Mackenzie's current boss, David Goulet.

On March 25, 1993, Mackenzie was "invited" to Miller's law library. There, two Miller attorneys confronted him about the conversation with Best. An hour later, Goulet escorted Mackenzie out of the building and told him never to return.

Soon after he was fired, Mackenzie began working indirectly for Miller under a contract with a corporate organization consultant, Michael J. Mazzoni of Boston. Mackenzie alleged that once Miller learned that he had contacted an attorney to sue Miller, the company forced him out of the contract.

Mackenzie's lawyer Gerald P. Boyle, who had defended serial murderer Jeffrey Dahmer, argued in Mackenzie's civil trial that top Miller officials were "out to get" his client. They used a false complaint by a devious coworker to fire him and ruin his reputation.

Miller's attorneys argued that Mackenzie had past problems with female employees. In 1989, after a secretary claimed that Mackenzie had made sexual advances toward her, Mackenzie settled out of court for $16,000. Miller also argued that Mackenzie had difficulties managing employees. After the 1989 harassment complaint, the company warned Mackenzie that any future problems would mean dismissal.

Boyle in turn claimed that Miller's failure to tell the truth ruined his client's chance to reach his coveted grade 15.

"To fail to tell a man is total and complete deceit," Boyle said. "And for that they must be made to pay."

In a damage award unprecedented in size in the state of Wisconsin, the jury in a unanimous verdict demanded Miller pay Mackenzie $25 million.

The Appeals Begin

Miller appealed the judgment to Wisconsin's 1st District Court of Appeals. The company alleged Mackenzie had failed to prove that anyone at Miller had lied to him. Moreover, Mackenzie, now 56, had not looked for a job since his dismissal.

In 1998, Mackenzie and his wife Bonnie moved to Washington State, where he eventually found work with a Seattle construction company.

In a 2–1 decision on February 22, 2000, the appeals court agreed with Miller but conceded some limits. The court said at-will workers (those who work without contracts) have no legal basis to sue if their bosses lie about their job status. However, employers cannot lie in certain situations, for example, to induce someone to take a job.

Presiding Judge Ted Wedemeyer, Jr., dissented. He wrote in his dissent, "Truthfulness and integrity in an employee-employer relationship form a foundation that allows all to thrive." Mackenzie appealed to the state supreme court.

The Wisconsin Supreme Court agreed in the summer of 2000 to review the case and heard oral arguments in November 2000. Miller lawyers said upholding the verdict in Mackenzie's favor would leave Wisconsin employers more vulnerable to lawsuits. Employers would be forced to guess what information they should disclose to employees. They added that the appeals court acted entirely within prior legal limits set by the state supreme court.

"If you're terminated and you can think of something later that your employers didn't tell you, you're a millionaire," attorney Frank Daily told reporters after the arguments.

The Wisconsin Supreme Court was expected to render its decision in late 2001.

—*B.J. Welborn*

Suggestions for Further Reading

"Fired Miller Executive Awarded $26 Million; Jury Decides Discharging Official in 'Seinfeld' Case Was Improper." *Milwaukee Journal Sentinel Online* (July 16, 1997).

"Jerold J. Mackenzie vs. Miller Brewing Co., Patricia G. Best and Robert L. Smith." *Wisconsin Court System Online.*

"Mackenzie v. Miller Brewing Co." *Court TV Library Online* (1999).

Vincent Doan Trial: 1997

Defendant: Vincent Doan **Crimes Charged:** Murder, kidnapping
Chief Defense Lawyers: John H. Rion, Jon Paul Rion (criminal trial); John H.
Rion, Kort Gatterdam (sentencing hearing) **Chief Prosecutor:** William Peelle
Judge: William McCracken **Place:** Wilmington, Ohio **Date of Trial:** July 21,
1997–August 7, 1997 **Verdict:** Guilty on one count of aggravated murder and
three counts of kidnapping; not guilty on one count of aggravated murder and
one count of kidnapping **Sentence:** Life imprisonment without parole

SIGNIFICANCE

Not for the first time, this case demonstrates that a conviction for murder does not
require the victim's body or any conclusive proof of the victim's death when there
is strong circumstantial evidence that a murder has been committed and the
accused did the crime.

It seemed as if Vincent Doan was two people. Friends and relatives described him as an extremely polite individual who, as a boy, cried at movies like *The Wizard of Oz* and later, as an adult, would buy a puppy for a friend. However, when it came to Clarissa Ann ("Carrie") Culberson, 22, Doan was a different man.

Doan and Culberson lived in Blanchester, Ohio, a rural community of fewer than 5,000 residents about 30 miles northeast of Cincinnati. At the time of her disappearance, Culberson resided with her divorced mother, Debra Culberson, and her 15-year-old sister, Christina. She worked part-time as a nail technician at two hair studios. After high school she lived in neighboring Midland with a female friend. It was then that she started to date Doan.

The couple's 3-year relationship was violent. Doan was known to push and punch Culberson and to drag her by her hair. Culberson once filed assault charges against Doan, alleging that he hit her in the head with a space heater. Doan also called Culberson at work at least five times every day and beat her when he caught her talking to male friends. Then, on August 29, 1996, Culberson disappeared.

Culberson's Disappearance

At about 6 A.M. on August 29, 1996, Debra Culberson noticed that Carrie and Carrie's red Honda CRX were gone. She and Christina drove around town to find her. Carrie's father, Roger Culberson, and two friends who had been with Carrie the night before soon joined the search. Nine days later, more than 300 volunteers spent the weekend looking through the forests, fields, and abandoned buildings in and around Blanchester. The Culberson family offered a $10,000 reward for information leading to the arrest and conviction of anyone responsible for Carrie's disappearance. Television programs such as *Inside Edition* and *The Oprah Winfrey Show* featured stories about the case. Still, neither Culberson nor her car was ever found. Then, in March 1997, Doan was indicted on four counts of kidnapping Culberson. Three months later, two counts of aggravated murder were added.

The trial began on July 21, 1997, at the Clinton County Courthouse in Wilmington, Ohio. During the trial, the prosecution called 23 people to the stand; the defense, 28. Despite the lack of a body or any decisive proof that Carrie Culberson was dead, the prosecution presented two theories to the jury. The first was that Doan was obsessed with Culberson and he murdered her when he found that he could not control her. The second was that Doan kidnapped and killed Culberson to prevent her from pursuing the assault charges she filed after he hit her with the space heater.

The first of the prosecution's key witnesses was Jessica Williams, a friend of Culberson's. Williams testified that on the evening before Culberson's disappearance, the two participated in a volleyball game in Morrow, about 10 miles away from Blanchester. During the game, Doan showed up and tried to get Culberson to leave, but she refused. After the game, Williams and Culberson returned to Blanchester and, at Carrie's request, they drove by Doan's residence twice before Williams dropped her off.

Kimberly Lannerd, a neighbor of the Culbersons who had a habit of sitting on her porch on late summer evenings, testified that Carrie was dropped off at the Culberson home at about 11:45 P.M. on August 28, 1996. Shortly afterward Lannerd saw Carrie's car backing out of the driveway without its headlights on. "The headlights being off stayed in my mind" she said. "They were put on about halfway down the street."

A third witness, Billie Jo Brown, lived across the street from Doan. Getting off work at around 11:40 P.M. on August 28, 1996, she walked home and went to bed about 50 minutes later. Just as she was lying down, Brown heard loud voices outside. Looking out her bedroom window, she saw a little red car parked at the intersection between her and Doan's house. Going to her kitchen window, Brown then saw a young woman in her yard running away from a man. Due to both the brightness of the street light in her front yard and a full moon, Brown recognized the couple as Doan and a lady that Brown had seen at Doan's residence a few times every week. According to Brown, the woman was screaming, "Help me!" while Doan shouted, "I told you next time I'd kill you, you fucking bitch." Once Doan caught up with the woman, he continually punched her while she used her fist to try to get away. Brown, who did not have a phone in her house, immediately alerted her husband, who told her not to worry because there was probably drinking involved. Brown heard tires squealing and when she looked out the window, the couple and the car were gone.

Also on the witness stand were Vicki Watson and Lori Baker, the former sister-in-law and former wife of Doan's half-brother, Tracy Baker.

Watson testified that she slept at the Baker residence during the night of Culberson's disappearance. At about 3:15 A.M., Watson heard a knock on the door. She did not answer it, but peered through the blinds. Outside on the lit deck was Doan with no shirt on, his right hand holding his left arm, and his hair messed up. She did not see any blood. Doan and Tracy Baker were talking, but Watson could not hear what was said. One half hour later, Doan and Tracy Baker left. Shortly afterward, Lori Baker took Watson to work.

On the witness stand, Lori confirmed that when Doan appeared at her home at 3:15 that morning, he was wearing only jeans and that his right hand was holding his left arm. She added that Doan's chest was smeared with blood. According to Baker, Doan and Tracy Baker talked awhile before Tracy Baker came inside and asked if there were any garbage bags. Doan took a shower before he left with Tracy Baker and the garbage bags and a gun at 3:30 or 3:45 A.M.

According to Lori Baker, Doan and her husband were back at the Baker residence by 5:50 A.M. Lori gave Tracy some bleach and a scrub brush and he took them to Doan who was again showering. Lori testified that there was blood on Tracy's clothes and that she saw him wipe off some blood from his boots. (Blood samples taken from Tracy Baker's boots, truck, and towel were too degraded for testing.)

Past Physical Abuse

There was also testimony about Doan's previously abusive treatment of Culberson. Culberson's boss at G & G Hair Studio, Desiree Gruber, told the jury that Carrie once came to work with a black eye. On another occasion, Culberson had bruises on her temple and fingerprint marks on her neck. One month before Carrie disappeared, Gruber testified that while shampooing Culberson's hair, she discovered medical staples on the back of Carrie's head. Culberson told Gruber that Doan had hit her with a space heater and that she was pressing charges.

Mitchell Epperson, Doan's jailmate while Doan was at the Queensgate Correctional Facility in November 1996 on traffic charges, testified that the two of them talked about girlfriends. That's when Doan said, "You can't let them walk. You got to make them pay." Doan also told Epperson that, concerning Culberson, he would "lie awake at night and think of a 100 different ways to kill her before I did."

The prosecution's final witness was Debra Culberson. One time, according to Debra, Doan said, "I've always slapped her [Carrie] around. I never hit her with my fist, I just slapped her." Debra also told the jury of how she approached Doan three times on August 29, 1996. Each time, Doan gave a different story about when he had last seen her. First, he told Debra that he had not seen Carrie for three days. A few hours later, Doan said that Carrie had come by his house at about 12:30 that morning. According to Doan, Carrie was honking her car horn and weaving inside her vehicle. He believed that she was drunk, so he closed the door to his house and ignored her until she left. The third time that he spoke to Debra, Doan told her that Carrie had arrived at about 12:30 A.M. and that he and Carrie went into his house. They argued and Carrie drove away after Doan told her that he did not love her anymore.

The defense tried to argue that there was nothing unusual about the relationship between Doan and Culberson. They also relied on the fact that there was no body or any other solid evidence that Culberson was dead. Indeed, Doan's lawyers argued that Culberson was still alive and called several witnesses who claimed to have seen her or her car since her disappearance.

Three women who were travelling together picked up a female hitchhiker on August 31, 1996, in Mount Orab (about 20 miles from Blanchester). They all testified that the woman resembled the picture of Culberson that was televised that weekend, but two of them also stated that the hitchhiker never mentioned Blanchester.

This same hitchhiker supposedly bought a soft drink at a store on August 31, but one of the store clerks couldn't remember what the young woman looked liked.

Other witnesses who claimed to have seen Culberson included one woman who spotted a red Honda CRX a week after Carrie's disappearance and said that the first four characters on the license plate was ROL 4. Culberson's missing car had the license plate number ROL 402. This witness admitted, however, that she had poor vision in one eye and that, when she was following the car, she was "hoping" that it was Culberson.

Kenneth Lancaster, a police officer from Norwood, Ohio, reported that he had observed a small red speeding car at about 4:30 A.M. on May 16, 1997. He only got a "quick glance" of the vehicle because it was traveling at a "full rate of speed" and, after a 30- or 40-minute search, he was unable to find the car. When Lancaster reported the vehicle to the police dispatcher, he wasn't sure about its license plate number, so he gave two, ROL 402 and RQL 402. By the time of Doan's trial, Lancaster had concluded that he had made a mistake. At no time before or during the trial did Lancaster say that he could identify the model of the car or its occupants.

Doan's stepfather, Lawrence Baker, testified to a possible alibi, saying that at about 1 A.M. on August 29 he and his wife, Betty, had received a call from their son who was calling from a friend's home in nearby Clermont County. (Phone records confirmed the timing of the call. The person from whose residence the call was made had earlier testified he observed no blood or bruises on Doan. The prosecution contended that Doan murdered Carrie after this call was made.)

Baker told the jury that, according to his stepson, a truck that Doan had borrowed from him had broken down about 15 miles away from Blanchester in Marathon. Baker suggested that Doan let the vehicle sit idle for a few minutes and, if the truck did not start then, to call back. Baker also stated that this particular truck could not travel faster than 45 or 50 miles an hour. Mr. and Mrs. Baker then waited about 15 or 20 minutes and, not hearing anything from Doan, they went to the other end of Blanchester to pick up another vehicle. On their way back, the couple stopped by Doan's house at about 1:30 A.M. and found Doan asleep on the couch with his front door open and his lights and TV on. However, when the prosecuting attorney cross-examined Baker and questioned how Doan could have driven from Marathon in a truck that could go only 45 or 50 miles an hour and still be home and asleep by 1:30, Baker pushed back his estimate of when he saw his son to 2 A.M.

Jury deliberations began on August 4, 1997. For four days, the six-man, six-woman jury deliberated. On August 7, Doan was found not guilty of premeditated murder. However, it did find Doan guilty of the charge that he had killed Culberson after he had kidnapped her and on three of the four kidnapping charges.

Three months later, the jury met to decide Doan's fate. He faced the death penalty, but the jury recommended life imprisonment without parole.

—Mark A. Thorburn

Suggestions for Further Reading

West's North Eastern Reporter. 2nd series, vol. 731. St. Paul, Minn.: West Group, 2000, 1139.

"Ohio v. Doan." *Court TV Online.* www.courttv.com/casefiles/verdicts/doan.html

Marv Albert Trial: 1997

Defendant: Marv Albert   **Crime Charged:** Forcible sodomy and assault and battery   **Chief Defense Lawyer:** Roy Black   **Chief Prosecutor:** Richard Trodden   **Judge:** Benjamin Kendrick   **Place:** Arlington, Virginia   **Dates of Trial:** September 22–October 24, 1997   **Verdict:** Guilty   **Sentence:** 1-year suspended sentence

SIGNIFICANCE

A celebrity defendant, steamy sex allegations, and surprise testimony made this one of the most closely watched trials in recent years.

In 1997, Marv Albert was an NBC sportscaster who, for 10 years, had conducted an on-again, off-again relationship with a former telephone operator named Vanessa Perhach. On February 12, 1997, the couple agreed to meet at the Ritz-Carlton Hotel in Alexandria, Virginia. Following the tryst, Albert was arrested and, on September 22, found himself in an Arlington courtroom facing charges of sexual and physical abuse.

At the trial, the state's prosecutor, Richard Trodden, painted Albert as a person with bizarre sexual appetites, who had become violent with Perhach when those cravings went unsatisfied at their Ritz-Carlton meeting.

Not so, according to defense attorney Roy Black. The encounter had been entirely consensual, and these charges were Perhach's way of lashing back at Albert, after he had told her that he intended to marry another woman.

From the prosecution's point of view, everything hinged on Perhach's testimony. Under questioning by Trodden, she described her relationship with Albert as conventional at first, but soon his darker side surfaced and he began pestering her to recruit other men to join them in sexual liaisons, which she did.

On this particular occasion, however, Perhach said she had been unable to obtain the promised third partner. Albert lost his temper. "You've been a bad girl," he said. "You didn't bring anybody." Then he threw her on the bed and began biting her back. When she complained that he was hurting her and told him to stop, Albert refused, saying, "You know you like this. . . . You enjoy rough sex." Perhach said that Albert next forced her to perform oral sex.

However, during cross-examination by Black, Perhach admitted that she had hugged and kissed Albert—signs of affection, not fear—before she left the hotel room. And why, Black inquired, did she not lock herself in the bathroom and call security if she felt threatened by Albert that night? Either unwilling or unable to respond, Perhach fell silent.

The Tape

Then Black produced an incredible piece of evidence: a taped conversation between Perhach and a taxicab driver, in which she appeared to coax the driver into supporting her allegations against Albert. "You know what to say . . . that when you went to pick him up, that he [Albert] wanted to get a boy. We gotta get tight on that."

On the tape the cab driver responded, "I'm getting too old for this. You owe me $50,000 and a new car." Both Perhach and the cab driver laughed as she told him, "Okay baby."

Stunned by the tape, Perhach denied trying to coach the cab driver, saying she was only joking with him about the promised money and car.

At this point most trial observers felt that Albert would be acquitted, but the prosecution had an ace of its own.

Surprise Witness

Up to this point, Perhach's accusations about Albert's sexual habits had remained uncorroborated. Now, out of the blue, the prosecution produced Patricia Masten, a liaison worker with Hyatt Hotels, who testified that twice she had to fend off Albert's unwanted advances—first in 1993 and again

Sportscaster Marv Albert. (AP/Wide World Photos)

the following year when he had attempted to bite her and force her to engage in oral sex. On the second occasion, she said, Albert had emerged from his hotel bathroom wearing panties and a garter belt. In the struggle to evade his clutches, she accidentally dislodged his toupee. After fleeing Albert's room, Masten had reported the incident immediately to her supervisor.

Roy Black tried to have Masten's testimony suppressed; however, Judge Benjamin Kendrick felt it proved a pattern of behavior on the part of Albert and therefore allowed it to be introduced as evidence.

This decision abruptly changed the course of the trial. By the next day, September 25, a plea bargain had been worked out: Albert agreed to plead guilty to misdemeanor assault and battery, while the felony charge of forcible sodomy would be dropped. Just hours later, NBC fired him.

Sentencing was set for October 24, at which time Albert was given a 12-month suspended sentence and ordered to undergo counseling. A little more than two years later, on December 15, 1999, NBC announced it had rehired Albert.

By modern standards this was a very brief trial, but in terms of roller-coaster emotions and switchback courtroom strategy, it packed more surprises into three days than most trials manage in several months.

—Colin Evans

Suggestions for Further Reading

New York Daily News: September 23, 1997, 1; September 24, 1997, 1; September 25, 1997. 1; September 26, 1997. 1.

www.CourtTv.com/verdicts.

Louise Woodward Trial: 1997

Defendant: Louise Woodward   **Crime Charged:** Murder
Chief Defense Lawyers: Barry Scheck, Andrew Good, and Harvey Silverglate
Chief Prosecutors: Gerard Leone, Jr. and Martha Coakley   **Judge:** Hiller
Zobel   **Place:** Cambridge, Massachusetts   **Dates of Trial:** October 7–31,
1997   **Verdict:** Guilty of second-degree murder (later reduced to involuntary
manslaughter)   **Sentence:** Life imprisonment (later reduced to time served)

SIGNIFICANCE
This was a sensational trial, followed intently on both sides of the Atlantic, that
employed a landmark use of modern technology—the Internet—to reveal the
outcome.

On February 4, 1997, teenaged nanny Louise Woodward called 911 and said
that the eight-month-old baby she was tending, Matthew Eappen, was
having difficulty breathing. When paramedics arrived at the Eappen household
in the Boston suburb of Newton, they found the baby had suffered a head injury
and his eyes were bulging, a possible sign of "shaken-baby syndrome." After
four days in intensive care, Matthew died. Louise, working in America but
British by birth, had already been accused of assault, but was now charged with
first-degree murder.

When the trial opened in Cambridge, Massachusetts, on October 7, 1997,
the defendant's age, nationality, and the crime she was charged with generated
headline media coverage. Back in her hometown of Elton, England, Louise's
supporters gathered in a pub to watch the proceedings on TV. They listened as
chief prosecutor Gerard Leone, Jr. described her as being more interested in
enjoying Boston nightlife than providing proper care for the Eappen children,
two-year-old Brendan and infant Matthew.

Family Warning

In late January 1997, the Eappens had issued an ultimatum to Louise:
shape up or ship out. Just five days later, Matthew was in the hospital.

"We are not saying . . . that the defendant woke up on February 4
specifically intending to kill Matthew Eappen," Leone told the jury. "What

we're saying . . . is that on February 4, the defendant, in a frustrated, resentful, unhappy attitude, slammed the baby into a hard object and shook him, causing his death—actions that anyone would know would result in death. In this commonwealth, that is murder."

An early prosecution witness, Dr. Kenneth Mandl, who had treated Matthew in the emergency room, described the infant as unresponsive and comatose, with enlarged pupils and evidence of retinal hemorrhaging—all signs of severe head trauma.

Under vigorous cross-examination from celebrated attorney Barry Scheck, however, Mandl conceded that he had found no physical evidence to suggest that Matthew had been shaken. Scheck pressed hard. Was there anything to support the prosecution's claim that Matthew's head had been slammed down "with the force of dropping a child 15 feet onto hard concrete"? Again Mandl had to concede. "There were no findings to specifically indicate that, no."

Dr. Joseph Madsen, who had operated on Matthew, said the injuries had caused the brain to swell "like a loaf of bread rising in an oven," and he rebuffed Scheck's suggestion—which would form the cornerstone of the defense—that the brain trauma was the result of a previous head injury.

Nanny Louise Woodward on trial in the death of eight-month-old Matthew left in her charge. (AP/ Wide World Photos)

Deadly Fall?

A string of medical experts testified for the prosecution that, in their opinion, Matthew's injuries were clearly indicative of "shaken-baby syndrome," although Scheck did make some minor headway when Dr. Gerald Feigin, who had performed the autopsy on Matthew, admitted that his much-quoted grand jury testimony about the baby's skull fracture resulting from the equivalent of a 15-foot fall was incorrect. A fall, Feigin acknowledged, of just two or three feet could cause such injuries.

Detective William Byrne, who had interviewed Louise after the incident, stated that she had admitted being "a little rough" with Matthew, angered by his nonstop crying, and that she had tossed him on a bed. Later, she said she had dropped Matthew onto the bathroom floor and that he may have struck his head on the side of the tub.

Some of the sharpest exchanges came when prosecution witness Dr. Eli Newberger, another pediatrician who had examined Matthew, was being cross-examined. He accused Scheck of attempting to distort his testimony, saying forcibly, ". . . this child was violently shaken for a prolonged period."

Deborah Eappen, Matthew's mother, was in a grimly ironic position: bereaved parent and qualified ophthalmologist. At the hospital she had examined her injured son's eyes and had seen extensive retinal hemorrhaging, a sign of shaken-baby syndrome.

"I knew what that meant," Mrs. Eappen said. "I was shocked. . . . I couldn't believe it." She also described the deteriorating relationship between Louise and herself.

Matthew's father, Sunil Eappen, the final prosecution witness, tried to convey an image of Louise as irresponsible and careless. "I can't remember a single evening when she was home . . . the mornings after were a problem," Mr. Eappen said, a reference to Louise's alleged inability to get up to care for their children after partying the night before.

Defendant Stays Cool

Although the defense began by producing several character witnesses for Louise, it was clear that this trial would be fought on medical grounds. In that respect the defense was just as well armed as the prosecution had been. Numerous defense experts testified that Matthew's injuries were inconsistent with "shaken-baby syndrome," and that they were the result of an old injury. Under Scheck's deft guidance this alternative theory gradually assumed credibility.

Then came testimony from Louise herself. Choking back tears, she described how she had tried to revive Matthew after finding him gasping in his crib. She also denied ever having told the police that she had been "rough" with Matthew. "I said maybe I was not as gentle with him as I could have been."

Louise stood up well under cross-examination, brushing aside Leone's suggestion that she had been upset with the Eappens on the day of the incident. Nor, she stated, had she told police that she had "dropped" Matthew on the bathroom floor, but rather "popped" him on the bathroom floor, explaining that "pop" is an English term that means to "lay" or "place."

Throughout her testimony, Louise remained calm. Too calm for Leone. In his peroration, he portrayed Louise as an "aspiring little actress," who told her employers "half-truths." He dismissed the "theatrical, high-priced" medical evidence presented by the defense, adding, "These injuries were caused by Louise Woodward in Matthew Eappen's own home while she was responsible for his care. To believe otherwise, you would have to believe that little falls kill little kids. They don't."

Defense attorney Andrew Good, in his summation, tried to make the defendant out to be the victim. "Louise Woodward had the colossal misfortune to be with Matthew when this old injury caused him to fall and the bleeding would not stop. . . . She has been vilified, she has been accused and now she has been proven innocent."

Scheck hammered home the "previous-injury" defense. Brandishing copies of X rays of the skull fracture, he argued that the absence of obvious swelling—which would have indicated that the injury was recent—destroyed the prosecution's case. "We may never know exactly how this incident occurred but, if this is an old injury—case over," he said. "It did not happen on February 4. And if it didn't happen on February 4, that's the end of the case."

Prosecution Switch

At this point the prosecution requested that the jury be allowed to consider alternative charges of voluntary and involuntary manslaughter, as well as murder, a move rigorously opposed by the defense. So far as they were concerned, it was murder or nothing. In the end Judge Zobel agreed with the defense; the jury could consider only first- or second-degree murder.

On October 30, after deliberating for 30 hours, the jury convicted Woodward of second-degree murder. The next day she was sentenced to life imprisonment.

But that was not the end of the story. On November 7, Judge Zobel heard a three-part defense motion: first, asking that the verdict be set aside and the case dismissed; second, setting aside the verdict and holding a new trial; or third, reducing the charge to manslaughter.

In light of the intense media interest, Judge Zobel took the unusual step of announcing that his ruling would be released on the Internet on November 10.

When it came, his decision was explosive. Not only did Judge Zobel reduce Louise's conviction to involuntary manslaughter, but he reduced the sentence to time served, which meant immediate freedom for the British teenager. She had spent just 279 days behind bars.

On June 16, 1998, the Massachusetts Supreme Judicial Court upheld Louise's reduced conviction of involuntary manslaughter and she returned to England, where she began studies as a law student.

A subsequent wrongful-death suit brought by the Eappens against Louise was settled out of court. Details of the settlement were not released to the public.

Throughout the trial, Louise's supporters in England maintained a vocal and publicly organized belief in her innocence that owed more to emotion than it did to evidence, prompting suspicions that, in this case at least, sympathy for a young woman in jeopardy appeared to outweigh concern for a child that lay dead.

—Colin Evans

Suggestions for Further Reading

Electronic Telegraph: February 11, 1997, issue 627; February 13, 1997, issue 630; October 11, 1997, issue 870; October 17, 1997, issue 876; October 29, 1997, issue 888.

Los Angeles Times: October 24, 1997, A11; October 28, 1997, A27; November 13, 1997, A17; November 13, 1997, A17.

Sunday Times Magazine (February 15, 1998): 38–45.

www.CourtTV.com/verdicts.

Pagones v. Sharpton, Maddox, & Mason: 1997–98

Plaintiff: Steven Pagones **Defendants:** Al Sharpton, Alton H. Maddox, Jr., and C. Vernon Mason **Plaintiff Claim:** Defamation of character
Chief Defense Lawyers: Sharpton: Michael Hardy; Alton Maddox; Mason: Stephen C. Jackson **Chief Lawyer for Plaintiffs:** William Stanton
Judge: S. Barrett Hickman **Place:** Poughkeepsie, New York
Dates of Trial: November 18, 1997–July 13, 1998 **Verdict:** Against all defendants; Pagones awarded $345,000 in damages

SIGNIFICANCE

Ordinarily, public figures have little recourse to libel. This case revealed that, on occasion, accusations can be so egregious that public figures must have the ability to have their name cleared in court.

On the afternoon of November 28, 1987, a black high school student named Tawana Brawley, 15, who had been missing from home for four days, was found outside an apartment complex in Wappingers Falls, New York, wrapped in a plastic bag, with racial epithets scrawled on her chest and feces smeared on her body. In her statement to the police, she claimed to have been kidnapped and raped by six white men, one of whom flashed a badge. A medical examination found no evidence of sexual abuse. On November 30, she made another statement to the police. It would be the last time she ever spoke to anyone in authority.

The unrelated suicide next day of a local police officer, Harry Crist, Jr., was seized upon by Brawley's supporters and family as evidence of a cover-up, sparking a rash of public accusations. In response to community concerns, New York governor Mario Cuomo appointed State Attorney General Robert Abrams as a special prosecutor and, on February 29, 1988, a grand jury was impaneled to investigate the case. At this time, the Reverend Al Sharpton, who had been in close consultation with the Brawley family, accused Dutchess County Assistant District Attorney Steven Pagones of being involved in the attack and demanded his arrest.

On October 6, 1998, the grand jury released its verdict: Tawana Brawley's entire story had been a fabrication. Following this decision, Pagones filed suit against Sharpton and two associates, Alton H. Maddox, Jr., and C. Vernon Mason, alleging defamation of character. Tawana was also named in the original suit, but after defying numerous subpoenas, she was eventually removed from the action in 1991 and Pagones won a default judgment against her.

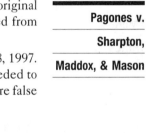
After almost 10 years, the case finally went to trial on November 18, 1997. Pagones faced a tough task—being a public figure, to win his case he needed to prove that Sharpton, Maddox, and Mason had known their statements were false or that they had recklessly disregarded the truth.

When opening arguments began, Maddox, who represented himself, told the jury he was convinced that Tawana had been telling the truth about what had happened to her in 1987. "If we had thought that Tawana Brawley was lying, we would have taken her to the woodshed and whipped the daylights out of her."

Tawana Brawley with Alton Maddox (left) speaks to supporters before the defamation lawsuit against the men who had advised her. (AP/Wide World Photos)

For William Stanton, representing Pagones, the issues were cut and dried. "The evidence will show that each of them defamed and slandered Steve Pagones," he said. "The Brawley family hatched the story. These defendants were the screenwriters."

Fistfights in Court

The trial was long and bitter; often the jury had to be excused from the courtroom as yelling matches and even fistfights broke out among the rival factions. Sharpton used the witness stand as a pulpit, insisting that it was his duty as a civil rights activist and a Brawley family spokesman to call for the arrest of the men the family accused of rape.

Stanton questioned Sharpton, inquiring, "Had she [Tawana] ever told you what happened to her?"

"In terms of details, I would not engage in sex talk with a 15-year-old girl," Sharpton replied. "I would have thought it would have been the height of ignorance to go to Tawana and say, 'Is your mother and father lying?' . . . That's absolutely ridiculous."

An extraordinary moment came during the cross-examination of Tommy Young, a police officer who had interviewed Tawana after the alleged incident and later concluded it was a hoax: Irked by the trial's slow pace, Judge Hickman asked the attorneys to work late to finish questioning Young. Sharpton's lawyer, Michael Hardy, complained that such a move would prejudice the jurors against himself. "I don't think that's appropriate judicial conduct," he said—whereupon Maddox joined in, "You can't give people respect," he yelled at Hickman, adding that he was not "tolerant."

"I've been as tolerant of you as any judge would be!" Hickman roared back.

When Stephen Jackson, attorney for Mason, also joined in the judge baiting, Hickman rose up, banged his gavel, shouted, "Stop it! Stop it! I've had enough! I've had enough!" and stormed out of the courtroom.

Eventually calm was restored, and the trial continued. And then, finally, Pagones got a chance to tell his side of the story.

A Ten-Year Delay

"Are you ready to testify?" Stanton asked his client as the former assistant district attorney took the stand.

"I've been ready for 10 years," Pagones said.

With a few simple questions, Stanton got down to the nuts and bolts of the case. "Did you rape Tawana Brawley?"

"No," replied Pagones, adding that he had never even met her in person.

"Did you conspire with Robert Abrams to obstruct justice?"

"No."

"Did you have Harry Crist [killed]?"

"No."

During Pagones' cross-examination, Hardy stressed the precise legal requirements that a public figure must meet in order to prove libel, asking, "Is there a witness that has testified that they knew for a fact that when Reverend Sharpton made those statements, he did not believe them?"

"Indirectly. I believe Sharpton said that himself when he took the stand and lied for days," Pagones answered. "I believe that every witness that has taken the stand has contradicted what Sharpton, Mason, and Maddox said. . . . Sharpton knew he was lying. Make no mistake about that.''

During Pagones' testimony, another outburst from Stephen Jackson resulted in him spending a night in jail for arguing with the judge. Finally, after 24 days of being questioned and cross-examined, Pagones left the witness stand.

In his final summation Stanton got to the crux of the matter, attacking the defendants' motives as well as their character. "These men are dangerous. They're bad. They're evil," he told the jury. "Don't let them get away with this. . . . They don't care who they stepped on and who they stepped over. . . . They destroyed lives for their own self-advancement.''

Jackson, in a furious counterattack, thundered that Pagones was "lucky he is not in jail" for rape and kidnap, and urged the jurors to "correct history" by dismissing the defamation claim.

Labeling the suit "three judicial lynchings," Maddox sought to portray the defendants as martyrs. "We are here because we stood up for the oppressed. . . . We have stood up for the poor, and now it's time to be persecuted.''

Almost eight contentious months after the trial began, the case finally went to the jury for deliberation on July 9, 1998. Four days later the jury decided that Pagones had been defamed by the defendants, and he was subsequently awarded $345,000 in damages.

Tawana Brawley did not avoid punishment for her roll in the affair. On October 9, 1998, Judge Hickman ordered her to pay Pagones $185,000 in damages resulting from her 1991 default. During his sentencing, he publicly upbraided her, saying she had ". . . thumbed her nose at the jury by not appearing to testify under oath . . . in the history of this state, never has a teenager turned the prosecutorial and judicial systems literally upside down with such false claims.''

—*Colin Evans*

Suggestions for Further Reading

Los Angeles Times: February 11, 1998, A12; February 12, 1998, A22; March 27, 1998, A18; July 9, 1998, A14; July 14, 1998, A12; July 28, 1998, A9; July 30, 1998, A11; November 22, 1998, A26.

McFadden, Robert D., ed. *Outrage—The Story behind the Tawana Brawley Hoax*. New York: Bantam, 1990.

Sharpton, Al and Anthony Walton. *Go and Tell Pharaoh*. New York: Doubleday, 1996.

Oncale v. Sundowner Offshore Services, Inc.: 1998

Appellant: Joseph Oncale **Defendant:** Sundowner Offshore Services, Inc.
Appellant's Claim: Sexual harassment **Chief Defense Lawyer:** Harry M.
Reasoner **Chief Lawyers for Appellant:** Nicholas Canaday III, Edwin S.
Kneedler, and U.S. Department of Justice *(amicus curiae)*
Justices: Stephen G. Breyer, Ruth Bader Ginsburg, Anthony M. Kennedy,
Sandra Day O'Connor, William H. Rehnquist, Antonin Scalia, David H. Souter,
John Paul Stevens, and Clarence Thomas **Place:** Washington, D.C.
Date of Decision: March 4, 1998 **Decision:** Reversal of the lower federal
courts, holding that the Civil Rights Act of 1964 prohibited same-sex sexual
harassment.

SIGNIFICANCE
The Oncale case applied the concept of sexual discrimination to include the idea
of same-gender sexual harassment.

The Civil Rights Act of 1964 was designed mainly to prevent discrimination
based on race. During congressional debate on the measure, a Southern
representative, trying to prevent its passage, added a clause at the 11th hour to
include a prohibition on discrimination "because of . . . sex." This representative was sure that sex-based discrimination would be too controversial for
Congress to consider. However, to his disappointment, the law was enacted
anyway.

In the 1960s women comprised only a small fraction of the workforce.
However, they soon began to use the act to fight discrimination in the workplace
including harassment from coworkers and supervisors, "quid pro quo" sexual
discrimination, and demands for sex in exchange for promotion or job security.
Eventually the courts also dealt with the issues involved with male workers
being sexually harassed by female coworkers and supervisors. By the early
1990s, sexual harassment was beginning to take a different form.

In 1991, 21-year-old Joseph Oncale took a job as a deckhand on a Louisiana off-shore oil rig. No women worked on the rig and Oncale was part of an
eight-man crew. Before long, he later claimed, some of the men began making

sexual threats and crude sexual advances that stopped short of rape, but which Oncale found frightening and humiliating. After an alleged assault that took place in the shower, Oncale finally quit. He later said that he feared that if he did not leave his job "I would be forced to have sex . . . if I didn't get off the rig . . . I would be sexually violated."

If Oncale had been a woman—or if his alleged tormentors had been female—he would have had a strong case for harassment under the Civil Rights Act. But in 1995, the federal District Court for the Eastern District of Louisiana dismissed his case, finding that Congress had never intended the act to bar same-sex sexual discrimination. Oncale took his case before the U.S. Court of Appeals for the Fifth Circuit, which affirmed the district court, and then finally before the U.S. Supreme in 1997. Up to then, federal courts throughout the country had handled the issue of "male-on-male" sexual harassment in different ways, and the Supreme Court was now apparently ready to end the confusion.

Court Rules Same-Sex Harassment Illegal

Oncale's attorney, Nicholas Canaday III, faced some hard questioning from the justices. The problem, in their view, was that the harassers' gender might not matter, but that the victim had to show that he—or she—had received the offensive treatment because of his—or her—own sex. Only if the harassers would have treated a member of the opposite sex differently than they treated the victim would the harassment then be "because of . . . sex." But for an all-male oil rig crew—with no easy way of comparing Oncale's treatment to that of what a woman would have received—such a thing would be hard for him to prove.

Finally, however, in a unanimous opinion rendered on March 4, 1998, the Court sided with Oncale. Justice Antonin Scalia, one of the Court's most conservative members, approvingly quoted Justice Ruth Bader Ginsburg (herself a specialist in sex discrimination law: "The critical issue," he pointed out, "is whether members of one sex are exposed to disadvantageous terms or conditions of employment to which members of the other sex are not exposed." In other words, the sex of offender and victim did not matter, and Congress' lack of specificity in so mentioning also was not an issue, regardless of what it had intended. Indeed, in his judicial opinions, Scalia rarely relied on what Congress intended, focusing instead on what the law actually stated. This approach made him an excellent choice—given the odd history of the Civil Rights Act's passage—to write the opinion concluding that Oncale should have had the chance to prove that he had been sexually harassed.

The Oncale case revealed that sexual discrimination in American society was becoming far more multifaceted and complex than that of traditional male harassment of women. It also revealed that the courts were growing aware of this fact, adapting a nebulous statute to the needs of society in response.

—Buckner F. Melton, Jr.

Suggestions for Further Reading

Smallets, Sonya. "Oncale v. Sundowner Offshore Services: A Victory for Gay and Lesbian Rights?" *Berkeley Women's Law Journal* (1999): 136–148.

Ware, Dabney D. and Bradley R. Johnson. "Oncale v. Sundowner Offshore Services, Inc.: Perverted Behavior Leads to a Perverse Ruling." *Florida Law Review* (July 1999): 489–509.

Casey Martin Trial and Appeals:
1998–2001

Plaintiff: Casey Martin **Defendants:** Professional Golfers' Association (PGA) Tour **Plaintiff Claim:** Violation of the Americans with Disabilities Act (1990) by refusing to adapt tournament rules to accommodate his disability
Chief Lawyers for Plaintiff: Trial: William Wiswall, Martha Walters; Supreme Court: Roy L. Reardon **Chief Defense Lawyers:** Trial: William Maledon; Supreme Court: H. Bartow Farr III **Judge:** Trial: Thomas M. Coffin; Final Appeal: U.S. Supreme Court, William Rehnquist presiding **Place:** Trial: Eugene, Oregon. Final Appeal: Washington, DC **Dates of Trials:** Trial: February 2–10, 1998; Final Appeal: January 17, 2001; Decision: May 29, 2001 **Decisions:** Trial: Martin's suit upheld; Supreme Court: The PGA's appeal denied

SIGNIFICANCE
In an era when people with physical disabilities of all kinds were gaining access to many areas and activities hitherto closed to them, this was the first case in which an athlete with a disability took legal action to demand a special arrangement so that he could compete with professionals. The issue then became whether professional sports should be allowed to impose and maintain their own requirements and regulations or whether they were to be subject to the same regulations as all public organizations.

During the last quarter of the twentieth century, Americans came to be increasingly sensitive to the needs of people with physical disabilities of all kinds. This culminated in 1990 with President George Bush's signing of the Americans with Disabilities Act, which banned discrimination against the disabled in housing, employment, and public accommodations. The most tangible results of this law included such things as the installation of ramps and special toilet facilities. Meanwhile, alongside this kind of legal remedy, individuals with physical disabilities had begun on their own to participate in sports of all kinds, so that Americans came to accept marathoners in wheelchairs, blind skiers, and competitors with prosthetic limbs in many sports. None of these disabled individuals, however, attempted to participate in organized professional competitions until 1997, when Casey Martin, a golfer, demanded to be allowed to compete in the Professional Golfers' Association (PGA) Tour.

The Challenger

Casey Martin was born in 1972 with a congenital defect in his right leg known as the Klippel-Trenaunay-Weber Syndrome. He lacked the vein that runs along the bone in the lower right leg, so that blood must return back to the heart by a jumble of veins near the surface of the leg. This condition degenerated as he grew and made it extremely painful for him to walk; for normal walking he wore an especially strong support stocking to keep the swelling down, but his right leg gradually atrophied. Even so, Martin took up golf and by the time he was at Stanford University, he was good enough to become a teammate of Tiger Woods.

Casey Martin, suffering a birth defect in his leg, is the only player on the PGA tour allowed to ride in a cart. (AP/Wide World Photos)

Walking the long distances of a golf course, however, eventually became too painful and by his junior year he took to riding a golf cart—a common practice of amateur golfers but not accepted in professional competitions (although it is allowed on the PGA's Senior Tour). In November 1997, Martin decided to sue the Professional Golfers' Association Tour, the sponsor and organizer of many of the major big-money golf tournaments in the United States. Martin argued that golf courses are "public accommodations" as defined by the 1990 Americans with Disabilities Act and that the PGA Tour, as a commercial enterprise, must obey all its rules. At once the case caught the public's attention, and this was further enhanced when in January 1998, while awaiting trial, Martin won the Nike Tour's season-opening Lakeland Classic, which allowed him to ride in his golf cart.

After winning this, Martin assumed celebrity status, appearing on televison and signing a generous endorsement contract with Nike. Meanwhile, as the trial approached, the PGA Tour was increasingly made to look like a spoilsport. Senator Tom Harkin and former Senator Robert Dole, who had sponsored the disabilities act of 1990, invited Martin to Congress; editorial pages took positions; sports columnists had a field day; and golfers and fans of every level took sides— the most notable being Jack Niklaus and Arnold Palmer, who opposed the use of carts. In general, Americans remained equally divided on the subject.

Walking the Course

The trial opened on February 2, 1998, in a packed courtroom of the U.S. District Court of Eugene, Oregon, Martin's hometown. It began with a video-tape showing Martin's disfigured leg, undoubtedly a powerful appeal for his case. His lawyer then opened by contending that the PGA had never claimed that "walking is fundamental to the game." The PGA's lawyer denied this, insisting that walking the 20 to 25 miles during a major 72-hole tournament involves a physical exertion that is part of the contest. Martin's lawyers were ready for this and called as witness a physiologist who contended that "because of the low level of activity in golf, it is not especially taxing." He estimated that 18 holes of golf would expend some 500 calories, "Nutritionally less than a Big Mac." Meanwhile, a charge by Martin's lawyer that the PGA Tour banned carts mainly because they do not look good on television was dismissed by the PGA lawyer as "a ludicrous comment!"

When the PGA came to open its defense, it employed videotapes of golf greats Jack Niklaus and Arnold Palmer, both of whom insisted that they were not taking any position *against* Martin, but rather *for* the game. "I'm more interested," said Palmer, "in the fact that I've always felt and been taught that golf is a game of stamina." Just as crucial was the testimony of two professional golfers who had themselves played tournaments with physical problems. Ken Venturi had won the U.S. Open in 1974 after walking the last 18 holes while suffering severe heat exhaustion. And Scott Verplank, a diabetic who tired easily, said that he had greatly benefited from riding a cart when it was allowed. The PGA Tour concluded its case by calling in its own commissioner, Tim Finchem, who testified that, "If walking were not an integral part of our competition, we would have found a way toward settlement." As the trial entered its final phase, it was revealed that the PGA Tour's position was being supported by the governing bodies of many of the world's major golf organiza-tions: The United States Golf Association; the Ladies Professional Golf Associa-tion; the PGA of America, which oversees the Ryder Cup; Augusta National, which governs the Masters tournament; the PGA European tour; the PGA of South Africa; and the Australasia Tour.

Given such an imposing opposition, it was all the more remarkable, that the presiding judge, Magistrate Thomas M. Coffin, ruled on the last day, February 10, in favor of Martin. "Mr. Marin is entitled to his modification because he is disabled. It will not alter what's taking place out there in the course." But well aware that his decision was not the last word, Judge Coffin went on to say, "The ultimate disposition of this case will have significant impact, not just at the level of professional golf, but also at all levels of athletic competition."

The Next Rounds

After Martin won his suit, the PGA immediately welcomed him into the tour and he continued to use his cart while playing in various matches, including the 1998 U.S. Open. But the issues were by no means resolved and the debate continued in the media, and in May 1998, the PGA announced that it was going to appeal the decision. In May 1999, oral arguments were held before the U.S. Court of Appeals for the Ninth Circuit, which announced its decision on March 6, 2000, upholding the lower court's ruling. Once more, the PGA, although realizing that many people would regard it as "picking on" this disabled man, weighed the issues, then on May 31 announced it would appeal this new decision to the Supreme Court.

Meanwhile, in November 1998, Martin had failed to qualify for the PGA Tour for the 1999 season—the court's decision had allowed him to ride while competing, but did not relieve him from winning the matches and/or money required to qualify. However, he did continue to play in non-PGA golf matches throughout 1999, and by October 24, 1999, he had won enough money to qualify for the 2000 season.

On September 26, 2000, the PGA passed the next hurdle when the Supreme Court announced that it would hear the case. The oral arguments were presented on January 17, 2001 (only three days after Martin signed a multimillion-dollar endorsement contract with Nike). To the court, there were only two main legal issues: Is a golf course when used for a tournament a "place of public accommodation"? Is making an exception to the walking rule the kind of accommodation required by the federal law? The lawyers inevitably argued on more emotional issues. H. Bartow Farr III, arguing on behalf of the PGA, insisted that the previous judges had failed to recognize that all top-level professional sports, including golf, "are simply tests of excellence, of who can perform the best on a set of physical tasks. Those tasks are defined by the rules of the sport." Martin's lawyer, Roy L. Reardon, countered that "walking is not the game . . . The game is hitting the ball." He pointed out that Martin had earned $143,248 on the PGA Tour in 2000 while never asking, "for any modification of any rule affecting where he hit the ball, how big the hole is, or anything else." To bolster his case, Martin also filed supporting briefs from the Clinton administration and former Senator Robert Dole, himself with a hand and arm disabled in World War II.

There were several light moments during the hearing. At one point, Justice Antonin Scalia said that if some justices knew as little about baseball as they did about golf, "the former would be a much greater sin." When Justice Sandra Day O'Connor—a golfer who had shot a hole in one only the month before—objected, "Wait a minute!" Justice John Paul Stevens chimed in, "In dissent again."

On May 29, 2001, the Supreme Court ruled against the PGA in a 7–2 vote. The Court ruled that the federal anti-discrimination law required that Martin be allowed to ride in a golf cart between shots. In writing for the majority, Justice Stevens wrote that the Americans with Disabilities Act prohibited the PGA from denying Martin equal access to its tours based on his disability. Stevens added that allowing Martin to ride a golf cart during a PGA tournament would not fundamentally alter the rules of the PGA Tour. Stevens rejected the PGA's argument that the walking requirement in tour events was an integral part of PGA tournaments. Stevens cited a federal judge's ruling that Martin endured greater fatigue by riding in a cart because of his medical condition than his able-bodied competitors did by walking the golf course.

—John S. Bowman

Suggestions for Further Reading

Cuneff, Tom. *Walk a Mile in My Shoes: The Casey Martin Story.* Nashville, Tenn: Rutledge Hill Press, 1998.

Francis, Leslie Pickering, and Anita Silvers, eds. *Americans with Disabilities.* New York: Routledge, 2000.

Henriod, Lorraine. *Special Olympics and Paralympics.* New York: Franklin Watts, 1979.

New York Times. January 12, 14, 15, 17, 18, 24, 27, 29, 1998; February 1, 2, 3, 4, 5, 6, 8, 10, 11, 12, 13, 14, 1998; March 31, 1998; May 21, 1998; June 9, 17, 20, 1998; July 3, 1998; November 12, 1998; May 5, 18, 19, 21, 1999; October 25, 1999; December 8, 1999; March 7, 2000; June 1, 2000; September 27, 2000; January 18, 2001.

Pelker, Fred. *ABC-Clio Companion to the Disability Rights Movement.* Santa Barbara Calif.: ABC-Clio, 1997.

Robert Johnson Estate: 1998

Claim: That Claud Johnson was the biological son and sole heir of Robert L. Johnson **Claimant:** Claud L. Johnson **Contestants:** Robert M. Harris, Annye C. Anderson **Claimant's Lawyers:** James W. Kitchens, Nancy A. Olson **Contestants' Lawyers:** Stephen E. Nevas, Karla Kithcart **Judge:** Jon M. Barnwell **Place:** Greenwood, Mississippi **Dates of Hearing:** October 12–15, 1998 **Decision:** In favor of claimant

SIGNIFICANCE

Mississippi probate and paternity laws helped to settle the estate of a major figure in American folklore.

When Robert Johnson was buried in a pauper's grave, it seemed unlikely that the itinerant musician would be remembered by anyone but the working people he had entertained at country dances and juke joints. In fact, Johnson's music and mysterious life became one of the enduring legends of American musical history, but not until decades after his death. The question of who should profit from his genius took even longer to answer.

Johnson was not well known outside of the Mississippi delta during his lifetime. His astonishing musical talent, coupled with the low opinion of blues musicians held by church going members of the African American community, stoked rumors that Johnson had sold his soul to the devil in order to play and sing so well. After he was poisoned by a jealous husband at a dance near Greenwood, Mississippi, and died horribly a few days later on August 16, 1938, it was whispered that Satan had claimed Johnson's soul. The 27-year old musician's entire known legacy consisted of 29 recorded songs. As country blues faded with the advent of other musical styles, so did interest in Robert Johnson.

In the 1960s, a resurgent interest in rural American music made the blues popular again. Johnson's mastery of the guitar and the imagery of his lyrics distinguished him from his contemporaries, creating plenty of curiosity about his mysterious life. The rediscovery also began generating a lot of money, not only from sales of Johnson's small but influential body of recordings, but also from enormous publishing and performance royalties generated whenever musicians like Eric Clapton and the Rolling Stones recorded new versions of his songs.

It was assumed that Johnson had died without leaving any heirs. In the 1970s, however, blues researcher Stephen LaVere located Johnson's half-sister, Carrie Thompson, who was living in Maryland, unaware of her long-dead brother's influence on popular music. By contrast, LaVere was aware of the profits inherent in a claim to Johnson's as yet unprobated estate, as well as the publishing rights to two photographs of the musician, whose likeness had never

been seen by modern admirers. On November 20, 1974, Thompson assigned all of her rights to Robert Johnson's works, the photographs, and any other materials concerning Johnson she possessed over to LaVere. In return, LaVere agreed to pay Thompson 50 percent of all royalties collected by him as a result of his efforts to capitalize on Johnson's musical and artistic legacy. Thompson's claim to be Johnson's only surviving heir was legally assumed to be true. If any other descendants should come forward, sharing profits with them would be her responsibility, not LaVere's.

In 1981, as Thompson's health failed, she granted power of attorney over her affairs to Annye Anderson, a half-sister by her father Charles Dodds' second marriage. In 1982, Anderson's lawyer advised her to choose an attorney in Mississippi, the place of Johnson's death, so that his estate could be officially probated. Thompson died in 1983, leaving Anderson and Thompson's

Claude Johnson (left), claimant to be the biological son and sole heir of legendary bluesman Robert Johnson. (AP/Wide World Photos)

grandson, Robert Harris, as the only known heirs to Johnson's legacy and revenue from the LaVere agreement. When a formal petition to open the estate of Robert L. Johnson in the chancery court of Leflore County, Mississippi, was finally filed on June 1, 1989, Anderson was appointed administratrix.

An Unknown Heir

Anderson's control of the Johnson estate seemed secure. On February 19, 1992, however, a retired gravel truck driver from Crystal Springs, Mississippi, filed a petition in which he claimed to be the son and sole heir of the dead guitarist. Claud Johnson swore that his mother had told him throughout his childhood that Robert Johnson was his father.

Claud Johnson's initial claim was dismissed after Anderson's attorneys argued that Johnson had missed a statutory deadline for presenting himself as an heir. Under a Mississippi law designed to equitably settle all existing pre-1981 claims by "illegitimate" children seeking inheritances from intestate fathers, such claims were required to be filed and adjudicated within three years of July 1, 1981. Claud Johnson's claim was filed years after the 1984 deadline.

When Johnson appealed, the court focused on his contention that Anderson had not performed her administrative duties properly. Appellate judges agreed that Anderson's failure to properly open the Johnson estate in 1982 and seek out possible heirs had benefited her, to the detriment of Claud Johnson. On March 26, 1996, the court reversed the earlier ruling. Waiving the 1984 deadline in the interest of fairness, the court allowed Claud to prosecute his claim to be Robert L. Johnson's son and heir.

The paternity issue came before the Leflore County Court on October 12, 1998. Claud Johnson's birth certificate, which identified his father as "R. L. Johnson, laborer," was introduced to establish that Claud was born on December 16, 1931. His mother, Virgie Jane Cain (formerly Smith), testified in a videotaped deposition that she had been intimate with Robert Johnson—and Johnson alone—in March 1931, nine months before Claud was born. The tryst, Cain said, took place in a wooded area by a Copiah County road.

Elderly witnesses agreed that there had been a relationship between Virgie Smith and Robert Johnson. Eighty-year-old Eula Mae Williams startled the court when she testified that she had watched Virgie and Robert making love in the woods in March of 1931. Williams unapologetically testified that she too had been in the woods with a man, with whom she witnessed what must have been Claud Johnson's conception.

On October 15, 1998, Judge Jon Barnwell declared that Claud was the son of Robert Johnson. The judgment entitled Claud to an inheritance of over $1.3 million. Lawyers for Anderson and Harris contested the ruling, questioning the identity of the "R. L. Johnson" listed on Claud's birth certificate and arguing that a note on Robert Johnson's death certificate suggested that he suffered from syphilis and was therefore sterile. Despite uncertainty about where the musician was actually buried, attorneys also wanted DNA proof of kinship between Claud and Robert Johnson.

On June 15, 2000, the Mississippi Supreme Court upheld the Leflore County decision, ruling that Claud Johnson was in all likelihood the son of the blues master. The court dismissed the scribble on the back of the death certificate as unreliable. Robert Johnson's 1931 marriage to a woman who died giving birth to a stillborn child further suggested to the court that he had not been sterile. In rebuffing the demand for DNA evidence, the court borrowed an image from Johnson's "Me and the Devil Blues."

Such proof "would be nigh impossible to obtain since Johnson's grave site is unknown," wrote Justice Mike Mills. "As far as we know, Johnson is buried down by the highway side, so 'his old evil spirit can get a Greyhound bus and ride.'"

— *Tom Smith*

Suggestions for Further Reading

Bragg, Rick. "Court Rules Father of the Blues Has a Son." *New York Times* (June 17, 2000): A1.

"Court Says Son Is Sole Heir of Robert Johnson." *Billboard* (July 1, 2000): 6.

Guralnick, Peter. *Searching for Robert Johnson*. New York: E.P. Dutton, 1989.

The Microsoft Trial: 1998–2001

Defendant: Microsoft Corporation   **Offenses Charged:** Violations of the Sherman Antitrust Acts. Two counts under Section 1: exclusive dealing and unlawful tying; two counts under Section 2: monopoly maintenance in the operating systems market, and attempted monopolization of the Internet browser market   **Chief Defense Lawyers:** Bill Neukom, John Warden   **Chief Prosecutors:** David Boies and lawyers of the U.S. Department of Justice   **Judge:** Thomas Penfield Jackson   **Place:** Washington, D.C.   **Dates of Trial:** October 1998–July 2001   **Verdict:** Guilty of violating antitrust laws   **Penalty:** Microsoft to be broken into two companies, and conduct restrictions imposed, pending outcome of appeals

SIGNIFICANCE

The United States government's prosecution of America's largest and most successful computer software company for violations of the antitrust laws was the most important and controversial use of these laws by the Department of Justice in the latter part of the twentieth century.

The origins and growth of the Microsoft Corporation had become the stuff of legend in America by the end of the twentieth century. Founded in 1975 by Bill Gates and his friend Paul Allen when the former left Harvard University as a sophomore, it rapidly outpaced all its competitors in the computer software business. By 1988 it was the world's largest software company; by 1998 its Windows operating system was to be found in 90 percent of the personal computers in America, and 50 percent of all homes possessed one. That same year, Microsoft's profits of nearly $4.5 billion were double those of General Motors, the world's largest corporation.

In May 1998 the U.S. Department of Justice charged Microsoft with four counts of violating the Sherman Act: two under Section 1, exclusive dealing and unlawful "tying"; and two under section 2, monopoly maintenance in the operating systems market, and attempted monopolization of the Internet browser market. Congress passed the Sherman Act in 1890 as a result of an upsurge of public opinion against the arrogance and power of corporate "trusts." The domain of the law was expanded by the Clayton Antitrust Act of 1914, and in that year Congress created the Federal Trade Commission (FTC) and empowered it to conduct ongoing policing of unfair trade practices. The use of the acts against Microsoft has been likened to their use to achieve the breakup of the monopoly held by the Standard Oil Company in the first decade of the twentieth century and the voluntary breakup of the telephone monopoly in the 1980s. Antitrust law, however, has become complex and controversial since its application. By its very nature, it involves the making of fine distinctions between the legitimate consequences of an aggressively competitive spirit, so highly valued in an entrepreneurial market economy, and practices which subvert or eliminate the environment of free competition which is essential to the capitalist system.

FTC Begins Investigation of Microsoft in 1990

The 1998 decision to prosecute Microsoft is perhaps best seen as a major escalation of the U.S. government's regulatory engagement with the company which had begun in 1990 when the FTC launched an investigation, into the company's business practices. As a result of that investigation, the Justice Department and Microsoft signed a consent decree in July 1994 by which the government agreed to drop its antitrust action; and Microsoft agreed to cease certain specific practices related primarily to the type of licensing agreements and royalty payment contracts that it had entered into with computer manufacturers. Microsoft, however, denied all charges of illegally exercising monopoly powers, and Bill Gates was successful in insisting that the agreement, which has been criticized as having been vaguely worded, contained a clause that allowed the company to develop "integrated products," a condition which was to become a crucial element in Microsoft's vigorous rejection of the 1998 charges. In February 1995 Federal District Court judge Stanley Sporkin ruled the consent decree to be an "ineffective remedy" to constrain Microsoft, but he was overruled within months by the U.S. Court of Appeals, which reinstated the consent decree and replaced Judge Sporkin with Judge Thomas Penfield Jackson as the judge administering it.

Bill Gates, founder of Microsoft. (Microsoft Corporation)

Department of Justice Decides to Prosecute

In October 1997 the Justice Department filed a motion charging Microsoft with violating the consent decree by "tying" Internet Explorer, its own Internet browser software, into its popular operating system, Windows 95, thus forcing computer makers to choose its browser. Microsoft's response was that this was an "integrated product" permitted by the consent decree. Judge Jackson issued a preliminary injunction ordering Microsoft to separate Internet Explorer from Windows. At about the same time the Justice Department retained David Boies to lead a prosecution against Microsoft. Boies had an outstanding reputation as a lawyer and successful litigator; particularly relevant to this case was his experience in successfully representing IBM against government antitrust action in the 1970s and 1980s. In the early months of 1998, the Department of Justice engaged in protracted negotiations with Microsoft in an attempt to arrive at an out-of-court settlement, but Microsoft was intransigent, and when the talks collapsed, the Justice Department and 20 states filed suit under the Sherman Act on May 18. An additional factor in the decision to take the antitrust action was a brief filed by antitrust lawyers, who, working with representatives of leading companies in the various arms of the computer industry, had presented the Justice Department with a 200-page document outlining the damaging effects of Microsoft's anti-competitive practices.

Microsoft Raked at Trial

Working to an unexpected and accelerated schedule decreed by Judge Jackson, which also limited each side to twelve witnesses, the trial opened a year earlier than had been anticipated on October 19, 1998, in the same federal courtroom in which Judge John Sirica had presided over the Watergate trials twenty years earlier. David Boies opened the presentation of the government's case, making extensive use of a lengthy videotaped deposition given by Bill Gates. Boies would return frequently to segments of this tape as he examined his witnesses. As Boies presented it, the testimony not only showed Gates making statements which he apparently knew were false, particularly about his lack of knowledge of the activities of other companies, but also revealed a pattern of prevarication and obfuscation that Boise claimed displayed an arrogant contempt for the requirements of federal law. Boies suggested that this disregard for the law permeated the corporate culture of Microsoft and that this atmosphere was created by the attitude and behavior of the company's founder, Bill Gates. The government's witnesses testified for the next two months. They included senior executives of other businesses in the computer industry, many of them celebrated pioneers in the new technology: Jim Barksdale of Netscape, Avie Tevanian of Apple Computers, and Steve McGeady of Intel.

Microsoft's defense began in January 1999. It's first witness was an economist, Professor Richard Schmalensee of the Massachusetts Institute of Technology, whose task was to support Microsoft's position that it did not hold a monopoly. Court observers felt that Boies effectively showed Schmalensee to have held contradictory opinions in recent publications and statements regarding competition in the computer industry, which weakened his testimony. Most of the other witnesses were Microsoft executives and employees who testified to the more arcane aspects of software technology, particularly as it related to Microsoft's claim that Internet Explorer was an integral part of Windows. Boies displayed great skill as a cross-examiner, in at least one instance reducing the Microsoft witness to pleading with the judge to be allowed to re-prepare his demonstration.

Towards the end of February, as Microsoft neared the end of its presentation Judge Jackson's remarks from the bench indicated that he felt that Microsoft's defense had collapsed. At the end of March, while the trial was in recess in preparation for rebuttals, Judge Jackson announced that he would divide his conclusion of the case into two parts: the first, "findings of fact"; the second, "conclusions of law." This was seen as a way of exerting pressure on Microsoft to arrive at a settlement, but although negotiations went on throughout the rebuttal stage, no agreement was arrived at, and the findings of fact were published on November 5, 1999. In a document of more than 200 pages, Judge Jackson declared Microsoft to be a monopolist which had "harmed consumers in ways that are immediate and easily discernible" and had been shown to be willing to "use its prodigious market power and immense profits to harm any firm that insists on pursuing initiatives that could intensify competition against one of Microsoft's core products"; its success in hurting such companies had deterred investment in technologies and businesses which exhibited any potential of threatening Microsoft.

Mediation Fails; Microsoft Is Ordered Broken Up

Judge Jackson then took another unexpected step: he announced that he was initiating a formal mediation process and that he had recruited Judge Richard Posner to act as the mediator. A former law professor at the University of Chicago, Posner had joined the Seventh Circuit Court of Appeals in 1981. A prolific author, he had a formidable reputation as a scholar of antitrust law. Although there would be 18 drafts of an agreement between the parties over the next several months, Microsoft refused to accept the government's terms, and the mediation collapsed in April 2000. Judge Jackson then delivered his findings of law, ruling against Microsoft on three of the four charges, the only favorable finding being on the "exclusive dealing" charge under Section 1. On May 24 Judge Jackson affirmed the government's proposal for the breakup of Microsoft into two companies, one restricted to operating systems, and the other to applications software. There was also an extensive list of conduct constraints. The federal Court of Appeals immediately announced that it would hear the anticipated appeal *en banc*—that is, with all justices sitting (three recused themselves). Judge Jackson then took the unusual step of invoking the 1974 Antitrust Expediting Act to request the U.S. Supreme Court to take up review of the case directly. However, in September 2000, the Supreme Court rejected this request, sending the case back to the Court of Appeals.

On June 28, 2001, the U.S. Court of Appeals for the District of Columbia vacated Judge Jackson's order to break-up Microsoft. The Court of Appeals upheld several findings of fact, including that the company violated federal antitrust laws. But the unanimous decision cited Judge Jackson's conduct as the reason for vacating his decision that Microsoft should be broken into two smaller companies. The court said that Jackson's secret interviews with members of the media and several offensive comments about Microsoft in public statements outside of the courtroom gave the appearance of partiality on Jackson's part. The Court of Appeals remanded the case back to a lower court for reassignment to a different judge.

—David I. Petts

Suggestions for Further Reading

Auletta, Ken. *World War 3.0: Microsoft and Its Enemies*. New York: Random House, 2001.

Heilemann, John. *Pride before the Fall: The Trials of Bill Gates and the End of the Microsoft Era*. New York: Harper Collins, 2001.

Charles Chitat Ng Trial: 1998–99

Defendant: Charles Chitat Ng   **Crimes Charged:** Murder, kidnapping, unlawful restraint   **Chief Defense Lawyers:** Allyn Jaffrey, Carl C. Holmes, William Kelley   **Chief Prosecutor:** Sharlene Honnaka   **Judges:** Robert R. Fitzgerald, John J. Ryan   **Place:** Santa Ana, California
Date of Trial: October 26, 1998–February 24, 1999   **Verdict:** Guilty
Sentence: Death

SIGNIFICANCE
At stake was whether a truly monstrous criminal, who would almost certainly get the death penalty if convicted, could escape extradition by fleeing to Canada, which has no death penalty. This case established that he couldn't.

A customer in a South San Francisco hardware store on June 2, 1985, saw an Oriental-looking man stuff a $75 bench vise under his jacket and walk out. He told a clerk, who called the police and followed the man out. The shoplifter put the vise in the trunk of a car and, after glancing back, quickly walked away. The police arrived minutes later. In the car the clerk pointed out, they found a burly man who looked like an aging "hippy." The man said he didn't want any trouble and offered to pay for the vise. He said a friend of his, who was Chinese and didn't know any better, had stolen the vise.

But when the officers looked in the trunk, they found, besides the vise, a loaded pistol with a silencer. The car's license plate had been issued for a Buick owned by a Lonnie Bond. This car was a Honda. The driver showed them a driver's license issued to a Robin Stapley. The Honda's vehicle identification number was for a car owned by a Paul Cosner, a San Francisco auto dealer reported missing almost nine months before. The police took the driver to headquarters.

Further checks showed that Bond and Stapley were also missing. The driver admitted that his real name was Leonard Lake. His companion was named Charles Ng. Lake said he was thirsty and asked for a glass of water, a pen, and a piece of paper. He drank the water and on the paper wrote a note to his ex-wife, Claralyn Balasz: "I love you. Please forgive me. Please tell Mama, Fern and Patty I'm sorry." (Fern and Patty turned out to be Lake's sisters.) Then he passed out. He had taken two cyanide capsules with the water.

The police rushed Lake to a hospital, where he was put on life support. Meanwhile, they searched the car thoroughly. They found blood stains and bullet holes in the car, as well as a utility bill addressed to Claralyn Balasz in Wilseyville, California, a hamlet in the foothills of the Sierra Nevada range.

The Wilseyville Horror

Police checked the Wilseyville address and found a cabin Balasz's parents had purchased as a retirement home. Balasz did not live there. In the cabin they found Lake's belongings, including a 250-page diary. In it, Lake detailed his plans for surviving a nuclear holocaust: he'd build bunkers and stock them with food and weapons. He'd also capture young, nubile females to be his slaves. With them he'd repopulate the world. The cops also found evidence in the diary that he'd been doing his best to depopulate the world. They found human remains in shallow graves around the property. A few were complete. The first remains identified were those of a homeless man police believe had helped Lake and Ng build a cinderblock shack next to the cabin. Most were fragmentary: charred bits of bone no more than three inches long. Lake and Ng had chopped up bodies and burned them in an incinerator. The police dug up 45 pounds of bone fragments.

Charles Ng, jailed in Canada, unsuccessfully fought extradition to the United States to face trial for murder charges. (AP/ Wide World Photos)

They also dug up a videotape showing two shackled young women being stripped and threatened by Lake and Ng. One was begging for her baby. Two of the bodies found were later identified as theirs. Behind a bookcase in the cinder block shack, police found a secret door to a torture chamber. In addition to handcuffs, leg irons, a whip, and other torture devices, the torture chamber contained a score of photos of naked young women.

Checking lists of missing persons, police found that at least 25 of them had known Lake or Ng. But it seemed later that many of the pair's victims were homeless people who had never been reported missing.

"Every time this guy [Lake] met somebody," said Calaveras County deputy Jim Stenquist, "they wound up gone." Ng was gone, too. So was Lake. Lake survived four days, alive, but brain dead. Then the hospital pulled the plug. Lake and Ng were the only two people who could explain the Wilseyville Horror.

"If Mr. Ng isn't caught," said Calaveras County coroner Terry Parker, "this is going to be impossible to solve."

Charles Ng Captured in Canada

Ng was caught. He was shoplifting again, this time in Calgary, Canada. A security guard grabbed him. Ng shot the guard in the hand, but another guard wrestled him down. He was convicted of robbery and assault and sentenced to 4 and one-half years in prison. Canadian authorities ruled that he'd have to finish his sentence in Canada before he could be extradited. Meanwhile, California authorities filed charges of murder and kidnapping against Ng. Digging at the cabin continued, with 11 more-or-less intact remains found in addition to the pile of bone fragments.

Ng spent his prison time studying Canadian and U.S. law. Son of a wealthy Hong Kong businessman, he had been expelled from several schools, including a private boarding school in England. He came to the United States but joined the Marines after a hit-and-run accident. He stole a number of guns from the Marine Corps, deserted, was caught but escaped from the marine brig. He met Lake, a former marine, through a survivalist magazine and moved in with him and Balasz.

Extradition Problems

The United States and Canada had an extradition treaty. Under it, neither country was obliged to extradite someone who might face the death penalty. At the time it was signed, Canada had the death penalty, but U.S Supreme Court decisions had made the death penalty almost impossible to apply in the United States. Since then, Canada had abolished the death penalty and the U.S. Supreme Court had relaxed its restrictions on executions. California again had the death penalty. If American authorities had guaranteed that Ng would not be executed, he could have been swiftly extradited. But with what was known of Ng's crimes, no California official would dare to give such a guarantee.

On October 26, 1989, Justice Minister Douglas C. Lewis of Canada said Ng would be extradited. Ng's Canadian lawyer, Donald MacLeod, said he'd fight extradition. The Ng extradition became a major civil rights case in Canada. Opponents maintained that the law forbade extraditing a person who could be executed as a result. The government said it had a choice, and with someone accused of Ng's crimes, the choice was not difficult. The fight went on up to Canada's Supreme Court. On September 26, 1991, the Court voted 4 to 3 to send Ng back. Within minutes, he was on a plane to California.

That was hardly the end of the story. Ng filed motion after motion from his cell. One was for a million dollar suit against his current defense attorneys. Another was to dispense with counsel and defend himself—a motion he withdrew within a week. He tried to sue the state over conditions of his imprisonment. The Ng case went to the California Supreme Court five times and involved a dozen judges.

Change of Venue

On April 8, 1994, Ng got a change of venue from Calaveras County, in Northern California's "Mother Lode" country, to Orange County, between Los Angeles and San Diego. A poll had shown that 98 percent of the population of Calaveras County was familiar with the case, and most of them thought Ng was guilty.

But soon after the change of venue, affluent Orange County went bankrupt as a result of financial mismanagement. Ng's lawyer, Allyn Jaffrey, a public defender, told Judge Robert Fitzgerald, "This is a case that will cost the public millions upon millions of dollars" that were not available. The case could not be tried in Orange County, she said. By this time, the murders were 10 years old. California attorney general Dan Lundgren demanded that the county try Ng. But there was no money. Eventually, the state agreed to pay all expenses. William Kelley, the public defender who was to try the case, said that with the volume of records involved, it would take the defense at least 2 and one-half years to prepare its case. There were 350 boxes of documents, containing 100,000 pages and weighing six tons.

When the trial began on October 26, 1998, Ng pleaded not guilty. He contended he was only helping Lake, and didn't know anything about the murders. Lake was the leader in everything, he said. A psychiatrist, Dr. Stuart Grassian, testified that Ng was "a classic dependent personality." But jurors also heard from Richard Carrazza, who was shot and saw his roommate murdered by Ng in a robbery that did not involve Lake. Shown the videotapes by Prosecutor Sharlene Honnaka, Ng contended the threats he made to the victims on tape were only bluffs.

On February 24, 1999, the jury deadlocked on one of the 12 murders Ng was charged with, but found him guilty of the other 11. They also found that the circumstances warranted the death penalty. On June 30, Ng was sentenced to death for the murder of six men, three women and two babies. By that time, the case had cost $6.6 million, making it the most expensive homicide prosecution—even including the O.J. Simpson case—in California history.

—William Weir

Suggestions for Further Reading

Harrington, Joseph, and Robert Burger. *Justice Denied: The Ng Case, the Most Infamous and Expensive Murder Case in History.* New York: Perseus Publishing, 1999.

Owens, Greg. *The Shocking True Story of Charles Ng.* New York: Red Deer Press, 2001.

Thomas Capano Trial: 1998–99

Defendant: Thomas Capano **Crime Charged:** Murder
Chief Defense Lawyers: Joseph S. Oteri, Eugene Maurer and Charles M. Oberly III **Chief Prosecutors:** Colm Connolly and Ferris W. Wharton
Judge: William Swain Lee **Place:** Wilmington, Delaware
Dates of Trial: October 26, 1998–January 18, 1999 **Verdict:** Guilty
Sentence: Death

SIGNIFICANCE

The notorious murder trial of one of the state's most prominent attorneys stunned Delaware's legal and political establishment.

On June 27, 1996, Anne Marie Fahey, a 30-year-old scheduling secretary working for Delaware Governor Tom Carper, vanished. On the night of her baffling disappearance, Fahey had been seen in a restaurant with noted Wilmington lawyer and political wheeler-dealer, Thomas Capano. Capano, 47 years old, married with four children, had been dating Fahey since 1993. She was just one of his many ongoing affairs. Capano was charged with Fahey's murder despite the fact that her body was not found.

The Trial

At Capano's trial, which began October 26, 1998, prosecutor Ferris Wharton in his opening address described Capano as becoming incensed because Fahey had ditched him for another man. "Tom Capano had determined that if Anne Marie Fahey could not be manipulated into being with him, she would be with no one else forever."

Responding for the defense, Joseph Oteri brought gasps to the packed courtroom as he presented that Capano now admitted being present when Fahey had died at his home—despite his previous denials of complicity in Fahey's disappearance—but that he had not killed her. "Anne Marie Fahey died as the result of an outrageous, horrible, tragic accident," said Oteri, adding that one other person was present at Capano's home that night and knew the whole story.

During the course of the trial it became apparent that the prosecution had built a strong forensic and circumstantial case against Capano. A search of his home had revealed the presence of two tiny bloodstains, which matched a donor sample given by Fahey in April 1996. Alan Giusti, a DNA analyst at the FBI laboratory, said Fahey "could be the donor" of the blood found in the two bloodstains, with only a 1 in 11,000 chance that they had come from another white American.

Additionally, Gerard Capano, the defendant's brother, testified that he and Capano had dumped Fahey's body, stuffed in a cooler, 60 miles off the New Jersey coast. Astonishingly, this same cooler—empty but full of bullet holes—was later recovered by a fisherman. A credit card receipt showed that Capano had bought an identical cooler on April 20, 1996.

The testimony of Deborah MacIntyre, a 48-year-old school administrator and Capano's longtime mistress, would prove to be pivotal. She admitted buying Capano a .22 caliber Beretta pistol on May 13, 1996, but had not seen it since. This, combined with the purchase of the cooler, was evidence, the prosecution claimed, that Capano had been planning Fahey's murder for some time.

Attorney Eugene J. Maurer's cross-examination of MacIntyre revealed the strategy behind the defense's case. Hadn't she been at Capano's house when Fahey was killed?

"No," said MacIntyre.

"You deny you discharged that firearm?"

"I don't know what happened to that firearm," MacIntyre responded indignantly.

Maurer pushed hard and extracted an admission from MacIntyre that she was testifying for the prosecution under a promise of immunity from her earlier perjury to the grand jury. "You're scot-free," he said, implying that Fahey's real killer was going to go unpunished.

Thomas Capano escorted from the courthouse during his trial for the murder of Anne Marie Fahey. (AP/Wide World Photos)

"I'm fortunate," MacIntyre replied.

Accident or Murder?

Two and a half years after Fahey's disappearance, Thomas Capano took the stand—against the advice of his lawyers. The former state prosecutor wove an incredible tale. He and Fahey had been watching TV at his house on the night of June 27, 1996, when MacIntyre called and asked to come over. Explaining that he had company, Capano hung up.

"The next thing I know, Debbie MacIntyre [had come over and] is in the room. . . . She was pretty ballistic." Babbling threats of suicide, according to

Capano's story, MacIntyre suddenly grabbed a gun from her bag. "Debbie was off the wall. I thought, 'Oh my god, she's going to shoot herself.'" As he grabbed MacIntyre's arm, the gun discharged, hitting Fahey, who had stood up to leave. "She [Fahey] was motionless on the sofa. I said, 'No, this can't be possible.'"

Capano went on. "That's when . . . I basically made the wrong decision, a cowardly decision, to get rid of the body." To protect MacIntyre, he said, he put Fahey's body in a cooler, which MacIntyre helped him move into his garage the next day.

He then recruited his brother Gerard and borrowed his boat to dump the body. When Capano and his brother threw the cooler containing Fahey into the Atlantic, they thought it would sink immediately. It didn't. "That's when Gerry shot it," Capano said. "Even after Gerry shot it, it still would not sink."

During cross-examination by prosecutor Colm Connolly, Capano was barraged with questions trying to unravel the tale he had woven together. Connolly accused him of manipulating family members in order to back up his story. "Let's talk about your daughters."

"Don't ask me questions about my children!" Capano yelled. He then flew into a rage, calling Connolly a "heartless, gutless, soulless disgrace of a human being."

This outburst by the defendant was too much for Judge Lee, who told guards, "Please take Mr. Capano out of the courtroom."

"He's a liar!" Capano screamed at Connolly as he was hauled away.

Connolly's closing speech to the jury was a scornful diatribe on Capano's outlandish description of how Fahey had died. "Ladies and gentlemen, this story is ludicrous. It defies common sense. . . . The defendant thought he would get away with murder. If anybody was going to be given the benefit of the doubt, it was the defendant with his political connections."

On January 18, 1999, the jury decided against the defendant and convicted Capano of murder. Ten days later, they handed down his sentence: death by lethal injection. On March 16, Judge Lee upheld this sentence, stating, "The defendant fully expected to get away with it, and if not for his arrogant and controlling nature, he may have succeeded. . . . He is a ruthless murderer."

As a lawyer Capano should have appreciated the value of silence, but his decision to testify, against the advice of counsel, was ruinous. Hubris got the better of him, and his punishment was of the severest kind.

—Colin Evans

Suggestions for Further Reading

Los Angeles Times: October 27, 1998, A18; December 17, 1998, A32; December 22, 1998, A38; January 18, 1999, A12.

Rule, Ann. *And Never Let Her Go.* New York: Simon & Schuster, 1999.

www.CourtTV. com.

Justin A. Volpe et al. Trials: 1999 & 2000

Defendants: Michael Bellomo, Thomas Bruder, Charles Schwarz, Justin A. Volpe, and Thomas Wiese   **Crimes Charged:** First trial: Bellomo: False statements; Bruder, Schwarz, Volpe, and Wiese: Violation of civil rights (i.e., aggravated harassment based on race, color, religion or national origin); second trial: Bruder, Schwarz, and Wiese: Conspiracy to obstruct justice   **Chief Defense Lawyers:** Bellomo: John Patten; Bruder: Stuart London; Schwarz: Stephen C. Worth and Ronald P. Fischetti; Volpe: Marvyn M. Kornberg; Wiese: Joseph Tacopina   **Chief Prosecutors:** Alan Vinegard, Lauren Resnick, and Kenneth P. Thompson   **Judge:** Eugene H. Nickerson   **Place:** Brooklyn, New York   **Dates of Trials:** First trial: May 6–June 9, 1999; second trial: February 7–March 6, 2000   **Verdicts:** First trial: Bellomo: Not guilty of cover-up; Bruder and Wiese: Not guilty of assault; Schwarz: Guilty; Volpe: Pleaded guilty during trial; second trial: Bruder, Schwarz, and Wiese: Guilty   **Sentences:** First trial: Volpe: 30 years imprisonment, $277,495 restitution; Schwarz: 15 years, 8 months imprisonment; Bruder and Wiese: 5 years imprisonment

SIGNIFICANCE

In these trials, four New York City police officers testified against a fellow officer, revealing a rare crack in the supposed "blue wall of silence" among law enforcement officials. Some legal experts still believe most policemen and women are reluctant to turn against fellow officers accused of brutality or corruption. This case gained national and international prominence, drawing attention to a problem that many consider commonplace in America: police violence against minority citizens.

On Tuesday morning, August 12, 1997, a voice on the answering machine of New York *Daily News* reporter Mike McAlary said,

You don't know me, but I am calling because in the Seven-O Precinct in Brooklyn, on August the ninth at 0400 hours, they, the cops there, sodomized a prisoner. They took a nightstick and shoved it up his behind and into his bladder. The patient is at Coney Island Hospital. His last name is L-O-U-I-M-A. Now they are trying to cover this up, because it was two white officers. And they did this to a black guy who they locked up for disorderly conduct. And now they are charging him with assault in the second. All this information can be verified if you call Coney Island Hospital or the Seven-O Precinct. I will not call you again.

Like any veteran police reporter, McAlary knew enough to take an anonymous call with a huge grain of salt, but a quick check of addresses confirmed the identity of the Louimas, a family of Haitian immigrants. A call to the hospital revealed that a prisoner-patient named Abner Louima was in critical but stable condition.

"... on tomorrow's front page. ..."

McAlary found the Louima family and their lawyer, Brian Figeroux, at the hospital. Using his reporter's savvy to get to Louima's bedside despite a posted police guard, McAlary took notes for an hour as he interviewed the prisoner, who was handcuffed to his bed. He learned that Louima, a bank security guard, had been arrested early Saturday morning after a fight broke out between two women at a Brooklyn nightclub. He also learned that when Louima was brought in a hospital nurse had called the New York Police Department (NYPD) Internal Affairs Bureau (IAB)—the unit in charge of police discipline—to report the serious injuries, but Internal Affairs had not followed up. Later evidence revealed that the first complaint logged officially by the IAB wasn't until 36 hours after the nurse's call. Nor was the complaint submitted to the district attorney's office, as the law required.

McAlary told the Louima's lawyer to call the Brooklyn district attorney. "Tell him," he said, "I'm going to put this on tomorrow's front page."

Within five hours, NYPD Internal Affairs officers and assistant district attorneys were at the hospital. The next day, New York Mayor Rudolph Giuliani and Police Commissioner Howard Safir both went to Louima's bedside and denounced the attack during press conferences as television news crews besieged the hospital. Doctors detailed Louima's injuries: a wooden stick shoved into his rectum had ripped into his bladder and punctured his colon and had then been jammed into his mouth, breaking his front teeth. The police, after holding him for three hours, had called an ambulance and sent him to the hospital only after other inmates complained of his bleeding. Emergency surgery had repaired both the bladder and his lower intestine.

Cops Reassigned, Suspended, Arrested

Within a week, the 70th Precinct's commanding and executive officers were reassigned. Fourteen cops were transferred, put on desk duty, suspended, or arrested. Of the 14, Justin A. Volpe, 25, and Charles Schwarz, 31, were arrested and indicted under New York State law, charged with aggravated sexual abuse and first-degree sexual assault. Thomas Bruder, 31, and Thomas Wiese, 33, were charged with beating the victim.

Volpe was the son of a former New York police detective and had won decorations for his police work. He had also been accused once before of using excessive force while on duty, but the accusation had never been proven. Volpe maintained his innocence regarding the assault on Abner Louima. Schwarz was accused of holding down the victim while Volpe raped him with the stick.

Police Torture

Michael Bellomo   Thomas Bruder   Charles Schwarz   Thomas Wiese   Justin Volpe

New York police officers' trials revealed crack in the "blue wall of silence." (AP/Wide World Photos)

During the 1990s, Mayor Giuliani had often heralded the rebirth of his city, citing its renewed vibrancy and civility. One reason for that improvement had been a drop in crime following the mayor's "get-tough" attitude with lawbreakers. But not all New Yorkers welcomed the new visibility and authority given to the city's police force. Some African Americans and other minority groups believed they were often unfairly targeted for police harassment and brutality. After the Louima case hit the media, anger over the perceived mistreatment of black New Yorkers erupted in full force. African-American leaders, including the Reverend Al Sharpton, attacked the NYPD for racism, and organized protest marches. At one point, thousands marched to the 70th Precinct carrying toilet plungers—the alleged weapon Volpe used during the assault.

On August 18, 1997, the U.S. Justice Department began a civil investigation of the NYPD, and in February 1998 federal prosecutors took over. (The original state charges filed against Volpe and the others were subsequently dropped.) They produced a grand jury indictment of all four officers on charges of violation of civil rights in assaulting Louima in the patrol car as they took him to headquarters. Volpe and Schwarz were also accused of kicking Louima and shoving a stick into his rectum and mouth while his hands were cuffed behind his back, with Schwarz specifically accused of holding Louima down in the bathroom while Volpe used the stick. Bruder and Wiese were also charged with criminal possession of a weapon—a portable radio with which they were alleged to have beaten Louima so severely that the patrol car's backseat became stained with blood. Sergeant Michael Bellomo, 37, was indicted on a charge of attempting to cover up the incident.

By November 1998, a new federal indictment had charged Bruder, Schwarz, and Wiese with conspiring to obstruct justice by lying to investigators from the NYPD Internal Affairs Bureau and the Brooklyn D.A.'s office in a plot to cover up the incident. A court document quoted Bruder and Wiese as singling out Volpe as the instigator.

A Breach in the "Blue Wall"

The trial opened on May 6, 1999. In his opening statement, Volpe's lawyer, Marvyn Kornberg, started an aggressive defense, accusing Louima of lying and suggesting the victim's injuries had come from consensual homosexual sex that had taken place at the nightclub. However, testimony soon revealed that the famed "blue wall of silence," with which police officers traditionally surrounded and protected their fellow cops who were in trouble, had been breached by the severe brutality alleged and now evidenced in the courtroom.

Detective Eric Turetzky, who was on duty when Louima was brought in, testified that he saw officer Schwarz lead the Haitian, whose hands were cuffed and whose trousers and underpants were around his knees, down the hallway toward the men's room where the assault with the stick occurred. City officials hailed Turetzky as a hero for breaking the code of silence. The detective said, "I knew I had information. I couldn't sleep. I couldn't eat. I made a decision to come forward."

Officer Mark Schofield said Schwarz led Louima toward the hallway and Volpe had borrowed a pair of gloves, taken them into the bathroom with the prisoner, and that they were bloody when he came out. Sergeant Kenneth Wernick testified that Volpe had boasted that "I took a man down tonight," and had walked around the station house displaying a broken broomstick covered with blood and excrement.

Then, on May 25, after denying the charges and pleading not guilty for 21 months, Volpe asked Kornberg to enter a plea of guilty. Hoping to avoid the maximum sentence of life in prison, the defendant admitted, "While in the bathroom of the precinct, in the presence of another officer, I sodomized Mr. Louima with a stick." Weeping, Volpe added, "I told him if you tell anyone, I will find you and I will kill you."

The former officer explained that, in the fray outside the nightclub, he had thought Louima had punched him. At the station house, he said, he had taken the prisoner to the restroom to demand an answer as to why Louima had hit him; Louima had cursed him repeatedly he claimed, and he had gone into "an animal rage."

"The next thing I knew," said Volpe, "the stick was in. My actions were wrong." Later, he admitted, he had realized he had been mistaken about who punched him.

As Volpe went to a cell to await sentencing, the trial resumed. On June 9, after 18 hours of deliberation, the jury found Charles Schwarz guilty of beating Louima, then holding him down during the torture. Thomas Bruder and Thomas Wiese were found not guilty of the assault in the police car; Sergeant Michael Bellomo was acquitted in the cover-up charge.

Volpe, however, changed his story at this point, telling both a psychologist and a probation officer that Schwarz had been wrongfully convicted because he had not helped in the assault. Schwarz awaited sentencing as his lawyer tried to appeal the conviction.

In a crowded courtroom on December 13, 1999, Judge Eugene H. Nickerson sentenced Volpe to 30 years imprisonment and also ordered him to pay $277,495 in restitution, at a rate—questioned by courtroom skeptics—of $25 a month. Handing down the sentence, Judge Nickerson declared, "Short of intentional murder, one cannot imagine a more barbarous misuse of power than Volpe's."

The Conspiracy Trial Opens

At his sentencing for his conviction at the first trial, Volpe claimed that Wiese, not Schwarz, had been the other police officer in the restroom during the assault. The question of which policeman helped brutalize Abner Louima was crucial as the second trial, for conspiracy to cover up the crime, began on February 7, 2000, in Brooklyn Federal District Court. If Schwarz, who had now been convicted, was not directly involved in the bathroom torture after all, how could he be charged with covering up his part? If Wiese, instead, had been there, charges should now be brought against him. And if Volpe alone was responsible, the case should be closed as a single charge covered Schwarz, Wiese, and Bruder.

The three men were equally charged with lying to authorities in an attempt to clear Schwarz of the crime he had been convicted of in the first trial.

More than 100 pieces of evidence and some 23 witnesses, several of whom had testified at the first trial, were produced to support prosecutor Alan Vinegard's theory that Wiese had lied early in the investigation when he said he saw only Volpe and the victim, and not Schwarz, in the bathroom just after the attack. And, Vinegard asserted, Bruder lied months later by telling federal agents he concurred with Wiese.

"Sit Tight"

Key prosecutorial evidence included flurries of telephone calls among the accused officers in the hours and days immediately after the attack. And prosecution witness Michael Immitt, a trustee of the Patrolmen's Benevolent Association (the police union), angrily conceded on the witness stand that, in a closed-door meeting for four days after the attack, he had counseled the defendants to keep silent, saying, "Sit tight, don't talk about it. Don't talk to anyone unless something official comes down."

On Monday, March 6, 2000, after deliberating four days, the six white and six nonwhite jury panelists found the three defendants guilty, accepting the prosecution's argument that Schwarz had recruited Bruder and Wiese to help cover up Schwarz's role in the assault. The conviction came even though Volpe testified at the second trial that Schwarz had not been in the bathroom during the attack. Schwarz, Bruder, and Wiese faced a jail sentence of up to five years, while Volpe planned to appeal his 30-year sentence.

Abner Louima also wanted another day in court, filing a $155 million civil lawsuit against the police officers, their union, the NYPD, and the city of New York.

—Bernard Ryan, Jr. and Michael Burgan

Suggestions for Further Reading

Bartollas, Clemens, and Larry D. Hahn. *Policing in America.* Needham Heights, Mass.: Allyn & Bacon, 1998.

Barry, Dan. "Officer Charged in Man's Torture at Station House." *New York Times* (August 14, 1997): A1.

Burris, John L. and Catherine Whitney. *Blue versus Black: Let's End the Conflict between Cops and Minorities.* New York: St. Martin's, 1999.

Crawshaw, Ralph, Tom Williamson, and Barry Devlin. *Human Rights and Policing: Standards for Good Behavior and a Strategy for Change.* New York: Kluwer, 1998.

DeSantis, John. *The New Untouchables: How America Sanctions Police Violence.* Chicago: Noble Press, 1994.

Fried, Joseph P. "Volpe Sentenced to a 30-Year Term in Louima Torture." *New York Times* (December 14, 1999): A1.

Geller, William A. and Hans Toch, eds. *Police Violence: Understanding and Controlling Police Abuse of Force.* New Haven, Conn.: Yale University Press, 1996.

Kappeler, Victor E., Geoffrey P. Alpert, and Richard D. Sluder. *Forces of Deviance: Understanding the Dark Side of Policing.* Prospect Heights, Ill.: Waveland Press, 1998.

Levitt, Leonard. "The Louima Verdicts: Some Splits, but Blue Wall Stands." *Newsday* (June 9, 1999): A4.

McFadden, Robert D. and Joseph P. Fried. "In Harsh Testimony's Wake, Officer Accused in Torture of Louima to Plead Guilty." *New York Times* (May 25, 1999): B4.

Roleff, Tamara L., ed. *Police Brutality.* San Diego: Greenhaven, 1999.

Skolnick, Jerome H. and James Fyfe. *Above the Law: Police and the Excessive Use of Force.* New York: The Free Press (Simon & Schuster), 1994.

"Volpe Recounts Night of Brutality, Threats and Rage." *New York Times* (May 26, 1999): B5.

Mark Crawford Trial: 1999

Defendant: Mark Crawford   **Crimes Charged:** Murder in aid of racketeering, racketeering, racketeering conspiracy, kidnapping, conspiracy to embezzle, embezzlement, wire fraud, money laundering, conspiracy to distribute marijuana, perjury, obstruction of justice by killing a witness, obstruction of justice by retaliating against a witness, conspiracy to threaten to commit a crime of violence against an individual

Chief Defense Lawyer: William May   **Chief Prosecutor:** Mark E. Cullers

Judge: Oliver W. Wanger   **Place:** Fresno, California   **Date of Trial:** June 22–August 20, 1999   **Verdict:** Guilty   **Sentence:** Life in prison

SIGNIFICANCE

Crawford was acquitted of murder in a state court but convicted of murder of a federal witness in federal court. The same person was murdered, but the two crimes were different, the court held, and therefore Crawford was not subjected to double jeopardy.

Mark Crawford looked like a poster boy for hard work and rectitude. Born dirt-poor in Maryland, he joined the army at 17. After two hitches, he and his wife moved to Ingleside, Texas, where he became a welder. He made a lot of friends in Ingleside, a small Gulf Coast town across the bay from Corpus Christi, taught Sunday school, and for the first time in his life was making a good income. In 1988, to the consternation of his wife, he quit his job and ran for mayor. Surprisingly, he won at the age of 33—mostly, according to the former mayor, because of his righteous image.

Crawford also started a construction business, but that venture was less fortunate. It failed. Undiscouraged, he started a new business, an employee leasing firm called Superior Staffing. The new business prospered.

Crawford began buying fancy cars, a boat and a beach house. People began to talk. For the first time, it seems, a substantial number of people in the area began to have their doubts about Crawford. After his second term as mayor, Crawford ran for the state senate but was defeated. The defeat didn't slow him down. He dropped out of politics and bought another business, Viking Casualty Co., that he operated in partnership with a Houston entrepreneur named Nick Brueggan. Tongues really began wagging when the IRS closed down Superior

Staffing and seized Crawford's assets. The IRS said the former mayor had been cheating the federal government out of tax money. But Crawford just acquired new assets. There seemed to be no end to his money.

Evidence of a Body

Then on June 1, 1996, a weight lifter named Kirk Johnson, employed as a bodyguard by Crawford, came to the Aransas County sheriff with a wild story. He said he and another Crawford bodyguard, Michael Beckcom, had helped Crawford murder Nick Brueggan. He led officers to a grave containing Brueggan's body. According to Johnson, they had forced Brueggan into a metal tool box, then attached a hose to a hole in the box and filled it from exhaust from a minivan. When Ingleside police and Texas Rangers went looking for Crawford, he had disappeared. Six weeks later, they found him in Biloxi, Mississippi.

The reason for the murder, Johnson said, was that federal agents were investigating Viking Casualty and a financial network Crawford had built up. It involved insurance companies that never paid claims, corporations that pocketed employees' income taxes, large-scale embezzlement, and marijuana selling. The organization's members referred to it as "the family" and wore gold rings engraved with the Chinese symbol for "family." Crawford's "family" operated illegal enterprises in Texas, Mississippi, Colorado, and California.

The second bodyguard, Mike Beckcom, pleaded guilty and agreed to testify against Crawford in return for a lighter sentence. Texas charged the former mayor with murder. The state prosecutors had two problems, however.

Suppressed Evidence and Conflicting Testimony

The state's biggest problem was that it couldn't present a motive for Brueggan's murder. At this point, there were no indictments against Viking Casualty or any of its subsidiaries or against Crawford, Brueggan, or anyone else in connection with the alleged activities of the "family." Because of that, no evidence concerning the federal investigation could be introduced. The second problem was that while Johnson and Beckcom both testified against Crawford, they told different stories. In both his cross-examinations and summation, Crawford's lawyer, Bill May, pointed up the inconsistencies.

The jury was deadlocked 10–2 in favor of a guilty verdict. In spite of the weakness of the state's case, there was a lot of suspicion of Crawford in Aransas County. But there wasn't enough for a unanimous verdict.

The state moved for a new trial. But this time in was held in San Antonio, Texas, in Bexar County. The people there had no feeling about Crawford one way or the other. The testimony of Johnson and Beckcom did not impress them.

"One of them said one thing, then the other said something else," May commented later. "The jury couldn't believe either one."

The jury found him not guilty.

Enter the Feds

Crawford was not released, however. By this time, federal prosecutors had secured indictments. They charged not only murder but a whole string of felonies. On January 26, 1999, May moved to have the case dismissed. The court rejected his motion to dismiss because of double jeopardy, because the federal murder charge concerned a different crime than the state charge although the same person was murdered. It also rejected motions to dismiss on several other grounds, such as overly vague charges.

The federal trial was held in Fresno, California, because Crawford was alleged to have defrauded Ararat International, a Fresno-based firm. Six months earlier, the CEO of Ararat had pleaded guilty to embezzlement himself.

At the trial the government piled up evidence showing that millions of illegal dollars had flowed into Crawford's enterprises. This time, Kirk Johnson was charged with a variety of felonies, including murder and kidnapping in aid of racketeering, and did not testify about the murder. (In return for his testimony in the state trials, Johnson had been given 10 years probation after pleading guilty to murder.) This time there was no chance of the jury getting conflicting stories.

After deliberating a week, the jury found Crawford guilty on all counts. Judge Oliver Wanger sentenced him to life in prison without possibility of parole.

— William Weir

Suggestions for Further Reading

Corpus Christi Caller Times. (Oct 15, 21, 1998; January 26, June 14, 22, 23, 25, 1999; Aug. 5, 6, 7, 11, 21, 1999; Dec. 9, 1999; June 13, 2000).

Dallas Morning News (June 21, 2000).

City Confidential: Ingleside, TX. Arts and Entertainment (A&E) Videocassette.

Kevin Mitnick Case: 1999

Defendant: Kevin D. Mitnick   **Crimes Charged:** Wire fraud (14 counts), possession of unauthorized access devices (8 counts), interception of wire or electronic communications, unauthorized access to a federal computer, and causing damage to a computer   **Chief Defense Lawyers:** Donald Randolph and Gregory Vincent   **Chief Prosecutors:** Christopher Painter and David Schindler   **Judge:** Marianna Pfaelzer   **Place:** Los Angeles, California   **Date of Sentencing after Plea Agreement:** August 10, 1999   **Plea:** Guilty   **Sentence:** 3 years and 10 months imprisonment, plus 3 years probation with strict limitations on use of computer equipment

SIGNIFICANCE
The federal prosecution of computer "hacker" Kevin Mitnick was the first case to focus international attention on computer security issues.

When the FBI arrested him on February 15, 1995, in a Raleigh, North Carolina, apartment, Kevin Mitnick was either a master of victimless computer trespassing or a dangerous vandal whose intrusions into commercial computer sites had cost international companies millions of dollars. The argument over whether Mitnick was a felon or a mere nuisance would outlast his confrontation with the justice system.

Prior to his North Carolina arrest, Mitnick was already well known to the authorities and had previously been prosecuted numerous times for "hacking" or using the Internet to gain unauthorized access to computers. In 1981, as a teenager, he was convicted of burgling computer manuals from Pacific Bell and sentenced to probation. He served six months in jail in 1983 for breaking into computers at the University of Southern California. In 1987 he was arrested for hacking into the computers of a Santa Cruz software publisher and sentenced at that time to three years probation. In 1988, Mitnick was arrested for illegally copying software from Digital Equipment Corporation. During that trial, his defense attorneys argued that his hacking activities were an "addiction" and he was sentenced to a year in jail and six months in a halfway house.

In 1992, authorities planned to arrest Mitnick for hacking into Pacific Bell computers and for violating the terms of his parole by associating with Lewis DePayne, a longtime friend and also a convicted hacker. Alerted to the impending arrest, Mitnick disappeared. His hacking, however, continued. After he attacked the computers of California computer security expert Tsutomu Shimomura, Shimomura assisted the FBI in tracking Mitnick to North Carolina.

By the time Mitnick and DePayne were taken into custody in 1995, the federal government had compiled a substantial indictment against them: 25 counts of computer crimes including possession of unauthorized access devices, computer fraud, causing damage to computers, wire fraud, and interception of wire or electronic communications. The indictment accused the pair of fraudulently obtaining unauthorized access to computers belonging to software and operating systems manufacturers, cellular telephone manufacturers, internet service providers, and educational institutions. They allegedly used the information to steal and copy proprietary computer software from Motorola, Nokia, Fujitsu, Novell, NEC, and Sun Microsystems. Mitnick and DePayne were also charged with fraudulent acquisition and possession of hundreds of confidential computer passwords.

Prosecution of computer hacker Kevin Mitnick was the first case to focus attention on computer security. (Archive Photos)

No Bail, No Computer

When Mitnick was arraigned in Los Angeles on September 30, 1996, he pleaded not guilty. He was denied bail. Mitnick and his lawyer, Donald Randolph, protested that Mitnick should not be denied bail for what they considered to be a benign violation of the law, but prosecutors continued to convincingly portray him as a "flight" risk. Although Randolph appealed the denial of bail all the way to the U.S. Supreme Court, Mitnick remained in prison for nearly five years.

The two sides also fought over Mitnick's right to use a laptop computer in jail to review the voluminous evidence prosecutors planned to use against him. The government argued that Mitnick's facility with computers made him too dangerous to be trusted with one. After over a year of ruling for the prosecution on the matter, Judge Marianna Pfaelzer eventually allowed Mitnick to use a laptop without a modem to review evidence on unalterable CD-ROM discs. The arguing continued, however, over the government's refusal to allow Mitnick access to encrypted data found in his computers at the time of his arrest.

As procedural disputes continued for years, public support for Mitnick among the hacker community grew, highlighting the division of opinion over the exact nature of his offenses. Mitnick's supporters accused the government of persecuting him for what they viewed as a victimless crime. They correctly pointed out that, unlike some hackers, Mitnick had merely copied the information he had accessed and had never used his intrusions into computer systems for financial profit. The companies whose systems he had entered, the government, and his detractors in the computer world, however, accused Mitnick of costing his victims millions of dollars in repairs by breaching their security systems. Supporters cynically responded that Mitnick had done the companies a favor by forcing them to fix the security flaws. Mitnick's defense attorneys accused the government of inflating alleged damage estimates to strengthen the prosecution's case.

Hacker Pleads Guilty

A month before Mitnick's trial was finally scheduled to begin on April 20, 1999, he agreed to plead guilty to 5 of the 25 felony counts against him. While Mitnick awaited sentencing, DePayne also agreed to a plea bargain. On April 26, he pleaded guilty to 1 count of wire fraud and agreed to cooperate with computer security investigators working on the case. He was sentenced to six months of detention at his home.

Although Mitnick's plea was sure to reduce the prison time he risked serving had he been convicted in a federal trial, he still faced a state charge of illegally accessing California Department of Motor Vehicles computers in 1992 to obtain confidential information. On August 6, however, the Los Angeles district attorney's office reversed their long-standing intention to prosecute and dropped the case, saying that Mitnick had been "mischarged." Mitnick had obtained the information over the telephone by simply misidentifying himself as a welfare fraud inspector. Since he had not used a computer, the case against him was unprosecutable and was dismissed upon the request of the D.A.'s office.

His guilty plea in the federal case was ultimately unaffected by the disposition of the unrelated state charge. On August 10, 1999, Judge Pfaelzer sentenced Mitnick to three years and 10 months in prison, granting him credit for time served, to be followed by three years of probation. Prosecutors wanted Mitnick to pay $1.5 million in damages to the companies in whose computer systems he had created so much havoc. The judge instead ordered Mitnick to pay a "token restitution" of $4,125.

Most significant, the terms of Mitnick's three-year probation prohibited him from having any contact with Internet access, computers, software, or cellular telephones. He was also prohibited from working as a computer consultant. Mitnick and his lawyers protested that this would deny him the ability to earn a living, not only in the field that he knew best, but also in a world where computers were increasingly used everywhere, even in the lowliest retail jobs. The judge was unmoved. Mitnick returned to prison to serve the remainder of his sentence.

After being paroled and released on January 21, 2000, Mitnick continued to insist that his hacking activities stemmed from intellectual curiosity about telephone systems and computer security, rather than any fraudulent intentions. And even on parole, his expertise was sufficient for him to be called upon by the media and even the government for his opinions on crimes by less-benign hackers.

— Tom Smith

Suggestions for Further Reading

Littman, Jonathan. *The Fugitive Game.* New York: Little Brown, 1996.

Markoff, John. "Cyberspace's Most Wanted: Hacker Eludes F.B.I. Pursuit." *New York Times* (July 4, 1994): A1.

Miller, Greg. "Hacking Legend's Sign-Off." *Los Angeles Times* (March 18, 1999): A1.

Penenberg, Adam L. "The Troubled Path of Kevin Mitnick." *Forbes* (April 19, 1999): 50–1.

Matthew Shepard Beating Death Trial: 1999

Defendant: Aaron James McKinney   **Crimes Charged:** Murder, kidnapping, robbery   **Chief Defense Lawyers:** Dion Custis, Jason Tangeman
Chief Prosecutor: Calvin Rerucha   **Judge:** Barton Voigt   **Place:** Laramie, Wyoming   **Date of Trial:** October 25–November 4, 1999   **Verdict:** Guilty
Sentence: Two life terms with no possibility of parole

SIGNIFICANCE

The murder of Matthew Shepard, an openly gay college student, by Aaron McKinney and Russell Henderson was publicized worldwide and gave a tremendous impetus to the drive to include hate crimes in criminal statutes.

After downing what they admitted were "several pitchers of beer," two 21-year-old high school dropouts, Aaron McKinney and Russell Henderson, decided to rob another patron of the Laramie, Wyoming, bar they were in. The mark, Matthew Shepard, 21, looked good because he was small—5′2″ and 105 pounds—and homosexual. McKinney hated "queers." The two got into a conversation with Shepard, a freshman at the University of Wyoming, told him they were gay, and invited him to ride with them. In McKinney's father's pickup, Shepard told them he had just left a planning meeting for a Gay Awareness Week celebration.

"Guess what—we're not gay," McKinney said. "This is Gay Awareness Week." He hit the student with a stolen revolver. He hit him again, and again. He told Henderson, driving the truck, to pull over at a spot outside the city. He got out, pulled Shepard out of the truck, and hit him again. While beating the student, he told Henderson to get a rope from the truck and tie Shepard to a fence. He hit and kicked the bound student a few more times and stole his wallet and shoes.

Then the two dropouts drove off, leaving Shepard tied to the fence.

It was the night of October 6, 1998. Winter comes early to the high plains of Wyoming. The temperature dropped to well below freezing.

Back in town, the two young thugs picked a fight with two Mexican-American teenagers. That didn't go as well for McKinney as his encounter with

Shepard: he got a cut on his head. In a way, though, it was lucky. When police stopped the fight, McKinney told them the blood on his clothes came from that cut. But there was a lot of blood. Police became suspicious. When, the next day, a bicyclist reported seeing the unconscious Shepard tied to a fence—18 hours after the attack—Detective Sergeant Robert DeBree went after McKinney and Henderson. He found the stolen revolver, covered with blood, plus Shepard's credit card and shoes in the truck. He found the student's wallet at McKinney's home. Police also arrested Kristen Price, 18, who lived with McKinney and Chastity Paisley, 20, who lived with Henderson. The women had helped dispose of the bloody clothing.

Four days later, Shepard died without regaining consciousness. His attackers were charged with murder as well as kidnapping and robbery.

Worldwide Publicity

The attack and Shepard's death got worldwide publicity. The *New York Times*, which seldom notices news from Wyoming, ran more than 50 items about the murder. The *Times* could not resist throwing in a bit of bogus Old West lore, comparing Shepard's being tied to the fence to the "practice of nailing a dead coyote to a ranch fence as a warning to future intruders." Coyotes, among the most observant of creatures in nature, can spot real danger hidden in high grass, but will not be deterred by canine scarecrows.

The Shepard case also generated at least 27 national magazine articles and numerous websites. President Bill Clinton and Attorney General Janet Reno both called for more hate crime laws. There were demonstrations against hate crime, particularly crime against homosexuals, in cities from San Francisco to New York. In New York, the demonstration turned into a riot, in which 120 persons were arrested.

A cross of stones lies below the fence where gay student Matthew Shepard was tied and beaten to death. (AP/Wide World Photos)

State Seeks Death

In Laramie, County Attorney Cal Rerucha, locally famous as a hard-nosed prosecutor, said he would seek the death penalty. Not everyone agreed. The National Gay and Lesbian Task Force, a coalition of a dozen gay rights groups, adopted a resolution saying the death penalty is not a deterrent and would not reduce hate crimes. The victim's parents, Dennis and Judy Shepard, however, said they favored the death penalty for such crimes as the recent murder of a black man, James Byrd, Jr., by bigots in Texas.

When he came to trial April 5, 1999, Henderson pleaded guilty and testified against McKinney. It was said that he had made a deal with the prosecution to avoid execution. He received two life terms, one for murder and one for kidnapping, to run consecutively.

Surprise Ending

When McKinney came to trial, October 25, his court-appointed attorney, Jason Tangeman, tried the "gay panic" defense. In his opening statement, he said that McKinney had suffered homosexual abuse as a child. When Shepard made a homosexual advance to him, the lawyer said, it drove him to an insane rage. "Gay panic" has no place in statute or case law, but it has been used successfully to reduce charges in several cases. Judge Barton Voigt, however, ruled that what Tangeman was trying to prove was temporary insanity, which is no defense in Wyoming.

Tangeman and McKinney's other court-appointed lawyer, Dion Custis, then tried to show that their client was less responsible because he had been taking drugs and was drinking heavily the night of the attack.

The jury found McKinney guilty of both kidnapping and murder. The next day, it was to consider whether or not to recommend the death penalty. But when it met, there was a surprise.

Dennis Shepard, the dead man's father, stood up and addressed the murderer.

"I would like nothing better than to see you die, Mr. McKinney," he said. "However, this is the time to begin the healing process, to show mercy to someone who refused to show any mercy."

The *Washington Post* said, "Judy and Dennis Shepard tempered justice with mercy and may have spared the life of the man who killed their son."

"Parents of gay obtain mercy for his killer," headlined the *New York Times*.

The situation, however, was a bit more complicated. The day before Dennis Shepard made his statement, when the jury delivered its guilty verdict, it had not agreed with the prosecution that the murder was premeditated. In that case, most Wyoming legal experts agreed, there was little chance that McKinney would be sentenced to death.

McKinney's lawyers, however, did not want to risk even a small chance. Tangeman approached Rerucha to see if the family would agree to a life sentence instead of death. Rerucha was flabbergasted and outraged. He denounced the audacity of the defense team—lawyers he personally disliked—in asking mercy of the parents of the dead man.

Two other members of the state team looked at the situation more realistically. Sergeant DeBree, who made the arrests, and his superior officer, Commander David O'Malley, knew that McKinney would probably get life anyway. And in that case, there was a chance he might again be turned loose on society. They brokered the meeting between the defense team and the Shepards. Rerucha went, too, but he walked out after five minutes. What Tangeman and Custis finally offered was two consecutive life terms, with no appeals allowed and no possibility of parole. After some discussion, Judy Shepard agreed. Dennis didn't. Neither did Rerucha, who had the final decision. Eventually, Judy Shepard's arguments and the police officers' cool assessment won over Dennis Shepard. Rerucha reluctantly agreed to forgo asking for death.

Judge Voigt sentenced McKinney to two consecutive life terms. There could be no appeal. McKinney will never leave the prison.

—William Weir

Suggestions for Further Reading

Loffreda, Beth. *Losing Matt Shepard*. New York: Columbia University Press, 2000.

Swigonski, Mary E., ed. *From Hate Crimes to Human Rights: A Tribute to Matthew Shepard*. New York: Vintage Press, 2000.

Nathaniel Abraham Trial: 1999

Defendant: Nathaniel Abraham   **Crimes Charged:** Murder, assault with intent to murder, and felony use of a firearm
Chief Defense Lawyer: Geoffrey Fieger   **Chief Prosecutor:** Lisa Halushka
Judge: Eugene A. Moore   **Place:** Pontiac, Michigan
Dates of Trial: October 29–November 16, 1999   **Verdict:** Guilty of second-degree murder   **Sentence:** Placement in a juvenile detention center until the age of 21

SIGNIFICANCE

Only 11 years old at the time of his arrest, Nathaniel Abraham became the youngest American convicted of murder as an adult. His trial spotlighted the controversial issue of trying juvenile offenders in adult court.

During the 1980s, the number of violent crimes committed by juveniles in the United States began to rise. In response, a growing number of states passed laws stipulating that children under 17 could be tried as adults for certain crimes. The slogan "adult crime, adult time" captured the sentiments of supporters of these juvenile justice statutes. By 1992, more than 40 states had passed laws for trying children as adults.

Some civil libertarians and juvenile justice experts argued against the tough measures, saying the juvenile justice system had a better chance of rehabilitating young criminals than the adult system did. Those arguments held little sway in Michigan, which passed its version of the juvenile justice law in 1996. The law was one of the strictest in the nation, allowing a child of any age to be tried as an adult. Three years later, the state was the setting for the country's most controversial juvenile murder trial.

Two years before, police in Pontiac, Michigan, had arrested 11-year-old Nathaniel Abraham for the October 29, 1997 murder of an 18-year-old man who was shot while standing outside a party store. He died a day later from a single .22 caliber bullet wound to the head. Nathaniel admitted that he had been firing a .22 caliber rifle in the direction of the store on the day of the shooting. The boy insisted though that he had not meant to shoot anyone; he had merely been firing randomly at some trees. But Oakland County prosecutors argued that

Nathaniel had deliberately set out to kill someone that day and had later bragged about the shooting.

Prosecutors received permission to charge Nathaniel with first-degree murder and several other felonies and try him as an adult.

Murderer or Troubled Youth?

Nathaniel hardly presented the image of a deadly killer. Wearing oversized prison garb, the 65-pound boy appeared tearful and bewildered at pre-trial hearings. But prosecutors argued that Nathaniel was exactly the type of juvenile offender the 1996 law had meant to target. Police had previously suspected him in almost two dozen crimes, including burglary and assault. For a variety of reasons, however, the boy had never been formally charged.

11-year-old Nathaniel Abraham became the youngest American convicted of murder as an adult. (AP/Wide World Photos)

Nathaniel's case drew the attention of attorney Geoffrey Fieger, who had previously defended "Dr. Death," Jack Kervorkian. Fieger took on the job pro bono and began a series of motions and appeals that delayed the trial until October 1999.

When the trial finally opened on October 29, prosecutor Lisa Halushka wrote down these words for the jury to read: "I'm gonna shoot somebody." This, she claimed, was what Nathaniel had said to his girlfriend days before the killing. As the trial progressed, Halushka called witnesses who supported the idea that Nathaniel's act had been a premeditated murder. He had stolen the rifle, then practiced target shooting at balloons. He had also fired the gun at a neighbor's house, barely missing the occupant, just before the fatal shooting. Later, Halushka noted that Nathaniel had told police conflicting stories about the shootings—proof that he knew what he had done, and that it was wrong.

Defense attorney Fieger argued that the shooting was an unfortunate accident. Nathaniel did fire the gun, yes, but was not trying to hit anyone. Fieger also introduced testimony from an expert marksman. The witness said that it would be almost impossible to deliberately hit a small target from more than 200 feet—the distance Nathaniel was from the victim—using the old, battered rifle the boy had fired.

Fieger also called on child psychologists to describe Nathaniel's mental state. The boy, these experts testified, had an IQ of 70, and at the time of the murder, his thought processes were like those of a seven-year-old. Fieger tried to prove that Nathaniel lacked the mental capacity to form the intent to kill. A prosecution psychologist witness, however, testified to rebut this claim.

Outside the courtroom, the trial provoked massive public interest. The CBS television magazine *60 Minutes* profiled the case, and Oakland County Prosecutor David Gorcyca admitted the Michigan social system had failed to help Nathaniel in the past, despite his impaired intelligence and previous brushes with the law. Gorcyca said he owed the boy's mother, Gloria, an apology. An upset Mrs. Abraham replied, "Owe me an apology! To say the system failed but they still want to try my child as an adult? This is ridiculous."

Controversial Sentence

Although Nathaniel was charged with first-degree murder, prosecutors asked Judge Eugene A. Moore to allow the jury to consider lesser offenses. Moore did so, and on November 16, 1999, the jury found Nathaniel guilty of second-degree murder. He was believed to be the youngest American ever convicted of murder as an adult. Moore had three options for the sentence. The harshest was a prison term of 8 to 25 years. Prosecutors favored a more moderate, "blended" sentence: Nathaniel would go to a juvenile detention center, and then be reviewed between the ages of 18 and 21 to see if he had been rehabilitated. If so, he would be released. If not, he would go to an adult prison after turning 21. Moore, however, surprised the prosecutors by choosing the most lenient sentence. He ruled that Nathaniel be sent to a maximum-security juvenile detention center until the age of 21, and then freed.

As he handed down his sentence, Moore attacked the harsh Michigan juvenile justice law. The state, he said, "has responded to juvenile criminal activity not by helping to prevent and rehabilitate." However, most Michigan lawmakers and prosecutors continued to support the law. And across America, no states seemed ready to change their own statutes, even as some experts questioned their benefits.

—Michael Burgan

Suggestions for Further Reading

Bradsher, Keith. "Boy Who Killed Gets Seven Years; Judge Says Law Is Too Harsh" *New York Times* (January 14, 2000): A1.

——. "Michigan Boy Who Killed at 11 Is Convicted of Murder as Adult." *New York Times* (November 17, 1999): A1.

——. "Murder Trial of 13-Year-Old Puts Focus on Michigan Law." *New York Times* (October 31, 1999): 22.

Hewitt, Bill, Champ Clark, and Amy Mindell. "A Life in the Balance." *People* (November 22, 1999): 197–99.

Michigan v. Abraham. Court TV Online (September 19, 1999): http://www.courttv.com/trials/abraham101999_ctv.hml.

Edwin Edwards, et al. Trial: 2000

Defendants: Edwin Edwards, Stephen Edwards, Andrew Martin, Greg Tarver, Ecotry Fuller, Bobby Johnson, Cecil Brown   **Crimes Charged:** Extortion, mail fraud, wire fraud, money laundering, interstate travel and communication in aid of racketeering, false statements, illegal wiretapping, Racketeer-Influenced Corrupt Organizations (RICO) Act violations, conspiracy
Chief Defense Lawyers: Edwin Edwards: Daniel Small; Stephen Edwards: James Cole; Andrew Martin: S.C. Garcia, III, Ryan J. Roemershauser; Greg Tarver: Mary Olive Pierson, Hillar C. Moore, III; Ecotry Fuller: Kenneth Craig Smith; Bobby Johnson: Patrick Fanning, Ernest Johnson; Cecil Brown: Rebecca Hudsmith   **Chief Prosecutors:** Eddie Jordan, Jim Letten, Michael Magner, Peter Strasser, Todd Greenberg, Fred Harper   **Judge:** Frank Polozola   **Place:** Baton Rouge, Louisiana   **Dates of Trial:** January 10–May 9, 2000   **Verdicts:** Edwin Edwards, Stephen Edwards, Andrew Martin, Cecil Brown, Bobby Johnson: guilty (Cecil Brown convicted March 21, 2001 of seven additional counts in separate extortion schemes); Greg Tarver and Ecotry Fuller: not guilty   **Sentences:** Edwin Edwards: 10 years in prison, $250,000 fine; Stephen Edwards: 7 years in prison, $60,000 fine; Andrew Martin: 5 years, 8 months, $50,000 fine; Cecil Brown: 5 years, 6 months, $50,000 fine; Bobby Johnson: 5 years, 4 months, $50,000 fine

SIGNIFICANCE

Former governor Edwin Edwards, who had served four terms as Louisiana governor (1972–1980, 1984–1988, and 1992–1996), was convicted of heading an extensive conspiracy during and after his last term, to extort bribes in the awarding of riverboat gambling licenses. The four-month federal trial of a popular state governor was marked by intensive local media coverage, an anonymous jury, and by the fact that the mail fraud charges that linked the crimes were dismissed.

Governor Edwin Edwards had established a record over four decades as a successful and popular Democratic politician in Louisiana. His first three terms were marked by numerous achievements, including revision of the complex state constitution in 1974, reduction of taxes, and a vast increase in state services. Nevertheless, the fun-loving and popular politician was enmeshed in several scandals, including accusations that his wife had received a $100,000 gift while he served a term in Congress.

Edwards was accused in 1999 of having managed a scheme to extort bribes in exchange for riverboat casino licenses. Although federal prosecutors claimed that at least four casino companies paid the bribes, only two casino owners admitted to making payments.

The Louisiana Riverboat Gaming Commission, from 1992 through early 1996, consisted of a seven-member panel appointed by the governor. This commission evaluated applications for a total of 15 riverboat casino gaming licenses provided for by state law. The commission did not grant the licenses, but would issue certificates of preliminary approval. The commission was empowered to award 15 certificates. The Riverboat Gaming Division of the Louisiana State Police would grant the actual licenses, after conducting its own investigation and hearing to determine the suitability of an applicant. In March 1993, the commission awarded eight preliminary certificates, and in June 1993, the commission awarded seven more. The second round was highly competitive and received wide media attention. Fourteen of the 15 applicants that received preliminary certification were granted licenses by the State Police. The 15th applicant was at first denied by the police, but awarded after appeal.

Governor Edwin Edwards and his wife Candy enter the courthouse where he was found guilty of extortion. (AP/Wide World Photos)

In early 1996, after Governor Edwards completed his fourth term, the state legislature created the Louisiana Gaming Control Board, with six members appointed by the new governor. The new board had one riverboat license to grant, and it received five applications for the single license that remained to be awarded.

Bribery Conspiracy Alleged

The FBI and the Justice Department alleged that former governor Edwards and his son Stephen, through their law practice in Baton Rouge, were at the center of a criminal conspiracy to extort bribes from applicants seeking gambling licenses. Playing on their supposed influence with the original Riverboat Gaming Commission and with the new gaming board, the two received attorney's fees and other payments from both successful and unsuccessful riverboat applicants. Stephen set up a company to sell merchandise to the casino operators as a channel for some of the payoffs. Cecil Brown, Andrew Martin, and Bobby Johnson were accused of serving as contact persons with the extortion victims, soliciting bribes. All three had served as aides or staff to Edwards when he had been governor.

Eddie DeBartolo, Jr., former owner of the National Football League's San Francisco Forty-Niners, and Robert Guidry, who owned the Treasure Chest Casino in Kenner, Louisiana, both explained how they had made large payoffs to win casino licenses. Guidry stated that he paid $1.5 million over the period 1996–1997 to the Edwards ring, while DeBartolo claimed he paid $400,000. The owner of The Belle of Baton Rouge Riverboat Casino, granted a license on July 18, 1994, agreed to cooperate with federal authorities in their investigation. The casino was jointly owned by Jazz Enterprises, Incorporated, and Argosy Gaming, Inc. Mark Bradley, vice president of Jazz, along with other principals and employees of the company, worked with the FBI, helping to record conversations with Edwards and his associates. Testimony indicated that another successful applicant for a license, Players Lake Charles, Incorporated, had also made pay-offs, through a friend of the Edwards, Richard Shelter.

Several unsuccessful applicant companies were also named in the indictment against Edwards. These included the Louisiana Riverboat Gaming Corporation (LRGC), the New Orleans River Corporation (NORC), and the Gretna Belle. The government alleged that funds were extorted from all of these unsuccessful applicants.

According to the indictment, Edwards and his associates obtained $350,000 in cash and an ownership interest in the two firms, LRGC and NORC. The cash and interest were extorted in exchange for support for their license applications, although both applications failed. The cash payments tracked through bank wire transfers were in the form of consulting fees to Cecil Brown.

Furthermore, the group extorted money from Jazz enterprises, Incorporated, and from Players. Working with Richard Shelter, Stephen Edwards demanded money from Players, from the Coushatta Indian Tribe, and from a third party in relation to the Players Casino. The Edwards group also extorted money from Robert Guidry in relation to the Treasure Chest Casino. Both Shelter, as go-between, and Guidry, as victim, gave evidence against the Edwards group.

The government's case was supported by explicit testimony from DeBartolo, Guidry, and Shelter. Although each was apparently guilty of either giving or receiving bribes, all three were granted immunity in exchange for testimony against Edwards and his conspirators.

Three Months of Testimony

Members of the state Gaming Control Board, and the former Riverboat Gaming Commission, denied that anyone had tried to influence their decisions. Even so, the government introduced testimony and wiretap evidence demonstrating that Edwin Edwards had made many telephone calls in connection with the extortion scheme. Specific acts of extortion against LRGC, NORC, Jazz Enterprises, Belle of Baton Rouge, Players Lake Charles Riverboat, Treasure Chest Riverboat Casino, and Hollywood/DeBartolo Riverboat Casino were charged. Tape-recorded conversations made it clear that Edwards's associates claimed that no license could be granted without his consent, and that payments and/or participation in the casino operations would have to be arranged if he were to support the applications.

Testimony and evidence stretched over three months in early 2000. Don Semesky, an Internal Revenue Service agent, used a chart to demonstrate that Edwards spent $872,000 more in cash than he reported as income in the period 1986–1997. Using Edwards' own testimony in an unrelated trial, Semesky claimed that Edwards spent at least $704,000 more than he could account for. His increased 1996 spending coincided with the extortion payments reported by Guidry. Part of the surplus cash was $383,500 seized from Edwards's safe deposit box. His defense claimed that amount was a legitimate payment from DeBartolo. Prosecutors and defense attorneys disputed whether the $400,000 payment, which DeBartolo had reported to the IRS, could be regarded as legitimate or not.

The defense attorneys argued that the federal government used its power to construct a case built on wiretaps and testimony from individuals who plea-bargained in exchange for their testimony. Bugged offices, paid expert witnesses, testimony from people who admittedly broke the law, and FBI tails on suspects added up to a government conspiracy, the defense charged. Tape recordings were edited and played out of context to construct a plot for the jury, and a known criminal made at least one set of tapes. According to the defense, the payments from Richard Shelter to Stephen Edwards were merely legitimate repayments on an investment in a failed pizza venture. Shelter had ledgers that included evidence of other transactions, some apparently illegal, and the defense charged that Shelter testified for the government in exchange for immunity.

Jury deliberations stretched over several weeks, and the judge dismissed one juror for smuggling notes and documents into the deliberation room. Ultimately, however, the jury appeared convinced by the testimony of Eddie DeBartolo and Robert Guidry, who both testified that Edwards extorted money from them, and from Richard Shelter who claimed he funneled over $500,000 to the Edwards group from the Lake Charles Players Casino. Five of the seven accused were found guilty on May 9, 2000. Judge Polozola handed down sentences on January 8, 2001. Former governor Edwards was visibly shocked when the judge sentenced him to 10 years plus a $250,000 fine. His son Stephen received the second most severe sentence: seven years and a $60,000 fine.

Although Judge Polozola originally intended for the convicted conspirators to begin serving their sentences immediately, another judge granted Edwards and the others freedom while their appeals were pending. Edwards claimed 21 grounds for appeal, including the fact that the mail fraud charges that linked all of the convictions were themselves dismissed. While the appeals were pending, Brown and Edwards were accused in a separate corruption case for having arranged a favorable settlement for Cascade Insurance Company, which had been declared insolvent, in exchange for payoffs.

As of mid-2001, the appeals of the convictions in the casino bribery case were still pending.

— *Rodney Carlisle*

Suggestions for Further Reading

Bridges, Tyler. *Bad Bet on the Bayou: The Rise of Gambling in Louisiana and the Fall of Governor Edwin Edwards*. New York: Farrar, Strauss & Giroux, 2001.

Brotherton, John. *A Fistful of Kings*. Shear's Group, 2000.

Amadou Diallo/NYPD Trial: 2000

Defendants: Kenneth Boss, Sean Carroll, Edward McMellon, and Richard Murphy **Crime Charged:** Murder **Chief Defense Lawyers:** Boss: Steven Brounstein and Ben Herzweig; Carroll: Bennett Epstein, Marvin Kornberg, and John Patten; McMellon: Stephen Worth; Murphy: James Culleton **Chief Prosecutors:** Robert T. Johnson, Donald Levin, and Eric Warner **Judge:** Joseph Teresi **Place:** Albany, New York **Dates of Trial:** February 2–25, 2000 **Verdict:** Not guilty

SIGNIFICANCE

This case focused world attention on the issue of racial profiling, as the tragic killing of an unarmed African immigrant by four plainclothes police officers became the symbol of wrongful suspicion of an entire ethnic group by cops. Experts noted that the case mirrored the minority community's resentment of aggressive police tactics designed to reduce crime even at the expense of civil liberties. The verdict further aggravated the situation, with police brutality becoming a major political issue in New York City and elsewhere.

On the evening of February 4, 1999, four plainclothes officers of the New York City Police Department's (NYPD's) Street Crime Unit were patrolling in an unmarked car in the Bronx. Their elite 438-member squad, whose motto was "We Own the Night," boasted a record of 2,500 guns removed from the streets since 1997—far more than any unit their size.

The four—Kenneth Boss, 27; Sean Carroll, 35; Edward McMellon, 26; and Richard Murphy, also 26—were looking for a suspect alleged to have committed rapes, robberies, and murder. The officers wore jeans, sweaters, and sneakers or boots, and bullet-proof vests. Two carried more than one gun.

The officers drove south on Wheeler Avenue. At number 1157, they saw a man lingering in the doorway. They stopped. Guns drawn, McMellon and Carroll crossed the sidewalk and mounted the steps. Murphy stood back on the sidewalk. Boss crouched behind a parked car.

Suddenly, shots were fired. McMellon fell backward off the steps. Carroll also fell off the steps. Both emptied their 16-bullet magazines. Murphy fired four times. Boss, five.

The accosted man lay face up in the vestibule, his black wallet beside him. A fatal shot had perforated his aorta. Others had punctured his spinal cord, lungs, liver, spleen, kidney, and intestines. Eleven bullets pierced his legs.

Unarmed and Law Abiding

Investigators learned that the man was a 22-year-old immigrant from Guinea named Amadou Diallo who sold videos, CDs, and tapes on East 14th Street in Manhattan and had a reputation as a devout, law-abiding Muslim. He did not have a gun. He died on his own doorstep.

A Bronx grand jury began probing the 41-bullet barrage. Police statistics showed that in 1998 the Street Crime Unit had frisked 22,414 law-abiding people prompting a rash of citizen protests, led by the Reverend Al Sharpton. On March 25, 1999, the four officers, all white, were indicted for second-degree murder.

Rev. Al Sharpton addresses the crowd along with Saikou Diallo, father of police shooting victim Amadou Diallo. (AP/Wide World Photos)

For eight months, the protests continued—in the Bronx, at City Hall, in Wall Street, and at NYPD Headquarters, resulting in nearly 800 civil-disobedience arrests. Arguing that a fair trial in New York City was impossible in view of the intensive protests and negative news coverage, defense lawyers filed a motion in the Appellate Division of the New York State Supreme Court to move the trial out of town. On December 16, five appellate judges—Richard Andrias,

John Buckley, David Friedman, Alfred Lerner, and David Saxe—unanimously decided to move the trial to Albany.

"This case has been deluged by a tidal wave of prejudicial publicity," concluded the judges, who cited a poll showing that 81 percent of Bronx residents saw no justification for firing 41 bullets at an unarmed man. "Even an attempt to select an unbiased jury would be fruitless."

Jury selection began before Judge Joseph Teresi in Albany on the last day of January. Four black and two white women, and six white men were chosen, with four white male alternates.

Outside the Albany County Courthouse, some 600 protesters, mostly bussed from New York City, thronged the snow-packed streets. The judge permitted television cameras into the courtroom.

"Every Police Officer's Nightmare"

Opening for the prosecution on February 2, Bronx Assistant District Attorney Eric Warner stated, "We will prove this man was cornered and killed in the vestibule of his home." Officer Carroll's defense attorney Bennett Epstein's opening countered that Diallo had ignored police orders to halt and that the police had opened fire, believing Diallo had a gun. "Mr. Diallo," he said, "had taken the officers into the no-man's land that is every police officer's nightmare. Had Mr. Diallo stopped to answer the officer's questions, the whole thing would have ended peacefully."

The bullets were introduced as evidence. Coroner Joseph Cohen described the wounds that had been inflicted after the victim had been brought down by a bullet through his aorta. Detective Joseph Flannino testified that the vestibule was well lit enough for him to do his work at the crime scene. Using photos that, on the contrary, showed how dark the area was, the defense argued how easy it was for the officers to have mistaken Diallo's black wallet for a gun. A 22-year-old neighbor of Diallo's, Debbie Rivera, testified that she had heard a momentary pause in the volley of 41 shots, supporting the prosecution's claim that the police had had time to see that Diallo was unarmed and had briefly stopped shooting.

An embarrassing moment for the defense came when Wheeler Avenue resident Schrrie Elliott testified that she had seen the shooting from across the street. (She later told television interviewers she had heard one of the cops shout "Gun!" If true, this supported the officers' position that they thought the victim had been armed.) On the witness stand, however, she said she couldn't be sure who had shouted—it could have been Diallo. Cross-examined by prosecutor Donald Levin, she said Diallo had had his back to the officers as they approached, and she hadn't heard anyone yell "stop" or "freeze" or "show your hands." Someone, she couldn't be sure who, yelled, "Gun!" and the firing started. The next day, shown her TV interviews where she described one of the officers yelling "Gun!" she admitted her story had changed. The jury was not present for this disclosure, having previously been excused. In the meantime, an investigation disclosed that she had a rap sheet that included an arrest and conviction for the possession and sale of drugs. The next time she was put on the witness stand, the defense asked the judge to declare her a hostile witness, then proceeded to cross-examined her. At this time she changed her story yet again, saying one of the officers had, indeed, shouted "Gun!"

"Gun! He's Got a Gun!"

The defense put each of the officers on the witness stand. Sean Carroll testified about the unmarked police car's cruise down Wheeler Avenue. He related that he had seen a man who stepped back into the vestibule as if he didn't want to be seen. He told how he and McMellon approached, asking for a word with the man and telling Diallo to "Show me your hands." Then, said Carroll, Diallo "started removing a black object from his right side" and "it appeared he had pulled a weapon on my partner." Carroll said he shouted, "Gun! He's got a gun!" And when he saw McMellon fall backward off the steps, he thought Diallo was shooting.

McMellon testified, "All I knew at that moment was that he was pointing a weapon in my direction and Sean and I were going to die."

Sobbing as he testified, Carroll said that after the shooting he looked at what was in Diallo's hand, "And I seen it was just a wallet." He held Diallo's hand, rubbed his face, and said, "Don't die, keep breathing. Please don't die."

A window of the stuffy courtroom was partly open as officers Boss and Murphy testified. Four floors below, some 100 protestors chanted, "No justice, no peace." The judge ordered the window closed as the officers backed up their partners' story that Diallo had had a gun and that they had feared for their lives. The defense cited state law that permits killing in self-defense by police or anyone else. Murphy, who fired the fewest number of shots—four—said that he was sure he would find a gun when the smoke cleared. "Over and over," he testified, "I said, I can't believe there's no gun."

Textbook Policing

The last defense witness, Dr. James Fyfe, an expert in police training, testified that the officers had practiced textbook policing that night. The prosecution decided not to cross-examine him and to not put on a rebuttal case. Both sides rested.

After his four-hour charge and before deliberations began, Judge Teresi dismissed one juror for discussing the case out of court. The panel was now one white and four black women, and seven white men. After deliberating for three days, the jury decided the policemen had reasonably thought Diallo was armed and had fired in self-defense. It found them not guilty of second-degree murder.

Judge Teresi's charge had made it clear the jury could also consider convicting the defendants on several lower charges, such as manslaughter. The jury deliberated on the alternate charge but decided that the evidence did not support a guilty verdict on any criminal charges. Following the verdict, Diallo's family announced it would file a wrongful-death civil suit against the four officers and the city of New York.

—Bernard Ryan, Jr.

Suggestions for Further Reading

Donner, Frank. *Protectors of Privilege: Red Squads and Police Repression in Urban America*. Berkeley, Calif.: University of California Press, 1990.

Grossman, Lieutenant Colonel Dave. *On Killing: The Psychological Cost of Learning to Kill in War and Society*. Boston: Back Bay Books, 1996.

Lowry, Richard. "Protest Too Much." *National Review* (April 19, 1999): 10.

Morales, Frank. "The Militarization of the Police." *CovertAction Quarterly* (Spring-Summer 1999): 15.

Ruchelman, Leonard. *Who Rules the Police?* New York: New York University Press, 1973.

Sante and Kenneth Kimes Trial: 2000

Defendants: Sante and Kenneth Kimes   **Crimes Charged:** Murder, criminal possession of a weapon, conspiracy, forgery, robbery, burglary, grand larceny, eavesdropping   **Chief Defense Lawyers:** Sante Kimes: Michael Hardy; Kenneth Kimes: Mel Sachs   **Chief Prosecutors:** Owen Heimer, Connie Fernandez   **Judge:** Rena Uviller   **Place:** New York, New York **Date of Trial:** February 15–May 18, 2000   **Verdicts:** Sante Kimes: guilty on 58 criminal counts; Kenneth Kimes: guilty on 60 criminal counts **Sentences:** Sante Kimes: 120 years, 8 months; Kenneth Kimes: 125 years, 4 months

SIGNIFICANCE

No trace of the body of the murder victim, Irene Silverman, was ever found, and neither accused ever confessed. The decision represents perhaps the heaviest sentence handed down in the United States in a case built entirely on circumstantial evidence. Sante Kimes and her son, Kenneth, were accused of a long string of crimes in connection with the disappearance of Irene Silverman, and evidence mounted that they had been involved in a bizarre series of frauds, schemes, and earlier possible murders in other jurisdictions. Their strange case became the subject of at least three books and two television documentaries.

S ante Kimes was married to wealthy motel owner and land developer Kenneth Kimes, Sr. During her marriage, she became involved in several legal turmoils. In 1986, she was accused and then convicted of 14 counts of enslaving a number of maids, holding them against their will, physically abusing them, and not paying them. She was sentenced to 14 five-year terms to run concurrently in that case. In the same year she was convicted of stealing a fur coat from another customer in a Washington, D.C., restaurant. She was also suspected of arranging the arson of a home in Hawaii in order to collect the insurance.

On the death of her husband, she concealed the fact of his death from his family, apparently out of concern that they would contest her claim to the estate. However, Kenneth Kimes had sequestered much of his fortune in an offshore account in the Cayman Islands, and she was unable to access those funds. She was suspected in the disappearance of a banker in the Bahamas, in the death of a hired man in Los Angeles, and a warrant was issued for writing a bad check for $14,793.50 to purchase an automobile in Utah.

Irene Silverman

Sante Kimes, now aged 65, and her son Kenneth, Jr., 24, moved to New York City and took up residence in a small, but extremely elegant, apartment house owned by former ballerina Irene Silverman, 82. Kenneth rented the apartment under the assumed name of "Manny Guerin." Silverman's apartment house, valued at between $4 million and $10 million, became the object of the Kimeses's next scheme. Obtaining Silverman's passport, and a false Social Security card for her, the Kimes's had a deed to the property made out to them.

Sante and Kenneth Kimes found guilty of the murder of missing millionaire Irene Silverman. (AP/Wide World Photos)

Their behavior at the apartment house aroused Silverman's suspicions. For example, "Guerin" refused to complete a credit application and always avoided the security cameras in the lobby and hallways. The Kimeses refused to allow access to maintenance personnel. Concerned with their unusual behavior, and apparently suspicious, Silverman began eviction proceedings.

On July 4, 1998, when New York City was relatively quiet and emptied for the holiday weekend, Silverman vanished.

Arrest of Sante and Kenneth Kimes

On July 5, 1998, the Kimeses were arrested on an entirely separate matter. An outstanding warrant for them had been issued in Utah on the charge of using a bad check to buy the Lincoln Towncar. When police searched the car, they found an odd assortment of evidence: two loaded pistols, a .9 millimeter and a .22 caliber; several wigs and fright masks; a set of plastic handcuffs; and about $30,000 in cash. A container of a pink liquid that later turned out to be a so-called "date rape" drug was also found, along with a box that had once contained a stun gun. Silverman's keys were in the pockets of Kenneth Kimes. The phony Social Security card and the forged deed to the property were also in the car.

Several hours after the arrest on the check charge, police connected the Kimeses with the report that Silverman was missing. On searching their apartment, a number of other incriminating pieces of evidence turned up. Several taped telephone calls, apparently from a wiretap, contained Silverman's conversations. Notes and lists appeared to suggest that the Kimeses had planned a crime.

Los Angeles authorities wanted to extradite the Kimeses in connection with the murder of David Kazdin in March 1998, and in the mysterious disappearance of a vagrant they had hired to work at their home there. Kazdin was found dead in a trash bin near the L.A. airport. However, the New York district attorney's office decided to proceed with a murder charge against Sante and Kenneth Kimes, even though they could not find Irene Silverman's body and police had no blood or other physical evidence of a murder.

The Trial

When the trial opened, February 15, 2000, Connie Fernandez, assistant district attorney, outlined the charges, describing an elaborate plot in which the Kimeses sought to steal the townhouse-apartment building. Evidence included testimony that Sante had called a title company and checked liens on the property. Testimony demonstrated that Sante, posing as Silverman, duped a notary into approving the fraudulent deed that transferred the ownership of the townhouse to a Kimes-owned corporation in Florida for a payment of $395,000, a fraction of its value.

Fernandez argued that they decided to kill Silverman when she sought to have them evicted. Their hope was to dispose of the body and to buy enough time to complete the transfer of the property. A fraud investigator testified that the Social Security card used by Sante Kimes to establish her identity as Silverman for the notary had originally been issued two years before to an infant. A former employee of the Kimeses learned that he was named as the head of the firm set up in Florida as a part of the conspiracy.

Although all of the evidence appeared to support the convoluted scheme outlined by the prosecution, there was no direct proof that the Kimeses had committed a murder. The Kimeses's attorneys denied all charges. The strongest element of the defense was that no murder could be proven. There was no blood, no DNA evidence. The motive for the killing was not clear, and none could be proven. If there had been a scheme to defraud Silverman of her townhouse, her unexplained disappearance did not appear to be a logical part of such a scheme. Neither Sante nor Kenneth testified at the trial. Frequently they held hands, but were admonished by the judge to desist.

When prosecutors introduced testimony that Kenneth Kimes had been involved in a fraud in the Bahamas, both defense attorneys and prosecutors sought to separate the trial of Kenneth and Sante Kimes.

However, Judge Rena Uviller denied the motions.

Conviction, Sentencing, and Aftermath

After three months of lurid testimony, during which the mother and son became known as "grifters" in the press, the jury handed down verdicts on May 18, 2000. Kenneth Kimes was found guilty on 60 separate charges; Sante Kimes was convicted on 58 charges. On June 27, Judge Uviller pronounced sentences: 125 years, 4 months for Kenneth; 120 years, 8 months for Sante.

The case had many other strange twists, and took on a vigorous afterlife in print, television, and Internet media. Sante's older son, Kent Walker, published an account, *Son of a Grifter*, a year later, suggesting that his mother had sought to engage him in several of her schemes. Kenneth gave numerous interviews in prison, but at one point, he took a reporter hostage by holding a pen to her neck. He demanded that extradition proceedings against his mother be dropped in Los Angeles, as a conviction in that case would carry a death penalty. Guards finally wrestled the pen away from him and freed the reporter. Another book on the case, *Like Mother, Like Son: The Strange Story of Sante and Kenny Kimes*, was made into a film for television, starring Mary Tyler Moore. The film aired about one year after their conviction.

—*Rodney P. Carlisle*

Suggestions for Further Reading

Havill, Adrian. *The Mother, the Son, and the Socialite.* New York: St. Martin's Press, 2001.

McQuillan, Alice. *They Call Them Grifters: The True Story of Sante and Kenneth Kimes.* New York: New American Library, 2000.

Walker, Kent, and Mark Schone. *Son of a Grifter: The Twisted Tale of Sante and Kenneth Kimes, the Most Notorious Con Artists in America: A Memoir by the Other Son.* New York: William Morrow, 2001.

Sandy Murphy and Rick Tabish Trial: 2000

Defendants: Sandra "Sandy" Murphy, Richard B. "Rick" Tabish
Crime Charged: Murder, grand larceny, burglary
Chief Defense Lawyers: John Momot, Louis Palazzo
Chief Prosecutor: David Roger **Judge:** Joseph Bonaventure **Place:** Las Vegas, Nevada **Date of Trial:** March 27–May 18, 2000 (Appeal pending before Nevada Supreme Court) **Verdict:** Guilty **Sentence:** Life in prison with possibility of parole

SIGNIFICANCE

The outcome of this high-profile trial ultimately hinged on how jurors believed Ted Binion died. Did he commit suicide by a drug overdose or was he smothered to death after being forced to ingest heroin and Xanax by his live-in girlfriend and her cash-strapped secret lover? The publicity drenched case touched off a media frenzy outside the courtroom and fueled fears that unprecedented public relations ploys could influence what goes on inside a courtroom, especially when a jury is not sequestered.

For two years, the mysterious death of casino millionaire Lonnie "Ted" Binion and the subsequent trial of his former girlfriend Sandy Murphy and her lover Rick Tabish mesmerized Las Vegas. This bizarre story of lust, addiction, buried treasure, blackmail, greed, celebrity, murder—not to mention unprecedented public relations ploys outside the courtroom—burnished the glitzy gambling capital's worldwide reputation for tackiness.

During her murder trial, former exotic dancer Murphy, 27, would claim that when she left the mansion she shared with boyfriend Binion on the morning of September 18, 1998, he was sleeping off a heroin-induced stupor. Upon returning, she found the 55-year-old gambling mogul dead on the den floor. Distraught, she dialed 911.

Authorities arrested 34-year-old Rick Tabish and two alleged accomplices two days after Binion's death, as they were digging up 46,000 pounds of silver bars Binion had buried in a desert vault. Tabish told police that he was following

Binion's earlier instructions that the $7 million treasure be safeguarded for his teenage daughter Bonnie.

Sandy Murphy Becomes a Suspect

Sandy Murphy, who had lived with Binion for 3 and one-half stormy years before his death, was soon busy in civil court chasing what she claimed was her share of Binion's $50 million estate. Murphy was initially awarded a share, but the Binion estate appealed and that case went to the Nevada Supreme Court.

Sandy Murphy and Rick Tabish found guilty for the murder of gambling figure Ted Binion. (AP/Wide World Photos)

For months following Binion's death, Murphy appeared to be the emotionally overwrought girlfriend, devastated at finding her lover dead in their home. Intense media coverage, augmented by a public relations team, seemed to rally the public to her side. Chief Clark County Medical Examiner Lary Simms initially ruled that Binion had died of an accidental overdose of heroin and Xanax intoxication while suggesting suicide was a possibility. Binion had recently lost his gaming license because of his drug use and association with a mob figure.

None of this rang true for Binion's sister, Becky Behnen, who ran the family's Horseshoe Club. She hired a private investigator, Tom Dillard. Dillard dug up incriminating evidence against Murphy and Tabish, a debt-ridden Montana father of two fighting to save his contracting business, who Binion had befriended after a chance meeting in a Las Vegas motel bathroom. According to Dillard, the two had begun an affair behind Binion's back in the summer of 1998. Dillard further found that the day before his murder, Binion had cut Murphy out of his will. Right after Binion died Murphy and Tabish looted Binion's home of rare coins, silver and cash stashed in closets, pants pockets, and even in the engine compartment of a boat stored in his garage.

Based on Dillard's findings, a new theory emerged that the levels of heroin and Xanax in Binion's body were so lethal that he could only be a victim of a forced overdose. Police began to investigate the death as a homicide. Medical examiner Simms later concurred that Binion had been murdered.

On June 24, 1999, police arrested Murphy and the 34-year-old Tabish. They were charged with first-degree murder, grand larceny, and burglary.

During a 13-day preliminary hearing in September 1999, Chief Deputy District Attorney David Roger revealed a new theory to explain Binion's death: He was suffocated. The prosecution brought to the case a New York pathologist of national repute, Dr. Michael Baden, who also had testified in the well-publicized O.J. Simpson case. Baden testified that he believed the levels of heroin and Xanax in Binion's system were not enough to kill him, as the local medical examiner had concluded.

Baden, who had conducted more than 40,000 autopsies in his 40-year career, said congestion under Binion's eyelids and abrasions on his chest and back indicated he was suffocated in a nineteenth-century method called ''burking.'' This occurs when someone sits on the victim's chest while covering his mouth and nose. Prosecutors built their circumstantial case around Baden's testimony. They contended that when Binion's gardener had unexpectedly arrived at the mansion, Murphy and Tabish were forced to suffocate Binion instead of letting the lethal drug cocktail work.

The defense, not to be outdone, brought in a well-known Milwaukee attorney, James Shellow, specifically to demean and discredit Baden. This ploy may have backfired. News reports indicate that Shellow's abrasive style may have alienated jurors, some of whom appeared to bond with Baden.

The defense also called on a pathologist with a national reputation, Pittsburgh's Cyril Wecht, who took the stand to contradict the prosecution's chief medical witness. Wecht, calling on 43 years of experience, disputed Baden's findings point by point. He testified that the ruptured blood vessels under Binion's eyelids were linear in fashion, not circular, which meant Binion was not suffocated. He said the discolorations around the victim's mouth and nose were not a result of being smothered to death, but more likely were caused by shaving. The marks on his chest possibly occurred in attempts to revive him.

The Trial Attracts Publicity

During the six-week murder trial, which began March 27, 2000, more than 100 witnesses testified. The courtroom simmered with legal maneuvering: a discordant parade of character witnesses, conflicting testimony over who saw what where, and a dizzying array of physical evidence. (The Binion family had offered generous rewards for information leading to a conviction.) Reporters swarmed the courtroom, passing on every bizarre turn of the trial to an eager public.

But the real theatrics that caused television ratings to soar took place outside the courtroom. Binion's sister went on the television show *20/20* to declare that Murphy and Tabish murdered her brother. Defense lawyers John Momot and Louis Palazzo made regular appearances on national television shows, spinning the case as a good-versus-evil drama: the bullying Binion money machine versus the kind, loving girlfriend, twice raped as a teen. The defense also hired a public relations team, which ran unprecedented television ads soliciting public input. The team then publicized the poll results (more thought the defendants innocent than before the trial began), and backed a tacky public seance. As cameras rolled, 11 psychics tried to contact Binion. Did he take his life or was he murdered? Binion did not respond.

Although presiding Judge Joseph Bonaventure did issue a gag order during the trial, he never sequestered the jury. He said he wanted to save taxpayer money in the $7,400-per-day trial.

Despite unprecedented publicity, the trial ultimately turned on the conflicting testimony of the famous and handsomely compensated medical experts. The jury evidently believed Baden. Jurors deliberated eight days before finding both Murphy and Tabish guilty of first-degree murder, on May 18, 2000. They were sentenced to life with the possibility of parole—for Murphy after serving a minimum of 22 years and for Tabish after 25 years.

In a companion case that unfolded during the Binion murder saga, Tabish's alleged accomplice David Mattsen and his business partner Michael Milot were tried and sentenced on charges of burglary, grand larceny, and conspiracy in the theft of the silver bars that Binion had buried. (Authorities had arrested Mattsen and Milot as they helped Tabish unearth the loot.)

Two other men, Steven Wadkins and John B. Joseph, eventually pleaded no contest to charges of conspiring to commit extortion, which stemmed from their assisting Tabish in torturing the owner of a sand pit tied to Tabish's contracting business to force the man to turn over his interest in the pit. They were sentenced to 200 hours community service or $2,000 fines.

Also, David Mattsen was found not guilty in federal court on 11 unrelated firearms charges a month before the Murphy-Tabish trial began.

Ruling on the appeal of the contested will, the Nevada Supreme Court ruled on October 9, 2000, that Binion had legally cut Murphy out of his will the day before he died.

The final roll of dice in this Las Vegas-style trial has yet to take place. On October 12, 2000 the defense team filed notice of appeal. It is expected that the Nevada Supreme Court will not act on the murder case before 2002.

—*B.J. Welborn*

Suggestions for Further Reading

Barandes, Laura. "Binion Jurors Hand Down Life with Possibility of Parole." *Court TV Online* (May 24, 2000).

German, Jeff. "Analysis: Binion Murder Case Being Fought on Five Fronts." *Las Vegas Sun Online* (October 14, 1999).

German, Jeff. "Sides Are Ready for Long-Awaited Start of Binion Murder Case." *Las Vegas Sun Online* (March 30, 2000).

Macy, Robert. "Jury Finds Pair Guilty in Death of Well-Known Gambler." *Associated Press Online* (May 19, 2000).

Smith, Kim. "Judge Gavels an End to Ted Binion Murder Trail." *Las Vegas Sun Online* (October 6, 2000).

Ray Lewis Trial: 2000

Defendant: Ray Lewis **Crimes Charged:** Murder, assault with a deadly weapon **Defense Lawyers:** Ed Garland, Jana Harris, Max Richardson **Prosecutor:** Paul Howard **Judge:** Alice D. Bonner **Place:** Atlanta, Georgia **Dates of Trial:** May–June 2000 **Verdict:** Guilty of obstruction of justice; other charges dropped

SIGNIFICANCE

The arrest of Ray Lewis, a National Football League (NFL) linebacker with the Baltimore Ravens, on murder charges, coming just weeks after the indictment of another professional football player, Rae Carruth of the Carolina Panthers, on first-degree murder charges, focussed national attention on the issue of violence by professional athletes.

Ray Lewis grew up in Lakeland, Florida, and played football for the University of Miami. He left after his junior year and was selected by Baltimore in the first round of the 1996 draft. He led the Ravens in tackles each of his four seasons, and led the league in tackles in 1997 and 1999. In 1998 he signed a four-year contract extension with the Ravens for $26 million, making him the highest paid middle linebacker in the National Football League.

Victims Stabbed during Brawl

At the end of January 2000, Lewis traveled from Baltimore to Atlanta, Georgia, in a Lincoln Navigator stretch limousine to participate in various activities associated with Super Bowl 2000, in which the St. Louis Rams defeated the Tennessee Titans. On the evening of January 30, Lewis and a number of friends engaged in post-game celebrations, which took them in the early hours of the next morning to a nightclub called the Cobalt Lounge in the Buckhead neighborhood of Atlanta. There were arguments inside the club between members of Lewis's party and other patrons, and these continued in the parking lot as they were leaving. A brawl began when Reginald Oakley, an old friend of Ray Lewis, was hit on the head with a champagne bottle by Jacinth Baker, a 21-year-old man from Decatur, Georgia. In the fight Baker and Richard Lollar, aged 24, also from Decatur, were stabbed to death. The Fulton County medical examiner was later to give the opinion that they must have been stabbed by someone with a knowledge of anatomy, because the wounds were directly to vital organs, causing them to bleed to death very quickly.

Lewis fled from the scene in his limousine, along with some 11 others, including Reginald Oakley and another old friend, Joseph Sweeting, both of Miami. Witnesses reported that some five shots were fired as the limousine left, but it was unclear whether they were fired from the vehicle, or at it. Police found the limousine a few hours later, parked behind the hotel in which Lewis was staying. He was arrested on suspicion of first-degree murder and held without bail. Sweeting and Oakley had disappeared. Within hours Max Richardson, an attorney representing Lewis, issued a statement denying any direct involvement in the deaths and claiming that it was just a case of a well-known public figure being in the wrong place at the wrong time.

The Case Against Ray Lewis

On February 2 the lead role in Lewis's defense was taken over by Ed Garland of Atlanta, described in the press as "a noted criminal lawyer who is known in the region for a certain flamboyance while representing the rich and famous." On February 7 Atlanta police searched Lewis's Baltimore home, and on February 10 there was a news conference given by Atlanta deputy police chief Carter Jackson and Fulton County district attorney Paul Howard, at which they gave the details of the case as they saw it. Reginald Oakley and Joseph Sweeting were also principal suspects in the murder. Both had extensive criminal records, were still fugitives, and were considered armed and dangerous. The authorities said Lewis and two acquaintances had purchased knives at an Atlanta sporting goods store on January 29. Howard stated that witnesses would testify that Lewis had been active in the brawl. The chief prosecution witness would be the driver of the limousine, Duane Fassett. Two days later Lewis was indicted by a grand jury and charged with two counts of malicious murder, two counts of felonious murder, and two counts of assault with a deadly weapon.

Baltimore Ravens linebacker Ray Lewis listens to testimony during his murder trial. (AP/Wide World Photos)

The next day Ed Garland gave the defense's version of the incident, claiming that Lewis had attempted to be a peacemaker in the brawl and to break up the fight, trying to pull his acquaintances away. The shots that were fired were aimed at the limousine as it left.

On February 14 Joseph Sweeting turned himself into police, and Reginald Oakley did so the following day. That same day Lewis was released on $1 million bail, ordered to stay in his Maryland home, and to use no alcohol or drugs.

The case was assigned to Fulton County Superior Court judge Alice D. Bonner, and Lewis formally entered a not guilty plea. In pretrial motions Judge Bonner ruled that the results of the search of Lewis's home could be used in the trial, but that previous allegations of assault could not. Twice during Ray Lewis's college days Coral Gables police had investigated Lewis following allegations of battery made by different girlfriends, but no charges were brought. In November 1999 a woman had brought second-degree assault charges against Lewis, alleging that he had punched her in the face during an incident at a Baltimore area nightclub. These charges were dropped in late March 2000 because of conflicting testimony from witnesses.

Prosecution's Murder Case Collapses

Jury selection for the trial began on May 15. Before opening statements were made Judge Bonner ruled that a statement given to police by Ray Lewis after the incident, and now acknowledged to be false, could be introduced in evidence against him. The prosecution, led by Fulton County district attorney Paul Howard, began the presentation of its case on May 27. Howard acknowledged that no witness would testify to having seen Ray Lewis with a knife, but that the testimony would show involvement in the fighting that resulted in the deaths of Jacinth Baker and Richard Lollar. The defense emphasized that no witnesses saw any of the three defendants with a knife, that two men known to have fled in the limousine had never been traced, and that defense witnesses would contradict the testimony of Duane Fassett, the limousine driver and chief prosecution witness. Lewis, the defense would argue, was only trying to stop the fight.

In the second week of the trial the prosecution case was weakened when four of its witnesses failed to identify Lewis as an aggressor in the fight, and it disintegrated when Duane Fassett took the stand. In a statement to police Fassett had said that he saw Lewis punch one of the victims, and that in the limousine as it left he had heard Oakley say, "I stabbed mine" and heard Sweeting reply, "I stabbed mine too." But on the witness stand Fassett said that he had never seen Lewis throw a punch, and that he appeared to be trying to break up the fight. To the surprise of legal observers, District Attorney Howard didn't even attempt to impeach the witness by confronting him with his earlier statement.

Murder and Assault Charges Dropped

On Monday, June 5 the prosecution dropped the murder and assault charges against Lewis, in return for his agreeing to plead guilty to a misdemeanor (obstruction of justice) for making false, incomplete, and misleading statements to police after his arrest, and to testify against his codefendants. Lewis was given one year's probation, during which he was to continue to be employed; ordered to pay one-third of the court costs; and forbidden to use drugs or alcohol during the period of his probation.

In testimony the following day, Lewis told the court that Sweeting had shown him afterwards how he had concealed the knife in his fist and jabbed with it, but that he could not tell whether either Sweeting or Oakley had stabbed anyone. Oakley, he said, had been the aggressor in the fight. He had seen no blood on Sweeting's knife or clothing. The jury acquitted both men on June 12.

District Attorney Howard expressed his disappointment that the evidence given in court by several prosecution witnesses differed from their statements to police. But legal observers noted that Howard may have made strategic errors: by pursuing a quick indictment he had circumvented a preliminary hearing, which might have revealed the prosecution's strategy, but this had enabled the defense to demand a speedy trial, which the prosecution seemed unprepared for. Moreover, Paul Howard had not tried a case in four years and was in the middle of a reelection campaign. The anticipated media attention the trial would receive was seen by many as a factor in Howard's decision to personally lead the prosecution team.

Ray Lewis was fined $250,000 by the National Football League for lying to the police, but resumed his successful career as a football player, helped lead the Ravens to victory in the 2001 Super Bowl, and won the game's Most Valuable Player Award.

—David I. Petts

Suggestions for Further Reading

New York Times, Atlanta Constitution (February-June, 2000).

Edmund Ko Trial: 2000

Defendant: Edmund Ko **Crime Charged:** Murder
Chief Defense Lawyer: Jack Litman **Chief Prosecutors:** Ann Prunty, Lisa
Friel **Judge:** Harold B. Beeler **Place:** New York, New York
Date of Trial: May 31–July 27, 2000 **Verdict:** Guilty **Sentence:** 25 years
to life

SIGNIFICANCE

The right to silence is enshrined in the American constitution. Here, two individuals availed themselves of this right, with drastically different outcomes.

When Edmund Ko split up with his girlfriend Hyesung Lynda Hong in 1997, the break was amicable, good-natured even. The three-year romance that had blossomed in their graduate days at Cornell University had run its course, and it was now time to move on. For Ko this meant a slot on the executive training program at Macy's department store, valuable preparation for when he took over his family's multimillion-dollar leather goods business in Korea; while Hong pursued her career dreams at Columbia Law School.

Hong was an excellent student with a big future, but it never came to pass. On March 20, 1998, a close friend, baffled by Hong's unusual telephone silence, called at her Morningside Heights apartment. Unable to get an answer he picked the lock. What he found inside the blood-spattered apartment was the stuff of slasher movies.

Within 24 hours Ko was arrested and later charged with murder.

When the trial finally came to court on May 31, 2000, Assistant District Attorney Ann Prunty painted a lurid picture of Hong's death. "Her body was cold, stiff and hard; dried blood marked her bed, her carpet, her clothes . . . [Ko] carried out a cold-blooded and premeditated murder by slitting her throat from one side to the other."

If that were not enough, over strident defense objections, Prunty then played a harrowing police video of the crime scene that showed Hong, lying face down on the floor of her apartment, amidst blood-drenched textbooks and papers. "The crime scene alone will prove to you that Edmund Ko killed her," said Prunty.

Jealous Rival

In reply, chief defense lawyer Jack Litman urged the jury to "scrutinize this case . . . [because] we believe the wrong person has been arrested." The real killer, according to Litman, was Ko's "pathologically" jealous current girlfriend, Claudia Seong, a 33-year-old aspiring fashion designer. "Claudia Seong was making all the rules," said Litman. "She wanted Lynda Hong dead. When she learned that Hong had called her a prostitute, she sought revenge."

Litman alleged Seong had ordered a henchman, Jae Young Shin, to murder Hong. Certainly, Shin had been untruthful when questioned by police officers shortly after the murder, and then, when the investigation became more heated, he had fled to his native Korea in November 1998.

While Prunty didn't dispute Seong's hold over Ko, she poured cold water on defense claims that he was merely an innocent pawn of this scheming, older woman. At the time of his arrest, Ko had already been bailed out of jail for his part in yet another sadistic attack on an ex-girlfriend. Diane Kim told the court how, just months before Hong's murder, she had herself been held down by Ko and Seong's sister, while Seong, in a jealous frenzy, slashed her across the face, legs and head.

Poignant testimony came from Hong's best friend, Se Ok, who described talking on the phone to Hong just minutes before her alleged time of death, only for Hong to abruptly terminate the call by saying, "It's Ed [at the door] I have to go."

Litman said Ko didn't deny being at Hong's apartment that night, but "he didn't kill her. He spoke to her. He left in about half-an-hour."

In this sketch Edmund Ko listens in court during his murder trial. (AP/Wide World Photos)

When they had first charged Ko, the district attorney's office had trumpeted the fact that a bloodstained knife had been found at his parents' home. Now Prunty revealed an abrupt change of prosecutorial heart, saying, "We will not be offering [into evidence] the knives recovered from his parents' apartment," admitting that no murder weapon had been found.

The reason for this U-turn became clear when Nagy Bekhit, a fingerprint expert, testified. He admitted that he might have accidentally contaminated the knife with blood from other evidence samples. Asked by Prunty if he could have used the same brush on the knives that he had used to dust the bloodied papers, Bekhit said, "Maybe." The witness explained that he did not always clean or change brushes after using them to dust an item for fingerprints.

"Could you have transferred dried blood from one item to another?" Prunty asked.

"It's a possibility," Bekhit admitted.

All of which was meat and drink to Litman, who seized upon Bekhit's admission as further evidence that Ko had been the victim of a conspiracy, in which the police and the FBI had planted blood and hair evidence to bolster their flabby case.

Litman had far less success explaining away a bloodstained black sweatshirt found next to Hong's body. It was identified as belonging to Ko.

Ominous Silence

Ordinarily the high-point of a major trial comes when the defendant takes the stand, but on this occasion Ko chose to exercise his right to silence, leaving Claudia Seong to take center stage: except that the jury never got to hear what she said—or rather didn't say. In the early days of the investigation, Seong had cooperated with police, claiming that Ko had confessed the murder to her, even brandishing Hong's wallet as a crime scene trophy. But when a grand jury began investigating her own involvement—if any—in the death of Lynda Hong, Seong had suddenly clammed up.

Anxious to safeguard Seong's interests in light of any subsequent charges, Judge Harold Beeler ruled she could only be questioned out of the jury's hearing. Litman was furious. Beeler rejected his pleas to have jurors present, saying Seong's already well-reported reticence would not help jurors to decide the current case and could "create the impression" that Seong was guilty of the crime.

Diminutive and dressed in black, Seong proved to be as difficult as anticipated, parrying everything counsel threw at her.

"Did you falsely incriminate Edmund Ko to the police to shift the blame away from yourself in the murder of Lynda Hong?" demanded Litman.

In a whisper, Seong replied, "I take the Fifth Amendment," invoking her right against self-incrimination. When Litman accused her of having conspired with Jae Young Shin to murder Hong, she again took the Fifth; and again when Litman pushed her on allegations that she had become "enraged at Lynda Hong" for calling Seong "a prostitute."

Prunty fared no better. She wanted to know about Ko's alleged confession, and whether Seong was living with Ko and intending to marry him at the time of the killing. Again and again Seong fell back on the protection of the Fifth Amendment. It was a ploy she used no fewer than 37 times before stepping down from the stand.

What bearing Seong's testimony might have had on the trial's outcome had the jury been present is unknowable: what is certain is that on July 27 they convicted Ko of second-degree murder.

On October 16, 2000, following an emotion-packed hearing at which the deceased's relatives hurled invective at Ko, Judge Beeler said he was imposing the maximum sentence because the murder was a display of "great heinousness and depravity . . . This young woman was a remarkable person for many, many people . . . a shining light . . . He extinguished her life without any reason."

Ko received a prison term of 25 years to life.

—Colin Evans

Suggestions for Further Reading

New York Times. See Hong, Hyesung Lynda, in the *New York Times Index* (June 1–July 28, 2000).

Senior, Jennifer. *New York Magazine* (June 1, 1998).

David Brock Impeachment Trial: 2000

Defendant: David Brock **Crime Charged:** Four articles of impeachment
Chief Defense Lawyers: David Barry, Michael Madigan
Chief Prosecutor: Joseph Steinfield **Judges:** The Senate of the State of
New Hampshire **Place:** Concord, New Hampshire
Date of Trial: September 18–October 10, 2000 **Verdict:** Not guilty

SIGNIFICANCE

This was the first impeachment trial of a chief justice of a state supreme court in U.S. history. The only other New Hampshire state official ever impeached was Supreme Court judge Woodbury Langdon, who in 1790 was described as "arbitrary and haughty" and was charged with failing to appear in court. He resigned rather than face a Senate trial. The impeachment process raised two questions: when is it appropriate for a legislature to intervene in court procedures, and when does such intervention constitute a violation of the separation of powers? As a result of this impeachment trial, the New Hampshire Supreme Court revised its Code of Judicial Conduct to set standards for determining the appearance of impropriety.

Early in 2000, the New Hampshire Supreme Court faced an unusual situation: It had to consider the appeal of a divorce decision by the ex-wife of one of its members, Stephen Thayer. In a court meeting on February 4, Chief Justice David Brock announced his appointments of substitute justices to stand in for those who had to recuse themselves because they knew both parties to the appeal. Justice Thayer objected strenuously to one of the appointments.

Court Clerk Howard Zibel, knowing it was a violation of court procedures for a judge to discuss a case involving a fellow judge when the fellow judge was present, reported the incident in a memo to state attorney general Philip McLaughlin. The resulting investigation led to Thayer's resignation from the bench in March and to McLaughlin's alleging to the state's House Judiciary Committee that other violations of ethics had been committed by members of the court.

The Chief Justice Impeached

The committee interviewed witnesses and debated whether to recommend impeachment of three justices, then decided to bring articles of impeachment only against the chief justice. Following seven hours of debate, the House voted 253–95 for the Senate to try Chief Justice Brock on four articles of impeachment:

Article I. Seeking to influence a case by improperly phoning a lower-court judge in 1987 and failing to report the call to his colleagues who were considering the case's appeal.

New Hampshire Supreme Court justices (left to right), S. Horton, J. Broderick, W. Batchelder, W. Johnson, and Chief David Brock. (AP/Wide World Photos)

Article II. Engaging in communications with fellow justices, all of whom had been recused, regarding judges to be appointed to hear the divorce appeal of a fellow justice, and discussing the selection of judges, outside the presence of fellow justices, with the justice whose appeal was pending.

Article III. Improperly permitting justices to comment on cases from which they had recused themselves because of conflicts of interest. (This article, while not originated by the Judiciary Committee, was adopted on the House floor.)

Article IV. Lying under oath to the House Judiciary Committee during the investigations of these matters.

Before the trial could begin, the Senate, never having held an impeachment trial, had to set its own rules. It voted on August 22 to require a two-thirds vote for conviction. Since two of its 24 members were disqualifying themselves, a guilty verdict would require at least 15 votes.

As the trial opened on September 18, prosecutor Joseph Steinfield promised that Article I would prove to be "a case of someone being given special treatment." The defense attorney, Michael Madigan, noting that a key witness had said he could be wrong, contended, "We're going to impeach a man on a maybe?" Madigan pointed out that the constitutional grounds for impeachment—bribery, corruption, malpractice, and maladministration—demanded evil intent or personal gain as motives. Those grounds, he insisted, were not evident.

Testimony on Article I

Prosecution witness Clerk Zibel reviewed a memo he wrote to then-justice David Souter in May 1987. It concerned an appeal from a lower-court ruling by then-Senate majority leader Edward Dupont, whose fuel company had been sued in a contract dispute by a competitor, Home Gas. The memo alleged that Chief Justice Brock had made an improper call to Superior Court Judge Douglas Gray to discuss the case.

The prosecution added that investigators found that Brock's call was to remind Gray that Senator Dupont could help pass a bill to raise judges' salaries.

While Brock contended that Gray called him, Gray testified he "never, ever, period" initiated the call and "I think it was a lapse in ethics." But he added, "Is David Brock unethical? No."

Gray also said that, while at the time he thought the call unusual, he did not consider it improper but had changed his mind since then.

Superior Court Judge Kenneth McHugh then testified that Gray told him about the call from Brock just after it occurred.

On the stand himself, Brock said, "I didn't call Judge Gray. Absolutely not." He did admit calling the court clerk about the case's status, but said such calls, while "fraught with risk," were part of his job as administrator of the court.

Testimony on Article II

Testifying for the prosecution, former justice Thayer said Brock permitted him to influence the selection of judges for his own divorce appeal. Defense attorney Madigan urged him to admit he was angry with Brock and the court clerk for filing a report that ended his career. "You're trying to build up this vindictive thing," responded Thayer, insisting Brock was a trusted friend.

Thayer then supported the prosecution by testifying that the chief justice invited his reaction by announcing his choices for the divorce appeals panel and then speaking privately with him about them. He said he blurted out an objection to one judge only when Brock asked him what he thought.

Brock's testimony countered, "When I made that announcement, I had no expectation anyone was going to respond. I was shocked by that." But, he added, "Justice Thayer immediately pushed down the arm rails of his chair, he jumped halfway up and yelled, 'No, no, you can't do that.'"

Testimony on Article III

On the charge that Brock routinely permitted judges to comment on cases from which they were disqualified, retired Supreme Court Justice William Johnson was the key witness. He admitted himself using suggestions from disqualified judges when writing his opinions, defending the long-standing practice and countering a judicial ethics expert who criticized it.

Testimony on Article IV

Questioned on the stand about whether he lied to the House investigators when asked about certain documents, Brock said he found the questions of House attorney Steinfield confusing. He added that, before appearing for his interview by the House Judiciary Committee, he had been warned by his lawyer not to violate court confidentiality. He said he gave copies to his attorney in April, skimmed them before his interview, but was reluctant to discuss them because of the confidentiality. "I guess looking back you could say my answers weren't complete," he admitted, "but they were truthful and not intended to mislead. I did the best I could at the time. I never intentionally misled the House Judiciary Committee in its investigation."

The Senate Votes Acquittal

Over five hours, 17 of the 22 senators made statements of their opinions on whether the charges were serious enough to warrant impeachment or the evidence was persuasive enough. Then, on October 10, they voted acquittal: 18–4 on Article I; 17–5 on Article II; 18–4 on Article III; and 14–8 on Article IV.

On October 12, Chief Justice Brock, who had been temporarily replaced during the impeachment and trial, returned to the bench of the New Hampshire Supreme Court.

—Bernard Ryan, Jr.

Suggestions for Further Reading

Tebo, Margaret Graham. "Equal Justice: New Hampshire Case Highlights Ongoing Problems of Gender Bias in the Courts." *American Bar Association Journal* (September 2000).

Robert Bierenbaum Trial: 2000

Defendant: Robert Bierenbaum   **Crime Charged:** Murder
Chief Defense Lawyers: Scott Greenfield, David Lewis
Chief Prosecutor: Daniel Bibb   **Judge:** Leslie Crocker Snyder
Place: Manhattan, New York   **Date of Trial:** October 2–24, 2000
Verdict: Guilty   **Sentence:** 20 years to life

SIGNIFICANCE

Fourteen years after the disappearance of his wife, a prominent New York City doctor was tried and convicted for her murder, although her body was never found.

D r. Robert Bierenbaum moved after his wife's July 7, 1985, disappearance from their New York City apartment—first to Reno, Nevada, in 1989, and then in 1996, to Minot, North Dakota. Fourteen years later prosecutors would charge that Bierenbaum had murdered Gail Katz Bierenbaum, packaged her body, and then dumped it from a Cessna 172, flying over the Atlantic Ocean somewhere between Montauk, New York, and Cape May, New Jersey.

After Gail vanished, her husband told police that she had left their apartment on East 85th Street in Manhattan following a fight, stating she was going to Central Park to calm down. A friend would later testify that Bierenbaum had speculated that his wife had been abducted or murdered by drug dealers with whom she was acquainted. As all their friends knew—and Bierenbaum acknowledged then and would later—their relationship had been a troubled one.

In Nevada and in North Dakota, by all accounts, Bierenbaum led an exemplary life. His medical practice flourished and, from 1990 on, he frequently flew his own plane to El Fuerte, Mexico, to perform free reconstructive surgery on poor children with cleft palates. He remarried and his new wife, Dr. Janet A. Chollet-Bierenbaum, praised him as a caring and loving husband. Friends believed that the first time around he simply had had the misfortune to marry a tormented, manipulative, and suicidal woman.

Growing Suspicions

Police investigators and Alayne Katz, Gail's sister, never bought into the picture of Robert Bierenbaum as a put-upon husband. They suspected him of murder from the beginning, even if there wasn't much evidence or even a corpse. Immediately after Gail's disappearance, Alayne launched a campaign against him, writing letters to his New York neighbors and to hospitals where he worked, and would take credit for driving him from New York. In 1989, she believed that a female torso washed ashore on Staten Island was that of her dead sister. However, in 1997, when Alayne and her brother Steven had the body exhumed, a DNA test revealed the body was not Gail's.

Alayne told reporters that her sister had confided to her that Bierenbaum once dunked her cat in a toilet boil and was often violent. Indeed, on November 12, 1983, Gail had filed a police report claiming that her husband had choked her until she lost consciousness. Later, police investigators traveled to Las Vegas where they questioned acquaintances of Bierenbaum, some of whom fed their suspicions with hearsay comments. But what finally convinced police and prosecutors they had enough evidence to make a murder case was what Bierenbaum hadn't told them—that he had taken an airplane out for a two-hour flight on the day his wife disappeared. Moreover, although airport records later verified the trip, it appeared he had attempted to alter the flight log. Brought back from North Dakota, Bierenbaum was arraigned in New York City on December 8, 1999, and freed on bail to await trial.

The Trial

When the trial opened on October 2, 2000, the press was focused on how the prosecutors would solve the problem of the "missing body." Basically, the law demands that the prosecution of any crime must pass the *corpus delecti* test, which refers to the "body of the crime," not a human corpse,

Dr. Robert Bierenbaum and his wife Janet leave court during his trial for the murder of his first wife Gail. (AP/Wide World Photos)

proving that the crime actually took place. Normally, the prosecution does base a murder case on a dead body, or on other physical evidence, but legal history is replete with murder convictions won by prosecutors who built the "body of the crime" without such traces, effectively demonstrating that a crime had taken place by circumstantial evidence. Although there are always obstacles to such a presentation, the prosecution built that argument brick-by-brick in the Bierenbaum case.

Without any trace of her corpse, prosecutors had to prove that there had been no sign of Gail Bierenbaum's existence since the date of her disappearance. That required testimony from friends and family members who claimed not to have heard from Gail since she disappeared. Investigators also explained how they had combed through records across the United States without finding any trace of her. There had been no subsequent activity in her bank, credit card, or Social Security accounts.

Prosecutors also had to present a theory of the case illustrating the circumstances under which the murder could have happened and explaining what the defendant's motive might have been, including evidence of a troubled relationship. Gail Bierenbaum had had affairs with at least two men and had separated more than once from her husband. The prosecution claimed that on the weekend of her disappearance she intended to tell her husband that she was leaving permanently for another man.

Prosecutor Daniel Bibb claimed that Bierenbaum had strangled his wife after she told him she was ending the marriage. The prosecution contended he then placed her body in a duffel bag and put it in the trunk of his father's Cadillac. Next, according to Bibb, he drove to the Essex County Airport in Fairfield, New Jersey, where he rented a plane, flew out, low over the ocean, and disposed of the body. A police reenactment was videotaped and shown to the jury, demonstrating how bags could be dumped from an identical airplane.

The prosecution showed that Bierenbaum had lied repeatedly and had given conflicting versions of specific events. For example, Bierenbaum had falsely claimed that a private detective had spotted his wife as a waitress in a California resort after her disappearance. Another lie was that Gail's psychotherapist, Dr. Sybil Baran, had told him his wife was suicidal. Dr. Baran testified that she had never reported such a thing. Baran also noted that Gail had gone apartment hunting and had bought birth control devices just before she disappeared, hardly the acts of someone contemplating suicide.

But the most damning lie was one of omission—that Bierenbaum had never disclosed to the police a two-hour flight on the day his wife disappeared and then had apparently attempted to cover up the flight by altering the log.

Three psychiatrists had warned Gail Bierenbaum that her husband was homicidal, but Judge Leslie Snyder ruled that they could not testify because of patient confidentiality. The judge said she was distressed that she had to exclude testimony of the three psychiatrists who were impressed by the danger posed by the defendant, but that she had to balance that against the protections afforded by the law to patient-doctor relationships. Prosecutors argued that Dr. Bierenbaum had waived his right to confidentiality by allowing his own psychiatrists to speak about his treatment with his parents and his wife. However, two groups opposing the testimony, the New York State Psychiatric Association and the American Psychoanalytic Association, argued in a brief that the waiver of confidentiality that allows psychiatrists to warn third parties of potential harm by a patient ends when that threat ends. The "goal of warning," argued the attorney for the psychiatric association, "is to protect people, not to prosecute them." Therapists feared that use of such evidence in court would discourage patients from sharing feelings of violence in the future.

The defense strategy was based on shooting holes in the prosecution case, rather than risk putting Bierenbaum on the stand to testify in his own defense. Defense attorney David Lewis claimed the prosecution's case was based entirely on guesswork. There were no eyewitnesses and no physical evidence. Lewis admitted that Gail's disappearance with no trace did suggest she was dead, but he claimed no one could possibly know how she died. The defense also pointed to her risky behavior, including her love affairs with drug users. Under the defense's theory of the case, Gail's many threats to leave her husband suggested she might have done so and then met with foul play. Moreover, the defense argued that she had a background of erratic behavior and had once attempted suicide.

After two weeks of testimony and two days of deliberation, on October 24, the jury found Bierenbaum guilty of second-degree murder. State sentencing rules called for a minimum sentence of 15 years to life and a maximum of 25 years to life. On November 30, 2000, Judge Snyder sentenced Bierenbaum to 20 years to life. Bierenbaum's appeal is pending.

— Rodney Carlisle

Suggestions for Further Reading

De Paulo, Lisa. "Intimations of Murder." *Vanity Fair* (September 2000): 148.

Friend, Tad. "Letters from Las Vegas: The Harriet-the-Spy-Club." *The New Yorker* (July 31, 2000): 36.

LAPD Rampart Division Trial: 2000

Defendants: Michael Buchanan, Paul Harper, Brian Liddy, Edward Ortiz
Crimes Charged: Conspiracy to obstruct justice, filing false police reports, lying under oath   **Chief Defense Lawyers:** Harland Braun (Buchanan), Joel Isaacson (Harper), Paul DePasquale (Liddy), Barry Levin (Ortiz)
Chief Prosecutors: Laura Laesecke, Anne Ingalls   **Judge:** Jacqueline Conner   **Place:** Los Angeles, California   **Date of Trial:** October 4– November 15, 2000   **Verdicts:** Harper: not guilty on all charges; Buchanan: guilty of conspiracy to obstruct justice and of two counts of perjury; not guilty on the other charges; Liddy and Ortiz: guilty of conspiracy to obstruct justice and of filing false police reports; not guilty on the other charges
Sentences: None. On December 22, 2000, Judge Conner overturned the convictions on the basis of jury misconduct. As of March, 2001, her decision is under appeal

SIGNIFICANCE

The arrest in 1996 of a crooked cop who was assigned to the Los Angeles Police Department's (LAPD) Rampart station led to one of the largest police scandals in American history. It also served to confirm the belief of many who feel that the entire LAPD is corrupt and can't be trusted.

Rampart is an eight-square mile area in Los Angeles west of the city's downtown core. Densely populated, it is home to approximately 375,000 residents, most of whom are working class immigrants or members of a racial minority. Rampart is also one of the busiest and most dangerous beats for the Los Angeles Police. However, not all of the officers who patrol the area play by the book.

A Crooked Cop's Arrest Opens the Floodgates

During the 1980s, gang violence dramatically rose in Los Angeles. Various factors caused this problem, including high unemployment, a dramatic increase in rent and other living expenses, cutbacks in education and health care, and a 40 percent poverty rate among the city's youth. To combat the violence, the

LAPD formed anti-gang units at each of its divisions, including the one in Rampart. These units were known as CRASH (Community Resources Against Street Hoodlums). The officers assigned to CRASH were to be the elite of the city's police force.

In 1996 Rafael Perez, a six-year veteran of the Los Angeles Police, joined the Rampart Division's CRASH unit. However, he was arrested two years later for stealing eight pounds of cocaine (worth approximately $1 million) from the Rampart station's evidence locker. On September 15, 1999, Perez pleaded guilty to the charge. In exchange for a reduced sentence and immunity for other crimes he participated in, Perez agreed to help investigators uncover widespread abuse in the Los Angeles Police Department's CRASH units.

Perez admitted to witnessing or participating in unjustified arrests, shootings, and beatings of suspects. He also claimed to have seen or taken part in the planting of drugs, guns, and other evidence on suspects, filing false police reports, witness intimidation, and giving false testimony in court to obtain convictions. Perez indicated that he and his partner, Nino Durden, framed up to 99 people for crimes that they did not commit. He also said that 75 percent of the convictions arising from the arrests by the Rampart Division's CRASH unit were tainted by police misconduct. Furthermore, according to Perez, such abuses happened not just at the Rampart Division, but at all of the CRASH units and that up to 90 percent of the officers assigned to CRASH were involved. (Indeed, the investigators quickly expanded their scope to look into the actions of the other LAPD divisions.)

According to Perez, he and the others who broke the law did so to wipe out gang violence in the city's toughest neighborhoods. "What we did was wrong" he admitted, but "we were out there fighting a war. . . . We felt that in our own way we saved lives." In one court hearing, Perez testified that "our mentality was, it's us against them. . . . They didn't play fair, so we didn't play fair. . . . One way or another, we were going to get the Rampart crime rate down."

During the next 18 months, over 100 criminal convictions were overturned and several people were released from prison on the grounds that, according to Perez' allegations, they did not commit the crimes that they were convicted of. (Some experts predict that, in the end, up to 30,000 other convictions may have to be reexamined and that the entire process will take years and millions of dollars to complete.) In addition, the city of Los Angeles agreed in November 2000 to pay $15 million to Javier Francisco Ovando for being unjustifiably shot and then falsely accused by Perez and Durden of assaulting a police officer. (Ovando was sentenced to 23 years imprisonment for that alleged crime and he served 30 months before his conviction was overturned.) That same month, the Los Angeles City Attorney's office agreed to pay $10.9 million to 29 other people who had been falsely imprisoned for up to three years because of tainted evidence or perjured testimony from officers in the LAPD's Rampart Division. As of the end of 2000, 64 other lawsuits had been filed related to the scandal, more were being prepared, and up to 200 others are expected. Estimates of the eventual total of civil damages against the city go as high as $200 million.

Perez's revelations also raised the possibility that civil actions in federal court may be brought against the city of Los Angeles and the Los Angeles Police. On August 29, 2000, a U.S. District Court judge ruled that people whose civil rights have been violated by officers at the Rampart Division could sue the LAPD under the federal Racketeer Influenced and Corrupt Organizations (RICO) Act. One month later, the city agreed to allow the U.S. Department of Justice to review the LAPD's administration, training, and street operations for five years in order to avoid a lawsuit by the federal government against the Los Angeles Police for civil rights abuses and police wrongdoing.

Indictments and Trials for Only a Handful

In addition, over 70 officers have been investigated as a result of the scandal and dozens have been fired, suspended, or have resigned. However, as of mid-2001, only eight have been indicted. Critics have charged that the District Attorney's Office has not acted quickly enough to bring the rogue officers to justice and these allegations played a large role in District Attorney Gil Garcetti's defeat for reelection in 2000.

Of the eight, Manuel Chavez has pleaded no contest to assault while Shawn Gomez entered the same plea to a charge of filing a false police report. Perez's former partner, Nino Durden, entered into an agreement whereby he pleaded guilty to six felonies, including obstruction of justice, perjury, and filing a false police report. This plea was in exchange for the dismissal of a charge of attempted murder and Durden's promise to cooperate with the authorities in their investigation of other officers. (Durden has since been sentenced to seven years and eight months in prison for those six charges.) Ethan Cohan pleaded not guilty on March 28, 2001, to charges of attacking a suspect and then trying to cover it; he is currently awaiting trial.

The remaining four officers (Michael Buchanan, Paul Harper, Brian Liddy, and Edward Ortiz) all pleaded not guilty to charges of unjustifiably shooting suspects, planting evidence, filing false police reports, and perjury. The charges specifically dealt with the alleged planting of a gun on a reputed gang member, Allan Lobos, in April 1996 and of a conspiracy to falsely arrest two gang members, Cesar Natividad and Raul Munoz, in July 1996, for an alleged assault on Buchanan and Liddy. The four officers were tried jointly in Los Angeles before California Superior Court judge Jacqueline Conner, a jurist who is regarded by some local commentators as pro-police. The trial began on October 4, 2000.

During the following month, 27 people testified for the prosecution. In contrast, the only defense witnesses were the defendants themselves and an accident reconstruction expert. Most of the prosecution's witnesses had credibility problems in that they were gang members with their own criminal past. Many of them were also reluctant to provide any incriminating evidence against their friends and, thus, limited the scope of what they would testify about in court. A number of the prosecution's other witnesses were police officers who were similarly hesitant to testify against their colleagues.

A Key Witness Unable to Testify

One key person who was not at the trial was Perez. Four days before the trial began, Perez's former girlfriend, Sonya Flores, claimed that Perez murdered two people in a botched drug deal and then, with the help of another officer, buried the bodies in a ravine near Tijuana, Mexico. Despite a search by both American and Mexican authorities, no remains were ever found and Flores later admitted that her allegations were a lie. (On February 26, 2001, Flores was

(Left to right) Officer Paul Harper, his lawyer Joel Isaacson, Sgt. Edward Ortiz, Sgt. Brian Liddy appearing in court for arraignment for their role in the Rampart Scandal. (The Gamma Liaison Network)

sentenced to 14 months in prison after pleading guilty to one felony count of making a false statement to an FBI agent.) However, Flores's admission that she concocted the story did not come until after the trial of the four officers, and Perez's immunity agreement did not cover any murders that he may have committed. As a result, if Perez were to take the witness stand and one of the defense attorneys brought up the murder allegations to discredit him, Perez would have had to exercise his constitutional right not to testify under the Fifth Amendment and that would put the credibility of the rest of his testimony in great doubt.

In the end, the jury delivered a mixed verdict. Buchanan, Liddy, and Ortiz were all found guilty of conspiracy to obstruct justice. In addition, Buchanan was found guilty of two counts of perjury and Liddy and Ortiz were each found guilty of filing a false police report. All of these verdicts related to the July 1996 arrest of Natividad and Munoz. Harper was acquitted of all charges and

Buchanan, Liddy, and Ortiz were found not guilty of the charges involving Allan Lobos.

Convictions Overturned

The three convicted officers were to be sentenced on January 16, 2001. However, on December 22, 2000, Judge Conner overturned their convictions after a series of hearings in which she investigated allegations of juror misconduct and the use of flawed evidence during the jury's deliberations. According to the judge, the jurors considered the wrong evidence and failed to decide a key issue in the case, i.e., whether Buchanan and Liddy were struck by a vehicle driven by a gang member in July 1996. As Conner stated in her ruling:

> While recognizing the enormous pressure on the community, on the police force, on the district attorney's office, and on the courts to 'fix' the Rampart scandal, this court is only interested in evaluating the fairness of the proceedings and determining whether justice was done in this case. . . . This court cannot simply look the other way and ignore the improprieties, innocent or not, intentional or unintentional, that served to deny a fair trial in this case.

On January 11, 2001, the Los Angeles County District Attorney's Office announced its decision to appeal Judge Conner's ruling. The matter is currently pending before the California Court of Appeals. In the meantime, prosecutors hope that whatever information Perez's former partner, Nino Durden, has will help bring further indictments and encourage other officers to cooperate with their investigation.

—Mark Thorburn

Suggestions for Further Reading

Los Angeles Times (September 15, 1999–March 2001).

Kristen Gilbert Trial: 2000–01

Defendant: Kristen H. Gilbert   **Crimes Charged:** Murder, attempted murder
Chief Defense Lawyers: David P. Hoose, Harry L. Miles, Paul Weinberg
Chief Prosecutors: William M. Welch, Ariane D. Vuono   **Judge:** Michael A.
Ponsor   **Place:** Springfield, Massachusetts   **Date of Trial:** October 16,
2000–March 26, 2001   **Verdict:** Guilty of three cases of first-degree murder
and of one case of second-degree murder; also guilty of two cases of intent
to murder   **Sentence:** Life imprisonment with no chance for parole

SIGNIFICANCE

Aside from the seriousness of the charge and an aura of scandal in elements of
this case, there was a broader issue: Was it appropriate for the federal authorities
to seek a first-degree conviction under a federal law that carried the death
sentence when the state—in this instance, Massachusetts—did not allow the
death penalty?

Between January 1995 and February 1996, a disturbing pattern of deaths began to emerge at the Veterans Administration (VA) Hospital in Northampton, Massachusetts. Patients, all male veterans of a variety of ages and medical conditions, were dying suddenly and unexpectedly—in some instances, in fact, with no apparent links to their diagnosed medical condition. The pattern included the fact that these patients would appear one moment to be resting comfortably, however serious their condition, and then suddenly go into cardiac arrest. Despite the quick and best efforts of a team of personnel trained for such emergencies, most of these patients died.

Then some of the staff began to be aware of another part of the pattern. One particular nurse seemed to be on duty during a disproportionate number of these crises. Not only on duty—she would often be reported as the last member of the hospital staff to have been alone with the patient. Then she was often among the first to respond to the emergency, during which she would seem to be making heroic efforts to save the patient.

Eventually three nurses went to their superiors and expressed their suspicions. They believed that this nurse was involved somehow in creating these medical crises. When the government pursued these suspicions, exhumations and autopsies of a number of the dead followed, and traces of a dangerous drug allegedly were found in their body tissue. This drug, epinephrine, is used by doctors in emergencies to stimulate a heart that has stopped; however, used in an overdose or when there is no actual threat of cardiac arrest, epinephrine causes the heart to beat uncontrollably and then stop abruptly. On the basis of various alleged links between the nurse and vials of epinephrine in the hospital, federal authorities charged 31-year-old Kristen Gilbert with murdering four patients and attempting to murder three more. In fact, during the seven years she worked at the VA Hospital (March 1989 to February 1996), one-half of the deaths there occurred in her ward, and she was known to have been present at the death of 37 patients during about a one-year period (January 1995 to February 1996). The government chose to focus on seven cases.

Kristen Gilbert, a nurse at Veterans Administration Hospital, charged with killing patients at the hospital. (AP/Wide World Photos)

Prosecutors Seek Death Sentence

A grand jury indicted Gilbert on November 18, 1998, and an extended series of motions and hearings and appeals followed. Multiple charges of murder would have been fought by any defense lawyers, but what gave this particular case its special edge—and high profile in the media—was the fact that the federal government had chosen to go for a first-degree murder conviction that carried the possibility of the death penalty. (It was a federal case because the alleged crimes occurred on federal property.) In any jurisdiction, this would have caused some comment, but in Massachusetts, it was the occasion for special controversy: Massachusetts did not have the death penalty (and had not executed anyone since 1946). Even among those who believed Gilbert guilty, many felt that, if she had done what she was charged with doing, she was a seriously disturbed individual. In fact, in 1998 she had been found guilty in a related case—namely, telephoning bomb threats to the VA hospital—which to some suggested that she was at the very least an unbalanced person.

Nurse Accused of Murdering to Impress Lover

In the end, the judge and the appeals court handed down a series of rulings that finally allowed the trial to begin on October 16, 2000, at the federal courthouse in Springfield, Massachusetts. The selection of a jury was complicated because it was a capital case that would almost certainly go on for several months, which meant that large numbers of potential jurors would be excused. After an exhaustive process, which included having hundreds of potential jurors fill out a 17-page questionnaire, a jury of 12 and six alternates was seated on November 17. The proceedings then began on November 20.

In its opening statement, the government claimed that Gilbert had injected epinephrine in order to induce medical crises in these patients so that she could then appear instantly at their bedside to participate in attempts to save these men. Her motive for doing so? To "show off" in front of her new boyfriend, James Perrault, a policeman on the staff at the VA Hospital who, in line with hospital policy, was required to be present during such an emergency. The defense said it would establish that there was simply not enough proof that these men had died from the epinephrine injections, and that in any case, there was not enough proof that Gilbert had been the one to inject them with it.

Anticipating that it was going to be a long trial, Judge Michael A. Ponsor had advised all the lawyers involved to exercise regularly: "It's a marathon, not a sprint." His premonition proved correct. Week after week the government called its witnesses to the stand as it tried to build up a "compelling wall of guilt," as the chief prosecutor called it, one that would hold up against reasonable doubt. Doctors testified that the alleged victims had not shown indications of being in risk of dying. Medical specialists testified to the effects of epinephrine. Nurses testified to their growing suspicions about Gilbert's actions, particularly about the empty epinephrine vials at the bedside of dead patients after she had been present.

But the prosecution's case took a dramatic turn on January 5, 2001, when the government admitted that the results of tests from a toxicology laboratory, which had analyzed the amounts of epinephrine in the alleged victims, were in error. The results did not, after all, establish the presence of the high levels on which the charges were based. The government agreed that it would no longer use these results as the basis of their case. Once the prosecution admitted this, the defense moved to stop certain witnesses from giving any testimony, but Judge Ponsor, although admitting it was an "extremely disturbing development," chose instead to advise the jurors that the now discredited toxicology evidence was being withdrawn. Further complicating the prosecution's case was the fact that two of the alleged victims had been given epinephrine during the unsuccessful efforts to resuscitate them.

Most of the prosecution's case was based on rather technical testimony, but some of the more human testimony came from relatives of the dead veterans who described how suddenly and inexplicably their loved ones had died. Two of the more dramatic witnesses were Gilbert's ex-husband and James Perrault, the policeman with whom she was having an affair at the time of the incidents. Glenn Gilbert claimed that on two occasions she had confessed to the murders; Perrault told a similar story, that she had told him she "killed all those guys."

There were few light moments in such a trial, but one came when Dr. Michael Baden, a nationally recognized forensic pathologist, was correcting a mistake he had made in referring to the condition of one of the alleged victim's heart. He said the mistake was merely a "senile moment"—he had meant to say "senior moment." The defense inevitably jumped on this second misstatement to challenge Baden's testimony.

After 10 weeks of the prosecution's case, the defense took over. In cross-examinations, they had already attacked the motives of various witnesses for the prosecution, charging for instance, that Perrault hoped to get a promotion by testifying on behalf of the hospital's authorities. Now the defense offered their own witnesses who testified to Gilbert's reputation as a competent, caring nurse; they tried to turn the prosecution's case inside out, claiming that her frequent presence at the side of patients with cardiac arrest demonstrated her expertise.

Gilbert herself did not take the stand. But the defense called on various medical specialists who cast doubt on whether these men had in fact died from epinephrine—even claiming that the records showed they had died of natural causes. Under cross-examination by the prosecution, however, the chief medical expert for the defense conceded that, although the deaths were most likely natural, "anything is possible."

Jury Convicts But Spares Nurse's Life

When the arguments ended on February 22, 2001, Judge Ponsor, in his charge to the jury, did something quite significant. He told the jury that they need not limit themselves to a finding of first-degree murder—they could find Gilbert guilty of second-degree murder, which meant life imprisonment but no threat of execution. In any case, if they were to find her guilty of first-degree murder, the jury would have to sit on another session to decide whether she should be executed or imprisoned for life.

After 83 hours of deliberation during 12 days, the jury returned with their verdict on March 14, finding Gilbert guilty of first-degree murder in three cases, and second-degree murder in the other; she was also found guilty of assault with intent to kill in two of the three other cases. Because of the first-degree murder finding, under federal law the jury then had to go back into new sessions to determine the punishment. They returned with this decision on March 26, announcing that they could not reach a unanimous decision required for the death penalty. The judge then sentenced Gilbert to three consecutive terms for life imprisonment without any chance of parole. Inevitably, Gilbert's attorneys announced they would appeal the conviction, but it appeared that Kristen Gilbert was going to spend the rest of her life in prison.

—John S. Bowman

Suggestions for Further Reading

Daily Hampshire Gazette (March 30, 2000; July 14, 2000; October 4,17, 21, 2000; November 13, 17, 18, 20, 21, 27 2000; December 14, 21, 2000; January 6, 12, 22, 26, 27, 29, 2001; February 5, 12, 13, 17, 22, 23, 2001; March 15, 27, 28, 2001).

"Gilbert Trial Timeline." http://www.gazettenet.com

Gabriel Gomez Trial: 2000

Defendant: Gabriel Gomez **Crimes Charged:** Murder, kidnapping
Chief Defense Lawyer: Antonio Bestard **Chief Prosecutor:** Donald J. Clem
Judge: Robert Martinez **Place:** Pomona, California **Date of Trial:** October
23–31, 2000 **Verdict:** Guilty **Sentence:** Life imprisonment without parole,
plus 22 years

SIGNIFICANCE

The disappearance of Sandra Rosas, wife of Los Lobos cofounder Cesar Rosas, was immediately linked to her half-brother Gabriel Gomez. Although family members had no doubts that Gomez had kidnapped and murdered her, the lack of a body forced prosecutors to attempt to convict Gomez with circumstantial evidence.

On October 23, 1999, the popular band Los Lobos was about to go onstage in Louisiana when guitarist Cesar Rosas received devastating news from the West Coast. His wife, Sandy, was missing from their home in Rowland Heights, a Los Angeles suburb. Rosas rushed home to California to learn that police were holding and questioning his wife's half-brother, Gabriel Gomez.

Victim's Half-Brother Arrested

What little hard evidence police had suggested that Gomez was the last person to see Sandra Ann Rosas alive. When her daughters arrived home at 11 P.M. on the night she disappeared, they had found the front door open and broken windshield glass scattered in the driveway. The family's van was missing. The daughters frantically dialed their mother's cell phone number. Although no one seemed to answer the call, a phone connection opened and they could hear the voices of their mother and uncle. Two days later, police found the empty Rosas van in nearby La Puente. Gomez was arrested and detained without bail on charges that he had violated the terms of parole he was serving for a 1989 arson conviction. Authorities tried to reason with the ex-convict, attempting to get some idea of where the missing woman might be. Gomez denied having anything to do with her disappearance. As the Rosas family's excruciating wait turned into days, police expressed increasingly less hope that she might be found alive.

The Los Angeles County District Attorney's Office charged Gomez with kidnapping and first-degree murder. The murder charge was filed "with special circumstances"—if found guilty of a murder occurring during the commission of a felony, such as kidnapping, Gomez would be eligible for the death penalty. When Gomez was charged and arraigned, he pleaded not guilty, continuing to deny taking part in any crime.

Circumstantial Evidence Weighed

Gomez's trial began on October 23, 2000, a year to the day of Rosas' disappearance. The prosecution's primary obstacle was proving that a murder had occurred when no body had been found. Their strategy relied heavily on the circumstantial evidence that led police to arrest Gomez in the first place.

Sandra Ann Rosas, wife of singer-songwriter Cesar Rosas, was kidnapped and murderd by her half-brother, Gabriel Gomez. (AP/Wide World Photos)

"Sandra's generosity is what got her kidnapped and murdered," Deputy District Attorney Donald Clem told the jury in his opening statement. Rosas, an adopted child, had met Gomez while searching for her biological parents in the mid-1990s. She allowed her half-brother to move in with her own family. She also helped find him work, including a stint on the road crew of her husband's band, Los Lobos, a critically acclaimed rock group widely known for their soundtrack work on the 1987 film "La Bamba." When relations between the Rosas family and Gomez began to sour, he was asked to move out. Rosas helped Gomez find an apartment and a new job, but increasingly distanced her half-brother from her own family. The prosecution theorized that Gomez was afraid the family might cut him off completely. As prosecutor Clem put it, "He saw his meal ticket slipping away."

When Cesar Rosas took the stand, he described how his kind-hearted wife had attempted to take Gomez under her wing. Her eldest daughter, Amber Steljes, recalled the cell phone call and testified that she heard Gomez say, "You can never leave me. I'm going to make mad, passionate love to you. I'm going to rape you. I'm going to strangle you." Blood traces found in Rosas' abandoned van were matched to both Rosas and Gomez through DNA analyses. A Los Angeles County sheriff testified that he found Gomez crying hysterically in his cell a week after the disappearance. "I don't know why everyone is bugging me," Gomez sobbed to the sheriff. "I can't remember where the body is."

Antonio Bestard, Gomez's court-appointed defender, offered a scenario in which Gomez had broken the van's window to retrieve her keys after she accidentally locked them inside. Bestard offered no theory as to what might have become of Rosas, but argued that no proof existed that his client had kidnapped her, let alone raped or murdered her as the prosecution was suggesting. The prosecution brushed aside the fact that Rosas' body had not been discovered. "The fact that a murderer successfully disposes of a body does not entitle him to an acquittal," Clem told the jury in his closing statement.

Gomez Reveals Burial Site

After two hours of deliberations, the jury found Gomez guilty on October 31. Outside the court, Cesar Rosas tearfully told reporters that Gomez "didn't just hurt me. He hurt hundreds of people." In spite of his family's suffering, Rosas expressed relief that Gomez would no longer be in a position to harm anyone else. On November 16, Gomez was sentenced to life imprisonment without parole on the murder charge, plus an additional 16 years for the kidnapping conviction. Judge Robert Martinez also added five years to the sentence for Gomez's unfulfilled 1989 arson sentence and a year for a drug arrest, for which he was liable due to his parole violation and conviction on the Rosas felonies. Judge Martinez told Gomez to consider helping investigators find Sandra Rosas' body to offer her family some closure from their trauma.

As soon as the sentencing was over, Gomez told a *San Gabriel Valley Tribune* reporter that if he had indeed killed Rosas, he had been too intoxicated with alcohol and cocaine to recall a murder or a burial. Yet within minutes, Gomez suddenly agreed to lead police to Rosas' body. Investigators spent the evening searching for a gravesite in Schabarum Regional Park near the Rosas home, without success. A few days later, Gomez told Judge Martinez that the body might be in a different park in rural Santa Clarita, 50 miles northwest of where he originally had steered investigators. On November 22, police and canine search squads discovered human bones in a shallow Sand Park grave. Family members identified jewelry, a hair clip, and nail polish found with the remains. Five days later, dental records officially confirmed that the bones were those of Sandra Rosas. She was buried in a private service soon thereafter, allowing her family the opportunity to heal, denied them by her killer for a year.

—Tom Smith

Suggestions for Further Reading

"About the Sandra Rosas Case: The Basic Story." http://www.loslobos.org/sandra.asp.

Cain, Stephanie. "Killer of Rosas Given Life, No Parole." *San Gabriel Valley Tribune.* http://www.sgvtribune.com.

Cholo, Ann Beatriz. "Jury Convicts Man in Slaying of Singer's Wife." *Los Angeles Times* (November 1, 2000): B2.

Rae Carruth Trial: 2000–01

Defendant: Rae Lamar Theotis Wiggins, a.k.a. Rae Carruth
Crimes Charged: Murder, conspiracy to commit murder, shooting into an occupied vehicle, using a gun to attempt to kill an unborn child
Chief Defense Lawyers: David Rudolph, Christopher Fialko
Chief Prosecutor: Gentry Caudill **Judge:** Charles Lamm **Place:** Charlotte, North Carolina **Date of Trial:** October 23, 2000–January 19, 2001
Verdict: Not guilty of first-degree murder; guilty on all other counts
Sentence: 18–24 years imprisonment

SIGNIFICANCE

The trial of a member of the Carolina Panthers football team for arranging the murder of his pregnant woman friend captured national attention at a time when other incidents raised public concerns about violent acts by professional athletes.

At about half an hour after midnight on the morning of Tuesday, October 16, 1999, Cherica Adams, 24 year years old and six months pregnant, was driving home through a middle-class suburban neighborhood in south Charlotte, North Carolina, when she was shot four times from a car which pulled alongside her. Seriously wounded, she drove her BMW off the road onto the lawn of a private home, and was able to make an emergency call on her car phone. In the phone call, she identified the driver of a car that had pulled in front of her and caused her to slow down immediately before the shooting as Rae Carruth, a member of the Carolina Panthers football team, who had just spent the evening at a movie theater with her. At Carolinas Medical Center, Cherica Adams's baby boy was delivered by emergency Caesarean section and survived; Adams remained in critical condition.

A Promising Football Career Shattered

Rae Carruth grew up in Sacramento, California, and played football for the University of Colorado. He was picked by the Carolina Panthers as a wide receiver in the 1997 National Football League draft, and signed a four-year contract for a total of almost three and three-quarter million dollars.

The police investigation immediately focussed on Carruth because of Cherica Adams's 911 call, statements she made to police at the scene, and notes she wrote a few hours after being admitted to the hospital. On Friday, November 19, police arrested Michael Eugene Kennedy, 24, of Charlotte, who was alleged to have rented and driven the car from which the shots were fired. Kennedy had a lengthy arrest record on assault and drug-related charges extending back to 1994. Carruth was arrested on November 25, charged with conspiracy to commit murder, and taken into custody. Also arrested on the same day on the same charge was William Edward (Van Brett) Watkins, 40, of New York. Frequently referred to as a career criminal, Watkins had a long record of violent offenses, and was believed to have fired the shots that hit Cherica Adams. Stanley Drew Abraham, 19, of Charlotte, believed to have been a passenger in the car with Watkins and Kennedy, was arrested on December 2.

Cherica Adams Dies and Rae Carruth Flees

Carruth was released on a $3 million bond on December 6. Eight days later Cherica Adams died of multiple organ system failure resulting from the gunshot wounds, and the charge of first-degree murder was added to others faced by Carruth and the other three codefendants. Instead of turning himself into police, as it had been arranged that he would do in this situation, Rae Carruth disappeared. His flight, however, was short-lived; the following day FBI agents, acting on information from his mother, discovered him hiding in the trunk of a car in the parking lot of a motel in Wildersville, Tennessee. He was returned to North Carolina and held in jail until his trial. At the end of December what had been generally supposed was confirmed: tests showed that Rae Carruth was the father of Cherica Adams's child.

Defense attorney shows documents to Theodry Carruth, mother of professional football player, Rae Carruth, on trial for murdering his pregnant girlfriend. (AP/Wide World Photos)

Carruth retained David Rudolph, a founder of the Chapel Hill firm of Rudolph, Maher, Widenhouse, and Fialko. Rudolph had a strong reputation as a criminal defense lawyer and had successfully represented several clients in high-profile cases. He would be assisted by his partner, Christopher Fialko. The prosecution was headed by Mecklenburg County assistant district attorney Gentry Caudill; a veteran prosecutor, this would be his last case before becoming a judge. Van Brett Watkins accepted a plea bargain, confessing that he had shot Cherica Adams and pleading guilty to second-degree murder and the other charges. He agreed to testify against Carruth and the other defendants. In pretrial motions Rudolph was unsuccessful in attempting to exclude as evidence the tape of Cherica Adams's 911 call, the notes she had written in the hospital, and testimony regarding Carruth's flight to Tennessee.

In a separate proceeding in civil court in August 2000, Carruth was found to be indigent, his house having been sold at foreclosure and his other assets disposed of. This ruling, however, was sealed at the request of Judge Charles Lamm, who had been assigned the criminal case. In a decision, which was controversial in the local legal community when it became known, Judge Lamm instructed Rudolph and Fialko to continue to represent Carruth as public defenders. None of this became public knowledge until the closing days of the ensuing trial.

Recording of 911 Call Is Played in Opening Statements

Jury selection began on October 23, 2000, and lasted almost a month, resulting in a panel of seven men and five women. As a part of its opening statement on November 20, the prosecution played the tape of Cherica Adams' emergency call. Their case centered on the fact, as subsequent witnesses were called to confirm, that she had identified Rae Carruth to the dispatcher, again to police at the scene in the hearing of a paramedic witness, and again at the hospital in the presence of a nurse. Carruth, the prosecution would show, had recruited Watkins and Kennedy to kill Adams because he did not want to pay support for her child, on top of the child support of $3,000 per month that he already was paying for a child he had fathered in California. The defense would argue that Carruth had not been involved in any plot to kill Cherica Adams, that the motive presented was implausible, given the fact that Carruth was earning $650,000 a year at the time of the shooting, and that the shooting was an indirect consequence of Carruth's refusal to finance a drug deal.

The first of several unexpected developments in the trial occurred the following day when the prosecution presented Michael Eugene Kennedy as its first witness. Although still facing his own capital murder trial, Kennedy testified without having entered into a formal or informal plea bargain arrangement with the prosecution. Kennedy told the court that he had rented and driven the car from which the shooting occurred, that Carruth had given him $100 to buy the gun, and that Carruth's reason was his unwillingness to pay child support. The prosecution then called another former girlfriend of Carruth who also testified that Carruth had confessed to her that he had been involved in the shooting.

After calling several of Carruth's friends to testify that he wanted the baby, and had no ill-will towards Cherica Adams, the defense took the unusual step of bringing Brett Watkins to the stand. Such was Watkins's reputation for impulsive violence that a deputy was positioned between the witness box and Judge Lamm, on the one side, and another between Watkins and the jury on the other. During a full day of confrontational examination, Rudolph attempted to get Watkins to admit that the killing had occurred because Carruth had refused to finance a drug deal. Watkins, however, insisted that he had been hired by Carruth, first with the idea of beating up Cherica so that she would lose the baby, but then to kill her.

The next day the defense introduced testimony from a prison officer, Sergeant Shirley Riddle, who testified that she had had a conversation with Watkins in jail at the time of Cherica Adams's death. In this conversation he had confessed to the shooting, but had also told her that he had pulled alongside Cherica Adams's car in order to try to get her to tell him where Carruth was going. When she made an obscene gesture at him, he said that he had "just lost it," and started shooting. According to Sergeant Riddle, Watkins had indicated that it was all about a drug purchase, and that if Carruth had given them the money they wanted, the shooting would not have occurred. Rae Carruth did not testify.

In its rebuttal the prosecution called another former girlfriend of Carruth from Colorado, Amber Turner, who admitted to having had an abortion after Carruth had threatened her life. Turner had been originally listed as a defense witness. Michelle Wright, the mother of Carruth's six-year-old son, also testified to having been threatened by Carruth.

The Jury Deliberates

After 11 weeks and 70 witnesses, closing arguments were heard on January 15, 2001. The prosecution played the 911 tape again, and emphasized the record of the long series of phone calls between Carruth and Van Brett Watkins during the weeks before the shooting. For the defense, David Rudolph laid out 10 points, all of which, he argued, presented reasonable doubt about the plausibility of the prosecution case.

The jury began deliberations the following day, but two days later, after 11 hours of discussion, the foreman reported to Judge Lamm that they were split on all four charges. After repeating jury instructions, he told them to keep trying, and on Friday, January 19, the jury returned its verdict, finding Rae Carruth not guilty of first-degree murder, but guilty on the other three charges. He was sentenced to not less than 18 years, 11 months, and not more than 24 years, four months in prison. Under North Carolina sentencing law, apart from credit for any time spent in jail awaiting trial, actual time served cannot be reduced to less than the minimum specified by the judge. Van Brett Watkins was subsequently sentenced to not less than 40 years and five months or more than 50 years and eight months. Michael Kennedy pled guilty to second-degree murder and received a minimum of 11 years and eight months. Abraham pled guilty to lesser charges as an accessory and received 90 days in jail and five years probation.

—David I. Petts

Suggestions for Further Reading

Charlotte Observer Online. www.charlotte.com/observer/specials

Schmitz, Brian. "In Wake of Rae Carruth, has Ray Lewis Learned His Lesson?" *Orlando Sentinel* (January 19, 2001).

Presidential Election Trials: 2000

Plaintiff: Al Gore   **Defendants:** George W. Bush, Katherine Harris
Chief Lawyers for Plaintiff: David Boies, W. Dexter Douglas, Bruce Rogow, Laurence H. Tribe, Stephen Zack   **Chief Defense Lawyers:** Philip Beck, Benjamin L. Ginsberg, Theodore B. Olson, Barry Richard, George Terwilliger (Bush); Joseph P. Klock, Jr. (Harris)   **Judges:** Leon County, Florida, Circuit Court: Terry P. Lewis, N. Sanders Sauls; Broward County, Florida, Circuit Court: John Miller; U.S. District Court: Donald Middlebrooks; Supreme Court of the State of Florida: Charles T. Wells, Harry Lee Anstead, Major B. Harding, R. Fred Lewis, Barbara J. Pariente, Peggy A. Quince, Leander J. Shaw, Jr.; Supreme Court of the United States: William H. Rehnquist, Stephen G. Breyer, Ruth Bader Ginsburg, Anthony M. Kennedy, Sandra Day O'Connor, Antonin Scalia, David H. Souter, John Paul Stevens, Clarence Thomas   **Places:** Atlanta, Georgia; Miami and Tallahassee, Florida; Washington, D.C.
Dates of Hearings and Trials: November 11–13, 2000 (Judge Middlebrooks); November 14, 2000 (Judge Lewis); November 14, 2000 (Judge Miller); November 15–16, 2000 (Florida Supreme Court); November 16–17, 2000 (U.S. Court of Appeals, Atlanta); November 17, 2000 (Judge Lewis); November 20–21, 2000 (Florida Supreme Court); December 1–4, 2000 (U.S. Supreme Court); December 2–4, 2000 (Judge Sauls); December 7–8, 2000 (Florida Supreme Court); December 9–12, 2000 (U.S. Supreme Court)

SIGNIFICANCE

After all the dates of hearings and trials and appeals, with all their specifics of fact and expressions of opinion, have long been forgotten, the world will still know that the 36 days of the 2000 presidential election trials amount to but one significance: The rule of law endures. The extraordinary U.S. system of legal institutions—a system, someone once said, "designed by geniuses so it could be run by idiots"—maintains its strength regardless of political pressures.

It all began on election day, Tuesday, November 7, 2000. That evening, before polls were closed in all 50 of the United States or even Florida's western panhandle, television news reporters projected Democratic presidential candidate Al Gore as the winner in the state of Florida over Republican candidate

George W. Bush. Later, they retracted the projection. By early next morning, they said the lead in Florida hinged on a few hundred votes, and by this time it was clear that Florida's 25 electoral votes would be decisive in the national outcome. With several news organizations declaring Bush the winner, Gore called the Texas governor to concede the election. Then, upon hearing later projections, he retracted the concession before dawn on Wednesday. A day-by-day, court-by-court drama followed.

Thursday, November 9

Forty-eight hours after the polls closed, a still-incomplete count gave Bush the lead by 1,784 votes. Election officials in 67 Florida counties ordered recounts of their machine votes.

Manual Recounts Requested

Friday, November 10

Complete in all but one county, recounts now gave Bush a lead of just 327. The Democrats formally requested manual recounts in Miami-Dade, Broward, Palm Beach, and Volusia counties, all four of which voted heavily Democratic.

Saturday, November 11

Palm Beach County announced it would manually recount all 462,657 ballots cast there. Bush sued in U.S. District Court in Miami to halt the manual counting. His lawyers argued that voters would not be treated equally (the Constitution's Fourteenth Amendment guarantees everyone equal protection of voting rights) because no uniform standard governs hand counts.

Monday, November 13

Judge Donald Middlebrooks rejected the Bush contention, declaring that election mechanics are a state, not federal, issue. Now Florida election officials announced that they would certify the statewide results, except for overseas absentee ballots, by 5:00 P.M. next day. The Gore campaign, along with Palm Beach and Volusia counties, immediately sued to extend that deadline.

Tuesday, November 14

Leon County Circuit Court judge Terry P. Lewis upheld the official deadline but said Florida's Republican secretary of state Katherine Harris was not to disregard hand recounts that might arrive after the deadline.

Broward County Circuit Court judge John Miller refused to grant an injunction, sought by Republican lawyers, to keep Broward County from conducting a manual recount. A recount of machine votes and of Volusia County's hand ballots put Bush ahead by 300 votes. At 5:00 P.M., the secretary of state certified this result but said it did not include overseas absentee ballots legally entitled to arrive later. She also gave counties doing hand counts until 2:00 P.M. next day to revise their results.

Manual Recounts Begin

Wednesday, November 15

The Broward County canvassing board decided to start manually re-counting all 587,928 ballots cast there. At the same time, Secretary of State Harris rebuffed requests that recounts in Broward and Palm Beach counties be included in her statewide certification. The Gore campaign appealed that turn-down to the Florida Supreme Court, all seven of whose members had been appointed by Democratic governors.

Thursday, November 16

The state supreme court said manual recounts in Palm Beach and Broward counties would be permitted.

Before the U.S. Court of Appeals in Atlanta, the Bush campaign argued that hand counts are unconstitutional, while the Gore campaign insisted the matter was a state, not federal, issue.

Friday, November 17

The federal court in Atlanta refused the Bush request to stop hand counts, and the Miami-Dade County election board voted to go ahead with its hand recount.

As the nation became educated about "chads," the bits of paper punched out of ballots by voters so machines could count the holes, Broward County judge John Miller decided the county canvassing board could count such a punch-card ballot as a vote, even when no hole was punched, if a "dimple" showed that the voter had tried to punch the hole. Television news now endlessly depicted board members holding ballots up to the light or squinting at them inches from their noses.

Leon County Circuit Court Judge Terry P. Lewis decided the Secretary of State was permitted to certify the election results and declare a winner without hand recounts. Gore again appealed.

The Florida Supreme Court, acting on its own motion and pending its consideration of the appeal, put a hold on Judge Lewis's decision.

Monday, November 20

The Florida Supreme Court listened to arguments by Bush and Gore attorneys on whether hand counts should be included in the final tally of votes, and on Secretary of State Harris's claim that she was authorized to ignore all late returns.

Florida Supreme Court Rules

Tuesday, November 21

Ruling unanimously, the seven Florida justices decided hand counts must be included in final voting results unless they were "submitted so late that their inclusion will preclude Florida's voters from participating fully in the federal electoral process." They set 5:00 P.M. Sunday, November 26, for the secretary of state's certification of the winner of Florida's electoral college votes.

Wednesday, November 22

In Washington, Bush attorneys filed an appeal to the U.S. Supreme Court. Their brief argued that the Florida Supreme Court had rewritten state election statutes following the election.

Back in Florida, Miami-Dade County, insisting that it could not complete its recount by the November 26 deadline, stopped counting.

Thursday, November 23 (Thanksgiving Day)

The Gore campaign asked the Florida Supreme Court to order Miami-Dade to keep counting. The court refused.

Sunday, November 26

At 5:00 P.M., Florida Secretary of State Harris officially certified that Bush had won Florida by 537 votes.

Monday, November 27

The Gore campaign, before Leon County Circuit Court judge N. Sanders Sauls, filed a request for immediate hand recounts in Palm Beach and Miami-Dade counties.

Tuesday, November 28

Judge Sauls turned down the Gore request but said he would hold a hearing.

Wednesday, November 29

The Gore team asked the Florida Supreme Court to order the hand recount to proceed while Judge Sauls's hearing was pending.

An Hour and a Half in Washington

Friday, December 1

For 90 minutes, the U.S. Supreme Court heard the Bush and Gore arguments. It focussed on a seldom-noticed statute, the Electoral Count Act of 1887, enacted by Congress following the disputed 1876 election contest between Rutherford B. Hayes and Samuel J. Tilden. Title 3, Section 5, of the U.S. Code states that if any state, before choosing its presidential electors, has passed laws on the handling of any contest "by judicial or other methods," determinations under those laws shall be conclusive in counting the electoral vote.

Bush attorney Theodore B. Olson argued that the Florida Supreme Court, in its November 21 decision permitting manual recounts to continue and setting November 26 for certification, had rewritten the law of Florida and violated the U.S. Code. The decision, he said, rewrote a Florida statute that set a December 14 deadline for election boards to report their totals.

Attorney Laurence H. Tribe, arguing the Gore side, said the Florida Supreme Court had not written new law but only interpreted differing Florida statutes, one of which sets a close deadline for certification while the other permits time-consuming hand recounts. And, he added, the 1887 law merely proposes incentives to states that follow it, but does not penalize them for failure to do so.

Both Chief Justice William Rehnquist and Justice Sandra Day O'Connor pointed out that Section 5 of the U.S. Code appeared to be a direction to Congress for resolving disputes over electoral votes, but not a rule to be enforced by the courts. "We're looking for a federal issue," said Justice Anthony Kennedy. Justice Ruth Bader Ginsburg challenged Bush attorney Olson: "I do not know of any case where we have impugned a state supreme court the way you are doing in this case," she said. "I mean, in case after case, we have said we owe the highest respect to what the state says is the state's law."

Before Judge Sauls: Chads and Patents

Saturday, December 2

Back in Florida, before Leon County Circuit Court judge N. Sanders Sauls, Gore attorneys urged the judge to order the hand counting of some 14,000 ballots that were considered "undervoted" or disqualified. Over nine grueling hours, they presented only two witnesses: an expert on voting machines, and a statistician. Judge Sauls plowed through lengthy and detailed descriptions of how chads do or don't become dimpled, how they may build up in the voting apparatus so they block a hole from being entirely punched from a ballot, how they can "hang" by one or more corners. Bush attorney Philip Beck cross-examined the statistician, Yale professor Nicolas Hengartner, who testified on the likely problems in punch-card voting. Beck's persistence brought an admission from the professor that he had not, in fact, examined a certain ballot that, in his affidavit, he said he had inspected.

Sunday, December 3

The slow-moving testimony in the Sauls courtroom sped up. For an hour, Bush witness John Ahmann, who some 35 years earlier helped design the punch-card system still used in several Florida counties and across the United States, spent more than an hour explaining why ballots that were only partly punched did not result from failures of the machines. "I seriously doubt," he said, "that a voter would be unable to push a chad through on a normal voting device."

In cross-examination, Gore attorney Stephen Zack read from a patent application filed by Ahmann for a new voting-machine design. It said that the old design, which was still used in Miami-Dade County, could make ballots unreadable by leaving chads hanging and that it "can cause serious errors to occur" by becoming so filled with chads that voters could not punch ballots all the way through.

Ahmann also revealed that he had tried but failed to sell Miami-Dade County on a new stylus designed to help the voter punch the ballot all the way through. The current stylus, he said, did not punch as dependably as the new design.

This witness called by the Bush side, said Gore lawyer David Boies afterward, was the Democrats' best witness. "He made every point we were trying to make," said Boies.

A Bush statistician, Dr. Laurentius Marais, rebutted the Gore statistician's statement that counties using optical voting machines recorded fewer non-votes than those using punch cards. This, he said, reflected the age-old fallacy of assuming a causal relationship where none existed, as in the classic example in which a statistician notes an increase in storks' nests in a town at the same time as an increase in human births and assumes cause and effect.

Marais also cited studies showing that a confusing ballot design, such as Palm Beach County's controversial "butterfly" ballot, could turn voters away from the polls without voting.

It was almost 11:00 Sunday night when Judge Sauls, promising to issue a ruling the next morning, recessed the court.

Decision "Vacated"

Monday, December 4

In Washington, D.C., the U.S. Supreme Court issued a unanimous six-page ruling. It told the Florida Supreme Court to clarify its November 21st ruling that allowed recounts to continue beyond the deadline set by statute. Technically, the U.S. justices "vacated" the Florida court's decision.

In Tallahassee several hours later, Judge Sauls read his ruling aloud. It dismissed every legal argument the Gore lawyers had offered. Mr. Gore had not proved, said the judge, a "reasonable probability" that the election would have turned out differently had there been no problems counting ballots. Furthermore, he said, to contest the election properly, every ballot in Florida—not just in the three counties under dispute—would have to be counted.

Thursday, December 7

While the judge was still speaking, Gore lawyers had filed an appeal to the Florida Supreme Court. As attorney Boies opened for plaintiff Gore, Chief Justice Charles T. Wells asked, "Why is not judicial review given to the circuit court and not this court?" The justice explained that state law gave the hearing of contests of elections to the circuit court and did not say they could be appealed. Boies contended that the case could be appealed like any other because the U.S. Constitution authorized the legislature to enact basic laws but not to act as a judicial body.

Justice Leander J. Shaw, Jr., questioned how this court could overrule Judge Sauls's findings of fact. Boies responded that Judge Sauls had refused to look at important evidence: the 14,000 punch-card ballots, rejected by tabulating machines that might change the election outcome if manually counted. Three justices—Major B. Harding, R. Fred Lewis, and Peggy A. Quince—asked why the Democrats wanted to count manually in only Palm Beach and Miami-Dade counties rather than everywhere. The losing candidate, said Boies, had the right to choose where to contest the vote, and, indeed, the Bush side had rejected the chance for a statewide manual recount.

As Bush lawyer Barry Richard addressed the court, Justice Harry Lee Anstead asked, "Isn't it highly unusual for a trial court to admit into evidence certain documents that one party claims will be controlling and yet never examine those documents before making their decision?" Justice Barbara J. Pariente added that the state election law requires the circuit court "to do whatever is necessary to ensure that each allegation in the complaint is investigated, examined, or checked." What does that mean, she asked, if it doesn't mean counting disputed ballots?

Richard responded that the plaintiffs had not established "an abuse of discretion by any of the challenged canvassing boards" even though counting is at the discretion of election boards.

Justice Quince questioned Judge Sauls's test that Gore had to show a "reasonable probability" of a recount making a change in the election outcome. "Where in the statute is that standard," demanded the justice, "that you have to show that a mistake was made through no fault of the voter?" She added that she was "really having a problem" with the Sauls probability standard.

Manual Recount Ordered

Friday, December 8

At day's end, a four-member majority of the court (Justices Anstead, Lewis, Pariente, and Quince) decided that all so-called "undervotes"—i.e., ballots on which no votes for president had been recorded, estimated at 45,000 statewide—must be manually recounted. The court ordered that Florida's 25 electoral votes be awarded to whichever candidate won the recount. It also said that Judge Sauls had set too high a standard in deciding that Gore had not proved that disputed ballots should be counted. And it ordered hand counting of 9,000 Miami-Dade ballots that machines failed to read—as well as similar ballots statewide.

As election boards rushed to organize recounts, attorneys for Bush raced to the U.S. Supreme Court to appeal.

Recount Stopped

Saturday, December 9

Just before 3:00 P.M., the U.S. Supreme Court, voting 5–4, ordered Florida to stop counting votes. It set Monday morning to hear the Bush appeal.

Monday, December 11

Bush attorney Olson was only 54 seconds into his opening statement before the U.S. Supreme Court when Justice Anthony M. Kennedy interrupted, asking, "What's the federal question here?" He said the proposition that a state legislature should not be guided by the courts "seems to me a holding that has grave implications for our republican theory of government." Olson responded that the Constitution gave state legislatures the authority to appoint electors and that legislatures were empowered to use the executive as well as judicial branch to implement election procedures. In Florida, he explained, the legislature designated the executive branch, in the secretary of state, to enforce the election law. It also assigned the Circuit Court as trial court to judge any election contests. "There is no reference," said Olson, "to an appellate jurisdiction."

Justice Breyer tried more than once to get Olson to state what he considered a "fair standard" for counting ballots on which the machine had found no vote for president. Finally, Olson said, "That is the job for a legislature."

The justice insisted on getting Olson's opinion.

"A reasonable standard," said Olson, "would have to be, at minimum, a penetration of the chad in the ballot because indentations are no standards at all."

Justice Stevens followed up: "And can we possibly infer from the failure of the secretary of state to promulgate a statewide standard that she might have inferred that the intent of the voter is an adequate standard?"

Olson said that was not a fair inference. Justice Breyer asked what would be a basically fair standard. "I would hold that you have to punch the chad through on a ballot," said Olson. "The only problem we have here is created by people who did not follow instructions."

Representing Gore, attorney Boies's task was to convince the court that the Florida Supreme Court had not exceeded its authority by ordering the manual recount. He argued that it was entitled to the deference usually shown to state courts by the nation's highest court. "You are responding," said Justice O'Connor, "as though there were no special burden to show some deference to legislative choices." Citing the U.S. Constitution's Article II, she noted that state legislatures have the authority to determine the manner of choosing the state's presidential electors. "In the context of selection of presidential electors," she added, "isn't there a big red flag up there, 'Watch out'?"

Justice O'Connor next commented on the Florida court's failure to respond to the justices' unanimous order, a week earlier, vacating the Florida court's previous decision to extend the deadline for certifying presidential vote totals. The Florida Supreme Court, she said, "just seemed to kind of bypass it and assume that all those changes and deadlines were just fine and they could go ahead and adhere to them. And I found that troublesome."

Supreme Court Ends It

Tuesday, December 12

At 10:00 P.M., the U.S. Supreme Court ruled, 5–4, that the counting of Florida's disputed presidential votes must end. The majority justices were Rehnquist, O'Connor, Scalia, Kennedy, and Thomas. Their ruling said the immediacy of the December 12 deadline for immunizing Florida's electors from a challenge in Congress made it impossible to find a way to count the votes that would meet "minimal constitutional standards" and meet the deadline that "is upon us."

Dissenters Breyer and Souter agreed with the majority that varying standards for counting the punch-card ballots in the Florida counties offered problems of due process and of equal protection. The answer, they said, was not to end the recount but to extend it to December 18, the date of the electoral college meeting. Such a recount would be a "tall order," said Souter, but "there is no justification for denying the state the opportunity to try to count all the disputed ballots now."

Justice Ginsburg was more outspoken. "The court's conclusion that a constitutionally adequate recount is impractical," she wrote, "is a prophecy the court's own judgment will not allow to be tested. Such an untested prophecy should not decide the Presidency of the United States."

Justice Stevens was equally perturbed. "Although we may never know with complete certainty the identity of the winner of this year's presidential election," he wrote, "the identity of the loser is perfectly clear. It is the nation's confidence in the judge as an impartial guardian of the rule of law."

— Bernard Ryan, Jr.

Suggestions for Further Reading

Achenbach, Joel. *It Looks Like a President Only Smaller: Trailing Campaign 2000.* New York: Simon & Schuster, 2001.

Apple, R.W., Jr. *et al* (political reporters of the New York Times). *36 Days: The Complete Chronicle of the 2000 Presidential Election Crisis.* New York: Times Books, 2001.

Bleich, Jeff, and Kelly Klaus. "The Road from Tallahassee." *Oregon State Bar Bulletin* (February/March 2001).

Dionne, E.J., ed. *Bush v. Gore: The Court Cases and the Commentary.* Washington: Brookings Institution, 2001.

Milbank, Dana. *Smashmouth: Two Years in the Gutter with Al Gore and George W. Bush.* New York: Basic Books, 2001.

Tapper, Jake. *Down and Dirty: The Plot to Steal the Presidency.* Boston: Little, Brown, 2001.

Sean "Puff Daddy" Combs, Jamaal "Shyne" Barrow, and Anthony Jones Trial: 2001

Defendants: Sean "Puff Daddy" Combs, Jamaal "Shyne" Barrow, Anthony Jones   **Crimes Charged:** Combs and Jones: Criminal possession of a firearm, bribing a witness; Barrow: Attempted murder, assault, criminal use and possession of a firearm, reckless endangerment
Chief Defense Lawyers: Combs: Benjamin Brafman, Johnnie Cochran, Jr.; Jones: Michael Bachner; Barrow: Ian Niles, Murray Richman
Chief Prosecutor: Matthew Bogdanos   **Judge:** Charles Solomon
Place: New York, New York   **Date of Trial:** January 17–March 16, 2001
Verdict: Combs and Jones: acquitted; Barrow: acquitted of attempted murder and on one count of assault, guilty of all other charges   **Sentence:** Barrow: 10 years imprisonment

SIGNIFICANCE
In one of the twenty-first century's first "celebrity trials," attorneys, pundits, and the public argued over whether hip-hop music star Sean "Puff Daddy" Combs was a wealthy bully trying to bribe his way out of a possible 15-year prison sentence or a mild-mannered multimillionaire being persecuted for rap music's frequent association with violence.

A round 2:30 A.M. on December 27, 1999, gunfire exploded inside Club New York, a midtown Manhattan nightclub. As ambulances were dispatched to the club to treat wounded patrons, police surrounded a sport utility vehicle that had raced away through red traffic lights. When a 9mm pistol was discovered in the car, the passengers were arrested. They included music executive Sean Combs and his retinue, including film and music star Jennifer Lopez, bodyguard Anthony "Wolf" Jones, and chauffeur Wardell Fenderson. Jamaal "Shyne" Barrow, an aspiring rap singer Combs was grooming for his Bad Boy Records label, was arrested at Club New York.

The incident was traced to an exchange between the arrested men and Matthew "Scar" Allen, who had thrown a wad of cash at Combs as an insult after

Allen's drink was spilled at the crowded bar. The case immediately drew headlines, not because of the three people wounded in the shooting, but because of the celebrity of those arrested. Combs, also known as "Puff Daddy" or "Puffy," was one of the wealthiest executives and performers in the music business. Lopez, Combs's girlfriend and a well-known actress and singer, was released without being charged. After hours of questioning, however, gun possession and assault charges were filed against Combs, Jones, and Barrow. Combs and Jones were further charged with trying to bribe Fenderson by offering him $50,000 to tell police that the pistol found in the vehicle was his.

Barrow, who faced attempted murder, assault, gun possession, and reckless endangerment charges, was clearly in the most serious trouble with the law. Due to Combs's celebrity, however, the case would become known as "the Puff Daddy trial." Combs had become famous as a rap singer, producer, songwriter, and talent scout. Contrary to the tough persona of his records, his attorneys began portraying him as a fatherless young man who had left college to build a multimillion-dollar business empire, which included his own recording, clothing, restaurant, and film concerns. In the courts of law and public opinion, battles raged over whether the real Combs was a gangster or a CEO. His legal record was not spotless. In 1999, he was arrested for beating a record executive and had been sentenced to one day in an anger management program after pleading guilty to a lesser charge. He was also being sued by a television show host he had allegedly assaulted and faced a weapons charge over an incident at another New York nightclub.

2001

Sean "Puff

Daddy" Combs,

Jamaal "Shyne"

Barrow, and

Anthony Jones

Trial

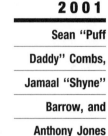

Hip-Hop music star Sean "Puff Daddy" Combs. (AP/Wide World Photos)

Tainted Witnesses or a Bad Case?

When testimony began on January 29, 2001, prosecutor Matthew Bogdanos proposed that Combs was responsible for the shooting because his celebrity status had allowed his party to enter Club New York without being searched for weapons. Bogdanos also accused Combs of firing a gun into the club's ceiling during the fight. Combs's lawyer, Benjamin Brafman, loudly accused the prosecution of persecuting his client despite a lack of factual evidence.

The trial quickly became a contest over the quality of witness testimony. Two prosecution witnesses, both of whom had testified before a grand jury that they witnessed an argument between Combs and Allen, changed their stories on the stand, infuriating prosecutor Bogdanos. They denied being able to identify Combs as a participant in the scuffle or seeing him with a gun. A third witness admitted that she was unsure what she might have seen in Combs's hand as he ran from the club. By contrast, numerous witnesses placed a gun in Barrow's hand.

The first witness claiming to have seen a gun in Combs's hand was Natania Ruben, who was shot in the face during the incident. Ruben testified that she saw both Combs and Barrow fire. When Ruben stuck to her story, defense attorney Brafman accused her of trying to malign Combs's reputation to aid her multimillion-dollar damages lawsuit against him. The second witness to place a gun in Combs's possession was chauffeur Wardell Fenderson, who testified that he saw Combs slip a pistol into his waistband before entering Club New York. The driver described Combs and Jones fumbling with a hidden compartment in the vehicle, trying to hide the weapon as police chased them from the club. Fenderson assumed that Jones or Combs had thrown a weapon from the SUV, for he had seen light stream through an opening window. Fenderson also accused Combs of offering him a diamond ring as part of a $50,000 payment for claiming ownership of the gun found in the vehicle. "Listen, you know, I'm Puff Daddy. I can't take the gun," Combs allegedly told the driver. Fenderson testified that he was tempted by the offer and accepted, but later declined it.

While Judge Charles Solomon was refereeing daily shouted objections from both sides, the media commented on everything from Combs's mother's wardrobe to the possibility that Jennifer Lopez might appear as a witness. Amid reports that Lopez and Combs had ended their relationship, speculators wondered which side might call her as a witness. Ultimately, she did not testify at all.

When the defense began its case, it concentrated on claims that Combs had been seen with a weapon at all, let alone firing one. Most damaging to the prosecution was security guard Cherise Myers, who recalled "Scar" Allen throwing money in Combs's face and being jostled as club customers grappled for the cash. Myers was advising Combs to leave the club rather than argue with Allen when she saw Barrow firing twice. She fell on top of Combs to protect him. Other people then tumbled on top of them. Myers testified that she never saw a gun in Combs's hands. Several witnesses recalled Combs dancing on a coffee table at the club with his arms raised. None saw a gun in his exposed waistband. When Combs took the stand in his own defense, his attorney asked him if he had a gun at any time on the night of the incident. "Absolutely not," Combs replied.

Lawyers Battle in Closing Arguments

Closing arguments were as acrimonious as the rest of the trial. Prosecutor Bogdanos reminded the jury that there were shooting victims in the case and insinuated that Combs had actively tried to bribe witnesses to change their testimony. Attorney Brafman responded with a full assault on the prosecution's witnesses. "Bad people came into this courtroom and made bad accusations because they wanted to get rich," Brafman said. He reminded jurors that Fenderson had a $3 million suit pending against Combs for emotional stress, implying that the driver was hoping to get enough money to pay off thousands of dollars in outstanding child support payments. Brafman pointed out that another shooting victim who testified for the prosecution claimed on the witness stand that he was suing for $17,000 in medical expenses, when in fact the suit sought $700 million from Combs. The other defense lawyers disputed the prosecution's scenario. Jones's attorney Michael Bachner claimed that the gun found in the vehicle belonged to Wardell Fenderson, not his client. Barrow's attorney Ian Niles admitted that his client had a gun, but argued that Barrow had fired in self-defense and to clear an escape route through the packed room.

The courtroom was tense when verdicts were delivered on March 16. Combs and Jones were acquitted of all charges. Barrow was acquitted of attempted murder and on one count of assault, but was found guilty of all the remaining charges against him. As Barrow was taken into custody, Combs left court quietly, thanking God and his mother for supporting him throughout the trial.

At his sentencing on June 1, Barrow apologized to the shooting victims and said that he had fired his gun in a panic. He was sentenced to 10 years imprisonment. Although "Puffy" Combs still faced civil suits seeking millions in damages, his acquittal ended the threat of his imprisonment for the Club New York fracas.

— Tom Smith

Suggestions for Further Reading

Finkelstein, Katherine E. "Defense Calls Combs Trial 'Stupid' Case." *New York Time* (March 13, 2001): B3.

——. "Hip-Hop Star Cleared of Charges In Shooting at a Manhattan Club." *New York Times* (March 17, 2001): A1, B2.

Italiano, Laura. "Getaway Driver: I Saw Gun in His Hand." *New York Post, (February 16, 2001): 2–3.*

Kenyan and Tanzanian Embassy Bombers Trial: 2001

Defendants: Mohamed Rashed Daoud al-'Owhali, Wadih El-Hage, Khalfan Khamis Mohamed, Mohamed Saddiq Odeh   **Crimes Charged:** al-'Owhali, Mohamed, Odeh: Conspiracy and murder; El-Hage: Conspiracy and perjury
Chief Defense Lawyers: al-'Owhali: David P. Baugh, Frederick H. Cohn; Odeh: Anthony L. Ricco, Edward D. Wilford; El-Hage: Joshua L. Dratel, Sam A. Schmidt; Mohamed: David A. Ruhnke, Jeremy Schneider
Chief Prosecutors: Paul Butler, Patrick J. Fitzgerald, Michael J. Garcia, Kenneth M. Karas   **Judge:** Leonard B. Sand   **Place:** New York, New York
Dates of Trial: February 5–May 29, 2001   **Verdicts:** All guilty of all charges   **Sentences:** al-'Owhali, El-Hage, Mohamed, Odeh: life imprisonment

SIGNIFICANCE

The trial in Federal District Court in New York of men accused of terrorist bombings in East Africa proves that a carefully and well-developed prosecution, with protection of the rights of the accused and with conclusive evidence, can produce justice even in the most appalling crimes.

In Nairobi, Kenya, on Friday morning, August 7, 1998, Prudence Bushnell, U.S. Ambassador to Kenya, was attending a meeting with Kenya's trade minister on the top floor of a bank building next door to the American embassy. Suddenly a huge explosion destroyed the seven-story building and ripped off the back of the embassy. It killed 213 people, including 12 Americans, and injured more than 4,000 others.

At almost the same moment, in the U.S. embassy in Dar es Salaam, Tanzania, U.S. charge d'affaires John Lange was holding a staff meeting in his third-floor office when a bomb blasted walls and windows. It killed 11 Tanzanians and injured 85 people, including Americans. Both bombings occurred on the eighth anniversary of the arrival of U.S. troops in Saudi Arabia in the Persian Gulf War.

Linked to bin Laden

Within days, the Federal Bureau of Investigation (FBI) linked the bombings to Saudi exile Osama bin Laden, leader of a worldwide conspiracy to destroy U.S. government property and kill Americans. Bin Laden and 16 members of his terrorist organization, Al Qaeda, were indicted. Eleven members remained fugitives as four were arrested and brought to trial in Federal District Court in New York City. The trial was held 7,000 miles from the bombed embassies because the conspiracy was alleged to have grown from a Muslim refugee group centered, among other worldwide locations, in Brooklyn. Some of its members had been convicted in the 1993 World Trade Center bombing.

As the trial opened on February 5, 2001, before Judge Leonard B. Sand, assistant U.S. attorney Paul Butler told the jury of seven women and five men that "all four defendants entered into an illegal agreement with Osama bin Laden and others to kill Americans anywhere in the world. And in the end, 224 men, women, and children lost their lives." The 302-count charge included individual indictments for murder for each death.

Defense attorney Jeremy Schneider, representing Khalfan Khamis Mohamed, conceded his client participated in the bombings but said he was a "pawn" who simply took orders. Attorneys for Mohamed Saddiq Odeh and Wadih El-Hage admitted their clients' ties to bin Laden but denied any violent activity. Mohamed Rashed Daoud al-'Owhali's attorney, Frederick H. Cohn, offered no opening statement.

"The Snake is America"

The first witness was a government informant. Jamal Ahmed Mohamed Al-Fadl testified he heard bin Laden say, "The snake is America and we have to cut their head off and stop what they are doing in the Horn of Africa."

Questioned by prosecutor Patrick J. Fitzgerald, Al-Fadl said Al Qaeda was "for focusing on jihad"—a declaration of a holy war—and implicated El-Hage in the violence. Cross-examining, El-Hage's attorney, Sam S. Schmidt, claiming his client was only a nonviolent business associate of bin Laden, tried to undermine Al-Fadl's credibility.

Over several days, the jury heard witnesses describe bin Laden's anti-American fatwahs, or religious declarations, and his group's responsibility for the deaths of American soldiers in Mogadishu, Somalia, in 1993. One witness said El-Hage, a naturalized American citizen in Texas, helped bin Laden buy a used jet plane in Dallas to fly anti-aircraft missiles from Pakistan to his Sudan headquarters.

Now the prosecutors read aloud the 52-page English translation of bin Laden's 1996 fatwah declaring holy war against the U.S. as he opposed the deployment of non-Islamic American troops to protect the holy Muslim shrines of his oil-rich Saudi peninsula after Iraq invaded Kuwait.

Prosecution witness L'Houssaine Kherchtou testified that Odeh and El-Hage had known each other in Kenya in the mid-1990s. He named other indicted fugitives as Al Qaeda members, saying Odeh traveled with them to oppose a United Nations mission that included American troops. On cross-examination, however, Kherchtou said he could not be sure of El-Hage's association with Al Qaeda.

Bombing a "Blunder"

The prosecutors introduced FBI agents who had interrogated the defendants. Special Agent John Anticev testified that Odeh said the Nairobi bombing was a "blunder" that killed so many Kenyans because the truck's drivers headed nose-first into the embassy, rather than backing in, so the explosion burst toward the adjacent building. Anticev said Odeh admitted membership in Al Qaeda and that in its military camps he learned how to use explosives.

The trial's most dramatic testimony came as Ambassador Bushnell gave details on the Nairobi explosion. As the ceiling caved in, she said, "I thought the building was going to collapse, and I was going to die." Descending the stairwell, she added, "there was blood everywhere. I could feel the person behind me bleeding onto my back."

FBI special agent Stephen Gaudin told the jury that defendant al-'Owhali agreed to describe his involvement if he could be guaranteed trial in the United States. The defendant, said the agent, called the Nairobi embassy "an easy target," with the bombing planned for late Friday morning when observant Muslims would be moving toward mosques and thus out of danger, and was targeted also because it had a female ambassador whose death would generate extra publicity. (A report filed after the bombing revealed that Ambassador Bushnell had earlier requested security improvements from the State Department and Defense Department, but none were made.)

Agent Gaudin added that al-'Owhali rode as a passenger in the bomb truck, carrying stun grenades. At the embassy gate, he jumped off, threw a grenade at the security guard so the truck could get past, then ran.

FBI special agent Donald Sachtleben described how the Toyota Dyna pickup truck's rear axle was hurled more than 700 meters as the blast blew out all embassy windows, produced major structural damage of the building, and reduced the seven-story building next door to rubble.

The Second Blast

Next, the prosecutors introduced survivors of the Dar es Salaam blast. Charge d'affaires Lange told how the explosion rocked his office during his meeting. Embassy translator Justine Mdobilu, whose braided hair filled with bits of flying glass, said, "I thought I was dreaming. When I looked around, people were bleeding." Information officer Elizabeth Slater, who was pulled from the rubble of a collapsed wall, said, "Coming down the stairwell, there were all kinds of body parts."

Witnesses described the Tanzania bomb truck, a Nissan Atlas sold by a Tanzanian driver to Ahmed Ghailani and Sheik Ahmed Salim Swedan, two of the indicted fugitives. Swedan had earlier been identified as the buyer of the Toyota Dyna that carried the Kenya bomb. A Tanzanian welder said Swedan paid him to alter it to hold batteries in the rear.

Evidence against Mohamed showed he had been seen meeting with the buyers of the Nissan Atlas, that his passport had been found in the home of one buyer, and that he rented the house where the Tanzania bomb was built. FBI agent Abigail Perkins testified that Mohamed told her he owned the bombers' Suzuki utility car and was responsible for helping grind the TNT that was loaded into the truck. He participated, he told her, "to help his Muslim brothers."

The Perjury Trail

The prosecutors turned to the 21 counts of perjury against El-Hage. They produced a trail of phone calls, faxes, and letters indicating El-Hage was in contact with bin Laden people he denied knowing. They revealed his finger-prints on a letter to bin Laden's military commander, whom El-Hage had told the grand jury he did not know. They introduced receipts on shipments of goods from El-Hage to Odeh, whom El-Hage claimed he never knew.

FBI forensic chemist Kelly Mount testified that a T-shirt, a pair of jeans, and a bed sheet found in Odeh's travel bag carried traces of explosives TNT or PETN. Cross-examined, Mount said it was possible but not probable that bomb residue was transferred to the clothing by bomb-scene investigators.

Closing their presentation after 92 witnesses and 1,700 exhibits, the prosecutors read claims of responsibility for the bombings that had been faxed to media outlets in Qatar, the United Arab Emirates, and France. The "Islamic Army for the Liberation of Holy Places," said the faxes, promised "to strike at American interests everywhere" until U.S. troops were withdrawn from Saudi Arabia.

Defense lawyers opened their case on April 16 with British forensic scientist Dr. John Lloyd testifying for Odeh. He said the explosive residue found on Odeh's clothing could have been as small as a speck of dust transferred by a handshake and was impossible to trace.

Supporting El-Hage's position that he worked for bin Laden but had nothing to do with terrorist activities, his lawyers presented a Nairobi business-man named Odeh who engaged El-Hage in gemstone trading and other ven-tures. The witness said his name was spelled and pronounced "Oudeh" in Arabic. This rebutted the prosecution's contention that shipments from El-Hage to someone named Oudeh went to defendant Odeh.

Calling no further witnesses, the defense rested. No defendant testified. In closing arguments, prosecutor Kenneth M. Karas charged El-Hage with repeated lying "to protect the Al Qaeda conspiracy," and El-Hage defense attorney Schmidt charged prosecution witness Al-Fadl with repeated lying to protect himself. Odeh lawyer Anthony L. Ricco said his client's "association with Al Qaeda is based on religious beliefs," not violence.

Mohamed attorney David A. Ruhnke cited his client's cooperation with the FBI, without which "there would be very little evidence," and contended "he never met Osama bin Laden." Al-'Owhali lawyer Cohn said his client should be acquitted because his confession was coerced as he was imprisoned "in terrible conditions, in fear of his life from jailers who had to hate him."

The jury deliberated from May 10 to May 29. It found all four men guilty on all 302 counts. It then met to consider, one at a time, what penalty to impose on each. All four men received sentences of life imprisonment.

—Bernard Ryan, Jr.

Suggestions for Further Reading

Bodansky, Yossef. *Bin Laden: The Man Who Declared War on America*. Rocklin, Calif.: Prima Publishing, 1999.

Grosscup, Beau. *The Newest Explosions of Terrorism: Latest Sites of Terrorism in the 1990s and Beyond*. Far Hills, N.J.: New Horizon, 1998.

Hoffman, Bruce. *Inside Terrorism*. New York: Columbia University Press, 1999.

Huband, Mark. *Warriors of the Prophet: The Struggle for Islam*. Boulder, Colo.: Westview Press, 1999.

Labeviere, Richard, and Martin DeMers, trans. *Dollars for Terror: The United States and Islam*. New York: Algora Publishing, 2000.

Reeve, Simon. *The New Jackals: Ranzi Yousef, Osama bin Laden, and the Future of Terrorism*. Boston: Northeastern University Press, 1999.

Tripp, Aili Mari. *Changing the Rules: The Politics of Liberalization and the Urban Informal Economy in Tanzania*. Berkeley: University of California Press, 1997.

Thomas E. Blanton Trial (Alabama Church Bombing): 2001

Defendant: Thomas E. Blanton, Jr.   **Crime Charged:** Murder
Chief Defense Lawyer: John C. Robbins   **Chief Prosecutors:** Doug Jones,
Robert Posey, Jeff Wallace   **Judge:** James Garrett   **Place:** Birmingham,
Alabama   **Date of Trial:** April 15–May 1, 2001   **Verdict:** Guilty
Sentence: Life imprisonment, four terms

SIGNIFICANCE

The bombing deaths of four black girls in a Birmingham, Alabama, church in 1963 brought additional support for the civil rights movement, and was a catalyst for the passage of the Civil Rights Act of 1964, but Thomas Blanton was not tried for the murders until 38 years after the event.

On the morning of Sunday, September 15, 1963, a bomb placed under an outside stairway of the 16th Street Baptist Church in Birmingham, Alabama, was detonated as the congregation inside prepared for services. The blast killed four girls who were in the basement of the church: Carole Robertson, Cynthia Wesley, and Addie Mae Collins, all age 14, and Denise McNair, age 11. Many others, including relatives of the girls, were severely injured. Birmingham had become a center of civil rights activities and protests in the early 1960s, and the 16th Street Baptist Church was known to be a place where young activists gathered. The attack occurred just months after Birmingham gained international notoriety as a result of news coverage showing the police using attack dogs and water cannons against civil rights marchers led by Martin Luther King, Jr.

FBI Quickly Identifies Suspects, but Does Not Pursue Prosecution

Within a few weeks investigators from the Federal Bureau of Investigation (FBI) had identified four members of local Ku Klux Klan groups as suspects. They were Robert Chambliss, known as "Dynamite Bob," and thought to be the ringleader, Thomas E. Blanton, Herman Cash, and Bobby Frank Cherry. Using electronic surveillance and assisted by a Klan member, Mitchell Burns, who had become a paid informant, the FBI gathered taped recordings of conversations among these men and their friends and families which implicated them in the bombing, and which would eventually provide the evidence crucial for the convictions. However, ignoring the express wishes of President John F. Kennedy, and subsequently President Lyndon B. Johnson, then-FBI director J. Edgar Hoover overrode his agents in the field and ordered that they not proceed with prosecutions, ostensibly on the grounds that the case was circumstantial, and it would not be possible to convict white men of killing blacks in Birmingham at the time. Hoover also ordered the records of the investigation to be sealed.

In the mid-1970s, Alabama attorney general Bill Baxley was able to obtain FBI records pertaining to Robert Chambliss, and in 1977 Chambliss was convicted of murder in the bombing; he died in prison in 1985. Herman Cash died in 1994; he was never charged in the case. In 1993 Birmingham civic leaders persuaded the FBI to re-open the case, which resulted in the production of 9,000 tapes and documents collected by the FBI in the 1960s, only a portion of which had been seen by prosecutors in the Chambliss trial. Several other successful prosecutions in the 1990s for acts committed against blacks and civil rights leaders decades earlier encouraged Birmingham leaders to press the case against Blanton and Cherry. These included the conviction in 1994 of Byron De La Beckwith for the assassination of Medgar Evers in 1963, and the conviction of former Klan imperial wizard Sam Bowers (see Price and Bowers trial) for the firebomb death of an NAACP leader in Mississippi in 1966. In May 2000 a Birmingham grand jury indicted Blanton and Cherry for the murder of the four girls killed in the 16th Street Baptist Church.

Blanton and Cherry were scheduled to be tried together, but two weeks before the trial was set to begin Circuit Court judge James Garrett postponed the trial of Cherry indefinitely, following a psychiatric finding that he was not mentally competent to assist in his own defense. Jury selection began on April 15, 2001, and took a week. The panel chosen from an unusually large pool consisted of eight white women, two white men, three black women, and three black men. The prosecution faced, by its own acknowledgement, a difficult task, made so largely by the number of years that had elapsed since the bombing. One key witness who had earlier testified to seeing a car resembling Blanton's Chevrolet near the church in the early hours of the morning of the bombing had died. Another witness who had testified to the grand jury that he had seen a man resembling Blanton carrying a black bag near the stairwell of the church at 1 A.M. on the morning of the blast had since suffered a stroke and was unable to give evidence. There was no physical evidence linking Blanton to the manufacture, transportation, or detonation of the bomb.

A Short Trial and a Quick Verdict

On the first day of testimony the prosecution, led by Doug Jones, a U.S. attorney who had been deputized to prosecute the case in state court, presented numerous witnesses who were present at the time of the bombing. These witnesses included the mother of Denise McNair, who was teaching a Sunday school class, and the pastor, the Reverend John Cross, who described digging through the rubble to find the bodies of the girls. Other prosecution witnesses included the FBI agents who had interviewed Blanton after the bombing and who had investigated the case over the following months, the informant Mitchell Burns, and others who described the surveillance and secret taping of Blanton. Others testified to the virulence of Blanton's segregationist views and to his involvement in Ku Klux Klan activities.

On April 27 in a crowded courtroom the jurors first heard segments of the FBI tapes. Some were made on a tape recorder which the FBI had placed in the trunk of Burns's car; others were obtained by the use of a microphone implanted in a wall of the kitchen of Blanton's apartment by FBI technicians, who, posing as truck drivers, had rented the adjoining unit. The defense was unsuccessful in seeking to prevent the playing of the tapes, which were made in 1964 and 1965 before Congress restricted such secret taping without a court order. In crucial sections of the tapes Blanton tells Burns that the bombing of the 16th St. Church "wasn't easy," and in a conversation with his then-wife, Blanton talks of going to a meeting "to plan the bomb." However, at no time did Blanton explicitly admit to having carried out the bombing, and Mitchell Burns acknowledged under cross-examination that in none of the many conversations he had had with Blanton had he ever done so.

A court-appointed attorney, John C. Robbins, represented Blanton. In his statements to the jury Robbins acknowledged Blanton's racist views, but exhorted jurors not to be influenced by the historical significance of the bombing, or by the emotional testimony of eyewitnesses. He reiterated that the prosecution's case was entirely circumstantial, and that there was no evidence proving that his client was responsible for the bombing. During cross-examination Robbins was able to expose flaws in the memories of some witnesses, and to cast some doubt on the reliability and credibility of others. Blanton did not testify, and the defense called only two witnesses.

The trial lasted only a little over a week, and the case went to the jury on May 1. They deliberated for only a little over two hours before returning a verdict of guilty on all four counts. Jurors subsequently acknowledged that the FBI tapes were the evidence that led them to convict. Thomas Blanton was sentenced to a term of life imprisonment for each of the four murders.

— David I. Petts

Suggestions for Further Reading

Kosof, Anna. *The Civil Rights Movement and Its Legacy.* New York: Franklin Watts, 1989.

Lee, Spike. *Four Little Girls.* Documentary film, 1997.

Wexler, Sanford. *The Civil Rights Movement: An Eyewitness History.* New York: Facts On File, 1993.

GLOSSARY

Note: References to other defined terms are set in bold type.

Accessory after the fact. one who obstructs justice by giving comfort or assistance to the felon (*see* **felony**), knowing that the felon has committed a crime or is sought by authorities in connection with a serious crime

Accessory before the fact. one who aids in the commission of a **felony** by ordering or encouraging it, but who is not present when the crime is perpetrated

Accomplice. one who voluntarily engages with another in the commission or attempted commission of a crime

Amicus curiae. literally, "friend of the court," an individual or entity not party to the lawsuit whose role is to provide the court with information, typically a legal brief, which might not otherwise be considered by the court

Annulment. a nullification, as of a marriage; when a marriage is annulled, it is as if it never existed, whereas divorce terminates the legal status of the marriage from that point forward

Appellant. the party appealing a decision to a higher, appellate court

Appellate jurisdiction. the power of a superior court or other tribunal to review the judicial actions of lower courts, particularly for legal errors, and to revise their judgments accordingly

Appellee. the party who prevailed in the court below the appellate court and who argues on appeal against setting aside the judgment of the lower court

Aranda rule. a 1965 ruling by the Supreme Court that forbids testimony in which one codefendant implicates another

Arraignment. the procedure by which a criminal defendant is brought before the trial court and informed of the charges against him or her and the pleas (guilty, not guilty, or no contest) he or she may enter in response

Bench warrant. an order from the court empowering legal authorities to seize an individual, usually to compel attendance to answer a contempt charge or when a **subpoena** has been ignored

Change of venue. the removal of a lawsuit from a county or district to another for trial, often permitted in criminal cases where the court finds that the defendant would not receive a fair trial in the first location because of adverse publicity

Circumstantial evidence. indirect, secondary facts from which the existence or non-existence of a fact at issue in a case may be inferred

Claimant. the party, customarily the **plaintiff**, asserting a right, usually to money or property

Clemency. the act, usually by a chief executive such as a president or governor, of forgiving a criminal liability for his or her actions, as when a **pardon** is granted

Co-conspirator. one who engages in a **conspiracy** with others; the acts and declarations of any one conspirator are admissible as evidence against all his or her co-conspirators

Common law. principles and rules of action derived from past judicial decisions, as distinct from laws created solely through legislative enactment

Commutation. alteration or substitution, such as when one criminal punishment is substituted for another, more severe one

Compensatory damages. monetary damages the law awards to compensate an injured party solely for the injury sustained because of the action of another (cf. **punitive damages**)

Conspiracy. the agreement of two or more individuals to commit, through their joint efforts, an unlawful act

Coroner's inquest. an examination by the coroner, often with the aid of a jury, into the causes of a death occurring under suspicious circumstances

Corpus delicti. objective proof that a crime has been committed, which ordinarily includes evidence of the criminal act and evidence of who is responsible for its commission

Cross-examination. questioning a witness, by a party or a lawyer other than the one who is called the witness, about testimony the witness gave on **direct examination**

Court of chancery. courts that follow rules of equity, or general rules of fairness, rather than strictly formulated common law; distinctions between courts of equity and courts of law have essentially disappeared at both the state and federal levels

Declarative judgment of relief. a binding adjudication of the rights and status of parties that does not require any further action or relief

Defamation. speech (**slander**) or writings (**libel**) that damages the reputation of another

Direct evidence. testimony at trial by a witness who actually heard the words or saw the actions that, if believed by the trier of fact, conclusively establish a fact at issue

Direct examination. initial questioning of a witness by the lawyer who called him or her, the purpose of which is to present testimony regarding the facts of the examining party's case

Diversity jurisdiction. one basis for granting federal courts the power to hear and determine cases, applicable to controversies arising between citizens of different states or between a citizen of a state and an alien

Double jeopardy. a bar against double prosecution or double punishment for the same offense, operational only in criminal cases and only if there is no appeal of a conviction

Due process. applicable only to actions of state or federal governments and their officials, it guarantees procedural fairness when the state deprives an individual of property or liberty; also, substantive due process requires that all legislation be enacted solely to further legitimate governmental objectives

Ex parte. literally, "on behalf of"; a judicial proceeding brought for the benefit of one party without notice to the adverse party, who does not participate

Extortion. a criminal offense, usually punished as a **felony**, consisting of obtaining property from another through use or threat of force, or through illegitimate use of official power

Extradition. the surrender by one state or country of an individual who is accused or convicted of an offense outside the borders of that state or country

Expert witness. a witness, such as a psychological statistician or ballistics expert, with special knowledge concerning the subject he or she will testify about

Felony. high crimes, such as burglary, rape, or homicide, which unlike misdemeanors, are often punishable by lengthy jail terms or death

Gag order. a court order restricting dissemination, by attorneys and witnesses, of information about a case (such orders directed at the press are unconstitutional); also, an order to restrain an unruly defendant who is disrupting his or her trial

Grand jury. traditionally consisting of twenty-three (as opposed to twelve- or six-member **petit juries**) individuals empaneled to determine whether the facts and accusations presented by prosecutors in criminal proceedings warrant an **indictment** and trial of the accused

Guardian ad litem. a guardian appointed by the court to represent the interests of an infant or incompetent in legal proceedings

Habeas corpus. a procedure for a judicial ruling on the legality of an individual's custody, used in a criminal context to challenge a convict's confinement and in a civil context to challenge child custody, deportation, and commitment to a mental institution

Hearsay. a statement, other than one made by a witness at a hearing or trial, offered to prove the truth of a matter asserted at the hearing or trial; such statements are inadmissable as evidence except under certain circumstances

Immunity. exemption from a duty or penalty; witnesses are often granted immunity from prosecution in order to compel them to respond to questions they might otherwise refuse to answer based on the Fifth Amendment's privilege against self-incrimination

Impeach. to call into question the truthfulness of a witness's testimony by offering evidence of his or her lack of veracity

Impeachment. criminal proceedings against a public official, such as a president or a supreme court justice, accused of wrongdoing while in office

Indictment. a formal written accusation drawn up by a public prosecuting attorney and issued by a grand jury against a party charged with a crime

Injunction. a judicial remedy requiring a party to cease or refrain from some specified action

In re. literally, "in the matter of"; used to signify a legal proceeding where there are no adversaries, but merely a matter, such as an estate, requiring judicial action

Interspousal immunity. a state common law rule, now largely abolished, prohibiting tort actions, or lawsuits concerning certain civil wrongs, between husbands and wives

Judicial notice. recognition by a court during trial of certain facts that are so universally acknowledged or easily verifiable (e.g., historical facts, geographical features) that they do not require the production of evidence as proof of their existence

Judicial review. review of a trial court decision by an appellate court; power and responsibility of the U.S. Supreme Court and the highest state courts to determine the constitutionality of the acts of the legislatures and executive branches of their respective jurisdictions

Jury tampering. a criminal offense consisting of attempting to improperly influence one or more jurors' vote(s) by threats, bribes, etc.

Justifiable homicide. the killing of another in self-defense or in the lawful defense of one's property; killing another when the law demands it, such as in execution for a capital crime

Libel. a method of defamation expressed by false and malicious publication in print for the purpose of damaging the reputation of another

Libelant. formerly, the party who filed a complaint in an admiralty or ecclesiastical case; a **plaintiff**

Manslaughter. unlawful killing of another without malice, aforethought, or an intent to cause death, it calls for less severe penalties than murder; most jurisdictions distinguish between voluntary, or intentional manslaughter, and involuntary manslaughter, such as a death resulting from an automobile accident

Misdemeanor. any criminal offense less serious than a **felony,** generally punishable by a fine or imprisonment other than in a penitentiary and for a shorter period than would be imposed for a **felony**

Mistrial. a trial declared void before a verdict is returned, usually because the jury is deadlocked or because some incurable and fundamental error that is prejudicial to the defendant

M'Naghten Rule. a test to be applied to the insanity defense under which the accused will be found not criminally liable if, at the time he or she committed the act in question, the accused was incapable of knowing that it was wrong

Nol. pros. (*nolle prosequi*). a formal declaration, usually by the prosecutor in a criminal case, that the state will not prosecute a given defendant or case any further

Obstruction of justice. the offense of attempting to interfere with the administration of justice through such acts as **jury tampering** or attempting to influence an officer of the court

Original jurisdiction. the authority to hear a case at its inception and to pass judgment on its law and facts, as opposed to **appellate jurisdiction,** which grants the power to review the decisions of lower tribunals, which can then be affirmed, reversed, or modified

Parole. a conditional release of a prisoner after he or she has served part of a sentence

Pardon. an act, usually of a chief executive such as a president or governor, that relieves a convicted individual from the punishment imposed for his or her crime and restores rights and privileges that have been forfeited because of it

Perjury. the criminal offense of making false statements while under oath

Petit jury. an ordinary trial jury, as opposed to a **grand jury,** traditionally composed of twelve (in some jurisdictions six) persons whose job it is to determine issues of fact in civil and criminal proceedings

Plaintiff. the party who initiates a lawsuit, seeking a remedy for an injury to his or her rights

Police power of the state. the power of state and local governments to impose upon private rights restrictions that are necessary to the general public welfare

Prima facie case. a case that, because it is supported by the requisite minimum of evidence and is free of obvious defects, can go to the jury; thus the defendant is required to proceed with its case rather than move for dismissal or a directed verdict

Punitive damages. compensation in excess of actual losses awarded to a successful **plaintiff** who was injured under circumstances involving malicious and willful misconduct on the part of the defendant (cf. **compensatory damages**)

Reasonable doubt. the degree of certainty required for a juror to find a criminal defendant guilty, meaning that proof of guilt must be so clear that an ordinary person would have no reasonable doubt as to the guilt of the defendant

Recusation. the act whereby a judge is disqualified, or disqualifies himself or herself, from a case because of the potential for bias or a conflict of interest

Reprieve. a temporary relief or postponement of a criminal punishment or sentence

Remand. to send a matter back to the tribunal from which it was appealed; when an appellate court reverses a judgment, the case is usually remanded to the lower court for a new trial

RICO laws. "Racketeer Influenced and Corrupt Organization Act," federal statute designed to prosecute organized crime; many states have enacted similar statutes

Sedition. any illegal action intended to disrupt or overthrow the government

Seditious libel. publication of words intended to excite public sentiment against the government (cf. **sedition**)

Slander. oral defamation; false and malicious words spoken with the intent to damage another's reputation

Statutory rape. the crime of having sexual intercourse with a female under an age set by the state statute

Subornation of perjury. the criminal offense of procuring another to commit **perjury**

Subpoena. a written order issued under court authority compelling the appearance of a witness at a judicial proceeding

Talesman. a court bystander summoned to serve as a juror

Temporary insanity. a criminal defense asserting that, because the accused was legally insane at the time the crime was committed, he or she did not have the necessary mental state to commit it and is therefore not responsible for the alleged criminal conduct

Venireman. one of a panel of jurors

Voir dire. examination by the court or by lawyers for the parties of prospective jurors; also, a hearing by the court during trial out of the jury's presence to determine initially a question of law

Writ of *certiorari.* a means of gaining appellate review; a written order issued by an appellate court to an inferior tribunal, commanding the latter to forward the record of the proceedings below in a particular case

Writ of *habeas corpus.* a procedure used in criminal contexts to bring a petitioning prisoner before the court to determine the legality of his or her confinement (*see* **habeas corpus**)

Writ of *mandamus.* an order issued by a court, usually to an inferior tribunal, commanding performance of some ministerial act or mandatory duty, or directing the restoration to the petitioner of rights and privileges that have been illegally denied

Subject Index

The roman numerals, in bold, identify which volume each reference appears in. The numbers following the roman numerals and colons are the actual page numbers.

I

S

U